FRANK SMYTHE

THE SIX ALPINE / HIMALAYAN CLIMBING BOOKS

FRANK SMYTHE

the six alpine/himalayan climbing books

Climbs and Ski Runs
The Kangchenjunga Adventure
Kamet Conquered
Camp Six
The Valley of Flowers
Mountaineering Holiday

BÂTON WICKS • LONDON
THE MOUNTAINEERS • SEATTLE

Also in this series

H.W. TILMAN
THE SEVEN MOUNTAIN-TRAVEL BOOKS

ERIC SHIPTON
THE SIX MOUNTAIN-TRAVEL BOOKS

H.W. TILMAN
THE EIGHT SAILING / MOUNTAIN-EXPLORATION BOOKS

JOHN MUIR
THE EIGHT WILDERNESS-DISCOVERY BOOKS

JOHN MUIR
HIS LIFE AND LETTERS AND OTHER WRITINGS

Published simultaneously in 2000 in Great Britain and the United States
by Bâton Wicks, London and The Mountaineers, Seattle.

All trade enquiries in U.K., Europe and the Commonwealth (except Canada)
to Cordee, 3a DeMontfort Street, Leicester LE1 7HD

All trade enquiries in the U.S.A. and Canada to
The Mountaineers, 1001 S.W. Klickitat Way, Suite 201, Seattle, Washington 98134

British Library Cataloguing in Publication Data:
A catalogue entry for this book can be obtained from the British Library.
ISBN 1-898573-37-9

U.S. Library of Congress Cataloging in Publication Data:
Catalog Card No. ISBN 0-89886-740-1

Printed and bound in Great Britain by M.P.G. Books, Bodmin

Contents

Photographs in the Text

Illustrations used at the beginning of each book

Also in the text

ACKNOWLEDGEMENTS The Publisher and Copyright Holders wish to thank the following for their help, advice and contributions to this book: Pete Horsfall and Nick Clinch for their initial advice on book selection; John Millar for a range of editorial advice, research and assistance which was particularly valuable in assembling the appendices; Robin Hodgkin, Charles Houston, Douglas Scott, Robin Campbell, Bill MacKenzie, J.H. Emlyn Jones, Norman Dyhrenfurth, Charles Warren, Lord Hunt (the latter two now deceased) for historical background information; Graham Cook, Maggie Body, Richard Hale, Margaret Ecclestone, Sheila Scott, Bob Lawford, Sheila Harrison, Livia Gollancz, Charles Black, Steve Dean and Harry Calvert for publishing and editorial assistance; Peter Lunn for permission to publish his father's article on Smythe; Mirella Tenderini, Lindsay Griffin, Hermann Reisach, Audrey Salkeld, Harish Kapadia, Katsumi Hino, John Bowles and Geoff Milburn for further research and enquiries; finally the institutions of the *Alpine Journal*, the *Fell and Rock Journal*, the *Himalayan Journal* and other publications whose reliable recording of mountaineering events was ever valuable.

The photographic credits are given with each photograph but the following are thanked for particular efforts made for the book: John Cleare for a number of the introductory photos and other illustrations; Norman Dyhrenfurth for photographs of the 1930 Kangchenjunga expedition, Jonathan Somervell, Mike Papworth, Wil Hurford, Roger Payne, John Jackson, Leo Dickinson, Doug Scott, John Allen, Graham Little and Mick Fowler – all of whom made particular efforts to improve the photographic coverage of the book. To all of the above, the credited photographers, and anyone we may have overlooked we offer our sincere thanks.

The aforementioned credits give some idea of the efforts made in compiling this omnibus. The central control has been a partnership exercise between Ken Wilson (Bâton Wicks) and Tony Smythe, Frank Smythe's second son.* The introductory note, various appendix matters, and the photo captions etc were jointly finalised by this partnership. In addition editorial comments, clarifications and footnotes have been added where suitable. These are either in [square brackets] or with asterisked footnotes to distinguish them from the numbered footnotes of the original books.

* Tony Smythe, an accomplished mountaineer, made a rapid ascent of the Route Major (with Barry Annette) in 1961.

INTRODUCTION

Frank Smythe was one of the leading mountaineers of the interwar period. His name can be placed alongside those of Mallory, Schneider, Welzenbach, Cassin, Heckmair, Schmaderer, Lauper, Amstutz, Lambert, Gervasutti and Roch. It is therefore a belated privilege to present here six of his finest books which collectively celebrate a great mountaineering career.

The astounding thing about Smythe is that he gained such distinction in his sport without excelling in any technical or athletic sense. He was considered to have rather a frail constitution and poor physique for the great demands of alpinism and particularly, Himalayan climbing.* Despite these handicaps he still managed to become a first class alpinist, superbly proficient on ice and mixed ground, and competent on rock. He was cautious, patient and shrewd in his mountaineering judgement, yet astonishingly bold when the situation was right. He built up an exemplary mountaineering career that is notable not only for its string of important ascents but also for its episodes of sheer ability, on mountains in all areas, and in all seasons. He is the exemplar of wise mountaineering. Apart from one notable occasion, Smythe never climbed with guides having learned his alpinism from impecunious youth. In the 1920s many keen climbers still used guides and guideless climbing, particularly on the harder routes was considered foolhardy.

Smythe was, perhaps, the first professional climber in a modern sense. He did not seek to become a guide but he found that literature, journalism, broadcasting, photography and lecturing provided for his needs. In this he was a precursor for many – e.g. Diemberger, Bonington, Scott, Messner. Smythe's astonishing output of twenty-seven books in twenty years matched his mountaineering energy. The books were very popular and probably influential in shaping emerging public perceptions about climbing during a period of frequent Alpine and Himalayan tragedies.

In this omnibus six of Smythe's finest narratives have been selected. These have been chosen to portray his climbing activity during his most active period in the 1920s and 1930s. He did not aim to present his adventures in strict chronological sequence. *Climbs and Ski Runs*, the first book of the collection, has stories about alpine climbs, winter ski trips, Dolomite adventures, a month of peak bagging in Corsica, and new route explorations in North Wales. The book ends with his great alpine seasons of 1927 and 1928 each of which culminated in first ascents on the unclimbed Brenva Face of Mont Blanc – the Sentinelle Rouge and the Route Major – classic climbs, which he did in partnership with T. Graham Brown, that still take their place among the finest alpine expeditions in the world.

His four main expedition books (published here) were best sellers. But a word of caution might be useful here. *The Kangchenjunga Adventure* and *Kamet Conquered*, though stirring and adventurous, also contain hints of colonial superiority and in *Camp Six*, Smythe is critical of the squalor in Tibet. Against

* Smythe was deemed unfit for strenuous sport at school and was invalided out of the RAF in 1927.

this, in *The Valley of Flowers* he shows that he has come to understand the ways of locals and porters and that he has developed respect and affection for the men he employs. *Mountaineering Holiday*, the final book, deals with a single very active alpine climbing season during the weeks before World War II. Ironically the final climb, the Innominata Ridge of Mont Blanc, is made in the company of four young German climbers during the last days of peacetime.

Although he loved the Alps it was as an expedition climber and as a high-altitude pioneer that Smythe was to find his true calling. On Kangchenjunga he was with a talented international group of climbers led by Professor Günter Oskar Dyhrenfurth. After a catastrophe on what was to become the main route of ascent in later years, they went on make the first ascent of Jonsong Peak (24,344ft) and reached several other high unclimbed summits.

A year later Smythe put his Kangchenjunga experiences to good use in the Garhwal, leading a happy team to success on Kamet (25,447ft), the highest peak to be climbed at that time. The party then completed a comprehensive exploration of the ranges on the Gangotri/Alaknanda watershed.

Two years later came the first (and most successful) of his three Everest expeditions on which Smythe, to the agreement of all, excelled. Alone, when Shipton was forced to retreat, he reached the highpoint of Norton, Wager and Wyn Harris. He was going well, with time in hand, and was only defeated by tricky but not impossible snow conditions where a roped party might have progressed to the final slopes and, possibly, pressed on to the top. In physiological terms, it can be argued that this was the most notable performance on Everest until Reinhold Messner made his solo ascent nearly fifty years later.

Any suggestion that Smythe was merely a "big expedition man" was firmly countered by his lightweight trip to the Garhwal in 1937 in which his ascents of Nilgiri Parbat and Mana Peak were outstanding. The first was made with two Sherpas, Wangdi and Nurbu, whom Smythe effectively trained as they made the ascent. On Mana Peak he was partnered by the not-fully-fit Peter Oliver, who tired, leaving Smythe to make an inspired solo ascent of the final 800ft rock buttress to a summit of nearly 24,000ft.

Smythe has the rare knack of taking you with him on his adventures. The rigours of climbing in the days of primitive equipment and clothing have an uncomfortable realism, although the author usually ends his accounts with a sigh of acceptance and a wry joke at his own expense. For years some hardened mountaineers have tended to dismiss him as a merely a well publicised "professional", writing for an armchair audience. But Smythe made honest efforts to record the emotional and reflective moments of climbing, and maybe unconsciously, tried to counter the cynicism, materialism and ruthless ambition he saw in the emerging mountaineering culture of the 1930s. His restrained, indeed humble, descriptions forged a bond between him and his readers. Above all he loved mountains and his pen captured some of the most poignant and joyful moments in climbing.

We might look back and wonder what dreams and inspirations drove Smythe. We might also ponder whether in today's pressurised and hectic climbing scene such dreams are not, in their simplicity, moving beyond our grasp.

CLIMBS AND SKI RUNS

Climbs and Ski Runs

First published by Blackwood, Edinburgh, 1929

Contents

* Taken from *The Adventures of a Mountaineer* Dent, London, 1940.

INTRODUCTORY NOTE

*Geoffrey Winthrop Young**

Mountains ... are a single large and natural field for a good kind of human activity; and their problems only vary superficially as the season or the weather alter their surface condition ...

By a mountaineer we mean, fundamentally, one who has the *feeling* for mountains, who has the undefined and unreasonable impulse to see mountains and to try conclusions with them at any season and in every fashion; and that he has the best understanding of mountaineering to whom any and every method of approach seems equally sympathetic, provided that the motive be a genuine desire to be among hills, and that the object remains the mountain and not a personal vanity of success in one or the other technical fashion of approach.

Happily there have been, in every climbing generation, mountaineers of this larger view. Among the younger generation of mountaineers no one has earned a better hearing than Mr. Frank Smythe. Not in a startling season or two, but progressively and thoroughly he has mastered mountain climbing in all its branches. His magnificent ascents of the South Face of Mont Blanc – to mention only two among many – are the greatest climbs which have been made since the war. They are models of the correct adjustment of the measure of human strength and endurance to the calculable elements of time, chance, and detectable circumstance.

He is also a winter climber, and an expert on ski. He has not only visited other less known ranges, he has shown himself equally enterprising, and original, in designing ascents upon our own much-climbed British cliffs. Further, he has devoted an equal enthusiasm to mastering the arts by which he might reproduce for us the beauty and adventure of the mountains with his camera and his pen.

We know that he, if anyone, can give us the wider view, and not only of mountain climbing, but also of mountains as they are, and as they offer us delightful adventure.

It is in this spirit that his book has been written, and that it should be read.

* Abridged from the original Foreword. Young's failure to mention Graham Brown's contribution to the Brenva ascents in this commentary may, inadvertently (?), have added fuel to the later dispute. (See Appendix notes.)

CHAPTER ONE

A Child's Hills

THE FIRST HILLS I saw were the East Downs, the "Backbone of Kent" we used to call them. Long and high and blue they were, and on them dwelt fairies, gnomes, and goblins.

Sometimes we picnicked. That was a rare joy. From Maidstone we would set out in a "growler" laden with all the paraphernalia ladies take with them on these occasions and trot leisurely through the quiet lanes. And at last there came a long hill so steep that we had to get out and walk, which exercise always had a powerful effect on the old coachman, for we would learn on the top of the hill that he was 'very dry'.

Fortunately, the fairies had placed by the roadside a neat little ivy-clad house with a weather-beaten sign and old gnarled benches outside, and a stout jolly-faced man inside. There we could leave the old coachman with strict injunctions to the jolly-faced man as to his welfare and, carrying the paraphernalia, walk along the downs.

As soon as the picnic spot had been selected, I liked to steal away on my own to some vantage point far from the unsympathetic pryings of nurse and relatives, where I could see far across the fair "Garden of England" with its meandering Medway and many an oast house in view – surely the hall-mark of Kent.

There was much to see and wonder at. The villages, hedgerows, woods and doll-like houses. Then the threads of roads leading away into the distance. I often wondered where they led, but anyway into the beyond, a land of mystery and glorious adventure. To the childish mind nothing is impossible so long as there is a suitable channel through which to steer the frail craft of imagination.

Thus, even so early, I began to feel the magic of the hill, the freedom of distance, the joy of being able to look down on a humdrum world and see that what seemed so big and important when one was there was very small when seen from the hill.

When I was eight years old I went to Switzerland.

It is curious how the memory of certain incidents, often trivial, survives the scour of time. In those days it was one of my dreams to travel by the "Continental Express". How grand to be in a train on which were important red boards with white lettering announcing "Continental Express – London, Folkestone, Dover". One felt infinitely superior to people in mere local trains.

I remember well the fields between Tonbridge and Ashford flying by, but nothing of the voyage over the Channel to France. But I recollect vividly a fidgety dreary wait in a great railway station where the hands of a sad-looking clock overhead moved in solemn jerks of maddening persistency.

Yet another scene occurs to me. It is that of a child leaning from a railway carriage window looking towards the dawn, while mother and nurse sleep and the "Foreign Man" in the corner snores lustily. And as the child gazes there appears something that is not of the Earth as the child knows it, something wonderful, something nearer Heaven.

We were at Chateaux d'Oex in the autumn. One day in September or October we ascended a hill – the Mont Cray it is called – only a grassy hill, and an easy walk. But to me it was my first peak. From its summit I saw a vast procession of snow-capped peaks to the south; also there comes to mind a delicious drink of milk on a small flat alp where there was a grey wooden chalet, a cheery herd-boy, and a host of dappled brown cows, each with a bell.

Later there was snow – more than I had ever seen before – and happy days of luging. There was one boy with ski; I regarded him with awe, and begged to be allowed a pair, but it was not to be, and authority decreed the dangers of luging as sufficient. Once we were caught in a blizzard, and had to walk back along the road in its teeth. The driving snow stung my face like a whip, but even at that age I experienced a fierce unreasoning enjoyment in struggling against the blast.

In the spring we were at Glion. The fields were white with narcissus and the waters of Geneva the deepest blue, but the scene was too tame to an adventurously minded child; I chafed and begged for return to the high mountains.

Every afternoon there was a low thunder on the air. People said that it was avalanches from the Dent du Midi, the tall mountain at the end of the lake. Towards sundown the noise was loudest of all, like a lion growling for its prey, but then died away into the evening. I worried the visitors as to the Dent du Midi. 'Was it possible to go up it? Could I ever do so?' It looked impregnable.

One day we went over the Chateau de Chillon, a cold dreadful place full of ghosts and gloom. My mother had previously primed me with the story of its tragic inmate, and, even at that age, I could appreciate the feelings of the patriot as freed at last from the vile pillar he could look through the grated window over the lake towards his beloved mountains.

> 'I saw them and they were the same,
> They were not changed like me in frame.
> I saw their thousand years of snow
> On high. Their wide long lake below,
> And the blue Rhone in fullest flow.'

In June we went to Wengen. There for the first time I saw the High Alps, the tremendous wall of the Oberland overhanging gloomy Lauterbrunnen.

Childish fancy wove many a fantasy around the "Maiden", the "Monk", and the "Ogre". We sometimes walked up to the Wengern Alp and watched the ice avalanches crashing down from the "Maiden" over the way. Once we ventured nearer to her, but she was shy, and hid herself in mist. But out of the mist came the roar of the falling masses, somehow harmonising with the tinkle of the cow-bells from the pastures below.

I began to appreciate the scale of the Alps. It was difficult to realise that the white smear of an avalanche on the face of the "Black Monk" could induce the thunder that boomed along the valley long after its appearance.

Once or twice I saw parties of climbers sunburnt and cheery. The heroes of "Grimm" and "Andersen" were as naught compared to these.

Later we left Wengen for Berne. I was terribly bored; even the bear-pit and the famous clock aroused no enthusiasm. I looked yearningly at the white range in the sky so far away and pleaded for return, but a little later we travelled back to England.

England seemed very flat and dull; the "Backbone of Kent", once so mighty, had shrunk to a mere wrinkle; there was no snow peak to beckon one from bed in the morning. Winter came dismal and foggy, but brought with it Christmas and a cheap edition of *Scrambles Amongst the Alps*. This I dipped into, but only dipped. A year or so later I chanced on the book, then almost forgotten, and read with increased understanding. The book enthralled me, and became my most treasured possession.

On the day war broke out we travelled down to Tintagel, where we had taken a cottage. Our cottage was perched on the side of a wooded valley. Behind it was a pinewood where we would often sit. It was fragrant in the sunlight, but mysterious and sighing when the night winds came in from the Atlantic. Pines are naturally associated with hills. Seen in a town they are grim melancholy things, but I like to sit beneath them for their presence, their odour, and the sound of the wind in their branches whispers gladly of hills.

The valley beyond our cottage stretched upwards into a cup of bare heathery moors. It was strange how these moors could change.

When the sun shone they smiled and the cloud shadows raced each other along the rim of the cup, but often grey mists would descend, with rain trailing at their skirts. Then they became dark and sullen and streaked with angry torrents. On these occasions the stream below the cottage roared lustily under its burden and hastened towards the sea.

It was an ambition of mine to get to close quarters with the clouds that stalked the moor, but somehow I never did.

The high cliffs overlooking the sea were another fascination. I could spend hours looking down them to the swelling combers beneath and watching the screaming gulls' intricate flight. It was these cliffs that prompted my first rock climb – a desperate affair known only to myself a crag facing King Arthur's castle. The Providence that watches over a reckless schoolboy is generous, and I hauled myself over the top vowing that I would never do such a thing again. But when I came to think of it afterwards, I remembered only an inexplicable if fearful joy.

CHAPTER TWO

Almscliff Crag

ABOUT MIDWAY between Harrogate and Otley, half a mile north of the main road connecting these two towns, a defiant outcrop of gritstone rises from the grassy slopes on the edge of the long brown moorlands that sweep north-westwards towards Simon's Seat. From a distance it is strongly suggestive of a robbers' castle, but the curious who approach it on a Sunday in winter are more likely to form a view that they have penetrated by accident into the grounds of a lunatic asylum. Why, they argue, after a simple walk to the flat summit of this eminence should man expend his energies and risk his neck by climbing up what is obviously the wrong side of the crags? And if they are ignorant they will peer down and shout, 'Hey, lad! There's an easy way oop round t'other side!'

This crag is Almscliff, the happy hunting ground of the Yorkshire Ramblers' Club, and a training gymnasium for those who would learn something of the art and craft of rock-climbing. It was here that I learnt the finer points of rock-climbing, the gradual balance to balance, the insinuations and sinuosities of the art of back-and-knee struggles up chimneys, the curious and varied tricks for overcoming special problems when lungs gasp and finger-holds are scanty. There are easy climbs on Almscliff and difficult climbs, climbs exacting to the uttermost, and climbs bordering on the impossible, varying from a few feet high to fully fifty feet on the northernmost side of the crags. It is up this latter face that the Green Chimney runs, a route that the late C.D. Frankland alone could lead. I have watched him go up it with an ease, grace and finish that I have never seen before or since on rock in Great Britain or the Alps. It would be interesting to bring the guides of Chamonix or St Niklaus to the foot of this "problem".

Almscliff is not a solid homogeneous mass. There are several subsidiary out-crops, and lying around the foot of the crags are many boulders, large and small. Here are all manner of problems. Greatest boulder of all, and one larger than a cottage, is the "Virgin Boulder". It is difficult to climb by any route, and I have distinct recollections of an unpleasant receptive sort of rock spike over which I once dangled feebly on a rope. Then there is the "Matterhorn" boulder, with its outside route, where one, and one only, diminutive "toe scrape" prevents a rasping slither down the rough millstone grit, and the "Whisky" climb, so named, I believe, by its conquerors after a particularly cold ascent on a winter's day followed by warming libations afterwards. But undoubtedly the most classical ascent on Almscliff is known as the "Fat Man's Agony". De Quincey, had he seen it, would have found inspiration in the spectacle of respectable middle-aged gentlemen groaning and writhing within its determined limits on a Sunday afternoon.

Almscliff teaches the novice much. It accustoms him to the sensational – a forty feet drop can be just as unnerving as four hundred feet, and some people find it more so – and, above all, it teaches him what he can do with safety and what he cannot. In other words, it defines the limits of his strength, and no man is safe on rocks until he has gauged his capabilities in this respect. What Almscliff does not teach is rapid climbing up and down on easy or moderately difficult rocks, the use of the rope, and route finding.

I owe a debt of gratitude to Almscliff and to the other gritstone crags of the Pennines, and especially to Mr. E.E. Roberts, a member of The Yorkshire Ramblers' Club and the Alpine Club whose wise counsel and help served to place the feet of a reckless youngster into the path of true mountain virtue and righteousness.

It is true that much of the technique acquired on English and Welsh crags had to be unlearnt in the Alps, where the slow deliberate movements of the home-trained cragsman are of little avail, and where the watchword is "speed, speed, and yet more speed". In the Alps there is no time save on the shorter and more difficult rock peaks such as the Chamonix Aiguilles, where the standard of difficulty equals that of Britain, to spend minutes hunting for suitable belays for the rope, or of moving one at a time with the slowness necessitated by the British crags. The capacity of the Anglo-Saxon for specialisation in sport has evolved a technique of its own on the home rocks, a technique which is fascinating and complete in itself.

Sound mountaineering experience of the utmost value is to be gained among the British hills, but it is not to be gained by a party confining itself to rubber-shoe climbing on exceptionally severe courses, but rather by deliberately setting out to gain that peculiar knack of moving "as one man" in ordinary nailed boots up and down passages of moderate difficulty, and regarding the rope not as the playmate of the devil, but as a trusty if eccentric friend, whose little foibles must be learnt and humoured.

Let it not be thought for a moment that I am in any way disparaging the severes of rock-climbing. I am only endeavouring to define their relationship to mountaineering. Personally I find no greater pleasure than in spending a pleasant sunny day on the bare facets of Gimmer Crag or the Pillar Rock, and I am merely tendering a truism to those who would go well equipped in mountain lore to the Alps.

I have mentioned Frankland. 'What will Chamonix say!' wailed old Peter Taugwalder after the Matterhorn disaster of 1865, when Michel Croz, the finest guide of his generation, and three others fell to their deaths.

'He meant,' wrote Edward Whymper, 'who would believe that Croz could fall?'

So with Frankland who lost his life on the crags of Great Gable in July 1927. Almscliff can never be the same without him.

CHAPTER THREE

The British Hills

THE AFTERNOON was showery as I stood on Loughrigg Terrace. Beyond Rydal Water a grey cloud whisked a blue haze of rain over Helvellyn; around, the sun glanced on the wet rocks or discovered jewels of water in the heather; a fresh breeze brought a sweet scent of damp earth and heather.

It was my first visit to Lakeland; for one weekend I had escaped toil amid the vapours of Bradford. I was armed with an ice axe, rope, nailed boots and rucksack. True, the ice axe was but a lady's model with a weak shaft and pitiful little head, but it was my first and I was proud of it. It would have been less trouble to have carried the rope in the rucksack, but worn around the shoulder it at once elevated me to the dignity of a "climbing man". Already I had been greeted with remarks such as: 'Eh now! There goes one of they climbing lads', and 'Going to 'ang yerself, guv'nor?' My only regret was my clothes. But a day or two's climbing should bring them to the proper degree of raggedness.

Near the top of Loughrigg Terrace I fell in with a party of climbers who congratulated me on my first view of Lakeland, and gently chaffed me on my poor little ice axe. They generously insisted on my sharing their lunch, and afterwards accompanied me over the brow of the hill to Langdale.

The 1920 Easter climbing meet of the Yorkshire Ramblers' Club was held at the Old Dungeon Ghyll Hotel in Langdale. To a psychologist a British hill climbers' meet provides an interesting study, for many and varied professions and interests are united for a while in the common bond of the hills. Men normally conventional, revel for a time in the unconventional delights of odd meals and old clothes. The hall of the hotel is wreathed with ropes and redolent with oily boots and strong tobacco. During the day the silence of the heather slopes, the tarns, and the crag-girt hollows is broken with the sound of laughter, and in the evening the walls of the smoking-room resound to the roaring choruses of songs known and beloved by all.

I am not going to describe climbing details. This has been done so well and often before. Are they not all written in those admirable little red books of the Fell and Rock Climbing Club?

My first rock climb was the Little Gully on Pavey Ark – a mere novice's climb, but to me supremely enjoyable. I remember only vignettes: a thin mist that clung to the crags of Pavey Ark or poured inquiringly into the hollows, a downward glimpse between the dark walls of the gully to the waters of Stickle Tarn, and far beyond a dim brood of distant hills.

One rock climb is very like another. Each is a different combination of contortions, yet each is a separate joy. Perhaps the real charm is in the varying emotions inspired by it. There is the emotion when you are not in form – an emotion pickled in fear; and there is the emotion when you *are* in form, with nerve and muscle uniting in a perfect harmony of rhythmic movement. Then there is the emotion of adverse circumstance, when numbed fingers cannot feel the holds, the rain lashes and the wind whips cruelly. But to my mind the best emotion of all is to halt and laze away a sunny hour on the warm heather of a wide ledge secluded high up on the face of the precipice. The true philosophy of hills lies neither in physical exertions or lazy contemplation, but in a combination of both, and the genuine lover of mountains finds in them both an outlet for his strength and a clear window to his soul.

The hours are charmed away on our homeland hills; soon the evening shadows steal over the moorlands, and the great crags facing the sea blush a little before sinking to rest.

There is seldom an element of the dramatic or spectacular in a British hill sunset. There is nothing resembling the wild glare that steeps the spires of the Dolomites, or the roseate hues of the alpine glow. There is no riot of fierce tropical colourings. But rather a gradual merging of the delicate blues and purples of the earth with the tender greens, saffrons, and oranges of the heavens, while always there is the suggestion of distant sea with its burnish of silver and gold. There is no striving for effect, no blatantcy in such a sunset, yet it possesses a beauty and dignity beyond the power of the pen or brush to interpret. In the High Alps you may stand on the threshold of a hut and say "wonderful", "marvellous" or "superb", but on a fell-side you will gaze without a word, for no words can describe the loveliness and peacefulness of the day's end.

There are days of rage, too, on the British hills, days when the salt gusts hurl themselves out of the west, gusts that strive to pluck the walker from his feet and spurn him from the ridges. He is blinded and confused by volleys of torrential rain. The mist tears past him, never-ending battalions of it, shredding through the rocks, rushing over the edge of the precipice, reeling into the depths, its ranks riven, attenuated, annihilated; reforming again, closing up, caring nothing for losses, like a robot army bent on some senseless errand of destruction.

And the wind: is there any sound to compare with its sudden thunderclap on the edge of the crag, or its long-drawn snarl of fury as it hunts like some mad pack of Baskavillian hounds around the cwms or corries?

Yet the mountaineer faces the elements gladly, revelling in their fierce caress. For is not the weather a part of our hills? Without its rain how could we feel the delicious yield of the turf and moss beneath our feet? When could we halt to bury our faces in the little streams that carve a channel through the peat? How could we fling ourselves down on a couch of springy heather, or slip our bodies into the cold waters of the tarn?

The Alps are not like the British hills. They strike many chords – inspiration, hope, fear, joy – but you cannot love them as you love the British hills. They are too vast, too austere, too far removed from the ken of common man. The British hills are different; they teach a brotherly love, a fatherly respect. You get to know their moods, and though their moods may be terrible at times they do not possess the relentless severity of the High Alps.

The British hills are capricious, sometimes astounding in their temper changes, yet they are great hearted; they will not seek to exact an unjust toll.

I see that I have been led into the old and timeworn theme of comparing the British hills with the Alps. There is no justifiable comparison. It is a waste of time to endeavour to laud one at the expense of the other. One cannot compare a dwarf to a giant save only in nobility or baseness of character. It is a common trick to compare British rock-climbing to Alpine rock-climbing. The respective difficulties of Kern Knots Crack and the Mummery Crack on the Grépon are discussed with as much seriousness as the morals and manners of the vicar at a ladies' tea-fight. Yet to compare what is only an incident on a great rock climb with a complete "climb" in itself is assuredly futile.

Much of my early scrambling and rambling, was perforce solitary, for I knew no one who craved for the hills as I did. Climbing alone is to be condemned from the point of view of risk and the trouble or anxiety it may cause others, but there is no question that walks and rough scrambles over the British hills in all weathers and seasons is the finest preliminary training for mountaineering a man can have. It breeds self-reliance, it cultivates observation and quickens the perception and appreciation of beauty. Never have I experienced a greater loneliness than when wandering alone on a misty day over the fells. One is cut off from one's fellow-men in another world – a misty world full of strange imaginings like one of those vague half-formed nebula that hurtle through the infinite on some pre-destined path. Yet it is not the dreary loneliness of a man alone in civilisation, or the loneliness of desert or ocean, but a subtle loneliness, half-sad, half-wistful, kind and tolerant to those who seek it.

Youth is ever rash, but who shall censure it? If I was to shudder every time I thought of the occasions when I have quite unjustifiably risked my neck I should spend a considerable portion of my life shuddering. There was the day when I found myself at the foot of a gaunt backbone of rock. It looked good to climb; it *was* good. I learnt afterwards that it was the Eagle's Nest Ridge. And there was the occasion when I tried to descend the East Peak of Lliwedd, but perhaps the most untoward incident occurred on the West Peak of that grand rock face. I had pulled myself up on to a broad ledge to find myself a yard from a sheep that had somehow strayed there. For perhaps a second the creature gazed at me idiotically with its glassy eyes, and then, suddenly, fear supervened. It leapt for a ledge, below and to my left. The leap was well judged, but how should the wretched beast know that instead of flat turf the ledge was formed of a sloping glacis of rock treacherously masked by heather? It happened in an instant, even while I clung to my holds. The sheep's feet struck the ledge and glanced helplessly outwards from the smooth slab. With a convulsive wriggle the body slid gently off into space. Then followed a fall of perhaps fifteen feet to a smaller ledge, from which the poor brute bounded far out into space with a horrible soft sort of thud. Fascinatedly I watched it as it turned over and over in a ridiculous fashion before vanishing from sight, a mere white speck in the shadowy depths. Never before or since has anything I have seen on a mountain made a more profound impression. Gravity is the simplest, the most elemental, of Nature's forces, and the end it exacts is simple too. I date a more scrupulous care and attention to detail from the moment when the sheep's body was battered to pulp on those brutal crags of Lliwedd.

This book is non-technical; it is merely a record of days spent on the hills. Therefore, I will not try and raise the perennial argument – Are the British hills worthy of attention by the mountaineer? Some speak contemptuously of them, discussing their humble crags with scorn; others magnify their climbing merits beyond their true worth. To me they are something more than climbing problems, a holiday rambling ground or a training gymnasium for the Alps, they are quite definitely a part of that religion, that reasoned devotion to the hills without which I should not care to exist.

CHAPTER FOUR

An Ascent of the Tödi

NO SWISS VALLEY I have seen surpasses the Lintal of Canton Glarus in grandeur of scenery and boldness of mountain architecture, and it is difficult to translate to the dull medium of print the magnificence of its cliffs, the beauty of its torrents and waterfalls, the charm of its old world hamlets, and the tenderness of its green valley swards.

Linthal is but seldom visited by the tourist. The narrowness of the valley and the height of the mountains on either hand oppress the traveller with a sense of gloom and foreboding, a feeling of imprisonment and a desire to escape to more open places. Beyond the rock peaks that enclose the head of the valley rise high snow mountains, whose torn glaciers constrict savagely between precipitous walls, and finally empty their waters tumultuously through deep gorges.

Monarch of the district, the Tödi rises 11,890 feet above the sea. Curiously enough, in spite of the awe-inspiring approaches and the broods of dragons that were confidently supposed to have infested the neighbourhood in the Middle Ages, it was one of the first of the greater mountains to be climbed in the Alps, and its grand square-topped peak is for ever linked with the name of that enterprising priest, Father Placidus, à Spescha. As early as 1824, when over seventy years old, he made two attempts on the mountain, and on the last attained a point within a thousand feet of the summit, whence he sent ahead his companions, two chamois hunters, to complete the ascent.

Like Father Placidus, I have a particular affection for the Tödi, for it was the first big mountain that I ever climbed. On this account I should be loth to visit it again lest, perchance, a more sophisticated worship should dim the memories of that early conquest. A later love of mountains is founded on sympathy and understanding, but that love, though strong and enduring to the end, can never attain to the rapturous passions of youth, when we looked upon the hills, not as comrades or foes, but as brides to be won by the swing of our unskilfully wielded ice axes. We may still climb mountains but never in the same fine spirit of pilgrimage as those early days.

My friend Mr. G.N. Hewett and I had often gazed longingly from the gentle slopes of the hills around Baden and Zürich towards the High Alps. Perhaps of an evening we would stroll to some eminence, and peering over the blue veils of distance watch the sunset lights flame and die on the snows of Glarus and the Oberland like plucked rose petals scattered along the horizon's verge, picked out by Night's Dustman and consigned to the infinite. But it was a long time before we were able to escape the toils of civilisation and obey the call of the snows. However, on the afternoon of 31 May 1922 a very slow train from Zürich drew up with a last defiant jerk at Linthal railway station depositing sundry rucksacks and ice axes into the waistcoat of a stout Swiss gentleman sitting opposite us. We were too late to reach either the Grünhorn or Fridolin Huts by nightfall, but we determined to push on to the Sand Alp and sleep in one of the cattle huts that our map marked there.

The weather was perfect as we trudged happily up the valley with high hopes that this, our 'first real climb', was to be successful.

At this time of the year the streams were in full flow, and from every cliff a cataract dashed, or a dreamy ethereal veil of water hung like a fairy curtain in the sunlight.

Soon the path passes the last level meadow and writhes into the jaws of a gloomy gorge, where strive the angry waters of the Biferten Glacier, in savage contrast to their well-ordered progress through the lower pastures.

The sturdy mass of the Tödi steeped in the setting sun confronted us as we emerged from the gorge on to the Sand Alp. But there was little time to stop and admire if we were to find shelter for the night and we hurried on in the gathering gloom.

It was almost dark when a darker patch loomed ahead, and we hailed with joy a hay-hut. Thus early in the year we expected to find it unoccupied, and we were startled on entering to hear a rustle of straw in the loft above and a hoarse growl of interrogation.

We announced ourselves, and the owner of the voice presently appeared with a lantern and a friendly offer to make us as comfortable as possible for the night.

Half an hour later a good hot supper, cooked over a spirit stove, was inside two hungry youths, and we turned in to sleep in the clean fragrant hay.

With the coming of dawn we arose, ate a frugal breakfast, and stole out along the Sand Alp. We followed an excellent path for some distance, but an ingrained preference for short-cuts on my part led to a suggestion that caused us to forsake it, and finally landed us on some awkward rocks by the side of the Biferten Glacier in a rainstorm.

Finally, however, we reached the Fridolin Hut, where we found two cheery young Swiss, whose optimism chased away our pessimism even as the sun presently routed the vagrant rainstorm.

We spent a pleasant two hours sitting outside the hut while our sodden clothes dried, and later pushed uphill to the higher Grünhorn Hut, from which we hoped to ascend the Tödi on the morrow.

A number of other parties had appeared, all apparently bound for the same objective, and we laboured quickly uphill anxious to stake a claim in the little box-like hut, which was only built to hold twelve persons.

The hut is finely situated above the shattered Biferten Glacier, and we spent a pleasant afternoon basking in the sun and wandering among the séracs of the glacier.

The official complement of twelve had arrived by teatime, but as dusk was falling five more figures were seen coming up from the Fridolin Hut. As one man the inhabitants turned out and roared discouragement at the oncomers. Time and again a heartrending 'Zu Viel' was wafted down the slopes; but the advancing five were deaf to these suggestions, and somehow seventeen climbers managed to pack themselves into the miserable little hut for the night.

We had no guidebook, and hoped that the route was too simple to need one, but as we ate our supper we were regaled with stories of the horrors to be expected on the morrow. We were told, between large mouthfuls of salami, that the *pièce de la résistance* consisted of a certain all but hopeless precipice known as the Gelbwand, traversed by a ledge so narrow that it certainly seemed that the protrudance of but an eyelid must court a backward fall into the abyss. We were not the only ones to listen to the description of these perils. Another party, obviously as inexperienced as we, regarded the speaker with blanched cheeks and feebly ejaculated 'Herr Gott' at intervals. Fortunately, our small knowledge of the German language was only sufficient to enable us to understand the general trend of the conversation, and not all the horrors, which the other party was so patently absorbing.

It was a crowded night, and the 'crowd' did not entirely consist of our fellow-climbers. I can as a rule only fall off to sleep when reclining upon my right side, but the reverse seemed to apply to my immediate neighbour, and as he had partaken freely of salami, I found that a sleepless night upon my left side was preferable to an attempt at sleep on my right side.

We were the first to get up and disentangle ourselves from the packed bodies of our neighbours. Drowsily we made hot tea, ate an uncompromising sardine, and at 1.45 a.m. faced the chill breeze and the darkness of the starry night.

It was good to leave the vitiated atmosphere of the hut and tread the frozen snow, even though we had but the feeble glimmer of a candle lantern to light us down the rocks to the Biferten Glacier.

Without any difficulty we picked our way between the crevasses of the glacier and reached the foot of the gully we must ascend in order to gain the ledge that traverses the Gelbwand. The gully is steep, and the base of it was littered with the debris of ice avalanches that fall from an unstable wall of tottery séracs at the top of the couloir. With thoughts of these we kicked steps as quickly as possible in the hard icy snow, but soon the increasing angle necessitated the use of the axe.

The first hint of dawn came as we were cutting steps up the side of the couloir, and was greeted by a crash from above and a terrible roar. A great mass of ice had split away and was descending upon us! There was little we could do, and naught that we could see in the gloom. For an instant – an unpleasant instant – the roar grew louder, but in another second it had subsided to a muffled rumble that finally died away in the recesses of the mountain. The fall was evidently down a neighbouring couloir.

The dawn, at first casual, determined on a new lease of life, and the light was increasing fast as we continued on our way.

As soon as possible we crept out of the couloir in preference for the rocks on the left. These were moderately easy and broken, and we ascended quickly, looking for the passage across the Gelbwand. But what was this broad terrace that appeared to run right across the Gelbwand to the easy snow of the glacier above the icefall? Surely not the terrible ledge? It was though, and we strolled along it with much the same feelings as the tourist who discovers that the path up the mountain recommended by the guide-book as fit for 'experts only with reliable guides' is in reality a broad mule-track picked out by red paint.

From the end of this traverse a narrow snow edge between two crevasses took us on to the gentle slopes above the icefall.

Sunrise held out a hand of fair promise, and we beat down the snow for a breakfast platform. From our position there was but little view, save to the north, whence we gazed down over the brink of the icefall to where shadowed Linthal lay as yet unknown to the sun.

There is no meal like breakfast on a high snowfield; one sits down to it in a virtuous glow of work done. Gone are the early doubts and fears, the ugly doubts that assail the mountaineer in the hours before dawn, when sluggish blood courses slowly in limbs that are stiffened with sleep. These are the hours when life is at its lowest ebb, when the brain is a numbed machine of ponderous uncertain action, the stomach disordered and acutely miserable. By the time second breakfast is partaken of the early fears have faded like mist wraiths in the sun; body and brain are braced and strung for action. Defeated one may be in the future, for who knows what the day may bring forth; but if defeat is to be our lot, it is a defeat to which we can go down to, knowing that we have done all that skill and physique can do to combat it. And if victory is to be our reward, remember that it was really won before second breakfast, and that the conquest of those drear early hours was the thing that mattered.

The snow was soft, and we were not sorry to be overtaken by the two young Swiss, who obligingly went ahead to make a track up the long monotonous slopes that make the Tödi a good skiing mountain to those energetic enough to carry ski over the Gelbwand.

At 6.45 a.m. we stood on the summit, shivering in the teeth of a cold north wind, which blew gusts of stinging snow in our faces.

The Tödi is a fine view-point, and between an occasional mist we could distinguish the silvery ridges of the Pennine Alps, whilst far, far beyond, floating like a dome of alabaster in a translucent sea of purest blue, the summit of Mont Blanc gleamed in the sun.

It was our first big peak, and we tried hard to realise the romance of those unforgettable moments. But as Leslie Stephen said, 'Bodily fatigue and appreciation of natural scenery are simply incompatible'. The cold wind dominated all; the joy we should have experienced on the summit evaporated in our chattering teeth and trembling limbs, and we hurried down to a sheltered place where, without more ado, we brewed a jorum of hot punch.

In the hills it is memories that count most and it is these memories that will sustain us in our old age when the voice of the high mountains whispers back through the span of years.

We wandered gently down, meeting on the way a stout gentleman, who was making heavy going of it in the soft snow. Sad indeed is the plight of those afflicted with a surplus of adipose tissue upon a mountain side; grand and noble their bravery and determination.

We avoided the initial avalanche-swept couloir by climbing directly down the face of the Gelbwand, but our descent was rendered dangerous by a clumsy party above, unversed in mountain etiquette, who refused to remain still for a few minutes, and thus dislodged many stones that caused us some anxious moments. Curses and entreaties being alike ineffective, we hurried down at a great pace, ran across a dangerous zone that was liable to be swept by falling séracs, and at 9 a.m., when a goodly portion of the world's population were toying with their eggs and bacon, arrived back at the hut.

The day was before us and we basked in the sun on the rocks near the hut. This I was foolish enough to do without a hat, with the result that I was suddenly stricken with a species of sunstroke, the symptoms being nausea headache and at one stage incapability of movement. Thanks to the excellent doctoring of Hewett and repeated applications of snow to the forehead, the attack passed away as suddenly as it came.

Our intention was not to descend to the Lintal, but to cross the Planura pass to the Maderanertal and Amsteg, so in the afternoon we traversed round the northern lower slopes of the Tödi and descended to the Ober Sand Alp. The snow lay deep on the alp, the cow-huts were deserted, and the hay inside them damp and odorous.

Seen in the evening, with the sunset flaring on the ice-draped cliffs of the Tödi and dusk falling in the wild upland valley, bare and devoid of trees, the Ober Sand Alp is a melancholy spot. Later on in the summer, when the slowly dissolving snow patches have been absorbed in the flower-gay turf, and the grave brown cows lazily clang their bells, it becomes lively and smiling and important with cheese-making.

The night was chilly, and we were glad to step forth early next morning and set off for our pass. It is a weary grind, and the day was hot. The dregs of winter had been flung from the loving cup of summer, and it was with perspiring thankfulness that we breasted the last slopes of the pass, and gazed down the long gentle reaches of the Hufi Glacier.

Descending the glacier towards the Hufi Hut, we were forced to run the gauntlet of a hanging glacier that discharged some hundreds of tons of ice right across our tracks shortly after we passed. Finally, we left the glare of the snows for the restful green of the Maderanertal – one of the most beautiful of all Alpine valleys – where June had come to her kingdom of gay flowers and winter's tears were splashing down the cliffs in innumerable waterfalls.

A pleasant path took us down to the dusty road in the Reusstal and Amsteg, where we caught the train to Zürich.

CHAPTER FIVE

Night Adventure in the Dolomites

THE DOLOMITES, contrary to the "Dear Old Lady's" confident belief, are not a religious sect, but a group of rock peaks, situated between the main range of the Eastern Alps and the plain of Venetia. Those who have stood on the snowy summits of the Zillertal or Hohe Tauern and looked to the south must have wondered what freak of nature was responsible for the weird saw edge of pinnacles jagging the languorous heat hazes of Italy, for the Dolomites are not ordinary peaks, and conform to no ordinary standards of mountain architecture; they are extravagantly formed futuresque pinnacles and fit subjects for the phantasmagoria of a magician's dream.

Picture an English countryside – the rolling hills between Guildford and Dorking, for example. Populate its pastures with flowers – gentians, anemones and primulas – and on the gentle ridges dump a series of rock escarpments and pinnacles of extraordinary outline and terrific aspect. Paint these an indefinable yellow, and add splashes and daubs of rusty red and black. Then sit down and await the sunset to accentuate these colourings, until they flame with a lurid crimson as though they had been dipped in blood.

Curious legends, queer fancies, old romances haunt these strange peaks and are woven about their cliffs. A simple, kindly folk live at their feet to whom political intrigue is of little consequence, so long as they may attend to their daily needs, gather their hay, and garner their crops in peace.

One hot afternoon in July 1922, Mr. J.H.B. Bell of Auchtermuchty, Fife, and I sat outside the Poste Hotel in the little town of Klausen (now called Chiusa) languidly sipping the warm red wine of South Tirol. We were *en route* to the Dolomites, and had to wait some three hours for the connecting train up the Grödnertal, the last stage of our journey from Innsbruck.

Bad weather in the High Alps had sent us south in search of more settled conditions, and the relentless sun blazing from a cobalt sky and the parched vineyards seemed to justify our speculation.

Klausen is a picturesque gateway to the Dolomites, German in speech and Italian in architecture, with narrow twisting streets, disseminating varied and powerful odours. In 1921, however, Nature subjected it to a spring cleaning in the form of a cloudburst. The rain fell on the hills behind the town, and the floodwaters, rushing through a deeply cut gorge, inundated the town, but without causing much damage or loss of life. Nevertheless, it was a great event, and to the inquiring the inhabitants will proudly point to certain marks on the walls of their houses registering the height of the floodwaters. It is not tactful, however, to draw attention to the obvious competition existing between these on various houses. The old axiom that 'water finds its own level' has received but scant encouragement in Klausen.

The journey on the narrow-gauge railway from Klausen to the head of the Grödnertal is the most charming mode of introduction to the Dolomites, and the cheapest. For the sum of four lire (about tenpence) we were conveyed from sub-tropical sultriness to alpine pastures and coolness 4,000 feet above in a distance of some twenty miles.

No one hurries on this line. Each station seemed inseparable from a drink and a stretching of legs by officials and passengers – and there are many stations.

The evening was a perfect one as the train laboured up the heavy gradients. The air was fragrant with the delicious scent of new-mown hay, whilst above the throb and rattle of the primitive coaches came the hum of innumerable grass-hoppers and crickets. Presently ere the day was completely spent, a full moon arose and, sailing up from behind a pine-clad hill, swung majestically into the starry arena.

In the lower portion of the Grödnertal there is little to suggest the proximity of great rock peaks, and the valley sides sweep uniformly upwards to a gentle wooded sky-line. It was on turning a corner that we saw a vision. Far up the valley above the peaceful pine forests something vast arose that seemed creature of neither earth nor sky – unsubstantial and ghostly, a dream castle whose moonlit minarets flouted the stars.

It was long before we realised that it was our first Dolomite, the Langkofel.

We arrived at St. Christina after 10 p.m. but a good supper was forthcoming at the Hotel Poste, where we were greeted as the first visitors of the season.

The comparison between the treatment of belated travellers at a continental inn and their treatment at a British inn would be farcical were it not tragic. The man who seeks supper and bed at a British inn after 10 p.m. is greeted with suspicion, and everything possible done to make him realise that his presence is thoroughly undesirable. Cold unappetising meat, accompanied by the inevitable pickles, is placed grudgingly before him, followed by cold stewed fruit, covered with a sickly yellow shuddering glutinous substance called by courtesy "custard". Finally, he spends a night on a bed reminiscent of the stone one in the Chateau de Chillon on which criminals condemned to die spent their last hours and awakes stiff and aching in every limb.

Arrive late at a Tirolese inn and you will at once realise that you are welcome. As if by magic a hot meal is produced – a delicious omelette, steaming and savoury, cutlets of "kalbfleisch" or "Kaiserschmarren", with hot vegetables, and the wine of the country. And then when ready for bed, you are shown to a scrupulously clean room with scrubbed pine floor smelling pleasantly of resin, with wide windows to admit the hill breezes, and a comfortable spring bed to soothe the slumbers.

We awoke next morning to watch the crags of the Langkofel – no longer ghostlike but ethereally beautiful – peering through silver mists, and every sign of good weather in prospect. With high hopes of redeeming our reverses in the High Alps, we set off after breakfast to the Langkofel Hut.

It was one of those brilliant mornings of early summer: a morning of vivid colouring even in a land where colouring is of a superlative quality. The dew gleamed on the petals of the unfurling gentian; the streams chattered inconsequently, full of a riotous merriment in the dancing sunlight, whilst ever ahead were tantalising glimpses of enchanting peaks between the mists.

Gustave Doré would have found inspiration in the situation of the Langkofel Hut, with its gaunt, hemming precipices and their frieze of fantastic rock spires. It is a grim melancholy spot even in the bright light of mid-day, suggestive of some slow, never-ending symphony of sadness, solitude, and death. To the north the peaks are breached, and we looked through a gloomy portal, formed by the cliffs of the Langkofel and the Plattkofel, to the smiling pastures of the Grödnertal, far over orderly regiments of blue hills to the old snow guard of the distant Alps.

We were surprised to find that the hut had suffered severely during the war. Its interior was ruined. Doors had been torn off their hinges, shutters from their fastenings and the floors were littered with filth and rubble. But in one room we found hay enough for a bed, and with an ingenious arrangement of woodwork contrived to fit shutters to the windows.

We had arrived at the hut soon after midday and were anxious for a taste of Dolomite rock climbing. So at 3 p.m. we set off for a practice scramble on the Langkofelkarspitze. This peak, which must not be confused with its larger neighbour, the Langkofel, rises directly behind the hut, in the very centre of the great rock amphitheatre sweeping round from the Plattkofel to the Langkofel.

For the subsequent events I am alone to blame. Our sole guidebook was "Baedeker", who described the Langkofelkar as being an easy walk of half an hour to the west of the hut. So it is, but the Langkofelkar is the screefilled hollow to the west of the Langkofelkarspitze and a very different proposition from the latter. My mistake was in thinking that, having attained the summit, a walk down to the west would bring us back to the hut.

Once on the rocks, Bell went ahead at a great pace. He is always in good rock-climbing form, but personally I must confess to a certain temperamentality at the start of a difficult rock climb. Like a motor car, I require to be warmed up – a condition that requires nursing for a while. In this particular instance we had not proceeded far before I had insisted that we should don the rope.

Dolomite climbing has certain peculiarities, dangers, and fascinations all its own. In British or Alpine rock climbing the difficulty above the angle of adhesion (*i.e.*, the greatest angle up which it is possible to crawl, utilising friction only) is limited by the number, distribution, and size of the holds. In the Dolomites the difficulty of a climb usually depends upon the angle, for the rock is extraordinarily rough and the holds embarrassing in their profusion. The roughness of the rock is also responsible for a certain tenderness in the tips of the fingers after a day or two, often developing to a painful rawness like frostbite.

Owing to its brittle nature, Dolomite rock is unsound in the most dangerous sense of the word, and it is often impossible to tell whether or not a hold will break away until the whole weight is upon it, whilst masses of unstable rock, ready to come away at a touch, are common on seldom climbed routes. Perhaps the most subtle trap that I have ever encountered was on the ordinary route up the most famous of Dolomite peaks, the Fünffingerspitze, where a hold, which I had tested, as I thought, in every direction, slid away from its parent rock like a drawer. Only a fingerhold with the other hand prevented me from joining it in its flight through space.

The fascination of Dolomite climbing lies in its steepness and complexity. There is an allurement beyond words in these immense peaks that soar from the emerald pastures – in their intricacies of detail: the chimneys, cracks, ledges, ribs, ridges, and edges hidden on their apparently featureless precipices. There is a joy in the direct defiance of nature's primary law; in the confident uplifting of the body by well-trained nerve and sinew; of balancing, edging, crawling, clambering up and up the lofty yellow walls.

The rocks of the Langkofelkarspitze afford typical Dolomite climbing. In some places they are steep and exposed, in others loose and easy. Vertical pitchers alternate with ledges, chimneys, faces, and traverses, admitting of much variation, but always interesting.

The last difficulty was a sheer wall. A little ledge ran across; a steep crack led upwards from the end of the ledge – an airy place with an immense cliff below. A knife-edged ridge followed. We scrambled along it and stepped on to a tiny summit. But what were we on? A deep cleft separated us from the main mass of the Langkofelkarspitze, which rose two or three hundred feet above us. Our summit was only a subsidiary summit – the north-west peak, as we discovered afterwards. We looked at our watches and were amazed to find it 6 p.m. Time is surely bewitched on the mountains. To us an hour at most had passed. There was less than two hours of daylight left, and no time to lose if we were to get off the peak by nightfall.

We were loth to descend by the way we had come. A little insistent demon whispered 'An easy way! An easy way!' But where? Evidently to the west, where long stretches of broken rocks, set at a moderate angle, seemed to offer little more than a scramble. It was a carefully baited trap, and our eventual decision to descend them was one which neither of us has since been able to understand. To attempt the descent of an unknown rock face with less than two hours of daylight remaining is at variance with the most elementary principles of common sense and rank bad mountaineering withal. Perhaps we were subconsciously influenced by the guide book; perhaps the ease with which we had ascended had gone to our heads; perhaps … But why moralise?

I have a recollection, as we turned to descend, of glancing round at peaks warming in the glow of the westering sun, of fairy pinnacles and fretted spires rising from dusky depths. Most extraordinary peak of all is the overhanging Zahnkofel, lurching over like a monstrous tidal wave about to break on some doomed shore.

At first all went well, and keeping close together we scrambled rapidly down long stretches of easy broken rocks. But presently the angle steepened to a wall dropping far away into the depths of a gully. We now had a first sight of what lay in store, and, had we still not been possessed with a species of madness, we should have returned and spent the night on the line of ascent. The wall was impossible, and a traverse to the right necessary to avoid it. It was an exposed and difficult piece of work on nearly vertical and treacherously loose rocks.

Bell went first, climbing in his ever neat and methodical way, testing every hold, moving with a perfect precision. And as I watched, holding the rope, the last flare of sunset died around us, and a cold deathly greyness came to the world.

There is but little twilight in these latitudes; night's hosts follow hard on the chariot of the setting sun; and it was almost dark by the time we were reunited on easier ground. There we halted a few moments to decide on our plan of campaign. We were on a sloping shelf – an excellent site for a bivouac – and the wisest thing was to have stopped there, but not only had we had nothing to eat since midday, but we had foolishly brought no food with us, and a night of enforced abstinence might well leave us in unfit condition for severe rock climbing on the morrow. We could not be far now from the foot of the peak; a few hundred feet more would see us safely down. So we argued, and continued the descent.

There were two alternatives: to keep to the face, or to take to the gully that falls from the gap between the north-west and main peaks of the Langkofelkarspitze. It was almost completely dark now, but the great rift of the gully seemed darker still, whilst the sounds of a falling stream in its depths spoke eloquently of large and probably impossible pitches. The face, on the other hand, offered less restriction of movement and more alternatives. We were soon undeceived. Below the stretch of easy rocks the angle steepened again – steepened to the vertical – and finally dropped, a hopeless overhang, into the gully.

Sitting on a ledge, I slowly paid out the rope as Bell descended out of sight. Presently I heard him shout –

'I'm on a small ledge from which we can rope down into the gully – come on!'

I came on. The climbing was terribly steep and exposed, and I was glad to place the doubled rope around a small knob of rock and use it as a handhold. I soon reached the ledge, which was about thirty feet below, where I found that Bell had moved along it some ten yards to the right and was firmly secured to a large rock spike. The ledge is but a few inches broad and formed the one wrinkle in the wall.

Holding on to the rocks with one hand, I jerked the doubled rope with the other to detach it from the knob of rock above, but it refused to come. This was exceedingly serious; without it, further progress was impossible. I jerked harder, sending waves up the rope, but still it obstinately adhered to the knob. Suddenly, after a particularly vicious jerk, there was a clatter above. I heard a shout of 'Look out – stone!' from Bell. Nothing was visible in the gloom, and there was no time to do anything save to duck my head down close to the rocks so that the chunk of dolomite, instead of braining me, merely grazed the back of my head. But it was a stunning blow, and for an instant I swayed back. There were some twenty feet of slack rope between me and the knob, and had I fallen over the overhang the rope must inevitably have broken or been pulled off the knob. Neither could Bell, from his position horizontally ten yards away, have held me, and he would have been left alone in as desperate a situation as could be imagined. Our guardian angels were very near us that night. As though from a great distance, I heard Bell's voice –

'Are you all right?'

A minute or two's rest, and I could assure him that I was. Curiously enough, there were no nervous or physical effects either then or afterwards.

But the problem of the rope remained. The only solution was to climb up, loosen it, and return without its aid. Bell could not pass me on the ledge, and the job rested with me.

The moon had risen behind our peak, and the reflected light revealed the way to some extent. For the rest it was grope, and feel, and test, step by step, and from balance to balance.

I shall not easily forget that solitary climb in the dark. Perhaps it was the blow from the stone, or the innate capacity for resignation possessed by man, for I remember no excitement or fear but rather an extraordinary detached sensation: things seemed to be moving in a dream. The black gulf of the gully beneath; the pinnacles and cliffs of the Plattkofel steeped in moonlight; the ghostly sheen of the snow patches in the Langkofelkar like uneasy spirits; the utter peace and stillness of that July night gave me a feeling of unreality – I had only to let go to awake in bed. Yet through these false imaginings a little voice whispered, 'You've got to get down! You've got to get down!'

It was impossible, of course, to use the rope as a handhold; it might well be on the point of coming off the knob after the jerkings it had undergone. Without further adventure I reached the knob, released the rope, climbed down to the ledge again, and, moving along, joined Bell. As far as we could judge, the doubled 100-foot rope just reached the sloping bed of the gully, and there was a substantial rock to put it round. This time there seemed nothing to prevent the rope from being jerked off the spike from below, but nevertheless it would have been wiser, had we thought of it, to have cut a small portion and made a loop through which the rope could have been pulled with certainty.

It was an eerie business sliding down the rope into the black maw of the gully with its invisible splashing water. There was little rope to spare but it just reached, and soon we stood together in the damp streambed, feeling that the worst was over. But our luck was tempered by a devil of misfortune. We had tested the rope in every conceivable way before the descent, yet once again it resolutely refused to be jerked off the belay, and this time there was no return.

Three hundred feet of climbing remained, and for this we took off our boots and, tying them together by their laces, hung them around our necks.

A few feet lower the gully dropped in an overhang, and from far beneath came the sound of its dashing stream. The only hope was on the left, where a long and steep rib of rock slanted down. This was difficult, but climbable; but darkness has one advantage – it eliminates the sensational. Slowly and methodically we groped our way down to safety, stockinged feet feeling for holds at every step, and at long last jumped down to the snow and scree at the foot of the peak. There we halted a moment.

Our sensations are difficult to describe. We were not elated, nor yet – at the time – thankful. The detached impersonal impression dominated all. It was almost as though we had been acting as the unwilling puppets of some satanic stage manager to the audience of demons, goblins, and witches who haunt the craggy amphitheatre. How they must have jeered at our discomfiture! But now they were very silent – no doubt our 'turn' was a poor one. But listen! What was that faint murmuring in the 'whispering galleries' of the rocks? – That undercurrent of sound as though from some vast uneasy concourse, part hushed, but not silent? Nothing more than the splash of a stream from the gaunt bastions behind us. Hark! A sudden crash, a mad roar of fiendish merriment, a thousand chuckles pulse and die around the cirque. An invisible curtain falls on – Silence.

What foolish fancies are these – have you never heard a falling stone?

Down we ran to the hut.

CHAPTER SIX

Langkofel's North-East Face and other Dolomite Climbs

A DAY OR TWO later Bell and I attempted the ascent of the Fünffingerspitze. As the name suggests, this peak resembles an up-thrust hand, and is famous among the Dolomites on account of the difficulty and interest of its climbing. Our plan was to climb it by the Schmitt Kamin – a terrific chimney/crack, which rifts the South Face of the peak from top to bottom.

At any time this is a difficult peak, but the difficulty was increased considerably by patches of melting snow in the bed of the crack, which sent down a fair-sized stream of water. All went well until we reached the most formidable obstacle of all, where a boulder wedged in the chimney forces the climber into making a difficult movement on one wall; then he must grasp the wedged boulder and haul himself over it. Normally this is a difficult and strenuous pull, and with an ice-cold stream and wet and greasy rocks it proved impossible, at all events to us, and we were forced to retire defeated.

There is, however, another and easier route up the peak. It runs up a gully to the Daumenscharte, the gap between the Thumb and the Index Finger. From this the climber must scale the wall above the gap and climb round the Index Finger into the gap between it and the Middle Finger, which is the highest point.

It was a bitterly cold day when we did this. An icy wind tore through the Daumenscharte and the rocks of the wall above had a treacherous coating of ice; to this day I can remember my numbed and nerveless fingers. But we got to the top at length, after a grand scramble, and there, miraculously, the sun was warm and genial and we spent an hour basking in its rays and looking out upon a panorama of pastureland and peak.

The following year I again visited the Dolomites in the company of Dr T.H.

Somervell, who was putting in a season of energetic mountaineering between the Mount Everest expeditions of 1922 and 1924. Our longest and finest climb was up the North-East Face/North Ridge of the Langkofel [Sassolungo], a precipice some three thousand feet in height, one of the greatest in the Dolomites. We were climbing without guides, and route-finding in the Dolomites without professional help is no easy matter, as the rope- or felt-soled boots used by climbers leave no scratches on the rocks. The guideless climber is therefore dependent on his own resources, his skill in route-finding, and ability to interpret the elaborate, and at times vague, guidebook descriptions of the routes. The Langkofel's great face is especially complicated and more than one party has got into trouble on it.*

The evening before our climb was spent at the inn on the Sella Pass, elucidating a description of the route we proposed to follow. We were away early next morning, the party consisting of three, Somervell, his brother Leslie, and myself. The weather was perfect, and as we mounted the dew soaked pastures above the inn the rising sun fired the great battlements of the Langkofel so that we felt like medieval knights setting out to storm some well-nigh-impregnable fortress.

Presently we stood at the foot of the three thousand feet high fortress wall. The first problem, which was to reach a terrace running for about one-third of a mile across the face of the precipice and several hundred feet from its base, was easily solved, and we mounted quickly over easy rocks without even bothering to rope. Once on the terrace we followed it to its northernmost extremity; this was simple enough, but not without an element of danger. In one place we had to cross the mouth of a wide gully that rises almost vertically to the summit ridge of the Langkofel. This gully is a natural chute for stones, and as we hurried across there was a bullet-like whizzing and whirring in our ears. The falling stones were no larger than pebbles, but they had fallen more than a thousand feet without touching anything and were moving so fast as to be invisible.

* First climbed by Eduard Pichl and Rolf Waizer in August, 1918 – one of the great Dolomite climbs of the day.

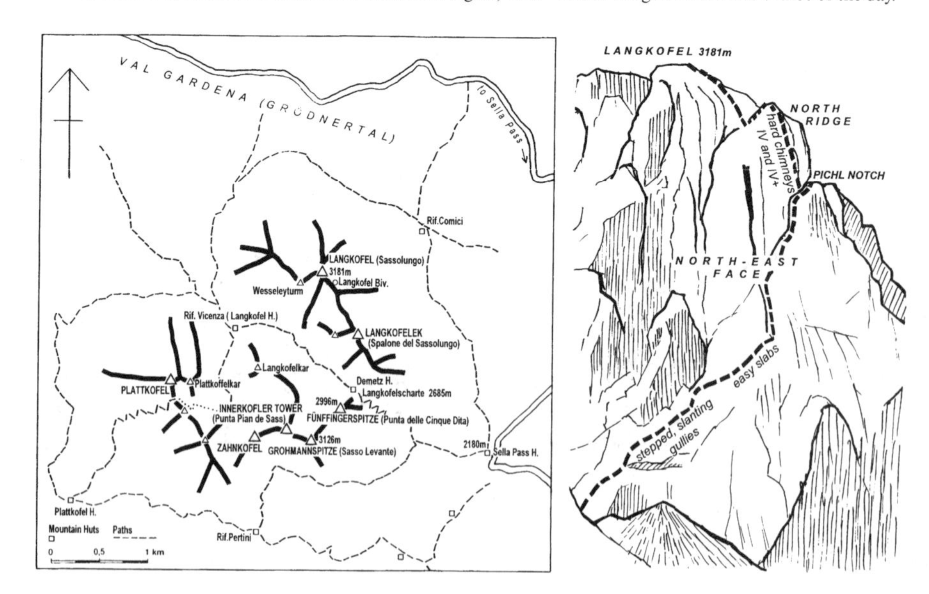

We next mounted a deeply cut gully, where the rocks were treacherously loose, to gain the crest of an ill-defined buttress. We were now bathed in sunlight and climbing was delightful. The rocks were warming up every instant and we mounted happily, moving for much of the way all together. It was much easier climbing than we had anticipated, but we knew that sooner or later we must encounter a serious difficulty. We were right. The buttress ended against an overhanging precipice; there was no avoiding it; the cliff had to be climbed. An absolutely direct route was impossible, and the only chance of success lay in a diagonal route to the left.

Dr Somervell and I both tried the route, but neither of us liked it at all. In climbing parlance the exposure was terrific, that is to say, after progressing a few feet upwards to the left, we found ourselves over a gulf as sheer as any I have ever looked down. The climber becomes accustomed to vertical cliffs in the Dolomites, but they never fail to influence him to some extent and, given two places of equal difficulty to climb, it is the one with the sheerest drop from it that proves the most difficult. So steep was the wall that strength as well as skill was needed to hold the body in position, and in the event of the fingers failing to hold, the body would have instantly toppled backwards into space.

Such places are best climbed quickly or not at all and this required both nerve and determination. It was Leslie Somervell who brought these very necessary qualities to bear on the problem. As there was little of hope for him if the rope broke, we tied an additional rope to his waist, a spare rope carried for emergency or in case we had any double roping to do. Up he went, step by step, with scarcely a pause, yet taking no risks, and testing every hold before putting his weight on it. Now he was at the worst place. His body was not even vertical – it was shoved outwards and backwards by the overhanging rocks, and his weight came on his arms. What lay above? Would it 'go'? Would he have the strength to return if it did not? All these things he had to decide for himself, there was nothing that we could do to help him.

On he went. Ah! He was past it, up and over that terrible overhang of yellow rock. The way ahead was clear. We shouted our congratulations.

For Dr Somervell and me climbing the overhang was an easy matter, for we had a stout rope above us; but even so I was thankful to be up it. It was a place where one would at least bounce once or twice in a fall of a thousand feet or so.

Thenceforward the climbing was difficult, but never so difficult as the wall. Up and up we went over ribs, ridges, and minor buttresses. What exhilarating work it was! In no sport is the combination of strength and skill, rhythm and harmony of movement, so apparent as it is in mountaineering. Every limb is exercised, every muscle attuned to the work, and every inspiration fills the lungs with clean, pure, mountain air. Gone are the cobwebs of civilisation, there is nothing dingy here, nothing but clean rocks and pure snow.

On and on, until the shattered rocks of the summit were before us. A last scramble; we were there and the Langkofel was won.

It was the finest Dolomites climb we had done, full of interest and with plenty of difficulty. It was a splendid climax to sit on the summit after a hard, exacting climb. Taut muscles were relaxed in repose; our gaze, no longer intent on the problems of the ascent, was released to wander afar, down to the valley pastures with their little villages and hamlets tiny and toy-like, the smoke of their wood fires lazily threading the still air, and over ridges, peaks, and ranges, square-topped bastions of rock, and isolated airy pinnacles, to the horizon's brim where the snows of the Eastern Alps shone like a great ice barrier in the northern sky.

For an hour we lazed in the sun, then turned to the problem of the descent. This was to be by the ordinary route, which lies on the west side of the Langkofel. Although much easier than the eastern precipice, it is nevertheless complicated, and we spent some time in studying the guidebook. This told us that we had to follow the summit ridge for some distance, then turn off from it on to the West Face by a conspicuous yellow pinnacle. The difficulty was that the Langkofel boasts innumerable yellow pinnacles, all of which seemed equally conspicuous. However, it was no use speculating, for time was getting on and we had no wish to spend the night out on the mountain, and we set off down. As far as I was concerned it was not a pleasant descent. I had been climbing in a pair of rope-soled boots, and the rough rock had torn these to pieces, so that soon after leaving the summit I was reduced to climbing in stockinged feet. Thus my progress along the ridge resembled that of the cat on the proverbial hot bricks.

After traversing the ridge for some distance we abandoned it and after passing several conspicuous yellow pinnacles entered a steep gully some eight hundred feet in length. This gully is normally filled with snow, and guidebooks recommend climbers to take an ice axe in case the snow is hard and step cutting is necessary. It was as well that we had followed this advice, for the snow was very hard and many steps had to be cut; tedious work, but we had the satisfaction of knowing that we were on the right route. It was a chilly descent for me; gloves, handkerchiefs, and puttees were requisitioned, but even so my feet soon became blue and numbed and it was a great relief to reach rocks again. It was a complicated route, and we descended a labyrinth of gullies, pinnacles, ridges, and buttresses.

The afternoon shadows had lengthened into dusk when at length we reached the base of the peak. Our difficulties were over.

Lastly, to regain the inn on the Sella Pass we had to cross the Langkofeljoch, a boulder-strewn gap between the Fünffingerspitze and the Langkofel. There was nothing left with which to protect my feet, everything had been torn to shreds on the sharp dolomite, and my soles were so sore that I doubted my ability to cross the pass. Seeing this, Howard Somervell, one of the most tirelessly energetic men I have ever known, generously insisted on going on ahead over the pass to the inn and returning with my leather climbing boots. His brother and I followed slowly, I hobbling along as best as I could. By the time we reached the pass it was completely dark, save for a continual flickering of lightning, which illumined weirdly the great pinnacles and peaks above us. We had not descended far from the pass when Somervell appeared with my boots, and, helped by a constant blaze of lightning, we picked our way down the slope and at about ten o'clock entered the inn, after a day's mountaineering of seventeen hours.

Another climb, which I did with the Somervells, was the Zahnkofel, a peak, which as the name tells, resembles a tooth. It was neither a long nor a difficult climb, though, like most Dolomite peaks, it was continuously steep, and required, as Baedeker's guide put it, 'a perfectly steady head' During the ascent we were followed by a solitary Austrian climber. The weather was uncertain, and as one climbed clouds quickly gathered. We had barely reached the summit when there was a lightning flash and a peal of thunder. As might be supposed, sharp Dolomite peaks form natural lightning conductors and are struck repeatedly during thunderstorms. We had no desire to offer ourselves as lightning conductors and immediately began the descent. We asked the young Austrian to rope on to us; it was safer as far as he was concerned, whilst, on our part, we did not want him descending behind us and knocking stones down on to our heads.

However, he politely refused our suggestion. He had climbed the mountain alone and he was going to descend it alone; so reasoned vanity and foolhardiness.

Although there were three of us we descended more quickly than he did and soon he was some way above, and, as was only to be expected, dislodged stones which whizzed close to us. There was only one place of genuine difficulty; a wall some twenty feet in height, almost vertical, and with small holds. We descended this one by one, and were soon down it. I was last on the rope and we were moving for the most part all together down the rocks beneath, when I saw the young Austrian begin to descend. It was at once evident that he was not at all happy and that he would have been far safer tied to a rope held from above. But it was too late now to do anything, and we could only hope that he would descend safely.

Presently he stuck; he seemed unable to move up or down. Then to my alarm I saw his legs and arms begin to tremble uncontrollably, a sure sign of unsteadiness on rocks. I was immediately beneath him but could do nothing to help him, whilst Dr Somervell and his brother were not close enough to see what was actually occurring. Suddenly he slipped. It was only a small slip, not more than a few inches, but he was within an ace of toppling off backwards. Next moment he had somehow contrived to reach lower holds. In climbing parlance, he scrabbled down.

I have always felt certain that a fatal accident nearly occurred on that occasion and that had he fallen the odds were that he would have swept us down with him, for we were all directly beneath him. It is in this way that mountaineering accidents occur; ignorance, selfishness, carelessness, vanity; many bad human traits are responsible for the great majority of disasters. Of course there are genuine accidents, which no human skill or power can avert, such as stones falling unexpectedly, or sudden bad weather, or the breaking away of an apparently firm handhold or foothold, but the great majority of accidents are avoidable, and occur primarily through recklessness and inexperience.

Later in the summer of 1923 I was an unwilling actor in one such accident, and as it was one of the closest shaves I have ever had, it may be of interest to narrate it here.

After climbing with the Somervells, I was joined by Mr E.E. Roberts. Without guides we accomplished a number of difficult climbs, and it was during an ascent of the Grohmannspitze that the accident befell us.

It was a misty morning when we left the inn of the Sella Pass, but presently, as we strolled up the pastures, we rose above the mist and looked over its vast sunlit expanse as though over a billowy sea, a particularly beautiful sight.

Before us rose the Grohmannspitze, a wall-sided mountain built up of massive buttresses and precipices fretted above by airy spires and pinnacles. Without difficulty we reached the col between the peak and the Fünffingerspitze. Above this the climbing begins. First of all we scrambled up easy broken rocks to a terrace. We should have followed this terrace for some distance, but we were tempted to climb directly upwards via a gully, which leads to a point high up in the summit ridge of the peak. This was a cardinal mistake, and we were entirely deceived by the appearance of the gully, which proved far steeper and more difficult than we had supposed. Nevertheless, all went well and we mounted slowly, if with considerable difficulty, until we came to a point where the gully narrowed and ended in a wall some hundred and fifty feet in height. It was a fearsome place; the gully was strangled to a mere thread-like overhanging crack, black and slimy from seeping water. There was no climbing that crack, nor was there any chance of climbing the overhanging wall to the right of it. There was only one hope; it appeared just possible to scale the wall to the left of the impasse. This was vertical, or nearly so, but the rocks were more broken and seemed to offer sufficient holds to make an ascent at least justifiable. Once we were up we had only to follow a ridge to the top of the Grohmannspitze.*

Fortunately, at the foot of the wall there was a wide ledge, and here Roberts secured himself whilst I went on to tackle the former. Immediately above the ledge the rocks bulged out in an overhang. It was impossible to scale this direct, but by climbing up to the right was able to traverse above it on to rocks which seemed to offer the line of least resistance to the ridge above. Something made me very suspicious of the overhanging bulge and as far as possible I avoided it, for Roberts was directly beneath and the mass of rock must have weighed a ton or more. Having successfully negotiated this doubtful bit I was able to climb directly upwards. It was an excessively steep and exposed climb, yet it is in such places, where the climber is dependent entirely on his own resources, where he knows that a slip simply must not happen, that the supreme joy of mountaineering is experienced, the joy of well-trained muscles working in unison, the joy derived from a perfect harmony between mind and matter, which is the essence of enjoyment and efficiency in all great sports. Step by step the climber progresses, calmly, confidently testing, each hold, measuring his force against the force of the mountain, his skill against the inert matter opposing him, his every movement measured against the relentless pull of gravity. He is very lonely; his is the battle, and his alone; no mechanical contrivance can help him; success does not depend upon the pulling of a lever or the turning of a wheel; safety, his life, is in his own hands; the pull on a single finger may differentiate safety from disaster; he is face to face with grand and elemental things. This is no mere recklessness, no foolhardy hazarding of life against death for some ulterior motive; it is life, and all the adventure that life can offer is momentarily concentrated for him in the slow, deliberate upward balance on the face of the precipice.

The last twenty feet were the most difficult; here the holds were very small, mere nicks and protuberances just sufficient for fingers and toes, and no more. Then my upward exploring hands grasped the rough crest of the ridge above, and I could haul lustily. The next moment I sprawled, panting, on the crest of the ridge in the hot sun. Beneath were the dark jaws of the gully from which I had emerged, and out of them, hollow, echoing, and remote, came Roberts's voice congratulating me on having climbed the wall. It was a good moment.

* Smythe and Roberts appear to have been following the Dimai / Eötvös / Summermatter route.

It was a steep sheep-backed ridge on which I stood, and the rocks were unusually smooth. There was no ledge on which to ensconce myself firmly, and no belay for the rope that I could discover. Yet, failing a ledge, a belay was essential, as I could not possibly hold my companion in the event of a slip, standing as I was on small, sloping holds. Roberts had not yet divined this difficulty, for I heard him shout: 'Shall I come up?' I replied 'No, wait,' and continued my search for a belay. It was some minutes before I found it and it was not a good one, merely a small flake rock large enough to accommodate the rope and no more.

It was in belaying the rope that I made the mistake that very nearly cost me my life. Roberts and I were tied to either end of a hundred foot length of rope. In ascending to the belay I had run out about eighty feet of this, leaving some twenty feet to spare. What I ought to have done was to have belayed myself as closely as possible to the rock, and then, thus secured, taken in Roberts's rope as he ascended. What I actually did was to take in the slack of the rope until I could feel Roberts and then belay it. This meant that between my waist and the belay there were twenty feet of slack rope.

In cases where the leader is not firmly placed it is best for him to take in the rope of the second man directly round the rock. In the present instance the belay was so small that there was no room for two ropes, and I deemed it advisable to do as I have then brace myself as firmly as possible on the slabby ridge and take in Roberts's rope over my shoulder. I did not for an instant anticipate a slip or, indeed, an accident of any kind, for no steadier mountaineer ever trod a mountainside than my companion. Having done this I shouted down to him: 'Come on' He did so, and an instant later I was taking in the rope foot by foot as he progressed. All seemed to be going well; the rope was steadily coming in and Roberts was obviously climbing with his usual care and precision. I remember reflecting that we were as good as on the summit of the Grohmannspitze, that we were having a grand climb and that the weather was perfect. I glanced also across the great lake of mist that stretched in all directions obscuring all but the higher peaks, which stood up out above it like fairy islands. There was not a breath of wind and the sun blazed down from a sky of cobalt blue.

And then, of a sudden, it happened. From the depths of the gully at my feet there was a startled shout off 'Look out!' followed the next instant by a terrific crash of falling rocks. An instant before, the rope had been coming in calmly and quietly as I drew it round my shoulder. Now, like a sleeping snake stirred by a stick, it sprang into horrible activity. I saw it whip across the rocks to the right, and realised in a flash that Roberts was not directly beneath me, and that the strain would come sideways as well as downwards. The next instant it tore through my hands, and there came an irresistible tug, which I was wholly unable to withstand. I was dragged sideways and downwards from my holds, and in another moment was sliding down the slabs of the ridge, at first on my side and then on my back. My first thought was the rope had come off the belay, for I expected to be stopped at once. Desperately I drove my heels, elbows, forearms, and the palms of my hands against the rocks, endeavouring to stop myself For ten or twelve feet I slid down the ridge, then shot off it sideways over the edge of the precipice.

It has been said that death by falling on a mountain is a painless end. This is true. The initial shock was terrible and it seemed to tauten every nerve and muscle of my body to an unimagined degree of tenseness. But in another instant this passed and was superseded by an extraordinary feeling of detachment. I bumped against the rocks, but I did not feel the bumps. I seemed, as I fell, to be standing farther and farther away from myself watching, as it were, my own body falling with little more interest in it than I should have felt for a cast-off suit of clothes; and it seemed that when that body had been smashed to pulp I should still be there, a disinterested witness of some purely mechanical process. If this is death, then it is not at all to be feared, and I can only say that the experience went far to convince me as to the reality of survival beyond the grave.

I found myself hanging on the rope a few feet below the crest of the ridge. I must have fallen the last few feet through the air without touching anything, yet I remember no jerk, though the strain on my waist was terrific, as bruising subsequently testified. I had fallen about twenty feet and the rope, a new one, had held.

I turned myself round, snatched at holds, and clawed my way back to the ridge. There I experienced what I had not felt during the fall – sheer naked fear!

As I regained the ridge I heard a shout from Roberts: 'I'm all right.' Thank God, he was safe and sound. Just as he was stepping across the overhang it had collapsed beneath him, and not having good handholds he had gone with it, fortunately alighting on the ledge uninjured while a ton of rock crashed down the mountainside with a roar that was heard at the inn on the Sella Pass.

After this I took in Roberts's rope directly round the belay, a method which I still believe is best in Dolomite climbing, unless the leader has a really secure ledge and is himself well tied to a belay. Presently Roberts joined me and I was able to inspect my personal damages; these were not serious, and; except for skinned elbows, and bruises to another and more prominent portion of the anatomy, I was unhurt. I did not then tell Roberts exactly what had happened; I was too ashamed of myself for my carelessness over the rope might have brought disaster to us both. At the time I had no thought of proceeding farther, but Roberts was of a different mind. 'We are going to get to the top of this —— mountain,' he said, and the epithet he applied to the Grohmannspitze was not at all complimentary to that peak. In this determination he was perfectly right. In the same way, the pilot of an aeroplane who is uninjured does well to go up again immediately, as by so doing his nervous reaction is minimised.

After a few minutes we continued with the climb. The remaining rocks were comparatively easy, and we were soon on the summit of the Grohmannspitze.

A considerable portion of skin had been removed from my anatomy, but I forgot this as we sat in the sun. The mist sea had dissolved and we gazed from our lofty vantage point on the tangled ranges of Dolomite peaks and bright green meadows thousands of feet beneath. There was not a cloud, not a breath of wind, and the day was perfect. Before descending we wrote our names in the summit book, which we found in a zinc case embedded in a cairn of stones. Lastly, with the solemnity due to the occasion, we added a stone to the cairn, thereby increasing the stature of the Grohmannspitze a few inches.

The descent was uneventful. There had been enough excitement for one day. When we reached the point at which the accident had occurred we discovered a much easier route, obviously the route by which the mountain is normally ascended. We had made a new route, but it is not one that I can recommend.

An hour or two later we were at the foot of the rocks, and all difficulty was over. Lastly came a stroll down the edelweiss-starred pastures to the inn on the Sella Pass. Subsequently we did various other Dolomite climbs, and on more than one of them I was reminded forcibly of the hardness of the rocks on the Grohmannspitze when I came to dispose myself on that portion of the body on which it was intended that man should rest.

To conclude, I can only say that safe and successful climbing in the Dolomites depends primarily on route-finding ability, coupled with never-failing care in the treatment of treacherous rocks. The fact that mountaineers often reach a ripe old age is proof of the healthfulness of climbing, not of its safety. It is not possible to reach a ripe old age when you are dead, and those who climb in the Dolomites would do well to remember this fact.

CHAPTER SEVEN

Five Days Alone in the Arlberg

ONE PERFECT MAY MORNING shortly before Whitsuntide 1923 I set off alone from the little village of Anton am Arlberg for my last ski expedition of that season.

I was heavily laden. My rucksack bulged with five days' food and climbing equipment, including a volume of "Pickwick Papers" to wile away dull hours at the Darmstädter Hut, which I intended to make my centre. In addition, ski had to be carried, for the snow line had crept two thousand feet out of the valley.

I crossed the boisterous torrent of the Rosanna, and strolled up the dew-spangled pastures. Below, the smoke from the clustered chalets rose lazily in the golden air; around, the goats released from winter imprisonment were frisking joyfully in their new-found freedom, a thousand little bells ringing merrily. Shy gentians peeped forth from the moist turf to kiss the sun. Yet there was a hint of frost in the shadows, and the peaks rose white in the deep blue sky. Everywhere water ran; noble torrents in the valleys; dashing streams down the hillsides; and an infinity of new-born brooks sparkling in the sun. The air was fragrant with damp earth and mosses; a morning fit for immortals. My load became lighter, my rucksack seemed not full of bloated devils, but rather of noble thoughts striving to elevate me to the mountain's brow; my ski were as fairy wings, so lightly they rested on my shoulder.

The way to the Darmstädter Hut lies up the Madauntal, a valley reminiscent of a Highland glen. The stream there is not a sorry thing full of glacier mud, but crystal clear and pure in its flashing surges and quiet rock-hemmed pools.

I halted for lunch a little below the snow-line and lazed in the sun. Spring lay behind; the lower pastures had yielded their load to the sun and were now dotted with sheep and goats. Around was 'No Man's Land' littered with the dirty debris of the avalanche barrage. Beyond, where the high peaks were smothered in snow, winter held despotic sway.

Later in the afternoon as I pushed on up the valley snow mists gathered, and I reached the hut in company with a desultory snowstorm. I found it shuttered and forlorn save for mice, which scurried before me as I walked through the *gastzimmer* to the kitchen. Hill mice are more friendly, or is it more curious, than valley mice, and I was conscious of undergoing a critical inspection from many pairs of sharp eyes. Apparently reassured, their owners stole out to gather what they might.

Snow showers ushered the day out, but ere night had completely fallen the mists parted disclosing a cirque of peaks clear cut in a cold green sky.

Supper in the small cosy kitchen was a jolly affair. There was plenty of fuel, and a cheery fire bid defiance to the cold without. If I remained still for a moment the mice crept out, and gathered expectantly around for crumbs. Without them the hut would have been almost lonely.

Wind moaned fretfully during the night, and the day broke in snow squalls. By 9 a.m. the weather had quieted, and I left the hut on foot for the Faselfadspitze. The best way lies along the South Ridge, which falls to a small col separating the peak from a minor summit. I reached the col without difficulty from the east, and found myself confronted by some formidable rock pinnacles. These I skirted on the west. An icy little chimney, where the axe was called into play, led back to the crest of the ridge.

To a solitary climber this ridge is ideal. There is no portion giving rise to hesitation, but the ascent is not dull. For my part I find no real pleasure in climbing alone a mountain where I have no sense of security. The factor of safety becomes all too small and fear supervenes. Fear has no place on a mountain; interpreted, it is only another term for danger. Solitary mountaineering within its proper limits is the most glorious of all forms of climbing. The day is yours to do what you like with, the halts are yours to linger over, and the hills are yours to lie and dream upon.

Snow greeted me on the summit, but blew away, revealing grey cloud drifts piled up to heaven, and a blaze of snow showers beneath them. Here and there a vagrant shaft of sunlight challenged, and falling upon a hill brought forth a little pool of colour where it struck; but for the most part the peaks gloomed in sullen shawls of mist. A storm was brewing.

I descended by the ridge to within 200 feet of the col, and by way of variation turned directly down the south face of the peak. The rocks were firm, steep, and dry, and afforded an amusing scramble. Near their foot the holds were scarce, and my efforts to descend resembled the alighting from a continental train of an infirm invalid.

The day was young; I was loth to return to the hut; so I scrambled up the subsidiary peak from the col, and with no difficulty ahead slept in a sheltered place below the summit.

A cold wind charged with damp snowflakes awoke me, and I returned to the hut.

The day waned dismally in sleet and snow. Wind arose later, and a furious blizzard raged through the halls of night.

It is pleasurable at these times to lie cosily in one's blankets, with naught but the walls of the hut between one and the wild fury of the elements outside. It is good to hear the demoniacal screaming of the storm, the roar of the gusts, and the lash of the snow about the stout defences. On these lonely occasions far above the civilised world, strange fancies are liable to assail one. The yell of the *tourmente* becomes the yell of the furies that ride on the wings of the wind, the boom of a gust and the shrilling of its eddies, the voice of the Mountain King and his goblin chorus. Sometimes after a particularly savage assault the Storm Fiend withdraws his forces for a while, and there ensues a strange calm, broken perhaps by a solitary moan as of some lost soul in torment. It is easy to understand the superstitions of the simple peasant folk. The spirits of the damned would seem to be abroad in the hours of the storm.

I awoke to a cold calm dawn filtering through snow-powdered windows. Flour-like snow, a foot deep, lay outside. Now was the time for my ski to justify their existence. Strapping them on I set off for the Kuchen Joch.

Sunrise colourful and ominous, came as I traversed the moraine of the Kuchen Glacier. There is a small lake here. In summer its deep green waters mirror the beauties of the hills around. In winter it forms a snow floor so delicately smooth, it could only be the "Palais de Dance" for the whispering feet of the elusive snow maidens who dwell in the ice caves of the glacier.

An hour took me over the gentle bosom of the uncrevassed glacier to the pass. A bitter wind blew through the gap, raising clouds of stinging snow. Leaving my ski, I turned to the right, and started an uninteresting trudge up the Scheibler. Normally the ascent is a simple walk of twenty minutes or so. Now, the incoherent snow lay over everything and the going was heavy. The wind hustled across the ridge, whirling little spiculæ of snow that shone like fairy spear-points in the sun. As is often the case, however, the summit was comparatively windless, and finding a sheltered spot for the spirit cooker I sat down prepared to enjoy the view for an hour or two.

Opposite, on the other side of the Ferwall valley, rises the Pateriol, a mountain whose massive buttresses support, like the Wetterhorn, a delicately soaring summit. Lower than the Kuchen or Küchel Spitzen, it is yet the undisputed Monarch of Ferwall. In the east stood the cheeky twin summits of the Seekopf and the higher but unimpressive Saumspitze, with its glacier robe curving deliberately down to the north. Yet it was not to these that the eye turned, but rather to the west, where the ranges stretched in jumbled waves to beat an ineffective sea on the bastions of the Oberland. Over them I strained my eye for a sight of my first love, the Tödi; and as I looked the sun, released from a cloud, illumined for a moment a beautiful mountain, whose pure snow peak shone through the trembling distance like the white wing of an albatross over the dark blue waters of the Southern Ocean.

An hour later I became sensible of a change in the weather. The distant peaks had vanished. A grey pall was spreading over the sky, a mere filmy cobweb at first, approaching from no definite direction, but coming as mysteriously to the World as "Challenger's Poison Belt".

Mountaineers are accustomed to bad weather in the Alps, and would have the weather fine throughout the season, but what is the result? 1923 was a dry summer. As compared with their usual selves the great peaks were ugly. Stark they stood from their dirt-riddled glaciers, black glared the stone-scarred ice slopes; grimy and treacherous were the remnants of snow clinging to the ice. Rock normally protected stuck through the snow like the ribs of the ill-fated ships revealed at low tide on the Goodwins. At such times even the Matterhorn must experience a vague uneasiness as he feels his pedestal of glaciers dissolving beneath him. Like a Southern belle the peaks age prematurely under a sun that seems to have sucked the heat of the Levant to expel upon their attenuated snows. Their cheeks are furrowed by a stony sweat, and their glacier torrents boil with rage. How terrible the Alps would become were they to be exposed for a year to the fury of the North African sun. How they would crave that cloud 'no bigger than a man's hand'. Let those who would have every season a perfect season climb the peaks that rise from the desert. There they will realise the greater meaning of running water, grass white with dew in the morning. a snow-slope framed between dark pines. The hills of the desert are hills of death; indestructible for there is naught to destroy them, unless it be the slow grind of the sandstorms on their weary facets; lifeless, soulless altars to the relentless Sun God, who waxes to decline without let or hindrance through æons of time.

In the winter the great peaks renew the bloom of youth, and I, from my lonely post in Nature's beauty parlour, was about to witness one of her lavish and periodical applications in the form of a blizzard.

The wind died to a whisper, and from a whisper to a dead calm. The sun from a bright lively orb faded to a dull thing, struggling feebly against its inevitable fate; and was slowly swallowed in the greyness that gathered above as yet contemptuous of the Earth. Light and shadow were lost, and the peaks became drab and flat like the inferior daub of an art student. Dark against the livid snows stood the forest ranks, and darker the fangs of the rocky ridges. The ranges of Arlberg disappeared, blotted out one by one in the leaden void. One minute they were there, the next they were not; engulfed in the rising tide of the storm.

In the valley beneath a puff of smoky mist came suddenly into being. Slowly it stole up the hillside, stretching ghost-like fingers among the pines. Lonely at first, it lurked far below, but soon, becoming bolder, it strode upwards, growing amazingly to a seething cloud that stalked majestically over the forest's brow and came charging up the mountain-side. A dimness came to the Pateriol over the way, and as I watched deepened to a slate-coloured murk into which the peak faded, reluctantly away. The dimness approached. A snowflake from nowhere came sailing down, twisting slowly. Another followed, and another, and finally countless millions. A gust of wind sobbed over the summit shepherding the snowflakes before it in a frightened hurrying multitude, as a handful. of policemen by *force majeure* rout an undisciplined mob.

It was time to be moving if I was to enjoy my run back. I had barely started when the van of the storm struck with a roar. For a few moments I could barely advance against its blast. The snow from harmless gently falling flakes became icy spits, stinging my cheeks and sheeting my clothes in a clammy armour. The ridge from a broad easy affair seemed to narrow abruptly, and I trod it more carefully than the ridge of many a first-class peak. True there was neither danger nor difficulty in return, but what is the position of a party on difficult ground? The paralysing force of these spring storms is hard to exaggerate, but at least they usually give warning of their approach.

Buffetted and beaten by the blizzard I plunged down through the soft snow to the Kuchen Joch. A ferocious wind snarled through the pass, sending the snow writhing before it, and booming along the cliffs of the Kuchen Spitze above. Strapping on my ski, I was glad to turn my back on it and set off for the hut. In a second or so I was on the lee of the col in a region of calm. My climbing track was distinct and I could safely follow it in one glorious swoop down the glacier.

There is no sensation like a straight run on ski down an unbroken stretch of glacier. It is the world that moves. Distant objects grow larger, slip past, and disappear; the parted snow hisses behind the ski; the wind croons in the ears. The humped moraine rushes to meet one. Swish——! And the ski swing round, raising a cloud of sparkling snow-dust. Within a few minutes – seconds it seemed – I was mechanically knocking the snow from my ski and boots on the threshold of the hut.

The bad weather lasted all day and well into the night. I sat up late reading of Mr. Jingle's artifices, until at last I began to speculate drowsily as to that gentleman's proficiency on ski. It seemed that he was arguing fiercely with Mr. Snodgrass on the advantages of the stem Christiania over the telemark, and I caught fragments such as, 'Magnificent feeling – always use it – sharp swing – no bone breaker – good turn – very!' While Mr. Pickwick, clad in his gaiters, smiled benignantly over an ice axe in the background …

I awoke later to a guttering candle and the moan of the storm without, and forthwith tumbled sleepily into my blankets. Did I take rum punch with me on that occasion? I wonder.

New snow lay piled on the window ledges and mist enwrapped the hut when I awoke the next morning. It was not until mid-day that the curtain was raised and the company of peaks stood revealed in their raiments of snow and ice. Yet there was little that could escape the May sun, and all the afternoon the growl of avalanches echoed fearfully round the cirque. Even the glittering armour of the Kuchen Spitze was ruthlessly stripped from his cliffs and hurled in thundering ruin on the glacier beneath.

With nightfall the cannonade dropped, and frosty peace came to the darkening hills.

The weather was perfect when I strolled outside after supper. No wind stirred, frost crackled and the dark forms of the peaks rode beneath a canopy of flashing stars.

There is a measure of sympathy to be found among the hills at night. In the day they may be proud, boastful, challenging – even cruel sometimes. But in the evening their harsher features relent. The terrors of height and depth, exemplified by the precipice or the gaping maw of the crevasse are smoothed away. When night enfolds the hills they become friendly. The stars above them speak of immeasurable space, cold and infinitely desolate; the hills by comparison are neighbourly. Towns are often more lonely than hills.

I was up betimes next morning, leaving the hut in the first hint of approaching dawn, my ski edging hard frozen snowcrust. Crossing the snout of the Kuchen Glacier, I climbed upwards to the little glacier that falls from the East Ridge of the Küchel Spitze, my objective. A mountain of 10,315 feet, it is second in height to the Kuchen Spitze and rises in a bold and graceful rock pyramid from the incipient glaciers at its feet.

My only guide was "Baedeker", who affirmed in his broad way that the peak was 'For experts only, with perfectly steady heads'. I have often wondered of what type the "Baedeker" 'expert' really is. Is he one of the three stout gentlemen I saw the previous summer essaying a broad snow ridge on their ample waistcoats? Or is he a beavered gentleman, usually a Herr Doktor, Direktor, or Professor with a capacity for beer that taxes sadly the most comprehensively "bewirtschaftet" hut, and an undying passion for "palatschinken"?[1]

The sole information vouchsafed by "Baedeker" as to the route was that the peak was best ascended from the Raute Jöchl, one of the gaps separating the Küchel Spitze from the Seekopf.

I left my ski at the foot of a short steep slope separating the pass from the glacier and proceeded on foot, floundering through soft deep snow.

Golden dawn met me on the pass. Below, an early morning crawl of cloud concealed the valleys. No breeze stirred to shatter the delicate frost flowers on the rocks.

A nearly horizontal ridge separated me from the final peak. I looked at the latter not very hopefully it was still heavily iced.

The initial ridge gave me a foretaste of what to expect, but the first two or three hundred feet of the final peak were easy. Then the angle steepened, and I found myself cut off from the summit ridge by a wall to which clung ugly ice, glittering evilly in the sun. To avoid it I attempted a traverse to the left by a ledge.

At first wide, the ledge narrowed and narrowed, finally petering out against a precipice. But the ledge seemed intended for better things than mere muscular effort.

On it the sun shone, and it was dry and warm. No breath of wind whispered around the gaunt crags; no cloud shadow stole across to chill. Above the sun-kissed face rose in an overhang, whence descended the melted snow in a silver rain. Below, the grey rocks fell away in a fearful slice to a gully from depths of which came a constant hissing, like a brood of serpents as the slush from above slid to destruction.

Down I sat, feet dangling, back to the cliff. Tobacco leapt from one pocket, pipe from another, united in perfect harmony at the whisper of a match. A conciliatory curl of blue smoke lofted gently up the precipice in peace-offering to the Mountain King; eyes closed in luxurious enjoyment … opened with a terrified start, fingers clutched convulsively. It was no place to doze. I returned to the foot of the wall. There was no avoiding it. But now the sun was breathing fiercely. Already in places the thick ice shivered and broke away at the stroke of the axe; in others it adhered tenaciously.

The wall was not more than thirty feet high. Where the ice could be hacked away in sheets the holds revealed were capacious, but where it adhered careful balance was required in the shallow steps. I found myself timing my blows to the rhythm of an absurd music-hall ditty – Tum ti ti, tum ti ti, tum tum Tum – and a piece of ice tinkled down. It was easier than it looked, and I was soon on the ridge above.

The ridge was narrow and the snow bevelled to a blade so fragile it seemed a shame to smash it down with the axe.

[1] Large jam omelettes – a Tirolese delicacy.

A rocky gap separated the ridge from the final rock tower on the mountain. The rocks were free of snow, and I scrambled happily over the warm rough slabs to the summit. Off came my rucksack, out came the spirit-cooker, and in a minute a lump of snow was slithering uneasily in the saucepan. I have occasionally encountered misguided people who profess to despise a spirit-cooker. Let it be said at once, and almost sadly, for I am not a teetotaler, that champagne itself is not the equal of a cup of hot tea on a hill top.

It was not yet mid-day and the weather was ideal. The longer I delayed the greater the work of the sun, and the easier the return. But now it was not necessary to return by the same way. Falling from the gap just below the summit tower was the most obvious of snow couloirs. True the angle was steep, and the ripple of a choked crevasse defended its junction with the glacier; but its sunless position favoured descent late in the afternoon. As for the crevasse, a glissade would shoot it. The sole difficulty was at the top, where the snow had slipped away exposing smooth slabs; but even a slither down these could hardly be attended by anything worse than an undignified descent to the glacier, unless one or two rock teeth projecting lower down relieved one of one's trousers.

Comforted by these reflections I settled down to a lazy time. Under the influence of an excellent lunch the world, and everything in it, seemed raised to a plane of almost celestial dimension. I forgot to revile "Baedeker". After all, why should I?, He had provided an amusing climb. The icy wall had served as just that necessary *hors d'oeuvres* that now made the summit so desirable. What did it matter if "Baedeker", in his sweeping way, had airily neglected to mention the easy couloir that I proposed to descend?

I cannot describe the view in any detail. Like a general surveying an army I was conscious of no particular unit. Not that it was dull, but it contained some subtle quality lulling the observer to a passive contemplation of the whole. The only tangible memory I carried away with me was that of a little round cloud many miles away resting importantly in the hollow of a peak. For the rest I have a hazy recollection of many mountains shining in the sunlight; of silver slope and delicate ridge vanguard of pine forest crawling reluctantly from dim shadowy depths; hill upon hill to the horizon's brim.

Dozing and dreaming the hours sped by. The westering sun flung ever-deepening shadows; the valley blues changed to purple. It was time to descend.

The couloir went well. Once past the teeth of trouser destructive tendency I glissaded merrily, shooting the choked crevasse with ease, and so reached the glacier.

Half an hour's wade through soft snow brought me to my ski. With them on I became a being of delightful locomotion, and quickly glided back to my hermitage.

It was my last day. Provisions were running low, luxuries had vanished. All but the bare means of another day's subsistence was gone.

That evening I stood long outside the hut watching the last light fading from peaks and sky, until the peaks were cold and grey, and all that was left was one bright slash of cirrus cloud hung like a fairy banner above the World. Finally that faded too, and was lost amid the stars.

The weather was good when I left the hut next morning. There was no occasion to hurry, and I prolonged the luncheon rest late into the afternoon before pottering hotel-wards down the valley.

Evening was falling and lights, of the village shining across the meadows as I strolled down the last slopes, the old patched rucksack swinging light, and my good ski groaning at the thought of the idleness that was to be theirs.

CHAPTER EIGHT

A Storm on the "Peak of Terror"

TO BE CAUGHT in a thunderstorm on a high mountain is an impressive and terrifying experience, for this is a mood of nature we know little about. Wind, hail, rain and snow we understand both in origin and effect; these we can contend with, though the fight is sometimes a stern one; but the mountaineer in the focus of a thunderstorm on an alpine peak experiences a feeling of complete helplessness and a very near danger.

Fortunately the death roll directly attributable to lightning in the Alps is a comparatively small one. The worst disaster on record was that in which a party of four were killed on the Wetterhorn in the Bernese Oberland. Thus did the "Peak of Storms" live up to its reputation. The Oberland peaks have always struck me as possessing a singularly apt nomenclature. What more fitting than the "Maiden", the "Monk", or the "Ogre", whose battlements frown down on the villages of Lauterbrunnen and Grindelwald?

The last great Oberland peak to be climbed was the Schreckhorn, or "Peak of Terror", whose summit rises 13,385 feet above the sea. It was in 1861 that Sir Leslie Stephen, 'fleetest of foot of the alpine brotherhood', made the first ascent, accompanied by three Grindelwald guides. He described his experiences in that charming mountaineering classic, *The Playground of Europe*.

The Schreckhorn is now frequently climbed, but it has never become a popular tourist ascent like the Matterhorn or the Jungfrau; one reason for this being its isolation in the heart of the snowy wastes forming the core of the Oberland; yet there are few finer peaks and none offering a more worthy or interesting ascent in this district.

The mountain has always exercised a fascination for me, and has twice suffered me to stand on her sharp rock summit. On both occasions the weather conditions were good, and on the first a lighted match scarcely flickered, so calm was the day.

The weather in 1925 was uncertain. Storm succeeded storm, and my climbing companion, Mr. J.H.B. Bell, and I were able to make but few ascents. For some days we made our headquarters at the Strahlegg Hut of the Swiss Alpine Club, which stands by the Eismeer Glacier some 5,000 feet above Grindelwald, and for the first three days of our stay were subjected to every variety of bad weather. On 27 July, however, we were able to make a traverse of the Schreckhorn and its neighbouring peak, the Lauteraarhorn. This expedition, which is among the longest in the Alps, took nineteen hours, and the following day was, of necessity, an 'off day'. The weather was now glorious, and we basked in the sun, admiring the cirque of beautiful snow peaks and glaciers in which the Strahlegg hut is situated.

The sunset that evening was one of the finest it has been my privilege to witness in the High Alps. Bars of cirrus cloud lay athwart the heavens glowing with indescribable colours, and long after the sun had disappeared behind the ridges of the Eiger their light was reflected downwards, until the peaks were lit by the weirdest afterglow that we had ever seen. Long we stood outside the hut watching the aerial pageantry as the last lights died from the peaks and the cloudy banners melted mysteriously into the stars.

Who would suspect evil to lurk in such a sunset? We went to bed feeling assured of fine weather on the morrow.

We arose at 3 a.m. next morning intending to attempt a previously planned route up the peak of the Klein Fiescherhorn, but Bell discovered that one of his ankles had mysteriously swollen up to nearly twice its normal size during the night. Try as he would, he found it impossible to don his boot, and we were forced to admit defeat.

Meanwhile two other climbing acquaintances, Mr. C.K.M. Douglas of the Meteorological Department of the Air Ministry, and Mr. Alexander Harrison of Edinburgh, who arrived on the previous day, had set off for the Schreckhorn, and Bell suggested that I should join forces with them. Unwilling to miss what promised to be a perfect day I accepted his proposal, and hastily packing my rucksack set off from the hut after them.

Going hard, I scrambled up the easy rock slopes above the hut, and soon caught them up. They were bound for the ordinary route up the Schreckhorn but I suggested that we should ascend by the rocky and more difficult South-West Rock – the route Bell and I had followed two days previously. They gladly agreed to this, and we forthwith started traversing the Schreck Glacier towards the ridge.

The morning was fine and calm as we trudged over the glacier. Yet there was a warmth in the air boding ill. The dawn was wild and hurried, and scarcely had the sun's first rays lit the snow wall of the Fiescherhörner when it was superseded by a weird greenish glow. Douglas is a meteorological expert, and I asked him what it meant. He did not know. None of us had seen such a sunrise. Far beyond the foothills of the Oberland the plain of Bern was drowned in a green haze. Everywhere we looked the green colour predominated. It was a portent beautiful but evil. We were foolish to disregard it. I have since spoken to Dr. A. Russell, F.R.S., the noted expert on thunderstorms and their attendant phenomena. He told me that these 'green ray sunrises', as he termed them, are not unknown to scientists, who do not, however, understand their cause. One thing is certain, they invariably precede exceptionally bad weather. It is a curious fact that the colour in question was identical with that emitted by a "Crookes" vacuum tube, though whether there is any connection it is yet impossible to say.

The weather appeared reasonably good otherwise; only a few smooth oily clouds, far detached from the world, suggested evil, while away in the far south a massive range of cumuli brooded over the Pennine Alps.

The South-West Ridge of the Schreckhorn falls steeply from the summit of the mountain for a considerable distance, before ending abruptly in a huge precipice. It is necessary, therefore, to attain the crest of the ridge high up above this precipice. A wide gully, set at a steep angle and over a thousand feet in height, affords the quickest and easiest route.

A gaping bergschrund defended the foot of the couloir, but the recent heavy falls of snow had slipped down from above, bridging the formidable obstacle. Over this we moved delicately, while admiring the baleful green depths, beneath us fringed with giant icicles.

Above lay ice, and we proceeded to cut steps up and across to the gully over the steep little rock wall at its base. Conditions had changed considerably during the two days since my previous ascent. Where Bell and I had found easy snow and dry rocks, there was now far too much ice. Progress over the slabs forming the bed of the gully was slow. It was a place not so much technically difficult as requiring unremitting care. A slip on such ground is difficult to arrest, and may result in destruction to the whole party. We mounted steadily to the foot of a long snow patch. This snow patch helped us considerably for a while, but eventually thinned down to ice. The rocks at the top of the gully were more pleasant than the slabs lower down, but they were steeper and more difficult, and though there was far less ice, what there was usually concealed the best holds.

At 7 a.m. we gained the crest of the ridge and sat down to a meal. The weather did not look promising. In the south the clouds were massing in ugly grey battalions, but over the Oberland the sun smiled kindly as yet. Bad weather was undoubtedly in the offing, but everything pointed to its holding off for some hours. By the time it did come we confidently expected to have traversed the mountain and be off all difficulties. The morning was still remarkably warm and windless.

We did not linger over our meal, and were soon off again. The South-West Ridge of the Schreckhorn is composed of sound and rough rock. It is indeed a joy to climb. In places it is steep, but the holds are always there in bountiful profusion. Climbing quickly and, for the most part, all together, progress was rapid on this splendid ridge.

The storm came with incredible rapidity. We were less than 500 feet from the summit when we heard the first roll of thunder, and looking round saw a dark wall of cloud, with leaden hail trailing at its skirts, rushing up from the north west. We at once looked round for shelter, and were able to climb down to a small ledge, partially protected by an overhanging rock, a few feet below the crest of the ridge. Our ice axes – an obvious source of danger – we left behind lying in a patch of snow.

Within ten minutes the storm was upon us. First we heard the bombardment as the storm clouds reached the isolated peak of the Eiger. Without a pause they rushed across to wreak their fury on the Schreckhorn. They came with an insane squall of hail and tremendous cracks of thunder. Every few seconds the lightning struck the ridge a few feet above with a rending tearing BANG! After one particularly brilliant flash that flamed all round us, accompanied by a terrific report, there was another crash, and a mass of rock – dislodged by the lightning – fell to the left of us. We looked at each other and smiled – a trifle wanly. All we could do was to hope for the best. An appreciable time after the initial bang of the discharge would come the long roll of echoes from peak to peak, booming in tremendous waves of sound from the cliffs of the Lauteraarhorn. It was terrible, but it was also magnificent.

Meanwhile hail fell steadily. The air was full of it; we could see but a few yards. Our ledge afforded but slight protection, but the weather as yet was warm, and we were reasonably comfortable.

The storm lasted for about an hour. When it had gone we climbed back to the ridge, where we were greeted by a glimpse of blue sky and a fugitive sun. Our ice axes we found uninjured much to our relief.

On the ridge we held a short council of war. If we went on we should have an easier descent, but we would be on an exposed ridge for at least two hours. To be caught by another thunderstorm on or near the summit of the Schreckhorn was not to be thought of. The rocks, moreover, were covered with newly fallen hail, and progress must of necessity be slow. To retreat by the way we had come would be the more difficult but shorter. We therefore started down the ridge moving as fast as possible.

We had nearly reached the point where it is necessary to turn down off the ridge into the gully, when again storm clouds blew up from the north-west. We had barely time to leave the crest of the ridge when the storm was upon us in a blinding *tourmente* of snow and hail, snarling wind, and crashing thunder. There was no previous indication of the electrical tension. Ice axes and metal objects did not hiss as they usually do. The charged clouds were blown at great speed against the mountain and, as soon as they were near enough, discharged their electrical energy.

Douglas and Harrison were below me, moving carefully over the difficult rocks, when there was a blinding glare and a terrible explosion. I received a stunning blow on the head as if I had been sandbagged. For a second or so I was completely knocked out, and but for the rope, which I had previously fastened securely round a rock, I might have fallen and dragged the party to disaster. When I had recovered my wits sufficiently to move down, fits of trembling supervened, and it was only with difficulty that I could control my limbs. No doubt the nerve centres were affected. Considering the violence of the discharge, and the terrific report that accompanied it, the shock I received was without doubt only the secondary effect of the flash. A direct hit must have been fatal. Even the secondary or "corona" effects of a lightning discharge may be fatal. Dr. Russell tells me that had my clothes been dry, I would in all probability not have survived such a powerful shock. Fortunately we had been well damped by the first storm, and the electrical fluid naturally ran down my wet clothes in preference to my body. As is well-known, a high frequency current utilises only the surface of a conductor. This peculiarity is known to engineers as the "skin effect". In my case my "skin", for electrical purposes, was represented by my clothes.

For the next hour or so our progress was painfully slow, perhaps less on my account than the ferocity of the storm, which reached a pitch that I had never before experienced in such a situation. We were in imminent danger of being blown off the mountain, and for minutes at a time we could barely cling on, while the wind roared by beating us with hail and snow until we were sheathed in ice from head to foot. Worst of all, the hail left by the first storm had partially melted, and now the bitter wind was freezing it on the rocks in sheets of ice which, in turn, were being covered by evil flour-like snow. The only alternative to the horrible icy slabs was the ridge forming the west wall of the gully, but this, the lightning was hitting with unfailing regularity, and the wind would have blown us off like flies. No, the gully was the sole way. There, at least, was a certain amount of shelter, though there was always the risk of falling stones dislodged by lightning. Once we were not in direct danger of being hit by the lightning, we gave up worrying over it. Yet never shall I forget the fearful rending bangs, for all the world like Mills' bombs magnified many times, a few feet above or to the left of us. Suddenly, above the howl of the *tourmente*, came the crash of falling rocks in the gully below us. We barely noticed it, but had we been a hundred feet farther down we must have been wiped out.

A slip was not to be thought of; steadiness was essential. Never did Douglas or Harrison falter; their progress was mechanical rather than human in its certainty. It is only thus that a party, caught by weather of this description on an exposed and difficult mountain, can hope to get down in safety. Whether we could stick it out was not so much the question as whether the storm would *allow* us to stick it out.

Often we were dependent on the rope. Several times I could neither find a hold nor feel what I was hanging on to. On these occasions I let myself slide, braking with my ice axe on the icy slabs; and always Harrison was below, a tower of strength, to gather me to his bosom at the end of the slide.

At length we were off the rocks and could cut across an ice slope to the long patch of snow, which had helped us on the ascent. There we could kick steps and move all together. The exercise was more warming than crawling down the slabs. The storm, however, increased in fury. We were unable to see where we were going, or each other, owing to the blinding clouds of powdery snow that came pouring down from the cliffs above, until they would be caught by the hurricane and whirled furiously back in writhing suffocating columns.

Knowing the route better than the others, I undertook to go first. With faces to the slope and axes well driven home at every step, we slowly struggled down to the safety that seemed so far away. So blinding was the drift that the holds kicked by me were immediately obliterated and Harrison and Douglas had perforce to make their own. We were often unable to see each other though separated by only a yard or so, and two or three times I felt Harrison's boot on my head as he moved down a step, quite unaware that I was immediately below.

We were not more than halfway down. In three hours we had not descended 500 feet of the gully. The storm was increasing rather than decreasing in fury. It was bitterly cold. Finally we could barely move at all, and for minutes at a time it was as much as we could do to prevent ourselves from being blown from our holds. I remember well the weird noise the wind made as it came rushing up the gully. Sometimes it fell upon us with a furious demented screech. At others it approached with the roar of an express train in a tunnel. Now and again it struck with a boom like thunder. Our chances of survival were nil if things went on as they did. The forced inaction was telling. Soon the wind would numb unless we could keep on moving.

Then Providence intervened. The wind suddenly moderated; the mist swept away for a few moments. We could see the route down. Somebody suggested some chocolate. The effect was magical. It brought warmth and renewed determination to get down come what might. So on we went, leaving the snow for the interminable ice-sheeted slabs where nearly every hold had to be hacked out with the axe.

Presently the storm came roaring back like a giant in anger, but not with the same fury as before. We were able to go on moving, albeit with difficulty. So for a total of six hours we fought our way down a gully not more than an a thousand feet high, reaching at last the easy rocks and the ice slope above the bergschrund. On the ice slope our steps had been obliterated and we had to cut them anew; but what a joy to be able to cut into good honest ice after the hours of hacking, scraping, and groping on the slabs.

Not worrying about finding the bridge over the bergschrund we sat down, and one by one slid down and over, subsiding ungracefully on the soft snow of the Schreck Glacier. There, with nothing but easy ground separating us from the hut, we shook hands not without feeling, for it had been a close thing, and turned for a moment to listen to the wild orchestra of the storm in the great crags above.

We were soon at the hut, where we found Bell anxiously awaiting us. Had we not returned he was fully prepared to organise a search party before nightfall. As it was, he was able to turn his organising abilities into the preparation of a truly superb stew.

We were walking down the path to Grindelwald next day when we met a cavalcade of trippers led by an old guide. And as we passed we heard one of them question the old guide: 'Where do you think they have been?' The old guide looked at us sternly. 'I think,' he replied, 'they have made the excursion on the glacier.'

NOTE ON THE "GREEN RAY" SUNRISE

In the foregoing chapter I mentioned a curious sunrise of a vivid green colour which preceded an electrical storm of exceptional violence, accompanied by a high wind and heavy snow. Some time after this incident I had a conversation with Dr. A. Russell, F.R.S., the noted authority on thunderstorms and their attendant phenomena. He informed me that the "Green Ray Sunrise", as he termed it, is not unknown to scientists, who are, however, unable to offer any explanation as to its cause.

Since the Schreckhorn climb I have observed two similar "green ray" sunrises, both of which I was able to watch more closely than that seen from the Schreckhorn

The first of these occurred during a traverse of the well-known easy glacier pass of the Grünhorn Lücke in the Bernese Oberland. Mr. J.H.B. Bell and I had left the Concordia hut shortly before dawn in weather conditions very similar to those of the Schreckhorn – *i.e.*, a moderately clear sky, with high cirrus clouds here and there, and a suspicious warmth in the air. Owing to the surrounding peaks our view was limited, and the eastern horizon was not visible.

As we ascended towards the pass we remarked the same greenish tinge of the snow which we had seen on the Schreckhorn and which appeared to be reflected from the sky. Even the rocks possessed a dull greenish colour. Yet there was nothing unusual about the sky, though we were unable to see the sun owing to a ridge ahead.

When we arrived on the pass about an hour after dawn, it was obvious that a storm was brewing. The accompanying photograph, taken looking south-east, shows the wildness of the sky. Like the storm on the Schreckhorn this storm approached with extraordinary rapidity. I say extraordinary because never have I seen storms approach at a greater speed than those, following a "green ray" sunrise. As on the Schreckhorn, the storm approached from the north-west and its origin was outside the mountains. A storm that gathers on a mountain is less to be feared than one which approaches from the outside, as it forms slowly, and the mountaineer is thus warned of the oncoming of bad weather. In the case of the Schreckhorn the sharp line of approaching storm-clouds were certainly not more than fifteen degrees above the horizon when first seen, in fact probably only ten degrees, but the storm reached us in a quarter of an hour or twenty minutes. The air currents bearing the cloud cannot thus have been travelling at less than sixty miles per hour at a conservative estimate.

The storm clouds in the present instance appeared to be in the main the ordinary cumuli and nimbus common to thunderstorms, but they were quickly augmented by local clouds as soon as they reached the Oberland massif.

Our original intention had been to traverse the Agassiz Joch, but we at once gave up this idea and descended to the Finsteraarhorn Hut. So rapidly did the storm develop that though the descent to the hut took us not longer than half an hour it was snowing, blowing and thundering by the time we had arrived. The storm continued all that day and all the night without, however, much thunder, though it is very probable that amid the noise of the wind it was not audible from the ridges high above. This storm was certainly one of midwinter severity, and within twenty-four hours over two feet of snow fell. A guided party on the Jungfrau who had not turned back was overtaken by it and benighted near the Rottal Sattel. The guide survived, but his employer, a German, died of exposure.

The third and last occasion when I saw the "green ray" sunrise was during the summer of 1928.

On 9 August Professor Graham Brown and I left the Lognon Hotel with the intention of attempting Les Droites. On this occasion a sharp frost and clear sky seemed to promise perfect weather. At dawn, however, we observed a few cirrus clouds which somehow reminded me of the last two occasions when I had seen a "green ray" sunrise, or perhaps it was because of the curious quality in the colour of the sky which seemed to possess an indefinable green tone. Shortly after sunrise the whole basin of the Argentière Glacier was flooded with a sort of phosphorescent green which pervaded both snow and rock of a colour exactly similar to the ultra-violet emanissions of a "Crookes Tube" employed in "X-ray" work. We abandoned the proposed attempt on Les Droites and decided to ascend the Aiguille d'Argentière, an easy peak from which we could return in the event of bad weather. For my part, from the first moment that I saw the "green ray" sunrise I had not the faintest shadow of doubt that bad weather must come – it is far too obvious and rare to be ignored.

As we ascended the glacier towards the final ridge of our peak I kept a careful observation on the weather. The green tinge lasted for over an hour, and did not even then completely disappear, but became less intense. Then, about three hours after dawn, we saw a line of cloud approaching from the north-west as on the two previous occasions. It was a perfectly regular formation of cloud and came up the sky almost like a curtain. When first seen it was barely visible, being but a degree or so above the horizon, but it approached with such speed that when about 1,500 feet from the summit we were obliged to turn and commence the descent. Actually about an hour and a half elapsed between our first seeing the cloud and the arrival of the storm. As before, it was accompanied by thunder and a sudden wind of a line squall nature. In fact, save for their prolonged severity, these storms bear a distinct resemblance to a line squall.

In the present case the storm lasted only an hour and passed almost as suddenly as it arrived, leaving a clear sky in its wake. The weather, however, showed that it had by no means finished its activities, and the sunset we watched that evening from the Gallois Hut was a wild one. At about midnight we were roused by thunder, and going outside the hut were rewarded by a magnificent lightning display to the north-west over the Aiguilles Rouges on the opposite side of the Chamonix valley. The storm then left the Aiguilles Rouges and came directly up the Argentière Glacier, moving with extraordinary rapidity. Then, as we watched the lightning playing among the peaks, we were startled to hear a deep booming rushing noise approaching us. Never in our experience had we listened to such a noise, and coming out of the night it was impressive and not a little disturbing. A few moments later a terrific squall of wind and hail struck the hut, and for a few moments we thought that the roof might be carried away. It soon dropped, however, to a more normal wind. The lightning, meanwhile, was tremendous, and there seemed almost a continuous blaze of it. Though this storm approached some sixteen hours after the "green ray" sunrise, there seems but little doubt that the "green ray" sunrise heralded its coming, for in every respect, including the new snow and hail that fell on the peaks, it resembled the storms following the previous two "green ray" sunrises.

These three experiences resemble each other too closely to be disregarded. What deductions are to be made from them? One thing is certain; that if I see a sunrise with a distinct greenish tinge in the shadows on the snow and the rocks I shall go back to the hut if I am starting for a difficult climb. I dare venture that even an experienced meteorologist might be deceived by the harmlessness of the sky at dawn, but if that dawn is green he may, without any other reason or data, confidently forecast bad weather within twenty-four hours.

To me the most significant point is that the colour resembles that of a "Crookes Tube". This seems to suggest that some tensional electrical quality is at work in the atmosphere. Also, that the green tinge should be only reflected and not so easily visible in the sky itself, is interesting. Possibly the colour bears some relation with the brush discharge preceding an electrical discharge.

At all events, the subject deserves to be recorded; it is possible that some one who reads this may be saved from undergoing such an experience as did Mr. Douglas, Mr. Harrison and I on the Schreckhorn.

CHAPTER NINE

The Mountains of Corsica

Even may nights can be cold in the North Mediterranean when the blazing southern sun is replaced by a rush of air from alpine snows. This Mr. F.H. Slingsby and I discovered, as we lay and shivered in our sleeping bags on the fo'castle of the paquebôt *en route* from Marseilles to Ajaccio; and we were glad when towards dawn a tireless light, blinking nervously from a grey spot of land, announced our goal – Corsica. A little later we slid into a bay where the white houses of Ajaccio clustered, and after some intricate manœuvring, accompanied by an excited clatter of tongues, drew up alongside the wharf.

We had breakfast at the Hotel de France, and afterwards sallied forth on the irksome task of buying provisions. The morning was sultry, and a leaden sirocco-clouded sky beat down the moist heat in stifling waves. Among other articles, we were unable to obtain maps, and for the whole holiday the "Carte Taride" was to be our sole mentor. Its most charming feature is a sturdy independence, and we were soon to learn the joy of standing in body on one mountain with spiritual intention on another.

At length the task was completed and we set off for the station. The voluble brother of the hotel porter carried our luggage, and on arrival at the station demanded an extortionate sum. We refused; negotiations were broken off, and a wordy battle ensued, Slingsby acting as spokesman. Somehow, during lulls, our luggage was got on the train. Eventually we compromised; but the porter still screamed his 'grievances'. A priest on the platform was appealed to. 'What! It is two days' wages for a labourer in the fields.' We were fools, and we knew it. The porter knew it too. He followed us into the train and continued his peroration. Finding it useless he played his trump card. As the train was about to leave he seized my rucksack and made as though to remove it. Up to then I had remained a passive though interested spectator, but this was too much. Grasping my ice axe I brandished it, at the same time indicating the probable point of contact with the porter's anatomy. It was the turning-point. Vendettas, knives and pistols the porter understood. These he could combat with. But an ice axe? No! A vile and uncivilised weapon in the hands of a mad Englishman. The tables were turned. Letting go of my rucksack he retreated. A stentorian voice bellowed, 'En voiture! En voiture!'

A whistle shrilled; the engine shrieked; a horn blared; the engine shrieked again; and the little train jolted leisurely out of the station. Our consolation was in the thought of the priest. There had been a speculative gleam in that dignitary's eye, when Slingsby told of the sum the porter had extracted, that boded ill for the latter. I have not the slightest doubt that the church benefited materially.

The train climbed slowly through forests of chestnuts and beeches. Heavy on the thunderous air was the sweet scent of maquis. Above, a pall of cloud drooped wrathfully on dim hills.

Gradually, as we crawled higher, the semitropical vegetation gave way to the sedate pine. A wild hollow opened out to the west, whence rose dark rock pinnacles into slowly writhing storm clouds. It was a scene of melancholy grandeur. Under its soothing influence the trials of travel were forgotten; we thought almost kindly of the porter of Ajaccio; we had reached the gateway of hills. What matter if at the end of the long tunnel that burrows beneath the pass of Vizzavona we alighted at Vizzavona in a slashing rain-storm and grumbling thunder? The tang in the air was grand after the heat of Ajaccio.

We scurried cheerfully through the deluge to the Hotel Modern, where we were made warmly welcome, and were soon ensconced before a roaring log fire doing justice to chestnut pudding and other Corsican delicacies.

Later the rain ceased, and we walked through the dripping forest up the lower slopes of Monte d'Oro (the Peak of Gold), which we hoped to ascend on the morrow.

Perhaps the greatest charm of Corsica lies in its forests. Never had we seen such stately pines, whilst groves of beech trees in bright spring green contrasted oddly with the winter snows.

We left at 4 a.m. next morning in sullen weather, and trudged up through a hushed forest that seemed to hold the threat of storm.

Vizzavona is 2,970 feet and Monte d'Oro 7,845 feet. We had, therefore, nearly 5,000 feet to climb.

Mist and rain greeted us on the open mountainside above the trees, but we pressed on and after a short scramble over broken rocks reached the south peak only to find that a long broken ridge separated us from the north and higher peak. It was now raining, snowing, and hailing. Our clothing was heavy and drenched; malicious trickles invaded our necks; we wondered vaguely whether we had chanced on some Mediterranean Lake District but we were determined on traversing the mountain.

A long traverse over steep snow-slopes on the East Face brought us to a point beneath the North Summit. We were plodding up the snow when my axe suddenly began a vicious hissing indicative of electrical tension. We at once hurried down to the shelter of some rocks and waited clammily for a storm that never materialised. Finally, we returned and hurried up to the summit. Once again the axes sang their weird *chanson*. Touching the summit we retreated at once.

A wide couloir cleaves the east face of the mountain. In it we glissaded joyfully, but roped. Half-way down smooth wet slabs intervened. To avoid them we kept to the right, where the snow continued in a subsidiary couloir. This couloir steepened and narrowed to a ribbon of snow inlaid between rock walls. At its narrowest point its continuity was broken by a deep crevasse, formed by the action of a waterfall dropping from the left wall. Descending cautiously, we looked down into the abysmal cleft, into the depths of which the waterfall rushed with many gurglings and subterranean rumblings. The place had to be jumped – somehow. Not from the snow above – the distance both downwards and outwards was too great – but from the waterfall wall itself. Driving my axe into the snow I paid out the rope as Slingsby descended. Soon he was beneath the waterfall and there, with enough water pouring upon him to work a small power station, turned, a happy smile on his face, and announced that it reminded him of pot-holing. Then he jumped. His jump was admirable, his landing awkward. Edward Whymper's description of Monsieur Reynaud's passage of an alpine crevasse is not entirely inapplicable. 'We saw Reynaud a flying body. We heard a thud as if a bundle of carpets had been pitched from a window.' But here the conditions were different. Slingsby hit a slope of hard steep snow at a tangent, and flew off down it. For a second I allowed the rope to whirr round the driven-in axe, tightened gradually, and held.

Slingsby, having removed snow from his neck, leered up, or so it seemed, and said, 'Your turn now'. I advanced. From my upper position the jump had looked a bagatelle; from beneath the waterfall it looked distinctly formidable. But at last I jumped. My landing also resembled Monsieur Reynaud's, and, like Slingsby, I shot off down the steep hard snow, vainly endeavouring to brake myself with my ice axe. Slingsby could have held me with ease, but I preferred to stop myself by more constitutional methods. And so on passing him I made a quick brief grab at his nether garments. I seized them, they held, we were safely reunited, and the crevasse conquered.

In our sodden condition we were glad to get clear of the wearisome lower slopes of boulders and trees. Our squelching advent was witnessed by Madame la Propriétaire in wide-eyed amazement doubtless it served to enhance the reputation for insanity borne by Englishmen abroad.

The following day we wandered gently through the woods to the east of the village, and ascending by a good path reached a pleasant spot, with a view over many shades of blue hills down the valley to the heat-stricken lowlands and the far sea shimmer. There on a couch of soft grass we lazed the hours away, with the notes of the cuckoo in our ears and the gracious woodlands around. It might have been a Surrey ridge, and one had to raise the eyes to where the dark rock fangs of Monte d'Oro grinned from a lowering mist to dispel the illusion.

Leaden clouds crept up from the south as we jogged down the hillside, and a wild sunset glared over the pass of Vizzavona. But we had yet to learn that bad weather in Corsica is only a sneak thief in the palace of good King Sol, not a feared and despotic tyrant as in the Alps, or a luckless institution as in this country.

For our next expedition we chose the ridge to the south-east of Vizzavona. The highest point is Monte Renoso, 7,735 feet; but the "Carte Taride" is a trifle vague as to its situation. When we told the proprietor of our intentions, he was aghast. 'It is impossible, Messieurs! Impossible! No one can go over the snow, and there is only one way; you will never find it without a guide – yes, you must have a guide.' We protested, but nevertheless the guide appeared. To him we reiterated our intention to go alone. The guide, however, seemed relieved; nor is this to be wondered at, for he was a cripple with only one serviceable arm. The proprietor, seeing that we were determined, good-naturedly drew us a sketch-map.

The morning was misty and the mournful wind of dawn sobbed distressingly in the tall pine tops as we walked up the road towards the pass of Vizzavona. Turning to the south at the top of the pass we ascended through scrub and trees. Gradually the light grew, until suddenly we breasted the mist waves and stepped full into a perfect morning. Below, the mist still clung to the pass, but elsewhere all was royal blue, silver and gold – the royal blue of the hills and distant sea, the silver of sun-flecked mist, and gold where the crest of the Peak of Gold (Monte d'Oro) shone in the rising sun.

We passed some bergerie and trudged uphill to the crest of a neighbouring grassy ridge. This was a mistake; had we followed the proprietor's sketch-map correctly we should have turned right at the bergerie and contoured towards Monte Renoso.

Brilliant sun and a biting west wind greeted us on the grassy ridge. The morning was cloudless, but suddenly in the frost-bound depths to the west a shuddering witch hag beladled her cauldron. A mist whirled up, poured over the ridge, and was instantly lost in the steely blue. And then the witch herself, tired of her chill gully, rode up on the cauldron's breath and stood, a ghostly haloed figure, opposite. I waved my axe; she waved a spectral broomstick. It was, of course, the "Brocken Spectre", for which the conditions were ideal, and I hastened to unpack my camera. But the witch scenting, no doubt, my base motive exercised her spell. The mist vanished, and she with it.

We continued on up the ridge, which presently became more definite. A steep slope of hard snow and a few feet of rocks brought us to a summit. Here we realised our mistake, for Monte Renoso rose some three miles to the south east, and separating us from it was a long jagged ridge with several intervening summits. The point we were on was evidently the Punta Orientale. There was no time to attempt Monte Renoso, and the biting west wind forbade a prolonged halt, so we decided to descend to the cosier beechwoods 2,000 feet beneath. A long couloir filled with glissading snow provided the connecting link, and in a few minutes we were basking in a blazing sun.

As we descended to Vizzavona we were able to examine the havoc wrought by the largest snow avalanche that had fallen in Corsica within living memory. Two miles of dense beech and pine forest had been laid flat over an area a quarter of a mile wide.

We left next morning for Calacuccia, a very slow train jolting us down to the baking vineyards of Corte, a quaint little town, and the scene of many bloody combats in the Middle Ages. Here we expected to find poverty and the primitive: we found silk stockings and motor cars. A luxurious charabanc conveyed us from the station to the town, where we were just in time to catch the daily motor diligence to Calacuccia.

The journey was not uneventful. For company we had peasants and the odour of garlic. For a diversion other than the scenery we carried one who was learning to drive. A narrow road, hairpin bends, and precipitous drops afforded him excellent opportunities for displaying his prowess. Some miles on our way, we rounded a corner to find a lanky dog comfortably asleep in the middle of the road. The brakes were applied, the horn gave an agonised toot, both drivers grappled with the wheel, we swerved violently, escaped disaster by an ace and proceeded merrily, every one roaring with laughter. Thus does the Latin temperament rise to the occasion. As for the dog, it rose slowly with an effort, its tail drooped, a sad hurt expression was on its countenance as much as to say, 'Is there nowhere on this island where I can take my noonday nap without unmannerly interruption?'

We halted at Francardo for lunch, and were there introduced to the most remarkable cheese I have ever met. Its flavour was unique, and remained an unhallowed and tangible memory for days . Slingsby said that it was made from donkey's milk, but subsequent inquiry revealed that it was the product of sheep's milk.

We were waiting for the motor to start again, when an Eastern-looking gentleman with a large smile and a selection of "gold" watches and rugs accosted us. 'Ullo, Charlie,' he said, 'you wanta buy a gold watch? I know you Eenglish towns "Leeverpool" and "Bummingham".'

The road from Francardo to Calacuccia passes through the wild gorge of the Golo stream, winding along above precipices, and we were glad to see that the wheel was now in the hands of the official driver.

The gorge continues for several miles, and eventually opens out into the pastures of Niolo. Once we stopped at a tumble-down shanty and were surprised to see a well dressed man step forth. He was a doctor, and this lonely out of the way spot was his occasional surgery.

At the Hotel des Touristes Calacuccia, we were hospitably received by Monsieur and Madame Vecchini-Lupi, who at once inquired whether we knew "La Grande Capitaine".[1]

Fortunately one of us did, and we were henceforth treated as princes.

The following morning we left at 5 a.m. with no definite idea as to the mountain to be climbed, but desirous of obtaining some better knowledge of the district

[1] Capt. G.I. Finch, one of the pioneers of Corsican mountaineering.

than that vouchsafed by the "Carte Taride" and the old pock-marked piece of cloth on rollers treasured by Monsieur Vecchini.

A long ragged ridge descends from Monte Falo towards Calacuccia. Along this we lounged, meet prey to an enervating morning, whose mists swayed uncertainly out of the valley and gathered about the hillsides. Up and down we scrambled over firm granite. Presently the ridge became more difficult. Cliffs dropped away to the north into a desolate boulder-strewn valley on the far side of which rose Monte Cinto 8,890 feet, the highest mountain in Corsica.

Finally a big rock tower blocked the way, a grim fellow, lurching towards us in a sneering yellow overhang. A short descent to the north and an airy traverse brought us to a charming little ledge set shyly in the lean sweep of slabs. The climbing above was delightful, and reminiscent of Sron na Ciche in Skye. The rock was rough and firm, and boots gripped it well; the work was steep and exposed. On such rock is the true delight of climbing to be found. For there is no need for 'muscle and will braced tense as steel', but the climber experiences that contemplative rhythm of upward progression in which lies the peculiar fascination of the 'great grey slabs bending up through immeasurable space'.

It was 4 p.m. when we reached the summit of the tower, and we turned regretfully valleywards.

A stony valley took us down to Calasima, the highest village in Corsica, as rain and darkness were falling. Beyond it we missed the path, and wallowed awhile in rank vegetation on a steep hillside, which Slingsby seemed to imagine was somebody's garden. But we found the path at last, and were soon bestirring the kitchen of the Hotel des Touristes to a sense of responsibility to its guests.

The following day we loaded up with five days' food and camping equipment and at 4 p.m. set off for the Grotto des Anges. We were passing along the village street when a familiar voice fell upon our ears.

'Ullo, Charlie,' it said, 'ow are you?' and turning we encountered the broad smile of the itinerant vendor of Francardo.

The road up the Golo valley was hot and dusty, and we were glad to leave it for the Calasima path. Calasima is the "highest" village in Corsica in more senses than one and its "highness" is most perceptible at the end of a hot day. We hurried through it, but the people were friendly and curious as to our doings. A hearty old gentleman, taking the evening "odours" on his front-door step, bade us 'Bon Voyage', and a crowd of children escorted us out of the village.

We walked up the Viro valley in the calm of a beautiful evening, and as the rapid Mediterranean night was falling sought for the Grotto des Anges. We found it, but inspection showed it to have been occupied by any but Heavenly beings, and we preferred a large boulder by the stream which overhung sufficiently to protect both of us comfortably.

An abundance of fuel lay around. It was dry as tinder and needed but a match; we had to be careful not to set the forest alight.

Supper was soon cooked and eaten. Afterwards we sat by the fire in that peace and contentment that can only bless the mountaineer with an appeased appetite. It was the ideal bivouac; no better is possible. Nearby the stream spoke with a friendly voice, telling of its release from winter snows, its short turbulent life, and eventual repose in the calm Mediterranean. No breath of wind stirred in the pine tops; no uneasy sound came from the hushed forest. The communion of hills was around. The fire roared and crackled gladly, illumining the pine trunks in a little oasis of dancing light. Presently a full moon rose, and from a place of black slumber the forest awakened to silver radiance and mysterious shadows. A sweet perfume stole across the air; a friendly wistful presence seemed abroad like that of shy children.

We slept fitfully, as is usually the case during the first night in the open. Towards dawn the temperature dropped suddenly, and we were glad to get up and blow the dying embers into flame.

We arose at 4 a.m. and crossing the torrent with difficulty walked up the valley towards, the Col Foggiale. Far above, the crest of the Paglia Orba saluted the sun. Truly does this noble peak deserve its title as the "Matterhorn of Corsica". There is none to dispute it in boldness of form or beauty of outline. We had come to regard Corsican granite with something of disdain, so we looked at the Paglia Orba and said arrogantly, 'We will go up the East Ridge, it looks amusing'. We were destined to return with very different views.

We passed some bergerie and turned uphill to the foot of the rocks of the south face of the mountain. There is singularly little amusement to be gained from reading a detailed description of an obscure rock climb, so I will say but little of our route. We had lunch on the rocks in company with a lizard, who discovered a great liking for the dripping in the lid of a bully-beef tin. The remainder of the day was spent in ascending to the ridge above by a remarkably steep snow gully, attempting the ridge itself, retreating, and attempting to break out of the gully lower down. After some difficult rock climbing we found ourselves quite 600 feet from the summit, the day drawing to a close and impossible cliffs ahead, crowned by a bulging lid of rock honeycombed with holes like a gigantic sponge.

There was nothing for it but to own an ignominious defeat, but we scuttled down in the gloom of eventide vowing that we had had a first-rate day, which indeed we had, and waded the stream to our camp. Two days later we had our revenge on the Paglia Orba. Starting soon after dawn we traversed the Punta Casteluccia – a pleasant scramble by the east face – and descending to the Col Foggiale attacked the South Face of the Paglia Orba. Less than two hundred feet of steep rough slabs brought us to the summit ridge, up which we walked without difficulty to the mist-enwrapped top of the mountain.

The mists prevented any but an occasional downward glimpse, but now and again we could glimpse the woods and pastures of the beautiful Viro valley at our feet, whilst the sense of isolation from the world was complete.

Our last expedition together was Monte Cinto, as in honour bound we felt obliged to climb the highest mountain on the island. Perhaps it was this undue sense of duty, but I must confess to having found the ascent by the ordinary way from Calacuccia thoroughly dull. The weather contributed to the general depression, and all we saw from the summit was a few yards of rain-soaked mist. Yet Monte Cinto is not to be lightly dismissed; it affords scope for some first-rate mountaineering, and many interesting routes await the enterprising seeker after the "impossible".

Slingsby left for England after this, and I was left alone for a week before going on to Chamonix.

With no companion the only alternative to some solitary climbing was the local guide, a charming old gentleman who peered benevolently through dark-tinted spectacles. As if anticipating my need he accosted me in the street.

'You want a guide? Then I will guide you. I will take you up Monte Cinto, but,' here he waggled his finger knowingly, 'only as far as the snow. Over the snow no man may go. What! You have been up Monte Cinto already?' He chuckled heartily for a minute. 'No, no! You only *think* you have climbed Monte Cinto. No man may go over the snow.'

I was greatly tempted to engage the old gentleman, it would have been an amusing experience, but as I was anxious to get some more climbing done I decided to go alone and unhampered by his services. The horror of snow possessed by all Corsicans is interesting. It is probably due to the fact that when the first heavy snowfall comes in late autumn the shepherds have to rescue their flocks. The snow then is soft and they sink deeply into it.

Returning to our bivouac I spent four nights there. I devoted two days to scrambling on the range of needle-like peaks to the north of the Paglia Orba, where I enjoyed the most difficult and interesting climbing I had as yet encountered in Corsica. The rock hereabouts is excellent, and rubber shoes grip it well. The topography of this range is so intricate that to attempt any explanation as to the exact situation of its peaks without an accurate map would convey little or nothing to the reader.

My last expedition was the Capo Tafonata. This is a narrow wedge-like peak to the west of the Paglia Orba, which is pierced by an enormous hole some 400 feet below the summit. It is easily reached by crossing the Col Foggiale and traversing the lower slopes of the Paglia Orba into the desolate boulder-strewn hollow at the foot of the peak.

I knew nothing of the way up beyond a somewhat vague memory of Captain Finch's description, but the route to the summit is unmistakable. It lies almost entirely up a series of ledges of the type so often depicted by artists but so seldom encountered on mountains. Climbing first to the left, and, then directly upwards over steep but easy rocks, I gained a ledge which led horizontally to the eastern end of the hole. This is certainly unique in my recollection. From afar it appears insignificant, a mere incident in the wall-like face of the mountain, but from close at hand it is so vast that the mountain seems to stride it like some Colossus, and one marvels that it does not fall. Long before I got there I became aware of a weird groaning sound made by the wind as it came rushing through the mountain. The view looking through the hole is the most impressive of any I saw in Corsica. One peers through the dark arch down to the green depths of a narrow fertile valley which winds placidly away to the sea coast some twelve miles distant, whilst falling away at the feet is the 6,000 feet high western face of the Capo Tafonata.

The ledge continues beyond the hole right round the end of the mountain, until the astonished climber finds himself on the western side. Here I encountered a steep slope of hard snow, in which not having my ice axe with me, I was forced to hack out steps with a knife. Above this a little scramble brought me to the northern summit. The southern summit, which is about equally high, is separated from the northern by the acute edge of the peak. It looked a fascinating scramble, and had it not been for the strong west wind I should have attempted it. But finding a sheltered place I sat down and dozed for an hour or so. It was my last climb, and I was anxious to store in my memory some of the many colourful scenes that delight the wanderer in Corsica.

The Capo Tafonata is a fine viewpoint. It stands nearer to the sea than any other peak of its altitude. There is a contrast of savage foreground, of dark forbidding peaks and precipices, with the emerald green of luxuriant valleys, and the cornflower blue of the Mediterranean. Even snow was not lacking to complete the colour scheme. Near at hand the Paglia Orba raised its lion-like head, snow crowned above the shadowed walls of its northern cliffs. Yet there was nothing of harshness in the colour renderings; the delicate merging of the blues and greens and purples was suggestive of the Hebrides or the elusive tones of Skye. There was so much beauty to see and so feeble a memory to store it. The minutes, the hours were charmed away; the sun swung round, dipping towards the sea; the valleys became dusky and mysterious, the breeze dropped to a murmur among the grey rocks. The coming of evening saw me strolling back to my solitary bivouac.

Two days later I was on that same blue sea *en route* to Marseilles, and my last glimpse of Corsica was of the snowy crests of Monte Cinto and the Paglia Orba, fifty miles away, lit by the sunset glow, like dim elfin lamps in a hall of waters hung with the curtains of night.

CHAPTER TEN

A First Ascent on Clogwyn Du'r Arddu

IT WAS A DROWSY DAY in August 1921 as I trudged up the interminable zigzags of the Gwynant track. Above, a clack of voices, the popping of bottles and the pantof a train spoke of Britain's most vulgar hilltop, Snowdon. I breasted the last rubbish-strewn slopes and paused for an instant amid the summit hubbub. The sun warmed; in the west a silver sea streak gleamed over hazed hill masses; on either hand Crib Goch and Lliwedd stretched austere arms embracing the sombre, waters of Glaslyn and Llydaw. The clamour triumphed; I bolted down the Llanberis path and turning westwards, along the Rangers track regained quietude. I followed the track and presently turned right – expectantly. The ground was level for a few yards; suddenly it fell away; the breeze soughed gently over an edge. A grey precipice connected the sunny breast of the mountain with a shadowed hollow where slept a little llyn in a maze of glacier-born boulders. An article in the Rucksack Club journal by Mr. H.R.C. Carr first attracted me to the crags of Clogwyn Du'r Arddu. There are four buttresses – the Far East, the East, the West, and the Far West. In 1920 only the last named had been climbed, though Messrs. Abrahams had made a short route up the east wall of the West Buttress. The Far East Buttress is broken and indefinite but the East and West Buttresses present the most formidable rock faces in Wales.

The continuity of the East Buttress is broken by a wide grass ledge running across the buttress at about two-thirds of its height, the sole break in the smooth sweep of slabs. The West Buttress is equally unrelenting and looks completely unassailable. The Far West Buttress slants back at an amenable angle, and its expanse of rough slabs affords delightful climbing of a quality comparable to the Idwal Slabs on Glyder Fawr. There are several distinct routes, but given a dry warm day and rubber shoes it is possible to wander almost anywhere. In such wanderings lies the joy of solitary scrambling, and I was soon at the foot of the crags.

There was a twenty-foot wall to start with, and a stiff groove; firm slabs followed. Little exertion was required; delicate treading took me up; dry turfy ledges prompted an occasional laze; the sun on the summit, a pipe. I finished the day by girdling the buttress.

I visited the crags on two other occasions and girdled the East Buttress by the grass ledge – an expedition of no difficulty, but which served to emphasise the grandeur of the rock architecture on which Clogwyn Du'r Arddu is built, and the apparent impregnability of the East and West Buttresses.

In September 1921 Mr. E.E. Roberts and I stayed at the Quellyn Arms, Rhydd Ddu, a cosy little inn between Beddgelert and Caernarfon, where we were hospitably entertained by Mrs. Owen, who is an excellent cook by virtue of previous hospital experience.

The weather was good, and we spent three days on Clogwyn Du'r Arddu. The first was devoted to the Far West Buttress and a curious route up the rocks between the West and Far West terraces. It lies up a sloping shelf, and involves some awkward and sensational climbing in its lower portion, where the shelf is narrow and slopes outwards. It is a worthy little scramble, and we named it the "Giant's Trod".

The following day we attempted the East Buttress in a half-hearted vague fashion by a great chimney that appeared to run up to the grass ledge. We failed, and retired to take our revenge on the crags by ascending Messrs. Abraham's route. This includes an exhilarating chimney and an exit behind a large wedged stone which we shared with a stream. Roberts enjoyed it – it reminded him of pot holing – but personally I thought it a detestable place.

Later we made the first ascent of the Far East Buttress. It is a disappointing climb, and was rendered unpleasant by a horde of trippers who collected at the Clogwyn station of the Snowdon Mountain railway and howled at us. The rocks are indeterminate, evil, and untrustworthy, but there was a crack that we named the "Non Such" which contained the only clean rock on the climb. We topped the crags to a shriek of execration from the assembled tourists.

We examined the West Buttress and walked round its overhanging base. At one place only did there appear any possibility of obtaining lodgement on the rocks, and that was from a point a short distance from the foot of the Eastern Terrace which runs down to the east of the buttress. A turf ledge ran out to the buttress crest, but so impracticable did the face appear above the recess in which the ledge ended that we did not investigate it. Afterwards I remembered the place, and regretted having made no attempt upon it.

Impressions survive, and in Easter 1928 when I next visited Wales, it was with the intention of proving beyond all shadow of doubt the practibility or impossibility of the West Buttress.

The East Buttress, meanwhile, had fallen to the efforts and ingenuity of Messrs. A. S. Pigott and Morley Wood. They had gained the grass ledge two-thirds of the way up the buttress by one of the fearsome cracks cleaving the lower wall, though the upper face above the ledge proved beyond even *their* powers. The West Buttress remained, therefore, the last great problem in Wales.

A grey sky, a spit of rain, and a roaring gale greeted us as we passed over the Llanberis ridge of Snowdon by the track from Pen-y-Pass. We were a large party, but none save myself had seen Clogwyn Du'r Arddu.

The furies were abroad that day; the cwm beneath the crags provided scope for their rage. Roaring round it they seized the waters of the llyn, whipped it into angry surf and hurled it upwards in sheets of foam, whose spindrift beat the crest of the crags 500 feet above. Several times we were forced to throw ourselves flat, clutching at turf and rocks, as the gusts howled past.

We descended the easy screes to the west of the crags, and passing around the foot of the West Buttress gained the Eastern Terrace. Meanwhile Mr. J.L. Longland, who had taken a short-cut by climbing the steep rock wall at the foot of the Eastern Terrace, had reached an easy corner, where stands a large block of rock, and continuing round the corner had gained the grassy recess. Returning, he assured me that he thought the rocks were possible above the recess, and together we climbed up to look at them.

I found myself gazing up the most impressive slab that I have seen in Britain. Two hundred and fifty feet high, it slants up to the left in one great sweep, sloping slightly outwards in the same direction. On the right it is bounded by an overhanging wall; and in the angle thus formed is a narrow cleft of terrific aspect. The left hand and outer edge of the slab overhangs another and even more formidable slab. The average width of the slab is about twenty feet, and the inclination between seventy and eighty degrees. Up it the eye wandered fascinatedly while the mind speculated half-dreamily, awed to passivity. I experienced a feeling that I have not encountered elsewhere in Britain, the feeling of all mountaineers who look for the first time up an unclimbed mountain face, a gamut of emotion impossible to analyse. But even suppose the slab to be vanquished, what then? It ended in a small ledge crowned by a quartz-sprinkled block and above that the buttress leaned out majestically. We scrambled up the Eastern Terrace and scanned it for a connection with the easier rocks above, but our scanning revealed nothing save a traverse that was only possible to the eye of faith, and the eye of faith is not always the servant of cold reason.

The attempt was made two days later by Longland, Professor T. Graham Brown, Mr. C. Wakefield, and myself. The weather was not propitious, and ere we reached the foot of the crack a drizzling rain was falling.

There is nothing of ease about the climb; it is difficult at the start, and the difficulty is sustained. First came a narrow chimney. Longland made light of this, and it was evident that he was in good training. At the top of the chimney is a smooth section, to which clung decrepit masses of turf. Now all the best works on mountaineering deplore the use of grass and heather as hand or footholds. Be that as it may, I must confess to deriving great satisfaction from the vegetation decorating the slab, and so I believe did the leader.

Another very steep and exposed piece of work brought Longland to a small stance where it was possible to thread the rope behind a small stone wedged in the crack. Graham Brown was now at the foot of the crack, and Wakefield out of sight below at the corner by the big block. Suddenly – how I do not know – a mass of turf was dislodged and went hurtling down. It harboured in its bosom a large stone, which made straight for Graham Brown's head. He had barely time to raise his arm to defend himself when it struck him, fortunately upon the forearm, bruising him severely. Apologies crept down in due course; undoubtedly the climb was in need of "gardening".

Longland, having secured himself by the threaded rope, invited me to pass him and try the next section. It was formidable work, how formidable then those who follow will have no conception. One advanced a foot or so at a time digging for holds and removing turf piecemeal; yet the rock beneath was sound, and we were only experiencing what all the early pioneers of British rock-climbing experienced. In a year or so ladies will climb the West Buttress of Clogwyn Du'r Arddu and marvel at the difficulties we encountered.

Higher up the overhanging wall on the right bulged out repulsively. An awkward movement to the left was necessary, and an upward pull, on the arms to a small stance. A pebble was wedged in the crack at this point, and after many laborious efforts I managed to thread the rope behind it and thus protect my ascent. The pull was a strenuous one; the overhanging bulge gripped my back lovingly. A haul, a heave, a gasp, a sinuous straining, and it was done. I found myself accommodated in a little corner where dwelt a friendly rock leaf, which would obviously serve both as an excellent belay and a means of descending on a doubled rope.

We became alive to the fact that rain was falling steadily; malicious trickles were beginning to course down the slab and crack; the holds were becoming slimy, and wet holds have a curious knack of dwindling to half the size they appear when dry. There were murmurs from beneath; the tail of the rope, hitherto patient and stoically silent, began to voice its grievances. Longland and I were sheltered and comparatively dry; Graham Brown and Wakefield were wet and cold through inactivity. Retreat was unanimously decided upon; but before retiring Longland climbed past me to a point where he could see something of the route ahead. He returned with the glad news that it would undoubtedly "go", but that rubber shoes and dry rocks were essential.

As last man down I had no intention of climbing the wet and slippery rocks. I cut off a length of rope, looped it around the rock leaf, threaded the rope through, and after the usual contortions managed to get into a double-roping position and slide off my perch down the airy reaches of the great slab.

Normally there is a certain pleasure to be derived from descending a doubled rope over a steep rock face, but on this occasion the rope was possessed of seven harsh devils, and instead of a dignified progression I proceeded in a series of profane jerks. The wet hemp clung to my breeches and cut cruelly into my thighs, and when I arrived eventually at the grassy recess it was with a feeling of thankfulness that I was still homogeneous flesh and bone and not sawn into two portions.

Thus ended the first round with the West Buttress but if it had defeated us, it had only done so with the assistance of a perfidious ally – the weather.

Two days later Mr. C.A. Elliott, Graham Brown and I returned to the attack, with the intention of exploring from above. The weather was bad a chill mist enveloped the crags, a biting wind numbed both ambition and fingers, but we gained some valuable knowledge.

The upper portion of the buttress is easy, and we descended with but little trouble to a point some twenty feet above the quartz-crowned ledge at the top of the great slab. From a rocky platform above we gazed down an overhang fifteen feet high to the ledge. The rocks are rough and firm, but there seemed small chance of climbing the overhang, even if the great slab succumbed and the quartz-crowned ledge was attained. The alternative lay in a traverse to the west from the latter round a corner and thence across a steep slab, but it looked a most sensational and tricky piece of work. Yet another alternative was to swing the leader from the end of the ledge down to a shallow groove which appeared feasible. Thence he could ascend and hold the remainder of the party over the traverse from above.

Easter passed and Whitsun came, but the genius of bad weather presided over Clogwyn Du'r Arddu. Once more a fierce wind goaded the Llyn to fury and rain slashed the crags. Mr. R. Ogier Ward, Graham Brown and I, setting out from Beddgelert, explored downwards once more, but got no farther.

On Whit-Monday Graham Brown and Ward unfortunately had to leave. That evening there were rumours of three men having been seen on the West Buttress. On Tuesday a party of us left Pen-y-Pass in two motorcars, and after sundry adventures, in which a climbing rope was called upon to haul one car out of a ditch, reached the last cottages of Hafotty Newydd above Llanberis.

Mr. G.W. Young accompanied us. The previous day he had ascended the East Peak of Lliwedd by Route II – a great feat and one indicative of his extraordinary arm power and skill.[1] We would have given much to have had him with us on Clogwyn Du'rArddu. In addition to Longland were Messrs. P. Bicknell and I. Waller, but they were present as spectators and not to accompany us on the climb.

As one approaches Clogwyn Du'r Arddu from Llanberis, the crags rise seductively over the desolate upland valley of Arddu. For once the weather was fine and warm. We laboured over the boulder-strewn slopes, perspiring gladly and scanning the West Buttress for signs of renewed activity. As we gained the well-defined moraine to the north of Llyn Arddu we saw three figures clamber up to the Eastern Terrace to the foot of the climb. There they halted, sat down, and appeared to regard us.

The steep sixty feet high wall at the foot of the Eastern Terrace is a wet, loose, turfy, and unpleasant place. Up it Longland proceeded nonchalantly, but when my turn came I must confess that my bad climbing condition, combined with a heavy rucksack, resulted in ignominious failure. Bicknell and I therefore, scrambled round by the ordinary easy way.

We found Messrs. W. Eversden, Pigott, and Morley Wood sitting on the terrace. It was they who had attempted the buttress on the previous day, and they had been very surprised to find the rope sling that we had left behind at Easter. They had got some twenty feet higher than we, and had spent three and a half hours in intensive "gardening". They considered the rocks possible above the point they had reached, and had driven in a piton as a belay. But unfortunately the piton

[1] Mr. G.W. Young lost a leg during the war, amputated above the knee.

had been dislodged, and, unwilling to tackle the section above with no support, they had retreated. Now, and most unselfishly, they advised us to try it, but this we were unwilling to do without them. Lounging on the terrace we expatiated – between mouthfuls of sandwiches – upon the obvious advantages of combining the two parties; it would be happier in every way. They had attempted the buttress and failed, so had we. Clogwyn Du'r Arddu could hardly stand the shock from a combined attack by a combination of both defeated armies thirsting for revenge.

We started in the following order – Longland leading, Pigott, myself, Eversden, and Morley Wood as sheet anchor bringing up the rear.

Conditions were very different from those on our last attempt. The day was warm and the rocks were dry. Longland went ahead in great style, and was soon up to the second stance, with Pigott ensconced above the first awkward slab. Soon came a pull on the rope and a cheery, 'Come on!' indicative of a hoped-for advance on my part.

When Pigott, Morley Wood, and Eversden retire from their professions they will always be able to pick up a comfortable living as landscape gardeners of the severe type. The climb was unrecognisable; where previously one had grasped substantial masses of turf, there was now smooth and uncompromising rock.

'How on earth do you get up this?' I inquired of Pigott, as I scrabbled about on the lower slab above the initial chimney.

'Well, you'll have to use that tuft,' he replied, pointing to a sparse and limp beard of grass hanging over, the edge of the slab.

'Glad you've left *something*,' I growled to myself and, pulling viciously at the beard, sprawled over the edge.

Within twenty minutes Longland passed the stance where our rope-loop of Easter still dangled.

Pigott joined him, and Longland progressed to a tiny turfy ledge set some twenty feet higher on the lean face of the slab. Above was the section that had stopped the others on the previous day. There was a long wait; the place would hardly yield softly. I advanced to the rope ring, and Pigott went up to join Longland on his diminutive ledge. There came another long wait. I looked up – two pairs of dissimilar breeches were actively defying gravity above; Eversden, who had joined me, was quietly contemplative; Morley Wood's appreciative grin illumined the depths. Now and again remarks and instructions floated down. 'In there; test it; now stick the rope through; take it gently, and if you get tired come back.' What had actually transpired was that Pigott had thoughtfully carried up two stones in his rucksack; one of them had been cunningly inserted into the crack and a loop of rope cut off and tied to it.

Longland had meanwhile with great difficulty changed into rubber shoes; but even with their aid his lead of the section above was a brilliant piece of climbing. To my mind it is the hardest bit of the ascent, and consists of an overhanging splayed-out chimney from the top of which it is necessary to step far out to the right. It is a long stride, the balance is critical, the handholds mere finger-scrapes, the exposure and the precipice beneath terrific. Only a man at the top of his form with nerve and skill working in perfect unison, could safely make it. Above was another slab; and if any particular portions of the climb are to be named I respectfully suggest as a suitable title the "Faith and Friction Slab". As I vacated the comfortable little hold at its foot I gazed downwards for a moment, and remarked Bicknell and Waller disporting themselves like two tiny pink frogs in the transparent waters of the llyn; whilst on the opposite bank two other pink patches told of Geoffrey Young and his shirt, though at that distance it was impossible to tell which was which.

'Have you got the matches?' inquired Pigott from above. These matches were throughout the climb a constant source of anxiety to Pigott, but on every occasion that we were together we forgot them, only to remember them when we were far apart again. There is, in fact, no portion of the climb, which is not associated to my mind with Pigott's craving to smoke and his demands for matches.

The air was breathless and hot; a smooth slate-coloured cloud underhung with coppery billows of cumuli slid lazily over Snowdon; a dusky purple swept down the cwm. Undoubtedly a storm was brewing, and rain was the last thing we wanted on the climb.

Above the "Faith and Friction Slab" Longland had, in the absence of a good belay, driven in a piton. It was the first that had ever gladdened my eye on a British rock climb; indeed, I understand that at Wasdale Head the hand that can drive a piton into British rock is regarded as capable of pulling a trigger upon a fox. Be that as it may, I have never seen a place, either at home or abroad, that called more for a piton; and I must own to a vast feeling of satisfaction on finding myself attached to it.

Why describe the remainder of the great slab in detail? It is a job for the guidebook writers. No doubt every handhold and foothold will be earmarked and catalogued in the future, because this route is unique so far as I know in Britain. The slab fought to the end – there was never a bit that was not difficult – and finished in a defiant overhang of turf clods. Below this overhang there was a section which was better climbed quickly, for the holds were small, and a man cannot hang indefinitely upon the tips of his fingers. Up it Longland floated with effortless ease and grace. Suddenly there was a shout of joy; he had reached the quartz-crowned ledge; the great slab was vanquished! The shout was taken up by each member of the party, and echoed joyfully around the cwm; our friends by the lake beneath clapped vigorously.

As I followed there came the ominous rumble of moving boulders, and I rebuked Longland and Pigott for thus rudely disturbing the peace of mind of those yet on the Great Slab.

The final section is very difficult, but at the last moment the wandering hand grasps a hold at least as comforting as the 'Thank God' hold on Lliwedd. A stout heave and the body writhes over the top; nothing remains save a few feet of easy work to the quartz-crowned ledge.

The ledge is actually a detached pinnacle separated from its parent cliff by a cleft which is choked with boulders. It was the movement of these that had interrupted my philosophical abstractions on the final section of the Great Slab. The ledge is only a few feet wide, but after the inch-wide holds of the last 250 feet it appeared as a veritable promenade. The situation upon it is amazing; the wall beneath is all but vertical down to the base of the cliff the face above overhangs. It is the ideal eagle's eyrie of fact or fiction.

Then did Pigott produce his cigarettes, and lo! the matches were forthcoming.

A little later we were all united on the ledge, struggling to extricate ourselves from the cobweb of rope that ensnared us.

The fates had been generous; it was not until the ledge was attained that the deluge was released. Had we been caught half-way up the Great Slab our position would have been distinctly unpleasant, especially in view of the leader's rubber shoes and we should have been forced to double-rope down again, always a tedious business for a large party. But Clogwyn Du'r Arddu had dozed that languorous May afternoon, and had awakened too late to preserve its dignity by invoking the aid of the weather. True we were not yet up, but we were within fifteen feet of the point we had reached when exploring from above. Certainly those fifteen feet were overhanging; but more than fifteen feet of overhang were required to stop Longland at this stage. Personally I had half-hoped that the previously considered and old-fashioned manoeuvre of "swinging the leader" from the end of the ledge into the groove up which we had planned to go might be essential. Longland, however, settled the question in arbitrary fashion by clinging up the overhang – the solitary piece of pure gymnastics on the climb – and gaining the platform above. The rest of us were in no particular hurry to follow, and we crouched down out of the rain contentedly smoking, in the pleasant consciousness that Longland was sitting above and getting wet. Finally one by one we strained up the overhang to the familiar ground above.

Some twenty minutes later, and four and a half hours from the foot of the buttress, we were grasping Longland's hand on the summit of the crags and congratulating him upon his magnificent leadership. It had been a great, a grand climb, and a very happily combined party. Now as we stood on the summit the storm was easing. In the east dim hills peered unsubstantially through a mist veil; overhead the rearguard of fat cumuli shook the last raindrops from their skirts; a steady line of washed blue advanced hard on the cloudy legions of the retreating storm. In the west a bushel of golden sun sovereigns gleamed on the distant sea. Turning, we plunged down into the shadowed cwm.

CHAPTER ELEVEN

Winter in the Oberland

THERE IS A BEND in the railway line near Thun where the traveller *en route* to Brig or Interlaken suddenly sees the snowy battlements of the Bernese Oberland rising above the deep blue waters of the Lake of Thun. There is an ethereal quality in the beauty of this mountain stronghold. It seems suspended in mid-air over a green sea of nearer pastural hills, and the most hardened mountaineers will feel their hearts quicken at the thought of winning to summits where the sunlit clouds pass in slow procession.

From this distance the scale is appreciated. The highest summits, such as the Finsteraarhorn, the Schreckhorn, or that trinity of grandeur the Jungfrau,

Mönch, and Eiger, are but points set above an elevated waste of eternal snows. From close at hand the eye is overpowered; it finds difficulty in estimating the relative size of glacier, precipice, and snowfield. To the visitor staying at Mürren, the cliffs of the "Black Monk", which face him across the Lauterbrunnen valley, might be two thousand feet or four thousand feet high, but mere thousands of feet convey little to his mind, and he will return to England with a feeling of having witnessed something sublime, but with few more definite impressions than those acquired by the visitor to the late Wembley Exhibition.

Like Sir Leslie Stephen, I must confess to an affection for the Oberland. It was the first high mountain range I saw. At the age of eight I wandered about its pastures, and gazed with childish longing at its snows. Even nowadays it is delightful to return to the Wengern Alp and, lying on the flower-gay turf, try to recapture the romance of those early days.

Of the three peaks which overlook the Wengern Alp the Jungfrau is the most beautiful. Her long flowing glaciers, with their network of crevasses, suggest the robes of a Grecian maiden, whilst her dark precipices, friezed with gleaming ice, are symbolical of an unapproachable virginity. The Mönch is more staid: he suggests his name, and stands aloof from the affairs of life, his firm square summit in commune with the stars. And lastly, the Eiger or "Ogre" springs from the pastures of Grindelwald and the Little Scheidegg in one tigerish sweep of rock and ice. Not even the Wetterhorn, the "Peak of Storms", can show more savage cliffs than these.

Prior to the winter of 1928–29 my acquaintance with the Oberland was limited to one spring skiing holiday and two summer holidays, but in December 1928 Dr. G. Graham Macphee and I arrived at Mürren with the intention of skiing on its glaciers and attempting some of the higher peaks.

Winter mountaineering conditions are very different to those of summer. Intense cold, sudden blizzards and short days combine to keep all but a few mountaineers from the High Alps during this season. But to the true lover of nature in her sternest moods, there are compensations. In the summer the mountains are crowded, but in the winter the mountaineer will have them to himself. He will find quietude in the shelter huts, and will experience a loneliness comparable to Arctic wastes. He will discover new beauties of colour and distance, new grandeurs in vast horizons free from haze. He does not trudge up the dirty guttered ice of the glacier as in summer, but his ski bear him lightly over its snow-cloaked bosom. He will hear nothing save the soft swish of the parted snow and the occasional growl of an avalanche. These are but a tithe of the charms of high mountains in winter.

At Mürren we became acquainted with Mr. Flurscheim, a former member of the Cambridge University Mountaineering Club, and it was arranged that he should accompany us for two days. Our intention was to travel by the Jungfrau Railway to the Jungfraujoch, and make the hotel there our centre for a few days before attempting the classic high level traverse of the Oberland Glaciers to the Grimsel Pass and Meiringen. Accordingly, on 27 December we left Mürren, laden with a week's provisions, which together with our ski, ice axes, rope, and other equipment, made up a load of some 70 lb. per man.

Christmas Day had been followed by a bout of warm Föhn wind, and the conditions were as dismal as the spirits of the winter sportsmen at Mürren. Under these circumstances we were not altogether sorry to escape to altitudes beyond the influence of the Föhn, even though they entailed discomfort after the luxury of Mürren.

We descended to Lauterbrunnen by the railway. For my part, I must confess that a mountain railway of the type that drags its passengers from Lauterbrunnen to Grütsch and Mürren, has greater capacities for inspiring a dread of mountains than any ordinary incident, such as an avalanche or blizzard. However, the efficiency of this mode of travelling is now accepted, and it is only nervous folk like mountaineers who object to being locked up in a sort of tramcar which ascends an angle of at least half the vertical.

It was raining at Lauterbrunnen, and grey clouds sagged into the gloomy valley. We changed trains and commenced the long upward journey, which transports the tourist from a height of little more than 2,000 feet above the sea to the 11,400-foot high Jungfrau Joch.

Two hours later we changed again at Kleine Scheidegg, and commenced the last stage of the journey. We had not proceeded far when the unwelcome order came to get out and walk. Ahead, the line was blocked with snowdrifts, so shouldering our burdens we trudged up to the Eigergletscher station, passing gangs of workmen who were busy shovelling the line clear. The snow lay fifteen feet deep, too much even for the rotary snow ploughs of the electric locomotives, but the hardy Swiss workmen made light of their task and the weather. It needs but a slight wind to drift snow into the cutting and it is only by unremitting toil that this section of the line can be kept open in winter.

Another train was waiting at the Eigergletscher station. Above this station the line plunges into the six miles long tunnel which terminates at the Jungfraujoch.

It is a queer experience to travel on this railway. It burrows through the vitals of the Eiger and Mönch, and is not unlike the London Underground save that the sides of the tunnel are of rough-hewn rock, which is plastered here and there with black ice. It requires imagination to picture the hazardous toil, the money spent, and the engineering skill entailed in the construction of these Alpine tunnels. Few of those who yawn drowsily in the electrically heated coaches can be aware of these things and of the lives sacrificed for their pleasure.

There are two stations *en route*, the Eigerwand and the Eismeer. The first is but a shaft driven outwards through the northern precipices of the Eiger. Through thick plate-glass windows the tourist can gaze down to Grindelwald lying in its hill-girt basin, thousands of feet beneath. At the Eismeer station we changed trains for the last time, and twenty minutes later arrived at the Jungfrau Joch.

The hotel, which is combined with the station, is built into the solid rock of the ridge connecting the Jungfrau with the Mönch, It projects but a short distance from the rock, and is equipped with many devices that electricity renders possible, such as electrically heated walls and floors and electric cooking arrangements. It is strange to find modern invention at these inhospitable altitudes, and, owing to the peculiarities of its design, the hotel suggests some curious underground building in a far distant "Metropolis".

The weather was bad below, but up here a furious blizzard was raging. Nothing was to be seen outside save writhing clouds of winddriven snow, while a continuous screaming and roaring spoke of wind of exceptional violence. According to Herr Marti, who combines the posts of stationmaster and meteorologist, the wind speed reached the terrific velocity of 166 kilometres per hour.

That evening we were hospitably entertained by the hotel and railway staff. Herr Sommer, the genial English speaking proprietor of the hotel, possesses so large a stock of anecdotes and stories that no blizzard-bound mountaineer need fear boredom. In addition, Herr Marti, who is no mean exponent on the concertina, regaled us with old Swiss songs, to which the blizzard howled a fitting accompaniment.

Perhaps it was the altitude or our overheated bedroom, but we awoke next morning with splitting headaches. The wind had dropped considerably, but still blew in petulant gusts. Later the mists lifted a little, and the sun struggled through, illuminating the long reaches of the Jungfrau Firn and the Great Aletsch Glacier stretching away for fifteen miles beneath us.

Towards midday we ventured forth for a short expedition. The cold was intense, and the wind blew spitefully as we dug our way out through a small snow-choked door on to the Jungfraujoch, where we gazed for the first time to the north. A dun-coloured sea of cloud swamped all Northern Switzerland; as far as the eye could see it stretched to lap the level line of the Jura nearly a hundred miles away.

Carrying our ski, we descended a short steep slope to the Jungfrau Firn whence long gradual slopes lead up to the Ober Mönchjoch.

Another blizzard was brewing ere we gained the pass; the wind was rising, and the Jungfrau behind began to draw a diaphanous drapery of snow about her shoulders. But we were vouchsafed one glimpse which I shall treasure in my store of mountain memories. Boiling clouds filled the abysses of Eismeer on the eastern side of the pass, but as though ordered by some invisible jinn, they suddenly swayed asunder to disclose the beautiful peak of the Schreckhorn shining in brilliant sunlight. Solitary and aloof it rose, backed by a curtain of scowling mists. Then the sunlight died, the mists swept back, and in an instant it was gone. It is these vignettes that the mountaineer remembers, not the panoramas which the memory is incapable of grasping.

Snow was beginning to fall as we turned our ski homewards, and the Jungfrau had vanished in the advancing tide of the blizzard.

There is little sensation of speed in skiing down a glacier. So vast is the scale that the peaks on either hand appear stationary. Only by falling does one realise that the speed is twenty miles an hour or more. It is a queer dreamy sensation; a gentle drifting through space, with the song of the wind in the ears, and the world sliding smoothly away beneath. The slope to the Ober Mönch Joch had taken us an hour to ascend it took us perhaps five minutes to slide down.

A blizzard raged again that night, but we countered it by broaching a precious bottle of rum and making merry with a hot punch.

Next morning Flurscheim had to return to Mürren, but Macphee and I decided to stay on, despite the fact that the stationmaster's self-registering barograph had all but reached the bottom of the scale.

Our reward came when towards mid-day the mists dissolved, and a glorious sun burst through, disclosing a world of dazzling whiteness. Yet the wind still blew strongly, driving clouds of icy spindrift over the Jungfrau Firn and tearing the new snow from the ridges, until the peaks smoked like volcanoes.

We decided to attempt the Gespensterhorn, a peak of 12,415 feet situated to the south of the Jungfrau and Rottalhorn, and forming a point on the mountain wall which dominates the head of Lauterbrunnen.

Curiously enough, there was no mention of the peak in the Alpine Ski Club guide-book; perhaps due to its sinister reputation, for its name, being translated, means the Ghost Peak, and local superstition has it that the spirits of the damned flock out of the gloomy depths of Lauterbrunnen and the Rottal. Perhaps we were lucky, for we encountered no supernatural manifestations, and our only regret was in not having provided ourselves with spirits of a more tangible nature as fortification against the intense cold. Had we done so, we might have returned with tales which would have formed notable additions to Herr Sommer's repertoire.

A steep glacier, cleft by some large but well covered crevasses, took us up to the Lauithor. This pass was first crossed from the Lauterbrunnen side by Professor Tyndall and his Oberland guides. It has since fallen into disuse, but it remains one of the classic Alpine passes.

Another fifteen minutes sufficed to place us on the summit, where we greeted with enthusiasm the Monarch of all the Alps, Mont Blanc. Though seventy miles away, he rose faultlessly distinct, his shining dome clear-cut in a hazeless sky. From the Italian valleys to the Col du Midi every detail was visible, and even at that distance we could distinguish the intricate steeps of the Brenva face up which Professor Graham Brown and I had twice forced our way.

The conditions were ideal for photography, and with cold gloveless fingers fumbling at the manifold and irritating gadgets of the modern camera, I took photograph after photograph, until a complete numbness and an unpleasant sticking of bare flesh to the metal portions of the camera forced me to desist. Photography has its limitations in a temperature of –25° Centigrade, plus a strong wind.

The descent of the Gespensterhorn was a perfect ski run over deep crystalline powder snow.

Telemarks, Christianias, everything is easy in such snow. It is the snow that the ski runner dreams of but seldom encounters. Neither Macphee nor I have any illusions as to our lack of skiing skill, yet slopes that had taken us nearly two hours to ascend were descended in a few minutes of joyous running. Like wraiths we flitted down our peak, first in the sun, with the parted snow flying up behind in a million scintillating points of light; then over an edge, plunging into a cold well of shadowed glacier, swinging now to the right, and now to the left, and then in one swift straight rush. Has the world a greater magic to offer than that which lies latent in the slender wooden runners? Theirs is the poetry of motion to command at will.

The peaks were golden as we trudged up the last slopes to the Jungfraujoch and the sky was of that clear wind-swept greenish-purple peculiar to cold latitudes. There is a quality of sadness and death in this colouring: a suggestion of the infinite, the passionless and terrible depths of space. I am minded of an oil painting possessed by a friend. It depicts a frozen sea. Jumbled ice floes stretch into the far distance. The sky above is just the same inexorable greenish-purple. A thin shriven moon peers down on a scene of unvarying desolation and solitude. There is nothing to relieve the monotony, save only the twisted hull of a small craft broken in the grip of the floes. In the foreground are the torn and shredded remnants of a tent, and a few items of gear lie scattered around. A polar bear is crouched among them eating something.

Why is it that man should adventure thus far from the warmth and comforts of the world?

The following morning dawned brightly, and we decided to set out for the Jungfrau. Easy slopes brought us to the foot of the steep snow and ice face leading up to the Rottal Sattel. Up this we climbed on ski to the foot of a formidable wall of ice. Here we left our ski and proceeded on foot wearing Eckenstein crampons. At one point the ice wall lay back at an amenable angle, but the ice was hard, and required a staircase cut with the axe.

Once again the weather threatened a blizzard. Behind us the Mönch assumed a gauzy snow veil; a grey blankness stole up the zenith, stifling the sun; a sullen "inkpot" drowned the Plain of Bern, leaving only the hilltops hard and livid in the fading light.

My axe swung less resolutely, wavered, and stopped. Turning to Macphee, I pronounced for retreat. He agreed; and 'Most distressing' was his considered opinion of good work dissipated in the melting pot of defeat.

It was snowing by the time we had regained our ski – a fine snow of light particles, which fell with a crepitating, rustling sound as though tiny fairy brooms were brushing the snow. All shadow had gone, and the slopes were devoid of detail. In bad light, when it is impossible to distinguish the nature of the slopes, the ski runner feels bewilderment, and, unless he is a fool, proceeds with care. If he does not, he may find himself running unawares over a cliff or into a crevasse.

The blizzard came up apace, and within a few minutes our tracks had disappeared in the drifting snow. But the Jungfraujoch remained dimly visible, and we were soon roasting within its super-heated precincts. A quarter of an hour after our arrival a storm of Arctic severity was raging.

So far our plans of running to the Grimsel Pass *viâ* the Concordia Hut had not materialised; the weather was too treacherous. To descend to the Concordia Hut was to risk being blizzard-bound for several days. This is the misfortune that overtook Messrs Fox and Dalrymple and their guide Fritz Fuchs of Wengen the previous winter. Their food supply gave out, and they were forced to choose between descent to the Rhone Valley or ascent to the Jungfraujoch in doubtful weather and dangerous snow conditions. They were overtaken by an avalanche on the slopes of the Eggishorn, and Mr. Dalrymple lost his life. The other two escaped, and after a miserable night in the open succeeded in reaching safety.

In the present instance, the unusual lowness of the barometer was a sufficient indication of the weather's intentions, and we decided to remain at the Jungfraujoch.

The blizzard blew itself out during the night, and fine weather next day tempted us to tackle the Mönch.

A party of two, a man and a woman followed us when we left *en route* to the Ober Mönchjoch. They intended, they told us, to descend to the Concordia hut, and asked us whether the way was sign-posted. This was a somewhat naïve query, and they possessed no equipment, no rope, and no food. Their evident enthusiasm for mountains was so touching that we could hardly allow them to depart thus to their probable deaths, and with all the knowledge of German at my command I poured forth a stream of persuasive argument against this scheme. They listened politely, but it was plain that I made but little impression on them.

'Rope?' 'What matter?' 'Ice axes?'

'We do not need them.' 'The barometer?'

'Piff!' In despair I played my trump card. 'You have no food. You will starve.' It was the turning point. For rope, ice axes, barometer, they cared little. But to starve! 'Donnerwetter! We cannot starve!' For a few minutes they whispered together; then we observed with relief that they were following docilely in our wake. We could imagine them saying, 'Doubtless these Englishmen are mad, but to starve!'

For once it was a windless morning. The snow-fields were bathed in warm sunlight; the peaks had furled their snow banners. The Mönch rose on our left, a massive pile of rock and snow, its South-East Face defended by a regular escarpment of ice, from which occasional avalanches are detached to feed the ever-hungry Jungfrau Glacier beneath.

We reached the foot of the South Ridge, which falls a little to the west of the Ober Mönchjoch. There we took off ski and donned crampons and rope. The others who had followed behind now joined us, and we observed with some anxiety that they had evidently made up their minds to attach themselves to us. Their enthusiasm, as I have before remarked, was admirable, but when the lady started to climb alone up the initial slopes of the ridge above, our anxiety increased. However, she did not go far, and we passed her a few minutes later seated contentedly on a rock waiting for her companion.

Hard snow and scattered rocks took us rapidly up to the point where the ridge narrows abruptly. There we paused and glanced back. The others were slowly following unroped. Soon they would get into difficulties, and we should have to rescue them; the day would be wasted and our peak lost. Such were our selfish but not wholly inexcusable thoughts. But presently, to our great relief, we saw them turn and commence to descend.

Ten years ago, when a complete novice at mountaineering, I read a thrilling account entitled, "Up the Mönch, in a Storm", and as we ascended certain passages from this occurred to me, such as –

'High up on the ridge-pole of our peak the gale flung itself upon us.' And 'There was a wild plunge for foothold, it collapsed, and I toppled over the icy precipice with uninterrupted views of a vaporous nether world.' And 'It was the work of a desperate instant to spring backwards to the solid part of the mountain.' And '… sinister memories of great climbers flung to their doom …'

I hasten to add that nothing so exciting befell us. We certainly crossed one narrow snow edge, which the softness of the snow made hard work. Above this we wandered happily up to the summit ridge. Here we found ice, but our ten-point "Eckensteins" gripped it well. Cornices forced us to traverse low down across the ice slope. The angle was steep, and we moved carefully, for there is little security to be obtained when traversing ice.

Twenty minutes later we stood on the summit beside two spades sticking into the snow. We wondered what they were doing there, until we remembered that during the summer certain enthusiasts dug themselves an ice cave under the summit, in which they lived while making scientific observations. There was no sign of the cave now, and the flat summit was an unbroken expanse.

The Mönch, is 13,463 feet high, and we were rewarded by an extensive view. From Mont Blanc to the Ortler, and from the Black Forest to the Italian Apennines we gazed. Such views are unrealisable; even a cartographer can scarcely comprehend them. Distance becomes almost meaningless; the ranges appear as mere wrinkles on the earth's surface, yet between each wrinkle lies a valley, and in the valley are little villages, where dwell little communities immersed in the everyday affairs of life. Over them the eye passes languidly to the horizon until, tired with multifarious detail, it returns for rest to nearer objects.

The Mönch, is a better viewpoint in summer. Then it combines the beauty of valley pastures with glacier and snowfield. There is the superb sweep of the Great Aletsch Glacier and the humble pastures of the Wengern Alp or Grindelwald; the spotless serenity of the Ewigschneefeld and the violet waters of Thun. But in the winter, when snow covers lowlands and highlands impartially the scene is of unvarying and almost tedious sublimity. Contrast is the keynote to all true beauty.

A biting breeze forbade more than a few minutes halt on the summit, and soon we retraced our steps across the ice slope. Here occurred the solitary untoward incident of the day. In the middle of the traverse one of my crampons came partially off, and I was forced to balance awkwardly on the other foot and readjust it with fumbling half-frozen fingers.

Within an hour we had descended the ridge, regained our ski, and slid down to the Jungfraujoch. There was no sign of the other party, and we heard that they had descended by train, a sorry ending to their schemes, but possibly the happiest.

It was New Year's Eve, and after dark there were festivities at the Jungfraujoch. I must speak guardedly of these festivities, for I fear that they were of a distinctly alcoholic, not to say jovial, nature. Herr Sommer is the possessor of a cellar which he informed us houses liquid sufficient to last for five years, though at what rate of consumption he did not say. All I dare venture is that it must be an exceptionally large cellar, and must occupy a considerable portion of the Jungfrau's interior.

At midnight we all went outside. It was a clear starlit night and intensely cold, but I for one was glad of the cold. A large bonfire had been prepared, and this was drenched with petrol and paraffin. At twelve o'clock the stationmaster applied a match. In an instant a column of flame shot up which must have been seen over most of Northern Switzerland. Laughing and shivering, we clustered around it, the highest party of revellers in all Europe.

Presently, when the fire died low, the stationmaster produced a large tin filled with calcium carbide. Water was poured on to it, and the resultant gas lit. Up it went, a great sheet of white flame. Finally, in an access of enthusiasm, it was seized and hurled over the precipice, but some way down it lodged and lit the curtains of rock and ice with a weird flicker, as though some ghostly nocturnal orgy were taking place beneath us. This item all but ended in tragedy, for one of the staff, impatient to see what had become of it, scrambled over the low protecting fence, apparently forgetting about the precipice. We had him by the coat tails none too soon.

The closing incident of the out-of-door festivities was the bomb. This was a home-made affair of dangerous appearance that any anarchist might have been proud of. By order of the stationmaster we took cover behind the observatory, and there waited in breathless suspense. But it was a poor affair, and instead of a shattering explosion, all that happened was a feeble whoosh like a damp cracker.

This ended the pyrotechnic display, and we adjourned indoors for further revelry.

We had hoped to ascend the Gross Fiescherhorn next day, but less than an hour after starting the weather threatened another blizzard, and we retreated. A further drop of the barometer and worsening weather decided us to return to Mürren, which we reached on the evening of 2 January.

We had not done as much as we had hoped for, but at least we had ascended two peaks, and had enjoyed the hospitality of the highest hotel in Europe.

Macphee, unfortunately, had to return to England, and as there seemed no possibility of further ascents I was about to follow him when I met Mr. T.Y. Kagami of Tokyo, a member of the Cambridge University Mountaineering Club, who agreed to join forces.

We were both anxious to attempt the Eiger. This peak has been seldom climbed in winter for the ordinary route up the North-West Face is usually iced and impregnable. This snowy season the rocks were draped in snow and ice from top to bottom, and it needed but a glance from Mürren, to show the hopelessness of assaulting it. There remained but one alternative, by the North Eigerjoch, and the South Ridge of the mountain.

The North Eigerjoch was reached as far back as 1859 by a large party, consisting of Sir Leslie Stephen, George and William Mathews, and their guides. Apart from the complexity of the route, which lies up the broken icefall of the Eiger Glacier, their principal difficulties were due to dissensions among the guides. Stephen was accompanied by Ulrich Lauener of Grindelwald, and the Mathews by JeanBaptiste Croz and Charlet of Chamonix, Lauener was, perhaps naturally, apt to take a disparaging view of the Chamonix guides when in his own district on the other hand, the Chamonix guides were in the majority.

The Chamonix guides commenced by involving the party in great difficulties in the icefall, the ice pinnacles of which appeared so insecure that they earnestly cautioned the remainder of the party not to speak, lest the vibration brought down the delicately poised masses above them. 'On my translating this well-meant piece of advice to Lauener,' wrote Sir Leslie Stephen, 'he immediately selected the most dangerous looking pinnacle in sight, and mounting to the top of it, sent forth a series of screams loud enough, I should have thought, to bring down the top of the Mönch.'

After this Lauener took the lead, and they at length reached the North Eiger Joch. Here they found themselves gazing down the precipices that fall to the Eismeer, which Lauener proposed, and nobody seconded, they should descend. 'This proposition produced a subdued shudder from the travellers, and a volley of unreportable language from the Chamonix guides.' In the end, not liking the appearance of the ridge connecting the North and South Eigerjochs, they were forced to retrace their steps and cut directly up the long steep ice slope to the latter pass. Thence they descended to the Rhone valley, having accomplished an expedition which even nowadays ranks as one of the finest ice climbs in the Alps. Incidentally, no one has hitherto succeeded in ascending or descending the steep eastern side of the North Eigerjoch.

Our object was, therefore, to reach the North Eiger Joch and complete the ascent of the Eiger by its South Ridge. This ridge was tolerably familiar to me, as in 1923 a large party of us had ascended the Eiger by the ordinary way and descended the South Ridge to the North Eigerjoch whence we had traversed the ridge to the South Eigerjoch. On that occasion we were burdened with a sample of the new Everest oxygen apparatus, which we were testing for comfort. Doubtless it possessed its virtues, but comfort was certainly not one of them, and, apart from its weight of 42 lb., it resulted in some picturesque and imaginative language on the descent of the steep South Ridge, particularly at the point where it wedged its owner – myself – into a narrow rocky chimney.

The weather was unpromising when we left Mürren, snow was falling slightly, and a thick mist enveloped everything. We were inclined to scout the assertion of an official at the Eigergletscher station, who, in response to a telephone inquiry, had declared the weather to be "Wunderschön".

At Wengen it was dull and snowing fast, but as the train crawled upwards towards the Wengern Alp the light gradually improved, the sun became faintly visible, and we rose out of the mist into a perfect morning. Above stood the Eiger, clear-cut in a stainless blue sky unmarred by a single speck of cloud. Below was the mist sea from which we had emerged, its level sunlit surface covering all Northern Switzerland.

At Kleine Scheidegg we learnt that the Eigergletscher Hotel was closed, but we were fortunate in meeting Herr Sommer, who kindly arranged accommodation for us at the railway staff quarters.

On arrival at the Eigergletscher station we at once set out to prospect the route of the morrow. The snow of the Eiger Glacier proved hard and unskiable, so strapping on crampons we proceeded on foot.

Even without the aid of glasses it was obvious from Mürren, that the icefall was not only practicable but easy. Just below the northern rock face of the Mönch, started the most obvious of snowy corridors, which zigzagged without a break through the icefall. Mr. Arnold Lunn had ascended it partly on ski in May 1924, but encountered difficulties in surmounting an ice wall which barred the passage. But in this winter of heavy snowfall the irregularities had been smoothed over, and we were confident that no check awaited us.

Our first objective was the foot of the Mönch's northern rock face. The slope above us was badly crevassed, but at one point falling ice avalanches from a hanging glacier perched on the side of the Mönch had worn a smooth channel, filling the crevasses. Nevertheless, we should have preferred a less exposed if more intricate route in preference to running the gauntlet of this hanging glacier, as it was only too plain that at intervals huge avalanches sweep the channel. Our anxiety was enhanced by one semi-detached block of ice as substantial as Bush House in Kingsway, which leaned unpleasantly outwards from the main mass of the hanging glacier. However, all mountaineers are fatalists, and we proceeded cheerfully on our way, reflecting that, in the event of its failing, our end would be at least catastrophic and painless.

We had almost reached safety when there came a sharp crack from above, followed by a roar, and looking up we saw a small quantity of ice – a mere hundred tons or so – detach itself from the hanging glacier and pour down the cliff. It might be the prelude to something bigger, or it might well be big enough in itself. We did not wait to consider these things, however, but dashed to the left as hard as possible. Our haste was unnecessary, for the fall stopped above us.

Not long afterwards we returned, well satisfied to have explored the route to the foot of the corridor, and regained our quarters as the sun was firing the peaks with golden promise for the morrow.

We left next morning at 5.15 a.m. A thin moon was up, but the Jungfrau effectually concealed her, and we followed our previous route by lantern light. The weather was brilliantly clear, save for a moon-tinted mist which lay over Grindelwald and Lauterbrunnen, and a cold of perhaps –20° Centigrade gripped us rigidly.

We had barely started when there came the ominous growl of an ice avalanche from somewhere on the Eiger, answered, almost immediately, by a louder growl from the Mönch. Perhaps the "Ogre" had got news of our coming and was voicing his views to his brother the "Monk". There was something very disturbing in these long thunderous rolls from the dark maw of the night. It was as though the great peaks were issuing a warning to rash mortals about to violate their sanctuaries of snow. Mountaineering is not a sport for the superstitious or the believer in omens.

Dawn came as we attained the commencement of the corridor, and the pale brows of a thousand peaks in the west blushed to her caress. We did not stop to admire; time and cold are exacting opponents, and our brief halts were spent in vigorous kicking and stamping, in attempts to induce sluggish circulation to course through feet numbed with cold and tight crampon straps.

A steep slope, broken by half-choked crevasses, led up between a huddle of snow-crowned séracs. This brought us to the corridor, which surpassed our utmost expectations. There were many crevasses but no impassable ones, and the snow bridges were hard and firm. Our sole anxiety was the likelihood of being overwhelmed at any instant by a mass of tottering ice pinnacles above.

Mounting quickly, we bore across towards the cliffs of the Klein Eiger, and then doubled back again until under the northern face of the Mönch.

If the climbing was easy, the work was hard. Sometimes we could walk on hard snow crust, at others we would break through the crust into soft snow beneath; often we waded up to the calves in powdery snow. However, we made fairly rapid progress, and divided the labour of making the steps between us.

The scenery gained in grandeur as we ascended. To the right rose the terrific northern face of the Mönch, its cold lustreless ice grinning in the fangs of its avalanche-swept couloirs. On our left was tier upon tier of immense ice pinnacles, which seemed not unlike a horde of inebriated giants frozen in the act of descending to the lower regions. Before us were the sunny parabola of the North Eiger Joch and the bold final peak of the Eiger.

A long tedious grind up steep slopes brought us at last to the secluded little plain of snow at the head of the icefall. Over it we trudged, and at the end mounted a snow slope which brought us to the long-desired-for pass. My first proceeding was to let forth an enthusiastic Banzai! – in deference to my companion's nationality. It was Kagami's first guide-less expedition and his first big winter ascent. In spite of a lack of training he had gone remarkably well, and we had ascended over 4,000 feet in less than five hours.

Sitting down on the rocks, we investigated the good things in our rucksacks. Everything was frozen: butter was brick-like; chicken and ham were a mass of ice crystals. But one thing the cold had not affected: I have seldom imbibed any fluid more gratefully than the hot tea from Kagami's thermos flask.

The mists had retreated from Lauterbrunnen, and Mürren lay clear in the sunlight. Doubtless we were providing excellent material for the numerous telescopes there and at the Wengern Alp.[1] That, indeed, is the disadvantage of climbing on the northern wall of the Oberland the mountaineer always has an uncomfortable feeling that his every movement is being watched and commented on.

Like Sir Leslie Stephen, we looked down the precipices to Eismeer. They were armoured in ice and wreathed in snow which had been blown by the wind into forms of delicate beauty, whilst the very crest of the Joch was decorated by a cornice, which curled far outwards in an extravagant volute. Beyond rose the Schreckhorn and its neighbour the Lauteraarhorn, ice plastered and hoary. More to the south, over the reaches of the Ewigschneefeld, the "Field of Eternal Snow", the Finsteraarhorn's acute peak wedged the blue.

Twenty minutes passed, and we turned to the real work of the day.

A steep snow slope leads upwards from the North Eiger Joch for 300 feet before merging into the final rock ridge of the Eiger. The snow was in good condition, and we mounted quickly. So far our route had lain entirely over snow. The rock ridge was a very different proposition. It was heavily iced. Wind and blizzard had attached ice to every excrescence. Numberless glass-like daggers of it were laid in parallel rows across the slabs, thick at their point of attachment, and tapering out into a blade often a foot or more in length. Afterwards it occurred to me that the sight was an unusually beautiful one, but at the time I must confess to have reviled it, for it rendered 'a direct ascent of the ridge impossible'. We looked for an alternative. The only hope was to the left on to the North-West Face; a traverse would bring us to a long, steep, snow slope leading, apparently, to the summit. But to gain this slope we had to descend from the ridge we were on for some distance before a horizontal traverse to it was possible. This descent was, in many ways, the nastiest bit of mountaineering that I remember to have undertaken. It was not that it was very difficult, but it was a place requiring unremitting care and attention to detail.

The angle was perhaps 55° certainly not less, and the smooth rocks were of little use, even as a means of securing the rope. All their interstices were ice-filled, and to climb them was impossible. Our route lay down a shallow chimney filled with loose and powdery snow a foot deep concealing ice-glazed rocks. The snow was only just firm enough to hold the foot in position, and it was a place where a slip of one must inevitably bring catastrophe on both. I went first, kicking and scraping for hold with my crampons, and Kagami followed in the all responsible position of last man, moving with the care and skill of the mountaineer who has acquired his craft behind first-rate guides.

1 We learnt afterwards that visitors at Mürren, were charged one franc per look. I greatly regret being a party to such extortion.

One of the most interesting psychological phases of a mountain climb is the capacity for resignation it can inspire. It is a much too uncomfortable business to get nervous, yet I must confess to a momentary qualm as I looked down the pitiless steeps below, and reflected on the long preliminary slide before 3,000 feet of precipices ended consciousness and life together.

I must even admit that I jammed myself as securely as possible in the chimney, and relieved my feelings by a little quiet swearing. On such occasions I discover a vocabulary that surprises me.

At last we were down the chimney, and could traverse towards the snow. We reached it, but here came a bitter disappointment. Not only were there rock slabs beneath, but the slope, being more exposed to the sun than the one that we had descended, was becoming avalanchy. Perhaps 500 feet below a large slice of it had already broken away and poured down the mountainside. We were but 400 feet from the summit, but the Eiger had beaten us. Retreat was inevitable.

The best line of descent appeared to be directly downwards to the ridge connecting the Eiger to the Klein Eiger. Thence, after a short ascent, we would be able to rejoin our upward tracks.

Once again we found ourselves on evil rock slabs thinly disguised by snow. There was one particularly unpleasant place – a steep descent followed by a traverse around a slabby corner. On it we deemed extra security of some kind advisable. Accordingly we spent a quarter of an hour scratching and burrowing like rabbits into the pastry-like rock, removing large chunks piecemeal in an endeavour to find something to place the rope around. But, quarry though we might, we could unearth nothing of more than moral support, and it was obvious that in the event of a jerk the rope must be pulled off. However, on such occasions the moral support is distinctly valuable. We learnt subsequently that these proceedings were watched with great interest through the telescopes, and that for once we puzzled the worthy folk at their ends.

At long last the slabs gave place to honest snow – honest, that is, to a point, for it was getting perilously near the avalanchy stage. Digging our feet well in, we hurried down as fast as possible, and were soon treading our original tracks, not without a certain feeling of thankfulness at being off such dangerous ground.

Then the laze on the Joch with plenty of time in hand, while the sun stole round and the shadow of the Mönch crept towards us. It had been a fair defeat, and a fair defeat does not rankle. On the other hand, we had reached the North Eiger Joch for the first time in winter, and the route up the Eiger Glacier had worked out exactly according to plan, despite certain gloomy prognostications from Olympian quarters at Mürren. Now, for a sunny hour, we could enjoy rest and meditation amid some of the grandest scenery in the Alps.

At 3.30 p.m. we commenced the descent, and had soon entered the chilling shadows of the glacier. On the North Eigerjoch and the upper slopes of the Eiger we had climbed in a hot sun, and our boots had thawed a little. My own boots had done more than thaw; they had leaked shamelessly and wetted my stockings, with the result that in the frigidity of the corridor both froze hard. This, combined with tight crampon straps across the uppers, stopped the circulation in the toes, which became suspiciously numb. Kagami was more fortunate with his boots, but he informed me that his toes also had lost sensation.

A gleam of reluctant sun had penetrated the glacier, and the crests of the séracs were aglow, but his presence was for once undesirable, as his warming rays might at any moment bring down the unstable pinnacles about our heads.

Suddenly our former tracks disappeared beneath a mass of tumbled ice blocks. For 200 yards our line of ascent had been swept by an immense ice avalanche. And another might come at any instant. There was no need to counsel speed. As one man we rushed across the dangerous area, scrambling over blocks of ice and halted panting in comparative safety.

There remained one more danger. "Bush House", as we had dubbed the hanging ice mass on the Mönch, appeared more unstable than before. The crack between it and its parent glacier had widened considerably. During our ascent we had not hurried unduly. Not because we had no desire to, but because we were going uphill. Our philosophical resignation was merely due to lack of wind. Coming down, I need hardly say, we bolted like scared rabbits.

Our haste was not unjustified. We were trudging up the last slope to our quarters when a long-drawn-out sullen roar rent the evening quietude, and looking back we saw a white cloud of ice debris, like smoke from a cannon shoot from the cliffs of the Mönch, and sweep with fearful speed the slopes we had descended. "Bush House" had fallen at last.

A few minutes later we were tenderly examining toes which were destined to remind us of the Eiger for some weeks to come.

I fear that this account has ended on a note of defeat, but defeat on a mountain is good for the soul. It teaches the mountaineer to respect and love the hills that an all-seeing Creator has raised for his inspiration and delight.

NOTE It is interesting to note that Mr. Arnold Lunn's party, which included Dr. Walter Amstutz and the late Willy Richardet, narrowly escaped disaster from an ice avalanche which fell from this same hanging glacier on the Mönch. Only a desperately quick and skilful piece of skiing saved Amstutz and Richardet. An admirable account of Mr. Lunn's expedition is included in his charming book, *The Mountains of Youth*.

CHAPTER TWELVE

Some Thoughts on Avalanches

THE QUESTION as to whether or not a slope will avalanche is the most vital problem the ski-runner has to face. A considerable amount has been written on the subject, but avalanches are still regarded by the majority of winter visitors to the Alps as haphazard affairs, to be classed with the "pine-tree's withered branch" in their behaviour, and only avoidable by good luck or attention to the warnings on the hotel notice board. During several seasons' skiing experience I have only met one or two ski-runners who possessed any but elementary ideas on the subject of avalanches; yet avalanches are an exact science and one which to my mind is one of the most fascinating branches of mountain-craft.

Avalanches do not affect the mountaineer on foot to nearly the same extent as the ski-runner. At the moment I can only recall the classic disaster resulting in the death of Bennen, while accidents to skiing parties flock into the mind. The reasons for this are –

1. That comparatively few climb on foot in winter.
2. That ski in themselves are definitely a more dangerous medium of progression than boots or raquettes.
3. That the man on foot necessarily follows a safer route than the man on ski. He instinctively follows the crests of ridges where the snow is usually hard and safe, while the man on ski naturally prefers smoother and more unbroken snow slopes where the risk of avalanches is considerably greater.

I can give some concrete examples to illustrate this thesis.

Once during a bout of spring Föhn, when staying at the Darmstädter Hut near St. Anton, I spent an afternoon experimenting on the relative safety of boots and ski. Near the hut was a short and steep slope of snow well sodden by the Föhn. First of all I traversed it on foot. There was no tendency of the slope to avalanche. Then, returning, I repeated the traverse on ski. The difference was striking. I had barely got half way across when the slope split away at the track of the ski and started to slide. The upper portion of the slope being no longer supported, followed the lower immediately. Thus, I was neatly imprisoned in the centre of the avalanche. As previously remarked, the slope was not long enough to present any possible danger, but it was an instructive little experiment for all that.

As regards "3", the accident near Zürs in 1926 is a very fair example. I know the place well, and have traversed the Valluga three times. A man climbing the peak on foot would instinctively avoid the steep slope of the Trittkopf, where the accident took place, as a route to the Paziel Glacier. To him the direct ascent of the terminal moraine would be much less wearying, quite apart from the question of relative safety. If he had mountaineering experience he would doubly avoid the Trittkopf slope, for not only is it long and steep, but its crest is heavily corniched in winter and presents the most obvious avalanche trap. Yet what ski-runner would undertake the trudge on foot up the rocky slope of the terminal moraine carrying his ski in preference to the less fatiguing but dangerous skiing route across the Trittkopf slope? This instance is repeated in numberless examples all over the Alps, and I will go so far as to say that, on the whole, the natural route for the ski-runner is very often an unsound one as compared with the natural route of the man on foot or raquettes. I am sure that the majority of avalanche accidents were not so much due to avalanchy conditions as to the following of the incorrect route in the "mountaineering" sense, which the employment of ski necessitated. Given two men, one on ski and one on foot, both equally ignorant of snowcraft, the man on foot would instinctively follow the safer route, for the simple reason that a ridge is his natural route, whereas a face is the natural route of the ski-runner.

It is simply and solely the development of skiing that has made snow-craft of such vital importance; the man who climbs on foot does not need such exhaustive knowledge because he is much less likely to detach an avalanche and does not need to venture upon such dangerous routes as the ski-runner.

Guides of olden days, such as Christian Almer, probably did not know as much about snowcraft as the modern ski-runner *ought* to know, but they knew all the snowcraft necessary to enable them to climb safely on foot or raquettes.

Thus it comes about that owing to ski and the unsound routes, which their use often entails, the science of avalanche detection has reached – on paper – a higher degree than it would otherwise have done. To say that skiing has done much to develop this is undoubtedly true, but ski-runners can hardly claim this with pride, for had it not been for the introduction of ski the number of avalanche accidents – and in justice to the ski-runner, the number of great peaks climbed in winter – would have remained infinitesimal. All ski-runners owe a debt of gratitude to Mr. Arnold Lunn, the author of *Alpine Skiing at all Heights and Seasons*, in which avalanche craft is very lucidly dealt with, and to Herr Wilhelm Paulke for his valuable exposition in *Die Gefahren die Alpen*.

The efforts of the Ski Club of Great Britain to instil snowcraft into ski-runners are admirable, but the vital point is that this most intricate branch of mountain craft can only be acquired by a long apprenticeship of the mountains in all their moods. However, the idea is excellent and the foundation of knowledge of snow-craft can be thus acquired.

The science of avalanches is an exact science depending upon definite physical laws, and my only excuse for this chapter is to place on record some observations extending over several seasons of winter mountaineering and skiing.

It may be of interest to go through the successive stages of avalanches. Snow when it first falls is crystalline. Each flake resembles a number of tiny ice feathers radiating from an apex. If the new snowfall falls on loose powder snow it quickly becomes consolidated with it, but if it falls on to crusted snow a considerable period may elapse before the two become homogeneous. In both cases before homogeneity takes place the slope may avalanche of its own volition, or as the result of some outward disturbance such as the cutting effect of a ski track. This homogeneity of the new snow with the old is produced by consolidation. In the case of crusted surface: the numberless crystals of new snow that fall on to it form millions of minute points of contact, but these points of contact are not sufficient to bind the two layers securely together. But soon the new snow begins to settle, and its weight tends to break the underlying crystals and press the new layer more firmly against the old layer. Sun and frost are the quickest agents of consolidation, but it is a mistake to suppose that fresh winter snow requires these. Consolidation proceeds independently from the constant shrinking of the snow-layer. As every one knows, by pressing two pieces of ice together one can cause them to unite. The same applies here. Pressure is sufficient to unite the numberless little ice crystals on the underside of the upper layer of newly fallen snow with the old snow beneath.

Wind is another factor that aids consolidation, and one which I have never seen mentioned. It has been stated that no ice can form at over 10,000 feet in mid-winter. This is not quite accurate. Sun may have no influence at all, but wind is an enormous factor. Board hard wind-crust is merely wind-consolidated snow in the first stages of ice. During some recent ascents in the Bernese Oberland some blizzards of great severity were experienced, and afterwards the rock ridges at heights of over 12,000 feet were plastered in ice consisting of long-drawn out ice crystals as much as a foot long and six inches in diameter. Nothing but wind-pressure could have produced this ice, and the influence of wind-pressure on a slope of newly fallen snow must always exercise a consolidating effect.

Whether or not the newly fallen snow is wet or dry makes a considerable difference. Wet snow obviously falls at a temperature round about freezing point, and its crystals are less feathery than dry snow. That is to say, they are larger and fewer in number. They are like a tree with trimmed branches, whilst dry snow crystals are of far more complicated construction. The result of this is that there are even less contact points between the two layers with less adhesion and a consequent tendency to avalanche. Owing to the high temperature the two layers cannot unite, while the wetness of the new snow acts as a lubricant between the two layers. Directly the temperature falls, however, consolidation takes place with celerity, and not only does the new layer freeze firmly to the old but the slope is now one homogeneous mass safe enough to bear any number of ski-runners.

When snow falls with a wind two different factors enter into the situation. In the first case the snowflakes are blown directly against a slope, where they are consolidated by the pressure of the wind into a hard compact cake adhering by pressure to the underlying surface. This is wind-crust, and may vary from the slightest, barely noticeable crust, to a crust in the first stages of ice and hard enough to walk on. Owing to its consolidation by wind-pressure to the old layer beneath, it *cannot* avalanche.

The other variety of wind-blown snow is more subtle, and forms an avalanche trap which is the most difficult and unforeseen of all avalanche forms that the ski-runner has to contend with. It is known as *Schnee Brett* or windslab, and there still prevails a considerable diversity of opinion as to how it forms. I give my own observations and experiences for what they are worth.

When snow falls with a wind the snowflakes are blown along the surface of the snow or carried through the air until they meet rising ground. The snowflakes are blown up the slope and their delicate crystals are shattered by contact and friction, so that one snowflake may be resolved into a number of minute icy pellets. These are hurried up the slope, becoming even more rounded and icy in the process, and are finally driven over a ridge to fall or be blown downwards on the lee side. In the case of ordinary snowflakes unaffected by this wearing process the flakes are like feathers and have little weight in proportion to the area they occupy. Before consolidation they resemble a mass of feathers or spillikins piled upon one another, and their weight per volume is small. In the case of windblown snow, however, its tiny ice pellets occupy but a small volume relative to their weight, and when compacted are of a density many times greater than ordinary snowflakes. As mentioned, these little pellets pour over a ridge and settle in a compact cake on the lee side. The under surface of this cake instead of consisting of spiky feathery crystals, tending to bind it to the old snow-layer, is rounded and smooth. They resemble numberless minute ball-bearings tightly packed together. Now suppose that the consolidating process is still acting on the old snow-layer. It is still shrinking slightly and sinking in the process. The newly formed wind-slab, on the other hand, is so tightly compacted that it is unable to sink with it. An analogy is the apple dumpling. The apple under the influence of cooking shrinks, leaving a gap between the pastry which, being of a different consistency tightly compacted, cannot shrink with it. That is precisely the case with the wind-slab. The hard cake of the tightly compacted slab is left with an appreciable gap between it and the old snow-layer with only a few points of support and but little friction to prevent it avalanching. Nevertheless, unlike pastry the wind-slab is capable of consolidating with the under snowlayer. The process is a slow one, and depends entirely on the stage of consolidation of the under layer. If this be ordinary old snow or consolidated wind-slab, the process is a comparatively rapid one. No gap can appear between the two layers, and in the course of a day or so the consolidation of the wind-slab will bind it to the under snow-layer and it will be safe. But where the under snow-layer is itself comparatively new and is still consolidating it is obvious that the process is a much longer one, and it may be days or even weeks before the windslab becomes safe, unless it is assisted materially in its consolidation by the sun.

Until consolidation has taken place the danger of an avalanche remains, and the wind-slab, provided it has not fallen of its own volition, lies in wait for the ski-runner or mountaineer. It is a form of avalanche of incalculable effect. Nothing at first sight can appear safer than a slope of snow which may be hard enough to walk upon. But suddenly with a booming roar the whole slope splits away, and, aided by the slight caving-in effect breaks up into a mass of hard blocks, sometimes feet thick, which imprison the ski-runner in an iron grasp. It needs but a slope of only 200 to 300 feet to prove fatal, and any one unfortunate enough to be caught in a wind-slab is as likely to be crushed by the weight of the hard snow-blocks as suffocated beneath them.

It has been my good fortune never to have been involved accidentally in a wind-slab or any other form of avalanche, but last winter I got a friend to photograph me while I traversed on ski a short slope of obvious wind-slab. This again was an instructive experiment. As previously mentioned the slope split, first at the ski track, and then above. It caved in and broke up at the same moment into the characteristic blocks of hard snow. Even on that small slope, which was not more than 50 feet long, I experienced a feeling of complete helplessness and was irresistibly borne downwards, while the weight of the snow-blocks on the ski twisted my legs and ankles uncomfortably. It is not the object of this chapter to describe the appearance of avalanchy snow, that is to be found in the textbooks, but I do not think that any textbook can adequately describe a wind-slab's appearance. It is discoverable only to the experienced eye by the texture of its surface, plus a knowledge of the direction of the wind which formed it, and the lie of the ground. It is also interesting to note that new snow is not necessary to form a wind-slab. Mere wind and blown loose snow is sufficient.

With the exception of the wet snow avalanche, which is too simple and obvious to mention here both in cause and effect, there is only one other main type of avalanche.

The *staublawine* or powder-snow avalanche is of little danger to the ski-runner, for no one in their senses would venture into a rocky, steeply-sided, narrow valley after a heavy snow-fall. Limestone valleys are especially liable to this form of avalanche. Large quantities of loose snow collect on the large broad sloping terraces, and in the incipient gullies peculiar to limestone. A movement is started and the incoherent snow begins to pour downwards like sugar. New snow has always a considerable amount of air imprisoned in it, and this air is released and flung before the downward pouring snow-stream. At least that is the accepted theory, but it is one which I have always regarded with suspicion. At all events the snow quickly gathers volume and rushes downwards pouring like a cascade over the cliffs, denuding every terrace of its snow, and finally, meeting the less steep lower slopes, shoots outwards across the valley, flinging a furious wind before it, sometimes strong enough to uproot dozens of trees. It is this wind which gives rise to the supposition that the snow contains imprisoned air. It does, but this wind is more probably the displacement of air by the avalanche. A large *staublawine* by virtue of its great volume necessarily displaces more air than a large wet snow avalanche which is of less volume but greater density.

Twenty-three degrees is the angle which has been agreed upon as the least angle at which an avalanche can take place, but in the case of a *staublawine* a much greater angle is required to set snow in motion; probably round about 50°. Thus it is that only slopes of a very high average angle are liable to this avalanche.

There is always something new to be learnt about snowcraft. This winter our party were turned back from an expedition by a long and steep slope composed of three feet of perfectly safe and consolidated powdery snow overlying an unsafe unconsolidated wind-slab. It would be difficult to imagine anything more treacherous and harder to foresee.

As I have said, snowcraft is a fascinating and absorbing study. If only ski-runners would realise this, the daily papers would be hard put to it for their usual and tragical winter "material".

CHAPTER THIRTEEN

The East Face of Aiguille du Plan: My Hardest Rock Climb

THE SNOWY DOME of Mont Blanc has often been compared to the cupola of some mid-aerial cathedral rising above a host of attendant Gothic spires. But so vast is the general scale of the range that the surrounding pinnacles seem insignificant against the immaculate breast of the monarch.

From the Montenvers Hotel above Chamonix, however, Mont Blanc is hidden behind his truculent supporters, and the true scale of the "Aiguilles", as they are termed, becomes apparent. The mountaineer will feel his heart quicken at his first sight of these grim rock peaks, sweeping up in 4,000 feet of clean granite precipices above the Mer de Glace.

It has taken two generations of mountaineers to unravel the problems offered by the Aiguilles and to tread their sharp summits. The Grépon once 'the most difficult climb in the Alps' and now 'an easy day for a lady', was first conquered by the late A.F. Mummery and his guides, Burgener and Venetz, as was also the Grands Charmoz; the Dru fell to Messrs. C.T. Dent and J. Walker Hartley, guided by Burgener and Maurer; whilst a more recent generation of rock climbers have ascended practically every peaklet and pinnacle.

Round about 1905 another factor was brought to bear in Mr. V.J.E. Ryan and his incomparable guides, the two Lochmatter brothers, who, not content with the standard routes up the Aiguilles, must needs choose the most difficult and inaccessible-looking of their sides and ridges as a playground for their inexhaustible energy. Even nowadays, when rock climbing has been brought to so fine an art that it has practically attained the limits of possibility, some of Ryan's routes stand unrepeated.

Highest of the Aiguilles to the west of the Mer de Glace rises the Aiguille du Plan, 12,050 feet. From the Requin hut the ascent is comparatively simple and lies for the most part up snow and glacier slopes. The northern side is famous for the *tour de force* by Mummery's party in 1892, which was described to the Alpine Club by Mr. Ellis Carr in a graphic paper entitled "Two Days on an Ice Slope". Their attempt failed after approaching very near success, and the climb was eventually completed by those fine French mountaineers, MM. Jacques Lagarde, Jacques de Lépiney, and Henry de Ségogne, But Mummery's leadership up the terrific ice slopes of the North Face must always rank as one of the finest feats of mountaineering determination and skill. The East Face of the mountain was ascended by Ryan and the Lochmatters in June 1906. No details were published, for Ryan was always reticent regarding his routes, but Franz Lochmatter wrote that he considered it to be the finest climb among the Aiguilles. The very fast time of the party, who only took twelve hours forty minutes from the Montenvers to gain the summit, testifies to the extraordinary climbing ability of Franz Lochmatter, who led the climb. This route had, prior to 1927, not been repeated.

So much has been written and said about the weather of 1927 that it is beyond my powers to invent any new expression or improve upon any old one. The only ingenious explanation that I have ever heard was that of an hotelkeeper during a heavy thaw at a popular winter sports resort. He said that Englishmen were responsible for the warm *Föhn* wind, and when I asked him why, replied. 'Because zey opens all ze windows and so, alas! lets ze 'ot air outside.'

When, on 21 July, my climbing companion, Mr. J.H.B. Bell, and I arrived at the Montenvers Hotel the weather on Mont Blanc seemed almost to reflect the unsettled conditions then existing on the Italian frontier.

Two days later, however, it cleared, and we spent a happy day in the sun prospecting a route up the icefall of the Glacier d'Envers de Blaitière to the foot of the East Face of the Aiguille du Plan. We found an easy way up the rocks of the north side, but at one point were forced on to the glacier and wriggled through a gritty hole in the ice under a sérac.

We left at 1.40 a.m. the following morning, armed with the admirable electric lighting contrivances advocated by Mr. P.J.H. Unna, the Alpine equipment expert, and wended our way up the Mer de Glace. Presently a shy moon arose from a couch of snowy mountains and smiled upon us in a friendly confidential sort of way, which could only mean fine weather.

Constraining once more through the gritty hole we were soon above the icefall.

Before us, over the gentle upper slopes of the glacier, the Aiguille du Plan shook the night from its shoulders, the deathly pallor of its cliffs changing imperceptibly to a dull crimson. On either hand the cliff curtains swept round magnificently from the Dent du Requin to the Grépon.

The Plan is supported on this side by a narrow scimitar-shaped buttress, and it was by this buttress that Captain Ryan and the Lochmatters made the first and only ascent of the East Face of the mountain.

Three great crevasses defended the foot of the buttress. The lower two were easily crossed, but the top one, or true bergschrund, proved more awkward. But, on the extreme right, the cleft was bridged, and we were able to gain the steep ice slope under the rocks of the Dent du Crocodile.

Ryan's party gained the crest of the buttress low down, but now the rocks were heavily iced. The only alternative was to ascend the couloir between the Plan and the Crocodile and break out on to the crest of the buttress at the earliest opportunity. For the next hour or so the couloir should be safe from falling stones or snow avalanches but it was obvious that once the sun warmed the face of the mountain above, the chute would become a trap of the deadliest description.

To gain the rocks at the foot of the couloir we must traverse the steep slope above the bergschrund. The avalanches from the couloir had worn out a deep channel several yards wide at this point; lower down this channel was strangled to a chimney of polished ice which emptied into the greedy maw of the bergschrund.

Bell was admirably placed under the rocks, and as I started to cross the couloir I laughingly remarked, 'You can hold me there all right.' Never was truer word spoken in jest. I had taken several steps across the couloir when something made me glance up to see if anything was falling as I was now directly in the line of fire. At the same instant I took a forward step. Up to then I had been traversing firm snow, but the moment I put my weight on to my forward foot I felt it sink through an inch or two of snow, strike hard ice, and slip. Events happened quickly. Unable to transfer my weight back upon my hindmost foot, I was forced to let my front foot slip. At the same instant I yelled, 'Look out!' to Bell, and throwing myself face downwards upon the slope drove the pick of my axe into the ice. But in the fraction of a second required to turn on my face and drive in my axe point I had acquired momentum. The in-driven axe point failed to check. But if it did not check the movement altogether it arrested the acceleration for perhaps a second – a second that might be of vital consequence in a case where a party are all together on an exposed slope. In the present instance I knew that Bell was so placed that he could easily hold me, and my action was purely instinctive. So for an instant I slid slowly with the pick of my axe grinding through the thin coating of snow into the ice beneath. But soon the coating of snow ceased and I reached pure ice, polished black and hard by the passage of falling debris. In an instant I flew off at a terrific velocity into the depths of the icy chimney; then there was a violent jerk on the rope to my waist swinging me violently, nose first, against the wall of the chimney, and I hung suspended. Well and truly had Bell held. It was the work of but a few moments to cut a small step with my ice axe and rest for a few moments, before commencing to cut a staircase up to the point of my undignified departure. It was my first slip on snow or ice, and I was deeply humiliated at the thought of my inexcusable carelessness. In all I suppose I fell some forty feet, the length of the fall being due to the fact of Bell being horizontally from me and a long length of rope connecting us.

Presently and without further incident we were reunited at the foot of the slabs forming the bed of the couloir. At once we saw the difficulty of the work confronting us; steep slabs covered with floury snow formed an unpromising means of progression, and it was only the hope of ultimate deliverance that took us within the confines of this evil place.

The climbing did not belie its appearance. Holds had to be scoured of their chilly load of snow; feet had to kick and scrape for the joints in the slabs. Early on we were forced into the bed of the couloir, where the only break in the smooth slabs was a crack down which soused a malevolent little stream.

It is the fashion nowadays to underestimate both difficulty and danger in mountaineering, but I cannot too strongly impress the difficulty and danger of this couloir, and the memory of this portion of the ascent detracts considerably from the sum total of one of the finest climbs in the Alps.

We were much longer than we had anticipated; the sun grew hotter as we laboured up the couloir, and the danger from avalanches became apparent. I was leading, and had just left the actual bed of the couloir in favour of the rocks to the left when I heard a sudden crack, followed by a grating roar, and looking to my right was horrified to see a large slab of solidified snow sliding down straight for Bell. There was no time to place the rope around anything, and nothing left for me to do save remain where I was, and hope that Bell was securely attached to the rocks by the rope in the event of him being swept off. The thing happened in an instant. Bell ducked down close beneath a small rock immediately above him the snow slab shot down clean over him, and an instant later, smashed to fragments, thundered away down the couloir sweeping it from end to end. Then, and not until the clamour of the avalanche had subsided, quietly and deliberately in his methodical Scottish, fashion, Bell proceeded to air his views about avalanches in general, the mountain we were on, and the incredible follies of mountaineering. His voice came up to me monotonously as I commenced the ascent once more, but there was nothing monotonous or hackneyed in his phraseology.

The rocks petered out into ice, not ordinary ice, but ice formed by water from above, almost black and unrelentingly hard. We looked for a way of escape to the crest of the buttress, but there was as yet no possibility and we resigned ourselves to the ice slope. About two hours later we found a niche on the left under an overhanging rock and there consumed a thoughtful meal; it was now 11.30 a.m. our progress had been funereal.

Our luncheon spot was not a comfortable one; we sat on an awkwardly tilted shelf with our legs dangling down the chill ice, and gazed into the depths of the couloir. These depths were grumbling with avalanches and falling stones, but we were safe now and they held no terrors for us.

Our immediate troubles were by no means at an end. Above our resting-place the ice slope swept up at an ever-increasing angle, and it was not even certain that it led to the buttress crest.

Continuing on our way, we were cheered by a patch of firm snow perhaps 100 feet long, but it gave way all too soon to the ice.

The slope became a veritable wall; handholds were necessary, and cutting became a constricted and tiring business. Mummery's party met with much the same thing on the North Face of the mountain. I do not know what the angle of the slope is, but I should place it as 60°. Here and there rocks projected through the ice, and we linked them as well as we could, but it was seldom that they proved of service either as temporary resting-places or belays for the rope.

There was recently a discussion at a meeting of The Alpine Club on the possibilities of arresting a fall by any member of a party on an ice slope, and many instances were quoted where men have been held by their comrades after a slip from their steps. It seems to me, however, that the question hinges on two vital factors – the hardness and steepness of the ice. On ice of hardness and steepness similar to that of the Plan, there is no question that a slip by any member of a party involves all in catastrophe.

The sun could not reach us, and if it was warm enough work for me cutting for hour after hour, it was a bitterly cold and uncomfortable business for Bell. During the five hours it took us to overcome the slope he was exposed to a constant bombardment of ice chips dislodged by my axe, and ice chips acquire a considerable velocity on such a steep slope, especially when the leader is some distance above the second man, as was often the case. But he endured it without complaint, while his numbed hands were cut and bruised by the ceaseless cannonade.

At last we emerged into the sunshine on the crest of the buttress, and, turning round for an instant to look at the slope beneath, murmured 'Impossible!' We were triumphant, but it was 3 p.m.

After the work we had undergone, the climbing ahead looked mild and friendly by comparison. Sunny slabs beckoned us up in a lean curving crest. Optimism bloomed afresh. 'In three hours we will be on the summit.' Never was man more utterly deceived.

The point at which we struck the buttress crest is, perhaps 1,200 feet below the summit, and this 1,200 feet took us nearly twelve hours of actual climbing time. We had not done the Mer de Glace face of the Grépon and comparison is not possible with that great climb. My own judgement may be biased – nine hours' work of the type we had undergone is a poor preliminary to severe rock climbing – but Bell and I are of the opinion that Ryan's route up the Plan is the most exacting climb that we have ever tackled.

We heaved ourselves to our feet and commenced the climb up the rocks of the buttress. These were by no means as dry as we had hoped, and we were often opposed by unstable snow edges set in airy disregard of the right of-way. These had to be flogged down with the axe before advance was possible.

Above was a prominent pinnacle. A sharp crest led to it, followed by a series of steep chimneys. These chimneys afforded us with a foretaste of what to expect. The buttress consists of a series of clean-cut granite slabs set at a high angle. These slabs are smooth and holdless, but weathering had caused them to split into sharp-edged cracks, also practically holdless, and it is up these cracks that the climber must go. Often they are so narrow that it is only possible to insert the toe of the boot and progression is made by jamming in the hand and pulling, often to the detriment of skin and knuckles. The cracks are seldom less than 60 feet in height, and often the whole of our 100-foot rope was requisitioned by the leader. Our difficulties were added to by the weight of our rucksacks, which had to be hauled up separately, as they tended to pull one backwards, so steep and exposed is the work.

Above the first pinnacle we came to a gap beyond which the difficulties increased. However, there was one guiding rule – an insuperable obstacle could usually be turned by traversing to the south.

Above the gap was a chimney, and here an incident occurred which might have resulted in very serious consequences. Near the top of the chimney was wedged a large stone. It looked insecure: and I very cautiously reached up with my hand to test it. But it was more than insecure: it had lodged by the veriest miracle, and at the first touch of my exploring fingers down it came with brutal force, jamming my knee against the wall of the chimney. The pain was considerable, and I tried vainly to loosen it with one hand, while clinging on as best I could with the other, at the same time yelling to Bell for help. To let go with both hands meant a backward fall and the certainty of a broken leg or worse. My leg was numb, and it was only a matter of time before my arms would relax their grip. With extraordinary promptitude, speed, and presence of mind Bell worked his way up underneath and oscillated the stone until, just as my strength was going, it toppled away and crashed down, a hundredweight of hate, into the depths of the couloir beneath.

Beyond bruising and skinning no damage had been done, but the nervous and physical effects made me little more than a passenger for the remainder of the day.

An even more unfortunate occurrence was the loss of Bell's ice axe. The lead finally changed hands after the chimney incident and, with the exception of one or two short stretches remained with Bell for the rest of the climb. The most difficult problem we had had so far was an 80-foot thin crack into which it was just possible to jam the toe and the hand. Bell led this in magnificent style, but near the top accidentally dislodged his axe, which he had wedged for a moment in the crack. Down it clattered into the depths of the crack, irretrievably lost. As he explains it himself: 'I had a great affection for that axe: it was beautifully balanced and had befriended me on many a peak, and yet I was too tired to feel either great grief or annoyance. The whole incident was due to a muddle-headed indecision as to whether the axe was any use as a foothold or should be hauled up with the rest of the gear.'

An easier passage stretched ahead, and we made good progress to the foot of a very steep chimney. After the wriggling methods employed in negotiating the narrow cracks it was a relief to place the back against one wall of the chimney, the feet against the other, and progress by time-honoured methods.

Above the chimney a traverse on the left led nowhere; one to the right was no better: it was 7 p.m. and we were clearly benighted.

At the top of the chimney, and just to the right of it, was a ledge about four feet broad and twelve feet long. It was not as commodious as we could have desired, but it was the only ledge we had seen large enough to lie upon and we greeted it with a pæan of praise and thanksgiving. At one end it ended abruptly over the depths of the Plan-Crocodile Couloir; the other sloped off uncomfortably into the mouth of the chimney we had last ascended. As regards the drop from the outside edge of it – we hastened to tie the rope in such a way as to prevent any involuntary sleepwalking in *that* direction.

By moving a large boulder we managed to arrange matters, and soon had the spirit-cooker in action brewing soup. And what soup it was! We lingered gratefully over each gulp; we luxuriated in the warmth that stole through our tired limbs;

we licked and scraped the last precious drops from the pan with the avidity of starved cats. Finally we stretched our cramped limbs, leaned back contentedly in our Zdarsky tent-sack, lit our pipes, and settled down to watch the pageantry of sunset.

The shadow sea had long since engulfed the Mer de Glace and was now lapping the crags of the Aiguille Verte. Slowly, insistently, the tide of night arose, pushing before it the crimson lees of day. The glorious northern precipices of the Grandes Jorasses glowed like a red-hot casting from a titan's forge. Above, the sky was a daffodil yellow, but over the long ridges of the Talèfre the night appeared marching swiftly in legion after legion with a skirmishing fringe of flashing stars.

Now the last blush had faded, and a cold deathly pallor came to the snows. Night had triumphed, and we gazed down in vain attempt to catch a glimpse of light from the Couvercle Hut to assure us that we were not the sole inhabitants of a forgotten world.

The night was very still, with scarcely a puff of wind, but now and again the silence was broken by the distant rumble of an avalanche or cracking noises from the glaciers beneath.

Finally we slept, to awake cramped, stiff, and shivering. As the hours passed the temperature dropped, it froze hard, and we became restless from cold and the numbing effects of cramp in our aching limbs. There was also an unpleasant tendency for the tent-sack to gradually work downwards towards the mouth of the chimney, and at frequent intervals we were forced to edge it back again by a series of wriggles. Perhaps I was luckier than Bell, for a large lump of ice and snow which occupied a part of the ledge formed a convenient pillow.

So we lay, sometimes dozing, sometimes watching the slow procession of stars. There were no lights to gladden us or arouse envious thoughts of other people sleeping in warm beds. We looked down upon a world of rock, and ice, and snow, governed only by the relentless law of gravity.

We spoke but little, beyond the conventional growls of quasi-humorous discontent proper to the occasion.

The moon was due to rise an hour or so before dawn, but it seemed an uncommonly long time in making an appearance and we reviled it for its tardiness. But at long last it slyly insinuated itself into the sky from behind the Talèfre, to be followed in due course by the feeble glimmer of dawn.

At 5 a.m. the sun rose in a cloudless sky, and we luxuriated in its life-giving rays for two hours before continuing on our way.

To fresh men the work was easier, but an awkward snow bulge and unstable snow edges took a long time to negotiate. Finally, we found further progress barred by a 100-foot pitch in the buttress. Further advance seemed hopeless at first sight, but a fearsome overhanging crack straight up the nose of the buttress offered a forlorn hope and Bell went at it with a will. For some minutes I saw him methodically working his way up, but then he paused and the mournful information that 'It wont go' was wafted down. Another way to the right seemed possible, but here the leaf of rock along which Bell started so hopefully thinned and thinned and finally ended altogether in a sheer slice of granite overhanging the depths of the Plan-Crocodile couloir.

The solution lay in a traverse low down to the left, and for this Bell removed his boots. I have never seen a more delicate and exposed traverse, and I realised as I watched Bell's progress that I was watching the finest piece of climbing that I had ever seen. Picture a smooth rock wall dropping without a break for perhaps a thousand feet, a wall whose hand and footholds consisted of the merest excrescences which on an ordinary climb would pass unnoticed. As I clawed, and dangled, and swung round myself on the rope I began to suspect Bell of becoming a sort of climbing "Faust" and of making certain arrangements with "Mephistopheles".

Chimney after chimney and crack after crack followed, always difficult and often bordering the impossible. At mid-day we sat down to lunch and watched several parties disporting themselves on the Dent du Requin. I think we both wished that we could exchange places with them, for as yet we saw no hope of deliverance, and the rocks immediately above us looked of the most hostile nature. Otherwise we might have enjoyed to the full the hour in the warm sun and the delicious repose after our severe contortions in the cracks and chimneys. At all events we judged ourselves to be within two or three hundred feet of the top.

On we went, hauling, wedging, and wriggling up the everlasting series of cracks. At every crack the rucksacks and ice axe had to be tied into a bundle and hauled up the rocks, an awkward and tiring business for Bell.

At length we realised with joy that we were indeed beneath the final buttress sweeping up to the summit rocks. But, seemingly, the only way was up an ugly narrow vertical crack, which appeared to ease off in slope some fifteen feet higher. To the right of the crack was a comfortable platform, but at the point where the crack commenced the platform petered out into the precipice.

Once again Bell took off his boots and standing as well as I could on the thin end of the platform and bracing myself against the rock I gave him a shoulder. It was a desperate place and I watched his efforts with great anxiety. If he fell I could not possibly hold him, and there was no belay for the rope; we would both go. For several minutes he strained and strained to gain the easier ground which was not more than a few feet above him. Another man might have overreached his strength and been unable to retreat. Not so Bell; I have never seen him climb a place from which he could not retreat safely if need be. At last after a terrible struggle, I heard him say, 'I can't do it,' and commenced to retire. Moving with the same safety and deliberation which characterises his climbing he came slowly down, until I was able to help him down over the last few feet on to the platform.

The question was, did Franz Lochmatter actually climb the crack? To us it seemed the only break in the cliff. On either hand the precipice appeared smooth and unbroken.

The situation was becoming serious. It was long after midday and we discussed the chances of another bivouac; the weather showed indications of a change. 'I've never seen such a mountain,' said Bell, 'but it's got to go!'

We descended and traversed to the right. It was a last forlorn hope. I was first and shouted to Bell, 'There's a chimney ahead, looks not too good, full of ice, but it might go.'

Ignoring this gem of logic. Bell joined me and started up the chimney. It was certainly a bad place; ice filled its interior, and a crack up the right wall afforded the sole alternative. Fifty feet up, the chimney thinned out into a wicked overhanging crack, which leant out and leered down upon us. But now came one of those dramatic surprises the mountains reserve for the mountaineer. Right across the hopeless looking wall to the left and unseen from below ran a narrow ledge. Half-wondering what further 'frightfulness' the mountains might have in store for us we passed along it. The ledge broadened. We walked. There was snow ahead and on it three people, two guides and voyageur, were descending by the ordinary easy way. We threw off the rope, raced past them, and a minute or two later stood on the summit of our peak.

NOTE

Since writing this account I have received a letter from Mr. Ryan which, in view of the fact that he published no details concerning his ascent, is of interest. He says:

> 'It is twenty-two years ago now, but I distinctly remember a long narrow crack just below the summit which, I think, brought us out practically on the top. It was the hardest climb I ever did; though we had it in perfect condition. All the climbs I did in 1905 and 1906 from the Mer de Glace were much of a muchness – *i.e.*, Grépon, Charmoz, Blaitière, Plan, but on the Plan the difficulties were longer. In 1914 I repeated Young's route on the Grépon, which was a great improvement on mine of 1905, but again not so long as the Plan.'

In view of these remarks, plus our own experiences, Bell and I see no reason to reverse our opinion that the East Face of the Aiguille du Plan is an ascent of something more than ordinary difficulty. It is in fact, the hardest rock climb I have ever done.

CHAPTER FOURTEEN

A Storm on the Aiguille Blanche

AT 9 A.M., 10 August 1927, Dr. G. Graham Macphee and I swung on weighty rucksacks and stepped out along the dusty road from Courmayeur to the Val Veni.

We were bound for the traverse of Mont Blanc by the Peuterey Ridge from the Brêche des Dames Anglaises. This great traverse, which is one of the longest climbs in the Alps, had been accomplished for the first time in its entirety by Herren Obersteiner and Schneider of Graz, Austria, but ten days previously and repeated on 4 August by Herr von Kehl, with two Grindelwald guides and a Courmayeur porter.

The Peuterey Ridge is itself broken into a series of peaks and pinnacles. Of these the principal summits are the Aiguille Noire de Peuterey, 12,380 feet, and the Aiguille Blanche de Peuterey, 13,480 feet culminating in Mont Blanc de Courmayeur and Mont Blanc, 15,780 feet.

In the deep brêche between the Aiguille Noire and the Aiguille Blanche rise a collection of grim pinnacles of extravagant Gothic aspect known as the Dames Anglaises, whereas separating the Aiguille Blanche from the main mass of Mont Blanc is another and far less deep gap, the Col de Peuterey. It will be seen, therefore,

1 Almscliff Crag in Yorkshire, the fierce gritstone outcrop where Smythe made some of his first rock climbs.
Photo: Ken Wilson

2 *(inset)* C.D. Frankland, one of the great Almscliff pioneers, whose famous Green Crack climb left a lasting impression on Smythe (the right slanting line, with ropes, just left and above the large boulder).
Archive photo

3 *(right)* On the Far West Buttress of Clogwyn Du'r Arddu. Smythe was an early explorer of this great Welsh cliff, adding three new routes and repeating the existing climbs. *Photo: Frank Smythe*

THE FIRST ASCENT OF THE WEST BUTTRESS OF CLOGWYN DU'R ARDDU

After his "Cloggy" explorations of 1920–21, Smythe returned to the cliff in 1928 with Jack Longland and others to attempt the unclimbed West Buttress. The most promising line was a slender groove/slab just right of the deep black chimney on the left flank. After a number of forays and attempts Smythe and Longland eventually teamed up with the Rucksack Club trio of Fred Pigott, Morley Wood and Bill Eversden to make the historic first ascent.

4 *(top left)* T. Graham Brown, Ivan Waller, Smythe and Longland (standing) prior to their first attempt.

5 *(lower left)* A supporting climber in full pioneering rig (nailed boots, ice axe etc) – the climb involved sustained "gardening" and cleaning of loose rocks.

6 *(lower centre)* Fred Pigott, who led the first ascent of the East Buttress in 1927 and courteously belayed Longland throughout the West Buttress ascent.

7 *(this page)* The left flank of the West Buttress. A party can be seen near the top of Longland's Climb (as the climb became known), just below the crevasse stance and the final steep wall.

Photos: Archive pictures and Ken Wilson (7)

8, 9 *(left and above)* The north side of Tödi (3614m/11,853ft) one of the main peaks of eastern Switzerland. This was Smythe's first significant summit climbed (by the Biferten Glacier route on the left) with G.N. Hewett (above) in June, 1922.

10 *(right)* George Bower on the Vire à Bicyclette on the Grépon, looking towards the summit block. The Venetz Crack splits the sunlit face, the Z Crack faces the camera and the Knubel Crack is further left on the East Face beyond the left skyline.

11 *(lower left)* Paglia Orba 2525m / 8282ft, the "Matterhorn of Corsica", which Smythe climbed with F.H. Slingsby in May, 1927.

12 *(near left)* Near Ober Mönchjoch after Christmas 1928, with the Jungfrau in the background. Smythe and Graham Macphee used the hotel on Jungfraujoch as a base to make ascents of Mönch and Gespensterhorn [Lauihorn?].

13 *(below)* T.J. Kagami at the Eigerjoch during the Eiger South Ridge attempt of New Year 1929.

Photos: Frank Smythe or Smythe archive

16 *(right)* Three of th Dolomite peaks climbed by Smythe in 1922–1923 – Grohmannspitze, Fünffingerspitze and Langkofel – seen from above Sella Pass. *Photo: John Cleare*

17, 18 Interwar climbers used primitive equipment and techniques. Abseils were made in a very basic classic style *(below)*. Nailed boots *(right)* were the norm (felt-soled scarpetti gave an option for hard climbs though they wore out quickly). Puttees served as crude gaitors. Ten-point crampons (lacking front points) did not remove the need for step-cuttin though the most efficien climbers (usually guides mastered skills that removed the step-cuttin chore on easier-angled ice slopes.

14, 15 *(above)* The thunderstorms that hit Smythe, Harrison and Douglas on the Schreckhorn (at A and B), prompted a hazardous retreat. Similar epics on Aig. Blanche and *(below)* after a Mont Maudit bivouac (with Parry and Harrison) made Smythe ever wary of the menace of alpine storms.

All uncredited photos: Frank Smythe

19, 20, 21, 22, 23 In 1923 Smythe joined Leslie and Howard Somervell *(centre insets)* for an ascent of the 3000ft N.E. Face of the Langkofel. Eduard Pichl and Rolf Waizer – Austrian soldiers stationed in the Val Gardena – had climbed this great Dolomite face in August 1918. Howard Somervell (in uniform) had this route planned for his training season prior to the 1924 Everest bid. The initial slabs *(inset right)* led to the Pichl Notch (the obvious skyline step). Above this a rising traverse *(left)* defeated two attempts before being led by Leslie Somervell. Further hard climbing and a long descent completed a memorable early repeat (probable 4th). *Photos: Smythe, Somervell archive (2), J.F. Burton and Wolf Jürgen Winkler*

24, 25, 26, 27, 28 Frank Smythe regarded his ascent of the East Face of the Plan with J.H.B. Bell as his hardest rock climb. The main picture shows Aiguille du Plan on the left and Dent du Crocodile on the right. In the action sequence Tony Smythe is seen leading some of the main pitches during a 1959 ascent. In 1927 the bergschrund was only bridgeable on the right forcing the climbers into the icy Plan/Crocodile Couloir (top left) until the main buttess could be gained. The other photos depict typical corner pitches on the buttress where Bell *(inset)* led the harder passages. *Photos: John Cleare and Frank Smythe (inset)*

29 *(left)* The Brenva Face: the original 1865 route follows the obvious diagonal ice ridge. The sunlit bulge of the Twisting Rib (Sentinelle Rouge) and the upper buttress of the Route Major can also be identified. *Photo: Wolf Jürgen Winkler*

30 *(above)* An "arranged marriage" – Edwin Herbert (Lord Tangley) introduces T. Graham Brown (centre) to Smythe (right) in 1927. *Photo: Graham Macphee*

31 *(right)* The annotated photo from *Brenva* of the upper buttress of the Route Major. C marks the crucial 1928 diversion to avoid the "Unclimbable Corner" (B). *Photo: T. Graham Brown*

32 The South-East (Brenva) Face of Mont Blanc seen from the summit of Tour Ronde. The Grande Pilier d'Angle (Eckpfeiler) and the Peuterey Ridge, that leads to Mont Blanc de Courmayeur, define the face on the left. The Old Brenva Route (or Brenva Spur) flanks the face on the right.

The buttresses are heavily snow-covered. The steep Red Sentinel buttress is seen clearly to the right of the lower narrows of the Great Couloir. The shadowy walls of the upper ice cliffs disgorge the periodic avalanches that make ascents of the face so serious.
Photo: Tony Riley

Scenes during the 1933 repeat ascent of the Route Major:
33 *(left)* Alexander Graven moving up from the "Unclimbable Corner". The ice in the corner is about three feet higher than in 1928; 34 *(above)* Alfred Aufdenblatten on the rib above the "Unclimbable Corner". The 1928 diversion finished up a steep ice slope to the left of the rib. *Photos: T. Graham Brown*

that the ascent of Mont Blanc from the Brêche des Dames Anglaises involves the traverse of the whole ridge of the Aiguille Blanche, itself one of the most formidable peaks in the Alps.

Conditions promised well. The weather of late had been bad, but many days of waiting and disappointment seemed on the eve of being rewarded, for the sun shone brilliantly and only a silver lock of cloud trailed from the summit of Mont Blanc.

The ugliness of grey skies and sullen cloud roofs was gone, and all was gay in the sunlight. We felt gay, too, but with a gayness tempered by doubt; would it, could it possibly last? The sum of many grievous failures was not to be easily dissipated.

As we trudged along the military road in the Val Veni we looked upon the great ramparts whose intricacies we hoped to unravel; the black precipices of the Aiguille Noire; the mass of the Aiguille Blanche, so elusively foreshortened. How vast they look, and yet that vastness is but a tithe of their real majesty.

Before entering on the wilderness of boulders below the slopes leading up to the Gamba Hut we rested and feasted on luscious bilberries. Placed between slabs of bread and butter they form a delicious dish undreamt of in the philosophy of Mrs. Beeton.

The slopes leading up to the Gamba Hut are wearisome; the sun shone with vigour on our backs and did his best to annihilate the more perishable articles in our sacks.

The Gamba Hut of the Club Alpino Italiano is situated on a little oasis of greenery enclosed by the jaws of the Brouillard and Peuterey Ridges. Glaciers riven and torn crawl down on either hand. Uneasy sounds of mountain strife, the forces of gravity and decay, come ceaselessly to the ear; the harsh roar of stones and the growl of ice avalanches echo threateningly around the cirque of precipices.

To the south the pastures of the Val Veni and Courmayeur are at the feet, and beyond gentle hills stretch to the snowy peaks of Cogne.

Long hard work was in front, and we stretched ourselves on the bunks for two hours of temporary luxuriance.

Other parties had meanwhile arrived. Mr. Eustace Thomas and Herr Zürcher with their guides, Josef Knubel and Lerjen; Dr. Hugo Müller with some friends; and an Italian party. A pleasant hour was spent in their company. We drank tea, packed our kit, and at 5.15 p.m. set off with the 'Good luck's' and 'Gute reise's' of our friends in our ears. In order to reach the foot of the Aiguille Blanche it is necessary to cross the Col de l'Innominata and traverse the broken and complicated Frêney Glacier. Macphee led off at a great pace and at 6.30 we stood on the Col de l'Innominata.

The day was almost spent and the wall of the Peuterey Ridge opposite looked terribly forbidding in the half-light. The livid huddle of séracs beneath seemed like some ghostly gathering, the sliced precipices of the Aiguille Noire a dungeon wall. The solemn stillness, the silence of great mountains at eventide, was unbroken save for one vagabond stone. But once it crashed and the echoes chuckled around; we listened in vain for the next crash, but heard instead the thin-drawn wail of its flight through space followed by a dull thud of relegation to the slow bosom of the glacier.

I know of no scene more dominating, more damning to hope and optimism, than the Peuterey Ridge viewed from the Col de l'Innominata. But one avenue of advance is visible, and that is the slender ribbon of snow couloir from the Frêney Glacier to the Brêche des Dames Anglaises. This we had planned to follow, but before we could attain the bergschrund at the foot we had to work out a route across the Frêney Glacier.

The descent to the glacier from the Col de l'Innominata is over a disagreeably loose rock face and a vile little crumbling gully half-filled with ice. Hard things were said here by the first man down, for however carefully we moved it was difficult not to dislodge stones.

A little later we stood on the summit of a square-topped ice pinnacle in a waste of shattered ice. The best way across the glacier was higher up, but how to get there? A wall of ice at least fifty feet high appeared to traverse the whole width of the glacier. There was nothing for it but to skulk in the maze of icy pinnacles and debris below this wall.

Already the first star shone tranquilly, far removed from our absurd problems; the last glow flamed on the peaks; we must hurry.

Momentary indecision gave place to fierce energy as we struggled and scrambled around, over, and between the tumbled blocks lying piled like the discarded bricks of the Ice King's children. Now across a half-choked crevasse, now leaping an abysmal cleft, now balancing on a slender edge, or crawling like rats through narrow corridors of polished ice. And at length the labyrinth was behind and we stamped our "Eckenstein" crampons into more sedate ground beneath the bergschrund at the foot of the couloir. The fortress is unassailable to direct assault; the dripping upper lip of the great bergschrund overhung the lower by twenty feet. But at one point on the left the moat was bridged, and we passed carefully over the icicle-fringed depths to the snow slope above. The snow, in the grip of the frost, was hard and we traversed quickly above the bergschrund into the couloir.

At the first rocks we halted for a meal. It had long seemed evident that we were carrying far too much; our sacks were unduly heavy. This I pointed out to Macphee, and to give weight to the assertion seized a large and unnecessary lump of cheese and hurled it viciously down the slope into the bergschrund. For once Macphee was startled out of his usual equanimity and he reproached me bitterly for the deed.

A full moon had now seized the torch of day and shone straight into the couloir. Climbing by moonlight produces a strange effect on the mind. One moves in another world, a dreamlike world, full of strange imaginings, mysterious and beautiful.

About two-thirds of the way up the couloir forks into a Y, the arms of which contain the rock pinnacle of the Isolée. We mounted by the left arm, which is narrow and deeply cut. No moonlight reached us here, but reflection served to light the way.

The angle steepened; the snow thinned and thinned; ice supervened.

The silence was broken by the ring of the axe; little fragments hissed away into the void; the goblins, if there were any, came forth to inquire at this disturbance of their nocturnal revels.

We sought for an alternative and found it on the rocks to the left; but it was an unpleasant alternative and gave us a foretaste of the many hours of climbing to follow. The rocks were treacherous, not merely unsound, but ready to come away at a touch, layer on layer like pastry; unstable debris covered every ledge. The point at which we left the couloir is perhaps 150 feet below the Brêche des Dames Anglaises, and as it is not possible to climb directly up the overhanging commencement of the South-East Ridge of the Aiguille Blanche from the brêche, it is necessary to traverse far out on the West Face of the mountain and gain the ridge higher up above the impasse.

The bad rock enforced extreme caution, and as far as possible we climbed in zigzags so that the leader should not dislodge stones upon the second man. Higher up the angle steepened, and the climbing became exposed and difficult in the waning moonlight. At 2 a.m. the moonlight failed, inky shadows leapt out upon us. A bivouac site was imperative. We found it on a neck connecting the main face of the mountain to an outstanding pinnacle. It was a chilly place – a bitter wind sighed through the gap – but it served. We made a hot drink with our spirit-cooker and crawled into our Zdarsky tent.

We slept little. The cold was intense, the interior of the tent was damp and clammy from condensation. I lay most of the time with the edge raised and drowsily watched the slow passage of the stars past the lean dark outline of the pinnacle. It was Macphee's first bivouac in the High Alps, but I did not altogether envy him his sensations; it was too cold for a proper appreciation of our magnificent situation far up the grandest ridge of the Alps.

Bodily discomfort and a mental appreciation of mountain scenery may be incompatible, but the greatest gifts of the hills are memories and sitting in reminiscent mood by the fireside it is not the discomforts, the trials, and hardships of a mountain climb that one remembers, but the scenery through which one has moved, the joys that one has discovered, the laughter, freedom and good fellowship of mountaineering.

Grey cheerless light stirred us to action. Frozen and fumbling we made hot tea and duly blessed its life-giving calories. At 5.30 a.m. we started, and commenced clambering, a trifle stiffly at first, up the slabs to the ridge.

Dawn broke as we reached the ridge – an evil dawn of smooth grey cloud zeppelins and fierce bars of scarlet, but presently the sun forced his way up and smiled kindly upon us. We welcomed him with breakfast, and seated on the ridge debated the problem of advance or retreat.

The Aiguille Blanche is the least known of the great alpine peaks, less on account of its technical difficulties than its complexity, length, and the dangers of enforced retreat. There is no mountain more stone-swept. Taking these facts into consideration, I think that it may be fairly described as the most difficult mountain in the Alps. We discussed the possibility of retreat by the way we had come, but the dangers of the stone-raked couloir make it an impossible avenue of escape except in early morning or late evening. The known alternative was the east face and down to the Brenva Glacier, but already this was alive with falling stones. In the end we decided to push on to the Col de Peuterey and, in the event of the bad weather developing, somehow force a way down to the Frêney Glacier.

Projecting from the South-East Ridge of the Aiguille Blanche is the rock tower known as the Grand Gendarme. Several hundred feet high, it rivals the Grépon in size, yet, such is the scale of the Peuterey Ridge, it is but an incident – an insignificant item of architecture. To avoid it, it is necessary to contour around its base on the east face of the mountain and regain the ridge above it.

On account of falling stones we kept too high and paid for it in an ice-filled chimney, a bad place, deeply cut, difficult to get into, and worse to climb out of. It cost us valuable, nay vital, time, for the weather, no longer undecided, was thickening up for evil, and there was now no further doubt as to its intentions.

At top speed we laboured on. The scale of this mountain is amazing. Up and up we climbed over interminable stretches of loose rocks, and at length reached the ridge once more above the Grand Gendarme. Snowflakes, the first harbingers of the storm, came flying out of the west to meet us. A sudden wind arose whipping them into our faces, then dropped to a momentary silence – the silence of brooding storm and expectancy of ill; rose again, this time on a note of unrestraint, a wine-bibbing giant's roar of rage.

On and on we scrambled, and at 1 p.m. stood on the summit of the Aiguille Blanche. The mists had parted slightly and we looked down into a dreary colourless world like a fogged negative, whence all contrast, all beauty, had vanished. In the depths beneath livid mists were born and came writhing silently up; now brought to a standstill; now torn by some inward dissension; now entering upon a stern resolve – the undisciplined armies of the storm marshalling to the attack.

The descent to the Col de Peuterey was slow work; the wind made movement difficult at times; the rocks were plastered in ice and snow. Fortunately our crampons saved us much step-cutting on the ice slope above the col.

At 3 p.m. we reached the col. A hurricane was now blowing on Mont Blanc and the noise of it resembled the deepest note of a cathedral organ. The Col de Peuterey itself was a fearful sight. The snow came whirling through the gap in a furious *tourmente*, whilst ever and anon came the mad crash of rocks from the crumbling precipices on the Brenva side.

We knew nothing of the route down to the Frêney Glacier, and were not even aware that it had never been descended, but we realised all through, by some curious inexplicable instinct, that it offered the best avenue of escape, and we were determined to get down somehow.

A bastion of rock 1,500 feet high falls from the gentle slopes beneath the col to the Frêney Glacier, and it was by this that at we made the descent. High up the rocks are smooth and slabby and offer no belays or support. It is easy to understand how Professor Balfour, F.R.S. and his guide, Johann Petrus, met with disaster in attempting to descend, as it is thought by this route. A slip by one member of a rope party must result in destruction to all.*

We were frequently in danger from falling stones *blown* off from above, whilst now and again gusts of enormous hailstones beat down upon us. At such times we could only crouch in close to the rocks. It was no time for half-measures. We cut up our rope and made a number of loops, and using our hundred feet of spare rope swung ourselves down the pitches, drawing our rope after us. But I believe these rocks to be climbable, and there is no question that a party retreating from the Peuterey Ridge in bad weather will be well advised to follow

* The bastion became known as the Rochers Gruber – Macphee was later complimentary about Smythe's skill during this difficult descent.

this route, in preference to the East Face of the Aiguille Blanche where that brilliant young Swiss mountaineer Willy Richardet was killed by falling stones.

The descent from the Col de Peuterey to the Frêney Glacier took us four hours, but our troubles were by no means at an end on the glacier. We had still the icefall to negotiate before we could rejoin our line of ascent at the Col de l'Innominata, and the light was failing. But fortune favoured us; we came suddenly upon footsteps and a neat little staircase cut up a cunning recess in the ice-wall. It was the work of Josef Knubel in prospecting the route to the Col de Peuterey for Mr. Eustace Thomas' party. So down we went and presently climbed the weary little couloir and loose rock face to the Col de l'Innominata.

It was almost dark when we stood on the col where, with nothing but easy ground, separating us from the Gamba Hut, we paused to watch a baleful lightning flicker. With incredible rapidity the storm approached. Never had we seen such a storm; its ferocity surpassed even those of the Argentine. The huge ramparts of the Brouillard and Peuterey flamed with a continuous mauve fire, while the hollow roll of thunder was flung from precipice to precipice in tremendous waves of sound, until it seemed that we were enclosed within the jaws of some monstrous dragon breathing hate upon the world.

We heard afterwards that there was a cloudburst over Montreux and a storm of unprecedented violence over the Italian Lakes; but Mont Blanc was the presiding genius, and we stumbled down the moraine half-blinded by the hail and electrical discharges.

At 9 p.m., just thirty-six hours after we started out from Courmayeur, we reached the hut. Our entry savoured of the best old-fashioned drama. The door opened to a blaze of lightning and a crash of thunder and in we went. As one man the occupants arose from the bunks and cheered. Kindly hands pulled our sopping clothes off our backs, our boots from our feet. Exciting liquids were poured down our throats, a hot meal prepared. The return of the 'Prodigal Son' was a poor affair compared to ours. And when at last our friends had ceased their ministrations we turned in, to listen thankfully to the straining of the stoutly built little hut and the wild raving of the storm outside.

CHAPTER FIFTEEN

The Red Sentinel of Mont Blanc

TO A MOUNTAINEER an Alpine peak is rather more than a mass of rock, snow and ice rising to inhospitable altitudes, and however much those who gaze from below may rhapsodise at beauty of form, grace of outline, and richness of colouring, they cannot experience the feelings of the climber setting forth to the attack; his doubts and fears; the fierce joy of conquest; the downwards glimpse through a breaking mist; the relaxation of taut muscles and strung nerves on the summit.

A great peak is only to be wooed and won after much preparation, toil and ofttimes, tribulation, and it is hardly surprising, therefore, to find in the caprices of mountains a close analogy to human nature. There are lucky mountains and unlucky mountains, mountains that repulse and mountains that welcome, beautiful mountains and ugly mountains. Let those without superstition, defy the Zmutt Ridge of the Matterhorn, and those who believe in luck and not probability the stone-swept couloir of the Col du Lion.

This temperamentality of mountains may be summed up in one word – weather; and of all Alpine peaks Mont Blanc is the most temperamental. I remember well the words of an old and famous guide.

'Ah, monsieur,' he said, 'there are many mountains, but only one Mont Blanc. He is king of all, but cruel and fickle; in the morning he may smile but in the afternoon he may kill you.'

The tourist, accompanied by guides, who ascends Mont Blanc in good weather by the ordinary snow route from Chamonix via the Grands Mulets, may return with the idea that the mountain is an easy snow promenade; but let him be caught on the summit ridge, or the complicated upper snow-fields, by one of the sudden storms that approach with but little warning, and he will have a very different story to tell – a story of roaring hurricane charged with numbing cold, paralysing to body and brain, suffocating wind-driven snow writhing in furious *tourmente*, and a slow plod for hours through a blankness where naught is visible. Under these conditions it is fatally easy for the most experienced mountaineers to diverge from the correct route, and many men despairing of finding the way, and tired of placing one foot before another, have sat down to rest – and died.

Yet sometimes the forces of unrest are stilled, and one may sit on the, summit with only the faintest of zephyrs whispering by, and a glorious sun blazing from a sky of deepest indigo blue.

Thus Mont Blanc by the ordinary way – a route by which any able-bodied man may under fair conditions, and with guides, gain the Alps' highest summit. Modern mountaineering, seeking to exercise its skill, has invented many alternative ways, until it seemed that every possible route had been made up the mountain.

As was the case elsewhere among the Alps, Englishmen played a great part in opening up the routes on Mont Blanc, and two of the finest mountaineering expeditions in the world, the Peuterey and Brenva Ridges, were first ascended by Englishmen and their guides. The traverse of the Peuterey Ridge, first made by the late Mr. Eccles and his guides, is now regarded as the blue riband of mountaineering achievement; whilst the Brenva route, the classic snow and ice expedition of the Alps – conquered more than sixty years ago by Messrs. Moore, Walker, and Matthews and their guides – has since been immortalised by Mr. A.E.W. Mason in his novel *Running Water*.

All these routes lie up the southern Italian face of Mont Blanc, grandest of all Alpine mountain-sides, which rises above the meadows of Courmayeur and the Val Veni in 12,000 feet of shattered glaciers, savage precipices, and icy steeps. So great is the scale of its ridges that the time necessary to overcome the climbs is reckoned not in hours but in days, and the possibility of bad weather overtaking a party high up is one to be seriously considered.

Mountaineering exacts its toll, and this great side of Mont Blanc has claimed valuable lives. Professor Balfour, F.R.S., was killed with his guide, Petrus, in an attempt on the Aiguille Blanche de Peuterey; H.O. Jones, his wife, and guide, Truffer, were killed on the Aiguille Rouge de Peuterey; and lastly, that splendid young Swiss mountaineer, Willy Richardet, was killed by falling stones in 1925 on the Aiguille Blanche de Peuterey, while retreating in bad weather and thick mist.

Dr. G. Graham Macphee of Ulverston and I have vivid recollections of our traverse of the Aiguille Blanche de Peuterey in an attempt without guides on Mont Blanc by the Peuterey Ridge; for we were overtaken by the same storm that inflicted widespread damage by cloudburst in lower Switzerland and the Italian Lakes on 11 August 1927. It is impossible to describe such weather at an altitude of 13,000 feet, and it was only by climbing continuously for sixteen hours without a halt that we were able to fight our way down to safety. As it was, our total time from Courmayeur was no less than thirty-six hours – a time which may convey some idea of the length of these expeditions on the southern flanks of Mont Blanc.

With the ascent of the Innominata face, which is enclosed between the Brouillard and Peuterey Ridges, by the Gugliermina brothers and Signor Ravelli in 1921, it appeared as though every possible route had been wrested from Mont Blanc. But one section – the greatest of all – remained inviolable. This was the South-East Face, which is bounded by the Brenva Ridge to the east, and the Peuterey Ridge to the west. So impregnable is it in appearance, that prior to 1927 not one single attempt had been made upon it. There is indeed no Alpine face, not even the eastern precipices of Monte Rosa to compare with this grand wall of rock and ice, which rises in a final sweep of 5,300 feet at an average angle of over 50° from the upper basin of the Brenva Glacier.

Many were those who had gazed upon it from the well-known tourist highway of the Col du Géant; some even had planned, and Mr. G.W. Young tells me that he and the late Mr. G.H.L. Mallory, who perished on Everest, examined a possible route; it was an ambition of Dr. Preuss, most skilful of the younger generation of German mountaineers, who was later killed in the Eastern Alps; Dr. Güssfeldt had studied it, and so, had others; but with one exception no one had actually ventured upon the face. The exception was the late Mr. A.F. Mummery's party, who diverged from the ordinary Brenva route to the left, and after cutting steps for many hours in hard ice were forced to retreat. Their route was, however, but a variation of the Brenva route, and later inspection has shown that its continuation is impossible on account of the formidable 200 feet high ice-wall which protects the brow of Mont Blanc. Professor Norman Collie, F.R.S., who was a member of the party, tells me that what impressed him most was the extraordinary steepness of the ice-swept couloirs, which seam the face. It was undoubtedly the threat of the impending wall of ice running along the crest of the face that prevented any attempt being made.

The mountaineer spends the winter in eating dinners and making plans for the summer and such is the optimism engendered by assimilation of the former that the latter are invariably made assuming perfect weather. It is a rash assumption, and my first visit to the range of Mont Blanc accompanied by Mr. T.S. Blakeney in June 1927 was fraught with two weeks of the most continuously foul weather that I have experienced.

There was little that we could do, save to trudge up to the Col de Géant and gaze regretfully at Mont Blanc scowling beneath a mantle of ashen *tourmente*.

Previously Blakeney had suggested the possibility of an attack on the South-East Face, and we had plotted routes on photographs, but my first view of the face plastered with snow and ice confirmed a certain scepticism for the project.

We retreated to Chamonix in tempest, snow, hail, rain – every weapon Mont Blanc thought fit to utilise to the completion of our discomfiture – and returned to England. During a fortnight's holiday we had not climbed a peak or crossed a pass.

But in spite of Mont Blanc's ungenerosity, I conceived a fascination for the great peak. The Oberland I know and love, Tyrol has always charmed, the Engadine and the Zermatt giants I shall return to, but 'There is only one Mont Blanc. He is king of all –' And all that is finest in mountain architecture and mountaineering is to be found on the range he rules.

In July I returned to the attack, and in company with Dr. R.Ogier Ward and Mr. G.S. Bower, ascended the Brenva route.

The weather had improved a little since June, but was unsettled enough to cause anxiety on every long climb. We were lucky on the Brenva, and laboured up its interminable slopes under a grilling sun. Owing to the snowy nature of the summer, the ice, which usually necessitates much tedious step-cutting, was overlaid with good snow, and instead of straddling the well-known ice-ridge *à cheval*, as did Mr. A.E.W. Mason's hero, we were able to walk upon its crest. It is exceedingly sharp nevertheless, and we moved along, with our "Eckenstein" crampons carefully implanted at every step and toes pointed out, not unlike a procession of Charlie Chaplins.

It was the condition of the snow which prompted reconsideration of the South-East Face. If this snow which lay uniformly on the Brenva route extended along the whole mountainside, there might well be justification in an assault. But, as always, thought and imagination would be brought to a dead stop against the final ice-wall defending the summit of Mont Blanc. To reach it, after perhaps two days of difficult and exacting climbing, and then have to return was unthinkable.

As August wore on storm succeeded storm with monotonous regularity, and one by one my friends returned to the even more doubtful humours of the British climate. It was at this stage, when everything seemed against any attempt on the climb on which I had now set my heart, that I was fortunate in discovering that Professor T. Graham Brown, F.R.S., who was also climbing with the Montenvers Hotel as his centre, was able and willing to stay on until the middle of September, if necessary. I accordingly suggested that we should join forces in an attempt to scale the South-East Face, and I was more than delighted when he agreed to do so. Indeed, I soon found that he shared my enthusiasm for this unclimbed side of Mont Blanc, and had examined it from the Col du Géant.

But as day after day passed and the high peaks whitened and whitened under the merciless lash of the blizzards, our spirits wilted with the enforced inactivity. We were reduced to planning desperate ascents on the peaks, traced out by the hotel barograph. Helped by a judicious bang the unfortunate instrument would always rise nobly to the occasion, only to sink lower than before. The other relaxation was the rotary gambling machine – a remarkable source of revenue to the proprietor. My friend, Mr. J.H.B. Bell, of Auchtermuchty, Fife, had, I should add, previously spent a considerable time in working out the odds on every colour, and finding them heavily in favour of the machine, wisely resisted its blandishments.

On 21 August a temporary clearance in the weather tempted us up the Petite Aiguille Verte, an easy peak of 11,400 feet. Deep new snow covered everything, and a biting wind whirled stinging ice particles in our faces. Winter appeared to have come into her own, and our pessimism, born of much disappointment, decreed weeks of good weather to put Mont Blanc into safe climbing condition. The weather on the 22 again brought discouragement, which was confirmed by even worse weather on the 23, when new snow lay on the veranda of the Montenvers Hotel, and the last visitors of the season went shivering down to Chamonix.

There appeared no alternative but ignominious retreat to England or the Italian Lakes. Our position resembled that of two swains mooning around the skirts of a mistress who repulsed with every weapon of primitive savagery. At this crucial stage Graham Brown was seized with a brilliant idea. We could at least go for a walking tour on the lower hills to the west of Mont Blanc, until such time as the mountain thought fit to receive us. The idea was good, for anything was better to mountaineers in training than the languors of the Italian Lakes or the leaden skies of Britain, and the same day saw us strolling leisurely over the pleasant pastures between Sallanches and Mégève.

We spent the night at the latter village, and for the first time that season found ourselves in an hotel that was not monopolised by our fellow-countrymen. The prices, too, were a revelation after the cosmopolitan tariffs of Chamonix. At dinner we were entertained by a swarthy Italian minstrel who accompanied himself well on a mandoline. He sang Neapolitan songs in a rich tenor, and wound up with the traditional "Funiculi funicula", in which the audience, forgetting their dinner, joined lustily. After dinner we were amused by a strolling acrobat, and our eardrums sorely tried by his small daughter, who sang in a piercing falsetto. Those who tire of the Anglicised table d'hotes of Chamonix or Zermatt should visit these charming uplands and quaint old villages to the west of Mont Blanc.

It rained hard next day, but we were by now well inured, and trudged over the hills to the south-west of Mégève. But as the day drew on, the mist drooped low upon the grassy hills, a mournful wind sobbed through the dripping pines and the rain descended in a deluge worthy of Cumberland. To escape a complete soaking we sought shelter in a deserted cattle hut, and spent a warm night in its snug hayloft, which, strangely enough, harboured neither mice, rats, nor fleas.

The weather improved the following morning, and as we tramped over the gentle pine-clad ridges, the clouds to the east were drawn back as though from some titanic stage, to reveal Mont Blanc aloof and stately in a sky of ominous steely blue. Later it rained again, but not maliciously, and in the golden calm of a perfect evening we descended to the little village of La Giettaz, on the southern slopes of the Col des Aravis.

For some reason we both felt unaccountably depressed. Perhaps the village itself is depressing in situation, lying as it does at the entrance to a gloomy gorge, and girt around by lofty craggy hills, whose abrupt precipices are darkly stained as though the mountains' life-blood had oozed from their veins. Edgar Allan Poe would have found inspiration in the old post inn. Never had we stayed in so dismal an habitation. No one spoke, and black-cowled monks from the neighbouring monastery crept noiselessly about on their sandals. Most mysterious of all, the bells and clocks struck not once but twice.

In spite of an excellent dinner and a bottle of good vintage wine, we went to bed behind a locked and barricaded door. Once I awoke from a horrid dream to hear the deep-toned monastery bell strike midnight, each reverberating boom echoing solemnly around the encircling hills, followed by a minute's silence and repetition.

We laughed at our unreasonable fears next morning, and set off in drenching rain to the inn on the Col des Aravis ; but we did not laugh when we reached the inn and learnt from a newspaper of the disaster on the Montenvers railway, in which twenty-three persons lost their lives. It is strange that the accident occurred in phase with our extraordinary feeling of depression during the evening that we spent at the "Sinister Inn", as we called it.

The same evening that we arrived at the Col des Aravis we watched Mont Blanc disentangle itself from a cloudy drapery and sink peacefully into a cold bath of stars. We did not then know that two parties, consisting altogether of five men, had been done to death by a blizzard the same day. Of these Dr. Grünwald and Herr Bickhoff, whom I had previously met at Courmayeur, were actually spending their climbing holiday on the range of Mont Blanc with the object, unknown to us, of attempting the South-East Face. Uncertain weather had forced the abandonment of their scheme, and they had crossed Mont Blanc by a conventional route to Chamonix, only to lose their lives on the Aiguille de Bionnassay. The other party of three young Italians disappeared in endeavouring to traverse the Col du Géant. The irony of their fate lay in the fact that they were remonstrated with, and every attempt was made to prevent them from starting; but they declared that if they did not return to Italy within a stipulated time they would be liable to imprisonment and loss of nationality. High mountains care little for State regulations, and Mont Blanc exacted the ultimate penalty on these three unfortunate young men. Their bodies remained undiscovered, and lie hidden in the ice of the "Glacier of the Giant".

On August 29 we returned to Chamonix in perfect weather, to find the town burying the dead of the railway disaster. As we walked up to the Montenvers Hotel we stopped to examine the wreck of the train.

Just below the hotel the railway bends round over an S-shaped viaduct and it was from the second bend of the S that the train left the metals. The gradient is steep at this point – about 1:8 – and the acceleration of the train must have been terrific once the cogwheels of the engine mounted out of the rack. The maximum speed of the trains on the line is nine kilometres per hour, and this speed is governed by an automatic braking arrangement on the locomotive. The latter utilises its steam as a brake on the descent by compressing it in the cylinders against the movements of the pistons. The driver, however, accidentally turned on full steam ahead instead of reversing the steam flow, with the result that the automatic braking arrangement, unable to withstand the sudden strain, broke down and the two cog-wheels mounted out of the centrally-placed rack, enabling the train to career down completely out of control.

Once the cogwheels had disengaged from the rack the driver was powerless, and there was nothing left for him to do to avert catastrophe.

Owing to rain and snow the blinds in both the coaches were securely fastened down, and none of the passengers were able to jump out to safety. The fireman saved himself, as did also the conductor of the first coach; the driver bravely remained at his post and was killed. The conductor of the second coach could have saved himself also, but instead he crawled along the footboard of his coach, uncoupled it from the first coach, crawled back again, and putting on the brake pulled the coach up as it was about to follow the fore part of the train over the edge of the viaduct. For this act of surpassing courage and promptitude of mind he was awarded the Legion of Honour.

The engine left the rails, as already stated, at the second bend of the S-shaped viaduct, and plunged through the parapet, dragging with it the first coachful of passengers. The drop at that point is about thirty feet on to the steep boulder-strewn mountainside, and the coach was practically dashed to pieces upon a large pointed boulder.

The weather was now perfect; there was not a cloud in the sky, and best of all the north wind – a sure sign of fair weather in the Alps – was blowing. At last we had the conditions for our climb.

Four days' provisions at least were necessary, and we spent a long time in cutting down the weight of food and equipment to the absolute minimum. Every article and luxury that was not an essential was ruthlessly ejected from our rucksacks, with the one exception of a small camera, until our burdens were reduced to a weight of some thirty pounds per man.

On the afternoon of August 30 we walked up the Mer de Glace to the Requin Hut. The weather was beautiful that evening, and we stood long outside the hut watching the calm passage of sunset along the peaks. Two other Englishmen, Mr. E.V. Slater and Mr. G.S. Sansom, were also stopping at the hut, and we enjoyed a pleasant evening in their company.

We slept but little, not on account of the excitement that always precedes a great climb, but because of torture from innumerable fleas and insects of even lower orders, and we were thankful to leave the hut at an early hour and trudge up the Géant Glacier to the inn on the Col du Géant.

The weather was irreproachable, but the north wind kept us moving briskly until the sun smiled from over the Dent du Géant.

We sat down to second breakfast under the rocks of the Vierge, the lonely "Virgin" who stands watch and ward over the snowfields of the Géant Glacier. A little distance away a large party of men were wandering, apparently aimlessly, among the labyrinth of crevasses. We could not understand their object, until we suddenly realised that they were searching for the three lost Italians.

From the point where we halted, the upper portion of Mont Blanc's South-East Face was in full view over the intermediate crest of the Tour Ronde Ridge. Long and earnestly we studied it through the small but excellent monocular carried by Graham Brown.

Could the ice-wall running across the brow of the mountain be surmounted or turned? In places this was up to 200 feet high. Unless we were assured that there was some possibility of overcoming it we were resolved not to attempt the climb. In such circumstances it would degenerate from legitimate mountaineering to a gamble, and mountains have no sympathy with the gambler. But, as we gazed, we were overjoyed to see that at one point the wall petered out into a smooth unbroken ice-slope – the sole breach in the fortification. 'But the decision,' wrote Graham Brown in his private account of the climb, 'must rest with the larger telescope at the Torino Hut. Not the final decision – that must be left to the process of trial and error – *absit omen ...*'

We arrived at the inn at 10.15 a.m., and occupied the remainder of the morning and most of the afternoon in careful examination of the visible part of our route.

A magnificent couloir descends from under the summit of Mont Blanc to the most westerly bay of the Upper Brenva Glacier. High up, this couloir is split into two arms by a bending rock ridge. The right fork of the Y so formed is comparatively short. The ridge ends above in the steep ice-slopes beneath the point where the ice wall is breached. In order to reach the bending ridge we must traverse across the foot of the right-hand branch couloir to the lower extremity of the bending ridge. Thence it looked possible to follow the ridge up to the point where the upper ice-slopes appeared feasible. Through the telescope these upper ice-slopes seemed of an easy angle, but the telescope lied to us. Once on the bending ridge, however, we should be safe from the avalanches of ice and stones that sweep down the two couloirs on either side of it. But the branch couloir must be crossed early if we were not to run the gauntlet from these ice and stone avalanches, which the sun would detach as soon as it touched the upper part of the mountain. To do this a secure bivouac place as high as possible was essential, and to discover this bivouac was our problem for the morrow.

All the afternoon we were faced, by that terrible view: the enormous ramparts of the Peuterey Ridge to Mont Blanc de Courmayeur, the Italian summit of Mont Blanc, and the 5,300-foot wall of Mont Blanc sweeping round to the Col de la Brenva. How cold and repelling it looked when the sun had left it, and the fear of it sank into both of us. Had one of us weakened then, the resolution of both would have failed, but neither of us liked to voice his fears to the other. We tore ourselves away, and passing round to the other side of the hut, rested our minds on the sunny prospect of green hills stretching away at the foot, and the afternoon light changing imperceptibly to gold on the distant snows of Monte Rosa. So the day passed, with not a solitary cloud pennon to usher it out.

We slept comfortably in real beds until we were awakened at 2.30 a.m. by the hateful clamour of an alarm clock. Glum and silent we ate the breakfast the obliging and kindly proprietor prepared for us, packed our rucksacks, strapped on our "Eckenstein" crampons, and at 3.30 a.m. stepped out into the night.

There was no moon, and far beneath the lights of Courmayeur blinked in feeble contrast to the ghostly banner of the Milky Way drawn across the breadth of Heaven.

In order to approach the foot of Mont Blanc, it was necessary to cross the Tour Ronde Ridge to the west of the Tour Ronde and descend to the upper basin of the Brenva Glacier. The Col du Trident, by which we intended to traverse the ridge, is itself a first-class expedition and had provided me with a stiff bout of step-cutting in steep hard ice on the occasion when I had ascended the Brenva route. We had therefore, many hours of hard work in front of us before we reached the foot of our climb.

According to doctors a man's vitality is lowest in the hours immediately preceding dawn, and the majority of deaths and suicides occur then. With this theory I entirely concur. More will power and mental effort is required, by the mountaineer at this period than at any other. There should be a feeling of excitement and elation at the thought of what the day may bring forth, and there are those who pretend that they experience it, in much the same way that the recruit pretends a love of battle. Personally I tramp behind a lantern apathetically, marvelling at the incredible folly of mountaineering in general and myself in particular. But after an hour or so of slogging along the brain awakens to a sense of responsibility to the body, and I gradually begin to take an interest in my surroundings.

The snow was soft and the wind warm as we breasted the Col des Flambeaux and struck over the western bay of the Géant Glacier towards the Col du Trident. The snow became ever softer as we progressed, and soon, from merely stamping a track, we were sinking in up to our knees at every step.

We waded on until we realised the immense time and labour involved in reaching the Col du Trident. We sat down hopelessly. In the end there was little to be done or said, and it was certain that we must postpone the climb. But at all events we were determined on obtaining a view of the lower part of our route, and with this object in view decided to spend the whole day, if needful, in ascending to the crest of the Tour Ronde Ridge, the nearest point of which was the Aiguille de Toule immediately above us.

It was still very dark, and as the ice we must cross looked considerably crevassed, we decided to await the dawn.

The next hour of sitting on the snow was the dreariest that I have ever spent on a mountain. All our hopes had been dashed by this unexpected contretemps of soft snow, all our preparations seemed to have been made in vain; for who could expect the fine weather to continue to hold out indefinitely and even the ever wonderful dawn tinge on the peaks was dismissed with a contemptuous snarl.

At last it was light enough to see, and we proceeded uphill towards the Aiguille de Toule.

We gained the peak without difficulty, but found that we must ascend to the summit of the Tour Ronde to obtain a satisfactory view of Mont Blanc. Seated on slabs of gneiss we munched our second breakfast; with the coming of the sun our grumpiness evaporated, and we set off in better spirits for the Tour Ronde.

The Tour Ronde is beset on this, the eastern side, by an extensive sore of rotten rock, which is eating into the very vitals of the mountain, and scarcely did a minute pass but a mass was detached to thunder down to the Géant Glacier. We gave the locality a wide berth, for many tons fall daily, and the peak was visibly and continually rotting before our eyes.

A steep ice-slope of considerable length leads up to the eastern ridge of the Tour Ronde, but our sharp crampons, helped by the well-cut steps of a former party, saved us much labour with the ice axe.

As we topped the ridge Mont Blanc burst upon us in all its magnificence. Far beneath the riven Brenva Glacier crawls down to the meadows of the Val Veni. All day long and all night its shattered ice-falls rage at the imperious behest of gravity, and the grumble of their discontent echoes sullenly around the gaunt precipices that enclose them. Higher up the glacier relents, and at the head of the icefalls is a little bay of snow, set like a peaceful strand 'twixt the frozen ice-billows and the huge face behind.

To the right of the great couloir, at the point where it narrows, a conspicuous red buttress projects from the face. It looked perpendicular, and we were at once assured that here – at its base – was the ideal situation for our bivouac. Not only was it placed in an exactly suitable position for a rapid traverse of the branch couloir early in the morning but it appeared to offer one of the few safe sites for a bivouac on the South East Face of Mont Blanc. Everywhere else was likely to be swept by ice avalanches from the fringe of hanging glaciers and ice walls above.

Two routes to the foot of it appeared possible. The first, by an upward traverse from the little col at the foot of the Brenva Ridge; the second, directly from below. In either case this small col, which we have since named Col Moore in honour of the first conqueror of the Brenva route, must previously be reached. This red buttress is the key to the climb; without its friendly protection the ascent would hardly be justifiable, and so delighted were we with it that we named it the "Red Sentinel", or "la Sentinelle Rouge".

We had reached the East Ridge of the Tour Ronde at 10 a.m. Many hours of daylight lay before us; the snow on all southerly slopes was good and hard; the weather was perfect. As one man we exclaimed, 'We will go on.'

The Tour Ronde is no part of a rapid or easy route from the Col du Géant to the upper Brenva Glacier, and from the point on the ridge where we halted on first seeing Mont Blanc, a long broken ridge confronted us, offering the prospect of several hours' climbing. The alternative was a direct horizontal traverse over the southern slopes of the Tour Ronde, which would have the advantage of taking us to the Col Oriental de la Tour Ronde, whence it is possible to descend to the Brenva Glacier. The excellent condition of the snow enabled us to walk with confidence over slopes of fully 50° in angle. The last wavering doubt was dissipated; we were coming to grips with things.

With our crampons biting well into the icy snow at every step, we passed steadily over the face of the Tour Ronde, probably the first party to undertake what would under icy conditions be a most hazardous route, but which was now perfectly safe, and an hour later found ourselves on the Col Oriental de la Tour Ronde, with nothing but steep snow slopes separating us from the Brenva Glacier and the base of our objective.

Soon we reached the snow bay at the head of the Brenva Glacier, and walked across its gentle expanses to the foot of the Col Moore at the commencement, of the Brenva Ridge.

The Col was protected by a half-choked crevasse and a wall of ice, perhaps sixty feet high, artfully overlaid with slushy snow. It was cold work for the leader; at every step the snow had to be shovelled and scraped away in order that a sound foothold could be cut into the solid substratum of ice. Cutting with one, hand whilst clinging to an ice handhold with the other is slow work, but our blood was up; axes swung viciously, and a little later we were straddling the knife-edged parabola of snow forming the summit of the col.

The snow ridge above the Col Moore leading to the lowest rocks of the ordinary Brenva route is remarkably acute, and the interested spectator, had he been present, would have observed two ordinarily rational men take up the burden of the serpent on its unstable crest. To put it more bluntly, we were forced to worm our way, inch by inch, on our bellies.

At 2 p.m. we gained the friendly rocks and sat down to a well-earned meal. We now saw that the route to the Red Sentinel was impossible, and to reach it we must traverse across the face. This traverse, which lies over ground of unrelenting steepness, involves the passage of no less than four couloirs. Of these, three were constantly swept by falling stones, and one formed the chute for the enormous ice avalanches that fall from a mass of tottering ice-pinnacles, hundreds of feet high, at the edge of a small hanging glacier perched up on the side of the mountain. To attempt a crossing while the hot sun was shining on the face would be suicidal; we must wait for it to pass, and for frost to curb the activities of the stone and avalanche fiends.

We had over two hours to wait, and we set to work to dry our clothes and stockings, which had become sodden from our crawl along the snow ridge.

We were now confident and happy. 'A very strange feeling of confidence,' wrote Graham Brown in his account. I experienced the same feeling. The unknown lower part of the route, which we had feared most, was now known; our early misgivings and fears had vanished. So we lazed a sunny hour away at the foot of the grandest mountain-side in the Alps, sometimes chatting, more often in silent contemplation of our surroundings, whilst the smoke from our pipes stole up the red granite crags in peace offering to the Mountain King whose inmost sanctuary we were about to invade.

Slowly the sun swung down behind Mont Blanc; cold purple shadows welled up the precipices; the ice of the Brenva Glacier changed in colour to a daffodil yellow.

The previous evening when the sun had set, Mont Blanc had appalled us, but now the shadow armies were our allies and friends.

The sun left us at 3.52 p.m., but we waited for the snow to harden properly.

At 4.50 p.m. we knocked out our pipes, strapped on our heavy rucksacks, and set off for the Red Sentinel.

The first of the four couloirs was simple – our crampons gave good purchase in the hard frozen snow – but the second couloir was seared by an ugly ice-groove ten feet deep, formed by the continual action of falling debris. Graham Brown drove in his axe to the head, and slowly paid out the rope, as I cut steps down the vertical side of the groove, then over its bed, and up the other side, keeping a careful look out meanwhile for falling stones. But the whole mountain-side was now silent as the grave, and we did not see the smallest stone fall.

The third couloir was easy, but the last is the one that may be swept at any moment by thousands of tons of ice-blocks. We raced across its slabby bed at the utmost speed, and flung ourselves panting down beneath the friendly protection of some overhanging rocks.

The Red Sentinel was now almost immediately above us, and we quickly climbed the steep slopes of rock, ice, and snow to its foot.

Our guardian is perhaps two hundred feet high, and projects defiantly from the mountainside in a smooth buttress of warm red granite. So pronounced is the overhang, that however great the avalanche that may fall from the hanging glaciers above, the debris cannot possibly harm any one at the base of it. In addition to this, the summit of the Sentinel is connected to the mountain-side by a sharp horizontal ridge of snow, and anything that falls from above is divided and sweeps the couloirs on either side.

A large inward-tilted slab lay at the base of it, covered by a cone of snow and ice. Twenty minutes chipping and scraping with our ice axes sufficed to fashion an alcove in the ice about three feet wide and seven feet long, protected at both ends, which was large enough for our Zdarsky tent-sack. To prevent any possibility of a nightmare roll from our narrow perch to the Brenva Glacier 1,500 feet beneath, we drove our ice axes in above and securely fastened the rope thereto.

We unpacked our rucksacks, made a hot soup over the spirit-cooker, and settled down to await the night. This was not long in coming. As the sun set, we saw the beautiful phenomenon described by Sir Leslie Stephen in his classic essay, "Sunset from Mont Blanc" – the immense shadow of the Monarch sweeping the ranges and finally mounting the sky. Like Stephen, we were privileged to witness the other sun, whose rays are shafts of darkness, but which are actually the parallel shadows of Mont Blanc, apparently converging on the horizon.

Yet day lingered awhile and long after the fires were quenched and the pageant passed on its way, a weird ashen glow steeped some stately cloud pillars brooding in the south. We expected to see them lightning-lit later, but on this most perfect of late summer nights even the Thunder God slept in his couch of cumuli.

The air was very still. Not a breath of wind whispered around the stern figure of the Sentinel above. It seems absurd to invest a mere rock with the attributes of sympathy and understanding; but all that night a friendly presence encompassed us, watching over the two little things that were men, who shivered and kicked on that hitherto untrodden mountain-side.

On these occasions amid the sublimity of Nature's innermost sanctuaries, where no human being has stood before, the mind is capable of asserting itself above the discomforts of the body, and the most prosaic of men will find his thoughts wandering in realms of strange fancy. The forces of the world are vast, and sometimes inexorably cruel; they care little for weaklings; but to those who deliberately set themselves to wrest from them their secrets they are often kind.

We estimated our height at 12,300 feet, and the clear starlit night was bitterly cold. No comfort was to be found in our Zdarsky tent-sack. As a means of refined torture these tent-sacks are admirable. They are so designed that the two victims sit inside facing one another, and supporting the fabric with their heads. A few minutes of partial suffocation follow until at length, unable to gasp longer without fresh stimulus, the lower edge is raised, and a gush of cold fresh air forces its way into the carbon-dioxidised interior. Meanwhile, the inside of the tent is saturated with condensed moisture, which drips unpleasantly down the neck. In fairness, however, it must be admitted that one of these tents might be of the greatest service to a party forced to bivouac high up in bad weather.

All night long the growl of avalanches was almost continuous, chiefly from the direction of the Peuterey Ridge and the crumbling rocks of the Tour Ronde; but between each growl of wrath there was complete and utter silence.

We were soon to learn the might of the Red Sentinel. Suddenly there came a crash from above, the increasing roar of thousands of tons of falling ice bearing downwards upon us. Then happened as we had foretold. The mass of the avalanche was divided by the Sentinel, and its two streams poured down the couloirs on either side a few yards away. So secure were we in the knowledge of our complete safety that we could appreciate to the full this unique experience, and our only regret was in not witnessing the spectacle.

For a few moments the masses went thundering past; then the noise subsided to a mutter, and finally died as the ice, ground to fragments in its fall, came to rest on the Brenva Glacier beneath.

One other incident of that eventful night I remember vividly. To induce warmth we brewed several cups of tea, and during one brewing we were startled to hear three long-drawn moans come up from the Brenva Glacier. Each moan was several seconds in duration, and seemed expressive of the utmost agony. They were inhuman in tone, and yet unlike any mechanical noise or syren that we had ever heard. I can offer no explanation. Glacier ice, under pressure, makes curious noises; it sometimes cracks, grates, and booms in the night, but I have never before heard a noise resembling those three extraordinary moans. The effect was weird in the extreme, and to us it seemed as though the very spirits of the lost or the damned were abroad that night.

Apart from these two excitements, sleep was impossible owing to the intense cold. Graham Brown endured it more philosophically than I, but suffered slight frostbite in his toes as a consequence. I spent most of the night in kicking my feet together, and periodically crawling out of the tent-sack for indulgence in the excellent exercise favoured among cab-drivers.

The night seemed endless and the World given over to perpetual darkness and cold, but at long last grey dawn filtered up from far Tyrol. We welcomed it with tea, ate some chocolate, and painfully strapped on crampons over the boots we had not removed all night. The iron stuck to our fingers with cold.

At 5.30 a.m. we passed out from beneath the Red Sentinel into the couloir on the west of it. With memories of the ice-avalanche that had swept it in the night, we climbed up and across this at the greatest possible speed, and soon gained the rock ridge on the edge of the main couloir. There can be no finer couloir in the Alps than this 5,000-foot chute. In the middle runs an enormous groove of ice 20 feet wide and 12 feet deep, writhing down like some evil serpent, and polished black by the passage of ice-avalanches and falling stones.

We descended into the couloir, and keeping close under the ridge, commenced the ascent. No falling material could touch us, for a friendly rock promontory projected ahead, and the hard snow at the side over which we mounted was smooth and unscored.

Our safety and the success of the expedition depended upon our crossing the branch couloir to the bending rock ridge before the sun obtained sufficient power to unleash the avalanches from the grip of the frost; and already the first glow of dawn was lighting the crest of Mont Blanc.

Gone now was the stiffness in our limbs engendered by our overnight chilling; the sweat poured from us as we laboured up the snow. To have met with hard ice here must have been fatal – the angle of the couloir is about 55°. But the good firm snow we had anticipated covered the ice, and our crampons ground well home into its frozen surface at every step.

Up and up we panted, until we were level with the lowest rocks of the bending ridge which splits the main couloir into two branches. Without a pause we rushed across the right hand branch couloir towards them, finding with thankfulness that a deep avalanche channel in the centre could be crossed without difficulty. At length we were on the bending ridge in perfect safety. Everything had worked out exactly to plan, and not a pebble had fallen.

Our previous examination through the telescope had shown that, once having attained the crest of the bending ridge, we were safe from avalanches for the remainder of the climb. We sat down on a slab of rock. Our exertions had been severe; for a few minutes we allowed mind and muscle to relax in infinite repose. Security is only worth while if one must fight and scheme to win it; it is moments like these that justify the motto, 'Live dangerously.'

We untied our rucksacks and ate the good things that we had been too numbed and stiff to assimilate beneath the Red Sentinel.

The morning was brilliantly clear, save for a few vagabond cloudlets floating about the distant Grivola; 10,000 feet beneath the meadows of Courmayeur drowsed in the morning shadow. An hour passed like an idle thought, and we turned once more to the ascent. As we did so we observed the first stones, loosened by the hot sun, whizzing down the couloirs on either side of the ridge. Our margin of safety had proved substantial, and we were well content.

We thought that above the climbing would become progressively easier, but here the telescope had entirely misled us, and we found the exact opposite to be actually the case. 'There was in fact,' wrote Graham Brown, 'only one short portion on which we were not moving one at a time. Such is the reality that perspective may clothe with fantasy on high mountains.'

The rock was unexpectedly sound, a grey red granite affording delightful climbing; it was a joy to grip its clean-cut holds and crawl up the friendly sun-warmed slabs.

A wall of rock perhaps 150 feet high cuts across the ridge, separating the lower portion from the upper. We avoided it on the right, and gained the crest of the ridge above over very steep ice. An edge of snow followed, moulded by the wind to a thin blade of fairylike beauty. It seemed a sacrilege to flog it down with the axe and to leave it mutilated by our clumsy passage.

Once again we were forced off the ridge by its difficulty on to an exposed ice-traverse under some rocks – ice so steep that we were forced to cut handholds as well as footholds. I have in mind an awkward corner, round which it was necessary to swing by gripping a leaf of rock with the hands into a little gully of pure ice. We regained the ridge, and continued along it over easier rocks to the point where it becomes horizontal and abuts against the mountainside. Here we noted with some anxiety that a 100-foot high rock face separated us from the upper ice-slopes leading up to the final ice-wall.

It was 10.30 a.m. and we sat down to another meal. Some way below on a ledge lay a piece of wood, and we speculated with interest as to how it could have come there. In shape it was similar to an aeroplane strut, but Graham Brown's suggestion that it was a piece of the old Jansen Observatory come down through the ice cap of Mont Blanc was probably the correct one.

The view was now superb. The ice-ridge of the Brenva had, sunk below us; the torn Brenva Glacier resembled the wrinkled countenance of an old man. We scanned the steeps for a view of the Red Sentinel, but it was now fully 1,500 feet below and out of sight. A violet haze filled the Italian valleys over which the distant snow peaks of Cogne rose like fairy castles from a sea of dreams. Far above, in grim reality, loomed the final ice-wall.

After building a cairn and leaving our names in a jam tin, we set off again at 11.45. Without trouble we passed along the horizontal crest of the ridge to the foot of the 100-foot rock face. There, to our relief we found that a beneficent Nature had placed a feasible chimney at precisely the spot where it was essential. Up to this point everything had gone marvellously well. Not once had we had to retrace our steps, no insuperable obstacle had presented itself, the curious unreasoning instinct that every mountaineer knows had proved infallible.

We were climbing on a rope-length of 100 feet, and at the top of the chimney I sat down on a ledge and proceeded to take in the rope as Graham Brown ascended. As I sat I allowed my gaze to wander over the expanses our height commanded until, out of the corner of my eye, I perceived a figure coming over the edge of the cliff at the top of the chimney. Graham Brown had evidently made short work of the chimney, and I turned to remark on the fact, but saw to my amazement that there was no one there. At the same time I heard Graham Brown's voice some distance below, and saw the piece of ribbon tied round the rope marking its mid-point just appearing out of the chimney. Hallucinations are not uncommon when body and brain are working at their utmost capacity, and the mental stress of a great climb is a very real factor, as apart from the purely physical. On this account the incident produced but little impression on me at the time, and was submerged beneath more practical considerations. I might even have forgotten it, had it not been for a remark of Graham Brown's when we were afterwards discussing the climb. He said –

'You know, Smythe, throughout the climb I always had the most curious feeling that there was a third man on the rope, and I couldn't rid myself of it all the way up. I think the feeling was strongest of all during the night beneath the "Red Sentinel".'

Above the rock wall we found ourselves on very steep ice-slopes, covered by a thin layer of slushy snow. And it was ice of exceptional hardness. The axe sank in with a dull thud, often without bringing away a chip. Many strokes were required to fashion a step, and every step represented a definite piece of hard work. The ice near the top of the Brenva route is of much the same consistency, and Dr. Claude Wilson described it in the *Alpine Journal* as 'Steep slippery ice, of a hardness unknown to us before, and with a curious quality unique in our experience, born probably of great cold and enormous pressure – a quality of viscosity which gave the impression of cutting into something which would not chip, but whose particles clung together like stiff tar, almost as hard as marble and tough as rubber.'

Some scattered rocks projecting through the ice were to the right of us, and we cut across towards them. We moved with the greatest care, yet had one of us slipped the rope would have served but to pull the other man from his steps. Personally the thought of a slip on the part of Graham Brown never entered my head, and I like to think that he felt the same. Mutual confidence in such a situation is the finest asset a climbing party can possess, and to my mind this confidence is one of the factors elevating mountaineering above the physical plane. There is nothing that promotes a greater understanding and friendship than a danger equally shared.

We gained the rocks and climbed them for a few feet until we were forced once more on to the ice-slope. Scattered about were other rocks, and we linked these as best we could by ascending traverses to right and left.

Against our will, we were gradually forced to the right, beneath the impending ice-wall, where it sweeps round a shoulder in the direction of Mont Blanc. Danger, however, there was none, for this portion of the wall was solidly built. Finally we turned left again, and clambered up to the highest rocks. We were now approaching the crux of the climb. Had the telescope spoken the truth, or was the fortress unassailable?

From our position we looked right along the mighty natural fortification. A veil of ice javelins hung from the upper edge glittering in the sun, and beneath the wall was sheared away as though cut by a knife of a skilled workman. We looked to the left and at once saw that the wall gradually decreased in height, and finally petered out altogether for a short distance in the ice-slope we had seen through the telescope. Once above it and we should be within the inmost keep of the Monarch.

We pressed on to the attack. On our left an ill-defined rib of ice, rounded and exceedingly steep, ran up the ice-slope at the point where the ice-wall is breached. To reach it involved a traverse across very steep ice. With hope in our hearts, our axes swung hard to their task, the fragments of ice went skipping into the depths beneath, and we were soon across.

We found the rib to consist of the usual glutinous ice. Up and up it swept at a pitiless angle, and many hours of continuous hacking seemed in prospect. But at all events, uncertainty as to the route was now at an end.

Once again fortune – the incredible fortune that had never forsaken us through all those strenuous hours – smiled. To the right of the ice-rib, and sheltered from the sun, two or three inches of hard snow clung to the ice sufficiently frozen to hold our crampons. Step cutting was unnecessary and we could walk up, albeit carefully, and with the picks of our axes firmly implanted at every step.

We climbed rapidly and passed between some bulges that evidently formed the remains of the ice-wall. Up and up we pressed, excitement growing at each foot gained. A small cornice curled over above, sun-kissed against the blue of Heaven. We halted a moment for breath, then fell upon it furiously and flogged it down. At 3.30 p.m. we crawled over and grasped hands. Nothing remained save a few hundred feet of easy snow to the summit of Mont Blanc.

Up went our arms and axes, and roars of joy were flung over the edge into Italy. For many hours we had been chained to the wall of the citadel; now that wall, terribly forbidding in the afternoon shadow, lay well below.

Unless I can carry the reader with me to that final cornice of Mont Blanc, how can I hope to convey an impression of those unforgettable moments? All I remember now was a vast shadowed gulf from the maw of which we had stepped into the sun; the snow breast of Mont Blanc above, curving deliberately into a sky of deepest blue; an insignificant evening breeze that murmured a welcome; silver foreground and blue distance shot tenderly with gold.

At 4.15 p.m. we stood on the summit of Mont Blanc.

The last party had gone, and on top at that late hour we were alone. A catalogue of peaks was ours to identify; 200 miles of distance ours to roam over; but we dreamt, and for a while trod space with the Gods.

Sunlit cloud genii stood out of the valleys; the haze over Italy had deepened to purple; we turned and tramped down the ordinary way to the Vallot Hut.

We had the hut to ourselves and slept well, despite the filth which defiles its shelter, until we were awakened in the morning by a tourist with a thermometer hung round his neck, and three guides bound for Mont Blanc.

We descended, not by the usual way, but by the Tête Rousse route, and in the evening arrived back at the Montenvers Hotel.

The proprietor and Josef Knubel joined us over a bottle of champagne. We were very happy. Before passing into sleep that night we both realised that rain was falling in torrents, and a furious storm raging on Mont Blanc.

CHAPTER SIXTEEN

Route Major

To appreciate fully the beauty and majesty of high mountains they should be viewed from afar. The visitor to the Alps, who is able to free himself from the hurry and bustle of Continental travel and "conducted tours", cannot do better than break his journey at some point northward of the Jura, and thence walking to their crest, discover the revelation of the High Alps seen over fifty miles of plain and hill. And if the day is clear he will see Mont Blanc rising in superb aloofness above the blue foothills of Geneva.

Prior to 1927 I had often gazed upon Mont Blanc from the peaks of the Pennine Alps, the Bernese Oberland, and Eastern Switzerland. I had glimpsed him as a steady cloud floating above clouds, or watched the sunset lights flame and die on his snowfields, long after the legions of the Alps had sunk to rest, until only the summit dome remained illumined, hung like a fairy lantern above the world and I have seen him scowling, ashen and grey, over the storm clouds sweeping up from Italy.

Mont Blanc possesses two summits; Mont Blanc itself, the highest point (15,780 feet), which is in French territory, and Mont Blanc de Courmayeur (15,595 feet), which is in Italy. A nearly horizontal ridge connects the two, sharp and jagged with rock teeth where it rises to the summit of Mont Blanc de Courmayeur, but gentle and snowy where it merges imperceptibly into the final dome of Mont Blanc.

Few venture downwards from Mont Blanc towards Mont Blanc de Courmayeur, for the average tourist is fully satisfied to have ascended by the ordinary easy route from Chamonix and trodden the highest point of the mountain. Untrained, bewildered with fatigue, altitude, cold, and the immensity of the view, it is doubtful whether he notices the ridge beneath him with its volute of snow curling delicately over an edge 12,000 feet above the bright pastures of Courmayeur and the Val Veni. But to mountaineers Mont Blanc de Courmayeur signifies much that is fine in mountaineering history. It is the culminating point of the grandest mountain-side in the Alps, the southernmost side of Mont Blanc, and the meeting-place of two of the Alps' longest ridges, the Peuterey Ridge and the Brouillard or "Misty Ridge", and until recently the indefinable glamour of the unknown clung to the gaunt precipices hemming the savage glaciers that creep down to the meadows of the Val Veni. Names famous in mountaineering history are linked with these southern facets of Mont Blanc. James Eccles, A.W. Moore, Dr. Güssfeldt, Mummery, the brothers Gugliermina, Captain Farrar, Messrs. Courtauld and Oliver, H.O. Jones, and G.W. Young, to mention but a few. To read of their struggles and conquests is to read of achievement, not only against natural difficulties and treacherous weather, but against the demon of supposed inaccessibility. Mont Blanc de Courmayeur! I cannot write the name without an instinctive tightening of heart and muscle. It is a sonorous, dignified, and beautiful name worthy of the high summit it adorns.

In 1927 as we climbed up and up the long rock and ice-slopes above the Red Sentinel towards Mont Blanc, we could not fail to notice a ridge to our left. In sickle-like curves of thin edged snow and ice it stretched, to abut against a steep buttress of rock surmounted by an ice wall hundreds of feet high. It was the largest ice wall that I have ever seen, greater even than those on the Jungfrau. To the right, the buttress appeared possible, and at the top the steep rocks sprang up into the ice-wall shouldering it aside, until at one place it rose but a mere thirty feet or so above the buttress. Once over it nothing remained save easy slopes cleft by a few crevasses to the summit ridge of Mont Blanc de Courmayeur. If this ridge was possible, it solved the problem of making the first route to the summit of Mont Blanc de Courmayeur from the Brenva Glacier and, incidentally, a new route up Mont Blanc itself.

All the winter we were haunted by thoughts of it. I dreamt of those untrodden ice-ridges, their narrow knife-like edges, and that final buttress of dark rock with its defending bastions of gleaming ice. Those were the difficulties; the danger was lower down. Mont Blanc is cleft on this side by a couloir as ferocious as the well-known Marinelli Couloir on Monte Rosa. It receives everything that falls from the cirque of hanging glaciers above; avalanches weighing thousands of tons crash down it, and in 1927, when we climbed for a while up its easternmost bank, its bed was of pure ice polished black and hard by the falling debris. This couloir we must cross to gain the safety of the ridge.

The season of 1928 will long be remembered as an exceptionally fine and dry one. Not since 1911 had the peaks appeared so bare of snow, and never do I remember glaciers so complicated and crevassed. Even the ordinary tourist route to the Col du Géant was denuded of its snow and became a maze of crevasses, becoming more intricate every day as the fierce sun melted away the snow bridges. Worst of all were the stone-falls. Several snowy seasons had combined to protect the rocks with a coverlet of snow, but now this was stripped from them by the sun to expose them to the ravening agents of decay. All day long, and sometimes all night, stones fell, not merely solitary stones or a few at a time, but thousands of tons of them. The precipices of the Droites and Verte smoked and groaned under the cannonade, and every couloir became a trap to the unwary. Let those who declare the mountains to be eternal see them in the nakedness of a dry season, and they will gain some idea of the forces that are ever at work levelling this rough world in which we live.

Graham Brown and I arrived at the Montenvers Hotel above Chamonix in the middle of July. Our advent was not a happy one. That first day as we sat outside the hotel on the terrace drinking in the joy of a peaceful evening we saw two men coming down the path with a shapeless sack-covered bundle slung upon a stout pole that rested upon their shoulders, followed by another two men with a similar bundle. For a moment I wondered idly as to the nature of their burdens, until I suddenly realised that they were the bodies of two French mountaineers, a man and his wife, who fell from the Aiguille Verte. But their accident was sheer bad luck: the woman had slipped, and her husband had planted his axe firmly into the snow. He had held, but the axe had broken, and he was dragged from his holds. Indeed, a party of guides found the broken shaft of the axe in the snow. It is interesting to note that the axe broke at the point where a leather band had been attached to prevent the arm sling slipping off the shaft; the wood had rotted and succumbed to the strain imposed upon it.

The evening seemed to grow cold and grey; the peaks, our friends of a few minutes before, became cruel; a chill arose from the glacier-people who had risen sat down awkwardly or passed indoors. A few minutes later a special train of one coach was chugging down to Chamonix.

Men must be exceptionally fit for long and arduous mountain climbs; the question of exhaustion high up on those pitiless ice-slopes of Mont Blanc had to be eliminated from the score of possible contingencies. And we were not fit. We realised it a day or two later on the cracks of the Grépon, up which we were ably led by one of the younger school of British rock climbers, Mr. Ivan Waller. But at all events the applied gymnastics and mechanics on the steep rocks of "Le Grand Diable" knit together muscles flabby from sedentary life in cities.

On 20 July we were joined by Mr. T.S. Blakeney. To him is due the credit for the conquest of the Brenva face of Mont Blanc in 1927. He was the first to suggest to me the possibility of ascending Mont Blanc by this side, and he had actually indicated on a photograph the charms of the two ridges on either side of the great couloir. It was cruel luck that prevented him from accompanying us on the climb, and sharing the joy of solving the greatest problem of all. And, in addition, I should like to mention how much we younger generation of mountaineers owe to the late Captain J.P. Farrar's encouragement and enthusiasm.

Three days later we sat and sunned ourselves on the warm summit slabs of the Trident de la Brenva. Superlatives obtrude with a fatal facility when writing of mountains, but it is impossible to say anything conveying a remote idea of the Brenva face of Mont Blanc seen across the upper basin of the Brenva Glacier. In fascinated wonderment the vision ascends its steeps, now pausing on the brink of some stark precipice, now hovering uncertainly on the sunless ice of an avalanche-swept couloir, up and ever up, until the neck is strained backwards, and the gaze seeks a way over that terrible wall of ice guarding the crest of Mont Blanc. In 1927 snow had predominated, but the fine weather of 1928 had stripped it from the rocks and ice, and even through a monocular we could distinguish a certain greenish gleam on the slopes above and in the couloirs below, whilst the slopes we must traverse to the Red Sentinel were scored with deep grooves cut by falling stones. We had hoped first of all to force a new way up the southern precipices of Mont Maudit, but here again the risk of falling stones and the impassable-looking bergschrunds deterred any attempt. Undoubtedly, new snow and colder weather were needed to put Mont Blanc into a suitable condition.

Next day we descended the hot and dusty slopes to Courmayeur, stopping *en route* in the green valley to bathe our tired feet in a little stream of deliciously cool and clear water. In Courmayeur we met Mr. Eustace Thomas, who had just completed the most extraordinary climbing feat of endurance and energy I know. Accompanied by his guide Josef Knubel, he had ascended four of the southernmost routes of Mont Blanc in a fortnight. He had traversed the Peuterey, Brouillard, and Brenva Ridges, and descended the great Innominata face of the mountain, all of them among the longest expeditions in the Alps. Those who consider themselves old at fifty-eight should take heart from this feat, which a young man at the zenith of his powers and training might well feel proud of. Under the influence of his boundless energy and enthusiasm we rallied; our plans were changed, and we decided forthwith to ascend to the bivouac place on the Brenva Glacier and attempt the climb. It was a happy party that forgathered that evening at the open-air cafe. The hot languorous air and the strains of the orchestra made it difficult to realise that in a day or so we should be shivering in a bivouac on the flanks of Mont Blanc. Alpine climbing is a curious admixture of civilisation and savagery.

We left at 8 a.m. the following morning for the ordinary Brenva bivouac. Two porters accompanied us one of whom, Proment by name, had acquired distinction the previous year by ascending the Peuterey Ridge with Herr von Kehl.

The snout of the Brenva Glacier looks out of place; it crawls across the meadows of the Val Veni, a mass of dirty grey-green ice disfigured by moraines and half-buried beneath the debris of the great rock and ice-avalanche that fell from the Peuterey Ridge in 1920. Boulders as large as cottages are poised precariously on the edge of its steep sides, until the ice beneath them melts and, their equilibrium disturbed, they hurtle madly down, crushing shrubs and smashing trees to matchwood, and even rendering dangerous the path between Entréves and the Brenva Chalets.

The heat was excessive that morning, and the blazing southern sun exulted from a sky of steely blue. The porters, stripped to their shirts, streamed with sweat; undoubtedly they earned their pay. We with our lighter loads toiled and sweated likewise in their wake. We halted at a chalet, and drank deep draughts of rich iced milk. It was long ere we could heave ourselves to our feet and swing our loads to shoulder once more.

We passed by the side of the restless glacier with its grumbling stone-falls and entered a pinewood. Sweet scents permeated the warm still air; a carpet of soft pine needles muffled our tread; ripe strawberries and bilberries invited us to halt. We emerged from the last weather-gnarled outposts of the forest on to the open mountainside. Ahead rose the Peuterey Ridge. First came the dark carnivorous-like fang of the Aiguille Noire de Peuterey, followed by the clustered spires of the grim "English Ladies" (Dames Anglaises). And the immense mass of the Aiguille

Blanche de Peuterey, most complicated and treacherous of Alpine peaks with a diadem of wind-carved snow resting upon the crest of its stone-swept precipices; and finally the upper portion of the great ridge to Mont, Blanc de Courmayeur and Mont Blanc.

We reached water, the first we had seen for a long time. It was dirty water, brown with glacial mud, but the thirsty porters assured us that it was good, and drank copiously. We followed their example – who could resist it? – and burying our faces, sucked in the welcome liquid. But it was an unwise indulgence, and an hour later Blakeney was attacked by a mild colic, nothing to worry about he assured us, but disquieting nevertheless in view of the long tough job we anticipated on the morrow.

After trudging up a buttress of broken rocks to the west of the stream, we came to a long wearying slope of loose stones, apparently arranged by the skilful hand of some diabolical demon, whose reward was barked shins and strong language. Half-way up the porters hesitated, and finally turned to the right on to an even worse slope, but we soon saw the reason for this move. High above, the side of the Brenva Glacier curved round in a wall of ice, whose crest was decorated with enormous boulders. Even as we ground upwards a rock weighing several tons heeled over. Plunging down the ice-cliff, it crashed with wild force and uproar down the very slope we would have been on had we continued straight ahead. As Graham Brown remarked, 'local knowledge is often useful,' and unguided parties ascending to the Brenva bivouac will do well to remember the existence of this subtle trap.

Some distance higher we gained the lower bivouac. Here we dismissed the porters and sat down for a rest. A quantity of aged newspapers paved the floor of the bivouac, among them being a year-old copy of "The Times" describing the sun's eclipse in 1927.

The weather had shown signs of a change, and now a brief shower was ushered in by a cannonade of thunder. Presently the sun reappeared, but it was a watery sun peering diffidently between purposeful masses of giant cumuli.

We decided to push on to the higher bivouac site without delay, and leaving the moraine, traversed the branch of the main Brenva Glacier flowing from the Aiguille de la Brenva. This branch glacier was easy and so uncrevassed as to make a rope unnecessary, but as regards the main ice-stream of the Brenva Glacier, a more broken glacier is inconceivable. There is nothing reposeful in it like the Great Aletsch: it is seamed with crevasses, and split into fantastic ice-pinnacles, and it groans and cracks like an old man in the throes of acute rheumatism.

The upper bivouac place is some two hours' walk above the lower. It is the best bivouac site that I have seen, well placed beneath the overhang of a rock nearly a hundred feet high, and sheltered from all but the most violent gusts of wind and rain. A couch of soft earth protected on the outside by a low wall of stones formed our "bedroom", whilst an adjoining space, also well-sheltered and littered with an abundance of old firewood, was the "kitchen". Soon we had collected all the wood and placed it under cover, enlarged the stone wall, and arranged the spirit-cooker in a convenient corner of the "kitchen".

Distant thunder growled as we ate our supper, and a stormy night seemed in prospect. The sunset was wildly beautiful. Westwards, Wotan fanned the fires of Aurora into flames; a fierce glare broke out behind Mont Blanc, bursting through prison bars of livid thunder clouds. Long bloody fingers of light poured rays upon spectral cloud pennons writhing upwards on the wings of an unsuspected hurricane. Forming, disappearing, they tore over the Peuterey Ridge, pouring affrightedly through the jagged gap of the Brêche des Dames Anglaises until, caught by an upward air current, they were whirled up the cliffs of the Dames Anglaises and the Aiguille Noire de Peuterey to melt into the leaden pall spreading slowly over the zenith. Yet with us all was still. Not a breath of wind hinted of this stormy rage thousands of feet above us. Suddenly the furnace was quenched; the lights died; lightning flickered and thunder boomed, like the growl of a giant from some far dungeon.

We hastened to arrange ourselves in our waterproof sleeping sacks, and settled down to await the storm. And even though it ruined our carefully prepared plans for the morrow, we could hardly regret so unique an experience as watching the oncoming of a tremendous thunderstorm 10,000 feet up on Mont Blanc.

As we sat under our sheltering rock we reflected on the numbers of famous mountaineers and guides who had bivouacked there for the classic route to the Col de la Brenva and Mont Blanc. First of all that party of great mountaineers, George S. Matthews, A.W. Moore, Frank and Horace Walker, with their guides, Jakob and Melchior Anderegg, and later Mummery's brilliant guideless party, including G. Hastings and Professor Norman Collie. This bivouac place is seldom used nowadays, and the old weather-seasoned wood lying around might well have been left by parties that contributed to mountaineering history. But surely none of these encountered such weather as we did that night.

It was dark now; a cloudy broom had scoured the sky of stars; and the lightning was ever nearer. The outlines of Mont Blanc and the Peuterey Ridge were wedged from the night by its quivering blue flames. We heard the storm strike the massif of Mont Blanc. The Brouillard Ridge was the first to receive its fury; then, without pause, it swept across towards us.

Weird beads of faint greenish light, like the watch fires of goblins, danced and trembled on the spires of the Dames Anglaises: it was the brush discharge preceding the storm, a phenomenon known to sailors as St. Elmo's Fires. I experienced a faint tingling of the scalp and a feeling as though light cobwebs were brushing my face. ... A curtain of mauve fire descended; a crooked sword of intense light stabbed the crest of the Aiguille Noire de Peuterey; a tearing crack of thunder was flung from precipice to precipice, but before the echoes had been stifled amid the cirque of peaks the lightning slashed again. From individual reports the thunder resolved itself into a continual barrage of sound in which only the first report was distinguishable, the rest was one prolonged and mighty reverberation.

In a few minutes the storm was around us. Time and again the lightning struck but a few feet distant. It forsook the ridges and darted like fiery serpents into the Brenva Glacier. We counted twenty-five flashes a minute; a number I have not seen equalled in the storms of the Argentine pampas. The Peuterey Ridge disappeared, drowned in a torrent of hail and rain that burst furiously upon us. Hail as large as marbles rattled about us; a gusty wind strove to pluck us from our shelter. We wedged ourselves closer together, and cowered into our sleeping bags. Fortunately, we remained sufficiently warm to appreciate our position, but

I fear that Blakeney's colic marred his enjoyment to some degree. Through the curtains of rain we no longer saw the lightning's spiteful stabs, but a confused and blinding glare. The interval between the lightning and thunder was now seldom more than a second or so, and often it was practically simultaneous, indicating that the lightning must have struck very close at hand.

For perhaps two hours the storm raged without intermission and Mont Blanc bore the brunt of its fury. Then the lightning became less frequent, and we saw what none of us had ever seen before. Shaken by lightning, hail, and rain, the Aiguille Blanche de Peuterey poured forth its avalanches of rocks, and through the darkness we saw torrents of fire streaming down its cliffs as the rocks ground and crashed together on their flight to the Brenva Glacier.

Towards midnight the storm relinquished its hold on Mont Blanc. The battalions of cumuli, lit now by the rising moon, passed away to the south-east, and moved in stately procession with drumming roll of thunder towards the plain of Lombardy.

Much later there was a straggling storm that hurried by with a few thunder-blasts, and hastened onwards to join the main body, now many miles away. For the rest of the night the moon and stars waxed and waned unhindered. It became cold, and we were thankful for our store of wood and a roaring fire.

Mont Blanc was hoary with new snow next morning, and the weather showed signs of renewing its activities. We returned to Courmayeur in rainstorms, where Blakeney, who was not feeling at all fit, decided to our great regret that he would return by motor coach to the Montenvers and thence go home to England.

So ended our first duel with Mont Blanc, a duel in which the mountain had arrayed against us forces that none might withstand. But defeat had but increased our eagerness for the assault.

A day later Graham Brown and I braved the 7,000-foot trudge to the Col du Géant. On the way up Graham Brown expressed fears that the crevasses above the final ice-wall might prove impossible to cross. Personally, I had no fears for this part of the route, for such an authority as Captain Farrar had stated that once over the ice-wall no further difficulty would present itself.

The question was definitely settled by a glance through the powerful telescope outside the Torino Hut, which revealed easy unbroken snow-slopes leading up to the summit of Mont Blanc de Courmayeur and Mont Blanc. Once upon them we felt assured of victory, but so much lay before. The 500-foot high upper buttress was plastered in snow and ice from the previous storms, and only two or three days of hot sun could tilt a spear sufficiently strong to rend its chilly armour. We resolved to descend to the Montenvers Hotel forthwith, re-equip, and return to the Col du Géant for the climb. But before doing so we ascended the sharp rock needle of the Dent du Géant, and from its superior altitude examined the route. Well satisfied, we threaded our way through the Géant Icefall, and strolled down the Mer de Glace in the sober light of a perfect evening.

We rested the following day. I discovered a sheltered rocky cove above the hotel, lapped by a sea of grass and flowers, with pine trees above and around. Leslie Stephen once wrote an essay entitled "An Off-day in the Alps". Truly, an off day is a precious thing to the mountaineer. Then he sees the mountains as they should be seen, not troubled by externals, but lying in delicious repose upon the springy turf, with the fragrant scents of flowers and sun-warmed pines to soothe an occasional doze, broken by dreamy contemplation of far white cloudlets, blue valley depths, and the dazzle of high snows betwixt half-closed eyelids.

That evening we discussed equipment. Equipping an expedition, whether it be to Everest or Mont Blanc, resolves itself into a war between the gods of Addition and Subtraction. My own method is simple. After filling my rucksack with everything that I am sure to need, including spare pants and a mouth organ, I grasp it, and raising it tentatively from the ground, remark that on mountains a man must travel light. Accordingly the mouth organ, pants, and other "essentials" are remorselessly ejected, until my sack has been brought down to a weight comparable to a Tommy's full marching kit. Precisely the same process is then repeated in a sterner degree. In the present instance, the most debatable items of equipment were eiderdown sleeping bags plus extra waterproof covers. But with memories of our last bivouac beneath the Red Sentinel, we decided to take them, a decision we sometimes upheld and sometimes regretted subsequently, according to circumstances.

The weather was doubtful next morning as we zigzagged through the maze of crevasses to the Col du Géant. The sun gleamed fitfully between scuds of grey clouds hustling over Mont Blanc, and the monarch smoked a wrathful pipe of wind-blown snow.

Herr Hoerlin, one of Germany's most enterprising young mountaineers, was also staying at the hut. I had first met him and his friend Herr Hardek the previous year, and now I learnt to my sorrow that Hardek had fallen but a short time previously from a difficult climb on the Wetterstein Gebirge in the Eastern Alps. It was a climb of exceptional severity, and rope-soled shoes had been employed. Hardek had slipped from an exposed traverse and fallen clear of the rocks; the rope, belayed round a rock, had broken. Thus do these limestone peaks of the Eastern Alps take the lives of the daring young University students who are forever vying with one another to discover new routes up their precipices.

The weather remained unsettled for four days, and all we could do was to make minor ascents in the vicinity of the Col du Géant. One of these was the Pic de la Brenva, an abrupt little rock peak, which we climbed in the hope of obtaining a view of the Brenva face and finding an easier route to the Brenva Glacier than the traverse of the Tour Ronde Ridge. But Mont Blanc was in bad humour that day, and but a vestige of the Brenva face was visible beneath the lowering mists. As to the 'alternative route', one look down the crumbling western precipices of the Pic de la Brenva was sufficient.

Later on that same day, 5 August, we lounged on the warm summit rocks of the Petit Flambeaux, watching a strong dry north wind combating a warm moist wind from the Italian valleys. Division after division of woolly clouds the north wind poured at his foe. They came marching up the Mer de Glace to meet the air currents from Italy on the crest of the frontier ridge. Wheeling in incipient whirl-winds they met in a savage mêlée, until at last the north wind triumphed and, content with victory, disbanded his armies into the evening. All the peaks stood revealed, and Mont Blanc rose serene and untroubled against a peaceful sunset.

Three days' food at least was required, and our rucksacks, when packed, weighed well over 30 lb. each. We told the kindly proprietor of our intention, bade farewell to various friends, and at 8.15 a.m. set forth on our venture. On the previous year we had left in the dark, our minds full of doubts and misgivings, but this year we tramped the snows of the Géant Glacier cheerfully, for who could entertain defeatist thoughts on a morning when a myriad snow jewels sparkled in a benevolent sun, and even Mont Blanc looked kind. Last year, too, a halo of mystery and inaccessibility had surrounded the Brenva side of Mont Blanc, and now, though we were essaying a climb of difficulty so great that it was by no means certain that it was possible, we had no fears as to the lower portion of the route, and was not our guardian the Red Sentinel waiting to welcome and shelter us at the end of the day?

We crossed the Col des Flambeaux, descended to the Géant Glacier, and walked uphill to the Col d'Entrèves.

The stone batteries were already at work. Sometimes rattling and banging, and sometimes as loudly as heavy guns, the rocks poured continually from the cliffs of the Tour Ronde, scarring the glacier beneath with their unsightly debris. It is sad to see a noble mountain like the Tour Ronde in the throes of ruin and decay, with sun and frost tearing at its crags and laying bare its vitals. The day is not far distant when the summit will be undermined and fall, for destruction proceeds apace, and the rocks of the eastern cliff have no cohesion or stability.

We reached the Col d'Entrèves without difficulty, and continued on up the South-East Ridge of the Tour Ronde. We now began to realise that a warm night in sleeping bags, with spirit cooker, fuel, plenty of food, spare clothing, and photographic luxuries must be paid for in sweat and hard labour, for the rocks of the Tour Ronde, though easy, were steep, and upward balancing was no easy matter with a heavy load on the back. We soon determined on leaving as much as we could spare beneath the Red Sentinel, and travelling lightly on the harder part of the climb.

As in 1927, we left the South-East Ridge of the Tour Ronde in favour of a horizontal traverse across the south face of the mountain to the Col Oriental de la Tour Ronde. This route, though longer than the ordinary passage of the Frontier Ridge by the Cols de la Fourche, Trident, or Tour Ronde, does not involve the hard step-cutting of these cols. Energy must be conserved as far as possible at the commencement of a long climb, and a long easy way with a heavy load is preferable to a short and difficult one.

From the point where we gained the West Ridge of the Tour Ronde we passed along the frontier ridge to the Col Oriental de la Tour Ronde, scrambling over or around upflung slabs of riven granite. And all the time Mont Blanc rose in front over the Brenva Glacier, gaining in grandeur as we approached.

The westernmost bay of the Brenva Glacier has never been trodden, and perhaps never will be, for it is protected by a hopeless jumble of crevasses, and its snows are sacred to the winds and avalanches. But the easternmost bay of the glacier is more tractable, and it we must cross to the Col Moore and the foot of our climb.

A steep snow-slope led us downwards from the Col Oriental de la Tour Ronde, split at its base by a bergschrund, which we descended into with some little trouble, and crossed by a crazy snow-bridge. We had lunch below, lolling in the wet snow, content to know that there was no hurry, that the work of getting to our climb had been accomplished, and that the real interest lay before. Not until the sun had left the face of Mont Blanc would it be safe to cross the avalanche-swept couloirs, and we spent a happy hour in the blazing sun before continuing on our way.

We descended to the Brenva Glacier, and passed between its wide crevasses to the foot of the Col Moore.

The slope to the Col Moore is a mere fifty feet high, but it is practically an ice-wall, and cleft by a bergschrund half-choked with snow, but wide enough in places to swallow a falling body. Personally I like nothing better than a strenuous piece of ice-work at the commencement of a climb. It warms heart and blood and loosens stiff muscles. We braced ourselves to the attack. 'Now for it,' we exclaimed, and the axe of the leader swung to its task.

Sitting astride the knife-like parabola of snow forming the crest of the col, I took in the rope as Graham Brown advanced. He joined me, and we continued along the narrow edge *à cheval*. A little higher the ridge broadened and swept up to a rock tower. This we climbed by a short crack, lamenting bitterly – I know that I was – on the "Sins of the World", as we had dubbed our heavy rucksacks.

Just beneath the first abrupt wall in Moore's Ridge of the ordinary Brenva route we turned to the west, following our route of last year. On that occasion we had traversed steep snow and ice-slopes to the Red Sentinel, practically all the way in "Eckenstein" crampons, but now we found broken easy rocks for the most part. In one place only did we encounter ice, but that was a bad place. Falling stones are, on the whole, conservative in their habits, and keep to well-defined channels. The stones at this particular point were possessed of so little initiative as to have all followed the same route to the glacier, with the result that they had worn out a groove quite fifteen feet deep in the ice of a narrow couloir. The lip of this groove overhung to such an extent that to climb down was impossible, and the only alternative lay in a long descent of the face to some lower rocks – a detour which would take far too long. Accordingly, I asked Graham Brown to drive his ice axe into the snow at the side, and paying out the rope round the shaft, lower me into the icy bed of the groove. But before abandoning myself altogether to the "sweet persuasion" of the rope I drove in my own axe up to the head, and lowered myself gingerly over the edge. The next moment the overhanging snow-lip collapsed, and I with it. Try as I would I could obtain no purchase for my feet in the hard slippery side of the groove, and I was left hanging entirely on my hands and the rope. This was very awkward. There was nothing for it but to leave go of my axe with my hands and gently oscillate, while Graham Brown secured the rope around his axe with one hand and handed me down my ice axe with the other. It has been said that there is a limit to a man's capacity for rope dangling. I can endorse this. The rope cuts cruelly into the body, restricting the expansion of the lungs, and it is only a matter of time before unconsciousness and suffocation supervene. Speaking physiologically, it is no doubt a most instructive experiment; speaking practically ... but I should not care to repeat my remarks on the occasion in question.

Swinging on a rope while cutting a step in hard ice is undoubtedly invigorating, but it is productive of too much forceful effort to be supremely enjoyable, and I was glad to find my weight resting on an honest ice-step once more and no longer "infernally dangling". Fortunately, the opposite side of the groove was not overhanging, and a staircase was soon made up it. At this point the intelligent reader will exclaim, 'So far so good, but what about Graham Brown? There is no one to lower him.' The solution was simple. Climbing to the full length of the rope up my side of the groove, I drove in my axe and belaying the groove, rope firmly, thereto, invited him to jump in and trust to the rope. The angle of the rope was such that I was almost directly above him, but not enough to prevent him from a nasty swing across the groove. It was the only way, and had to be done, but Graham Brown did not hesitate. Next moment a slither a swing, a taut rope, and a gasping sound told that the introduction to the icy embrace of the groove had been safely made. It was the solitary excitement of the day's climbing, and the only tricky bit on the way to the Red Sentinel. For the rest, we traversed easy broken rocks by convenient ledges, and scrambling at express speed across the rocky bed of two couloirs, which are occasionally swept by ice-avalanches from a hanging glacier above, climbed simple rocks direct to the base of the Red Sentinel.

It was good to see his ruddy countenance again, to feel his rough honest rock, and sit beneath his protective bulwarks. In 1927 we had only fashioned a bivouac place by hewing out an alcove in the solid ice, but in this year of dry weather the snows had melted, disclosing a perfect little site which Graham Brown was soon levelling and enlarging, while I struggled manfully with the spirit cooker and a wind which sought out the most cunning recesses into which it was wedged. Finally, after much coaxing, a tinful of hot tea was forthcoming, and placing it between us we crawled into our sleeping bags as a preliminary to a comfortable supper, consisting of an impressive mixture of tinned tongue, bread, butter, jam, chocolate, and raisins.

The few clouds of the afternoon had long since vanished, and save for an uneasy wind blowing in petulant gusts, the evening was full of calm promise for the morrow. 8,000 feet beneath the lights of Entrèves and Courmayeur shone out like fireflies in the dusk. It was freezing hard now, and we must inevitably shiver, yet no envious thoughts disturbed us as we pictured the warm garden cafés of Courmayeur with their bands and throngs of gay dancers.

The snows were pallid in an afterglow that lingered on the shapely crests of the Grivola and Paradiso, but in the east Monte Rosa was already lost, though we could still distinguish the defiant spire of the Matterhorn – a small but perfectly proportioned wedge rising over the mass of the Grand Combin.

During our last bivouac beneath the Red Sentinel the avalanches had roared all night, but this time we heard but little. The forces seemed spent for the time, though now and again a growl came from the Peuterey Ridge or the Brenva Glacier at our feet. Yet we were glad to have the Sentinel above, and lying in our sleeping bags see his clean breastplate of rock sweep up into the stars. Considering the cold wind, we were remarkably warm in our eiderdown sleeping bags. With an additional waterproof and windproof outer covering of jaconet they weigh but 2 lb. 10 oz., and are far superior to any light tent that I have experimented with. Indeed, I will go so far as to say that they solve the problem of bivouacking in any weather – a problem of vital importance to the mountaineer.

Warmed by a good supper we dozed and slept a little, our heads tucked well inside our sleeping bags. Later I awoke, and wondering for a few drowsy moments where I was, lifted the edge of the sleeping bag. In the east from the ranks of the Pennine Alps the blood-red disc of the moon was sliding up behind the Matterhorn. Moving perceptibly it swung up the heavens, changing as it did so from its first lurid red to a quieter orange, and finally to a cold steadfast radiance as it soared above the mists and humours of the world.

Dawn is not tardy when one is warm and comfortable, and the curtain of night was being raised behind the footlights of day by the time we had reluctantly crept out of our sleeping bags. Shivering, we ate a scanty breakfast, stamping our sluggish circulation into activity meanwhile, and afterwards dumped as many provisions as we dared in a rocky niche. There they remain, and anyone who cares to take the trouble to climb up is welcome to them. Even so our loads were very heavy, and Graham Brown had suggested previously the possibility of abandoning the sleeping bags. But now it seemed that another bivouac was by no means improbable. Thus it was that we left the Red Sentinel at 5 a.m. with loads which in themselves were all but responsible for a second and very much more unpleasant bivouac high up near the summit of Mont Blanc.

Haste was essential if we were to cross the Great Couloir before the sun detached the stones and ice-avalanches from above. Moving fast we passed across a steep narrow couloir to the west of the Red Sentinel, and traversed easier rocky ledges to the edge of the Great Couloir. There we sat down, and for the first time on the climb strapped on our ten-point Eckenstein crampons. As we did so we looked anxiously up at the stealing fires of dawn illumining the upper snows of Mont Blanc. Cross the couloir within the next half-hour we must or retreat from the climb.

I know of no mountain detail more impressive than the "Great Couloir of Mont Blanc", as we termed it. It is the natural chute down which pours all the debris from the ice-becastled precipices above. Its polished black ice speaks eloquently of the cataracts of crashing ice that hurtle down to the Brenva Glacier thousands of feet beneath. The average angle of it must be fully 55°, but at the point where we gained it, it sloped at a gentler angle for a few feet before making its final plunge over the cliffs to the glacier. This was also its narrowest point, and but 200 feet separated us from the safety of the ridge we hoped to climb. But what a 200 feet! The bed consisted of rock slabs, worn smooth by the polishing and grinding of avalanches, and covered in a thick sheet of ugly verglas formed by water trickling down from above during the day and freezing at night. It is difficult to conceive how any party without the aid of crampons could cross under these conditions, but with our sharp Eckensteins it was a comparatively simple matter. Securely placed on a ledge, Graham Brown paid out the rope round a large rock spike as I advanced towards the middle. There was no question of cutting steps, and fortunately no necessity; the thing had to be done quickly or not at all. We had already noticed an ominous fuzziness about the crest of Mont Blanc telling of wind, and in the middle of the couloir a small and harmless stream of snow poured down, whilst in addition an occasional fragment of ice passed with a vicious Whut! – going so fast that it was invisible [see note on p. 134].

In a minute or two the full length of our 120-foot rope was out, and I shouted to Graham Brown to follow. Moving both together at express speed we raced across. There was little chance of slipping as our crampons bit well into the ice, but had a stone fallen and struck one of us the rope would have served but to pull both to destruction. 'Why use the rope under such circumstances?' exclaim the uninitiated. Because the rope is instrumental in forming that mutual trust and comradeship without which no party has any business to be on a mountain. On a place where a slip of one means disaster to all, the moral value of this common link of hemp is inestimable. Remember also, that even when a slip occurs the miracle may happen, and a kindly fate place the rope around a minute projection of rock, thus holding a party. It has happened time and again, and will continue to happen. I have been saved myself thus by a knob of rock no larger than the tip of a little finger [see p. 928].

A few minutes later we stood panting on the rocks of the ridge. Danger lay behind, and difficulty only now confronted us. But we saw immediately that the difficulties were of no mean order. There was no hesitation in the ridge before us. A few broken rocks and it sprang up in a 150-foot wall of pale-red granite. Under the wall we halted for a few moments and craned our necks, but all we saw was a crack, crooked, overhanging, and repulsive. The only alternative was to descend into the Great Couloir, cut up its side, and regain the crest of the ridge above the impasse. A convenient shelf sloped downwards into the couloir, and there Graham Brown ensconced himself and paid out the rope as I descended into the couloir. Danger there was none, as long as the extreme edge of the couloir was followed, but the ice was hard and very steep. Cutting steps thus early in the day was a pleasure. The axe swung backwards and leapt forwards, hitting the ice with that ringing thump the iceman loves so well. The chips and flakes of dislodged ice skipped and hissed into the depths. Much later in the day, when muscles were fatigued and the first fineness of the task had worn off, cutting in the ice became a hard labour, from which joy had been ousted by the loads on our backs.

Fifty feet higher and we were able to clamber out of the couloir, and ascending steep rocks gain the crest of the ridge once more. There we sat down and removed our crampons, after which Graham Brown went ahead, leading up a long stretch of broken rocks. Firm rough granite slabs followed to the foot of an ice-slope besprinkled with rock slabs leading to the commencement of the first of the series of ice-ridges, which are the unique feature of the climb. Here, at 8.40 a.m. we sat down to a meal. Out came the inevitable sardine tin with its pitiful little key, followed by the conventional profanity, the stronger tin-opener, the unexpected oil gush, and at long last peace, with jaws moving in just appreciation of the hard-won contents.

It was a long and happy hour we spent in the cheery sun. The morning was beautiful, but we glanced a trifle uneasily towards the upper slopes of Mont Blanc. High up on the edge of the final ice-walls and parapets of the monarch the wind was busy. The fuzziness we had noted lower down had resolved itself into a *tourmente* of wind-blown snow, and we could plainly see the blasts sweeping the crest of the ice-wall we must climb over. Spiral after spiral of snow powder rose into the blue sky like restless ghosts, and swept impetuously upwards towards the placid dome of Mont Blanc. Elsewhere all was calm and still, and as far as the eye could roam there was no wind devil to torment the host of peaks rising above the diaphanous hazes of Italy. Truly, 'mountains make their own weather'.

An hour and ten minutes passed with wilful speed, and strapping on crampons once more and swinging to back our ponderous rucksacks, we braced ourselves for the real work of the day.

Strictly speaking, there are four ice-ridges, but the lower three succeed each other, and form one practically continuous ridge. The highest and fourth ridge is distinct from these three lower ridges, and is separated from them by a short steep rock pitch. For length, difficulty, and interest these ridges are unique in my recollection, and I cannot do better than describe in detail the work and artifices required to overcome them.

The first and lowest ridge was short, but steep and sharp. Fortunately the snow that had fallen during the previous unsettled weather still adhered to the ice sufficiently to enable us to proceed without cutting steps. Keeping at first on the crest and later below it, we kicked and stamped a staircase.

Fashioned by wind and storm into fragile blades of snow and ice, these ridges had remained virgin and untrodden since the very beginnings of Mont Blanc. Now for the first time they were being trampled and defiled by ubiquitous man. To place foot where no foot has been placed before, to crush unknown snows beneath the feet and grasp unhandled rocks, are joys beyond the diction of the written page.

So we mounted like insects on the whetted edge of a great sword, mere atoms on the cold passionless ice.

We gained the second ridge and passed along it, but almost immediately it merged into the third ridge, and this was very different from the first or second.

At the commencement of it we advanced confidently, our feet sinking through the snow, but gradually the snow thinned, it no longer supported the boot, and our crampons ground into hard ice. The angle steepened, and here the snow had slipped away altogether, exposing pure ice. For a while we climbed on or as near as possible to the crest of the ridge, but when it became ice we were forced off it on to the right-hand slope falling into the depths of the Great Couloir. Anything is better than a traverse on steep ice, and had it been possible to have kept to the crest, even with great difficulty, we should have done so, but the angle was too great even for the ungraceful manoeuvre usually described as *à cheval*, and the thinness of this ridge was such that in places we could see the light glinting through it a foot below the crest. It was hard ice too, ice of the viscous quality that predominates on this side of Mont Blanc, tough to chip like glue, yet coming away unexpectedly in large flakes, all of which made the work of fashioning a safe step exceedingly arduous. It was little use pecking at it with the axe it had to be hit hard. Furthermore, the weight of our rucksacks, and the strain of the straps on the shoulders, added greatly to the difficulty of balancing in the steps, and restricted the easy movement of the arms. Indeed, I will go so far as to say that no man should carry so great a load when cutting steps at 14,000 feet in steep ice; to do so is to court exhaustion, and exhaustion on a climb of this magnitude is but a synonym for disaster. Another factor to struggle against was the necessity of running out a long length of the 120-foot rope, which meant an additional drag of several pounds to the leader, but it seemed safer to move one at a time and not both together, though there is, of course no hope of arresting the fall of the leader should he slip.

As might be supposed, in view of the labour, I cut the steps as far apart as possible, helping myself from step to step by a scraped out handhold; but Graham Brown's shorter stride was unable to accommodate itself to these, and he was forced to cut alternate steps. This added to the fact that we only moved one at a time, and that he cut his steps after I had cut mine and not at the same time, made our progress terribly slow and laborious.

We gained the foot of the rock pitch separating the third ice-ridge from the fourth and highest, and climbed eighty feet of steep rocks to the commencement of the latter. We raised a glad shout, as we looked up its broad comfortable beginnings, but the shout died on our lips as we gazed at its narrowing crest and higher the wicked sheen of ice. Even so, the ridge looked comparatively short, but we were deceived by foreshortening; it is actually the longest ice-ridge of all.

Lower down at the commencement of the ice-ridges we had begun to experience wind, but now harsh gusts laden with stinging ice-particles smote us without warning – a bitterly cold wind making a longed-for halt impossible.

Ice again; the same glutinous stuff, the same hard-swinging axe, the same dull thud, thud as the pick drove home. Yet I would have enjoyed the work had it not been for that devil's load on my back with its constant threat of overbalancing me from my steps as I wielded my axe. Over and across to a rock tongue we went, but the rocks were smooth and unclimbable, offering not even a knob around which to place the rope. Up the ice to the left we backed, and here as elsewhere on the final ice-ridge the steepness and the gusty wind made handholds essential.

Graham Brown was now about fifty feet directly beneath me and his lot was not a pleasant one. Ice falling down ice acquires considerable velocity in a distance of fifty feet. Every ice-chip spun down towards him, and sometimes flakes as large as plates whizzed past, but lying against the slope with both arms protecting his head he endured the bombardment with splendid fortitude. Soon I could traverse to the right, and he was no longer in the line of fire. At last a rock spike projecting through the ice provided an excellent belay for the rope and a resting-place. There I halted until Graham Brown joined me. A few more steps above this and the last of the ice-ridges was vanquished, and we were at the foot of the final 500-foot rock buttress.

A short chimney led up to snow; there we halted and discussed the route. In front and on the west the buttress rose sheer, its granite slabs sheeted in ice. The sole hope was to traverse the ice-slope to the east of the buttress. Here the ice lay in what I can only describe as transparent shields; black and glazed like a frozen waterfall. Above and below were precipices. We glanced down into the head of the Great Couloir and its hemming bastions of glittering ice, and it was an effort to bring the eye back from those terrific depths; we stared up at the bulging ice-draped crags above; and lastly, we gazed along the pitiless ice. The wind hustled round the corner like a snarling wolf. Once more came the measured thudding of the axe.

The slope was not broad, a mere 120 feet, but every foot of the way had to be won, and much of it by one-handed cutting, for handholds were very necessary when the wind was ever trying to pluck one from the steps. About three-quarters of the way across my arm became numb through cramp, and my fingers refused to grasp the shaft of my axe. Cramp, whether it takes place in the water or on a mountain, is an unpleasant affliction, and I was forced to halt a few moments and rest my arm by hanging it at my side. It was the first time that I have experienced cramp while cutting steps in ice, and it was probably due to stoppage of the circulation by the straps of my rucksack, which tended to slip downwards over my arms as I cut steps.

A tongue of ice led up to a corner with an overhanging crack in it, which appeared to lead to easier ground. Here Graham Brown joined me, and I attempted to climb the crack, which was reminiscent of a crack in the Lake District which goes by the expressive name of Amen Corner. But whereas you may fall from Amen Corner in perfect comfort on to a broad grassy ledge, a fall from this crack meant hitting an ice-slope of perhaps 55°, and there was no belay for the rope. Apart from these trivialities, the landing above the crack was on to a steep shelf bulging with ice. The first effort failed, and I asked Graham Brown for a shoulder, which he accorded willingly, despite the fact that I was wearing crampons. Another desperate struggle ended in a complete repulse. It was then Graham Brown's turn to groan in the crack while I groaned below, as the sharp ten-point "Eckensteins" ground through layers of clothes into the flesh beneath. But all these strenuosities were of no avail.

The only alternative was to descend the ice slope and cut round a corner under some rocks. Accordingly, Graham Brown descended and cut round the corner. After some half-dozen steps I heard a faint shout of relief. I descended and joined him. There was indeed cause for relief. We found ourselves on good firm snow, and the everlasting ice-cutting had come to an end – for the time being at any rate. What a pleasure it was to ascend the snow after those hours of chopping! But Mont Blanc allows little latitude on these Brenva precipices; and soon we were confronted by a steep rock-wall. A narrow couloir, half-rock and half-ice, appeared to offer the line of least resistance, but at its base the rocks were impossible. To enter it we must climb up to the right and traverse into it. This involved climbing some steep rocks half-sheeted in verglas. The most difficult bit was an overhang perhaps 10 feet high to overcome, which meant an arm pull. This I attempted with my rucksack, but finding my arms tired with the hours of step-cutting, asked Graham Brown to pass me and tackle it without a rucksack. It was an awkward business, as the ledge I was standing on was a small one, and I had to manage his rucksack in addition to my own. But presently he was able to pass me, and after a good lusty haul sprawled triumphantly over the top.

The traverse to the left into the chimney lay over a bulge of ice resting on a ledge, but soon we were across and wrestling with the intricacies of the chimney.

The wind was cruel in the chimney. It poured down upon us in snow-laden gusts, and the chimney seemed to provide a natural funnel for its hateful spitefulness. The sun had long since departed, and the cold became intense. I think that the possibility of another bivouac must have occurred to both of us at this stage, for it was by now about 5 p.m. Yet, when we looked at each other, and reflected on the manner with which our clothes were being whitened with wind-blown snow and sheeted in ice, we realised that a bivouac in that terrible north wind would be stark misery in spite of sleeping bags and plenty of food. Besides, we had not seen a single place on those unrelenting slopes where we might bivouac, and not so much as a ledge where we could have sat in comfort. No, we *had* to get up come what difficulties there might.

The ice-chimney continued for some distance with great difficulty and our fears became less real as we realised that we were nearly halfway up the buttress. But a little higher hope was dashed with bitter suddenness from our lips. The chimney steepened to the vertical, and finally leant outwards in a bulge of solid ice. It was with considerable labour that I was able to back up between the vertical walls beneath the ice-bulge, but an inspection of the bulge disclosed no hope of overcoming it short of spending hours in chopping the whole thing away. We must try another route, but where? A crack on the left led nowhere, but to make sure Graham Brown climbed up for some distance before returning. The sole remaining possibility was a horizontal traverse over a sloping ice-glazed shelf to the right. It looked a bad place – in boots it would have been difficult indeed – but our crampons, though blunted, sufficed. Rounding a corner we reached snow again, unsuspected snow that took us rapidly upwards.

The great ice-wall was now full in sight. We were beneath it, but exposed to no risk, for it rose clean-cut, solid, and apparently immovable, the sheer edge of Mont Blanc's snow dome. And all the time the fierce wind swept along it, flinging clouds of snow-spray over its crest like the spume from the Atlantic breakers on the ironbound coasts of the west.

The snow-slope that we were on narrowed to a thread; the thread sprang up into a 200-foot shallow chimney set in the glacis of smooth slabs below the ice-wall. It was easier than the last ice-chimney. Foot by foot we worked up it, iced gloves grasping iced rocks, crampons kicking and scraping through loose incoherent snow into the substratum of ice beneath.

Gone now were thoughts of defeat and retreat. My mind was in that state of detached resignation peculiar to hard work coming after many hours of hard work at high altitudes. It is this capacity for detachment that enables man to endure the horrors of war or the long-drawn-out hardships of Polar exploration or Everest. In it lies the secret of achievement and the conquest of mind over matter; it enables man to go on, and on, and on.

If I live to be an old man I shall sit by the fire and looking into the embers see two specks creeping up that vast mountain-side, mere microcosms of flesh and blood on the frozen face of Eternity. Slowly they crawl up that last buttress of rock, buffeted and beaten by the cruel wind, gaining a little every hour. And at last one of them is up. Hand over hand he takes in the slack of the frost-stiffened rope. The other is up. Together they wave arms and ice axes in the air.

Far away below at the Torino Hut they saw us. For five hours they had lost us on the rocks, and their anxiety grew. But at 5.55 p.m. the high-powered telescope revealed us on the summit of the buttress

The ice-wall remained, but here Mont Blanc relented. The buttress was his real defence, and no doubt he had not anticipated a direct assault. Like a castle built on a high hill, he had only troubled to protect the precipitous side with paltry defences. On either hand the main defences rose proudly, utterly impregnable, but on the summit of the buttress they had sunk to a mere 30 feet of blue ice. We went at it with a will. The axe swung for the last time. A few steps and the angle steepened, but inserting my ice axe in a crack I hauled myself over the top. There Graham Brown joined me.

The difficulties were over, and we turned and gazed for a few moments.

The evening was cloudless, and from Monte Rosa to the Paradiso the peaks glowed warmly over the deepening hazes of the Italian valleys. But around us the snows were pallid like death, and the wind-pack snarled in purposeless hunt over the austere dome of Mont Blanc. For eight-and-a-half hours their harrying had kept us on the run, and the need for rest and food was urgent. Yet to halt in the wind was to court frostbite, and we trudged wearily through the snow towards our goal. But presently we came to a large crevasse that petered out in a grotto beneath the snow. We entered the grotto, and sitting down munched hard unappetising chocolate. For many hours we had looked forward to a meal, and now when it was possible to have one we could eat but little. Even the grotto was not immune from the wind, and powdery snow was blown down upon us in clouds. We did not dare to venture too far in case the roof might fall, but the dim light of evening penetrating the entrance revealed a hall of ice, flanked and supported by icicles as large in girth as young firs. As far as we could see it stretched, a veritable snow palace, and fit habitation for the Mountain King and his attendant snow-maidens.

We halted but a quarter of an hour before continuing on our way. We moved slowly, taking it in turn to stamp a trail through the soft deep snow. The wind became fiercer as we rose, and two or three times sent us staggering. Behind, the peaks changed from daffodil to gold, and the dusky tide of night creeping over the edge of the world poured into the deep valleys. Above, the wind-blown snow was caught by the setting sun, until Mont Blanc seemed like a great iced birthday-cake lit by the shivering flames of expiring candles.

We gained the summit ridge but a few yards north of Mont Blanc de Courmayeur. The full force of the wind met us here, and for a minute or two, we could barely struggle against its insensate blasts. A few easy rocks and two little gendarmes followed, and at 7.45 p.m. we stepped on to the summit of Mont Blanc de Courmayeur. Somewhere in the dimness beneath a minute spot of light flashed out. We were not forgotten. Herr Zürcher and his guides, Josef Knubel and Graven, were waving a lantern. It was a kindly thought. Man's effort on a mountain is not yelped at by a gallery of thousands; the stage set for his activities is a lonely one; the forces of encouragement, laudation, or execration are locked within his own soul; he moves in a stern world ordered by inexorable forces, knowing neither love nor hate. That is not the least charm of high mountains. But that minute speck of light telling us that through those many strenuous hours friends had watched us was a happy inspiration indeed.

We turned and set off along the ridge to Mont Blanc.

The peaks were all livid now, and night advanced swiftly over the green fields of the sky, sowing an infinitude of stars. Only the wind still raged in unbridled fury; elsewhere all was calm.

We tacked up the last slope, and at 8.15 p.m. Europe was beneath us.

The sunset fires were very low now; they trailed redly over the calm line of the Jura. We stamped our feet and beat our hands together. The job was done. Ahead stretched the well-trodden way to the Vallot Hut and Chamonix.

So we paused, careless of the cold and the wind, striving through the medium of vision to memorise a moment of supreme joy and beauty.

[NOTE: Any doubts about the serious nature of this climb will be removed by reference to Rob Ferguson's essay "Why" in *The Games Climbers Play* p. 207.]

CHAPTER SEVENTEEN

The Philosophy of a Mountaineer

MOST PHILOSOPHIES are really the attempts of egotistical man to probe and analyse his soul and to discover the whys and wherefores of its reactions to varying circumstances. I will say at once, and frankly, that this chapter falls within this category. I want to know why I love the hills, why I climb them, why I experience certain emotions upon them.

In bygone days the philosophy of hills lay dormant in man. Hills were reviled as useless appendages upon the Earth's surface; they provoked loathing or fear in the hearts of those who were forced to pass over or between them. Yet there lived men whose thoughts and ideals rose above the superstitions and prejudices of their age, whose love of nature went far towards elevating the minds of their fellows above the material, although it was given to few to experience the urge to accomplish more than to admire hills from afar. If the hills were beautiful they were also, terrible.

This attitude of mind lasted well into the previous century. Even Ruskin was not immune from its limitations, and although he discovered many hitherto undiscovered beauties in high mountains, he had not the imagination to realise that the peaks at which he was content to gaze from below were something more than natural impressionisms, whose inmost beauties were only revealed to those hardy and energetic enough to seek them. Pictorial art, however beautiful, only appeals to one sense – the vision, and it was Ruskin's failure to realise the fact that mountains offered scope to many more senses than the merely artistic that led him to such a bitter denunciation against the early mountaineers. For this he has since been described as a snob, but let us take the broader and more charitable view that it was only an ignorance that had its roots in jealousy. If only Ruskin had climbed.

Though I were stricken with blindness I would still go to the mountains. I would lie on the turf of a quiet alp in the morning, when the dew is drying, and the light breezes are fragrant with flowers and moist earth. I would breathe long breaths of pine-scented airs. I would harken to the lazy jangle of cowbells from distant pastures, the boom of glacier torrents, and the solemn roll of avalanches. And, maybe, the "Lordly Folk who dwell in the Hollow Hills" would take pity upon me I would hear their friendly chuckles in the near-by stream, their elfin whispers in the grass, and their murmured chorus in the pine-tops.

Or I would ask to be led to some high hut and, lying on its straw-filled bunks, listen to the deep voice of the night wind, and in the early morning open the door and going forth meet the keen dawn-breath with its indefinable promise of delight.

Or possibly I would be content with the homeland hills, and sitting on a windy edge inhale deeply the salt tang of the sea, or spend a day on a soft couch of heather in some silent cwm or glen, and share the confidences of the small hill-stream on its journey to the sea.

A full appreciation of mountains is not to be experienced by merely looking; that is why men climb. On this Earth the physical is an essential complement of the spiritual.

At first sight there appears some justification in Ruskin's charges of 'greasy pole' mountaineering in the spectacle of a climber's contortions in the "Mummery Crack" of the Aiguille du Grépon. But what are the feelings of the climber himself? If he be an ordinary man, not endowed with especially good nerves or physique – and there are many such who climb – he may undergo a certain anxiety of achievement. He will puff and pant, strain and sweat. But when he reaches the long-desired little stance above the lower portion of the crack he will halt for a few moments, and while thus halted his gaze will stray away from the prospect of his continued labours. He will glance far down the grey slices of precipice into the sunless depths of the long couloir he has ascended to the foot of the crack, and his eyes will seek the Mer de Glace, which appears from above not unlike some monstrous dragon, frozen in the act of wriggling from its lair to devour Chamonix. He will look downwards into violet depths and upwards to shining heights, or peer between fugitive mists that are ever vignetting some new enchantment of form or colour.

These things he will see, while his breast heaves with his previous exertions. Yet, at the time, they are meaningless to him. His thoughts are concentrated upon his position and the problem before him.

But all the time his brain is registering his visions, and months later as he sits by the winter fireside these visions will recur. For a few minutes he will be lost to his surroundings. Once more he will find himself high up on the sunny precipice, remembering, not the discomforts, the anxieties, or the physical stresses of the climb, but the beauties and grandeurs that were around him. He will see again the thin-edged spires splintering the blue sky, the silvery blades of wind-carved snow, the stern rock-towers threatening his progression, the lacery and tracery of glaciers at his feet. He will remember the pure joy of conquest unattended by mean rivalry, bloodshed or the feverish clamour of his fellow men. His muscles will tauten a little at the recollection of fierce upward struggle in crack or chimney, or delicately balanced tread on the warm red granite. He will rediscover a deeper inspiration at the thought of airs untainted by factory and city. And not least, he will share again the company of friends, responsibility, and the common fund of interest. These are but a tithe of his dreams.

There are many other aspects of mountaineering. Englishmen are afraid to let themselves express their feelings lest they bring ridicule upon themselves, but is not philosophy a genuine and analytical revelation of thought? I do not mean a senseless ranting or a phraseful rhapsodising, but a sober statement of those emotions stirred into being by mountains and mountaineering. As the late Donald Robertson wrote in his paper to the Alpine Club on "Alpine Humour" –

'... there is room in our generation for a new *Peaks Passes, and Glaciers* by the best pens in the Club, telling freely and fully, without false shame, each for himself, the story of a day among the mountains.'

There is a phrase common among journalists and film producers, the 'gamut of emotion'. I have used it myself in connection with mountaineering, but what does it mean? The whole range of emotion? If so, what is that range? Does it begin on a note of love and end on a note of hate, or is it bounded by hope and fear? Who can say? There may be emotions outside the human scale which we are incapable of appreciating, chords beyond the range of emotional audibility as it were. It has often seemed to me that mountains strike very near a territory of thought as yet unexplored by the philosopher.

It is curious how certain trivial incidents are remembered long after more important events are forgotten. Is it because the brain is like a camera and that the exposure, or wavelength, or whatever actuated the memory was synchronised exactly with the memory? At all events, the capacity for remembering the smaller details is not the least charming thing in mountaineering. For instance, I remember vividly a certain spring morning on a small mountain called the Speer above the lake of Wallenstadt. I had spent a night alone in the snug hayloft of a chalet on the edge of the retreating snow line, and awakened to the song of a small bird singing his paean of praise to the Goddess of Dawn. And as I came outside into the crisp morning, yawning and drowsy, the first thing that caught my eye was a platoon of crocuses facing the doorway of the hut. They stood in a little ragged woe-begone row; their petals were closed and their heads drooped pathetically. In the half-light they appeared like naughty children after a scolding. Or there is the noise the hail made as we sat in the old Brenva bivouac and watched the most terrific thunderstorm that I have ever seen venting its rage on the great massif of Mont Blanc. In the silences as the storm waned it sounded 'exactly like the slow tread of a mountaineer walking up the scree beneath us, with the point of his ice axe clinking against the loose stones.

'Why do you climb?' The mountaineer has no answer to this question. The best things in the world cannot adequately be expressed in speech or print; they are part of the soul. The love of hills is indefinable; it is like a clear stream passing through rough country. Sometimes it runs eagerly over the pebbles, and sometimes it halts to dream in deep pools. Sometimes it is vivacious and sparkling and sometimes sullen and quiescent. Circumstances vary it; it may be agitated by flood, or reduced by drought yet it continues to flow. So with the mountaineer. He is subject to the whims of fate; he is scorched by fierce suns and shriven by bitter blizzards; he freezes in the morning and sweats in the afternoon. Discomfort, doubt, anxiety and weariness are often his lot; he eats food he would scorn to eat at home, and eats it at all manner of absurd hours; his ablutions are scanty and perfunctory, if they take place at all; he omits to shave; his clothes become worn – even odorously reminiscent of sardines and rancid butter; his general appearance, reckoned by civilised and social standards, is beastly. Yet, why he could not possibly explain, he goes back to the mountains next season.

To remember well is to have lived well. Mountaineering stores a fund of memories that will endure through a man's lifetime. Seen through the mists of time its harsher features are smoothed away. We still see the struggle with the *tourmente* on the ice-glazed slabs; we hear the furious howl of the wind, and smell the dank mist wreathes. But we do not feel the pain of numbed fingers, the ache of cheeks slashed by the hail, the weariness that assails the joints.

We remember, too, the vistas that have delighted our gaze; the host of peaks raising their silver shields to heaven; a solitude and sadness infinitely restful.

Our muscles clench instinctively at memories of some tussle with the fierce red granite slabs; or the slow never-ending chop, chop to win a passage up the icy steep. We see again the bivouac on some hospitable ledge, where the melody of distant waters lulled us to a fitful doze; and hear the slow percussion of thunder from precipice to precipice. And best of all we remember the friends who have shared with us the vigils of the mountains.

No thinking man who has lived in lonely places or travelled the rough spaces of the Earth cannot but find his thoughts, straying to the manner of his end.

Men find religion in different ways, and some on a mountain. The religion of the mountain is not one of cant or ritual, but a leaning towards a power of infinite wisdom. Thoughts, music, the things we call inspiration spring from the mysterious reservoirs of Nature. Never does a man approach nearer the line bordering life and death as on a mountain. He holds in his fingertips the power of either; his very toes are arbiters of his destiny.

And how small an organism he is, a mere atom amid forces that may arise and crush him, yet a dominant atom for a time, of a wider orbit than his fellows of plain and city.

Man cannot exist without a philosophy of some kind. However hard he may try to keep awake he must always find something to lay his muddled head upon. Civilised life is too complex, too full of superficialities and false doctrines. The philosophy of the hills is a simple one. On them we approach a little nearer to the ends of the Earth and the beginnings of Heaven. Over the hills the spirit of man passes towards his Maker.

THE KANGCHENJUNGA ADVENTURE

The Kangchenjunga Adventure

First published by Victor Gollancz, 1930

THIS BOOK is a personal account of the attempt made in 1930 to climb Kangchenjunga, 28,156 feet, and the successful ascent of Jonsong Peak, 24,344 feet, and other great peaks of the Eastern Himalayas, by a party of mountaineers from four nations, Germany, Austria, Switzerland and Great Britain, under the leadership of Professor G.O. Dyhrenfurth. I have endeavoured to record my own personal impressions of what was primarily an adventure. It is now no longer necessary to disguise adventure shamefacedly under the cloak of science. The scientific side of the expedition was well attended to, and interesting and important data has been gained. We went, however, to Kangchenjunga in response not to the dictates of science, but in obedience to that indefinable urge men call adventure, an urge which, in spite of easy living and "Safety First", still has its roots deep in the human race.

[The author goes on to thank: *The Times*; The Indian Government; the Maharajahs of Nepal and Sikkim; Alpine Club members – Bruce, Strutt, Spencer, Somervell and Seligman; Himalayan Club members – Mackworth, Young and Gourlay. In addition there was the usual list of commercial sponsors who were thanked for their support.]

Contents

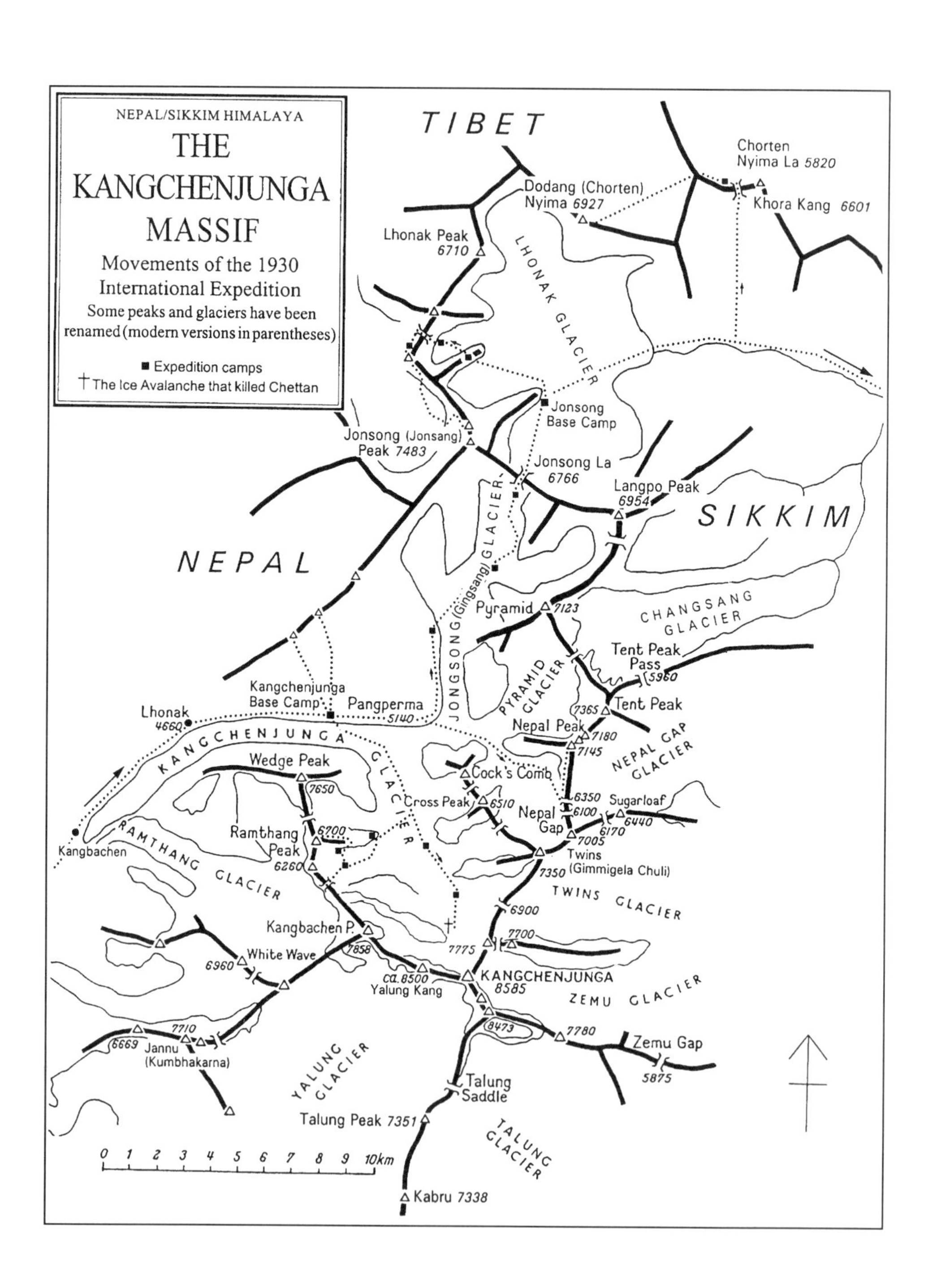
NEPAL/SIKKIM HIMALAYA
THE KANGCHENJUNGA MASSIF
Movements of the 1930 International Expedition
Some peaks and glaciers have been renamed (modern versions in parentheses)
Expedition camps
The Ice Avalanche that killed Chettan
TIBET
NEPAL
SIKKIM
Chorten Nyima La 5820
Khora Kang 6601
Dodang (Chorten) Nyima 6927
Lhonak Peak 6710
LHONAK GLACIER
Jonsong Base Camp
Jonsong (Jonsang) Peak 7483
Jonsong La 6766
Langpo Peak 6954
JONGSONG (Gingsang) GLACIER
Pyramid 7123
CHANGSANG GLACIER
Tent Peak Pass 5960
PYRAMID GLACIER
Tent Peak
7365
Nepal Peak
7180
7145
NEPAL GAP GLACIER
Kangchenjunga Base Camp
Pangperma 5140
Lhonak 4660
KANGCHENJUNGA GLACIER
Wedge Peak
7650
Cock's Comb
Cross Peak
6510
Nepal Gap
6350
6100
Sugarloaf
6440
6170
7005
Twins
7350 (Gimmigela Chuli)
Ramthang Peak 6260
6700
Kangbachen
RAMTHANG GLACIER
TWINS GLACIER
6900
Kangbachen P.
7858
7700
7775
White Wave
6960
ca. 8500 Yalung Kang
KANGCHENJUNGA 8585
ZEMU GLACIER
8473
7780
Zemu Gap
5875
7710
6669
Jannu (Kumbhakarna)
YALUNG GLACIER
Talung Saddle
Talung Peak 7351
TALUNG GLACIER
Kabru 7338
0 1 2 3 4 5 6 7 8 9 10km

CHAPTER ONE

Ambitions and Dreams

IN THE GEOGRAPHY class at school we knew on paper, three kinds of mountain ranges. There was the mountain range represented by a long line supported on either side by little legs, which straggled pathetically across the page of our freehand geography drawing books, like some starved mediæval dragon. This method of mountain delineation is technically known as hachuring, but our Geography Master generally referred to mountain ranges drawn thus contemptuously as "centipedes" and awarded but a low mark to home-made maps drawn in, as he rightly considered, such a slovenly fashion. Then there was the shading method. The idea of this was in imagining the sun to be shining on one side only of the range, the other side being in funereal shadow. Well done it is quite effective, and as there are few schoolboys who can resist rubbing a pencil lead up and down a piece of paper, it was universally popular. Yet, if giving some vague impression of form and relief, the mountain ranges we drew were grim sad affairs as desolate and unattractive as the airless vistas of the moon. And lastly, there was the contour method. This was popular among few owing to the time and labour involved, for unless approximate accuracy was achieved, a map drawn thus was sure to incur the teacher's wrath.

Personally, I found much satisfaction in laboriously drawing out and colouring any mountain range portion of the map, sometimes to the exclusion of all else on the map and other items of homework. Geography, was indeed, one of the few subjects in which I took any interest whatever at school, and had it been the only subject necessary to qualify for promotion I *might* have reached the "Sixth". As it was, I was relegated for the remainder of my natural school life to the "Fifth Modern", a polite term for "Remove", the pupils of which were taught handicrafts on the apparent assumption that their mental equipment was such as to render it impossible for them to make their living otherwise than with their hands.

The green lowlands of the map had little fascination for me. Mentally, I was ever seeking escape from the plains of commerce into those regions, which by virtue of their height, their inaccessibility and their distance from the centres of civilisation were marked, "Barren Regions Incapable of Commercial Development". My gods were Scott, Shackleton and Edward Whymper.

There was one portion of the Earth's surface at which I would gaze more often than at any other, the indeterminate masses of reds and browns in the map which sprawl over Central Asia. For hours I would pore over the names of ranges, deserts and cities until they were at my fingertips. By comparison with distances – I knew the distance to the seaside, or to London – I tried to gain some idea of a mountain range the length of which is measured in thousands of miles, the Himalayas.

In imagination I would start from the green plains, and, follow the straggling line of a river up through the light browns of the map to the dark browns, to halt finally on one of the white bits that represented the snowy summits of the highest peaks. There I would stop and dream, trying to picture great mountain ranges lifting far above the world: the dull walls of the schoolroom would recede, and vanish, great peaks of dazzling white surrounded me, the airs of heaven caressed me, the blizzards lashed me. And so I would dream until the harsh voice of the Geography Master broke in with its threats and promises of punishment for slackness and gross inattention. If he had known, perhaps he would have left me there on my dream summits, for he was an understanding soul.

If I had learnt, as much about other branches of geography as I knew about mountains I should, indeed, have been a paragon. As it was, the knowledge gained from every book on the subject on which I could lay my hands had its drawbacks, and I have a distinct recollection of being sent to the bottom of the form for daring to argue that the Dom and not Mont Blanc was the highest mountain entirely in Switzerland.[1]

Three Himalayan names stood out before everything else, Mount Everest, Mount Godwin Austin (now called K2) and Kangchenjunga. Once the knowledge that Everest was 29,002 feet high, instead of a mere 29,000 feet, resulted in my promotion to the top of the form, where for a short time I remained, basking in the sun of the Geography Master's approval (for he was a discriminating man) before sinking steadily to my own level, which was seldom far from the bottom.

For years my ambitions were centred about the hills and crags of Britain; the Alps followed naturally. They were satisfying, if not supremely satisfying, for they enabled me to erect a more solid castle of imagination upon the foundations of my early dreams. On their peaks I learnt the art and craft of mountaineering, and the brotherhood of the hillside. To some the British hills are an end in themselves, and to others the Alps, but the "Journey's End" of the mountaineer is the summit of Everest.

'Is mountaineering worthwhile?' many ask. Not to them, but to others. Adventure has its roots deep in the heart of man. Had man not been imbued with it from the beginning of his existence, he could not have survived, for he could never have subdued his environment, and were that spirit ever to die out, the human race would retrogress. By "adventure" I do not necessarily mean the taking of physical risks. Every new thought, or new invention of the mind is adventure. But the highest form of adventure is the blending of the mental with the physical. It may be a mental adventure to sit in a chair and think out some new invention, but the perfect adventure is that in which the measure of achievement is so great that life itself must be risked. A life so risked is not risked uselessly, and sacrifice is not to be measured in terms of lucre.

Mental alertness is dependent on physical virility, and an inscrutable Nature decrees that man shall ever war against the elemental powers of her Universe. If man were to acknowledge defeat, he would descend in the scale of life and sink once more to the animal. But there has been given to him that "something" which

[1] The peak of Mont Blanc is equally portioned between France and Italy. Only the extreme eastern end of the Mont Blanc *range* being in Switzerland.

is called the "Spirit of Adventure". It was this spirit that sustained Captain Scott and his companions, and Mallory and Irvine. Even in their last harsh moments, the crew of the R.101 knew that they did not perish uselessly. Mr. G. Winthrop Young wrote, 'Will the impulse to adventure – which has coincided so happily for a time with that "feeling" for mountains – die with its opportunity? Or will new outlets be found during yet another stage in our conquest of the elements?' I think they will when man has conquered the Earth, he will turn his eyes to the stars.

CHAPTER TWO

Kangchenjunga: its Nature and History

ROUGHLY SPEAKING, there are two types of mountains. There is the mountain, which forms a point projecting from a range, ridge, or glacier system, and there is the mountain, which stands apart from other ridges or ranges, and possesses its own glacier system. A good example of the former type is afforded by the peaks of the Bernese Oberland. Magnificent though they are individually, especially when seen from Mürren or the Wengern Alp, they are in reality but elevated points above an interlinking system of snowy plateaux and glaciers. Another good example is the great Himalayan peak, K2. Though in many respects one of the most wonderful peaks in the world, it is, properly speaking, but a solitary spire of rock and ice rising above the glaciers and snowfields of the Karakoram Range.

Of independent mountains, there is no finer example than Kangchenjunga. It is a mountain great enough to possess its own glaciers radiating from its several summits, and though surrounded by many vassal peaks, which add their quota to the ice rivers radiating from the main massif, the glaciers which flow far down to the fringe of the tropical forests cloaking the lower valleys are the undisputed possession of the Monarch. Of the world's first half dozen peaks, Kangchenjunga is the only one that displays its glories to the world at large. Only those who can afford the time and expense necessary to penetrate the remote fastnesses from which they spring can view the glories of Everest or the Karakorams, but Kangchenjunga is to be seen by anyone who cares to visit the hill town of Darjeeling, or climb one of the lower foot-hills. Thus man is able to turn his tired eyes towards the snows, and reflect that there are still worlds unconquered towards which he can gaze for inspiration and hope.

Whether or not Kangchenjunga is the second or the third highest mountain in the world is not yet certain, for its height is approximately equal to that of K2, and it is still a matter of argument as to which should take pride of place. As determined by the Survey of India K2 is 28,250 feet high, 194 feet higher than Kangchenjunga. These heights have been estimated by the most accurate trigonometrical processes possible. So many slight errors are, however, liable to creep into the most elaborate calculations that they can be regarded as approximate only. Sir Thomas Holditch, one of the greatest of survey authorities, held that there are bound to be errors owing to refraction. For instance, the rays of the sun passing through rarified air over snow-covered areas are liable to cause an error of refraction. Another difficulty is the attractive forces exercised by such a great mountain range as the Himalayas. It is well known that in the vicinity of the range there is a slight dip in the surface of water. It can hardly be doubted therefore, that instrumental levels are affected.

With these factors taken into account, the heights of the three highest peaks in the world were worked out by Colonel S.G. Burrard, Superintendent of the Trigonometrical Survey of India, who arrived at the following: Everest, 29,041 feet; Kangchenjunga, 28,225 feet; K2, 28,191 feet. Thus Kangchenjunga is made 34 feet higher than K2. This slight difference is scarcely worthy of note and taking into account fluctuations of height due to seasonal snowfall on the summits, it may be assumed that there is a dead heat for second place.

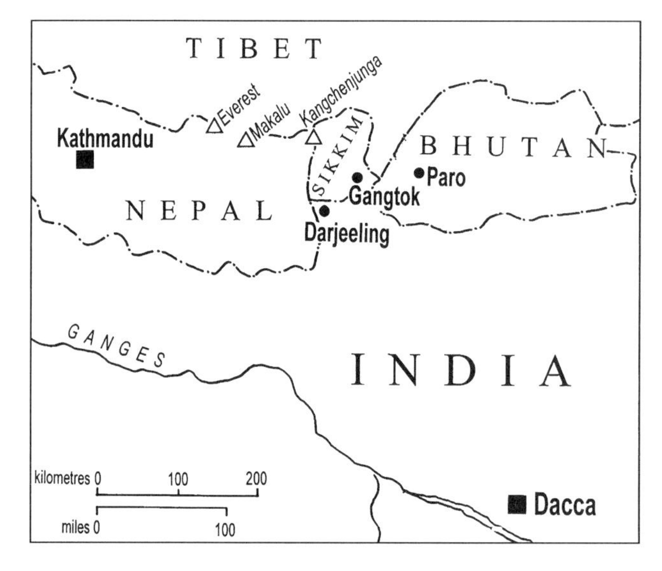

Kangchenjunga is situated to the north-east of Nepal, an independent state, and to the north-west of Sikkim, a state under British mandate. Its main ridges, which run from N.N.E. to S.S.W., form a natural boundary between these two states, as well as a watershed to several important rivers. Twelve miles north of Kangchenjunga is the Tibetan frontier. This runs along what is strictly speaking the main watershed of the Himalayas, which separates the arid plateaux of Tibet on the north from the more fertile and rain-washed country on the south. On this watershed, however, there are no elevations to rival Kangchenjunga, so that the mountain and its satellite peaks form a huge mountain massif pushed southwards from the main Himalayan Range.

Generally speaking, the more isolated a mountain or mountain group, the greater are its fluctuations of climate. Kangchenjunga is large enough not only to make its own weather, but also to catch the full force of ready-made weather in addition. Only low foothills separate it from the Plain of Bengal, and these are not high enough to afford it protection from the south-west monsoon. The result of this is an annual precipitation of snow that is probably greater than that of any other peak in the Himalayas. Because of this Kangchenjunga boasts some of the most magnificent snow and ice scenery in the world.

Kangchenjunga not only breaks the force of the monsoon, but also protects the main watershed to the north from its onslaught to a great extent. The result of this is an extraordinary variation of scenery and climate within a small area. The dry, almost dusty hills at the head of the Lhonak Valley, the Dodang Nyima range, and the plateaux of Tibet beyond are in striking contrast to the valleys radiating southwards from Kangchenjunga, for here is a dry reddish brown country with a snow level appreciably higher and glaciers considerably smaller than those of Kangchenjunga and its immediate neighbours.

The huge annual precipitation of snow on Kangchenjunga is, from the mountaineer's point of view; a disadvantage, for it plasters itself on the mountain, and fills every hollow with clinging masses of ice. Owing to this quantity of snow, that is ever building up, plus the tug of gravity, these icy masses move downwards to join the main glaciers, which they feed. Frequently, they are perched high up on the mountainside, and are unable to flow down the steep, rock precipices beneath, so they break off in chunks hundreds of feet thick, which fall thousands of feet to the glaciers beneath in terrible ice avalanches. These ice avalanches are Kangchenjunga's deadliest weapons.

There is probably no other mountain where the mountaineer is exposed to greater dangers than he is on Kangchenjunga, for not only has he ice avalanches to contend with, but uncertain weather as well, weather incalculable both in cause and effect.

With such a mountain before their eyes, it is perhaps small wonder that the peoples inhabiting the valleys round Kangchenjunga have become impregnated with the grandeur and mystery of the great mountain. To them its five summits are the "Five Treasures of the Snow", and on them rests the throne of an all-powerful god. Their prosperity, and even their lives, depend on the good humour of this god, for he is able to blast their crops with his storms, or destroy their villages with his floods and avalanches. There are even dark tales of human sacrifices to this powerful deity handed down from the remote past.

Roughly speaking, there are four main lines of approach to Kangchenjunga, up the valley of the Tamar River in Nepal, passing Khunza and Kangbachen, up the Yalung Valley in Nepal, up the valley of the Teesta River in Sikkim, and up the Talung Valley also in Sikkim. Between the Yalung and Talung Valleys there is also the Rangit River, which has its sources in the glaciers of Kabru, 24,002 feet, one of Kangchenjunga's outpost peaks to the south. But compared to the first two, this is but a subsidiary valley, and does not form a main line of approach.

The first European to undertake serious exploration in the neighbourhood of Kangchenjunga was the famous botanist and explorer, Sir Joseph Hooker. Eighty years ago the valleys round Kangchenjunga, were unknown and unexplored.[1] Dense, trackless jungle covered them, through which trails had to be cut, whilst

[1] Mr. Douglas Freshfield in his book, *Round Kangchenjunga*, included an interesting chapter on the early history of Kangchenjunga. The subject was also dealt with more recently in Vol. II of the *Himalayan Journal* by Lieutenant-Colonel H.W. Tobin.

transportation was very difficult. In 1848, Hooker traversed the Tamar Valley, and visited the Walung and Yangma Passes, which lead from north-eastern Nepal into Tibet, north of Mount Nango. He then passed through Kangbachen and back to Darjeeling, via the Yalung Valley and the Singalila Ridge. In January 1849, he reached Dzongri via the Rathong Valley, but was unable to go farther owing to snow. In April he ascended the Teesta Valley to Lachen, and made several attempts to climb Lamgebo Peak, 19,250 feet. Thence, he ascended the Poki River, and after bridging it near its junction with the Tumrachen River, tried to reach the Zemu Glacier. Failing to do this, he explored the Lachen and Lachung Valleys and made attempts on Kangchenjau, and the Pauhunri, 22,700 feet and 23,180 feet respectively.

Unsuccessful though these attempts were, they deserve something more than passing notice. At this date mountaineering had scarcely begun even in the Alps, and it was not until sixteen years later that the Matterhorn was climbed, yet here was an explorer attempting peaks 8,000 feet higher than the Zermatt giant. As it was, Hooker ascended to the Cholamo Lake at the head of the Lachen Valley, whence he ascended a small peak, and crossed the Dongkya La, 18,130 feet, into the head of the Lachung Valley.

Hooker, and Dr. Campbell, Superintendent of Darjeeling, who accompanied him, were seized and imprisoned at Tumlong on their way back to Darjeeling, at the orders of Namgay, Prime Minister of Sikkim, and it was some time before they were released. As retribution for this outrage, a portion of Sikkim, south of the Great Rangit Valley, was annexed by the British Government. This district had once belonged to Nepal, but after the Gurkha war of 1817; it was restored to the Sikkim Government, who in the same year ceded to us Darjeeling. It is now covered in valuable tea plantations.

Hooker made a small scale map of Sikkim to illustrate his wanderings, but this remained untouched until 1861, when Lieutenant Carter made a reconnaissance survey between Darjeeling and Tumlong during the march of Colonel Gawler's force. It was not until 1878 that the survey of Sikkim was resumed by Captain H.J. Harman, R.E., of the Survey of India. Harman made several journeys, which included an attempt to reach the Monastery of Tulung, but he was forced to return owing to the hostility of the inhabitants. He tried to reach the foot of Kangchenjunga, but his health suffered in the tropical valleys, and he was forced to return. Colonel H.C.V. Tanner undertook the continuance of the survey. It is thought that he was responsible for the survey training of the three Indian surveyors, "Pundits", signing themselves S.C.D., U.G., and R.N., who performed such valuable work in this district. The actual triangulation was undertaken by Tanner and his assistant, Robert, whilst the "Pundits" added topographical details.

In 1879, S.C.D. (Babu Sarat Chandra Das), the best known of the "Pundits", crossed the Kang La, 16,373 feet, from Sikkim into Nepal, passed up the valley of Kangbachen, traversed the Jonsong La, 20,200 feet, and the Choten Nyima La to Tashi Lhunpo in Tibet. This is certainly one of the boldest journeys on record in that part of the world, and the crossing of the Jonsong La, a high glacier pass, was a great feat. Two years later, in 1881, he crossed the Nango La, north of Kangbachen, and continued to Lhasa. In 1883, another bold journey was undertaken by a native, Lama Ugyen Gyatso of Pemayangtse Monastery, who travelled to Lhasa by the Teesta and Lachung Valleys, and over the Dongkya La, making valuable sketches *en route*.

In October to December of the same year, the survey of the more accessible parts of Sikkim was completed by Robert and his assistant, Rinzin Namgyal (Rinsing of Mr. Freshfield's *Round Kangchenjunga*) who explored the Talung Valley to the Tulung Monastery. In October 1884, he crossed the Kang La into Nepal, explored the Taung Glacier, and followed Sarat Chandra Das's route over the Jonsong La. But instead of crossing the Choten Nyima La, he descended the Lhonak Valley to its junction with the Lachen Valley, returning to Darjeeling on January 31, 1885.

I mentioned these preliminary explorations in the neighbourhood of Kangchenjunga if only to show how little was known but a short time ago of the approaches to the mountain. Had this preliminary exploration work not been carried out, and the way cleared for future mountaineers, one of the most beautiful and interesting climbing districts in the world might still be accessible only with great difficulty. It would be as well therefore, for future parties who may attempt Kangchenjunga, to remember that no route on the mountain can be considered as a *preserve* for any one party.

What may be called the first purely mountaineering party made its appearance in 1883, in which year Mr. W.W. Graham began his ascents in Sikkim. He first visited Dzongri at the beginning of April, and climbed a peak of about 18,000 feet on the Singalila Ridge. After a week he was forced to return to Darjeeling on April 12. Later in October, he ascended Jubonu, 19,350 feet, a peak in the Kabru Range that he gave as about 20,000 feet, and a peak west of the Kang La, which he gave as 19,000 feet. Finally came his climb of Kabru, 24,002 feet, the summit of which, he claimed to have reached. This ascent has been the subject of much controversy, and whether or not he actually climbed Kabru is still doubtful. Possibly, he may have mistaken it for the Forked Peak.

Graham made one interesting remark: he said that May was the avalanche month. Furthermore, it should be noted that nearly all the big climbs in Sikkim have been done during or after the monsoon.

The most valuable mountain exploration ever carried out in the Sikkim Himalayas was that of Mr. Freshfield's party in 1899. Leaving Darjeeling on September 5, the party ascended the Teesta Valley and Zemu Glacier, crossed into the head of the Lhonak Valley, and traversed the Jonsong La. Owing to a heavy snow-fall, they were greatly hampered in their plans, and descended to Kangbachen without having attempted Kangchenjunga or one of its neighbours as had been their original intention. But though unable to do any climbing, Mr. Freshfield made many valuable speculations and observations as to the possibility of peaks, whilst Signor Vittoria Sella, who accompanied him, took many beautiful and instructive photographs.

Mr. Freshfield was the first mountaineer ever to examine the great western face of Kangchenjunga, rising from the Kangchenjunga Glacier. Speaking of this glacier he writes: 'It has its origin in a snow-plateau, or rather terrace, lying under the highest peak at an elevation of about 27,000 feet, that is only some 1,200 feet below the top, the final rock-ridges leading to which look very accessible. Below this terrace however, stretches a most formidable horseshoe of precipices, or what at least the ordinary traveller would describe as precipices. Since however, this glacier affords what is in my opinion the only direct route to Kangchenjunga, which is not impracticable, I must qualify the word.' He goes on to say, 'But – and it is a "but" I desire to emphasise – the routes I can discern by careful study of my companions' photographs are more or less exposed to the worst, because the least avoidable by human skill, of all mountain risks. Steep places will have to be surmounted by a series of slopes, in which the crevasses and séracs have been filled or beaten down by avalanches from hanging ice-cliffs above, and when the peril of this staircase has been run, a way must be found along a shelf similarly exposed.'

After passing through Khunza, Mr. Freshfield crossed the Mirgin La and the Kang La to Dzongri and Darjeeling. He describes his experiences in his classic book *Round Kangchenjunga*, a book which is unfortunately out of print.[2] During this expedition, one of Mr. Freshfield's companions, Professor E. Garwood, constructed a map of Kangchenjunga and its environs, which still remains of great value. It is, indeed, an extraordinarily accurate work, considering the difficult conditions under which it was made.

Between the years 1889 and 1902, the late Mr. Claude White, Political Officer in Sikkim, made various explorations, of which he has unfortunately left but few details. He was the first to investigate the gorges between the Pandim and Simvu mountains, and in 1890 crossed the Guicha La, and ascended the Talung and Teesta valleys. He ascended the Zemu Glacier to about 17,500 feet, and crossed the Tangchang La and the The La into the Lhonak Valley.

Of all mountaineering pioneers in the Kangchenjunga district, and for that matter in the Himalayas, Dr. A.M. Kellas's name will stand pre-eminent. He was perhaps the first mountaineer to regard the Himalayas in the same way that the modern mountaineer regards the Alps – as a playground. Topographical and scientific considerations, while being important to him, were nevertheless of secondary importance as compared to mountaineering, yet, in the course of a number of purely climbing expeditions into north-eastern and north-western Sikkim, he could not fail to acquire much valuable topographical knowledge which will be of much value to mountaineers in the future when Sikkim has been opened up, as it is bound to be one day, as the "Playground" of the Himalayas.

Kellas's climbs are too many to mention in detail, but among the many peaks and passes of 20,000 to 23,000 feet that he ascended or attempted in the immediate neighbourhood of Kangchenjunga, must be mentioned the Nepal Gap, 21,000 feet, separating the Zemu and Kangchenjunga Glaciers, which he attempted four times from the former glacier, nearly reaching the crest of the pass; Simvu, 22,360 feet, which he attempted three times with European guides in 1907, but failed owing to bad weather and snow conditions to reach the summit; the Simvu Saddle, 17,700 feet, and the Zemu Gap, 19,300 feet, which he ascended from the Zemu Glacier in May 1910; the Langpo Peak, 22,800 feet, ascended in September 1909; the Sentinel Peak, 21,240 (or 21,700 feet), east of the Choten Nyima La, ascended in May 1910, and the Jonsong Peak, 24,344 feet, on which he was beaten by bad weather after ascending in December, 1909, to 21,000 feet on the North-West Ridge.

[2] *Round Kangchenjunga* was published in 1903 by Edward Arnold, but owing to a disastrous fire, all copies in stock were subsequently burnt.

Kellas's last expedition prior to his death on the first Everest Expedition was made in 1921 when he conquered Narsingh, 19,130 feet. His mountaineering has had far-reaching effects. He was the first systematically to employ and train Sherpa and Bhutia porters. On one occasion only, in 1907, was he accompanied by Europeans, at other times natives climbed with him. That he was able from such raw material as untrained natives to train men who subsequently worked and climbed so splendidly on Everest and Kangchenjunga expeditions shows how great a mountaineer he was. As one who has humbly followed in his footsteps on the Jonsong Peak, I can safely say that from the technical point of view of route-finding and mountaineering Dr. Kellas will stand out as the greatest pioneer of Himalayan mountaineering. Apart from climbing, he contributed valuable papers on the physiological and physical aspects of high mountaineering to various scientific journals. If in place of his occasional scanty notes and articles, he had written a detailed account of his climbs, posterity and the literature of mountaineering would have been the richer.

One more ascent must be mentioned before turning to the attempts on Kangchenjunga itself, and that was the attempt made in October 1907, by two Norwegians, Messrs. C.W. Rubenson and Monrad Aas on Kabru, 24,002 feet. They tackled the mountain via the Kabru Glacier, which is broken into a great icefall, and had to cut their way for five days through a complicated maze of ice pinnacles and crevasses. These difficulties came to an end at about 21,500 feet, and they camped on the plateau above the icefall between the two peaks, which is so plainly visible from Darjeeling. From there they attempted to reach the eastern summit. Their first attempt was beaten by lack of time due to a late start. They advanced their camp to 22,000 feet on October 20, and tried again. Owing to intense cold they were not able to start until 8.30 a.m. At 6 p.m. they were only about 200 feet below the summit, although separated from it by a considerable distance horizontally. Here they were exposed to the full force of the terrible west wind, against which advance was almost impossible. At sundown the cold became so intense, that to save themselves from frostbite they were forced to retreat.

The descent was marred by a bad slip on the part of Rubenson, who was last man down. Monrad Aas held him on the rope, but the shock was so great that four of its five strands actually parted. When at last they reached camp, Monrad Aas's feet were frost-bitten.

Thus ended a most plucky attempt, especially plucky in view of the fact that Rubenson had never been on a mountain prior to the expedition. The party, though failing to reach the top, made the valuable discovery that it was possible for men to spend a considerable time (in this case twelve days) at an altitude above 20,000 feet, and there to eat well and sleep well and generally keep fit and acclimatise without noticeable physical deterioration.

PREVIOUS ATTEMPTS ON KANGCHENJUNGA

With the exploration of the lower valleys and peaks round Kangchenjunga it was only a matter of time before an attempt was made on the mountain. The first attempt was made in August 1905, by a party consisting of three Swiss, Dr. Jacot-Guillarmod, M. Reymond, and Lieutenant Pache, who put themselves under the leadership of an Englishman, Mr. Aleister Crowley, who had been one of the companions of Dr. Jacot-Guillarmod during an expedition to the Karakorams in 1892. To help with commissariat arrangements, an Italian hotel-keeper from Darjeeling named De Righi was added to the expedition.

Leaving Darjeeling, the expedition proceeded by the Singalila Ridge and the Chumbab La Pass to the Yalung Valley, and having ascended the Yalung Glacier, attacked the South-West Face of Kangchenjunga. This face is exceedingly steep, and consists for the most part of granite precipices. At one point, however, there is a snowy shelf, conspicuous from Darjeeling, which leads up to the ridge, falling in a westerly direction from the third highest summit of Kangchenjunga. This appears to be the only breach in the great curtain of precipices hemming in the head of the Yalung Glacier. Even supposing this face to be climbed, it would still be necessary for the mountaineer to traverse a long distance from the third highest summit to the highest summit, a distance which, in the opinion of all who have seen the intervening ridge and noted its exposure to the west wind, is too great. The snowy shelf looks, and probably is, desperately dangerous owing to falling stones and avalanches, and its dangers must be considerably increased by its southern and consequently warm aspect.

The party established a camp at 20,343 feet, and some of them appeared to have climbed 1,000 feet higher. Disaster overtook them on September 1. On that day the party was assembled at midday at the highest camp. In the afternoon Dr. Guillarmod, Lieutenant Pache, and De Righi with three porters decided to descend to a lower camp, leaving Crowley and Reymond at the higher. The danger of descending steep snow slopes in the heat of the day should have been obvious, and Crowley states that he warned them of the danger that they were incurring by doing so. While traversing a snow slope, two of the porters who were in the middle, slipped, dragging with them Pache and the third porter who were behind, and Guillarmod and De Righi who were in front. This slip in itself might not have proved fatal, had it not started a large avalanche of snow. Guillarmod and De Righi escaped with a severe shaking, but their four companions, Pache and the three porters, were buried and suffocated by the avalanche.

The cries of the survivors soon summoned Reymond, who, apparently, found no difficulty in descending alone from the upper camp. Crowley remained in his tent, and on the same evening wrote a letter printed in *The Pioneer* on September 11, 1905, from which the following is an extract: 'As it was I could do nothing more than send out Reymond on the forlorn hope. Not that I was over anxious in the circumstances to render help. A mountain "accident" of this sort is one of the things for which I have no sympathy whatever. ... Tomorrow I hope to go down and find out how things stand.' In another letter, written three days later, and published on September 15, he explains that it would have taken him ten minutes to dress, and that he had told Reymond to call him if more help was wanted, which he did not do.

The first search for the bodies was in vain, and they were not found until three days later (after Crowley had left the party) buried under ten feet of snow. Thus ended a truly lamentable affair.

From such an expedition it is not easy to draw conclusions as to the dangers and difficulties of an ascent of Kangchenjunga from the Yalung Glacier. Yet, these dangers, even so far as they are revealed by telescope at Darjeeling, are great, and though the Yalung Glacier is well worth investigating both from the point of view of the magnificent scenery at its head and other routes up the great peaks bounding it, there would seem little justification for a further attempt on Kangchenjunga from it.

Kangchenjunga remained untouched until eleven years after the war. British mountaineers had devoted their energies to overcoming Everest, and it was left to other nations to attempt Kangchenjunga. The Everest expeditions produced far-reaching effects. They showed that men could stand, without extraneous aid in the form of oxygen, an altitude as great as 28,000 feet. The lessons learned in transport organisation and climbing equipment were invaluable, and perhaps what is most important of all, they proved that high Himalayan climbing depends on having the right mentality as well as the right physique.

The second attempt on Kangchenjunga was made, like the first, from the Yalung Glacier and like the first, it ended in tragedy. Early in May 1929, an American, Mr E.F. Farmer, of New York, left Darjeeling. He was accompanied by native porters, his sirdar being Lobsang, whose work was to be so invaluable to our expedition. Farmer's climbing experience was limited to the Rockies, and he had never before visited the Himalayas. He told no one of his plans, and having obtained a pass to enable him to go into Sikkim, and signing an undertaking that, he would enter neither Tibet nor Nepal, he left on May 6, with reliable Sherpa and Bhutia porters. He did not return. The porters' story, which has been carefully probed and tested in every particular, is as follows:

He first of all visited the Guicha La; then crossed the Kang La into Nepal. In order not to arouse suspicion, he avoided the little village of Tseram in the Yalung Valley by traversing the rhododendron-clad slopes on the eastern side of the valley. He camped on the same site as the late Mr. Harold Raeburn and Mr. C.G. Crawford, who prospected this district in 1920.[3] Farmer's party found graves which must have been those of the victims of the first attempt on Kangchenjunga.

On May 26, Farmer and three ex-Everest porters started up towards the Talung Saddle. Farmer was warmly clad and wearing crampons, but the porters were poorly shod, and had no crampons. In view of this Lobsang advised turning back, and it was agreed to do this at noon. Climbing became difficult, and the porters found it impossible to proceed in their poor quality boots. Accordingly, Farmer ordered them to halt, while he continued a little higher for photographic purposes. The porters did their best to dissuade him, but, apparently, oblivious of all risk, he climbed up and up, through drifting mists. Now and again when the mists cleared he appeared, and the porters waved to him to descend. At 5 p.m. he was still seen to be climbing, then the mist came down and he was seen no more. The porters remained where they had halted until dusk, then they descended to the

[3] Mr. Raeburn made two visits to the southern walls of Kangchenjunga. The first, on which he was accompanied by Lieutenant-Colonel H.W. Tobin, was made in order to investigate the south-east outlying peaks of Kangchenjunga and possible routes up the South-East Face of Kangchenjunga itself, and to explore the Talung Glacier. Later Raeburn and Crawford ascended the Yalung Glacier and examined the Talung Saddle, which lies on the ridge between Kabru and Kangchenjunga, separating the Yalung and Talung Glaciers. According to Raeburn, it looked "vicious in the extreme, defended everywhere by overhanging masses of ice". Failing in this object, they descended to Upper Tseram, were able to cross the ridge just south of little Kabru, and thus descended the Rathong Valley.

camp, and waited in vain for his return. They signalled at intervals during the night with an electric torch and Meta fuel, but to no purpose. The next morning they climbed up to a point from which his route was visible, and caught a glimpse of him soon after dawn far up on a steep snow slope. He seemed to be moving jerkily, with arms outstretched. Of course, this may have been imagination on the part of the porters, but if true, it may well have been due to snow blindness. They kept up their vigil throughout the day, and it was not until the morning of May 28 that hunger forced them down to Tseram.

In order that any suspicion as to foul play should be eliminated from the score of possible contingencies, the narrative of each porter was taken down and checked. Investigation and minute cross-examination convinced those that enquired into this sad disaster that the whole truth was told, and that no blame whatever attached to the porters, whose conduct had been of an unimpeachable character throughout.

Kangchenjunga had scored heavily. Two attempts had been repulsed with merciless severity, but it must be confessed that the attempts were of so weak a nature that the great mountain had no need to call in its real weapons of defence, storm and altitude. Serene and untroubled, it had not even attempted to kill its attackers; it had let them kill themselves. But its complacency was to be rudely shaken in the autumn of the same year, 1929, in which Farmer met his death.

In view of the fact that no published account has appeared in this country of this attempt which was made by Munich mountaineers, I make no apology for giving a detailed description of one of the most brilliantly resourceful and courageous attempts in mountaineering history, an attempt which has been described by the Editor of the *Alpine Journal* as 'a feat without parallel, perhaps, in all the annals of mountaineering'.

As all mountaineers know, Munich is the home of one of the most enterprising schools of young mountaineers there is. The men who attempted Kangchenjunga were the pick of this school. The leader was Dr. Paul Bauer and his companions were Herren E. Allwein, one of the conquerors of Mount Kaufmann in the Pamirs, Peter Aufschnaiter, E. Beigel, Julius Brenner, W. Fendt, Karl von Kraus, Joachim Leupold, and Alexander Thoenes. The expedition on arriving at Darjeeling was helped in their transport arrangements by Colonel Tobin, the Darjeeling Secretary of the Himalayan Club, and Mr. E.O. Shebbeare, Transport Officer of the 1924 Everest Expedition. So well planned were their transport arrangements, that three days after their arrival, the first half of the expedition was able to leave Darjeeling. The second half followed two days later, together with Colonel Tobin. Eighty-six porters were employed. Eight days later they reached Lachen and ten days later, August 18, established their Base Camp (Camp Three[4]) on Green Lake Plain at a height of 14,126 feet.

Exploration of the north-east side of Kangchenjunga was immediately begun. One party ascended to the Simvu Saddle, whence an attempt, beaten by bad weather, was made on the Simvu Peak, 22,760 feet. The other party explored the possibilities of reaching the East Ridge of Kangchenjunga. As the terrific precipices leading upwards to the lowest point in the North Ridge between

[4] Permanent camps were established from Yaktang at the end of the Zemu Valley and numbered from that point.

Kangchenjunga and the Twins were quite hopeless, they decided to attack a spur, or ridge which leads up to the North Ridge, and joins it at the point where a conspicuous snowy terrace runs across the north-west face of Kangchenjunga about 1,500 feet below the summit. This ridge is heavily armoured in ice and its knife-like crest is broken up into towers and spires of pure ice. Great masses hang precariously from it and huge precipices fall on either side to the glacier, down which thunder great avalanches. No such formidable route had ever been tackled by any other party on any other peak in the world.

Owing to the weather, the snowfall, the great variations of temperature, and the quality of the ice, these ice ridges of Kangchenjunga are completely different from those encountered in the Alps. Mr. Freshfield had seen this ridge too, and there is an excellent photograph in *Round Kangchenjunga*, but he did not mention it as a possible route to the summit of Kangchenjunga, and small wonder. All one can say is that though the technique of icemanship may not have advanced far since pre-war days, the will of man to conquer the greater summits of the Himalayas has developed beyond all expectation. The Munich attempt on Kangchenjunga proves this.

Actually, the ice ridge has one advantage over the main ridges and in particular the North Ridge of Kangchenjunga: it is sheltered from the prevailing western winds, which blow with such paralysing force. If the upper part of this ice ridge could be gained, the party thought that they would have a chance of reaching the summit. But to do so, many and terrible difficulties had to be overcome. Yet, as Dr. Bauer wrote. 'With mountaineers, it is the one remaining possibility of access to Kangchenjunga.'

On August 24 and 25 the party had assembled at the Base Camp, and were ready to make the attempt. The porters had proved themselves worthy of the confidence that was to be reposed in them, and the party had become well acclimatised to altitude. The only drawback was the weather, which was stormy. But considering that the monsoon season had not yet finished, that was only to be expected.

The first difficulty was a 700-foot icefall, which had to be surmounted in order to reach the base of the ice ridge. From Camp Six, 18,696 feet; the party endeavoured to storm the 2,800-foot wall leading to the crest of the ice ridge. The way proved very dangerous; falling boulders a cubic yard in size swept the route, compelling a sharp lookout. They had nearly attained the crest of the ridge when bad weather necessitated return. The following day a stronger party, four Germans and three porters equipped with bivouac necessities and food, returned to the attack in better weather. The slopes leading to the ridge were ribbed with ice flutings common to the Himalayas, between which rose sharp, serrated, and cornice crowned edges of rock. The party was spread-eagled one above the other on the smooth ice slopes without security, and the fall of one would have meant disaster to all. Also, there was a grave danger of stone falls. Once more they were forced to retreat.

On the following day, Allwein and Thoenes reached the ridge by climbing a steep ice gully. This gully was so difficult, however, that it was a question whether porters could be got up it. Indeed, so great were the difficulties proving, that it was nearly decided then and there to abandon the attack in favour of the East

Ridge from the Zemu Gap, but this ridge is so long, and the obstacles so many, that there seems little chance of reaching the summit of Kangchenjunga by it. Incidentally, it does not even lead directly to the highest summit, but to the second highest summit, 27,820 feet, between which and the highest summit stretches a formidable ridge. But before abandoning the ice ridge, one more attempt was decided upon. Camp was pitched 900 feet higher up the wall. The following day dawned sulkily, and the weather was none too good, yet it was decided to make one last effort to hew a breach in the snow bosses, and force a way to the crest of the ice ridge.

The difficulties were immense. They slowly hacked away at the ice curtain; everything that could be utilised as a help to the sorely-tried party was employed and even icicles as thick as a man's arm were used to hitch a rope round. Height was gained; hope replaced despair; the party turned back rejoicing at the thought that they had discovered the necessary ice-technique for making a formidable slope possible for laden porters.

But Kangchenjunga prepared to resist the onslaught. A snowfall compelled a retreat to Camp Six. Another attempt to reach the ridge was made but another snowfall occurred, and avalanches drove the party down again. Camp Seven was rendered unsafe by these avalanches, and all the equipment had to be carried down through deep new snow to Camp Six.

On September 13, the weather cleared, and the assault was renewed. Two days of strenuous step cutting brought the party to the crest of the ridge. A scene of incomparable splendour opened out before their eyes. 'Nearly vertically below lay the Twins Glacier, while slopes of 60 degrees led downwards, on the farther side, to the Zemu Glacier. Icy and shining pinnacles led upwards for 6,500 feet. In a wide cirque above us towered the ice slopes of the Tent Peak, the Twins, Kangchenjunga, Simvu, above the two mighty glacier basins. Avalanches thundered in continuous icy cascades down these faces. Behind us swept endless glacier shapes into the dim and cloudy distance.'[5]

Three great towers interposed, barring their advance. For two days they toiled and struggled in conquering them. Beyond these towers the ice ridge rose in a precipitous step. They had hoped to reach a snowy ledge on the step, and establish Camp Eight, but they were overtaken by night before they had reached this level. 'Bivouac material and provisions were dumped where we stood. The porters belayed to a well-buried axe watched us with astonishment scooping out a place for the camp in a cornice on the dizzy ridge. Then Aufschnaiter and Kraus descended with them to Camp Seven, while Beigel and Dr. Bauer settled down in our tiny tent. The spot was not altogether trustworthy since in one place, where the axe had been deeply driven; we could look down through a hole on to the Twins Glacier. We slept well, but at dawn great care was necessary in distributing our stiffened limbs properly while wriggling gingerly out of the insecurely pitched tent. Hardly had the sun begun to thaw us than we started on the first gendarme hacking out layer after layer of ice from its flanks, till we could force a way past it on the left and attain a névé slope at an angle of fully 70 degrees. Two hours later this also lay below and we had cut a good deep zigzag track through it

[5] From Dr. Paul Bauer's account in the *Alpine Journal*, translated into English by Lieutenant-Colonel E.L. Strutt, the Editor.

connecting each icy boss with the next. A hundred feet below us lay the little tent; above us rose more ice pinnacles. A little ice crevice, enlarged by us into a chimney, brought us some twenty feet higher up the steepest part of the névé, much hampered here by many cornices. By the early afternoon we stood at length at the base of the last pinnacle separating us from the first platform in the spur. We saw the "shock troops", Nos. 2 and 3 parties, approaching from below with their porters; quickly we levelled out a space on the terrace for our friends' camp, and then turned downwards as the spur now lay in shadow. Soon it grew so cold that danger of frostbite became threatening. We met the other contingent, Allwein and Thoenes, with the porters Chettan and Lewa, just as they attained the terrace.'

Above Camp eight there were more pinnacles, or perhaps it would be more correct to say perpendicular steps or pitches in the ridge. These had to be stormed by the crest. The first was not so difficult. An overhanging crack filled with powdery snow led diagonally upwards to the left. The second pinnacle was harder. A short, nearly vertical ice runnel had to be negotiated followed by a traverse to the left of it. A steep ascent to the right brought them to the crest. The next pinnacle hung over the ridge like an enormous mushroom some 120 feet high. 'On the Twins side rose a wall formed of wind-blown powdery snow above the overhanging bulge. It was dreadful work crawling up on the treacherous powdery mass poised above the nearly perpendicular Twins Glacier slope.'

The pinnacle above this gave them the longest work of all. Allwein's report reads as follows: 'On reaching the fourth tower on September 23, we were at first completely at a loss, the crest appeared vertical or even overhanging, so was the slope falling towards the Twins Glacier, and so indeed was the left flank as well. Yet on this latter flank depended our only hopes, for a tiny ledge led upwards in the face crowned with a huge cornice furnished with a deep recess hollowed out of the ice in its centre. Higher up the ledge soon ended under impossible ice overhangs, leaving no other alternative but from the said recess to burrow a shaft perpendicularly upwards through the wide, stretching cornice. We worked away the whole day at this tunnel, but on returning to camp at 4 p.m. the work lay still unfinished.'

On the following days they were able to improve this route, until finally this originally difficult and dangerous pinnacle became the easiest of all.

Such hard work as this has never before been accomplished at such an altitude. Its technique opens out an entirely new method of overcoming these terrific Himalayan ice ridges, though only time will show whether routes of this difficulty will ever lead to victory on the greater peaks of the Himalayas.

On September 25, they traversed along the edge of a dizzy snow rib corniced on both sides to the bottom of a long-dreaded 200-foot gap. So soft was the snow and so narrow the rib, which was not more than two feet wide, that no proper route could be made, and they could only beg the porters to follow exactly in their footsteps. Beyond the gap rose another great tower. The lower part of this was comparatively easy, but necessitated very hard work. Above rose a steep snow runnel, on which it was a severe struggle clearing away the soft snow and cutting steps in the underlying firm ice. The party forgathered on a little shoulder half way up. A hundred feet of more difficult work led to the foot of a wall of fearful steepness, crowned by a huge cornice. The base of this was masked by masses of rock and snow, and it was difficult to fashion reliable footholds from which the cornice could be flogged down, but at last a way was forced through the eaves of over-hanging snow, and the party stood on the crest of the ridge.

The great tower had been conquered; slowly, but surely, the gallant party were winning their way up this terrific ice ridge. The fight was a fair one until Kangchenjunga called in its ally, the weather. Snow began to fall nearly every day, and on the following morning after the conquest of the tower, lay fully a foot deep. The most difficult part of the route had been done, but it had cost two valuable weeks. Fresh obstacles were always cropping up; disappointments had been many, and until the conquest of the gap and the great tower was accomplished, it had seemed problematical whether progress was possible at all. Now, however, the party was sufficiently far advanced to push hard for the summit.

In lieu of tents, ice caves were carved in the solid ice at Camps Eight and Nine, large enough to hold six to eight persons. The entrance to these was as small as possible, and the temperature inside rarely sank below 26° to 28°F., whilst outside it was usually about 14°F. by day and 10° to 25° below zero Fahrenheit by night. Future Everest expeditions would do well to investigate the technique of ice cave making. Ice caves properly constructed below and on the North Col of Everest would most likely prove more efficient than tents. Above the North Col only tents could be used, for the climbing lies entirely over rocks.

Above Camp Nine, 21,646 feet, the difficulties dwindled. Two easier ice towers were soon stormed. Snow slab avalanches broke away under the leader, but it was always possible to secure him so that he could not slip far. One snow slope entailed caution, but once firm steps had been made it became safe. Camp Ten, 22,288 feet, was pitched on easy and open snow. Here, as below, an ice cave was scooped out. Preparations were made for the final assault, communication was established between all camps and food and equipment sent up with the utmost speed.

Theoretically, October should bring settled weather, practically, the weather was doubtful; it was not exactly stormy, but aggravated by continual snow flurries. On October 3, Allwein and Kraus set out to reconnoitre and track out the route above Camp Ten for the next stage on the following day. The snow was not good, and they often sank in knee-deep, but they were able in an hour to ascend about 350 feet, which was very fair going. They turned back at about 24,272 feet. As a result of their exploration, they considered that no more difficulties were to be expected, but that owing to the soft, powdery snow, two more camps would have to be pitched. Was this optimism justified in the light of previous Himalayan experience? I think not.

This was the highest point reached. That night hopes ran high in the ice cave. What they had hardly dared to expect, the summit, seemed to lie within their grasp.

October 14 dawned evilly. The sky was cloud covered a cold wind was blowing and light snow falling. The snow thickened; by 8 a.m. it was coming down hard. Plans had to be altered, and preparations for a siege made. Kraus and Thoenes with two porters, Lewa and Chettan, left, and descended in order to save food, and help with the transport. The snow continued; by the evening of October 15 things looked black. 'We began to realise with heavy hearts that the ascent of Kangchenjunga was now hardly possible. Only a deliberate abandonment of our hitherto "safety-first" tactics for a desperate assault might result in success. This would entail a complete break-up of our lines of communication and result in "every man for himself". The "summit" party could no longer, as hitherto, be supported by a reserve party ready to "leap-frog" in case of necessity. Even with instant improvement of the weather it would take days for a relief party to fight its way through from below to our support.'

As the weather appeared too bad for an attempt on the summit, they decided at least to make an attempt to reach the North Ridge and gaze down the unknown north-west side of the mountain. Even this proved impossible. After two hours' hard work they had risen not more than 250 feet. The wind-blown, crusted slopes of snow continually collapsed beneath them, letting them sink in thigh-deep. Abandoning their loads, they struggled upwards for an hour and a half. They reached a height of about 24,000 feet and then decided to retreat.

As they sat again by their ice cave, they were startled by the extraordinary appearance of the sky to the south. A huge cloud bank over 30,000 feet high was forming, whilst above it the sky was of an extraordinary sea-green colour, 'a most threatening and terrible sight'.[6]

The following day they awoke to find the cave entrance completely blocked with snow. The snowfall continued, and many times during the day they had to sweep the entrance clear. By nightfall no less than seven feet of snow had fallen, and it was still snowing. 'A cataclysm of nature seemed to foreshadow our doom.' There was now no thought of advance. Communications had been cut off, they did not know what was happening below, and those below did not know what was the fate of those above. It was a terrible position to be in. To stay meant starvation. 'The Storm God was still piling snow on us, yet, on the following morning, trusting to our powers and experience, we determined to "Wrestle one more fall". The descent appeared humanly impossible, but an attempt had to be made.'

So deep was the snow that they fought their way down leaving behind a furrow a man's height in depth. A slightly *ascending* bit not 150 feet high took them over two hours. The porters behaved magnificently, though laden with some eighty pounds each. They had frequently to be jerked from the holes into which they sank, but they continued to struggle gallantly on.

Steeper slopes peeled off in avalanches as the leader, tightly held on a rope, stepped on them. The most dangerous slope had fortunately already avalanched. They descended in the actual groove made by the avalanche, thus saving a good two hours. Disaster nearly overtook them when another slope with Allwein and two porters on it avalanched, and only a desperate effort on the part of Dr. Bauer saved them. So great an effort was it for all concerned, that for ten minutes or more they lay motionless and exhausted before they could resume the fight.

On their arrival at Camp Nine they had to clear the ice cave entrance from beneath seven feet of snow. They lay there all night, recovering their strength for the tussle with the most difficult portion of the descent.

The next day things went wrong. The porters, not unnaturally, were nervous.

[6] In *Round Kangchenjunga*, p. 114, Mr. Freshfield describes a similar strange atmospheric appearance, which heralded the great storm of September. 1899, during which no less than 27 inches of rain fell in 28 hours in Darjeeling, occasioning considerable loss of life and damage to property. See also my own description in my book *Climbs and Ski Runs* of the green ray sunrise which preceded a terrible storm on the Schreckhorn.

To face such difficulties with heavy loads was impossible. They were brought back to the cave, and the Europeans without packs set out to clear footsteps in the newly fallen snow, and thus make possible the traverse of the great ice towers.

The following day, a good half of the loads were jettisoned, and thrown down the 5,000 feet precipice to the Twins Glacier. Thus relieved, the party could renew the struggle.

For once wayward Fortune smiled on them – the weather became fine. They gazed down, but could see no sign of any living beings either on the ice ridge or on the Zemu Glacier. It was not until two days later that they learned that all the ice ridge party were still alive.

Each of the two communication parties had had a great struggle in retreating. The exhausted porters continually fell, and avalanches poured down. Beigel and Aufschnaiter had suffered the worst. Between Camps Nine and Eight they were swept off their feet by small avalanches. Once the leader slipped when traversing slightly below the crest of a ridge; in another instant all must have been pulled off, and hurled down the precipices, but the party were saved by the presence of mind of the second man, who had time to leap into space on the reverse side of the ridge, and thus held his companions on the rope. This mishap resulted in the loss of both rucksacks, provisions and bivouac material, and a miserable night had to be spent on the ridge under a cornice without shelter of any kind. As a result Beigel was severely frost-bitten in the feet.

At last with joy the upper party reached Camp Six. Communications had been severed from below. It took four days to plough down through snow many feet deep to the Base Camp. Everyone carried as great a load as possible. The sahibs broke the trail, sinking in below their knees. The porters followed, while last of the exhausted procession came Beigel, carried on a rough stretcher made from two tent poles, 'silent and uttering no complaint'. Even at the snout of the Zemu Glacier another weather catastrophe overtook the worn-out party. For three days it snowed and rained, and the snow covered bamboos and rhododendrons proved almost impassable. Poor Beigel, who had been carried, had perforce to walk. The mountainsides were alive with landslides; mud-shoots did their best to annihilate the party. 'Dishevelled, dead-beat, our nerves worn out with the wild struggle against nature, with unkempt beards and covered with mud, we trod with heavy feet into the brilliantly lit dining room of the Lachen bungalow.'

Thus ended one of the most gallant mountaineering enterprises ever carried out.

In one respect only is criticism justified. When they reached their highest camp at an altitude of 24,000 feet, they considered that they had overcome the worst difficulties. Such, however, is far from the case. These difficulties had scarcely begun. Altitude and its effects only begin to be serious over 24,000 feet, and being on the sheltered side of the mountain they had not yet begun to experience the terrible west wind which sweeps the upper part of the North Ridge with such merciless severity, and last, but not least, is the final pyramid, of which the climbing difficulties are certainly greater than those of the final pyramid of Everest. Colonel E.F. Norton, in an interesting letter in the *Himalayan Journal* analysing the respective difficulties of Kangchenjunga and Everest, lays stress on the time factor. He writes:

'*Exclusive of false starts* it took the party just under a month from the foot of the ridge (17,060 feet) to Camp Ten at 23,290 feet. This includes the establishment of Camp Ten for six sahibs and four porters equipped "for the fight for the eight thousanders". (The meaning of this expression is not quite clear to me. 8,000 metres equals 26,600 odd feet, equals 1,500 feet below the summit, so I am not certain if they were equipped for the whole distance to the top.) This represented a climb of 6,230 feet.

'Compare Mount Everest; in 1924 we estimated to establish a similar party (equipped to lay out one more camp and reach the top) at Camp Five (25,000 feet) in 15 days from the Base Camp (16,500 feet). This represented a climb of 8,500 feet.

'We failed; but that this was not an unreasonable estimate is proved by the fact that we established Camp Five in 1922 (including a four-day reconnaissance of the East Rongbuk Glacier – up and back again) with four sahibs in 19 days from first leaving the base camp, largely over an unknown route.

'Camp Five on Mount Everest was 4,000 feet from the top – an easy rock climb.

'Camp Ten on Kangchenjunga was 5,000 feet from the top, and judging from what Mr. Bauer says, the condition of the snow even at this height necessitated "stamping a track".

'Now the difficulties imposed by altitude only begin to be really serious from about 24,000 or 25,000 feet onwards, both as regards condition of the snow and rarity of the air.

'Next consider the time available on Kangchenjunga.

'Mr. Bauer's party started presumably in the tail of the monsoon (August 26), and got badly caught high up on the mountain by the first winter snowfall on October 3 – after five and a half weeks. A party trying it in the spring can hardly kick off from the foot of the mountain until April 15 on account of the spring cold; the monsoon is due to arrive by May 21 (I am writing from memory) – again five and a half weeks.

'On Everest we reckoned on a season of from four to six weeks, i.e. from May 1 to the arrival of the monsoon on the north face of the mountain – any time between June 1 and 15. The penalty for being caught high on Everest in soft new snow is the danger of avalanches on only about 1,500 feet of descent from the North Col. On Kangchenjunga there must be thousands of feet of such dangers – as Mr. Bauer found.

'Events may well prove me wrong: but on the face of it, Kangchenjunga appears to me a more formidable and more dangerous proposition than Mount Everest.'

One cannot but concur with this admirable analysis. Time will always be the most important factor in any attempt on Kangchenjunga. Five and a half weeks is the maximum period during which weather and conditions suitable for climbing can be expected. It is significant also to notice that at their highest camp the Bavarians had begun to experience the west wind.

I mention these facts in no carping spirit, but merely to point out the difficulties to be expected. Given sufficient time, and weather of the right type, there is a remote probability that Kangchenjunga can be climbed by present day methods. But does a sufficiently long enough spell of good weather *ever* occur on the mountain? Can men acclimatise sufficiently to climb even moderately difficult rocks and the upper rocks may be more than moderately difficult, between 27,000 and 28,000 feet?

There is no need to analyse further possible routes on Kangchenjunga. Every side has now been explored, photographed and mapped, and further reconnaissance is unnecessary. The mountain may require methods to overcome it which are at present not known to mountaineers, but even supposing medical science discovers means artificially to acclimatise the body so that as much work can be put out at 28,000 feet as at a much lower altitude, Kangchenjunga will still remain something more than a formidable antagonist.

CHAPTER THREE

Plans and Preparations

ONLY BY COMPARISON is it possible to obtain any idea of the scale of the world's greatest mountain range. Yet, even this method is unsatisfactory, for whether the mountaineer is toiling up Mont Blanc or Everest, his feelings, apart from those imposed by altitude and the desire to achieve are very similar; he is but a microcosm on the vast mountainside. Suffice to say that Mont Blanc is little more than half the height of Mount Everest, 29,002 feet, Kilimanjaro, 19,700 feet and Mount McKinley, 20,454 feet. The highest peaks of Africa and North America would rank as minor peaks in the Sikkim Himalayas; and even Aconcagua, 23,000 feet, the monarch of the Andes, is no higher than the North Col on Everest.

Each group of the greater peaks has its own type of scenery, but none is finer than the magnificent massif that culminates at 28,156 feet above sea level in the summit of Kangchenjunga. The visitor to Darjeeling who climbs to the top of Observatory Hill sees it fifty miles away over range upon range of lower ridges, split with deep, gorge-like valleys, incredibly remote and icily aloof, lifting its glaciers like silver shields to the sky. There is no scale by which the observer can appreciate the size of what he sees. The apparently insignificant ridges over which his gaze passes are themselves as high as, or higher than, the Alps. The slit-like valleys and gorges are disclosed only by the mists, born of their steamy, tropical heat, that form towards noon and writhe slowly upwards in columns of massive cumuli. There is no standard of comparison, and experience alone can teach that the heights, depths, and distances are twice or three times as great as those in the Alps.

The eye can pass at a glance over these leagues of ridges and valleys between Darjeeling and Kangchenjunga, but the foot of man cannot take them at a stride. The problems of reaching the base of the greater peaks and of carrying sufficient food and equipment are second only to the problems of scaling the peaks themselves. It is largely due to these initial difficulties, and to the expense of organising and maintaining a large bandobast[1] of native porters that so few expeditions are undertaken in the high Himalayas. Yet, in an age when mountaineering in the

[1] Bandobast – a common Indian term meaning organisation, arrangement, party, etc.

Alps is said to have reached technical perfection, it is indeed remarkable that not one of the greater Himalayan peaks has been climbed.

Yet, if the summits of Everest and other giants over 25,000 feet remain untrodden, man has not been idle; he has climbed thousands of minor peaks and several expeditions that have been carried out in the Himalayas have taught valuable lessons as regards the right personnel, the best kinds of food and equipment, and the easiest and most efficient methods of porterage. The three Everest expeditions and the 1929 Kangchenjunga expedition taught invaluable lessons. It is over the graves of former mistakes, and not on the wings of new ideas that the climber will at length tread the highest summits in the world.

Though it may sound "a glimpse of the obvious" there is only one way of learning Himalayan mountaineering, and that is to climb among the Himalayas. Useful asset though it is, a brilliant Alpine mountaineering record is no "Open Sesame" to a brilliant Himalayan record, the conditions are so different. In the selection of the personnel and equipment it was unfortunate that not one of the party that left Europe had experience of Himalayan expeditions. Schneider certainly had climbed in the Pamirs, but the conditions prevailing there are not the same as those of the Eastern Himalayas. Had it been possible, it would have been the wisest move to have invited at least one or two British or German mountaineers at the outset with past Himalayan experience. Apart from this vital omission, the party selected by Professor Dyhrenfurth was an exceptionally strong one. It possessed one important advantage over most other British parties that have visited the Himalayas – all its members had experience in winter mountaineering and ski running, as well as summer mountaineering in the Alps. This was important because snow conditions approximating to alpine winter conditions are frequently encountered in the Himalayas.

Climbing is mental as well as physical work. Mr. G. Winthrop Young devotes a whole chapter to the mental aspects of Alpine mountaineering in *Mountain Craft*. All that he wrote applies with even greater force to Himalayan mountaineering. The climbing party must be something more than a collection of expert mountaineers, it must be a team, and like a team of Test cricketers, one that pulls together in every department of the game; and if it is a good team, it should also be a happy family. In no other pursuit is the best or the worst in a man brought out as it is in mountaineering. An old friend of civilisation may be a useless companion on a mountain. The 1929 Munich expedition had one great advantage over our own; they were all friends before they started from Europe. We were not, and the fact that everything went so smoothly must be set down to luck. There have in fact been other Himalayan expeditions the members of which were acquaintances, if not friends, which did not go so smoothly as our expedition.

In Professor Dyhrenfurth, the expedition possessed a leader of wide mountaineering experience as well as an accomplished geologist. He has ascended more than seven hundred peaks in the Alps and Hohe Tatra. He is forty-four years of age, and comes of a hardy mountaineering stock, for his father, Dr. Oskar Dyhrenfurth climbed the Jungfrau at the age of sixty-nine,[2] and at the age of

[2] This is by no means an unusual age for mountaineers to make ascents. Many members of the Alpine Club have made greater ascents at considerably greater ages. The late Captain J.P. Farrar at the age of seventy-one climbed many first class peaks in the last year of his life. Mountaineering begets longevity and longevity mountaineering.

seventy-four made a solitary climb on the Dachstein, in which he fell badly, but recovered. Professor Dyhrenfurth made his first climb at the age of nine, and at the age of thirteen, ascended the Rosengartenspitze, the well-known peak in the western Dolomites. He was severely injured in 1921, when he fell twenty-one feet owing to a rope breaking when ascending the Drusenfluh. During the War he commanded a corps of mountain guides on the Italian frontier, and spent summer and winter at heights of over 10,000 feet in redoubts among the Ortler mountains, and in dugouts cut in the solid ice of glaciers. These experiences were of more use to him from a Himalayan point of view than any ordinary alpine mountaineering.

Frau Hettie Dyhrenfurth is perhaps best known as an international lawn tennis player. She is one of the best players in mixed doubles in Switzerland. She has accompanied her husband on many expeditions, but few women have taken part in great climbs in the Himalayas, and by accompanying the expedition, she joined that select little band of Himalayan lady mountaineers, including Mrs. Bullock Workman, Mrs. Ruttledge and Frau Visser.

The second in command of the expedition was Monsieur Marcel Kurz, who besides being a climbing member, was our cartographer. He is the greatest living Continental authority on winter mountaineering, and his record of first winter ascents and difficult climbs is unique. His climbs included, the first winter ascents of the Ober Gabelhorn and Täschhorn in the Zermatt district, the last two peaks in the Alps of Valais to be unclimbed in winter. He is an expert on snow-craft and avalanches, particularly from the point of view of ski running. When climbing with Mr. H.E.L. Porter in the Southern Alps of New Zealand in 1927, he made a new route up Mount Tasman by the East Ridge, and also ascended Mount Cook, 12,349 feet, the highest peak in the New Zealand Alps, by a long and difficult route. He revised and brought up to date the famous Kurz guide-books on Mont Blanc and the Pennine Alps written by his father, and has also written *Alpinisme Hivernal* and a guide to the Alps of Valais. He has mapped Mount Olympus for the Greek Government, and published a monograph on the mountain from both historical and topographical aspects.

Herren Hermann Hoerlin and Erwin Schneider joined the expedition with as brilliant a record of great climbs as any young mountaineers in Europe. The number of great ascents made by them rivals that of the famous Swiss pair, Dr. Walter Amstutz and Herr Schumacher. In 1929, they carried out a series of climbs on the range of Mont Blanc which included the first winter ascents of the Aiguille Noire de Peuterey and the Aiguille Blanche de Peuterey, as well as a ski traverse of Mont Blanc. They are an extraordinarily fast pair; their time for their winter ascent of the Aiguille Blanche de Peuterey, one of the most dangerous climbs in the Alps, was actually faster than that for the summer ascent of the peak by Mr. Eustace Thomas and Josef Knubel, Mr. Winthrop Young's famous guide. They also ascended the Aiguille Verte and Les Droites in winter. Herr Schneider comes from Hall, in Tyrol, and is a geologist. In 1929 he took part in the Alai Pamir expedition led by Herr Wilhelm Rickmer Rickmers, in the course of which he climbed some fifteen peaks in the neighbourhood of 17,000 feet, eight 20,000 feet peaks and Mount Kaufmann (renamed Pic Lenin by the Soviets) the highest peak ascended in Central Asia. Herr Ulrich Wieland, though not so experienced as his compatriots, is nevertheless one of the keenest of the younger German mountaineers.

Herr Hoerlin is a student of medicine. Though he only started to climb in 1922, he is recognised as one of the leading young German mountaineers, and is the president of the Akademischer Alpen Club, Berlin; the most exclusive mountaineering club in Northern Germany.

Dr. Helmuth Richter was to act not only as surgeon, but also as reporter to the German newspapers. He is a German army doctor, and though his experience of climbing was limited, he had had considerable experience of skiing, and was an excellent runner. He is a keen physiologist and hoped to obtain valuable data in connection with the effects of high altitudes on the bodily functions.

In order to ensure bringing back a first-rate film record of the expedition, Professor Dyhrenfurth engaged Monsieur Charles Duvanel, who had previously made a number of aerial films for the Swiss Government, as well as instructional films of Alpine climbing and skiing. He is, like Kurz, a French-speaking Swiss, and comes from Lausanne.

The importance of having expert transport officers with a Himalayan expedition can hardly be over-estimated. It is one thing to climb a mountain but it is quite another thing to get to the foot of the mountain and having got there maintain an efficient line of communication. The expedition were fortunate in obtaining as chief transport officer Lieutenant-Colonel H.W. Tobin, D.S.O., O.B.E.. the Darjeeling secretary of the Himalayan Club whose experience not only of Himalayan mountaineering generally but also of local Darjeeling conditions made him an invaluable asset to the expedition. Upon him devolved responsibility for the enlistment of porters and the arrangement of the multifarious expedition details at Darjeeling, many of which though seemingly trivial in themselves are vital to the efficient working of a transport organisation.

In order to strengthen not only the transport organisation but also the climbing party as well, Mr. George Wood Johnson was invited to join the expedition. Like Colonel Tobin he is well acquainted with local conditions. His enthusiasm for mountaineering may be gauged by the fact that he had come to India not only to learn tea-planting but to learn how to manage local workers and speak Nepali in order to fit himself for a future Everest expedition. In these things he had prospered exceedingly under the able tuition of Mr. McKean his manager. Though he had then no previous alpine experience he was a member of the Fell and Rock-Climbing Club and an expert rock climber. Alpine experience counts for little in the Himalayas without knowledge of travelling conditions, and an expedition undertaken by him in 1929 to peaks around Dzongri was to prove of more value to our expedition than any amount of Alpine experience.

Having chosen the personnel of a Himalayan expedition, the next thing to do is to equip it. Himalayan mountaineering falls naturally into two categories. There is the expedition that has for its object the conquest of peaks up to 23,000 feet high, and for this ordinary alpine clothing and footgear are sufficient. Then there is the expedition that sets out to attempt the greater peaks of the Himalayas. This requires more specialised equipment, for owing to the effects of altitude and subsequent lowering of the vitality and bodily wastage, the winds that mercilessly sweep the upper ridges, and intense cold, it is essential to prevent frostbite.

There is only one way of efficiently clothing an expedition, and that is to study the lessons of the past, and to take heed of the lessons learnt, often at considerable cost, on expeditions such as Sir Martin Conway's in the Karakorams and the three Everest expeditions. These lessons and the recommendations derived from them are all laid down and should be studied with the utmost care. Nor should the late Sir Ernest Shackleton and the clothing which he provided for his expeditions into the Antarctic be neglected, for he was one of the first to make a scientific study of *light* wind-and-cold-resisting clothing.

Professor Dyhrenfurth was fortunate in having the advice of Brigadier-General the Hon. C.G. Bruce, C.B., M.V.O., Lieutenant-Colonel E.L. Strutt, C.B.E., D.S.O., who accompanied the 1922 Everest expedition, and others. In the light of their experiences on Everest they were unhesitating in their recommendation that light clothing and light boots should be worn of a type similar to that advocated by Shackleton. On Everest, the best clothing was found to consist of woollen underclothes, Shetland wool sweaters, and outside a light jacket of wind-proof material. Boots were similar to those used in ordinary Alpine work, only lightly nailed and sufficiently roomy to take two or three pairs of stockings and socks. It is interesting to note that the porters who went highest, about 27,000 feet, did so in Army ammunition boots brought out from England and costing 15/6 [77p] a pair. Thus, in a properly equipped expedition, frostbite is usually due to the carelessness of the climber.

Bearing these things in mind, it was unfortunate that Professor Dyhrenfurth did not follow advice founded on many years experience, of equipping his expedition with light clothing and boots. He chose rather to adopt the diametrically opposed theory that one layer of heavy material is warmer than two or more layers of lighter material.

The following is a list of clothing that was supplied. A tricot coat weighing six pounds; breeches, three pounds, six ounces; sweater, two pounds, ten ounces; outer wind-jacket, three pounds. I can only describe the boots as portmanteaux. They weighed six and a half pounds a pair and each was nailed with sixty clinker and tricouni nails. The soles were built up of layers of felt, rubber and leather and the uppers, which came halfway to the knee, were felt-lined. Crampons supplied with these boots were proportionately heavy and weighed four pounds a pair. Allowing an additional two pounds for an ice axe, and five pounds for under-clothing, head-gear, socks, stockings and puttees, but not including gear and equipment such as is normally carried in a rucksack or rope, we were, therefore, expected to carry a total of thirty-two and a half pounds to the summit of Kangchenjunga. This, together with other equipment, etc., would in my case be *nearly a quarter of my own normal weight*. It goes without saying that this equipment proved totally unsatisfactory. The only occasion on which I wore the expedition boots was on the Ramthang Peak, and I shall not easily forget the effort of lifting them at an altitude of 23,000 feet. What would they and the clothing be like to the climber dependent on his last dregs of energy between 27,000 and 28,000 feet near the summit of Kangchenjunga?

It was with some inkling as to what was likely to be provided that caused me to purchase some equipment in England in addition to that with which Professor Dyhrenfurth was providing me. This consisted principally of Shetland woollies and Jaeger underclothing. Of the former, I had four sweaters weighing four ounces each purchased from W. Bill of Great Portland Street, London.

I never found it necessary to wear more than three of these and these three worn in conjunction with Jaeger combinations and a wind-proof jacket were definitely warmer than the tricot jacket, and the two pounds ten ounces single sweater. Unfortunately, the boots came as a complete surprise, and, like some of the other members of the expedition, I was forced to wear a pair of boots which I used to tramp from Darjeeling to the Base Camp, boots which would only take two pairs of stockings and that at a squeeze, but which nevertheless proved perfectly satisfactory with a dozen or more tricouni nails knocked into each.

I know that in making such challenging statements I may arouse the wrath of my continental friends, who believe that weight and thickness alone spell warmth, but apart from my own former experiences in the Alps, during which I have made a close study of clothing and equipment, and apart from the experiences of former Himalayan and Polar expeditions, it cannot be doubted that several layers of light clothing are preferable to one layer of thick, heavy clothing, and that clothing one third of the weight of that which I have mentioned would be heavy enough, and warm enough for a man to reach without fear of frostbite the highest peaks in the world.

There is another thing that must be considered besides mere warmth – the ventilation of the body. Though the air temperature may be many degrees below freezing, the sun temperature is enormous at high altitudes. If the body is not sufficiently ventilated, perspiration cannot evaporate, and a sudden lowering of body temperature by wind, or the withdrawal of the sun may result in a severe chill. A single layer of thick material, while being wind-proof, is also ventilation proof. It is possible to have clothing which will both ventilate the body and protect it from the wind, and in this respect there is nothing better than several layers of Shetland wool.

The head and ears must be well protected, and here again one cannot do better than to wear two or three Shetland wool Balaclava helmets, while in the event of a severe wind, a leather flying helmet can be worn outside, although this again tends to retard ventilation.

Snow blindness must be guarded against. At high altitudes the ultra-violet rays of the sun are so intense that even on rocks it is possible to suffer snow blindness. No special protection, other than the ordinary bottle green or dark yellow snow-glasses that can be purchased in Switzerland at one franc a pair, is necessary. Personally, I found Crookes' glass more restful, as it does not distort colour, and eliminates all glare by cutting out the ultraviolet rays. The sun also shines with such power that it strips the skin off the face like paper, a process which, incidentally, is assisted by the wind only too effectually. The best kind of protective face cream is that which both lubricates tne skin and absorbs the ultra-violet rays, which are principally responsible for the painful stripping process.

Excellent gloves were provided. They were of the leather fingerless variety fleece-lined. Puttees have many opponents among mountaineers, but the Kashmiri puttees as recommended by General Bruce do not impede the circulation in the least degree and are wonderfully warm. Not only do they prevent the snow getting in, but they afford excellent protection against the inroads of leeches. Incidentally, while on this last subject, it is a useful tip to put tobacco leaves in the stockings. Although leeches enjoy one's blood, they object to having to chew tobacco first in order to get it.

Professor Dyhrenfurth did a wise thing when he decided to have separate tents for each European member of the expedition. Later on, I shall have occasion to remark on the psychological importance of this. Suffice to say that these tents made by Schuster of Munich were excellent, and stood up well to wind and rain. The only criticism that might be made is that there was not sufficient overlap in the flaps.

The best thing of all among the camping equipment was the synthetic rubber ground sheets. These were about one third of an inch thick. Not only do they keep one dry, but also they insulate one from the cold ground or snow, and are soft enough to eliminate the "inevitable stone".

Wise is the mountaineer who fusses over his sleeping bag as a cricketer fusses over his particular brand of bat. Individual taste should be satisfied, for the Himalayan mountaineer spends an appreciable portion of his life lying in his sleeping bag. Here again the lessons of the past are not to be ignored. It has been said of Everest sleeping bags that they were too narrow, and that at great altitudes. the climber had to wriggle, strain and pant in order to insinuate himself into his bag, an effort so great at 25,000 feet or more that he would lie for minutes exhausted by the effort. The warmest sleeping bag is not a tightly fitting one, but one in which there is plenty of room to change the position. Warmth also depends upon having sufficient air space round the body. Several years experimenting in Alpine conditions have convinced me that quilted eiderdown is superior to all other forms of material for a sleeping bag. Also that an outer covering of jaconet is advantageous. A plain sleeping bag, open only at one end is better than one slit down the side for however well the side may be laced up, and the finicky business of lacing is, incidentally a labour, the slit is sure to coincide with the middle of the back during the night, and chilliness will result.

Unwilling to be standardised on this matter, I had a sleeping bag made by Mr. R. Burns, of 5 Lever Street, Manchester, to my own design. It was seven feet long, thirty-two inches wide at the head end, tapering to seventeen inches at the feet end, and weighing eight pounds, fourteen ounces. It consisted of two quilted eiderdown bags, one inside the other. The inner one was lined with Jaeger fleece, and the two bags were enclosed in an outer covering of jaconet. Both bags and the outer covering were fitted at the head end with a string-bag arrangement. The length was so ample that I was able to snuggle up right inside it with only my nose and mouth projecting through the drawn up opening.

The advantage of having two bags was a great one. It meant that in the lower tropical forests I could utilise the outer of the two eiderdown bags only, and sleep comfortably without being too hot. Higher up, the second bag could be utilised with its fleece lining, and on the snows both bags together with or without the outer covering. Thus it was easily possible to regulate through a wide range of temperature the degree of warmth required.

It is interesting to note that when only one bag and the jaconet cover are utilised, the latter tends to condense the vapours of the body and wet the eiderdown, but with two bags this does not occur, owing to the air space between the bags. I slept for six weeks using both bags and the cover without the bag becoming damp. I slept well too; in fact, during the whole expedition I do not remember shivering once during the night, and that fact, coupled with the excellent sleep I was able to enjoy, was of no small importance, and was undoubtedly responsible for my keeping fit during the expedition. I can unhesitatingly recommend these bags to other expeditions, and particularly those whose route takes them through a variety of climates.

The expedition bag was about the same weight, and was enclosed in a heavy canvas cover weighing five or six times more than the jaconet cover. It was narrow and slit down the side. The slit was done up with little wooden crosspieces which had to be fitted through string loops, an awkward and irritating business, whilst the bag was so narrow, that more than once I heard my companions groaning as they strove to get into it.

The expedition took with it one large "Debrie" cinecamera with its manifold gadgets, including various telephoto lenses, three "Kinamo" cine-cameras, which take one hundred feet of film and can be loaded in a daylight charger, and no less than 60,000 feet of standard size film. In addition, practically everyone had his own camera, the majority of which were fitted for film packs. Of the latter we took an enormous quantity made by Messrs. Agfa, Ltd., each in an air-tight tin, and I am happy to add that they gave every possible satisfaction, and admirably stood the manifold changes of humidity and temperature they had to undergo between exposure and development. My own pet cameras were two thin pocket "Etui" cameras, one 6 x 9 centimetres, and the other 9 x 12 centimetres. Of the work done by them, I need only say that it was of the finest possible quality, and photographs taken by these little cameras appeared in newspapers all over the world. Both cameras were very light, and either could be slipped into the pocket. They were supplied by Sands, Hunter, Ltd. The disadvantage of cinematographic and photographic work on a large scale is the number of additional porters this entailed. I do not think that less than fifty porters were utilised in carrying our cinematographic and photographic apparatus and materials.

A large quantity of continental and English rope was taken, and regarding this all members of the expedition were agreed that the Alpine Club rope manufactured by Beale's was far the superior both in strength and general handiness.

There is no space here to mention the manifold items of equipment necessary for an expedition of this nature. I think a good deal of what we took might have come under the heading of luxuries rather than necessities, and had our subsequent transport difficulties been realised at the outset, it is safe to say that there would have been a drastic cutting down of individual and general equipment, and this without imperilling the party in any way. The seeker after information regarding Himalayan equipment should refer to the Alpine Club equipment report.

Turning to food, the importance of correct feeding can hardly be overestimated. The mountaineer climbing at high altitudes should look after his stomach with as much care as most American millionaires are forced to look after theirs. Up to the Base Camp, normal eating and foods can be indulged in. Above that the health, and therefore the success of a Himalayan expedition, depends upon eating the right kind of food. Sugar is to the mountaineer climbing over

20,000 feet as petrol is to an internal combustion engine. Thanks to the generosity of many firms the expedition was able to leave Europe with enough food and chocolate to start a grocery store and confectioner's shop. Unfortunately, however, much of this food came under the heading of luxuries, and included such substances as caviare, paté de foie gras, tinned gherkins, Christmas puddings, tinned mushrooms and so forth. If in place of these, sugary foods had been taken, the subsequent ill health and upset stomachs which afflicted the expedition members at various times might have been avoided. As a substitute for bread, which is not to be obtained in most parts of the Himalayas, we took Swedish biscuits. These proved excellent, not only as a food, but also as an aid to the digestion. The effect of high altitude is to make the stomach very acid, and food tends to ferment rather than be absorbed by the normal processes of digestion. Bismuth tablets are a splendid neutraliser of this uncomfortable condition. Owing to low pressure at high altitudes water boils at lower temperatures than at sea level. In order to facilitate boiling we took with us a patent high-pressure boiler. Though there was often some doubt as to whether or not it would blow up it was on the whole a great success.

No physiological subject during recent years has provided a greater controversy than whether oxygen is useful or not at great altitudes. In spite of the fact that Norton and Somervell reached 28,000 feet on Everest without oxygen, there are those who still declare that oxygen is of value despite the weight of the cylinders, and the apparatus to distribute it. Personally, I think a compromise will be reached so that the future climbers of Everest will carry one or two small oxygen cylinders as a reserve to boost their strength up for that last terrible few hundred feet. We compromised, but in a different way, and took with us oxygen cylinders, not for inhalation on the actual climb, but for use in tents, as it was thought that this "English air", as the natives called it, would serve as an excellent "bracer" to the day's work at a high altitude, and might be of use in resuscitating an exhausted man. It was certainly found to be useful in both these departments, but whether the expense of porterage and the apparatus was worth it is doubtful. I think however, that for Everest or Kangchenjunga oxygen should be taken as a medicine, for its effect on an exhausted man is superior to that of alcohol.

Apart from oxygen, Dr. Richter took with him a special physiological apparatus in addition to the usual implements of his profession.

The foregoing is necessarily little more than an allusion to a few among many of the details that must be considered before an expedition can so much as set sail from Europe. It is intended only to give the reader some idea of the manifold things the leader of an expedition has to consider. No one could have worked harder than Professor and Frau Dyhrenfurth, and their work was inspired by the fact that in going to Kangchenjunga they were fulfilling a lifetime's ambition.

As regards the Press, it was arranged that I should act as Special Correspondent and Photographer to *The Times*. Messages were to be sent back by runners from the expedition and thence telegraphed to Europe through the *Statesman* newspaper in Calcutta, the Editor of which, Mr. Alfred Watson, was of great service to the expedition. So at last, on February 24, 1930, the first party consisting of Professor and Frau Dyhrenfurth, Dr. Richter, Duvanel and myself left Europe on the S.S. *Gange* of the Lloyd Triestino Navigation Company.

On our arrival at Bombay, we sent off six and a half tons of goods to Darjeeling. Our first task was to apply to His Highness the Maharajah of Nepal for permission to pass through his country. That that permission was granted was due partly to the kind offices of Mr. Howell, Foreign Secretary, and Colonel Dawkes, the British Envoy at Kathmandu the capital of Nepal. It was considered also that an English-speaking Gurkha N.C.O. would be most useful to us, and thanks to the kindness of Field-Marshal Sir William Birdwood, Bart., we were able to obtain the services of Naik Tikeram Thapa of the 2/8th Gurkha Rifles, who was specially selected by his Commanding Officer, Lieutenant-Colonel C.D. Noe.

These things being accomplished, we toured through India, visiting such show places as Delhi, Agra, and Benares. But the plains were hot and dusty, and we longed, all of us, to sense the keen air from the snows of Kangchenjunga and the High Himalayas.

CHAPTER FOUR

A First Glimpse of the Himalayas

IN ORDER TO MEET Wood Johnson and make some of the preliminary arrangements for the expedition, I left the first party at Agra, and travelled on alone to Siliguri. The "Darjeeling Mail" from Calcutta arrived there soon after dawn. The night in the train had been a stifling one, and intense heat had not improved a slight attack of dysentery contracted at Agra. Yet, it was impossible not to experience a thrill, for Siliguri lies at the foot of the Himalayas, and I craned my head out of the window to try and catch a glimpse of the great mountain range we had come so far to see. But nothing was visible save a few miles of the monotonous heat-soaked Plain of Bengal.

Alighting on the platform, I found my hand clasped by Wood Johnson. He said, 'I knew it was you, because you are obviously a climber.' I replied that at the moment I certainly did not feel like one, as my stomach appeared to be full of gnawing rats. 'Oh! That's nothing,' was the comforting reply, 'everyone gets these little "tummy" troubles out here.'

It was during breakfast that I learned that I was expected to accompany Wood Johnson on the pillion of his motorcycle to his tea plantation at Rangli Rangliot, 5,000 feet up, thirty miles from Siliguri and twenty from Darjeeling. Three years previously I had risen from a muddy ditch by the side of a remote road in Wales whither I had been hurled at a speed of forty-five miles per hour vowing that I would never again ride a motorcycle. Now, this vow must perforce be broken.

I will not mention the make of the motorcycle, as this might be considered derogatory by the makers. We had not proceeded a mile from Siliguri when a portion of the horn fell off. Many bullock carts were on the road, and vigorous blasting on the horn was required to move them. After a search, we retrieved the lost portion, and proceeded on our way.

The road from Siliguri is flat and straight, as straight as a Roman road, and with a fair metalled surface. On either hand is dense jungle; tangled, knotted masses of trees and undergrowth, interspersed with tall, coarse elephant grass. Here are to be found elephant, leopard and tiger. Indeed, Wood Johnson told me that a man eater of the last species had recently caused considerable alarm in the district. The road we were on is a unique highway. It is the connecting link between India and Tibet, the great trade-way along which Tibetans pass to sell their goods in India, and the route followed by three Everest expeditions. After the sullen-eyed Bengalis of Calcutta and the plains, it was a relief to see alert little men from Tibet and Nepal, with their wide, cheery grins.

As we chugged and exploded through the silent forest, dim, unsubstantial shapes far overhead began to loom through the haze, the Himalayas. In no other mountain range that I have seen is the transition from plain to mountain so abrupt. One minute we were on the Plain of Bengal, as flat as a golfing green, the next the wooded jaws of the great Teesta Valley had enclosed us.

The Teesta Valley is one of the most superb valleys in the world. Though no snow peaks are visible from its lower portion, the traveller realises that he has entered the Himalayas. Above him the valley sides rise for thousands of feet at such a steep angle, it seems almost impossible that the dense tropical vegetation can cling to them. Below, in a rocky bed of giant boulders carried down by the turbulence of the monsoon rains, thunder the melted snow waters of Kangchenjunga, and the glaciers of Northern Sikkim.

Where it debouches on to the Plain of Bengal, the valley floor is but a few feet above sea level. Luxuriously beautiful though the forests are at this low altitude, they serve but to breed one of the most malignant malarial mosquitoes known to exist. It is said of Teesta Valley malaria that once it is fairly in the blood, the victim will never entirely rid himself of it. That this is a truism is shown by the poor physique of the Sikkim Lepchas, who inhabit the valley. This race of gentle mild-eyed people is being gradually, but ruthlessly exterminated by disease and malaria. Their plight is not helped by a strict conservatism regarding marriage, which decrees that they shall not marry Tibetans, their hereditary enemies. Thus the evils of inter-marriage are added to those of disease, evils that increase as the population decreases. It is only fresh and healthy blood that can save the Lepchas from extinction.

Soon after entering the valley, the road began to climb in a series of hairpin bends. These Wood Johnson negotiated at a high speed, while relating to me how the previous year he had run off the road, fallen a considerable distance with the motorcycle on top of him, and had to spend three months in hospital. Fortunately, it was on a straight section that the tyre elected to go suddenly flat. The valve was at fault, although had the tyre been punctured, it would have made little difference, as Wood Johnson possessed no repair outfit.

We were five miles from the nearest village where help could be obtained. First of all, we attempted to continue as before, but even at a slow speed the motorcycle slewed unpleasantly about the road, and after I had received a bruise on the shin, I suggested to Wood Johnson that he should go on alone, repair the valve, and return. With no weight on the pillion this was possible, and a few minutes later he was out of sight.

To one who had but recently escaped from the cold, damp vapours of a London February, the heat seemed terrific. From all sides came a shrill symposium of innumerable insects, and the harsh clatter of frogs. It was my first experience of a tropical forest, and as I wished to see more of the Teesta Valley, I decided to continue walking along the road.

For the most part the hillside rises steeply and directly from the road, but at one part there was a comparatively level intervening stretch of forest. It was while passing this that I was suddenly startled by an unpleasantly malevolent snarl. Looking to the left I could clearly distinguish between the matted undergrowth the form of a large tiger, not more than five yards away. Apart from Zoos and circuses, it was the first time that I had ever seen a tiger, and I must confess that Wood Johnson's story of the man-eater recurred unpleasantly in my mind. My only weapon, a pocket-knife, seemed a poor defence. It was a situation requiring tact. If I ran, the tiger might regard this as an indication of timidity, and follow me. If I stood still, he might assume me to be an attacker, and himself attack. The best compromise was to continue quietly walking down the road. Once I heard a rustle as though the brute was following me through the jungle, but after two hundred yards the flat jungle gave place to a buttress of crags abutting against the road. I could breathe more freely, for the tiger was scarcely likely to follow me along the open road. It was, of course, much to be regretted that I had not a rifle, for to have shot one's first tiger in such circumstances would have been unusual. The fact that farther along the road several Lepchas passed me showed that in this district, at least, nothing is to be feared from tigers.

A mile or so farther on was a native hamlet, consisting of thatched, wooden houses resting on log piles. Here the road divided, one branch climbing the hill towards Darjeeling, the other continuing along the valley, after crossing a tributary of the main Teesta River by a well-made suspension bridge. By the bridge, I sat down to wait for Wood Johnson. At length, he arrived, and we continued, once more on our journey.

I told him of my encounter with the tiger, and gathered that I should consider myself lucky seeing one so soon after arriving in India. Other men had been out for years, and had not seen a tiger. He, Wood Johnson, would have given a month's pay to have seen that tiger at the business end of a rifle. The tiger had already killed deer, and other animals. There was, of course, no question of it attacking human beings unless itself attacked. All this I gathered as I bumped painfully up and down on the pillion of Wood Johnson's motorcycle.

Presently, we left the road in favour of a narrow lane that winds up the hillside to Rangli Rangliot, 4,500 feet above the Teesta Valley. In England, this lane would be much in demand by motorcycling clubs as a test hill. People would line its one in three gradient and hairpin bends to cheer the intrepidity of the riders, but in this part of the world it is only one among many other hills of a similar character habitually traversed by the Austin Seven cars and motorcycles of the tea planters. Wood Johnson said his record was twenty minutes for this particular ascent, but that out of consideration for my stomach he would not try to break it. Anyway, Fate willed otherwise. We had climbed but two or three hundred feet above the main road when the engine, after a few splutters and a sharp cough, stopped dead.

This time it was a twist-grip throttle control that had broken. A caravan of laden ponies under the charge of some natives was coming up the path. They wished to pass us, but this Wood Johnson would not allow. He said they would interfere with our future progress. First of all, we endeavoured by an ingenious arrangement of string to manipulate the throttle from the handlebars, then Wood Johnson in the saddle, and myself and two natives shoving, the motorcycle was pushed up the hill. After several attempts the engine suddenly elected to start with a gallant roar. I sprang on behind, Wood Johnson let in the clutch, and once more we shot up the hill. But we had not gone more than a few yards when the engine again spluttered and coughed to a standstill. The same laborious process was then repeated, after which we sat down exhausted amid a circle of interested natives.

The noonday heat was appalling. Divesting ourselves of the majority of our clothes, and giving them to one of the natives with instructions to bring them up, we once more attacked the problem of our recalcitrant mount. First of all I thought of something ingenious and then Wood Johnson thought of something even more ingenious. The result was always the same, a vulgar splutter and a sarcastic cough. An hour or two later we hurled the contraption to the side of the road, and sat down to consider the situation. We were very hot, Wood Johnson's hand was bleeding from contact with one of the sharp edges common to all motorcycles, my stomach had not been improved. The motorcycle tilted over by the side of the road at an inelegant angle, with its horn tied together by string and lurching drunkenly over one handlebar, seemed to leer at us. There was nothing for it but to walk uphill. Luck was with us. We had not got halfway when we met some unladen ponies coming in the opposite direction, two of which we at once commandeered.

It was now possible for the first time since leaving Siliguri to appreciate the surroundings. As we climbed, the tropical heat of the Teesta Valley was gradually superseded by a temperature comparable to that of a warm English summer day. The jungle thinned, and abruptly we emerged from it on to open slopes covered in tea. A fresh evening breeze greeted us, seeming to whisper of high places and the snows. Thousands of feet below now was the Teesta Valley with its argent river thread. Northwards, rolling hills stretched like grass-grown slag-heaps towards the factories of the snows. These grass and forest-clad hills are but the foothills of the Himalayan wall, yet they are as great in scale as the main range of the Alps. In the Alps one may gaze down into a valley and see trim, neatly laid out little villages and fields, roads, railways, and electric power lines, but these give to the mountains an artificial taint, and even on the summit of Mont Blanc or the Matterhorn the mountaineer cannot escape entirely from civilisation. But amid these lower foothills of the Himalayas there are few signs of commercialism. True, man has hacked a way here, and scraped a clearing there, but generally speaking the country is the same as it always has been. Up there, in the evening stillness of the tea-gardens I experienced for the first time in my life that subtle feeling of joy and sorrow intermixed which comes to all who are born with the love for mountains, joy for the vision and hope of the unknown and sorrow in realising how many adventures there are to seek, and how pitifully short is the life in which to seek them.

Gielle Tea Estate, where Wood Johnson works, is one of the most beautifully situated among the Darjeeling district tea gardens, and commands a view up the Teesta Valley towards the snows. A pleasant evening was spent there as the guest of Mr. McKean, Wood Johnson's manager, who had kindly given permission for the latter to accompany the expedition, although it meant single-handed work on the plantation for the next three months.

McKean had lived twenty years at Gielle, and it was largely due to his expert tuition in the handling of native labour that made Wood Johnson so invaluable to the expedition.

He presented me with a kukri as a memento of the occasion. The cutting powers of this heavy, curved knife in the hands of an expert Gurkha is amazing. It is said that with one blow a bullock's head can be severed from its body, whilst during the war it was a favourite amusement among men of Gurkha regiments to crawl across "No Man's Land" at night, lie "doggo" on the parapet of the enemy trench, and lop off the head of the unfortunate sentry or anyone else who happened to pass. But apart from its unique cutting powers, the kukri is useful in many other ways, and during the expedition I saw it employed in cutting up firewood opening packing-cases, sharpening pencils, hewing down vegetation and other varied, if menial tasks.

That evening a number of tea garden coolies came in with baskets of freshly plucked tea. Most of them were women; sturdy little Nepalis with gay coloured head-dresses, necklaces and earrings. In spite of a heavy day's work, for which they are paid but a few annas, they have always a smile at the end of it and they stood outside the factory laughing and chattering like school children starting out for a treat. The gaiety of these hill people is indeed infectious and one cannot but compare these lively little women of the hills to the morose Hindu women of the plains.

It was late when Wood Johnson and I left McKean's hospitable roof. Innumerable fireflies flitted round us as we passed through the silent plantation. Somewhere in the direction of the Himalayas lightning flickered restlessly. The profound quietude of the hills was broken only by the distant throbbing of a native band.

CHAPTER FIVE

Superstitions and Storms

GREAT MOUNTAIN peaks usually excite superstitious awe in the minds of the simple peasantry who dwell in the valleys beneath them. Their height, their isolation from the everyday affairs of life and their grandeur impress men with a sense of their insignificance, persuading them against all judgement and reason that there are forces abroad beyond human ken.

During the Middle Ages the Alps were popularly reputed to be the abode of monstrous dragons; the uneasy ghost of Pontius Pilate was believed to haunt the slopes of Mount Pilatus above Lucerne, and as late as the latter half of the last century, Edward Whymper wrote of the Matterhorn: 'There seemed to be a cordon drawn around it, up to which one might go, but no farther. Within that invisible line gins and effreets were supposed to exist – the Wandering Jew and the spirits of the damned. The superstitious natives in the surrounding valleys (many of whom firmly believed it to be not only the highest mountain in the Alps, but in the world) spoke of a ruined city on its summit wherein spirits dwelt; and if you laughed, they gravely shook their heads; told you to look yourself to see the castles and the walls, and warned one against a rash approach, lest the infuriate demons from their impregnable heights might hurl down vengeance for one's derision.'

With the advance of civilisation, however, most Alpine superstitions became legendary. Sturdy guides haul tourists to the summit of the Matterhorn, the ghost of Pontius Pilate is enjoying a well-earned repose, and the dragons have fled before the hosts of Mr. Thomas Cook and the Polytechnic Institute.

Yet even in such an accessible mountain range as the Alps superstitions die hard, and the traveller who forsakes the tourist highways will still find ancient beliefs that have been handed down through countless generations. How much more, therefore, must superstitions be rife among the stupendous ranges of the Himalayas? The fact that their greatest peaks have defied the best efforts of skilled mountaineers, and that, of the sixty odd peaks over 25,000 feet, not one has been scaled, is in itself a justification of the belief that a cordon is drawn round the summits beyond which man may not enter, where dwell the gods in icy detachment from the world.

The most rationally-minded of men cannot gaze from Darjeeling upon Kangchenjunga without experiencing something of the same emotions of the simpler-minded Sherpas and Lepchas who dwell in the valleys below. He will find himself wondering half in shame whether there is anything in the tales told him of the powerful god whose sacred throne rests upon its summits, the "Five Treasures of the Snow", and whether the snow-fields and glaciers suspended in mid-air above a misty ocean are indeed the abiding places of the Mi-go, the Abominable Snow Men. He will gaze on Siniolchuo and reflect that if there is a God of Inaccessibility, his unapproachable halls and palaces must be fashioned beneath the icy flutings and sweeping scimitar-like ridges of that amazing peak.

It is easy to understand the superstitions of those who live round Kangchenjunga. Their fears and fancies are merely an outward expression of a primitive instinct that recognises in Kangchenjunga something beyond human understanding; a world apart, akin both to Heaven and to Hell; something to be revered, feared and worshipped.

At first sight it seems strange that men should flock so willingly to the banners of expeditions such as have attempted Everest and Kangchenjunga. The reason is not far to seek; there is prestige and honour to be gained in daring the inaccessible and braving the wrath of the gods. The Sherpas may be the prey to superstitious fears, but they are strong-minded enough to be able to conquer them.

Mountain superstitions are much the same the world over; it is, therefore, curious to find such a unique superstition as the Abominable Snow Men so firmly implanted in the native mind. Our porters, even the most educated among them, swore that they had seen them, and described them as being white-skinned and naked, but covered with thick hair. Whence did this belief originate? Was there once a wild tribe that roamed the Himalayas – a tribe, perhaps, of white nomads from Southern Siberia, half ape and half man, to give to this superstition a foundation of fact? During the last Everest expedition wild rumours were afloat that the expedition actually encountered these beings. Actually, however, no European has set eyes on a snowman. The nearest approach to fact was the experience of Mr. E.O. Shebbeare, who accompanied the 1929 Bavarian expedition to Kangchenjunga. He relates that when ascending to the Base Camp his porters begged him to come with them to see the footprints of a Snow Man in the snow. When, however, he arrived at the spot a fresh fall of snow had covered the ground.

Thunderstorms are common among the Himalayas. Most fine mornings see the cloudy galleons sweeping up from the steamy Plain of Bengal. Slowly they sail over the green foothills or float in lazy stateliness on the blue hazes of the deep valleys, their keels in shadow, their sails of massive cumuli bellying thousands of feet aloft in the sunlight. As they advance, they are augmented by the warm, moist air currents from the valleys. Magically they grow larger; their girth and height increases every moment; they are sifted by the upward breezes, broken and distorted into all manner of queer forms by vagrant winds; momentarily dissipated by unexpected blasts. They become a mighty fleet and pass in splendid line ahead towards the huge wall of the Himalayas, where they assault in misty surges the snowy bastions of Kangchenjunga.

Towards midday the first thunder echoes in deep growls along the valleys. A smooth slaty pall of nimbus, underhung with billows of cumuli, slides up the zenith. The thunder becomes louder; its solemn booms are resolved into an angrier crackle. Spiteful lightning spears the whale-backed crests of the foothills and leaps among the clouds. A veil of rain is borne along by the thundercloud trailing hill and valley, blotting out the sunny hillsides, sweeping over the ridges.

Local thunderstorms occur almost every day among the foothills of the Himalayas; they seldom attack the great peaks, and usually expend their wrath before the evening, their apparently indissoluble clouds melting into the night. But, occasionally, there are storms which are neither local nor confined to the foothills. I saw such a storm at Darjeeling.

The afternoon had been thunderous, and storm after storm had stalked over the hills, their hailstones bringing dismay to the tea planters whose leaves were ready for plucking. The sunset was wild as I climbed Observatory Hill. Long, tendrous clouds, bridging a gap between the dense curtains of cumuli, had been twisted by the wind until they appeared like bloodstained claws groping in the sky. The sky between was that ominous cat's eye green, a colour that mountaineers and seamen instinctively distrust. One doresque shaft of ruddy light striking through the turmoil of mists fell upon the Singalila ridge. Day was dying as I gained the summit of Observatory Hill, and sullen draperies had been drawn across the sunset. In the south lightning flicked a restless whip over Tiger Hill; in the east, towers of cloud were occasionally revealed by fountains of lightning. Once again came thunder, long heavy vibrations shaking the earth; lightning blue and vivid slashed the peaks of the Singalila ridge and Nepal.

On the summit of Observatory Hill there is a Tibetan temple, not a building, but a forest of prayer flags ringing a small space in which is set a primitive altar. Here, as though to propitiate the gods, and perhaps, in particular the great God of Kangchenjunga, the lamas began to pray, a low mutter breaking forth into a wail of religious fervour, accompanied by the monotonous ringing of a hand bell. I felt that indefinable sensation that every visitor to the East feels sooner or later – that time and space are limitless, that man is but the puppet of fate, a mere plaything of elemental forces beyond his comprehension or control.

Tibetan music is the epitome of that strange mountain land of the Himalayas. Its weird dirge-like monotone, its occasional passionate crescendo, suggests infinity, the presence of great mountains and limitless spaces, the fears and hardships of those foredoomed to dwell on bitter windswept plateaux and gaze for ever on the barren slopes and inhospitable solitudes of Central Asia.

The praying ceased; between two rolls of thunder no sound disturbed the hilltop save the sigh of an awakened wind among the prayer flags and the distant clamour of Darjeeling.

The storm came up apace with glares of bluish lightning and staccato thunder that flung in waves of sound across the valleys or rolled and grumbled like immense engines on the ridges. Rain and hail swept the hill; the lightning leapt in furious confused brilliance. Thunder, crashing and majestic came hard on its heels. In a few minutes the storm was gone, its turbulence swallowed in the night. A small star gleamed tentatively, was extinguished by a cloud scud, and gleamed again more confidently. The subsiding groan of the wind among the prayer flags broke a heavy silence.

Other and more distant storms took up the tale. In the direction of Everest sudden floods of white light soundlessly illuminated the cloudy pavements of the sky, picking out in faultless detail the towers, minarets and cupolas of a cathedral of mist towering above the world. As though jealous of his supreme neighbour, the God of Kangchenjunga struck out with fierce blue swords and vicious darts of forked lightning. Somewhere over Bhutan and Tibet another cloud winked with bibulous persistence like some lesser mountain god delighting in this fiery combat of Himalayan giants.

No thunder was to be heard. From the depths of the Rangit Valley beneath, mist wraiths swayed upwards like jinns from the confines of a monstrous bottle. The moon was rising as I turned to go; her calm radiance seemed to quell the stormy disputes between earth and sky. Beneath her contemptuous gaze the distant lightning became desultory and wan. The clouds were withdrawn from Kangchenjunga. Far up in the awakened stars something white gleamed steadfastly – the summit.

CHAPTER SIX

Approach: Through Nepal or Sikkim?

BY THE END OF March all members of the expedition were assembled in Darjeeling. While in Delhi we had written letters to the Maharajah of Nepal, and to Colonel Dawkes, C.I.E., British Envoy at Kathmandu, requesting permission to attack Kangchenjunga from the Nepalese side. Owing, however, to political friction existing then between Nepal and Tibet, it seemed advisable not to worry the Nepalese authorities until matters had quieted down. The letter was left, therefore, with Mr. Howell, the Foreign Secretary, who had kindly undertaken to forward it at an appropriate date. The previous year, the Munich expedition had also applied for permission to enter Nepal, but though this permission had been eventually given, it had arrived far too late for them to avail themselves of it. Bearing these things in mind, we had no option but to plan an attempt on Kangchenjunga via Sikkim, and the eastern face of the mountain.

Apart from Colonel Tobin, who as previously mentioned, was appointed Transport Officer, Mr. J.S. Hannah, of the Bengal and Nagpur Railway, was invited to join the expedition. Hannah had had considerable experience of Indian travel, and had also climbed in the Alps. Most important of all he spoke Hindustani, and this, combined with the efficient way in which he handled transport and porters, was to make him an invaluable member of the expedition.

By whichever route we went, we hoped to leave Darjeeling early in April. The time during which an attempt can be made either before or after the monsoon is so short, that it was essential to be at the foot of the mountain, if possible, by the middle of April. This would allow some six weeks. But as General Bruce pointed out, the monsoon *might* come by the middle of May, and that this was possible was borne out by the experience of the tea planters and others living in the Darjeeling district. Assuming that the difficulties would be comparable to those encountered by the Munich expedition, four weeks was definitely too short a time in which to make the attempt. On the other hand, so far as could be seen from Darjeeling the Kang La, the 16,373 feet pass we must traverse into Nepal was still so deeply snow-covered at the beginning of April that to have started earlier would have been impossible.

Attempting any great Himalayan peak must always mean a gamble with the weather. Had we decided in the beginning to tackle the eastern face of the mountain by the same route as the Munich expedition, we could have established our Base Camp early in April, and commenced to have attacked the mountain without delay. But Professor Dyhrenfurth had other objects in view besides attempting Kangchenjunga. North-east Nepal was practically unknown. No European had passed along the valleys to the west and south-west of Kangchenjunga since 1899, when Mr. Douglas Freshfield passed round Kangchenjunga. The upper branches of the Kangchenjunga Glacier were still unexplored. No one had seen the head of the Ramthang Glacier which falls from the western face of Kangchenjunga. There were valleys unknown, and peaks untrodden, and the district might confidently be expected to provide topographical and geological data of considerable interest.

Directly on arrival at Bombay we had dispatched the expedition's goods, weighing some 61 tons, in a special truck by passenger train to Darjeeling. Though this cost £135, and should have taken no longer than four or five days in transit, over two weeks had elapsed, and still there was no sign of the truck. Imploring telegrams were sent to high officials, eliciting non-committal replies. The truck had been seen here, and seen there, but not one of the railways could tell us exactly where it was at the moment. Finally, as we were in despair, the goods arrived, but the expedition had been delayed two or three days, and every day was of vital importance.

A store-room was hired, and the 180 crates containing food and equipment unpacked under the supervision of Frau Dyhrenfurth. She was in her element, as clad in a neat apron, and armed with a pencil and notebook, she superintended operations, amid stacks of various foodstuffs, tins, rucksacks, boots, films, patent hot-water bottles, dangerous looking magnesium flares, and a multitude of other things all heaped up amid a labyrinth of packing-cases and crates. There was one tragedy, a German firm had presented the expedition with a large quantity of honey. This had been packed in cardboard containers. Travel and heat had done their worst, and it had arrived a glutinous mass. It was not, however, entirely wasted, for it was much appreciated by the porters and countless children who gathered around the crate and licked the honey as it oozed through the cracks.

General Bruce had been emphatic on one thing in particular. 'Don't forget to worm your porters,' he had whispered into my ear at Victoria Station. Worms are a curse in India, and the strongest Himalayan porter may become anaemic and weak from them. Actually, Dr. Richter discovered but few porters who were suffering from this particular ailment. Possibly the Medical Officers of previous Everest expeditions taught them how to cure themselves with santonin and castor oil. More prevalent among the porters was a species of scurvy, due most likely to under-nourishment that showed itself in the form of skin breakings, and boils. A number of porters were so badly affected by this that we considered it impossible to take them.

Owing to recent cases of smallpox locally, it was deemed advisable to vaccinate all porters. We anticipated some trouble here, and Frau Dyhrenfurth heroically offered herself as the first victim and example. But her public-spirited offer was unnecessary. The porters took to vaccination with alacrity, and they roared with laughter at the lengthening of the faces of those being vaccinated as their arms were scratched.

Not warning Darjeeling of our coming had been a serious error, and meant much additional work for Colonel Tobin in enlisting every available porter. It was an exceedingly busy time for most members of the expedition and especially so for Colonel Tobin, who laboured with all his might to get the manifold preparations completed in time. About 400 porters were necessary if we were to attack

Kangchenjunga from Nepal, and 400 good porters are not obtainable normally in Darjeeling. As had been proved previously on Everest and Kangchenjunga, the best types of Himalayan porters are Sherpas, Bhutias, and Tibetans. There is little to choose between these hardy races for carrying powers and endurance, but the Sherpa is the best mountaineer. Like the Bhutia, they dwell in the remote valleys of Northern Nepal, and have both Nepalese and Tibetan blood in them. They are used to withstanding cold and hardships on some of the most inhospitable portions of the world's surface, and are natural mountaineers. The men who did so well on Everest and Kangchenjunga were known as "Tigers", for their work in carrying loads at immense altitudes was tigerish in its strength and courage.

It may appear extraordinary that these men should so readily leave their homes and rickshaws in Darjeeling, where many of them make a comfortable living during the tourist season. Perhaps it is because of a born instinct for adventure, perhaps because of the prestige that is to be gained by being chosen to accompany an expedition to the greatest peaks of the world, and perhaps because they love the mountains with a primitive unreasoning devotion which finds expression in the belief that they are the abiding places of the gods. Whatever it is, and it would be interesting to get behind their minds in the matter, it is not entirely the prospect of monetary reward that impels these men to risk life and limb on Everest and Kangchenjunga.

There are many good men in Darjeeling, "rickshaw wallahs", most of them, but there are also many good men living in far-away hill villages, who, had they known, would have been only too willing to come too. As it was, during the fortnight we were at Darjeeling, a number of men came in from the hills anxious to join the expedition, including two from Nepal, who said that they had traversed the Kang La. So long as these men remain unspoilt in a world where commercial gain is becoming the only thing that matters, future expeditions, with mountaineering as their aim, will have no difficulty in finding the right men to help them on their enterprise.

Thus it was, that though the expedition was able to enlist a nucleus of keen, reliable men, it was forced also to enlist others who had no interest in its objects, "bazar wallahs" who were merely out to serve their own ends, and who had no intention of working or serving the expedition faithfully.

Four sirdars were engaged, Naspati, Gyaljen, Narsang and Lobsang. Of these, Lobsang was incomparably the best. Though only an ordinary "rickshaw wallah" of humble origin, and affecting none of the European clothes and manners of the other sirdars, and of little experience, having only recently been promoted from coolie to sirdar, he was a born commander of men. A Bhutia by birth, he was yet liked and respected by the Sherpas and Tibetans. His pock-marked, rugged countenance was the hardest I have ever seen in a native, and indicated a masterful personality. Perhaps it was this very personality that was responsible for adverse criticisms from some quarters, for Lobsang was of that rare native type which prefers being left to itself, to act largely on its own initiative. He was a genuine "tough" in the best sense of that word, and as Wood Johnson remarked, his work was equal to that of a sahib. Unfortunately, he was now too old to climb to the highest camps, but as commander of the general coolie organisation at the base, in the lower camps and on the march he would be invaluable.

Of the other sirdars, Naspati and Gyaljen were excellent men, especially in keeping payrolls, management of stores, and "office jobs", but for sheer drive and personality they were not to be compared to Lobsang.

Minor worries are to be avoided at all costs on a Himalayan expedition, and a good personal servant can do much to alleviate the trials and discomforts of life. General Bruce had given me a letter to his own personal servant, Lhakpa Chede, who accompanied him on the Everest Expedition. In this letter General Bruce flatteringly if inaccurately referred to me as his grandson. It is needless here to enlarge upon the admiration, affection and respect with which the leader of two Everest expeditions is regarded in Darjeeling. On many occasions natives stopped me in the streets of Darjeeling to ask whether the General Burra-sahib was leading the expedition. This charming fiction was of inestimable advantage to me personally, and I was soon known among our porters as the Nati-sahib (Grandson).

Lhakpa Chede had taken a post as a waiter, and was unable to come. Mr. Kydd, of St. Paul's School, suggested his own "rickshaw wallah", Nemu. It was a happy suggestion. Nemu had been Sandy Irvine's servant on Everest, and had ascended as high as Camp Five, a height of 25,000 feet. But that was six years ago, and Nemu was now thirty-six. For Europeans this should be the prime of life, but it must be remembered that these men are frequently old at thirty, whilst the majority of them die in the neighbourhood of fifty. Was Nemu therefore too old, was his strength, and power of resistance to cold, still equal to the task, did he really want to leave a comfortable and easy job in favour of the hardships and rigours of high mountaineering? Nemu's keenness to come was in itself an answer to these questions.

I took an instant liking to the man. Clad as he was in a ragged and patched old coat, a dirty pair of aged corduroy breeches, frayed puttees, probably relics of the last Everest expedition, and a pair of apparently cast off boots, he looked at first glance a thorough old vagabond, but his face was broad and good-humoured, and his eyes were those of a hillman, possessing that subtle, far-away look of those accustomed to gaze great distances. Hazel brown, and set far apart, they were eyes indicative of honesty and trustworthiness. So I engaged Nemu, and had no cause ever to regret it.

There were many other seasoned veterans of Everest and Kangchenjunga who were anxious to come. "Satan" Chettan was secured by Schneider as his servant. Of all Himalayan porters he was the most experienced in mountaineering, for he had accompanied all three Everest expeditions, climbed with Dr. T.G. Longstaff and Mr. H. Ruttledge in Garhwal, and as the servant of Dr. Paul Bauer, the leader of the Bavarian expedition, performed miracles of endurance on Kangchenjunga the previous year. There was also Lewa, who put up a magnificent performance on the Bavarian expedition. Perhaps most important of all were the cooks, for on their efficiency much depended. The Bavarians had sung the praises of Tencheddar, so we engaged him. He spoke a little English, and among his favourite expressions which we soon learnt by heart was 'sometime coming'. To him everything was always "sometime coming" – even death itself. There is a whole philosophy in "sometime coming".

Many of these porters produced tattered and dirty letters of recommendation from General Bruce and other members of the Everest expeditions, testifying to their courage and loyalty. One of the first questions was often whether the General Burra-sahib was coming. Happy indeed the man who can win the respect and affection of such men.

As nothing had been heard from Nepal, it was necessary to plan a provisional scheme to attempt Kangchenjunga via Sikkim and the Zemu Glacier. It was arranged that Wood Johnson and myself should leave Darjeeling about April 1, and proceed via Gangtok, the capital town of Sikkim and Lachen; and blaze a trail up to the Zemu Glacier. It is possible to take ponies as far as Lachen, but above that, dense jungle would probably necessitate arduous trail making. It would also be the task of this advance party to find three camping sites between Lachen and the Base Camp, which we proposed to establish on Green Lake Plain on the north bank of the Zemu Glacier. With the way thus prepared, the main body of 150 porters and about 60 pack ponies would start from Darjeeling under the charge of Hannah, where they would be joined at Gangtok by the climbing party, who would travel in motorcars from Darjeeling.

From Gangtok the main body would proceed on foot or ponies to Lachen, where a provision dump under the supervision of Colonel Tobin would be made. The three temporary camps between Lachen and the Base Camp would be a day's march between, and would be used as stages in the relaying of loads from Lachen to the Base Camp. By this means we estimated to reach the Base Camp with 67 porters. Of these 25 would be sent back, leaving 42 porters to do the work of establishing the Base Camp, and the first two high camps on Kangchenjunga. By this method it would be the work of only eight or ten days to bring all the expedition's food and equipment from Lachen to the Base Camp.

Professor Dyhrenfurth was naturally loth to attack Kangchenjunga by the same route as that of the Bavarians the previous year so long as there was a possibility of climbing the mountain by any other route, but it was obvious that the ice ridge leading to the North Ridge was the only line that offered any possibility on the Sikkim side of the mountain.

It was at this stage, when all preparations had been completed, that the following charming letter was received from the Maharajah of Nepal

Kathmandu,
Nepal.
29th March, 1930.

To Professor Dr. G.O. Dyhrenfurth,
Darjeeling.

Dear Sir, – I beg to acknowledge the receipt of your letter of the 16th March. 1930, giving information of the formation of an International Expedition to attempt an ascent of and make scientific observations on Kangchenjunga, and requesting permission for the expedition to enter Nepalese territory and approach the said mountain via Kang La, Chumbab La, Tseram, Mirgin La, Khunza and Kangbachen, using the same route on return with the possibility of one party going over to Sikkim by way of Jonsong La.

His Highness appreciates your remarks about the international character of the expedition which has for its object the cementation of international friendship and goodwill among the countries concerned, coupled with the augmentation of human aesthetical and scientific knowledge, and desires me to inform you that he gladly accedes to your request. The Nepalese local authorities concerned are being ordered to permit the party the use of the routes mentioned in Nepalese territory.

His Highness hopes that the expedition will be a great success in every way, and sends to you as the worthy leader of the expeditionary party the best wishes for that.

I remain,

Your obedient servant,

(Signed) MARICHI MAN SINGH,

Bada Kaji,

Private Secretary to his Highness the Maharajah, Nepal.

Although a complete change of plans was necessary, no time was lost in rearranging matters. Had, however, we realised the difficulties confronting us, I do not think we should so willingly have abandoned the original scheme. The route to the Zemu Glacier is a relatively easy one compared to that to the Kangchenjunga Glacier and good paths along low valleys lead four-fifths of the way from Darjeeling. The road to the Kangchenjunga Glacier via the Kang La and Mirgin La passes is much more difficult. Most important point of all – the winter was a late one, and snow lay low on the Kang La.

Mules could be employed only as far as Yoksam, five marches from Darjeeling. Thenceforward, we must rely entirely on porters, and as previously stated, 400 of these were necessary. We estimated that it would take us three weeks to reach the foot of the mountain, and once the base camp was established, communications had to be maintained, and fresh supplies for the porters obtained. Obviously, we must rely to a large extent on local help in Nepal. A telegram was sent to the Maharajah asking whether we could buy porters' food at Tseram or Khunza, two Nepalese villages we must pass through. We received a very courteous answer, informing us that everything possible would be done to help us, and that we could employ local porters and obtain local supplies. Thus was solved the greatest difficulty of all, for without local help, this route would have been absolutely impossible.

In order to avoid overcrowding at the camping sites, Colonel Tobin considered it necessary to split the expedition up into three parties. Wood Johnson and Hannah were to be transport officers of the first and second parties respectively, whilst Colonel Tobin was to bring up the rear with eighty mule loads of provisions and equipment, which he would transport to Yoksam, where he would be met by 150 porters sent back from the first and second parties to carry his loads over the Kang La.[1] This arrangement was made assuming that local help in the shape of porters and food was to be obtained by the first and second parties on the Nepalese side of the Kang La.

It was an excellent scheme, but it was perhaps not sufficiently elastic in its allowance for failures. How were we to be certain that porters and supplies would be immediately forthcoming in Nepal. The Maharajah's commands would take some time to infiltrate from Kathmandu into a remote corner of North-east Nepal. Little time would be available for the Subadar appointed by him to look after our needs, and to collect porters' food and porters from the sparsely populated valleys. The weather was another important factor. Anything might

[1] This arrangement was known only to Professor Dyhrenfurth and Colonel Tobin and the fact that neither the transport officers, Wood Johnson and Hannah, of the first and second parties respectively, knew anything about it was largely responsible for subsequent transport difficulties.

happen on a pass as high as the Kang La. Even now, the beginning of April, almost daily storms were depositing snow at levels far below the summit of the pass, and boots were available for but a few of our porters, principally the "Tigers" intended for the work of establishing the high camps on Kangchenjunga. Was it wise to split up the party into three separate groups over such a difficult route? The discomforts of overcrowding in camping sites would have been well worth cohesion and unity. If I have dealt at length with this problem of transport, it is because it is a very real problem, and one on the solving of which the success of any Himalayan expedition depends.

The three Everest expeditions had a far easier task, for in spite of the length of their route from Darjeeling to Everest, they were able to take ponies and mules the whole distance. This meant employment of less than 100 porters, and these were all picked men. We had 400 porters, some very good, others very bad. In addition to attempting Kangchenjunga from the Kangchenjunga Glacier, it was proposed first of all to explore the southern face of the mountain above the Yalung Glacier, the face attempted by the ill-fated Crowley party, but like Mark Twain, our exploration got no farther than an examination through the powerful telescope at the Planters' Club at Darjeeling.

To appreciate the beauty and dignity of Kangchenjunga, the apparently smooth, sickle-like sweep of its ridges, the pale red of its granite precipices gleaming like a sun-caressed Devonian sea cliff through a blue Atlantic haze, it should be viewed with the naked eye. Seeing it thus it is impossible to grasp the scale of the mountain and the mountaineer's analytical mind is peacefully submerged in a quiet ocean of meditation. But seen through a telescope Kangchenjunga ceases to be an object of restful meditation. It is revealed in all its cruelty. The pale red precipices are resolved into fearful slices of unrelenting granite; the apparently smooth ridges resemble the blade of a knife seen through a microscope; broken and jagged, torn and hewn by wind and weather into edges, gaps and towers of fantastic and terrible beauty; what appear as straggling thin white threads are terrific ice-armoured couloirs, down which crash stones, and ice avalanches from disintegrating cliffs of rock and ice. Even looking through a telescope it was impossible not to gain some idea of Nature's forces that are ever at work slowly destroying the greatest peaks of the world.

But a minute's examination was needed to assure us that it was futile to seek a way from the Yalung Glacier. Though only the upper part of the route was visible, the long sloping icy shelf the mountaineer would have to ascend is exposed to avalanches of snow, ice and stones, while the ice-fall up which the party would have to go to reach the shelf, looked unassailable. The telescope effectively dispelled any schemes we had of attempting this side of the mountain.*

At last the preparations were completed. On the night of April 5, the last load was packed and weighed by Frau Dyhrenfurth, assisted by many willing helpers. We had planned to reach the dak-bungalow at Chakung in one day by motoring to Singla Bazar, and from there riding to Chakung 4,000 feet higher. This was, however, a long march for the porters, so it was decided to send them off a day beforehand.

* The subsequent first ascent route of 1955.

It is interesting to remember that there are days during every month when it is considered by the natives extremely unlucky to start on a journey. However, should a native find it absolutely essential to leave on one of these unlucky days, it is usual for him to send on his hat on a lucky day beforehand by a servant or friend. In this way the gods are deluded into thinking that he has actually started on a lucky day, and he may escape the consequences of his rash act.

It was important to have someone in Darjeeling who would look after our mails, and arrange for the sending of dispatches to Mr. Alfred Watson, Editor of the *Statesman*, of Calcutta, whence they would be forwarded to *The Times* in London. We were extremely fortunate in obtaining the services of Mr. W.J. Kydd, of St. Paul's School, Darjeeling. Mr. Kydd had been in the Secret Service during the War, and we felt we could not leave the work in more competent hands.

It was arranged that Herr Eberl, the German Vice-Consul at Calcutta, should accompany the expedition part of the way. Before leaving Calcutta he was able to arrange to have weather reports broadcasted for us by the courtesy of the Meteorological and Broadcasting Departments, and he brought with him a suitable receiving set complete with masts. He also loaned us some useful porters' tents, and presented to the expedition a number of records.

April 6 was a day of bustle and activity at Darjeeling. Each porter and his load was checked by Colonel Tobin. This was facilitated by the issue to each porter of a metal disc stamped with a number. The native population of Darjeeling was agog with excitement. Crowds lined the roads; porters' wives were there to see their husbands off, some to give them a final cup of tea, others to wag an admonitory finger. The porters themselves swelled with conscious pride.

Kangchenjunga sympathised but little with these preparations for its discomfiture. It sulked behind sullen clouds, dispatching now and again sudden rainstorms, destined apparently for the express purpose of drenching and damping the ardour of the expedition.

That night before turning in, Wood Johnson and I took a final stroll along the terrace of the Mount Everest Hotel. The weather boded ill. Lightning glared every few seconds through a rain-charged murk. Ghostlike swathes of mist eddied evilly from the valleys. From the direction of the Himalayas came long low growls of thunder.

CHAPTER SEVEN

Through Tropical Sikkim

APRIL 7 DAWNED MISTILY but as the sun got up, the dense blanket of white, wet fog enwrapping Darjeeling quickly dissolved. Rifts were torn in the curtain disclosing Kangchenjunga, silvered, blue-shadowed, and remote. It was a morning full of a calm promise.

There were many friends and strangers to see us off, including an American lady, who seemed particularly anxious for our welfare, and asked us whether we did not expect to find it "turrible slippery" on Kangchenjunga.

Four Austin Seven motor cars had been engaged for the first stage of our journey to Singla. There we were to be met by ponies and continue on them to Chakung. From Darjeeling to Singla a rough track descends tortuously 6,000 feet, in a distance as the crow flies of about five miles. Frequently the gradient is as much as 1:3 or 1:4, and hairpin bends are such as to necessitate reversing, with the wheels but a few inches from the unprotected edge of precipitous drops.

"Baby" cars have done much to improve the social amenities of the Darjeeling district. A few years ago the tea planters, whose estates are scattered about the hillsides, were forced to use ponies or mules for transport. As a result, their existence was frequently a lonely one, for many of the plantations are twenty or thirty miles from Darjeeling. Recently, however, one of the planters bought a "baby" car as an experiment. He found to his surprise and delight that it was capable of negotiating the narrow zig-zagging tracks, and terrific hills of the district. Now practically every tea planter owns one, and the social life of the district has been vastly improved thereby.

The climate of Darjeeling is temperate, and comparable to that of England, the temperature seldom rising above 70°. That of Singla in the Rangit Valley is definitely tropical. At first we passed through woods and glades of oaks, firs, and beeches reminiscent of the hillsides of Shropshire. Then came more open slopes covered in dark green terraces of tea, and clumps of tall bamboos.

Kurz, Wood Johnson, and myself were in the first car of the little procession. We had not gone more than a mile or so from Darjeeling when we overtook a number of our porters scattered along the road, who had obviously only left Darjeeling that morning instead of the previous day. In reply to our query as to why they had not started, several of them said they were not feeling well. The cause of this was not far to seek. The advance pay intended for the upkeep of their wives and children in their absence had been spent in one last "beano" the previous night at Darjeeling. It was essential to get these men to Chakung the same day, and to Wood Johnson, as transport officer of our party, fell the unwelcome task of staying behind to see that they *did* get there.

As we descended, we were vouchsafed occasional glimpses of the snows. Below was the floor of the Rangit Valley, 2,000 feet above sea level, whilst forty-five miles away remote in heaven rose the summit of Kangchenjunga, 28,156 feet, a vertical height difference of over 26,000 feet!

Once we were stopped by a tea planter who cheerily wished us good luck, and insisted on taking a photograph. It became hotter and hotter. Several of us were wearing Terai hats, double wide-awakes with broad brims. These are worn mostly by tea planters, and afford excellent protection from the sun. The pith solar topi soon goes to pieces in rain, but the Terai stands up to any amount of hard wear.

A peculiarity of tea is that given the right soil, and the requisite amount of rainfall, it seems to grow satisfactorily in any climate, varying from the temperate to the tropical. The highest Darjeeling tea garden is over 6,000 feet above sea level, and the lowest descends to the bottom of the Rangit Valley. We passed garden after garden, all picturesque and forming charming deep green foregrounds to the procession of woolly white clouds masking the distant wall of the Himalaya.

At Singla we were hospitably greeted by the planters of one of these lower plantations, and spent a pleasant hour sipping cool drinks in a shady bungalow.

Apparently on the principle that walking was good for us, only four ponies had been ordered and we had to take turns in riding them. No doubt, the intention was a good one, but in the enervating heat of the Rangit Valley, such mortification of the flesh seemed both unpleasant and unnecessary.

At Singla Bazar a dismal tale awaited us. According to Narsang, one of our sirdars, a large number of coolies had not yet arrived, and they could not possibly get to Chakung that day. We would have to wait a day for them to catch up. There was much that was unintelligible, and little that was useful in his declarations, poured out as they were in weird and wonderful English learnt during service with a Gurkha regiment in France. And what had happened to the cook? Why was he not there waiting for us with lunch prepared? "The cook? He is gone on somewhere," and Narsang waved a hand with characteristic native vagueness.

In my rucksack was a large lump of dry gingerbread. This was broken up and handed round. Suddenly, Wood Johnson arrived. 'Not get to Chakung?' Nonsense! Of course, the porters would, all of them. Within five minutes the peaceful serenity of Singla Bazar was replaced by a feverish activity. The lazier of the porters who had settled down for the day and the night at the village, found themselves, much to their surprise, on the road to Chakung. Our sheet anchor, Lobsang, was behind, bringing on the stragglers. The majority of the good porters, the Sherpas and Bhutias, had left the previous day, and were well *en route* to Chakung, it was only the Nepali "bazar wallahs" who were exhibiting such early slackness.

After leaving Singla Bazar we came to a suspension bridge across the Ramman River, a tributary of the Rangit River. The former forms the frontier of Bengal and Sikkim, and there was a native frontier post at one end of the bridge, with a corporal in charge. To him we showed the passes that had been given us in Darjeeling. Unfortunately, Dr. Richter and Eberl had left their passes in their rucksacks, which had been sent on ahead, whilst Wood Johnson, whom we had left at Singla Bazar; had forgotten his altogether. The former two had to wait until their rucksacks were returned, but Wood Johnson, we knew, would get across without a pass whether he was given permission or not. It transpired later that when the pass had been demanded of him, he had looked the corporal up and down until that unfortunate man had apologised for daring to insult the sahib by asking for the pass, and had humbly escorted Wood Johnson across the frontier.

The suspension bridge had tied to it numbers of little prayer flags, or perhaps more literally, prayer rags. All bridges in this part of the world are decorated thus in order to propitiate the river gods. It is usual, also, to throw a coin or two into the river when crossing to help, presumably, towards the upkeep of the river gods.

From the suspension bridge the path wound steeply uphill through dense jungle. The afternoon was close and boilingly hot, and a heavy slumberous silence was broken only by the whirring of insects. We turned a corner; a small spring of pure water was bubbling from a bank. By the side of the path in an orange garden a meal had been laid out on the grass, presided over by the grinning face of Tencheddar. Famished, we greeted it with a paeon of praise and thanksgiving, forgetting in the ecstasy of the moment to revile Tencheddar for his idiocy in having come this absurd distance before stopping to prepare a meal.

The orange garden is the property of the Maharajah of Sikkim. There are many such scattered about this fertile countryside, for orange-growing is the most important industry in Sikkim, and the revenue brought in from these scattered estates is surprisingly large.

With appeased appetites we lay back at last contentedly. Already we felt ourselves to be far from civilisation. Dotted about the hillside below were primitive little houses, above rude terraces of rice, irrigated by roughly cut channels along which flowed water from the mountain streams and springs. The day was drawing to a close, and between the blue cloud shadows moving across the broad bosomed hills, the forests were daffodil gold in the declining sun. Somehow I was reminded of an evening I once spent on Bowfell, in the English Lake District, one of those perfect evenings, still and peaceful, with soft colourful distances. Seated on a grey boulder I had watched just such a peaceful sunset and seen the hills imperceptibly annexed by the Kingdom of Night. But here everything was greater. In the Lake District, you may run down a hill into a valley and up another hill in an hour or so. In the foothills of the Himalayas, it is a day's hard work. The country over which we were looking was vaster than any of us had imagined. It produced in us almost a feeling of impotence. We were not ants, or flies, but mere microcosms toiling over the age-worn wrinkles of the earth.

Night was falling rapidly as we continued on our way. Now and again we passed porters. In the heat, they were making heavy weather of it, but a few days' marching would soon sweat out the fatty accumulations of soft living, and knit together muscles and sinew in preparation for the hard work ahead.

Presently the path rounded a shoulder and passed into the Ratho Valley, contouring along its southern side. The others were ahead, and I found myself alone. Night trod hard on the heels of day. Soon it was dark. Fireflies flitted out from the forest on either hand, like minute lamps in the hands of hurrying elves. Rain began to fall, each heavy drop drumming on the still leaves of the silent forest. The path divided, but my pony unhesitatingly took the left branch. A few minutes later I arrived at the dak bungalow, just in time to escape a tropical deluge.

The dak-bungalows of Sikkim are theoretically run by the Government of that State, but actually it is the British Government that is primarily responsible for their upkeep. Each bungalow is in charge of a native caretaker. All those at which we stayed were clean and comfortable. Their situation is admirable, and the sites of many of them were obviously chosen by someone with an eye for scenic beauty. The bungalow at Chakung stands on a wooded ridge separating the Ramman and Ratho Valleys close to the ruins of an ancient shrine, which was most likely formerly employed for the worship of some local deity.

The supper that evening was a merry one. Wood Johnson arrived in the middle of it, and later Eberl and Dr. Richter. Just as we were thinking of turning in, the corporal of the police put in a belated appearance. Recovering from his surprise at the suspension bridge, he had followed Wood Johnson with a tenacity worthy of the "Flying Squad". As he had no wish to get the man into trouble, Wood Johnson gave him a note to take to the Commissioner at Darjeeling. With this in his pocket, plus substantial *baksheesh*, the corporal returned to his post a happy man.

Heavy rain fell all night, and was succeeded by a dull grey morning and low sluggish mists. Already some of the Nepali porters had come to the conclusion that loafing in Darjeeling was preferable to work, and it was only with difficulty that we were able to get some of the more miserable specimens to start at all.

Our next stage was to Rinchenpung. From Chakung the route descended into the Ratho Valley, and crossing a stream climbed over a low ridge bounding the northern side of the valley. The path was bog-like in places, and the morning was as depressingly dismal and damp as an August day in the Highlands.

We had not gone far before we saw our first leech. Soon the path was swarming with them. Apparently they had their own telegraph system, and leeches all along the route had been warned of our coming. These pests are the most unpleasant feature of journeying through the tropical valleys of Sikkim. Ungorged they are about the thickness of a match, and a little shorter. Gorged, they attain the dimensions of a large slug. They are blind, and attack by scent alone, but their nasal acuteness more than compensates for their blindness. Stop for but a few moments, and they approach from all directions.

Their method of progress is peculiar and comical. Raising their heads in the air, they bend forward and attach themselves, apparently by the mouth, to the ground in front. The tail is then brought up against the head with the body arched between and the head makes another forward lunge. Had it not been annoying, it would have been amusing to see these eager little blood-suckers standing with their heads upright, like tiny serpents, waiting to affix themselves to their prey.

The powers of insinuation and penetration of a leech are great. They can insinuate themselves into an eyehole of a boot with the greatest of ease, whilst their drill-like head is capable of boring through at least one layer of a puttee. Personally, I found that the Kashmiri puttees given to me by General Bruce afforded excellent protection, and I was not once bitten on either foot. But the persevering little devils are not easily baulked of their prey. I was just beginning to congratulate myself on my immunity, when I discovered two large ones firmly attached to my scalp. It is a mistake to pick a leech off once it has become attached to the skin, as its head will be left in the wound, and this may lead to blood poisoning, or at least a nasty festering sore. The usual way of forcing them to release their hold is by dipping a bag of salt in water and letting the brine drip on to the leech, which soon drops off. Another excellent method is to apply a burning cigarette.

If, by virtue of boots and puttees, we were comparatively immune it was a different matter for the porters and ponies. The majority of the porters preferred walking in their bare feet, and the leeches made the most of them. The ponies' legs streamed with blood, and it was necessary to keep a sharp look-out to see that the leeches did not crawl into their nostrils and ears. In the absence of human beings and beasts, how do leeches manage to exist?

From the ridge north of the Ratho Valley, we descended into the Rishi Valley. Both these valleys are side valleys of the main Rangit Valley, and are comparatively small and glen-like. A primitive little bridge of logs spans the Rishi River, and large boulders near by afforded a luncheon site free from leeches, for a leech hates a dry surface, and only lives in swampy ground, or comes out after rain.

It was a delightful spot, almost like a valley in South Devon. The water of the torrent was sweet and clear, and despite a formal protest on the part of Dr. Richter, we did not hesitate to drink it. It is only from these smaller streams that pass through villages that there is danger of typhoid or dysentery.

If there had been any doubts as to how Frau Dyhrenfurth would stand the strain of these marches through Sikkim, they were soon set at rest, for the "Memsahib" as she was soon respectfully and affectionately known by all the members of the expedition, not only insisted on taking a man's share of the work, but was usually among the first to finish the day's march.

From the Rishi Valley, the path rose steeply to the ridge on which stands the Rinchenpung dak-bungalow. This is one of the prettiest bungalows in Sikkim, and from its well kept lawn and creeper-clad veranda, there is an enchanting view up the Rangit Valley towards the snows. Once again, the day ended in rainstorms of monsoonish intensity.

There were two other visitors at the bungalow. They told us that they were on a world tour, and had been 'taking the Himalayas' as part of their Indian itinerary. The weather, they said, had been continuously bad, and they were now returning to Darjeeling without having had one satisfactory view of Kangchenjunga.

Wood Johnson and I preferred the fresh air of the veranda to the crowded little rooms of the bungalow. I woke at dawn next morning. The rain had ceased. From the still woodlands came the song of the coppersmith bird, a musical, yet monotonous note, like someone beating a sheet of copper with a metal hammer. As I raised myself in my sleeping bag, I saw between a gap in the nearer mists the crest of a great cloud high up in the sky aglow with the first pale light of day. But was it a cloud? It was too steadfast, too immovable. I rubbed the dimming sleepiness from my eyes. It was no cloud, but a snowy mountain. Even as I watched, the dawn came up fiercely, ruddily, a titanic conflagration sweeping the upper regions of the sky. The nearer mists dissolved; other peaks became visible, their summits glowing like the white tents of a besieging army reflecting the glare from some burning city.

I roused our tourist friends. Now, at last, they had seen the snows. I wonder whether they still remember that glimpse of them?

The morning was one of sparkle and freshness as we set out for Pemayangtse. Improving weather raised the spirits of the porters, and for once in their lives even the Nepalis seemed cheerful and willing.

I left well in advance of the party to try to take some photographs before the usual morning clouds concealed the peaks. I did not go unrewarded. For a little distance the path descended through woods, but in one place a landslip had swept out a clearance. Framed between the trees, and thirty miles away, I saw Kabru and Kangchenjunga. It was a view so overwhelming in its magnificence as would cause the most ardent photographer to despair of reproducing one tithe of its grandeur. The morning clouds gathering about the crests of intervening hills, or, rising from the valleys, served but to increase the visual impression of height and depth. How is a photographer to transfer such an impression to a film? Only by comparison can he hope to convey to the unsophisticated any suggestion of the real scale, and what method of comparison is there? The forests covering the lower hills are but a dark green cloak, over which the eye passes at a casual glance. The river in the valley beneath was a mere thread. The greatest works of man, his towns, his cathedrals, and his factories, would be lost in such a landscape. Place St. Paul's on the crest of one of the intervening hills; to the eye it would appear as a mere dot; on a photographic film it would be invisible. Only physically can one learn to appreciate the scale of the Himalayan foot-hills, and that by toiling over them.

Mentally, a man is lost in this country. Like an astronomer he can estimate distance only in figures. His brain is too small, too tied to the little houses, towns, villages, and hedgerows among which he is accustomed to live, to grasp the real magnitude of these immense landscapes.

As I came out of the forest on to the open hillside, the snows had all but vanished behind growing masses of cumuli. Only the summit of the nearest snow peak, Narsingh, was visible, and I had barely time to take a photograph before it, too, vanished.

The path passed along a ridge, decorated by a row of chortens (prayer shrines), at which it is customary to pray and give thanks to the gods, and then plunged in steep zig-zags down a precipitous hillside.

At the junction of the Kalet and Rangit Valleys we found ourselves once more in tropical heat. The Rangit Valley here becomes gorge-like, yet so fertile is the soil, trees and other vegetation somehow manage to eke out a precarious existence on ledges and crannies of precipitous cliffs and crags.

Some women from a neighbouring hamlet were washing clothes in the river.

Their method was to dip the clothes in the water, then, holding them up beat them violently with a piece of flat wood. This must be the method employed by my local laundry when washing my dress shirts.

Thanks to the efficiency of Mr. Kydd, we were overtaken here by a runner, and spent a pleasant half-hour in the shade reading letters from home, and the latest sensations and French railway accidents in newspapers.

Some members of the party had seen a large snake, the markings of which they described to Wood Johnson. He said it was probably a king cobra. If so, they were lucky not to be attacked, for the king cobra is one of the snakes that attack human beings without provocation. It is said that it can overtake a running man.

We lunched near a small hamlet, at which Duvanel and his ciné camera created considerable excitement, and afterwards trudged up to Pemayangtse. It was scorchingly hot, but the gradually increasing coolness as we gained height was well worth the effort.

The dak-bungalow at Pemayangtse is admirably situated on a grassy sparsely wooded ridge, and commands superb views to the north and south. We had barely arrived when we were greeted by an imposing little procession of Lamas from the neighbouring monastery. They were bare-footed, and clad in long gowns of a dingy red colour, on which was the "patched robe", the emblem of poverty. From the girdle encircling their waist were suspended various sacred instruments and relics, such as holders, knives, and purses. Their heads were close cropped like black flue brushes, but the tropical sun seemed to have little effect on them. Most of them were young, with somewhat vacuous faces, dull, unintelligent eyes and loose lipped smiles. There was, however, one old monk of dignified carriage, who was most likely the Proctor of the monastery, for his face bore the stamp of character and intelligence. Standing before the bungalow, they commenced a low, monotonous intoning, possibly praying for our souls, while the old man came forward and burst forth into a torrent of Nepali and Tibetan. After considerable difficulty, we were at last able to get his meaning. Yes, they were glad to greet us, but we had only come in the nick of time. Had we a Doctor Sahib? Then would he cure them of this terrible thing that was afflicting the monastery? 'What was the terrible thing?' we enquired. His answer was simple and expressive, 'Worms!' And as for himself, for his sins, he was possessed of a terrible ear-ache.

A little later, a number of Holy Men might have been seen imbibing large quantities of castor oil and santonin with every appearance of gusto and enjoyment, whilst the old monk lay on the ground in order to have oil poured into his bad ear. Gratitude in the form of eggs and skinny chickens arrived later, and it was arranged that they should give us a devil dance the following morning.

Devil dances are a religious observation. They are usually given in honour or propitiation of some deity. In this particular instance, the deity was the God of Kangchenjunga.

That evening we made merry with the gramophone. This was always a never-ending source of amusement to the porters. Scarcely had the first record been put on, when the doorway of the dining room was filled with dirty faces grinning appreciatively. The classical masters were little appreciated, but Messrs. Layton and Johnstone, and the bass voiced vocalist in 'Give Yourself a Pat on the Back' never failed to produce roars of merriment.

Before turning in, we sat on the veranda, arguing as to whether something white far up among the stars, lit by the rising moon, was a mountain top or a cloud. Most argued cloud, but when hours later I woke in the middle of the night, and looked out, the "cloud" was still there, watched over by trembling stars.

We rose early next morning, and passed up the roughly paved road leading to the monastery. The approach to the monastery was lined with high poles decorated with prayer flags, consisting of long, multi-coloured strips, inscribed with prayers, nailed longitudinally to the poles. These prayer flags are common all over Tibet, Sikkim, and Nepal, and are supposed to have been originated by Asoka, the Constantine of Buddhism, who ordered pillars to be erected, inscribed with prayers and extracts from Buddhistic laws. Planted in the ground more than twenty centuries ago (B.C. 253–251) there are six set up by him in India still standing. Sometimes prayer flags display the dragon-headed horse, one of the great mythical animals of China.

The Pemayangtse Monastery stands on a wooded ridge about 7,000 feet above sea level. So fierce are the storms that sweep across the Himalayas, that its wooden roof was once carried away. It is now secured by iron wires to the ground. It is a tall building of stone and wood, gaudily painted in red and yellow, the two holy colours of Tibet.

The Lamas were waiting to receive us grouped round the Head Lama, a charming old gentleman who greeted us with a warm smile of welcome. While not engaged in conversing with Wood Johnson, our transport officer, who spoke Nepali, he was ceaselessly engaged in telling his rosary of yellow beads, keeping up a low, monotonous mumble at the same time, which is appropriately called "purring like a cat".

General Bruce relates that on one occasion when visiting the Pemayangtse Monastery he was for some reason put under a spell by the Head Lama. The spell took the form of a severe stomach-ache, which General Bruce was told would last until midday. It did, in spite of efforts made to cure it, but punctually at midday it disappeared as "miraculously" as it came.

Telling beads is one convenient method of praying, but perhaps the best of all methods, as it gets through the greatest number of prayers in the shortest possible time, is the prayer wheel. This consists of a copper or brass cylinder, which is made to revolve on a wooden handle. Inside the cylinder is a roll of paper or parchment on which are written as many prayers as can be squeezed in. As every revolution is equivalent to reciting all the prayers inside, it is possible, by assiduously revolving this apparatus, to get through some millions of prayers a day.

The Head Lama told us that he would be pleased to offer up a prayer to the God of Kangchenjunga for the safety of the expedition, and also volunteered the information that the weather would remain fine. This was an excellent idea, as we knew it would put great heart into our porters. If he possessed such powers over General Bruce's internal economy, the ordering of meteorological conditions should present little difficulty.

Before the monastery was a large grass-covered quadrangle, enclosed by pavilions and outhouses on three sides, whilst a flight of steps leading up to the imposing and fantastically painted portico of the monastery, overhung with tapestries, formed the fourth. Arranged in a line before the monastery was the band. The instruments consisted of two long metal-chased and ornamented horns, from twelve to fifteen feet in length, smaller horns, flutes, drums, and cymbals. Some of the bandsmen wore cowls, which gave to them a curiously Ku Klux Klannish appearance, and others a curved, cockatoo-like crest to their hats.

Shortly after our arrival, the band crashed forth into what was presumably a welcome. My first impression was of a hideous medley of sound, which, judged by European standards, was completely tuneless and unintelligible. Yet, as my ears became accustomed to the din, I became aware of a perceptible rhythm. The music began to take shape and form in my mind. Gradually, I felt myself borne away, as it were, mentally, from the Twentieth Century, conveyed on the wings of this strange music into the very heart of this mystic mountain land, where time and space are limitless, and man is re-incarnated through eternity. The bass note of the great horns, surely the deepest note of any known musical instrument, seemed to boom of the might of the gods, the thunder of their avalanches, the roar of their torrents, the solemn roll of the thunderstorms that beat about the buttresses of their mid-aerial thrones.

The music dropped into a dirge-like monotone, then rose suddenly into a passionate crescendo. Two hideously masked figures appeared in the portico of the monastery. Leaping down the steps they dashed into the quadrangle, spinning round and round with wide-spread arms and swirling silken robes.

The band had previously taken up a position in the pavilion. Seated in front was the Head Lama amid a horde of acolytes. In one hand he held a bell which he occasionally rang vigorously as a signal for changes of music, or to call in more devil dancers.

The duty of these first two devils was apparently only to announce the more important devil participants in the dance. Suddenly the band, which had stopped for a rest, blared forth again, and four figures slowly descended the steps, and commenced to dance.

They wore long silken robes, beautifully embroidered, and on their heads the most fantastic masks we had ever seen. Intended primarily to represent animals, fowls, yaks, eagles, goats, horses, and sheep, they were yet ghastly mockeries of nature – the phantasmagoria of a madman's imagination. At first the music was dirge-like, and the dancers' movements correspondingly slow. It quickened gradually. Other dancers joined in. Lines, circles, and squares were formed as in folk dancing. Movements became more rapid, arms were flung wide with gestures of abandon, legs kicked high in time with the banging of the drums, and the boom of the great horns. They pirouetted round and round with incredible speed, their heavy garments flying upwards and outwards like human catherine wheels. The music mounted to a terrific pitch of frenzy. Suddenly, above the din, came the sharp ringing of the Head Lama's bell. The music dropped, the dancers retired after a final twirl and obeisance and sprang quickly up the steps into the monastery.

Duvanel was naturally anxious to secure "shots" of the dancing, but at first it was plain that his machinations were regarded as savouring of black magic. However, directly he commenced to turn the handle of his camera the Lamas appeared considerably relieved. Obviously this complicated machine was nothing but a new and improved form of prayer wheel.

Lastly, there appeared several monsters of ferocious aspect, accompanied by two small boys dressed to represent demons. Possibly, they were intended to represent the devils which worry beasts in the form of insect pests and leeches, for armed with long yak-hair whisks, they proceeded to goad the monsters into fury until they reared, stamped, and charged about the quadrangle, whilst once again the band obliged with a crashing crescendo of sound.

As though in answer to this demonstration in its honour, the cloudy draperies of morning were drawn aside, disclosing Kangchenjunga. One silver banner of cloud trailed from its crest. The attendant fairies of the great God were "baking their bread".

From Pemayangtse to Tingling was an easy march, but a hot one. Once again, we descended into and across the upper Rangit Valley. On the descent we passed a well-built, modern looking temple. It was here that the Dalai Lama stayed during a tour of Sikkim. As, in view of his extreme holiness, it was thought necessary to erect a temple at every place at which he spent a night such a tour must be something of a drain on the purses of the local taxpayers. Several members stopped to bathe in the Rangit River. The current of these mountain torrents is dangerously strong, and Dr. Richter was nearly carried away. Had he been so, he would certainly have been drowned.

We gathered for lunch in a cool, shady spot by a small brook, afterwards dozing and resting during the heat of the day. But cool, shady spots in Sikkim are only too liable to harbour leeches, and it was not long before Schneider had a large one affixed to his bare arm.

At Tingling we camped for the first time. It was a charming site for a camp. Close at hand was the little village of Tingling, which stands on one of the few flat bits in Sikkim, and we pitched our tents at the edge of a wheatfield.

Prior to the expedition, Professor Dyhrenfurth had had tents made for each member. Actually, they were two-men tents, so that there was plenty of room for one man. The dweller in civilisation may argue that for each man to have his own tent is unnecessary and unsociable. Travellers and explorers, however, know the psychological value of privacy. During the months of monotony and hardship of a Polar expedition – and the same thing applies in a lesser degree to Himalayan expeditions – the best friends may become sick of the sight of each other, and little habits of speech and manner that count for nothing in civilisation may jar intolerably. Only by being able to escape for a while is a man able to tolerate things which normally he would not give a care to.

Nemu, my servant, was an expert in the art of camping. He was usually among the first to arrive at the end of a day's march, and had an unerring eye as to the best place to pitch a tent. This, combined with a never failing capacity for looking after his master's interests, made him an invaluable servant. He was an old soldier, and had the North-West Frontier Medal, and like most old soldiers, he was an adept in the gentle art of scrounging. Not that I ever missed so much as a cigarette, but in the event of my breaking or losing anything, it was sure to be replaced in some mysterious way. Both on the march and on the mountains Nemu proved a tower of strength, and I can see now his broad good-natured face, with its philosophical eyes, and occasional broad grin, that flashed out always when least expected.

At Tingling an unpleasant incident occurred. One of the coolies ran amok with a *kukri*, and before anyone could stop him, had run another porter – one of our best men through the chest. The wound was a serious one below the heart, and had it not been for the skilful treatment of Dr. Richter, the injured man would probably have lost his life.

His assailant was brought along to the Mess Tent, under the charge of Tikeram Thapa, to be interrogated by Wood Johnson. While doing so, he managed to pick up a large stone, and made as though to try and brain me as I was standing back to him outside the Mess Tent, but was fortunately promptly collared by Tikeram. The man was obviously demented, and we were forced to tie him up, hand him over to the Head Man of Tingling, and send a runner to the police at Gangtok.

Apart from this unpleasant incident. Tingling will always remain in my mind as one of our most charming camping sites. There is no view of the snows from it, but perhaps that is as well, for the gentle verdure-clad hills around are reminiscent of Glen Affric, and any intrusion on such a scene by the more restless forms of nature would tend to detract from the peaceful beauty of the landscape.

Late that evening, several of us went to the Head Man's house to see after our injured porter who had been lodged there. Climbing a rickety, wooden ladder, we entered a low-roofed room, like the upper story of a Swiss cowherd's chalet. In the middle was an open stone fireplace, in which crackled a log fire, the flames of which lit the wrinkled face of the Head Man and his friends, as they squatted round. The atmosphere was close and heavy, even the pungent smoke not altogether successfully combating the odour of bodies unwashed since birth. The injured man had been wrapped in rugs, and placed on a bed of straw. He appeared comfortable. We ordered hot milk to be given to him at intervals throughout the night. Such is the toughness of these people, that despite the severe injury, and the obvious risk of subsequent infection and blood poisoning, we heard later that he was on his feet again in less than a fortnight.

It was good to be in a tent again beneath the stars, and I lay long in my sleeping bag that night looking between the flaps at the sentinel trees on a neighbouring ridge dimly outlined against the sky.

From Tingling to Yoksam was a longer march than that of the previous day, although the horizontal distance was no greater. A sharp ascent brought us to the crest of a wooded ridge north of Tingling. As we breasted the last rise, we were surprised to be met by a sudden blare from a band. The monks of the neighbouring Kachoperi Monastery had come to greet us, and had erected two little shelters of gay chintz-like material, for all the world like little beach bathing tents, in which fruit and tea were pressed upon us. The latter appeared to be made from aromatic herbs and was rich, thick, and buttery. The day was very hot, and we were thirsty; I, for one, drank several cups of the sickly stuff, and for the remainder of the day wished I had not. The monastery band, complete with long poles to which were fastened various prayer flags and pennants, lined along the path outside the tent and did honour to us in a crashing crescendo of sound.

From the ridge we glimpsed the summits of Kangchenjunga and Kabru. A silver lock of cloud was trailing from Kangchenjunga. Standing there in the still morning, perspiring gently under a fierce sun, it was difficult to realise that had we been up there we might have been fighting for our lives in death dealing cold and a *tourmente* of wind-flung snow.

From the ridge we had to descend once more into the Rangit Valley. The valley here begins to narrow, and bold crags jut out through a tangle of vegetation on its steepening sides.

The trudge up to Yoksam was a hot one but we were fanned by a fresh southerly breeze. As we progressed, we were puzzled to hear a series of pistol-like reports, and an intermittent crackling, like rifle fire. Turning a corner, we saw that the jungle was ablaze. Dull red flames were leaping high into the air, amid a pall of black smoke. Hastened by the breeze, the fire was sweeping with great velocity along the hillside. One moment some majestic tree would stand defiantly in its path, the next it would disappear in a smother of flame and smoke, reappearing as a gaunt, blackened corpse. Owing to the clearings made by the natives of Yoksam, the scope of the fire was limited, but its fierceness and the speed with which it swept the hillside reminded me of boyhood tales of prairies and pampas.

Like Tingling, Yoksam is situated on a shelf clothed in pasture land, rice and wheat-fields. We pitched our camp on the terraces of a rice-field. Soon after we arrived we received word that the second party, under the charge of Hannah and Wieland, was two marches behind and that the convoy of mules under Colonel Tobin had left Darjeeling.

Yoksam is the last village. Thenceforward our way must lie through wilder country, and along rougher tracks towards Dzongri and the Kang La. Soon we would be at grips with things. Already the veneer of civilisation had lost its polish, despite the restraining and elevating influence of the "Memsahib". Table manners were already at a discount. Beards were growing steadily, and it was a matter of speculation as to who would win the race for length and bushiness. At present the honours were fairly evenly distributed between Professor Dyhrenfarth, Dr. Richter, and Duvanel. My own particular effort promised to develop into what I believe is technically known as a "King Beaver", or a beard bright red in colour.

The following morning, April 12, saw us strolling across the open pastures of Yoksam, or between fields of ripening grain. Then the path degenerated into a narrow, rough track and the forest enclosed us once again.

The paths in this part of the world are a fair indication of the character of those who make them. The native, of course, lives only in the present; the future holds no interest for him. Therefore he goes about everything in the easiest possible way, the thought that by a little extra trouble he might save himself work in the future never occurring to him. It would not have been difficult to have made the path north of Yoksam contour the eastern side of the Rangit Valley. It would never have occurred to a Swiss Verschonerungs Verein to have done otherwise. But generations of native yak-herds and travellers over the Kang La have thought fit always to follow the line of least resistance, irrespective of time and future convenience. Thus, the path was continually climbing up, or dropping down to avoid the direct traverse of a steep piece of hillside. It was an extremely irritating path to the ordered and practical mind of a European.

But passing through this magnificent primaeval forest cloaking the Upper Rangit Valley one can forgive the path its vagaries. None of us had ever seen an Amazonian forest, but it can scarcely be finer than the forests that line the trench-like valleys of the Himalayas. Yet, to one who finds pleasure in tramping the windy moors, fells, and bens of the North Country, there is something indescribably depressing about such a forest. The dense walls of vegetation on either side of the narrow straggling track and the interlacing canopy of vegetation far above the head shut out the health-giving sunlight and breezes. An awed silence seems somehow to hold in its arms a breathless suspense. There exists undefined menace, suggested perhaps by the dank odours of rotting vegetation. I experienced a feeling of being imprisoned in a vault, and longed to escape into more open places, to breathe air untainted by the miasmal odours of decay. Even the creepers that writhe about the trunks of the trees, or hang snakelike from the branches, appear ready to grip the traveller, and drag him to some horrible death in the gloomy recesses of the forest. There is little of good, and much of evil about such a place, and as Wood Johnson said, its impenetrable depths might hide anything, even the dreaded Snow Men.

To the botanist, however, there is much of interest and beauty in the flora of these forests. Quoting from Sir Joseph Hooker: 'The vegetation consisted of oak, maple, birch, laurel, rhododendron, white Daphne, Jessamine, Arum, Begonias, Cyrtandaceae pepper, fig, Menispermum, wild cinnamon. Scitamineae several epiphytic orchids, vines, and ferns in great abundance.'

As the path progressed it became worse. Here and there it was built up of bamboos and logs against the sides of precipitous crags. Mr. Freshfield found it 'a great trial of temper.' So, too, did we, or perhaps I should say, the porters. For loads such as ski and tent poles are a considerable nuisance in such a place.

Professor Dyhrenfurth was anxious to make a double march and reach Dzongri in two days instead of three from Yoksam. But these three stages had not been arranged without reason, and Wood Johnson, who had traversed this same route the previous year, pointed out the inadvisability of a double march under such difficult conditions for transport. We accordingly camped in the usual camping place at the end of the first day's march, where there is a flat shelf and the forest is not too dense to allow of tents being pitched. This camping place harboured an unpleasant form of tick, a crablike insect about the size of a little finger nail, the bite of which was both painful and poisonous.

The scene at night was a curious one. Every flat Place on the hillside above the camp was occupied by the porters. Their fires twinkled through the gloom like the fires of goblins. Like us, they were depressed by the forests, but their depression found adequate expression in the simple belief that devils and other unpleasant characters dwelt therein. That is, perhaps, the chief difference between the workings of the native mind and the European mind. Scenery may depress or exhilarate the European mind in exactly the same way as it does the native mind, but the European mind is educated sufficiently to be able to analyse consciously, or subconsciously, the reason for its reactions. The European tells himself that his feeling of depression is due to the gloom, the smell, or the appearance of what he sees, but the native mind is too clogged with superstition to be able to reason out its reactions. It must look for a simpler and more direct explanation, and such an explanation usually takes the form of belief in devils, gods, or other figments of the imagination. These he is able to propitiate and thus set his fears at rest. Thus, where the European is able to conquer his feelings by the exercise of will power, and so remain mentally superior to his environment, the native is able to arrive at exactly the same result by completely different means. Thus, that evening it was thought necessary to propitiate the devils of the jungle, but this having been accomplished, our porters settled down for the night perfectly happily, with no fears that anything untowards was likely to occur.

Mists hung low in the great ravine up which we were passing as we set off the following morning. The path became gradually worse and worse. In some places it was blocked by fallen tree trunks. Sometimes it was necessary to jump from one boulder to another across turbulent torrents. For a considerable distance the path vanished altogether beneath the debris of a landslip of considerable size. Here shattered tree trunks were piled in an inextricable confusion, and dense undergrowth that had sprung up between made progress fatiguing and difficult.

The way had to be cleared with *kukris*, and it was interesting to watch how quickly and neatly these were wielded by expert hands. Many who are reading this will have seen the batting of Frank Woolley, the great Kent cricketer. Seemingly little force is put into the stroke, yet the ball is at the boundary before the spectators have realised what has happened. The secret is hitting the ball exactly in the driving centre of the bat, combined with perfect timing of the stroke. The same methods apply to cutting with a *kukri*, and it was interesting to watch the dexterity with which heavy branches were lopped cleanly off, and a way cleared through the undergrowth.

It was during this march that I began to feel ill. The forest had repaid my dislike for it by presenting me with a severe chill. Of course, it was my own fault – a chill always is the fault of its victim in the tropics. I did not have to cast back far in my mind to remember how the previous evening I had neglected to change damp clothes until I had been actually shivering. The tropics allow no latitude for foolishness, and to look after one's physical well-being with scrupulous care is the first essential of Himalayan travelling.

We crossed the eastern branch of the Rangit River, where it divides south of Dzongri. It was a wild spot. Mountain and cloud seemed to roof us in; the air was damp and chill. Far above we could just discern streaks of snow projecting like white fangs through the lowering mists. The glacier-born river roared sullenly over its rocky bed; cold spray beat upwards from its grey waters. Even more than in the forest did we feel enclosed and shut in. As Eberl said, it might have been the end of the world.

Into the forest again, and up the hillside, where the feet sank into leaves rotting into leaf mould, or crushed into blackened debris, and decayed branches. A storm was threatening as we camped on a slope under dismal trees. No doubt my recollections are prejudiced, for my voice had completely disappeared, and I crawled into my sleeping bag ill and feverish, but this camping site remains in my memory as the most depressing one at which it had been my ill fortune to spend a night. Fortunately, Dr. Richter gave me some excellent medicine and throat spray which considerably relieved me, but sleep was impossible. The weather broke that night in a thunderstorm accompanied by torrential rain. Though lying ill in a sleeping bag, with the rain from a leaky patch in the tent oozing through, there was an element of magnificence in listening to this warring of the elements on the very edge of the Himalayas. The blue glares of lightning were answered by majestic crashes of thunder that seemed to be precipitated from hill to hill and peak to peak in volleys and waves of sound like music in the nave of some immense cathedral. The very echoes were indicative of vastness. In a flat country the thunder seems to dominate, but in the Himalayas, it is but the mouth-organ of the giants.

The storm died of its own fury, and morning dawned clear and cold. The forests above were dusted with new-fallen snow which extended down to as low as 8,000 feet. Such weather boded ill for the crossing of the Kang La.

My lungs had been touched by the chill, and breathing was painful and difficult when walking uphill. Had it not been for the encouragement of Wood Johnson, who stayed with me during this trying time, I do not think I could have struggled up the 5,000 feet to Dzongri.

As we ascended, oaks and chestnuts gradually gave place to firs. The dense tropical tree roof under which we had been marching for the past two days thinned. Shafts of sunlight illuminated a ground covered no longer in the rotting debris of tropical vegetation but in fir cones and needles. The fresher and purer air from the snows brought with it a fragrance of sun-warmed resin. Beneath the firs were clumps of giant rhododendrons already budding, and as we got higher, these thickened, and the path twisted tortuously between their snaky mangrove-like stems. The sun melted the snow on the fir branches above, sending it down in little showers of water drops, that filled the forest with patterings and murmurings.

Wood Johnson and I rested in a hillside glade, but before we had sat down for more than a minute we saw dozens of malignant leeches making for us with a stern resolution. At this height, above 8,000 feet, we had expected to be rid of the pests, but they seemed to thrive in spite of the cold. Actually, they were the last we saw until returning to Darjeeling.

The snow-drifts became more frequent. At length the path was completely snow covered, in places to a depth of two or three feet. Only a small portion of this snow had fallen in the night, and what we were encountering was obviously the last of winter snow. To find such deep snow below 10,000 feet was disquieting, and doubts as to getting barefooted porters over the Kang La returned with redoubled force.

The rhododendron belt seemed interminable, but at length we emerged from it on to an open hillside clad only in dwarf rhododendrons, which are but two or three feet high, as compared to giant rhododendrons which attain a height of fifteen to twenty feet. The scene was more Alpine than Himalayan in character. The gentle snowy summits of the Singalila Ridge to the west put me in mind of the summits around Kitzbühel in Tyrol. Normally, at this time of the year these slopes should have been mostly grass covered, but now, so large was the amount of snow on them, they suggested skiing rather than walking.

The trudge, or perhaps it would be more correct to say stagger in my case, up to Dzongri remains in my mind as the most severe physical effort I have ever been called upon to do. As we breasted the last slope, on the summit of which flutter a few forlorn prayer flags, we were met by a biting wind from the north, bringing with it a hurrying swarm of snow-flakes.

The sky was greying as we walked over the bleak upland pastures on which stand the huts of Dzongri. The few remaining blue pools of sky were engulfed in the advancing tide of a blizzard. Wood Johnson went on ahead to look after the porters. On arriving at the camp he at once ordered a Thermos flask full of hot tea to be sent back. Narsang also carried my rucksack. Thus, I was able to reach Dzongri without having to be carried.

The two primitive stone huts of Dzongri which afford shelter to the yak-herds later in the summer, stand on a rolling upland, the crest of which separates the Praig Chu and Rathong Valleys. Though Dzongri would appear to be a prey to every wind that blows, it is the obvious climbing centre for this part of the Kangchenjunga Range, and its comparative easiness of access from Darjeeling demands that a proper shelter hut, run on the same lines as a Swiss Alpine Club hut, should be built. There are a number of fine peaks, for the ascent of which Dzongri would make an excellent starting point: Kabru, 24,002 feet, Little Kabru, 22,000 feet, Simvu, 22,360 feet, Pandim, 22,010 feet, and the rugged range to the south of it. All these peaks would appear to be possible to a strong mountaineering party.

Dzongri itself stands at 13,200 feet, and immediately to the north of it is 15,480 feet Kabur, the culminating point of the Dzongri Ridge. The great gneissic boulders that are strewn about the slopes hereabouts form an interesting geological problem. How came they to be there? Sir Joseph Hooker's theory that ice once covered the whole spur, and in moving downwards transported these boulders from the upper crags to other parts of the spur is most likely the correct explanation. At all events, it is curious to find these grassy, rolling downs littered with boulders lying in the midst of savage snow and rock peaks.

That evening the threatened blizzard broke. Once again I lay sleepless listening to the fury of the elements. Two days before we had slept in the moist, enervating heat of a tropical forest, now the snow slashed our tents, and the mercury of the thermometer shrank into its bulb.

CHAPTER EIGHT

Over the Kang La to Nepal

A CALM MORNING succeeded an angry night. Winter had ousted spring and snow lay over six inches deep. The sky was a clear washed blue, and far to the south blue hazes indicated the heat stricken Plain of Bengal. The crests of Pandim, and the peaks to the south of it were fringed with a faint iridescence as the rising sun shone through their delicate eaves, cornices and flutings of snow and ice. We had little time or inclination to admire the beauties of the scene, for the blizzard had done something more than transform the hillsides; it had turned the hearts of the Nepali porters into water. They refused to go on. Wrapping their blankets round them they cowered in the snow, weak, miserable specimens of humanity.[1]

Cajolery and argument were useless. It was necessary to separate the good men from the bad. Even though it meant delay in bringing some of the loads over the Kang La, it was better that we should get rid of these poor creatures now, rather than find ourselves at their mercy in a less favourable position. Wood Johnson,

[1] Considering that they were clad only in cotton clothing and were unequipped with boots they are scarcely to be blamed for refusing to traverse the snow-covered Kang La.

accordingly, ordered those men who wished to go back to stand to one side. They were indeed a sorry looking crew. The Sherpas and Bhutias eyed them contemptuously. The deserters numbered fifty, and the abandonment of their loads was a serious matter. It meant that they would have to be brought over the Kang La by relays of porters. Such a *modus operandum* had little to recommend in it in view of the uncertain weather, late winter and low snow line. Having sent back the shirkers, and issued snow goggles to our faithful porters, we were at length able to start, not forgetting to leave a reliable man in charge of the dumped loads.

For some distance the path contoured along the south-western slopes of Kabru, then dropped in a series of steep zig-zags into the Rathong Valley. In places it was deeply snowed under, and trail making was tiring work for those in front. It was here that we began to appreciate the surefootedness of the Sherpas and Bhutias. Though many of them wore rope soled Tibetan boots without any nails, whilst others had no boots at all, they descended with that easy gait characteristic of hill men.

Somehow the Rathong Valley reminded me of the upper reaches of Glen Nevis. There was the same luxuriant vegetation, sky line of crags and firs, and clear torrents hurrying down the hillsides, or hanging in thin, gauzelike water veils from beetling cliffs.

Much to our relief we saw that the lower part of the valley leading up towards the Kang La contained but little snow. The Kang La itself and the peaks north and south of it were buried in clouds suggestive of another blizzard. Snowflakes were falling as we mounted rhododendron-clad slopes into the Kang La valley, but presently the bleak sky was tempered by a fugitive sun, and the clouds rolled back.

We pitched camp on a bed of dwarf rhododendrons.

Apart from these, the valley was distinctly Alpine in character, and the stern rock walls on either hand dark stained by oozing water, turf-crowned slopes above and below, interspersed with occasional slopes of scree and drifts of snow provided scenery of a type typical to the Alpine gneissic ranges.

Thanks to Dr. Richter's treatment, plus a tough constitution, my chill was already better, and I was able to take my place at mess that evening. Seated on packing cases, we ate our supper in the open, warmed by the sun's last gleams. Up to date Tencheddar's cooking had met with approval, although not always unqualified approval. We were getting used to the varieties of food and cooking he expected us to stomach. It is indeed strange what men can get accustomed to in the wilds. Even the assistant cook's confirmed habit of pulling his shirt out of his trousers, and wiping the plates with it met with no more than a conventional grunt of disapproval. Our servants waited upon us, and it was a point of honour with each one of them to see that his own particular sahib got more than anyone else. As time went on, we would endeavour to vary the monotony. At this Schneider displayed most aptitude, and his favourite concoction consisting of toasted cheese, salad dressing, Worcester sauce and gherkins remains an unholy memory.

One unfortunate result of splitting up the expedition into three parties was the absence of alcohol in our own party, and it was not until we had crossed the Kang La that we discovered that Tencheddar had accidentally packed some bottles of rum in mistake for Worcester sauce. It was the only mistake he ever made that ended happily.

As soon as the sun disappeared it became very cold, and a bitter wind got up, hustling down the valley from the snows. It was necessary to let the world know something of our doings, and I sat up late that night hammering on a portable typewriter, until numb fingers no longer functioned and an overwhelming desire for sleep, after two bad nights, submerged journalistic considerations.

The porters had now been marching for ten days without a rest, and an off day was certainly theirs by right, but the unsettled weather, and the possibility of another snowstorm decided Professor Dyhrenfurth to push on over the Kang La without delay, and not only this, but to try to cross it in one day from our present camp. In view of the quantity of snow on the pass, one day certainly meant a very long and tiring march, for our camp was not more than 13,000 feet, and the Kang La is 16,373 feet. In addition, none of the sahibs or porters were acclimatised yet to altitude, and 16,000 feet to an unacclimatised body is more of a strain than 20,000 feet to an acclimatised body. Porters, also, were carrying a load of sixty to eighty pounds each. Taking all these considerations into account, it was doubtful whether such a long march was advisable.

To our delight and relief, the following morning dawned brilliantly. The wind had dropped, and a benevolent sun warmed the chill air of the upland valley. Our porters were if anything more susceptible bodily and mentally to weather conditions than we, and on this occasion they started off in great heart.

For a short distance above the camping site the valley floor is almost level, and covered in loose stones. We mounted over an ancient and steep terminal moraine. Thenceforward, the way lay entirely over snow.

The direct heat of the sun and the reflected glare of it from the snow were terrific. Unfortunately, protective glacier face cream was not available, and all we had were some tubes of ordinary cold cream. These proved almost completely useless and despite liberal applications, we could feel our skin becoming dried up, scorched and burnt. As we gained height, there were backward and enchanting views. The great foot-hills that had enclosed us during our march through the tropical forests to the snows seemed now mere rucks and folds in the earth's surface. The deep valleys along which we had laboured had sunk out of sight; their presence indicated by belts and bands of translucent blue haze, from which white cumuli clouds born of steamy earthen heat were beginning to nose their way upwards. It was as though we were gazing out upon some ocean from a viewpoint of few miles inland, the nearer peaks forming the broken edges of the coastal cliffs overlooking the long rollers of the foot-hills.

Hoerlin and Schneider with their usual indefatigable energy left early with the intention of climbing the Kang Peak, 18,280 feet. This rises south of the Kang La, and if Mr. Graham's description is correct would appear to have been climbed by him. Their ascent would act as an excellent spur to the porters.

On the Sikkim side of the Kang La there is a small uncrevassed glacier, which is joined by another glacier from the north. This northern glacier, which boasts a considerable ice fall, leads up to the foot of a symmetrical snow peak, the delicately pointed summit and sharp ridges of which invite exploration and conquest. Southwards, were a number of rock peaks and ridges, one of which bears a striking similarity to the well-known Dent du Géant and Rochefort Ridge, on the range of Mont Blanc.

As we plodded through the soft snow we experienced for the first time that Himalayan malady known as glacier lassitude. In our case, this lassitude, the mental and physical weariness induced by climbing the long snow slopes, was due probably to the fact that in six days we had ascended no less than 13,000 feet. But glacier lassitude is due to something more than mere lack of acclimatisation; sun and glare have much to do with it, as does also a curious lifelessness in the air. In the snowy trough we were ascending the air seemed dead and incapable of vitalising lungs and body. It lacked oxygen, and was as depressing to breathe as flat soda-water is to drink. In Himalayan glacier hollows evaporation in the tropical sun is so rapid that maybe the air is deprived by absorption of some of its oxygen. Only in snow and glacier hollows does lassitude attack the mountaineer, and by climbing a ridge he may rid himself of its baneful effects in a few minutes. It is also interesting to note that lassitude only makes itself felt on windless days, and that wind always restores energy to the apparently fatigued body.

We halted for lunch on a level place some 500 feet below the crest of the pass. Directly above rose the steep slopes of the Kang Peak, and on them were the minute figures of Hoerlin and Schneider. How slowly they seemed to move. In the soft snow they were finding the going very laborious. They were making for one of the ribs falling from the summit ridge, and by the time we had finished lunch they had gained it. Thenceforward, the way looked less exacting physically, though more difficult from a climbing standpoint. The porters watched interestedly, forgetting their own tiredness.

The last slopes of the Kang La remain in my memory as entailing something more than a weary trudge. I was, of course, still weak from fever, and every upward step meant an expenditure of will power as well as physical energy. At long last the slope eased off, and stepping on to an outcrop of rocks, I gazed down into Nepal. Little was to be seen save battalions of fleecy clouds struggling up the snow-filled and desolate valley leading to Tseram.

From a scenic standpoint the Kang La is not an attractive pass. Like some of the passes across the Alps, such as the Brenner, the Simplon and St. Gotthard, it is fatiguing without being particularly interesting. Perhaps its greatest charm is the sense of isolation and remoteness from the world of men inspired by it. It is suggestive of some Arctic landscape, frigid and hostile to flesh and blood. Looking down the way we had come, I could see the men strung out in a long line of slowly moving dots. It was difficult to realise that these dots on the vast counterpane of snow were indeed men, and each man, in addition to the load he was carrying, carried another load of care and trouble, joy and sorrow.

Did I really soliloquise thus? I doubt it. It is only now, seated in a comfortable chair, and breathing the air of Primrose Hill approximately 200 feet above sea level that I can think of what I ought to have thought of on the Kang La, and forgetting for a moment the grumble of traffic, and a distant yet audible inferno of pneumatic drills, conjure up in my mind's eye that string of little men toiling up the weary snow-slopes.

After a short steep slope on the Nepal side of the pass, the snow-filled valley curved gently downwards. After the labour of the ascent it was an easy matter descending through soft deep snow. It was an interesting fact that however much altitude may effect a man climbing in the Himalayas, he can, given easy ground, descend almost at an Alpine pace. Some remarkable instances of this occurred on Everest where slopes that had taken hours to ascend were descended in a few minutes.

The "Memsahib" was as usual well to the front of the party, and we congratulated her on being the first European woman to cross the Kang La. After a short distance, the valley floor dropped in a steep boulder strewn pitch. Below this was another level section, and there, among stones and patches of snow we pitched camp.

Two or three of us arrived with jarring headaches. It was the first and last time on the whole expedition that I was affected thus, and it is tolerably certain that the headaches, which seemed to strike through the head from the back of the neck to the eyes, were induced by intense sun glare plus an altitude to which our bodies were not yet acclimatised. We found aspirin tablets the best remedy and under their influence the headaches disappeared in a few minutes.

The northern side of the valley on which we were camping, had been almost denuded of snow by the sun, but the unbroken snow covering the valley floor on the opposite slopes seemed to offer possibilities of ski-running. Actually, ski would have made the traverse of the Kang La much easier, but it seemed hardly fair to use them in view of the laden coolies, and it was necessary, too, for the Europeans to stamp out a track through the soft snow. Descending, however, we had no such scruples, and Dr. Richter set an example by running down the upper slopes on ski, which in lieu of bindings, he had tied on with odd bits of string.

Scraggy dwarf rhododendrons were growing on the slopes above the camp, and soon a dozen or more little fires were smoking on the ledges and crannies, as the coolies cooked their evening meal. The day had been a hard one, an exceptionally hard one, even for our toughest Bhutias and Sherpas. The Alpine porter seldom carries more than a load of forty of fifty pounds, and this as a rule only along paths up to huts; on mountain ascents he carries considerably less. Our men had carried sixty to eighty pounds each over a pass higher than the summit of Mont Blanc. They had, of course, been used to carrying heavy loads from early childhood, but even so their work that day had been simply magnificent.

An hour or two after we had arrived Schneider and Hoerlin rejoined us. Their attempt on the Kang Peak had been crowned with success, albeit the ascent had been scarcely enjoyable in view of the bad snow conditions. The view had been marred by mist, but once they caught a glimpse of Jannu, 25,294 feet, which had impressed them as being a magnificent mountain.

We had camped at about 4 p.m., but as the evening drew on stragglers were still coming in, some of them very tired. Of Wood Johnson, who was bringing up the rear, there was no sign. As it was likely that he was experiencing difficulty in getting the last of these stragglers over the pass, I set off alone from the camp to meet him.

Night was falling swiftly as I plugged uphill. The evening was a calm one, and there was not even the faintest whisper of wind. For some distance I could hear the murmur of the camp beneath, and smell faintly the odour of burning rhododendrons, but soon nothing was to be heard. The gaunt, craggy sides of the mountains enclosed me. The murmurous trickles released by the sun had been clenched by frost to their channels. The silence of the high mountains at eventide was unbroken. I felt very lonely. Had it not been for the track stretching before me, a mere thread drawn across the snowy waste, I might have felt myself the sole inhabitant of a frigid planet. There was indeed an element of unearthliness about the scene. In the High Alps a man may find himself temporarily removed from civilisation, but always at the back of his mind is the thought that he has but to turn downhill, and in a few hours at the most he will regain civilisation. But in the High Himalayas such subconscious knowledge does not exist, and the wanderer experiences the genuine meaning of solitude. Above me the sun glowed redly, cruelly, on the peaks, but round me the snows were livid, deathlike, and the black rocks jutted through like unburnt coals amid the white ashes of the world.

So I trudged on, conscious only of the pounding of my heart, and the crunch of the crusted snow beneath my nailed boots. Far above, on the last slopes of the pass, some black figures appeared, moving slowly and jerkily, like marionettes operated by tired hands. They approached a sorry little procession of exhausted men. Wood Johnson was with them to cheer them on. He, too, was very tired. He said it had been necessary to *drive* them over the pass. They were so tired, he said, that they had sat down and asked to be left there to die in the snow. He had himself been forced to carry loads up the last slope to the pass. Both physically and mentally he was worn out with the strain. If we others had known difficulties of this sort were likely to arise, we would, of course, have remained behind to help, but we had not known, although in view of the trying day it had been even for unladen Europeans we might have guessed.

Three or four of the porters could hardly stagger, but we supported them as well as we could, cheering them on and telling them that they had but a short distance to go. Several loads had been abandoned on the pass, but there was one grey-haired old man, who looked the oldest of our porters, who, although in bare feet and as exhausted as any, steadfastly refused to abandon his load. To him it was a point of honour to get it to camp at any cost. I wish I could remember his name. So we continued down the snow slopes towards the camp, a little army of exhausted men.

All the peaks were livid now, and the reflected glare of the sunken sun illuminated the snow-fields in a weird opalesque afterglow.

Leaving the others, I hurried on to the camp, and rousing it, returned with men carrying lanterns. It was quite dark by the time we had got back to the tired porters. Willing hands relieved them of their loads or supported their faltering steps. It was bitterly cold as we stumbled down the last ice-glazed rocks to the camp.

The poor old man's bare feet were frost-bitten, happily not seriously, and he and the remaining stragglers were completely exhausted. It was only due to Wood Johnson that the casualties were not more serious. Thus ended the march over the Kang La.

The weather maintained its promise, and the next day dawned fine. Eberl decided he would take advantage of it, and return to Darjeeling and Calcutta. His leave of absence was not long enough to permit of him coming to the Base Camp, and he could not afford to take the risk of being held up by bad weather returning over the Kang La. We parted from him with regret.

The sun glare of the previous day had done its work only too efficiently, and I awoke conscious that my face was a temporary ruin. Edward Whymper in

Scrambles Amongst the Alps gives a harrowing description of the effects of sunburn:

> They have been scorched on rocks and roasted on glaciers. Their cheeks – first puffed, then cracked – have exuded a turpentine-like matter, which has coursed down their faces, and has dried in patches like the resin on the trunks of pines. They have removed it, and at the same time have pulled off large flakes of their skin. They have gone from bad to worse – their case has become hopeless – knives and scissors have been called into play; tenderly and daintily, they have endeavoured to reduce their cheeks to one uniform hue. It is not to be done. But they have gone on, fascinated, and at last have brought their unhappy countenances to a state of helpless and complete ruin. Their lips are cracked; their cheeks are swollen; their eyes are blood-shot; their noses are peeled and indescribable.

Wood Johnson had not unnaturally suffered most, for he had been far longer exposed to the sun, and in his anxiety for the porters had neglected to look after his face. The non-mountaineering reader may think I am making a lot of this affliction, but those who gently brown, either artificially or naturally on the sands of Margate or the Lido, have little conception of the truly dreadful state that the Himalayan sun reduces the countenance to. Anyone who has ever experienced the agony of eating and smiling, or the sleepless nights it may cause will have good cause to remember it. As a Doctor once remarked to me: 'Take a man straight from England, and sit him for a few hours without clothes on in the middle of a snowfield in the sun, and he would most probably die.' I believe he would.

The previous evening I had eyed the snow-fields around with that sort of longing that every ski-runner knows. Now I determined to try my luck on ski. We had brought with us ski for every European member of the party. Made by Schuster of Munich, they were a compromise in length and weight between ultra short and summer ski as used in the High Alps, and standard length winter ski. The wood was hickory, and the bindings detachable clip-on ones, of a breed not familiar to me, a compromise between Huitfeldt and Alpina.

Unfortunately, however, these bindings had already left in one of the porter loads by the time I was ready to start, and like Dr. Richter I had recourse to string, and odd lengths of yak-hide thongs. The porters watched my preparations with intense interest. I think they thought that the ski constituted part of some flying machine by the aid of which the sahibs would alight on the summit of Kangchenjunga. In the narrow forest paths, their porterage had been an irritating and difficult business, but the porter carrying them had treated them with the utmost care and respect. Had he known that they were not part of a flying machine he might possibly have been tempted to throw them away.

Dirty faces grinned expectantly as I fastened them on. Willing hands helped to tie the cat's cradle-like bindings of odd bits of string. At length I was off, shooting down the slopes into the middle of the snow-filled valley. The snow was board hard, with a delightful loose crystalline surface into which ski could be edged. It was very similar to early morning spring snow in the Alps, but in the Alps a two or three inches deep surface of crystals is only experienced after a snowfall; normally, the surface is conducive to skidding, and the traverse of steep slopes is tiring. But on this Himalayan snow which gains its crystalline surface from the heat of the midday sun, any swing is possible, from the Telemark to the stem Christiania.

The running was of its kind the most perfect that I have ever experienced. Would that it had been longer. As I glided down the valley I was scarcely conscious of movement only the procession of mountains on either hand, the gentle slush of the snow beneath my ski, and the breeze meeting my face suggested it. I felt Einsteinian. It was I who was stationary, and the world that was slipping away beneath me.

The valley floor dropped in another pitch; it was necessary to make downhill swings. I became more conscious of movement, and movement swift, fierce, exhilarating. Some porters were marching down the side of the snow. I swooped past them in tremendous style, leaving them gaping in wonder. My triumphant progress was short lived. Suddenly both ski came off together. The world ceased to slip; it revolved with great velocity and in revolving dealt my nose a shrewd blow. I arose; my neck was full of snow, and my mouth full of hard words. From above was borne down faintly a roar of laughter; the prestige of the flying machine had vanished for ever.

We descended from winter into spring. A softer air lubricated our tortured countenances. There were patches of grass and dwarf rhododendrons, whereon we flung ourselves down for a few moments of delightful repose. We turned a corner. Below was the emerald green Alp above Tseram, where Mr. Freshfield pitched his camp thirty years previously. Behind were the snow-clad peaks of the Kang La. Over the ridge to the north we could see some glittering summits in the neighbourhood of Jannu, forming the culminating points of acute ice ridges, defended beneath by ribbed curtains of blue ice. They looked, and probably are, unassailable.

The vegetation became more luxuriant as we descended. Small flowers peeped shyly out between the boulders of an ancient moraine. Everything was green and glad in the sunlight. A rough path led us gently downwards to Freshfield's camping site.

Since Yoksam, our camping sites had been poor ones. It was pleasant, therefore, to find a level pasture of dry, springy turf on which to pitch our tents. Around were woods of firs and giant rhododendrons. The air was permeated with sweet scents. Near at hand the voice of a crystal clear stream babbled a friendly welcome. Majestic snow-clad peaks stood watch and ward over this little Eden.

At one end of the pasture a new hut, constructed of rough-hewn timbers, intended for yaks and their herds, had been built, but of the yaks and herdmen, or more important, the Nepalese Subadar, whom we had hoped to find waiting or us with coolie food, there was no sign. Doubtless, our coming had not been observed, and it was possible that the Subadar might be waiting for us in the hamlet of Tseram, which was some twenty minutes' walk farther on. But it was not so much the beauty of our surroundings to which we first turned our attention, as to the great wall of snow- covered peaks to the north of Tseram and the Yalung Valley, peaks very similar in steepness and general appearance to those hemming in the Gastern Valley, near Kandersteg in the Bernese Oberland. Did the way via the Mirgin La to Khunza lie over this wall? We knew that we must cross the Mirgin La, but the map and Mr. Freshfield's description had not led us to expect anything so formidable in appearance. Already, the Kang La had forced us to realise how great was the task that we had embarked upon in attacking the Nepalese side of Kangchenjunga.

Coolie food was running short, and it was imperative to find the Subadar without delay. Accordingly, that afternoon, Wood Johnson and I set off for Tseram.

A rough path oozing with snow-drifts led down the mountainside, through a tangle of giant rhododendrons into the Yalung Valley. Less than a year previously, the young American, Farmer, had passed this way with his porters *en route* to the Yalung Glacier, whence he made his attempt on Kangchenjunga which ended so tragically. We had received a telegram asking us to make every possible enquiry and search for him, and in particular to visit the Decherol Monastery, which, according to the map, was situated some distance up the Yalung Valley, below the terminal moraine of the Yalung Glacier. A quarter of an hour's walk brought us down to a muddy torrent, flowing from the Yalung Glacier, which we crossed by a small bridge. During the flood season, Himalayan torrents must be immense. The width of the torrent bed, and the jumbled confusion of great boulders carried down by the flood waters bear witness to what the Yalung River is capable of, but now it was no bigger than an Alpine torrent from a glacier of moderate size.[2]

As we ascended the north bank of the stream, a head rose cautiously over a large boulder. We shouted a greeting, but it abruptly disappeared, and its owner, a boy, bolted precipitately as though all the devils of the district were at his heels. There came a furious clamour of dogs, and a few instants later we approached a rude hut, long and wide-eaved, with the boards of its roof weighted down with stones. A wizen-faced old man wearing high Tibetan boots and a dirty black robe girdled at the waist came forth to greet us. Behind him was his wife, twisting her fingers in shyness and embarrassment, while eyeing us half fearfully with narrow, dark, restless eyes, under a tattered fringe of hair. Close at hand, two savage Tibetan sheep dogs strained at the cords with which they were fastened to stakes in the ground.

The old man was the yak-herd of this remote valley, and if being dirty constituted good yak-herd-man-ship, he was certainly efficient at his job. There was no question of any high-water mark round his neck, for no tide had ever penetrated as far. Yaks were obviously his great enthusiasm in life. He smelt of them too. His wife was, if anything, dirtier and more odorous.

From them we learned that the Nepali Subadar had been staying at Tseram waiting for our arrival for some time, but not hearing anything of us, he had gone down the valley the previous day. This was most unfortunate we must find him and obtain coolie food at all costs. The best man for the job was our Gurkha, Tikeram Thapa, and we arranged with the old man for the loan of his son as a guide. Meanwhile, should our coolie food run out entirely, there were always the yaks. We were told that their owner, who lived in the lowlands, had kindly sent up a message to say that if necessary we could slaughter one. If possible, however, we wished to avoid feeding our coolies on meat, as they are vegetarians, and meat has a deleterious effect on them.

We asked the yak-herd for information regarding Farmer. He was not able to tell us much. Farmer and his porters had not passed through Tseram itself, being unwilling to attract attention owing to the fact that they had crossed the Nepalese frontier without permission. They had avoided Tseram by traversing the rhododendron-clad hillside above that hamlet. As for the Decherol Monastery, that had been a ruin for thirty years or more. This was all he could tell us, but we decided if we had time, we would go some distance up the valley and attempt to discover traces of Farmer.

The evening was chilly, and we adjourned into the yak-herd's hut. One end of it was reserved for yaks, the other end for the yak-herd and his family. A mass of dirty straw, alive with fleas, was the family couch. At one corner were piled some sacks of grain, rough cooking utensils, and wooden drinking cups. The rough and uneven floor was paved with stones and dried mud. A fire of rhododendron wood was burning on a primitive stone hearth, but as there was no chimney the smoke had to find its way out through chinks in the roof, a process more efficient in theory than in practice.

The old man and his wife, and two or three of our porters, who had come down from the camp, squatted round the fire, and a greasy looking concoction was brewed, but fortunately, we were spared having to drink it. It was a scene simple and primitive, that will live in my memory. The last gleams of sunset filtered through the cracks; there was a glimpse of forest and mountain. Is happiness to be measured in terms of modern invention? Was not this old man in his old hut, through the chinks of which he could watch the sunset and the stars, with his simple philosophy and his yaks, happier than many dwellers in a city?

In the last light we walked back to camp. A profound quietude enwrapped mountain and valleys. Below, the lazy smoke from the yak-herd's hut lifted gently upwards, mingling imperceptibly with the night. For the yak-herd and his family it was just the end of another day, the passing of another spoke in the wheel of life.

That evening after dinner we sent for Tikeram, and acquainted him with the urgency of the situation. He was keen and willing to start at once. 'I am here to help,' he said, and set off at once on his journey through the night, guided by the yak-herd's son with a lantern.

Whether or not we were forced to remain at Tseram until food arrived, it was essential to rest the porters. It is not too much to say that we had arrived, a dilapidated party in health and morale. Several of the porters had bruised or cut feet, and one or two, including the plucky old man who had refused to abandon his load, minor frostbites. Worst of all, a number of them were suffering from snow blindness. There was no real excuse for this, for they had been issued with snow glasses, but the native is sometimes both careless and improvident. Snow blindness is, as I know from personal experience, extremely painful. Its first effect is by straining the optic nerve to put the vision out of focus. A profuse discharge follows, and the eyes ache abominably. It is impossible to open them in the light without severe pain, as the light seems to strike them almost like a blow. Fortunately, ordinary snow blindness is as brief in its effects as it is painful, and two or three days' rest and treatment are usually sufficient to effect a complete recovery. Our porters, however, did not know this. They thought they were dying, or about to become completely blind, and it was a pitiable sight to see them cowering beneath their blankets, pathetic bundles of humanity, outside Dr. Richter's tent.

News came that Hannah and Wieland were in difficulties. Their porters, not unnaturally, had refused to traverse the Kang La without boots. The next day, therefore, we called for volunteers to return over the Kang La to carry boots to their help. Thirty-seven of our best men immediately responded, and were sent off under the charge of Lobsang.

The situation was certainly not promising. Every day was of vital importance, and here we were relegated to Tseram for an indefinite period.

That morning, Kurz left early to map the lower portion of the Yalung Glacier and Valley. He returned later, confirming the statement of the yak-herd that the Decherol Monastery was indeed a complete ruin.

Had it not been for our anxiety over the transport, and the painful state of our faces which made eating a misery, and sleeping difficult, we might have enjoyed our four days enforced rest at Tseram. To while away the time we rigged tape between two upright poles, made a quoit from rope, and played deck tennis. Even at such a moderate elevation as 10,000 feet, we found this somewhat strenuous, but exercise had the excellent effect of quickening acclimatisation.

That evening Wieland arrived, and acquainted us with the situation on the other side of the Kang La. It was not a good one, but we knew that we could rely upon Hannah and Lobsang to get their men across. For the rest, everything depended on the weather. Actually some of Hannah's men had already arrived, carrying light loads, having marched direct from Dzongri.

On April 20, Wood Johnson and I, with Nemu, who had accompanied Farmer, to show us the way, visited the Yalung Valley to search for traces of Farmer. From Tseram a rough track traverses the north side of the valley. It was evidently the former route to the monastery, for we passed a number of rude walls and shrines covered in inscriptions.

Like most large Himalayan glaciers, the Yalung Glacier terminates in a great moraine some 1,000 feet high. Above this, the glacier is moraine covered for so great a distance that Lobsang, who was with Farmer, told us that they had had to march for three days before they trod ice.

It was while resting after lunch on the slopes of the valley near the terminal moraine of the glacier, that two curious incidents occurred. The first was an earthquake shock, the same shock I believe, that was experienced in Turkestan and which we afterwards saw mentioned in the newspapers.

The second incident was an amusing one. As we sat smoking, we saw something moving in the valley beneath, half hidden by a huge boulder. Whatever it was, it seemed too large for any animal likely to be met with thereabouts. Nemu, however, had no doubts upon the matter, and fell on his belly with a frightened whisper of 'Bad Manshi, Sahib! Bad Manshi!' (Bad Men, Sir! Bad Men!)

This was interesting; were we at last to meet one of the redoubtable Snow Men in person? Lying flat and motionless behind the rocks we peered intently down into the valley. For perhaps ten minutes we gazed, and we were beginning to wonder whether what we had seen had been a mere figment of imagination, when suddenly with majestic tread out walked – an enormous yak. Needless to say, we burst into a roar of laughter at poor Nemu, who had been trembling with terror, but his superstitions were not to be so easily over-ruled. He declared that like other of our porters he had on several occasions actually seen the Bad Manshi, and described them as being huge men, white skinned and naked, but covered with thick hair.

Native temperament is childlike in many respects. Given work to do, or some object in life to fulfil, our porters were happy, but after having been left to their own devices for two or three days, they were only too liable to get into mischief, or work up some imaginary grievance. Among our porters were one or two men who, had they lived in England, would make admirable paid labour agitators or "tub thumpers" in Hyde Park. As it was they did their best to stir up strife among the rest of the porters, and to a small extent they succeeded in deluding the more credulous.

That evening, we were eating our supper in the Mess Tent, when there came an excited babble of voices. We took no notice of them until we had finished our meal, then Wood Johnson went outside. As usual, the trouble had originated with a few of our more unreliable porters. The Sherpas and Bhutias stood eyeing the scene passively, if curiously. A few minutes later, thanks to Wood Johnson, the agitators were slinking away amid the laughter and jeers of the remainder of the porters. The trouble had arisen simply owing to Narsang forgetting to issue a ration of sugar. To get behind the native mind would indeed be to get behind the mind of a child.

Late that evening, Tikeram Thapa arrived with the welcome news that he had found the Nepali Subadar, and that the latter was coming up to Tseram the next day, bringing a few local porters with loads of coolie food. Tikeram, told us that he had marched over twenty miles down the valley in the night, guided by the yak-herd's son, although he had fallen and damaged a knee. It was a capital bit of work.

The same evening we made the discovery of the bottle of rum which as previously mentioned had been accidentally substituted by Tencheddar for a bottle of Worcester Sauce. Despite the transport thorns besetting our way, we went to bed happy that night.

The following day we decided to shift the camp to Tseram, and carry as many loads as possible up the mountainside above in preparation for the start to Khunza. Diplomatically, we had made friends with the yak-herd by presenting him with a number of empty tins, which he had obviously coveted, and as a result he was willing to guide us to Khunza by a route over the Mirgin La that was well known to him. In such a remote part of the world an empty condensed milk or bully beef tin obviously possesses a very definite value.

The hillside above Tseram scarcely belies its apparent steepness. It is steep, but nowhere dangerously so. We returned to find the Subadar had arrived. He proved to be a thin-faced, sad, somewhat anaemic-looking man with a long, straggling, and ill-nourished moustache. He was clothed in baggy white breeches and a black jacket. The only indication of any rank was the Nepalese coat of arms in gold above his turban. He seemed a cultured and educated man. We told him of our labour agitators, and he proceeded to tell them exactly what he thought of them. Making a number of comments on their ancestry, their personal appearance, and their chances of future salvation which, if he was to be believed, were nil, he ended up by telling them that the Maharajah of Nepal, whose country they were now in, had given orders that every assistance should be given to the expedition, and that he, the Maharajah's representative, was there to see it done. If, he concluded, it was not done, there was always the time-honoured custom of chopping off a few heads. There were no more labour troubles.

CHAPTER NINE

In Unknown Nepal

WE BROKE CAMP ON April 22. After the enforced inaction of the past few days, it was a relief to be again on the march. It was a brilliant morning and fragrant odours of sun-warmed firs and flowers permeated the still air as we trudged up the hillside. We emerged from the forest on to open slopes of grass and boulders. There we were greeted by Kabru, and for the first time found ourselves gazing at its eastern face. Thus early in the morning it was in deep blue shadow, but the reflected light from the snow-fields of the peaks opposite across the Yalung Valley revealed the clean-cut edges of its hanging glaciers, and lit with a greenish sheen its icy steeps and snowy mouldings.

If Kabru turns a serene and benevolent countenance towards Darjeeling it has, like a two-headed giant, another face, and this face which overlooks the Yalung Glacier is savage and cruel. Even as I watched there came a distant roar, the snowy lips of the giant writhed back, and an avalanche was spat out from between its teeth. A mere puff of white dust it seemed at that distance, and only the thunderous roll of its falling told of the tens of thousands of tons of grinding ice blocks crashing down thousands of feet to the Yalung Glacier. As though ashamed at the meaningless ferocity of its twin brother, a cloud was detached from the warm, sunny face of the mountain, and was wafted gently over the ridge. Dispassionately, it slid along the precipices, growing larger as it did so and finally wrapped the mountain in a soft, grey shroud.

It was not long before we came to the snow. It was still frozen hard, and I determined to hurry on to try and obtain a glimpse, and if possible, a photograph of Everest. The mountainside which appears from Tseram a smooth, unbroken face topped by small, rocky summits, is in reality broken up into subsidiary ridges and valleys, and rounding a shoulder, I found myself in one of these snow-filled valleys leading upwards to the first of a series of snowy cols we must cross.[1]

As I mounted the snow slopes, I saw over a low ridge to the left a solitary peak rising above a sea of woolly clouds. In shape its summit was a symmetrical sugar loaf like the Zermatt Weisshorn, and to the north and south its ridges swept down in graceful parabolas to perfectly proportioned shoulders. It was Makalu, Everest's 27,790 foot neighbour. When Everest has been climbed, Makalu may defy many generations of future mountaineers, for it is one of the most terrific peaks in the world. By the time I had reached the col it had disappeared behind clouds welling up from the warm depths of the Arun Valley. Of Everest there was nothing to be seen.

[1] This first col is actually the highest point traversed between Tseram and Khuna and is 15,361 feet high.

From the col I looked across a desolate snow-clad hillside, broken into rounded shoulders and stony hollows. Here and there the snow had melted disclosing grass and straggling patches of dwarf rhododendrons. On one of these I had my lunch. The day was sunny, and the grey rocks warm to the touch. I was alone. Some may not appreciate the charm of solitude, but the true mountaineer, even if temperamentally of a gregarious nature, realises the value of occasionally parting from his companions in order to contemplate mountains as they should be contemplated, alone. On an expedition escape from one's fellows is seldom possible, not that one often desires it, but there are times when an inexplicable and fierce desire demands temporary release from the bonds of sociability.

I sat down, ate my lunch, and afterwards inhaled a contemplative cigarette, lolling among the dwarf rhododendrons, with my back fitting comfortably into a hollow of a rock. For a while I was merely a body clogged with an excellent lunch, gazing with peaceful digestion and bovine appreciation at the landscape. But presently and unexpectedly the dull pudding of my mind was stirred by the spoon of inspiration. I seemed to become a part of the hillside on which I was resting. I felt very old, and yet eternally young. The hills had been my companions through aeons of time. I had seen them created, raised, and fashioned by the forces of the earth. I had seen vegetation clothe them, and snow cloak them, ruin overtake their more fanciful and extravagant constructions. I felt that I had always lived with the hills, and on the hills, and that the hills had treated me kindly. How else could a man be born with the love for hills? There is eternity both ways.

Men came over the col, one after another, a string of them. The silence was broken by the clatter of voices. I did not resent their presence, for I had had my hour alone on the mountain.

The snow was soft and fatiguing to march through. For some distance the path to the Mirgin La contours the mountainside. It was a long, hard day for the porters, especially for those who had had to carry loads all the way from camp. Once I came across Nemu. From somewhere he had acquired a pair of truly remarkable breeches. As there were no fifty-shilling outfitters at Tseram, I was at a loss to imagine how he had got them, and Nemu himself never enlightened me on the subject. I say that they were remarkable breeches, because they did not look as if they were intended to be breeches at all. They were made of some curious balloon-like cloth, that hung down in loose folds like a collapsed parachute, and as Nemu walked, the breeches gave forth an important sort of swishing noise.

I think he experienced some mental strain in wearing them at first, for sahibs and coolies would gape at them, laugh, or make uncomplimentary remarks, but nevertheless he wore them in, as it were, until they became as much part of the expedition as Duvanel's beard, or Wieland's sunskinned nose.

But Nemu was by no means alone as regards eccentricity of costume. One porter boasted an officer's khaki tunic, another a bandsman's jacket, then there was a villainous looking fellow with what might have been once an old Etonian tie, and two or three who sported engineers' overalls. Everest equipment was still greatly prized, and one man possessed a pair of Everest puttees, ragged and worn, sacred relics of which he was very proud. Like ladies, they allowed their imagination to run riot in the matter of headgear. My own impression as to the constructive principles underlying the latest shapes in ladies' hats is that you take a perfectly ordinary hat, such as a Homburg, and then proceed to knock, kick, crush, and cut it in a fit of berserk fury. After such treatment, it is styled the latest mode or shape. This is precisely the treatment meted out by our porters to their own headgear. Any fashionable Paris hat designer, desirous of obtaining new ideas, can hardly do better than go on an expedition into the Himalayas, taking with him Sherpa and Bhutia porters.

We reached the Mirgin La, 14,853 feet, under a greying sky. Hailstones were falling, and from the east came an occasional thunder growl. Below, the snow slopes fell away into a desolate valley, ribbed with ancient moraines, like the embankments of a railroad fallen into disrepair. A few tattered prayer flags fluttered on the summit of the pass.

Viewed thus under a leaden sky, with light and shadow merged into one universal monotone, black-jawed crags jutting from livid featureless snow slopes, and a chill wind sighing through the gap, it was a depressing scene.

No depressing thoughts occurred to the porters as they breasted the pass, and they grinned broadly at the prospect of descent. Among them were several women, who had been with Wieland's party. In weight-carrying powers they were the equal of a man, and their powers of endurance were prodigious. These women did much to keep up the spirits of the porters, and relieved the tedium of the march with many verbal leg-pulls and jokes which, according to Wood Johnson, it was fortunate the "Memsahib" did not understand. Now, one of these women, with a load on her back, sat herself down in the snow, and commenced a glissade down the steep snow slopes. For a few yards all went well, and she slid slowly and with dignity, then suddenly a hard icy patch of snow supervened. She uttered a shrill scream as her speed suddenly increased. The next moment she spun round, something happened, and her skirt was blown up over her head. Her load went one way and she another, both rolling over and over to the bottom of the slope. A roar of laughter followed her from the assembled porters.

It was an easy matter descending these upper slopes, but tedious work lower down. There we encountered for the first time a type of soft snow that is fortunately seldom met with in the Alps, but which is, however, all too common in the Himalayas. It is not that it is simply soft, but the direct heat of the sun appears to have the effect of shrinking the snow beneath the surface, so that holes are formed into which the climber may sink up to the waist. For a few steps the surface crust may bear, and then, all at once, it collapses.

Walking under these conditions is extremely tiring and irritating, especially for laden porters, who sink in at almost every step. The Nepali Subadar, who was in front, was making very heavy weather of it. I came across him energetically digging in the snow with his hands to retrieve one of his shoes that had been left in a hole. Snow passes were evidently not to his liking and the wan smile with which he greeted me was in sad contrast to his magnificent bearing on the previous day. I offered him a chocolate biscuit as solace for his woes, but he was unable to eat it owing to his religious principles, which forbade the eating of food handled by anyone outside his own particular caste. Nevertheless, he eyed it wistfully. It must have been about this time that he got severe frostbite, which resulted in his nearly losing a foot.

Perhaps, it would be as well to explain here that there are three stages of frostbite. The first is merely a temporary numbness, a loss of circulation, which may be restored by rubbing or warmth. In the second stage frostbite manifests itself in blisters and swellings charged with fluid. And lastly there is the worst stage of all, in which the whole area affected usually the extremities, becomes gangrenous. In this case, amputation may be necessary. The Subadar most likely came from one of the warm valleys or plains in Southern Nepal, and was not able to resist the cold, as were our porters, with their more active circulation and thicker blood. Perhaps he had not even realised that he was being frost-bitten when one foot lost sensation.

As we stood in the snow, Dr. Richter and Kurz shot by on ski. Their progress was to be envied. At the same time, someone had to make a track for the porters. To have to walk oneself at the expense of considerable effort, and to be passed by someone else travelling with but little effort rouses the worst passions. It is like trudging along one of those incredibly dull by-pass roads on the outskirts of London, and being passed by fat, opulent men in luxurious motor vehicles. Of course, if you are one of the fat, opulent ones, your viewpoint is different.

Dense, black clouds were massing as we struggled down the valley. Spiteful stilettos of lightning stabbed the peaks, and thunder crackled like a giant shelling walnuts. Once I descended into a hole up to my chest between two boulders. One foot jammed, and I was unable to extricate it for a quarter of an hour. I mention this purely as a point worthy of note among solitary climbers. I have seen a man so trapped that it took half an hour or more of hard work, plus considerable ingenuity, to get his feet out from between two boulders. Death by starvation thus would not be pleasant.

We pitched camp on a miserable spot on the north side of the valley. Had it not been for the porters, we should have continued the descent, and camped below the tree line, but the day had been a heavy one for them, and it was necessary to camp at the first available place.

From our camp we looked across the Kangbachen Valley, in which, out of sight, lay Khunza, to a range of peaks rising to 21,000 feet. They were for the most part massive mountains, with indeterminate ridges, between which flowed steep and broken glaciers. Owing to a lack of definite ridges, and the consequent difficulty of finding a continuous route to their summits, they looked decidedly awkward of access.

The day ended wretchedly in a heavy snowstorm, whilst a miserable supper turned out by Tencheddar did little to alleviate the general gloom.

The clouds snowed themselves out during the night, and morning dawned clear and cold. With memories of Signor Sella's wonderful photograph of Jannu in Mr. Freshfield's book in our minds, we set off up to the ridge running southeast from the Sinon La, the last pass we must cross to reach Khunza. We found, however, that the ridge above the camp was only a subsidiary ridge of the main ridge. Some decided to go on, but Schneider and I favoured descent to the "flesh-pots" of Khunza.

A good path led up to the Sinon La, but we found that on the north side of the pass formed the head of a long and steep couloir filled with hard snow, which must be descended some distance. It was a place where a slip might well end fatally, and we stamped secure steps for the porters. A number of other snow-filled couloirs had to be traversed, after which we found ourselves in rhododendrons. Somehow, I was irresistibly reminded of the descent to Chamonix from the Grands Mulets. Not that there was much in common between the Chamonix and Kangbachen Valleys, except a certain trench-like monotony. The Kangbachen Valley is far wilder than the Chamonix Valley, and on either side rise peaks to an altitude of 20,000 feet or more.

We strolled down sunny slopes to the crest of an indeterminate ridge from which we looked down to Khunza, a little cluster of brown dolls' houses thousands of feet beneath, and far up the valley we must go towards the Kangchenjunga Glacier. But this view, fine though it was, had not the dramatic quality of the view up the Yamatari Valley to the east. Curving round the corner were the moraines of the glacier, which has its sources in the southernmost recesses of Jannu, and above rose a range of rock and ice peaks of terrific aspect.

One of the curses of being a mountaineer is that an analytical mind, trained as it is in seeking routes and estimating their relative difficulty, tends to detract from aesthetic enjoyment. In other words, the humble tourist, unversed in the art of mountaineering, is sometimes more able to appreciate the beauty and magnificence of a scene than is the mountaineer with his mind clogged with technicalities. But here was a scene so magnificent as to submerge the sharp, ugly rocks of analysis and technical considerations beneath the smooth rollers of pure contemplation. The thought of how these peaks might be climbed did not intrude. I did not see couloir or ridge and did not endeavour to win a theoretical way to a summit. Even Mark Twain would have put aside his telescope and been content to gaze up that sylvan valley with its background of stupendous ice peaks.

As I lay on the flat summit of a moss-clad boulder, something of my boyhood's simple adoration of the hills returned to me, that half wild yearning for an unattainable "something". It is a yearning that becomes dulled by time and experience. But such is the magical influence of the hills that sometimes they are able to recall it at unexpected moments, and this was one of them. However much a man may delude himself into thinking the contrary; he becomes as expert in his mental appreciation for the hills as he does in his physical appreciation for them. The unsophisticated moments of youth are to be prized and cherished.

We lunched and lounged in the sun, then plunged down through the rhododendrons by a steep zig-zagging path. Soon we were among the firs, strolling by the side of the torrent from the Yamatari Glacier. The path entered on to an open grassy glade, a smooth sward as flat as a cricket ground. What a cricket ground it would make too! With the dark fir woods as a natural boundary, and snowy mountaintops as pavilions – surely more conducive to century making than the dingy villas and gasometers of the Oval, or the sulphurous vapours of Bramall Lane.

We had found our way to this delightful spot easily enough, for the path had ended there, but we could not find any way out and down to Khunza for some time. Yet who would wish to escape from such a fairy glade? However, presently we crossed a little bridge over a stream, and found ourselves on a good track. At a turn of the path we could gaze down to the village, a trim little place, with neatly laid-out fields. It was strange to think that no European had passed through here for thirty years. It might have been a village in Switzerland or Tyrol.

Porters passed us. They were tired after two days hard marching, but they were cheerful at descending from the snows once more.

As we ran down the last part of the path, we were puzzled to see various little water wheels revolving in the streams. They seemed to have no practical use. Then it dawned upon us that they were prayer wheels. The inhabitants of Khunza are lazy but ingenious. Unwilling to expend time and energy in revolving prayer wheels by hand, they utilise the abundant water power of the vicinity, and had rigged up a number of water-wheels, on which are carved many prayers. Every time a wheel revolves, so many prayers are "said" for the village. Literally millions must go out every twenty-four hours, and if these prayers mean anything, the gods that dwell on the mountains round Khunza must look very favourably on its inhabitants.

Our camp was pitched on a flat field at the southern end of the village. The inhabitants eyed us with curiosity; small children stood round, sucking their thumbs in round-eyed wonder at these strange reincarnations of something or other that had come down from the mountains.

The Subadar had arrived early that morning; he had not camped with us, but lower down in the woods. We did not then know that he was frostbitten, and it was not until later that a gangrenous sore developed. Narsang was there too, having preceded us to arrange about food. Actually, he had done nothing, and the reason was plain to see; the hospitality of Khunza had proved too much for him. With magnificent optimism he declared that though no food had come up from lower down the valley, we could have as much food as we wanted, and unlimited coolies from Khunza. That no food had come up was a serious matter. We had hardly one day's coolie food left, and whether enough would be forthcoming from Khunza with which to carry on to the Base Camp was doubtful. The fact that there was no food or coolies available, as kindly promised us by the Maharajah of Nepal, was partly due to the slackness of the Subadar who had been sent up to arrange for it. He was aware of our intended route, and all he had done was to collect some food in the lower valleys several marches away. It was exasperating to be confronted with such difficulties when within easy reach of our goal, and Wood Johnson told the Subadar that if coolies and food were not forthcoming, we should have no option but to report him to the Maharajah. This threat had an immediate effect on the Subadar, and he at once informed the Head Man of Khunza of our requirements. We had no wish to deplete the village of food, but the Subadar said there was plenty to spare, and that to take it would mean no hardship to the villagers. We were, of course, prepared to pay a good price for it. The Head Man was, therefore, given a day in which to collect the food.

That evening several of us decided to call upon the Head Man, the principal reason being that Wood Johnson had promised us a drink of an intoxicating liquor known as marwa. The Head Man's house was a large building constructed on the chalet principle. Built of sturdy timbers, with a wide-eaved roof weighted down with large stones, it looked fully capable of withstanding any storm. On entering, we found that half the inhabitants of the village were present. In the middle of the floor a large log fire was burning, and round this we squatted, cross-legged on rugs. Presently, a mixture of water and fermented hemp seeds was brewed in a large cauldron, presided over by a withered old hag, whose wrinkled face and claw-like hands, illuminated by the ruddy glow of the fire, were positively witch-like. The atmosphere was heavy and close and a strong reek of smoke from burning rhododendron branches fought a losing battle against a stronger reek of unwashed bodies. Presently, the concoction was brewed, and was ladled out into cylindrical wooden metal-bound pots. These had a lid, in the centre of which was a metal cone, with a round hole through the top. Through this hole was thrust a bamboo stick up which the liquor had to be sucked. I cannot pretend to describe the taste of this drink, it is enough to say that it is by no means unpleasant and, taken in sufficient quantities, is decidedly intoxicating.

Heavy rain was roaring on the roof by the time we had finished, but we splashed back along the village "High Street" to camp happily enough singing the latest music hall airs.

Theoretically, the following day, April 24, was a rest day, but not for Wood Johnson, His was the disagreeable task of getting blood out of a stone, or in other words, food out of the Head Man. That individual, lulled doubtless into a sense of security by the patronage of his house by the sahibs the previous evening, had done nothing. Probably, this was due not so much to wilful neglect, as to native inability to appreciate the value of time. What mattered a week or two weeks, or even a month to the sahibs? What was their hurry? Why were they so anxious to undergo hardships on the mountains when every day was bringing the summer nearer? Such was his philosophy – the same sort of philosophy in these regions that decrees that when you are invited to a wedding you find it usually more convenient to turn up two or three months after the ceremony.

We repaired to the Head Man's house to find him peacefully tilling his garden. The Subadar was furious. He saw his reputation being destroyed; his authority set at nought, possibly even his head removed on his return to Khatmandu. After a volley of invectives, he grasped the cowering Head Man, seized some rope lying handy, and proceeded to lash him up to a post. 'Produce the food, or have your head cut off' – that appeared to be the gist of the conversation for the next few minutes. Of course we interceded. We had no wish for our way through Nepal to be littered with the heads of Head Men. Nevertheless, the situation was not without its humour. Imagine a portly and worshipful mayor of some British provincial town tied to a post in his own back garden, and told to supply a party of complete strangers with food, or have his head cut off in the event of not doing so. So the Head Man was released from his bonds. The thunder clouds disappeared from the brow of the Subadar, and Khunza slumbered peacefully in the sunlight once more.

That afternoon we visited the Khunza Monastery. This is situated outside the village on the West Bank of the Kangchen River. A rickety suspension bridge, the safety factor of which it would be scarcely wise to enquire into, spans the river. Entering a stone gateway, on which were carved the usual prayers, we passed through a forest of dilapidated prayer flags.

Khunza Monastery is a branch of the famous Khampa Dzong Monastery in Tibet. Normally, the Buddhistic religion imposes celibacy upon the Lamas, but so lax have conditions become at Khunza that from the Head Lama downwards, they intermarry with the villagers. There were also chortens. These are stone monuments erected in honour of some former Lama saint. On the summit there is usually a crescent moon, sun, or lotus, whilst sacred relics, such as the ashes of Lamas, are placed in a niche.

A Tibetan monastery is more in the nature of a village than a single group of buildings. For instance, about 8,000 monks reside at the De-pung (Rice-heap) Monastery near Lhasa. Compared to the great Tibetan monasteries, Khunza Monastery is, of course, small. Its wooden buildings are primitive, and display none of the grandeur of the great Tibetan monasteries. Passing along a narrow street, bounded by primitive two-storied houses, where circulated many varied and powerful odours, we were ushered through a doorway and up a flight of wooden steps, deeply furrowed with the passage of countless feet, into the monastery temple. As our eyes became accustomed to the gloom, we found ourselves to be in a barn-like room with uneven wooden floor. At one end gleamed little Aladdin-like oil lamps on altars, lighting the enigmatical face of a carved Buddha and effigies of former lamastic saints. The decorations were of the usual garish mixture of red and yellow, the beams across the roof and the pillars supporting it red and the tapestries and friezes yellow. Dozens of little lockers filled with sacred books lined the walls. Presently, the stairs creaked beneath a heavy tread, and the Chief Lama, a very fat man with a dough-like face and crafty smile, entered the temple.

On this occasion the hospitality consisted of some conventional devil dancing by a number of Lamas, but this was only the preliminary to a religious ceremony the purport of which was difficult to understand. Possibly it was intended as a blessing upon our expedition, but this was doubtful in view of our unpopular demands in the matter of food and coolies.

The ceremony consisted of numerous incantations by the Head Lama, accompanied by the monastery band, and repeated by the Lamas, varied by an occasional vigorous ringing of a small bell by the Head Lama. Sometimes the band would stop, and only the low mutter and wailing of the praying Lamas would be audible, like the rise and fall of wind in the rocks of a mountain-top. Put such a scene on the stage of a London music hall and it would scarcely induce anything but boredom, but here, many marches from the nearest outpost of civilisation, it produced a strange impression upon us. The crowding cares of the Twentieth Century seemed to fade away. We were back in a medieval land caring nothing for progress, a land fiercely jealous of its ancient rights, its conservatism looking askance upon modernity and the outer world. Perhaps it is happier so.

At the conclusion of the ceremony everyone was handed small quantities of rice and seeds which were cast into the middle of the floor. Among other things, the Head Lama showed us a knotted raw-hide whip, stained with blood, with which the Lamas are accustomed to keep order among the villagers, for they have the powers of life and death over the inhabitants of the district.

Much of the power wielded by the Lamas over the destinies of Tibet, Nepal, and Sikkim is due to their preying on the superstitious beliefs of the people. While on the expedition there was related to us a story concerning a certain high dignitary. The dignitary who owned a large and scattered estate decided to visit an outlying portion of it. There were, however, strong reasons why he should not do so. It appeared that a considerable portion of the revenue accruing from the estate had been pocketed by the Lamas of a neighbouring monastery. Therefore, he was told that there was a large and thoroughly malevolent devil who had taken possession of this portion of the estate, and that should its shadow fall upon him he would die an agonising and lingering death. Naturally the dignitary was loth to come to such an unpleasant end, and decided to postpone his visit. It was then that some ingenious person suggested that if he carried an umbrella the devil would be unable to cast its shadow over him. This idea was seized upon gladly, and the estate was visited under the devil-proof shelter of an enormous umbrella. It is to be hoped that the embezzling Lamas were brought to book.

We had with us our portable gramophone, and suggested that the Head Lama might care to hear some white man's tinned music. Thus it came about that for the first time in its history the religious gloom of the monastery was broken by Messrs. Layton and Johnstone and 'Sunny Side Up'. The Lamas gazed open mouthed for none of them had ever seen or heard a gramophone before, while the Head Lama forgetting his dignity squatted on the floor and gazed with great curiosity up the horn, seemingly under the impression that Messrs. Layton and Johnstone were the reincarnated voices of two holy English Lamas.

Before we departed our host insisted on our drinking large quantities of marwa. It was a more intoxicating brand than the Head Man's and the suspension bridge seemed to sway unpleasantly to more than one member of the expedition.

It was necessary to establish a provision depot at Khunza, and we decided to leave Tikeram Thapa in charge, for he had displayed considerable aptitude in the making up and paying of accounts. Meanwhile, the Subadar would go down the valley, and arrange for food to be sent up on the backs of local coolies. Such was the procrastination of the Head Man that the porters' food did not arrive until late that night. Fortunately, its quantity exceeded our expectations, and we finally turned in happy in the knowledge that with eight maunds[2] we had sufficient food to feed our porters for at least a week, and could carry on without further delay to the Base Camp.

The majority of the party were away early the next morning *en route* to Kangbachen. It was a perfect morning ; a myriad water jewels gleamed on the pastures of Khunza ; the peaks rose serenely into a stainless blue sky, little puffs of mist eddying enquiringly from their shadowed hollows and meeting with annihilation from a brilliant sun. Wood Johnson, remained behind to supervise the transport, and see that all the coolies were evacuated from the village. This last was important, because our men had not unnaturally made the most of their rest at Khunza. If the Sherpa or Bhutia has any vices, the only one I know is predilection to strong liquor at any and every opportunity. But this is not so much a vice as another indication of their childlike disposition, for, like a child, they will eat and drink more than is good for them, without a thought as to the consequences. Unfortunately, they are liable to become quarrelsome when intoxicated, and at such times like an Irishman at a race meeting, they pick up the nearest weapon and proceed to run happily amok. Luckily, we had no serious damage done in this way, save for the porter stabbed at Tingling, and Dr. Richter was spared having to stay up all night, as did Mr. Somervell in the last Everest expedition, sewing up scalp wounds.

[2] One maund = eighty lbs.

The march promised to be a long one, but Wood Johnson, had the brilliant idea that he and I would ride on yaks. Accordingly, the Head Man was summoned, and told to parade the local yaks.

A yak was produced for Wood Johnson, Never have I seen a more inoffensive looking beast, and with its long hair and mild brown eyes, it might have been a child's toy. Personally, I felt a little doubtful about it, and remarked to Wood Johnson, that yak-riding was not numbered among my accomplishments. I also suggested that it would be unpleasant to be thrown over the edge of a mountain path. Wood Johnson's reply was contemptuous. He said: 'Walk if you like, *I* am going to ride. No tea planter has ever been known to have been thrown by a yak.' Suiting his actions to his words, he vaulted with Wild West abandon on to the back of the yak. Watching him do it, I felt that there was nothing that he did not know about yaks, and that he had ridden them since infancy.

For a few moments the yak stood peacefully. It turned its head and looked at Wood Johnson in a gentle, enquiring, pleading sort of way. Wood Johnson, sat nonchalantly, but then with the idea of getting the yak to move, he hit it. The yak *did* move. From a gentle, doormat-like creature it became suddenly possessed of seven devils. It commenced to tear rapidly round and round in circles and in the middle of one of these circles its back arched bow-like and Wood Johnson sailed through the air, alighting heavily on his back. He got up. The yak had stopped, it was nibbling a bit of grass, its mild brown eyes contemplating Wood Johnson, with a sort of gentle, pitying, reproachful look. In the background stood the Head Man, his face a mask of Eastern passivity.

A few minutes later I was walking along the path, having declined the yak that had been thrust upon me, leaving Wood Johnson, swearing that he would ride a yak that day, or perish in the attempt.

It was a delightful walk. The path lay through pinewoods and glades yellow with primulas. Pine tops vignetted glimpses of cathedral-like peaks. It was a morning overflowing with jollity and good humour. The little brooks hastening down the hillside towards the river gurgled and chuckled with merriment. Below in its rocky bed the river laughed more ponderously. The Pipes of Pan played softly in the treetops.

The path was so good for the first few miles that I was always half expecting to come across a Beer Garden full of fat men in shorts noisily drinking beer. Certainly, in Switzerland such a sylvan valley would have been so defiled every kilometre or so. There would have been red paint on the trees to guide the tourist from Beer Garden to Beer Garden. There would have been benches for them to rest upon, the pinewoods would have been cut down and laid bare in order that a view should be obtained from these seats, though this would have been unnecessary, for you could have bought picture postcards of the mountains, the coloured ones costing five centimes more than the plain. But here was a Switzerland unspoilt, Alpine beauty on a loftier, nobler scale, its paths traversed only by yaks and their herds.

Presently the path descended into the torrent bed, which is here nearly a quarter of a mile wide. Great boulders, some of them as large as cottages, are piled in it, their rounded smoothness telling of terrific floods that have carried them down like pebbles, rolling them over and over. Once the path passed through a considerable stretch of forest that had been blasted by fire, indicating that long spells of dry weather sometimes occur in these parts.

Some four miles from Khunza the stream was bridged. It would have shortened the day's march to have crossed it, and continued up the western side of the river, but not unnaturally we followed the route marked in Professor Garwood's map. judging from the stony banks of the torrent, the floor of the valley was composed of an ancient moraine, in which the present stream is busily engaged in carving out a larger and larger channel. We were given an unpleasant example of the speed at which this old moraine is being eroded when crossing a steep slope of loose stones more than one hundred feet high above the river, for boulders, large and small, were constantly falling down this slope, while some blocks of rock, weighing many tons, seemed ready to come down at any moment. It was not a place to linger in.

The path got worse and worse as we ascended, in places it was so overgrown with giant rhododendrons that it had to be cleared with *kukris*. Once we passed an enormous boulder fifty feet high at least, under which there was a cave with a fire blackened roof, and a small patch of cultivated ground outside which suggested that it was possibly inhabited by a hermit, for there was no grazing ground handy for yaks.

Finally, the path emerged from the forest, and we found ourselves confronted by the snout of the Jannu Glacier, which pushes a huge dyke of ice and moraine almost across the valley. Should this glacier advance and dam the streams from the Kangchenjunga Glacier and those of north-eastern Nepal, the consequences might be disastrous for villages lower down the valley.

The glacier snout is fully 1,000 feet high, and it was weary work clambering up its high moraine. Curiously enough, we were all feeling the effects of altitude, though the altitude was less than 15,000 feet. Mr. Freshfield remarked the same feeling of tiredness and listlessness between 14,000 and 17,000 feet. Is it because at this altitude the body undergoes a definite physical change? Acclimatisation would appear not to be gradual, but taking place in stages, though these stages are not necessarily at the same heights for everyone. There should now be enough evidence for physicists to be able to draw some conclusions. Personally, I was in addition still suffering from the effects of my chill, and I could scarcely drag my unwilling body up the wearying slopes of loose stones.

The afternoon mists had long since gathered, and cold, clammy vapours swirled over the drab stone covered hills of the glacier. It might have been difficult in the mist to have found the way over the moraine mounds, but for Tencheddar who had gone on ahead and built cairns every few yards. At length we reached the other side. The mists lifted. and we gazed down to the flat valley floor where stood the huddled chalets of Kangbachen. Seen thus beneath the mists, this barren and treeless valley, unrelieved by a single shaft of sunlight, appeared inexpressibly dreary. It was a scene that recalled to mind a similar evening in the Pass of Glencoe, when a low roof of mist divorced the world from its good wife the sun, and seemed to oppress me with a sense of gloom, foreboding, and death, so that I hurried through the grim defile, unwilling to linger on a spot rendered ghastly by its association with a fiendish crime.

But as I slithered down the moraine, a light pierced the gloom. A tiny window of blue sky was disclosed, and in it was thrust a summit, red hot from the furnace of the setting sun. It was Jannu, 10,000 feet above me. Even as I watched, the glow faded from it. For a few seconds, before the mists closed in again, it gleamed down palely white, like some nun, disdainful of the world, yet peering curiously upon it from some high window of an unapproachable convent.

There came a sound of yak-bells, a sound, at once homely and calling up memories of Switzerland. Gloom was replaced by cheerfulness. A small boy was driving the yaks back to Kangbachen from the neighbouring pastures. He was crooning a song to himself as he did so, a monotonous little tune of infinite repetitions. At Kangbachen, one day is but a repetition of the last, and music is but an echo of life itself. When he saw me the tune froze on his lips. I did not blame him, for what he saw was a villainous looking fellow, with a stubbly red beard, an old slouch hat, and an aged pair of plus fours. He might have been forgiven for thinking me an apparition, a Mi-go, or some other unpleasant and undesirable character. Having, however, after a critical scrutiny, assured himself that I was in reality, perfectly harmless, he jumped on to a yak, which splashed through the torrent leaving me wondering whether the latter would have suffered Wood Johnson.

I followed and arriving at the camping site found our servants had mostly got in before us, and my own tent already pitched. I was surprised to see Nemu washing something in the stream. On inspection, it proved to be a dishcloth with which he was wont to clean my plate, knife, and fork. As this dishcloth had already reached saturation point as regards grease and dirt, I wondered by what process of reasoning Nemu had decided to wash it at this particular hour and place, even though he had always a capacity for doing the unexpected. As one of the porters carrying some of my luggage had not arrived, and did not arrive until the next morning, it is possible that the washing of the dishcloth may have been simply to propitiate my probable wrath. The workings of the native mind are curious.

A number of the porters did not get into camp that night. This was largely due to the carousals at Khunza, and their inevitable aftermath of headaches. However they were quite happy bivouacking out in the woods around fires. Wood Johnson, arrived proud and happy, having with characteristic bulldog determination succeeded in mastering the yak and actually ridden it for the first few miles.

We awoke next morning, April 26, to see Jannu, and its attendant peaks, in all their magnificence. From this side there is no possibility of climbing Jannu, and nothing I have seen is more hopelessly unassailable than the terrific sweep of its northern precipices. The peaks to the south of the Jannu, Glacier and to the west of Jannu, though considerably lower, look equally hopeless. They are but acute wedges of rock, the ribs and ridges of which are plastered in ice that has been fashioned by time and weather into mere blades and biscuits. These peaks possess no main ridges, they are up-flung indeterminate wedges of extraordinary steepness and complexity and their ribs and ridges usually end in complete cut-offs, consisting of rock precipices, or hanging glaciers. Looking at such peaks, one is forcibly reminded of the geological newness of the Himalayas as compared to the Alps and other mountain ranges. They have not weathered sufficiently to present the mountaineer with feasible routes. They are still elemental and savage masses spat out by fire and eruption. Time has had little softening influence on them. Restless looking, inhospitable peaks they are, grand to look upon but evil to climb.

Kangbachen is situated at the junction of the Kangchenjunga and Thangchen rivers. The last named flows down a valley, which was formerly traversed by traders between Tibet and Nepal, but owing to political friction between these two countries, it would appear to have fallen into disuse. During what must have been more profitable days, Kangbachen must have flourished, and its inhabitants were most likely of good physique, but with the closing of this trade route, it was cut off from the world. Among so small a population, the evils of intermarriage soon manifested themselves, and at the present time a number of its inhabitants are cretins, not quite the ghastly type as depicted and described in Whymper's *Scrambles Amongst the Alps*, but nevertheless stunted, dwarf-like and seemingly possessed of but little intelligence. Several of them collected round our camp, and eyed it with curiosity. Two, a man and his wife, were but three feet high, and the woman carried on her back a baby almost as large as herself, which seems to show that physical development is arrested at an early age, judging from this couple, at the age of five or six. By no means all the inhabitants were thus stunted, and several of the children appeared quite normal and healthy.

It was desirable, if possible, to replenish our larder. Wild sheep were known to be in the vicinity, and as local knowledge might be helpful, we engaged an old gentleman, who styled himself the village Shikari.

Before breaking camp, I went a short way up the valley for some photographs. I had not walked more than two hundred yards from the village when, on turning a corner, I found myself face to face with a wild sheep. He was a fine specimen, with a splendid head, and had I taken with me a rifle, I could have shot him easily, as he stood staring at me without moving for more than a minute. But soon fear overcame his astonishment and curiosity. With a tremendous and agile leap he was away up the hillside, and in a few seconds was lost to sight among the grey boulders.

It was impossible to leave Kangbachen early that morning, owing to many of the bivouacking porters not having arrived. The march from Khunza to Kangbachen had been a hard one for them, and it was necessary to give them an off-day, or at least a very short and easy march. At Wood Johnson's suggestion, therefore, it was agreed that they should have no more than three hours marching. This does not sound much, but with full loads of sixty to eighty pounds carried at a height of 15,000 feet, it was enough for tired men. The porters, having been told of this through Lobsang, were perfectly willing to go on.

Passing through the evil smelling, refuse strewn main street of Kangbachen, we found ourselves on an excellent path running along the western side of the valley. As yet, we had had no glimpse of Kangchenjunga, but some of its snow-clad neighbours were now visible far ahead up the valley. The snowfields of one peak in particular aroused our skiing enthusiasm. The path, in keeping with the usual evil habit of paths in this part of the world, presently petered out into a stony waste formed by the terminal moraine of the Kangchenjunga Glacier. In order to save time we had engaged several locals from Kangbachen who knew every inch of the way to the upper pastures by the side of the glacier where they are accustomed to graze their yak herds. Among these was the local milkman, or

Dhudwallah of Kangbachen whom we had engaged to bring up fresh milk to the Base Camp at regular intervals. This old man, who was to prove distinctly useful to us later on, was a picturesque figure. With his lined, seamed and weather-beaten face, he might have been any age, but his bright eye, and the speed with which he walked up the hillside on broken ground betokened the born hill-man. He was *exceptionally* dirty, and exuded a strong odour of yaks and other things, and more than one of us had qualms in entrusting the milk to his care. Also, he expectorated, a vice not common among natives, and expectorated with an accuracy of range, which I have seldom seen surpassed. This accuracy we hoped would save the milk.

As in the valley lower down, denudation had worn a deep rift in the old valley floor, but here the slopes of loose, insecure boulders were much larger – in places over a hundred feet high – and the danger of traversing beneath them was proportionately greater. Above these slopes, the mountainside at one place appeared dangerously unstable, owing to an outward dipping strata of rock. Rock falls were obviously not uncommon, and one of many tens of thousands of tons had only recently taken place. For more than a hundred yards we scrambled as quickly as possible over masses of scarred boulders. It was a relief to leave the vicinity, for though the risk of crossing such a place is small, it exists, nevertheless. In view of the communications that must be maintained and constant passage of porters up and down between the Base Camp and Kangbachen, it would perhaps have been better to have gone a longer if more fatiguing way round.

Wood Johnson, and I were last, and with such an easy march in prospect, we sat ourselves down on every convenient grassy patch, and lounged in the sun.

In its lower portion, the Kangchenjunga Glacier is so moraine-covered that the inexperienced might be forgiven for thinking that there was no glacier there at all. This stony camouflage has, indeed, often led travellers, and even surveyors, into the mistake of thinking that Himalayan glaciers are much shorter than they actually are. These moraines tell a tale of destruction, and their size alone is eloquent of nature's forces that are ever engaged in pulling down the proud peaks of the Himalayas.

As we ascended the valley, the scenery became wilder and the ridges on either side rose in height. Farther up the valley we caught a glimpse of Wedge Peak, with its amazing rock and ice precipices. Heavy clouds began to gather, the sun was obscured, the temperature dropped, and a bitter wind charged with snowflakes smote down from the snows.

The porters, believing that the march was to be a short one, had taken things easily, and Wood Johnson and I hurried anxiously on. But there was no sign of the others having stopped to camp. The weather worsened, it began to snow heavily. Evening was drawing on apace as we reached a little group of huts marked in the map as Ramthang, 15,431 feet. There camp had been made. The actual marching time for unladen Europeans had been about five hours.

The day ended with a heavy blizzard. Less than half the porters arrived, the remainder spending the night in the blizzard, many of them without shelter.

The snow lay over six inches deep next morning. Above the huts of Ramthang, the way lay over flat, stony pastures. With the new snow covering the ground, plus the hot sun piercing the dissolving mists, our faces were threatened once again with disaster. In a desperate attempt to save mine from further destruction, I donned a white cotton veil. I found little to recommend in it. It tended to produce a feeling of breathlessness, whilst it was apt to strain the eyes, thereby producing a headache. The latter disadvantage was, however, overcome by cutting holes for the goggles.

Presently, the mountainside became so steep that it forced us down to the Kangchenjunga Glacier. Himalayan glaciers have usually a convenient trough between the ice and the mountainside. Were it not for this trough, the ascent of most of them would be very tiring as they are usually very bumpy. To give some idea of the moraine-covered portion of the Kangchenjunga Glacier, I can only say that it resembles a road-mender's paradise, or a London thoroughfare that has been erupted by pneumatic drills.

It was curious how badly we were going at this moderate altitude. Kurz and I had our lunch together, and we both agreed that though we were only about equal in height to the summit of Mont Blanc, we were feeling the altitude more than we had ever done on that mountain. Possibly, it was because glacier lassitude is at its maximum in a glacier trough. Members of the Everest expeditions remarked the same thing in the trough of the East Rongbuk Glacier.

After lunch we toiled on again. The trough was lost in a maze of moraine mounds, and we toiled over miniature summits, and along stony valleys. Once more, with the coming of afternoon, the sky had clouded. It grew leaden, and a strong, biting wind hinted at another blizzard as we ground up a stony slope. Above was a flat shelf of coarse grass. Here we decided to make the Base Camp.

Wind and snow harassed us as we pitched our tents on the leeward side of a little knoll. It was a dreary welcome. All the porters got in that evening but they exhibited little enthusiasm at so doing, they were too tired. We crept into our sleeping bags with a flurry of snow beating on the tents. As I lay in mine, I thought over the events of the past three weeks. We had met and overcome certain transport difficulties, but these were by no means at an end. Difficulties of the route, and lack of time, had meant working the porters very hard indeed. On the last Everest Expedition they had been given one rest day in every four or five working days, whenever possible or circumstances justified it. Our porters had been marched for the first eleven days without a rest day, including a double march over the Kang La, a march, which must have stretched the physique of the fittest of them. The march from Khunza had also been a tiring one, whilst the march from Kangbachen to Ramthang is better forgotten. Would even our best men, the "Tigers", on whom so much depended stand up to the strains and hardships of Kangchenjunga?

CHAPTER TEN

Establishing Base Camp and Assessing the Task

THE TEMPERATURE DROPPED to zero Fahrenheit in the night, and the morning of May 27 dawned cold and clear. As I pulled aside the frozen tent flaps discomfort was forgotten. It was a morning of silver and blue; silver where the rising sun sparkled on the crystals of newly formed snow, blue in the shadows. Opposite the Base Camp, rising in one clean sweep of 8,000 feet above the Kangchenjunga Glacier, was Wedge Peak. It is appropriately named. Other mountains may be termed fanged, or sugar loafed, but Wedge Peak seen from the north is nothing more or less than a gigantic elemental wedge. It is a brutal mountain, possessing neither the structural massiveness of Kangchenjunga, nor the fairy-like ethereal remoteness of Siniolchum. The last named mountain has been called the "Embodiment of Inaccessibility", yet who would think of Siniolchum in terms of accessibility or inaccessibility? It is too beautiful to be defiled by man. Wedge Peak is different; its very aggressiveness challenges the mountaineer to pit himself against it, yet what mountaineer would accept that challenge? Even as I watched, it flung an icy gauntlet to the glacier, and the still morning air trembled to the dull boom of an avalanche.

Look at it through glasses, if you will, and seek a way up the sliced granite precipices, but when your gaze has passed up these, it will halt aghast upon the ice slopes above. Even imagination will boggle at the thought of having to climb them, at cutting and cutting for hour after hour, and getting – nowhere. Even imagination slips and is cast headlong down the precipices. Turn to the skyline.

There ice, not ordinary ice, sharp-edged and unbroken, but ice hacked and tortured by the winds, clings to the ridges; thin flakes of ice through which the sun gleams with a cold fire; pinnacles of fairy-like delicacy, elegant busts, daring minarets, extravagant mushrooms; a strange goblinesque procession, drunken and tottering, frozen in a downward march.

I tore eye and mind away. Eastwards rose The Twins peaks, more staid and comfortable, not merely elemental and savage, but displaying that dignity and grandeur of the nobly proportioned and adequately buttressed. Framed in this magnificent gateway is Kangchenjunga. It is farther away, but distance enhances rather than detracts from its intrinsic grandeur, so great is its scale. It is built up of icy terraces one above the other. Rock cliffs separate each terrace. Glaciers rest on the terraces, their lower edges forming ice walls anything up to 1,000 feet in height – tiers of fortifications guarding the precipices from assault.

If the difficulties of Wedge Peak are blatantly obvious, those of Kangchenjunga are less obvious. At first sight, the difficulties of Kangchenjunga on this side fail to impress. Glancing at the apparent angle of the mountain, with its sloping snow-covered terraces, one tended to exclaim involuntarily 'It will go!' But, gradually, as first general impressions were superseded by a closer analysis, optimism was ruthlessly uprooted; the easy became difficult, the difficult impossible, and the impossible appalling.

The face of the mountain is nearly 10,000 feet in height. Compare this to some of the greatest alpine mountainsides. The southern side of Mont Blanc rises 11,000 feet from the Val Veni, yet compared to Kangchenjunga, this cannot strictly be called a genuine mountain face, for the lower part of it is grass and forest covered, whilst it is broken up into a series of ribs and ridges radiating from the summit of Mont Blanc. The west face of Kangehenjunga is a mountain wall of almost equal height, rising not from a green valley, but from a glacier, and cloaked in snow and ice. To compare Kangchenjunga with the Alps is like comparing a pygmy with a giant. But it is the only possible form of comparison, and the only one, which the reader unacquainted with Himalayan conditions will be able to appreciate. It is a better comparison than to state that it is equal to so many Snowdons piled one on top of another, a comparison which only vaguely suggests height. Height and scale can only be thought of in terms of a more direct comparison.

The view we were looking at was similar to that seen by Mr. Freshfield. His camp, however, was a little farther up the glacier, on the corner he calls Pangperma, where the Jonsong Glacier unites with the Kangchenjunga Glacier. One thing was very clearly impressed upon us at the start, and that was that if such an expert mountaineer as Mr. Freshfield considered that Kangchenjunga offered the greatest chance of attack on this side, it must indeed be a formidable mountain.

There is probably no great peak in the Himalayas on which so much snow is precipitated every year. Strictly speaking, it is not on the main watershed of the Himalayas which separates the arid plateaux of Tibet from the northern states of India, it juts out like a rugged peninsula from the main mountain coast. The Everest group is on the main coastal watershed, and by reason of the intervention between it and the plains of India of many inferior ridges, receives the south-west monsoon after much of its fury has been spent. Such hills as there are separating Kangchenjunga from the plains are not high enough to break the monsoon, and the mountain, and its satellite peaks, receives almost the full force of it. It would be interesting to know what the annual precipitation is on Kangchenjunga as compared to Mont Blanc. It is possible that the amount of snow that falls on the upper part of the mountain is two or three times greater than that of the Alpine giant. Only evaporation prevents the glaciers of Kangchenjunga from extending far down into the lower valleys.

Mr. Freshfield's analysis of the possibilities of this side of Kangchenjunga, was a shrewd one. He considered that the greatest difficulties would be experienced on the lower part of the mountain. Once the upper terrace immediately under the highest summit had been gained, he considered that the final climb would be practicable. 'The mountaineer,' he writes, 'should search to the left between the saddle, which connects Kangchenjunga and The Twins.' Unfortunately, this saddle is hidden by the shoulder of The Twins, and he did not see it. Had he done so, his report could not have been anything but a pessimistic one, and we, in all probability, would not have planned an attack on this side of the mountain. As it was, we hoped to find a way on to the North Ridge, which connects the highest summit to The Twins.

Though Mr. Freshfield considered that the Kangchenjunga Glacier was the most likely line of attack, he was seriously under-estimating the difficulty of the mountain when he wrote that 'the peak is hardly likely to be gained with less than two nights spent on its actual face.' We estimated that a minimum of six camps would be required. It is necessary to add, however, that when Mr. Freshfield made his journey, little was known about the effects of great altitude upon climbers, or the difficulties of snow, ice and weather above 23,000 feet. On Everest six camps were established above the Base Camp, and Everest is, technically speaking, an easy mountain. Kangchenjunga is in everything but actual height an infinitely more difficult mountain than Everest.

The Base Camp was separated some five miles from the foot of the western face. At this distance it is difficult to form a just estimate of mountain difficulties and dangers. Also, we were not far enough away to escape the illusive effects of foreshortening, or near enough to be able to see whether or not a route might be found even up the glacier, that was not likely to be swept by avalanches from the huge hanging glaciers of Kangchenjunga and The Twins. Mr. Freshfield found himself in a similar predicament when examining Kangchenjunga, and although of the opinion that the most practicable route existed on this side, wisely committed himself to no definite statement. While admitting that 'the whole face of the mountain might be imagined to have been constructed by the Demon of Kangchenjunga for the express purpose of defence against human assault, so skilfully is each comparatively weak spot raked by ice and rock batteries,' he was yet not prepared to say Kangchenjunga was not possible. 'Perseverance and good judgement may meet their reward.'

Our plan, then, boiled down to this, we must reach the North Ridge, if possible, at the lowest point – the col between Kangchenjunga and The Twins. We must climb this ridge, and make our last camp on the upper of three glacier-covered terraces, about 1,500 feet, beneath the summit under the final rock pyramid.*

There was one alternative, to gain the first or lowest terrace, and from it climb directly up the mountain face, past the second to the upper terrace.** If the first terrace could be gained, the upper difficulties did not appear to be insuperable. It was by no means certain, however, what sort of climbing would be found on the rocks and ice between the three terraces. Also, in the event of a heavy snowfall, retreat would be impossible, owing to the danger of snow avalanches for the obvious route between the terraces formed a natural funnel down which they might be expected to sweep. But the chief difficulty would be in gaining the lower terrace. So far as we could see from the Base Camp, the ice wall forming the lower edge of this ran without a break across the mountainside. Only on the extreme right did there seem any possibility of getting up to it, but even if this was accomplished, the mountaineer would be exposed for over a mile to the risk of ice avalanches while traversing to the left towards the second terrace.

Kurz had previously suggested this route, but one glance at the mountain was enough, it was hopelessly and desperately dangerous. Owing to the interposing

* The way followed by the 1979 party (Doug Scott, Peter Boardman, Joe Tasker and Georges Bettembourg).

** The face taken by several ascent groups in the 1980s and now considered the Normal Route.

shoulder of The Twins, we could not tell whether or not the lower ice wall petered out to the left, but the general lie and form of the mountainside suggested that it swept right round to beneath the col between Kangchenjunga and The Twins. A prolonged examination revealed the disturbing truth that there was no chance of successfully attacking any portion of the mountainside visible from the Base Camp, and that any direct assault on the face from the head of the main Kangchenjunga Glacier was foredoomed to failure. The only hope was that held out by Mr. Freshfield, that rocky shelves might lead easily upwards from the Eastern Tributary of the Kangchenjunga Glacier to the col between Kangchenjunga and The Twins. The fate of the expedition would be decided by what lay round the shoulder of The Twins.

It was a fascinating, yet depressing view. It was fascinating to let eye and mind wander over that huge mountain wall, to pass up the granite precipices, and over the defending bastions of gleaming ice, resting finally on the summit where the streamers of wind-blown snow were being torn off by the westerly wind. But it was depressing to think that where the eye wandered easily, the body could not follow.

The weather had relapsed into a capricious vein. The morning was a beautiful one, and under the warm sun the snow vanished as one looked at it. But towards midday dank, snow-charged clouds began to gather. A cold and hostile wind was signalled, and came rushing up the valley; snow began to whip across, frothing the ground.

A Base Camp must be something more than a starting point, it must be the G.H.Q., the hospital, and provision dump of an expedition, and not least, the peaceful haven at which tired and worn-out climbers can recuperate their strength. In fact, the psychological importance of a good base camp to a Himalayan climbing party is great both to Europeans and porters.

The thick, peaty turf lent itself admirably to the building of huts for the porters. Duvanel, Wood Johnson, and myself were the leading surveyors, architects, and builders. A piece of ground was levelled, and the construction of a building that was to serve both as a cookhouse and porters' quarters was commenced.

The methods adopted by Wood Johnson and myself were primitive. Having prised out stones, we piled them on top of each other filling up the intervening spaces with clods of earth. Duvanel, however, was not so easily pleased. He displayed a praiseworthy and unexpected aptitude for the work. With that meticulous accuracy and attention to detail that are such admirable qualities in the Swiss, he proceeded to build a wall that will stand through all time. Not for him clods of earth piled higgledy piggledy, but stones that fitted into one another; and corners that *were* corners, and not tottering masses of stones and turf.

At length the task was completed. With a large sheet of canvas stretched from wall to wall as a roof, and with a low front, it presented such a curious pavilion-like appearance that it inspired me to nail to it a notice that read, "MCC Members Only".* Then we stood back with a sigh of satisfaction to admire the result of our labours. But the next moment a puff of wind came up the valley, and the whole front of the pavilion, which had been constructed by Wood Johnson and myself, collapsed, leaving Duvanel's wall alone standing. Perhaps our type of architecture was too Gothic in its conception; Duvanel's was Norman, and so

* Marylebone Cricket Club – a hallowed British institution.

his wall stood. Generations hence, when the descendants of Sir Henry Lunn and Mr. George Lunn run fortnightly tours to the Pangperma Palace Hotel and Kangchenjunga, people on their way to the Helicopterdrome for the ascent of Kangchenjunga will pause and gaze in astonishment on Duvanel's Wall. Honeymoon couples will sit under it in the moonlight, and hoarse-voiced local guides will bellow opinions and lies as to its origin and antiquity.

A day or two after we had dug ourselves in, a large pole was carried up from below Kangbachen and various prayer flags were affixed to it, not only as a propitiation to the gods in the future, but in expiation for our crimes in the past. Most important of these latter was the releasing of sundry devils by the rash removal of stones during our building operations. It appeared that the sole function of stones is to act as a shelter for devils, and by moving stones we had evicted any number of them. As a result they were highly indignant with us, and unless propitiated might wreak dire vengeance upon us.

A special medicinal tent was allotted to Dr. Richter, the atmosphere of which soon became impregnated with the unpleasant and insidious odours associated with the profession of medicine. During the march Richter had trained one of the porters in elementary first aid. This man had been presented with a Red Cross armlet, the psychological effect of which, combined with Richter's teaching, had produced such an excellent effect, that he had become quite expert in the art of applying iodine and bandaging.

Soon after we arrived at the Base Camp we were submitted to the usual tests of breath holding, pulse rate, lung pressure and capacity, etc. Though the height was but 16,500 feet, I found that I was still unacclimatised, and could only hold my breath for twenty-five seconds. It is interesting to note that three weeks later, at a height of 20,000, I was able to manage thirty-five seconds.

Acclimatisation is, of course, one of the most important factors in high Himalayan climbing. In the short season available for attempting peaks such as Kangchenjunga and Everest. It is very desirable that the climber should become acclimatised as quickly as possible. Whether a climber climbs better after he has become quickly acclimatised or slowly acclimatised is doubtful. Experience on Everest would seem to show that the likeliest man to reach the summit is not the man who acclimatises quickly early on in the expedition, but the man who acclimatises so slowly that he is at his best towards the end of the expedition. The experience of Mr. Odell on the last Everest Expedition affords an interesting example of a man who acclimatised so slowly that he was not at his best until nearly the end of the expedition, at which stage he was fitter than those who acclimatised earlier.

Against slow acclimatisation on Everest and Kangchenjunga must always be set the all-important factor of time. We could not reasonably expect more than a month of good weather in which to attempt Kangchenjunga, and even, this short period might well be curtailed by the early breaking of the monsoon.

It was with this in mind that Dr. Richter had devised two methods, which he hoped, would aid the climbers in acclimatising quickly. The first was by withdrawing 200 cubic centimetres of blood from each climber. The object of this was to lessen the blood pressure, in order to counteract to some extent the low pressure of the atmosphere.

Mountain sickness (lack of acclimatisation) is due not only to lack of sufficient oxygen in the air, but to the low pressure of the atmosphere as compared to that to which the body is accustomed normally. This low pressure reacts unfavourably on the blood and nervous centres, producing headaches, general lassitude, and in some cases, nausea.

These ill effects are automatically countered by the body, which increases the number of haemoglobins in the red corpuscles of the blood. So far as it is known, it is only by increasing the number of these haemoglobins that the body is able to adapt itself to the low pressure and lack of oxygen at high altitudes. It was difficult, therefore, to see what practical use withdrawal of blood could be. For one thing, taking such a large quantity of blood away must inevitably result in a temporary weakening of the body, and therefore the climber's powers. Also, it is well known that the body quickly remakes and replaces any blood that has been lost. At all events, I refused to part with my blood, and so, too, did the rest of the party with the exception of Professor Dyhrenfurth and Duvanel. The first, no doubt, through a sense of duty towards the scientific objects of the expedition, and the latter because he seemed to like it. The remaining members withstood the doctor's vampirish entreaties for their blood.

There was more to be said for the second experiment. The state of an acclimatised body at a high altitude closely resembles the effect of anaemia at a normal altitude. Anaemia is a poverty of blood due to the lack of red corpuscles and haemoglobins, but it has been found that ordinary liver eaten by the patient has the effect of increasing these, and thereby the quantity of blood. The mountaineer at a high altitude suffers not so much from poverty of blood, but from a lack of the essential haemoglobins. It was hoped that eating a concentrated liver preparation would have the effect of increasing these haemoglobins and hastening acclimatisation. High altitude also induces wastage of the body, so that anything which would strengthen the blood is advantageous. Therefore, each climber was presented with a bottle filled with tablets of concentrated liver, three of which had to be taken three times a day. I regret to say that being somewhat absentminded by nature, I took mine for only two days, after which I usually forgot to take them at all. Sometimes, however, I would find the bottle in my pocket, or at the bottom of my rucksack, and I would then swallow a large number of tablets at once in an endeavour to make up for what I had forgotten. Such irregularities are to be deplored, and it is to be feared that the liver tablets were not so beneficial as they might have been had I taken them more regularly. Schneider was, however, meticulous as to taking them, and I used to see him rolling his ration meditatively round his tongue, instead of swallowing them as per instructions, after meals.

In the evening we would gather in the mess tent, where, muffled up to the ears in sweaters, we would eat our dinner and endeavour to preserve some semblance of cheerfulness while wind and snow beat without. In order to delude ourselves into thinking that we were really enjoying life a porter would be told off every evening to work the gramophone, which he would keep in full blast for the duration of the meal. Once or twice the temperature was so low that it froze up the vitals of the gramophone, which after slowing down into a dismal dirge, would finally stop altogether with a protesting groan.

It was necessary to remain at the Base Camp some days in order to rest the porters, and prepare the plan of campaign. As yet, owing to the non-arrival of the second and third parties, we were still without much necessary equipment, and what news there was as to the state of the transport was not altogether satisfactory. In fact it seemed probable that the delay to Colonel Tobin's bandobast on the Kang La, which had been caused by bad weather and lack of porters, owing to desertions from our party and our consequent inability to send back sufficient help, might result in a serious shortage of food. It was, therefore, decided to slaughter a yak, which had been sent up from Kangbachen. I felt sorry for this yak, for it was a depressed looking beast, and its sad brown eyes seemed always to follow us about piteously, as though aware of its impending fate. Wood Johnson was its executioner, and the fell deed was done with Professor Dyhrenfurth's rifle. Although Wood Johnson tried on several occasions to get near to wild sheep it must be confessed that this was the only useful rifle shooting accomplished, unless the assassination of a tame pigeon at Khunza is included.

On April 29, we decided to explore two peaks, both of about 20,000 feet, to the north of the Base Camp. It was arranged that Wieland should tackle one and Wood Johnson and myself the other. The weather was good when Wood Johnson and I set off up the stony moraine slopes above the Base Camp. From the crest we had an excellent view of our objective, a cone-like peak with a sharp summit of snow, which formed the culminating point of a long rock ridge set at a comparatively easy angle.

We halted for some minutes in the sun to enjoy the glorious panorama of Kangchenjunga and its neighbouring peaks and glaciers. From the Tent Peak to Wedge Peak nothing was hidden, save only the two upper tributaries of the Kangchenjunga Glacier, and in particular, the bay of the Eastern Tributary Glacier and the slopes to the North Ridge, on the feasibility of which so much depended. The upper ridges were smoking with blown snow telling of a fierce westerly wind. One silvery banner from the crest of Kangchenjunga streamed far out against the blue sky. Since we had arrived at the Base Camp we had not seen the mountain unassailed by wind. Was it always so, we wondered. The chances of climbing the North Ridge in the face of such a relentless opponent would be nil.

Himalayan peaks are cruel. The Alps are the "Playground of Europe", the Himalayas the Playground of the Gods. The Alps provide physical and aesthetic enjoyment, the Himalayas, the fiercer joys of achievement. In the Alps, when you have climbed a mountain you want to climb it by other routes, to explore every ridge, tramp every glacier to make a friend of it. You get to know its moods, learn to appreciate its weather vagaries. There is nothing friendly about a Himalayan peak. You feel that it is coldly hostile, that it resents intrusion. It allows no latitude and seizes upon the slightest mistake. It will kill you if it can. And so if you climb it, you climb it only to conquer it for the sake of achievement. To do so you may have to mortify the flesh, steeling yourself to overcome bodily and mental weariness. When you have reached its summit you have finished with it. There is no desire to renew acquaintances, or make a friend of Himalayan peaks, they resent familiarity. And always they will kill you – if they can.

How is it that the mountaineer should gain such an impression? Is it merely the height, the scale, the distance from civilisation, the weather, and the clearness of the atmosphere, the unknown? Theoretically, I suppose a combination of all these things. Actually, you cannot help feeling that these peaks are imbued with a fanatical hatred towards the intruder. They are as conservative in their attitude towards modernity and progress as the humans who dwell in the valleys beneath them.

We continued on our way, passing under the snout of a small glacier that descends from the north-west slopes of Cone Peak, as we subsequently called it. This glacier is very broken, yet there were a few crevasses in it. The ice, which is curiously stratified, was hummocked and pinnacled, for its surface had been raised and broken by internal pressure. There were few actual crevasses, and many of the ice pinnacles were markedly bent. In the Alps such bending would be impossible without a fracture, and one is led to the conclusion that Himalayan ice is more plastic than Alpine ice. This plasticity is doubtless due to an enormous range of temperature.

Toiling up a slope of scree, we found ourselves on the crest of an easy rounded ridge of loose stones, leading upwards towards the summit. We began to experience wind, and worse still, the weather began to cloud up for the usual afternoon snowstorm.

Wood Johnson and our two servants, Ondi and Nemu, whom we had taken with us, were going slowly, but my own progress, was funereal. Though we were but 18,000 feet or so above sea level, I was feeling the height severely. Every step was an effort, and every flat stone suggested a rest.

Snowflakes began to whip across, stinging our cheeks with their icy particles. Grey mist rags writhed over the ridge. We donned our spare clothing and gloves, and with heads bowed to the blast, struggled on.

The hog-backed ridge narrowed to a nearly horizontal ice ridge, abutting against the summit cone of rock and ice, which rose steeply for perhaps 200 feet. With crampons it would have been an easy matter to have walked along the crest, or on one side of this ice ridge, but without them we had to cut steps. The ridge was not possible on the side sheltered from the wind, and the crest bore the brunt of its fury. We were forced, therefore, to cut along the exposed side, which consisted of steep unbroken ice slopes falling to the glacier beneath.

We tied on the rope, and leaving the porters in a sheltered place under some boulders, advanced to the attack. There was nothing to break the cruel force of the wind. But if it was cruel it possessed one good attribute, it completely banished my lassitude. I felt fit for anything, fit enough to cut steps for hours in the ice.

I cut steps as quickly as possible, until the whole length of rope between us was out. It was Wood Johnson's first experience of ice-work, but he is an excellent rock climber and his sure-footedness precluded a slip. The wind was no longer blowing steadily; it was coming in gusts of increasing strength that threatened to blow us from our steps. Our clothes were becoming sheeted in ice, and our fingers were rapidly losing sensation. Retreat was inevitable. With axe picks driven well in at every step, we slowly descended the ice to the friendly rocks. According to an aneroid, we had reached a height of 20,000 feet, about 150 feet from the summit.

Our servants were glad to see us back, for sheltered from the wind, as they were, it had nevertheless been a chilly wait for them. After slow movement on the ice, it was a relief to feel the blood circulating again in tingling fingertips. We rattled down the easy ridge. It had been an interesting experience. If this wind at 20,000 feet had been sufficiently strong and cold to turn us back; what would such a wind be like on the summit ridge of Kangchenjunga?

We arrived back in camp to find that Hannah and his porters had come up that day. Wieland had been more successful than us. His peak had proved a lower and easier one, and he had reached the top without difficulty, and descended before the storm broke. As this peak was to the west of ours, he had been able to look into the Eastern Tributary of the Kangchenjunga Glacier, but his report of what he had seen was not encouraging. There were no easy rock shelves leading to the North Ridge. A cirque of sheer cliffs and hanging glaciers walled in the head of the glacier, apparently barring approach to the North Ridge. With the arrival of Hannah and much of the vital equipment necessary for establishing the high camps, Professor Dyhrenfurth decided to start on the morrow. He hoped to establish Camps One and Two. The route to the North Ridge would have to wait until a closer inspection would enable us to estimate its difficulties and dangers.

The weather would have to improve a lot. At present, it was still wintry. Only with its aid would Kangchenjunga be climbed.

That evening, Wood Johnson harangued the porters. He said, 'You have had a hard time, you will have a much harder time, and you will be faced with privations and dangers. Let any man who wants, go back to Darjeeling.' None did. They replied with burst after burst of cheers.

CHAPTER ELEVEN

The Great Ice Wall

WE LEFT THE NEXT MORNING, May 1, in good weather. The party consisted of Professor Dyhrenfurth, Kurz, Woodland, Duvanel, Wood Johnson, and myself. Hoerlin, Schneider and Dr. Richter were to follow in a few days; the first two were not fit, and had been bothered by stomach trouble, whilst Richter was suffering from a strained heart. Hannah also was to follow in a day or so, and remain in charge of Camp One.

Whether or not the rest at the Base Camp had been as beneficial to the health of the party as had been hoped was doubtful. It is a curious fact that during the whole expedition we never felt really fit at the Base Camp. Probably, it was not so much the altitude as the damp and boggy ground on which it had been pitched, and the relentless winds and snowstorms that chilled us every afternoon. At all events, we were glad to leave it, and get to grips with our opponent.

In order to get on to the middle of the glacier, we had to thread our way through moraine mounds; the route had, however, been facilitated by the cairns made the previous day by Schneider and Kurz, who had visited the glacier for mapping purposes.

For a considerable distance the gradient of the Kangchenjunga Glacier is a gentle one, and in five miles it does not rise more than 1,500 feet. The day before, Wood Johnson and I had noted a snowy corridor running up the middle of the glacier, which seemed to offer an easy route and this we gained after negotiating the maze of moraines.

As we marched on up the glacier, the mountain wall began gradually to shut us in on either hand. We were passing through the portals of an immense gateway into another world. Kangchenjunga gained in magnificence as we approached the foot of its northern face. From the Base Camp the edges of its hanging glaciers had looked but a few feet high, but now we began to appreciate their real scale – huge walls of ice hundreds of feet in height. Once there came the sound of an avalanche from the icy recesses of the great mountain; its deep growl echoing menacingly from peak to peak seemed to threaten us for our invasion of these solitudes.

The corridor, at first wide, became a narrow trough through ice hummocks. The sun poured down upon us a fierce heat in which the snow became more abominable every hour. Once again we experienced the energy sapping effects of glacier lassitude.

Progress was slow, but there was no need for hurry, save at one place, where we were forced by the roughness of the glacier under the cliffs of The Twins. Here, the glacier was liable to be swept occasionally by ice avalanches discharged from a hanging glacier and we hurried across a level stretch, which was strewn with fallen ice blocks.

The way became rougher. Presently, there came into view an unknown mountain to the west, about 23,000 feet high, situated between Wedge Peak and the North-West Ridge of Kangchenjunga, on the watershed of the western tributary of the Kangchenjunga Glacier and the Ramthang Glacier. Between it and Wedge Peak a steep glacier flows downwards to join the main ice stream of the Kangchenjunga Glacier. It is a serene and stately mountain, with icy ridges converging to a summit of purest snow. So impressed were we by its beauty, that we named it Madonna Peak. This name was, however, subsequently changed by Professor Dyhrenfurth to Ramthang Peak.

The Indian Survey authorities have wisely decided to adhere to native nomenclature in the Himalayas. They are justified in doing so by the fate that has overtaken the peaks of the American and Canadian Rockies, where anyone with any pretensions to fame, and sometimes none at all save to be the first to tread a summit, has dubbed his name (or it has been dubbed by admirers) to inoffensive mountain tops. Only in very exceptional cases is there any justification for this. Among these may be mentioned the case of a member of the Alpine Club (Mr L.S. Amery), who, hearing that a peak had been named after him, considered it his duty to make the first ascent.

We were anxious to see round the corner of The Twins, and up the Eastern Tributary Glacier to the North Ridge, but soon we saw that the glacier dropped so steeply above its junction with the main ice stream of the Kangchenjunga Glacier that no view would be obtained until we had mounted some distance up it.

The first object was to find a suitable place for Camp One. It was necessary to camp out of range of ice avalanches from The Twins and Kangchenjunga. The most level site for a camp was under the cliffs of The Twins, but as this was by no means safe, we were forced to pitch camp some way out on the glacier itself. Here the glacier was very rough, and there were several crevasses near the camp artfully concealed by snow. Professor Dyhrenfurth fell into one of them up to the waist. It was a deep one, and he was unroped. Had all the snow-bridge given way, the odds are he would have been killed.

A few yards from the camp we discovered another deep crevasse running in the direction of the camp itself. Determined probing, however, failed to reveal any crevasse actually under the camp, so that there seemed reasonable hope that we would not disappear into the bowels of the glacier in the middle of the night.

We were a happy party in camp that evening. Happier than we had ever been at the Base Camp. The feeling of lassitude so often experienced at the Base Camp had disappeared; we felt fitter and stronger. Most important of all, we were sheltered by Ramthang and Wedge Peaks from the abominable afternoon winds. Only an occasional puff stirred along the snowy surface of the glacier. Higher it was different. Far above, the icy bastions of Kangchenjunga jutting defiantly out into space thousands of feet above our heads like the prows of some ghostly mid-aerial fleet were being lashed by tortuous columns of snow spray. Thin shreds and sinuous tendrils of blown snow writhed from the crest of the North Ridge. Sometimes they would rise steadily, like smoke from a factory chimney on a calm day, the next moment they would be captured by the vortex of a local whirlwind, and drawn upwards convulsively, to vanish into the deepening purple of the evening sky.

For once the weather was kind to us. The evening snowstorm was a mild, desultory affair, lacking its usual venom. The sun gleamed through the gently falling snow, illuminating its crystals, until they gleamed like showers of diamonds distributed by the prodigal hands of the mountain fairies. At sunset, the clouds rolled back, leaving only light grey skirts of mist that clung to the knees of the peaks. The peaks took to themselves the splendours of evening, and the snow around us gleamed opalescently with their reflected glories. We stood outside our tents entranced, and mindless of the cold. Blue deepened to purple, purple to inkpot. Stars glittered frostily; the low mists dissolved into the night. It was very silent, yet not quite silent. From somewhere came a sound, more felt than heard, like the distant surge of Atlantic breakers heard from far inland – the wind.

There was no mess tent, and we ate our dinner lying in our sleeping bags. A candle placed on my tin-box served to illuminate my own abode. At regular intervals the honest face of Nemu, with its habitual slightly worried expression, thrust itself between the flaps, and two horny hands would press upon me such delicacies as the cook thought fit to inflict upon us. These included portions of the yak Wood Johnson had shot, but I found them only suitable to sharpen a knife on for the next course.

I awoke next morning to see the sun stealing across the glacier, pushing before it the cold shadow of The Twins. With a short march in prospect, nothing was to be gained by starting until we were thoroughly warmed up. During the expedition, we did not once have occasion to leave a high camp before the sun had risen. To have done so on many occasions would have been to have courted frostbite, and it was doubtful whether the porters could have been induced to start until the life-giving rays of the sun had cheered them.

Professor Dyhrenfurth had brought with him a small horn, of a pattern not unlike those used on foreign railways as a signal for the train to start. With this horn he was wont to arouse the camp in the morning. In theory, the three blasts which he used to blow on it were the signal for climbers and porters to tear themselves from their sleeping bags. In practice, Wood Johnson and I would, if it happened to wake us, turn over with a sleepy curse and enjoy another forty winks. Finally, Wood Johnson managed to steal it, but shortly afterwards another one was produced. However admirable the intention, there is something abhorrent in being awoken thus on a mountainside in the morning. A more human method is for the leader himself to go round to the tents shouting into each one, 'Get up, you lazy louts,' or some such appropriate remark.

Leaving Camp One, we set out up the glacier, and soon reached the foot of the Eastern Tributary Glacier, which rises steeply from the main Kangchenjunga Glacier for some distance. Under the cliffs of Kangchenjunga it is considerably broken, and pours over a low rock cliff, down which the unstable ice topples hourly with thunderous roars. Under the cliffs of The Twins it was less broken, and extensively moraine covered, and we mounted it without difficulty.

Wieland and I were leading. Anxious to see the head of the glacier, and solve the problem that had been exercising our minds, we climbed as fast as possible. The going was simple, nothing worse than an occasional step to chop out. The slope eased off, and we stepped on to a level terrace of snow.

Leaning on our ice axes, we regained our breath, gazing upwards at the same time. What we saw was doubly disappointing. Before us, the glacier rose in unbroken snow slopes set at a moderate angle, yet steep enough to obscure all but the crest of the ridge connecting Kangchenjunga, to The Twins – the ridge we must gain. But what was visible was very unpromising. Here were no easy rock shelves and snow slopes, but sheer ice-armoured precipices. Only the north-westerly angled part of the face, directly beneath the highest summit of Kangchenjunga seemed to offer any hope. If the lower terrace could be reached, it might be possible to establish a camp there, traverse to the left, and climb a slope of 1,600 to 2,000 feet to the crest of the North Ridge. The slopes leading upwards from the end of the terrace did not seem so excessively steep as those dropping directly from the North Ridge to the glacier. Yet, we were looking up and foreshortening had to be taken into account, so it was likely that the climbing would be decidedly difficult.

But how to reach the terrace? Did the ice wall defend its whole length? If so, what was the alternative? We were in a horseshoe of mountains. From Kangchenjunga on the east to The Twins on the west, the precipices swept round without a break. The sole alternative to attacking the North Ridge via the terrace was to retreat. Discussions and opinions were unnecessary. Optimism's flower was already withered as we trudged up the snow slopes.*

The glacier here forms a trough into which the sun was beating with piercing intensity. To have gone up its centre would have meant lassitude in its most disagreeable form. On those concave snow slopes we would be like flies in the middle

* Following the first ascent of this flank in 1979, by way of the North Col Couloir (Smythe's 'ice-armoured precipes') and the North Ridge (the third ascent of the mountain), three separate lines have been established up the North-West Face. In 1981 a Japanese expedition forced a line directly up the face with a start roughly the same as the Great Ice Wall (a.k.a. "Ice Building") line tried in 1930; the "Ice Building" start was used in 1981 by the Chandler/Bremer-Kampf team, and also in 1982 by the Messner/Mutschlechner/Ang Dorje trio, but both these groups then moved up to join the North Ridge (the 1930 plan). In 1983 a German group led by Hermann Warth established a new start up the mixed face left of the "Ice Building" but right of the North Col Couloir (which they considered too dangerous). When above the initial ice cliffs they took a high right-trending diagonal line following couloirs and a final rock wall to join the 1979 line at the highest of the three great terraces.

of a burning glass. Accordingly, we traversed the northern slopes of the trough. Even on these the heat was bad enough, but it was relieved now and again by puffs of cold wind. We came to crevasses, only occasional ones, but cunningly concealed in places, with only a slight ripple or depression in the snow to indicate their presence, and once or twice, not even that. The snow was soft, and stamping a trail was hard work. We took turns at it; a quarter of an hour at a time was enough.

Already we were beginning to learn something of the secret that makes for good uphill walking at high altitudes; it is rhythm. Heart and lungs must keep in time with the movements of the legs. Each upward step must synchronise with the breathing. It does not matter how many breaths are taken to each step, as long as always the same number are taken. Once let this synchronisation fail, and it is necessary to stop and puff. The secret of maintaining it is a pace not varying by a fraction of a second in the interval of time elapsing between each step. To begin with, it is necessary to concentrate on the maintaining of this rhythm, but soon it becomes automatic. This is one reason why ground calling for a variety of pace is much more tiring to negotiate at a high altitude than ground on which the same pace can be kept up continuously. Above 20,000 feet it is much easier to ascend a snow slope in good condition than the easiest rocks, provided, of course, steps do not have to be kicked or cut.

As we rose, we were able to gaze up the Western Tributary Glacier. Like the Eastern Tributary Glacier, it falls in a steep icefall in its lower portion, but above the icefall unbroken snowfields rise gently to a low col separating Ramthang Peak from Kangbachen, the western summit of Kangchenjunga. Ramthang Peak itself rises gracefully, but seen from this direction Wedge Peak is less impressive.

Our pace was painfully slow, for quite apart from rhythm, or the lack of it, we were by no means acclimatised. Like the lower slope, the one we were on eased off on to an almost level terrace. Above the terrace the glacier rose again, but this time it was broken into an icefall which appeared to extend its whole width. We decided to camp on the terrace, for there seemed little chance of getting through the icefall the same day, and the porters, like us, were making heavy weather of it in the soft snow under the broiling sun.

Now at last we could see the whole of the face separating the North Ridge from the Eastern Tributary Glacier. Our hearts – I know that mine did – sank, as we gazed at it. There was no question of climbing it. The only possibility, if "possibility" it can be called, was directly over the ice wall, under the face of Kangchenjunga. This runs as a clean-cut barrier 600-800 feet high for some three miles across the face of the mountain, but under the North Ridge it is broken up into a series of ice waves and subsidiary walls. At one place a steep shelf sloped upwards from left to right, but above it towered a huge mass of unstable pinnacles that were liable to fall at any moment and sweep the shelf from end to end with their debris. Indeed debris lying on the shelf and below it showed that such falls were a frequent occurrence. Even had the shelf offered an easy climb, the steep ice of its lower and most dangerous portion would necessitate a staircase being cut. The sole remaining "possibility" was directly over the ice wall, where it was most broken, but I must confess that until it was pointed out to me as such I had not given it a second thought.

It was a pleasant spot for a camp. The sun lingered long upon us. The only drawback were one or two concealed crevasses in the vicinity, but we gave the porters strict orders not to go more than a yard or two from the tents.

Afternoon merged into evening, and the sun fought its daily battle with grey snow clouds. The cook was preparing the evening meal, and tempting odours were being wafted across the snow as, anxious to obtain some photographs, I strolled down the track for a short distance. Far beneath, the last half-dozen porters under the charge of Wood Johnson were toiling up the snow slopes. How small they looked, how painfully slow their progress. They halted; I heard a faint shout. Doubtless they were glad to be within sight of camp. Now they were moving again. I heard another shout, and then another; not so much a shout, as a curious high-pitched cry. This immediately struck me as strange. Men going uphill at nearly 20,000 feet do not waste their, hard-won breath in shouting. There came a whole series of these cries. They seemed to come from a distance of a mile or so away, in the direction of the cliff of The Twins. But between me and these cliffs the snow stretched unbroken, with no sign of any living thing on them. And still these strangely insistent, almost eerie cries came.

Wieland joined me, and we both listened. An eagle perhaps? Wood Johnson approached, and calling down we asked him if he heard them too. 'Perhaps it is a Mi-go,' he said, half jokingly, and then asked if Ondi, his servant, had arrived. I went back to the camp. Yes, Ondi had arrived, said the others. But where was he now? There was no sign of him. At that the truth began to dawn upon us and Wieland and I hurried across the snow in the direction of the cries. Soon we came across a single track, coming from the camp; there were no returning footmarks. We followed it cautiously. After a few yards the track ended in a small hole, not more than two feet across. Approaching it, we gazed down between the jaws of a crevasse. From the depths came a moan and a faint despairing cry.

We hastened back to camp. While Wieland returned with ropes and porters, I strapped on crampons in order to be ready to go down, if necessary. By the time I returned, a rope had been lowered. Fortunately, Ondi still retained sufficient presence of mind and strength to tie himself to it. With half a dozen sturdy porters hauling on the rope, he was soon dragged out. We quickly ascertained that he had no bones broken, but he had been badly bruised, his back and hands were skinned and bleeding, and he was half frozen and suffering severely from shock. He had fallen fully thirty feet before wedging between the walls of the crevasse, and had been down there for fully two hours. His extremities were white and numb, but we managed to prevent frostbite by massaging them. So severely was he suffering from shock, that, in the absence of Dr. Richter, I took upon myself the responsibility of giving him a double dose of belladonna. Whether or not this was the right treatment I do not know; at all events, it sent him to sleep in a few minutes, and when he woke up next morning, he was much better and no longer suffering from the physical effects of shock.

It must have been a terrible experience for him, and many men less tough would most likely have succumbed. The next day he was sent down to the Base Camp, but after two days there he insisted on returning. Such was the spirit of the man. But the accident had a lasting effect on him. Prior to it he had been an excellent servant in every way, after it he became morose and sullen, dirty and careless in his work. It was only towards the end of the expedition that he began to recover something of his old spirit. I hope that by now he has completely recovered from his terrible experience.

Night fell, accompanied by the usual snow flurry, but the weather next morning was perfect. Unfortunately, Kurz, who had been afflicted with ear-ache and general altitude debility which had rendered him unable to sleep, decided to return to the Base Camp. This he did for a large part of the way on ski. Professor Dyhrenfurth, also, was not feeling well enough to continue. This left only Wieland, Wood Johnson and myself.

As Professor Dyhrenfurth was anxious to attack the ice wall, it was necessary to establish a camp at the head of the glacier. It was, therefore, arranged that a day should be spent in working out a route through the icefall to the upper plateau of the glacier. With this end in view we set off in two parties, Wood Johnson and myself on the leading rope, with Wieland and a porter carrying a cine camera on the second.

Traversing first of all towards the cliffs of Kangchenjunga, we turned up a snowy corridor. The difficulties and complexities of the icefall proved far greater than they had appeared from a distance. First came a short, steep wall of ice. This ice, like all ice we subsequently encountered on Kangchenjunga, was of a rubber-like toughness, and many blows of the ice axe were needed to fashion a step. The work served to remind us once again that we were by no means acclimatised to even this moderate altitude, 19,500 feet, and I felt my ice-man-ship lacking in vim as Wieland, with a wicked grin, proceeded to post himself on a snowy hump and film my efforts.

Above this pitch we found ourselves on the lower lip of a huge crevasse, which appeared to traverse the whole width of the icefall. It was a formidable moat, several yards wide and not bridged by a single tongue of snow. Even supposing we got across it, it was by no means the only difficulty, for there were wider crevasses beyond equally formidable. As there was no possibility of crossing it on the left, I told Wood Johnson to anchor himself, whilst I explored as far as the rope would allow me to the right. The ice lip I was on writhed upwards sneeringly. There seemed little object in going on, but I gingerly ascended to its delicate crest. It was a happy move; for but a short distance farther did the icefall continue towards Kangchenjunga, before becoming lost in smooth snow-slopes offering no difficulty whatever, which led easily up to the plateau above.

We retraced our steps, and passing along the foot of the icefall, gained these snow slopes. There was certainly no difficulty in circumventing the icefall by this route, and a gentle walk took us quickly uphill. It was, however, not quite certain whether these slopes were entirely free from danger. Though we were separated by nearly half a mile of level snow-field from the foot of Kangchenjunga, the huge masses of hanging glaciers suspended on the great face of the mountain told of forces held in check which if released must result in avalanches of cataclysmic dimensions which might well sweep the whole breadth of the snow-field. Indeed, one solitary block of ice lying near at hand and projecting through the newly fallen snow seemed to make this unpleasant possibility very real.

The reader may think that I am making much of the problematical, but one of the first lessons the Himalayan mountaineer learns is that exceptional forms of danger are more likely to encompass his disaster than ordinary forms of danger.

In the Alps accidents usually occur through ordinary causes and neglect of ordinary rules. There is a certain mediocrity in alpine dangers; the mountaineer knows that in one place he may be in danger from falling ice or stones, and in another he is not. In a word, the Alps are a well-regulated mountain range. They have passed through so many geological epochs that they have acquired a certain staidness of demeanour. The Himalayas are different; they are not entirely divorced from their catastrophic epoch. Their scale is so vast, their weather conditions so different that they are still capable of producing the exceptional. Thus, I think it may truly be said that until the mountaineer has learnt to appreciate the huge scale of things and the catastrophic size of ice avalanches his chances of annihilation are infinitely greater than on the most difficult Alpine climbs.

Tacking up the snow slopes, we reached the little plateau above the icefall. Having satisfied ourselves that it was the obvious site for a camp we continued on up towards the ice wall. We had not gone far before we came across more artfully concealed crevasses. Wood Johnson went through into one, but I had him so tightly on a rope that I was able to jerk him outwards and backwards almost at the same instant. The snow was soft and fatiguing, and we decided that it would be best to return and save our strength for the morrow.

We descended quickly, and in less than an hour were back in camp. We had done what we had set out to do, to discover a camping site as high up the glacier as possible. We had also ascertained that there was no possible way to the North Ridge save over the ice wall and the lower terrace.

That night I was awakened several times by the sound of great ice avalanches. Heard thus, through the darkness, there was something indescribably menacing in their deep growls. It was terrifying to be disturbed from sleep in this way; one felt pitifully small and helpless amid these vast and wrathful mountains. The porters felt something of the same, but in a different way. In the avalanche they heard the voices of the gods, in the moan of the night wind the jeering of the Snow Men. Once I heard a mutter from their tent, a low intonation rising and falling – they were praying.

The morning of May 4 was warm, sunny, and windless. Professor Dyhrenfurth was not well; he was suffering from severe high altitude throat, and could only speak in a whisper. These throats are induced by the dryness of the air, and the necessity for breathing through the mouth. The throat becomes painful and congested. At its best it is a nasty infliction, and reduces climbing efficiency considerably; at its worst, it may be really serious. On Everest, Mr. Somervell's throat became so congested that he could scarcely breathe, and had he not been able to cough away the obstructing matter he might have been suffocated.

Professor Dyhrenfurth decided to return to the Base Camp. Before leaving he gave us his instructions. As the route over the ice wall was the only way to the North Ridge offering any hope, we were to make every effort to overcome it. We were to establish a camp on the terrace, and attack the slopes above it leading to the North Ridge. Once on the latter, there were two routes worthy of consideration to the upper terrace immediately beneath the final rock pyramid. The first lay directly up the ridge. Immediately below the terrace, however, which at its junction with the ridge formed an extensive scree shelf, the ridge rose in an abrupt step, which looked far from easy. The other route left the ridge below the step in favour of steep, crevasse-riven slopes on the east face overlooking the Zemu Glacier. By crossing these, the upper and easy portion of the great rib attempted by the Munich party would be reached, and this followed to thc tcrracc above the step. This route possessed the advantage of being on the leeward side of the mountain, and not exposed to the terrible west wind that constantly harries the North Ridge. On the other hand, the possibility of avalanches was not to be disregarded on this traverse, and the loose snow blowing over and off the North Ridge might well form wind slabs[2] of the most dangerous nature. If this was so, it would be best to keep to the crest of the ridge, but the great step below the upper terrace suggested something more than ordinary rock climbing difficulties, and by "ordinary", I mean the difficulties that a mountaineer may be expected to tackle with some degree of confidence at a height of 26,000 feet.

The reader must forgive me if the pictures I paint in his mind are done so with a brush steeped in the blues of pessimism, but the more we examined that huge mountain face, the more difficult and dangerous did it appear. Retreat in the face of such obvious difficulties and dangers would have been dishonourable neither to ourselves nor to mountaineering. After all, mountaineering is not to be classed with one of the modern crazes for sensationalism and record breaking at the possible cost of life and limb. It is an exact science, a perfect blending of the physical and the spiritual. It is not, and should not become, a desperate enterprise. There is no sport worthy of the name that has not its own peculiar risks, but no one has any business to walk deliberately into danger, and if risks are to be taken, they should be taken only by those who are fully alive to them.

Following our tracks of the previous day, we were soon up on the plateau. Leaving the majority of our porters to make camp there, and taking with us our personal servants only, we started off to the foot of the ice wall, accompanied by Duvanel with his little cohort of porters carrying various cinematographic apparatus and gadgets.

The snow had not improved since the previous day, and we sank in almost knee deep as we ploughed up the slopes. We kept as far as possible to the left, for the danger of ice avalanches sweeping the slopes to the right was obvious, and the ice blocks of former avalanches were strewn about them. Higher up, we were forced by some crevasses to the right for a short distance, but were soon able to traverse back to the left again.

As we approached the ice wall its magnificence increased. It towered over our heads, cold and green, in tier on tier of ice, laced and friezed with snow. Immediately beneath it was an almost level terrace of snow about a hundred yards in breadth intersected longitudinally by a large crevasse. As far as we could see there was only one bridge over the crevasse, and that did not appear particularly solid. Driving two spare ice axes into the snow, one on either side of the crevasse, we fixed a rope between them, which would serve as a safety handrail in the event of the bridge collapsing.

Beneath the lowest point of the wall was a clean-cut mass of ice some fifty feet high, under the shelter of which we sat down for a few minutes. It seemed a safe

2 The most treacherous form of avalanche: often found in the Alps during the winter months. The whole slope of wind-compacted snow comes away in a solid slab, which breaks up into a cataract of hard snow blocks.

place in the event of anything falling from above. This lower mass could hardly count as a part of the main wall, and we were able to circumvent it on the right, and mount to its crest up an easy snow slope. It was at this point that the real work began.

Immediately above us rose an overhang of ice some eighty feet high. Above this was an icy shelf sloping upwards to the left and outwards to the edge of the overhang at an angle of at least fifty degrees. Above this shelf rose another sheer wall of ice. The shelf was the only break; we must gain it, and traverse it to the left to an easier slope that bore up to the foot of another ice pitch about one third of the distance up the ice wall.

The slope to the right afforded convenient access to the shelf. At first sight it appeared to be a snow slope, but actually it consisted of an ice slope evilly overlaid with a foot or more of floury snow. This snow had to be shovelled away, and firm steps cut in the ice substratum. It was an easy enough place and a snow avalanche was not to be feared, but it took time.

The ice was, as usual, tough and glue-like, and an altitude of 21,000 feet discountenanced severe exertion. Wieland and I took turns at the cutting, whilst Wood Johnson and the porters enlarged the steps to the dimensions of Wapping Old Stairs. We drove three pitons in, and fixed ropes thereto to assist the loaded porters in the future. These pitons were of a special type advocated by that great German mountaineer, Herr Welzenbach. They are barbed like an arrow, and we drove them into the ice with a broad-headed metal mallet. This type of piton has fastened to its head an iron ring. In addition to pitons, we carried a number of clip-on oval rings. These we could attach to the permanent ring on the piton, and afterwards fix a rope through them without the bother, and possibly the danger, of having to unrope. The procedure was for the leader to advance, drive the piton into the ice, clip on to its ring one of the detachable oval rings, and clip the rope through the oval ring. Thus, he could be securely held on the rope at every stage of the step cutting. The detachable oval rings were not, of course, used to thread the rope as a permanent handrail. In this case, the rope was threaded through the piton ring and then tied.

By the time we reached the shelf it was beginning to snow. The hours had passed like magic, and the afternoon was well advanced. Thus far, the work had been easy; it now became very different. First of all, it was necessary to cut out a secure "jumping off" place in the ice at the end of the shelf from which the party could be securely held if need be. Duvanel took this task in hand, and soon fashioned a platform sufficiently broad on which to stand his ciné camera tripod.

It was while commencing to cut steps along the shelf that Wood Johnson's voice came up from below informing me that a hundred feet or so higher a large semi-detached flake of ice weighing a hundred tons or so was leaning unpleasantly over the route. I had already noticed this, and I am afraid, therefore, that I did not take Wood Johnson's information in the spirit in which it was meant, and after growling something about keeping up the morale of the leader and sundry damaging remarks about the ice flake, which might justifiably have retaliated by falling upon me, I addressed myself once more to the task of step-cutting.

We were in a curious frame of mind. We knew that the place was dangerous.

Had it been in the Alps, we should have gone back, but as the route was the only possible chink in the armour of Kangchenjunga the attack was persisted in, and the risks tacitly accepted. It was an understandable, yet false attitude of mind, but it is one that has warped the judgement of Himalayan parties in the past and will continue to exert its evil influence on other parties in the future. Suffice to say, that there will be many and terrible disasters before the greater Himalayan peaks are conquered, and before Himalayan mountaineering attains to any standard of sobriety.

Step-cutting on the shelf was weary work. First of all, the snow had to be cleared away, and beneath that a sort of flaky coating of ice before a step could be cut into the honest ice beneath. As in walking up-hill at high altitudes, so with cutting-rhythm. As each upward step in walking must be attuned to the breathing, so must each swing of the ice axe. It has often been said that Mallory had some trick of climbing at a high altitude. I wonder if this was a scientific cultivation of rhythm. Mallory was one of the most graceful climbers that ever lived, and grace is the child of rhythm. It may be that the rhythmical grace with which he was wont to climb on the most difficult rocks of Great Britain or the Alps proved of inestimable value to him on Everest.

A spell of twenty minutes' cutting was sufficient. I returned, and Wieland took my place. Twenty minutes' cutting, a few hard-won steps; it was not much. It was now snowing hard, but fortunately there was no wind, and it was reasonably warm.

Through the murk the great ice wall loomed coldly hostile. I have experienced fear many times on many mountains, but never quite the same dull, hopeless sort of fear inspired by this terrible wall of ice. I have often had occasion to remark how like men mountains are; some are friendly and others unfriendly. Kangchenjunga is something more than unfriendly, it is imbued with a blind unreasoning hatred towards the mountaineer. Sir Leslie Stephen once wrote: 'But we should hardly estimate the greatness of men or mountains by the length of their butcher's bill.' Kangchenjunga has every claim to majesty, and though the mere slaughter of those who attempt to reach its summit can scarcely add to it, the deaths that have occurred, and will occur testify to the greatness of the mountain, and its supreme contempt for its wooers. The beautiful is often dangerous. Strip Kangchenjunga of its icy robes, and it would become weak and defenceless, a mere rocky skeleton. In its dangers lie its beauties, and no right thinking mountaineer would have it otherwise.

As we turned to descend, the mists thinned for a few moments. As though signalled by the rise of a curtain, a great ice avalanche blasted forth on to the snowy stage. Dimly, to the left, we could see clouds of wind-blown snow belch out from the mountainside, and the echoes boomed and crashed from precipice to precipice like the thunderous applause of some huge audience.

We returned to camp. Bad news awaited us. Owing to lack of local porters and our being unable to send back enough men to help him, Colonel Tobin was experiencing great difficulty in getting the transport to the Base Camp. We had sent back as many porters from Khunza as possible, but these were unreliable men. Not only had they refused to help Colonel Tobin, but also they had looted a dump of stores at Dzongri, and stolen many articles of value. Colonel Tobin wrote that as far as Yoksam everything had gone well. There he had engaged local porters to bring his loads on to Dzongri, but these had refused to traverse the Kang La. He had experienced bad weather, and his assistant sirdar, Phuri, had died of exposure on the Kang La, whilst his chief sirdar, Naspati, had proved physically unequal to the task, and had returned ill to Darjeeling. Lobsang, whom we had sent back from Tseram, was now working with relays of men to get the loads over the Kang La. Colonel Tobin had laboured heroically against great odds, and as a result was physically worn out, and had lain ill for some days at Tseram. Also he had fallen and hurt his arm. He did not feel equal to the task of coming on to the Base Camp and had decided to return to Darjeeling as soon as adequate arrangements had been made to send on the remainder of the expedition's stores and equipment.

No one could have worked more for the expedition than Colonel Tobin, but the task that had been set him was an impossible one, and he was in no way responsible for transport delays. With only a few porters at his disposal, he could not be expected to get his transport to the Base Camp. Worst of all, Wood Johnson and I were unaware of the arrangements that had been made between him and Professor Dyhrenfurth regarding the sending back of porters, otherwise such a situation could hardly have arisen as Wood Johnson would have arranged to send back local porters from Khunza. Thus, a serious situation had arisen.

Something had to be done, and done quickly. Already sahibs' food was running short; there was only about a week's supply left, and we were lacking many vital necessities, to say nothing of those little luxuries, which help to alleviate the rigours of high altitude climbing. At sea level yak meat should be an excellent diet for those gifted with a cast-iron digestion, but at a high altitude it is totally unsuitable and difficult to digest. At the Base Camp, even Schneider had expressed a dislike for it, and had turned with obvious relief to Welsh rarebit, salad dressing, and Worcester sauce. We were still without many items of equipment; the wireless set had not arrived, and it was sad to think that every evening weather reports for our especial benefit were being broadcast from Calcutta.

There was nothing for it but for Wood Johnson and Hannah to leave Kangchenjunga, collect local porters at Khunza with the assistance of the Nepali Subadar, and return over the Mirgin La to the help of Colonel Tobin at Tseram. It was extremely hard luck for them to have to leave Kangchenjunga when at grips with it, but it was some consolation for them to know that the work they would be doing would be of the utmost value to the expedition. Hannah had already come up to Camp One, and had moved it to a site a little farther up the glacier where it was less exposed to ice avalanches from The Twins. He had returned to the Base Camp directly he had received news of the transport difficulties. We had got back to camp too late from work on the ice wall for Wood Johnson to do likewise, nor could he be expected to do so after such a heavy day. Some time later, when he returned, after successfully helping to solve the transport problem, he told me that though it had seemed hard to have to abandon climbing he had somehow felt that what had transpired was all for the best. And perhaps that is so, for had he remained with the climbing party, he might have lost his life.

We slept fitfully that night, awakened at frequent intervals by the thunder of ice avalanches. During the nineteen days that we were on Kangchenjunga ice avalanches seemed to fall more frequently at night than in the daytime. At first sight, this may appear strange. The coldest period of the twenty-four hours should serve to knit together the unstable masses of ice. Actually, this tendency for avalanches to fall during the coldest hours is probably due to expansion owing to water freezing in cracks in the ice and forcing the masses asunder. Another avalanche period is in the early morning. In cases where freezing water has wedged the ice apart without forcing a fall, the frozen water tends to bind the ice together. Thus, a mass on the edge of a hanging glacier may not be forced to part from its parent glacier until it is well past the point of unstable equilibrium, owing to the ice mortar that is binding it to its parent glacier. It may be just a matter of a few pounds that prevents it from falling. When the sun penetrates the crack the restraining influence of the ice mortar may be removed, and the mass of ice, with nothing left to support it, topples to destruction.

A striking illustration of this thesis occurred on Mont Blanc. We were ascending by the classic Brenva route, and halted on the Col du Trident to watch the red glow of the dawn sun creeping down Mont Blanc. We were debating as to the advisability of following a French party who were making a short cut to the crest of the Brenva Ridge, or of going the longer and safer way round via the Col Moore, when the rising sun touched a mass of hanging glacier above this route. Almost at the same instant that it did so a great avalanche was let loose, which swept the route between us and the French party. The slight warmth of the sun had been just sufficient to tear the unstable mass of ice from its parent glacier. After that we went the longer way round.

The next day, May 5, dawned gloriously. It was with great regret that we parted from Wood Johnson. Only Wieland, Duvanel, and I were now left to continue with the work of making a route up the ice wall. Carrying with us several hundreds of feet of rope, and two or three dozen pitons, we returned to the attack.

The previous day we had cut steps to a point about half way along the shelf. The work was useful in one respect for we were becoming acclimatised, and were climbing every day with increasing vigour.

We went to work on the shelf with a will, the leader cutting fair sized steps, the second man enlarging them, and lastly the porters, who seemed positively to enjoy the work, hacking out platforms large enough for an elephant to stand on. An hour or two's strenuous work and the traverse to the shelf was completed. From a snowy ridge at its end we could gaze back with satisfaction at the long line of steps, and a comforting hempen handrail of fixed rope. The most formidable ice slope loses much of its terrors when so decorated.

The snowy ridge we were on led upwards for one hundred feet without difficulty. It was a gift from the gods of the ice wall, and we accepted it gratefully. Our gratitude was a trifle ill timed. We should have realised that the gods, like the morbid inventor of a crossword puzzle, had only invented this easy bit for a joke. The joy departed from our hearts as we stood on an almost level ledge of snow. Above the ledge, the ice wall rose in what a mountaineer, despairing of a suitable descriptive term, might call a "vertical overhang". It was certainly vertical for twenty-five feet, and, about fifteen feet up, the ice bulged out forming a genuine overhang. To left and right the ledge thinned out into precipices of ice. Only from the point where we were standing was there the remotest possibility of climbing the wall. Twenty-five feet above our heads it "eased off" to an angle of about 70-degree. This "eased off" portion extended through a vertical height of about two hundred and fifty feet; crowning this slope and leering down upon us, rose a final and vertical barrier of ice fifty feet high.

As we stood, gazing silently, I tried to recall to my mind climbing of a similar nature in the Alps. I was unable to do so. In fact, it is probably safe to say that ice work of this nature had never been tackled in the Alps. Why should it be when it can always be avoided? The most continuously exacting ice climbing on record is that done by the Munich expedition on Kangchenjunga, but some of our porters, who had been with that expedition, assured us that though the work had been much longer, there had been nothing to equal this ice wall for *continuous* difficulty.

It is a well-known optical illusion that a slope looked at from below appears considerably less steep than looked at from above. The ice wall before us was a notable exception; it looked steep and it *was* steep.

A few mouthfuls of food, a drink of hot tea from a Thermos flask, and we set to work. At one place, a shallow splayed out chimney ran up the ice wall. It was too shallow to be of any use for body-wedging purposes, but we preferred it to the more exposed walls of ice on either side. Higher up, however, it became overhanging, and an upward and outward traverse to the right would be necessary. We debated whether crampons would be of any assistance, but decided that they would destroy the steps and would generally be more dangerous than useful, especially in view of the possibility of the leader falling off and spiking any unfortunates who happened to be beneath.

It was on Mont Blanc that I had undergone the exquisite torment of having a man stand on my shoulders in crampons. Even tricouni nails are bad enough, and I can sympathise with Wieland, and his request for me to be as quick as possible, as I stood on his shoulders. Reaching upwards. I hammered a piton into the ice, and clipped the rope into the oval ring. Supported by the rope running through the ring, I cut steps from the bottom of the wall. The easiest method of doing so was to place the feet in the steps already made, and leaning outwards and backwards on the rope, cut the next step above. Having reached the level of the piton, a fresh piton was driven in above, and the rope clipped into another oval ring. The lower piton could then be removed.

It was hard work; two or three steps at a time was as much as a man could manage. Leaning back on the rope did not improve matters, for it compressed the upper part of the body and made breathing difficult. The ice was white and flaky on the surface, but underneath of a blue-black transparency, like the cold depths of the ocean. It was difficult to swing the axe effectively, and we had to peck at the ice like an aged chicken seeking grubs in a farmyard. At this altitude, every stroke represented a definite piece of work and every step a stage in a day's hard labour.

To the mountaineer who revels in the art and craft of ice-man-ship, there is no music finer to his ears than the ringing thump with which an ice axe meets the yielding ice, and the swish and tinkle of the dislodged chips beneath him. But aesthetical and poetical sentiments were not for us. We wearied of the dull thud, thud, as the pick struck the ice. The musical ring of pitons driven well home found no answering ring in our hearts. We felt no excitement, no enthusiasm, no hope, and no fear. We became mere dull automatons, as dull and as automatic as the driver of a racing car towards the end of an attempt on a non-stop distance record. Such is difficult ice work at 21,000 feet.

The day was drawing to a dull close, and the usual snowstorm was pouring vials of snow powder on the world, as we stood together at the foot of the pitch, eyeing the scene of our labours. We had done eighteen feet, no more, but the steps were good ones. We would finish the lower wall on the morrow, and the day after that get up to the foot of the last wall. Yet one more day should see us up the final wall. Five days for five hundred feet of ascent! Was it worth it? Even with fixed ropes could laden porters ever be got up to the terrace above?

We returned to camp tired and dispirited, there to meet Schneider who had come up that day from the Base Camp, and a Schneider brimful of energy and enthusiasm. To me his presence was doubly welcome, for, as the most experienced member of the party, I had felt myself to be saddled with more responsibility than I cared for. The difficulties and dangers were too obvious to be ignored. The porters realised the former, but did they understand the latter?

The next morning, May 6, found us once more at the foot of the ice wall. Wieland and I were tired mentally and physically, and it was a relief to us to see the businesslike way with which Schneider went to work. He is a splendid iceman, cutting steps with a methodical neatness and quickness equal to that of a first-class Alpine guide. He uses a short ice axe with such a long and heavy pick that only a man with his strength of wrist and forearm could wield it effectively.

Even with three men on the job, it was a day's work to climb the last few feet of vertical or overhanging ice.

From the top of the shallow chimney it was necessary to traverse across a slightly overhanging bulge to the right. Here the ice was of a slightly more flaky nature than lower down, and it was not altogether pleasant leaning outwards, trusting that the piton would remain firm, and not pull away from the ice. Duvanel had come up with us, and took a number of "shots" of our struggles on the ice. Surely no film camera has ever been used in quite such a situation. We might have got farther that day, but we were hampered by a heavy snowstorm that set in soon after midday. So thickly did the snow fall that within an hour or so it was six to eight inches deep.

By the time we turned to descend, so much snow had fallen that our upward steps and fixed ropes had been obliterated completely. The steps along the shelf were difficult to find. Duvanel and his porters carrying the cinema apparatus were the first to descend. They were about halfway across when Duvanel slipped, and slid quickly downwards towards the eighty feet overhang beneath. Apparently, he had not reached the handrail when he slipped. It seemed that the three porters with him must be pulled off too, but the porter next to him, I think it was Sonam, an old Everest "Tiger", had such a tight rope that he was able to hold him and stop him before he had slid more than ten feet. It was a splendid bit of work – none of us could have done it better – and shows to what a state of mountaineering efficiency these porters have been brought by their experiences with former expeditions. But the slip had the effect of unnerving the remainder of the porters on the traverse, and one of them promptly followed Duvanel's example. This man had no ice axe, but fortunately he was held from the platform at the end of the traverse, and was drawn up on the rope wriggling like a fish by two lusty porters.

Roping on to Nemu, I followed the first party. The new snow made the traverse treacherous. Unfortunately, the fixed rope did not extend the whole distance across, but only stretched across the steeper portion. For several yards the passage had to be made without its aid. The newly fallen snow made the going distinctly tricky; not in all cases did the steps made by the descending porters correspond with the ice steps below, and one of them collapsed beneath me. I was well supported by my ice axe pick, and driving it in, was able to arrest the slip before it was properly started. But never shall I forget Nemu's agonised 'Oh, sahib, sahib!' It was a relief to get hold of the fixed rope, and walk across the remainder of the shelf.

The snowstorm was an unusually heavy one, and looked as though it might continue all night. But as we ploughed down the snow slopes towards the camp, the snow stopped falling, and the clouds, relieved of their burden, began to dissolve. Below, grey mists swirled and eddied in the glacier valley; and above, the peaks stood forth in the radiance of a perfect evening. It was one of those transformation scenes that mean so much to the mountaineer. For hours we had wrestled with the ice wall, wrestled in gloom and snowstorm, and now, like love in a world of hate, the sun shone through to cheer our downward march.

The mists beneath became less turbulent and ceased their eddyings and swirlings, lying in the valley like November vapours over a sodden meadow. The last cloudy rags were being thrown into the purple dustbin of the evening sky as we reached camp.

As I stood outside my tent after supper, watching the unity of earth and sky in the bonds of night, the harsh labours of the day were forgotten. Strange imaginings possessed me. In the profound quietude I heard the whisper of small voices; the liquid notes of some strange harmony stole across the glacier, seeming to rise from the very snow I was standing on, then – a shattering, bellowing roar from Kangchenjunga; snow whirling upwards and outwards; a grinding thunder of echoes rolling and crashing from peak to peak, booming, murmuring, dying into an affrighted silence. But the voices and the music I heard no more.

The party had been further strengthened by the arrival of Hoerlin, and Wieland and I felt that we could justifiably leave him and Schneider to continue with the attack on the ice wall. Since leaving the Base Camp, we had worked solidly for six days, and a rest was necessary if we were not to crock. Such ice work at high altitudes as we had been doing is not of a type that can be kept up indefinitely, and coming thus early in the expedition, we were both feeling the strain of it.

Hoerlin and Schneider put forth a great effort, and climbed the slope to the foot of the final wall. During the day we watched them, mere specks crawling upwards with the slowness of an hour hand. While they were at work, a large avalanche broke away from the left-hand extremity of the wall, and swept the lower part of the sloping terrace, which we had decided was too dangerous to be climbed.

They returned with the news that there were two possibilities of getting over the final wall. One was directly up it and the other by engineering a way up a crack, which separated the lower portion of the ice wall from the ice of the terrace. It would be necessary to keep as far to the right as possible, in order to avoid getting beneath some unstable-looking ice pinnacles on the terrace. On the other hand, they regarded with disfavour the crack, which seemed to suggest that the portion of the ice wall outlined by it to the right was breaking away from its parent glacier. They considered that the work would be completed on the morrow, and the terrace reached, and proposed to take up all the porters with loads, to establish Camp Three on the terrace. If the upper wall turned out to be harder than was anticipated, the loads would be dumped as high as possible. They had roped up all the upper part of the route, but it remained to be seen whether the porters could go safely up and down. Even if they could, keeping up the communications would be a much harder task than on Everest, where porters were able to go up and down unaccompanied between camps. Here every convoy must be under the charge of a European.

But would it be possible to maintain such communications at all? As we had seen two days previously, a slight fall of snow had altered the complexion of things completely. A heavy fall would undoubtedly isolate Camp Three. And what of the other camps above that? At least six were anticipated between the Base Camp and the summit, and this number might well be increased by the difficulties of the climbing and the altitude to eight. With the beanstalk severed just above the root, it would both cease to climb and die.

Apart from snowstorms, something worse than an awkward situation might be created by the collapse of any part of the ice wall involving the route. Even supposing no immediate deaths resulted, it might be difficult, or even impossible, to descend.

One primary fact had not been realised, and that was that Kangchenjunga is something more than an Alpine peak on a large scale. Not one of the party could deny that the route was liable to be swept by ice avalanches, but it was not realised exactly to what extent risks were being taken. A party in the Alps sometimes deliberately incurs a risk of being overwhelmed by an ice avalanche when passing beneath a hanging glacier, or under an unstable ice pinnacle in an ice face, but such a risk is seldom incurred for longer than a few minutes. We had been exposed to these risks for four consecutive days, and were to be exposed to the same risk for yet another day. And this was not all; the risk would last as long as we were on the mountain. Communications between camps must be maintained, and porters go to and fro. Thus, the ice wall and the slopes beneath would have to be traversed not once, but many times, and the probability of accident was greatly increased thereby. As I have pointed out, Himalayan porters appreciate difficulty, but not danger. They place implicit confidence in their sahibs, whom they are prepared to follow anywhere. This confidence should not be abused.

That day, and late into the night, I sat in my tent writing up a sadly overdue diary, and also a dispatch to *The Times*, which last was sent down the same day to the Base Camp. In the former I wrote:

> Our camp is pitched on the only safe place in the cirque, for the hanging glaciers that cling precariously to the hollows of precipices frequently let loose enormous ice avalanches that sweep the snow slopes beneath with cataracts of ice blocks. Yet were one of these catastrophic ice avalanches – the collapse of a hanging glacier – such as are common among the Himalayas, to take place, we would be brushed like a speck of dust from the earth. Even as I write there comes at almost regular intervals, the boom and roar of ice avalanches from Kangchenjunga. It is almost as though the mountain was pulsating to the fierce beats of her restless heart. Unhurriedly masses of ice are riven by the downward motion of the ice fields from the edges of the red

> rock cliffs. They totter forward, masses as great as the Houses of Parliament, breaking up into disintegrating ice masonry, which strikes the precipices beneath with an appalling crash, and pours down in an irresistible torrent of ice, concealed by billowing clouds of snow dust flung before it.

My dispatch to *The Times* concluded with these words:

'As I write, avalanche after avalanche is roaring off Kangchenjunga, each one seeming to proclaim defiance and warning.'

CHAPTER TWELVE

The Ice Avalanche: the Death of Chettan

I LAY LONG in my tent that evening writing, and it was nearly midnight before I blew out the candle, and composed myself to sleep. But sleep would not come. I was quite comfortable, my digestive organs were in good order, and acclimatisation had reduced my pulse-rate to nearly normal. The night was curiously warm, in fact, the warmest night we had had since we arrived at the Base Camp. Now and again came the long-drawn-out thunder of avalanches.

Perhaps it was the atmosphere, or maybe some trick of the imagination, but the sound of the avalanches seemed dull and muffled. It was as though Kangchenjunga was choking with suppressed wrath. My body was ready for sleep, but my mind was not. It was troubled and restless, groping in a catacomb of doubt and fear. I have known fear before on a mountain, but that was fear of a different nature, sharp and sudden in the face of an immediate danger, but I have never known what it was to lie awake before a climb tortured by the devils of misgiving.

Some people may call this a premonition, but I do not think it can be so defined. Premonition of danger is, after all, an anticipation of danger, where, theoretically, danger ought not to exist. That danger existed in this case cannot be denied. The mind had brooded over it consciously and subconsciously to the detriment of the nerves, and these had become temporarily unstrung. That is a more logical explanation than the acceptance of the premonition theory, which is more dependent upon a belief in psychical phenomena.

When, at last, I fell asleep; I was troubled with terrible dreams. These dreams were not dreams of personal danger, but of danger to the porters. They were always getting into an impossible position, and would turn to me appealingly for help. But I was unable to help. Afterwards, Wood Johnson told me he used frequently to dream this too. Possibly it was due to an innate sense of responsibility. Others on Himalayan expeditions have probably experienced the same sort of dreams. It was a bad night.

I crawled out of my tent the next morning, dull, heavy, and unrefreshed. I looked at the ice wall, and the weary track leading up through the snow to it, with loathing. Neither mentally nor physically did I feel fit to start.

The morning was ominously warm and a steamy heat beat down through sluggish mists. The sun was obscured, but for the first time on the mountain we were able to sit outside and keep reasonably warm without its rays on us.

It was decided that the scheme arranged the previous day should be adhered to. All except the cook and myself were to leave and try to establish Camp Three on the terrace.

Schneider with his usual boundless energy was the first to leave. He was accompanied by his servant, "Satan" Chettan, who was carrying a considerable load.

There was no porter in the expedition of a finer physique than Chettan, and I remember watching him swing on his load with effortless ease, and start off in the wake of his master, his legs propelling him uphill in shambling powerful strides, the gait of a born hillman and mountaineer.

Duvanel and three porters carrying cinematograph apparatus came next, as the former wished to obtain "shots" of the last party, which consisted of Hoerlin, Wieland, and eight porters carrying heavy loads. For a while I sat on a packing case, watching them as they slowly plodded up the slopes of soft snow, then I adjourned to my tent in order to write some letters.

Perhaps half an hour later I was startled by a tremendous roar. Two thoughts flashed through my mind. Firstly, that only an exceptionally large ice avalanche falling close at hand could make such a din, and secondly, with a sudden clutch of horror at my heart, that the noise came, not from the usual direction of Kangchenjunga's face, but from the ice wall!

I dashed outside. What I saw is indelibly engraved on my memory.

An enormous portion of the ice wall had collapsed. Huge masses of ice as high as cathedrals, were still toppling to destruction; billowing clouds of snow spray were rushing upwards and outwards in the van of a huge avalanche. On the slope below was the party, mere black dots, strung out in a straggling line. They were not moving. For an instant, during which I suppose my brain must have been stunned, the scene was stamped on my mind like a still photograph, or perhaps a more apt comparison would be a cine film that has jammed for a fraction of a second. Then everything jerked on again. I remember feeling no surprise it was almost like a fantastic solution to something that had been puzzling me.

Now the dots were moving, moving to the left; they were running, but how slowly, how uselessly before the reeling clouds of death that had already far outflanked them. The next moment the avalanche had swept down upon them; they were engulfed and blotted out like insects beneath a tidal wave.

In the tent I had been conscious of noise, but now I was no longer aware of it. The clouds of snow swept nearer. At first they had seemed to move slowly, but now they were shooting forwards with incredible velocity. Vicious tongues of ice licked out under them. Here and there solitary blocks broke free from the pall; behind them I caught a glimpse of a confused jumble of ice blocks, grinding together like the boulders in a streambed caught up by the floodwaters of a cloudburst.

The thought of personal danger had not occurred to me at first, but now, suddenly, came the realisation that the avalanche might sweep the camp away. I glanced round for the cook – he was standing outside the cooking tent – and yelled to him to run for it.

I had stood and watched the avalanche like one rooted to the spot in a nightmare. Running was nightmarish too. The feet sank deeply into the snow; at the height (20,000 feet) every step was an effort. We floundered along for perhaps twenty yards, then heart and lungs gave out, and neither of us could continue. We looked round; the avalanche was stopping two hundred yards away. Though I had not been conscious of any noise after the initial roar, I was paradoxically conscious of it ceasing.

The avalanche stopped, only the clouds of snow, driven by the wind displaced by the falling masses, writhed far into the air. There was no sign of my companions. I turned to the cook: 'They are all killed, but we must do what we can.' We retraced our steps to the camp, seized ice axes, and set out for the scene of the disaster. We tried to move quickly, but it was impossible at the altitude, it was better to go slowly and steadily, and how slow this was.

The clouds of snow began to settle, the veil thinned. It was a terrible moment. I expected to see no sign of the party. Then, to my immense relief, I saw dimly a figure away to the left, and then some more figures. We toiled upwards, skirting the edge of the avalanche; it was sharply defined, and the ice blocks were piled several feet high. Beyond it the snow was untouched, save where it had been scored by solitary blocks flung forwards from the main mass of ice.

Two hundred yards from the camp the track vanished beneath the debris of the avalanche. We reached a little group of porters. They were standing stupidly, without moving or speaking, on the edge of the debris; all save one, who was probing energetically with an ice axe between the ice blocks. It was Nemu. I asked him what he was doing, whether there was a man buried there, and he replied, 'Load, sahib, I look for load.' In order to run and escape from the avalanche he had dropped his load, and this was seriously worrying him. Who were alive and who were dead did not concern him, he had dropped his load, the load entrusted to him by the sahibs.

I counted the party, two were missing. Hoerlin, Wieland, and Duvanel I could see above me. The missing ones were Schneider and Chettan. Two hundred feet higher I saw Wieland approaching something sticking out between the ice blocks. It was Chettan's hand. By the time I had climbed up he had been dug out. He was dead, having been carried down at least three hundred feet, and crushed in the torrent of ice blocks. His head was severely injured, but as a forlorn hope we administered artificial respiration for over an hour. In the middle of it Schneider reappeared. He had had a marvellous escape. He had actually been under the ice wall when it came down. He said: 'I heard a crack; then down it came, huge masses of ice from hundreds of feet above. I thought I was dead, but I ran to the left, and the avalanche missed me by five metres.' Chettan had been too far behind Schneider to save himself.

The remainder of the party had amazing luck. They had been on the track where it ran farthest to the left. Had they been ten minutes earlier or later, nothing could have saved them. Even so, they had had to run for their lives, and the track was swept almost from end to end. Duvanel told me that when he saw it coming, the thought of being able to escape never even occurred to him. But, like the others, he had run to the left as it seemed better to be killed *doing something* than waiting for apparently certain death. So narrow had been the escape of the main body of the porters that some of them had actually been bruised by blocks of ice on the edge of the avalanche. The escape of the party can only be called a miracle of the mountains.

The portion of the wall that had fallen had been that outlined by the crack noted by Hoerlin and Schneider the previous day. In falling it swept the route on the ice wall diagonally, completely obliterating the lower part of the route that Wieland and I had made, destroying the snow bridge over the crevasse and the ice hump under which we had sat. In fact, the topography of the route we had made at the expense of so much labour had been altered completely. The area of snow slopes covered by the debris must have been nearly a mile square, and the avalanche can scarcely have weighed less than a million tons.

We returned to camp, two of the porters taking turns at carrying Chettan. According to those who had been highest, another crack had opened up above the ice and there was a strong possibility of another possibly greater even than the first, which might conceivably sweep away the camp. It was advisable to retire to Camp One with all speed. But before doing so we buried Chettan.

It was a simple, yet impressive ceremony. A hole was dug in the snow, and the body, dressed as it was in climbing clothes, laid within with folded arms. A handful of rice was roasted by the porters, and this was scattered over the body to the accompaniment of muttered prayers. We stood round with bared heads. Then someone gave an order, and snow was quickly shovelled into the grave. As this was done the mists dispersed, and the sun shone through for a few instants. Almost one could see the brave soul winging its way over the mountains. We drove in an ice axe to mark the spot, and silently turned away. We had lost not a porter, but a valued friend. We left him buried amid one of the grandest mountain cirques in the world.

So died a genuine lover of the mountains, a real adventurer at heart, and one whom members of several Himalayan expeditions will mourn.

We descended to Camp One in a wet and soaking snowstorm, that later developed into a blizzard. Word was sent down to the Base Camp of the disaster, requesting that Professor Dyhrenfurth and Kurz should come up and discuss matters.

Wind was howling, and snow lashing the tents, as we ate supper and crept miserably into our sleeping bags.

CHAPTER THIRTEEN

The North-West Ridge: Attempt on Kangbachen

ON MAY 10 the day after the accident, Dyhrenfurth, Kurz and Dr. Richter arrived from the Camp, and a conference was held on the situation. "Conference" is perhaps a little misleading. It is a word conjuring up a picture of frock-coated gentlemen round a long mahogany table, the highly polished surface of which reflects waistcoats ornamented with gold chains and earnest countenances on which responsibility and a heavy lunch sit heavily. In the present instance I must ask the reader to imagine the sombre interior of the large porters' tent, the thick canvas of which reduces the light within to a faint depressing green, whilst a pungent reek of smoke struggles with a faint, yet perceptible odour of unwashed bodies that have lain there during the previous night. In the middle, a heterogeneous collection of packing cases do duty as a table. Seated on other cases are a number of unsavoury looking ragamuffins with unkempt hair, frowsy beards, cracked sun-scorched countenances, and eyes bleared by the snow glare.

The first suggestion made by those who had remained at the Base Camp was that the attack on the ice wall should be renewed, but this was very properly rejected by all those who had shared in the attack. The sole remaining alternative was to attempt the North-West Ridge which rises from the western tributary of the Kangchenjunga Glacier. This ridge ends in a snow and ice terrace beneath Kangbachen, 25,782 feet, one of the main summits of Kangchenjunga. Even supposing the terrace to be reached, however, the most we could hope for was to ascend Kangbachen, as there was no possibility of traversing to the highest summit, as both distance and difficulty were too great. Personally, I must confess to a longing to flee from the mountain altogether, and be able to lie in a sleeping bag at night and sleep undisturbed by the fear of annihilation from ice avalanches. I suggested, therefore, that we should retire, cross the Jonsong La, and attempt Jonsong Peak, 24,344 feet. This idea met with no support, and it was decided to attempt the North-West Ridge. Should we fail, as it seemed certain we must do, judging from appearances, at all events we could ascend the Western Tributary Glacier, explore its head, and possibly climb Ramthang Peak.

In order to do this it was decided to move Camp One across the glacier to the foot of the rocky spur separating the Western Tributary Glacier from the glacier falling between Wedge Peak and Ramthang Peak. This new site would have the advantage of being considerably safer than the present one, for it was by no means certain that we were safe in the event of an exceptionally large ice avalanche falling from Kangchenjunga, or The Twins. This uncertainty was emphasised the same afternoon in a startling fashion.

We were aroused from an after-lunch siesta by the thunderclap of a great avalanche. We issued from our tents in alarm. Thousands of feet above us on the face of Kangchenjunga masses of hanging glacier were collapsing. Sweeping the precipices with appalling violence, the avalanche crashed down to the glacier, and roared straight across at us.

Huge clouds of snow were raised by the windblast from the surface of the glacier, and came rushing down upon the camp. They concealed the falling ice, and it was hard to tell whether the camp was safe or not. My own inclination was to run for it and I was about to bolt precipitately when I saw Duvanel calmly turning the handle of his ciné camera with that sang-froid peculiar to his calling, the tradition of which demands that the handle of a ciné camera shall be turned in the face of charging elephants, and at shipwrecks, fires, explosions, earthquakes and other catastrophes. Fired by his example, I pulled my own folding camera from my pocket, and took a hurried snap. As will be seen from the accompanying illustration the avalanche resembled the white clouds of some new and deadly form of gas attack. The God of Kangchenjunga is evidently well up in the technique of modern warfare. The roar of the avalanche subsided. We knew that we were safe from ice debris, but the clouds of snow continued to pour down the glacier towards the camp with extraordinary velocity. The next moment a wind-blast struck the camp, and a blizzard of snow sent us scuttling into shelter.

The blizzard lasted some minutes, and when it had cleared the upper part of the glacier was seen to be covered in nearly an in inch of wind-blown snow. The actual ice debris of the avalanche had stopped well short of the camp, but it had swept quite half a mile down the glacier. This was not the only avalanche; other lesser ones fell, but none of such terrifying dimensions. It was obvious, however, that it was a mere question of volume and momentum whether or not the camp was to be swept away by a future avalanche. If it was a rest day for tired bodies, it was scarcely so for nerve-racked minds.

It was a simple matter moving camp the next day, and the new site on the other side of the glacier was safer than any we had yet discovered. We had not been able to bring down all our equipment from Camp Two, so some porters under the charge of Kurz went up to fetch it. Schneider and Duvanel, meanwhile, descended to the Base Camp, the former in order to make a new track up the glacier to our new Camp, the latter to develop some ciné film. I was left in charge of the evacuation of the old camp, and took the opportunity of donning a pair of ski, and making short runs on the glacier. The snow was excellent and similar to late spring alpine snow.

The new Camp One was pitched in a fine situation. There was a delightful view northwards up the moraine-stacked Jonsong Glacier winding sinuously up towards the little notch of the Jonsong La. The background was dominated by the rocky mass of Jonsong Peak. Farther to the east, rose a ridge of icy peaks running northwards from Kangchenjunga and The Twins, from which Tent Peak, 24,089 feet, rose head and shoulders above everything else. It is as aptly named as Wedge Peak, for its horizontal summit ridge with its small points at either end resembles a tent, the ridge of which sags between its supporting poles.

Some useful stores arrived from the Base Camp that day, among them being synthetic rubber ground sheets for the tents. Though light and spongy, and weighing but a pound or so each, the difference they made to our comfort was amazing, and we were able to sleep then and afterwards far more warmly and comfortably than we would have done otherwise, insulated as we were from the snow. There is no question that they are far superior to any ground sheet, and form an item of equipment that no future Himalayan expedition can afford to leave out, for they induce the sleep which is so essential if climbers are to keep fit.

Relieved by the thought that we were tolerably safe from avalanches, we slept well that night. It would have been wise to have started early the next morning while the snow was still hard from the overnight frost, but we did not get away until the sun had thawed its crust sufficiently to let it break beneath our weight. The obvious route up the Western Tributary Glacier was a trough between the glacier and the rock ridge forming its northern containing wall. The trough was snow-filled for most of its distance, except for one section where a scree slope interposed. These troughs, which form such a convenient line of least resistance up the glaciers of this district are perhaps the only thing vouchsafed by Kangchenjunga which seems to have been intended for the benefit of the long suffering mountaineer.

Wieland and I, with some porters, were the first to set off. Hoerlin, Kurz, and some more porters were to follow, but at the last moment Kurz, who was again not feeling well, decided to return to the Base Camp.

The snow in the trough was in the worst possible condition. We floundered waist deep into holes between concealed snow covered boulders and wallowed in hollows where the snow was soft and watery. An hour passed; we had made but little progress. I suggested to Wieland that we should leave the trough in favour of the icefall of the glacier. In making this suggestion I was actuated by the fact that at one place the trough seemed likely to be swept by falling stones from the cliffs above. Hoerlin, however, was of a different mind; he would stick to the trough. As things transpired, he was right; the danger was more apparent than real.

Ascending the icefall was fatiguing work on account of the soft snow. Snow-shoes eased the porters' labours to some extent but there were not enough pairs to go round. Considering how broken was the ice, it was remarkable how few crevasses there were, but these few were dangerous ones, subtly concealed. We toiled up and down over hummocks, or threaded our way between pinnacles. The devil of doubt began to gnaw at our hearts; would we be able to get through the icefall? The sun beat down upon us mercilessly, and glacier lassitude sapped the strength of sahib and porter alike. At last we saw a sort of corridor leading from the icefall into the upper part of the trough. We could see that the trough was perfectly safe, but had it been dangerous, we should still have preferred it to the sweltering gullies and hollows of the icefall, for glacier lassitude tends to undermine the judgement and warp the conscience of the mountaineer.

A crevasse barred the way. We stepped gingerly on to a fragile snow bridge. Icicles were dislodged and went tinkling down into the green depths with a noise like the banging together of small chandeliers. The corridor stretched ahead; its smooth, snow floor looked innocuous, but Wieland suddenly disappeared up to his waist in a concealed crevasse: it was merely one of Kangchenjunga's little jokes.

At the top of the trough, where it debouches on to the glacier, above the worst of the icefall, there is a short section liable to be swept by ice avalanches from a hanging glacier forming the edge of a snow plateau on Ramthang Peak. While still within the danger area we were startled by a sudden crash, but all that came down were a few boulders and blocks of ice.

The porters were by now very tired, and they begged us to camp as soon as possible. We promised to do so as soon as we were out of range of ice avalanches. The sun was declining, and evening mists gathering around us as we reached the smooth slopes above the icefall, where stretched Hoerlin's straggling track, man's first score on these snowfields. Here we decided to camp, while Wieland went on with ski to bring down Hoerlin, who had camped some distance further up the glacier.

The evening was strangely still save for an undercurrent of sound, as though the goblins and witches who haunt the cliffs of Kangchenjunga above were murmuring at our coming. As usual, it was the wind. An upward glance disclosed the snow eddying and swirling from the polished ice cliffs defending the snowy terraces. The sun set calmly. Barely had its last rays faded when they were replaced by silver moon sheen behind the North Ridge of Kangchenjunga. The snow blown off the ridge by the wind was illumined from behind, and Kangchenjunga took to itself a glowing aureole of light. Imperceptibly the upper snow-slopes were resolved from the darkness; ghostlike, unreal, they shimmered far above the world. Mindless of the cold, we stood outside our tents entranced by the glorious spectacle. At long last the laggardly moon peered over the ridge in a shy, self-deprecating sort of way. It seemed to wither and shrivel as it mounted into the frosty sky and its radiance, at first soft and wan, became a hard, cold electric blue. Details stood forth as clearly as in daylight. Only the shadows were black, and in these lurked the darkness of a pit.

The cold gripped us. We crawled into our tents and with numbed fingers laced the flaps. As Sir Leslie Stephen wrote: 'Bodily fatigue and an appreciation of natural scenery are simply incompatible.' He might have added cold and discomfort.

The sun reached us early the next morning, and we were off betimes. Our first business was to move camp farther up the glacier to a site that would form a convenient upper base for operations against the North-West Ridge. As we marched up the glacier we were able to examine the latter. First impressions are not always accurate and it is never easy to assess the difficulties of a mountainside or ridge at their true worth. As that great mountaineer, Captain J.P. Farrar used to remark: 'You can never tell what rocks are like until you have rubbed your nose against them.' Yet even bearing these things in mind, no ridge I have ever examined affected me with the same feeling of utter and complete hopelessness as that of the North-West Ridge of Kangchenjunga. Picture a ridge rising 4,000 feet. Thin, trim and whittle down its edges until they are as keen as a Gurkha's *kukri*; then hack deep gaps into these edges and perch rocky towers hundreds of feet high on them. Armour every smooth bit with ice, and mask every ledge with snow, and you will perhaps obtain a faint glimmering of an idea of the North-West Ridge of Kangchenjunga. The ridge attempted by the Munich party is formidable, but it cannot compare to the North-West Ridge. Ice pinnacles alone had to be surmounted on the former; spiky rock pinnacles bar the way on the latter and between these are some of those extraordinary ice ridges peculiar to the Himalayas. In appearance and sensationalism they are comparable to those on Wedge Peak. There are the same tottering masses, the same biscuit-like flakes through which the sun gleams, the same extravagant forms, hacked and torn by the wind, lurching and tottering at the behest of gravity, and the same ice flutings to emphasise by their graceful lines the appalling steepness of the slopes they decorate. If we had been forced to attack the ridge from its base, I think we would have relinquished any idea of attempting it at the outset, for the lowest rock towers are hopeless from a climbing point of view. It looked possible, however, to gain the crest of the ridge above these initial pinnacles, by a steep snow-filled couloir about 600 feet high, leading upwards from the glacier to one of the gaps in the crest of the ridge.

Camp was pitched on the glacier, and leaving the porters to make it comfortable we set off to climb the couloir. The lower half was simple; then the angle steepened. It was not difficult, but care had to be taken that the footsteps kicked in the floury snow that masked rock slabs and ice did not collapse. The last hundred feet were very steep. The angle must have exceeded 60 degrees, but we were comforted by the thought that we could fix a rope to facilitate descent. A small cornice leaned over the summit. The leader, Hoerlin, hacked and flogged it down, and squirmed through and over to the gap, Wieland and I following one by one. The ascent had taken only forty-five minutes, indicating that we had become well acclimatised to altitude.

My first impression was probably somewhat similar to that experienced by a house-breaker, not a burglar, but one of those phlegmatic gentlemen who stand on the dizzy edges of aged and tottering walls knocking bricks off into space with a pick-axe. But surely no housebreaker has ever stood on top of such an unstable wall as we found ourselves on. A modern £25 down and balance in rent villa could scarcely be more "jerry-built" than the place on which we stood. On either side of us the rocks were piled in loose masses needing but a touch to send them crashing down on either side of the ridge below us. On the opposite side of the ridge to that which we had ascended loose yellowish precipices dropped to the head of the Ramthang Glacier. From our gap it appeared possible to descend to the glacier down another steep gully, scarred with falling debris. Such a descent would, however, involve unavoidable dangers. And far above this scene of perpetual decay rose the great ice slopes and ice walls of Kangchenjunga.

Is there any hope of ascending Kangchenjunga from the Ramthang Glacier? The answer must be, no, unless the climber is prepared to take his life, *and* the lives of his porters, in his hand. Like the face above the Kangchenjunga Glacier, that above the Ramthang Glacier is defended by enormous walls of ice running across the mountainside. At one point only is there any hope of climbing the *lowest* of these ice walls, and this point is also liable to be swept at any moment by ice avalanches from another and tottering ice wall above. Kangchenjunga was not built for the mountaineer.

Leaving rucksacks and spare rope, we commenced to climb along the unstable ridge. Almost immediately, we were forced off the crest to avoid a decrepit rocky tower. A traverse had to be made on the southern side of the ridge over steep, loose rocks, here and there treacherously covered in snow. It was a place not so much difficult as dangerous. There was not a reliable rock round which a rope could be placed to secure the party, and had a slip occurred, it would in all probability have been attended by the worst results.

From the traverse, an upward ascent brought us into the mouth of a loose gully, the head of which consisted of slippery slabs disagreeably covered by a few inches of unstable scree.

It is curious how on any climb the mental equilibrium, of the mountaineer is liable to be upset by bad rock. Difficulty is one thing, danger another. The nerve-stressed mountaineer needing a safety valve for his feelings frequently finds an outlet for them in forceful language. I make no excuses, therefore, for certain improper remarks when clambering up these rocks. I cannot remember what Hoerlin and Wieland said, I had not yet learned the English translation of the German epithets that they held in reserve for such occasions, but once, Hoerlin turned and remarked to me in perfect English, "These rocks are * * *!" sentiments which, happily, I was able to return with interest.

The principal advantage of taking photographs on a mountain is that the mountaineer is thus enabled to stop at frequent intervals and recover his breath. That is why most elderly mountaineers carry cameras. Taking a photograph is a much more convincing excuse for a halt than a bootlace or braces that need adjusting. All those liable to be touched in the wind should take a camera. With what the reader will no doubt consider admirable foresight, I had brought up my camera with me, and not left it at the gap. I was not blown, but the ridge beyond the top of the little gully appeared so uninviting that I decided to stop there and photograph Hoerlin and Wieland doing it.

Seated in a sheltered place, with the sun glancing warmly down upon me, I was able to appreciate the situation to the full. For a short distance the ridge appeared possible, and although extremely loose, not excessively difficult. But beyond the next tower it was very different. It rose abruptly in a huge pinnacle, quite three hundred feet high, and above this pinnacle, connecting it to the next pinnacle, was the first of those appalling ice ridges. As I sat there I tried to think of an alpine ridge comparable to it, but I could think of none. The Peuterey, the Brenva the East Ridge of the Jungfrau, none would fit.

How were porters to be got up? Even supposing ropes were to be fixed the whole way up the smooth slabs of the first great pinnacle, they would not be able to climb with anything but a light load; also we had lost so much rope, in the avalanche that we certainly had not enough spare for even this first pinnacle. There was, however, no necessity for experiencing renewed pessimism. What we were now seeing simply confirmed the opinion that some of us had formed when gazing from the glacier below.

Hoerlin and Wieland were moving slowly and carefully, but even so they could not avoid dislodging many rocks which thundered down the precipices of the Ramthang Glacier. They turned a corner, and disappeared from view, but presently I saw them on the top of another minor pinnacle. There they remained, and I conjectured that they could not advance farther.

The usual mists gathered, but without threatening anything beyond desultory snow flurries. Occasionally, they rolled aside to disclose a beautiful snow mountain, unknown and unnamed in a south-westerly direction, apparently on the ridge separating the Yalung and the Ramthang Glaciers. This peak was in shape something like the Ober Gabelhorn, and possessed the same sweeping lines as the graceful Zermatt Peak. Jannu should have been visible beyond, but mists obscured it. Almost immediately beneath us was the camp we had just established. We seemed to be looking almost vertically down upon it so steep were the precipices below. It seemed that a jump would have landed us on our tents. Above the camp, the Western Tributary Glacier swept up serenely to the col separating Ramthang Peak from the first rock towers of the ridge we were on. Ramthang Peak itself was playing hide-and-seek in a fitful mist but what was visible of it reminded me forcibly of the Mönch seen from the Jungfrau Glacier. There were the same graceful lines and flowing yet defiant massiveness. It was late when we returned to camp, where we found Professor Dyhrenfurth, Schneider and Duvanel, who had come up that day from Camp One. I fear none of us were particularly optimistic over the day's work, and it was refreshing to find that Professor Dyhrenfurth did not agree with an opinion that the ridge was hopelessly inaccessible and considered that we should continue with the attack towards the terrace above.

For once the afternoon clouds, instead of thickening for a snowstorm, dissolved. The evening was a calm and beautiful one, sky and world were unsullied by a single speck of cloud, a profound silence brooded over the sanctuaries of the snows and only an occasional streamer of wind-blown snow sallied into space from the upper reaches of Kangchenjunga. Slowly night's floods filled the valleys, and the peaks became steeped in gaudy hues, like waxen deities covering their countenances with rouge and lipstick. Imperceptibly, the aerial pageantry died, but its riot of colourings was superseded by an afterglow which released the peaks from night's bonds for a few instants revealing them as cold statues of purest alabaster against a sky of deepest indigo. It was of such a day's end that Mr. G. Winthrop Young once wrote:

When in the hour of mountain peace,
The tumult and the passion cease,
As the red sunfloods sink,
And the pale lords of sovereign height,
Watch the cold armies of the night
Mustering their first assault.

Who would suspect evil to lurk in such a sunset? Yet, somehow, its superlative colourings put me in mind of a sunset I had once watched from a tiny ledge 12,000 feet up on the South Face of Mont Maudit. *That* had been a sunset preceeding a heavy snowstorm in which retreat had been no easy matter.

I awoke some hours later to hear the pattering of snow on my tent. In the quietude it sounded like the light tread of fairy feet. Presently, I became aware of a faint under current of sound like the far off throb of a train down some pastoral valley. The train approached, its distant murmurings rising gradually to a booming crescendo of sound. A gust of wind struck the tent, hurling the snowflakes against it with rude fierce spatterings. The gust passed, but soon came another and stronger gust. In a few minutes the blizzard burst, furiously sweeping upon our encampment. I snuggled more closely into my sleeping bag, for strong though the tent fabric was, it was not entirely proof against this bitter onslaught at a height of 20,000 feet. We had thought to be sheltered by the North-West Ridge, but it afforded no protection, for the wind seemed to pour over it like a cataract, and descend almost vertically upon the camp.

The gusts grew stronger; they wailed and shrilled, rising to a roaring sort of boom like an express train racing through a tunnel. I could feel the tent floor rise as though malicious wind devils were undermining it with the object of my abode flying upwards into space. The wind dug viciously at the sides, or strove with strong fingers to tear apart the flaps, and burst the tent asunder. I prayed that Nemu had driven the pegs firmly and deeply into the snow, and then I recollected that the guy ropes were pitifully thin, no thicker than a sashline. There seemed every possibility of the tent carrying away; if it did, there would be little fun in being overtaken by such a disaster clad only in underclothes, so I struggled out of my sleeping bag, pulled on my climbing clothes, and packed my rucksack with some necessaries.

The storm had now reached a pitch of intensity I had never before experienced when camping, and the night was filled with thunderous volleyings. Sometimes the wind would sink to a mysterious calm, during which it was possible to hear the storm snarling and worrying on the North-West Ridge as a preliminary before gathering its forces for a fresh charge on the camp. It was during one of these temporary lulls that I heard a sort of wailing outside, a wailing more human than storm-like. Peering through the flaps, I could just perceive a figure crawling through the snow. It approached my tent. In the light of my electric torch I saw the white, frightened face of Nagpa, the cook.[1] 'Sahib! Sahib!' he cried, 'Tent go! Tent go!' Opening the flaps wider, I glanced out, the porters' tent was intact; the cook had merely lost his head. I was unwilling to have him for a bedfellow, and told him to go back. The cook, however, was completely demoralised, and shielding his face from the blast, he crawled down the line of tents with his constant wailing of 'Sahib! Sahib! Tent go! Tent go!' Eventually, he found sanctuary with Wieland and Schneider, but as they explained later, they took him in not for love or charity, but simply as additional ballast for their own tent! It was the solitary untoward incident of the storm. Well and truly had our tents been pitched.

An hour or two later the wind began to subside and ere dawn it withdrew with some last mutters and snarls, leaving a clean sky picked out with stars against which the windy banners of Kangchenjunga softly lit by moonlight, streamed in ghostly rivalry to the starry constellations.

We awoke to a warm sun glancing benevolently over The Twins. The North-West Ridge was plastered with new snow, and our steps in the couloir had been obliterated. As there was a possibility of avalanches occurring, we decided not to renew the attempt that day, and devoted the morning to building a wall of snow blocks on the windward side of the camp. Hoerlin was not feeling well; somehow he had contracted a severe chill. Duvanel was also by no means fit, and only his devotion to his cinematographic duties had torn him away from the Base Camp.

At the head of the glacier on the ridge separating Ramthang Peak from the North-West Ridge of Kangchenjunga is a small point about 20,800 feet high. This Wieland climbed by himself, using ski most of the way, and returned reporting that he had had a splendid view of Ramthang Glacier and the North-West Ridge. It was decided, therefore, that the whole party should ascend to this point the following day, and carefully examine the latter to see whether it was worth while persisting in the attempt to climb it.

The following morning, May 15, dawned fine. Unfortunately, Hoerlin was so ill that there was no option but for him to return to the Base Camp. This was a serious loss to the climbing party; at the same time, the prospect of getting any distance up the North-West Ridge was so utterly hopeless that it did not really matter.

After the experiences of the past fortnight, it was with something more than relief that we set out to climb something that could be climbed. It has been said that on Everest the climbing party were so heartily "fed up" with the mountain, its weather, and the effects of altitude that their sole wish was to get the job over and done with, no matter who did it. Our attitude towards Kangchenjunga was the same. I do not think there was one of us who was not sick to death of work on the mountain. At exactly what height mountaineering ceases to be pleasurable is not easily defined, the matter is rather one of individual temperament, but I do not think there is one mountaineer who has climbed on Everest or Kangchenjunga who can honestly say that he enjoyed the work. Achievement may be good for the soul, but it is not necessarily enjoyable. It was a relief to turn away from our exacting opponent for a day and *enjoy* ourselves.

[1] Tencheddar had been left at the Base Camp.

The 20,800 feet point is easily reached along the ridge connecting it to Ramthang Peak, but from sheer exuberance we chose to ascend by a little rock face rising from the glacier. We raced each other up by various routes, and subsided puffing and blowing on the summit. What a summit it is – one of the most extraordinary that I have ever stood upon. From the Western Tributary Glacier it appears a mere knob, an insignificant excrescence, but had we stood on the Ramthang Glacier we should have seen an "impossible" peak. Seldom have I gazed down such abysmal precipices as those falling to the Ramthang Glacier. They were as long as the South-East Face of the Finsteraarhorn, and as steep as the Dolomite wall of the Winklerturm. The seamed and wrinkled surface of the Ramthang Glacier was spread out beneath us like a relief map, and we gazed down upon it like pilots from the nose of a bombing aeroplane. The upper portion of the Ramthang Glacier rises very steeply in an almost continuous icefall. From the col we had reached in the North-west Ridge we had been separated by but a few hundred feet from it, but the drop from Point 20,800 must be at least 4,000 feet, and as this point is separated from the col by only about a mile, the inclination of the glacier is a steep one.

At its extreme head the Ramthang Glacier forms a snowy plain beneath the West Face of Kangbachen. This face resembles closely the North Face above the Kangchenjunga Glacier. There are the same impregnable ice walls stretching across it from which ice avalanches fall at least as big as those that fall from the North Face. At the southern end of the face, where it abuts against the main West Ridge of Kangchenjunga, which separates the head of the Ramthang Glacier from the Yalung Glacier, there appeared to be a remote possibility of ascending between the ice walls and gaining the West Ridge. But, like the route we had already tried to the North Ridge, the possibility of success was more than counterbalanced by the possibility of annihilation, for the whole of the route was liable to be swept at any moment by ice avalanches. Even if the West Ridge was gained, what then? At the best it could only lead to the summit of Kangbachen. To traverse the ridge between Kangbachen and Kangchenjunga's highest summit, over the third highest summit, would be beyond the powers of any party. Therefore, it can be said without hesitation that Kangchenjunga is definitely unassailable from the Ramthang Glacier.

But if this side of Kangchenjunga is disappointing as regards its climbing potentialities it is hardly so otherwise. Great tiers of ice, gleaming steeps, and terrific red granite precipices combine to form a mountain face of a magnificence and grandeur worthy of the high summits it defends.

We had looked upon the last portion of Kangchenjunga to be properly seen by man, and what we had seen but confirmed our opinion that there are no groups of mountain tops defended so impregnably as the "Five Treasures of the Snows". We tore our eyes away from those terrible ice walls and glanced, for relief along the winding trench down which flows the Ramthang Glacier, and up over the sea of peaks to the west. Woolly clouds were rising from the valleys and draping themselves about the shoulders of the peaks. Once the cloudy waves rolled back; in a distant trough a great peak rose in noble solitude above the world. Someone said, "Everest". Then the mists closed in, and we saw it no more.

We turned to the North-West Ridge. Our view of it was an end-on one, but if it was impossible to gauge its length, its height and difficulty were apparent. Below us on the glacier was the camp, a mere smudge on the immaculate expanse of snow. The terrace we must gain was 4,000 feet higher. The North-West Ridge was the connecting link. I have already described its knife-like edges of ice and its rocky towers. Seen thus, end- on, they were jumbled one against the other, and one gained but little idea of the real length of the ridge, perhaps it was this that deceived Professor Dyhrenfurth into deciding to continue with the attack. To those used only to Alpine scale, it is easy to be misled by the length of these Himalayan ridges. But if the length was not apparent, the difficulties were, and one could not but wonder how porters were to be got up, and camps established along that tremendous crest. There was no answer to this question. Even supposing the upper ice wall, against which the ridge abutted, to be climbed, and the terrace gained, what next? There was no possibility whatever of reaching any of Kangchenjunga's summits. The terrace did not extend right across the mountain to the North Ridge; there was a cut-off of impassable precipices. At the best, we could only hope to reach Kangbachen, and that was separated from the terrace by 1,600 feet at least of formidable granite precipices. The most we could do was to climb as high as possible, perhaps even as high as the Bavarians, but what was the practical use of that? I fear my companions thought me a pessimist, but what else could one be taking everything into consideration? Anyway, the decision was made. We were to go on. This settled, we sat and lazed two or three hours away in the warm sun, happy hours, but trammelled by the thought of the morrow. The evening mists saw us jogging down the glacier to the camp.

The party that left the next morning consisted of Professor Dyhrenfurth, Schneider, Wieland and myself, with two porters, Lewa and Nima, the last named not to be confused with Nemu, my servant, both experienced Everest men. The couloir was in bad condition, and steps had to be kicked or cut through an upper layer of powdery snow a foot deep. The porters were not happy; neither of them had experienced similar climbing before. Lewa stuck gamely to the task, but Nima was constantly slipping from his steps. I was next to him on the rope, and had several times to hold him. The ridge itself was also in a worse condition than it was during our reconnaissance.

We climbed on two ropes, Schneider, Wieland and Lewa on the first, and Professor Dyhrenfurth, Nima, and myself on the second. The duty of the second party was to drive in pitons and fix ropes to the rocks. Nima caused us some anxious moments. It made one shudder to see the way he climbed on the loose rocks, hauling himself up on his hands without testing loose holds. So poor a show did he put up that we decided to leave him on a broad and safe part of the ridge, a decision that relieved him as much as it did us. Lewa was, however, an excellent rock climber, and followed Schneider and Wieland without difficulty to the top of the pinnacle, which had been the farthest point reached during the reconnaissance.

From the top of the pinnacle a vertical and holdless slice of granite drops to a gap. The climber must descend the granite slice on the rope, and alight on a sharp edge of snow. A piton was driven into a crack on the pinnacle, and a double rope fixed to it. Schneider and Wieland then descended hand over hand down the fixed rope, while being held at the same time from above on another rope by the remainder of the party. It was the sort of place fiction writers would make much of. Their descriptions would bristle with "unfathomable abysses", "like a fly on a wall", "beetling precipices", and so forth. The mountaineering guidebook writer would, however, describe it simply as "a twenty feet absail (sic)"[2] and as a grudging compliment to the place add "sensational". In this case, however, the fiction writer would convey a better picture to the mind of even the most sophisticated reader than the guidebook writer. To add to the sensationalism might be added the fact that the cracked and disintegrating pinnacle on which we stood exhibited a distinct tremor if rudely handled. I distinctly remember thinking, a trifle morosely, what a grand finale it would make to the expedition if the thing collapsed, and toppled into the "unfathomable abyss" with its human load.

As Wieland swung over the edge, the dirty and battered topi he was accustomed to affect looked strangely incongruous in these surroundings of rock, snow and ice, and, as he bumped and rasped down the rough granite, I half hoped that it would be knocked from his head and go spinning down the precipices, arriving at the camp below a pulped and shapeless mass. No such diversion occurred, and soon he had joined Schneider in the gap on the snow ridge.

Professor Dyhrenfurth and I remained on the pinnacle for an hour or two. We were privileged in witnessing one of the finest feats of climbing we had ever seen. Immediately above the gap rose a semi-detached mass of rock; beyond was another small gap, above which rose the great pinnacle in three hundred feet of slabs set at an angle not far removed from the vertical. Ice in the interstices of these slabs had forced them apart in many places and dangerously unstable flakes rested against the face. Every ledge was loaded with snow or ice. On an alpine climb of exceptional severity the ascent of this pinnacle would be a formidable proposition; at 21,000 feet it bordered on the impossible.

Wieland ensconced himself on top of the semi-detached mass, and Schneider descended, without much difficulty, into the secondary gap, and began the ascent of the slabs. Methodically he worked his way upwards. The exertion of hard rock climbing at such an altitude was obviously severe, and after each upward heave he was forced to halt and rest. At length he reached a small stance, a tiny triangular recess, where Wieland joined him. Above this rose a slanting crack formed by the edge of a projecting flake the upper part of which bulged out unpleasantly. It was not a place to linger over and Schneider did not linger. A foot scrape on the wall, a hand wedged in the crack, a quick upward caterpillar-like movement with nought but tiny hand holds to prevent a backward topple, and the hardest part had been accomplished. In the silence, unbroken save by an occasional whisper of wind, I could hear the sibilant sucking in of breath by sorely stressed lungs. A few feet more of difficult, but not such exacting climbing brought him to a sloping shelf. Wieland followed, and although burdened by both ice axes and a rucksack, he came up without relying on the rope.

So far, so good. For a few feet the work was easier; then the slopes steepened once more. In places they were dangerously ice-glazed, and their sloping icy shelves were masked by snow. Ice axes were called into play to clear holds. Now and again loose flakes of rock were dislodged. Hurtling madly down the cliffs

[2] A German term for double roping. [Abseil – the term "absail" (pronounced "absale") has recently crept back into common usage in the English spoken-media, completely ignoring the German word seil (pronounced syle) meaning "rope".]

towards the Ramthang Glacier, they loosed other rocks until a perfect torrent of crags set the echoes thundering from the cliffs of Kangchenjunga.

Two hours work, two hundred feet of ascent, such was the climbing on the great pinnacle. Professor Dyhrenfurth and I watched the struggle with intense interest. It was, probably, the finest piece of rock climbing ever done at such an altitude. We forgot for the moment that the real problem was not the ascent of the ridge by the Europeans but the establishing of camps and the getting up of porters over this gaunt, inhospitable backbone of rock and ice.

The weather restored pessimism, grey mists came flying up from the west, a chill wind sobbed over the ridge, driving before it small moths of snow. Schneider and Wieland were out of sight now. Occasionally we could hear their voices, whilst an occasional stone crashed out news of their advance. We rose, stretched our cramped limbs, tied on Lewa, and started to descend.

We had collected Nima but were still above the col when we were startled by an enormous roar, millions of tons of ice had broken away from the ice wall and were thundering down to the Ramthang Glacier. Instantly, the whole upper basin of the glacier was filled with a writhing hurricane of snow. Whirling up at us, it enveloped us in a blizzard, that whitened and sheeted our clothes in snow. The sky was darkened; the whole district seemed to be filled with the wind-blown snow dislodged by this monstrous avalanche.

Such an avalanche, had it occurred in the Alps would command widespread attention, newspapers would refer to it as a "Cataclysm of Nature". and questions would be asked in the Swiss Parliament about it. But on Kangchenjunga, such avalanches are not the exception, but the rule – almost an everyday occurrence in their season.

Kangchenjunga is by no means the only Himalayan peak to discharge avalanches of such magnitude, but it is probably safe to say that there is no other Himalayan peak that discharges them with such frequency. This is due, of course, to its great snowfall, the quick downward movement of its glaciers. A good instance of the size of a Himalayan avalanche is that which occurred during the late A.F. Mummery's attempt on Nanga Parbat. The party had bivouacked on a rock rib, which projected some five hundred feet from the mountainside, but when they returned to their bivouac site after an unsuccessful attempt on the mountain, they found that their gear had been swept away by an ice avalanche. The avalanche had fallen diagonally and taken the five hundred feet rib in its stride! The size and destructive power of Himalayan avalanches is the first thing that should be studied when climbing in the Himalayas. A purely alpine trained mountaineer finds it difficult to appreciate the scale on which such avalanches occur. Mummery paid the penalty of not realising this when he made his final and disastrous attempt on Nanga Parbat. No trace of him and his two Gurkha followers was ever discovered. We narrowly missed paying the same penalty too, and had we been wiped out during our attempt to reach the North Ridge of Kangchenjunga, we should have received our just deserts.

It must be remembered that Himalayan ice avalanches *habitually* sweep the whole breadth of glaciers. To illustrate this I can but add that were the peaks in the vicinity of the well-known Concordia Hut in the Bernese Oberland enlarged to Himalayan scale, the mountaineer staying at the hut would not be safe from ice avalanches falling from the peaks on the opposite side of the Aletsch Glacier.

It was a relief to leave the rotten rocks, and to stand once more in the col; and it was pleasant to escape from the cutting wind, and seizing the fixed rope that hung down the steep upper part of the couloir step blithely down the capacious ladder of holds towards the camp.

We glissaded down the lower part of the couloir and for the first time that day Nima's worried expression gave place to a broad grin of delight. The porters are children at heart, and they have all the enthusiasm for a glissade down snow that a child has for a toboggan. For the benefit of the uninitiated I should explain that there are two methods of glissading. One is to stand upright, and the other is to sit down. The former is best employed on hard snow, the latter on soft snow. A certain degree of expertness is necessary for the stand-up glissade. Many commence in elegant style. With ever-increasing speed, they slide down the slope. Presently, as the speed becomes faster and faster, they become flustered. From stability, they are reduced to instability; their elegance, their dignified deportment is lost, their balance is upset, they struggle wildly to regain it, then the snow comes up and hits them on the nose. They go head over heels, their ice axes are snatched from their hands, their hats torn from their heads, their rucksacks wind themselves round their necks, endeavouring to strangle them, snow is forced down their collars, up their sleeves, and into their pockets and trousers. Over and over they go in a series of somersaults, to subside finally at the bottom where they rise to their feet vowing it was good fun. On this account, the inexpert and less venturesome prefer to glissade sitting.

There is one other variety of glissade worthy of mention, and that is glissading on a rope. This is one degree worse than skiing on a rope. What usually happens is this: the leader, without troubling to enquire whether the second man is ready, shoots off with great velocity, despite the agonised cries of the latter. In a moment or two, the rope tightens on the second man who has barely had time to start, snatching him forward on to his head, and squeezing the breath out of him. The jerk arrests the leader, who hurls an uncomplimentary remark over his shoulder at the unfortunate second man, who meanwhile slides, or somersaults pell mell past the leader. Then, before the leader has time to continue, he is in his turn dragged in the wake of the second man. And so it goes on a vicious cycle, until they have reached the bottom, where they sit side by side in the snow roundly abusing one another.

We reached camp in desultory snow squalls. Mists concealed the North-West Ridge, but now and again they blew aside and we scanned the rocks a little anxiously for signs of Schneider and Wieland. It was not until evening that we saw them descending, mere dots silhouetted against the jagged skyline. Dusk was falling when they returned. They reported immense difficulties, difficulties both of rocks and ice. Short of roping the great tower up from top to bottom, there was no possibility of getting the porters up it even with ropes, it would most likely prove impossible for laden men. The prospect of further advance beyond the tower was doubtful in the extreme. The whole crest of the first knife-like ice ridge would have to be hacked away before a passage could be won. At the end of this ridge, there was another tower, not so high as the first, but more difficult, in fact, probably impassable. Its summit was capped by a boss of ice, which flowed down its sides like icing on a cake. There was no avoiding this tower, for the precipices on either side were sheer and offered no hope of a traverse. Above this tower, other ice ridges rose, a whole series of them, up to the terrace. Nowhere, said Schneider was there a place on which a camp might be pitched. There were not even any ice pinnacles of a type suitable for bivouac caves. And the weather? What would be the position of a party caught high up on this great ridge in bad weather or high winds? The storm on the glacier three nights previously had been bad enough, but what would it have been like on the ridge? Retreat would be impossible. It would probably mean two weeks hard work to reach the terrace, even supposing camps could be established, and porters brought up and by then the monsoon would most likely have broken. Each of these facts taken separately was sufficiently weighty to militate against any attempt; accumulatively, they were overwhelming.

There was no alternative but to abandon the project and the following day Wieland and I accomplished the dreary task of collecting and bringing down the fixed ropes. Kangchenjunga had beaten us, beaten us not by bad weather, so much as by sheer difficulty. We had examined every portion of the faces above the Kangchenjunga and the Ramthang Glaciers. Nowhere was there a chink in the armour of the giant; nowhere was there a route at which the mountaineer might look and say, 'Well, it *might* go.' Others sceptical as to the truth of these assertions may follow in our footsteps, but they too will return disappointed, and like us they will lie awake at nights and tremble, even as the ground trembles, at the roar of the great ice avalanches that seek their destruction, and like us, their hope and optimism will be ruthlessly crushed beneath the icy heel of Kangchenjunga.

CHAPTER FOURTEEN

The First Ascent of Ramthang Peak

I HAVE ALREADY had occasion to mention the beautiful snow and ice summit rising from the head of the Western Tributary of the Kangchenjunga Glacier. This peak, which is about 23,000 feet high, had inspired the appellation of Madonna Peak, for its sweeping robes of snow and ice suggest an unapproachable virginity, but Professor Dyhrenfurth had, in the interests of topography, subsequently re-christened it Ramthang Peak in deference to the Ramthang Glacier which is fed by its southern snow-slopes.

On May 18, the day after our decisive and final defeat on the North-West Ridge of Kangbachen and Kangchenjunga, we decided to push camp as far as possible up Ramthang Peak and so bring the summit within reasonable reach. With this end in view, it was agreed that Schneider and I should start before the main body of the expedition, and explore the route, with a view to ascertaining whether it was possible to establish a camp on a snowy shoulder at the foot of the eastern ridge of the peak which we hoped to follow to the top.

I was the first to leave, and soon after the sun had struck the camp strapped on ski and started alone up the glacier, which in its upper portion is practically devoid of crevasses and perfectly safe for a solitary ski runner.

The morning was a lovely one; scarcely a zephyr of wind disturbed the delicate ice crystals formed by a sharp overnight's frost on the surface of the glacier; a host of hoary peaks lifted silvered heads into a sky of gentian blue. Slowly the sun flooded over the snowfields, his slanting rays revealing the most delicate folds and unsuspected wrinkles and undulations on the timeworn countenances of the peaks. I almost felt myself to be the invader of some moonscape, fantastic, unreal and beautiful.

A load of care had been lifted from my mind by the abandonment of the attempt on the North-West Ridge. Now at last we were to attempt something that offered some prospect of success. Even my ski seemed to hiss joyfully beneath me, like a carefree ostler grooming a horse, and my ski sticks drove into the crusted snow with a light triumphant plop at every forward lunge.

Impelled by sheer exuberance I climbed quickly, too quickly, for soon my lungs began to labour reminding me that I was not on the slopes of Mürren but 20,000 feet up in the Himalayas. Gladness departed; what was mere flesh and blood that it should stride about the mountains in this way?

I halted, and puffed myself into a more sedate frame of mind. Like walking uphill at great altitudes, so with skiing, rhythm. And, once cultivated, an easy rhythm. Despite the heavy hickory boards, I found myself climbing more steadily, and making height more quickly, than if I had been on foot. Unconsciously, I began to keep my upward lunges in time with the slow beats of an old and sentimental music-hall ditty. I had not heard it, or sung it, for years, yet now, high up on Ramthang Peak, it jogged through my brain in harmonious time with the forward movements of my ski.

Leaving Point 20,800 feet on my left, I climbed up and round in a wide arc, and began to ascend to the snowy shoulder. The slope I was traversing gradually steepened, and presently, on glancing down, I saw that an ice cliff two or three hundred feet high was below me. For fifty yards, where the snow was resting but a few inches deep on hard ice, a ski-jump down the ice cliff was the penalty of slipping, and I advanced cautiously, stamping my ski well in at every step.

The slope eased off, and I found myself on the shoulder. From beneath it had looked almost flat and a good site for a camp; actually, it was by no means flat and was, moreover, exposed to the full force of the wind. At all events, there was little object in advancing camp thus far, when only half an hour's extra work would be entailed on the morrow if we pitched it as high as possible up the glacier.

Above the shoulder rose an ice slope nearly 1,000 feet high, and forming a cut-off in the eastern ridge of the peak. The ice was too steep for crampons to be effectively used, whilst an evil glitter from its polished blue-black surface suggested a long and hard bout of step cutting.

Schneider joined me. Together we lazed in the sun. The view was an extensive one. The whole of Kangchenjunga's northern precipices were outspread before us. Our gaze swept along their granite facets, with their tiers of icy escarpments that stretched across the face of the mountain like the galleries of some colossal stadium. Now and again avalanches boomed through the still morning air telling of an ever restless and malignant activity.

South-westwards rose Jannu, 25,294 feet high. It would be difficult to conceive a more inaccessible looking mountain.

Like many Himalayan peaks it is wedge-like in formation, with two summits set at either end of an almost horizontal ridge. Once gain this ridge and the ascent of either summit should be feasible. But how to gain the ridge? On the side facing us the precipices lifted in one smooth, terrible facade of granite; on the other side, to judge by photographs, are equally fearsome cliffs. Can either summit be reached directly? The answer is, no! Both ends of the wedge end in hopeless precipices. Such is the problem presented to the mountaineer by Jannu, a rival of the famous Mustagh Tower in the Karakorams, and one of the most appalling rock peaks in the world.

Northwards, was the Jonsong Glacier, its irregular moraine strewn surface looking as though it had been riven by the picks and drills of a million mad navvies. These ugly moraines stretched far up the glacier, and it was only at its head that the forces of ruin and decay relinquished their grip, and gentle snow slopes stretched upwards to the snowy notch of the Jonsong La. West of the Jonsong La, Jonsong Peak, 24,344 feet, rises grandly, its massive summit forming the culminating point of the ranges of north-eastern Nepal and north-western Sikkim. On this side, the south-eastern face, it throws down great cliffs friezed like Kangchenjunga with hanging glaciers. Dr. Kellas had, we knew, attempted it from the north-west. Given sufficient time before the arrival of the monsoon, that would be also our line of attack.

Then the range of peaks directly to the north of the Base Camp attracted our attention: fine precipitous rock peaks standing out from torrential glaciers. One of them, with a horizontal roof-like ridge rising to an acute spire at one end, bore a curious resemblance to a church. At first we were observant and critical, but as we reclined in the snow, warmed by the sun, mind and muscles relaxed, and the peace of the high places laid soothing hands upon us. Through half closed eyelids I gazed at a world unsubstantial and dreamlike. Once again I seemed to hear music, but this time music solemn and slow, a majestic symphony from the massed orchestras of the hills. Its slow pulsating waves bore me away into space – the music was drowned in a sudden roll of drums. I tried to escape from the insistent din. I could not. It closed in on me, surrounded me. There was a thundering crash. I awoke. My opened eyes were dazzled by the snow glare, but the thunder still smote on my ears – a great avalanche was roaring off Kangchenjunga.

There is no peace to be found on these mountains. Solitude, yes, but peace, no. Every hour the mountaineer is reminded of the destructive forces that are ever at work ceaselessly endeavouring to reduce the grandeurs and beauties of the mountains to the uninspiring uniformity of the plains. To discover the peace that dwells upon hilltops you need go no farther than our homeland hills. On them, among their rocks and heather, you will be given something that not even the lords of the Himalayas are able to give.

We unclipped our sealskins, thrust them into our rucksacks, and strapping on ski set off down towards the little worm-like caravan of porters who were toiling up the glacier far beneath.

I had barely started when Schneider was half way down to the glacier. He is a splendid ski runner, combining the dash of the first-class racer with the shrewd judgement of the mountaineer. To him, as with me, ski are something more than wooden boards and skiing something more than a winter sport.

We had reached a height of between 21,000 and 22,000 feet and I found skiing downhill at this height more tiring than skiing downhill at Alpine levels. One good point about mountaineering on foot at high altitudes is that it is no more fatiguing to *descend* moderately easy ground than it is in the Alps. The same does not apply to skiing. Balancing at low levels is automatic, but at 20,000 feet a conscious effort is required, whilst a swing is distinctly hard work. After a few swings the knees tend to become weak, and balancing more difficult. For a moderate class runner like myself, really to enjoy a long descent, it is best to stop and rest now and then.

The snow was of a delightful quality, hard, but with a loose crystalline surface into which the ski edged well. On such a surface the jerked Christiania was a simple matter. So much for the technique and the drawbacks of skiing at high altitudes, how can I describe the delights? The swift rush with body tensed and crouched, the song of the wind, the slow procession of the mountains, the fierce exhilaration of pure speed, and far below a little line of laden porters ascending the glacier gazing up in amazement at these strange pranks, as I sped down towards them. As Mr. Arnold Lunn once remarked, 'Skiing is the finest form of locomotion known to man.'

Camp was pitched on the gently sloping glacier under Point 20,800 feet. Unfortunately, Professor Dyhrenfurth, Wieland and Duvanel were not fit, and it looked as if Schneider and I alone would be able to make the attempt on the morrow. Duvanel was worst; he had worked very hard on the taking of his film, and had not spared himself.

The unfitness of the party was due, partly, to the wrong kind of food, and partly to nerve strain. Owing to transport delays, we had been forced to exist for ten days on food scarcely suited to the peculiar requirements of high altitudes. Now, thanks to Colonel Tobin, Wood Johnson and Hannah, the transport had been reorganised and food cases were arriving every day at the Base Camp. But the harm had been done, stomachs had rebelled, and constitutions had been undermined. Yet, compared to nervous strain, food is of secondary importance. We had escaped annihilation on Kangchenjunga only by a miracle, and during the eighteen days we had been on the mountain we had never felt safe from ice avalanches. At the back of our minds there had been always the feeling that we were only there on sufferance, and did Kangchenjunga choose, it could kill us. However philosophical a man may be, and as regards danger he *does* become philosophical at high altitudes, such mental strain tells on the physique. The period spent on Kangchenjunga was the most nerve-racking that I have ever experienced. Wieland and I had been up the whole time, and we were both tired, mentally as well as physically. We were sick of the unvarying glare of snow, and longed to feast and rest our eyes once more on green grass. Schneider alone was brimful of energy, for he is of a type impervious to "nerves", besides being a man of extraordinary physique.

I spent the remainder of the afternoon seated on the snow ridge above the camp between Point 20,800 feet and the first rock towers of the North-West Ridge.

Among other dainties that had come up from the Base Camp, were some boxes of fruit jellies, and I lay contentedly in the snow eating them for hours, with the appreciative mechanical regularity of a small boy possessed of a generous, if misguided uncle.

Mists gathered ere evening, their light luminescent filaments serving to enhance the beauty of the peaks. Once again I thought I saw Everest, like a blue jewel resting on cotton-wool clouds.

Towards sundown a chill wind rose, and I was glad to retire to the camp. We had thought it to be protected from the wind, but that capricious element poured over the ridge above and descended on us in a bitterly cold douche. There were fifty degrees of frost as we vainly endeavoured to boil some hot tea over a Meta cooker, and so quickly did the heat radiate from the aluminium cooking pan, that it was impossible to get more than a lukewarm brew.

Among other good things that had arrived were some tins of cranberries. These mixed with condensed milk formed a delicious dish, and Duvanel, who had undertaken the onerous task of cooking, distributed them to us.

We were glad to get into our sleeping bags and warm numbed hands. The wind increased in force during the night, and once I awoke to hear the driven snow lashing my tent like rawhide whips.

At dawn the wind had not dropped, and the cold was still severe, but, nevertheless, Professor Dyhrenfurth gallantly blew the conventional three blasts on his horn. But for once he blew without effect; there was no competition among my companions to "show a leg". A few minutes later I heard him passing down the line of tents endeavouring to rouse their occupants to a sense of duty. Eventually he stood before mine. 'Herr Smythe, it is time we started.' No answer. Louder: 'Herr Smythe, it is time we started.' I emitted a lusty snore. A few minutes later the camp was slumbering peacefully again. It was not until eight, by which time the wind had abated and the sun was warm, that we were tempted outside.

By 9 a.m. Schneider and I were away. The wind had dropped completely, and the morning was as perfect as that of the previous day. Following our former tracks, we were soon on the shoulder. There we took off our skis and made preparations for the final climb.

More as an experiment than anything else I had brought with me the pair of expedition boots that had been supplied to me. These weighed no less than eight and a half pounds the pair, and each boot bristled with over sixty nails. So far during the expedition I had not been able to pluck up enough courage to put them on, except when camping, and I had worn ordinary light Swiss-made climbing boots, which had kept my feet perfectly warm. The expedition boots were designed to guard against frostbite, and their uppers, which came half-way to the knees, were lined thickly with felt, whilst their soles were constructed of layers of rubber, felt and leather. As regards weight, the same remarks might be applied to the climbing suits supplied to the expedition. These again were excellent for use in camp, but were too clumsy and heavy for difficult climbing on a mountain. My own favourite garb consisted of Jaeger combinations and shirts plus several light Shetland sweaters weighing about two or three ounces each, with a wind-proof jacket on top, a pair of strong tricot breeches, one pair of socks, and one pair of stockings, and as additional protection to the legs, a pair of light and warm Kashmiri puttees that I had got from General Bruce. Two or three light Balaclava helmets on the head afforded ample protection to the ears and neck, whilst in the event of a particularly strong, cold wind, a leather flying helmet could be added. Fleece-lined leather finger-less gloves are superior to all others.

In addition to the portmanteau-like expedition boots, it was necessary to wear crampons. These weighed about four pounds the pair. Thus, I was carrying a load of twelve and a half pounds on my feet, nearly an additional stone of weight, and I felt something like a cross between a leaden-footed diver, and one rooted to the spot in a nightmare after a heavy dinner. Thus attired, I began to lift my two-foot portmanteaux up the snow slopes, with a slow, treadmill-like action, trying to keep up with Schneider who was wearing ordinary light climbing boots. I felt fortunate in being with Schneider, for he exults in hard work on a mountain and would, I hoped, make all the steps. If he did, it might be just possible for me to raise myself, plus boots and crampons, to the top of the mountain.

The slope soon steepened, and step cutting became necessary. Schneider went at it with a will, swinging his heavy ice axe with that graceful yet vigorous style of the born iceman. The ice was blue-black, polished and hard. Step after step was hewn out. The slope seemed interminable, and it needed a glance backwards down the long ladder of steps to assure us that we had made progress.

Professor Dyhrenfurth, Wieland and Lewa arrived on the shoulder, and sunned themselves, while waiting for the work to be finished. Cutting went steadily on, the thud, thud, thud of the ice axe becoming gradually monotonous to the ears. I occupied myself with enlarging the holds.

Suddenly came a mighty roar. We looked round. Huge masses were falling from the edge of the upper terrace of Kangchenjunga. Sweeping downwards with fearful force, a million tons or more of ice poured on to the Eastern Tributary Glacier. Sweeping forwards with lightning speed, the avalanche seemed to leap across the glacier, obliterating our former route between upper and lower Camp Two, and so far as we could see the site of lower Camp Two. The clouds of snow raised by the wind shot cannon-like across the mile-wide glacier and beat furiously against the precipices of The Twins. It was a tremendous avalanche, the largest we had ever seen. It confirmed, if confirmation was needed, the fact that nowhere within a mile or so of Kangchenjunga's North Face is the mountaineer safe.

As quickly as possible I got my camera out of my pocket, and bracing myself firmly in my ice steps, took two hurried snaps. It shows the head of the avalanche about to sweep the route between upper and lower Camp Two. The roar subsided, but it was long before the clouds of wind-blown snow began to settle. We turned again without a word to our task.

About halfway up the slope we decided to try our luck by traversing to the left to where snow appeared to overlay the ice. Our speculation was justified, and to our delight we found ourselves on hard snow in which only a couple of good kicks were necessary to make a step. Without further difficulty, we gained a subsidiary ridge falling from the main east ridge of the mountain. The snow here was wind-blown, hard and icy, and without crampons another hour's cutting at least would have been required. As it was, we walked, our faithful spikes biting well home. The angle, at first steep, gradually eased off. We found ourselves on the main ridge. It was almost horizontal at its junction with the subsidiary ridge, and we sat down for a welcome rest. My legs felt as if they had been afflicted with varicose veins since birth, and I anathematised the foolish spirit of experimental inquiry that had led me to don the expedition boots.

If Schneider is included in a party, that party does not get much rest. Now, he was fairly bubbling with suppressed energy and enthusiasm, and unable to wait, untied the rope, and set off along the ridge, which appeared quite easy for a considerable distance. A minute or two later he disappeared over a snowy hump, and I was left to myself. I did not feel like going on, my calves ached abominably, but I supposed it had to be done, and so heaving myself to my feet, I set off on the wearying task of dragging the expedition boots up the final five hundred feet of ridge to the top.

With a superhuman effort I gained the crest of the hump, wondering vaguely whether it would be practical to take my foot luggage off, and proceed in stockinged feet. Schneider was halted some distance along the ridge, and he called to me urgently. Beyond him the ridge was obviously much more difficult, narrowing to a mere blade of ice, of a type so characteristic of the Himalayas. I gathered that without me he did not like to go on alone.

With an inward, if not outward groan, I galvanised the expedition boots into activity, and together we toiled along the ridge.

There certainly appeared to be one or two distinctly formidable pieces in the ridge. Immediately above Schneider it was split by a curious crevasse and above the crevasse was a nasty, unstable looking ice flake. Roping on to Schneider, I paid him out while he carefully bestrode the crevasse, and cut steps up and along one side of the flake. After a short upward traverse, he cut up directly to the top of the flake and commenced to hew its crest away with a cheerful abandon. The flake became thicker, and the work easier. Soon he reached a broader portion of the ridge, and there, comfortably seated in the snow, bade me cheerily to come on. I did so, cautiously propelling the expedition boots upwards from step to step.

To the non-mountaineering public, there are only three kinds of mountaineering difficulties. There is the vertical, or overhanging precipice, the dizzy ledge, and the knifelike ridge. All these figure conspicuously in novels purporting to present the thrills of mountaineering. In actual practice, however, they are seldom met with. The Matterhorn, for instance, can be climbed, and not one of them will be encountered, and it is necessary to go to special districts such as the Aiguilles of Mont Blanc, or the Dolomites to find plumb vertical, or overhanging precipices, and genuine dizzy ledges. The knife-like ice ridge scarcely exists at all in the Alps, and the only examples I can recollect are the ice ridges on the Brenva face of Mont Blanc, and in particular the classic ice ridge of the Col de la Brenva, along which Mr. A.E.W. Mason's heroes and villains crawled in *Running Water*. But even the Brenva ice ridges, airy though they are, cannot compare to the ice ridges adorning Himalayan peaks. It was with something of satisfaction, therefore, that I found myself on a ridge, the knife-like merits of which not even the most earnest seeker after the sensational could carp at.

On my left the slopes dropped with tremendous steepness towards the Western Tributary Glacier; on my right, I looked down the most extraordinary precipice I know of. Not extraordinary so much from the point of view of steepness – the Alps can produce a nearly vertical face of 4,000 feet in height – but in its appearance. Great uncouth lumps of ice clung to it, bulging outwards like the primitive sculptures of Mr. Epstein on the "Underground" building at St. James' Park. Leering, gargoyle-like heads suspended from thick, goitrous-like necks of ice peered over into the abyss; great boilerplates and sheets of black ice coated the smooth granite slabs; icy stalks, marrows and pumpkins, grew from every wrinkle, niche and cranny.

How ice could cling to rocks at such an angle passes the comprehension. Such formations are not seen in the Alps. Only once before have I seen anything to approach this precipice, and this was strangely enough on Ben Nevis during an Easter climbing holiday. In that case, however, the ice was due to freezing moisture-charged winds from the Atlantic beating against the sunless northern cliffs of the Ben. In the present instance, it was more likely temperature fluctuation that enabled the ice to stick glue-like to the all but vertical precipice.

Needless to say, I did not think of all these things at the time; my attention was concentrated on getting over the narrow bit as quickly as possible to the broader and more comfortable ridge on which Schneider was sitting. The ice was obviously tough, but the crest tended to curl slightly, but unpleasantly outwards over the right-hand precipice. This tendency was perhaps slightly exaggerated in my mind by Schneider's reference to *gefahrlichkeiten* and earnest exhortations to me to hurry. In a minute or two it was no longer essential to emulate the stealth of a cat burglar, and treading more boldly, I rejoined Schneider.

For a short distance the ridge was easier, then once more it narrowed. This time it was not so much a knife-edge as a leaf. The ice was curiously stratified, each stratum indicating a previous snowfall which had gone to help build up the leaf, but the latter was so thin and undernourished that it needed but a blow to knock a hole through it several feet below its tapering crest. There was no going along that crest; the sole way of negotiating it was to traverse below it on the Kangchenjunga side. It was steep work; handholds were as desirable as footholds. The expedition boots did not like it at all, and struggled clumsily to maintain a grip in the steps cut by Schneider. Given one good kick with them, the leaf would most likely have collapsed.

The length of the leaf was quite short, not more than twenty-five feet. It thickened gradually, and presently Schneider was able to cut directly up. He put his head over the top like an evil disposed small boy peeping cautiously over the wall of an orchard. Satisfied that the leaf was thick enough to support him, he hauled himself on to its crest, and advanced a few steps until it widened out considerably, and there was no longer any doubt as to its stability. There he halted, and shouted back that it was the last difficulty. I followed. Half way along I found myself opposite an awesome hole, a yard in diameter, through which I was able to put my head and shoulders, and gaze down the other side of the ridge. My sensations were no doubt similar to those of one who gazes out for the first time from the attic window of a New York skyscraper. One glance was sufficient, and I popped my head back again. The downward view from *my* side of the ridge was sufficiently nerve harrowing. Presently, with a tremendous effort, I hauled the expedition boots on to the crest, and a few instants later flopped down thankfully beside Schneider.

The difficulties had been conquered; snow slopes alone separated us from the summit. We grinned at each other, but my own grin was a trifle wan. Three hundred feet of soft snow slopes to do in the expedition boots at nearly 23,000 feet. The ascent had taken longer than we had anticipated, time was getting on, it was well after midday, and the afternoon mists were forming, and getting denser every instant. Leaving all our spare kit in our rucksacks, including, I regret to say, my camera, we set off on the last push to the top.

Dense mist concealed the way, and in its enveloping folds the snow slopes seemed to stretch never-endingly upwards. Fortunately, it was remarkably warm and windless.

On the way up the snow had been bad, but its vileness had been compensated for to some extent by the interest and excitement of the climbing. Now, with interest and excitement evaporated, and with nothing else to think about save getting to the top, we realised how vile it was, and what a purgatory we were undergoing. At every step Schneider sunk in well above the boots, but he persisted in leading, and his indomitable energy seemed in no whit abated. I plodded after him, cramp numbing my calves, my knees weak and trembling from the strain of raising the expedition boots.

It was not all plain sailing. At one point a half-choked crevasse rifted the slope, and its steep upper lip necessitated a few steps being cut. Above that the slope eased off.

We trudged resolutely, if slowly, upwards. The mist thinned. The sun glared down upon our labours; its suffocating heat scarcely served to lighten them, rather did it seem to sap all energy, so that despite well acclimatised bodies, every step became a gasping toil. We topped the slope, and found ourselves on an easy snow ridge sloping gently upwards. The summit became dimly visible. Schneider leapt forward; soon he was fifty yards ahead, plugging with the tireless regularity of a machine through the soft snow. The fitful mists closed in upon us as we trod that last remote ridgepole of the world.

We stood together on the summit. The mists lifted for a few seconds; once more sunlight and shadow chased about us. Below steamy clouds eddied and boiled from deep glacier cauldrons. A bitter breath of wind sallied out of the west, causing us to knock gloved hands together, and shuffle chilled feet. The world was not visible; we felt ourselves to be far removed from it. A picture flashed through my mind of civilisation, its hateful clamour, its sweatful heat. Up here, all was peace. When we had gone, the wind would fill our footsteps with snow, and remodel once more the serene crest of the snow ridge we had trampled under foot. All would be the same, and continue the same. When we die, may our spirits linger on the high places to which we have dedicated our youth.

We turned and strode downhill. An immense vitalising relief coursed through my tired body. I was no longer lifting the expedition boots, I was simply swinging them forwards, and allowing them to drop. How mercilessly long the ascent had seemed, how mercifully short and easy the descent.

In a few minutes we were sitting in the snow by our rucksacks. For a while we lazed, but time was drawing on, and the descent had perforce to be continued. The flake and the knife-edge were soon traversed, jumping the crevasse; we threw off the rope, and fairly raced along the ridge. At the end of it we found Professor Dyhrenfurth and Lewa. Though far from well, the Professor had pluckily climbed until he could go no farther. Wieland had ascended to the shoulder, and then turned back. A welcome drink from the Professor's flask, and we were off once more.

Facing inwards, and with picks driven well home, we carefully descended the long line of steps. Halfway down, where the snow gave place to ice, and the route traversed across the slope, we found a convenient streak of snow. Stamping our crampons well in, we pelted down to the shoulder.

During the latter part, at least, our haste had been induced not so much by the desire to get down as by the knowledge that a large tin of fruit had been left on the shoulder. We had been the prey to grim forebodings that they might no longer be there, but these proved to be without foundation, and soon parched mouths and throats were being lubricated by delicious Californian peaches and their accompanying juice.

We did not loiter, for the afternoon wind was increasing in strength every minute, and stinging particles of snow from a greying sky were whipping across the shoulder. With stiff fumbling fingers I pulled off crampons and expedition boots. The latter, with their armoury of nails, seemed to leer at me. I thrust them out of sight into my rucksack, registering at the same time a solemn vow never again to burden myself with them on a mountain. I strapped on ski, swung my heavy load on to my back, and turned downhill for home.

Schneider had decided to descend direct to the Base Camp, and he suggested that I should leave my load at Camp Two for the porters to bring down the following day. This was a first rate idea, for like him, I hungered for the comfort and luxury of the Base Camp. With no boots to change, Schneider was off first. Taking everything straight, he shot skilfully down the snow slopes, and was soon a mere insect on the vast counterpane of the glacier. I followed. For a while, all went well, but then, instead of being sensible, and kick turning at the end of every traverse. I essayed a downhill Christiania swing. Instantly, the expedition boots retaliated; the heavy rucksack swung me off my balance, and I pitched headfirst down the slope, where my nose, already raw and peeled, clove through the crusted snow like the prow of a ship. For a while I lay too winded even to curse, but then the humour of the situation suddenly dawned on me, and the breath I had regained was lost in an uncontrollable fit of laughter.

Kick turn by kick turn, I descended to Camp Two. A circle of grinning faces greeted me as I entered the porters' tent, and hurled the expedition boots to the ground. Somewhere in the gloom a Primus stove was roaring; a dirty hand pressed a large cup of steaming hot tea upon me. The porters were genuinely pleased that we had got to the top, as pleased as small boys would be at the success of their schoolmaster in an International rugger match. What splendid fellows they are! Their devotion to duty, their uncomplaining fortitude, and unvarying cheerfulness on Kangchenjunga can never be forgotten. The ground is well prepared for the corps of native Himalayan guides that General Bruce and the Himalayan Club are anxious to form.

The light was poor when Schneider and I started off for Camp One. The basin of the Western Tributary Glacier we were leaving seemed sombre and sad, the ice walls of Kangchenjunga shone greenly, malignantly in the fading light, and the jagged rock towers of the North-West Ridge stabbed the livid mists like grim watchful sentinels. How long will it be before man again visits this lonely corner of the World?

We skied in long smooth sweeps down the gentle breast of the glacier. Gradually, the angle steepened, the keen air tightened in nostrils, whooped past Balaclava-covered ears. Swish! A swing one way, a long sideways skid on the hard frozen surface, snow crystals raised in a scintillating shower. Swish! A swing the other way. The ski whipped round like live things. Walking up through the soft snow we had been exposed for perhaps half an hour to the risk of ice avalanches from the ice cliffs below the shoulder of Ramthang Peak. Skiing down, we swept across this dangerous area in a few seconds.

Schneider soon disappeared ahead; he had as usual, taken everything straight. My skiing is, however, not of the type that allows me to take steep slopes straight without disaster, or at least frequent and unpleasant crashes, and I entered the corridor alone. In it I was forced to tack to either side of Schneider's straight track several times. It was during one of these tacks that I went into a crevasse. In the dull light the slight concavity in the snow-crust concealing it was not visible. I was running moderately fast when the snow beneath me collapsed. There was no time in which to do anything, no fraction of a second in which to make a desperate spring forwards, my legs dropped into nothingness, my body, owing to its forward impetus was flung violently against the opposite lip of the crevasse. There I lay, half in and half out of the crevasse utterly and completely winded. My legs were numbed with the shock, and my back felt as though it were broken, as well as every other bone in my body. I certainly ought to have broken both ski and legs, yet, by some miracle, both were intact. It was a nasty moment that drop into space; I remember vividly the noise of dislodged fragments of snow and ice as they fell with a sort of shush, shush, shush, into the bowels of the crevasse. Minutes later I was able to make an effort and haul my legs and ski out on to *terra firma*, where for some time I lay, still partially winded and feeling not a little sick. As I lay I remembered the wise words of an American friend of mine who fell into a crevasse the first time he had been escorted on to a glacier. He said: 'Never again! I guess it's *terra firma* for me in future, less terror and more firmer.'

Taking off my ski, I walked down the remainder of the corridor, following the porters' tracks. Dr. Richter was at Camp One. He had some hot tea ready for me and, what was even better, rum. Both served to steady shaken nerves.

The way between the Base Camp and Camp One had been well prepared by Schneider and Duvanel; it was not only a good route for foot slogging, but first rate for skiing, and soon we had left Camp One far behind.

The angle at which the main ice stream of the Kangchenjunga Glacier rises is deceptive. From the Base Camp the glacier looks practically flat, but actually it slopes downwards at a much steeper angle than at first appears, and we skimmed gaily down it for quite three miles with scarcely a stop.

Dusk was falling as we reached the maze of moraines separating the snowy middle of the glacier from the grassy terraces of Pangperma and the Base Camp. Seated on a boulder, we gazed back towards the scene of the labours, bitternesses, hopes and fears of the past nineteen days. The evening was a still one; the glacier rivulets were already hushed and awed in the grip of frost; only the occasional slither and splash of a dislodged stone falling into a glacier pool broke a profound quietude. Through a window, where the mists were melting into the first stars, stood Kangchenjunga, its precipices aflame in the setting sun. Before us curved the great glacier down which we had come, like a ghostly road stretching to the foot of some Goblin fortress. All day long the avalanche juggernauts had roared down upon it; now they rested cold and silent in the garages of the hills, and "Policeman Day" retired wearily from his long beat.

We turned to go, leaving our ski and sticks on the stones. Two figures came scrambling over the moraines to meet us, Nemu and Nima with a thermos of hot tea for each of us. It was a kindly thought, something to remember when other and more grandiose events have passed into oblivion.

I had expected to feel very tired. On Ramthang Peak it had seemed an impossibility to get down to the Base Camp that day, but seven thousand feet of descent had stimulated muscle and will jaded by altitude, and I found myself trudging over the moraine feeling little more tired than at the end of an Alpine day.

Tropical night fell like the lowering of a curtain. As we stumbled over the last stones more figures emerged from the gloom and we clasped hands with our companions.

Though defeat on Kangchenjunga had been our lot, it was a cheery crowd that gathered in the mess tent that evening. What a joy to be able to sit and eat dinner with one's fellows once more, instead of "pigging" it cramped up in one's own tiny tent. Even Tencheddar's 'Soup sometime coming,' as we sat and waited hungrily for dinner, could not damp the general cheerfulness.

Transport difficulties had been solved, and Wood Johnson and Hannah were back from their arduous tasks, which they had accomplished so successfully. Wieland and Duvanel had come down that day; the latter was far from well. Only Professor Dyhrenfurth and Dr. Richter remained in the upper camps, and they with the remainder of the porters and equipment would be down next day.

Kangchenjunga had beaten us, and claimed a brave soul in so doing. That the toll was not greater was not due to any skill on our part, it was a Divine Providence.

CHAPTER FIFTEEN

The Jonsong La and Nepal Peak

ON MAY 20 the remaining camps on Kangchenjunga were evacuated, and all members of the expedition and porters assembled at the Base Camp. Rest and reorganisation were the first essentials. The general health and condition of the party was by no means what it should be; several members were still suffering from the relaxing effects of altitude throats and Hoerlin was weak from his chill. Our greatest anxiety was Duvanel, who was seriously ill with a chill on the lungs and severe altitude throat. It was a question whether or not he should be sent down straight away to the lower valleys, if not Darjeeling, but he was determined to carry on, if possible. Frau Dyhrenfurth had stood her trying time at the Base

Camp wonderfully well. She had organised the dispatch of stores and equipment to the other camps most efficiently and her untiring efforts, and especially her unvarying cheerfulness, had been real assets to the expedition.

In order to attack Jonsong Peak, 24,344 feet, which was now our main objective, we had to cross the Jonsong La, 20,200 feet. Though, technically speaking, an easy pass, the crossing of it was by no means an easy undertaking for two reasons, firstly, weather, and secondly, porterage. Every day was bringing the monsoon nearer, and on such a high pass heavy snowstorms and deep snow must be expected. Apart from the monsoon, purely local storms might well prove embarrassing. The question of porterage was, however, the most serious one. We had dismissed the majority of our porters, retaining eighty of the best, and two hundred and fifty loads had to be transported. A new Nepali Subadar had come up in place of the former one, whose feet had been severely frostbitten, and he promised to enlist for the expedition all the local porters available, but we knew that we could not rely upon obtaining more than twenty or thirty at the most. There was another factor, dissatisfaction among the porters, and this, it must be admitted, was not entirely without reason. During the expedition the porters had been worked very hard, harder, it is probably safe to say, than they had ever been worked before on any other expedition. On Everest, it was customary to give them one rest day in every four or five working days. These rest days naturally depended on circumstances, but they had been set aside whenever possible. Our porters had marched without a rest from Darjeeling to Tseram, eleven days' marching, with full loads of sixty to eighty pounds per man, which had included a total of something like 35,000 feet of uphill work, and marches in tropical heat. Since Tseram, owing to the breakdown of the transport arrangements and difficulty in obtaining sufficient local food, they had frequently been on short rations, or had to eat food to which they were not accustomed.

Furthermore, a quantity of clothes had been lost or stolen *en route*, and a number of Sherpas actually had worked on Kangchenjunga for several days before their full complement of high climbing clothes had turned up. Another grievance, confined to the Bhutias, was that clothes had been issued only to the Sherpas on the mountain, and the Bhutias, who had been alloted the donkey work of bringing up loads to the Base Camp, had not had the extra clothes that had been promised them. Naturally, we had no option but to clothe the high climbing Sherpas in preference to the Bhutias, but the latter's grievances were nevertheless easily understandable. An ugly situation that threatened to resolve itself into a strike and general desertion of the Bhutias was once more saved by the tactfulness of Wood Johnson, and the Bhutias agreed to cross the Jonsong La on the condition that the clothes promised them should be recompensed for by a cash equivalent on our return to Darjeeling.

As regards transport, Wood Johnson told me that when he and Hannah had gone back, Hannah had arrived at Khunza first, and took what coolies he could find over the Mirgin La to Tseram. Subsequently, Wood Johnson, who had followed him to Khunza, went through that place with a fine comb, and got women, boys, and men from villages below, in fact every available coolie in the district, and sent them to Tseram. As a result of these efforts, ninety-eight loads were got from the Kang La and Tseram to the Base Camp; the remaining loads were mostly looted. Incidentally, sixty-eight Darjeeling men and twenty-three Khunza men were sent back from the Base Camp the day after we arrived there, but as they did not reach Colonel Tobin, they must all have deserted. Fortunately, while at Khunza, Wood Johnson made arrangements to send up coolie rations, meat, eggs, and vegetables to the Base Camp. The situation had been got well in hand by May 11 when Colonel Tobin left Tseram for Darjeeling, after having sent on all loads to Khunza.

Wood Johnson now suggested that in view of the limited number of coolies available, only a small and light party should cross the Jonsong La and attempt the Jonsong Peak; the remainder of the expedition should return to Darjeeling, turning aside to attempt Kabru, 24,002 feet. The snow would have melted from the Mirgin La and the Kang La, and even during the monsoon there should be no difficulty in crossing these passes, as they were not high enough to be snowed under, while there would be little risk of the transport breaking down. The only other alternative was to get the loads over the Jonsong La by relays of porters. Such a scheme was all very well in theory, but there were grave objections to it in practice. In the event of a severe snowstorm, it was bound to break down, and we might find ourselves in the unpleasant position of having one half of the transport on one side of the pass and the other half on the other, with all intervening communication cut off. Bad weather might well result in a wholesale desertion of the porters, or at least the underclad Bhutias. In spite of these objections it was decided that this scheme should be proceeded with. That it succeeded was due entirely to luck, the greatest piece of luck the expedition was blessed with.

Owing to the expiration of his leave, Hannah had to return to Darjeeling, but before doing so he climbed with Wieland the 20,000-foot peak on which Wood Johnson and I had been beaten by bad weather. We parted from him with real regret. His work on behalf of the transport had been invaluable. In fact it is only fair to say that without him, Colonel Tobin, and Wood Johnson to do the spadework, the expedition would not have reached the Base Camp.

Now that the main object of the expedition had been frustrated, Professor Dyhrenfurth wisely decided to make all use of the large party under his command, and by splitting it up, explore as much new country as possible. With this end in view Schneider and Wieland went to explore the 21,000-foot high col known as the Nepal Gap, which forms the lowest point on the ridge separating the head of the Zemu Glacier from the Kangchenjunga Glacier. Dr. Kellas had attempted to reach it from the Zemu Glacier no less than four times. In 1907 he made two attempts; on the first he reached 18,000 feet and was forced to retreat by a thick mist, and on the second 19,000 feet, at which height impassable crevasses again enforced retreat. His third attempt in September 1909, was defeated by a heavy snowstorm 1,000 feet below the col, whilst on his fourth and last attempt in May 1910, he almost reached the col, but did not climb the small rock wall just beneath the summit.

I should have liked to accompany Schneider and Wieland, but the claims of journalism and photography relegated me to the Base Camp. It was arranged that the Nepal Gap party should leave on May 23 and the main party for the Jonsong La the following day. Dr. Richter and Duvanel, who was now recovering from his chill, were to remain at the Base Camp until it had been cleared of all loads. Meanwhile, an urgent message had been sent to Tikeram Thapa at Khunza, telling him to collect and bring up as many local porters as possible.

The few days' rest at the Base Camp had been most welcome. It had been good to feel the soft turf beneath the feet again, and to rest eyes strained from the glare of glaciers and snowfields. The weather was now very warm, an ominous warmth, which seemed to herald the monsoon.

Unfortunately, the wireless set had arrived completely shattered, and we were unable to obtain news as to when the monsoon might be expected. It was small consolation to know that every evening messages were being broadcast for our especial benefit, from Calcutta. Among the loads that had arrived intact was the dark room photographic tent, a sinister looking affair, like the lair of a fortune-teller, in which we developed a number of negatives and cinematograph films. For the interest of photographers I need only remark that so brilliant was the light at 20,000 feet that an exposure of 1/50 of a second at an aperture of f.22 was sufficient, save during the early morning or late afternoon.

Given good weather, no one can fail to get over the Jonsong La. Whether the passage is to be a fatiguing one, or a relatively easy one depends largely on finding the best way through the labyrinth of moraines covering the Jonsong Glacier. Mr. Freshfield found it a troublesome business descending on this, the Nepal side, and camped twice between the pass and Pangperma. He was, however, much hampered by snow covering the glacier. In former times the pass was frequently used by salt traders between Khunza and Lachen, and we were astonished to learn that the Dhudwallah, who had been engaged in bringing milk up to us regularly from Kangbachen, was fully conversant with the route. We engaged him, therefore, as our guide.

In order to find a good camping place for our first camp, Hoerlin and Wood Johnson went up the Jonsong Glacier the day before the party left. They returned after having found a grassy shelf on the west bank where tents might be pitched.

The morning of May 24 was a beautiful one, and Wood Johnson and I strolled up the grassy moraines feeling at peace with the world. On the way we passed Nemu, who was laden with a miscellaneous assortment of my luggage, including my aluminium washing basin which jerked up and down with a mournful clang at every step. For some distance we followed a well-defined path which seemed to show that the Jonsong La was frequently crossed in the past, or that yaks were brought up to graze on the stony pastures of Pangperma. Possibly, it was the latter speculation that caused me to halt and sniff, and remark that there was a strong smell of yaks. Wood Johnson however, seemed to take this as a personal reflection.

Between the moraines and the mountainside were a number of old snowdrifts, composed probably of avalanche debris. These had been resolved by the hot sun and dry atmosphere into groups of beautiful little snow pinnacles a foot or two high. These are known in the Andes of South America as *nieves penitentes*, owing to their resemblance to a penitent congregation. The most common explanation as to how they are formed is that winter and spring snowstorms form snowdrifts, which are blown into ridges. As the snow of these ridges is not of the same consistency throughout, the less dense snow tends to melt and evaporate, leaving the denser masses, which are subsequently sculptured into pinnacles by sun and evaporation. As with ice pinnacles on Himalayan glaciers, the origin of *nieves penitentes* is also influenced by temperature fluctuation. I have only once seen anything to approach them in the Alps, and that was in the exceptionally hot summer of 1928, when the snow on the surface of the glaciers became so rough and spiky in the broiling sun, that one could only assume it to be in the first stage of being formed into *nieves penitentes*.

In the corner of Pangperma where the Jonsong and Kangchenjunga glaciers unite, we sat down and rested awhile. Are there grander or nobler peaks than those surrounding the head of the Kangchenjunga Glacier? A snowstorm was raging on Kangchenjunga, and dark slate-coloured clouds sailing up from the south were adding their quota to the snowfields and glaciers. A few clouds detached themselves from the main masses, and sailed inquisitively up the glacier, strewing snowflakes in their wake, before being disrupted and annihilated by the dry Tibetan winds from the Jonsong La. Other and heavier clouds pouring over the ridges from the south advanced to the attack. Wedge Peak received their first furious assault, and became impenetrably shrouded in the murk of a snowstorm. The storm clouds advanced in a solid phalanx, but the north wind counter-attacked vigorously. A writhing mêlée took place above the glacier basins. The storm clouds were held, but now and again they sallied desperately forward, bombarding us with hasty flurries of snow. Impotent against the north wind, they retreated sullenly; the latter pressed its advantage irresistibly and, sweeping through their once proud ranks, forced them back in a confused and hopeless rout. A searchlight of sun pierced the gloom. Like the floodlit summit of a lofty spire, Wedge Peak stood forth from the blue veils of snow. Once through the shifting murk concealing Kangchenjunga came the deep growl of an ice avalanche. The great mountain was bidding us begone.

We gazed up the glacier towards the Nepal Gap, arguing as to which was the most probable route taken by Schneider and Wieland. Was it a trick of the imagination, or did we see two minute dots descending the broken glacier from the ridge north-west of the Gap? Some porters were passing, and Wood Johnson directed their keen eyes to the place. Yes, they saw the dots too. Schneider and Wieland were evidently busy at their task of finding a way over the Gap.

Continuing on our way, we passed the corner of Pangperma and looked up the stony reaches of the Jonsong Glacier. There are many peaks hereabouts that would yield to determined assault, and some look decidedly easy. Dr. Kellas must have realised this when he crossed the Jonsong La from the Lhonak Valley to climb Langpo Peak, 22,800 feet, at the head of the glacier.

The passage of many porters had trodden out a good path along the moraine. Turning the corner at Pangperma seemed to bring us into a different country and a different climate. Everything pointed to a much drier climate, the very ground was more dusty than at the Base Camp, whilst the defeat of the storm clouds suggested that the strong, dry winds of Tibet protect the Jonsong Glacier to a large extent from many of the snowstorms that attack Kangchenjunga. Were a number of meteorological stations to be installed between Kangchenjunga and the Jonsong La, they would most likely exhibit striking differences of precipitation and humidity.

Camp had been pitched on a charming spot – a small grassy shelf above the moraine of the glacier. The shelf ended in a spur on which a number of flat stones,

Members of the 1930 International Kangchenjunga Expedition

35 Standing *(l to r)*: Hermann Hoerlin, Erwin Schneider, Uli Wieland, Günter Oskar Dyhrenfurth (leader), Marcel Kurz and George Wood Johnson; (seated): Helmuth Richter, Hettie Dyhrenfurth, Charles Duvenal and Frank Smythe. Not shown: J.S. Hannah and H.W. Tobin. *Photo: Dyhrenfurth collection*

38, 39 *(right)* Kangchenjunga's then untried North-West Face (seen here from Drohmo) is menaced by ice cliffs across its full width. The 1930 plan was to gain the North Ridge on the left and follow this to the upper slopes. From the Base Camp B the route was pushed up the approach glacier to seek a way through the ice cliffs at the bottom left corner of the face, and thence up the snow slopes to gain the ridge. Reaching Base Camp from Darjeeling in India involved a major transportation effort crossing a 16,000ft col. The inset shows six of over four hundred porters arriving at the end of their long trek.
Photos: Dyhrenfurth collection and Doug Scott (right)

36, 37 Professor Günter Oskar Dyhrenfurth and his wife Hetti (an amateur tennis champion with tournament wins in Germany, Austria and Switzerland). Initially from Breslau they moved to Austria (1923) and Switzerland (1926) becoming Swiss citizens in 1932. When the Nazis came to power in 1933 Dyhrenfurth resigned his Breslau University seat (Geology) rather than take the required oath of allegiance to Hitler. In the 1936 Olympics, Gold Medals were awarded to the Dyhrenfurths for their "international" expedition exploits. In 1930, moving a major expedition to two Base Camps over two very high passes was a prodigious achievement in which both played a major role. In 1934 Hettie climbed Sia Kangri West (c.24,000ft) – a woman's height record at the time. Their son, Norman, a documentary film-maker, also led major Himalayan expeditions in 1955, 1963 and 1971.

B

40, 41, 42, 43, 44 *(above and lower right)* Avalanches from Kangchenjunga's North-West Face sweep across the Kangchenjunga Glacier. The other side of the glacier was similarly menaced making the positioning of the approach route and Camp 2 problematic. *(top right)* Steep ice climbing on the lower left ice-fall of the face (later known as "the Ice Building"). After the route had been advanced to the first terrace a group set out to establish Camp 3. Smythe's annotated photograph (taken from Camp 2) indicates their position when the critical avalanche fell. The experienced sherpa Chettan *(inset)* died in a catastrophe which might easily have killed them all. *Photos: Frank Smythe and Hugh Ruttledge (inset)*

NORTH RIDGE
PROPOSED SITE OF CAMP FOUR
STEEP ICE SLOPE
PROPOSED SITE OF CAMP THREE
UPPER WALL HIGHEST POINT REACHED 60°-70° SLOPE
600 FEET
OVERHANG
SHELF
POSITION OF SCHNEIDER WHEN AVALANCHE OCCURRED
CHETTAN KILLED HERE
EDGE OF AVALANCHE
POSITION OF PARTY WHEN AVALANCHE OCCURRED
AREA SWEPT BY ICE AVALANCHE
ROUTE

JONSONG PEAK
Dodang Nima Range
TIBET
Jonsong La
JONSONG GLACIER
Nepal Peak
First Base Camp
KANGCHENJUNGA GLACIER

44 *(far left)* Erwin Schneider, the most experienced climber on the trip, who made four major first ascents – Ramthang Peak, Nepal Peak, Jonsong Peak and Dodang Nyima – and several minor ones. His skill and energy greatly impressed Smythe.

45 *(near left)* Ramthang Peak and Wedge Peak seen from the Kanchenjunga Glacier below Camp 2. Ramthang Peak (left) was climbed by Schneider and Smythe. *Photo: Frank Smythe*

46 *(lower left)* The view from Kangchenjunga to the unprepossessing and distant Jonsong Peak. *Photo: Doug Scott*

47, 48, 49 *(right)* The route to Jongsong La (20,080ft / 6121m). The whole expedition moved over this high pass which, once crossed, reflected the climate change with isolated ice towers and pinnacles *(inset)*. In the lower photo Kangchenjunga can be seen above the intervening spur. *Photos: Frank Smythe*

50 *(left)* Preparing the steep ice face between Camps 2 and 3 on Jonsong Peak to enable it to be used by laden porters during the second attempt on the peak.
51 *(top right)* Hermann Hoerlin, George Wood Johnson and Erwin Schneider before the first attempt on Jonsong Peak.
Hoerlin and Schneider were successful but Smythe and Wood Johnson were unable to complete the long ascent. *Photos: Frank Smythe*

obviously arranged by the hand of man, suggested a former encampment, possibly Mr. Freshfield's. Ranged along the shelf was a drift of *nieves penitentes*. They occupied most of the width of the shelf, and there was but little room in which to pitch our tents. Had we known how this icy congregation was to protect us, we should scarcely have resented their usurping so much space. Opposite the camp rose a fine snow peak of about 22,000 feet, which appeared climbable. On this side, it lets fall a steep glacier to the Jonsong Glacier. Were it in the Alps, this glacier would by reason of its steepness be much crevassed, yet here, so plastic is the ice, and so capable is it of accommodating itself to the irregularities and steepness of the ground down which it flows without breaking or cracking, that though hummocked and lumpy, there was scarcely a crevasse to be seen in it.

Half a mile farther on up the glacier, another steep high glacier flowed down to join the main ice stream of the Jonsong Glacier, the pinnacles of which made a fitting foreground to the great southerly walls of Jonsong Peak. From our position the mountain appeared to full advantage. South-westwards from the summit, smooth unbroken snowfields descend for some distance, but like Kangchenjunga, they come to an end above precipices thousands of feet high, and like Kangchenjunga these snowfields, which are hundreds of feet thick, are constantly breaking away at their edges in huge ice avalanches, which set the echoes grumbling round the great cirque of peaks, whence the Jonsong Glacier draws its strength.

That afternoon the sky was covered with gossamer-like clouds, floating above the mountaintops. Wood Johnson eyed them suspiciously, and gave it as his opinion that they preceded the monsoon. He added a grain of comfort, however, by declaring that we need have no immediate fears, and that we might confidently expect another week of fine weather. We could well believe in the imminence of the monsoon, for these clouds were strongly reminiscent of those which forecast a bout of *föhn* in the Alps.

The majority of the porters were sent back the same day. Professor Dyhrenfurth's scheme was that they should leave the Base Camp early the following morning bringing up more loads, and continue with us up the glacier. Lobsang had been given instructions that this was to be done. The porters, however, not unnaturally, regarded such a procedure as being in the nature of a double march, and though they left the Base Camp early enough, they took good care not to arrive until it was too late to start another march up the glacier. This gave us no option but to postpone our advance for another day.

This attempt to double march the porters had an unfortunate effect on their morale. When at length they arrived, they gave it out as their intention to strike. Collecting in a sullen group, they declared they would not continue farther. Once more Wood Johnson was forced into the onerous position, in which he should never have been placed and over which he had no control, of having to placate our disgruntled labour. The porters were quite reasonable. They regarded the attempt to double march them as being the forerunner of other double marches and continual hard work without rests. Their experiences on the march out from Darjeeling, when they were marched for the first eleven days without rest, still rankled at the back of their minds. They were perfectly prepared to cross the Jonsong La, provided they were given one rest day in four working days. Naturally, this was agreed to, but it is a pity that such a situation should have arisen.

Late that afternoon Schneider and Wieland arrived. Their reconnaissance of the Nepal Gap had been most successful. Not only had they been able to solve the problem of the Gap, but Schneider had made a lone ascent of the unnamed 23,470 feet peak to the north of it. Thus, if Graham's claimed ascent of Kabru is not taken into account, it was the highest actual summit yet reached, for it was slightly higher than Mount Kaufmann [Pic Lenin] in the Pamirs, also climbed by Schneider in 1929, or Trisul, in the Garhwal, climbed by Dr. Longstaff in 1907.

The party had first of all ascended the tributary of the Kangchenjunga Glacier enclosed between The Twins and the 23,470 feet peak. They had made no attempt to reach the Gap directly from this glacier as the slopes are extremely steep, and consist for the most part of rotten rocks, but they had ascended a subsidiary glacier falling from the ridge between the Nepal Gap and the 23,470 feet peak. On this they had camped, and thence proceeded with little difficulty to the ridge. On the far side of this, and well to the north-west of the actual Nepal Gap, they had discovered a short, steep snow slope leading downwards towards the Zemu Glacier. They described it as being very similar to the south side of the Jungfraujoch in the Bernese Oberland. Thus, strictly speaking, the problem of the actual Gap remained unsolved, but a practicable way had been discovered over the main chain a little distance to the north-west of it, which is obviously much easier than the direct traverse of the Gap, even although the ridge traversed is a few hundred feet higher than the Gap.

Having made this important discovery, they decided to attack the 23,470 feet peak. Wieland was unwell, but the indefatigable Schneider climbed it alone, a truly splendid effort. Low down, he had to dodge an icefall that cut across the lower part of the ridge. Above this was a steep snow ridge. The snow was hard and icy, but with crampons, scaling it was an easy matter, and he had to cut no steps. The summit was attained without further difficulty, whence he enjoyed a glorious view of distant Everest and Makalu. The name of the 23,470 feet peak suggests itself, and we christened it Nepal Peak.

That evening we made merry in the camp. By some sleight of hand on the part of Frau Dyhrenfurth a small crate of champagne materialised. My mouth organ emerged from the seclusion forced upon it by cracked and sunburnt lips, and the peace of the Jonsong La was broken by the strains of "John Peel", the rousing chorus of which was rendered by Wood Johnson.

But the great peaks of the Himalayas take defeat hardly. That night I was sleeping peacefully, as a man should sleep after champagne, when I began to dream that I was involved in a railway accident. I could hear the coaches in front of mine telescoping, one after another, with a series of appalling crashes. My own was just about to smash when I awoke trembling with terror. The crashes continued, each one was nearer than the last. With an almost animal like quickness my mind grasped the danger – boulders were rolling down the slopes on to the camp! I struggled to get out of my sleeping bag and tent, but it was too late; the former gripped me lovingly, the flaps of the latter had been securely laced up by Nemu. I could do nothing but lie where I was and hope for the best. Some sort of curious sixth sense, a sense dependent entirely upon sound, told me that one boulder was coming straight for my tent. One side of the tent was occupied by my luggage, including a large tin box. Against this I rolled myself, hoping vaguely that it would break the force of the boulder. Actually, of course, it would have been crushed like an eggshell beneath the falling lump of granite. For what seemed an eternity I could hear the onrush of the boulder. It was travelling in bounds. One moment, with a crash, it would strike another rock, the next, it would fall with a dull thud into the yielding turf. There came a great thud not more than a few yards away, the next bound would assuredly bring it on top of me. It was a tense moment. Then came a mighty thudding splash, and silence. The boulder had plunged into the drift of *nieves penitentes* not three yards from my tent!

It had been the last to fall. I scrambled out of the tent wondering whether any damage had been done by the other boulders. There were perhaps half a dozen in all. The camp was awake, all save Wood Johnson. Bawling into his tent elicited nothing more than a sleepy 'Whasermarrer?' Happy indeed the man who can sleep thus, even after champagne.

The next morning I searched for and found my potential assassin. It was a rock about a foot and a half cube. A certain piquancy was added to the situation all unconsciously by Nemu. As he packed my kit, he glanced disparagingly at my tin box and remarked, 'Box, him come to pieces, Sahib, you get other box from cook.' He was right; the tin box certainly was on its last legs and on the point of collapsing from the ill usage of the past few weeks. I took his advice and surreptitiously exchanged it for a stronger one owned by the cook.

As this camp was to remain until everything had been transported over the Jonsong La, it should have been transferred to another and less dangerous spot. This would perforce have been on the glacier, which was here rough and moraine covered. That it was not, indicated the callous – one could scarcely call it philosophical – frame of mind into which we had dropped. The result of not moving the camp was evidenced a few days later when Frau Dyhrenfurth, who had been left by Professor Dyhrenfurth in charge, was nearly killed by another and larger fall of rocks. It was curious that these falls of rock should have occurred at precisely the same spot. The slope above the camp is by no means steep, and why two falls should have come down it when there were other and far more favourable slopes for falling rocks is a mystery. It almost seemed as though they had been uprooted and aimed at the camp by some malignant hand. The porters put them down to the Snowmen, and for once I was not inclined to disagree with them.

Explorers of the great Baltoro Glacier in the Karakorams relate that it takes no less than four days to march up the moraine-covered part of the glacier, before the ice is actually trodden. The Jonsong and Kangchenjunga glaciers combined cannot rival the Baltoro in size, yet in approaching the Jonsong La from Kangbachen the traveller marches a full three days on moraine before reaching open ice.

Leaving the camp we climbed up and down over the stony moraine. There is little of beauty about the lower portion of the Jonsong Glacier, but there is a certain impressiveness in the barren grimness of its stony reaches; it is nothing more than a gigantic refuse bin for the great peaks about it.

The Dhudwallah was a most useful acquisition to the expedition. Without him we should frequently have been at a loss as to the easiest route, and might have wasted much time in the stony labyrinth, but he picked out the way with the skill and aplomb of an Alpine guide, his leathery, wrinkled face with its deep-set hawk-like eyes frequently cracking into a broad grin of conscious importance.

Some distance above the camp was a small glacier lake. High parapets of ice surrounded it from which a frieze of javelin-like icicles were suspended. Miniature icebergs floated on it, and its deep green depths, as placid as a Scottish loch on a calm September morning, reflected the glories of the great peaks around. Presently, as we toiled over the wearying stones, a considerable glacier opened out to the west. This was the one explored by Dr. Kellas, when prospecting the South Face of Jonsong Peak. Half a mile above its junction with the main ice stream of the Jonsong Glacier this glacier thrusts out pinnacles similar to those of the Rongbuk Glacier on Everest. These ice pinnacles are not found on the Kangchenjunga Glacier, and are common only to those parts of the Himalaya exposed to the dry airs of Tibet. There is something attractively fantastic in them; their queer constructions, their cleanly chiselled walls, minarets and spires suggest a goblin city, the queer phantoms of a cubist's dream, or maybe a halted regiment of the Mountain King.

It was hard going for the porters. The glacier rose gently, but we must have climbed an additional two or three thousand feet up and down these moraine mounds. As we walked we searched for gemstones among the multi-coloured rocks, but all we found were gneissic stones inlaid with small garnets.

At last the most turbulent part of the glacier was passed, and we pitched camp thankfully in a small hollow near the middle of the glacier.

There are really two glaciers here flowing side by side, and sharing a common valley. That on the eastern side of the valley flows from the elevated snowfields dominated by Langpo Peak and The Pyramid. That on the western side has its source in the snows of the Jonsong La. Though coming together high up, the two glaciers maintain their individuality for two or three miles before becoming indistinguishable from one another. The Jonsong La branch resembles any ordinary Alpine glacier, but the Langpo branch exhibits a multitude of monstrous ice pinnacles of the same pattern as those to which I have alluded. So vast is the scale of the country hereabouts, that it is not until the mountaineer approaches close to these pinnacles that he is able to appreciate their size. Some of them, are nearly a hundred feet high. Our camp was near them, and Wood Johnson and I practised cutting steps up a minor one. We found the ice hard and tenacious, and it provided Wood Johnson with an excellent first lesson in icemanship.

As the sun sank, the scene became beautiful in the extreme. The foreground was set with the ice pinnacles, the background with Kangchenjunga. During the day the latter had sulked behind the clouds, now the clouds were absorbed into the evening and it rose serenely into a deep mauve sky. But it was plain that the bad weather had not left it unscathed, for the upper part of the mountain was powdered in new snow. It was some consolation to think that even had we been able to hack our way up to the North Ridge, and established higher camps, we should most likely have been beaten by the weather on the final push towards the top. Day died amid almost unearthly splendours. The pale ghostly pinnacles were faintly lit by the reflection of Kangchenjunga's sunset flare, and when night had at last cooled the red-hot castings of the peaks; bright-eyed stars glanced down on a world of awful desolation.

We were off early the next morning. After the irritations of the previous day, it was delightful to stroll along the nearly level crest of a medial moraine, which formed the boundary between the two ice streams.

The general condition of the party had greatly improved; better food, and improved "nerves", had worked wonders on our health. Wood Johnson and I pelted uphill almost as though we were on the fells above Wasdale, and not 2,000 feet higher than the summit of Mont Blanc. Kurz, who had gone on a day in advance of the main party to do some surveying, had pitched his camp where Kellas had pitched his, at the junction of the Langpo and Jonsong Glaciers. Passing him, we continued on up the latter glacier, accompanied by the Dhudwallah carrying my ski, building small cairns as we went for the benefit of the porters who were following.

At last, after two and a half days' marching, we trod snow and ice where Hoerlin joined us, having come by some mysterious short cut of his own, through the icefall, which here occupied the centre of the glacier. He and I put on ski, and continued up a snowy corridor contained between the icefall and the mountain-side. Wood Johnson had not skied before, and he continued on foot with the Dhudwallah. Every few yards there were undulations in the snow, suspiciously like concealed crevasses, and the suggestion was made that those on foot had better rope up. The Dhudwallah, however, greeted this with contempt, and declared there were no "holes". He was right; the undulations were merely due to the melting effects of the sun, or rivulets beneath the snow.

There is no doubt that with a little training the Dhudwallah would make a first-rate guide. As it was, the way he led us up the pass was remarkable in its mountaineering instinct and judgement; he seemed to know the Jonsong Glacier as well as a Zermatt guide knows the Matterhorn.

Ski were much quicker than foot slogging, and leaving Hoerlin to make some adjustment to his bindings, I went on ahead to find a suitable camping site. The corridor was the easy and obvious route, but at its upper end, where it debouched on to the unbroken glacier above the icefall, it was liable to be swept by ice avalanches from a hanging glacier on the mountainside above. It was only a small hanging glacier, the danger being limited to a few yards, and on ski one would have stood a sporting chance of dodging an avalanche. The dangerous area was traversed in a few seconds and I was soon sliding over the gently sloping upper snowfield of the glacier.

Camp was pitched in a shallow snow hollow. Above it rose a steep slope of snow about 2,000 feet high. I saw Schneider fasten his eyes on this slope with that half fanatical, half predatory gleam peculiar to ski-runners, The next instant, unable to withstand temptation, he was off. For half an hour he climbed vigorously, then, pointing his ski straight downhill, he descended like a thunderbolt on the camp.

The Jonsong La was close at hand, and I suggested to Wood Johnson that we might ascend to it on ski, and prospect the way for the morrow.

The shadows were lengthening as we started up the glacier, and the glaring arc lights of day were being dimmed by the stealthy hand of night. In another hour or two they would be switched off altogether, and tropical darkness would fall almost with the suddenness of a blow.

It was the first time that Wood Johnson had donned ski, but he made excellent progress; surely no one has ever taken their first lesson in skiing at 20,000 feet. The glacier led us gently upwards to the foot of a steep little snow slope falling from the pass. Frost had already hardened the snow into a crust and we found it easier to leave our ski, and climb the slope on foot.

A bitter wind met us on the pass, but we scarcely heeded its onslaught. We were looking down into a new world, a world of yellow brown and gold. The mountaineer experiences many dramatic views; there is the view from the summit of the Wetterhorn, with its fascinating and terrible glimpse down to the emerald pastures and doll-like châlets of Grindelwald; there is that backward glance down the Brenva face of Mont Blanc to the wrinkled surface of the Brenva Glacier curving over towards the heat-hazed meadows of Courmayeur; there is enough drama in the outlook from the Dolomite Vajolet Towers to satiate the most earnest seeker after the sensational. Yet, none of these views impressed me so much as that from the Jonsong La. We had come from a world of ice and snow; we were passing into a world of earth and rock. Our eyes, tired with the unrelenting glare of snowfields rested gratefully on the brown terraces and colourful scree of the Lhonak Valley. We even tried to delude ourselves into thinking that it was a warm country we were descending into, but we knew that it was not; these colourful slopes were on the edge of the bleak and inhospitable plateaux of Tibet.

Our soliloquies were cut short by the wind. Fingers and toes were numbing. Furious banners of snow were streaming from the ridges on either hand. We turned. The shadows had stolen across the smooth carpet of the glacier beneath, and were marching up the opposite slopes. Kangchenjunga was yellow and unearthly. Eastward night's purple band was mounting the sky, sowing the first stars in its wake.

Beating gloved hands together, we ran down the slope to our ski. I wish Wood Johnson could have enjoyed the run down as much as I. Perhaps he did, for skiing can be enjoyed equally well by the complete novice or the expert of experts, that is not the least of its charms.

Wood Johnson responded readily to tuition, and some distance down executed a manoeuvre, which he triumphantly described as a Stemming turn. When the camp was in view I regret to say I left him to his own devices. Perhaps it was selfish, but who could resist the long unbroken slopes, so hard, and yet with their crystalline surface so perfect for skiing. I took them straight. The wind roared at me; a fierce exultation gripped me. I felt as I did on my first solo flight when, with the engine shut off, and the wind crooning in the rigging wires, the old bus dived swiftly towards the little row of hangars that came rushing up to meet me. All was the same, only here, in place of hangars, the camp. An aerial dive, a perfect ski run, there is a close affinity. And so with a long, almost lingering Christiania to a standstill.

The weather was again good next morning. For photography's sake I started before the others, and from the pass was able to snap the party as it crawled worm-like up the glacier beneath. It is only by views containing figures that one is able to give to others any idea of the vast scale of mountain country. My thumb at arm's length before me sufficed to conceal the whole party from view.

A strong cold wind was blowing across the pass, this time from the south. About fifty feet down on the Sikkim side an outcrop of rocks formed a sheltered place. There I remained for nearly two hours basking in the sun, while awaiting the remainder of the party. Below this outcrop the slopes dropped steeply for five hundred feet, with rocks jagging from them here and there. Only in one place, immediately to the right of the outcrop, was there an unbroken run out. As the snow was hard and icy in places, and it was not certain whether a slip or slide might not be attended with unpleasant consequences, it seemed safest to fix a long rope down the steep upper portion for the porters. These seemed to think the descent a huge joke, and when they saw that there was no danger, many let themselves glissade before they had reached the end of the rope, and shot down loads and all, to the glacier.

The angle of the upper part of the slopes was at least fifty degrees, but apparently only the perpendicular can deter Schneider on ski. The only compliment he paid the slope was by not taking all of it straight, and he descended the first part in a series of miraculous swings before pointing his ski straight at the glacier. Other and less venturesome mortals preferred to put on their ski at the level where Schneider had disdained to make any more swings. It was a glorious run down the glacier, for the snow was of that delightful crystalline consistency commonly found in the Alps in spring. As we descended we slanted across to the left, taking care to give a wide berth to a hanging glacier on a subsidiary ridge of the Jonsong Peak, which is liable to discharge ice avalanches.

The difference of snow level between this, the Sikkim side of Jonsong La, and the Nepal side is striking. Even taking into account the steepness with which the glacier falls, the snow line is much higher than on the Nepal side and only a few minutes' running was necessary to bring us from snow to a waste of moraines.

As usual Nature, which obviously favours ski-runners in this part of the world, had provided a snow-filled corridor between the moraine and the mountainside to the west of the glacier. Down this we loitered, stopping every few minutes on the stones at the side for a siesta in the sun.

Far away now, was the pass with the descending porters strung up on it like a row of pendent black beads. I was reminded strongly of the opening scene in Charlie Chaplin's film *The Gold Rush*, which shows the seekers after wealth toiling in single file up the Chilkoot Pass.

Eastwards of the Jonsong La is a nameless peak of 22,160 feet, and Langpo Peak, 22,700 feet, which was climbed by Dr. Kellas. It was but one of many great ascents that he made in this district. Looking at it, and later at other peaks that he climbed, one could not but be impressed by his mountaineering judgement and route finding abilities. Climbing with only native porters as companions, he had to rely solely on an instinct and judgement that seldom, if ever, failed him. When the history of the Golden Age of Himalayan exploration comes to be written, Dr. Kellas's name will take a high place in the select little list of early mountaineers.

The snowy corridor petered out into a stony waste. To the west was a subsidiary glacier, and we traversed across to it, floundering through bog-like patches of snow between the rocks. The snow of this glacier was abominable, whole masses of it frequently collapsing beneath our ski, letting them sink into water-undermined cavities.

The glacier ended in an abrupt nose of ice. Beneath was a little lake, a blue-green gem in a sombre setting. It was an ideal spot for a camp, and Kurz and I returned with the welcome news to the porters who were finding it heavy going in the soft snow.

Our camping place was Arctic in its solitude and beauty. Above us towered the ice nose festooned with giant icicles, and sculptured into all manner of forms. There was the wrinkled face of an old witch, peering sardonically down upon us, and, in bas-relief, three classical figures linked hand in hand. Beneath was a hermit's cave, and above, a little balcony from which the fair-haired snow maidens could gaze rapturously, if not enviously, down upon us, as we munched our dinner of sardines and gherkins. All these things were reflected with faultless accuracy in the green blue depths of the little lake beneath. That evening, when frost stalked out with the shadows, freezing the surface of the lake into a smooth, white floor, the elves and fairies held a midnight ball, while we sophisticated mortals snored in our tents.

We were short of fuel, and it was essential to secure some without delay. The porters had had a trying day traversing the Jonsong La, and were entitled to a rest. We called, therefore, for volunteers, who, for an extra day's pay, would descend the Lhonak Valley and bring up rhododendron wood. Fortunately, sufficient were forthcoming. Also, we had none too much coolie food left, and runners were dispatched with notes to the Maharajah of Sikkim at Gangtok, and the Headman of Lachen, requesting immediate assistance.

Above the camp was a low ridge pushed into the Lhonak Valley by the Jonsong Massif. This rose to a little knob, which formed an ideal belvedere for viewing the head of the Lhonak Valley, its glaciers and surrounding peaks. Seated on the gaunt, granite slabs piled up like a ruined Stonehenge on the summit, we drank in the glories of this new country. There was much to interest and impress us; the brown upland valley; the lateral terraces 1,000 feet above the floor of the Lhonak Valley telling of a former Ice Age when a great glacier extended many miles down towards the plains; the rugged limestone peaks of the Dodang Nyima Range, governed by the graceful summit of Dodang Peak, 22,700 feet high; a sea of peaks to the north-west, above which projected two great combers, Chomiomo, 22,430 feet, and Kangchenjau, 22,700 feet, ascended by Dr. Kellas, in 1910 and 1912 respectively. But it was not these distant peaks that delighted our eyes so much as a beautiful snow peak, which stands watch and ward over the head of the Lhonak Valley. It is the Weisshorn of the district, possessing as it does all the gracefulness and elegance of the Zermatt peak. The superb sweep of its ridges culminates with mathematical preciseness in a slender spire of snow, and so well designed is it that it deceived us utterly as to its height, and we began to believe that it was actually higher than Jonsong Peak. Only the upper part of the last named was visible. Its south-east ridge immediately below the summit appeared easy, but could it be reached? Kellas, we knew, had attacked it from the north-west, and we had already learnt enough about him to realise that his judgement was likely to be sound.

Below us, two main tributaries of the Lhonak Glacier united to form a great ice stream, which stretched, far down the valley. This ice stream was, for a mile or two, broken up into similar pinnacles to those met with on the way to the Jonsong La. A weird procession they were, contrasting oddly with the browns and yellows of the scree slopes on either side of the valley.

That denudation as well as glacier ice plays an important part in shaping these valleys was evidenced by a collection of earth pyramids on the northern side of the valley resembling in general characteristics the well-known ones above Bozen (now called Bolzano) in South Tyrol. They are due to water forming deep runnels in the soft earth of the hillside. As these runnels become deeper, so do the ridges between them become sharper. Some parts of these ridges are more knit together by stones and harder than others. The soft parts fall, or are worn away; the hard parts remain, forming eventually these quaint pinnacles of earth and stones.

Jonsong Peak was now within our grasp. But would the weather hold, could we snatch it from the teeth of the monsoon? Westwards, battalions of cumuli cloud were flooding up from the Teesta Valley. Were they the advance guard of the monsoon? Wood Johnson thought they were, and pointed out inky black clouds, which floated detached from the main body of cumuli, saying that they were typical monsoon clouds. We had endured one great disappointment, were we to experience another? Time alone could tell.

CHAPTER SIXTEEN

The First Ascent of Jonsong Peak

THE DAY OF our little reconnaissance of the summit of the rocky point above the camp had ended in snow squalls, but monsoonish threats came to naught and the following morning, May 30, was calm and sunny. The party that was to make the first attempt on Jonsong Peak consisted of Schneider, Hoerlin, Wood Johnson and myself. It was decided that the Europeans should go on ahead of the porters and see if there was any possibility of reaching the South-East Ridge via the north face of the mountain. We knew that the ridge was possible if we could gain it, but the north face was cut off from view by a buttress and it remained to be seen what was round the corner.

Wood Johnson and I were the first away. Crossing the ridge above the camp, we descended the broad snowfield on the other side diagonally towards the Lhonak Glacier. The glacier is split in its upper portion into two streams, one fed by Jonsong Peak, and the other by Lhonak Peak and the Dodang Nyima range. A long lower ridge divides the two bending down from the North-West Ridge of Jonsong Peak. So far as we could ascertain from his description, Dr. Kellas when attempting Jonsong Peak had camped low down at, or near the end of this ridge. His second camp had been on the col between Jonsong Peak and an unnamed peak next to Lhonak Peak. This unnamed peak does not appear to advantage when looking up the Lhonak Glacier, for it is farther away than its more impressive neighbour, Lhonak Peak.* Yet, as we learned later, it is a worthy mountain.

There were no crevasses on the snowfield, and we walked down and across it

* Climbed later in 1930 by G.B. Gourlay and W. Eversden (one of the Longland's Climb team – see page 65).

unroped. The rocks of the buttress were easy but disagreeably loose, and we dislodged great masses that thundered down to the glacier amid clouds of sulphurous dust.

All hope of reaching the South-East Ridge was erased from our hearts as we turned the buttress. One glance at the great precipices falling from the ridge armoured and defended with hanging glaciers was sufficient. Farther along, the rock precipices ended, and directly beneath the peak there appeared to be a chance of reaching the South-East Ridge up the 7,000 feet of snow and ice slopes forming the North Face of the peak. But it was a very remote possibility, for the steep average angle of the slopes, plus confused masses of unstable ice pinnacles and hanging glaciers strewn indiscriminately over them suggested dangers at least as great as those of Kangchenjunga.

The reader may wonder why we continued considering attacking the South-East Ridge when we knew that Dr. Kellas thought the mountain to be accessible by the North-West Ridge. The answer is that it is the mountaineer's duty to consider every possibility however remote. Following blindly in the steps of his defeated predecessor is not the right attitude of mind in which to attack a great peak in the Himalayas. That was one reason why we had attempted the Nepal face of Kangchenjunga in preference to the better known Sikkim face. As regards Jonsong Peak another reason must be admitted, and that was the appearance of the North-West Ridge; it looked terribly long. From the col reached by Dr. Kellas, it swept up in ice edges over point after point before merging into the final rock and ice slopes of the peak. Earlier in the expedition we might have gone for it with cheerful *insouciance*, but Kangchenjunga had taught us wisdom. Length alone will forever militate against the ascent of the majority of the greater Himalayan ridges. Yet, Dr. Kellas had seen the peak from a better vantage point than we, for he had approached it directly up the Lhonak Valley and he was too good a mountaineer to waste his time attempting a hopelessly inaccessible route, or one beyond the powers of his expedition. We had already learned to respect his judgement, and the fact that he had tried the North-West Ridge of Jonsong Peak, though he had returned defeated from it, was practically a guarantee of its accessibility.

Scrambling down the slopes of loose boulders, we gained the side moraine of the south branch of the Lhonak Glacier, there we sat down to await Schneider and Hoerlin. They and the porters were not, long in coming. The latter were going well. There were only a dozen of them – all picked men – for we hoped to make a rapid push for the top. The porters left at the Base Camp were to relay the remaining loads over the Jonsong La the men we had were all hard-bitten "Tigers", as tough, hardy and weather-beaten as the Old Guard of Napoleon. They were not merely porters, but genuine mountaineers and adventurers, who enjoyed a tussle with a great mountain as much as we did, and were as keen as we were to get to the top.

The hanging glaciers on the North Face of Jonsong Peak were too obviously unstable to risk passing close beneath them. Fortunately, the broad upper part of the glacier was unbroken enough to enable us to keep in the middle out of range of their ice avalanches. For the most part we trod glacier ice, but here and there stretches of snow covered it. This snow seemed to have been laid down by some diabolical demon. If there were any watery hollows, they were concealed by innocent looking coverlets into which we floundered, sometimes up to the hips. The diabolical demon could seldom have laughed so heartily as he did that day.

The surface of the ice was curiously fretted with little *nieves penitentes*. This could only have been the work of the sun. Many little pinnacles, no more than a few inches high, were capped by stones, forming minute glacier tables. The stones, of course, had protected the ice from the sun, so that when the surrounding ice had melted away, a little stalk had been left on which rested the stone.

As we mounted the glacier, the snow and ice face immediately beneath the peak came into full view, and we saw what we had not seen lower down, that a possible route might be forced up it. But it was a route that would undoubtedly be exposed to unavoidable risks – risks of both snow and ice avalanches. Our last doubts were removed; it only remained for us to follow in the footsteps of Dr. Kellas. First of all we must cross the glacier, thence climb to the crest of the low ridge, where we would make Camp One.

For the first time on the expedition we found ourselves among large crevasses. It is easy enough to get off the Mer de Glace on Mont Blanc to the Mauvais Pas if you know the right way, but if you do not, you are liable to get hung up by crevasses at the edge of the glacier. Such was our position now. We could see the side moraine only fifty yards away, and an easy slanting shelf leading up from it to the crest of the ridge, but that fifty yards was riven and torn into huge crevasses, with knife-like blades of ice between. The climbers could, of course, have forced a way even though it involved some tricky ice work, but it was a different matter for the porters. An easy way must be found by which we could send them up and down between Camp One and the Base Camp unaccompanied by a climber. A way was found at last along a little horizontal gully of ice, which led out unexpectedly to the moraine. The shelf, as anticipated, offered no difficulty, and soon we had reached the crest of the ridge some five hundred feet above the glacier. There we camped.

The actual crest of the ridge consisted of a hog-backed gently inclined snow-field, but we preferred as a camping site a rocky edge almost flush with the snow.

The ridge was well sheltered from the wind by the main North-West Ridge of Jonsong Peak, and the evening was warm and calm. Far down the valley the setting sun dwelt on the brown slopes of stones and earth, transforming them into sheets of yellow and gold, or lingered on the crests of the ice pinnacles of the Lhonak Glacier. There was one pinnacle conspicuous among the rest, which formed a tapering neck, surmounted by a bird-like head with a cruel beak. As the sun set, and other and lower pinnacles had become cold and livid, one shaft of light, passing through a gap in some distant ridge, lit this pinnacle with a ruddy glare. I almost imagined myself to be looking down at some strange and terrible prehistoric monster steeped in the blood of its victims.

Day perished; brown changed to violet, violet to purple. The huddle of ice pinnacles became cold and ghostly. Above the world, a vein-like network of cloud tendrils glowed fiercely as though suspended over the blaze of a city's lights. Slowly, they faded, and were lost amid the stars.

On Kangchenjunga we had known no peace of mind, we had awakened in alarm to the roar of ice avalanches, but now we could sleep peacefully.

For the most part the night was a quiet one, with only the groaning and cracking of the glacier beneath to tell of its slow progress. Once came the bellow of an ice avalanche from Jonsong Peak, like the startled growl of an aroused watch dog.

Morning dawned mistily. Grey clouds roofed in the world; but the rising sun thinned them, and tore them apart. In its powerful rays they dissolved swiftly into a sky of Italian blue. I was reminded of a Whitsun morning up Langdale; when the turf is silvered with dew, the lambs cry through the low mists, and Pike O'Stickle and Bowfell take to themselves the dawn.

A friendly sun smiled down upon us, as we trudged over the marble-like surface of the snowfield above the camp. We had hoped that the ridge would lead us straight to the col reached by Dr. Kellas, and it was something of a disappointment to find that ahead it looked difficult. The alternative was to descend to the north branch of the Lhonak Glacier. I volunteered to go on ahead and prospect the ridge. A short scramble up a slope of boulders brought me to a point whence, so far as I could see, the ridge stretched without difficulty for a considerable distance. Seen thus, there seemed every hope that we should be able to follow it all the way and that it would merge eventually into the snow slopes directly beneath the col. Rather prematurely, therefore, I waved, on the others. This was a mistake. Only for a short distance was the ridge free from difficulties. Soon it became a conventional Himalayan knife-edge of ice, and writhed downwards evilly into a deep gap. We retreated. Some hard things were said, but they were deserved.

We descended a slope about 200 feet high to the glacier. Soon we were wallowing and floundering in soft snow, the most terrible snow we had ever experienced. The sun had softened a crust formed by an overnight's frost. For a step or two it would bear us, then a whole cake of it would collapse, and we would go knee-deep or even waist-deep into a hole.

But if it was trying or irritating work for the sahibs, it was much worse for heavily laden porters, Even though we stamped out the track, they, with their loads, frequently sank in to a much greater depth. Over the worst part of the glacier, I do not think we progressed more than 300 yards in an hour and that along the level.

We halted for lunch. The weather was not propitious, a snowstorm was brewing, and grey clouds brought with them a tide of scurrying snowflakes. The sun reappeared again for a few moments, but its smile was but a transitory one, and soon faded and died behind leaden mists.

Above our luncheon place the snow was less disagreeable, and we climbed thankfully out from the worst part of the glacial snow swamp to the foot of an icefall. We had come to regard Himalayan icefalls with something of disdain. They were usually much easier than they looked, due to the absence of big crevasses. This one gave us no reason to revise our opinion. It was a tame affair, so tame that we did not need to rope until above the steepest portion, and that only for a solitary crevasse with overhanging caves of snow necessitating an awkward step.

The storm clouds had rolled back, and a benevolent sun illuminated the long snowfield before us, that lifted gently up towards Kellas Col, as we had already learnt to call it. Dominating this snowfield rose a little peak. Sunlight and shadow chased across it, a wilful mist concealed it for a few instants. Without it the world seemed dull and lifeless. Then it reappeared, supremely arrogant, and important.

Actually, it was just an insignificant hump, on the great North-West Ridge of Jonsong Peak.

We took off the rope, which we had put on for the one crevasse, and trudged manfully up the soft snow slopes. Ahead, was a skyline, which we thought must be Kellas Col. We breasted it only to find more slopes ahead. Time was getting on; the day had been a hard one, for all concerned. Therefore, we were content to camp on a little platform beneath the humpy little peak. Only the tireless Schneider elected to go on, and prospect the way. For once his prospecting nearly led him into trouble. In the dull light, he was unable to see the slight depression formed by a solitary crevasse, treacherously bridged. He went through up to the waist, and was lucky not to go farther. Although a narrow crevasse, it was a deep one.

We awoke the next morning to hear the unpleasant sound of pattering snow on our tents. Enforced delay was something more than disappointing. We were short of food and fuel. In order to travel light, we had left as much as possible of the former at Camp One, and of the latter we had taken all the Meta solid fuel available at the Base Camp, the remainder had still to come over the Jonsong La. We estimated that if the snowstorm delayed us but one day, we would only have enough Meta to heat two cups of hot tea a day. How long would it last? Monsoonish opinions alternated with hopes of a clearance, but the snowfall continued without intermission.

Had we known, stern events were afoot. Frau Dyhrenfurth, who had been left in charge of transport organisation, on the Nepal side of the Jonsong La, having carried out her task of sending relays of porters off with the remainder of the loads, had left for the Jonsong La. As luck would have it, the day that she traversed the pass coincided with the snowstorm. Duvanel and Dr. Richter had come over before her, and she had no European companions. She was accompanied, however, by her servant, the Nepali Subadar, and a Subadar Major, who had recently come up from Khunza. In spite of the snowstorm, these last two escorted her to the actual frontier before turning back, another remarkable instance of the courtesy and help with which the Nepalese authorities had greeted us while we were in Nepal.

To traverse a pass 20,200 feet high in a snowstorm during which we, mere men, were cowering in our tents, was a fine effort, and one which, as regards height alone, has probably only been surpassed by women on two or three previous occasions. Luck had held, and the crossing of the Jonsong La had been successfully accomplished. Unfortunately, it had been marred by an unfortunate accident, and a glissading coolie had come to grief and broken an arm. Disaster had also overtaken some of the more fragile loads. Of the two typewriters on which I was wont to hammer out my dispatches one was no more. The box containing the gramophone records had broken loose from a porter's back, and bounded down the glacier. Only a number of strong and thick records that had been supplied by Eberl had survived, and these were strictly classical. Our souls, and our porters' souls, hungered not for Wagner or Beethoven, but for the bass-voiced gentleman who used to advise us every evening to give ourselves a pat on the back. Now he was lying shattered to fragments at the foot of the Jonsong La.

It was still snowing the next morning, and our spirits sank to zero. We had little enough food and fuel left, and could not afford to play a waiting game. We had to decide definitely whether we would advance, or retreat. The former was scarcely practicable, and the latter seemed inevitable. We were preparing to descend when the snow stopped. A bright light smote through the mist pall; a tiny patch of blue sky appeared. Miraculously it broadened and an eager sun burst through. The mists rolled back; a wind from the north-west completed their discomfiture; they had to relinquish their hold on our ridge, and retreat to the Lhonak Valley, where they congregated in sullen battalions ready for a further assault on the heights. Nearly two feet of new snow had obliterated our tracks, it would be hard but not dangerous work going on, for so far as we could see there was no fear of the gentle slopes we must climb avalanching.

It was certainly hard work, but not so strenuous as we had anticipated. The new snow was of a more or less uniform depth, and was light and powdery. We climbed roped, for there were several concealed crevasses, two or three of which were only discovered by "trial and error".

From the Lhonak Valley the North-West Ridge had appeared a definite edge all the way from Kellas' Col. In point of fact, for some considerable distance there is no ridge, and what appears to be a ridge from below is merely the edge of a gently sloping snow-field. This snowfield gradually narrows, until at a height of about 21,500 feet it does actually become a ridge.

One or two of the porters were feeling the effect of the altitude, and one of them, Nima, unroped himself from the rest. He was cautioned and tied up again. In the absence of an accredited sirdar, Nemu was put in charge. It was interesting to watch the psychological effect of responsibility. As Mr. Samuel Weller would have had it, he seemed to 'svell wisibly'. His countenance became even more earnest and worried, if such a thing were possible, and he fussed about like an old hen over a brood of chickens, but withal, he made a good sirdar, and one whom the men respected and obeyed.

At the head of the snowfield was a platform, on which we enjoyed lunch and a welcome rest. Immediately below the platform and to the west precipices dropped to a great glacier, which has its source in the snows of Jonsong Peak. This glacier at first runs in a north-westerly direction before curving round to the west. It is at least fifteen or twenty miles long, and its direction, and the ranges bounding it are delineated inaccurately on the Government map. Whence do its waters flow? Do they enter the Khunza Valley at Kangbachen, or do they flow northwards into Tibet, and join the headwaters of the Arun River? This was a question that we were unable definitely to solve, but it seems probable that the latter direction is the correct one. This glacier, like the Jonsong Glacier, only consists of bare ice for a few miles. Its lower portion is so moraine covered as to be invisible, but the ice continues for many miles under the stones. As Mr. Freshfield pointed out, many of the early travellers and surveyors utterly misjudged the length of the glaciers in this district owing to their thinking that the glacier ended at the point where the ice was no longer to be seen. In its upper portion this glacier rises in a great icefall. Rocky spurs jut out into it, and over these ice avalanches fall periodically with thunderous roars.

Beyond the glacier, we looked over ridge upon ridge of peaks, some easy looking snow mountains, others more difficult, and here and there carnivorous-like fangs of rock, forming summits which appeared hopelessly inaccessible. Our gaze passed far across these turbulent mountains, to where seventy miles away two superb summits stood aloof from the world – Everest and Makalu.

Everest has been described as a dull, if imposing mountain, when seen from the north and not to be compared with Makalu in grandeur or beauty. The latter is certainly a superb peak. Its delicately shaped summit based on two wide shoulders is as perfectly proportioned as the Lhonak Peak. Yet, grand mountain though it is, it somehow lacks the sovereign dignity of the World's highest summit. From our position we saw the North Ridge of Everest in profile, sweeping down in a graceful parabola to the North Col, to the right of which rose the little North Peak. But the most imposing face of the mountain is its southern or Nepal face. No European has ever stood beneath it. Were he to do so, he would find himself looking up the grandest mountain wall there is. The North-West Face of Nanga Parbat rises 22,000 feet from the Indus Valley. It is possible that Everest's southern face does not exceed this height, and it is probably less, but no other mountain can show a face to rival its unbroken general angle, combined with its length. We saw it in profile and seventy miles away though we were from it, it seemed to drop and drop for thousands of feet, to disappear finally into the flocks of cumuli cloud that browsed about its base.

We could have stopped long gazing upon that view, but our start had been a late one and the sun was well past its zenith. So far the foot slogging had been easy, if arduous, of a type Baedeker would class as, 'For adults only'. Immediately above us, the snowfield rose in steep waves, before narrowing into a sharp snow-ridge. Henceforward the climbing was, 'For experts only, with perfectly steady heads.' At the foot of the lowest wave was an incipient bergschrund. This was only visible on the right, on the left it was firmly bridged. The wind sweeping the slopes above it had compacted the snow into a hard icy cake. Luckily there was no ice, and a few slashes with the adze end of the axe sufficed to make a step. Above this lower wave, the slope eased off for a few yards; then came a similar wave but a few feet high, and easily surmounted.

We found ourselves on a level shelf, forming the lower lip of a long snowy trough. Above the trough rose the final wave. We looked at it with sinking hearts. Like the ice wall of Kangchenjunga, it was a brutal, elemental bulge of blue ice. Schneider thought there was a possibility of circumventing it, and quickly traversed along to the left like an old hound nosing out the trail. A minute or two later he returned with the glad news that he had found a way, and the advance was resumed.

At one point the lower lip of the trough we were traversing was split at right angles by an abysmal cleft. An insecure-looking tongue projected on our side, and from this we stepped gingerly across. At its westward end, the trough and the ice bulge petered out into an ice slope. To reach this we had to cross another crevasse. Now came the first real climbing of the day. The ice slope fell away to the right, like the roof of a house, ending in a sheer drop to the glacier we had discovered. Steps, and good steps, had to be cut. A slip on the part of the porters was not to be thought of. Schneider cut the steps, which Hoerlin; Wood Johnson and myself enlarged to the dimensions of buckets for the porters. Nevertheless, we gave the latter a tight rope. The slope was short, not more than 100 feet high; and soon we stepped on to the crest of the North-West Ridge. There we experienced a disagreeable surprise. For some way the ridge was level, then it rose to an icy point which formed a respectable peak in itself. So far the ridge was reasonably broad, and free from difficulty, but beyond the little peak it narrowed to a mere ice-blade of obvious and aggressive difficulty. Between this ridge and Jonsong Peak was a gently inclined glacier, forming one of the heads of the glacier flowing north-west. Could we but gain this glacier all would be well, for from its head we could attack the final slopes of Jonsong Peak.

There were two possibilities of descending to this glacier. One, by following the North-West Ridge to a point where it sank to within reasonable reach of the glacier, and the other, by descending the ice slopes directly beneath us. Both were possible, but to get porters over either route meant an extra day's work, and another camp, and for this we had neither sufficient food nor fuel. The only alternative was to camp where we were on the ridge, and leaving the porters, making a bid for the summit the following day. It would be a very long and strenuous day, and a race against time. Any real difficulty such as steep rock climbing, or step cutting, would defeat us, and enforce retreat if we were to escape being benighted. It was by no means certain that there were no real difficulties on the final 2,000 feet of snow slopes and rocks separating the head of the glacier from the summit. It certainly looked easy enough, but as we knew from bitter experience, apparent easiness in the Himalayas is too often apt to prove a delusion and a snare.

Another factor by no means to be neglected was altitude. We had been going slowly today in the soft snow and that from 19,500 feet to 21,700 feet. We would go more slowly on the morrow. Such was the problem, and like that of the Jonsong La, it was one that luck alone could solve.

The ridge was a poor place to camp upon, and we would have done better to have descended to the platform below, or to the trough. But every foot of height and minute of time was precious, and we decided, therefore, to stop where we were, even though forced to bear the brunt of the west wind.

It would be difficult to imagine a more superb camping site, and we lounged about in the sun enjoying every minute of the remainder of the day. As we did so, we studied the route to be followed, and after a prolonged argument as to the respective merits of the ridge and the ice slope, the former was adopted as affording the most convenient route to the glacier.

On the peak itself there were two possibilities. One up the crest of the North-west Ridge, which would mostly consist of rock climbing, and the other up snow slopes to the col between the highest point of the peak and a subsidiary summit to the west. The final decision, however, as to which was the better of these two routes would have to be left until we were actually at grips with the mountain, for it was difficult to tell by mere visual examination which was likely to prove the easiest.

From a geological standpoint, Jonsong Peak is very interesting. It forms the point at which the gneiss of Kangchenjunga and the limestone of Tibet meet. The upper part of the mountain is composed of stratified limestone, similar to the upper bands of rock of Everest, which we hoped would provide as easy climbing as it does on Everest. This limestone is based on gneiss. Where the two meet, there are alternate layers of gneiss and limestone, which run for a considerable distance across the mountainside.

For warmth and companionship's sake we placed our tents end to end. Hoerlin and Schneider shared one, and Wood Johnson and I the other. The porters were housed in a tent of Polar design, which had been found to withstand the fiercest winds. They had also a little Welzenbach tent, which in shape resembled a triangular slab of cheese, being head-high to a sitting man at one end and sloping wedge-like to the feet-end.

As the sun set, the west wind rose and howled with bitter venom across the ridge, blowing fine powdery snow through every chink between the laced-up flaps. Our little camp was bathed in a ruddy glare. So beautiful was the scene that Wood Johnson and I, peering through the gauze-covered ventilation square at the back of our tent, could not forbear to go outside and photograph it. For perhaps a minute I stood in the snow, fumbling with numbed fingers at my camera. The sun was sinking northwards of Everest. One stiletto of cloud spanned the ranges, its hilt reached to Everest, its acute point, so acute that it was hard to tell where it ended, stretched far over Tibet. The hilt was dark, the point afire, as though it was steeped in blood. Although seventy miles away, Everest was as sharp and clear as though it rose from the range across the nearest valley. The North Col and the weary East Ridge up which expeditions had fought their way were clearly distinguishable. As I gazed at the final cone, beneath which high hopes were shattered, I thought of Mallory and Irvine. Their last resting place is surely one to be envied. When all the other peaks were cold and grey, one steadfast cloud banner streamed from it, whilst below, the great mountain drew to itself night's purple folds, like the toga of some imperial Caesar.

The cold was intense. We had no thermometer, but there were at least fifty degrees of frost. I took two photographs, but my fingers became white and dead. I beat and rubbed them for fully a quarter of an hour inside the tent before the sluggish circulation returned. After cooking a cheerless and limited supper, we gulped down gratefully our one precious cup of hot tea, and wriggled into our sleeping bags.

The night was a wild one. The wind roared across the ridge, its snow-charged gusts flinging themselves on the camp with an insane fury. Once again our little tents held out nobly. Nevertheless, it was not altogether a comfortable feeling knowing that there were precipices on either hand. I thought of Captain G.I. Finch and Mr. Geoffrey Bruce's windy night on Everest, but their experience was a far worse one than ours.

Dawn broke; the sky was unclouded, and the sun rose unhindered, but the wind continued with unabated violence. We peered out of our tents. A *tourmente* of windblown snow was whirling past, and far up in the blue sky to the leeward of the ridge its crystals scintillated in the sun like a myriad elfin spear points. At the Base Camp they would be thinking about breakfast, basking in the sun, maybe. Possibly some observant eye would note a slight fuzziness about the ridges, but little would they realise what it really meant. To start was impossible, for to have faced the blast would have meant frostbite. The peak was within our grasp, yet we must retreat. With our limited supplies of food and fuel, we could not afford to wait another day. From Camp One we had sent back all the porters we could possibly spare. Instructions had been sent to the Base Camp to send up food and fuel at the earliest possible moment, but this was scarcely likely to arrive in time. The hard work of the past few days had been wasted. We had resigned ourselves to endure yet another bitter disappointment when with dramatic suddenness, at about 8.30 a.m. the canvas of our tents ceased to roar and smack – the wind had dropped! For some time we lay listening for its return, but save for a petulant gust or two, it did not return. We ate a hurried breakfast, while our servants thawed our frozen boots – I think Nemu took mine to bed with him – and packed our rucksacks with necessaries.

At 9 a.m. we were off, in two parties, Schneider and Hoerlin on one rope, Wood Johnson and myself on the other. We were all wearing crampons. Walking easily up the ridge we gained the summit of the ice peak which is about 150 feet above the camp and nearly 22,000 feet high. This marked the beginning of the difficult section of the ridge.

From the ice peak the ridge descended steeply for some distance in a series of sweeps to a col above which it rose again to another little peak. The col was only about 200 feet above the glacier, and once it was reached, the descent to the latter should be a comparatively easy matter. There was no possibility of keeping to the crest of the ridge, it was too sharp, whilst enormous cornices festooned with icicles overhanging the Lhonak side had to be avoided. We must traverse well below it on the south or Jonsong Peak side. Had we not had crampons, the mountain would not have been climbed that day, for without them the steep icy slopes would have involved several hours of step cutting. As it was, steps were seldom necessary although it was tiring work flexing the feet in order to drive the crampon spikes well home. But if crampons made it possible to succeed without step cutting, it was not altogether easy work. The slope was too steep to face outwards, we had to face sideways, and descend like crabs. Below, sharp shark's teeth of rock, projecting viciously from the slope and a bergschrund awaited a false step.

Schneider and Hoerlin moved for the most part both together, and were soon far ahead. Wood Johnson and I moved for the most part one at a time and were therefore very slow. This slowness was dictated partly by the fact that Wood Johnson had had little previous experience of snow and ice, and was actually wearing crampons for the first time. There was, however, another reason of which I was not aware at the time, he was not feeling fit. It is only fair and just to remark that considering his unfamiliarity with such work he put up a remarkably fine performance. The technique of crampons is not to be learned in a day.

Below the col, the ice was harder and steeper than above, and Schneider found step cutting essential. This enabled us to catch up to some extent, but even so by the time the first party had reached the glacier, we were still a long way behind. Schneider had cut a cunning zigzag staircase, which led to the one place where the bergschrund could be crossed without much difficulty. After flexing the ankles on the slopes above the col, it was a relief to tread in good honest steps. The upper lip of the bergschrund was steep, but this Schneider had facilitated by hacking out large buckets of steps.

Seated on the glacier, we ate a snack of chocolate. The weather was now perfect, and the sun burned down with a fierce intensity, untempered by a breath of wind. Before us, the glacier sloped gently upwards with scarcely a ripple to mar its smooth surface. Trudging up it, mere dots now, were Hoerlin and Schneider. They were at least an hour ahead of us. We started after them. Almost at once, I noticed that Wood Johnson was going very badly. We had not gone far before he said he was too tired to go on. He said he would sit down in the snow, and wait until I returned. Naturally, I thought that altitude alone was responsible. He was feeling what I felt on Ramthang Peak, when wearing the expedition boots, only worse. Under the circumstances a safe glacier, a windless day, and a broiling sun, I felt no scruples in agreeing to his suggestion that I should go on to the summit. Had I known, however, that he was suffering, not from altitude, but from a definite physical malady, there would have been no question of my going on. I should have returned with him then and there to the camp.

Would it be possible to overtake Schneider and Hoerlin? They were going very fast. Could I go faster? I thought I could, for I was feeling very fit. I said goodbye to Wood Johnson with deep regret. It was something more than hard luck for him, and no one was keener than he to do Jonsong Peak. Yet, he could console himself with the thought that should it be climbed, his share in its conquest would be as great as anyone's, for it was only his able management of the porters, which was every bit as important towards the success of the undertaking as the actual climbing, that had rendered the ascent possible.

Every man possesses his own natural pace on a mountain, and by natural pace I mean the pace at which he is able to conserve the greatest amount of energy. This pace is, of course, apart from the difficulty of the ground, dependent on general bodily and mental condition, combined with the limitations imposed by altitude. At 22,000 feet, pace and rhythm are synonymous. Increasing the pace, and breaking the rhythm, results in an output of energy far out of proportion to the time saved. This I discovered to my cost. At low altitudes, this loss of energy is negligible, and there is always a larger store of energy held in reserve than at high altitudes. The men who reach the summit of Everest will be drawing on their last dregs of reserve energy. My attempt to catch up Schneider and Hoerlin failed because by going faster than my natural pace I unfortunately exhausted myself by utilising my reserve energy.

Putting every ounce of energy into it I toiled up the glacier at a speed, which would not have been out of place on Mont Blanc. I got within 100 yards of them, as they sat resting prior to leaving the glacier in favour of a steep little couloir leading up into the rocks of the peak. Here I sat down in a state of tired inertness, from which I never fully recovered for the remainder of the day. It was fully half an hour before I could move, and during that time I had the mortification of seeing Schneider and Hoerlin continue on their way. Quite rightly, they could not afford to wait for me. The peak was, after all, the first thing.

I started again to follow them. The spurt had done me little good, for I was now almost as far behind as I had been when I left Wood Johnson, and now I had tired myself to such an extent that I could not go as fast as Schneider and Hoerlin.

If I have described at length the evil effects of hurrying at high altitudes, I have done so to save others who may be tempted to hurry. Rhythm will one day get men to the top of Everest, but hurry, such as a race against time or weather, will defeat them utterly, and perhaps even render them so exhausted as to bring about disaster. It is possible that Mallory and Irvine perished thus, for if Mr. Odell was not mistaken in thinking he saw them, they were so late in starting that their attempt must have been a race against time.

From the head of the glacier, there was no question as to which route should be followed. The apparently easy snow slopes leading up to the col between the two summits of Jonsong Peak were composed not of snow, but of ice, and ice set at a steeper angle than had appeared from the camp. The rocky North-West Ridge was by far the easiest route.

I plugged up the couloir. At first wide and fan-like, it gradually narrowed. Its western bank was formed by the ice slopes of the glacier falling from the ridge connecting the two summits. The other bank consisted of rocky shelves. On one of these shelves Schneider and Hoerlin had left every article of equipment they could spare. Obviously, they considered that time was of the utmost importance and that if they were to reach the summit without being benighted on the descent, they must climb to it as lightly laden as possible.

At the ledge, they had left the couloir in favour of the rocky shelves. I preferred to continue up the former, for the rocky shelves were ice glazed here and there. It was not altogether a wise choice, for it was fatiguing work kicking and cutting steps in the hard snow of the couloir, and after climbing it a short distance I left it in preference for the rocks.

A falling stone passed with the vicious buzz of a racing car. I looked up. Schneider and Hoerlin were fully 500 feet higher. They were now on the crest of the ridge and silhouetted on the skyline. They seemed to be moving quickly. I scrambled to the left out of range of anything they might send down. The mountain was patently rotten, a ruined mass of broken, shattered limestone. I looked at my watch, 3 p.m. My height was about 23,000 feet, approximately 1,500 feet from the top. It would take another three hours, at least, perhaps four hours. To go on meant being benighted. Great mountains have little sympathy for the solitary climber and the Himalayas none at all. The foolhardiness entailed in going on would be fair neither to my companions, nor to myself. So I sat down, and prepared to enjoy a quiet half-hour.

From my position I could see Wood Johnson seated on the glacier. He had followed me slowly for a short distance, and then returned and stopped near the foot of the ice-slope. Now that there was no question of going on, I felt contented and happy. The day had been something more than a disappointing one, but altitude has the beneficial effect of dulling disappointment in the same way as it dulls ambition, and ambition had sunk beneath the oily surface of lassitude. From my perch I gazed upon a view combining both interest and beauty. All the nearer peaks were below, and I could gaze over the Lhonak and Dodang summits.

Northwards, over the Dodang Nyima range was the brown plateau of Tibet, contrasting oddly with the nearer snowy summits. Little cloud nautilae sailed gently over its vast expanses; their undersides tinged brown from the reflected ruddiness of the earth. North-west of Lhonak Peak were rolling snow peaks and snowfields. What a paradise for the ski-runner or mountaineer they would make, for there are many summits between 20,000 and 23,000 feet that are assailable either on ski or foot.

I turned to descend. Schneider and Hoerlin were out of sight now. I could not even hear their voices. Eastwards of every peak and ridge, blue shadows were stealing over the snows, greedily gulping the sunlight, now and again a chill little wind puffed across and was gone. Here was a peace such as we had not experienced on Kangchenjunga, a peace unbroken by the grumble of ice avalanches. Quickly I scrambled down the rocks, and descended the couloir until it was possible to glissade safely. It had taken me nearly two hours to ascend to my highest point from the glacier; I scrambled and glissaded down in a few minutes.

I strolled down the glacier to Wood Johnson. His appearance shocked me. His face was drawn and haggard, and he showed every sign of being a sick man. I was even more shocked to learn that, some time after I had left him; he had had a stomach seizure, and had actually fainted. He recovered consciousness to find himself lying in the snow. I asked him whether he thought he would have the strength to ascend the ice ridge to the camp. He replied that he was game to try.

There were three things that might be done. I could return to camp and bring back porters. This I dismissed instantly as being impractical; the porters would be more of a hindrance than a help on the ice ridge and could never be got back before nightfall. Moreover, they were not used to crampons, and steps would have to be cut the whole way – hours of work. We might remain where we were until Schneider and Hoerlin returned, but they would most likely be back late, possibly after dark, and they would be tired. The sole remaining alternative was for Wood Johnson and myself to start as soon as possible and take things very easily in the hope that Wood Johnson would be able to muster up sufficient strength.

As we stood considering the situation, two minute dots passed slowly up the last snow slope towards the summit of Jonsong Peak. They traversed to the right and disappeared, but in a few minutes more, reappeared, toiling upwards. At last they stood on the summit, barely distinguishable against the deep blue sky. It was a great moment. Schneider and Hoerlin had accomplished a splendid feat of pluck and endurance. Taking into account the height lost in descending from the camp to the glacier, they had ascended about 3,000 feet in seven hours. Schneider had led magnificently whilst Hoerlin's performance, considering that not long before he had been ill with influenza, told of a splendid constitution.

Wood Johnson's strength must be kept up, and I insisted on him eating some chocolate. This put new life into him, and he decided to make an attempt to get back to camp then and there. It was a journey I shall not easily forget for he was very weak, and every upward step cost him an intense effort. He had reached the stage of not caring what happened to himself, and only the knowledge that he was roped to me, and that by slipping he would involve me, as well as himself, in disaster, prevented his complete collapse. It was one more example of how closely, spiritually as well as physically; two friends can be linked by a mere hempen line. I do not know how long we took to climb the ridge, the time seemed interminable. It was probably about three hours. Slowly, rope length by rope length we progressed. The declining sun flamed and died around us. A vivid furnace with bars of scarlet glared behind Everest; the tropic night rushed down upon us. The wind rose again, and began to numb our hands and feet.

A wall of mist gathered on the Lhonak side of the ridge. At one point near the crest of the ridge, the nearly horizontal sun thrust each man's shadow against it, in a beautiful Brocken Spectre. As I lifted my ice axe to plunge it into the icy snow, so did a ghostly figure, surrounded by a brilliant, prismatic halo, gesticulate, with a weird, eerie abandon. Slowly, the sun sank behind the ranges, its spear-like beams radiating far into the green heavens, like the spurts from some monstrous explosion.

The wind pack fell upon us, beating our faces with painful spiculae of snow and ice. A myriad stars looked down on a scene of intense effort and the snows around us had assumed a cold pallor as of death, as I took in the rope for the last time. We breasted the crest of the little ice peak, and looked down the broad easy snow ridge to the camp. Porters came rushing forth through the gloom to meet and greet us. Only then did Wood Johnson collapse. His effort had been one of which any mountaineer might be proud.

A minute or two later, our servants had pulled off our boots as we sat in our tents. Our feet had lost their feeling, my own had become encased in ice, for during the heat of the day, my boots had leaked, and my feet had become wet. In a trice, Nemu had my stockings off, and started to massage my toes with his horny hands. He proved himself an adept at it, and soon I was groaning under the exquisite torment of returning circulation.

Food and fuel had arrived that day in the shape of a chicken and coolie food, some petrol and a primus stove. How we poured down hot tea, and gnawed the tough chicken! A meal was prepared for Schneider and Hoerlin. It was not until some time after dark that they arrived: they were very tired, but by no means exhausted. When we had all assembled once more, and not until then, a bottle of rum began to circulate steadily between the occupants of the two tents. One day, many years hence, the bottle in which this rum was contained will come out at the end of the glacier beneath, perhaps to provide some future generation of airmen with material for speculation as to what sort of men were those who elected to climb on their flat feet before the helicopteral age.

The wind was blowing hard again the next morning, and our start was delayed, even later than on the previous morning. This was unfortunate as it meant that by the time we got down below Camp Two, the sun had done its worst and the snow was in vile condition. It was a curious fact that the principal precipitation of snow had been confined between 19,000 and 21,000 feet. Above and below that range of altitude there had been practically no new snow.

It was a trying descent for Wood Johnson. Once more he fainted, but soon recovered. It was a weary wade for him across the level glacier near Camp One, and it was a tired party that floundered through the snowy morass and plugged uphill to Camp One.

At Camp One a surprise awaited us. Professor Dyhrenfurth, Kurz, and Wieland had come up from the Base Camp with the intention also of climbing Jonsong Peak. Schneider, Hoerlin, and Wood Johnson were to descend to the Base Camp the next day for a rest, after which the first two were to ascend to the Choten Nyima La, the 18,500 foot pass on the frontier of Sikkim and Tibet, whence they hoped to ascend Dodang Peak, 22,700 feet, the highest point of the limestone Dodang Nyima Range, bounding the northern side of the Lhonak Valley. I should like to have accompanied them, but I naturally preferred to attempt Jonsong Peak once more, and although feeling in need of a rest, I decided to go back with Professor Dyhrenfurth's party next day.

Some cylinders of oxygen had been brought up from the Base Camp, more as an experiment than anything else, for there was certainly no necessity for oxygen. However, it can be extremely beneficial taken medicinally, as was demonstrated in the case of Wood Johnson. He had arrived practically exhausted at Camp One.

As is common with exhausted men, his pulse rate was a high one, 115, but after a few minutes' inhalation of oxygen it was found to be 95, and much of his strength had returned to him. Therefore, I would recommend that even if oxygen is not taken on future Everest expeditions as a help to actual climbing, it should be taken as a revivifier. Also it promotes warmth and may thus stimulate the circulation, or minimise the effects of frostbite. A dose taken in the morning before the start of a climb should prove a valuable preliminary to a hard day's work.

Plenty of food and fuel were now available, and that evening we did our best to make up for the privations of the last few days.

I cannot close this chapter without reference to the porters. Although on short commons, they had not once grumbled, but had carried out their arduous tasks with uncomplaining cheerfulness and fortitude. As a reward for their work, they were to be given three days' rest at the Base Camp, and a bonus on their pay. All save one of them were ready to descend. Nemu was not going to allow his sahib to return without someone to look after him; he would accompany me once again up Jonsong Peak.

CHAPTER SEVENTEEN

Jonsong Peak: A Repeat Ascent

THE FOLLOWING morning, June 4, dawned mistily. A slight sprinkling of snow had fallen overnight, but this vanished with the first lick of the kindly sun. The weather *felt* good, and the air was fresh, with that magical tang of the hills that presages a brilliant day. The frost crystals on the grey rocks round glittered defiantly, but slowly, insidiously, the sun absorbed them and relegated them to the Infinite. As on the last occasion when we had left Camp One, so with this; it was easy to imagine that somewhere hidden by the grey shawls of mist was a little llyn or loch, the still green waters of which had yet to be disturbed by the slim brown trout flashing upwards for their breakfast.

Wood Johnson was stronger, yet it was imperative that he should descend to the Base Camp for medical attention. What wretched luck! Of all of us he was the one who most deserved to reach the summit. Among the porters who had come up from the Base Camp were some of the Bhutias who had previously grumbled at not being equipped to the same extent as the Sherpas. Several of them now took the opportunity of renewing their grievances, and declared it as their intention not to go on. Fortunately, they were prevailed upon to do so. It was unfortunate that Lobsang was still at the Base Camp, for his influence over the porters was great. Recently, he had completed the arduous task of getting the remainder of the loads over the Jonsong La, and it had been arranged that as soon as he had had a rest, he should come up with a support party carrying food.

Our first ascent of Jonsong Peak had been dependent upon speed and good weather; now, with the arrival of food and fuel both over the Jonsong La and from Lachen we could afford to play a waiting game should the necessity arise, not an indefinite waiting game, but one that allowed for two or three days' bad weather.

To avoid having to wade through the glacier morass, we left early before the sun had time to soften the snow. The going was delightful. Of all sounds there is none more pleasant to the ear of the mountaineer than the musical creak of frozen snow beneath the nailed boot in the early morning. It is one that to me, at least, is charged with as much delight as the thud of an ice axe pick meeting ice or the soft silken swish of a pair of ski parting powdery snow. On our first ascent we had waded for hours across the glacier, and up the icefall above, now we strolled, conscious that each upward swing of the leg was bringing us with the minimum of effort towards our goal. The porters seemed to realise this too, and the importance of gaining as much height as possible before the snow was softened by the sun, for they came on well, their tireless gait telling of perfect training, coupled with a physique which makes them the finest natural mountaineers in the world.

In spite of the last few days of hard work, I felt in good training too, and found myself sufficiently far ahead to be able to lounge for an hour in the sun, on the former site of Camp Two. While doing so, I ate a meditative lunch, washing it down with long pulls from a large, new Thermos, flask, which had appeared mysteriously in place of my last one which had been broken on the first ascent. It was my fourth Thermos, for three had been broken, but in every case a new one had appeared in place of the smashed one. I did not think it politic to question Nemu as to the means or methods by which these miracles were accomplished.

Naturally of an untidy and careless disposition, I had lost or broken a number of articles, but replacements of these had invariably appeared. Once or twice, it is true, I seemed to detect growls of discontent from other members of the expedition, but it seemed to me tactful not to enquire into them. I preferred to think that Nemu had, in some mysterious manner, discovered the secret of reincarnating the spirits of broken Thermos flasks into newer and better Thermos flasks. In this particular instance the reincarnation had been so successfully accomplished, that I was now the proud possessor of the largest Thermos flask I had yet had. It was, in fact, the twin brother of one that I had seen Hoerlin using. While I was having my lunch, Nemu himself passed, carrying my tent and bedding. As he did so, I noted that his solemn brown eyes rested on the Thermos flask; they seemed to lighten a little, almost twinkle in fact; the creases in his forehead, which gave to him his habitual worried expression, were smoothed for an instant; something – was it a smile? – twitched at the corners of his broad mouth.

So good was the snow, and so easy the going, that Professor Dyhrenfurth decided not to camp at the site of the former Camp Two, but to push on up to Camp Three. In view of the fact that the porters were carrying very heavy loads, that the altitude was not inconsiderable, that the Bhutias had before resented attempts to double march them, and that we had plenty of food and fuel, it would have been wiser to have stopped at Camp Two. At all events, by the time the platform beneath the icy waves, or bulges, below the ridge had been gained, it was obvious that a number of porters would not, or could not, proceed farther that day, and the camp *had* to be pitched.

Kurz suggested that he and I should go on and prospect a way down the ice slopes from the ridge on which we had previously pitched Camp Three to the glacier we must ascend. This was necessary for two reasons. We hoped to make a shorter day of the final ascent by camping at the head of the glacier, for we were anxious to have enough time to carry out topographical, photographic, and cinematographic work from Jonsong Peak, then, while the ice ridge beyond Camp Three might be a reasonable traverse for the climbers, it was hardly suitable for laden porters. Whichever way we descended to the glacier a secure staircase and fixed ropes would be essential, and while we had enough rope for a direct descent to the glacier we had not enough for the ice ridge.

We ascended by the same route as last time until we came to the commencement of the roof-like ice slope. Across this we cut horizontally to join a steepish snow ridge falling from the main ridge just below the site of Camp Three. There I anchored myself, and payed out a long length of rope as Kurz descended in search of the easiest route to the glacier 500 feet beneath.

The slopes did not belie their appearance; they looked steep and they were steep, probably a good sixty degrees in angle. As I expected, Kurz returned with the news that a way could be forced down, but that it would entail hours of step cutting and necessitate fixed ropes for the porters.

The afternoon was drawing on, and the declining sun had lost its white heat and was slowly sinking, a red-hot ball, into the black abysses of night, as we descended to camp. The day had fulfilled its early promise. If only the good weather would hold.

As I gulped my plateful of soup I peered out between the flaps of my tent on the beauties of a mountain sunset. Below in the Lhonak Valley a cold broth of mist was brewing. The glaciers and slopes up which we had passed had been won over to the advancing hordes of night, but above, the beautiful Lhonak Peak stood out like a glowing beacon, as though warning the fatigued and retreating hosts of day of their impending dissolution. Much later, when night had triumphed, and all the peaks about us had pinned its dark cockade on their crests, Everest and Makalu, like two great citadels, stood between night and the fleeing remnants of day. But, finally, they too were lost, and night's hosts bivouacked on the ground they had won round a million starry fires.

But night had allied itself to our old and capricious enemy, the wind. Impetuously, savagely, it smote our tents, and several times I awoke to listen to its futile snarlings and worryings.

On our last ascent, the wind had had the decency to drop by 9 a.m., but on this occasion it evidently considered that such perfunctory politeness was no longer needed, and instead of dropping, it became if anything more violent, and joyfully seizing up the loose snow, hurled it with shrewd aim at the camp.

Eventually, we decided to make a start. I was first away, with the idea I must confess of finding a spot sheltered from the wind on one of the rocky outcrops projecting from the ice slope and lazing away an hour or so. But as I struggled against the buffeting onrushes of bitter wind across the roof-like slope, it seemed to me that I should have been wiser to have remained in my sleeping bag until the last moment. Descending, where Kurz had descended the previous day, I found what I was looking for, a little rock pinnacle with a sunny sheltered alcove on the leeward side, the floor of which was paved by a granite slab obviously intended for a lazy mountaineer. There I sat, smoking cigarette after cigarette. The wind moaned and sobbed above the pinnacle, but I listened to it with the complacent assurance of one immune from its scoldings. The sun was warm, and I leant languidly back. The mountain world floated unsubstantially between half closed eyelids; the smoke spiral of my cigarette ascended gently, until caught by the wind it was whirled into nothingness; the peace that is engendered by an ordered digestion and a warm body stole upon me ...

I glanced at my watch. Something must have gone wrong with the mainspring. Two hours had passed in a few minutes. Where were the others? They, too, seemed to have preferred to shelter from the wind, and were probably still in their sleeping bags. More anxious thoughts supervened. In the wind the roof-like slope would be no joke for laden porters; a slip there ... I hurried back.

My anxieties were relieved as I turned the corner. No one appeared to have left the camp. The situation was explained when I reached the camp. The long march on the previous day plus the wind had been too much for the porters, and they had refused to start.

The camp was in a peculiarly shelterless position, and even though a day's climbing was lost we could, at least, find a better place for it. Between us and our old camping site on the ridge was the trough mentioned in the last chapter. Although formed by a choked crevasse, the snow was good and solid for the most part, and within an hour after my return we had broken camp and remade it there. At all events, there would have been little object in taking on the porters that day, for their presence during the cutting of steps down the ice slopes to the glacier would have been more dangerous than useful. Professor Dyhrenfurth and Wieland decided to spend the remainder of the day cutting some of these steps; Kurz and I, meanwhile, dug ourselves in, and built a wall of snow blocks as some protection for the tents against the onslaught of the wind. I felt proud of the work of Nemu and myself, a horse-shoe shaped wall higher than the top of my tent, and I had just stepped back with a sigh of contentment to admire it when I went up to my knees in a crevasse. It was not a particularly dangerous crevasse, but it was unpleasantly near to the door of my tent. Stepping out of one's tent door into a crevasse would be tantamount to stepping out of the door of one of those economically constructed seaside lodging houses where the unsuspecting visitor steps out of his bedroom, not on to a landing, but straight down the stairs.

The evening meal had been cooked when Professor Dyhrenfurth and Wieland returned. They had done capital work, having cut steps about halfway down the slopes to the glacier.

The building of a snow wall was a cunning move, for shortly after it was completed the wind dropped, a phenomenon which reminded me of what promised to be a wet fortnight in the Isle of Skye, but which, after only two days of rain, had been changed to a dry fortnight by the zeal of two meteorologists, who planted a number of rain gauges round the district.

The atmosphere, if chilly, was calm when we left the next morning. Our camp had been a cold one, and we had started for once unwarmed by the sun, but that kindly orb made full amends for its tardiness on the slopes to the glacier. Indeed, it glared upon us so furiously that we felt our now leather-like face covering (it is scarcely correct to call it skin) regaining that unpleasant drum-like tightness which we knew only too well preceded the disruption of our countenances.

Professor Dyhrenfurth and Wieland had worked out a good route down to the glacier, and a straightforward bout of step cutting was all that remained to be done. They had descended the same route as Kurz and I for some distance, then leaving it, cut downwards and across to a rib of rocks; descending these as far as practicable, they had started to cut across steep and very hard ice towards a point where the bergschrund looked feasible. Wieland described the ice as being exceptionally tough and hard, a description that I was able to endorse as, held on the rope from the rock rib, I started on the task of continuing the staircase.

Whether a man is acclimatised to altitude or not, cutting in hard ice at nearly 22,000 feet will always be something more than a strenuous exercise. A minute or two's hard work, a few dozen blows, and the wind is *non est*. Altitude has, metaphorically speaking, given you a straight left in the solar plexus, and you double up gasping for life giving oxygen. Don't gasp shallowly, but deeply, using your will power to force the air into the lungs. In the Alps the respiratory organs function automatically, but in the Himalayas they have to be forced to work if they are to give of their best, and the same applies to other parts of the body. It is not a brainless machine, however efficient at a low level, that will get to the highest summits of the Himalayas, but a machine ordered and directed by will power, and not least, that other something we call the spirit.

The axe hit the ice with a dull thud. Several blows were often necessary to dislodge a chip or flake. A step meant several dozen blows. A few steps, it was enough. I retired and Wieland took my place. Both of us could, of course, have gone on for a long time with intervals of rest, but it was much quicker to take turns, even though it meant retreating each time back along the line of steps to the rocks.

For twenty yards the ice was tough and transparent. Frequently, the pick stuck in it as it might hard glue, and had to be wriggled and coaxed out. Gradually it became more flaky, and easier to cut into. At last came hard snow with a soft ice under-stratum, in which it was safest to cut a step, for the sun would soften the snow by midday. We unroped, and while Wieland and Kurz proceeded to enlarge the steps, drive in pitons, and fix ropes I continued to descend alone in order to discover the easiest way over the bergschrund.

The slope here was in excellent condition, and a couple of good kicks sufficed to make a secure step. In a quarter of an hour or so I had reached the bergschrund. At this point it was perfectly feasible for roped men, but if possible, I wanted to find a place where it could be crossed safely by an unroped man, or two men on one rope, in case we had to send porters back. I accordingly traversed to the left to a point where the moat seemed to be well bridged by a thick tongue of snow. The upper lip of the bergschrund was steep and icy, and I cut two or three large steps in it. Standing on these, I probed the snow tongue with my axe; it seemed safe enough. With the axe pick driven well in, I stepped down cautiously, holding on to the shaft with my left hand. It was fortunate I did so, for with startling suddenness my feet went through the snow tongue into nothingness. My whole weight came on my left arm and ice axe, and for an instant I swung free across the upper lip of the bergschrund. The next moment I pulled myself back into safety. The wrench upon my left arm and wrist had been considerable, and the twisting effect on the wrist as I oscillated for a moment on the lip had sprained the latter. It was not a bad sprain, but one that reminded me many times during the next week of a nasty moment.

A yard or two to the right, the bergschrund, although insecurely bridged, was so narrow that it was possible to jump it, and a few instants later I was gaily glissading down the snow slopes below it to the level floor of the glacier. There I sat down in the sun and watched Kurz and Wieland, followed by Professor Dyhrenfurth and the porters, enlarging the ice steps and fixing ropes. They came straight down, and crossed the snow-bridge at which I had first looked, which proved, despite its appearance, to be perfectly safe. Helped by fixed ropes as well as good steps, the porters soon descended, and the whole party forgathered on the glacier for lunch.

So far, so good. Everything, excluding my sprained wrist had gone splendidly, but the ice slopes had taken us a long time to descend, and evening was drawing on apace as we trudged up the glacier. We had hoped to make our camp on the glacier at its head, on or below the broad col in the North-West Ridge, but our old enemy, the wind, thought otherwise, and as the day declined, so did it, like an habitué of a night club, it girded up its loins and prepared to spend a night of revelry and devilry. But we were now used to its little tantrums, and its blasts elicited nothing more than a conventional curse or two as we approached the col, although, for comfort and warmth's sake, it was essential to find some place more or less sheltered from its venomous gusts.

The crest of the col was defended by two or three crevasses, over which the wind had laid a thin covering of pie-crust-like snow as innocent looking as the sands of Margate, but as treacherous as an elephant trap. Circumventing this, we reached the crest of the col and looked down the great ice face above Camp One. Just beneath us, and to the right, a little shelf ran along under an ice bulwark, below which the ice slopes dropped with appalling steepness for thousands of feet. It was the only break, and the only possible site for a camp where we might reasonably expect some shelter from the wind. We descended to it without difficulty, a shovel was produced, and we started to dig out platforms for our tents in a sloping snowdrift, as near to the protecting ice bulwark as possible.

If we thought to find shelter here from the wind, we had made a sad mistake, for our relentless opponent poured over the col and descended upon us with a merciless *joie de vivre*. There is something almost human in the way it seeks out every niche and cranny in these Himalayan mountainsides.

By the time the tents were pitched and the pegs driven firmly and deeply into the snow in expectation of a wild night, the sun was setting. It was invisible to us from our chilly shelf, but its rays lit the snow eddies as they were blown furiously over the ridge above us, until they resembled gossamer-like scarves of spun gold trailed negligently from the white shoulders of the snow maidens.

Wieland and I shared a tent, and after a chilly supper, Wieland, with characteristic enthusiasm, proceeded to indulge in what at first appeared to be some strange and mystic ceremony, but which he condescended to inform me is known as "Determination of Height by means of a Boiling-Point Thermometer".[1] For some reason this necessitated the use of alcohol, but it seemed to me that this

[1] The height determined was 6,620 metres=21,720 feet, 2,624 feet below the summit of Jonsong Peak.

alcohol could be more beneficially employed elsewhere. But Science must be served, even at the expense of numbed fingers in a small tent, which the wind is doing its best to carry away. Perhaps I should not speak so lightly of sacred things, but I must confess that at the time I was concerned not with the determination of height to three places of decimals, but to having a good night's rest preparatory to a strenuous day. However, to cheer Wieland, I gave a short recital on my mouth organ. Beneath the insidious influence of "She's got Hot Lips", the water boiled in great style round the thermometer, and the mercury rose to prodigious heights. Both performances ended in rum, and a sleep such as only rum can induce.

The wind was still blowing when we awoke next morning. My companions were pessimistic, but on the strength of our experiences on the first ascent, I ventured to indulge in a little optimism, and even went so far as to declare that it would drop by 9 a.m. The wind, however, objected to having its fortune foretold in this way, and instead of completely dropping, as it fully intended to do, it compromised with its dignity by only moderating.

Our start was a chilly one. We took with us our servants Lewa, Tsinabo, and Nemu: the name of Wieland's servant I do not remember.

Just before leaving the camp one or two of the party took a cocktail of oxygen to wet their appetite for the thin air of 24,000 feet. Personally, I refused this extraneous aid, as I wanted to convince myself that I was capable, not only of getting to the top of Jonsong Peak on my own lungs, but of going higher.

The camp was reasonably sheltered, and the morning sun shone brilliantly over a cloudy carpet that covered all but the highest peaks in the east, but on the col above we met the full force of the wind, which seemed to cut into our flesh like a knife in spite of every stitch of spare clothing.

On the first ascent, the little couloir leading up into the rocks had contained good snow, into which steps could be easily kicked, but since then the wind had done its worst and had blown its surface hard and icy and steps were necessary. I led; deriving some measure of warmth by slashing out steps as quickly as the altitude would permit.

We might have saved ourselves twenty minutes' work by wearing crampons, but on such a cold morning they would probably have numbed the feet, and circulation once lost is hard to regain over 22,000 feet.

Arriving on the rock ledge where Hoerlin and Schneider had dumped their kit, we started to climb up the rocks of the face towards the ridge. They were easy enough rocks, yet a slip would have been hard to stop. They reminded me strongly of the photograph taken by Mr. Somervell of Colonel Norton at 28,000 feet on Everest. There, as here, were the same tile-like slabs of limestone, as dark and forbidding as the rock of the Cuillin Hills in Skye. Only here the angle was steeper than on Everest, and powdery snow burdened every ledge, sometimes concealing a glaze of ice.

The wind was something more than unpleasant; it roared across the gaunt slabs, licking up the powdery snow, and beating us with its stinging particles. Sometimes advance was impossible, and we crouched in close to the rocks, with bowed heads and turning our backs to its fury. Nevertheless, we made good progress, although we knew that should the wind increase as we gained height, we would not be likely to reach the summit. The porters did not like it. At the best of times they hate wind, and no weapon that a Himalayan peak can produce demoralises them to a greater extent. Soon I noticed that Nemu was going badly. He was finding it hard to keep up with Kurz and myself, and was gradually dropping farther and farther behind. Obviously he was tired, and no wonder considering the work he had done on the expedition, especially since we had left our last Base Camp. In returning with me, instead of descending with the other porters of the first party to the Base Camp for a rest, he had shown of what stuff he was made. He was not one to spare himself, and he would, I knew, go on until he dropped if by so doing he could serve his master. I waited on the ledge until he had joined me, then, taking the rucksack he was carrying, which contained food, photographic apparatus, spare gloves, etc., I bade him go back. At first he pretended not to understand. I shouted at him again above the roaring wind that he must do so, and pointed downwards towards the camp. And Nemu went, after one reproachful look, like a faithful hound that has been ordered home for he knows not why. I felt really sorry for him, but Jonsong Peak is no mountain for a tired or exhausted man.

We had expected to find the wind worse on the ridge itself, but strangely enough, it was not nearly so strong. We could still see it sweeping the slopes below, driving the snow before it like sand. We seemed to have stepped from an area of storm into an area of comparative calm. In fact, once the ridge had been reached, there was no longer any doubt as to our gaining the summit so far as the weather was concerned.

For some distance the ridge formed a sharp snow edge, but Kurz and Tsinabo, who were first, had stamped an excellent trail. Above the snow, the ridge rose steeply for two or three hundred feet, forcing us out on to the western face. Never have I seen more rotten rocks. This part of the peak is nothing more than a festering sore of shale and limestone. There was scarcely a firm hold. The safest method of climbing such rock is to have always three points of attachment. This means that the climber should never trust to one hold only, but distribute his weight between at least three handholds and footholds. This may sound simple in theory, but it is not so simple in practice. Many accidents have resulted from yielding to the temptation to rely on one seemingly good hold.

For two hundred feet the climbing was steep, and the inadvisability of not using a rope might have been argued. But I think that the rope would have been more dangerous than useful, and Kurz had evidently assured himself that Tsinabo was sufficiently expert at rock climbing to climb without its aid. Tsinabo was certainly climbing in splendid style, and seemed to enjoy the work for its own sake, he and Lewa are excellent rock climbers and with their wonderful strength and agility would probably be capable of leading the most difficult rock climbs in the Alps.

Once or twice I glanced down the great mountainside. It was still in shadow, and looked terribly forbidding, its brutal black-jawed crags at savage variance with the peaceful serenity of the sunlit snowfields. The peaks that had recently dominated our outlook had sunk beneath us. Even Lhonak Peak looked formless and insignificant and our gaze passed over the Dodang Nyima Range into the brown fastnesses of Tibet.

The steep rocks eased off. We found ourselves on a slope of slabs similar to those below. We were now definitely feeling the altitude. Each upward step was an increasing effort. I felt strongly tempted to leave what now seemed an abominably heavy rucksack, but which only weighed about ten pounds, and climb to the top without it. Photographic scruples came to the rescue. Had I not taken the expedition boots to the summit of Ramthang Peak? And these with crampons had weighed nearly half as much again as my present rucksack. Heartened by this reflection, I toiled on.

The wind had by no means dropped, but it had lost much of its former venom, and the sun was shining with great power. Climbing at high altitudes is a "slow motion" of climbing at low altitudes. Movement is the same, but it is slowed down, and the climber concentrates upon performing every action with the minimum of effort. Thus, the man who is accustomed to climbing neatly and with a minimum expenditure of effort on Alpine peaks will, other things being equal, be a better climber at high altitudes than he who always relies on brute force rather than skill.

Major J.B.L. Noel in his book, *Through Tibet to Everest*, wrote: 'Collect an Olympic team of fine young men who represent the manhood of the world, and send them equipped with modem scientific appliances and devices. Let them not attack or assault Everest, but let them *walk up* the mountain and prove its conquest without loss, injury or suffering to themselves ... It would be a victory for modern man.' These are magnificent sentiments. Unfortunately, however, the Olympic athlete without mountaineering experience would be of little more use on Everest, or any other of the big peaks in the Himalayas, than Falstaff with gout. Mountaineering experience, and in this I include development and training of mental as well as physical powers, is the first essential. How often do young and brilliant batsmen fail when tried out in a Test Match? It is simply lack of experience. The skill is there, but the brain is incapable of utilising it advantageously. Precisely the same applies to Himalayan mountaineering. Everest will be climbed not on a record of super athleticism, but on a record of all-round mountaineering experience coupled to a suitable temperament.

The slabs petered out into a long slope of scree stretching up almost to the summit. Easy technically, it was yet trying work, for while the scree would delight the heart of a road-mender, or one of those evilly disposed Urban District Councils that cover up a perfectly good road with small sharp stones, it awakened no such response in our hearts, for it rested upon a frozen sub-stratum, and slipped back at every step. A few steps, a bout of panting while leaning on our ice axes, then another few steps, was our method of progression.

It is interesting to remember the thoughts that flash through the brain at such a time. My first thought was what an unutterably weary business it was, how 'fed up' I was, and what a fool I was toiling up there, when I might have been sitting in the Planters' Club at Darjeeling, admiring the Himalayas through a telescope. I sat down for a rest. And as I sat fatigue magically departed, and I experienced to the full the joys of my wonderful position. But always, at the back of my mind like a cloud, hung the thought that I had to go on. I heaved myself to my feet, and went on. Two steps and weariness returned, but this time I was able to counter it. I remember thinking that it would be quite easy if I could discipline my brain to think of the same things as when sitting down for a rest, but such a task the brain seemed incapable of performing. At rest, aesthetic enjoyment had predominated, but it was impossible to experience aesthetic enjoyment when heart and lungs were beating like sledge hammers, legs felt leaden, and knees ached at every upward step.

What the brain did was to compromise with the body and compromise so effectively that it made me more than half forget that I was toiling up a vile scree slope at a height of over 24,000 feet. It brought a power of mental detachment. Without bidding, a number of trivial thoughts and remembrances flashed through my mind. They are not worth repeating, even to a psychoanalyst, and not many of those are likely to read this book. They were quite trivial, quite ordinary, some of them absurd, so that I wanted to laugh, and lose the wind I was so carefully trying to husband. Then, quite suddenly, the little devils of weariness returned with redoubled force. I halted, but when I glanced back I was surprised to find how far I had climbed from my last halting-place.

I have mentioned these things because they are of interest to all who appreciate the real power of mind over body. I think the men who will eventually reach the summit of Everest will not be of the type accustomed to set teeth and "bullock" forwards unthinkingly, they will be men capable of detaching their minds from the physical work which their bodies are performing. Nowhere else is the power of the mind over the body demonstrated to a greater extent than at high altitudes. It is not sufficient for the mind deliberately to force the body into action, it must humour it, even delude it into thinking that it is not working so hard as it really is.

So far I have only mentioned the conscious control of mind over body. I have not mentioned the subconscious control, yet that is what really counts, for when all else has failed, and the conscious mind and the body are united in one desire to quit, it is this subconscious "something" that will drive a worn-out body beyond the ultimate limits of endurance.

The final slope was snow. Below it was a little outcrop of rocks on which we rested for a few minutes. Kurz and Tsinabo were first away. The summit was not more than a hundred feet above the rocks. After the stones it was a relief to kick steps into firm snow. The worst thing about the stones was that rhythmical movement was impossible, but now, in spite of the height I found myself going much more easily than I had lower down.

The slope steepened into a little lip a few feet high, forming the skyline. Kurz and Tsinabo climbed over it and disappeared. There came a thin faint shout. I followed. Even in the hard work of those moments there was borne upon me an intense feeling of excitement. On the stones there had been merely weariness, but now weariness forgotten. I had no longer consciously or subconsciously to force myself to go on, I *wanted* to. To see over that snowy lip was my one dominant idea. Something wonderful was the other side. As a small boy I had often longed to climb a hill behind the house where I lived. I was certain that a new and wonderful world lay the other side. One day I did climb it, to see – factory chimneys. The feeling now was much the same, only I knew that whatever I should see it would not be factory chimneys.

My legs levered me up, my head rose over the lip, my eyes peered across a flat tabletop of snow and stones to meet vast pillars of cloud, blue depths, silver heights – Kangchenjunga and Jannu. The next moment my gloved hands were grasping those of Kurz and Tsinabo. The ascent of 2,624 feet from the camp had taken a little over five hours, an average uphill speed of 500 feet an hour. This is fast going, especially taking into account the fact that the ascent had been by no means a walk, whilst we had been delayed a little by the wind on the lower portion of the climb. The wind had now dropped considerably, but what there was shortened a stay that will live in my memory.

A savage mountain world surrounded us; our gaze passed at a glance over inconceivable distances, resting on mountains and glaciers unknown to man, seeking languidly the infinitude of vast horizons in a subconscious attempt to escape from a nearer and an unvarying world of rock, snow, and ice. The atmosphere was wonderfully clear. Over the brown Tibetan plateau to the north-east rose two huge snowy peaks. Only their snow-covered upper parts were visible, their bases were beneath the horizon. We were 24,344 feet; the Tibetan plateau is about 12,000 feet, yet the lower half of these mountains was below the horizon. How far were they away, and what was their height? Their distance was so great that the tip of the little finger held out at arm's length would have covered them both.

I have seen Monte Viso from the summit of the Piz Bernina, a distance of about 180 miles as the crow flies, and these peaks were much farther. In direction, I should place them as being approximately in the same line as Lhasa. Lhasa is about 220 miles distant from Jonsong Peak, so that it is probable that they were some 50 miles or more beyond Lhasa. On the other hand, 150 miles away, and slightly to the south of this last line are the peaks of Nangkartse Dz, but I am positive that they cannot have been these. One hundred and fifty miles is no excessive distance to see in the clear air of Tibet. If these peaks were actually to the north-east of Lhasa, what could they have been? The only definite statement I can make is that a considerable portion of their height was concealed by the horizon consisting not of a high intervening range, but of the rolling hills and minor ranges common to this part of Tibet. Anyway, I will not commit myself to any statements as to their distance or height or exact direction, for we had no means of determining them. They looked immense mountains even at that great distance, and dominated everything.

Westwards, and much nearer, were Everest and Makalu. From our lower camps we had seen them between gaps in the nearer ridges and though these latter had not detracted from their magnificence, it was not so easy to appreciate their sovereignty over all other peaks. Seen from the summit of Jonsong Peak, one realised to the full that Everest is indeed the "Goddess Mother of the World".

The whole country to the south-east was covered by the cloudy pall of the monsoon, above which the highest peaks stood out like a fairy archipelago. For the first time we saw Kangchenjunga without being misled by foreshortening. Had Mr. Freshfield seen it from the same vantage point, I doubt very much whether he would have held out any hopes whatever as to the possibility of climbing it from the Nepal side. Of course, looking at this side as we were from directly in front of it, we were liable to be deceived in the opposite extreme. Edward Whymper never dreamed of climbing the Matterhorn by the East Face until he had seen it in profile, for looked at from Zermatt, or the Riffel, it looks fearfully steep. The same applies, no doubt, to some extent to our view of Kangchenjunga from Jonsong Peak, yet I am convinced that the impressions gained from what we saw were more accurate ones than those gained when viewing the mountain from Pangperma or the Jonsong Glacier.

For one thing, the terraces which had appeared flat, or gently sloping, were now seen to be set at a much steeper angle than we had supposed, whilst in many places they consisted, not of snow-covered glacier, but of bare ice. Furthermore, we saw the summit pyramid in its true proportions. It is not easy to climb, and is likely to prove much harder than the final pyramid of Everest. The Everest pyramid is about 800 feet high, that of Kangchenjunga about 1,500 feet high. It will not be possible for climbers, who may one day try to storm it, to keep to the crest of the North Ridge above the highest terrace, for this rises directly above the terrace in a Λ-shaped cut-off. They will be forced out on to the face on the western side of the ridge, where they are likely to experience little gullies and chimneys filled with incoherent, powdery snow and smooth granite slabs.

Because we failed, I have no wish to pour cold water on the aspirations of others, but let those who attempt the same route as the Munich expedition remember that the difficulties are *not* over when the upper and easier portion of the ice ridge is reached. Only the hardest of the *technical* difficulties are behind, the *real* difficulties, altitude, powdery snow, wind, and rocks are to come, and they will tax the climber to the uttermost limits of his powers. Only with the aid of exceptional and superlative good fortune can he hope to conquer them, and Kangchenjunga is not a mountain that bestows good fortune on those that woo it.

We could see that the monsoon had already broken on Kangchenjunga and the country to the south. Indeed, we heard later that during the time that we were attacking Jonsong Peak, rain poured for days on end at Darjeeling. It was difficult to believe that the sunny billows of cloud over which we gazed were in reality rain clouds, which were deluging the lower valleys. We were lucky to see Kangchenjunga, for it was smothered in new snow, and it was evident that the monsoon had already wreaked some of its fury on the great mountain. Even as we watched, we could see battalion after battalion of cloud marching up from the south endeavouring to encircle Kangchenjunga, and pour up the Jonsong Glacier. And the north wind was losing. Sullenly, doggedly, it was fighting a rearguard action. In a few days it would have been beaten back to its fortress keep, Tibet. There it would hold the monsoon, which would beat impotently on the ranges bounding the brown plateaux of that barren land.

The advancing tide of the monsoon was slowly creeping towards us; its streams were pouring up the Teesta Valley to the east, and the Arun Valley to the west, slowly outflanking the dry corners of north-east Nepal and north-west Sikkim. One could say definitely that two or three days' marching down the Lhonak Valley would bring one into the monsoon area. It was an interesting spectacle, and one which meteorologists would have given much to see.

Here and there above the cloudy carpet to the south, huge columns and towers of cumuli-nimbus projected far into the clear blue sky like scattered trees rising from a vast snow-covered prairie. One or two of them were drawn out at their crests like anvils by upper air currents, a typical thunder formation. Occasionally, bits would become detached, and swim placidly up into the blue heaven like Zeppelins. The mountaineer who sees these long fish-bellied, smooth-looking clouds in the Alps, knows that almost invariably they precede bad weather. Here they proceeded more than a mere storm, they were the forerunner of the south-west monsoon, the rains of which bring life to the sun-scorched plains of India.

To the cartoonist, who is frequently led by some strange reasoning process to associate mountaintops with politics, there is only one type of mountaintop. It is shaped like a dunce's hat, and its summit is a mathematical point, on which is seated, a trifle uncomfortably, a mountaineer, who usually takes the form of some striped-trousered politician, yodelling blithely some political profundity or sentiment. If there are other and more fearful mountaintops, they are assuredly those that emanate from the fertile brain of Mr. Heath Robinson. His are too sharp even to sit upon, and are usually tenanted by a stout gentleman with a silk hat and spats, who, balancing upon one leg, operates some fearful and wonderful magnetic mechanism which draws more stout gentlemen to the top. Exactly how they are to crowd together on the top is never explained.

There was nothing so thrilling about the summit of Jonsong Peak. It was, in fact tame and dull, consisting as it did of a long drift of snow and a bed of loose stones. The stones were all of the same size and were evidently intended as a reserve dump for the Borough Engineer, whose job it is to repair the ravages of climbing parties on the scree slopes below. We were even able to promenade up and down, while indulging in that vigorous arm exercise practised by the drivers of taxi cabs. In this way we preserved some semblance of warmth in face of the wind, which cut across the summit, jabbing us cruelly with its icy stilettos. But even arm exercises and promenading cannot be carried out as vigorously at 24,000 feet as at sea level, and soon we decided that we had had enough and after taking a number of photographs and swinging our vision along that marvellous panorama in a vain attempt to capture some of its beauties, we turned to go.

What a difference there is in the Himalayas between ascending and descending. On the ascent, the last little bit above the rocky outcrop had seemed by no means inconsiderable. Now, we strode down it like giants. How wearying the slope of scree had been to ascend, how ridiculously easy to descend. The mountains that had sunk below the horizon seemed almost to shoot up at us as we rattled down.

In a minute or two we were off the scree, and scrambling down the slopes. There we met Professor Dyhrenfurth and Lewa. We had taken only a few minutes from the top, it would take them over another hour at least to get there, and perhaps longer, for as I shouted a greeting, I perceived at the same instant that Professor Dyhrenfurth was wearing the expedition boots. In what spirit of selflessness had he done this? Was it in the same spirit that a scientifically minded friend of mine once declared that it was easier to climb a mountain with the climbing boots carried in the rucksack than on the feet? He urged me to ascend the precipitous slopes of Box Hill in this manner, first with boots, then without boots altogether, and then carrying the boots in the rucksack, while he timed my efforts with a stopwatch. In view of the broken bottles distributed there every weekend by motorists, I am happy to say that for some reason this experiment never materialised. Perhaps, therefore, it was something of the same spirit of scientific enquiry, which led Professor Dyhrenfurth to don the expedition boots. Knowing that they weighed eight and a half pounds, and that they had to be carried through a height of 2,624 feet, should provide a basis for a pretty calculation in horsepower and foot-pounds.

I discovered what I had been looking for, a sheltered place out of the wind, where I could enjoy the view to the full. It was only 300 or 400 feet beneath the summit, and the panorama extended from Everest to Chomolhari 23,930 feet, the holy peak of Eastern Tibet. On the summit aesthetic appreciation of the view had been numbed by the wind, now I could even take off my boots, and toast chilled feet in the sun. As I laid my boots carefully on a rock beside me, I could not help shuddering at the thought of accidentally knocking them down the mountainside. Once I had been with a friend on a long walk in the country. It was a hot day, and we had sat down on a river bank to dip our feet into the cold waters of a mountain torrent. We were many miles from the nearest village, and my friend remarked on the fact, and said what a terrible thing it would be to lose a boot. He had hardly said so when one of his boots was snatched, as if by magic, from his hand and dropped into the mountain torrent. He never saw it again. Fortunately, however, we were able to discover lying under a hedge an aged and enormous boot, which had apparently been discarded, after many years' wear by a fastidious tramp. I have not forgotten my friend's remarks on his return to civilisation, or the size of his blisters when at length he did get there. To lose a boot on a Himalayan peak would be a much more serious business, and the man who did so would stand a good chance of losing his foot from frostbite, if he got down at all. I put my boots on very, very carefully.

From my vantage point I looked down to the long, unknown glacier which flows in a north-westerly direction from Jonsong Peak. It is at least 15 miles long, but even from this height it was not possible to tell which river received its waters. In this corner of the Himalayas there are many peaks accessible to ordinary mountaineering parties, and it is certain that a party making the Lhonak Valley its headquarters could scale a dozen or more fine peaks in the course of a comparatively short holiday. Naturally, ambitious minded man is more anxious to climb the greater peaks of the Himalayas, but one cannot help thinking that he is beginning at the wrong end, that by neglecting the many fine mountains of 20,000 to 23,000 feet, he is denying himself the real pleasures of mountaineering. For instance, north-westwards of Lhonak Peak there are a number of fine snow mountains, all of which can be climbed, whilst in the north corner of Nepal itself are dozens upon dozens of accessible mountains.

Kurz had gone on down, but presently I was joined by Wieland, whose servant had deserted him at about the same place from which Nemu had returned. Together we continued the descent, rattling down the rocks at an almost Alpine rate. With the approach of evening the wind began to rise once more, and by the time we had reached the lower slopes it was snarling at us with ever increasing ferocity. But, as we glissaded down the couloir and trod once more the friendly glacier, we could forgive it its spitefulness, for taking all in all, it had been a wonderful day and the fates had been kind to us.

We stood for a few moments on the col above the camp bathed in the radiance of the reddening sun. Its gleams lit the steel heads of our trusty ice axes, and our shadows were thrown blue and spider-like across the wind rippled snow. Our eyes sought the long ridge we had descended for Professor Dyhrenfurth and Lewa. There was no sign of them; obviously they would be late, but should they be benighted, the moon would aid them on their descent.

Darkness fell; the wind steadily increased as we lay in our sleeping bags. Driven snow lashed the tent Wieland and I were sharing. At 8 p.m., there was still no sign of Professor Dyhrenfurth. We looked outside; the air was full of snowy spindrift. Above the camp the wind was roaring over the col in a deep symposium of sound, like the bass note of a huge organ. Our anxiety increased. Ought we to get together a rescue party? Even supposing we did, what could we do on such a night? It was nearly nine o'clock when we heard a whistle. An ice-sheeted figure sank down in the snow outside – Professor Dyhrenfurth.

He was very tired, and no wonder, for not content with having climbed the highest summit of Jonsong Peak his geological enthusiasm had caused him to traverse the ridge to the lower summit. He told us that the descent had been a terrible one. He had expected moonlight, but the moon had not risen sufficiently high to light the western face of the ridge. The wind had harried them continuously, and in the driving clouds of snow raised by it, the way had been hard to find. Lewa had done simply magnificently.

It had been a great effort for a man of forty-four years of age, especially in view of having climbed in the expedition boots. The boots had triumphantly vindicated themselves on the descent, for in spite of the wind and the cold, Professor Dyhrenfurth did not have frostbite. On the other hand, Lewa was wearing only ordinary boots, and he also had no frostbite. It is perhaps doubtful whether the party would have been benighted had Professor Dyhrenfurth not worn the expedition boots.

The wind had done its worst, and we awoke to a morning of perfect calm. Leisurely we prepared for the descent, basking in the sunlight the while. We left at 9 a.m. and strolled down the glacier. If only we had known that the weather would hold like this, we should have postponed the climb, for no snow streamers were being drawn from the mountain tops and Jonsong Peak rose calm and untroubled into the blue.

Up the ice slope we went, releasing the fixed ropes as we did so, and down the other side to our former camp. There we were greeted by Lobsang and several tins of Christmas pudding. Personally, I found the presence of the former more acceptable than the latter, for if there is one thing more calculated to disarrange the digestion at a high altitude, it is tinned Christmas pudding. So far as I remember there was only one member of the expedition who ever seemed to appreciate it and that was Schneider, but even he used to find it necessary to help it down with salad dressing and Worcester sauce.

Had the weather turned bad, the advent of Lobsang and his men with the Christmas puddings might have enabled us to have stuck it out, but I shudder to think of what life without exercise in a small tent would have been like on a diet of Christmas puddings. Full of Christmas pudding I glissaded with great velocity down the snow slopes.

The day ended in a struggle and a wade through the inevitable glacier morass which, despite the passage of many porters and the ploughing out of a deep track, seemed to be worse than ever. After camping on snow for four nights it was pleasant to get back on to the stony ridge where Camp One was pitched. Seated on a granite slab, I watched the last of the porters swinging down the snow slopes. The sun was setting in a transparent bank of mist, and its rays lighted the ice crust already formed by Jack Frost until the snow gleamed like beaten silver.

Slowly the last man came trudging in with his heavy load, yet as he sank gratefully on to his haunches, and slipped out of his headband, that cheery grin that knows no tiredness broke over his countenance. As he passed one ragged sleeve over his sweat-bedewed brow, his eyes swept upwards to Jonsong Peak, and the grin was replaced almost by a look of awe. Was it possible that he had been up there near that great summit, glowing in the declining sun with the sahibs, so near to the gods?

The following morning we packed up. After leaving two cairns that the porters had built ornamented with flags, and a number of empty oxygen cylinders, we set off for the Base Camp. With the arrival of all the loads over the Jonsong La the Base Camp had been shifted to the end of the Lhonak Glacier. It was better, therefore, to descend to the northern branch of the glacier instead of the southern up which we had approached Camp One. Easy snow slopes led us to the crest of a steep declivity some three hundred feet high, consisting of ice overlaid with soft snow. Had it been a little longer it would have been dangerous from avalanches. As it was, those detached by glissading porters were not large enough to harm anyone.

Nemu was the last down. Not for him the wild glissade with load bumping one way and its owner the other. He followed Wieland, who thoughtfully cut steps for such porters who had to descend carefully on account of fragile loads. It was not until nearly half way down that he permitted himself to slide, using my tin box as a toboggan descending with dignity and decorum.

Below these slopes were rocks, between which meandered a little rivulet fringed with flowers and mosses. They were the first flowers I had seen since I had left the Base Camp, and I greeted them gratefully. What would mountains or mountaineering be without its contrasts between the little things and the great things? These flowers were as important to me as Jonsong Peak, and perhaps even greater, for they were synonymous with the small and homely things of life, and these are the things, which the mountaineer turns to with rejoicing and gratitude. Only by knowing the ugly can we adore the beautiful, and only by seeing the small can we appreciate the great. I remained behind to sit down and dream for a few moments among the flowers.

We followed the side moraine of the glacier. Lower down we encountered some of the most lovely ice scenery upon which I have ever gazed. There was a little glacier lake bounded on three sides by walls of ice. Sun, evaporation and melting had sculptured these walls into fantastic forms. There was the Gothic, with its flying buttresses and daring minarets, the Roman, with its superb solidity, and not least, the Victorian, for many of the pillars ornamenting these walls bore a striking resemblance to those that flank the doorways of the more respectable houses in Kensington. In fact had M. Karel Capek seen one stretch of this ice wall he would most likely have compared it to the frozen respectability of Westbourne Grove.

Apart from these things, there was in one corner a fine organ of ice with keyboard and pipes complete, and even as we passed there seemed to come from it a deeply resonant note – no doubt due to the movement of the glacier.

After this the way became duller. The glacier was moraine covered, and included among the moraines were many stones of singular beauty, mostly from the reddish-veined limestone of the Dodang Nyima range. I appropriated several as paper weights.

Traversing the junction of the east and west branches of the glacier was a tiresome business. Up and down we went over enormous moraine mounds, and soon any joy we might have had at descending to the Base Camp had completely disappeared. The trudge became weary and uninteresting, although brightened once or twice by little clusters of Eidelweiss. We passed the pinnacled portion of the glacier, where I noticed that the beak-like structure, which I had seen from Camp One was still preserved.

Near the snout of the glacier Professor Dyhrenfurth and I left the main party in order to have a look at the curious earth pyramids which we had previously noted. They are indeed weird structures, and appeared so unstable that we did not linger beneath them longer than was necessary. This peregrination brought us opposite to the Base Camp, but on the wrong side of the glacier torrent. Fortunately, the latter here divides into a number of smaller streams. We waded across these, but the last stream, a deep and swift torrent daunted us. We shouted lustily. Our shouts were heard, and grinning porters soon arrived to carry us pick-a-back across. Not the least humorous spectacle of the expedition was the arrival of the leader at the Base Camp, clad in his pants.

Wood Johnson was much better, and that night, before turning in, he and I strolled away from the camp. The soft turf muffled our tread. How pleasant it was to feel it again and scent its elusive fragrance. The moon was rising. Her soft rays illuminated the great terminal moraine of the Lhonak Glacier and the weird earth pinnacles. Almost, we fancied ourselves looking up at a titanic cinder heap, ejected from some mountain hell.

Up and down we walked, yarning over the events of the past fortnight, and when at last we turned in, the moon rode high in the heavens and the great peaks around stood radiant against the stars.

CHAPTER EIGHTEEN

A Celebration Banquet in Sikkim

WE ARRIVED BACK at the Base Camp on June 10. The following day was necessarily a rest day, and we devoted it to lounging about the camp, writing letters to home, or making desperate endeavours to fill in many blank pages of our diaries.

For some time I dutifully hammered away at a dispatch on the portable typewriter, but soon I gave even that up, and sitting in the sun on the warm springy turf allowed my mind to wander back over the events of the past fortnight. From May 29 to June 12 there had been for me only one rest day, and that was on June 1 when we had lain in our tents unable to move owing to a snowstorm. Kangchenjunga had been too nerve-wracking for enjoyment, but though we had had some tough and trying times on Jonsong Peak we had enjoyed them, too; we had not been merely avalanche fodder, we had climbed free from nerve-strain and anxiety, and life had been very good. Staying on in the Lhonak Valley, as Professor Dyhrenfurth wanted to do might result in some useful exploration and geological work, but to me at least the thought of a hot bath submerged every other consideration. I looked at my hands; they were brown and wrinkled with the sun and wind, the hands of an old man. My fingers explored my face, pulling on the red beard sprouting therefrom with a feeling, not of pride at its luxuriant growth, but of loathing. Hoerlin had been the only one to escape a beard, and had been known as Pallas (Pallas Athene). Dr. Richter had weighed us that morning. The work of the past twelve weeks had told, and we had all lost a stone or more each, Professor Dyhrenfurth as much as twenty-two pounds.

That afternoon Schneider and Hoerlin returned from the Nyima Range. They had added yet another success to their splendid climbing achievements by ascending Dodang Peak, 22,700 feet. With characteristic modesty they had little to say about it, beyond the fact that the climbing had been of a most difficult nature. They had cut steps for many hours in the toughest ice they had ever encountered, and the picks of their ice axes bore striking witness to the toughness, for they were bent round out of alignment. First of all they had, descended to the Choten Nyima La, across which runs the Tibetan frontier; thence they had climbed Dodang Peak. It had cost them nearly a day to work through a difficult icefall and on the final climb they had only just escaped being benighted, so difficult had been the work.

Wood Johnson, who was much better, was anxious to return to his tea estate, as his leave was nearly up. Frau Dyhrenfurth, Dr. Richter, Duvanel and myself decided to accompany him, leaving the remainder of the party to attempt the ascent of Lhonak Peak, and afterwards cross over one of the passes into the Zemu Valley in order to view the great eastern precipices of Kangchenjunga and the ice ridge attempted by the Munich expedition. Whether or not they would be able to do this before the arrival of the monsoon was, however, doubtful. It needed only a glance down the valley to see the clouds flooding steadily up from the Teesta Valley, and it was practically certain that the latter part of their programme, at least, would be spoilt by the rains, as the Zemu Valley receives them earlier than the head of the Lhonak Valley.

One march from the Base Camp down the Lhonak Valley was a yak-grazing ground, and a runner was sent down ordering yaks to be sent up for our luggage. Perhaps it was memories of Wood Johnson's adventure with the Khunza yak that led Duvanel to object strongly to having his exposed films and cinematograph apparatus yak-borne down the valley. However, while even a Lhonak yak might have objected to the yak-man-ship of Wood Johnson, it apparently did not mind carrying Duvanel's films, and the matter was thus amicably settled. As a matter of fact, I noticed no desire on the part of Wood Johnson to "yak it" down the valley.

June 12 was another beautiful day, and Europeans, porters and yaks started off in great fettle. Frau Dyhrenfurth was left behind, typing Professor Dyhrenfurth's letters and articles, and was to follow with her servant later.

A mile or two down the valley we turned for one last look at the beauties we were leaving. The huge snout of the Lhonak Glacier was thrust down the valley like some tremendous earthwork of the gods. Far above rose Jonsong Peak, serene and peaceful. Had we really stood on that remote summit, so far above the world?

Dominating the head of the Lhonak Glacier stood Lhonak Peak, rising in perfect symmetry and superb simplicity. Northwards, was the brown reef of mountains separating us from Tibet. Silently we stood gazing at Jonsong Peak. It had taken and given some hard knocks. We had conquered it, but conquered not its spirit; it had merely suffered us. The true mountaineer does not regard a vanquished summit with contempt, but rather with increased respect. Kangchenjunga is terrible; it is difficult to think of it in any other way. It is a giant, with all a giant's meaningless passions and illogical rages. Jonsong Peak is a more tolerant mountain. In stature it cannot rival Kangchenjunga, therefore, it is more sober, less blatant. After being cast out from the precincts of Kangchenjunga, we had approached it with humility, and it had welcomed us.

One last regretful glance at brown valley, silver peak and gentian sky. We turned. Soon a corner had hidden peaks and glacier from view.

For some distance we strolled over turf and over the shoulders of rolling hills that put me in mind of the South Downs. We were well content with life; so too were the porters. Even the "Thundering Herd" of yaks seemed to sense the gaiety of the occasion, and increased their normal speed of two miles to nearly two and a half miles per hour.

We were short of coolie food, but word had been sent down to Lachen, and we were expecting to meet some loads. Unfortunately, they were sent on the other side of the glacier torrent, and it was only with considerable difficulty that a sack of coolie food was slung across on a rope, for it was impossible to ford the torrent.

We passed the end of the valley leading up towards the range running south from Langpo Peak. Looking up it we were rewarded with a fine view of the Tent Peak, with a plume of monsoon clouds tearing its summit.

The grass, at first dry and green, became greener and more luscious. Brooks of clear, cool water babbled down the hillside to join the turgid mountain torrent that followed the valley. Little flowers grew beside them, many of which were familiar Alpine friends, and for the first time since leaving Kangbachen we came upon dwarf rhododendrons.

The broad valley narrowed abruptly into a steeper defile. Just before it did so there was situated a little group of huts, marked on the map as Tancha.

A stiff wind was blowing down the valley, and we took good care to pitch our tents to the windward of the filthy hovels in which dwelt the yak-herds and their families. This portion of the Lhonak Valley reminded me of a valley in the Red Cuillins of Skye, only here the ground was not bog-like, there was no misty drizzle, and neither bannock cakes nor whisky were to be purchased at the yak-herds' huts. For the rest there were the same bare slopes, and colourful reddish rocks and broken crags, similar to those of the Red Cuillins. At eventide when the sun gilded the hill crests, I almost felt that I had only to walk to the crest of one of them to see the landlocked waters of the sea lochs, and the dim, blue isles of the Hebrides. The darkness fell more swiftly than it does over the Hebrides. Here was no lingering twilight, no gradual merging of blue and violet, violet and purple, but a sudden and brutal switch over from light to darkness.

We began to feel anxious as to the whereabouts of Frau Dyhrenfurth, but presently we espied two figures in the gloom, and went out to greet her. She had been kept longer than had been anticipated by her typing duties, and it was not until long after we had left that she was able to leave the Base Camp together with her servant, a youth of sixteen, named Kipa. She had forded the torrent under the impression that we had gone down the same route as that followed by the men carrying coolie food, and she had had to cross back. Kipa, who had carried her, had been nearly carried away and drowned by the swiftly running waters. As it was she was very wet and anyone with a less tough constitution might well have caught a severe chill.

My estimate as to the distance from the Base Camp at which we might expect to meet the monsoon rains was not far out for we had not marched more than a mile or so down the valley the following morning when we ran into a depressing drizzle and damp mists. Wood Johnson revelled in it, for being a North countryman it naturally reminded him of the purlieus of Manchester and Wasdale Head. I fear that for my part I found it merely depressing. It soon cleared up, however, and as we descended to a flat plain marked on the map as Langpo, the sun peered out again.

We were now on the north bank of the river, having forded it with some difficulty below Tancha. We began to encounter a number of side streams flowing from the main watershed of the Himalayas to the north, along which runs the Tibetan frontier. Sometimes, it was no easy matter fording these, but the porters were used to such work, and carrying us pick-a-back, picked their way sure-footedly through the rapids.

One of these streams, the Chaka Chu, flows down the valley at the head of which is the Nakpo La Pass on the frontier of Sikkim and Tibet. It is a pass probably not often used, but we came across an old man with his son and a yak. The yak was laden with an extraordinary variety of objects. Had Lewis Carroll seen it he might have mounted his White Knight on a yak instead of the more conventional war-horse. If the White Knight had been so mounted, he would not have needed to fall off; he would have been thrown off, and that frequently.

Tucking up their dirty robes, the old man and his son strove to coax the yak across the stream. First of all the son pulled on the bridle, while the old man shoved behind; then the old man pulled on the bridle while the son shoved behind. These proceedings seemed merely to bore the yak, and it turned its brown eyes upon the two in the same pitying way that Wood Johnson's yak had regarded him.

At last, after many efforts to budge the yak had failed, the old man and his son halted, too exhausted even for profanity. As they did so, the yak gave them one contemptuous glance, and with stately tread, crossed the stream of its own accord.

A little distance beyond this stream we camped. Though our height was only 14,000 feet, wet snow was falling heavily and the climate had degenerated into a rawness similar that of a November day in England. For the first time on the expedition we felt really chilly. Up high we had experienced occasional numbness and had narrowly escaped frostbite on two or three occasions, but though one might numb, one did not shiver. In order to experience a really unpleasant form of cold, it is unnecessary to leave Great Britain. Towards evening the sun broke through for a short time, but the snow instead of evaporating was resolved into a wet slush.

The next morning saw us tramping along a path of muddiness reminiscent of a clay valley in Surrey. Wood Johnson rejoiced in it, for it reminded him once more of Manchester. We were now in a delightful country "between the pinewoods and the snow", the alps of Kangchenjunga. I would that I were a botanist, and it was indeed unfortunate one was not included in the party. The whole hillside was covered in dwarf rhododendrons in full bloom; there were clumps of gorgeous blue poppies, and everywhere dwarf pines, to say nothing of many flowering mosses and rock flowers, some of which were familiar some were not.

The valley narrowed almost to a gorge. We ate our lunch near some great drifts of avalanche snow. Everything pointed to the fact that the rainfall and snowfall are far greater in the lower part of the Lhonak Valley than in the upper. The snow line was definitely lower, and the drifts still left on the hillside suggested a heavy winter snowfall.

As we had only been able to take yaks to our last camping place, word had previously been sent to Lachen for local coolies to carry our loads. We met some twenty-five of them both men and women. They had come up from Lachen the same day, and expected to reach our last camping site ere nightfall, a prodigious piece of walking. These Lachen people are remarkably handsome, with finely chiselled features and smooth, clear skins. Like most of the peoples who dwell in these upper valleys of Sikkim and Nepal they had emigrated from the bleak plateaux of Tibet to the more fertile valleys south of the main Himalayan watershed.

Shortly after passing them, we entered the gorge of the Zemu Chu.[1] We were on the north-eastern bank of the stream, and it was essential to cross to the south-west bank in order to reach the camping place at Yaktang at the junction of the Zemu and Lhonak valleys.[2] Former travellers have mentioned a huge boulder resting in the torrent bed, by utilising which it is possible to cross the torrent. This may be possible at normal times, but certainly not during the rains. A party of our own men, under the charge of Tikeram, who had been sent on ahead some days previously, and aided by the Lachen men had, however, constructed a bridge from pine trunks to which cross pieces were lashed with yak-hair rope. Though primitive in appearance, it was strong enough for its purpose, and worth the fifteen rupees charge for the yak-hair rope by the Head Man of Lachen. We crossed it gingerly, one by one, for to have fallen into the boiling torrent beneath would have meant certain death.

We were now down to the level of giant rhododendrons and coniferous trees. Beyond our home-made bridge the way had been prepared and a track hacked through snaky tangle of rhododendrons. Had it not been prepared, we could not possibly have got to Yaktang that day. The gorge was a wild gloomy place, and its gloominess enhanced by a low roof of cloud. We felt imprisoned. I found myself longing for the upland breezy slopes of the Lhonak Valley, for there is something terribly depressing about these great gorges that carry the melted snow waters of the Himalayas to the plains.

1 Chu equals River.

2 The nomenclature is here somewhat confusing. The Zemu Chu is not the stream from the Zemu Glacier, but the lower portion of the Lambo Chu which flows down the Lhonak valley.

The gorge opened out suddenly, dropping at the same time fully 1,000 feet to Yaktang. Down the pitch thus formed the swollen torrent of the Zemu Chu roared in a tremendous cataract. What a place for a hydro-electric station! A million or more horse power which could easily be harnessed are going to waste.

We found ourselves once more in the region of deciduous trees, and for the first time since we had left Yoksam a tropical forest enclosed us. Wild strawberries were growing everywhere, but they were watery and tasteless. The path became muddier and muddier. Wood Johnson and I were far ahead of the others, and we hurried on.

At the junction of the Zemu and Lhonak valleys there is a flat open space, where is situated the shepherd's hut dignified by the title of Yaktang. Here we found the assistant cook, comfortably ensconced before a roaring fire, and proceeded to arouse him to a sense of his duties. It was found that he had in his possession a large tin of strawberries: these, together with a tin of condensed milk, were opened and engulfed – there is no better word to express our hunger and greed – by Wood Johnson and myself. A day or two after this episode, Frau Dyhrenfurth, when checking her list of stores, announced with joy that so far as she could remember there was still a tin of strawberries unopened and uneaten. The cook was told to produce them. He could not, neither, fortunately, could he speak English or German. His jabber in Nepali was, however, translated by Wood Johnson to the effect that the cook regretted it, but the strawberries had been eaten. A more literal translation would, however, have been to the effect that Wood Johnson and I had eaten the strawberries and he the cook, did not see why he should be blamed. Now I fear, the "Memsahib" will know the disgraceful truth as to the fate of that tin of strawberries.

It was a dismal night, but despite the rain we preferred to camp on the wet grass outside the hut rather than on the years' old layers of offal comprising the floor of the hut. We had hoped to obtain a view of Siniolchum, but the monsoon had now this part of the Himalayas in its grip, and we marched down the valley squelching through glutinous mud under a leaden sky. We reached Lachen before midday and for the first time for over two months entered the door of a civilised dwelling.

At Lachen there are two lady missionaries, one of whom, Miss Konquist, a Swedish lady, has been there for thirty years. Their good work is evidenced by the neatness and cleanliness of the village, and the industry of its inhabitants. The latter had been taught weaving, and I brought back with me to England a handsome rug, dyed in natural colours from the flowers of the Teesta Valley, and a quantity of cloth, as superior in quality as the finest Harris homespun. The fact that anyone should spend thirty years in such a remote corner of the world bears testimony to the charm of Lachen. It is indeed a beautiful little place, nestling on a shelf of the Teesta Valley, 8,000 feet above sea level, amid charming woodlands, dells and glades where many varieties of fruit and vegetables, including the homely apple tree, flourish.

We were invited to tea at the Mission House. Surely it was never before invaded by such a set of blackguardly looking ruffians. I exclude, of course, the "Memsahib" whose appearance went far to redeem that of her be-whiskered companions. It was strange to be sitting in a drawing room again, balancing a cup of tea in one hand, and biting elegantly at a piece of bread and butter held in the other. I fear our bites were neither elegant nor few, and the excellent cakes and scones provided disappeared at almost an indecent speed.

From Lachen to Gangtok is four marches. The weather was kind to us for the first two marches, and we were able to enjoy the scenery and flora of one of the loveliest valleys in the Himalayas, the great valley of the Teesta River. Owing to landships, it was impossible to take ponies more than a few miles beyond Tsuntang, one march from Lachen. The rains had begun, so the missionaries told us at Lachen eleven days ago, when we had been enjoying fine weather on Jonsong Peak. They must have been very heavy indeed, amounting to a cloudburst, for between Tsuntang and Singhik the path had been obliterated in many places by landslides, which in some cases had swept broad tracks through the dense forests. We had expected to find many leeches, but curiously enough, we encountered hardly any, although in some places it was necessary to keep a sharp look-out.

Singhik bungalow is in a delightful situation, and admirably placed for a stay of several days for botanists who like to browse among the varied flora of this part of the Teesta Valley, but after my own experience there, I think I should prefer to give it a miss in the future.

In order to finish a dispatch to *The Times*, which was to be telegraphed from Gangtok, I sat up until after midnight writing. The job done, I took up the candle by the light of which I had been writing, and started off to the room I was sharing with Wood Johnson. In order to get there I had to walk along the verandah. I had hardly passed out of the sitting-room door on to the latter, when suddenly I received a heavy blow on the neck almost sufficient to stun me. Thinking I was being attacked by some robber or other evil disposed person, I let out a yell, and dropping the candle turned round to face my attacker. There was no one there, the verandah was deserted! Then came a horrid thought, above the verandah the roof was supported by rafters; perhaps a snake hanging from one of these had struck the blow! I put my hand to my neck, but there was no blood, neither was it bruised or sore, though the blow had seemed a heavy one. I took up the candle, relit it, and passing along the verandah, entered the bedroom. My yell had been sufficient to wake Wood Johnson, but not to get him out of bed – *that* would require nothing short of an earthquake, or some other natural cataclysm. The obvious explanation was a bat, owl or some other nocturnal rover; yet, one of these could scarcely have felt like a human fist. There would, in addition have been the beat of wings. Probably it was due to a lack of a suitable explanation but my sleep was a disturbed one. I dreamt that I was trying to escape from something malignant and horrible. Then the ground I was standing on began to rock in the grip of an earthquake. I awoke to find myself standing on the unfortunate Wood Johnson trying to climb out of the window. Altogether, it was a somewhat disturbed night.

Between Singhik and Dikchu the weather during the day was no longer able to contain itself, and broke wrathfully in what novelists writing of the tropics usually describe as "ropes of rain". I did not see anything that resembled "ropes of rain", and it will probably give a better idea to the scientifically minded reader of the rainfall to say that it probably fell at the rate of about one inch per hour.

The bungalow at Dikchu is in a bad situation, and is only 2,000 feet above sea level, near the Teesta River, and in the middle of dense jungle. It is well within the malarial area, and as I have before remarked Teesta malaria is one of the most virulent forms of malaria known. Also, the moist heat was unpleasant after the clear cold air we had been used to. Lightning flamed through the jungle canopy, and the rain roared down so loudly as almost to drown the crash of thunder. We had no mosquito nets, and we were badly bitten during the night. It was probably here that Dr. Richter and Kurz got a touch of malaria.

The weather rained itself out during the night, and we climbed up to the Penlong La in fine weather, save for a desultory shower or two. Near the pass we were met by servants of the Maharajah of Sikkim with the Maharajah's own racing ponies. It was a kindly thought and the ponies fairly flew along guided by the familiar Chu! Chu! which is successful above all exclamations in this part of the world in galvanising ponies and yaks into activity.

The first thing that encountered our gaze as we entered the dak-bungalow at Gangtok was a bottle of whisky standing like a Serjeant-Major before a row of tins containing various delicacies, a gift of the Maharajah's. We were greeted also by Mr. Dudley, the Maharajah's secretary, and his wife, whose hospitality we are never likely to forget.

Gangtok is something like Darjeeling on a smaller scale. There are the same terraced roads, and platforms for houses cut in the hillsides. The following morning we called upon the Maharajah and the Maharanee, and were shown round a temple that was being constructed in the Palace grounds. The interior was being painted by expert native artists. Though there appeared to be little in the nature of any preliminary plans or drawings, the work was being executed with extraordinary accuracy as regards spacing and attention to detail. The wonderful designs were Chinese in their conception, and were presumably intended to represent incidents in the life of Buddha and the beliefs of Buddhism. But in one corner was a squatting figure with a cruel countenance and sardonic grin, which we were told was the God of Kangchenjunga. Before we left I mentioned the little incident at Singhik to the Maharajah who told me that people avoid the bungalow as far as possible and even double march in preference to spending a night there. Possibly, however, he only told me this out of politeness to my story!

That evening the Maharajah entertained us to dinner. I fear that we were hardly dressed for the part, but any slight diffidence we may have felt regarding our beards and clothes was soon forgotten under the influence of an excellent dinner, including one or two strange Chinese dishes with which we were not familiar. Indeed, I found myself relating to the Maharanee, who speaks excellent English, my best stories, which were translated into Tibetan for the benefit of a stout gentleman who sat on my other side, who, I gathered, was the Holiest Lama of Sikkim. That evening his holiness was not proof against certain Welsh stories into which I endeavoured to impart as much as possible of that accent for which the leader of another great Himalayan expedition is renowned. It was a convivial evening. Among other things we were told that once a year a great dinner is given by the Maharajah to the Lamas of the Sikkim Monasteries, and that it is considered an insult to the hospitality of the Maharajah if the Lamas are able to leave the Palace on their own legs. I can believe that they never do.

The following morning we said good-bye to Gangtok, and to Mr. and Mrs. Dudley with regret. We had hoped to be able to travel in motor cars all the way to Darjeeling, but owing to floods and the main road bridge being down at Tsingtang we walked and rode. Riding proved something more than exciting, for our ponies had been trained as racing ponies, and one and all hated to see another pony in front of them. Their mouths were like iron, and at times it was impossible to hold them in. I shall not easily forget mine bolting at a point where the road was narrow and turned a sharp corner, below which sheer cliffs two or three hundred feet high fell to the torrent beneath. For a non-horseman like myself it was a relief to cross the temporary bridge at Tsingtang to find a little fleet of docile "baby" cars waiting to take us over the last stage of some forty miles to Darjeeling.

We stopped at Gielle Tea Estate, where we were hospitably received by Mr. McKean, Wood Johnson's Manager. Darkness and rain were falling as the gallant little cars, laden to overflowing, toiled up the steep hills to Darjeeling. A little later the fashionably dressed habitués of the ballroom at the Mount Everest Hotel were startled by the appearance of a number of ill-favoured tramps, the entrance of whom was greeted by the band with what some described as "Die Wache am Rhein" and others as "The Star-Spangled Banner" or was it the Froth-Blowers' Anthem?

Three days later we took leave of Wood Johnson and many hospitable friends at Darjeeling, and motored down to Siliguri. Our servants and porters said good-bye to us as we got into our cars and each of them slipped little cotton scarves over our shoulders as a mark of esteem. I shall always remember the grip of Nemu's horny hand.

Two glimpses with which we were rewarded on that journey are memorable. The first glimpse occurred as we came out of the monsoon mists which were enwrapping Darjeeling and the hills round with a grey shroud, to see the Plain of Bengal stretched out below us in the sunlight. For three months we had seen nothing but hills, and valleys, now we looked upon one of those vast fertile plains which had been vouchsafed by Nature for the use of man. Far into the dim blue distances it stretched its dark green forest blurs, and the silver thread of the great Teesta River, no longer turbulent, but calm and serene, bearing the melted snows of the Himalayas to the ocean. To appreciate life to its full, you must sample its contrasts. We had toiled amid the snows, our cheeks had felt their harsh coldness had been scorched by their burning suns and lashed by their bitter blizzards. Now the soft warm air of the plain came up to meet us. Tropical forests enclosed us, and above the purr of the car we could hear the *chanson* of innumerable insects.

The second view was later when we had left the hills, and were passing along the flat straight road near Siliguri. The last gleams of sunset were fading from earth and sky, the insect chorus had died away, and no sound came from the hushed forests on either hand. Before us stretched the plain, behind us rose the Himalayas. A range of towering cumuli clouds rested on the foothills, their crests sharply outlined against a saffron sky. Grand, solid, immovable, they rose; seemingly as eternal as the great mountain range over which they stood watch and ward.

CHAPTER NINETEEN

Lessons of the Expedition

BEFORE THE WAR little was known of the peculiar mountaineering problems presented by the greatest peaks of the Himalayas. Peaks of 22,000 feet and 23,000 feet had been conquered by such pioneers as Dr. Longstaff and Dr. Kellas, the Duke of the Abruzzi had reached a height of 24,000 feet in a bold but unsuccessful attempt on the Bride Peak in the Karakorams, and two of the giants, Kangchenjunga and Nanga Parbat, had been also vainly attempted. In the light of subsequent experience however, these attempts can only be regarded as tentative, if valuable reconnaissances into altitudes formerly deemed impossible of access. The lack of knowledge as to the special equipment, and the elaborate camping and transport organisation necessary, and the absence of real information of the effect of altitude on the bodily functions made attempts on the greater peaks in those days foredoomed to failure.

After the War, however, a new era of mountaineering was inaugurated by the three assaults on Everest, in which Colonel Norton and Mr. Somervell, by reaching a height of 28,000 feet, showed that man's body is capable of acclimatising itself to pressures of air as low as those into which Everest thrusts its crest. Curiously enough, Everest is the only great Himalayan peak which can definitely be said to be accessible to mountaineers. Other great peaks may defy all comers for many generations, and among these I would number Kangchenjunga.

Our attack on Kangchenjunga from the Nepal side was largely based on Mr. Douglas Freshfield's analysis of the most likely lines of attack in his book "Round Kangchenjunga". Photographs of Kangchenjunga from the Kangchenjunga Glacier appear to indicate a mountain face of reasonable angle. Actually, they give an entirely false impression of this huge face. Distortion and fore-shortening misrepresent the scale and steepness of the rock and ice slopes, while in place of the rocky shelves, which Mr. Freshfield thought might form the head of the Eastern Tributary of the Kangchenjunga Glacier leading upwards to the col in the North Ridge separating Kangchenjunga from The Twins, there is instead a rock and ice slope 4,000 feet high set at an impossible angle.

Considering that, with the exception of Colonel Tobin and Wood Johnson, not one of the party had had previous Himalayan experience, the project of approaching the Base Camp site through Nepal by way of two high passes, the Kang La (16,373 feet), and the Mirgin La (14,853 feet), was ambitious. Had we known what difficulties confronted us in particular the lateness of the winter and consequent lowness of the snow-line, we should certainly have preferred the alternative route by way of the Teesta and Lhonak valleys and the 20,200 feet pass of the Jonsong La. The Jonsong La would have been much less difficult in spite of its height, and, as we proved later, we could have worked our transport in relays of trustworthy porters.

There are two types of Himalayan expeditions, the large expedition with its correspondingly elaborate bandobast, and the small expedition burdened only with a light transport. The present expedition was probably the largest climbing expedition that has ever visited the Himalayas, and in its transport was unwieldy and top heavy. The chief advantage that a small expedition has over a large one is that it can live more on the country. Had it not been for the generous help of the Maharajah of Nepal our expedition would have been impossible, as not enough supplies could have been obtained from the sparsely populated valleys through which the expedition passed. The large expedition has, of course, several advantages over the small expedition. In the case of illness there is a reserve of climbers to carry on with the work, and the climbing party can be split up into two or more groups, one group undertaking the work of establishing high camps, leaving the others free to rest before their attempt on the summit.

But provided its members keep fit the small expedition has other advantages besides those of easier provisioning. It is mobile, it needs comparatively few porters, and it can take its pick from first-rate men, thus making its plans secure and free from labour troubles. The ascent of Jonsong Peak proved that four men backed up by good porters are capable of overcoming a great peak. The greater giants of the Himalayas, such as Everest and Kangchenjunga, demand the large expedition, if only on grounds of health, for altitude will surely weed out the climbing party, leaving perhaps from eight or ten men not more than two or three fit to make the final attempt on the summit.

Himalayan mountaineering only resembles alpine mountaineering so far as the actual technique of climbing is concerned. In scale, snow and weather conditions, route-finding, and general organisation, it is so different that only by experience can the alpine-trained mountaineer learn safely to tackle its manifold problems – and this experience is gained all too frequently at the cost of valuable lives.

Kangchenjunga is not merely a mountain built on greater scale than an alpine peak. It is a mountain that is a law unto itself. Its northern and western faces are among the most desperately dangerous mountainsides in the world. Had we realised how dangerous the western side of Kangchenjunga was we should have abandoned any attempt on it at the outset. But, not unnaturally, it was some time before we were able to accustom ourselves to conditions entirely different from those which any of us had previously experienced, and it was not until the mountain discharged an avalanche upon us of almost cataclysmic dimensions did we realise how utterly different was the work compared to that of the Alps. This, at least, was a bitter lesson, for it cost the life of Chettan, a porter of almost unparalleled Himalayan experience.

In the Alps the risk of being overwhelmed by an avalanche is sometimes taken, but such a risk is usually incurred only for a few minutes when passing beneath a hanging glacier or under unstable ice pinnacles in an ice face. On Kangchenjunga the risk lasts as long as the party is on the mountain. Communications must be maintained, and parties go to and fro between camps. Thus, one short stretch of ground exposed to avalanches may have to be traversed not once, but many times, and the probability of accident is greatly increased. Himalayan porters do not appreciate danger; they place implicit trust in their sahibs, whom they are prepared to follow anywhere. Thus the sahib incurs a grave responsibility by risking the lives of his porters and cannot afford to betray such magnificent confidence.

Ice avalanches are Kangchenjunga's deadliest weapon. Ice walls, forming the edge of hanging glaciers 1,000 feet thick and running for miles across the face of the mountain, bar approach. These hanging glaciers are in a constant state of downward movement. They break off in masses weighing millions of tons, which fall for thousands of feet down the granite precipices.

The avalanche that on May 9 ended our attempt to reach the North Ridge of Kangchenjunga covered about a square mile of snowfield with debris several feet thick, which weighed at a rough estimate about 1,000,000 tons. Other and greater avalanches fell later, in particular one that completely swept the route between Lower and Upper Camp Two, and, not content with this, the site of Lower Camp Two, fortunately evacuated a few days before, nearly a mile from the foot of the mountain face. It is difficult to appreciate the scale of such monstrous falls, and I shall always remember the period spent on Kangchenjunga as the most continually nerve-racking that I have ever experienced. In several of the camps one never felt secure, although everything possible was done to pitch them in protected sites. It is easy to be wise after the event, but even such a great mountaineer as Mummery was deceived by the "scale of things" and perished on Nanga Parbat, together with his two Gurkha followers.

The second attempt on Kangchenjunga by the North-West Ridge a week later taught lessons of a different kind. Owing to scale and deceptive foreshortening, the difficulty of this route was under-estimated, for its length alone militated against any attempt. Yet an attempt was made more as a forlorn hope than anything else and, as we expected, failed. Even if the knife edges of ice and rock, carved and split into icy towers, had proved practicable to the expert climbers of the expedition, the impossibility of establishing camps on the crest and of getting up laden porters would have made it a hopeless proposition. To tackle routes of advanced alpine difficulty on such peaks as Kangchenjunga is a mere waste of time.

Curiously enough, we seldom met with dangerous snow conditions and saw only a few snow avalanches. Generally speaking, conditions were similar to those of the Alps during late winter and early spring. Most of the party were expert winter mountaineers and ski runners, so that the danger of being involved in a snow avalanche was slight. As regards weather, Kangchenjunga is great enough to make its own local conditions and these are not favourable to the mountaineer. Sudden storms of wind and snow are liable to strike with but little warning. Wind, in particular, will ever be the climber's bitter enemy, and on the upper ridges blows for days on end with paralysing intensity. Porters will face most things but wind demoralises them completely. Perhaps in its fury they recognise the wrath of the gods.

Himalayan ice is frequently unusually tough, and cutting steps in it is a more gruelling task than in the Alps. This toughness or plasticity is probably due to rapid evaporation, combined with a great range of temperature, varying from an almost tropical sun heat during the day to zero temperature at night. It is this capacity for bending that is partly due to the size of ice avalanches. Where Alpine ice would break away in small quantities at a time, Himalayan ice does not fall until large overhanging masses of it are no longer able to resist the tug of gravity. The ice ridge encountered on Ramthang Peak afforded an interesting example of this peculiar tenaciousness. Though appearing to be precariously poised on the crest of the ridge, it was found possible to traverse edges and masses of ice that could not exist in Alpine ridges. It is undoubtedly this quality of elasticity and tenaciousness that results in the extraordinary ice ridges of many Himalayan peaks such as Siniolchum and Wedge Peak.

Will Kangchenjunga be climbed? The answer is 'yes', but most likely not in this generation and not by present day mountaineering methods. The only route offering any hope would appear to be that attempted in 1929 by the Munich Expedition. But the difficulties are likely to be so great on the final rock pyramid that, taken together with the effects of altitude and the inevitable wind, it is doubtful whether they can be overcome.*

In an analysis of the Munich Expedition as compared with the Everest Expedition in the *Himalayan Journal*, Colonel E.F. Norton compares the respective dangers and difficulties. Progress on Everest was more than twice as fast as that on Kangchenjunga, yet, whereas on Everest a height of 28,000 feet was reached, on Kangchenjunga but 24,400 feet was reached after five and a half weeks of gruelling work before bad weather enforced retreat. The Bavarians considered that they had overcome the principal difficulties. Such, however, is far from the case. These difficulties had scarcely begun. Altitude and its effects only begin to be really serious over 24,000 feet, and being on the sheltered side of the mountain they had not yet begun to experience that terrible west wind which sweeps the upper part of the North Ridge with such merciless severity. And last, but not least, is the final pyramid – a rock pile rivalling the upper part of the Matterhorn in its steepness and technical difficulty.

Present day oxygen apparatus is too heavy for such climbing as is offered by Kangchenjunga, and it is the conviction of the present expedition that only by some medical means which will artificially acclimatise the climber so that he is able to put forth the same effort at 25,000 feet as he would at sea level, or at least on Mont Blanc, will the upper part of Kangchenjunga be justifiably assailable. The present expedition was lucky to escape from an avalanche; the Munich Expedition was luckier still to escape with no loss of life after being overtaken by a snowstorm of great severity.

After we had abandoned the attack on Kangchenjunga, having been driven back by ice avalanches from the North Ridge, and by the sheer difficulty of the route from the North-West Ridge, we decided to cross the 20,200 feet Jonsong La. We were able to get over this pass by the efforts of Frau Dyhrenfurth and Wood Johnson, together with invaluable help in the shape of coolies from the Nepalese authorities. The number of loads far exceeded the number of porters available, so the transport had to operate in relays. Everything worked perfectly, but luck was with us. The season was well advanced and the monsoon imminent. Had the weather broken, the expedition might have found itself in a serious

* The mountain was climbed by the South (Yalung) Face in 1955 by a NZ/British Expedition led by Charles Evans. The Zemu side was climbed by an Indian Expedition in 1977 and the Kangchenjunga Glacier side was climbed by a Franco-British group in 1979.

predicament with some of its loads on one side and some on the other side of the pass, and faced, in addition, with a possible desertion *en masse* of the coolies. The move proved weatherwise, for shortly afterwards the monsoon broke on Kangchenjunga, covering it with new snow, while the district at the head of the Lhonak Valley remained untouched by bad weather.

In its topographical and geological work the expedition has added considerably to the previously little known country at the head of the Lhonak Valley and in North-eastern Nepal. The western and north-western glaciers of Kangchenjunga were thoroughly explored, while Schneider and Wieland found a practicable route over the Nepal Gap, thereby making a new pass between Sikkim and Nepal and solving a problem that had interested mountaineers for many years. The Dodang Nyima Range, separating the Lhonak Valley from Tibet, was also explored by Schneider and Hoerlin, who ascended its highest point, the 22,700-foot Dodang Peak, and traversed the Choten Nyima La.

Some idea of how little is known of the district to the west of the watershed at the head of the Lhonak Valley may be, gained from the fact that a glacier was observed at least fifteen miles long not marked in any map. When political prejudices and difficulties have been overcome, this district of Northern and North-eastern Nepal will offer an interesting field for the explorer and mountaineer. Geologically, the district is extremely interesting, as it forms the junction of the Tibetan limestone with the granite of which Kangchenjunga and its satellites are composed. Fossils were discovered in the limestone Dodang Nyima range at a height of about 20,000 feet.

There is indisputable evidence of a former ice age in huge terraces of the Lhonak Valley. The topographical data collected by Kurz and the geological work of Professor Dyhrenfurth have yet to be analysed and classified. Much valuable information will be at the disposal of the topographical and geological survey authorities. The meteorology of the district is remarkable. The difference of precipitation between that of Kangchenjunga and that of the Lhonak Valley is great, and the monsoon conditions quite different. Observations and photographs were made which should prove of interest in determining the approach and extent of the monsoon on this part of the Himalaya.

In addition to Duvanel's fine cinematograph work, Professor Dyhrenfurth took the highest film yet taken from the summit of Jonsong Peak. Probably nowhere else does the actinic value of the light vary so much as in the Himalayas, and the photographers of the expedition had much difficulty in judging the correct exposure. In the lower regions, though the sunlight is brilliant, its yellow quality demands an aperture as great as f.8. and an exposure of 1/25 second. On the snowfields, however, the ultra-violet rays demand an aperture as small as f.22. and an exposure of 1/50 second.

Much forethought was given to equipping the expedition. To guard against cold and frostbite, thick tricot suits were supplied. But these, together with the special high climbing boots, were found to be unnecessarily heavy, and to impede active movement on difficult ground. The climbing boots, weighing 6½ lbs. the pair and containing over sixty nails each, proved extremely fatiguing and most members climbed for preference in their ordinary Alpine boots. Incidentally, such a large number of nails is unsuitable in the Himalayas, as they conduct cold to the feet. On Everest comparatively light boots, sparsely nailed, proved effective, so long as they were large enough to hold several pairs of socks. Heavy clothing does not necessarily spell warmth, and several layers of light clothing is preferable to one layer of heavy clothing. The writer found that three or four light Shetland sweaters, weighing but a few ounces each, beneath a light water-proof jacket, withstood the coldest winds. No member suffered frostbite.

The feeding of climbers at high altitudes is a very real problem. A mountaineer climbs on his stomach even more than a soldier crawls on his. Altitude impairs the power of the stomach to assimilate food, and the strongest constitution may be laid low by gastritis and other "tummy troubles". The appetite must be kept up and the palate titillated if rapid deterioration of strength is to be prevented. At heights of over 20,000 feet light sugary foods were found most suitable, such as jams, biscuits, chocolate, sugar, tinned fish and fruit, and condensed milk. A little alcohol is a great aid to the digestion. Hot rum taken at bedtime is the best of all drinks to promote the sleep that is as essential as good feeding to the hard worked and mentally stressed mountaineer.

Owing to transport difficulties, the climbers during the early stages of the attempt on Kangchenjunga had to subsist on yak flesh and other mostly unsuitable foods. As a result a marked deterioration soon became evident, and it is practically certain that much of the subsequent illness that weakened the party was due to this. Later, with the arrival of good food, there was a rapid pick-up, and towards the end of the expedition on Jonsong Peak the climbers, though reduced by a stone or more in weight, were putting forth their best efforts.

The general health of the expedition was well cared for by Dr. Richter. Attempts to combat the deleterious effects of altitude were made by bloodletting, to relieve blood pressure, as it was considered that the high blood pressure relative to the low pressure of the atmosphere is responsible for headaches and mountain sickness.

Only two members, Professor Dyhrenfurth and Duvanel, submitted to having 200 cubic centimetres of blood withdrawn, and as they were both subsequently taken ill, Professor Dyhrenfurth within a few days, and Duvanel later, it is doubtful whether any good resulted from the experiment. More successful was the special liver preparation invented by Dr. Richter. This took the form of a pill, nine of which had to be swallowed daily. It is believed to have assisted the special formation of the essential haemoglobin corpuscles, which enable the climber to acclimatise to altitude. As on Everest, it was possible to form but few conclusions from physical tests made before the expedition. The capacity to hold the breath for a long period, or to blow up mercury to great heights has little or no bearing on the subsequent fitness of the climber on the mountain, where only genuine stamina, physique, and will power avail.

A certain amount of oxygen should always be taken by a Himalayan expedition, if only for medicinal purposes. When Wood Johnson returned ill to camp on Jonsong Peak, an inhalation of oxygen reduced the pulse rate from 115 to 95 in a few minutes. If oxygen could be continuously used on the upper part of a peak, its effects would be good, but used intermittently it serves only to stimulate the body for a short time, while the subsequent reaction is severe. The weight of the apparatus prohibits prolonged use and by tiring the climber neutralises the effect of the oxygen. The experience of the last Everest Expedition makes it clear that, provided the actual climbing offers no great physical difficulty, the highest summits of the earth can be reached without oxygen. The secret of high climbing is slow acclimatisation, and this is best effected by living for several weeks as comfortably as possible at a height of about 20,000 feet. At this height the appetite is unimpaired and sound sleep possible. A future Kangchenjunga or Everest expedition would do well to send its climbing party a month or so in advance of the date fixed for the attempt, build a substantial wooden hut, and make small expeditions to moderate altitudes and thus acclimatise to their task.

Himalayan mountaineering is mental as well as physical. Nowhere is the control, conscious and subconscious, of mind over matter better demonstrated than at great altitudes, and the reaction of the body to the processes of the mind is marked. The man who dislikes the work is more likely to become ill than the man who enjoys it, and, though the greatest mountaineering enthusiast is likely to crock, the finest physique is useless without a proper mental complement. The men who will force their way to the summits of Everest and Kangchenjunga will be men capable of disciplining their minds as well as their bodies, genuine philosophers at heart, who experience in mountaineering something far greater and finer than the mere physical joys of struggling with an inanimate opponent.

Apart from the difficulties of the country and the weather, some mistakes were made at the outset. Expeditions starting from Darjeeling should give long notice of their intended date of departure, in order that coolies may have time to come in from remote villages. Unfortunately, this was not done, and it was found necessary to recruit many coolies entirely unsuitable to the work. The best porters are Sherpas and Bhutias, and while in carrying power and endurance there is little to choose between these hardy races, the Sherpa is the better mountaineer on really difficult ground. Of those at Darjeeling, many are "rickshaw wallahs", and such was their keenness to join the expedition, that they were prepared to throw up easy and profitable work at the beginning of the season to face dangers and hardships of the nature of which they were fully aware.

To Colonel Tobin, the transport officer, who was in charge of the third party, fell the responsible task of getting the transport to the Base Camp. It is safe to say that without him and the two other British transport officers the expedition would have failed.

Owing to permission to enter Nepal coming at the last moment, a complete reorganisation had to be made. Apart from the difficulties of the route, which included two snow clad passes, numerous problems had to be solved, of which shortage of reliable porters, shortage of boots, shortage of snow goggles, and the uncertainty of obtaining even a limited number of local porters on the route were the most important. Most of these difficulties were foreseen and emphasised by Colonel Tobin before the start, but it was not easy to obviate, or even minimise them, and the leader decided to take the responsibility of facing all the risks involved.

The first party with Wood Johnson as transport officer left on April 6, with two hundred and twenty porters, the second party with about one hundred and sixty porters under the charge of Hannah left the following day, and Colonel Tobin, chief transport officer left with eighty mule loads on April 12. Between April 7 and April 12, twenty-five other porters started with loads that had arrived late in Darjeeling.

Darjeeling had been so denuded of porters that the only method of transporting the remaining porter loads was on mules. These loads would, of course, have to be transferred to porters for porterage over the Kang La, and it was arranged that as soon as the first two parties were over the Kang La, one hundred and fifty porters with a good sirdar should return to Dzongri. The farthest point to which mules could be taken was the bridge between Tingling and Yoksam. Colonel Tobin actually hoped that he would be able to get his loads to Dzongri by April 17 or 18, carried by local porters and the porters sent back. It was also understood that a European member of the expedition would remain at Khunza until the third party reached that place. Khunza was the most important point on the route, being the junction of the lines of supply from Darjeeling and Nepal.

If this part of the scheme had been carried out, the loads of the first two parties would have been worked from Tseram to the Base Camp with two hundred porters. It was anticipated that supplies and equipment would thus reach the Base Camp sufficient for the work of fifteen days or more on Kangchenjunga. Had this plan been carried out the first two parties, with about three hundred loads would have arrived at the Base Camp by about May 3. The first two hundred loads, would of course have reached the Base Camp by about April 23. This was sufficient to start climbing operations, and it was arranged that one hundred and twenty to two hundred and fifty porters would then be available to return to Tseram for the remaining loads.

Unforeseen circumstances prevented this plan from being carried out, with the result that it was not until May 3 that any of these men returned to Tseram. Meanwhile, Colonel Tobin had succeeded in working his loads by means of a few locally raised porters to Dzongri by April 20 but these men refused to work beyond that place. After a delay, twenty men were obtained from Yoksam and Tingling, which are three and four marches respectively below Dzongri, and these agreed to lift the Dzongri loads up to the snow-line on the Kang La, but no farther. This was completed by April 28, and on that date in very foul weather Colonel Tobin crossed the Kang La with the intention of raising porters in Nepal, as it seemed that there was no prospect of getting any Darjeeling porters for an indefinite time.

He reached Tseram on April 29, with only two of the nine men he had started with fit for anything. Of the remainder, two had deserted *en route*, two had left their loads in the snow, and three were snow-blind. On April 30, seventeen coolies from Khunza arrived. They included six women and five small boys, and they were despatched to the Kang La, but were driven back by the heavy snow and the strong winds. On the second occasion, they had to carry back four of the boys, but at the third attempt they were more successful.

Colonel Tobin sustained a fall on the Kang La. This, combined with the great physical and mental strain that he had been undergoing, made him unfit to go farther in the quest of transport. However, on May 3, seventy porters and a temporary sirdar arrived, and the clearing forward of the Kang La dump began in earnest, although the sirdar, Phuri, died on the pass.

By May 8, many of the loads began to reach Khunza and by May 11 they were arriving at the Base Camp. Further batches of porters meanwhile became available. Messrs. Wood Johnson and Hannah were sent down the line to assist for the food situation began to cause great anxiety. Indeed, the climbers had been on rather short commons. However, by the last named date, the situation had improved, and more local porters were being procured.

But the absence of a responsible sirdar, and the presence of certain disaffected coolies had resulted in looting on the Kang La, and on the upper route, so that many of the boxes reached the Base Camp depleted. The expedition was able to carry on, though at one time it was feared that a temporary withdrawal would be imposed on it.

The situation was greatly eased by the arrival of supplies ordered by the Maharajah of Nepal himself. Colonel Tobin gave over to Hannah at Tseram on May 12, and started back to Darjeeling down the Yalung Valley and through Nepal. By that date the Kang La dump was well on its way to the Base Camp. It was actually cleared by May 15.

There are many lessons to be learnt from the above story, and it may be remarked that it was fortunate that the expedition, though faced with a serious situation, had only a temporary setback.

Colonel Tobin made some interesting commentaries. He said that an expedition requiring an enormous quantity of stores and equipment should arrange for its transportation a long time beforehand. Food packed in zinc cases which have to be cut open are superior to easily opened boxes fastened with nails or insecure padlocks. For an expedition on such a large scale, it would be advisable to arrange a series of food and equipment dumps the previous autumn season. Other members of the expedition should understand the supplies and transportation arrangements. Actually, the arrangements for an attack on Kangchenjunga via the Zemu route had been put on paper, but owing to the eleventh hour change of route, the scheme of operations was not so carefully worked out, with the result that a serious situation nearly occurred.

It should have been realised at Khunza that it was an important point, and that the presence there of a European, at least until supplies were assured, was imperative. Bauer, the leader of the Bavarian Expedition in 1929, with a less vital line of communication, kept one of his members halfway between his Base Camp and Lachen arranging operations. Hard luck on the individual, no doubt, but each member of an expedition must remember that he is one of a team, and should have his definite job allotted. Large batches of coolies must be in the charge of a reliable sirdar. Failure to arrange this was not only the cause of bad work, but also of desertion and looting.

Until the expedition is concentrated, those engaged on transportation, at least, must be kept apprised of the local situation, as well as of the general position to ensure intelligent co-operation, which is essential. Moreover, the work behind is dull, and men engaged on it are liable to become apathetic unless they are told what is going on at the front.

An ample supply of good boots is necessary. Owing to the excessive number of coolies requiring these they were not available. On another occasion it would be better to issue these in Darjeeling, and risk the small loss due to desertion. Shortage of goggles was also due to so many coolies not being allowed for.

After Colonel Tobin had returned to Darjeeling, the responsibility for transport devolved entirely upon Wood Johnson. Though theoretically a climbing member of the expedition, he undertook the arduous task of looking after the porters and arranging for supplies of food. No man should have been expected to shoulder the responsibility and do the work he did as well as climb, but it was entirely due to his efficient organisation that the expedition was able to carry out its programme, and it was entirely due too to his unselfish and disinterested work on behalf of the expedition that he subsequently broke down on Jonsong Peak.

Nor must Frau Dyhrenfurth be forgotten. There were those who had said she would be little better than a passenger on the expedition. Her management of stores and supervising of communications, especially those over the Jonsong La, were invaluable to the expedition, and could not in its efficiency have been excelled by one well versed in the peculiar problems of commissariat in the Himalayas. And lastly, must be mentioned Naik Tikeram Thapa, who served as a valuable connecting link at Khunza and Lachen in the supply and dispatch of stores, added to which he supervised the porters' pay roll.

Did we make a mistake in attempting Kangchenjunga before the monsoon? Only time can tell. Heavy snowstorms appear more probable after the monsoon, and the Bavarian party narrowly escaped disaster from a snowfall of seven feet, while Mr. Freshfield was considerably hampered in his plans by a fall of similar severity. On the other hand these two parties experienced little or no wind and wind is the greatest enemy of the Himalayan mountaineer. The present expedition had to withstand fierce winds, which according to porters were as bad as or worse than those on Everest. Nothing is more demoralising or lowers the vitality more than wind at a great altitude. The danger of being overtaken by a heavy snowfall, plus the increasing cold with the approach of winter after the monsoon, is more than counterbalanced by the winds before the monsoon. On the whole, therefore, another party attacking Kangchenjunga will do better to go out after the monsoon.

No general summary of the work of the expedition, and the lessons learned from it would be complete that left out reference to the porters, without whom the expedition would have been impossible. It is absolutely essential that any Himalayan expedition should include transport officers who speak the language of the porters and understand them. The expedition was fortunate in having Colonel Tobin, who is well acquainted with local conditions, whilst Mr. Wood Johnson, by reason of tea-planting experience, speaks fluent Nepali, and thoroughly understands the child-like temperament of the splendid men to whom the expedition owes so much.

The work of the chief Sirdar, Lobsang, was invaluable, and was equal in intelligence and trustworthiness to that of a sahib. Less spectacular, but also useful, was that of Naspati and Gyaljen, who were engaged with Colonel Tobin on the transport. Among those who did so well – and they are but a few among many equally good – must be mentioned the names of Nemu, Lewa, Sonam, Tsinabo, Ondi, Narsang, Kipa, Nima and, not least, Tencheddar, the cook, who, if frequently reviled, certainly did his best to propitiate rebellious palates. May but a short time elapse before I see again their broad, homely faces, with their infectious grins, and share once more with them the thrills and delights of mountaineering on the great peaks of the Himalayas.

KAMET CONQUERED

Kamet Conquered

First published by Victor Gollancz, London, 1932

ACKNOWLEDGEMENTS I should like to express the sincere thanks of the expedition to the Yorkshire Ramblers Club and the Ski Club of Great Britain, who generously contributed towards the expenses. I must also express the gratitude of the expedition to the Government of India, who kindly allowed our equipment into India free of customs duty, and to the many officials, especially Mr. N.C. Stiffe, Commissioner for the Kumaun Division, who assisted the expedition in India. Before leaving England we were the recipients of valuable advice from Mr. C.F. Meade, Mr. H. Ruttledge, Doctor T.G. Longstaff, and Brigadier-General the Hon. C.G. Bruce, all of whom were intimately acquainted with the Kamet district, whilst General Sir William Beynon was instrumental in securing for the expedition two Gurkha N.C.O.s, who were selected by Captain Bradford, Commandant of the Third Gurkha Regiment at Almora. In India we owe much to the kind help and hospitality of Sir Malcolm Hailey, the Governor of the United Provinces, and to Lady Hailey. In Ranikhet we were entertained by Major and Mrs. Crowe, and elected honorary members of the club there, thanks to the courtesy of the hon. Secretary, Major Brown. Transport arrangements were facilitated in Bombay by Mr. Golding and Mr. Boreham, of the Army and Navy Co-operative Society Ltd., and by Mr. Osier; at Ranikhet by Captain J. Clarke; and at Calcutta by Mr. G.B. Gourlay; whilst Colonel H.W. Tobin selected and despatched porters from Darjeeling. Mr. Browne, Deputy Commissioner for Almora, and Mr. Smythies helped us *en route* to Kamet, and Mrs. Brown helped with arrangements for porterage by writing to the Rawal of Badrinath, who was most useful to the expedition.

It was arranged that the expedition's dispatches should be sent to *The Times*, the *Statesman* of Calcutta, the *New York Times*, the *Asahi* of Japan, and other newspapers. Thanks to the courtesy of the Indian Posts and Telegraphs, communications between the expedition and England were greatly facilitated, and I should like to express here our gratitude to its officials, especially Mr. Wears Taylor and Mr. Martin.

I should like also to testify here to the efficient work of the two Indian Assistant Commissioners, Hukam Singh Sahib and Ram Singh Sahib, who accompanied and assisted the expedition, and also to the Indian surgeon at Joshimath.

Contents

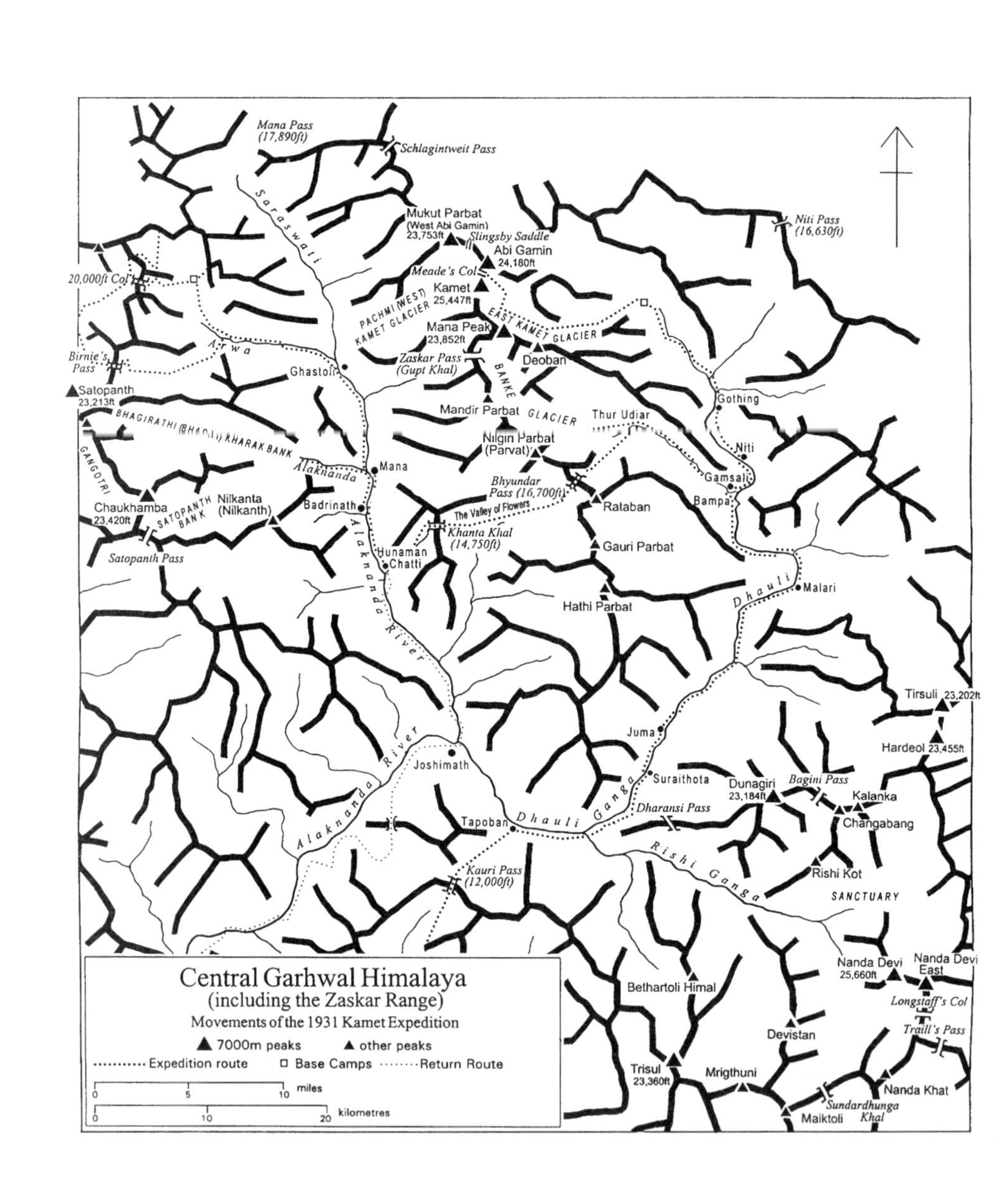
Mana Pass (17,890ft)
Schlagintweit Pass
Mukut Parbat (West Abi Gamin) 23,753ft
Slingsby Saddle
Abi Gamin 24,180ft
Niti Pass (16,630ft)
20,000ft Col
Meade's Col
Kamet 25,447ft
PACHMI (WEST) KAMET GLACIER
EAST KAMET GLACIER
Mana Peak 23,852ft
Saraswati
Arwa
Birnie's Pass
Zaskar Pass (Gupt Khal)
Deoban
BANKE GLACIER
Ghastoli
Satopanth 23,213ft
Mandir Parbat
Gothing
Thur Udiar
BHAGIRATHI (BHAGIT) KHARAK BANK
Nilgiri Parbat (Parvat)
Niti
GANGOTRI
Alaknanda
Mana
Bhyundar Pass (16,700ft)
Gamsali
Bampa
Rataban
Chaukhamba 23,420ft
SATOPANTH BANK
Nilkanta (Nilkanth)
Badrinath
The Valley of Flowers
Khanta Khal (14,750ft)
Gauri Parbat
Satopanth Pass
Hunaman Chatti
Alaknanda River
Dhauli
Malari
Hathi Parbat
Tirsuli 23,202ft
Juma
Hardeol 23,455ft
Joshimath
Suraithota
Dunagiri 23,184ft
Bagini Pass
Kalanka
Changabang
Dharansi Pass
Tapoban
Dhauli Ganga
Alaknanda River
Rishi Ganga
Rishi Kot
Kauri Pass (12,000ft)
SANCTUARY
Nanda Devi 25,660ft
Nanda Devi East
Bethartoli Himal
Longstaff's Col
Traill's Pass
Devistan
Trisul 23,360ft
Mrigthuni
Nanda Khat
Sundardhunga Khal
Maiktoli
Central Garhwal Himalaya
(including the Zaskar Range)
Movements of the 1931 Kamet Expedition
7000m peaks
other peaks
Expedition route
Base Camps
Return Route
0 5 10 miles
0 10 20 kilometres

CHAPTER ONE

The Himalaya

TWO HUNDRED YEARS ago mountains were regarded as useless and terrible masses of inert matter where dragons had their lairs and the spirits of the damned lay in wait to claim the unwary. But as man emerged from the superstitions and materialisms of the Middle Ages he began to realise that mountains were beautiful and their summits worthy of attainment. The nineteenth century saw the conquest of the Alps. Unknown difficulties and dangers had to be faced by the pioneers of mountaineering. Disasters occurred, lives were lost, and mountaineering thrown into disrepute. The mountaineer was not dismayed. He knew that beauty was his for the seeking; he rejoiced in a new-found comradeship and in the acquirement and exercise of a new craft.

The great alpine summits fell one by one; traditions were established; a technique was evolved; a literature was born. The ripples of alpine mountaineering radiated outwards, bearing with them mountaineers to other ranges: the Caucasus, the Rockies, the Andes, the New Zealand Alps. On their highest peaks the skill acquired in the Alps was sufficient to ensure success. But there remained one great range that defied invasion of its strongholds – the Himalaya. There, the technique acquired in the Alps was not sufficient. Height alone was a physical deterrent, and coupled to height was steepness and danger. Expeditions had to be organised to reach even the foot of the great peaks; time and money had to be found. Yet, despite these disadvantages, Himalayan mountaineering and exploration progressed steadily. Pioneers such as the Schlagintweit Brothers, Sir Joseph Hooker, The Duke of the Abruzzi, Mr. W.W. Graham, Lord Conway, Sir Francis Younghusband, Mr. D.W. Freshfield, Doctor T.G. Longstaff, Doctor A.M. Kellas, General Bruce, Mr. C.F. Meade, Doctor and Mrs. Bullock Workman, Messrs. Rubenson and Monrad Aas, and many other pre-war pioneers opened up a region unsurpassed for its beauty and grandeur, and by their experiences pointed the way to the highest summits.

Many people refer to the Himalaya as though their limitations in scenery and climate were similar to those of the Alps. The tourist who gazes upon Kangchenjunga, 28,226 feet, from Darjeeling returns home saying that he has seen the Himalaya. So he has, but how much of two thousand miles of mountains stretching from the Pamirs to the borders of Indo-China, and beyond these limits, in terms of mountains? A lifetime might be spent wandering about the Himalaya, yet the knowledge acquired would embrace but an infinitesimal portion of that vast labyrinth of peaks, valleys and plateaux scrawled across the map of Asia.

In climate alone there is an extraordinary variety. From hot steamy tropical valleys, filled with luxuriant vegetation, it is but a few horizontal miles to zero temperatures and the highest snows in the world. Between these two extremes is an immense range of climate, the common despot of which is a fierce sun. Added to the complexities of climate due to height alone is the added complexity of seasonal weather fluctuations, due directly or indirectly to the influence of the monsoons and weather conditions emanating from the plateaux of Central Asia.

Racial characteristics are as diversified as the climate. From the people of Hunza and Chitral to the Sherpas and Bhotias of Northern Nepal, the almost extinct Lepchas of Sikkim and the wild races of Bhutan, the Himalaya can show many different types, for they form a natural frontier between India and Tibet, and a pudding-bowl wherein is stirred a mixture of Mongolian and Indian blood.

Politically, only a comparatively small portion of the Himalaya is accessible to the mountaineer and explorer. Democracy is unknown in Tibet and Nepal, and both these countries have closed their frontiers to Europeans and resolutely set themselves against infiltration of European thought and ideas. Some of the finest peaks of the Himalaya lie within the borders of Nepal, including the southern side of Everest, 29,140 feet, Dhaulagiri, 26,795 feet, Gosainthan [Shisha Pangma], 26,305 feet, and many other great peaks. In addition there are other districts where the mountaineer is not always welcomed, owing to political and other objections. The three most interesting districts accessible to mountaineers and explorers are the Karakorams, the Kumaun and Garhwal Himalaya and the Sikkim Himalaya, including the eastern side of Kangchenjunga, and it is in these three districts that the most notable mountaineering expeditions have been carried out, with the exception of Everest (now barred politically) and the northern side of Nanga Parba (forbidden territory to expeditions at present). Each of these districts is magnificent in its own way. In the Karakoram there is no glacier to rival in grandeur the Baltoro, and no peaks surpassing in ferocity the terrific ice-armoured spires dominated by K2 (Mount Godwin Austin), 28,187 feet. From the Kumaun Himalaya rises Nanda Devi, 25,645 feet, the highest peak entirely within the confines of the British Empire, a mountain so difficult to approach that no one has yet succeeded in treading the glaciers at the foot of it, whilst Kamet, 25,447 feet, dominates the ranges of Northern Garhwal. In Sikkim, Kangchenjunga boasts the most wonderful snow and ice scenery in the Himalaya, owing to its exposure to the moisture-laden airs of the monsoon. It has defeated three determined attempts to climb it, in 1929, 1930 and 1931 by mountaineers well versed in the technique of high-altitude mountaineering. The highest point reached was 26,000 feet, by the gallant Bavarian expedition in 1931 and that only after incredible difficulty.[1]

Geologically, the Himalaya are a young mountain range, due to an uplift of the ancient seabed covering Central Asia. This uplift took place so slowly that rivers such as the Indus and the Brahmaputra, which have their sources to the north of the Himalaya, have been able to carve their way through the range as it rose. This is the only explanation that can account for the deep valleys cutting through from Tibet to India. According to geologists, the uplift is still proceeding,

[1] The former measurement of Kanchenjunga was 28,156 feet, and that of K2, 28,252 feet. The latest measurements of these mountains are Kanchenjunga, 28,226 feet, K2, 28,187 feet; the difference is so negligible and so dependent on the perfect accuracy of instruments, and even upon fluctuating snowfall, that it is best to assume equality in height. [Modern measurements give K2 26,260ft/8611m. and Kangchenjunga 28,146ft/8586m.]

but whether or not it is taking place at a greater speed than the lowering of the peaks by weathering is a matter for conjecture. Owing to their geological youth, the Himalaya have not weathered as have the Alps. Their peaks are often wedge-like in form, wall-sided, and with incipient ridges and buttresses. This formation is unsatisfactory from the mountaineer's standpoint, for it too often means that a summit cannot be reached by following a continuous ridge. A ridge is always the safest way up a mountain, and the modern alpine-trained mountaineer soon realises this truism in the Himalaya. It is a humbling experience, after climbing steep and difficult alpine mountainsides, to be confronted with a Himalayan giant. Putting aside the peculiar difficulties of altitude, the mountaineer finds himself confronted by difficulties and dangers, which can only be described as appalling in their frequency and magnitude.

The difficulties are due primarily to sheer length and steepness. In addition, ice-ridges are formed such as are never seen in the Alps, ridges so thin and steep that the sun may be seen gleaming through them many feet below their crests.

The principal dangers are avalanches and bad weather. Owing to an immense range of temperature,[2] Himalayan ice is more plastic in its consistency than alpine ice, and it can adhere to mountain-sides at an extraordinary angle. This ice is the product of countless snowfalls, which go to form hanging glaciers. These glaciers are frequently hundreds of feet thick, and on peaks such as Kangchenjunga may exceed 1,000 ft. Every hollow in the mountainside is plastered with them; gravity is ever dragging them downwards – a movement accelerated by snowfalls accumulating above them. When these hanging glaciers come to the edge of a precipice, they overhang it and then break away in masses of ice weighing tens of thousands of tons that crash with appalling force down the precipices and sweep the whole breadth of the main glaciers beneath. The mountaineer must discover a route, both in approaching the foot of the mountain and on the mountain itself, that is not exposed to this danger. In the Alps a chance is sometimes taken, even on standard routes, but in the Himalaya a chance should never be taken, for Himalayan ice avalanches are cataclysmic in their magnitude. It must be remembered, too, that where a portion of an alpine route is exposed to falling ice the risk of traversing it is not taken more than once, or at the most twice, on an expedition. In the Himalaya, however, it might be necessary to take the risk every day for weeks on end. Unless a line of communication from the base camp to the high camps on the mountain can he found that is free of this danger, the route is unjustifiable.

And then, there is the weather – the incalculable factor in mountaineering. If Himalayan weather was as consistently treacherous and evil as alpine weather, few parties would return alive from the great peaks. The Alpine mountaineer benighted in a storm and forced to bivouac has a chance of survival, but the Himalayan mountaineer knows that, to bivouac without protection in bad weather at a great altitude can have but one ending. At mid-day the sun's rays at great altitudes are sometimes almost paralysing in their intensity, but when the

[2] A temperature of 219° F. direct sun heat has been observed (*Alpine Journal*, Vol. XXIV, p. 141), whilst at night it may fall to –30° F. or lower – a range of about 250° F.

sun has set a coldness akin to the coldness of space comes to the upper world. In the Alps, mountaineering is a sport. The mountaineer starts from a hotel and ascends to a hut. The following day he climbs his mountain, and returns to the hut or the hotel. In the Himalayas he may have to march weeks to get to the foot of his mountain; then he may spend weeks in climbing his mountain. If it is a mountain such as Kangchenjunga, the chances are in favour of him returning defeated to Europe. It is not really fair to compare Alpine mountaineering with Himalayan mountaineering; they are so different that comparison is liable to become odious, but it is the only possible and understandable comparison.

Had it not been for the Alps, a great deal of what has been accomplished in the Himalaya would not have been accomplished. For, even though the mountaineer in the Himalaya must readjust his ideas if he would climb safely and successfully, the knowledge he has acquired on alpine peaks will be invaluable to him. But let him beware of approaching the Himalaya with preconceived and bigoted notions, for not only will he find conditions that are unintelligible to him until he has learnt to understand them, but he is liable, on the strength of his Alpine knowledge, to under-estimate the dangers. An Alpine mountaineer walking up to the Concordia Hut along the eastern bank of the Aletsch Glacier does not expect to be blotted out of existence by an ice avalanche falling from the cliffs of the Dreieckhorn, a mile away on the opposite side of the glacier, yet if the Aletsch Glacier was under the hanging glaciers of Kangchenjunga or Nanga Parbat, this is what he would have to expect. Such things are not to be learned by trial and error, they should be assumed beforehand, and heed taken of the experiences of others.

The Himalaya must be approached humbly. Respect their beauty, their majesty, and their power, and they will treat you as you deserve: approach them ignorantly or in a spirit of bravado, and they will destroy you. Other mountains forgive mistakes, but not the Himalaya.

CHAPTER TWO

The Early Attempts to Climb Kamet

THE PRIMARY OBJECT of our expedition was the ascent of Kamet, 25,447 feet, the great peak in the Central Himalaya; and the secondary object, exploration in the Badrinath range west of Kamet, which forms the watershed of the Gangotri and Alaknanda Rivers, the two parent tributaries of the Ganges.

Kamet has known various names. The Schlagintweit brothers, who in 1855 were the first to attempt its ascent, referred to it as the Central Ibi Gamin; it has been called Kangmen by surveyors, whilst it is known to the Tibetans as Kangmed (the "Lower Snows"), as distinct from the "Higher Snows" of Kailas, in Tibet, 110 miles east of Kamet, although this last range is lower than Kamet, the highest peak being Gurla Mandhata, 25,355 feet.

Strictly speaking, Kamet does not rise from the main Himalayan Chain, but is the culminating point of the Zaskar Range, which forms a northern bifurcation. It is situated in the extreme north of British Garhwal, on the watershed of the Upper Alaknanda and Dhaoli Rivers, and its summit is one mile south of the Tibetan border between the Mana and Niti Passes, which are traversed by trade routes between British India and Tibet.

Climatically, the mountain lies on the borderline between the dry westerly Tibetan winds and the area invaded by the Indian monsoon: it receives a heavy precipitation of snow during the winter months, but during the summer months, although subject to local bad weather, it is struck by an attenuated monsoon. Much of the moisture is precipitated on the intervening foothills, the Zaskar Range to the south of Kamet, and the main Himalayan chain; but the Upper Alaknanda Valley and the Dhaoli Valley, form funnels for the warm moisture-charged airs that survive their passage of the foothills or penetrate the Lower Alaknanda Valley, and it is left to the dry Tibetan westerly winds to exercise a sheering effect on the clouds and evaporate their moisture.

Snowfalls during the summer months, comparable to those of Kangchenjunga, 570 miles south-east of Kamet, are unknown, whilst winds seldom persist for long or rival in remorseless ferocity those that assail Everest, 500 miles to the south-east. Even during the height of the monsoon season, fine spells, when the hot Tibetan sun blazes down from cloudless skies, are common.

Another reason for Kamet's equable weather, as compared to that of Everest or Kangchenjunga, is that deep, hot tropical valleys do not lie close to the mountain, and convection air currents are therefore less strong.

In scenery and climate Garhwal is comparable to Switzerland at its best, and no district in the Himalaya can show scenery combining such tender beauties and savage grandeurs. From valleys carpeted in alpine flowers and lined with noble pine forests, the traveller passes through gorges of terrific aspect, where eagles wheel aloft, and the dark knees of the peaks bend down towards thundering glacier torrents. Then, in a few horizontal miles, he climbs up to the snows, where peaks unknown and unnamed stand watch and ward over untrodden glaciers. A simple, friendly people inhabit the upper valleys of Garhwal, varying in race from the Hindu to the Mongolian; a mixture of blood due to the linking of Garhwal to Tibet by the Niti and Mana Passes. Fate, if not choice, has decreed their existence to be a nomadic one. In the winter months, when snow and avalanches render impassable the upper valleys, they are forced to descend to lower and warmer levels, but, when the snows melt, they return to their primitive villages and pastures with their flocks of yaks, sheep, and goats, bearing grain, wool, cloth, and other commodities, which they barter with the Tibetans for salt, borax, and ornaments, of which they are inordinately fond.

Kamet, as the crow flies, is some ninety miles from the Indian hill station of Ranikhet, and nearly as far from Ranikhet's sister station Almora. Seen from these hill stations, it appears as an insignificant point, just peeping over the intervening foothill ranges, and not to be compared in size or magnificence with the main Himalayan Chain, that culminates in the great peak of Nanda Devi, 25,645 feet, 198 feet higher than Kamet, and the highest mountain entirely within the British Empire. Seen, however, from the Kuari Pass, other elevated points of the higher foothills, the valley of the Sutlej, and Tibet, its majestic pyramidal peak of reddish granitic schist forms a towering landmark.

Kamet is the highest of a group of four peaks which, ranged in order from north to south, are: the Western Ibi Gamin, 24,200 feet, the Eastern Ibi Gamin, 24, 170 feet; Kamet, 25,447 feet and Mana Peak, 23,860 feet.*

Owing to Kamet's apparent insignificance when viewed from the Indian side, it remained unmeasured until 1848, when Richard Strachey determined trigonometrically the height and position of its four peaks. The mountain was not again visited by Europeans until 1855. In the August of that year, however, a resolute attempt to climb it was made by the brothers Adolphe and Robert Schlagintweit, of the Magnetic Survey of India. Approaching from Tibet they ascended the Abi Gamin Glacier. Their highest camp was at 19,325 feet, and from this they reached an altitude of no less than 22,239 feet, after bivouacking continuously for ten days at altitudes over 17,000 feet. Theirs was an amazing performance, especially if it be remembered that at that date many of the great Alpine peaks had not been climbed, and not for another nine years was this altitude surpassed. One thing, however, is certain; the mountain the Schlagintweits attempted was not, strictly speaking, Kamet, but the Abi Gamin East, for to climb Kamet from the Tibetan side would be impossible without first traversing that mountain.

Three weeks later, Adolphe Schlagintweit made a panoramic drawing of the Kamet group from the Boko La, fifty-seven miles distant in Tibet, yet, although he correctly delineated East and West Abi Gamin, as well as Kamet itself, he apparently did not realise his original mistake. It was, however, a natural mistake, for the traveller approaching from Tibet cannot see Kamet, as it is hidden behind the Abi Gamin East.

No further expedition of importance to Kamet appears to have taken place until the survey of it under Mr. E.C. Ryall, of the Survey of India, in 1877. Kamet was then accurately fixed both for position and height, but the earlier trigonometrical observations relating to the Eastern and Western Ibi Gamin being considered doubtful, were rejected, and both those peaks remained unmeasured for some time.

During a topographical survey, Mr. I.S. Pocock, of the Survey of India, set up his plane table at 22,040 feet. As he approached from the Mana or western side of the group, his route must have lain up the slopes of East or West Abi Gamin. He reported that from the Mana side the illusion that the Abi Gamin East is merely an excrescence on the northern ridge of Kamet is extraordinarily strong.

No further attempt or reconnaissance of Kamet was made until 1907, when Doctor T.G. Longstaff, Major (now Brigadier-General) the Honourable C.G. Bruce, and Mr. A.L. Mumm, made a preliminary reconnaissance from both the Niti (east) and the Mana (west) sides. This expedition was fully reported in the *Alpine Journal,* vol. XXIV., page 125 *et seq*., and the *Geographical Journal*, vol. XXXI., P. 379 *et seq*. After a preliminary excursion up the Raikana Glacier, Doctor Longstaff and General Bruce started to reconnoitre Kamet, taking with

* Ibi Gamin is now known as Abi Gamin. For contemporary clarity these peaks are, from this point, referred to as Abi Gamin West and Abi Gamin East though the former is now known as Mukut Parbat.

them the Italian guides Alexis and Henri Brocherel, six Gurkhas, and ten coolies.

Crossing the Raikana Glacier from their base camp, which they had pitched at 15,350 feet, they: ascended the East Kamet Glacier and made a camp at 16,800 feet on its north lateral moraine. A mile beyond this point the East Kamet Glacier narrows abruptly and becomes little more than an ice-filled gorge, less than half a mile wide. The glacier is bounded on its southern side by a steep wall of peaks, that culminates in Mana Peak, 23,860 feet. Every hollow and shelf in this wall is filled with hanging glaciers hundreds of feet thick, which appear ready to discharge ice avalanches of appalling magnitude at any moment across the whole breadth of the East Kamet Glacier beneath.

As Doctor Longstaff considered the direct ascent of the glacier too dangerous, the party turned sharply to the north-west up steep moraine-clad slopes to the north of the glacier. This landed them on a glacier of a secondary order, which they followed upwards towards a snowy saddle at its head. They hoped that this saddle would prove the key to the situation, and lead them on to the slopes of Kamet. Mist enveloped them, but they pushed on up steep snow-slopes to the saddle, 20,180 feet. On their arrival, the mist cleared somewhat, and they saw below them the upper portion of the East Kamet Glacier, winding down from the foot of Kamet. But disappointment awaited them; they found themselves completely cut off from the slopes of Kamet by impracticable precipices, and what they saw of the East Kamet Glacier confirmed their opinion that it is horribly dangerous, lying in so narrow a gorge that it would be quite impossible to escape the ice avalanches which constantly fall on to it.

As the party considered it useless to attempt Kamet from the east, they decided to cross the Zaskar Range to the Alaknanda Valley. Utilising and reopening the Bhyundar Kanta Pass, 16,700 feet, and the Khanta Khal Pass, 14,750 feet, they reached the Bhotia village of Mana, to the west of Kamet. Thence, they ascended the Khaiam Glacier for some little distance, and climbed to the summit of a peak of 17,550 feet. They experienced very bad weather, with high winds and snow-storms, and their reconnaissance was cut short by the onset of the monsoon.

One result of their reconnaissance was that they came to the conclusion that the Khaiam Glacier was the most likely approach to Kamet.

Earlier in the same summer, and prior to this reconnaissance, Doctor Longstaff made his memorable ascent of Trisul, 23,406 feet, which, until the ascent of Jonsong Peak, 24,344 feet, in 1930 was the highest actual summit attained.

Unfortunately, no complete record exists of the determined attempts made to climb Kamet by the late Captain A. Morris Slingsby,* of the 56th Frontier Force Rifles, who was killed in 1916 at the head of his regiment in Mesopotamia. He bid fair to be a great mountaineer, and, had he lived, would undoubtedly have achieved much in the Himalaya, As few will have read the account of his attempt in Vol. IV of the *Yorkshire Ramblers' Club Journal*, I make no excuse for quoting it.

With Captain (now Lieut-Colonel) H. Ch. de Crespigny he set off from Ranikhet early in May 1911 with eighty coolies, carrying stores for two and a half months. It was an exceptionally late winter, and at Badrinath the party were delayed for two weeks owing to no Bhotia coolies being available.

* A relative of Cecil Slingsby, the famous pioneer climber – noted for his Norwegian ascents. See *AJ* 28, pp. 326–28.

Early in June, however, they set off up the Ghastoli Glacier with ten picked coolies, who were well provided with warm clothing, sleeping bags, and boots. They camped at 15,500 feet and next day continued on up the Glacier, having to toil knee deep through soft snow. They were overcome by mountain sickness, and had to halt and camp at a height of 18,000 feet. They gave up all idea of reaching the col below Kamet, at which they were aiming, and returned to Ghastoli with their stores.

A day spent in a comfortable camp aided acclimatisation, and Slingsby set out again with six coolies and double-marched up to the 18,000 foot camp in eight hours.

Next day he left the camp at 6 a.m. for the col between the Eastern and Western Abi Gamin, confident that the former peak was merely a minor pinnacle on a continuous ridge leading to the summit of Kamet. He now felt very fit, and the coolies also were going well. After two hours' walking, the foot of steep slopes leading up to the col was reached. The party found themselves standing in a snowfield almost surrounded by an amphitheatre of ice, snow, and ice-covered rocks, cleft by gullies stretching up to the col some 1,500 feet above them.

The slopes to the col were very steep, but a thin covering of frozen snow over the ice sufficed for footholds and saved them the exertion of step-cutting. At last however, step cutting became necessary.

A thick mist enshrouded them, and the Bhotia coolies became tired and dispirited after three hours' climbing, all but one were weeping bitterly and declaring that they could go no farther. They did not, however, dare to retreat, as Slingsby had taken off the rope. By way of cheering them up, he let them sit down, and went on ahead by himself to cut steps. He got above the snow, and had to climb steep ice. The rocks also were sheeted with ice, and the whole burden of chipping this off and making footholds fell upon him. At intervals of a hundred feet he halted to fix the rope round an ice axe or a rock and threw it down to the coolies, who, utilising it as a handrail, hauled themselves up one by one.

It was very slow work. Thick mist made it difficult to keep to the route that had been mapped out from below, and it was essential that this route should be adhered to owing to falling stones. As Slingsby wrote:

> ... We went on slowly like this, until, after ascending about 1,000 feet, we came to more rocks and ice, where we had to cross over to the main gully, and, after getting across it, climbed up by its easterly side. I had hoped the abundance of rocks would have made it easier, but they only added to the labour, for they were all covered with ice so hard that even at noon it was only with difficulty that I could chip off enough to get a foothold. Each coolie had to be carefully watched, for there would have been little hope of saving anyone who slipped, as there was nothing over which to hitch the rope. They were now very tired, dread of the unknown adding to their physical weariness, and it was only with the greatest difficulty that with the help of Gulab Khan, after nine hours spent in climbing some 1,500 feet, we reached the top of the col (21,000 feet) at 6.30 p.m., as the day was drawing to a close. The place was so steep that it was only with difficulty that I found a site for our Mummery tents. One coolie, overcome with weariness, sat down and, slipping his arms from the rope by which he held his load, stood up. Immediately, and without warning, the load slid away before

> he could stop it and went bumping down to the bottom of the gully, where we found it the next day.

In reaching this col, Slingsby had accomplished a splendid piece of mountaineering. His account in the *Yorkshire Ramblers' Club Journal* continues:

> After settling down in camp, I went on to the top of the pass and got a glimpse of Kamet and the country to the north. The mists slid away, and the panorama before me was magnificent. Just below the corniced slope of the col, a very high glacier, starting from the north-west side of Kamet, stretched away at our feet – and curved gradually north until it merged in the low grey hills of the distant Sutlej Valley. Beyond the untrodden summits of the Kailas Mountains rose tier after tier up into the skies, girt here and there with long straight lines of hovering clouds, which seemed to add considerably to their height. Turning from this vast upland view of Tibet, I looked eastwards on Kamet. From the col, a long snow-slope swept up to a great rock tower, itself a minor peak, some 2,000 feet above me, from which, if it were climbed, it would be necessary to drop down many hundreds of feet before again commencing to climb up the slopes of Kamet itself. By going more to the east, however, and avoiding it altogether, it would, I believe, be possible to get on to a long continuous snow-slope, and so to the top of Kamet. What manner of hidden crevasses lie between the col and this slope I cannot say, but the snow, of course, gets the full effect of the sun at the early dawn, and here undoubtedly would be the greatest difficulty. To the south and west were countless small peaks, and here and there a larger one that raised its head above its fellows, their eternal snows flushing pale yellow in the rays of the setting sun. As I gazed on this sea of peaks, as yet untrodden by man, the last parting rays of the sun lit up their upper slopes, the wind dropped, the peaks grew dim beneath the twinkling stars, the avalanches from Kamet ceased, and over all a great stillness reigned.
>
> Next morning, after a cold but windless night, I tried to get the coolies to come on, but they had all been somewhat affected by the altitude and their exertions of the previous day, and only one would accompany me. Though the reward of our efforts had seemed so close at hand, even within our grasp, I now began to realise that I could not go on and leave the coolies where they were, for they would surely have died. With the obstinacy of despair, I went on for about two hours, to a height of, I suppose, some 22,000 feet, and then returned to camp. The snow was very soft, and this served to confirm my misgivings of the previous evening and the effect it would have had on our further progress.

Retreat was imperative, and Slingsby returned to Ghastoli. Thus ended a gallant attempt to climb Kamet. If Slingsby had had expert Darjeeling porters with him, he would in all probability have reached the summit of the Abi Gamin East. He seemed to realise that this peak was a separate entity and that it would have been necessary to have descended many hundreds of feet before the ascent could have been resumed. Actually, a descent of over 700 feet. from the summit of Abi Gamin East to the col between it and Kamet would have been necessary.

It is even doubtful whether the summit above him was the summit of the Abi Gamin East. His proposal to go to the east and avoid the Abi Gamin East shows that he was misled by the nature of the ground. Such a traverse would have been quite impracticable, whilst a traverse across the western face would have been equally impracticable.

Any party approaching Kamet from Slingsby's Col would be bound to traverse the summit of Abi Gamin East. Such a traverse would be a very long one, and would involve at least another two camps above Slingsby's highest camp, whilst the position of a party exhausted on the final slopes of Kamet, or caught there, or on the col between Kamet and the Abi Gamin East, by bad weather, and faced with a re-ascent over the latter mountain, would be precarious in the extreme.

Undeterred by his reverse, this determined mountaineer returned to the attack during May and early June 1913. The same route was adhered to, but he was again dogged by bad luck. As before, he had difficulty in persuading the local coolies to accompany him at high altitudes; the weather was bad, and finally, a severe snowstorm put an end to his climb at a height of over 23,000 feet.

The credit for the eventual conquest of Kamet belongs to Mr. C.F. Meade, for he solved the perplexing problem as to the right route, and would undoubtedly have reached the summit had not luck been against him.

In 1910, Meade, with the Italian guide Alexis Brocherel and the French guide Pierre Blanc, prospected the western side of Kamet. They experienced very bad weather, and accomplished but little with the exception of an ascent of the Khaiam Glacier to the Khaiam Pass, 19,300 feet.

In 1912, Meade returned to the attack, this time with four alpine guides, Pierre Blanc, Franz Lochmatter, Justin Blanc and Jean Perrin.

The party left Mana on May 26, and two days later established their base camp on the Ghastoli Glacier. On May 31 they advanced a camp to 18,000 feet near the foot of the slopes leading to Slingsby's Col. Bad weather intervened, however, and enforced retreat to the base camp. The weather mending, they returned to their 18,000-foot camp, and on June 5 ascended to Slingsby's Col in three and half-hours. Like Slingsby, they found the slopes of snow above the col in very bad condition, and were not able to push their camp to a greater height than 21,000 feet. Next day, June 6, they continued to advance, finding the going very exhausting in the soft snow, but they struggled on to a height of over 23,000 feet. Deteriorating weather and mountain sickness again rendered retreat imperative. Fifty-two degrees of frost were registered that night.

They returned to Mana, but on June 19 again set out for Kamet, this time without Franz Lochmatter and Jean Perrin, who had to return to Europe to fulfil engagements. On June 20 they reached Slingsby's Col. Snow again fell, rendering the slopes exceedingly dangerous. Retreat down the steep face below Slingsby's Col under such conditions was no easy matter, but the descent was skilfully accomplished without accident.

Although he ascended but little higher than Slingsby, Meade was convinced by what he saw that the Eastern Abi Gamin was not a mere spur or point on a ridge leading to Kamet, but a separate and formidable peak. The view he obtained of the Raikana Glacier system also convinced him that, if there was a practicable route at all up Kamet, it must be sought for on the eastern and not the western side of the mountain.

Before crossing to the eastern side of the mountain, he carried out an interesting exploration up the Satopanth and Bhagat Kharak Glaciers, from the combined snouts of which issues the sacred Alaknanda River, the source of the Ganges. In both cases he discovered passes from the heads of these glaciers, a pass across the range from the head of the Satopanth Glacier leading to the Kedarnath Valley system, and a pass from near the head of the Bhagat Kharak Glacier, which appeared to lead into the head of the great Gangotri Glacier, which is about twenty miles long. He then explored a pass from the ice-filled valley above Mana from which flows the Kulhia Ganga. This pass he crossed without difficulty, and descended into the Bhyundar Valley, and, ascending to the Bhyundar Kanta Pass, 16,700 feet, descended to the Dhaoli Valley and Niti.

During July, he thoroughly explored the Raikana Glacier system to the east of Kamet, becoming convinced from what he saw that the only solution of the problem of ascending Kamet was to traverse the East Kamet Glacier, the route which Doctor Longstaff had so uncompromisingly condemned on account of the danger from ice avalanches.

In 1913, Meade proceeded with Pierre Blanc to test his theory. By this time, thanks to their tactful handling by former expeditions, experienced and willing porters, who had lost much of their fear of the heights, were available from Bhotia villages such as Niti and Mana. Meade established his Base Camp on the Raikana Glacier and Camp One in the same position where Dr. Longstaff pitched his camp. From Camp One he proceeded up the narrow trenchlike East Kamet Glacier. Though very forbidding in appearance, this glacier did not prove so dangerous as it looked and no ice avalanches menaced the party. Camp Two was pitched in a safe place at 18,500 feet, and Camp Three at about 20,600 feet. Above Camp Three the party's difficulties began. It was only after some difficult rock-climbing and heavy step-cutting in steep ice that they were able to gain easier slopes and pitch their fourth camp at about 22,000 feet. This was their highest camp. They had hoped to establish another camp on the broad and easy col, 23,500 feet, now known as Meade's Col, between Kamet and the Abi Gamin East, but, although they reached the col, they were unable to pitch a camp there, and were beaten by the weather and the terrible snow conditions. In addition to these troubles, they were not properly acclimatised to altitude, and suffered also from lassitude induced by the fierce glare of the sun.

Meade had accomplished great work. He had discovered the only practicable route up Kamet. From his highest point he saw that no insuperable obstacle intervened between him and the summit. That success should have eluded him at the last moment was cruel luck. Had he realised the importance of acclimatisation, and had the weather and snow conditions been better, there is no doubt that he would have gained the summit.

Owing to the war, no further attempt was made on Kamet until 1920. In that year Doctor A.M. Kellas, who died the following year while engaged on the first Everest Expedition, and Colonel H.T. Morshead, who was foully murdered in Burma in the summer of 1931, left Niti on August 29 with twenty-one yaks and forty porters. They established their Base Camp on the Raikana Glacier on August 31.

Owing to lack of acclimatisation and the incidence of malaria, they did not advance up the East Kamet Glacier until September 3. Having established Camp One, they were delayed owing to transport difficulties, and it was not until

September 8 that Camp Two was established. Here Kellas's servant was incapacitated through an accidental night out.

Their third camp was established on September 11. There they were delayed for another week by transport difficulties. The weather was fine, but very cold, temperatures below zero being registered. Owing to the effects of altitude and cold, their remaining servants were unable to go higher.

On September 19 they climbed the steep rocks and ice above Camp Three and camped at 22,000 feet. After a rest day for acclimatisation, they ascended to Meade's Col, 23,500 feet, with three Mana porters. They left their camp at 9 a.m., and reached the col at 3 p.m. From the col they pushed on for a short distance up the final slope of Kamet, and at 3.30 p.m. had attained an altitude estimated at 23,600 feet. This was their highest point. They were well acclimatised to altitude, and were fully fit enough to make an attempt on the summit, but their coolies flatly refused to continue on Kamet, or even to attempt Abi Gamin East, which seemed feasible. It was essential to establish a camp in the neighbourhood of Meade's Col, but the coolies refused to carry up their tents, equipment, and food from Camp Four.

Several reasons contributed to the coolies' lack of heart. They suffered from headaches, the stuffing was knocked out of them by a cold wind, and they were terrified by the thought that the first winter snowstorms were due. Another reason for the party's defeat – a small reason but a vital one – was the failure of their paraffin cooking stove to vaporise in the thin air of over 20,000 feet. Thus they were unable to cook for themselves or their coolies.

It is interesting to note the time taken by the party to ascend from their base camp to their highest point. No less than eighteen days were occupied in making the ascent. This was largely due to transport difficulties, and it is doubtful whether Doctor Kellas intended to spend so long a time on the mountain before making an attempt on the summit. Yet, I believe that his experiences on the many other Himalayan peaks that he had previously ascended had taught him the value of slow upward progression at great altitudes. Meade and Slingsby both suffered from the effects of altitude, but Kellas and Morshead were not seriously inconvenienced, and, had it not been for difficulties other than those of the actual mountain and its height, they might have reached the summit.

Doctor Kellas, besides being a great mountaineer, was a clever physicist and had contributed many valuable papers to various learned societies on the problems of acclimatisation. On this occasion he took with him oxygen apparatus, in order to carry out various experiments, and it was the non-arrival of this apparatus from England that delayed his attempt on Kamet. I think it may be assumed, therefore, that, unlike other parties that had attempted to climb Kamet, he realised the importance of besieging the mountain and of acclimatising at each camp before pushing on to the next camp.

No further attempt was made to climb Kamet until the present expedition in 1931.

From the foregoing it will be seen that ten expeditions prior to 1931 prospected routes on the mountain or attempted to climb it. No other great Himalayan peak has received so much attention by mountaineers. For the convenience of the reader, I append the following table setting out these reconnaissances and attempts.

Expedition	*Year*	*Route*	*Highest Point*
A. and R. Schlagintweit	1855	Tibetan side up Abi Gamin Glacier and Abi Gamin East	22,239 ft.
Dr. T.G. Longstaff and Brig.-General C.G. Bruce and A.L. Mumm with Alpine guides Alexis and Henri Brocherel	1907	Preliminary reconnaisance eastern and western sides. Highest point reached was above East Kamet Glacier	20,180 ft.
C.F. Meade with Alpine guides Alexis Brocherel and Pierre Blanc	1910	Preliminary reconnaisance western side: Khaiam Glacier and Khaiam Pass	19,300 ft.
Dr. A.M. Kellas	1911	Preliminary reconnaisance western side: Khaiam Glacier, Khaiam Pass and peak north of Khaiam	20,200 ft.
Capt. A.M. Slingsby	1911	Attempted Kamet on western side from Ghastoli Glacier via col between Abi Gamin West and East	22,000 ft.
C.F. Meade with Alpine guides Pierre Blanc, Franz Lochmatter, Justine Blanc and Jean Perrin	1912	Attempted Kamet by same route as Slingsby	23,000 ft.
Capt. A.M. Slingsby	1913	Attempted Kamet by same route as before	23,000 ft.
C.F. Meade with Alpine guide Pierre Blanc	1913	Attempted Kamet from eastern side via East Kamet Glacier and reached col between Kamet and Abi Gamin East	23,500 ft.
Dr. A.M. Kellas	1914	Another reconnaissance of which no record was published	–

NOTE: The above list does not include the early reconnaissances of Strachey and the Survey of India.

As regards the secondary object of the expedition, explorations in the Badrinath Range to the east of Kamet, which forms the watershed of the Alaknanda and Gangotri Rivers, the two parent tributaries of the Ganges, this possessed both human and topographical interest. What the Jordan was to the Jews, the Ganges is to the Hindus, for it irrigates and fertilises the northern plain of India and brings sustenance to millions of Indians. Because of this it is revered by all Hindus. As it flows past the sacred city of Benares it receives the living and the dead – the living, who enter it to be cleansed of their sins, and the dead, whose ashes are taken from the burning ghats and cast upon its waters. Yet, the devout Hindu does not consider himself to have completed his religious devotions by a visit to Benares; he must make a pilgrimage to Kedarnath and Badrinath and pay his respects to the holy and eternal snows whence the Ganges flows from the feet of the gods. Fifty thousand pilgrims toil annually to these places, of which Badrinath is the holier place and the seat of the Rawal, the high priest and the keeper of the temple.

Benares can be reached by train, but not so Kedarnath and Badrinath; the pilgrim must brave the heat and disease of the lower Himalayan valleys, and finally the freezing airs from the snows, before he can accomplish his pilgrimage. Some fall by the wayside, and many more perish of cholera, dysentery, typhoid, malaria and other tropical diseases. Yet, the greater the tribulation and the immolation the greater the virtue and the forgiveness. To gaze at the sacred image in the temple at Badrinath and purify the body by dipping it into the icy glacier waters of the Alaknanda River is worthy of much toil and suffering.

Unimaginative is he who can gaze upon the Himalaya from the lower foothills or the plains, and not sympathise with the simple, child-like adoration of the Hindus for the eternal reservoirs of snow, the gods of which despatch Mother Ganges to minister to their needs. Dull indeed is he who can gaze unmoved upon the snows – when the maiden of dawn fires them and the great peaks glow above the slumbering plains.

The explorer and mountaineer who visits northern Garhwal will find much to interest him in the religious mysticism, mythology and folk-lore associated with these holy snows of Himachal.[1] Parties of explorers and mountaineers have been few and far between in this district and a wealth of virgin peaks and glaciers remain to be climbed and explored. The upper reaches of the Gangotri Glacier, which is not only the greatest glacier in the district, but one of the greatest glaciers east of the Karakoram Himalaya,[2] are unexplored. The Indian Survey map, painstakingly accurate and uniformly excellent in its delineation of the main valleys and ranges of Garhwal is vague and sketchy in its delineation of the labyrinth of peaks and glaciers between the Gangotri and Alaknanda Rivers. The most ambitious explorations in this range were those undertaken by Mr. C.F. Meade in 1912. Although he only descended a few hundred feet on the western side of the range from his pass at the head of the Satopanth Glacier, he could see that the way was not difficult. The discovery of this pass is of particular interest in view of an existing legend that pilgrims in former times, when visiting Badrinath and Kedarnath, used to take a short cut across the range instead of making, as

[1] Himalaya.

[2] Possibly the greatest, unless there are glaciers of greater magnitude in Nepal.

they do now, a long roundabout journey via Joshimath and Chamoli. Meade, however, is of the opinion that the pass is not a practicable one for pilgrims, for it is about 20,000 feet high, and its traverse necessitates mountaineering knowledge. Having seen for myself the pitifully underclad, shivering pilgrims who toil up to Badrinath, I am inclined to agree with him. Yet, in India, a land of strange and subtle changes, both progressive and retrogressive, anything is possible, and it is not inconceivable that in bygone years a hardier type of pilgrim existed who thought nothing of crossing 20,000-foot glacier passes in the execution of his religious vows and devotions.

As regards Meade's exploration of the Bhagat Kharak Glacier, he discovered a pass, not from the extreme head of the glacier, but from the head of a side glacier leading southwards. If the map[3] is to be taken as being approximately accurate in its general indications, this pass was across the range where it runs almost due east and west, and, if the map is to be trusted still further, leads into the head of the Gangotri Glacier, which flows from south-east to north-west, but which in its upper portion bends round in an easterly direction. Descent was made a few hundred feet on the far side of the pass, and it is Meade's opinion that had he continued he would have found himself on the head of the Gangotri Glacier. He describes the scenery as being of a most magnificent character, and including many terrific peaks which appear to be hopelessly inaccessible.

One of our objects, therefore, in exploring the Badrinath Range was to traverse it from east to west, and cross the watershed of the Alaknanda and Gangotri Rivers, if possible descending to the Gangotri Glacier and thus making the first complete passage of the range.

CHAPTER THREE

The Conditions for Success

THE SUCCESSFUL carrying out of an expedition to the summit of a great Himalayan peak depends upon so many factors that it is difficult to enumerate them in order, yet, however well planned an expedition may be, and however well the plans are executed, there is always one link of strength unknown in the chain of circumstances, and that is – luck. That solitary link may be stretched unreasonably and not break; it may be strong and unyielding or pitifully weak; when apparently strong, it may develop an unexpected flaw, when apparently weak, it may continue to hold. Luck is blessed and cursed, but without it mountaineering would be a dull, mechanical pastime. Luck depends largely on the weather, and what the weather has done, or may do, to the mountain. Bow therefore to luck, accept it and forget it, making sure at the same time that all other links in the chain are as strong as human ingenuity and forethought can devise.

[3] Survey of India Map No. 53 N. Badrinath. Scale: 1 inch to four miles, or 1:253,440. The main range is shown bending at right angles from a direction approximately north to south to a direction approximately due west to east.

Himalayan mountaineering depends upon unselfish teamwork, and unselfish teamwork depends upon having a team of men who are temperamentally in phase. Your friend in civilisation may become your enemy on a mountain; his very snore assumes a new and repellent note; his tricks at the mess table, the sound of his mastication, the scarcely concealed triumph with which he appropriates the choicest tit-bits, the absurd manner in which he walks, even the cut of his clothes and the colour of the patch on the seat of his trousers, may induce an irritation and loathing almost beyond endurance. None of these things may matter at sea level, and why they should matter on a mountain is a problem more within the scope of physiologists and psychologists than the writer of this volume. But the whole success of an expedition depends upon them *not* mattering.

The ideal team is one that includes different interests; paradoxical though this may sound. It is a profound truth that men sharing identical interests seldom get on well together in the wilds. If they do, it is as much of a miracle as a happy marriage. Wide divergencies of opinion seldom matter. It is the small divergencies of opinions that count for so much. I cannot conceive a team of mountaineers composed exclusively of doctors, barristers or politicians.

In the present instance, I was extremely fortunate in securing as my companions men of widely diverse interests in life. I make no apology for putting on record the following scrap of conversation overheard at the end of the expedition. It emanated from Captain Birnie. He said, 'When I started on this show I expected that I should hate you all before the end of it, but, strangely enough, I can still tolerate you.'

The size of a Himalayan expedition depends largely upon the magnitude of the task to be attempted. For a peak such as Everest, where long and difficult communications must be maintained, where ill-health and high-altitude deterioration are certain to reduce the party and where it may be necessary to make two or three attempts on the summit and each one by a fresh party, a minimum of eight to ten climbers is essential. For a party who aim at summits no higher than 23,000 feet, four climbers, who can be split up into two parties of two, is ample. The next best number above four is six, which can be split up into three parties of two or two parties of three.

What is the best age for high altitude mountaineering? I believe it to be on the average between twenty-four and thirty-five years of age. Opinions differ as to whether men younger than twenty-four should expose themselves to the physical strain of high-altitude climbing. I am convinced they should not. Possibly, I am unduly prejudiced, for I know that at thirty-one I cannot go so fast as I did at twenty-one, but I can go farther and withstand cold and hardship better. There is another and subtler argument against *extreme* youth on Himalayan expeditions. The effort that must be put forth to climb the highest peaks in the world is a mental as well as a physical effort. It is something greater and finer than athleticism. The men who will one day reach the summit of Everest will be men capable of disciplining their minds as well as their bodies. Experience and skill, coupled to the right mental attitude towards a great task, are required of the men who would attempt the highest summits in the world and this is only gained by experience. Athleticism by itself is of no more use to the mountaineer than size and weight by themselves to a boxer. If I have stressed this point, it is because of a suggestion put to me by a well-known traveller and sportsman who ought to have known better. His suggestion was that an ideal Everest party should consist exclusively of the pick of University athletes!

The present party consisted of Wing Commander E.B. Beauman, of the Royal Air Force; Captain E. St. J. Birnie, of Sam Browne's Cavalry, and Adjutant to His Excellency the Governor of Bengal's Bodyguard; Doctor C.R. Greene; Mr. R.L. Holdsworth; Mr. E.E. Shipton and myself. We were fortunate in possessing both a doctor and transport officer who were also mountaineers.

Wing Commander Beauman is a mountaineer of many years' standing. He has a large number of first-class alpine climbs and ski expeditions to his credit. He served throughout the war, and holds an early flying certificate.

Captain Birnie, our transport officer, had not had a great deal of alpine experience, although he had some excellent climbs, to his credit, but he was experienced in Himalayan travelling both in Sikkim and the north-west frontier provinces. He speaks fluent Hindustani, and thoroughly understands the psychology of the primitive hill people whence we had to draw our porters. He is one of the best polo and squash racket players in the Indian Army, and an expert big game shot. His services were invaluable to the expedition.

Doctor Greene practises in Oxford. He is a former President of the Oxford University Mountaineering Club, and was editor of its *Journal* and the *Climbers' Club Journal*. He is a mountaineer possessing both Alpine and British rock-climbing experience. He stands six feet four, and required a specially extended sleeping bag. He joined the expedition in the triple capacity of doctor, physiologist, and mountaineer. In the second subject he is particularly interested, and has contributed a number of papers to scientific journals on the question of acclimatisation to high altitudes.*

Holdsworth is a classical master at Harrow School, and gained a double blue at Oxford for soccer and cricket. He is a fine ski-runner, and is the founder of a flourishing little mountaineering and ski-mountaineering club at Harrow known as the "Harrow Marmots". He was also the expedition's botanist.

Shipton, although the youngest member of the party, is a mountaineer of skill and experience. He plants coffee in Kenya Colony, and made, with Mr. P. Wynn Harris, the second ascent of Mount Kenya which had been attempted many times since the first ascent by Sir Halford Mackinder and two Alpine guides. He has also made first ascents of a number of subsidiary summits in the Kenya massif, and ascended Kilimanjaro, the highest mountain in Africa.

The next consideration after the formation of a team was the best time of the year during which to attempt the ascent of Kamet. Owing to the monsoon precipitating much of its moisture on the foothills and main range of the Himalaya, Kamet is subjected only to its strongest outbursts, and climbing in northern Garhwal is possible from May to the end of September and, under exceptional conditions, into October. During the monsoon season, which may last during the whole of July and August, bad weather lasting for a week or ten days at a stretch must be expected and provided for. It was decided, therefore, to attack Kamet before the monsoon in June. If the ascent was not completed before the onset of

* Raymond Greene was the brother of the novelist Graham Greene.

the monsoon, we hoped to be established at a considerable height, with plenty of stores and equipment, ready to seize upon any favourable weather that might occur during the monsoon season. It was, however, inadvisable to go too early, for, as Doctor Longstaff warned us, the Dhaoli Valley and its villages, which are deserted during the snowy winter months, are only repopulated by the nomadic Bhotias and their flocks of sheep, yaks and goats towards the end of May or the beginning of June. If we went too early we might find it impossible to obtain food for our coolies, whilst the bridges spanning the Dhaoli River, which are often swept away or damaged during the melting of the snows, might not be replaced or repaired. Reliable information is often hard to come by, and the expedition owes a debt of gratitude to Mr. Hugh Ruttledge for much invaluable advice on local conditions and travel. Mr. Ruttledge also sent a covering letter to Mr. N.C. Stiffe, the Commissioner of Kumaun. Mr. Stiffe replied in the friendliest terms, and generously offered to help the expedition to the best of his power. It may be perhaps as well to mention here that expeditions into the Himalaya are usually a source of trouble and anxiety to the officials administering the territory they are operating in. It behoves an expedition therefore, to cause the minimum of worry and trouble to those in authority, for an unfavourable impression left in the minds of officials and inhabitants may vastly increase the difficulties of future expeditions in the same district.

The most vital condition of success in Himalayan exploration or mountaineering is successful porterage. Travelling to the foot of a great peak, and establishing a Base Camp, is only less difficult than the task of climbing the peak. Successful porterage depends on employing a body of loyal and willing men, of interesting them in the objects of the expedition, of treating them fairly, and feeding them well. No amount of bullying or slave driving will make for successful porterage, and the smooth running of an expedition depends enormously upon the work of the transport officer. Thanks to expeditions to Everest, Kangchenjunga and the Sikkim Himalaya, there exists now at Darjeeling a body of men trained in the peculiar problems, hardships and difficulties of high altitude mountaineering. These men are Sherpas and Bhotias, and they come from the valleys of northern Nepal along the frontier of Tibet. They are half-Tibetans, half-Nepalese, and are the hardest, toughest natural mountaineers in the world. They are born adventurers at heart, and, whatever the hardships, difficulties or dangers, invariably come up smiling. To know them is to love them, and no expedition which intends serious mountaineering on the great peaks of the Himalaya should go without some of them as a backbone to its porterage.

Successful porterage also depends upon mobility, and mobility depends upon cutting down the size of an expedition to the absolute minimum. An expedition small enough to be able to feed its porters from the country is in a happy position, for it must be remembered that where an expedition is so large that this is impossible men must be engaged, to carry food for their fellows and those men who are carrying food must themselves be fed – a vicious circle. Whether local food is obtainable or not depends upon the country and its population. Fortunately, in the Kamet district food is available locally, but how much food depends upon previous harvests and stores of grain. It is essential to make careful enquiries beforehand before assuming that food will be available, even from villages where it is usually obtainable. The amount of food available is limited at the best of times in the upper valleys of the Himalaya, and the advantage of a small party over a large one is obvious. The 1930 Kangchenjunga expedition employed over four hundred porters to carry the expedition's goods to the base camp at the foot of Kangchenjunga. The difficulties of feeding these men were immense, and the consequent anxieties detracted considerably from the pleasure of the expedition for all members concerned, especially the transport officer. I had no intention of risking the same difficulties again, and went into the question of porterage very carefully. By rigorously excluding the unessential from the essential, it was found possible for six Europeans to manage with only seventy porters, and these included ten men carrying cinematographic and photographic apparatus. Thanks to previous arrangements, and the kind help of various officials, I made certain in advance that our men would be fed properly.

While on the question of food, the importance of adequate feeding on the right lines can hardly be overestimated.

As with polar expeditions, the essential vitamins must be carefully considered. I believe that the bodily deterioration supposed to be inseparable from high altitudes is accelerated by lack of vitamin C, the anti-scorbutic vitamin. Fresh fruit should be taken by expeditions, and, failing this, pure lime juice. Fresh meat and vegetables should be eaten whenever possible and tinned food only reverted to when necessary.

As regards the harmonious working of an expedition, much rests on food. The fads and fancies of each member must be considered, especially above the base camp. Like and dislike are sure guides to good or evil. Palates must be tickled with dainties. The higher the climber goes, the more he realises that his body is nothing more or less than an engine crying out for heat and yet more heat – and heat is sugar. Estimate for as much sugar as you think you will need, then double that estimate and you may with luck have enough. It is safer to treble the original estimate.

It is not proposed to deal here with questions of health, which in itself is a vital condition of success. Suffice to say that scrupulous attention to detail, both on the part of the medical officer of an expedition and of each individual member, is necessary, if fever is to be avoided in the tropical valleys of the Himalaya, and also those minor stomach disorders which are the bane of Himalayan travelling, and which lower the physical and mental stamina.

Assimilation of the experiences and lessons of previous expeditions is the first duty of an organiser of a Himalayan expedition. To make the same mistakes as one's predecessors is inexcusable. The lessons taught by previous expeditions including three Everest and two Kangchenjunga expeditions were invaluable to us. We knew that it is possible for man's body to acclimatise itself to heights greater than Kamet and the moral value of that knowledge was inestimable. Among the general public some misapprehension still exists as to the use of oxygen at great altitudes. There are even some people misguided enough to question the fairness of employing such an adventitious aid as oxygen on a mountain. I do not think, however, that those who have climbed in the Himalaya will have any doubts on this question. The odds are so much against the mountaineer that he is fully justified in exercising his mechanical ingenuity. It may be sacrilege to drive a piton into the rocks of Scafell, but it is common sense to drive it into a Himalayan peak if safety is increased thereby. "Safety first" may be a loathsome slogan, but it is worth remembering in the Himalaya. Were it possible to devise an oxygen apparatus weighing only a few pounds, and giving off gas for some days, no one but a fanatic would deprecate its use. Unfortunately, however, the weight of the apparatus, and consequent labour of porterage, counterbalances any benefit that may be derived from its use. Possibly, for the next assault on Everest, a compromise will be arrived at, and oxygen employed for the last 1,000 feet or so when the climber is too exhausted to continue without it. Yet, I believe that the summit of Everest can and will be reached without oxygen apparatus. Himalayan mountaineers of today are labouring under the same moral disadvantages as those who essayed the ascent of Mont Blanc over a hundred years ago. The bogey of altitude is always lurking at the back of their minds. It is safe to predict that in another hundred years, or even less, Himalayan mountaineers will regard with amazement the gasping struggles of their predecessors. They will be acclimatised to altitude physically and mentally and by then physiologists should have discovered some artificial means of adapting the body to the lack of oxygen at great altitudes. When that time comes, the bogey of altitude will be finally laid, and the greatest and grandest mountain range in the world will be fully opened up to the mountaineer.

Such are the principal conditions of success on a Himalayan peak, and it is to be hoped that from this fragmentary account the reader will be able to gain some idea of the preparations and forethought involved in planning a Himalayan expedition. Such planning is only less interesting than the expedition itself. We left England knowing that we had concentrated our whole attention on the problem before us. We knew that we had one link of unknown strength, luck, in our chain of reasoning, but should that snap we would have done our best.

CHAPTER FOUR

Preparations in Ranikhet

THE SMELL OF THE EAST came in at the window. Above the rattle of the train hummed and whirred myriad insects. Dawn came up over the great northern plain of India the sun swung over the level horizon like a huge blood orange, then, topping the low hazes, burst into white, eye-searing flame. Somewhere beyond that level horizon were the Himalaya.

Jungle, mile after mile of it, dank, steamy, malarious and then – a darkening of the heat haze – dim shapes – the foothills of the Himalaya.

Languid after two days of travelling in appalling heat Shipton and I stepped from the train at Kathgodam. We loaded our goods and ourselves into a lorry and set off on the last stage of our journey to Ranikhet, the hill station 6,000 feet up on a ridge of the Kumaun foothills, which was to be the starting-point of the expedition. Forest fires were raging on the foothills, and the atmosphere was blue with smoke. Up and up climbed the lorry. The air was cooler now; we no longer just lived; we enjoyed living.

Through a complicated maze of hills wound the road, now up over a ridge, now down into a valley where the heat clutched at us again, lifting itself from the dusty road in suffocating waves.

Along the side of vast-bosomed hills terraced with rice we climbed – an ugly country, with not even the saving grace of the desolate. If this was Ranikhet—! We turned a corner of the dusty hillside and miraculously found ourselves in a cool forest of deodars and chestnuts. Above the noise of our vehicle came the bell-like call of a cuckoo.

At Ranikhet we were met by Captain J. Clarke. He had kindly arranged for us to live at the forest bungalow while we made arrangements for the expedition.

Waiting for us were three of our Darjeeling men who had been sent by Colonel H.W. Tobin. Lewa was to be our sirdar. Nima Tendrup, the Old Soldier, had been my servant on Kangchenjunga in 1930. It was good to see again their merry eyes and broad grins. These Darjeeling men are Sherpas and Bhotias. They come from the valleys of northern Nepal, along the frontier of Tibet, and are Mongolian in type. They are natural mountaineers, and carried loads to over 26,000 feet on Everest. The third of the trio was Achung, our cook, a quaint, nervous little Lepcha from Sikkim. Lewa and the Old Soldier did not disguise their pleasure at seeing me again. We had had some great times together on Kangchenjunga and Jonsong Peak in 1930. Mountains can overcome barriers of race and language. Beneath the ragged and odorous exteriors of the Darjeeling Sherpas and Bhotias are hearts of gold. They are adventurers.

The bungalows of Ranikhet are scattered along the crests of wooded ridges. No other nation has such a genius as we for carrying its life and customs to the fringe of its empire. In Ranikhet there are motor roads, and a club, an inevitable adjunct of British life, from the veranda of which the eye can turn from the tennis-courts to the distant Himalaya.

Shipton and I had three weeks in which to make the final preparations – the hospitality we received while doing so will always remain a pleasant memory. We visited Naini Tal, where we were received by His Excellency Sir Malcolm Hailey, Governor of the United Provinces and President of the Himalayan Club, and Lady Hailey. Mr. N.C. Stiffe, the Commissioner for the Kumaun, loaned us fifty-five of his own Dotial porters to carry our goods to Niti, the last village on the route. Captain Bradford, the Commandant of the 3rd Gurkha Regiment, to whom General Sir William Beynon had written a letter of introduction, loaned us two Gurkha N.C.O.s who were to prove invaluable to the expedition. Meanwhile Birnie worked hard in the stifling heat of Calcutta, ordering and packing our stores, in which work he was greatly assisted by Mr. G.B. Gourlay, who had been invited to join the expedition but had unfortunately been unable to do so; and Mrs. Brown of Ranikhet arranged with the Rawal, the High Priest of Badrinath, to have porters' food ready for us. In England we had heard many pessimistic accounts as to the difficulty of obtaining porters. These difficulties may have existed before the war, but they no longer exist. The real difficulty is, and always will be, the feeding of porters, and for this reason we made careful enquiries as to the stores of grain available along the line of march.

The climate of Ranikhet in spring and early summer is delightful. Seldom does the shade temperature during the day exceed 85° Fahrenheit, and at night it sinks to 65°. The only disadvantage is the dust, which, before the monsoon, rises in clouds when the wind blows. This dust is largely composed of small particles of mica, which find their way into the water and food. The result is an unpleasant stomach disorder, a mild but weakening form of dysentery.

Shipton and I slept on the veranda of the forest bungalow undisturbed save for an occasional leopard and the monkeys, which used to prowl around the compound at night. I shall not easily forget how, on waking in the morning, we opened our eyes to the Himalaya. The view extended from the peaks of Nepal and the snowy cone of Nanda Kot to the snows of Badrinath, and the wonderful spire of Nilkanta. But the central glories in the wall were Trisul, 23,406 feet, and Nanda Devi, 25,660 feet, for these were only fifty or sixty miles distant.

Three weeks before I had opened my eyes every morning in a London flat. From my window I had gazed over a few square yards of smoke-grimed garden to a row of houses, a bilious yellow in colour, covered in that horrible stucco which defaces residential London. The roar of London's traffic, the rattle of the milkman's cans and the yowling of cats had been in my ears.

At Ranikhet I awoke to hear the call of a cuckoo vying with the flute of some far-off shepherd, and the tops of the deodars awaking with gentle sighs in the dawn breeze.

Below the veranda on which we slept the forest fell away, a dark green sheet, into the blue trough of a valley. The wooded hillside rose again half a score of miles away, and so continued ridge on ridge, like deep-sea rollers, breaking at last in foamy snow on the eternal peaks of the Himalaya.

Sometimes I would awake early and watch dawn's alchemist transmute the leaden snows to pearl and gold. In that magical hour of dawn, all that I knew of mountains was forgotten, and I saw them again as I had seen them when I was a boy. Once, while the dawn was coming thus gloriously to the world, I noticed my servant, the Old Soldier, standing in the compound gazing towards the snows. Like ourselves, the men from Darjeeling see more in a mountain than inanimate ice, snow and rock. Love and veneration for Nature is part of their Buddhist religion. That religion may be burdened with superstition, but it has one great doctrine; it teaches that God made all life, therefore life is a precious thing. We Christians pride ourselves on our societies for the prevention of cruelty to animals and children, but in Tibet there is no necessity for such societies. Small wonder that the Buddhist looks askance upon a religion that tolerates the disembowelling of horses by pain-maddened bulls and delights in the tearing to pieces of a fear-crazed stag by a pack of dogs.

The fine weather broke; vast clouds massed in the valleys. Thunder spoke from the Himalaya. Grey veils of rain were slashed by blue swords of lightning. Every afternoon storms stalked raging across the foothills. At night this cloudy combat over the Himalaya was weirdly magnificent. There is something intimidating and almost terrifying in such a vast horizon as that on which we gazed from Ranikhet. As I watched the daily miracles of dawn and sunset along the snows, I could feel that strange exaltation and mystification that comes to some in the presence of great mountains. I knew, as the Indians know when they turn their eyes towards the snows, that the mysteries of life and of death must be sought for there.

On May 10 Birnie arrived, looking remarkably fit considering that he had been living in the heat of Calcutta. He brought with him our stores and a gramophone and records. Next day we packed hard. The Dotial porters arrived under the charge of their "mates". We were immediately impressed by them – they were a cheery crowd. They come from southern Nepal, but, unlike the Gurkhas, have more Indian than Mongolian blood in them. On May 13 they left under the command of Lewa. The day after their departure, Beauman, Greene and Holdsworth arrived from England. The following three days were spent making our final preparations. We were to cover the first fifty miles in a motor-lorry which would take us to Baijnath, the terminus of the road. There we would overtake the Dotial porters and thenceforward proceed on foot as one party.

The night prior to our departure I felt that same queer thrill the adventurers of old must have felt when they slipped their cables to venture into the unknown. The plans, theories and preparations of months were to be put into practice. How futile and foolish they seemed that night. The world stretched limitless into the darkness. All along the Himalaya the lightning flamed wrathfully and the still air quivered to the vibration of thunder. I could feel then that 'the mystery and thrill of travel is always upon one in the Himalaya, but the mystery is awful and the thrill is sometimes a shudder.'

CHAPTER FIVE

The Foothills

MAY 18 DAWNED BRILLIANTLY. The recent thunderstorms had scoured the atmosphere of the dust blown up from the plains, and the great Himalayan wall stood out sharp and clear beyond the orderly ranges of foothills. I looked at it with a new feeling; for nearly a month Shipton and I had been unable to respond to its insistent call, and now, at last, the expedition was ready to start.

On those remote and shining peaks we were about to adventure. The plans, the theories of months, were to be tested.

I stood in the compound of our bungalow and gazed for a few moments between the deodars at Kamet. It was one hundred miles distant, yet every detail was distinct. Through glasses I could discern the sweep of its red granite precipices seamed by avalanche-swept gullies; the cold gleam of its icy ridges. A small scarf of snow trailed from its square-topped crest. A hurricane was raging, but where I stood only the gentlest of dawn breaths stirred the forest.

Would Kamet be kind to us? It was just such a morning that we had left Darjeeling last year to attempt Kangchenjunga. High hope had been ours, but we had returned defeated, and we had left one of our number buried in the snow beneath that terrible mountain.[1]

[1] Chettan, a Sherpa porter.

We had ordered the lorry that was to convey ourselves and our luggage to Baijnath, sixty miles distant, for 5 a.m., but it was not until 9 a.m. that we were ready to start.

We experienced a qualm of apprehension when confronted by our vehicle. It was very old and decrepit. Its body, which was absurdly large for its chassis, was constructed of three-ply wood, warped and cracked by tropical suns. But it was the tyres that caused us most anxiety. Of tread there was but little left and here and there the covers had worn through, exposing the inner tubes, which bulged out like sausages. In the worst places gaiters had been affixed, but in other places there was no such protection. The driver was a dark taciturn Moslem. He looked a soured and disappointed man.

Somehow, six Europeans, eight Darjeeling porters, Achung the cook, with his paraphernalia of clattering pots and pans and 2,000 lbs. of luggage were stowed away into the vehicle.

Before leaving Ranikhet, it was necessary to obtain a pass from the police. Apparently, our load was about three times the maximum allowed legally, but the police were solicitous neither for our safety nor for regulations. After all, if we did go down the *khud,*[2] why worry? It would be the will of God.

This difficulty removed, the clutch was engaged with a fearsome wrench, the gears jerked home with nerve-shattering crashes, and we went rattling, bumping and banging through the bazaar, the cynosure of all eyes. The first stage of our journey had commenced. We could only hope that it would not also prove the last.

We passed the Ranikhet golf-links. These links are both sporting and expensive. Sporting, because it is often necessary to drive off from the summit of one hill to a green on the summit of another, and expensive because a slice or pull may dispatch a ball into dense jungle or down a steep hillside. The links are superbly situated, and between rounds the golfer may find consolation for his misfortunes in the view, which embraces a considerable portion of the Garhwal Himalaya.

The road narrowed; its hairpin bends were sometimes so acute as to render reversing necessary. Where it traversed open hillsides, there were places where drops of over a thousand feet awaited an error on the part of the driver or the bursting of a tyre.

We smiled at each other – at times a trifle wanly – and strove to make light and airy conversation. Our porters, however, had no qualms, and chattered away merrily in the back of the lorry. Packed tightly as we were, we had perforce to stop at intervals and alight to stretch our cramped limbs.

Down hillsides terraced with rice and dotted with the primitive bamboo thatched huts of the peasants into the steamy heat of malarious valleys rattled our aged vehicle, to wind tortuously up once more to the cooler uplands.

Now and again we caught glimpses of distant peaks, but, though we were approaching them, the vast scale on which even the foothills of the Himalaya are constructed made them seem, if anything, farther away.

Once we were stopped by a native, and a colloquy ensued between him and our driver. The gist of it was that the former wanted a letter delivered, but this

[2] Hillside.

commission our driver resolutely refused to undertake until he had satisfied himself beyond all reasonable doubt that the deliverer was, like himself, a Moslem by faith.

It was a striking instance of the antagonism prevailing in India between Hindus and Moslems, for, had the deliverer of the letter been a Hindu, our driver would not have acceded to his request.

At the junction of our road with the Almora road, we found awaiting us the two Gurkha Lance-Naiks[3] who had been detailed off for service with the expedition by Captain Bradford, Commandant of the 3rd Gurkha Regiment at Almora. Their soldierly smartness and alertness was in itself a tribute to British army training. Their names were Budhibal Gurung and Randhoj Kan. Budhibal Gurung was a serious young man, which is unusual among Gurkhas. He seldom spoke unless addressed, but his speckless, tropical uniform, his wide-brimmed, rakish hat, and his quiet air of efficiency betokened a good soldier, and one who would serve us well. Randhoj Kan was of a very different type. Here was the typical Gurkha: broad-faced, thick-lipped, with a wide humorous mouth ready to expand at any moment into a smile and with merry twinkling eyes, he appeared to find life one perpetual joke, and to extract huge amusement from everything he saw or did.

During the halt to collect our Gurkhas, one of the tyres elected to go flat. The driver, with characteristic Oriental laziness, decided to try to pump it up rather than change the wheel for the spare, but happily, as we expected, he had to admit himself defeated and put on the spare wheel.

It was fortunate that the next puncture occurred, not on a sharp corner or above a precipitous hillside, but on a safe and level stretch of road. This time, there being no spare wheel, the puncture had to be repaired, and we took the opportunity to lunch in the shade of a wood beside a small stream in which we could see mahseer[4] swimming.

It was with profound sighs of relief that we stepped at last from our chariot at Baijnath.

Lewa was awaiting us, radiating his usual vim and energy. From him we learned the good news that the fifty-five Dotial porters in advance were marching well. Owing to some extra loads that we had brought with us, it was necessary to recruit five Garhwal porters. These men were not to be compared with our Sherpa or Dotial porters, either in physique or morale. They were weak, cringing creatures, and it obvious that our Darjeeling men regarded them with contempt.

Baijnath is situated in a wide open valley running south-east and north-west, enclosed by low forest-clad hills and grassy alps rising to gentle undulating skylines. The valley was brown and parched with drought, but here and there the bright green fronds of banana trees afforded a pleasing contrast to the prevailing aridness.

The village consisted of the usual collection of thatched and filthy hovels. The ground around these hovels was strewn with rotting garbage, black with flies, ready to rise in clouds at any moment and transfer their filth and disease to a newcomer. Mangy dogs prowled about the huts, and languid, dejected-looking cattle, which appeared to have given up all idea of obtaining nutriment, stood or lay on the withered, sun-scorched fields without the village.

[3] Lance-Corporals.

[4] Hill salmon.

It was late in the afternoon, and as soon as the Garhwal porters had been recruited we set out on the ten-mile walk to Gwaldam.

A well-constructed path passed over or between little tree-clad knolls. In the more open valleys between the low hills banana groves flourished, and their fruit, which could be purchased at the rate of a dozen for one anna, was a welcome lubricant to mouths parched by the heat.

Here and there small brooks chattered over the stones, but we dared not drink from them for fear of cholera, typhoid or dysentery.

As we progressed, the country became more and more like an English parkland. The hillsides were covered in well-spaced deodars, the resinous fragrance of which permeated the warm air, whilst their fallen needles softly carpeted the path. Now and again we sat down to rest in their shade. Only the diapason of insect life, so monotonous as to be almost unnoticeable, was there to remind us that we were within tropical latitudes.

Once from the crest of a hill we saw the summit of Trisul, its summit snows, tinged with gold in the declining sun, couched in lurid thunder-clouds.

Gradually the small and indefinite ridges were replaced by bolder forms. Dusk saw us trudging up a steep hillside, sweating profusely and afflicted with thirsts induced by the heat and our lack of training. As I endeavoured to lubricate my parched tongue with saliva, I reflected that, at this very moment, our friends in Ranikhet were reclining luxuriously in armchairs at the club, imbibing long iced drinks.

The sun withdrew into the cloudless west; the tops of the deodars were steeped in its soft glow. The insect chorus died away into the silence of the forest. From the deepening gloom above glanced a remote star.

Night fell swiftly. Darkness revealed a dozen twinkling points of light on a range of hills to the east. They were forest fires over thirty miles away. Fireflies darted about like minute lamps of palest blue in the hands of restless fairies.

To those unaccustomed to it, a tropical forest is terrible at night. During the daytime little is to be heard, save the whirr and hum of insects, but at night-time, when the insects are hushed, its potentialities for evil become apparent. There are furtive rustlings; a twig cracks suddenly with a report like a pistol-shot; perhaps there is some startling crash of undergrowth, followed by an agonised scream – a leopard has secured its prey. But this last is unusual; for the most part there is little to be heard save the continual furtive rustlings.

To the newcomer a night walk along a path through a jungle is both intriguing and terrifying. No doubt to those well versed in its lore the jungle loses many of its terrors. To the keen ear and trained intelligence of the shikari, its sounds are full not of menace but of interest, yet Birnie's experience with a tiger must have shaken even *his* nerve.

The usual method adopted in tiger shooting is to tie up a calf or goat a few yards from a tree the fork of which allows of a platform being constructed. Position on this platform may be taken up either before or after the tiger has killed the bait. In the one case, the tiger returns to the kill, and in the other it is a matter of luck as to whether the tiger appears on the night when the sportsman is ready for him. Birnie loves the jungle, and delights to wander alone in it. Perhaps it is for this reason that he disdains the conventional and safer method of shooting from a tree platform, and prefers to shoot his tiger from the ground seated in some concealed spot near the tied-up animal, with an electric torch tied along the barrel of his rifle. On one occasion, however, he let fly at his tiger when unable to obtain a perfect view of it. He wounded the tiger but not mortally, and the beast charged. Unluckily the shock of the discharging rifle had broken the bulb of his electric torch, and he was unable to see anything in the darkness. There was no time to run for it, and he sat there waiting to give the tiger his second barrel. It is not easy to picture such a situation, or to imagine the feelings of a man alone in the darkness of a tropical jungle at night charged by an infuriated tiger. Birnie says that the whole thing happened so quickly that he had no time to experience any other emotion than an intense excitement. He waited until he thought the tiger was a yard or two away, and then fired his second barrel. He missed completely. The next moment the tiger seized him.

He says his predominant thought at the moment was that it was a very poor way of being "outed" but, with instinctive self-preservation, he beat at the tiger with the stock of his rifle. This saved his life. It diverted the tiger's attention from him to the rifle and it snatched the weapon in its jaws and made off with it.

The next few minutes were mentally the worst for Birnie. He was badly mauled, for the tiger's teeth had met in his shoulder, and he expected the beast to come back and finish him. In the darkness it was not easy to find a tree which he could scale, but at length he discovered one, and, climbing it, passed the remainder of the night in a fork. His wound bled profusely and he was unable to bandage it, but so venomous were the tiger's jaws that within two hours suppuration set in and the bleeding stopped.

Next morning he was joined by his native shikari. Most men after such an experience would have returned there and then to civilisation, and Birnie, in addition, was badly mauled and weak from loss of blood. He decided, however, that the wounded tiger must be tracked down, so, accompanied by his shikari, he followed it for five miles and finally shot it. This delay in receiving medical attention nearly cost him his arm, for blood-poisoning set in, and when at last he reached hospital, it was touch and go whether it was amputated or not.

From ahead came a shout, and presently we were joined by Tikia, the mate of our Dotial porters. All the men and all the loads had arrived at Gwaldam. This was good news, as we had experienced a doubt when sending off the advance-party of Dotial porters from Ranikhet with no European in charge of them.

The path climbed steadily through the forest. At length a cool breath of wind denoted the crest of the ridge 6,000 feet high on which stands the dak bungalow of Gwaldam, and a minute or two later, the squat, dark mass of the bungalow loomed out of the darkness.

We groped our way round the unlit veranda in search of Achung. Tired, hungry men are liable to become both angry and impatient. Why was there no tea waiting for the sahibs? What was the good of having a cook if he didn't go on ahead and prepare a meal for his employers? Achung spread out his hands with a weak, hopeless gesture. 'No tea, no milk, no here,' he mumbled. The bungalow was not even unlocked. We roared for the chowkidar.[5] A miserable, ragged man

[5] Caretaker.

materialised from the darkness; he was the chowkidar, but he had lost the key of the bungalow he was supposed to look after.

With the arrival of Birnie matters assumed a different complexion. Milk was forthcoming, tea, and later food. Naturally, things were in a muddle, and in the darkness it was not easy sorting out from the rest of the baggage the load containing the required food. A kind friend in the person of Lieutenant Carr, who had camped in the compound of the bungalow, came to our rescue, and lent us necessaries, so that soon we were seated in the little dining room eating ravenously.

The Gwaldam dak bungalow is unprepossessing both within and without. On the spot where it stands there had once stood a large bungalow occupied by some tea planters. They had experimented with tea growing in the locality, but their experiments had not proved commercially successful, and in the end they had been forced to sell their bungalow to the Public Works Department who required a dak bungalow at Gwaldam. They received a good price for it, but as luck would have it, on the very day that the bungalow was paid for by the Public Works Department it was burnt to the ground. The Public Works Department, undismayed and with commendable economy, collected the remnants of their purchase, and constructed the present dak bungalow from the scraps thus obtained. Whitehall should be able to point the moral.

The one bedroom of the bungalow was small and dirty, so we pitched our tents in the compound. It was good to be in a tent once more; to sniff the faint odour of clean new canvas and the sweet scent of dewy grass; to peer through the doorway into the kindly night.

Long after I had blown my candle out, I lay in my sleeping bag, my brain busy with thoughts of the past and the future. The past was already remote. I could review its events almost with the detachment of a god. The remembrances of civilisation passed before me, a procession of phantasms. Of the future I could but speculate in vain. And, so at last, the peace of the hills laid gentle hands upon me and I fell into the deep, dreamless slumber that is the daily reward of those who live and travel in the open.

I awoke next morning to see the broad face of old Nima Tendrup, with its habitual worried expression, peering in at me from the door of the tent. I crawled outside. It was a glorious morning; water jewels gleamed on the grass; from the woodlands came the call of a cuckoo and the bell-like notes of the coppersmith bird. From the terrace on which our tents were pitched the forest-clad hills stretched northwards, ridge on ridge, lapping at last in dim blue waves against the ridges of Trisul from the snowy crest of which streamed a small tendril of wind-blown snow. In the limpid atmosphere of early morning as yet unpolluted by the heat-hazes from the valleys, details were faultlessly distinct, and every dell in the silvery snowfields was revealed by the slanting rays of the sun.

At breakfast, flies introduced themselves to us. We had been warned about these flies, but both in numbers and perseverance they exceeded our most pessimistic expectations. The food was black with them, the air droned with them; they swam in the milk and dragged their foul bodies over the butter; they struggled to extricate themselves from the jam. And there were other flies that bit, and bit viciously. These last were small and black, scarcely larger than sand-flies, and they drove their probosces into our arms and legs and, having sucked our blood, injected their poison, leaving us with itching sores. We could well understand the regret expressed by General Bruce when he travelled in Garhwal that, owing to a defect in the anatomy of these flies, he was unable to make them scream.

After breakfast Birnie re-allotted the loads. The porters were full of good cheer, and they strode off down the hill chattering gaily.

From Gwaldam we had to descend into the steamy valley of the Pindar River. Had it not been so hot we might have appreciated the beauties of the path, which passed through forests of firs and sub-tropical jungle. The Gwaldam dak bungalow is the last dak bungalow on this route, and at the village of Debal we pitched camp. Our tents stood on a grassy shelf above the Pindar River. Behind the camp were the filthy hovels of the village of Debal. Owing to the foul and unsanitary conditions, plus the presence of innumerable flies, disease is rife at Debal, and Greene had his hands full. Apart from venereal disease in its worst and most varied forms, he was asked to treat cases of cancer of the stomach, malaria, and intestinal ulcers. One poor little girl, about six years old, brought to him by her father, had a terribly septic leg, the oozing sores of which were battened on by swarms of vile flies. There was little he could do save advise the sufferers to go to the nearest hospital, a journey which they seemed loth to undertake. He might have administered morphia in some painful cases, but, as he said, it would not have been fair to let his patients realise that there was a means of affording them temporary relief from their pain, which was not available to them. It seemed strange and dreadful finding such misery so near the purity of the snows.

That evening we fished for mahseer in the Pindar River below the camp. Mahseer attain to the dimensions of salmon, and are quite good eating, although decidedly bony. We fished both with small and large spoons, and with fly, but, although we saw many rising fish, we were unlucky. The ragged villagers clustered around, grinning broadly at our unsuccess. Obviously, they considered fishing with rod and line a futile and foolish method, and one of them proceeded to demonstrate his skill with a net below the pool in which we were fishing. We did not see him catch anything, but later a fish weighing several pounds was brought to our camp.

Before turning in that evening we treated ourselves to a gramophone concert. Night brought in its train a delicious coolness, and relieved us of the horde of flies. We sat at peace outside our tents, with only the faintest of breezes rustling the fir tops above us. At such times it is always the old songs that are appreciated most, possibly because one does not wish to be reminded of the busy, teeming life of plain and city beyond the ranges. But some of these old favourites we were alas, to hear for the first and last time during the expedition, for in the middle of our concert there was an exclamation, a crack, and a crunch. Beauman had sat on the records!

Before leaving Debal, we were shown the village war memorial. On a simple stone slab let into the side of a rickety hut is an inscription, which reads 'From this village twenty-two men went to the Great War, 1914-1919. Of these, two gave up their lives.' Somehow that primitive little record in this remote corner of the Empire impressed me to a greater extent than have many elaborate memorials to the fallen that I have seen amid civilised surroundings.

The march from Debal to Lohajang is a long one. Officially, it is ten miles.

Actually, it is much farther for the path ascends more than 4,000 feet, and the tropical sun was on our backs. It was grillingly hot. Our lack of training was again manifest. How the porters, carrying 80 lbs. each did it I do not know, but they marched so well that many of them were waiting for us when we arrived at Lohajang.

Of our two Gurkhas, one, Budhibal Gurung, was in charge of the treasure chest, and it was amusing to see him striding along, immaculately clad, behind the sweating native who laboured under a box of rupees weighing 75 lbs. The other Gurkha, Randhoj Kan, was appointed a general whipper-in of straggling porters. Undoubtedly, the smartness and discipline exhibited by these men was a valuable example to our porters. For this reason we made no attempt to restrain their salutes or the clicking together of their heels whenever a sahib appeared.

Camp was pitched on a grassy ridge fanned by a cool and refreshing breeze. As we wanted to conserve our tinned meat as far as possible, Lewa was sent to buy a sheep. He returned later leading one on a halter, and explained that, as he had been unable to find the owner he had appropriated the sheep from the pasture on which it was grazing!

The sheep was slaughtered in a masterly fashion by Budhibal Gurung. We had often heard of what a kukri is capable. It is said that this heavy sickle-shaped knife can, in the hands of a skilful Gurkha, sever a bullock's head from its body at one stroke. I can well believe this. In the present instance a rope was tied to the sheep's horns, and, with one man holding it and another man the sheep's hind legs, the animal was held in position without movement.

The sun was setting over the hills, and in its dying gleams Budhibal Gurung, with his uplifted right arm grasping the kukri, looked like some Druidical figure about to perform a sacrifice. The next moment, in a curve of crimson light, the knife descended. There was a dull crunch, and the sheep's head rolled on the ground.

This had scarcely been done when we observed a gesticulating and agitated figure, its rags flying in the breeze, running along the ridge towards the camp. It was the shepherd of the flock! As soon as he reached us the floodgates of his eloquence were unloosed. What was he to do? The sahibs had taken his sheep. What would his master say? He had betrayed his trust. He was a ruined man.

Laughingly, Birnie took hold of his shoulders and forced him into a kneeling position.

'Now,' he said, 'be quiet or we will cut off your head too.' But this little pleasantry was lost on the shepherd he still chattered volubly. 'All right, then. Cut off his head,' Birnie ordered Budhibal Gurung. I looked at Budhibal Gurung. There was no trace of a smile in his eyes. 'Cut off his head,' reiterated Birnie. Budhibal Gurung's hand seemed to tighten on the hilt of his reeking kukri; there was a curious look in his eyes; these men are used to obeying orders. I don't think we realised at the time how near that order came to being carried out.

The shepherd's wrath waned; suddenly his weather beaten face cracked into a broad smile.

Yes, he would take money for the sheep. Seven rupees was the usual price, but we gave him eight annas extra for the insult. He was vastly pleased. After all, he could always tell his master that the sheep had died or had fallen down a precipice-and he was seven rupees eight annas to the good. 'If the sahibs would like another sheep ...?'

We dined well off the sheep's liver and kidneys, while our men gorged themselves on a fearsome concoction the principal ingredients in which were the sheep's entrails.

The next morning, before leaving camp, Greene was called upon to do some more work. One of his patients was a small boy, who complained, apparently, among other things, of a sore throat. Greene examined him, but could find nothing in particular wrong. He decided, however, that, as the boy's tonsils were none too healthy, it would be a good thing if they were to come out on the spot. He was preparing to perform this operation when the terrified boy explained that it was not he who was ill, but his father in the village below, and that he had come on his behalf, and had merely tried to enact his ailments.

The march to Wan was a charming one. The scorched ridges across which we had passed for the first three marches were behind, and we found ourselves on more fertile hillsides. The Himalayan oak predominated: its stocky, weather-beaten trunk and gnarled branches make it a fitting comrade to the great peaks beneath which it grows.

Shoots of bracken which were growing in the forest near the path were collected eagerly by our porters, for they are prized hereabouts as an excellent vegetable.

The valley, bent north-westwards, disclosing bolder ridges, no longer dominated by forests but bare and craggy with streaks of winter snow lingering in their gullies.

The sun beat relentlessly down upon us, but the breeze was sweet and clean, and brought with it a fragrance of woodlands and wild thyme. The stream below us was no longer the sullen thing we had fished in at Debal, but rushed joyously along its rocky bed, halting here and there to dream in quiet pools among the grey boulders.

In a glade beneath a hoary old oak, a shepherd-boy was sitting minding his flocks. Clad in ragged sackcloth, he made a picturesque figure, and I stopped to photograph him. He glanced at me shyly out of his dark, sloe-like eyes, and would have fled had it not been for a grin on the part of Nima Dorje and a voluble explanation as to the harmless nature of the proceedings.

Passing through fields of ripening maize, the path turned and zigzagged up the north-eastern side of the valley. Standing at a corner of the path were three villagers busily twirling their shuttles of wool, and regarding us curiously the while. We seldom saw a native in Garhwal without his shuttle of wool. In one hand he carries a mass of wool; from this he draws out a thread, which is wound on to a shuttle suspended by the thread itself and twirled so that the wool is both attenuated and woven into a compact strand before being wound on to the shuttle. Such of this wool as is not required for their own hand-looms they sell to the agents of the Cawnpore woollen mills, or trade it for salt and borax. They were a cheery and smiling trio, and were vastly intrigued with my cinema camera.

The majority of Garhwali men possess an abundant crop of hair. This they bob in feminine fashion until two knots of it project from under their tight-fitting little caps on either side of their heads. Although, as a rule, clad in clothes of the most ragged and disreputable description, they are fond of ornamenting themselves, their wives and children, and it is a common sight to see a woman clad entirely in rags hung around with a costly array of jewellery.

The path entered a grove of magnificent pines. They were the largest conifers that I have ever seen. Some of them must have been 150 ft. in height, and their timber would be most valuable were it possible to export it. As we passed through their dim-lit aisles, thunder boomed threateningly, and large drops of rain began to fall.

We had barely pitched camp on a grassy terrace beyond the pines when the storm burst. It was the first time our tents had been exposed to rain, and we were gratified to find that not a drop from the heavy deluge that accompanied the storm penetrated their fabric.

So delightful a spot is the camping-ground at Wan that Carr, who had accompanied us from Gwaldam, decided to stop there and make it his centre for some days; but, before we parted from him, he very kindly insisted on presenting us with some excellent large-scale maps of the Badrinath and Kamet districts.

We awoke to a morning of delightful freshness. The sun shone brilliantly. Overnight there had been a hint of frost and the air was sweet with the fragrance of resin and wild roses. Just such a morning may be experienced in the Lake District or the Scottish Highlands after rain.

In the valley beneath the camp, the blue smoke from the brown huts of Wan rose lazily above a patchwork of yellowing barley-fields. From the valley, noble forests swept upwards in a deep blue-green sheet, to straggle out at last in vain attempt to win the crests of the snow-friezed ridges.

From the camping-place a stony path passed between banks ablaze with creamy wild roses, and then mounted towards the ridge we must cross to reach Kanaul. Ram Singh, an Indian Assistant Commissioner, who had accompanied us as far as Wan, now parted from us. He had taken a lively interest in the expedition, and had helped us by arranging food for our coolies. His work was taken over by Hukam Singh. Both of these men were the finest types of Indian Assistant District Commissioner. Hukam Singh possessed that introspective, far-away look in the eyes peculiar to those who dwell among the hills, whilst his thin, almost ascetic countenance, seamed with innumerable wrinkles, was of that weather-beaten, leathery quality found only among those who expose themselves to hot suns and cold winds.

Shipton had left at dawn to ascend a peak of 13,357 feet to the south west of the pass between Wan and Kanaul. We envied him his view from the summit, but our envy was forgotten as we mounted the last slope, covered in oaks and rhododendrons, to the crest of the ridge we must cross.

A cold wind met us, rustling the gnarled and stunted oaks and rubbing their twisted branches like the bones of a skeleton hung from a gibbet on a windy heath. Before us were the snows of the Badrinath peaks, a confused jumble of mountains. Before them stood their queen, Nilkanta. It is one of the loveliest mountains in the world: above the broad buttresses from which it springs its graceful lines lead the eye upwards to a perfectly proportioned summit, a sheer spire of gleaming snow and ice. Nilkanta stands watch and ward over the snows of Himachal. It is from its flanks that the sacred Alaknanda River falls 'like the slender thread of a lotus flower.'

We descended through woodlands and glades gay with dwarf gentians to the pastures of Kanaul, where we camped beside some shepherds and their flocks.

Greene busied himself the same afternoon with blood-pressure tests, while some of us amused ourselves playing deck tennis, using a fir-cone in lieu of a quoit. As I reclined on the close cropped turf, I could not help comparing my companions to the immaculate young men they had once been. The ladies who had given us dances at Ranikhet would have looked askance could they have seen us now with our sun-tanned faces and rapidly growing beards.

It must not be thought that we grew beards out of sheer laziness. We did so because they afford protection from the ravages of the sun at high altitudes. But at this early stage in their development they presented an unpleasant spectacle. Greene, Shipton, and myself had so far developed little more than straggly fluff. Birnie's fiery red growth was, however, beginning to inspire respect, whilst the appearance of Beauman and Holdsworth, both of whom are dark-haired, can only be described as blackguardly.

That evening, Greene and I strolled up a small hill covered in barley-fields to watch the sunset. The tall cumulus clouds that had been built up fold on fold, layer on layer, and turret on turret by the moist warm valley airs during the afternoon were being dissipated, and their apparently solid bastions were melting into the evening sky. The summit of a peak stood forth. A cloud still hung to one of its supporting ridges, concealing it. The effect produced was that of a peak of height and breadth but of negligible thickness, something cut out from cardboard, or a photograph. A solitary pine-tree was pencilled darkly against a sky of vivid green. Long, zeppelin-shaped clouds flared and sank into the abysses of night.

As we turned downhill towards camp, there came to our nostrils the scent of burning pine and juniper and to our ears the carefree laughs of our porters.

CHAPTER SIX

The Kuari Pass: First View of Kamet

THE PATH BEYOND KANAUL descended into the Nandakna Valley. Banks of honeysuckle and wild roses lined the way. Flocks of horned and shaggy sheep were streaming up the path, many of them carrying little bags of grain, slung on either side of their backs for the nutriment of their shepherds and for trading purposes.

On entering the gorge down which rushes the torrent bearing the snow-waters from the western glaciers of Trisul to the Alaknanda River at Nandaprayag, we were made to realise for the first time that we were in the immediate presence of the High Himalaya. Looking up between the precipitous walls of the gorge, we could see the ice-crowned buttresses of Trisul, vignetted by the silvery mists of morning.

Crossing the torrent by a log bridge, we toiled up a steep path and then traversed horizontally along the northern slopes of the Nandakna Valley. The sun burned down with a piercing heat that presaged a storm. I developed a thirst of which a fireman might have been proud. This thirst was not relieved by Greene, who, looking at me sadly, murmured something about long iced lagers at Ranikhet.

We lunched by a stream in company with a large lizard, which took a great interest in us. Beyond our lunching place, the path passed across one of the steepest grass-clad hillsides that I have seen. The steepness of the valley sides is a feature of the higher Himalayan foothills. Formidable landslips occur frequently, whilst stone and mud avalanches render dangerous many of the paths between villages during the melting of the snows or the monsoon rains.

The camping place at Ramni was shadeless, and had been befouled by sheep and oxen. Shipton was taken ill, and, as there was a possibility that he was beginning an attack of dysentery, Greene injected a special anti dysentery serum he had procured from the military hospital at Ranikhet. Probably, he was only suffering from an acute form of the stomach disorder that so often afflicts travellers in the more unhealthy valleys of the Himalaya for in three days he had completely recovered.

The heat was relieved that evening by a sharp thunderstorm. From the west a smooth, dun-bellied pall of nimbus slid up over the hills. Battalion after battalion of giant cumuli followed. The hushed landscape seemed to quiver to the hollow bellow of thunder. Crooked blue swords of lightning drove at the crests of the wooded ridges. The thunder's clamorous roll was resolved into an angrier crackle. A giant rent strips of calico from mountain top to mountain top. Rain rushed down upon the camp with a roar.

The lightning was exceedingly vivid. One stream of mauve flame, that connected with a hilltop across the valley, seemed to last for at least one second: possibly the cloud from which it emanated discharged the whole of its energy in a single violent "flash-over".

The grey skirts of rain, lashed by furious lightning, swept up the valley towards Trisul. The storm was superseded by a calm sunset of vivid opalescent green, into which the foothills carved purple wedges. The crests of the retreating thunder-clouds were steeped in the glare of the setting sun; their bases, merged in the darkness of the storm, flamed wrathfully with lightning. Night fell; a delicious coolness and fragrance of moist turf ushered in her stars.

Ramni had been selected previously as a halting-place for our porters. The marches on this route are not long ones, but they involve tedious ascents. Load yourself with 80 lbs. and walk ten to fifteen miles in a day, included in which is an ascent of 3,000 feet in a shade temperature between 80° and 90° Fahrenheit, and you will be glad that you were not born a Dotial porter. And, if you believe in reincarnation, you will pray fervently that you are not born a Dotial porter in the next life. Load carrying over long distances is of course a matter of knack and experience, but this cannot alter the fact that it requires so many foot-pounds of energy to carry 80 lbs. a distance of fifteen miles and lift it through a height of 3,000 feet. There is probably no better load-carrier than the Himalayan Dotial porter, and even Lewa, ever jealous of the reputation for load-carrying of his Darjeeling men, told us that he had never seen a finer body of porters than our Dotials.

They had worked so well that on the following morning we gave them each eight annas *baksheesh,* and they departed happily in search of such pleasures as the ramshackle village below the camp might afford.

Greene, Holdsworth and I, unwilling to spend a day in the shadeless camp, with its filth and its swarms of pestering flies, climbed up to the ridge immediately to the north of Ramni, which separates the Nandakna and Gohna Valleys. As we topped the ridge we hailed with enthusiasm – Kamet. It was the first time we had seen it since leaving Ranikhet. It was no longer an insignificant point, but a great peak dominating the ranges of northern Garhwal.

To the west, Nilkanta stood out magnificently, whilst immediately to the east rose Kamet's sister mountain, Mana Peak. The massively proportioned peak of Dunagiri was visible in the extreme east, but minor peaks were hidden by the nearer range of Pilkhunta, over which we had to cross by the Kuari Pass, 12,000 feet. Almost immediately opposite, on the northern side of the Gohna Valley, was the great scar in the side of Maithana Hill caused by the landslip of 1893. As this landslip was the greatest that has occurred within living memory, a few details may be of interest.[1]

The portion of Maithana Hill which fell was a spur of 11,109 feet. The fall was due to several causes. The dip of the dolomite rock of which Maithana Hill is composed was the primary cause. The beds of rock are inclined at an angle of about 45° to 50°. As the dip of the rock on the northern side of the Gohna Valley is greater than the angle of repose of dolomite, sliding tends to take place when the necessary facilities are presented. As long as the slope of the surface of a mountain does not exceed in average angle the dip of its strata, there is no danger of a slip. In the present instance, however, the foot of the slope was undermined by the action of a river and of springs. Thus, the average angle of the slope was increased, and an enormous fall resulted. It is perhaps as well to mention that if rock beds are well cemented, and subject only to the influence of their own weight, the surface slope may greatly exceed the dip before sliding commences. In the landslip at Gohna, however, not only was the support removed by undermining at the foot of the slope and loosening of the beds; but the beds were impelled outwards by a series of changes following as a natural consequence of the processes which destroyed the originally compact nature of the strata. These causes combined to precipitate a mass of material, which dammed the Birahi Ganga and formed the Gohna Lake.

The causes producing a loosening of the strata were rainfall and melting snow, which resulted in a reduction of the coefficient of friction.

The southern side of Maithana Hill became thoroughly unsafe, and in September 1893 occurred the huge landslip that now blocks the Gohna Valley. Two falls took place. It is difficult even to imagine a fall estimated to contain 12,500,000 cubic feet of rock. The fall was catastrophic in its magnitude, and continued for three days with deafening noise and clouds of dust which darkened the neighbourhood and fell for miles around, whitening the ground and tree branches like snow. Great lumps of rock weighing tons were precipitated through the air like cannon-shots, striking far up on the slopes of the opposite side of the valley.

Providentially, the actual fall was unaccompanied by loss of life, only a few uninhabited fields being overwhelmed. Small wonder if the villagers thought that the end of the world had come. The Birahi Ganga was dammed by the huge mass

[1] I am indebted to His Excellency Sir Malcolm Hailey, Governor of the United Provinces for the following details, which are embodied in a Governmental report entitled Report on the Gohna Lake.

of debris. The dam was nearly 1,000 feet high, and formed an impenetrable barrier to the stream. Steadily the water collected behind the dam, forming a lake, which attained to a maximum length of about three miles. The rise of this lake against the dam was watched anxiously. There was little likelihood of the dam collapsing owing to its thickness, but a very real danger was to be apprehended when the lake finally overflowed it, as the water in the loose debris of the dam would soon form a deep channel through which the lake would quickly empty itself, with disastrous consequences to life and property in the Alaknanda Valley. Every precaution was taken by the authorities to prevent loss of life, so that when, at 11.30 p.m., on August 25, 1894, the waters of the lake overflowed the dam and started to carve a channel through it, every place along the path of the flood-waters had been evacuated and towns as far distant as Hardwar, 140 miles from the dam, were warned to expect a heavy flood.

Thanks to this prompt action of the authorities, the loss of life was limited to a man, his wife and three children, who were killed by a slip of debris from the dam some time before the water flowed over. The man was known as the Gohna Fakir, and he persisted in remaining in a very dangerous position below the dam, although he had been ordered to leave it. Twice he and his family had been forcibly removed to a safe place, but had returned each time.

The flood must have been a terrifying affair. The enormous mass of water released from the lake roared down the valley at a speed between twenty and thirty miles an hour, which stands at the junction of the Alaknanda and Birahi Rivers. The flood was estimated to be 280 feet deep at the point where it left the lake. At Chamoli it was 160 feet deep. The river bed was raised 50 feet by the mass of boulders borne down by the torrent. The bridge, abutments, temple, bazaar, and dispensary were washed away. All down the main Alaknanda Valley enormous damage was done. The entire city of Srinagar, including the Rajah's palace, dispensary, police station and dak bungalow, was destroyed.

Some idea of the volume of water released from the lake, and the rapid erosion of the dam, may be gauged from the fact that during the nights of August 25 and 26, the level of the lake fell 390 feet. The lake now left is 3,900 yards long and 400 yards broad. The depth averages about 300 feet. Recently; it has been experimentally stocked with trout, so that now it is possible to fish from waters covering what was once a dry valley floor.

While Greene and Holdsworth slept I wandered into the forest. These primeval forests that stretch along the feet of the Himalaya are grand, savage and untamed. Their great trees lift themselves proudly from a tangle of impenetrable undergrowth, draped with tendinous creepers, and their dim aisles are pregnant with mystery, I sat down in the shade. The afternoon was warm and slumbrous. Even the brain-fever birds had ceased to call. It was a relief to hear the buzz of a fatherly old bumblebee and to watch him fly with noisy importance through the undergrowth.

Next day we continued our march. It was a brilliant morning charged with freshness. As we walked uphill through groves of oaks we could almost fancy ourselves on a Sussex hillside. Shipton, who was still a little weak from his bout of stomach trouble, rode a pony, but he soon found walking preferable to the uncomfortable and primitive saddle.

Kamet welcomed us once more as we stepped on to the ridge above Ramni. It was the first time our porters had seen it since leaving Ranikhet, and, as each Darjeeling man breasted the ridge, he halted, doffed his hat, and muttered a few prayers. Even Nima Dorje's face assumed an unwonted solemnity. Of what were they thinking? Doubtless of the gods whom they believe dwell on the heights, and in particular of the god whose throne is the solitary pyramid of Kamet. Other gods had not been kind. Chomolungma,[2] Goddess Mother of the World, had swept six of them to destruction; Kang-mi, the vengeful snow god of Kangchenjunga, had claimed the life of "Satan" Chettan, bravest and best of Himalayan porters.[3] Prayers to these deities had been of small avail, but perhaps the god of Kamet might prove kinder; and so, facing the great mountain, they prayed.

On a pasture just below the ridge on which we were standing, a ragged shepherd was sitting minding his flock. Like many another shepherd of these hills, he was whiling away time on a flute. The air he played was the essence of the hills translated into sound. Like most Eastern music, it was rhythmical rather than tuneful. As in Tibetan music, there was a *motif* of mystery and sadness and acceptance of life, but, now and again, a cheerful upward trill seemed to denote courage and hope. Play the same music on the plains or in the city and it would sound but mean, but played on the slopes of the Himalaya, it spoke of the slow night wind, the torrent, and the little brook hastening between the ranks of golden kingcups. Two annas will purchase a shepherd's bamboo flute, but a king's ransom will not purchase its music.

Descending the northern side of the ridge, we entered a forest of oaks, pines and rhododendrons. Here and there were little glades blue with dwarf gentians. Holdsworth discovered a rare primula, and just before our camping place at Semkharak we passed a dell of creamy peonies.

Our tents were pitched on a grassy ridge fringed with pines. Between the pines we could see the graceful peak of Nanda Ghunti. The sky was no longer hazed by the dust from the plains, or by steamy vapours rising from low tropical valleys, but was a deep rich blue sprinkled with lazy galleons of cumulus cloud.

Near our camp was a shepherd's bivouac, from the filth of which the usual swarm of flies arose to pester us.

That evening we ate our supper seated by a fire built around a tree stump. After supper we opened one of our precious bottles of whisky, lit our pipes, and yarned. What happy evenings those were on the march! Even now it needs but a whiff of smoke from burning pine or juniper to take me back in spirit to the Himalayas.

Next morning I was awakened as usual by Greene's stentorian bellow of 'Passang! Passang! Garram pani!' The volume of his voice is commensurate with the inches of his frame. Beauman said that he had been awakened in the night by some animal sniffing at his tent. He thought it was a leopard, but it was more likely an inquisitive sheepdog, or possibly imagination stimulated by some horrific ghost stories narrated by Greene the previous evening.

We were now approaching the Kuari Pass. From Semkharak we descended to the Birahi Ganga which drains the western snows of Nanda Ghunti. The valley-

[2] Everest

[3] Passang a porter with the Bavarian 1931 expedition, has since perished on Kangchenjunga.

sides hereabouts are so steep that they have in places slipped away, exposing long slopes of loose rocks and rubble. During the rainy season or the melting of the snows, landslides occur frequently, and travellers and villagers traversing this route must be prepared to run the gauntlet of these as well as falling boulders and mud avalanches.

During the march Beauman attempted to photograph a small shepherdess, but narrowly escaped being stoned for his pains. Possibly, she mistook his camera lens for the evil eye.

It was a long, hot climb up the northern side of the valley. As we ascended, we saw large numbers of the little black beetles which infest the paths in this district. They are almost always to be found firmly fastened to the round dropping of a sheep at least twice as big as they are. This they roll down the path, clinging to it resolutely the while. The dung, doubtless forms their meal, though why they roll it about in this fashion must remain a mystery. Perhaps they do it to work up a satisfactory appetite.

The camping ground at Khaliaghat had been so befouled by the villagers that Hukam Singh gave orders for us to camp on one of the villagers' rice-fields. 'It is the villagers' duty,' he said, 'to preserve a clean camping site for such sahibs as may pass!'

The local shikari came from the village to greet us. He was a typical hill man, lean and stringy of figure, with deep, far seeing eyes set in a lined, cadaverous face. As he carried good *chits* from former travellers, it was arranged that Birnie and Holdsworth should start at dawn next morning and try their luck with the local bear, thar (wild goats) and bharhal (wild sheep).

That evening there was another heavy thunderstorm. Approaching from the south, it burst furiously upon a range of rock peaks above the camp. It was a scene of wild magnificence. We stood outside our tents watching the blue rapiers of lightning lunging at the crest of the rocky pinnacles. Now and again, the over-charged clouds seemed to deliver themselves of their electrical burden all along the crest of the ridge, and a curtain of flame would fall, followed by a tearing crash of thunder, that boomed and reverberated from peak to peak.

We left early next morning for the camping ground known as Dakwani, on the southern slope of the Kuari Pass.

Above Khaliaghat, the path meanders along the hillside and then zigzags upwards to the crest of a wooded ridge. It was again a glorious morning, with the faintest suggestion of frost in the air. We could see plainly the huge scar left by the Gohna landslip on the face of Maithana Hill, whilst reposing in the valley at our feet was the turquoise Gohna Lake.

We passed over the breast of an alp bright with buttercups, and descended through woods to a waterfall that leapt from the jaws of a rocky cleft. Birnie and Holdsworth joined us here. The shikari had shown them some thar, but they had not been able to get near enough for a good shot.

The hillside above the waterfall was clothed in rhododendrons, which early in the season must afford a gorgeous spectacle. Even now many were still flowering.

Budhibal Gurung approached with a baby musk deer he had found by the side of the path, a mile or two back. It was a pretty little beast, with a coat of iron grey and light brown. It had long ears, laid back like a rabbit's ears, and brown eyes barely opened, which stared pathetically upon the world. Its legs, which were long and gawky, could scarcely support it. I was annoyed with the Gurkha for stealing it from its mother, and would have returned it had it been possible, but to have done so now would have meant certain death for it. So we adopted the poor little beast as the expedition's mascot, naming it Rupert. It was doubtful whether Rupert had been weaned, and Greene's medical skill was called upon to combat the problem of feeding him. By means of a mugful of milk, a syringe and a rubber tube, he tried to inject nutriment down Rupert's unwilling throat, but Rupert objected strongly to this procedure, and his pitiful bleat showed that he considered a syringe a poor substitute for his mother.

Camp was pitched on a grassy terrace, mauve with dwarf irises, about 1,500 feet below the Kuari Pass. Behind us, a broad gully, set at a steep angle and half-choked with beds of slowly melting snow, led up to the parabolic notch of the pass.

Southwards, the foothills stretched wave upon wave towards the violet hazes of the distant plains. We were on the threshold of the High Himalaya.

There was the usual evening thunderstorm, but it did not approach near to us, and vented its wrath upon the foothills. Later, however, there was a sharp little hailstorm and a cold wind, which made us glad to employ for the first time both layers of our eiderdown sleeping bags.

As we wanted to view the magnificent panorama for which the Kuari Pass is famed before it was obscured by clouds, we arose early. It was a cold morning, and the grass was rime encrusted. For the first time since leaving Ranikhet, we were able to appreciate to the full the value of a plateful of hot porridge. Achung had a peculiar culinary knack of rendering the most palatable food tough and leathery. The liver that morning was no exception. Fortunately, however, the worst he could do to the porridge was to render it lumpy, or reduce it to an attenuated broth, and so we came to regard it as our stand-by on the march.

It was a goodly sight to see the long train of porters zigzagging up the last slope to the Kuari Pass. I must confess that of late I had experienced some misgivings as to our porterage – misgivings founded entirely on the experiences of Kangchenjunga in 1930, when difficulty succeeded difficulty. I had no fear that our Darjeeling men would let us down – they were picked men, as keen as we were for the success of the expedition. But our Dotial men were an unknown quantity had they chosen to "play up" or desert us, our position would have been an awkward one, for porters would have been difficult to replace from the scanty population of the district through which we had passed. But the Dotials had marched, and were marching, magnificently, and everything had gone without a hitch, thanks to Birnie's tactful handling of them.

We tramped upwards towards the pass in the frosty calm of a cloudless morning. We expected to be rewarded with a beautiful view, but what we did see exceeded our greatest expectations.

As we emerged from the head of the gully on the last grassy slope leading to the pass the sun crept up over a neighbouring spur. For a few moments the rime glittered like fairy spear-points on the grass, then was resolved into shining drops of water.

We breasted the slope and halted, silent, on the pass. No words could express our delight. The Himalaya were arrayed before us in a stupendous arc. Our vision swept from the gorges of Trisul to the peaks of Kedarnath. Was it from the Kuari that the Hindu sage of old gazed upon the Himalaya and penned those inspired lines:

> He who thinks of Himachal [the Himalayan snows], though he should not behold him, is greater than he who performs all worship in Kashi [Benares]. And he who thinks on Himachal shall have pardon for all sins, and all things that die on Himachal, and all things that in dying think of his snows, are freed from sin. In a thousand ages of the Gods I could not tell thee of the glories of Himachal where Siva lived, and where the Ganges falls from the foot of Vishnu like the slender thread of a lotus flower.

The snows before us were the snows of Himachal. A curving belt of purple haze marked the course of the Alaknanda River, sacred to every Hindu as the principal tributary of the Ganges. We saw Kamet as we had not seen it before – a queen among mountains. Nilkanta was draped in clouds, but to the west the square-topped summits of Gauri Parbat and Hathi Parbat rose like fabulous monsters from a sea of lesser ridges. Remote in the east, the icy crest of Dunagiri gleamed in the sun.

Clouds were forming, and one slid jealously athwart Kamet's pyramid of granite, concealing it from our gaze.

The path traversed for a while almost horizontally across beds of snow along the northern side of the Pilkhunta ridge. At one point a subsidiary spur jutted outwards, forming an ideal belvedere. On it we sat for a long time, all save Holdsworth, who was anxious to descend as soon as possible and look for flowers. It was the only occasion during the expedition that I was glad not to be a botanist.

So we lingered awhile on a couch of fragrant turf. Clouds were born in the valleys and floated slowly upwards, caressing the hillsides. I wish we could have camped there for a night, and watched the passage of eve and dawn along the ranges. Aurora must sometimes stand on the Kuari Pass to witness her handiwork.

We descended from the pass towards the Dhaoli Valley, passing flocks of sheep with their shepherds, toiling up to the pass. Soon the last snowdrift was behind, and we halted to lunch on an alp gay with flowers, the music from a dozen little brooks in our ears. Below us was the verge of the pine forest, with one sentinel weather-beaten tree standing out before the others. Above the forest were the peaks, smoky blue and mysterious in the mid-day haze.

As we descended into the heat we felt again the runnels of sweat coursing down our bodies. Pines gave way to peaches, plums, almonds and cherries, but none were ripe. The porters, who had arrived long before us, had pitched camp on the usual camping ground near the village of Tapoban. It was a foul spot, strewn with filth, swarming with flies and crawling with vermin, so our tents were removed half a mile up the valley and pitched on the grassy talus of a former landslip.

Birnie and Budhibal Gurung had parted from us below the Kuari Pass in order to go to Joshimath to fetch our mail, which had been sent there. They arrived late that evening bringing letters from home, and newspapers. As regards the world's news, I must confess that the first thing I turned to was the cricket reports. How Kent was faring in the county championship seemed of greater importance than the latest political crisis, divorce, scandal or arsenical poisoning. As a nation we are often accused of lacking a sense of proportion in regard to our love of the open air and of sport. In other words, the foreigner means that we enjoy fresh air and hard exercise more than we ought to. Obviously I must have been suffering from an excess of both, and as a result the things that ought to have mattered had ceased to matter. The things that mattered to us were the machinations of Achung, the length of a day's march, and our internal economy. The mountaineer, if not a throwback to the ape, is certainly a throwback to some sort of primitivism.

CHAPTER SEVEN

To Niti

We rested our porters for a day at Tapoban, and on May 30, set off on the last stage of our journey to Niti, which was now only four marches distant. The march over the foothills had been, save for flies and heat, a most enjoyable experience, but memories of the march up the beautiful Dhaoli Valley will remain bright when much else has passed into oblivion. We are likely also to remember a particularly bad smell which was encountered two or three miles from Tapoban. Our gaze was directed to the spot whence it emanated by the drone of a million flies. It was a dead bullock – a very dead bullock – that had died by the side of the path. Another smell of approximately the same wavelength was met with a mile farther on. Again it was a bullock, but in this case the animal had apparently been killed by falling from the path down the precipitous hillside.

But it is not of these unpleasant things that I would write, but of other scents and scenes: the scent of pines and dewy turf in a hot sun; little alps set in a chaos of giant crags; splendid precipices veiled in gauzy waterfalls or steaming with tumultuous torrents; and deep gorges where the overhanging crags flung back the voice of the torrent, so that we could imagine ourselves walking in some whispering-gallery of the gods.

We camped that evening on the grassy plain of Surai Thota, and were lulled into dreamland by the dull roar of Kamet's snow-waters hastening to join the Alaknanda at Joshimath.

Before leaving Surai Thota we were told of a belief which we were to hear repeatedly in the Kamet and Badrinath districts. When Doctor Longstaff climbed Trisul in 1907, one of his Gurkhas, Karbir by name, who accompanied him to the summit, was questioned by the villagers on his return as to the view he had seen from the top. Being of a somewhat inventive and mischievous turn of mind, Karbir replied with a grave face that they had seen far over the foothills to the great plain where they could see the cities of Delhi and Bareilly. And then, of course, it was easily possible to see Bombay, and beyond Bombay was the Black Ocean, and beyond that England and he knew it was England because he'd been there! Thus does folklore originate, and we were questioned more than once as to whether we were climbing Kamet in order to see England from the summit.

Another local belief is that on the summit of Kamet there is a palace of pure

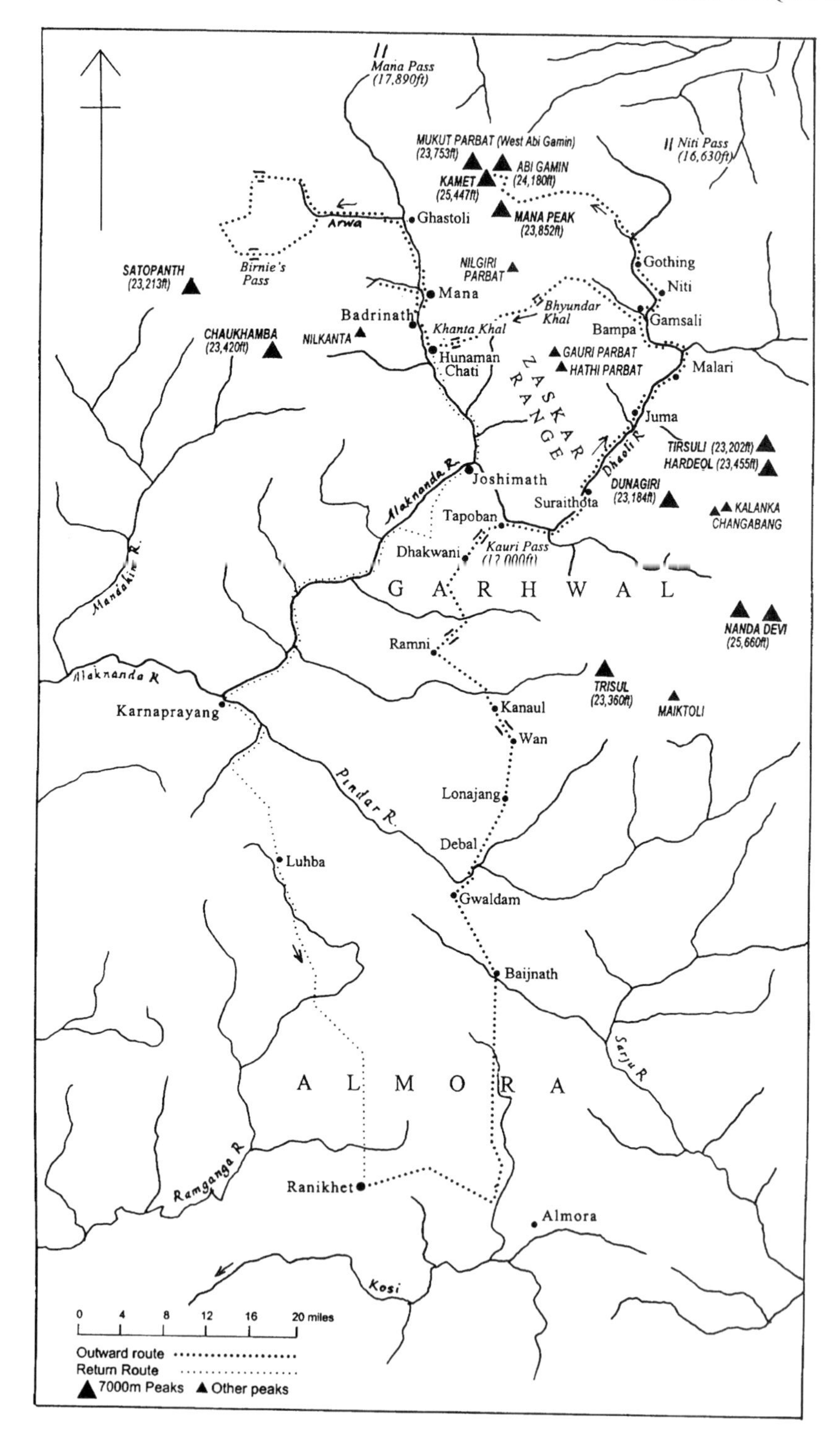

Mana Pass
(17,890ft)
MUKUT PARBAT (West Abi Gamin)
(23,753ft)
ABI GAMIN
(24,180ft)
KAMET
(25,447ft)
MANA PEAK
(23,852ft)
Niti Pass
(16,630ft)
Arwa
Ghastoli
Birnie's Pass
SATOPANTH
(23,213ft)
NILGIRI PARBAT
Gothing
Niti
Mana
Bhyundar Khal
Gamsali
Badrinath
Khanta Khal
Bampa
CHAUKHAMBA
(23,420ft)
NILKANTA
Hunaman Chati
GAURI PARBAT
HATHI PARBAT
Malari
ZASKAR RANGE
Juma
TIRSULI (23,202ft)
HARDEOL (23,455ft)
Dhaoli R.
Alaknanda R.
Joshimath
DUNAGIRI
(23,184ft)
Suraithota
KALANKA
CHANGABANG
Tapoban
Dhakwani
Kauri Pass
Mandakini R.
G A R H W A L
NANDA DEVI
(25,660ft)
Ramni
Alaknanda R.
TRISUL
(23,360ft)
MAIKTOLI
Karnaprayang
Kanaul
Wan
Pindar R.
Lonajang
Debal
Luhba
Gwaldam
Baijnath
Sarju R.
A L M O R A
Ramganga R.
Ranikhet
Almora
Kosi
0 4 8 12 16 20 miles
Outward route
Return Route
7000m Peaks
Other peaks

gold tenanted by a powerful god. It seems a pity that Mr. Snowden was not informed of this national asset before he decided to abandon the gold standard.*

During the night there was a storm that dusted the peaks with snow, but the morning dawned gloriously fine, and we walked along the path breathing keen, invigorating airs, so different now from the steamy, languorous vapours of the lower valleys. Only Rupert was unhappy, and he, obviously unwell, was bleating hoarsely and pitifully. During the marches he had been carefully carried in a small string bag similar to those borne by the sheep, slung to the belt of one of our porters. Now, his head drooped weakly from the mouth of the bag and his eyes were dull and glazed. I wish we had known what to do with the poor little beast, but there was little hope of its living separated from its mother. We were not surprised to learn, after an hour's march, that Rupert had died.

We buried our short-lived mascot by the side of a torrent beneath a sheer precipice of red granite that swept regally into the deep blue sky.

A short distance from Rupert's last resting-place, Greene and Shipton narrowly escaped being hit by falling rocks. At the spot where this occurred, the path traversed beneath vertical or overhanging cliffs, and the rocks fell free through the air with tremendous velocity, giving no warning of their approach save for sudden screams like shells. Greene was almost struck by a block as big as a man's head, that crashed to the ground beside him so viciously that his boots were covered with its dust and splinters.

Every half-mile or so we overtook families of Bhotias who were coming up the Dhaoli Valley to re-populate its villages, which are deserted during the winter months. They were driving before them herds of sheep and goats, carrying panniers laden with grain, home-spun cloth and other goods which they were taking over the Niti Pass into Tibet to trade for salt, borax and gold ornaments. These Bhotias have both Mongolian and Hindu blood in them. In appearance and temperament, however, they are more Mongolian than Hindu. They are friendly, happy-go-lucky people, with the same merry, twinkling, almond-shaped eyes as our Darjeeling porters. Like most nomadic people, they are fond of brightly coloured clothes and gay ornaments, and it was a pleasure to meet them.

Geologically, there is much of interest in the Dhaoli Valley. In its lower portion, for some ten miles above Joshimath, it passes between mountains, the strata of which has a dip of about 30° from south to north. This results in abrupt cut-offs on the southern sides of the peaks and inclined slopes on the northern sides, which in the case of the lower peaks are thickly wooded. There are abundant traces also of previous glaciation. Moraines issue from the mouths of side valleys, and in places line the main valley consisting usually of hardened mud in which are imbedded stones of all sizes, varying from a pebble to boulders weighing tons. Where the path passes beneath them, they form a danger to travellers, for boulders constantly fall from them, particularly during rain, when the cementing mud becomes softened. What might easily have been a fatal accident occurred but a few yards from our camping place at Juma, when one of our Dotial coolies was struck on the head by a falling stone. Fortunately, he only received a scalp wound, which was sewn up by Greene, an operation which vastly amused his comrades.

* Philip Snowden, Chancellor of the Exchequer 1924, 1929–31.

The fine weather we had so far enjoyed was steadily deteriorating. Heavy rainstorms were developing earlier every day and lasting well into the night; the peaks were becoming plastered with snow. We went to sleep at Juma with the patter of rain in our ears, and awoke next morning, June 1 to find the pines a thousand feet above the camp white with freshly fallen snow.

At Juma, we were joined by Alam Singh, who had been sent from Mana by the Rawal of Badrinath to help organise our local transport and secure for us coolie food. He had been Meade's servant during his expeditions to Kamet, and we expected to find him a great help to us in many ways. He was a man of medium height, spare and slightly stooping in figure; his hair was greying, and his face, which was long and sheep-like, was ornamented by a straggling, uneven and ill-nourished moustache. His most pronounced physical characteristic was what novelists describe as a "flashing smile". His greatest use to us lay in the fact that he had been appointed by the Rawal to look after our interests, for the Rawal, although not possessed of executive power, is the spiritual ruler of Garhwal and the high-priest of the Badrinath district. We therefore appointed him sirdar over our local men at a salary of sixty rupees a month.

Alam Singh is a Hindu, and Lewa a Sherpa Bhuddist and it was interesting to compare the two men. Lewa, the hard-visaged fighting man, abrupt, brutal in his diction, never giving an order which he was not prepared himself to carry out, a man of magnificent physique, tough, alert, wiry, loyal to the core, sparing neither himself nor his comrades in the service of his Sahibs. Alam Singh, willing yet weak, intelligent yet lacking initiative, shelving responsibility whenever possible, expecting the expedition machine to run of its own accord, helpless in the face of a small difficulty or danger, frightened of offending either his superiors or his inferiors, a passenger not a captain on stormy waters, leaving most things to chance and God, yet, withal, a likeable man, who faithfully did his best to help us, and one whose cheery smile will ever remain a pleasant memory.

In places the path disappeared beneath smashed and uprooted pines – brought down by spring avalanches. Small wonder that the Dhaoli Valley is uninhabited during the winter months, for, apart from the depth of snow, the paths between villages are swept by many avalanches.

It was an interesting walk to Malari. Every turn in the path revealed new beauties and grandeurs. Dunagiri was visible from our lunching place. Its delicate snow summit is formed by the intersection of ice ridges, ribbed in their turn with gleaming flutings of ice. Two of these ridges were visible – the North Ridge and the West Ridge. Neither appear practicable save to an expedition prepared to spend weeks of arduous work hacking a way up their thin, razor-like crests, and over their rickety pinnacles of ice. The West Ridge looks practicable in its upper portion, but is protected from assault in its lower portion by a cut-off. Probably the eastern side of the mountain is accessible from the Bagini Pass, traversed by Doctor Longstaff's party in 1907.

Our eyes, wearied of dazzling snows, sought relief in the green depths of the Dhaoli Valley, where a pleasing contrast was afforded by a number of rocky pinnacles crowned with sentinel fir trees.

Nima Dorje was unusually talkative as we tramped along the path after lunch. His knowledge of English was greater than I had imagined, and he chattered gaily about Everest and Kangchenjunga. Like Lewa, he was profoundly optimistic as to the eventual conquest of Everest. It was obvious that three Everest expeditions had done something more than inculcate a spirit of loyalty into the Darjeeling porters; they had stimulated in them an enthusiasm for mountaineering. Future expeditions should continue to foster this spirit. By doing so, they may eradicate some of the fears and superstitions these men have for the high snows.

Two miles below Malari, hundreds of cedars grow from the hillside. Possibly, they are the survivors of a forest felled before the advent of British Rule and the forest conservation laws. Among them are many lordly trees, hundreds and possibly thousands of years old. What inscrutable process of nature decreed their growth in this particular spot, far from their fellows of the lower valleys?

The sky darkened and the usual afternoon rain began to fall. Seen under a lowering mist, the slopes in the neighbourhood of Malari assumed a melancholy appearance suggestive of a Derbyshire moorland.

Malari is a quaint little village, the grey houses of which, clustered together as though for mutual protection, melt peaceably into a stony landscape.

Camp was pitched in pouring rain half a mile beyond the village. Shipton greeted us gloomily. Being in charge of our commissariat, he was always anxious to procure for us as much fresh food as possible. His most roseate dream was of the eggs and chickens awaiting us at the next village, dozens and dozens of chickens and hundred and hundreds of eggs. He would talk to us of chickens, roasted and succulent and of eggs – boiled eggs, poached eggs, curried eggs, scrambled eggs, fried eggs, and huge omelettes, steaming and savoury. Alas! These dreams had not materialised yet, despite disappointment after disappointment, Shipton remained undaunted. He had started out from Juma that morning with the stern light of a fixed resolve in his eyes. Malari was, he told us, the largest village in the Dhaoli Valley. There *must* be chickens and eggs. Now he was seated on a biscuit box. The light of stern resolve had died from his eyes and had been replaced by a look of settled gloom. There were no eggs and no chickens in Malari. But near the camp someone had caught and killed an unfortunate bird that was fluttering about with a broken wing. The remains were handed solemnly round, and, after a prolonged examination, declared by a majority to be those of a cuckoo. And so, as the corpse was much too small to divide among six, our dinner that evening started with cuckoo soup.

When making up our list of stores we had, as previously stated, made an allowance for food obtained locally. Our provisions of late had been disappearing at an alarming rate. Jam in particular was being consumed at the rate of a pot a meal. We deemed it advisable, therefore, to augment our larder by as much local food as possible. In lieu of porridge we had already sampled a kind of meal composed almost exclusively of husks. This had not proved a success. Hardened campaigners, such as General Bruce, who have travelled in Garhwal, are reputed to have lived almost exclusively on chupattees. Without desiring to cast any aspersion on the gastronomical integrity of these pioneers, I must confess that I find this as difficult to believe as I find chupattees are to digest.

It was for reasons of economy that dinner began with cuckoo soup and ended with a native meal called sattu. Both dishes were accompanied by chupattees, into which Achung had managed to impart a consistency and texture resembling well-seasoned boot leather. Holdsworth, who, up to this point, had been insistent that living on the country was essential, was enthusiastic as to the excellence of sattu. This enthusiasm was maintained, verbally, up to the last spoonful. It is remarkable, therefore, that on no future occasion was he observed to eat this excellent and nutritive food, nor did that pearl of Himalayan philosophy, "living on the country", again fall from his lips.

In appearance and taste, sattu resembles powdered cement. This comparison is not based on imagination.

A friend and I were ski-ing in the Austrian Alps. The weather was perfect, and we enjoyed excellent sport. Unfortunately, however, our provisions ran out, and it seemed necessary to return to civilisation from the remote hut which we had made our headquarters. To avoid doing this, we ransacked the hut for food. My friend was outside the hut attending to his ski when, in a corner of the kitchen, I discovered a sack, and, plunging my hand into it encountered a soft powder, which I took to be flour. Our problem was solved; we could subsist for another day or two. I took a large pinch of the flour to taste. It was certainly a harsh and gritty flour, and in flavour decidedly peculiar. Saying nothing to my friend, I proceeded to mix a quantity of it with water and knead the resulting pasty mixture into a number of little cakes, which I placed on the stove to cook. Then I went outside to declaim the joyful news to my friend. He came in, eyed the results of my labours hungrily for a moment, picked up one of the cakes, and took a hearty bite. But, alas! The paste had changed miraculously to stone. The bagful of "flour" I had discovered was a bagful of cement!

That evening it rained heavily. For some reason – probably because they were dirty – our tents leaked a little, and once or twice I was awakened by drops of water impinging on to my face with maddening accuracy. It was, however, the sole occasion during the expedition that the "Willesden" canvas displayed the least inclination to leak.

Next morning was again brilliantly fine. Snow lay low on the grass slopes above Malari, and the peaks gleamed virginal white in a sky of deepest blue. The hills north-east of Malari with their blue, brown and purple slopes merging into snow-crested ridges reminded me of the Scottish Highlands.

Presently, the path, after plunging through a pine forest, ran out on to fertile meadows hemmed in by savage rock peaks. General Bruce once told me that the Gastern Thal, near Kandersteg, in the Bernese Oberland, is Himalayan in the character of its scenery. I can bear him witness, for the Dhaoli Valley above Malari bears a striking resemblance to the Gastern Thal, only the Dhaoli Valley is on a more lavish and magnificent scale. The splintered rock peaks of reddish granite, of alpine size in themselves, are mere outposts of greater peaks behind.

Near the junction of the Dhaoli and Banke Valleys are the two little villages of Bampa and Gamsali. The former village actually boasts a post office. It is the last post office in the Dhaoli Valley and must be one of the highest post offices in India, standing, as it does, at an altitude of nearly 10,000 feet above sea level. That postal communication should extend so far up these remote valleys speaks well for the initiative of the authorities concerned.

At Bampa several of our Darjeeling porters prevailed upon the local natives to relieve them of their loads and to carry them, for a consideration, to Niti. I think, however, that they were not actuated solely by laziness, but because, in their own estimation, they were great men specially picked to climb Kamet, and also selected by the Sahibs as their personal servants. Strolling along like Sahibs, able to pay for substitutes to carry their loads, their prestige in the valley would be enormously enhanced; not only would the villagers offer them liquid refreshment, but they would find favour in the eyes of the village belles. I noticed that, among our Darjeeling men, Ondi, who was the first to find a substitute, invariably appeared to find favour with the feminine element of the villages through which we passed, although when we looked at him we used to wonder why, for he is by no means prepossessing in appearance.

We were no longer within range of Gandhi's activities, and, after the insolent stares of the "Congress Wallahs" of the lower hills and plains, it was pleasant to be greeted with a respectful and friendly 'Salaam, Sahib' or 'Salaam, Huzoor' from the villagers we met on the path.

A dozen or so ponies, driven by Tibetans, passed us, laden with merchandise. They were probably the first traders to cross the Niti Pass that year.

Half a mile above Gamsali, the Dhaoli Valley narrows to one of the grandest defiles in the Garhwal Himalaya. From either bank of the Dhaoli River the precipices rise smooth and sheer, as though sliced by a titan's knife. Here and there time and weathering have rifted the rocks into chimneys and clefts, which spring upwards as straight as spears for 1,000 feet or more. But, for the most part, the precipices are unbroken, and rise in a series of smooth "boiler-plate" slabs of terrific aspect.

Through this awesome rift the Dhaoli River rages in unbridled savagery, and its cold spray blasts upwards like smoke from a cannon. The path is in places a mere platform of wooden boards laid on iron stanchions driven into the side of the cliff, and a sheer drop of 300 feet into the boiling torrent awaits an unwary step.

We crossed a vibrating and swaying log bridge, turned a rocky corner, and emerged on to the stony fields of Niti. We had passed, as it were, through the gorge of the Styx to the pastures of Avalon.

Arriving at our camping site, which was at a height of nearly 11,000 feet, about one mile below the village of Niti, we were surprised to find another camp pitched not far away and be greeted by an English lady, Miss Gertrude Benham. She told us that she had already been several times round the world, and had chosen this quiet retreat in order to be alone and undisturbed while making some sketches of the country and the people; she hoped, later to obtain permission to cross the Niti Pass into Tibet and visit the sacred peak of Kailas.

On the hillside immediately above our camp several bharhal could be seen moving about among the patches of scrub on the long scree slopes. Bharhal are wild sheep, and some of them are larger than ordinary sheep. They have curved horns, and are almost as active as chamois. Owing to the fact that they are seldom stalked in the remoter parts of Garhwal, it is sometimes possible to approach within a hundred yards of them. Birnie and Holdsworth, who were first in camp, watched one of the Niti villagers stalking one along the mountainside above the camp. Finally he shot it, and it was rolled down the scree slope to the camp. The old axiom that "the mountain sheep are sweeter, but the valley sheep are fatter", does not apply to bharhal, for their flesh is tougher than that of ordinary sheep.

The mincing machine was our gastronomical stand-by, and often there would go up a paean of praise and thanksgiving to General Bruce. His last words whispered into my ear before I left England had been, 'Don't forget the mincing machine.' Was it chance or providence that, soon after Shipton and I had arrived at Ranikhet, we received a note from a lady: 'I understand that you require a mincing machine. I have for sale a second-hand one in excellent condition.' We bought it. Its operation, however, entailed a certain amount of work, and, because of this, Achung conceived a hatred for it. One day we were given chops for dinner instead of the usual minced meat. A Gurkha could have stropped his kukri on those chops. We summoned Achung and questioned him. Achung spread his hands helplessly; there was an unholy gleam in his eyes. 'Mincing machine no good. No go,' he replied. He had 'lost' a vital screw, and, as he said, the mincing machine would 'no go.' All the mechanical ingenuity of the expedition was called in to solve the urgent problem of making the mincing machine work again. It was finally solved by Shipton, who substituted an artfully carved plug of wood for the lost screw, and the digestion of the expedition saved. After that we would see Achung seated on the ground, turning the handle of the mincing machine round and round and round with the dull, hopeless look of a beaten man. He was a slave to the mincing machine.

It was a cheery party that congregated round a table built of packing cases in the mess tent for dinner that evening. Everything had gone well so far. Porterage had worked without a hitch and we had not lost a load; we had been blessed with glorious weather, and had enjoyed every mile of a march which, as Greene said, was worth an expedition in itself. We were lean, tanned and fit.

CHAPTER EIGHT

Stalking Bharhal

I ROSE AT DAWN the next morning and set off with Budhibal Gurung for a day's stalk after bharhal. It was a frosty and cloudless morning. My legs levered me uphill with that effortless gait that is the product of physical wellbeing; my lungs drew deep breaths of pure air. We mounted rapidly up the stone-strewn hillside, not halting until we were a good 2,000 feet above the sleeping camp.

The black carbons of night glowed redly in the current of dawn, then brightened to radiant white; blue shadows stole down brown hillsides. A small bird burst into twittering song. Only the valley slept beneath a tenuous shawl of chill, white mist.

No bharhal were to be seen, but Budhibal Gurung who was well versed in their habits, said that we must traverse the hillside in a northerly direction.

Traversing was not easy, for the mountainside was seamed with steep gullies, the earthen beds of which were hard frozen. Care was needed in crossing these gullies, for they were studded with sharp stones ready to rip the flesh to ribbons in the event of a slide.

A crag projecting from the mountainside was an obvious coign of vantage, and we made for it. As we clambered on to it, there was a sudden and startling rush, and a large eagle flew up from the rocks and circled round, obviously annoyed at our intrusion. We kept a wary eye on it for a minute or two, but it did not attack us, and presently made off. Had its nest been on the crag, we should have been in for a warm time of it, even though we had a rifle with which to defend ourselves.

Long we lay on the crag, scanning the rough hillside before us. No bharhal were visible, but presently I saw something moving across a patch of open ground half a mile away. It looked like a small brown bear, but, before I could get my monocular trained on to it, it disappeared into some bushes. We approached the spot carefully, but finding nothing, continued traversing the hillside, As we did so the sun swung up over the range we were on and glared down upon us with ever-increasing intensity.

The hillside bent round a corner. Budhibal Gurung was ahead. As he gained the corner, he sank down with a sharp warning hiss. I crawled up to him. 'Bharhal, Sahib!' he said. I gazed in the direction in which he was pointing, but could see nothing. Before us the ground sank into a deep hollow, the far slope of which rose some 2,000 feet to a gentle skyline. It was on this opposite slope, at least a mile away, that the bharhal were grazing. I strained my eyes, but still could not see them. It was not until Budhibal Gurung had sighted the rifle on the spot that I could make them out. Even then it required a long look through the monocular to convince me that what I at first took to be seven small white stones on the slope, amid many other similar stones, were indeed bharhal. Budhibal Gurung has eyes like a hawk.

To gain the far side of the hollow we had to cross the head of the widest and steepest gully we had so far encountered. We would have given much for ice axes. But we got across at last by clinging to tiny pebbles projecting from the frozen earth.

Taking advantage of the scanty cover afforded by scattered bushes two or three feet high, we toiled up the hillside.

Luck was against us. The morning air, which until that moment had been perfectly calm, began to stir. Light puffs came up out of the valley beneath us, wafting our scent straight to the noses of the bharhal. We were not surprised, when they retreated beyond the ridge, bounding the hollow far up the main mountainside above.

We were dripping with sweat, but we decided to follow them. The bharhal were clearly visible some 1,500 feet above us, congregated on a broad grass ledge, running across a minor buttress of the hillside. Their leader, a magnificent ram, was standing apart from the rest of the herd, doubtless on the *qui vive*, and was silhouetted sharply against the blue sky.

Direct approach was hopeless, both on account of the breeze and lack of cover. The best we could do was to make a wide circling movement to the right, and approach diagonally up the hillside. Had we the time and the energy, we might have made an even wider circling movement, climbed the steep hillside half a mile to the right of them, traversed it, and descended on to them. But we were climbing at 15,000 feet, and we should have been far too slow.

Utilising the scanty cover as well as we could we toiled on. Half an hour passed and the bharhal remained stationary. Four hundred yards, three hundred, two hundred and fifty. Suddenly, the big leader, who had been looking down into the valley, turned and gazed straight at us. The remainder of the herd did likewise. We "froze" immobile in our tracks. 'Shoot, Sahib!' whispered Budhibal Gurung. But to shoot was hopeless at such a range. I was panting and trembling from my exertions and for such a long shot steadiness was essential. I did not want to wound the quarry, for I was not prepared to follow up; I was tired; we had climbed over 4,000 feet – sun and altitude had done the rest. So I lay watching whilst heart and lungs gradually reassumed a quieter rhythm, hoping meanwhile that the suspicions of the bharhal might be allayed. But it was not to be. At first they were merely curious, but in a few moments fear supervened. The big ram turned suddenly and darted off, disappearing down the far side of the buttress. The remainder of the herd immediately followed his example.

As it was possible that their fear might be forgotten and they might stop when out of sight of us, we ascended another 500 feet of steep grass and broken rock on the opposite side of the buttress to which the bharhal had descended. Cautiously we poked our heads over the crest of the buttress. No living thing was to be seen on the expanse of mountainside before us. To make sure that they were not concealed in "dead ground", Budhibal Gurung climbed several hundred feet farther up the buttress, while I made myself comfortable in a convenient turfy hollow. Presently he returned without having seen any sign of them.

I had one regret. For me it is a greater pleasure to photograph wild animals than to shoot them. Had I taken a camera with me, equipped with telephoto lens, I might have obtained some interesting photographs.

Holdsworth had started soon after us to ascend on ski a peak of some 15,000 feet to the south of the camp. We could now see him descending, a tiny black speck, tracing out a wavering line on the northern snow slopes of the mountain. From where we sat, the summit of Dunagiri was visible. That this mountain, although placed well to the north of Trisul and Nanda Devi, receives a greater precipitation of snow than the Niti district is evidenced by a lower snow-line and the absence of rock. Dunagiri, like Kangchenjunga, is a beautiful mountain to look at, but, from the northern side at least, a dangerous one to climb, for its accumulated snows bulge out over its precipices in hanging glaciers, ready at any moment to sweep the glaciers beneath in huge avalanches.

It was now about midday, and towering thunderclouds were creeping up from the foothill valleys. Ere nightfall they would expend their energy on the main range. They were not likely to reach Niti, and, even should they do so, they would receive short shrift from the dry Tibetan wind.

For a long time we lay on our couch of turf while the hours sped and the shadows swung round to the east. I wondered of what Budhibal Gurung was thinking. Was his enjoyment of such a day merely an adventurous enjoyment? Was it only the excitement of the hunt that appealed to him, or could he see farther than the brown rocks and the blue sky?

We heaved and stretched ourselves to our feet, and raced each other down the long slopes of grass and scree. Late afternoon saw us back in camp.

CHAPTER NINE

With the Yaks to Base Camp

AT NITI, BIRNIE PAID OFF the Dotial coolies, and they departed happily on their long trek to their homes in the foothills.

Hukam Singh also left us at Niti. He had helped us considerably, particularly in regard to the feeding of our coolies along the line of march, and we parted from him with many expressions of goodwill.

Alam Singh, meanwhile, was busily recruiting Bhotias from Niti, Gamsali, Bampa and Malari. In addition to the men he collected, others had come from villages as far away as Mana, Alam Singh's own village, to offer their services to the expedition. At first appearance they seemed a wild, almost ruffianly-looking crowd. Their faces had never seen, or their bodies experienced, soap and water. They exuded strong odours of yaks and other things. Their tattered garments consisted for the most part of coarse sackcloth. They walked either barefoot or with their feet encased in clumsy cloth Tibetan boots or layers of sackcloth. But their gait was the gait of the hillman – slouching and slow on the level, rhythmical and deceptively fast uphill.

At first we were puzzled by their sullen and suspicious demeanour. Later, we discovered the reason for this. It was Lewa. Not only was as he anxious to demonstrate his own personal superiority, but he regarded the Garhwal Bhotias as being racially inferior to the Darjeeling Sherpas and Bhotias. Therefore, he adopted a bullying, truculent, parade ground attitude which he had been wont to use when dealing with the Dotials. But the Bhotias of northern Garhwal are a very different type of men to the submissive and easily cowed Dotials: not unnaturally they resented Lewa's attitude and their resentment caused them to shun their work. In the beginning Lewa would exclaim passionately, 'These men are no good!' and almost we believed him, for their morale did indeed seem poor. It was not until we had discovered their unspoken grievance, and warned Lewa to exercise more tact, that we won their confidence, and then we discovered that beneath their unsavoury exteriors beat hearts every whit as courageous and loyal as those of our own Darjeeling men.

So far, with the exception of Shipton's illness at Ramni and minor stomach disorders, we had all been very fit. At Niti, however, Greene went down with a sharp attack of fever, accompanied by a splitting headache, aching limbs and general lassitude. The attack passed away within thirty-six hours; it was probably a touch of the sun. In the coolness of the upper Himalayan valleys the traveller is liable to become careless of the sun, but its rays are, if anything, more penetrating than at lower elevations, and it is not safe even to sit in the shade of a tree without protecting the head. A great deal of nonsense is talked about sunstroke by those who have never experienced a tropical sun, or by those whose skulls are so thick that they can do without a solar topee and assume that others can do likewise. The ideal sun-hat for Himalayan mountaineering is the planter's terai, which consists of two wideawake hats, one within the other to ensure complete protection, a piece of red cotton may be inserted between the two hats. Birnie was not fit either. Possibly "living on the country" had something to do with it. At all events, we agreed that local food had better be left severely alone until we had finished with Kamet.

By June 4, thirty local coolies and thirty yaks and jhobus (half-bred yaks obtained by crossing yaks with oxen) were in readiness to start.

On the morning of June 5 we set out on the last stage of our march to the site of our base camp. The recent unsettled weather had mended, and the winter snows, although lying exceptionally low for this time of the year, were melting fast beneath a brilliant sun.

In some ways June 5 was the most anxious day of the whole expedition. Now that our willing and faithful Dotial porters had been dismissed, we relied upon the local men, the yaks and jhobus. Many of the former had been rendered sullen and resentful, thanks to Lewa's tactlessness. As to the latter …

At first sight, there is nothing more inoffensive in appearance than a yak. Its large brown eyes survey the world with the placidity of a White Knight. Its clumsy, lumbering body covered in long hair, which droops down concealing all but the lower portion of its legs, resembles a walking doormat, or one of those little yapping flat-nosed dogs, adored by some ladies. Never are appearances more deceptive. A yak will stand calmly contemplating the infinite while a heavy load is being laboriously strapped on to its back. Suddenly, however, it awakes from its day-dreams, and, finding to its surprise that there is something on top of it that it does not at all like the feel of, it proceeds to get rid of the encumbrance as quickly as possible. It tears itself free from those who are holding it and dashes away, bucking and jumping, until the ropes tying the boxes to its back are wrenched loose and the boxes distributed violently over the surrounding landscape. Directly the yak has freed itself from its load, the devil departs from it and it stands quite still, surveying the ruin it has wrought with a puzzled expression in its brown eyes, as though wondering how the boxes came to be lying on the ground.

The boxes, having been collected and any that have had their sides stoved in or their lids wrenched off repaired, are reloaded, to an accompaniment of many curses, by the yak drivers. But this time the yak displays not the slightest interest in the proceedings. Having registered its official protest and disapproval, it bows to the inevitable and moves peaceably off, maintaining an "all out" speed of one and a half miles per hour for the rest of the day.

Unfortunately, the yaks employed by us had done little or no load carrying for a long time, and continued to register protests throughout the day. The more fragile of our belongings seemed to have been placed on the backs of the most obstreperous yaks. Starting late from the camp, I was just in time to see a box containing my photographic plates and spare cinema camera crash to the ground, and all but roll down the steep hillside to total destruction.

The yak drivers were largely to blame for the frequent stampedes, for they did not seem to know how to tie on the loads securely, and the yaks were irritated into stampeding.

From Niti a stony track zigzagged upwards for about 1,500 feet and then traversed more or less horizontally across broken hillsides. The path was in places a mere goat-track, and had not yet been built up after the ravages wrought by avalanches and streams due to the melting of the winter snows. It was interesting to observe that all the devil departed from the yaks when the ground became difficult, and they walked across the dangerous bits with sober circumspection. There was one steep rocky gully where the path petered out altogether. Seated on the far side of the gully, I waited for the yaks. With their heavy loads, it seemed scarcely possible that they could safely negotiate such a place. The first of them appeared a lumbering, ungainly beast like a walking tank. It halted a moment, eyed the path critically, and proceeded to cross with stately *sang-froid*. Considering that its projecting load forced it to walk on the very edge of the rocky ledges, it was a remarkable piece of work. The remaining yaks and jhobus followed their leader, one by one, unaccompanied by their drivers, who evidently considered it the wisest policy to let their charges work out their own salvation. A slip would have resulted in a fall of a thousand feet or more, but not a yak faltered. It was not until they approached close to me that they showed any signs of perturbation. A European, particularly one with a reddish beard, appeared to unnerve them.

It was probably my appearance that caused a stampede. This occurred on a steep slope of loose stones. One yak bolted. Two or three others immediately followed its example. Beauman and I had to leap aside for our lives. In the general *mélée,* several boxes fell to the ground, and one of them rolled down the hillside. Lewa leapt after it in hot pursuit. The lid of the box was torn from its hinges and Shipton's pyjamas emerged; they were caught by a bush, and remained bravely fluttering in the breeze. The gramophone shot out and bounded valley-wards, but, before it had gone far, Lewa pounced upon it. We thought it must be irreparably damaged, but from another unbroken box we unpacked a record and placed it in the machine, scarcely expecting anything to happen. It was with profound thankfulness that we heard Caruso's passionate "O sole Mio". Whether this had a steadying influence on the yaks I do not know, but thenceforward they proceeded soberly.

We turned a corner and gazed into the gently inclined valley up which stretched the pastures of Goting. It was a desolate valley, and save for a solitary clump of scraggy, weather-beaten trees in its lower portion contained nothing but grass and stones. Above the Dhaoli River long slopes of reddish-brown screes swept upwards to cliffs of decaying rock and a frieze of shattered pinnacles that leant wearily against the sky. These valleys on the edge of Tibet suggest a slow, never-ending symphony of solitude and sadness. As the snows deepen and melt on their hillsides, so do nations and men wax and wane on the far-off plains, but on the borders of Tibet only the voice of the torrent, the occasional rattle of a falling stone, and the growl of avalanches breaks a silence that is akin to the silence of death.

Sharp and hard on the still air came the report of a rifle. Before its echoes had ceased clamouring there came another and another – nine in all. Budhibal Gurung, who had gone on ahead to look for bharhal, was having a merry time.

Camp was pitched on a stony pasture by the Dhaoli River. There, Budhibal Gurung turned up with the good news that he had shot two bharhal. We were particularly glad to hear this, because the Niti villagers had demanded ten rupees for a sheep – an exorbitant sum. We had refused to purchase one, and now the gods had provided us with two large bharhal, an object lesson to the villagers, illustrating not only the sagacity of the Sahibs, but the impartiality of the gods.

Budhibal Gurung said that he had sighted a herd of about a dozen bharhal, and had blazed away at a range of over two hundred yards, killing two of them. Both he and Randhoj Kan are in the army "marksman" class. One of the bharhal was deftly skinned by our Darjeeling men, and we supped off its liver and kidneys.

We were already beginning to learn something of our new porters. Living as they do on the Indian side of the Himalaya, the Garhwal Bhotias are, theoretically, Hindu by religion. But in practice, their creed is as accommodating as that of the Vicar of Bray, and it is probable that when in Tibet they revert for the time being to Buddhism. Alam Singh was the only one among them who showed signs of being a devout Hindu, and this was doubtless because he had been the servant of the Rawal of Badrinath.

Because of their religious unorthodoxy, the Garhwal Bhotias are less prone to superstitious terrors than are the Darjeeling Bhotias and Sherpas, whose orthodox Tibetan Buddhism is impregnated with Lamastic superstition. Yet, although the two had many traits in common, they would seldom mingle during the day or share a fire at night. The most intelligent among these local men was Natar Singh, who was capable of keeping written accounts and of exercising authority in some small degree over his undisciplined companions. One man, whom I remember vividly, was a crotchety old fellow, with weak watery eyes and a querulous mouth. He was seldom without some new grumble or complaint. His name was Pomo.

Garhwal Bhotias are simple and childlike in disposition. Most simple and childlike of all appeared Kesar Singh. We had yet to learn that behind his disingenuous and self-deprecating smirk lurked the brain of a schemer and a scrounger. Of all the local men, he is the one I remember best, not so much for his outstanding work on Kamet, but because of the disarming grin of conscious guilt with which he invariably met well-merited rebukes from Birnie.

We rose early next morning, for the march to the base campsite promised to be a long one. Old Pomo grumbled that it was two marches from Goting to the Raikana Glacier, but, as other parties had done it in one march, we saw no reason why we should not do likewise.

A hard day's marching had evacuated the devil from the yaks, and no one seeing them now as they lumped peaceably along would have attributed to them anything but the most harmless of dispositions. The Darjeeling men had purchased local cloth at Niti, and the Old Soldier had blossomed forth into a pair of remarkable breeches, made from a white cottonish material, the bagginess of which suggested a Zouave or an American baseball player. Some of the local men had affected broad-peaked caps, which lent to them a sportive and rakish appearance, whilst one, who had wrapped a dark blue scarf round his neck, might easily have been taken for an oarsman in an Oxford crew.

For two miles we followed the main Dhaoli Valley, which is almost flat above

Goting. It was a brilliantly clear, frosty morning, and as the sun lit the pinnacled ridges and slowly stole down the long slopes of reddish rock and screes, I was forcibly reminded of Mr. T. Howard Somervell's paintings of the valleys in the neighbourhood of Everest. There were the same crude, almost bizarre colourings, in which reds and yellows predominated. The shadows were hard-edged, like shadows thrown by an electric arc lamp. Such a scene would induce despair in a conventionally minded artist. To those accustomed to the diffused lighting and soft atmospheric effects of Europe, Somervell's paintings appear harsh and brutal in their lighting and colouring. Yet, were they to see the country for themselves, they would realise that only by brutal daubing can the spirit of these strange valleys on the edge of Tibet be transferred to canvas.

Above the junction of the Dhaoli River and the torrent from the Raikana Glacier we had to cross the former stream. Other parties had experienced difficulty here and had been forced to build bridges, but, luckily for us, the Dhaoli River was spanned by a great drift of avalanche snow.

At the lower end of the Raikana Valley is a stretch of level, grassy ground where spring onions flourished. We breasted a rise, and gazed for the first time at the Raikana Glacier and our base campsite. It was not an inspiring view. All the great peaks were hidden. The terminal of the Raikana Glacier blocked the valley like a vast slagheap from some demon mine.

According to their map, Kellas and Morshead followed the western bank of the Dhaoli River above Niti. Early in the season, however, the route is very dangerous, and we saw boulder after boulder leap down the hillside and dash into the river beneath.

Winter snow lay down to 12,000 feet, and soon we were trudging across wide drifts of it. Below the terminal moraine of the Raikana Glacier is a level alp on which the Niti shepherds graze their flocks. It was now mostly snow-covered, but the warm sun was already arousing many little flowers from the scanty patches of sodden turf,

We crossed a stream and trudged up the terminal moraine, noting with satisfaction that abundant fuel in the form of dwarf juniper bushes was present. The higher we went, the larger became the snow patches, until we were trudging through almost unbroken snow of the usual abominable type met with during a hot afternoon in the Himalaya. It was seldom of the same consistency for more than a few yards, and we sank sometimes boot-deep and sometimes knee-deep into it.

Nothing is more tedious to walk over than a Himalayan terminal moraine, and we toiled to the crest of ridges a hundred feet high only to find that we had to lose the height so laboriously gained by descending an equal distance into hollows on their far sides. Providence must provide Himalayan terminal moraines for the express purpose of humbling presumptuous mountaineers.

At the foot of the moraine we said arrogantly, 'We will be pitching the Base Camp within an hour.' But it was three hours before we swung our rucksacks from our backs on a boulder-strewn ridge projecting from the snow which we decided was the least uncomfortable of all the boulder-strewn ridges in the vicinity.

The Darjeeling porters set to work with such right good will that in less than an hour level platforms had been constructed for the tents, and walls built to protect them from the wind. It is surprising how the roughest and most desolate mountainside can be rendered habitable. The height was 15,500 feet, almost equal to the summit of Mont Blanc.

The local men and yaks arrived in fine fettle, despite a long day's marching, and the former, after a short rest, went back down the moraine to collect juniper wood. Towards evening, the clouds hanging about the peaks dispersed. Kamet appeared: only the summit was visible over an intervening ridge, and we were unable properly to appreciate its grandeur or to grasp its scale. Both the southern and northern faces were visible in profile. It was the northern face we must ascend from Meade's Col. The angle was steep – steeper than we had anticipated – and we realised immediately that it was going to be something more than a walk to the summit. Great bulges of ice on the upper slopes could be seen through glasses. They appeared to present ugly obstacles. It would, however, be rash to jump to any premature conclusions as to technical difficulties, for we could only see the slope in profile, and there was no telling how broad it was and how many opportunities it might present for out-flanking obstacles.

From the Base Camp we could gaze up the Raikana Glacier. For perhaps three miles the moraine debris stretched, a silent witness of the forces that disintegrate the great peaks, but beyond, the glacier stretched smooth and unbroken towards a wall of snowy peaks, which forms a natural frontier between Garhwal and Tibet. Many of these peaks invite the mountaineer to test his strength and skill. One of the most striking was a cone-like snow peak so simply constructed that it might have been drawn by a child.

The northward view was a fascinating one, but it was to the south that we turned at sunset, to watch the twisted masses of ashen thunder-clouds passing like tall ghosts into the night, and the summit of Nanda Devi glowing for a few minutes like a red-hot casting from a Titan's forge before being quenched in a cold bath of stars.

It was strangely silent; the avalanches were hushed; not a pebble fell. Night distributed her stars. And what stars! Stars that flashed and glittered a bright electric blue, stars that pulsated eagerly and fiercely. And across the stars stretched the Milky Way, a tenuous banner spanning the breadth of heaven.

The frost was a sharp one, and we were glad to don warm clothing. As we sat in the mess tent facing candles that no longer leaned wearily from the heat, it was strange to think that a few days previously we had laboured in tropical heat and that the sweat had rolled from our foreheads.

After dinner we celebrated the completion of one stage in our journey with a ration of rum apiece. Everything had gone well; porterage had worked without a hitch; despite the obstreperousness of the yaks, we had not lost a single load. Shipton manipulated the gramophone, and the well-remembered favourites floated out into the still night, whilst we sat around on packing cases puffing at our pipes, at peace with the world.

As I turned into my tent, I could see the fires of our porters about the camp. Soundless lightning was flickering in the south as I slipped into my sleeping bag.

Frost jewels were sparkling on the roof of my tent when I awoke next morning. The bass roll of a distant avalanche heralded the rising of the sun. It was a busy day. Time was vital now; in another month the monsoon would be upon us; we must take full advantage of the present fine weather. On the morrow we must establish Camp One.

The local men were paraded before Birnie, and volunteers were called for to work between the Base Camp and Camps One and Two. Thus far they could go without any special equipment save snow-glasses, for Camp One was to be pitched at a height of only 16,500 feet, and Camp Two at 18,500 feet. For the work of helping our Darjeeling men to establish the higher camps, six additional men were selected. These were doled out with the same warm clothing as supplied to the Darjeeling men.

The local men were now more cheery and confident than they had been at the outset. Even old Pomo ventured a smile – after he had been warned that any more grousings would ensure his instant dismissal. We could not afford to include an agitator in our little army.

The plan of attack was as follows. Our first object was to establish an Advanced Base Camp. At what height this would be depended on the condition of the mountain and the weather. We hoped, however, that it would be at a height of over 20,000 feet, and if conditions permitted, on Meade's Col, 23,500 feet. Relays of unequipped men were to work between the Base Camp and Camp Two, bringing up food and fuel, and relays of equipped men between Camp Two and the Advanced Base, until the latter had been fuelled and provisioned for at least a month. During the period while this was being done, the climbers would be acclimatising steadily to altitude. When this Advanced Base Camp was established we should be in a strong enough besieging position and capable of lasting out long periods of bad weather without having to retreat far down the mountain at the expense of valuable time and acclimatisation. Indeed, it would not be of vital consequence if, owing to bad weather, communications between the Base Camp and Advanced Base Camp broke down completely once the latter had been well stocked with provisions and fuel. We were even prepared to dig ourselves ice caves similar to those made and utilised so successfully by the Bavarians on Kangchenjunga.

As a halt at Camp One for acclimatisation was unnecessary we were to push on after one night there and establish Camp Two. At Camp Two, we were to remain some days to acclimatise before pushing on to Camp Three. At Camp Three there would be another halt for acclimatisation before pushing on to Camp Four, and the same would apply to Camps Four and Five. We must not rush Kamet. Success depended on acclimatisation to altitude. Even the temptation of pushing on owing to good weather must be resisted until we were acclimatised.

It was arranged that, on June 8, Greene, Holdsworth, Shipton and myself, with 36 men, including Lewa, Budhibal Gurung, and 12 high-camp men, were to establish Camp One. Directly this was done, 25 local men were to return to the Base Camp, leaving the remaining 11 men to continue with us to Camp Two. Birnie and Beauman were to remain at the Base Camp, and, on the same day that the advance party established Camp Two, ascend to Camp One with the 25 local men, carrying more loads. Twenty yaks and jhobus were to be retained by the expedition and kept on the nearest pastures, to graze until they were wanted again.

Both our Gurkhas were keen to go high. We told them that, if they did, they would have to carry loads, as we could not afford any passengers. To this they agreed with enthusiasm, and spent the remainder of the afternoon practising the use of rope and ice axe on the snow slopes around the camp. Meanwhile, Holdsworth and Shipton ascended a small eminence of 17,230 feet which stands near the junction of the East Kamet and Raikana Glaciers, from which they obtained a view of the East Kamet Glacier, up which we had to go to reach the foot of Kamet.

Our plan was simple, but, like all Himalayan plans, depended for its success on the weather. We watched the sky anxiously that evening, but the sun dipped into a cloudless west, flooding peak and snowfield with a peaceful rose. Even Greene's presumptuous announcement that any party he accompanied was always favoured with fine weather failed to arouse the wrath of the gods, and we turned in with high hopes of the morrow.

CHAPTER TEN

Avalanche on the East Kamet Glacier

JUNE 8 dawned brilliantly. The first task was the correct allotment of loads. Among our local men were some whose ambition was to carry a lighter load than their fellows. If they could escape observation with an empty box instead of a full one, they would do so without any qualms of conscience, believing, like children, that work existed only to be evaded. If they were not detected, well and good, the sahibs were to blame, but if they *were* detected they shrugged their shoulders philosophically, grinned broadly, and accepted without question a heavy load. We had already caught out one young man, who had been apparently bowed down beneath a load of empty petrol tins and food boxes. But now we were wary, and Birnie lined the men up and inspected every load.

Thanks to the muddling of Alam Singh, who had not understood properly which loads were to be taken and which left at the Base Camp, it was not until the sun was high in the sky that we bade farewell to Birnie and Beauman and set out for Camp One.

The snow was soft, and Holdsworth demonstrated the utility of ski on the Raikana Glacier; where Greene, Shipton and I sank in above the tops of our boots, he was able to slide along the surface.

From the Base Camp we slanted diagonally across the glacier, until we found ourselves beneath the cliffs of the little peak climbed the previous day by Shipton and Holdsworth.

It was grillingly hot, and a fierce sun beat down upon us with a glare that absorbed our energy like blotting paper. But if the snow was soft, it was at least consistent, and we advanced steadily.

Below its junction with the East Kamet Glacier the Raikana Glacier is concealed beneath a wilderness of moraine mounds, but these were now, for the most part, snow-covered. We had not expected to find so much snow, and we hoped that the tardy spring presaged a summer of exceptional fineness. Himalayan snow melts and evaporates at an astonishing rate, and the sun was now hard at work. Boulders the size of cottages were beginning to appear from beneath their winter covering; ice and snow were being stripped from the cliffs, and tumbling to the glacier in miniature avalanches, the ice with a silvery tinkle and the snow with a heavier thud.

We pressed on eagerly, anxious to obtain a view of the East Kamet Glacier. We turned a corner of the 17,230-foot. peak and saw the glacier spread out before us. At first sight it was not possible to appreciate Doctor Longstaff's reluctance to traverse it. Where we stood the glacier was at least a mile broad and only minor rock or snow avalanches could fall from the peaks on either side of it. Indeed, the mountains bounding the glacier to the north had long, unimpressive rubble-covered slopes which could easily be walked up. But some five miles higher the glacier narrowed to a gorge, less than half a mile wide. Here again the peaks bounding its northern side were gently inclined; those bounding its southern side were of a very different nature. Here was a mountain wall typical of the Himalaya. Six thousand feet above the glacier rises the range culminating in Mana Peak, 23,862 feet. It is a range that bears a slight resemblance in outline to the range bounding the south-eastern side of the Lauterbrunnen Valley, in the Bernese Oberland, the northern side of which forms one of the greatest mountain walls in the Alps. But there the resemblance ends. The angle of the Mana Wall is not Swiss, but Himalayan. Owing to plasticity induced by temperature range, Himalayan ice can cling to rocks set at a terrifically steep angle. Had this wall been in the Alps, where, owing to a lesser temperature range, ice is of a more brittle nature, there would have been few, if any, hanging glaciers adhering to the rocks. As it was, the precipices were crowned with walls of ice hundreds of feet thick, some as clean cut as though chiselled by an expert mason, others broken and tottering, with fantastic towers and pinnacles leaning precariously over the cliffs. It was a place that reminded me vividly of the Nepal side of Kangchenjunga, for here were the same forces held in leash ready at any moment to sweep the precipices in avalanches of ice-blocks weighing tens of thousands of tons, the momentum of which is sufficient to carry them far across the level glacier beneath. Even as we gazed, there came a deep growl that swelled to a thunderous roll.

Yet, the danger was not so great as I had expected to find. Ice avalanches and large ones must be expected to fall into the East Kamet Glacier, but it takes an avalanche of Kangchenjunga calibre to sweep a glacier over half a mile wide and although there were hanging glaciers fully capable of discharging avalanches sufficiently large to do this, there were no ice-walls so huge as those that defend Kangchenjunga and avalanches that traverse the breadth of the East Kamet Glacier can seldom fall. He who ascends the East Kamet Glacier must take a chance, but it is a fair and not an unjustifiable chance.

From the junction of the East Kamet and Raikana Glaciers we passed across to the northern side of the former glacier. It was irritating travelling. We were either climbing up the side of a moraine mound, or descending into the hollow between two of them. It must have taken us well over an hour to march a mile.

Along the northern side of the glacier stretched a convenient side moraine on the crest of which we were able to walk with comparative ease. Side moraines are a boon to the Himalayan mountaineer, as they enable him to avoid wearisome detours and ascents. Another useful line of least resistance is a trough between the glacier and the mountainside formed by the sun's heat and radiation from the rocks.

Here and there, the way along the sharp crest of the moraine was barred by great boulders many of which were so ill balanced and unstable that circumspection was needed when traversing beneath them.

We lunched on some slabs of Kamet's red granite. How many decades had passed since these rocks formed a part of the great mountain we were assailing? Time and weather are pulling the noblest mountains to destruction, but this destruction is so gradual that centuries hence, when civilisation as we know it now has crumbled to dust, the great peaks of the Himalaya will challenge the hardihood of man. After lunch we basked in the sun, watching lazily between half-closed eyelids the play of light and shadow on the peaks.

Continuing on our way, we tramped along the broken crest of the moraine until we came to a hollow in the mountainside just above the glacier, which the local men affirmed was the camping-site of "Kellas Sahib". Now it was half filled with snow, and we pitched our tents on a rock-strewn slope above it.

The local men were in fine fettle, and, putting down their loads, grinned farewell and started off for the Base Camp, chattering gaily among themselves. It seemed scarcely possible that they were the sullen, dispirited creatures we had engaged at Niti. They strode along the crest of the moraine as though they were at the beginning and not at the end of a day's work. We had won their confidence.

Platforms were constructed for the tents, but, before the tents had been pitched, slate-coloured clouds poured down the glacier, bringing a biting wind and a drift of snowflakes. The snowstorm was a mild, desultory affair, and at sunset the clouds rolled back, disclosing peaks wedging a cold sky of greenish purple. A solitary avalanche roared like a questing lion; the stars blazed forth; frost gripped the snowfields; the last zephyr of wind died away – and the world knew silence.

We supped luxuriously in our sleeping bags. Fortunately, Achung had been relegated to the Base Camp. We had parted from him without regret. His cooking of late had reached the ultimate zero of inefficiency, and no makeshift cooking on the mountain could be worse than his. As luck would have it, both Nima Dorje and Ondi displayed an unexpected talent for cooking, and the former at least should go far in that abused but profitable calling. Their inventiveness that evening was not taxed, for we supped off pemmican soup, tinned fish, fruit and biscuits. At periodic intervals, the broad countenance of the Old Soldier inserted itself between the flaps of my tent and his horny hand passed in some fresh delicacy. When the idea happened to occur to him, he would pull an *exceptionally* greasy rag from his pocket and solemnly wipe my knife and fork upon it.

Supper was followed by a steaming cup of "Ovaltine", and the last thing I remember was a bottle, which inserted itself at regular intervals into my tent. I believe its career ended in Greene's tent, where its remaining contents were taken care of until the following morning. As an example of the implicit confidence reposed by the layman in the medical profession, this deserves to be recorded.

A miniature snowstorm falling on to my face rudely awakened me next morning. The sun had risen, and its warm rays, striking the tent, were detaching the ice-cakes adhering to the inside of it, formed by the condensation and freezing of my breath.

We had decided the previous evening that an early start was undesirable. This decision was dictated by the possible danger of avalanches falling into the trench-like East Kamet Glacier. In my own experience, I have often noted that the greatest ice avalanches fall during the early hours of the day and some of these *within a few minutes of the sun first touching the peaks*. The explanation for this possibly lies in the fact that, though the downward movement of the hanging glacier due to gravity is constant, the internal tension of the ice is affected considerably by temperature change. Thus, a hanging glacier will continue to move down over the edge of a precipice during the night, but, though a large mass of it may be in unstable equilibrium, it will remain bound to the stable ice by frost. It often happens, however, that the first touch of the sun is sufficient to shatter the frost shackles and detach the unstable mass of ice. Frost is also responsible for detaching ice avalanches in the evening. In this case, the freezing and consequent expansion of any water in cracks may just give the necessary outward impetus to a mass of ice already on the point of reaching unstable equilibrium. If the mountaineer is forced to expose himself to the risk of ice avalanches, by traversing beneath hanging glaciers, he can minimise that risk considerably by avoiding the hours of dawn and sunset. Ice avalanches may occur at any hour of the day or night, but they are more likely to occur during these two periods. Two Himalayan expeditions have, however, gone some way towards teaching me that it is seldom wise to compare alpine conditions with Himalayan conditions. In the Alps, the number of avalanches falling at dawn and sunset is markedly greater than at any other period of the day, but on Himalayan peaks, where hanging glaciers are twice as thick as Alpine hanging glaciers, this is not so evident, as the ice is not so affected by temperature change. During the monsoon season, however, when the air temperature is appreciably higher than it is during the spring and autumn, avalanches are constantly occurring at all hours of the day and night and I am convinced that during that period of the year the traverse of the East Kamet Glacier would be very dangerous. Had we followed out the plan that was at one time mooted of attempting Kamet during August, it is more than likely that we should have run a grave risk. As things turned out, however, the danger during June was negligible, and, as was subsequently proved, our porters were able to proceed safely between Camps One and Two during all hours of the day. By starting early, when the snow was hard frozen they were able to traverse the East Kamet Glacier with the minimum of effort and so quickly that any slight additional risk they may have incurred by ascending it during the dawn hour was more than compensated for by the speed with which they traversed the dangerous area.

We left Camp One at 8.30 a.m. Descending slopes of loose rubble and frozen earth, we reached the East Kamet Glacier. Walking was considerably easier than on the previous day. Instead of being forced to toil up and down in a wilderness of moraine mounds, we progressed easily over the gentle undulating surface of the glacier, having to make only an occasional detour to avoid a crevasse or heap of boulders.

It was a lovely morning, and so long as we went reasonably slowly we could appreciate it to the full. But presently, when the snow, at first frozen hard, became softened by the sun, we sank in several inches at every step and pleasure degenerated into toil. Holdsworth, however, slid easily along upon his ski. Why were the whole party not equipped with this labour-saving device? The answer is that someone must make a track for the heavily laden porters. 'But,' argue my skiing friends, 'if ski conserve the energy, they should be taken by the Europeans, who will require all that energy at some later period.' One way out of this impasse is unladen porters who make the track for their fellows. The obvious disadvantage of this is that there are extra mouths to feed.

Holdsworth considers that these men's loads might be distributed among the Europeans, but in that case the advantage of ski becomes doubtful. Another suggestion is that every porter should carry a pair of short light ski, but this is open to the disadvantage that all the porters must know how to ski, and they would have to carry their ski up places where skiing is impossible in addition to their loads. I doubt also whether a Himalayan porter, who carries his load by a headband, would find ski practicable. Recently, there has come into prominence a snow raquette-cum-ski. I hope that some Himalayan expedition will give these a trial, for they appear to be an excellent compromise between ordinary snow-raquettes and ski. Long stretches of suitable skiing snow are, however, seldom encountered on the greater Himalayan peaks.

We halted to rest on some boulders. The backward view was an interesting one. We gazed down the East Kamet Glacier to the jumble of moraine mounds at its confluence with the Raikana Glacier. We were now as high as the little peak climbed by Shipton and Holdsworth. Next to it on the range of peaks forming the southerly retaining wall of the East Kamet Glacier was a graceful rock peak over 20,000 feet high, the dark precipices of which provided a welcome relief to the eye after the monotonous glare of the snow. This glare would, we expected, soon mutilate our countenances, and to counteract its ravages we generously smeared our faces with a special cream the Brick-red colour of which is said to eliminate the ultraviolet rays of the sun at high altitudes. So efficacious was this preparation that we experienced none of the facial misery usually inseparable from high-altitude mountaineering.

Above our resting-place the East Kamet Glacier narrowed abruptly into a huge gorge. Although we were nearly half a mile from this gorge, the great peaks rising 6,000 feet above it seemed almost to lean over us, and their precipices of reddish granite crowned with gleaming masses of ice threatened us with destruction. Suddenly, there came a thunderous roar, a small puff of snow-dust hung suspended for a few moments from the crest of a precipice and gradually melted away. The echoes reverberated sullenly from side to side of the glacier gorge, dying away at last in the distant recesses of Kamet. Only a small avalanche, a few hundred tons of ice-blocks, ground into powder before reaching the glacier, but it set my nerves quivering, for fresh in my memory was that terrible avalanche that killed poor Chettan on Kangchenjunga.[1] Was it a warning shot, fired across our bows, or was it the scornful laugh of the mountain gods at sight of this pitiful little cavalcade of men about to dare their stronghold?

We trudged onwards. It was heavy going. In that glacial trench the sun's heat,

[1] *The Kangchenjunga Adventure*, pp. 256–9.

reflected upon us from either side by snow-clad peaks, was almost suffocating. Our bodies and minds became the unwilling slaves to that insidious drug, glacier lassitude. But glacier lassitude, if it saps the energy from the limbs and renders each forward step a mental as well as a physical effort, has at least one good thing to be said for it – it dulls appreciation for danger. We looked at the wall above us and its suspended bastions of gleaming ice with indifference. The beauties and grandeurs of the immense defile through which we were passing appealed not one whit. Our eyes lifted not heavenwards, but sought the featureless snow before us. Our thoughts were concentrated, not on completing the day's work, but on the next halting-place where we might rest our leaden limbs. We longed for shade, but a sun almost vertically overhead scorched us relentlessly.

The distance to be covered was no more than five miles, but it seemed interminable. At last we reached the point where the glacier bends north-westwards. As we turned the corner, Kamet appeared. Lassitude was momentarily forgotten as we gazed upon it. From the Base Camp we had seen only the summit peeping over the nearer ridges, but now the mountain appeared in all its grandeur. The eastern precipice, nearly 7,000 feet in height, which falls in one sweep from the summit to the East Kamet Glacier, confronted us. Our gaze passed up and over escarpments of rock towards the level plateau of Meade's Col, and then continued to mount slopes of snow and ice to the summit. How remote was that final point! A small, gossamer-like cloud formed suddenly, rested there for a few instants, and was absorbed again into the deep blue sky.

Beyond the bend the glacier rises steeply. At the foot of the slope is a level plain. This was littered with ice-blocks. Many of them, weighing tons, had been cast right across the glacier, and it needed but an upward glance at the tottering walls of ice, thousands of feet higher, to assure us that others might be expected to fall at any instant. We did not linger, but toiled on. If this plain formed a bowling-ground for the gods, we could only hope that they would not make us their jacks.

We crossed the danger-zone and commenced to ascend the slope above. This was the most trying part of the day. In spite of the steps that we stamped out in the sodden snow, the porters were making very heavy weather of it and were halting every two or three hundred yards to rest. One man was so affected by glacier lassitude that he was unable to carry his load. Lewa refused to abandon it, and with indomitable energy insisted on shouldering it *in addition to his own*. He was already carrying about 50 lbs., though, being sirdar, he was not expected to carry anything. Thus, he bore on his back a total load, in the neighbourhood of 100 lbs.

I went on ahead to look for a camping-site. A block of rock the size of a cottage formed an excellent shelter for a kitchen. Water was obtainable from a hollow close by. This was important, as we must conserve our fuel, for the amount of heat required to melt snow is almost as much as the amount of heat required to raise water from freezing point to boiling point.

I expected to find that the porters after their heavy day were too tired to return to Camp One as arranged, but after a drink of tea they quickly recovered their vitality, and at about 4 p.m. Lewa, Budhibal Gurung and ten porters set off back to Camp One.

We, hoped that the Base Camp party, consisting of Birnie, Beauman, and 21 porters carrying rations for two days, had arrived at Camp One the same day. I felt doubtful however, whether the local men would be able to stand up to the gruelling march from Camp One to Camp Two, a march that had tired our strongest Darjeeling men, so I sent back a note by Lewa advising an early start when the snow of the glacier was hard and frozen, for the danger of ice avalanches had proved far less than anticipated. I also suggested that if, on the morrow, it was found impossible to get all the loads to Camp Two in one day, the men who were too tired to carry them the whole distance should dump them as far up the East Kamet Glacier as possible. Actually this proved unnecessary. We had yet to learn beneath the unprepossessing and unwashed exteriors of our local men beat valiant and strong hearts.

After Lewa, the best load-carrier among our Darjeeling porters was Passang, Greene's servant, who lumbered along with an ungainly gait. No one would credit him with intelligence or initiative, but, as Greene said, 'What he lacked in grey matter was more than compensated for by his prodigious strength.' On this occasion he arrived at the camping site no less than fifty minutes before any of the other porters. I fear that Passang's lot was not altogether a happy one. As I have said, he was not conspicuous for his intelligence, and for this reason his leg was pulled unmercifully by his comrades. I shall always remember Passang as the good-natured and willing horse of the expedition – one who never ventured a complaint, and who conscientiously strove to do his best. As Greene's servant he made many mistakes – he was no Jeeves – but he tried so hard that it was impossible to upbraid him for slow-wittedness. He was a pearl of great price.

Late that afternoon there was a drizzle of snow. Battalions of mist flooding up from the south-west poured over the ridges to the south of Kamet and assembled in the gloomy trench of the East Kamet Glacier. There they remained a sullen army, undecided as to their next move.

The sun passed behind Kamet; the mists rising uneasily from the crests of its ridges were illumined until it seemed that we gazed at some astral body fringed by the flames of the sun's corona. The ice walls of Mana Peak stood out redly like the fortifications of some aerial Verdun* steeped in the blood of stricken attackers.

The lights died. The clouds about Kamet shrank grey and wraith-like into the dusk. The ice walls relapsed from red to a cold, malevolent green. The snows about us assumed a deathly pallor. Frost gripped the world. We crawled into our tents and slipped into our sleeping bags.

Night enwrapped our small camp, her stars glancing down on a scene of stupendous desolation.

* A major battlefield in France in World War I.

CHAPTER ELEVEN

Camp Three: Advanced Base

I SLEPT BADLY, troubled by worrying dreams. The incidents I dreamed of were trivial, yet in my dreams they assumed an absurd importance. Strangely enough, these dreams were very similar to those I used to have on Kangchenjunga. For instance, I dreamt of a rucksack buckle that had broken, or some trivial object that I had lost. But the most worrying dream of all, and one that persistently recurred, was of the porters having got into some difficulty. In this dream I invariably had to stand by, powerless to extricate them from their plight. Such dreams are peculiar to high altitudes, yet, in my case, it was only at heights between 18,000 and 20,000 feet that I was troubled, either on Kangchenjunga or on Kamet. In addition I never felt well at these moderate altitudes, and apart from dreaming, slept badly. At higher camps I dreamt less, slept better and was undoubtedly fitter. It is interesting to note that two weeks later, when I descended to Camp Two from the higher camps, I dreamt exactly as I had done before. Mine is by no means an unusual case, for many Himalayan mountaineers have felt ill at moderate altitudes and some at heights as low as 15,000 feet. Are such things symptomatic of some physiological change that occurs at a certain altitude? Here is an interesting problem for physiologists, and one which may have an important bearing on acclimatisation.

At Camp Two also I was afflicted with jarring headaches for which aspirin proved a certain remedy. These headaches, unlike dreams, did not, however, recur on descending from higher camps to Camp Two; it is probable, therefore, that they were due purely to lack of acclimatisation and not to any physiological change independent of acclimatisation at a certain height.

Next morning we decided to move Camp Two farther up the East Kamet Glacier. This was rendered necessary by the hanging glaciers of Mana Peak. There were no indications that ice avalanches ever swept the whole width of the glacier at this point, but the Himalaya have a habit of producing the exceptional, and at all events the debris of avalanches soon disappears beneath snowfalls. A quarter of a mile farther up the glacier we should be safe from the largest ice avalanches that might fall from Mana Peak.

A good camping site was discovered beneath the rocky slopes of a peak about 21,500 ft., which forms a south-easterly spur of the Abi Gamin East. Above our camp the East Kamet Glacier broadened into a gently sloping plain that extended to the foot of Kamet's eastern precipice. After this plain, the main ice stream of the glacier narrows and bends in a west-south-westerly direction, finally widening out again into a series of snowfields, riven by ice-falls, which lead up towards the long western ridge of Mana Peak. One branch of this great reservoir whence the

East Kamet Glacier draws its strength ascends to a well-defined col in the ridge between Kamet and Mana Peak.

Beauman and Birnie turned up in good time. Their local porters were not nearly so tired as we had expected them to be. They had carried heavy loads, and had well earned the extra eight annas each which had been promised them if they went all the way from Camp One to Camp Two. They had left Camp One at 8 a.m. and arrived at Camp Two at 2 p.m.

All the unequipped local men and nine equipped men returned to Camp One the same day to join Lewa and Budhibal Gurung. Birnie reported that arrangements had been made for the relaying of wood and provisions between the Base Camp and Camps One and Two. Camp One was already well stocked with juniper wood. This was important, as wood was disappearing at an alarming rate. That evening we discovered that its rapid disappearance was due to the fact that the Darjeeling men and local men refused to share a common fire. For economy's sake this difficulty had to be adjusted. One of the local men was interrogated by Birnie.

'Why will you not share a fire with the Darjeeling men?' he was asked.

'Because we are of a different religion. They are Buddhists and we are Hindus,' was the reply.

We knew that this was not strictly true, for the Bhotias of northern Garhwal care little for religious differences. The schism was more likely due to a mutual distrust resulting from Lewa's contemptuous attitude towards the local men at Niti; the plaint of religious inequality was a mere excuse. Then Birnie asked a cunning question of the local men.

'How do you cook your food?'

'In cooking-pots,' was the reply.

'But you have none.'

'Oh, as to that, we borrow them from the Darjeeling men,' was the naïve answer.

'Well,' said Birnie, 'how can any devout Hindu refuse to share a fire with an unbeliever and at the same time eat from the pot he has defiled?'

There was no answer to this, and thenceforward our Darjeeling men and our local men shared a common fire. Prejudice and mistrust gradually vanished and were replaced by mutual esteem and respect. Mountains have a knack of bringing men together.

June 11 was a rest-day for everyone with the exception of 12 local men, who, as previously arranged, ascended from the Base Camp and stocked Camp One with wood. During the afternoon a postman arrived with our mail. Men had been specially selected as runners between our camps and the post and telegraph office at Joshimath. These men were well paid, and their reliability justified to the full the confidence reposed in them. We were shocked and saddened to read in the newspapers of Lieutenant-Colonel H.T. Morshead's tragic death in Burma. The association of mountaineering in the past with mountaineering in the present is a very real one. Those who climb the Matterhorn without remembering the pioneers who toiled and struggled against its at one time impregnable defences, and those who can gaze at Kangchenjunga or Everest without a thought for the hopes and fears and tragedies of the past are blind to that essence of the mystical and the romantic in which mountaineering has its roots. In the shadow of Kamet, in the silence and the loneliness about us, we felt that the pioneers who had crossed their "last pass" were watching our progress, even perhaps instilling into us their own determination, and passing on to us the bright torch of their pioneering. If success was to be ours, we should be completing work well begun, and in realising our own ambitions realise theirs.

Although it was a rest-day, Holdsworth's enthusiasm for skiing took him for an excursion up the glacier. I followed on foot for a short distance. I had just erected my cinema camera to take a film of his descent when there was a sudden roar. A mass of ice on the lower slopes of Mana Peak had collapsed and fallen from the edge of a hanging glacier. Its fall left unstable a still larger mass, and even as I watched, an enormous square chunk of ice, the size of a cathedral, slowly lent away from its parent glacier. With deliberate yet irresistible force and with the stateliness of a felled factory chimney, it toppled on to the slope below and, rent into a million fragments, thundered down to the East Kamet Glacier, preceded by whirling clouds of wind-driven snow-dust. Luckily, I had time to train my cine-camera on the spot and obtain a "shot" of the avalanche.

Holdsworth enjoyed an amusing little ski run, but he found the snow heavy and slow. We spent the remainder of the day lounging in the sun. We were already becoming acclimatised and though I slept no better that night and suffered from occasional headaches during the day, I felt my strength increasing so far as walking up hill was concerned.

The weather was none too promising. Snow-showers were frequent after midday, and as the rate at which snow was falling higher up was greater than the rate at which evaporation and melting were taking place, the rocks above 20,000 feet were becoming plastered. This was, however, of no immediate consequence to us, for we knew that the difficult climbing was to be expected *above* Camp Three and we anticipated no difficulty in establishing that camp unless exceptionally heavy snowstorms supervened.

Half a mile above Camp Two a wide snow gully was visible, running up between steep and broken rocks. At first sight it appeared an unpromising route to Camp Three, but we knew from Meade's and Morshead's accounts that it formed the only route leading up to the small glacier plateau on which Camp Three had to be pitched. From Camp Two this glacier plateau was invisible, and the precipices into which the gully cut seemed to run up unbroken to a great rock peak forming a buttress of the Eastern Abi Gamin. Were it not for this gully it would be a long and difficult rock climb to reach the glacier plateau. We could distinguish above the glacier plateau, the upper part of a steep rock and ice precipice crowned by a bulge of ice. On this bulge, at 22,000 feet, must be pitched Camp Four. We knew the 1,000-foot precipice of rock and ice between Camps Three and Four to be the crux of the climb so far as reaching Meade's Col was concerned.

With the exception of the difficult section between Camps Three and Four, the route to Meade's Col is a remarkable line of least resistance, and the greatest credit is due to Meade for its discovery. It is the one chink in the armour of a giant.

June 12 dawned brilliantly fine, but in my rough diary of the expedition I wrote 'Too cold to start until the sun reached us at 8.30 a.m. How one longed for it. Temperature 10° Fahrenheit in my tent.'

The first of these references applied to every camp on the mountain. The temperature might not be very low – to a polar explorer 20° or 30° of frost is negligible – but one effect of altitude is to render sluggish the circulation of the blood, so that it is possible to be frost-bitten in but a few degrees of frost. Another difficulty in high-altitude climbing is to induce porters to start off from camp when they are feeling cold, for, although a Sherpa porter feels the cold less than a European, he has not the strength of will nor the detachment of mind to combat what he does feel of it. He is even less able to withstand wind, and nothing paralyses his faculties or knocks all the stuffing out of him so quickly as the pitiless blasts, which sweep the upper regions of the Himalaya. It is scarcely to be wondered at that the Tibetan believes in a cold hell. Whether education will ever overcome these natural and inborn mental disabilities is doubtful. The intelligence of a Sherpa may be quickened, but as long as he glimpses his hell in the cold of the snows, and the wrath of the gods in the storm, he will be fit only to follow, not to lead, on a mountain.*

Greene, Holdsworth, Shipton and I were off soon after 9 a.m. leaving Beauman and Birnie to spend a complete rest day at Camp Two after their strenuous trudge the previous day.

We reached the foot of the gully without difficulty, although the glacier was somewhat rough, and choked crevasses insecurely bridged with snow necessitated small detours. The lower portion of the gully was wide, and filled with snow. The snow was soft, but we mounted with comparative ease. I noted, I must confess with a certain selfish satisfaction, that those on foot were making height more quickly than Holdsworth who was on ski. On the East Kamet Glacier he had had the laugh on us, but slopes of good snow steep enough to necessitate zig-zagging by a ski-runner can be ascended direct by the foot-slogger with less effort.

The gully led upwards into a rocky hollow. Sheer walls of rock rose to the right and to the left. In front, suspended over a low cliff of smooth "boiler-plate" slabs, was the snout of the little glacier covering the plateau on which was to be pitched Camp Three. Only a small quantity of broken-off ice lay at the foot of the snout, suggesting that the downward progression of this glacier is a slow one. The glacier snout was impervious to direct assault, but between it and the cliff to the east was a steep and narrow snow couloir. This couloir formed an obvious line of least resistance, but after a heavy fall of new snow it becomes a natural chute for any avalanches that may fall from the cliffs above. Even under normal conditions it cannot be described as absolutely safe, and as we sat resting on a rock we heard the vicious ping and whirr of a falling stone.

From our resting-place we gazed downwards and outwards between the walls of the gully across the East Kamet Glacier to the dazzling snowfields and icy steeps of Mana Peak. From Camp Two we had been unable to appreciate the vast scale of this mountain, and what we had taken for points on its summit ridge were now disclosed as subsidiary buttresses thousands of feet below the summit. Swelling snowfields, shattered ice-falls, tottering séracs, polished ice-slopes, knife-like edges, curling cornices, and granite precipices such is Mana Peak, one of the noblest and loveliest of mountains.

The snow in the couloir was in good condition, and taking it in turns we

* Subsequent developments soon disproved this theory.

advanced, kicking steps. Increasing shortness of breath, necessitating frequent halts, made us realise that we were climbing now at over 20,000 feet. The couloir was deceptively long, but its angle gradually eased off, and Holdsworth, who had been forced to carry his ski over his shoulder, was able to put them on again.

As we mounted we were aware of a low booming, rushing sound in the cliffs above, like distant breakers on a rocky coast. Now, on gaining the gently sloping surface of the glacier plateau, we were met by a spiteful gust of wind that seized the loose snow and flung it stingingly into our faces. In the couloir we had dripped with sweat, but that first gust of wind seemed to go through our ribs and out of our backs like a rapier-thrust, and we hastily donned every stitch of spare clothing, including balaclava helmets.

The Meade and Kellas expeditions had pitched their camps on or near the crest of the ridge which formed the southernmost retaining wall of the glacier plateau and also the crest of the precipices above the East Kamet Glacier.

It was a stern, hard plod up to the ridge, for we were now sinking above the boots at every step into crusted, powdery snow similar to that met with on Alpine peaks in winter. Shipton was going better than anyone, and broke the trail for most of the way.

As we slowly made height the wind assaulted us more vigorously, and we had to bow our heads to its gusts. The sky darkened, and clouds rushing out of the west brought in their van desultory flakes of snow.

We gained the crest of the ridge and gazed for a few moments at the East Kamet Glacier 1,800 foot below. Then we turned to seek a more sheltered spot for Camp Three. We found it in a snowy valley 200 feet below the crest of the ridge. Here the wind was unable to harry us, and we sat down and rested for a while.

The ascent of nearly 2,000 feet from Camp Two had taken us little more than two hours, a speed indicative of an increasing acclimatisation to altitude. There was no reason, therefore, for deferring the establishing of Camp Three. Whether or not it would be made our Advanced Base Camp depended upon the nature of the difficulties that must be overcome on the 1,000-foot rock and ice face separating the plateau from the top of the ice bulge on which Camp Four had to be pitched. From our resting-place this rock and ice face was in full view. It was heavily plastered with new snow and ice, and its ascent under such conditions was not going to be easy. Even should it prove possible to relay a month's provisions and fuel up to Camp Four the work of doing so would be excessively fatiguing, and might leave our porters incapable of carrying loads to Meade's Col, where we hoped to pitch Camp Five. Also, in the event of a heavy snowstorm, communication with Camp Four might be entirely disrupted for more than a week. But, assuming reasonable weather and a practicable route to the summit, the length of time spent above Camp Three depended upon our ability to acclimatise. Supposing all these things proved satisfactory, a day or two at Camps Four and Five should prove long enough for an attempt on the summit. At all events, the first thing to do was to get as much food and fuel as possible to Camp Three.

We returned to Camp Two in a mild snowstorm. I was suffering from a splitting headache, due, I think, more to wind than altitude, but under the influence of ten grains of aspirin it vanished in less than ten minutes.

The following day, June 13, we set out to establish Camp Three. Birnie volunteered to remain behind at Camp Two, in order to superintend transport arrangements, as another convoy of provisions and fuel was expected from Camp One. We set off gaily, expecting that an ascent of two hours would bring us to the camp, as it had done on the previous day, but now conditions were different. In my diary I wrote, 'Misty snowy day. Very trying. Heavy work for porters. Took hours. Arrived with severe headache. Pitched camp in driving powdery snow.' Much lies behind those terse phrases. The previous day we had ascended at an Alpine speed, but now glacier lassitude had us within its toils. Every step was an effort. We had frequently to halt and pant for breath. Only an inch or so of snow had fallen in the night, and, as we had our steps of the previous day to follow, walking should have been easy, especially as we were not tired from our previous exertions. It was simply and solely the climatic conditions. Sluggish shawls of mist draped the peaks. The air was lifeless. The sun shone through the mist with a blinding glare. Sunglare is particularly unpleasant at high altitudes, and no doubt contributes to lassitude, but the primary cause of the peculiar languor which affects both acclimatised and unacclimatised mountaineers is due to humidity, and, were observations to be taken, I believe they would disclose that it is on days and in places of marked humidity that the Himalayan mountaineer feels at his worst. The maximum humidity in the air is found in hollows and on slopes sheltered from the wind. Directly the mountaineer experiences a breeze or escapes on to a crest of a ridge his languor quickly disappears. When ascending for the first time to the site of Camp Three, a constant draught had been blowing up the gully, but now the air was close, breathless and heavy with water vapour.

It was a hard day for the porters. They cannot have taken less than six hours to make the ascent. The mists closed down upon us as we plodded up the last slope to the camp. The scene was inexpressibly dreary. The snows about us were dull, lustreless, shadowless; dark precipices scowled through rents in the shifting murk; pale green walls of ice seemed to regard us with feline malevolence. Wind rose and powdery snow began to fall heavily as we pitched our tents. I sank into my tent too tired, headachy and listless even to help Holdsworth and Shipton fetch some slabs of rock from the ridge above for our kitchen.

Our little tents were pitched in two regular lines, the snow between which was soon trampled down into a miniature high street. It is curious how the most inhospitable waste can be made homely by the addition of a few tents.

The wind rose in fury, and a blizzard whirled past the camp. We snuggled into our sleeping bags. I started to write a dispatch. But my brain seemed incapable of coherent thought, and preferred to dally lightly with general events rather than concentrate on their detail. So putting down the pencil I lay listening to the hurried tread of the snowflakes on the roof of my tent.

Towards sunset the snowstorm abated and I crawled outside. The scene was wintry in the extreme. Several inches of snow had fallen. The last wisps of grey scud were being absorbed into a cold green sky. In the fading light Kamet's huge precipices were terribly forbidding.

Shipton and I preferred the warmth of the cooking-fire to the coldness of our tents, and sat huddled around it with the porters. At periodic intervals the sinewy arm of Nima Dorje grasping a wooden ladle shot out to serve the "mess of pottage" that constituted our supper. The leaping flames of the juniper fire illuminated the faces of the porters squatting around it. If, in civilisation, I wish to recall the memories of those days in the Himalaya, I have only to sniff the smoke from burning juniper. Still more vivid memories will be recalled by the *taste* of juniper, for most of the things that we cooked over it were impregnated with its acrid smoke. The tea tasted of juniper; the porridge reeked of it; however strong the soup, juniper invariably won.

It was bitterly cold, and as I sat by the fire with the front part of me roasting and the back part of me freezing, I was forcibly reminded of winter evenings spent by the draughty firesides of England. A minute or two of that excellent exercise practised by cab and taxicab drivers revived sluggish circulation, although at that height it was impossible to persist for long.

The green fields of sunset had been long swamped by the dark floods of night as we crept once more into our tents.

CHAPTER TWELVE

Through the Rock Barrier to Camp Four

THE PORTERS WERE in poor shape next morning. Several of them were suffering from the effects of altitude. Among our veterans, the Old Soldier and Ondi were *hors de combat*, whilst Ang Nerbu was groaning from a severe headache. Nima Dorje, Nima and one or two others were their usual cheery selves, but it was obvious that the whole party needed acclimatising before pushing on farther. Personally, I felt reasonably fit, despite a night of broken sleep caused by a rebellious stomach. Beauman, however, was not feeling fit and was not so well acclimatised as were the rest of us.

Unwilling to face the boredom of a day in our tents, Shipton and I started out to prospect the route up the rock and ice precipice leading to the ice bulge on which we proposed to pitch Camp Four. The weather was dull and calm. To reach the foot of the precipice we had to traverse the glacier plateau for perhaps the third of a mile. It was hard work plugging through the soft snow, and we sank in halfway to the knees at every step.

Directly we left camp we began to realise the importance of rhythm in high-altitude mountaineering. Below Camp Three rhythm had mattered little, and we had walked uphill in much the same way as we were accustomed to walk in the Alps, albeit more slowly and with more halts. Apart from the necessity for walking slowly and systematically, it had been unnecessary to keep breathing in time with stepping. But over 20,500 feet we found that if we were to conserve our strength and proceed with the minimum expenditure of energy, we must consciously adopt a rhythm of breathing to stepping. The beneficial effect of rhythm in walking or climbing at high altitudes may be entirely psychological, for Greene told me that he could see no reason why it should be physiologically beneficial, but the fact remains that the adoption of a rhythmical progression benefits a man bodily as well as mentally. A conscious rhythm, of course, implies measured breathing, and measured breathing implies deep breathing. Possibly, therefore, the greater part of the benefit ascribed to rhythmical progression is due to increased oxygenation of the blood. On the other hand, deep breathing alone will not carry a man along with the minimum of effort. Breathing must be attuned to stepping if rhythmical progression is to be maintained with a minimum expenditure of effort.

One of the peculiarities of the Himalaya is that their mountainsides invariably prove to be steeper than they look, unless they have been viewed exactly in profile. This optical delusion is fostered by the vast scale on which Himalayan peaks are built, and consequent foreshortening; it is also due in part to an exceedingly, clear atmosphere. From the camp the rock and ice precipice had appeared moderately steep, and its only obvious difficulty was its plaster of freshly fallen snow. Now, as we approached the foot of it, it became more formidable every moment. What had appeared from the camp to be rock slabs set at an easy angle became rock slabs set at a steep angle, whilst steep but apparently climbable rocks were resolved into vertical or overhanging cliffs. The best route seemed at first sight to start from the left and then slant diagonally upwards to the right across the face to a point about half-way up it, then straight up the final slopes of snow or ice to the right of the steepest portion of the ice bulge.

We accordingly started to ascend a preliminary snowslope. The snow had been disagreeable enough on the glacier plateau, but it was even worse here, for wind had hardened its surface into a breakable crust. Our lack of acclimatisation was made evident by our breathlessness and need of frequent halts. As we slowly gained height, the view ahead of us appeared more and more unpromising. Could we but gain a ledge running across the face to a rocky corner the route we had planned should be possible. But how to gain the ledge? For it was separated from the snow-slopes up which we were climbing by a smooth and repellent rock cliff 100 feet in height. Even if the ledge were gained, further progress would be by no means easy, for it was laden with snow, piled at an angle of over 50°, whilst the appearance of the granite slabs projecting from the snow showed plainly that an icy glaze must be expected. Doubtless any pessimism we felt was induced by altitude, but we returned to camp as disgruntled as the weather, which ushered us into our tents with a brutal flurry of snow.

During our peregrinations above the camp Birnie had ascended from Camp Two with porters carrying food and fuel. Thus if our preliminary reconnaissance of the route to Camp Four had been unsuccessful we could at least console ourselves with the thought that time was not being wasted … thanks to Birnie's painstaking work, our position at Camp Three was being steadily consolidated.

June 15 dawned fine. We decided to make a determined attempt to find a route to Camp Four. Between the ice bulge and the red cliffs of Abi Gamin East the glacier flowing downwards from Meade's Col ends abruptly in an ice-fall which overhangs the rocks in walls of ice two or three hundred feet high. Occasionally, masses of the glacier are detached, which fall in cataracts of ice-blocks to the glacier plateau beneath. Our camp was well out of range of these avalanches, but it would be extremely perilous to venture upon the precipice beneath this hanging glacier. Between the hanging glacier and the cliffs of Abi Gamin East there was a breach formed by a long couloir which connected the glacier plateau to the upper slopes. In its lower portion this couloir was too steep to contain snow, whilst shelving rock slabs sloped awkwardly outwards. It appeared, however, as if this initial pitch could be avoided by an upward traverse from the right into the snow-filled bed of the couloir. From this point the couloir appeared practicable throughout its entire remaining length. Assuming safe snow conditions, the most serious objection to this route was the risk of stones falling from the great cliffs of Abi Gamin East into the couloir. From the camp these cliffs appeared to be built of firm material, and their reddish granite showed little signs of disintegration, whilst the glacier plateau at the foot of the couloir was unscored by falling stones. Owing, however, to the recent snowstorms which had probably concealed traces of debris, we could not be certain that this risk did not exist. The chief advantage of this route over a more direct route up the cliffs to the upper slopes was that it was less steep.

The party that left the camp consisted of Shipton, Holdsworth, Greene, Birnie and myself, with Nima Dorje as our only porter.

Crossing the glacier plateau was scarcely less trying than it had been on the previous day, for its concave formation caused it to radiate sun glare, and we felt like flies in the focus of a burning-glass.

At the foot of the rocks Birnie, who was not feeling too fit and who was still one day behind us in acclimatisation, decided to return to camp. Once more we discovered that we had been deceived as to the apparent angle of our proposed route. The couloir was much steeper than it had appeared from the camp. Its lower pitch of shelving slabs had, from the camp, appeared possible to climb but preferably avoided by an easy sloping terrace to the right. Actually, the lower pitch was completely unassailable, whilst the easy looking terrace to the right resolved itself into a steeply sloping shelf covered with snow banked at a fearsome angle.

We started up the shelf. If the snow had been avalanchy we should have turned back at once, but, despite the recent bad weather, it was reasonably firm. Its surface consisted of the loose powdery snow, which had fallen during yesterday's storm, but the snow beneath this had been consolidated by sun and frost and the boot could be plunged into it to make a firm step.

The angle of the banked-up snow was such that when standing upright, the slope could be touched with the outstretched hand. A slip was not to be thought of, and we moved one at a time with extreme caution, plunging our ice axes in up to their heads and belaying the rope whenever possible.

At the outset we were scarcely gratified to observe a block of rock the size of our portable gramophone fall from the cliffs of Abi Gamin East into the couloir, down which it rolled at a terrific rate before plunging into a patch of soft snow. This in itself was a damning indictment of the couloir, but before turning back we decided to satisfy ourselves beyond all reasonable doubt that no safe route could be made up it.

The shelf merged gradually into the bed of the couloir, which above its initial rock pitch was some fifty yards broad. It was no longer possible to drive in the ice axe to its head – there was ice beneath the snow. Had it not been for the security afforded by rocks around which the rope could be securely hitched, we should have turned back. The sun shone with relentless vigour upon our backs and our pace was funereal.

The angle steepened still more. Bidding Shipton to anchor himself securely, I advanced slowly up the snow, utilising the rocks as handholds. Turning a corner, I found that the rocks petered out, and that it was necessary to traverse the mouth of a subsidiary couloir descending from the precipices of Abi Gamin East. Wandering down this couloir was a ragged furrow caused by the falling rock we had seen. Here and there this furrow disclosed the gleam of ice. Plunging in my ice axe before me, I found that about a foot of soft avalanchy snow covered the ice. To have ventured upon such a slope would have been suicidal. If further evidence was needed as to the impracticability of the main couloir as a route we had merely to glance upwards to where in its upper portion it steepened still more. There the soft snow had slipped away altogether, disclosing a sheet of black ice hundreds of feet in length.

I glanced downwards. The couloir allowed little latitude for life but an overwhelming margin in favour of death and an unchecked slip or an avalanche would bring about certain destruction.

My companions' countenances expressed feelings similar to my own. The sooner we were out of the couloir the better, for the tropical sun was softening the snow every instant. Only Nima Dorje seemed unaware of the general pessimism, and his broad grin came up from the depths like a fine day in an English summer.

It was with considerable relief that two hours later, after a careful descent we found ourselves once more in safety on the glacier plateau. Our proposed route up the couloir had proved a fiasco, yet, curiously enough, we marched back to camp feeling by no means dispirited. As Shipton remarked, 'We have had a grand day's mountaineering.' It was our first piece of serious mountaineering on Kamet, and we felt that we had pulled, as a team should pull – together.

The sole alternative left to us now was the direct ascent of the precipice to the ice bulge. We were becoming well acclimatised – our strenuous efforts in the couloir had been an invaluable aid to this end – and it was with a certain feeling of determination that we set out next morning, June 16, to solve the problem of forcing a route to the site of Camp Four.

Opinions as to the most promising line of attack were not unanimous, so we decided to divide into two parties. Shipton and Holdsworth were to attempt a narrow couloir just to the left of that part of the precipice liable to be raked by falling ice from the hanging glacier above. This route had the initial disadvantage of commencing with a steep pitch formed by several jammed boulders, which had wedged themselves into the narrow neck of the couloir. Snow had piled up on this obstruction, and the effects of sun and frost had combined to form a bulge of green ice. From the bulge there projected one large boulder weighing a ton or more, the stability of which appeared doubtful. Higher, however, the route was more promising, and the couloir should take them a long way up the precipice. Leaving Shipton and Holdsworth to find a solution to this problem, Birnie, Greene and I turned our attention to the snow and rocks on the left of the couloir. The snow here was soft, but its consistency was not such as to render it liable to avalanche. Later in the season, when the precipice is free of snow, its broken granite slabs must afford a comparatively easy scramble. Now, every hold was masked treacherously by powdery snow, whilst an icy glaze on the slabs made extreme caution imperative. The work of clearing away snow from the holds with the gloved hand or the ice axe was slow and tedious. The first fifteen feet must have taken us as many minutes to climb. Even when the holds were discovered and cleared, raising the body by them was no easy matter. As Birnie and Greene followed, they improved the holds by scraping away additional snow or ice with their axes. We were now well acclimatised to altitude, but what would in the Alps have ranked as a simple piece of gymnastics was an effort that taxed the strength of both heart and lungs at 21,000 feet.

Above these preliminary rocks we found ourselves in a steep shallow couloir filled with snow. Climbing here was hard work, but not technically difficult. At the outset we trod the slope with extreme caution, but, although soft, it was not in a dangerous condi-tion and our feet plunged through a layer of loose powdery snow to firm consolidated snow beneath. Breaking the trail was an arduous business, and my companions must have chafed inwardly at my slowness, although their patience was commendable.

Toiling upwards, we reached the foot of a rocky wall cutting across the couloir. There was no avoiding this, for an outflanking movement was impossible – it had to be climbed. The wall was not more than 20 feet high, but it must have taken nearly half an hour to surmount. What rocks showed through the snow consisted entirely of granite slabs. Loose powdery snow had to be shovelled away with hand or axe. I retain vivid memories of the place. There was a splayed-out shallow groove from which the snow had to be cleared. The holds disclosed were barely sufficient. The upward movement was an awkward one, the landing on a sloping glacis of rock, snow and ice still more awkward. Friction was at a discount, and temporary exhaustion due to altitude tended to upset my balance. It was a great feeling to haul myself over the top, and plunge the axe up to the head in the firm snow above.

After my own heavings and strugglings it was somewhat disconcerting to see Greene ascend after a few moments' pause with leisurely elegance. True, the hard work of clearing the holds of snow and rendering the place climbable had been done, but Greene's six and a half feet of height, combined with a proportionately long reach, enables him to grasp holds far beyond the reach of ordinary mortals. Another stretch of snow followed, studded with small rocks. These rocks were of a friendlier nature than the smooth slabs below, and were broken into great blocks piled one on the other. Snow and ice had been stripped from them by the sun, and it was a joy to grasp their clean-cut edges and feel the nailed boot grind on their honest ledges. The rocks brought us with little difficulty to an easier snow-slope forming the crest of a broad ill-defined ridge. We sank thankfully down into the snow. It was the first place we had come to where a rest was possible on the precipice – and the going had been strenuous.

From our resting-place we gazed down to the glacier plateau across which we had trudged in the morning. The slopes fell away beneath us at a terrific angle. We had climbed them, and could climb them again, but what about the porters? Under such difficult conditions it would be no easy matter for them, even though ropes were fixed on all the difficult sections.

But worries as to the future could not long predominate during that few minutes of delicious repose. I found my gaze wandering dreamily along the irregular track we had scrawled across the glacier plateau to the dark blob of Camp Three, the sole evidence of man in a seemingly unending expanse of ice, snow and rock. My gaze passed over it and beyond, across the unseen trench of the East Kamet Glacier, from which little clouds were nosing upwards to the icy ramparts of Mana Peak, and still farther over range upon range to the violet hazes of the south where towering thunder-clouds were massing for their daily march along the foothills.

We heaved ourselves to our feet and turned once more to our task. Above, the snow-slopes on which we stood the granite precipice rose proudly. There was no climbing it; it was overhanging and impervious to direct assault. Somehow it must be turned; not to the left, where the rocks overhung, but to the right, where a slanting shelf piled steeply with snow led up to a corner. Had the snow not been in safe condition, the traverse of this shelf would have been impossible, but sun and frost had done their work well, and the substratum of snow was firmly consolidated.

We gained the corner and congregated on an almost level slab of rock. The next few feet reminded me vaguely of a section on the well-known North Climb up the Pillar Rock in Cumberland, known as the "stomach traverse". A slab some 12 feet high, slanting up to the right across the corner, had to be climbed. The slab presented no difficulty once a load of snow masking it had been cleared away, but the awkward angle at which it sloped outwards over the precipice to the right induced me to utilise a crack on the left into which I inserted my left knee and safely wriggled upwards in a painful and serpentine-like fashion. Later, when the snow had all been cleared away and fresh holds disclosed, the ascent of the slab was a surprisingly easy matter.

As we gained the easier rocks above the slab we heard voices, and discerned Shipton and Holdsworth on a snowslope to the right of us. We also noted with satisfaction that no impassable obstacle intervened between us and the top of the ice bulge on which Camp Four had to be placed.

Broken rock and a shallow gully filled with snow, brought us to the foot of the final slopes of snow and ice leading up to the bulge. There was no room to sit until we had scraped the snow away from a rock. This done we were able to investigate the edible contents of our rucksacks. But our lunch was marred by the activity of Shipton and Holdsworth who were now immediately above us. They decided that they had gone far enough and would join us. Descending the snow-slopes they dislodged masses of snow, which bounded down and bombarded us ruthlessly. They brought with them the news that, although the wedged stone in the ice of the gully they had ascended had proved perfectly safe, it was only after some difficult climbing that they had conquered the pitch. Above the pitch they had climbed, for the most part, up very steep snow. They were doubtful as to the feasibility of getting porters up by their route, and, as we felt the same pessimism about ours, we all agreed that it was essential to discover a route which, when roped up, would afford a relatively easy ascent for laden porters.

The slope down which Shipton and Holdsworth had descended consisted of ice overlaid with firm snow well frozen to the ice. But, above their highest point the snow thinned until it petered out on a forbidding slope of blue-black ice 300-feet high. To cut a staircase up this ice-slope was going to take time.

The afternoon clouds had blown up and flakes of snow were falling as we commenced to descend. The sole possibility of finding an easier route lay in making a downward traverse along a slanting shelf from the first resting-place on our upward route. This possibility we decided to investigate, although Shipton and I, remembering the view we had previously obtained of the precipice when we first prospected it, did not feel optimistic as to a satisfactory route being worked out.

As we had plenty of rope with us, we decided to leave as much as possible fixed to the precipice. A piton was driven into the rock at the upper resting-place and a long length of rope let down to the foot of the corner, the sloping slab of which was not easy to a laden man. Another length of rope was placed along the snow-covered shelf below the corner.

From the lower resting-place the route along the shelf did not, at first sight, appear promising. The banked-up snow on the shelf was exceedingly steep, whilst beneath the shelf the rocks fell sheer for 100 feet to the lower snow-slopes up which Shipton and I had made our reconnaissance. If only this cliff could be climbed, all would be well. But direct descent was hopeless, for the granite slabs were smooth and devoid of holds. Our one chance lay in finding a break in the cliff below the far end of the shelf.

The snow on the shelf was similar to that on the shelf leading up to the corner, and, although very steep, was in excellent condition. Save where it lay thinly over slabs, the ice axe could be plunged into it up to the head, and the rope firmly belayed.

Soon I had run out the whole length of the 100-foot rope to which I was attached. Below the point where I stopped a slabby section of no more than thirty feet separated the shelf from easy slopes of snow leading to the glacier plateau, but they were unclimbable slabs, smooth and repellent. Shipton came along and joined me, and I descended a few feet to investigate whether there was any possibility of climbing them, but as nothing short of a rope ladder would suffice, I returned. The sole remaining possibility was to traverse the shelf to its extreme end, though from where we stood the rock face appeared higher and, if anything, steeper than that immediately below us.

Leaving Shipton securely anchored, I continued traversing the shelf, The snow held well, and only in one place where some slab of rock lay a foot or so beneath it was the foot not able to make a secure step. Above me the red precipice rose sheer, and once I heard the whirr of a falling stone. On the shelf, however, there was little danger from stones, for the precipice deflected them outwards.

The shelf ended against a minor buttress of the overhanging precipice. Suddenly, and unexpectedly, I noticed a narrow snow-filled couloir between the rocks of the shelf and the buttress. It was an obvious and easy route between the lower snow-slopes and the shelf. Here was the last link in the route between Camp Three and Camp Four. The problem was solved! I could not restrain a delighted shout to the others. The reason for our not having previously noticed this couloir was that from the highest point reached on our first reconnaissance the couloir is not to be seen; it is cunningly concealed by the buttress, and the effect when the shelf is seen from below is of a smooth unbroken rock wall running across the whole width of the face beneath it. It was the first time in my experience that anything Himalayan had proved possible when it looked impossible, and I felt it to be a happy omen.

Pitons were driven in at either end of the shelf and a handrail of rope, 200 feet long, stretched between. Now the porters could ascend safely. It only remained to make the staircase in the upper ice-slopes and the crest of the bulge would be gained and Camp Four established.

One by one the others traversed the shelf, and, led by Birnie, kicked out a secure staircase down the snow of the narrow couloir. Once again the Fates were kind, for, although the couloir was very steep, and by rights should have been a sheet of ice, steps could be kicked throughout its whole length.

At the commencement of the descent the weather had threatened the usual afternoon snowstorm, but this for some reason had not materialised. As Shipton and I drove the lower piton into the rocks above the shelf, the last wisps of cloud were melting into a daffodil sky. It was strangely calm, and the dull thuds of the wooden mallet striking the piton sounded weak and muffled in the thin frosty air of 21,000 feet.

After some difficulty the piton was driven firmly into a crack, and the lower end of the rope securely tied to it. As we turned to go we glanced with satisfaction at the long line of steps and the slender handrail of rope suspended above them, mute evidence of work completed and another step forward in our venture.

We descended the couloir cautiously the frozen surface of the snow crunched and creaked beneath our feet. Once the slopes below were gained we moved quickly and easily.

Night was draining the red wine of day from the peaks as we trod the glacier plateau; in the half-light the great wall on which we had laboured all day looked terribly forbidding. Above and behind it rose the huge peak of Kamet, blazoned on a shield of awakening stars.

At Camp Three good news and bad news awaited us. The good news was that Dorje, Birnie's servant, who had been left at the Base Camp with stomach trouble, had arrived, having, according to his own account, ascended from the Base Camp in one day. It was an amazing performance, and showed what can be accomplished by a seasoned veteran of Everest and Kangchenjunga. It showed also his enthusiasm and keenness for the task of climbing Kamet.

The bad news was that several Darjeeling men were complaining of mountain sickness, and the Old Soldier, who had been relegated to Camp Two a day previously, for that complaint, was reported as being unfit to return to Camp Three. Fortunately, all the local men were working splendidly; already they had carried up enough provisions and fuel to last us a month.

Next morning, June 17, Holdsworth was feeling a little unwell, a sharp attack of earache having kept him awake most of the night. Beauman was still unacclimatised, and Greene felt in need of a rest after the exertions of the previous day. This left only Shipton, Birnie and myself to continue with the work of forcing a route up to the site of Camp Four. It was arranged that Shipton and I accompanied by Lewa, should go on ahead and commence the task of cutting steps up the final ice-slope. Birnie was to follow with four porters carrying provisions, which were to be dumped as far as possible up the precipice.

We left the camp early, while the snow of the glacier plateau was still frozen hard. After the gruelling work of the previous day, it was surprisingly easy to utilise the steps, on the making of which we had expended so much energy, whilst the handrail of rope was most comforting. Climbing rapidly, we soon reached the rocks on which we had halted the previous day for lunch. Here hard work began. The downhill track in the slope above made by Shipton and Holdsworth was of little use to us, as we had to make an uphill track, the steps of which were sufficiently close together for ascending porters to use comfortably. The snow was in excellent order, and, although hard ice lay two feet below its surface, it was unnecessary to cut any steps, as it was safely frozen to the ice.

Above the highest point reached by Shipton and Holdsworth, the snow began to thin; soon it was barely a foot deep, and it became questionable whether it was safe to proceed without cutting steps. To the left of us were some scattered patches of rock, and, turning aside to them, we sat down for a snack of food. The view ahead was both encouraging and discouraging; encouraging because it could be climbed, discouraging because of the length of time and the hard work that would be required to climb it. Above the granite slabs on which we were sitting the slope rose, unbroken by any projecting rocks, to the crest of the ice bulge on which must be placed Camp Four. But it was ice – green-black ice – that reflected the sun with a steely glitter. The slope was 300 feet high, and its steepness precluded anything but buckets of steps being cut for the porters. If, as appeared, cutting was necessary throughout its entire length, at least two days' toil were in prospect, and no light work at nearly 22,000 feet.

To the right of us snow concealed the ice, but it appeared to lie in too thin a layer over the ice to be utilised successfully. It seemed better to climb the slope where it was pure ice, rather than involve ourselves in the additional labour of having first to clear away snow before a step could be cut.

Leaving Shipton firmly anchored to the topmost rocks; I addressed myself to the task of cutting steps. The first half-dozen blows of the ice axe convinced me that it was one involving the hardest possible labour. The ice was hard, tough and rubbery, of a consistency similar to that encountered on the ice-wall of Kangchenjunga. The axe pick sank into it with a dull thud, frequently without releasing a flake or chip of ice, and had to be wriggled about in order to detach it for the next blow. Under such circumstances, rhythm, so important at high altitudes, was impossible, and I had to halt every few strokes and gasp for breath.

A quarter of an hour passed; I looked down. The steps I had made were adequate, but the height I had gained was pitifully inadequate; it was not more than a few feet; Shipton, comfortably ensconced on a granite slab, grinned encouragement. If my progress had been funereal in its slowness, he exhibited no sign of impatience, and only suggested that it was his turn to do some work. To this I assented readily, for the breathlessness of altitude and the sun blazing on my back had rendered me weary. But before I retraced my steps I glanced to the right, where the ice disappeared beneath the snow. Close to us the snow was only an inch or two deep – not deep enough for a step. The odds against it being deep enough and safe enough farther along were a hundred to one, for the slope appeared far too steep for snow to cling to it in any depth. Yet, when I rejoined Shipton, we both agreed that before committing ourselves to the ice, and the immense labour involved by cutting steps up it, we ought to investigate this new possibility. If the slope was dangerous, or threatened to become dangerous, we could but retreat. Apart from the time and labour required for the bare ice, several hundred feet of rope would have to be fixed if porters were to be got up and down in safety, and although we had plenty of spare rope, the accounts of the Meade and Kellas expeditions had not led us to believe that a thousand feet or more of fixed topes would be required between Camps Three and Four, and to sacrifice so much would leave us short of it. It was the bad conditions caused by a lingering winter and recent snowfalls that were responsible for the difficulties, especially those lower down, which obviously do not normally exist.

We traversed downwards and to the right along the topmost slabs of rock to the snow. At first it was a mere skin above the ice, but the farther we progressed to the right the deeper it became. Soon, to our delight, the ice axe could be driven into it almost up to the head. We kicked at it tentatively; unless it was firmly consolidated and frozen to the ice, we should have no option but to continue with the work which we had just abandoned. But sun and frost had done their work well. Here was not a loose layer of sloppy snow such as might have been expected after recent snowfalls, but snow firmly crusted two to three feet in depth, adhering tenaciously to the ice. I saw Shipton's eye light up, and next instant he went at the slope with the energy of the boxer who, after months of training, sees his opponent before him. I followed, barely able to keep up with him although I had merely to follow in the steps he kicked.

Progress directly upwards was impossible without step cutting, as the slope steepened high up, and the snow had slipped away, exposing bare ice. The obvious line of least resistance slanted diagonally upwards to the right. The snow gradually thinned inch by inch. Presently, we could only drive the axe in halfway before encountering ice, but so firm was the snow that it was still possible to climb without cutting steps. It was not until the snow was less than a foot deep that, with a sigh of resignation, we resigned ourselves to the task of cutting steps in the last hundred feet or so of the slope. Quickly now, the snow thinned and we found ourselves once more on bare ice, but it was not the tough, rubbery ice that we had at first encountered, but white, brittle and flaky, ice that had not long since been snow, and which had not yet been converted by pressure, and temperature change into glutinous ice.

With hope animating our hearts and putting new strength into our arms, we went to work with a will. There was no hesitation now. The ice axe met the slope with a firm, confident thump, the dislodged fragments of ice skipped and hissed continually down the slope; even our gasps had in them something of exultation. We were tasting the real joys of mountaineering, joys of work doing, of work done and its forthcoming reward.

Above us, the crest of the slope formed a silvery edge against the deep blue of the sky. A small cornice curled over the edge, sun caressed above and blue shadowed below. We avoided it easily on the right. The angle eased off. Steps were still necessary, and we chafed at the delay. At last nailed boots alone were sufficient to grip the flaky surface of the ice. We toiled upwards, breathing hard. The silvery skyline before us sank suddenly below the level of our vision and was replaced by the giant precipices of Kamet. We trod the soft snow of the little plateau forming the summit of the bulge. There we leaned on our ice axes and panted for breath.

We sat in the snow, untied our rucksacks and rummaged for our lunch. Out came the familiar tin of sardines. As usual, the key that is optimistically supposed to roll back the lid broke. Savagely, I drove my pocket tin opener into the portrait of the beautiful French lady who, surrounded by many elegant scrolls, ornamented the lid. How good those sardines were! How well their oil lubricated our parched throats! And after the sardines, a tin of Californian cling peaches and a cup of tea apiece from a vacuum flask made life seem good.

It was a day of superlative calm; not a zephyr whispered across the snow; the sun shone hotly from an unclouded sky. The world was at rest and peace; the smoke from my cigarette rose with scarcely a waver not even the growl of an avalanche broke the noonday quietude.

Our languid gaze passed for a few yards across the dazzling snows of the little plateau on which we sat, and then there was nothing – nothing save the depths from which we had emerged, more felt than seen, and beyond, mountains upon mountains, violet-shadowed and remote. Our gaze swept upwards. The sun was declining; stealthy shadows were stealing down the eastern precipice of Kamet. It is a precipice that might well cause the most hardened mountaineer to shudder. In sunlight it had looked forbidding; in shadow, it became appalling.

Owing to the recent bad weather, the upper part of Kamet was plastered with new snow and glazed with ice. We need expect but little more rock climbing between Camp Four and the summit, but this new snow was going to make tracking exceedingly laborious.

We had expected to find smooth, unbroken snow-slopes leading up from Camp Four to Meade's Col, but the slopes before us by no means justified this expectation. Some 500 feet above us, the slope was riven by huge crevasses and broken up into séracs. The former presented no difficulty so far as we could see, for they were mostly choked with snow, but the latter were composed of ice walls anything up to 100 feet high. The way through such a maze was by no means obvious, and though the Meade and Kellas expeditions experienced little difficulty in overcoming this portion of the route, conditions might well have changed. Ice conditions vary from year to year, and a glacier slope that is easy one year may be difficult or impassable the next year. In the present instance, the icefall could be outflanked, if need be, by an upward traverse across an ice-slope falling from Abi Gamin East. This alternative was, however, a disagreeable one, and would necessitate arduous step cutting.

But, try though I might to concentrate my attention on the problem before us, I soon found myself relapsing into a placid contemplation of the glories about us. We sat upon a promontory of snow and ice, from which the icy billows swept round towards Kamet, a tempestuous yet immobile sea. Green waves of ice, hundreds of feet high, gleaming in the slanting rays of the afternoon sun, lurched outwards over shadowed gulfs. Sometimes these waves break from their bonds, and Kamet shudders as avalanches weighing thousands of tons are hurled with dreadful uproar down its flanks.

The precious hours of delightful repose soon passed; we must return to camp. Sitting we had forgotten that we were 22,000 feet above the sea, but the effort of rising to our feet set heart and lungs clamouring for oxygen. There was no sign of Birnie and his convoy of porters, and, approaching the edge of the plateau, we shouted down the slope. There was a faint reply, but it came from far below; evidently, Birnie, had not thought it advisable to bring his porters up to the plateau in view of the hard work that would be required of them later.

We took one last glance round. The air about us was still calm, but from the serene skyline of Meade's Col little, "snow devils" wore rising against the deepening green of the evening sky. Placid weather in the Himalaya is short-lived.

The slopes up which we had come had been in shadow for the past two hours and our steps had frozen into a hard staircase. How easily we descended! It seemed incredible that it had cost us four days of hard work to make a route up the precipice. Yet, if the fixed ropes had been removed and the precipice reduced to its pristine condition, we should not have been in camp before dark.

Birnie's porters had dumped their loads of provisions on the topmost rocks, and it was only necessary to carry them up the final slope.

It was a perfect evening, and we descended happily, conscious both of physical fitness and ever-increasing acclimatisation to altitude.

At length the last fixed rope was behind and the steep little couloir below it descended. We almost ran down the snow-slopes to the glacier plateau.

That evening in camp we held a council of war. At the Base Camp we had vowed that under no circumstances would we rush Kamet until we were properly acclimatised to altitude, but now, after only ten days on the mountain, some of us at least were so well acclimatised, as had been proved by our ability to work hard from 20,600 feet to 22,000 feet, that we felt fit enough to make a push for the summit. It remained only to consider the weather – and the weather was good. How long would it remain good? Supposing the monsoon was earlier than usual? If we tarried to acclimatise still more, might we not be asking too much of the weather? If it should break, we should regret ever afterwards that we had made no attempt. Supposing that an immediate push made by those who were best acclimatised failed, those who were now not so well acclimatised should by then be sufficiently acclimatised to make a fresh assault. It is pleasant to record that those who were not yet acclimatised were unanimous in recommending an attempt on the summit by those who were acclimatised.

There was another point to be considered – porterage. Mountain sickness had so reduced our high camp porters that only ten men were available for carrying loads to Camps Four and Five. To establish Camp Five with equipment and provisions sufficient for an immediate summit attack by the whole party was an impossibility, for it was necessary to provision Camp Five with something more than the bare essentials of existence if an attack on the summit was to be carried out under favourable conditions. Not to provision Camp Five properly would be to court disaster, for even supposing Camp Four was properly provisioned a blizzard might isolate Camp Five.

At the moment Shipton and I were the fittest. Shipton had gone better than anyone and had participated in every climb. I possessed the incalculable mental and physical advantage of having climbed Jonsong Peak, 24,344 feet, in 1930. Mentally, my starting-point on Kamet was 24,344 feet. Physically, the experience in 1930 was valuable because, once the human body has learned to acclimatise itself to high altitudes, it will acclimatise more quickly and easily when called upon a second time. But, first of all, Camp Four must be established and provisioned. Only when this was done could a final decision as to the summit assault be made.

Thanks to Birnie's organisation and some splendid work by our porters, both on the part of the men working above Camp Two and the men working between the Base Camp and Camps One and Two, Camp Three was now provisioned and fuelled for about a month. We had at least established our Advanced Base Camp, and felt ourselves to be in a strong besieging position. We were even prepared to dig ourselves in, and had all the necessary shovels with which to do it should the weather deal hardly with us.

June 18 dawned brilliantly fine. Holdsworth, who had completely recovered from his earache, decided to accompany Shipton and myself. Owing to the limited number of porters available, we carried quite 20 lbs. each, ourselves, whilst Holdsworth, in addition to this load, burdened himself with a pair of ski and sticks, as he hoped to be able to ski at least part of the way from Camp Four to Meade's Col.

It was a heavy day. For once we could appreciate the lot of our high camp porters, even though we carried little more than half their load. Theirs is a heritage of service and hard work of the most exacting description. I cannot believe that it is entirely for pecuniary gain or for self-glorification that these men are prepared to undergo the toils, hardships and dangers that are inseparable from mountaineering on the greatest peaks in the world. I believe that, like their sahibs, they are born with that strange instinct men call "adventure".

At the upper rocks we added to our loads from the dump of provisions left by Birnie's party until we were carrying as much as we could manage. Fortunately, the upper slope was in excellent condition, but the treadmill-like action of stepping from hold to hold with a load on the back, so heavy that it threatened to overbalance one backwards, was fatiguing work, and it was with something more than ordinary relief that we gained the plateau.

The porters were far behind. They were too wise to ascend as quickly as we. Their slowness gave us time to drive an ice axe deep into the snow and soft ice of the plateau, tie a long length of rope to it, and let the end down the icy upper section of the slope as a handrail for the porters. This done, we sprawled in the snow for a delightful siesta. The weather was again perfect, and, in spite of the plateau's exposed position, a lighted match scarcely flickered. Yet, the "snow-devils" were sporting on Meade's Col and Kamet, and their uneasy spirals rose high into the sky.

Presently, we heard voices below, and going to the edge of the plateau looked down and saw the porters coming up. Wisely, they were taking their time and conserving their energy: a few steps, a halt, a few more steps, and another halt to lean on their ice axes and regain their breath. Yet, their progress, if slow, was inevitable and magnificently steady. On the previous day the local men who had accompanied Birnie had not unnaturally displayed some timidity for the steepness of the climbing – it was outside their experience. But now these same men were ascending with the sure-footed nonchalance of our Darjeeling men. It was a striking proof of their aptitude for mountaineering, for they are born mountaineers, and only experience is necessary to equip them for the most difficult and sensational climbs.

One by one the porters breasted the edge of the plateau and sank down into the snow breathing heavily, then, with broad grins, they set about erecting the tents. They were as pleased as we at the establishment of Camp Four.

The tents pitched, they set off back to Camp Three, leaving only Lewa and Nima Dorje. Holdsworth accompanied them, leaving his ski at the camp. After the work of carrying them up from Camp Three, his enthusiasm deserved to be rewarded above Camp Four.

The day ended cloudlessly, but the wind increased in force: it no longer confined its attentions to Meade's Col and Kamet, but swept down upon our camp. How cold were its gusts! It was as though Death himself breathed on us.

The sun sank behind Kamet, its red rays lighting the spirals of wind-tossed snow. Almost we could fancy ourselves gazing upon flames, not of heat, but of cold, rising from the cold hell which the Tibetans believe exists for the eternal damnation of the evildoer. A glimpse through my monocular disposed of this vagrant fancy. I could see the loose and powdery snow being torn off Meade's Col and the northern slopes of Kamet, whirled furiously into the air and beaten down on the lee side of the eastern precipice in a furious writhing *tourmente*.

Shuddering with cold, Shipton and I crawled into our little tent and slid into our sleeping bags. Presently, the grinning countenance of Nima Dorje thrust itself in upon us, accompanied by two plates of steaming soup. We supped well, even luxuriously, rounding off the meal with cups of hot "Ovaltine" that quickened sluggish circulation and wrapped us in a warm glow, then, lying side by side in our sleeping bags, we smoked and yarned. By the time that sleep claimed us we had come to the conclusion that the affairs of the British Empire should have been entrusted to a cabinet consisting exclusively of ourselves. It was not the first time we had reached such a conclusion.

I think we both slept well, although troubled by the usual worrying dreams. One of the curious facts relevant to high altitudes is that insomnia, so long as it is induced solely by altitude, matters but little. Rest and not sleep is the first essential, and although one may lie awake for hours at a high camp unable to sleep, this does not necessarily induce mental or physical weariness or restlessness. Provided one is warm one lies peaceably, scarcely conscious of the passage of time, and rises next morning feeling fit and refreshed. The reason for this is probably that sleeplessness is induced solely by altitude and not by physical or mental ill health, as is sleeplessness at low altitudes. Thus subconsciously the mind realising that there is no physical or mental disability does not worry, and the body can rest content. Actually, I cannot remember spending a sleepless night above Camp Two, nor can I find any mention in my diary of having done so, although I remember that on one or two nights sleep must have been hard to woo, but I am quite certain there must have been occasions when I slept intermittently, and the fact that I did not consider these worthy of mention in my diary goes to amplify my previous remarks. At Camp Four we found it necessary to sleep with the head considerably higher than we were normally used to, as this position allowed of easier chest expansion, and aided the flow of oxygen to the lungs. Possibly the greatest bar to sleep is what is known as "Cheyne Stokes breathing", which at sea level is symptomatic of heart affection. In its effect, it makes the mountaineer at high altitudes take a series of rapid short breaths followed by a deep easing deep breath. As regards dreams, I can only remember one in detail, and this was so ridiculous and absurd that it may possibly be of interest as an example of the type of dream experienced at high altitudes.

I dreamt that I was sitting among the crowd in the pavilion at Lord's on the occasion of a test match between England and Australia. The start of the match was already overdue when, of a sudden, a fat man, came rushing agitatedly down the steps of the pavilion looking to right and left of him. Suddenly, he espied me and jostling his way past the intervening people reached my side. 'We're a man short and you've got to play,' he whispered urgently.

'But I'm no good at cricket and I've no clothes or anything,' I protested.

'No, no, no! you must come,' he exclaimed and fairly dragging me from my seat pulled me through the throng of spectators into the pavilion. There I was able to borrow a flannel shirt, but there were no flannel trousers available and only one pad. A few minutes later, the huge crowd were doubtless much edified at perceiving Mr. K.S. Duleepsinhji correctly clad, and myself, clad in a white flannel shirt and a pair of dark striped morning trousers, on the left leg of which reposed the one dirty pad with which the M.C.C. had been able to provide me, and my feet encased in a pair of Mr. Carter's climbing boots ornamented with grey spats, emerge from the pavilion to open the batting for England. Just as we were about to pass through the pavilion gate, a tall, woebegone man, dressed in black like an undertaker, came up to me and said with a broad Yorkshire accent:

'Remember, laad, ——' – naming a well-known Australian fast bowler – 'either bowls at your brains or y' guuts. Keep tha baat straight, and tha end oop.'

As my partner and I walked across the expanse of green towards the wickets, we argued fiercely as to who should take the first ball. This was finally settled by our stopping halfway to the wicket and tossing a half-crown. I won and, to my immense relief, did not have to take the first ball.

We arrived at the wicket, but before play could commence, the umpire and I took a boiling point thermometer reading. The height above sea level of Lord's cricket ground having been determined to the satisfaction of the umpire, play was allowed to begin. The bowler, a tall man with arms like flails, retreated to the edge of the ground, then sprang forward in a series of huge leaps towards the wicket, but long before he got to it he swung his arm and delivered the ball. It missed the umpire by a fraction of an inch and struck the wicket at my end. Instantly, a tremendous shout of 'How's that!' went up. 'Hout!' said the umpire laconically. At this there came a savage scream from the pavilion, and I saw a number of old gentlemen wearing public school and college ties leap to their feet, shaking their fists. As I started to walk towards the pavilion, the uproar around the ground increased. Police with drawn truncheons and an armoured car filled with the "Flying Squad" appeared from behind the bowling screen. Then there came a series of staccato reports and I saw the umpire and the players begin to fall one by one upon the turf. Looking up, I perceived that one of the old gentlemen, red-faced, white-moustached, and with an Old Etonian tie, was perched on the pavilion weather vane, with a Lewis machine-gun with which he was sweeping the ground. I threw myself flat to escape the hail of bullets. Around me the uproar grew and grew and grew … and then I woke up. I make psychoanalysts a present of this dream.

The sun found us early next morning, and we breakfasted leisurely in its warm rays. It was delightful knowing that a whole day of ease was before us, whilst our satisfaction was increased by the knowledge that we had earned it. A week's hard labour was behind us. It was on June 13 that we had left Camp Two to prospect the route to the site of Camp Three; now we were almost within striking distance of the summit.

Lying at our ease on a tarpaulin laid over the snow; we could gaze up at Kamet. Today it looked almost kind. Its eastern precipice was not shadowed and terrible as it had been the previous afternoon, but its details were revealed by the sun. Our gaze passed up the broken slopes leading towards Meade's Col. Would their jumble of séracs and crevasses present any difficulty? And what of the final slope of Kamet? Long we gazed at it. Only the eastern edge of it was visible. Here and there it was broken by ice-walls which we could only hope did not traverse the whole width of the face.

Yet we experienced a feeling of confidence. Up to date everything had gone well. Our plans, which had materialised with scarcely a hitch, seemed but movements in some intricate symphony that would conclude inevitably on a note of triumph ... Yet might not Kamet be preparing a furious resistance? For ought we knew, a blizzard might be gathering its forces in the blue dome of the unclouded sky. Kangchenjunga had taught some bitter lessons. It had taught me that Himalayan weather is fickle, and that Himalayan peaks are ruthless and cunning. It had taught me, paradoxically, always to assume the unexpected. And so as I looked upwards at Kamet shining serenely in the morning sun, my confidence was tortured by devils of doubt and misgiving. Plan an attack on a Himalayan peak with all the experience and skill of mountaineering craft at your disposal, and you still depend on luck. In the pitiless frost of adverse weather conditions the most elaborately organised assault must wither and droop. Should the weather deal hardly with us now, not only should we fail to reach the summit, but we might be hard put to it to retreat to Camp Three. Yet against such forebodings had to be set the fact that so far we had not experienced snowstorms approaching in ferocity and precipitation those that assail Kangchenjunga. Another comforting reflection was that even if we were forced back to Camp Three, such a retreat would not necessarily spell defeat, for Camp Three was so well stocked with food and fuel that it would enable us to lay siege to Kamet.

When the brain is disturbed by such conflicting thoughts it is difficult to resign oneself to a day of inaction, yet inaction was necessary if we were to become acclimatised. For a while impatience predominated, but the brain, realising its futility, presently rejected it. Doubts and fears for the future vanished like wraiths; we dozed in the sunlight, until the world seemed unreal and unsubstantial, and the peace of the hills embraced us.

Soon after dawn we had espied the remainder of the party setting out from Camp Three; mere specks on the glacier plateau below. Now, towards midday, we heard voices, and from the edge of the ice-slope we could see them toiling upwards. The porters were all going well, and the local men in particular had mastered the rhythmical method of progression to which I have previously alluded. One by one they breasted the ice-slope, halted a moment leaning on their ice axes, breathing heavily the while, then sank down into the snow with guttural grunts of satisfaction. They had done well, and their grins when they had recovered their breath showed that they realised it.

Shipton and I were surprised and delighted to find that Beauman was with the others. When we had left Camp Three he was still unacclimatised, and we had not expected him to be fit enough to ascend to Camp Four for several days. Recently, Greene had experimented with ammonium chloride, and had administered this to himself and Beauman. The theory underlying this experiment is that ammonium chloride counteracts to some extent the diminution of acidity in the body which results from oxygen lack at high altitudes. Whether or not the experiment had the desired effect of hastening Beauman's acclimatisation must remain non-proven, but in its effects it was at least harmless, and, on the small evidence available, it would appear desirable to experiment further with it. An interesting point is raised by this question of diminution of acidity at high altitudes. It would seem to show that climbers whose tendency at sea level is towards acidosis will do better at high altitudes than those whose tendency is towards alkalosis.

Later in the day, Holdsworth, with his usual energy, ascended on ski the snow-slopes for a few hundred feet above the camp and ran back to the camp as steadily as though he was skiing on an Alpine peak and not at 22,000 feet. He found the consistency of the snow to be variable and running difficult, and that, owing to the altitude, swings necessitated a considerable expenditure of energy. The pleasure derived from skiing is, of course, inversely proportional to the altitude.

We spent the remainder of the day laying our plans for the morrow. A total of nine porters, including Lewa and Budhibal Gurung, were available. It was arranged that we should split up into two parties. Shipton, Holdsworth and I were to constitute the first party; on the morrow we should establish, if possible, Camp, Five on Meade's Col, taking with us the nine porters. Lewa and Nima Dorje were to remain with us at Camp Five, and the seven remaining porters return the same day to Camp Four. The following day the first party were to make an attempt on the summit, weather conditions and their physical fitness permitting.

The same day that the summit attempt was being made, the second party with the seven remaining porters were to ascend to Camp Five with provisions and fuel sufficient for several days.

So much for the plan, simple enough in itself, yet dependent for success on several factors: good weather, reasonably good snow conditions, lack of insuperable difficulties on Kamet, and the fitness of ourselves and our porters.

CHAPTER THIRTEEN

Meade's Col

I AWOKE EARLY next morning, June 20. It was very cold, and the roof of my tent sparkled with my condensed and frozen breath. Through the little window at the head end of the tent I could see that the sky was brilliantly clear. The dawn was stealing down Kamet, not a lurid dawn of riotous colourings presaging evil, but an ordained and gradual awakening.

Presently the sun's rays warmed the camp, and I arose in the midst of a miniature snowstorm falling from the roof of my tent. A few minutes before, everything had been in the grip of intense cold and now, miraculously, life had returned to the white corpse of the world.

Seated on packing cases, we crammed food into reluctant stomachs. A few minutes were needed for final preparations and, within an hour after the sun had risen; Shipton, Holdsworth and I with our nine porters were on our way to Meade's Col. We started with the 'good lucks' of our friends in our ears.

The surface of the snow-slope immediately above the camp had frozen into a hard crust, and we ascended easily for the first two or three hundred feet, except for Holdsworth, who found it difficult to edge his ski into the crust. But the crust could not long withstand the fierce rays of the sun, which poured upon our backs with a relentless fury that sapped both will power and energy. We began to sink in, at first only an inch or two, and then, as the snow became softer and softer, over the ankle and finally the top of the boot.

Taking it in turns to break the trail for the heavily laden porters, Shipton and I advanced slowly, while Holdsworth zigzagged easily now up the slope. For a man on ski there was no necessity for the rope, but Shipton and I deemed it advisable on account of sundry concealed crevasses. As we trudged upwards, we scanned anxiously the icefall ahead of us. Most prominent in our vision was an abrupt wall of ice that appeared to stretch across the whole width of the slope between Kamet's eastern precipice and Abi Gamin East. If it extended without a break and was impossible to climb, we should have no option but to outflank it on the steep ice slopes of Abi Gamin East. Such a course would be disagreeable in the extreme, owing to the amount of step cutting that would be required. Here and there fragments of ice fallen from the séracs above showed through the snow. But we need apprehend no danger from ice avalanches, for the séracs were stable, as evidenced by their smooth facets and clean cut edges.

The slope steepened and the snow thinned out. Ice supervened. A few steps landed us on to the lower lip of a crevasse twenty yards wide. This crevasse was choked with snow and formed a trough running horizontally across the slope. Its upper lip was formed by the ice wall we had previously noticed, varying between thirty and fifty feet in height.

Immediately facing us the ice wall rose vertically, and continued thus without a break across the whole width of the slope to the left, but to the right a portion of the wall had sagged outwards and downwards, forming a projecting bastion. In the angle between the bastion and the wall there was an obvious line of least resistance, for the slope at this point was not vertical, but between 40° and 60° in angle. It was the one breach in the fortification, and had it not existed, we should have had no option but recourse to the long and arduous traverse of Abi Gamin East ice-slope.

At the foot of the slope the snow was in good order, and step kicking only was necessary. Higher up, where the angle of the ice was too great to hold snow *in situ*, steps had to be cut. The ice was not tough and hard as it had been on the precipice below Camp Four, but brittle and flaky. Less than a dozen steps sufficed. Yet the work, if not technically difficult, provided us with a foretaste of what to expect near the summit of Kamet should step cutting be necessary. Altitude, a blazing sun and the soft snow-slopes had already sapped our energy, a few swings of the ice axe sufficed to set heart galloping and lungs gasping. As I stepped over the top and sank down into the snow, I saw to my great relief that, save for a crevasse or two, gently inclined snow slopes alone separated us from Meade's Col.

Shipton joined me, and together we sat basking contentedly in the sun. Presently, our peaceful contemplation of our surroundings was interrupted by an exclamation and a slithering sound. We peered over the edge in time to see Holdsworth drop his ski and sticks into the snowy trough of the choked crevasse at the foot of the ice-wall. We felt sorry for him as he descended to collect them, but we could scarcely repress a chuckle at this sudden tumbling of the gods head over heels, as it were, down their own Olympus. The ski were finally hauled up on the end of a rope.

We waited to see the porters safely up the ice wall, then continued on our way. A few yards above the ice wall the snow slopes were split by some crevasses, the largest of which was a huge rift of unknown depth. Fortunately, it was securely bridged with snow and, crossing it, we found ourselves on slopes leading without a break to Meade's Col.

If Shipton and I had found it hard work breaking a trail for the porters on the slopes below the ice wall, it was even harder work above. The snow became softer and softer, and at times we were sinking in halfway to the knees. In consistency the snow was not powdery, but heavy, wet and soggy. Every few yards it was necessary to halt and kick balled masses of it from the boot. Tricouni nails, excellent in many ways, are at their worst under such snow conditions, for the snow coagulates between them on the sole of the boot and soon forms a heavy and awkward ball.

Slowly we toiled on; taking turns at leading every few minutes. An almost vertical sun blazed down upon us with pitiless intensity. Its glare was reflected from the snow to such an extent that we halted to replace the face cream washed away by sweat, for without it the skin would have been stripped from our faces like paper. The porters were going very slowly. Even had they been physically capable of ascending more quickly, they were far too experienced in high climbing to do so. They knew that once Camp Five had been established they could return to Camp Four with little effort and in but a fraction of the time they were taking for the ascent.

The slope before us rose gradually to a horizon of snow, beyond which, and invisible, was the crest of Meade's Col. That horizon seemed always as far away. Halts became more and more frequent. It was not enough to lean on the ice axe and gasp; we had to sit in the snow until strength could be mustered for further advance. Soon after midday, a mist formed and swooped down upon us. Detail was obscured, and all we could see before us were a few yards of blinding snow slope. If this mist had been thick enough, it might have protected us to some degree from the sun, but its effect was to interpose a burning glass of vapour between us and our tormentor, thus increasing the glare and sapping our remaining dregs of energy.

Perhaps halfway up the slope, Budhibal Gurung found himself unable to carry his load another step. He was not a professional load-carrier like our Darjeeling men and he need not have ascended beyond the Base Camp. It was his own personal enthusiasm and desire to do his bit for the expedition that brought him thus far. Dogged determination and tenacity of purpose had alone kept him going. We found out later that his lack of experience in load carrying, coupled to an awkward load, had resulted in a badly flayed back, yet he had continued without a word of complaint. It appeared as though his load would have to be temporarily abandoned, but once again Lewa insisted on doing two men's work. He took on Budhibal Gurung's load in addition to his own! At that height it was a *superhuman* effort; there is no other word to describe it.

The slope gradually eased off. So far as we could see between rents in the shifting mists, we were not more than three hundred feet below the crest of Meade's Col. The porters were now far behind, and the afternoon was drawing on. If we continued farther, the porters might not be able to return to Camp Four in daylight, and it was essential that they should return the same day, for there was not enough food to feed them. Close by was a horizontal shelf running across the slope; on it we decided to pitch Camp Five. This decision made, we flopped down thankfully in the snow to await the porters. They were a long time in coming, but at length they appeared, a straggling line of weary men. Among them, and not behind them, was Lewa. He must have been carrying a load of about 80 lbs. on his back, and that at a height of over 23,000 feet. The men arrived and squatted apathetically in the snow, slipping their heavy loads from their backs and their sweat-soaked headbands from their foreheads. They had done a splendid day's work, but they were too tired at the moment to realise it. We expressed our admiration for their conduct as well as we could in the limited language at our command. A few minutes' rest served to restore them. An atmosphere of languor was dispelled as usual by Nima Dorje's inevitable grin. They busily set about erecting the tents and cooking some tea for themselves and for us. How good that tea was.

At length the men were ready to return to Camp Four. They swung their empty sacks on to their backs and strode off down the slope, leaving only Lewa and Nima Dorje behind with us. As the sun swung down, the mists began to melt away. Far up in the gauzy vapours a silvery crest stood out against the dark blue sky – the summit of Kamet. The cool alchemy of evening dissolved the lingering vapours and the white caves of the world were bathed in the golden radiance of the setting sun.

Above us rose the final slopes to the summit of Kamet. Long we gazed at them. There were two distinct possibilities of making an ascent. Rising directly from Meade's Col was a ridge set at a moderate angle. At a first casual glance, it appeared to afford an easy route to the summit, for it was not broken by any serious gap or obstacle, and its angle, although moderately steep, was not such as to suggest difficult climbing. Yet, when we came to examine it more closely, we saw that there was one fatal objection. For a considerable portion of its length it was heavily iced. The westerly wind, which rushes through Meade's Col and across Kamet strikes this ridge before anything else, and it had stripped the loose snow from it, exposing ice, black ice, gleaming evilly. There was no avoiding this ice. The crest of the ridge and the slope on the eastern side of it were both iced, whilst the western side of the ridge was, we judged, in all probability a sheer precipice. Hours of step cutting would be necessary.

The sole alternative was the slope rising directly above the camp. Here and there, this slope was broken into séracs, which limited the route high up to the eastern flank of the face not far from the edge forming the crest of the eastern precipice.

In form the slope was concave, and, although we were looking at it from a point directly in front where foreshortening and distortion would tend to make us underestimate its angle; it was apparent that in its upper portion it was very steep – far steeper than the ridge. In the afternoon shadow the last few hundred feet appeared to spring up in an almost sheer wall. Was this final slope possible? Long we scanned it. We could not assume that it was snow but only hope that it was not ice. If it was ice, we should in all probability be forced to establish another camp, and it was doubtful whether any spot could be found on that inhospitable mountainside on which tents could be pitched.

Another factor to be taken into consideration was the avalanches, but the weather had been fine now for some days, and the wind which we had seen almost every afternoon and evening sweeping the upper slopes of Kamet must have hardened the surface of the snow into a safe crust. The problem boiled down to this: the ridge from Meade's Col was possible, but its ascent would entail another camp; the direct ascent of the face was obviously possible to a point about 400 feet beneath the summit ridge, but whether or not the summit could be reached in one day from Camp Five depended on the state of the final 400-foot slope. We decided, therefore, to attack the face in preference to the ridge. Actually, we had left the Base Camp fully prepared to establish a camp above Meade's Col, and our decision to try and reach the summit in one day direct from Camp Five was influenced by unexpected physical fitness and acclimatisation, allied to perfect weather conditions. Another reason was lack of porters. With only the few men available it would take two or three days getting up enough food and fuel for another camp. Supposing that, after this had been done, the weather was to break, we might be robbed of the summit when it was almost within our grasp, and to retreat knowing that we had not seized an opportunity would be a bitter experience. Actually, the decision to go on next day and attempt the summit was an unspoken one. As soon as we had seen that there was no insuperable difficulty, we had tacitly assumed that we were to go on, and it had not been necessary to voice this decision.

If I have gone into some detail as to the pros and the cons of the final problem, it is because I would have the reader form some idea as to the many factors leading up to a decision in Himalayan mountaineering. Those who know mountaineering for the craft it is, know that one false move on a Himalayan peak may result in checkmate, with the mountain as master of the situation. I remember that after the decision was made to push on with the attack, I experienced a strange feeling of confidence and happiness, a feeling, I believe, shared by my companions.

As we packed our rucksacks with food, spare clothing and photographic and cinematographic apparatus in preparation for the morrow, Lewa and Nima Dorje busied themselves with the preparation of our supper: and the hiss of the pressure stove was the only sound in our ears, save for our own laboured breathing and the pumping of our hearts.

The sun slid downwards almost parallel to the crest of the ridge leading from Meade's Col to the summit of Kamet, and its rays lingered long upon us. The shadows lengthened; dusk stole from the valleys. No longer were the snows harsh, white and glaring, but every undulation was revealed by blue shadows. The beautiful Mana Peak was no longer a brutal fang of blank snow and black rock jagging a brazen sky as it had appeared in the noonday sun, but a queenlike mountain with perfectly proportioned shoulders, rising to a crest so fine and delicate that only the Great Architect himself could have chiselled it with His instruments of sun and frost. Far beyond, above orderly ranks of lesser ridges, rose Nanda Devi. Seen from this direction, it stands out as a symmetrical pile, not unlike Kamet, and no other peak challenges its sovereignty. Beyond it, huge masses of coppery cumuli towered above the foothills. Our vision swept eastwards, past an isolated and graceful snow peak, that rose above the mists concealing the valleys of western Nepal, to the snows of Gurla Mandhata, and Kailas, the sacred peak which Hindus believe to be the throne of Siva and the hub of the universe. North-west of Gurla Mandhata the Himalaya fell away in brown waves crested with snow into the golden plains of Tibet, which were just visible beyond a shoulder of Abi Gamin East. Were it not for that glimpse of Tibet the mountaineer standing on the slopes of Meade's Col might fancy himself in a world given over to an eternal and awful desolation. Our eyes feasted on that little strip of golden earth as the eyes of a shipwrecked mariner feast on a distant shore. On those plains of Tibet men dwelt and moved; we were not the sole inhabitants of a frozen planet.

Night welled from the valleys; the higher peaks stood from it, like fairy isles of rosy coral. The towering cumulus clouds in the far south flared up one by one as though ignited by some huge conflagration sweeping the far-off foothills. The lights died, the peaks sank pallidly into the night, and all save Nanda Devi, which, long after other summits were quenched, defied the darkness. The plains of Tibet changed from gold to daffodil, from daffodil to ochre, and from ochre to a weird greenish-blue. A wave of purple lifted itself from the east and swept up the sky, distributing myriad stars. Lightning began to flicker in the south. From one cloudy turret to another its darting spears were launched, whilst now and again the clouds burst asunder and fountains of mauve fire leapt from their cavernous recesses, illuminating for an instant some citadel of the sky. The snows about us reflected this conflict of the elements like chalk cliffs lit up by the flashes of a nocturnal naval engagement, yet so distant was the storm that no sound reached the ear, and the profound peace of high mountains at eventide was unbroken.

The cold was intense, and we sought refuge from it in our sleeping bags.

Holdsworth unselfishly occupied a small and uncomfortable Norwegian bivouac tent; Shipton and I shared a Meade tent. As we slipped into our sleeping bags, we blessed them for their capaciousness. After hearing tales of mountaineers, who had almost exhausted themselves at high altitudes by having to insinuate themselves inch by inch into tightly fitting bags, I had designed sleeping bags of generous width. Yet, even so, the slight effort required for settling down and making ourselves comfortable brought about temporary breathlessness.

A final hot drink put us in a warm glow, which lasted all night. We did not take off our clothes as we had done in the lower camps, for it was impossible to do so owing to the cold and consequent risk of frostbite. As a rule we took off our clothing, and donned pyjamas whenever possible, as heavy clothing at night tends to retard circulation. When sleeping in clothes, therefore it is advisable to relieve the body of pressure by releasing encumbrances such as braces and undoing buttons, for anything that retards circulation at high altitudes not only makes sleep impossible, but renders the affected portion of the anatomy sensitive to frostbite. Shipton, unfortunately, was not feeling at all well, but such was his enthusiasm for the morrow's task that I believe he already assumed himself as good as on the summit. It is such an assumption, so selfless as to rise superior to bodily infirmity, that will one day take mountaineers to the summit of Everest. I do not think Shipton slept much, but Holdsworth and I both enjoyed a tolerably good night. As I have mentioned before, it matters little whether or not a man sleeps at high altitudes, provided mind and body are untroubled by ill. At frequent intervals during the night I awoke and, lying placidly on my back, stared vacantly at the roof of the tent, taking little account of the passage of time. Now and again the green canvas was lit by distant lightning, and my mind was prodded from its lethargy: I remember thinking that we were sleeping higher that night than any of our fellow men.

CHAPTER FOURTEEN

To the Summit

THE NIGHT PASSED; the lightning became feeble and finally died away; petulant gusts of wind set the frost stiffened canvas rustling and crackling.

A cold dawn filtered into a cold world. With a conscious effort I heaved myself to my knees. The sleeping bag crackled sharply; it was sheeted with ice deposited by my congealed breath. With numbed fingers I fumbled at the frozen tapes securing the flaps of the tent and, parting them at last, peered outside. A cloudless sky was shot with green and orange; the peaks stood from the night like pallid statues. I glanced upwards. Dawn was gilding the crest of Kamet. Now was the time to start, but it was too cold – the coldest morning I ever remember in the Himalaya. The world almost creaked in the cold. To have left the comparative shelter of our tents would have meant certain frostbite. It was essential that we should start comfortably, with a hot breakfast inside us, and cooking and eating under such conditions were impossible. I slipped my hands back into my sleeping bag and busied myself restoring the circulation to my numbed fingertips. How easily circulation is lost at high altitudes, and how slowly and painfully it returns!

The sun was not long in coming, and we emerged thankfully from our tents into its life-giving rays.

Breakfast was a hurried affair. We craved sugar more than any other substance, but tinned fruit and sardines also went down well, and so did steaming cups of tea.

We spoke but little; our minds were busied by thoughts of what the day might bring forth. At 8 a.m. we started off, on our final push for the summit.

We climbed on two ropes, Shipton and Lewa on one, Holdsworth, Nima Dorje and I on the other. We carried rucksacks with food and spare clothes and Nima Dorje bore a heavy load consisting of some 20 lbs. of cinematograph apparatus.

Between Camp Five and the foot of the northern face of Kamet stretched an almost level expanse of snow. We had hoped against hope that the westerly winds which lash the upper regions of the mountain had hardened the surface of the snow into a crust sufficiently solid to enable us to walk comfortably without having to do anything more than kick steps. Our hopes were not fulfilled; we had not marched more than a few yards from the camp before we were sinking in boot deep.

The foot of the slope up which we must go was littered with ice blocks, fallen from a line of séracs 1,000 feet higher. Fortunately, by keeping well to the left we were able to avoid the danger zone, and were thus spared the ordeal of having to run the gauntlet of ice avalanches.

But the snow, if disagreeably soft, was at least consistent in its softness; it was possible to maintain a rhythm. I have already written of the importance of maintaining a rhythm in high-altitude mountaineering. It is better to have moderately soft snow consistent in its softness than a mixture of very soft and very hard snow on which rhythmical movement is impossible. Of course, when very soft snow is encountered, rhythm is equally impossible, owing to the difficulty and effort of lifting the foot, and had the snow between Camp Five and the summit of Kamet been very soft the whole way, there would have been no hope of reaching the summit in one day, and we should have been forced to pitch a higher camp.

Shipton, Holdsworth and I took it in turns to lead. We did about a quarter of an hour each. Had there been only two of us to stamp out the steps the work would have been very exhausting, but the difference between taking a turn every half an hour and taking it every quarter of an hour at such an altitude is enormous.

In its lower portion the slope was between 30° and 40° in angle: it steepened gradually.

We sat down for a rest. As we sat, our thudding hearts and hard-pressed lungs gradually eased to a more normal rhythm. We had climbed the first 500 feet in an hour and had reason to congratulate ourselves. Immediately below us were

Meade's Col and the camp – toy-like tents and snow crumpled with footmarks. Only Abi Gamin East overlooked us. To the right was the snowy edge of the eastern precipice. Fleecy clouds were beginning to twist up from the valleys. The plains of Tibet were opening out; their brown and yellow expanses melted into violet distances. Eastwards, Gurla Mandhata rose serenely.

We munched a little chocolate and sipped tea from a Thermos flask. It was gloriously hot in the sun, and as yet no wind had arisen to chill us. Lolling in the snow, I felt languid and sleepy. Further advance seemed unnecessary and even absurd. Why not continue to sit and drowse the day away in the warm sun? I forced myself to take some photographs and change a cinematograph film. It was simple and easy work, yet it involved expenditure of both physical and mental energy.

The few minutes we allowed ourselves soon passed. Shipton and Lewa rose to their feet and started up the slope. It was interesting to watch them. Shipton, a born mountaineer, has acquired to perfection the art of climbing a snow slope with the minimum of effort. Lewa, on the other hand, is so constituted that he tends to expend more of his magnificent energy than is necessary. So much fire and dash is his to command that he cannot properly control its tumultuous outflow, and his eager jerky movements contrasted oddly with the almost leisurely rhythm of Shipton. As they toiled through the soft snow, I trained the cine-camera on them and "shot" some film. I remember wishing as I did so that I had not burdened myself with the work of taking a film of the expedition, and I vowed that I would never do it again.

Holdsworth, Nima Dorje and I followed. One moment we had been sitting at ease, fully capable of appreciating the glorious panorama spread out before us; the next moment, almost with a suddenness of a blow, ease had been relegated to the past, and we became once more panting automatons of flesh and blood. Sitting, we had forgotten that we were breathing the thin air of nearly 25,000 feet but even the effort of rising to our feet served like the touch of a foot on the sensitive throttle of a powerful racing car, to set the machinery of heart and lungs pounding furiously.

The snow worsened. Previously, it had been merely soft, but now we encountered crusted snow of the most malignant type, crust which broke when the whole weight had been transferred to the forward foot, letting us sink helplessly into the soft powdery snow beneath.

Even had we taken snow-raquettes with us they would have been useless – the slope was too steep. Ski also would have been impracticable, for, although the crust was not sufficiently frozen to withstand the weight of a booted man; Ski would not have broken it and could not have been edged into it. Rhythmical movement was impossible, and we resigned ourselves to something worse than ordinary toil. Our speed of ascent dropped from 500 feet to about 300 feet an hour. From 100 feet at a stretch by the leader, we were reduced to 50 feet, jealously we glanced back at the square-topped summit of the Abi Gamin East, but it was long ere we overtopped it.

Here and there the slope had been riven by crevasses. These were now choked with snow over which we could pass safely, but in some cases the upper edges of the crevasses rose in steep lips, necessitating a few steps being cut. Step cutting over 24,000 feet is dreadfully fatiguing work, and every minute or two the leader had to stop and gasp and gasp for oxygen.

Perhaps 1,000 feet below the summit we encountered plate-like masses of hard snow, resembling shallow mushrooms several yards in diameter, that had been plastered to the slope by the wind. These plates cracked and slithered away when the foot was placed on them, and we sank knee deep into the powdery snow beneath.

During the ascent of the first 500 feet we had been content to halt only while the lead was being changed, but now, owing to the exhausting nature of the work, the leader found it necessary to sink down into the snow for a rest every few yards, whilst even those behind were glad to follow his example. During these frequent halts we could discern nearly 3,000 feet beneath us the second party mounting slowly towards Camp Five. If to us they appeared mere dots moving with the slowness of a clock's hour hand, how must we have appeared to them? It was good to see them, for we knew that they must be watching us, and were with us in spirit urging us on to success.

We arrived at a point where the slope steepened abruptly. Ice walls and soft snow forced us diagonally to the left towards the edge of the eastern precipice. Now, for the first time since leaving the camp, we could see the final slope separating us from the summit ridge. It was at this slope, 400 feet high, that we had gazed so doubtfully the evening before. Previous opinion as to its steepness needed no confirmation. From the camp it had looked steep, and we knew now that it *was* steep. Everything depended on its condition. Supposing that the rippled, wind-blown snow covering it concealed hard ice? If step cutting was necessary throughout its entire height it would be impossible to overcome it without pitching a higher camp. Time would defeat us; it would take many hours – a whole day's work at least. And supposing the slope consisted of snow ready to avalanche if disturbed? There was no avoiding it. Ice walls barred approach to the right; sheer precipices fell away to the left. Then indeed we should be conclusively beaten. Supposing it proved necessary to pitch a higher camp; was there a ledge on that inhospitable slope of Kamet where a camp could be pitched? We could see none. And were the porters capable of carrying up equipment? It was doubtful; they were already tired from their exertions between Camps Four and Five.

The edge of the eastern precipice abutted as an ill-defined ridge against the final slope. At the point where the ridge merged into the slope a large boulder of Kamet's reddish granite projected from the ice. It looked a welcome resting-place where we might recoup our energies for the final tussle. Up to it we started to climb. Perhaps 100 feet below the boulder, our feet struck ice beneath the snow. The snow thinned until it was no longer deep enough to hold the foot securely to the ice. Step cutting became necessary. The leader braced himself to the task. The axe swung back and leapt forward, meeting the ice with a dull thud.

In the Alps, the ringing thud of the axe and the swish and tinkle of dislodged fragments are music in my ears. The confident raising of the body from step to step, by limbs untired and in perfect training, brings happiness and contentment. But cutting steps in ice at 25,000 feet is a very different matter. The ice slope is not to be welcomed as providing a test of skill; it is an implacable enemy, mute yet savage, passive yet resistant. It hates.

Thud, thud, thud. A step is made. The foot lifts slowly; the nailed boot grinds into the ice.

Thud, thud, thud. There is a duller, less confident ring in the sound of the axe striking the ice. The work stops. Heart and lungs are striving desperately for oxygen; the snow slope swims uncertainly before the eyes of the exhausted mountaineer. He doubles up, and gasps, and gasps, and gasps.

Presently, his body ceases its clamouring for oxygen. He braces his tired and quivering muscles, grasps his axe, and swings it forward again into the green face of the ice.

Thud, thud, thud.

And so it goes on.

One hundred feet – an hour's unremitting toil. We approached the red boulder and, glancing gratefully at it, promised ourselves a long rest on its sun-warmed surface. But as we cut steps up the ice by the side of it our premature gratitude changed to disgust. The boulder was smooth and sloping and there was no place on it where we could sit. But, in one respect at least, fate was kind; the snow above the boulder lay a foot deep on the ice. One by one, we sank down into it.

Nima Dorje was last on the rope. He was going badly. His feet were slipping from the ice steps and he was using the rope as a handhold, a sure sign of exhaustion. As he approached, I could see that his eyes were dull and had lost their animation. His thick lips were parted widely and his lower jaw hung down. It was no surprise to us when, on joining us, he sank into the snow gasping out that he was finished, and could go on no farther. He had bravely done his best and had carried a load of cinematograph apparatus weighing 20 lbs. on his back to a height of over 25,000 feet. He soon recovered from his temporary exhaustion, and although it was impossible for him to continue, he was able to return alone safely, for the route was devoid of danger so long as he kept to the uphill track and a slip on the ice slope could be attended with no worse consequences than a slide into the soft snow beneath.

It was now 2 p.m. Six hours had passed since we had left Camp Five. The first 500 feet had been climbed in about an hour, but the last 1,300 feet had taken five hours, an average speed of well under 300 feet an hour. This slow rate of progress had been due to the terrible snow and the time spent hewing steps in the ice slope below the boulder. Anxiously we stared at the slope above us. There was no deception as to its steepness. The average angle was well over 50° – an angle at least as steep as that of the ice slopes on the Brenva face of Mont Blanc. Everything depended on the condition of the snow. Had the slope been pure ice from top to bottom there would have been no alternative but to retreat and devote our energies during the next two or three days to the difficult task of establishing a higher camp, or possibly of attempting the alternative route from Meade's Col.

As far as the boulder, a slip could not have mattered, but the final slope overlooked the great eastern precipice of Kamet, and a slip on it was not to be thought of. Heaving ourselves wearily to our feet, we recommenced the ascent. Again we found ourselves on mushroom-like plates of snow, but on the whole firmer snow than we had encountered lower down. Between these plates there was powder snow, and the foot sank into it encountering ice. Here step cutting was necessary. To do it we had to summon up the whole of our mental determination as well as our physical energy, and both were now dulled by fatigue and altitude. The temptation was to kick steps and trust to the snow holding. Luck had been with us so far, and we could scarcely afford to abuse it now. In places steps were necessary for safety, and I am glad to be able to record that those steps were cut.

The slope steepened until it was practically a wall. We advanced in turn. A few feet at a time was enough, and we would then stop to gasp for oxygen and renewed energy.

I remember that on these occasions, as I leaned forward to rest on my in-driven ice axe, I could see my feet, a few yards of wind-caked snow slope, and then the East Kamet Glacier, nearly 7,000 feet beneath. By the boulder sat the solitary figure of Nima Dorje. The sun was still shining on him, but already we were in chill shadow.

In with the ice axe and on. The plates of hard snow swished away into the abyss, a gentle sibilant whisper. When I was leading, there was naught but the blank slope before me. When my companions were leading, my vision was limited to their feet. I remember once experiencing a ridiculous feeling of annoyance at the sight of Holdsworth's boot, breaking away one of the evil snow-slabs. I thought savagely to myself, Why can't he kick a better step – why fiddle and fumble in that ridiculous manner? But, when my turn came to lead, my feet kicked just as clumsily. Directly above us the declining sun illuminated a small flake of snow projecting from the summit ridge with a calm gleam. The flake seemed always as far away. Then suddenly, to my surprise I could touch it. Driving my ice axe in before me, I hauled myself up on both arms, crushing the flake, beneath me. I found myself sprawling, exhausted with the effort, face downwards, across the summit ridge. My head was in the sun, my feet in the shadow. Huge columns of cloud were rising djinn-like from the blue depths into which I gazed. They swayed unsubstantially for a moment as I fought for oxygen. For perhaps a minute I lay gasping like a stranded fish, then, pulling myself together, swung astride the sharp roof-like ridge and began taking in Holdsworth's rope round the ice axe. Presently, we were all congregated on the ridge.

We had hoped to find ourselves on the summit, or within a few yards of it, but we saw immediately that we were separated from it by a knife-like crest of snow. As we gazed along the narrow path we must tread, we experienced a pang of apprehension. Some thirty yards distant the ridge rose up into a sharp point. Beyond this nothing was to be seen, but we realised instinctively that the point was not the summit. Slopes of rock and snow, which we could see sloping up beyond it, indicated something higher. Had Kamet a surprise in store for us? What if there was an impracticable cleft in the ridge between us and the summit? We would have given much for a rest, but to rest was impossible, until we had stood upon the point and seen what lay beyond.

We started to toil along the ridge. It was nearly horizontal and exceedingly sharp. On either hand the slopes fell away with great steepness; it seemed incredible that we could have ascended from those shadowy abysses to the right of us. I remember trampling and crushing the delicate snow edge with a careful yet savage deliberation. There must be no mistake now. On the slope below we had been mere automatons – toiling atoms incapable almost of reasoned and coherent thought – but now we were thinking men again, capable of realising our amazing position on this snowy edge of the world. Tiredness was replaced by a fierce exhilaration. The numbed brain leapt into renewed activity. The summit was almost within our grasp; surely it could not escape us now? We gained the point and gazed over and beyond it. At our feet the ridge sank down to a shallow gap. Beyond the gap it merged gently into a small cone of snow – the summit!

We seized hold of Lewa and shoved him on in front of us. As I clutched hold of him I could hear the breath jerking from him in wheezy gasps. I do not think that he quite understood what we were doing. And so he was first to tread the summit. It was the least compliment we could pay to those splendid men, our porters, to whom we owed the success of our expedition.

As we reached the summit we saw that there was another equally high summit a few yards away, so, to be quite sure, we trudged across to it. Nothing further disputed us and for the last time we sank down into the snow.

With numbed and fumbling hands, I manipulated my camera and cine-camera, photographing and filming the party, the view from the summit, and the summit itself from the range of a few yards. By the time I had finished, my fingers were stiff, white and dead. Fearing frostbite, I beat my hands together. Circulation returned sluggishly and so painfully that I could barely refrain from groaning.

We left Camp Five at 8 a.m. and arrived on the summit at 4.30 p.m.; eight and a half hours work for about 2,300 feet of ascent. As the first 500 feet had been climbed in a little over an hour, the ascent of the last 1,500 feet had taken no less than 7½ hours – an average climbing speed of little more than 200 feet an hour. Snow conditions, rather than altitude, had been responsible for this funereal rate of progress. As we lay in the snow, Holdsworth smoked half a pipe. We had often chaffed him for his devotion to his pipe, but we could scarcely do so after this. Whether or not he *enjoyed* smoking a pipe at 25,447 feet is another matter. At all events, this offering to the Goddess Nicotine deserves to be recorded.

The view? It is difficult to render any account of it. We were too far above the world. Our gaze passed almost contemptuously over mighty range upon mighty range, to seek repose in the violet hazes of illimitable horizons. Huge clouds, sun-crested above, purple-shadowed below, stood out from the valleys, but their top-most turrets could not attain to our level. The breeze fanning us was deathly cold, the silence and sense of isolation almost terrible. There were no green valleys to be seen; all about us were peaks of black rock and glaring ice and snow, frozen outposts of the infinite. Thousands of feet beneath curved the glacier flowing south-westwards of Kamet, ribbed and girded with moraines like some monstrous dragon crawling from one cloudy cavern to another. Our sole link with the world was the camp we had left, now a mere blob on the snow of Meade's Col. Perhaps our friends there were regarding us. We rose to our feet, waved ice axes, and let out a gasping shout. But our voices sounded pitifully weak through the thin air, and there came no response from the dotted tents.

In the far south, anvil-shaped plumes of coppery nimbus stood out from the foothills. Nanda Devi was buried in clouds and there was naught to challenge Kamet with the exception of Gurla Mandhata's glorious *massif*, 110 miles away. I have a dim recollection of a range on the extreme north-western horizon. Was it the eastern wing of the Karakorams? If so, it was 280 miles distant. Only in the north was relief to be found from a savage mountain world: there, barren hills, streaked untidily in snow, fell away into the golden plains of Tibet, tessellated, with blue cloud shadows.

It was 5 p.m., time was vital; in less than three hours we should be overtaken by night. We rose wearily and stiffly to our feet, and tramped back along the summit ridge.

When we came to the point where we had gained the ridge we halted a few instants. At our feet we could see the East Kamet Glacier curving in a serene arc through its gorge of peaks. I looked for Camp Two, but could not distinguish it. My vision swept upwards and over the ranges to the cloud-girdled south, where tall cumulus clouds passed, like ethereal ghosts, along the foothills of the Himalaya. The declining sun caressed us in its kindly glow.

We grasped our ice axes in a firmer grip, and one by one stepped from the ridge. Next instant the shadow of Kamet's northern face had engulfed us.

Now that the job was done, we began to realise how tired we were. It is at such times of mountaineering anticlimax that accidents occur. The oncoming of night, cold, fatigue and desire to return as quickly as possible to the comparative comfort of Camp Five all combined to tempt us to rush down the upper slope. To have done so would have been mountaineering folly of the most elementary character. Steadiness was imperative; impatience had to be curbed. We progressed slowly, rope length by rope length. How slow it was! Impatience and resignation flared up alternately. It seemed as though we were doomed forever to cling and crawl like snails to this snowy flank of Kamet.

We descended in two parties, as on the ascent, but found it quicker to take separate lines rather than for both parties to descend the upward track, even though occasional step cutting was necessary. Yet, if progress was slow, it was also certain and efficient. In drove the ice axe into the snow until it struck the ice beneath; the rope was hitched around it and down went the first man as quickly as possible, until the whole length of the rope was out; then he in turn anchored himself firmly, and took in the rope of the last man as he descended. In the Alps such tactics are seldom necessary even on the steepest snow slope, but we were not in the Alps; we were tired men at a height of 25,000 feet, and a slip must be expected at any moment.

Fortunately, we did not find it essential to adhere to our uphill tracks owing to the improved quality of the snow, and by keeping more to the west were able to make a route that in its lower portion did not overlook the eastern precipice.

At the foot of the final slope Holdsworth and I halted to await Shipton and Lewa. The latter was moving very slowly and was obviously distressed. His face was greenish in hue, his eyes rigid and staring from exhaustion. He groaned out that he was in great pain, and pointed to his stomach. There was nothing we could do for him save to encourage him to continued effort and to relieve him of his load. As I lifted the rucksack with its 20 lbs. or more of film apparatus, I was forcibly reminded of the amount of energy Nima Dorje and Lewa had expended getting it to the summit. Swinging it on to my back overbalanced me, and my tired legs almost collapsed beneath me. Yet, even at that moment, I said to myself that as the "damned thing" had been got to the summit, it somehow had to be got down again.[1]

[1] To those explorers and mountaineers who may be contemplating a cinematograph record of their achievements I can only say that they must remember that, if their picture is to be a success with the film magnates and the film going public they must contrive to include incidents faked or authentic at least as revolting as those that delighted the audiences of the Colosseum at Rome. The mentality that can tolerate pictures such as the Akron airship disaster when men were photographed falling to their death must be fed on lust and horror.

On the ice slopes below the boulder it was necessary to go carefully, for the rough surface of the ice was frozen so hard that an uncontrolled slide would have stripped a man's skin from him like paper.

Below the ice slope we unroped. We had hoped to descend the lower slopes quickly and easily, but the soft snow had frozen into a vicious breakable crust, and the hard snow had frozen into icy boards. In some places our feet broke through the crust into the powdery snow beneath, and had to be dragged out again; in other places we slithered unpleasantly. Once or twice we tried to glissade, but this proved impossible on the breakable crust or dangerously uncontrollable on the harder and icier slopes.

Slowly Abi Gamin East rose to the level of our vision. The camp below, a single blob when seen from the summit, resolved itself into the separate specks of our tents.

About 1,000 feet from the camp I decided to abandon the load of cinematograph apparatus, as its weight was delaying me, whilst the difficult snow made it an exhausting load to carry. At all events, it was left within range of the camp and could be recovered next day.

The cold became more severe, and the coldness of high altitudes is akin to the coldness of space itself.

The sun's last flare lit peak and snowfield. Night, a vast phalanx of purple, rushed up the sky. The slanting rays of the setting sun flooded the Tibetan plains, throwing into sharp relief numberless little crags and hills, that stood out like the fantastic buildings of some demon city.

Day drained quickly from the peaks. A cold pallor invested the world. And now we witnessed a strange spectacle. As the sun sank in the west another sun rose to rival it in the east, but a sun with rays, not of light, but of darkness, that radiated upward to the zenith of the evening sky. It was the parallel shadows of the peaks in the west cast by the real sun across the sky to such a distance, that they appeared to converge in a point above the eastern horizon.

I do not remember feeling exhausted, yet I do remember that my knees were so curiously weak that a stumble in the crusted snow or a slither on the hard crust was difficult to correct without falling.

Figures detached themselves from the camp beneath and came slowly through the dusk to meet us. A few minutes later I was grasping Birnie's hand and drinking hot liquid from a vacuum flask which he had thoughtfully brought with him. A glowing warmth spread through my tired limbs; a profound contentment permeated my whole being. A hundred yards more and the tents of Camp Five loomed up before us. The afterglow of a cloudless sunset saw us stumbling into camp.

We had not escaped scatheless. Intense cold during the descent had wreaked its will upon us. Poor Lewa was so exhausted that he could scarcely stagger. The removal of his boots and stockings revealed feet frozen and immovable, the whiteness of which was already changing to a dark purple. Men were immediately set to work to try to restore their circulation, but though they massaged for an hour or more his feet were far beyond the initial stages of frostbite, and circulation would not return. Holdsworth's right big toe was also frostbitten and Shipton's toe tips were slightly affected. I was the only one to escape, and I attribute my immunity, not to an exceptionally good circulation, but to the fact that when mountaineering and skiing in the Alps I have made it my invariable practice to keep my toes moving in my boots by bunching them up and straightening them out at periodical intervals throughout a cold day. This had become so much of a habit that, though I cannot remember doing so, I feel certain that I kept it up on Kamet.

Supper went down well that night, although we were too tired to eat much. Tinned beans and tinned fruit, followed by a jorum of hot rum, set us in a warm glow that lasted throughout a cold night. For some time Shipton and I lay cosily side by side in our sleeping bags, recalling the events of the day. Already they seemed a past chapter of life, and, as drowsiness gradually overcame me, they receded farther and farther into the forgotten. Quietness fell upon the camp. In the south, lightning winked and glimmered ceaselessly over the foothills.

CHAPTER FIFTEEN

The Second Ascent

THE SECOND PARTY decided not to climb Kamet the day after the first party, but to spend a day at Camp Five acclimatising, and, if weather conditions permitted, ascend on the following day. Another reason for this postponement was Lewa. His feet were so seriously frost-bitten that the sooner he was sent down to the Base Camp the better.

Greene said that he would not be answerable for the consequences if this was not done: in the denser air of lower altitudes and increased oxygenation of the blood lay the only chance of saving his feet.

During the day three local porters arrived with a mail, surely the highest postal delivery ever made? One of these men, Kesar Singh, was retained, and Budhibal Gurung was put in charge of the party detailed off to take Lewa from camp to camp down the mountain. We had already seen enough of him to know that he was to be relied upon absolutely. Another piece of work that had to be done was the recovery of the abandoned cinematograph apparatus. To begin with, not a Darjeeling man would volunteer for this. Superstition was rife among them, and they would not stir. According to the second party, Nima Dorje had returned to camp in a hysterical condition and babbling of gods and devils whom he affirmed had taken all the air away. And now the all-powerful god of Kamet had burnt Lewa's feet. At last Birnie managed to prevail upon his own servant, Dorje, to brave, for a consideration, the wrath of this outraged god and ascend to recover the apparatus.

The day was not a pleasurable one. Holdsworth, Shipton and I were experiencing a certain physical and mental reaction. The air was not so still as it had been previously, and the gentlest breeze at 23,300 feet is sufficient to send the mountaineer shivering into his sleeping bag. The weather appeared to be deteriorating, and leaden clouds massing in the south boded ill. In spite of these omens, the morning of June 23 dawned fine, except that the loose powdery snow was streaming in twisting clouds from Meade's Col and the final slopes of Kamet, whilst even Camp Five was not immune from the wind's hateful activity.

To the great regret of all, Beauman decided that he would not accompany the second party. He had not yet acclimatised properly and he doubted his ability to reach the summit. Unselfishly, therefore, he decided not to imperil the safety of success of his companions by risking exhaustion or collapse. It was a wise decision, and one made in accordance with the best traditions of mountaineering. How much disappointment it meant, I do not think any of us realised until afterwards. I am confident that, had it been possible for him to have spent another day or two at Camp Five, he would have acclimatised sufficiently to have made the ascent.

The second party were not burdened with cinematograph apparatus, but they decided to take a porter to carry their odds and ends, their clothes and food, etc. But a porter was not easy to obtain. Not a Darjeeling man would go. Nima Dorje had shaken them profoundly; Lewa's feet had demoralised them. To them Lewa was something more than a sirdar; he was a strong man, one whom the gods had endowed bountifully with strength far in excess of their own; if the gods had treated him thus, how should they escape even worse consequences for invading their sanctuaries of snow? And, after all, had not Kamet been ascended by the sahibs? Why worry, why risk life and limb by making a second ascent? Such were their arguments and convictions, and not even Birnie could shake them. It was indeed strange and pathetic to see these hardened veterans of Everest and Kangchenjunga, the prey to superstitious fears, crouched cowering in their tents.

But the Bhotias of Niti and Mana were not cursed by such fears and superstitions. Among them, Kesar Singh appeared to regard the expedition as one huge and continual joke and not even the thin air and cold of 23,300 feet had shrivelled his grin or quenched his natural cheerfulness. Gods and devils meant nothing to him. Of course, it was quite on the cards that there might be a few odd ones knocking about on the summit of Kamet. Was there not supposed to be a golden palace there, tenanted by a powerful god? Yet here he was, only a short distance from the summit, and there was no sign of any such thing. Women's tales! The imagination of fakirs, who had never seen Kamet, but who terrorised for their own pecuniary ends the villagers in the Alaknanda Valley. And it would be something to have seen England from the summit. Had not the Gurkha soldier with Longstaff Sahib said that it was visible? What a triumph it would be! He would be king of his village, of his valley. The village elders would sit at his feet in respectful admiration, and he would say, 'I, Kesar Singh, have been up with the sahibs to the palace of the gods. The sahibs singled me out from among many as being the strongest and best. Even their own Darjeeling wallahs would not go, and without me they could not have got to the summit of Kamet. Behold those whom the sahibs and gods favour,' etc., etc., etc. Thus Kesar Singh, a plausible and likeable rascal, and one with the lust for adventure in his veins. There are more of his type in the valleys of northern Garhwal, and, given the same opportunities as the Darjeeling men, they would, I am convinced, develop into even finer mountaineers, finer at all events in that they would not be cursed on a mountain with unnerving superstitions.

Kesar Singh had been equipped with the same clothing and boots as had the

Darjeeling men and other local high-climbing porters. He was thankful enough of the former, but refused to wear the latter. He preferred to don the local footwear, and wrapped layer after layer of sacking and cloth round his feet. It hardly seemed suitable footgear for 25,000 feet, but he so evidently preferred it to boots that he was allowed to wear it.

The second party started at 6.45 a.m. June 23 – more than an hour earlier than the first party, for the morning was not so cold as on June 21. Yet, an hour later, when the sun's warmth tempted us from our tents, they seemed to have covered but a short distance and were still near the camp.

Watching them, we could realise how slow our own progress must have been. There they were, mere dots fastened to the vast slopes of Kamet. We would go into our tents and spend an hour or two in our sleeping bags and come out again: there they were, the same place as before; no, just a little higher. As the morning wore on, one black dot detached itself from the other two and was left behind. We wondered whether it was Kesar Singh, but when the dot moved on again in determined pursuit of the first two dots we knew it must be either Birnie or Greene, for if Kesar Singh had been left behind he would hardly have had the initiative to try and catch up again.

As the day wore on the dots crept up the mountainside. The sun passed westwards, shadows engulfed them and they were lost to view.

It had been our intention to climb, if possible, the Abi Gamin East. Beauman suggested the ascent, but I fear that Holdsworth, Shipton and I did not greet the suggestion with the enthusiasm it deserved. It was not that we were lazy, but that we were tired. Lost energy is difficult to recoup at high altitudes. Holdsworth, however, despite his frostbitten big toe, visited Meade's Col on ski, 23,500 feet, the highest point to which ski have ever been taken. He reported on his return that the slopes fell sheer on the other side of the col and the ridge leading to Kamet, which we had first thought to be the easiest route to the summit. We realised now that, had we attempted to climb the ridge, it would have been impossible to have deviated from its crest on to its western side, and that the ice slopes would have had to be cut up.

During the afternoon, gusts of cold wind kept us in our sleeping bags most of the time, and in our brief excursions outside our tents we saw that clouds of snow were blowing off the summit of Kamet. Towards evening the wind dropped. We scanned the slope anxiously for signs of the returning party. At length we spotted them, and Holdsworth and I set out to meet them, carrying food and drink. Night was falling as we toiled up the snow slopes towards them.

Before proceeding further, I will quote Captain Birnie's own account written to *The Times*.

> After collecting raisins and chocolates for lunch, we roped and started at 6.45 a.m. We followed the tracks of the former party, Greene leading at a rhythmical pace, which kept us going for long periods without need for a rest.
>
> After two hours the lead was changed. This may have been a mistake, for after a further hour's work Greene feared the possibility of his not reaching the summit, and insisted on my continuing with Kesar Singh without him, saying he would rest and follow if he felt like it.
>
> After another hour's climbing we decided to abandon rucksacks and rope, in order

to lighten ourselves to the minimum. This was a big mistake, due to my not realising the steepness of the snow and ice slope to the summit ridge.

Our route continued up very steep snow, ice steps, cut by the former party, proving very welcome and greatly accelerating our progress. From time to time we saw Greene following half an hour behind.

As we rose, a magnificent view appeared. To the south and east only peaks over 20,000 feet broke through an ocean of white cloud. To the north the vast brown plateaux of Tibet stood out in contrast to the snow-clad peaks to the south, dominated by Nanda Devi. Far away to the north-west, a magnificent range of mountains must surely have been the Karakoram, over 250 miles away. Our immediate object was a big rock, 300 feet below the summit ridge, which we hoped to reach in two hours, but actually took three.

Progress was now extremely difficult. Looking down from the rock, we saw Greene still coming up, a splendid effort, as he was not feeling fit from the start. After a rest we began the final 300 feet to the summit ridge. This proved very hazardous, as the angle increased considerably, and the slope consisted of ice thinly covered with snow. Traces of Smythe's party had been completely spoiled by their downward tracks. This necessitated a long session of step cutting. Kesar Singh assisted splendidly, holding my feet to the slope while fresh steps were cut. Almost unconsciously the work continued, a feeling of despondency dominating everybody, a feeling that the summit would never be reached.

Greene was still following, and now called to me. It was heartening to hear him, and I shouted, 'The summit's quite close,' though actually despairing of ever reaching it.

Suddenly the ridge appeared six feet above. We were there! We climbed the distance in as many seconds, and gazed for the first time south from Kamet's ridge. But we were not yet on the summit, though only 150 yds. from it. We walked along the knife-like edge until we reached the two rounded domes which form the summit of Kamet.

The wind was bitterly cold, so we dropped down the mountain to the south for protection. Shortly afterwards Greene arrived, having made a splendid effort. We wasted no time on the summit owing to the cold.

On starting to descend, Kesar Singh for the first time demurred, saying that his cloth boots would not hold on the steps. Here was where my fault in leaving the rope behind was accentuated. We laughed him out of his temporary fright, Greene leading down the mountain. I came next, Kesar Singh following close behind. I ordered him to use me as a brake, which he did half-a-dozen times before the rock was reached, 300 feet below the summit. Thence he held the steps very well. Above the camp we were met by Smythe and Holdsworth, with rum and chocolate, a most welcome reviver, for we were all very tired and not at all ashamed to allow the offered arms to support us into camp. So ended an arduous climb – made pleasant by the wonderful attention of those in camp on our return.

Like the first party, the second party did not escape scatheless. Kesar Singh, thanks presumably to his cloth boots, escaped frostbite, but Birnie had a little toe badly frostbitten, and Greene's fingertips were slightly affected. He told me afterwards that he had removed his gloves for a few seconds to take a photograph, and in that few seconds the cold and wind had numbed and frostbitten his fingers. The mountaineer who climbs to such heights is made to realise that he is approaching that outside limit of the earth beyond which life cannot exist save under artificial conditions.

CHAPTER SIXTEEN

The Descent

JUNE 24 DAWNED EVILLY. The clouds that had been massing in the south for the past few days had now spread a menacing pall across the zenith, and the summit of Kamet was smoking a wrathful pipe of wind-driven snow. There was no question of remaining longer to climb the Abi Gamin East.* Provisions were running low, bad weather was impending, and the party, both sahibs and porters, were tired from their efforts of the past few days. Our thoughts turned not to further conquests but to rest and warmth. The Base Camp! The very words had a homely ring.

With fingers frozen by vicious flurries of wind-driven snow, we packed our tents. We turned to go. The scene was inexpressibly desolate. Fugitive patches of wan sunlight were chasing affrightedly across the upper slopes of Kamet. Through rifts in the massing clouds sawed menacing fangs of rock and ice. From above came a dull sound, more felt than heard – the orchestra of the storm.

The porters squatted down on their haunches, slipped on their headbands, heaved themselves to their feet, wriggled and shifted their loads into a position of comfort, and lumbered off in their ungainly way down the snow slopes.

Empty food tins, scraps of paper, and odds and ends were all that remained of our highest camp. Nature is an efficient scavenger. Soon the debris would be covered, the trampled snow smoothed, and again Kamet would know peace.

Save that our legs were still a trifle tired, it was an easy matter walking downhill, and we descended at an alpine pace. Holdsworth ran down on ski in a series of long, clean traverses and Christianias which even his frost-bitten toe did not prevent him from executing. Birnie, however, found that his little toe had swollen to such an extent that he could only limp slowly and painfully. The wind rushed at us spitefully as we stood on the crest of the ice-wall. Wind is always unpleasant on any mountain, but at high altitudes it is imbued with a quality of devilishness which must be experienced to be appreciated. It does not blow constantly nor even from the same direction, but thrusts venomously at the mountaineer just when he is congratulating himself on having escaped its attentions.

We hurried down the slopes beneath the ice-wall and gained Camp Four, where all six of us somehow managed to squeeze into the Meade tent standing there and eat some lunch in its shelter, while the porters pitched another tent and crammed themselves into it.

We had managed to bring all our equipment and remaining stores down from

* Climbed from the north in 1950 by Gabriel Chevalley, René Dittert, Alfred Tissieres and Dawa Thondup, supported by Kenneth Berrill.

Camp Five, but as there were not enough porters to carry the spare tent, provisions and equipment remaining at Camp Four, we decided to cast two or three loads down the precipices to the glacier plateau.

The falling loads afforded a horrid spectacle. In the way the bundles of tents and sleeping bags fell they might have been human. They slid sedately yet helplessly for the first few yards down the smooth ice slope. In a second or two their pace increased, they turned over, and commenced to roll. The rolling became faster and faster, increasing to such a fearful velocity that we could hear the rush and the wind of them. They struck the rocks at the foot of the snow and ice slopes hundreds of feet lower, leapt insanely into the air, and, turning over and over, disappeared into the depths. I could scarcely repress a shudder as I watched. Supposing they had been human bodies! I descended to Camp Three with something more than ordinary caution.

We had intended to unloose the fixed ropes during our descent, but the cold wind made us shun this task. We had plenty of rope to spare, and were not likely to require fixed ropes on other mountains.*

A dull afternoon was lapsing into a dismal evening as we tramped across the snow plateau to Camp Three. The jettisoned loads had arrived safely on the plateau, albeit torn and battered, and we were able to congratulate ourselves on having evacuated the high camps without abandoning anything of importance. The worst that could now befall us was a snowfall deep enough to render the upper part of the gully leading down to Camp Two dangerous. But the weather, if unpleasant, did not appear to have the heart to summon up a snowstorm.

At Camp Five, we had sent off Budhibal Gurung with a telegram telling of our successful assault on Kamet, but owing to the strain and difficulty of getting Lewa down, our Gurkha had forgotten it, and we had found it in the tent at Camp Four. Holdsworth, however, volunteered to take it from Camp Three to the Base Camp in one day on ski. Next morning, therefore, he started before the rest of us and accomplished this journey successfully. It was a long hard day, which none of us on foot would have cared to have faced, and demonstrated the utility of ski. As regards the rest of the party, it was arranged that Beauman and Shipton with two men should take Lewa from Camp Two, which he had reached on the day that we had descended from Camp Five to Camp Three, whilst Birnie, Greene and I stayed at Camp Two to supervise bringing down the remaining loads.

Descending from Camp Three, we were reminded of the recent fine weather and the approach of the monsoon. Rocks were peeping through the snow where formerly none were to be seen, but now the peaks were shrouded in sluggish mists, and desultory snowflakes told of bad weather above us.

The bed of the gully leading down to Camp Two and the East Kamet Glacier had been considerably altered by the sun, and it was possible to descend on broken rocks by the side of it for some distance. Falling stones had worn out a deep runnel in the snow of the gully. Porters who had ascended or descended it almost every day since we arrived at Camp Three must have narrowly escaped being hit, but as they seldom worry about anything until it actually happens, and none of them *had* been hit, we had heard nothing about it. Theirs is a fatalistic philosophy.

* Leaving fixed ropes on mountains is now considered very poor practice.

As we descended the steep, upper pitch of the gully there came a sudden clatter. I glanced hurriedly upwards, but before I had time to move there was a whirr and a whizz, followed by several dull thuds, as the stones plunged into the soft snow. I never saw the stones – they were moving too quickly to be visible. I shouted up to Randhoj Kan, who was behind me, to hurry up. My words had no effect, and the little Gurkha descended nonchalantly, with a broad grin; obviously he considered falling stones a huge joke and an occurrence calculated to add zest to an otherwise dull descent.

The East Kamet Glacier had changed considerably in appearance. When we ascended to Camp Two it had stretched white and unbroken; now it was split by crevasses and strewn by boulders as large as cottages.

It was extraordinarily warm, and the soft, moisture-charged airs and roof of grey fish-bellied clouds betokened the onset of the monsoon. I descended in my shirt-sleeves, and the sweat dripped from me.

We trod the glacier and zigzagged between the crevasses. In one place a snow bridge over a crevasse had given way, and an ominous black hole suggested that someone had made an intimate acquaintance with the depths of the glacier. We learnt later that this investigator of subglacial regions was none other than the Old Soldier. Fortunately, however, he had been pulled out again by a rope, uninjured.

As we approached Camp Two, the tents of which straggled between the boulders and crevasses, we saw a number of local porters, who had come up that day, seated smoking their usual villainous mixture of yak dung and charcoal. In the middle of the camp was a solitary figure.

It was Budhibal Gurung. He was standing at attention, as rigid and erect as a ramrod. His head was up-tilted, his chin thrust forward, and his eyes fixed unblinkingly on the infinite. I greeted him in English, but he did not answer, and remained standing stiffly at attention. I could not understand what was the matter with him until I suddenly realised the meaning of his strange behaviour. He had remembered his oversight in leaving the summit telegram at Camp Four, and this was his way of doing penance, a self-imposed fatigue drill for neglecting to carry out an order. It was not until Birnie had arrived and "dismissed" him that he allowed himself to execute an "about turn" and march off to his tent.

Lewa was at the camp. He had refused to go any farther as he wanted to wait for us. His feet were a dreadful sight and it was obvious that if they were to be saved he had to be got down to lower levels without delay. Mentally and physically he was a different man. Lying helpless, with his fierce impetuous spirit chained to a disabled body, unable to give orders, and forced to watch the inefficiency of his fellows without being able to intervene, was gall and wormwood to him. From Camp Five, he had been able to walk down most if not all of the way, but further walking was out of the question. Frostbite in its worst form is cumulative in its effects. To begin with, the part affected is frozen and it is only after it has thawed that the real trouble begins. The tissues have been destroyed, the corpuscles of the blood killed. Gangrene sets in and destroys the affected part. Fortunately, unlike other forms of gangrene, it is local and cannot spread provided sepsis does not supervene, and those portions of the limb or extremities capable of recovering recover, but cause great pain to the patient in so doing. Transportation of badly frostbitten men is no easy matter. Four men under the charge of Beauman and Shipton were detailed off for the work of carrying Lewa to Camp One. Where the East Kamet Glacier was snow-covered and reasonably smooth, he could be dragged along seated on a blanket, but this was only possible for the first mile and he had to be carried the remaining four miles. It was a long job, and it took them seven weary hours to Camp One.

It had taken us little more than an hour to descend from Camp Three to Camp Two, and, as the day was before us as many porters as could be mustered were sent back to Camp Three to fetch down the remainder of the loads. These men went under the command of the Old Soldier, who as temporary sirdar in place of Lewa, exhibited commendable alacrity in getting them together. They returned the same evening with all the loads.

The following day, June 26, Birnie, Greene and I set off to the Base Camp, taking with us all the porters. We had to leave some half-dozen loads, but these could easily be retrieved later by the local men. It was a dismal morning, and mists shrouding the peaks drooped down almost to the level of the East Kamet Glacier. For a while the sun shone feebly, then, giving up an unequal contest, disappeared.

As we trudged down the glacier into the jaws of its great gorge, the mountain walls on either side, concealed behind leaden mists, seemed full of an indescribable menace. If we could not see, we could at least visualise the hanging glaciers above us with their unstable walls of ice, waiting only for the monsoon's warmest breath to sweep the glacier in cataclysmic avalanches. I could not help thinking, that here was Kamet's last chance for revenge. For a while we walked downhill in mist, then, emerging from the mist, found ourselves on the level plain where the glacier bends round a corner before rising steeply towards Camp Two. On the way up to Camp Two we had kept as far as possible to the northern edge of this plain, but the local men who had been working between Camps One and Two had had no thought but to spare themselves work; they had ascended by the easiest route, and this lay across the middle of the plain. It showed their complete ignorance of mountaineering principles or contempt for danger, for the plain was strewn with blocks of ice, many of them weighing tons, which had recently fallen from the hanging glaciers perched thousands of feet above on the side of Mana Peak. We wasted no time hereabouts, and, hurrying across the dangerous area, gained the crest of the big side moraine running along the northern bank of the glacier, where we could breathe more freely.

The gloom increased. Snow began to fall, at first in desultory flakes, then in a heavy storm. We ate a cold, uncomfortable lunch in the lee of a boulder. We were no longer in the danger zone, and, as though to emphasise our safe deliverance, the clouds parted and pools of sunlight fell upon the glacier. By the time we were abreast of Camp One we were warm and dry.

There was no need to visit Camp One and we cut across to the southern side of the glacier, having to make many toilsome ascents over moraine mounds in the process. On the way up we had borne patiently with these, but now they exasperated us. Our thoughts were concentrated, not on the beauties and grandeurs about us, but on the sumptuous meal we were going to have at the Base Camp, and of how long and comfortably we would sleep.

At last we turned the corner under the little peak at the junction of the East Kamet and Raikana Glaciers. I said to myself, 'In another twenty minutes we shall be there.' It was more like two hours. Landmarks as we had known them had disappeared. The snow partially filling the hollows between the moraine mounds had melted. We wandered wearily and fretfully in a stony maze, soon losing touch with one another and taking different routes, each man convinced that his was the best route.

Evening was drawing on apace, and I was beginning to wonder whether we should find the Base Camp at all that day, and was thinking with a certain grim humour that it would be somewhat of a joke to have to bivouac on that vile moraine probably within a few hundred yards of it, when of a sudden there came a distant shout, and I perceived a figure standing on the summit of one of the moraine mounds. It waved an arm and disappeared like a jack-in-the-box. A minute or two later it reappeared, this time on the summit of a nearer moraine mound. After this process, had been repeated a number of times, the sheep-like face of Alam Singh, carved into a broad smile of welcome, suddenly shot up over the crest of a neighbouring stone ridge a few yards away. He pointed in the direction I must go, then went off to round up my companions. Even so it was difficult to find the Base Camp amid such a bewildering labyrinth of stony mounds. Once I saw its green tents seemingly only 100 yards or so away, but when, after toiling up to the crest of the next ridge the tents had mysteriously vanished, I began almost to imagine myself moving aimlessly about in some "Looking-glass" land, and I should scarcely have been surprised had I seen the grim-visaged Red Queen stumping towards me over the stones. And then, suddenly, I heard voices. I could sniff the familiar odour of burning juniper. There was the Base Camp below me not twenty yards away!

The porters did not turn up until after dark. They had wisely chosen a more circuitous but easier route from Camp One, which had been carefully cairned while we were on the mountain. Short cuts on a mountain seldom pay a dividend of saved time.

At the Base Camp we learnt that Beauman and Shipton had experienced considerable difficulty in getting Lewa down from Camp One. The local men had refused to carry him and had started up the East Kamet Glacier towards Camp Two, saying that they would rather bring down the remainder of the loads. Nima had been sent after them to expostulate with them and bring them back. There had never existed any particular love or sympathy between the local men and the Darjeeling men, and words had run high. Finally, Nima received somebody's fist in his eye. However, enough men were got together to carry Lewa. Apart from the natural antipathy liable to flare up at any moment between the local men and the Darjeeling men, the attitude adopted by the former towards Lewa was undoubtedly due to the treatment he had meted out to them in the first place. Driving-power, and not tact, was Lewa's strong suit.

It was a happy party that sat down to supper in the mess tent that evening. Not even a return to Achung could dim our cheerfulness. Even soup tasting of juniper and greasy dish cloths could be forgiven and forgotten when our last bottle of brandy went the round and when pipes and cigarettes had filled the little mess tent with a blue haze. Then Shipton got out the gramophone and records from the packing-case where they had lain during our sojourn on Kamet with the tenderness of a mother raising her child from its cot; and once more Frank Crumit,

Gracie Fields, Caruso, Paul Robeson, Kreisler, and other well-tried favourites made their bow to an uncritical assembly. Between whiles we yarned; yarned of incidents already almost forgotten, of delights and difficulties, of humours and of what we had done and what we might have done, of Piccadilly and Camp Five, of our favourite grill-room and the cooking of Nima Dorje. We were not the only ones to make merry. From the direction of the porters' quarters came a constant chatter of voices, punctuated with guttural laughs – the carefree laughs of men who had found happiness in the knowledge of work accomplished.

It was late when we turned in. The snow-charged clouds of the day had long relinquished their burden and melted away. The moon rode high; glacier, peak and snowfield were bathed in her radiance. No lightning flickered to disturb the serenity of the night. Remote from the world, the moonlit summit of Kamet was hung from the stars.

CHAPTER SEVENTEEN

To Gamsali

THE WEATHER, after harrying us during the descent, regained its former tranquillity. We spent three days resting. During that period the sun shone from cloudless skies and we basked in its rays. But on the peaks there was evidence of bad weather. The smoke from our cigarettes scarcely wavered in the still air, but we could see the banners of wind-blown snow streaming from Kamet. Peaceful days they were except for me, for I had to spend many hours every day chained mentally to a typewriter, thumping out a full account of our doings.

While we rested, the last loads came down from Camps One and Two and the yaks came up from the pastures where they had been grazing. On June 29 we packed up preparatory to descending to Niti and Gamsali.

On June 30 we left the Base Camp. On the way up to it we had trudged over snow for the last mile, but now, save for scattered drifts, it had melted. Stones and grass had taken its place, and many little brooks had been born that babbled over the red pebbles or paused to repose themselves in quiet pools which mirrored the peaks around. A soft moisture-charged breeze brought a fragrance of flowers. Between the boulders were little alps set green and level, like elfin bowling-grounds. Here perhaps the snow-maidens join hands with the "Lordly Ones" of the pastures. The shush of the wind in the grasses might almost have been their impish whisperings.

The yaks, after a long sojourn on the pastures and a life of luxury and ease, made it plain that they resented a renewal of work. Off went their loads one after another amid curses and entreaties from their drivers, but presently they resigned themselves grumpily to their task.

We lounged, downhill to the plain at the confluence of the Raikana and Dhaoli Rivers. Ascending, we had crossed the Dhaoli River by a snow bridge of avalanche debris, but the bridge had long since melted or been swept away and we found ourselves confronting an unfordable, raging torrent. Fortunately, it was possible for an active man to cross the torrent higher up, but this involved rock climbing and did not appear a feasible route for laden men. It seemed best to span the torrent by a rope bridge stretched between two large boulders that stood opposite to one another on either bank. Our local men were fully equal to such an emergency, and promised us that they would soon make the bridge. As it was already late in the afternoon and it would take many hours for ourselves and our loads to cross the torrent, we decided to camp.

Growing near the camp were spring onions, which made a welcome addition to the cooking-pot. The evening was wonderfully warm, and even night chilled the air but little; evidently, the monsoon was close at hand.

Early next morning a rope of five strands of alpine line was securely stretched between the two boulders. A sturdy V-shaped juniper root was trimmed and whittled until its surface offered the minimum of friction to the rope; this was placed inverted over the rope, and from it, suspended by various odd bits of rope, another root which had to bear the load or man. The contraption was then hauled along the rope across the torrent. It was a primitive form of the rope and breeches buoy arrangement by means of which shipwrecked mariners are rescued. Alam Singh stood on one side of the stream and screamed instructions; Natar Singh stood on the other side and screamed back; the men, taking no notice of either of their sirdars, pulled the loads one by one across the stream.

But if the contraption was able to transport men and loads, it was scarcely able to cope with a yak. The yaks, however, were fully capable of crossing the torrent without extraneous aid. Unladen, they were driven in a herd to the edge of the torrent at a point where it curved slightly, and with yells, shouts, imprecations, sticks and stones from the porters, urged into its raging waters. For a few seconds they struggled ineffectually to keep their feet – then they were swept helplessly away. It seemed as though some at least must perish in the turmoil of water, but all the time their sturdy feet were pawing at the bed of the torrent, and so, helped both by their own efforts and the bend in the torrent, they heaved themselves ponderously on to the other bank none the worse for their adventure. The only yak to require assistance was a half-grown one which for a while resolutely refused to enter the river, but, when a rope had been fixed to it as a safeguard, it seemed to realise that it must follow its elders, and set out resolutely for the opposite bank, which it reached without misadventure. In such a torrent a man would have been swept instantly from his feet and smashed to pulp on the boulders. The same fate would, in all probability, overtake a horse, but a yak, despite its ungainly appearance and ponderous body, is endowed with enormous strength, whilst its centre of gravity is so low that it cannot be capsized easily.

As to our own crossing of the river, if not as dangerous as the journey by lorry from Ranikhet to Baijnath it was at least as terrifying. The rope bridge sagged in the middle, so that the legs, and even the nether garments of the heavier members of the expedition, were immersed in the stream. It was an instance where the light-weights, Beauman, Birnie, Shipton and myself, scored over the heavy-weights, Holdsworth and Greene. It took many hours to get all the loads across, but the crossing was effected without casualty, save that a valuable camera outfit of

Birnie's broke away from its securing strap and was lost in the torrent.

We camped at Goting in drizzling rain, and next day, July 2, set out for Gamsali. It was a damp, hot day, with heavy clouds gathering in the south. On the way Budhibal Gurung managed to shoot two bharhal. As it was impossible to carry them down, the choicest and tenderest portions were separated and added to the loads.

Our porters were in great spirits, and I noticed that most of the Darjeeling men deviated from the path in order to visit Niti. Below the village we found Miss Benham encamped on the same spot where she had been when we left Niti. Local information had it that some English people were coming up the valley and were camped close at hand. As we saw some tents on the hillside we took these to be their camp, and were not a little disgusted when, on toiling up to them, we found that they were the tents of some nomadic Bhotias.

As we passed along the path through the Niti Gorge we endeavoured to cheer up Lewa. We had managed to procure a pony for him at Niti, and on it he now sat bowed and huddled like a dispirited Napoleon returning from Moscow. The tears were streaming down his cheeks, and he was sobbing bitterly not, I believe, so much from pain as from what he felt to be an undignified position and thoughts of the future. He was but a shadow of his former self, and we could not help but perceive in his moral breakdown and distress the essential difference between the European and the native. Had one of us been seriously frostbitten he would at least have *tried* to bear his misfortune with stoical calm and fortitude. But a native cannot control his feelings; he is a child; his mind cannot master pain or mental depression; he seeks not to know the whys and wherefores of a physical infirmity – he only knows that he is hurt or ill, that something is wrong with him, and that is sufficient to cause a moral breakdown which is all the more pitiful when it happens in the case of an otherwise strong man.

As Greene and I walked along the path we noticed one of our porters ahead of us. As we approached him we saw that his walking, both in execution and direction, was decidedly erratic. We watched him a trifle anxiously, for the edge of the path was unprotected and there was a sheer precipice of several hundred feet into the Dhaoli River. As we passed him, we received a foolish grin. It was Passang. And a Passang who had partaken of spirituous liquor. Passang, the stolid, the sober, the respectable, was drunk!

Now we knew why our porters had visited Niti. Passang was not the only one. As we neared the camping-ground at Gamsali we heard an uproar of angry voices. The bone of contention – and it was literally a bone – was the leg of one of the bharhal shot by Budhibal Gurung. Two or three Darjeeling men had hold of one end of it and two or three local men the other. It was a fine tug of war, and we only arrived in time to prevent an affray in which kukris might have done serious injury. The dispute was easily settled – if the porters could not decide whose property it was, the sahibs would have it. There were no more arguments as to the ownership of the meat. There were also some empty packing cases which were coveted by the local men. As we had no further use for them, we were disposed to give them away to the more deserving. As, however, the local men refused for some time to set about their task of collecting firewood, orders were given for the destruction of the boxes to start a fire. This brought the malcontents to their senses and they implored us to spare the boxes. It was the only occasion on which trouble occurred among our porters, and it was the result simply and solely of the local firewater, which fanned into flame the smouldering jealousy existing between the Darjeeling men and the local men. Order was soon restored, and the men set about erecting our tents. Passang hitting his thumb with the mallet in mistake for the tent peg, and the Old Soldier, always preternaturally solemn when under the influence of alcohol, entangled in the guy ropes of my tent were not the least amusing incidents of the day.

Apart from the necessity for a rest at a reasonable altitude in order to recoup strength and allow enlarged hearts to return to their normal size, it was necessary to reorganise our porterage and overhaul our stores. Men had to be engaged in place of yaks, and in this sparsely populated district they were not easy to find. Food was lasting out well. As however we were short of sugar and jam, a message was sent to Captain Clarke at Ranikhet asking him to send up to Badrinath a load of provisions including these commodities, and also golden syrup, the omission of which from our original stores was a grievous mistake, and had been often bemoaned.

Our next objective was Badrinath. The easiest and longest route was down the Dhaoli Valley to Joshimath, and then up the ordinary pilgrim route. We had resolved, however, to cross the Zaskar Range to the south of Kamet. Only one pass, the Bhyundar Kanta*, 16,790 feet, had been made across the watershed of this range. The date on which it was first traversed is not known, but it is known to have been crossed in 1862 by Colonel Edmund Smyth, who reopened it, when it had been disused and forgotten for many years. His Bhotia porters lost their way and he had to bivouac in the open on the pass. This pass leads into the fertile Bhyundar Valley, which joins the Alaknanda Valley some five miles north of Joshimath and ten miles south of Badrinath. When Doctor Longstaff's party crossed the pass in 1907, local information had it that a descent of the lower part of the Bhyundar Valley was impossible owing to steep and narrow gorges. He, therefore, climbed out of the Bhyundar Valley at the point where it bends in a southerly direction, and, crossing the easy grass pass of the Khanta Khal, 14,750 feet, descended to Hanuman Chatti, some five miles south of Badrinath, on the pilgrim route. Another route between the Alaknanda and Dhaoli Valleys was that made by Meade from Mana by the Kuhlia Ghata and Bhyundar Kanta Passes. A way has now been trodden up the gorge of the Bhyundar Valley by shepherds and their flocks, and it is no longer necessary to traverse the Khanta Khal in order to reach the Alaknanda Valley. Our object was to cross the range north of these passes and make as direct a line as possible between Gamsali, Badrinath and Mana. Doctor Longstaff mentioned that the late A.L. Mumm found unexpected indications of a pass at the head of the Banke Glacier which fills the upper part of the Gamsali Valley. These indications were not, however, followed up.[1] We intended to act on this information and make a new and more direct route to Badrinath and Mana from the head of the Banke Glacier. We hoped also to examine Kamet's southerly outpost, Mana Peak, 23,862 feet, with a view to attempting an ascent. Further, the head of the Banke Glacier and its tributary glaciers should repay exploration.

[1] *Alpine Journal, Vol.* xxiv, pp. 127–29.

* Now known as Bhiundhar Khal.

With these objects in view we decided to send our heavy luggage round by the lower route via Joshimath to Badrinath under the charge of Alam Singh, and proceed as a light mobile party across the Zaskar Range with a limited number of porters carrying only a small amount of food and light equipment. Lewa was to accompany the heavy baggage party to Joshimath, where there is a hospital at which his frostbitten feet could be looked after.

The monsoon had now arrived, and during the three days that we were at Gamsali warm drizzling rain alternated with sunny periods, and woolly grey clouds, hanging low on the peaks, seemed an earnest of worse weather to come.

One afternoon we spent visiting the village of Gamsali. It is a quaint little place, and its primitive houses are almost indistinguishable from the huge grey boulders among which they cluster. Like other villages in this part of the world, it is built anywhere and anyhow, and its streets, if such a name can be applied to the refuse-stinking channels between the houses, run in any and every direction. Yet, even this remote corner of the British Empire possesses its social amenities. There is a school, a collection of ragged little urchins every whit as impudent and potentially intelligent as their East End prototypes, ruled by a headmaster even more ragged and disreputable in appearance than they are. His shirt was torn, tattered and filthy, his trousers beyond repair, sacking in lieu of boots encased his feet, and his long melancholy face wore an expression of patient martyrdom. There was also a tailor who was the proud possessor of an aged sewing machine.

A mob of curious children followed us round. We were invited by the headman to partake of tea with him, but had not the courage to enter his filthy-looking abode. The inhabitants were mostly Hindu-Bhotias, Hinduism being evidenced by the number of girls and women with rings piercing their nostrils. Unlike the sullen-faced, suspicious Hindus of the plains, these Bhotias are a friendly, cheerful and happy-go-lucky people, reflecting in their broad grins and graceful salutations the freedom and *camaraderie* of the hills. Of a very different type was the itinerant fakir who visited our camp. He was on a pilgrimage, so he said, to the sacred peak of Kailas, though I suspect, like many others of his type, his pilgrimage was merely an excuse for beggary and extortion on religious grounds, from the villages along his route. Never have I gazed upon a more evil countenance; it made us shudder, and his fixed automatic smile could not disguise the calculating evil of his cruel eyes. He was a gymnast, and for the sum of one rupee stood on his head on the top of a large boulder and contorted himself into various attitudes, principal among which was a lithesome locking of the legs. He knew four words of English, one, two, three and four, and shouted these out like a sergeant major at every kick of the legs. We were not sorry to see the last of him, for he was the incarnation of evil and vice.

At length, on July 4, the loads had been made up by Shipton and Beauman, who sorted out from among a mountain of provisions the quantity required for the crossing of the range. The only commodity in which we were seriously short was sugar. We had left Ranikhet with 100 lbs. of it, and it had melted away like snow, for, as I have previously explained, sugar is the fuel on which the body works at high altitudes. Admittedly the amount was a miscalculation, but, even so, it had disappeared in an extraordinary way, and there is no doubt that the Sherpas' and Bhotias' predilection for anything sweet was in part responsible. Expeditions would do well to note this point, and to divide their sugar supply among small sealed and numbered bags, which can be easily checked. Fortunately, as a substitute we had the native goa, a coarse brown sugar both palatable and nourishing, which is sold in large lumps the size of a man's head, wrapped around with leaves as a protection from dirt.

At length all was ready and we bade farewell to poor Lewa and, leaving Birnie behind us for an extra day to complete the arrangements for the porterage of our heavy luggage, set off on July 5 up the Banke Valley.

CHAPTER EIGHTEEN

The Bhyundar Pass and the Valley of Flowers

JULY 5 HAD DAWNED FINE. It was a morning charged with a joyous freshness, and only gossamer remnants of the monsoon mists clung to the peaks, or explored, like tiny yachts, the deep blue ocean of the sky. From every hollow in the hillsides jaunty brooks poured, to add their quota to the thundering torrent from the Banke Glacier. The moist turf gave springily beneath our tread. Shining drops of water hung from every flower, as though numberless elfin glass blowers were practising their craft.

Doctor Longstaff compared the Banke Valley to "the Vale of Lauterbrunnen carved on a sublime scale, but without the forests". It does indeed bear a striking similarity to the great Oberland trench. Stern precipices hemmed us in on either side; the eye passed almost giddily up their sweeps to a skyline of jagged rock peaks around which the morning mists wove patterns of light and shadow. From the cavernous recesses of deep gullies the melted snow waters boomed sullenly. Here and there, where hollows permitted, rested small glaciers, the green tongues of which licked downwards towards the valley.

The Vale of Lauterbrunnen encloses the traveller between its limestone walls; it is gloomy and depressing at the best of times. The Banke Valley is wider and sunnier. It is open to the breezes that blow from the snows; it possesses the subtle charm of the little known. We could gaze up its cliffs and reflect that they do not serve as rubbish-chutes to hotels. There was no shriek of funicular, no honk of motor-horn, no hum of power station. Peaks climbed and unclimbed stand watch over pastures where brown-eyed yaks graze, and the ragged weather-beaten shepherds make music on their flutes.

For a while we traversed the southern slopes of the valley, then, crossing the stream where it was bridged by avalanche snow, gained an alp of luscious grass where the shepherds of Gamsali and Bampa graze their flocks. For nearly four miles above this alp the valley floor is almost level. We could just perceive the stone-covered snout of the Banke Glacier curving round a corner. The view up the valley was dominated by a beautiful peak. It is one of the few peaks that has been triangulated in this district, and its height is given as 19, 815 feet. It reminded me strongly of the Oberland Bietschhorn, for it has the same graceful shoulders supporting a delicately soaring peak. Shipton was particularly attracted by it, and I saw his eyes wandering over it with the speculative predatory gleam of the mountaineer who sights a foe worthy of his steel.

We ambled along the valley, passing, here and there rude encampments of piled-up stones beneath which the shepherds shelter when minding their flocks.

We camped on a level meadow by a brook. This camping-ground is named Thur Udiar, and Doctor Longstaff's party camped there in 1907. It is 12,000 feet, but the evening was so warm that we did not have to don extra clothing, and sat in comfort around the campfire. The following day, July 6, we continued on our way. After clambering over slopes of boulders forming the terminal moraine of the Banke Glacier, we gained the crest of that glacier's northerly side moraine, which afforded an easy and convenient route. This was the only day of the expedition which I did not in some measure enjoy. I was afflicted with a raging toothache. For a week or two past I had been forced to eat sugary substances and drink hot and cold liquids with circumspection, but now the tooth needed no such stimulant – it ached continuously – and not even the arrival of the mail by a runner, and the fact that it was my birthday, could alleviate my sufferings.

We camped on the grassy shelf a few feet above the glacier, known as "Eri Udiar" ("Cold Cave"). There, screwing up my courage to sticking-point, I asked Greene with a wan smile to remove the offending tooth.

'Certainly,' replied Greene, with a broad grin and offensive cheerfulness. 'But I'm afraid I've no cocaine or chloroform. It's gone round to Badrinath with the heavy luggage.'

A good many people are cowards where their teeth are concerned – I am one of them. Before the discovery of anaesthetics patients about to undergo an operation were wont to fortify themselves with rum. Our limited supply of rum had of necessity to be rationed sparingly. On this occasion, however, my companions generously offered no objections to my partaking of an extra ration of it. I must, however, question their veracity when they say that I lowered three-quarters of a bottle. I must also question another statement which they are strangely unanimous in making. They said that before the rum I pointed up the Banke Glacier to a fine ice peak that rises from the head of it and said, 'Look at that peak up there, typically Himalayan, hopelessly inaccessible. No one will ever climb those terrific ice ridges.' But after the rum I said: 'Look at that peak up there! Anyone could climb *that*.' My recollection is that I was stabbed in the chest with a morphia syringe, a gag artfully carved from a piece of juniper root was thrust between my teeth and then ... The tooth came out, removed with skill and dispatch by Greene. I remember nothing more until I awoke in my tent feeling somewhat the worse for wear. Rum and morphia do not go well together.

Three months later, after Greene had assisted in the removal of some more of my teeth under a general anaesthetic in London, he said that it was fortunate that the tooth he pulled out at Eri Udiar was not like the others, the pulling of which added considerably to the muscular development of the dentist's biceps.

The following morning, July 7, Shipton and Holdsworth set out at dawn to attempt the conquest of the 19,815 foot peak. During the day Birnie arrived with the good news that the heavy luggage had gone off safely under the charge of Alam Singh and our two Gurkhas, of whom Randhoj Kan was to remain at Joshimath to look after some baggage which was to be left there, and Budhibal Gurung accompany Alam Singh with the remaining baggage to Mana.

Shipton and Holdsworth did not return until dusk. They had got within 300 feet of the top of their peak after a long and difficult climb, involving both ice and rock work, and then had been forced to turn back owing to lack of time in which to complete the ascent. They were confident, however, now that the route had been worked out, that the peak could be climbed directly from the camp. As Eri Udiar is only 14,690 feet, to reach the summit in one day meant a climb of 5,125 feet – a formidable day at such an altitude.

As Shipton was bent on completing the ascent, he and Nima set out again next morning. Unfortunately, Holdsworth was experiencing trouble with his frost-bitten big toe and was unable to accompany them. This time the summit was reached, after a climb, that Shipton described as being equal in difficulty to a Cumberland "severe". That rocks of such difficulty were climbed at a height of nearly 20,000 feet was indicative of acclimatisation and freedom from deterioration. Kamet instead of weakening us had raised us to the pinnacle of fitness. There is no doubt that many Himalayan peaks now thought to be inaccessible will be proved accessible in the future by acclimatised men in the zenith of their powers.[1]

Shipton reported that the view had been obscured for the most part by clouds. Nima, he said, had climbed splendidly; it proved again that the best of the Darjeeling Sherpas and Bhotias are fit to accompany Europeans on the most difficult and exacting climbs.

The same day that Shipton and Nima ascended the 19,815-foot peak, Beauman and Greene explored the head of the Banke Glacier with a view to ascertaining whether a practicable pass existed across the range to Badrinath and Mana. They returned with the depressing news that the Banke Glacier was hemmed in by a wall of peaks across which there was no practicable route, at all events for laden porters. We had hoped that a pass might be found across the ridge to the north of a measured peak of 21,198 feet and between it and an unmeasured ice peak, as this was, presumably, where Mumm had noticed indications of a pass, but the face of the ridge, on this its eastern side, presents a sheer wall of ice, plastered above and below with hanging glaciers that constantly discharge avalanches. One look had been sufficient. From their farthest point they had gazed northwards into a cirque of peaks, some of which presented pinnacles and faces comparable in sharpness and steepness to the Chamonix Aiguilles. Mana Peak, they declared, was hopeless to attempt by its southern side or south-eastern face. If another reason was wanted for not attempting the difficult or impossible, it was the avalanches which were being detached by the monsoon from every peak. Throughout the day they roared and thundered like heavy guns – not only avalanches of ice, but avalanches of snow, for so warm was the weather that masses of old and consolidated snow were slipping periodically from every steep snow slope. Thus, we had no alternative but to abandon our scheme and revert to the

[1] Immense difficulties were overcome by the Bavarians on Kangchenjunga in 1929 and 1931 at a height of over 23,000 feet.

easy route across the range by the Bhyundar Kanta and Khanta Khal passes.

On June 9 we packed up and set off from Eri Udiar for the Bhyundar Kanta. It was a dull morning, and heavy mists blanketed the peaks. From Eri Udiar the route to the pass is by no means obvious. The Banke Glacier is bounded on its south-western side by a ridge from which spring two great peaks, Rataban, 21,198 feet, and a nameless peak to the north-west of Rataban, which, according to the map, is precisely the same altitude! Between these two peaks lies the pass, which is 16,700 feet high according to the measurement of Doctor Longstaff. Two glaciers lead up towards the pass, and the westerly of these appeared to us the one to follow. Our local porters, however, assured us that the proper route ascended the easterly glacier under the northern precipices of Rataban. They were so positive that we must follow this glacier that for once we decided that local advice must be trusted.

To cross the Banke Glacier meant the usual tedious ups and downs and detours, which are such an annoying feature of Himalayan glacier travelling. By the side moraine of the glacier was a small lake. In its icy waters Greene had mortified his flesh the previous day. The lake was over 15,000 feet above the sea. Few people can have bathed at such an altitude, whilst the number of people who want to bathe at such an altitude must be even more limited. The "fine frenzy" that induces a human being to break the ice of the Serpentine before breakfast, or to jump into a glacier lake is self-inflicted castigation akin to the religious craziness that causes Indians to slash themselves with knives, or Burmese to suspend themselves in mid air from meat-hooks.

A well-defined moraine led us easily up the small side glacier towards our pass. As we trudged uphill, the heavy mists drooped still lower and rain began to fall, a cold, penetrating rain that soaked through our climbing clothes to our skin. Now and again, between sombre mists we saw the northern precipices of Rataban, grooved with couloirs that swept up to the green lips of hanging glaciers. Once or twice our feet struck blocks of ice beneath the snow – we were just within range of the ice artillery.

After the brilliant weather to which we had become accustomed, such a day seemed unreasonably depressing, yet to appreciate mountains they must be seen in gloom as well as sun. When only the black ribs of the peaks glare through the mists, when the snow-slopes are blank and shadowless and not even the deadly ripple of the masked crevasse is visible, the mountaineer feels himself to be encompassed about by the forces of death, and the awful solemnity and majesty of his surroundings strikes at his very soul.

By keeping to the northern side of the glacier we were able to avoid the danger zone of ice avalanches from the cliffs of Rataban. The porters were going badly. They had not fully recovered from the effects of the local alcoholic poisons they had imbibed at Gamsali and Niti. As we rose, the rain changed to sleet, which was lashed into our faces by a biting wind. It was impossible to see more than a few yards ahead. More by luck than judgment we hit off the lowest and easiest point on the ridge forming the Bhyundar Kanta. We huddled shivering under the lee of a boulder and ate a little chocolate. We waited perhaps half an hour for Birnie and Beauman, who were a long way behind, and then, half frozen by the wind and soaked to the skin, started to descend the other side of the pass. This was a piece of neglect on my part, for however numbed and cold I was, I should have remained on the pass to see all the porters safely across it.

We knew from Doctor Longstaff's account that we had to slant diagonally downwards in a westerly direction. Owing to the mist, visibility was limited, but not sufficiently so to prevent us from glissading long and easy slopes of snow. As we descended, we left the wind behind us, and entered a region of calm. We sat down on the wet rocks to await the others. As we did so we saw that we had entered the Kingdom of Flowers. Barrenness was replaced by beauty. Our misery was forgotten as we gazed upon little clusters of light blue primulas, peeping from ledges and crannies, watered by melting snows. Presently we heard voices, and, traversing across the hillside, joined Birnie and Beauman, who had with them some of the porters.

No difficulty in descending was experienced, and soon we were treading the stone-strewn surface of what we took to be the Bhyundar Glacier, but which subsequently proved to be a tributary of that glacier which is not marked on the map. For a mile or so we tramped down through wet mists. A side moraine loomed out of the mist, and we climbed to the crest of it in search of a camping-site. When the moraine petered out into the hillside, we took to the latter. The mist thinned; the rain now was light and warm, like the rain of a spring day in a Devon combe. Lower down we entered what I can only describe as an Eden of flowers.[2] Growing among the rocks was the tiny stemless *Primula reptans*; the flowers of the commoner but beautiful *Primula denticulata* covered the hillside, and above the glacier were three varieties of androsace. Between clumps of creamy dwarf rhododendrons, the ground was purple with dwarf irises, and blue and yellow with pansies and fritillaries. As the track descended we came upon the most beautiful of all Himalayan flowers, the mecanopsis (blue poppy). Its petals are as blue as a glacier lake, and its stamens as golden as the glow on the great peaks beneath which it grows.

We camped on a small grassy shelf, gay with flowers. At the entrance to our tents grew creamy anemones, homely blue forget-me-nots, golden, white and red potentillas, purple primulas, androsace, blue and pink geraniums, and many other plants. The pipes of Pan could scarcely have surprised us here.

The porters arrived with disturbing news. One local man recently recruited had been taken mountain-sick and, abandoning his load, had returned to Eri Udiar. It was difficult to understand how a man used to spending the majority of his life at an altitude of 10,000 feet or more should be afflicted with mountain sickness on a pass of 16,700 feet. He was not the only one: three more men had not turned up, and it was to be presumed had bivouacked on the slopes below the pass. It had not been a heavy day – indeed an easy one – and our Darjeeling men were frankly scornful of our latest recruits. We could only presume them to be exceptionally poor specimens of Bhotias, or else soft from easy living and indulgence in the aforementioned spirituous poisons. Natar Singh, who had been appointed sirdar over the local men, was ordered to send some men back immediately. This was done despite grumblings and protestations. The men returned in the last daylight, declaring that their comrades were quite safe, though I suspected that this statement was prompted by imagination rather than observation.

[2] I am indebted to Holdsworth for the following names.

Next morning a strong body of men was sent out to bring in the errant ones and their loads, and also to recover the abandoned load on the far side of the pass. This was successfully accomplished, some men returning, with the news that the man who had abandoned his load had descended safely to Eri Udiar and Gamsali, whilst others brought down the loads of the three who had bivouacked out. The latter appeared to have had a comfortable night despite a lack of shelter. Bhotias of Garhwal think nothing of spending a night out in bad weather at 15,000 feet or more under conditions which would make a European quail.

The same afternoon we decided to move our camp farther down the Bhyundar Valley in order to shorten the march over the Khanta Khal Pass. The weather was mending. Shafts of sunlight piercing clouds lower down the valley disclosed green pastures and a dark wash of pine forest. Through rifts in the monsoon mists the dark bastions of Gauri Parbat stood out like the blunt rams of some mid-aerial battle-fleet.

As we descended, the flora became more and more luscious, until we were wading knee deep through an ocean of flowers, ranging in colour from the sky blue of the poppies to the deep wine red of the potentillas. We filled our buttonholes and adorned our hats. A stranger had he seen us might have mistaken us – at a distance – for a bevy of sylphs and nymphs. But had he taken a closer look he would have seen, beneath a canopy of flowers, beards sprouting from countenances browned, scorched and cracked by glacier suns. Nor are tricouni-nailed climbing boots an appropriate footwear for sylphs and nymphs.

Leaving the untidy, rubble-strewn Bhyundar Glacier behind us, we strolled on across the meadows until at length we discovered an ideal camping-ground of dry sandy soil near a clear-running brook.

To us the Bhyundar Valley will always remain the Valley of Flowers. It is a place of escape for those wearied of modern civilisation. The means of sustenance are to be found there. Rhubarb grows abundantly, an edible second only to eggs in Shipton's estimation, but one for which Holdsworth evidenced a strong dislike. Sheep are driven up to graze, and doubtless bharhal and other game are to be shot. It would be easily possible to secure an abundant supply of provisions from the Alaknanda Valley. True, it would be necessary to descend in the winter to warmer and less snowy levels, but for half a year the lover of beauty and solitude could find peace in the Valley of Flowers. He would discover joy and laughter in the meadows; the stars would be his nightly canopy; he would watch the slow passing of the clouds; he would share the sunset and the dawn with God.

Beyond the hills, nations might fly at one another's throats; Mussolinis rise and fall; anarchy and revolution rot the nations; but in the Valley of Flowers the only strife would be that of the elements, the only sounds the wind in the flowers, the voice of the stream, and the rumble of the avalanche.

Towards, evening, the sluggish monsoon mists drifted asunder. Summits peered through from immeasurable heights. Far up the valley the crest of Gauri Parbat glowed in the declining sun. Day's cold fires were drawn by the dark stokers of night.

Peace and contentment were ours as we sat around the cam fire. Felt rather than seen were the peaks about us. A million stars eyed us. The voice of the mountain torrent lulled us to sleep.

CHAPTER NINETEEN

Across the Khanta Khal to Mana and Badrinath

THE FOLLOWING MORNING dawned brilliantly, but soon soft grey clouds began to poke their noses up from the south. At breakfast, there was the usual rhubarb grouse, excluding of course Shipton, yet, when wild rhubarb was so plentiful, what could we do but eat it, for it is valuable as an anti-scorbutic.

From our camping-place we could see the route to the Khanta Khal Pass. From the Bhyundar Valley the way lay up a secondary valley and then over a grassy skyline cloaked in monsoon clouds. To enter this secondary valley covering we had to walk across meadows the flora covering which was the most luxuriant that I have seen. The hillsides were snowy with anemones; potentillas lifted delicate petals of deep wine and yellow; nomicharis mingled with crimson orchids. We saw pale blue borage, mauve polemonium, rosy-petalled cypripedium, dwarf larkspur, clumps of superb purple asters, and clustered primulas of the deepest purple. Fat bumble-bees satiated with honey buzzed languidly; fritillary butterflies, red brown and mother-of-pearl, fluttered from flower to flower; small birds raised a gay song; a gentle intermittent breeze stirring the flowers, wafted their fragrance abroad.

We encountered a flock of sheep. There evidently exists a well-trodden path up which the shepherds drive their flocks from the Alaknanda Valley to the rich upper pastures. The shepherds eyed us curiously. They were hardy, weather-beaten men with sinewy frames, and their far-seeing, deep-set eyes reflected the quietude and immensity of the mountains among which they spend their lives. They paused to bid us cheery *salaams*, and passed on their way, walking with a loose-limbed shambling gait.

Where the side valley debouches into the Bhyundar Valley it is narrow and steep, and the smoke-like spray of its falling torrent issued from between the silver birches lining its rocky banks.

A slope ablaze with flowers took us quickly uphill. Gradually, the valley opened out into rock-strewn slopes set at a lesser angle. Dirty masses of avalanche snow cluttered the way; between were little lawns of bright green grass; golden kingcups lined the streams. Once or twice we saw the blue poppy peeping out shyly from beneath overhanging boulders. The monsoon brought a warm, thin rain. Now and again the mists, sundered by vagrant winds, revealed snowy summits.

We came to the verge of a small rubble-strewn glacier; above it through the shifting mists a hanging glacier loomed. We did not linger within range of its missiles, but turning to the left, mounted grassy slopes towards our pass. It was an easy ascent, yet some of the local porters complained of the weight of their loads. Possibly, they thought they could hold us up for an increase of pay. Again, they may have resented the nonchalant and even swaggering manner in which our Darjeeling men, now tough and perfectly trained, carried their loads. They had no cause to complain, for, owing to the food that we had eaten, they were carrying lighter loads than those they had shouldered originally at Gamsali. We determined to dismiss most, if not all of them, at Mana, for many of them were fit only to cross easy grass passes and were obviously incapable of sustained exertion at higher altitudes.

We reached the pass bathed in the perspiration we had learnt to associate with monsoon weather even at 15,000 feet. Mists prevented us from seeing Nilkanta, but it was pleasant reclining on a soft couch of flowering turf, watching the play of light and shadow on the nearer peaks.

Scattered about on the grassy crest of the pass were some crooked whitish objects. These our porters pounced upon eagerly, declaring that they were the antlers of fairy deer which bring luck to the finder if they are burnt as incense to the gods. It was a charming thought, and the objects in question, which are probably some species of fungoid growth, do resemble minute antlers. Scarcely less eagerly did Holdsworth pounce upon yet another variety of primula, the ninth species that he had discovered since descending into the Bhyundar Valley.

The mists obstinately refusing to lift, we started to descend. For such an easy pass as is the Khanta Khal the descent is a steep one. The difference in height between the summit of the pass and Hanuman Chatti, in the Alaknanda Valley, is no less than 6,500 feet, and this in a horizontal distance of a little over two miles. Long glissades in snow-filled gullies took us expeditiously down the first 2,000 feet. The snow petered out, and we continued the descent on steep, vegetation-masked hillsides, following a rude track. Doctor Longstaff reached Hanuman Chatti in three hours from the pass. This was exceptionally fast going, and although we were not set on emulating him, we were congratulating ourselves at being as good as in the Alaknanda Valley when the track almost disappeared beneath vegetation including dense thickets of bamboos and, to cap its wilfulness, zigzagged sharply uphill.

The evening was hot, close, and thunderous, and sweat poured from us as we forced a way through the bushes.

At length the apology for a track became horizontal, and even began to descend slightly. We rounded a corner, and found ourselves forced to traverse a cliff face set at a formidable angle. Here the track had collapsed or been washed away, and considerable time was lost in negotiating a slimy outward-sloping slab.

By the time gentler slopes had been reached night was falling swiftly, and we had no option but to camp. Fortunately, we were able to find a grassy shelf on which to pitch our tents.

It was not a pleasant spot. The moist monsoon air was tainted with tropical odours – the stench of rotting undergrowth, rank grasses and shrubs. The vast vegetation cloaked valleys of the Himalaya come as a strange anticlimax after the snows, and their foetid airs reek of disease and death.

We were glad to get on the move again next morning. As we descended we congratulated ourselves that we had camped where we did and not tried to force our way down to the Alaknanda Valley the previous evening. Had we attempted this, we should most certainly have been benighted on precipitous slopes overgrown with dense vegetation. Conditions must have changed greatly since Doctor Longstaff descended by this route, for the vestige of a path we had been following now disappeared completely beneath a tangle of undergrowth and bamboos, and it was only with difficulty that we were able to force our way downhill. The porter carrying the ski had a sorry time of it here.

We crossed the valley torrent with some difficulty, and after traversing some loose and unpleasant slopes of detritus found that no further difficulties separated us from the floor of the Alaknanda Valley. Once I heard the thin piping of a marmot and saw the quaint little beast scurry under a boulder. Looking under the boulder, I saw it sitting there eyeing me fearfully. Next moment it rushed out again and sought a more secure refuge beneath another boulder.

We reached the end of the valley, where are some primitive huts, the inhabitants of which eke out a precarious existence from little fields of grain between the boulders. A horde of children eyed us shyly, energetically sucking their thumbs the while, and a ragged fellow whose clothes were not worth an anna grinned cheerily at us, and gabbled unintelligibly. We passed a natural stone basin in a boulder filled with water from the overflow of the stream, where the women of the village were washing clothes. The only laundering known to them is to soak their garments in the water and beat them energetically against a neighbouring slab, worn and polished by centuries of washerwomen.

We found ourselves at last on the pilgrim route to Badrinath. The first objects that attracted our attention were the telegraph-poles that bear a solitary wire from Chamoli to the telegraph office at Badrinath. Possibly, I ought here to pay a compliment to the Indian Posts and Telegraphs for their enterprise in carrying a line into this remote corner of the Himalaya, especially as the expedition was not slow to take advantage of the facilities afforded thereby; but we had come from the Valley of Flowers, and at first sight this evidence of civilisation grated horribly. As I gazed upon the ugly line of poles topped by white insulators gleaming like soulless eyes, my predominant thought was that soon we must follow them back to civilisation. It was a comfort to think that for a time at least we might turn our backs on the lower valleys from which the telegraph-poles straggled, and adventure once more among the snows.

The pilgrim path is so broad that a baby motor car might be driven along it for miles on end, but Heaven forbid that these solitudes of Himalaya should suffer such a fate: let civilisation cherish its noise and Himalaya its quietude.

Below the path rushed the Alaknanda River, its turbulence and volume reflecting the power and majesty of the peaks that gave it birth. At this season of the year, when warm monsoon airs are melting the snows on the highest peaks, the Alaknanda is in spate. A man who fell into it would be smashed to pulp in a few seconds. See how the great boulders in the bed of the torrent appear one moment and disappear the next beneath a furious gush of grey glacial water. It is almost as though the heart of the river responds tempestuously to the caress of the summer sun.

The pilgrim way was impregnated with what I can only describe as an odour of sanctity. It was not like other smells that I have smelt, but a special Eastern smell that includes in it an odour of spices, exhalations from unwashed bodies, and other things too unpleasant to enumerate.

Pilgrims, old and young, were toiling up the path. Maharajahs and Maharanees visit Badrinath and its sister pilgrim city Kedarnath, so also do miscreants who seek to escape from the law, and the filthiest beggars, odorous, unwashed, ragged, and whining for alms, who batten on the charity of the villages through which they pass. Educated Indians with university education and the lowliest "untouchables" from Calcutta, Madras and Bombay toil through the humid tropical heat of the lower valleys, braving cholera, dysentery, typhoid, malaria and other tropical diseases in order to pay their respects to the holy snows of Himachal, to see the sacred image of Vishnu in the temple at Badrinath, bathe in the sacred hot spring there, and cleanse soul and body in the icy waters of the Alaknanda. Some of the more fanatical seek to expiate their sins by falling on their faces, stretching out their arms before them, drawing a chalk line; standing on it and falling again. Such take many months to accomplish their pilgrimage. To Western ideas there is something inexplicable and almost terrible in such immolation. To appreciate political motives in India it is necessary to delve deep down to the basic root of all things, and that is religion. Europeans who listen with languid boredom to sermons preached on Sundays cannot understand how great are the powers of religion in India for good or evil. Fanaticisms and hatreds are always simmering, like a molten, subterranean lava lake, and it is only the firm rock of British rule that prevents explosion. Here and there they find a peaceable outlet for their turbulence, and the pilgrimage to Badrinath and Kedarnath is one, but once allow those imprisoning walls to collapse and India would become an unimaginable shambles. The law abiding Hindus toiling up the path to Badrinath would become fiends incarnate, seeking to tear the Moslem population of India limb from limb, sparing neither man, woman nor child; and down upon this shambles would come the tribesmen from the north-west, and the Gurkhas from Nepal, to carve their way through what was left of India.

India is not, and cannot be for centuries, fit to rule herself, and to abandon her would be equivalent to putting all the animals of the Zoo in one cage. The strong would survive, but the agonies of the weak would be too terrible to contemplate. With India would fall the British Empire. Let us, in the interests of humanity, maintain a just balance in that most complicated and passionate of lands.

We came to the little village of Hanuman Chatti, which, like other villages along the pilgrim route, consists largely of pilgrim rest houses. These are reminiscent of a hop-picker's temporary abode, but they are infinitely dirtier. There are a few straw-thatched shops which sell their wares to the pilgrims. Earlier in the expedition we should have turned with disgust from the dainties these displayed, if only on account of the flies that swarmed about them, but weeks of Achung's cooking had hardened us body and soul. I have heard it said that, in nine cases out of ten, no one would again visit a restaurant in London if he could peep behind the scenes. The same applies with tenfold force in India, but Achung had long since eliminated any scruples we might have possessed, and we turned with relish to food not cooked by him. And the food we got at Hanuman Chatti was surprisingly good. There were chupatties, warm, greasy and savoury, and sweets – the coarse local goa disguised in various ways. Of the latter, the ones which we most favoured were tapered masses of brown sugar speckled on the outside with "hundreds and thousands". In the back of each tumbledown shop the shopkeeper squatted, cross-legged, with a small charcoal fire before him, over which, in pans black with age and dirt, he prepared his delicacies.

We continued on our way, forging through the village in as few breaths as possible. The pilgrims huddled in the shade eyed us apathetically; most of them appeared worn out by travelling and privation, and exhibited no elation at being so near to their goal. One old man clad only in a loincloth, with stick-like arms and legs, and wild unkempt beard, rushed out in the middle of the street and, crouching there, raised trembling suppliant hands. He was, probably, one of the professional beggars who infest the pilgrim route. We emerged from the village with relief. It is strange that man, an intellectual superior to animals, can surround himself with filth that most animals would instinctively reject.

The Alaknanda Valley is worthy of the torrent that rages down it. Its precipitous sides spring up on either hand for thousands of feet. Cliffs, black and dripping with moisture lurch threateningly over the traveller; rocky pinnacles cleave the sky thousands of feet above him. It is a fitting pathway to Himachal and the foot of Vishnu.

In places the path disappeared beneath the dissolving and dirty remnants of spring snow-avalanches that had swept down gullies in the hillside. Some of these avalanches still spanned the Alaknanda with their debris. During the winter months Badrinath is snowed up and deserted, and its inhabitants retire to the lower and warmer valleys.

We lunched in the shade. Pilgrims passed us, ascending or descending the path, some with their wives and some without, the wealthier, the aged and infirm, being borne in palanquins by sweating bearers. The wives it was who carried the family goods and chattels, toiling in the wake of their husbands, who had nothing more to do than concentrate their thoughts on the sanctity of their pilgrimage and the absolution of their sins.

In the early afternoon we reached Badrinath. The first thing we saw was the ugly red corrugated iron roof of a bungalow that might have graced a south coast "resort". The second thing was an Indian gentleman clad in a saucy pullover and a pair of Oxford flannel trousers. He passed us without a salutation. Possibly he was a Congress wallah detailed off to spread the germ of unrest in this peaceful corner of the world. Another shock in store for us was an iron bridge, in the process of building, intended to span the Alaknanda River. As it was not yet completed, we had to cross by the existing bridge a short distance higher up the river. Whether, owing to the building of an improved bridge, this had been allowed to fall into disrepair, or whether the state in which we found it was its normal state, I am not prepared to say, but Mr. Heath Robinson in one of his lighter moments could scarcely have designed a more intriguing structure.

Theoretically, it was a suspension bridge; practically, it was an intricate network of wires, ropes and odd bits of cord and string overlaid with rotting wooden planks. Portions weary of cohesion had already collapsed, and hung from the underside of the bridge like seaweed from a pier. Even the Indians, whose casualness in such matters is usually beyond the comprehension of Europeans, had erected a notice advising a maximum load of four people. My own peace of mind was seriously disturbed by Holdsworth, who trod the bridge behind me so heavily and unexpectedly that the crazy structure trembled and swayed like an aspen-leaf in a gale.

Having safely crossed the bridge, we entered the main street of Badrinath. We were surprised to find ourselves passing between reputable-looking shops – book shops and trinket shops, tailors, fruiterers, grocers and so on. There was even a local photographer, whilst one member of the expedition was able to purchase a tube of toothpaste at a price far below that charged in the plains of India. Many shops advertised a drug known as Shilkret. Neither vendors nor manufacturers of this drug have anything to learn from Western advertising methods. Shilkret is the panacea for all ills, the elixir of youth, the essence of the gods; it will make the old young, and the weak strong; the germs of cholera, dysentery, typhoid and malaria wilt and die at sight of it. From rabies to housemaid's knee, there is nothing it cannot cure.

A large crowd soon collected around us, and we elbowed our way towards the temple through a throng, of pilgrims, shopkeepers, loungers and scroungers.

The temple is not the imposing affair that might he imagined, and compared to the magnificent edifices of the plains is a humble building. Inside it is a shrine dedicated to the sacred image of Vishnu.

The Rawal is the high priest, and his house stands between the temple and the Alaknanda Rivers. To reach it, we had to descend a flight of stone steps. These steps, worn and polished by the tread of countless pilgrims, offered but a little friction to tricouni bootnails, and first one member and then another of the expedition came a cropper down them. As conquerors of Kamet we can hardly have impressed the bystanders. Presently, the Rawal came out from a dark passageway to greet us. He was short of stature, and a typical plainsman in appearance. He had come from Madras, and, to judge from the heavy European overcoat he was wearing, found it chilly living so close to the snows. He is the keeper of the temple and temporal ruler of the Badrinath district. He greeted us shyly and eyed us a trifle askance, and small wonder for our appearance was positively terrifying. I saw his dark eyes fix themselves fascinatedly on Birnie's red beard. However, in a minute or two he appeared to realise that we were not quite so villainous as our appearance warranted, and invested us with garlands of flowers which had been awaiting our arrival. After thanking him for helping arrange our porters' food, we continued on our way to Mana, where we intended to pitch our camp, accompanied by two of his servants in scarlet sashes with large gilt buckles.

As we neared Mana we became aware of a confused medley of sound, and saw a procession wind down a steep path to the Alaknanda River, cross a crazy wooden bridge, and approach us to the accompaniment of much drum beating. The village had put itself *en fete*, but whether this was in honour of our advent, or whether it was merely a feast-day in honour of some deity, we could not imagine.

The procession approached us, drumming furiously and waving brightly coloured banners in the air. In the middle of it was carried a long and gaudily painted wooden idol. It was an attenuated and ill-nourished object; possibly, therefore, the proceedings were intended to propitiate the god of Famine who stalks occasionally through these valleys.

Mana is a Bhotia village, and the broad and cheery grins of its inhabitants vouched for the fact. The local Mr. Jack Hylton and his orchestra passed us, and, stationing themselves on the hillside above the Alaknanda, beat furiously on their drums. We were glad to cross the crazy bridge and leave the din behind us.

As we breasted the little plateau on which stands Mana, Alam Singh hurried to greet us, radiating huge grins and gabbling out many expressions of welcome, whilst Budhibal Gurung in the background clicked his heels together and drew himself rigidly to attention. From them we learnt that Lewa's feet were so bad that the doctor at Joshimath had insisted that he must remain there to be treated, and not continue to Ranikhet. All the heavy luggage had come safely round by the lower route, and Randhoj Kan was satisfactorily posted in charge of the luggage we no longer needed, at Joshimath.

We pitched our tents on a grassy shelf, well away from the village hovels and their attendant garbage. Huge boulders, fallen in some catastrophic landslide, surrounded us. A few minutes after our arrival, a messenger from the Rawal arrived, bearing the following delightful missive.

From His Holiness the Rawal Sahib.
Temple – Sri Badrinath.

DEAR SIR,

I and the public of Badrinath greatly admires and congratulates you on your brilliant victory in having succeeded in climbing the renowned Kamet peak for the first time in history.

I am therefore proposing to accord you and the party a most loyal welcome in a public meeting and to hear from you the romantic and heroic description of your expedition.

Would you therefore please accept this humble request and inform us the date and time for the purpose convenient to you. Further we will be highly interested to witness an expedition of the connected goods and implements with their use that you carried with you for helping in the achievement of your expedition, if you can possibly arrange it to be done side by side as well without any great inconvenience to you.

Thanking you in anticipation,
Yours sincerely,
(*Signed*) THE RAWAL.

Who could refuse such a charming request? Birnie was the only one among us who could speak Hindustani, and it was arranged, therefore, that he should give the Rawal and the public of Badrinath a lecture on the expedition after our return from our proposed explorations in the Badrinath Range.

As Shipton was again suffering from one of his attacks of egg-fever, a man was dispatched post haste to Badrinath with orders to go through that town with a small comb and bring back with him every egg he could find, irrespective of age or quality. Alas! his efforts were unsuccessful, but at least we were able to indulge in an orgy of mangoes: they were poor, small, coarse fruit, but to men who had been pining for fruit for weeks they seemed delicious.

Our tents pitched, and our goods unpacked, we could look about us. The scene suggested the stony savagery of the Dauphiny. We gazed into the heart of the Badrinath peaks through a portal of splendid precipices from which issued the turbulent glacier waters of the Alaknanda. Perhaps fifteen miles away, somewhere near the head of the Bhagat Kharak Glacier, two beautiful ice-draped peaks over 22,000 feet high were visible. In the sky eagles wheeled, mere specks that emphasised by their smallness the vast scale of the precipices on which they dwell.

Evening brought another messenger from the Rawal bearing a generous gift of mangoes, nuts, onions and goa.

Mana is 10,000 feet above sea level, but the night was remarkably warm and numberless small moths and other insects fluttered about us as we sat over our dinner in the mess tent. Our minds were occupied no longer with thoughts of the morrow and what the morrow might bring – on Kamet. The bogey of altitude had been laid, the problem solved; we could go on our way unmolested by doubt. The mountains about us were friendly mountains.

I was awakened in the night by the dull thumping of drums, accompanied by the plaintive wail of some primitive instrument and voices raised in tuneless song – our porters were making merry in Mana. Just as I was dropping off to sleep again I heard someone blundering about among the tents and voices raised in drunken argument – an argument brought to a premature conclusion by a fluent and pungent flow of Hindustani from Birnie's tent. After that, quiet settled down on the camp.

CHAPTER TWENTY

The Arwa Valley

NEXT MORNING, when I looked out of my tent, the first object I saw was the Old Soldier. He was seated on the ground, his head buried in his hands. A minute or two later he rose slowly, and with an obvious effort, to his feet and, tottering to the brook that ran down past the camp, immersed his head therein. Obviously, he was unfit to minister to my personal needs; this was done by Nima Dorje, who materialised from the direction of the cook-house with a broad grin and a cup of hot tea. 'Nima Tendrup no good, sir,' he informed me confidentially. Then, pointing to his forehead and stomach in turn, he explained significantly, 'Drink plenty chang, sir. Very strong, sir.' I was well able to appreciate the last part of this statement, for I knew from experience that the Old Soldier was usually impervious to the effects of local firewater. Others among our porters were in an even worse state, and Nima waited upon us at breakfast with a fixed, vacant and bloodshot glare in his eyes that was painful to see.

We decided to stay two whole days at Mana, as this would enable us to reorganise our porterage and plan our expedition into the Badrinath Range. As was usual on "rest days", so called, Birnie worked hard arranging details of our porterage, paying off porters, paying advances to new porters, and arranging for porters' food, while I had to hammer away on a typewriter at a dispatch to *The Times* and answer dozens of letters and telegrams. These proceedings were enlivened by funeral processions that passed and repassed the camp. Whether they were the outcome of last night's dissipation in the village I cannot say. As they were composed exclusively of drummers and wailing women and children, possibly they were professional mourners, but there was nothing professional about the drumming, which resounded from the village at all hours of the day, in an uproar indicative rather of the personal feelings of each drummer than of any attempt at timing or rhythm.

Moist grey clouds stole up from the south, but seemed incapable of precipitating anything more than an occasional drizzle of rain – they had vented their spleen on the foothills, and the Mana. Villagers told us that only ten or twelve days of rain need be expected during the height of the monsoon season.

Our plan was to cross the Badrinath Range, the watershed of the Alaknanda and Gangotri Rivers. As mentioned already, Meade had explored the Bhagat Kharak and Satopanth Glaciers and visited passes from them that appeared to lead across the range. We preferred not to follow in his footsteps, but to explore the next glacier valley to the north and parallel to the Upper Alaknanda Valley and Bhagat Kharak Glacier system, and try to find a pass from it leading to the Gangotri Glacier system. This is the Arwa Valley, and it is marked in the Indian Survey map as containing a glacier some twelve miles in length, extending to within three miles of the Sarsuti [Saraswati] Valley, which runs northwards from its junction with the Alaknanda Valley at Mana, to the Mana Pass, 17,890 feet. Vagueness in the map's delineation of the glaciers flowing into the Arwa Valley suggested that the northern end of the Badrinath Range would repay exploration. While criticising the existing map of this district I should like to make it plain that the survey work was done in the seventies and is not to be compared to the excellent work of the Indian Survey in other Himalayan districts. According to an old report, surveyors in Garhwal were ordered not to waste time on uninhabited districts, but to devote their energies to mapping the inhabited valleys and main lines of communication. Their triangulation of such is reliable, but the existing map of the Badrinath Range is not a topographical survey, and all that the surveyors did was to sketch in what they could see without ascending to the snow and glacier level. Thus is it hardly fair to criticise the crude delineation of the Badrinath Range. Perhaps the only justifiable criticism of the existing map is that it would have been wiser to have left unexplored districts a blank and not to have sketched in ridges and glaciers that do not exist, just to "complete" the map.

Owing to the stupidity of the Dak-wallah (postman), we nearly lost our mail while staying at Mana. Before he started from Badrinath he was told by the postmaster that we had already left Mana and gone up the Sarsuti Valley. He had seen our camp at Mana, and even spoken to one of our men, but in spite of this a misplaced devotion to duty had taken him many miles up the Sarsuti Valley toward the Tibetan frontier. It took all the eloquence of the man we sent after him to persuade him that we were still at Mana, and that an artfully prepared trap was not being laid for his destruction and the theft of the mail. His devotion to duty was praiseworthy, but, as Birnie said, he was a "poggle admi", which is a phonetically descriptive expression in Hindustani meaning fool or madman.

We were not sorry to see the last of the Gamsali men. Neither in stamina nor morale were they the equal of the Mana men whom we enrolled in their stead. We retained, of course, the six Niti high-camp men, for these were all first-rate porters, and also Natar Singh; he and the easygoing Alam Singh were poor substitutes for Lewa, but at least they did their best, and their cheerfulness was an asset. As far as possible we reduced baggage to a minimum and left a large dump of surplus stores and equipment at Mana under the charge of Alam Singh, who by virtue of being an inhabitant of the village could be expected to look after it.

On July 15 we left Mana, with 30 porters and food for two weeks. Little trading is carried on nowadays between Garhwal and Tibet over the Mana Pass, but we found the path along the Sarsuti Valley in good condition. Above Mana the Valley rises abruptly in a pitch nearly 1,000 feet high, in which the Sarsuti River has carved out an amazing slit-like gorge, so narrow that boulders fallen from the peaks above are wedged across its jaws. It is a fearful sight to see the torrent tear downwards a sheer two hundred feet into the gorge, where, strangled by the rocks, it roars and rages like a mad beast. Beneath a stone slab wedged across the gorge that does duty as a bridge the smooth water-worn rocks curve into unseen depths like cyclopian boiler-plates. Shouts and jeers, moans and thunderings, come from far below; the ground shakes to the tempestuous fury of the imprisoned waters. I could almost imagine myself standing on the brink of some watery hell, and it needed no imagination to picture the fate of anyone who fell from the unprotected bridge into the gorge. Gusts of spray, beating up like smoke from subterranean explosions, were lit by the sun until a fugitive rainbow danced and quivered on the brink of this awesome rift.

Above the gorge, the Sarsuti Valley is featureless and dull. Its stony hillsides were blanketed in mist from which swept down spasmodic showers of drenching rain. Presently the mists thinned, there was a sudden gleam, and we gazed astonished at a distant lake of blue sky, flooding the far-off foothills. Obviously we were experiencing, not monsoon rain, but merely local rain, for it was to the south that the monsoon should have been most in evidence.

The mists shrank into a peaceful evening. Unsuspected beauties were revealed by the declining sun; wine coloured potentillas lined the way and small rock plants lifted rain-bedewed petals.

It was a longer march than we had anticipated to the pasture at the junction of the Arwa and Sarsuti Valleys, marked on the map at Glastoli, and the porters began to grumble that there was no wood there, but we had heard this plaint before and disregarded it.

We camped on a gently sloping lawn a mile from the entrance to the Arwa Valley. Juniper bushes were growing abundantly in the vicinity, in a few minutes the porters had collected plenty of fuel. The evening was a calm one and the last tendrils of mist melted into a sky of deepest green. Our camp was in shadow, but from the other side of the valley rose a ridge of barren and stony peaks which reflected the crimson of the setting sun so brilliantly that each man's face glowed as he moved about the camp. Some miles down the valley and above Mana rose a delicately shaped snow-peak, the ridges of which met in a sharp point of pure snow. Long after the glow had left the rock peaks across the valley, this peak declined the night.

An easy walk next morning brought us to the entrance of the Arwa Valley. Potentillas formed a golden carpet on the floor of the valley, and we almost wished that we were not leaving such a joyful place for the sterility of the high peaks. Across the meadows meandered a brook of crystal purity. The source of which was a pool that might have been used as a mirror by the mountain elves. Greene bathed in it; it was gaspingly cold, and one plunge was sufficient. The porters were greatly impressed by his performance and there was no doubt that his stock rose several points in their estimation.

Two miles above its junction with the main valley the Arwa Valley is almost blocked by a moraine. According to the map, this was the terminal moraine of a glacier some twelve miles long flowing down the main valley, but as we neared it we saw that it was the terminal moraine of a side glacier descending from the south into the valley. To avoid it, it was necessary to contour round the base of it directly under the snout of the glacier, which was about 500 feet high. There was no difficulty in doing this, but many large boulders, some the size of cottages, perched on the very edge of the dirt-riddled ice above, warranted a sharp look out. It was no place to linger. The unstable boulders over which we scrambled were pock-marked and scarred, and now and again crashes from above, accompanied by puffs of rock dust, betokened fresh falls of boulders from the glacier snout. Boulders fall erratically down such a slope, and are deflected from rock to rock, so that it is impossible to anticipate the way they are coming until the last moment, and then they may be going so fast as to be difficult to dodge. We were lucky, but one mass of rock, weighing several hundredweight, came perilously near to Shipton. The side glacier from which they fell appears to be advancing and pushing its snout farther and farther across the Arwa Valley. It needs to advance but three or four hundred yards farther to dam the valley, with a wall of ice and stones several hundred feet high. If the stream was unable to percolate or force a passage through the barrier, a lake would form. As the Arwa Valley is practically flat for two or three miles above this point, the lake would be a large one. Should the dam holding it burst, ruin, in all probability on an even greater scale than that caused by the bursting of the Gohna dam in 1895, would overtake the Sarsuti and Alaknanda Valleys. This glacier should be periodically examined, for although it is unlikely to advance much farther, it is always the unexpected that happens in the Himalaya, and catastrophes brought about in such a way are by no means uncommon.

As there was no sign of any main valley glacier above the side glacier, we could only conclude that the surveyors had not ascended the Arwa Valley, but, seeing the terminal moraine of the side glacier apparently blocking the valley, had jumped to the conclusion that it was the terminal moraine of a main valley glacier. In this connection it is interesting to note that the height of insignificant points opposite to side valleys debouching into the Sarsuti and Alaknanda Valleys are usually given in the map, so that it would appear that the surveyors merely *looked up* the branch valleys from these points and made their sketches and deductions from what they saw.

Whether or not any European before us had been far up the Arwa Valley is a matter for speculation, but one of our local porters informed us that his brother had accompanied a Mr. Pigott (or Bigott) up the valley some twenty years previously, and had visited a pass at its head without, however, crossing the Badrinath Range to the Gangotri Glacier.

We lunched on a flowering slope and drank our fill from a brawling brook that emptied its clear water into the mud-fouled valley river. The weather was ideal, and we lay watching the white clouds trailing leisurely from the red rock peaks lining the valley.

Above our lunching-place the ground became stonier and stonier and walking correspondingly slow and laborious. Beauman seemed to bear a special grudge against the stones, and his epithets relating to them were almost as numerous as the stones themselves. He said they reminded him of the Dauphiny. I could only sympathise with him and register a mental vow to avoid the Dauphiny. We crossed the valley torrent by a bridge of avalanche debris and proceeded along its northern bank. Dank evening mists were veiling the hillsides as we pitched our tents near the last scattered clumps of dwarf juniper. A day's marching had sufficed to bring us but six miles up the stony valley. Though we had passed two or three other side glaciers, there were still no signs of any main valley glacier.

Contrary to their usual custom, the mists refused to dissolve at nightfall and discharged their moisture in a drizzle of rain that lasted well into the next morning.

In moist, enervating warmth we set out once more, and, negotiating an abominable slope composed of earth in which were lodged unstable boulders like plums in a Christmas pudding, gained the almost level floor of the valley. Still no signs of a main valley glacier could we see as we trudged over the never-ending fields of stones.

Gradually, the mists dissolved in the sunlight, and several glaciers flowing into the main Arwa Valley became visible.

The valley floor had been silted up by floods and moraine debris and was nearly level. The stream rushing down it was a strong one, and there was no possibility that we could see of fording it; there was no possibility either of our postman getting across to us. He had come up the valley the previous evening from Mana carrying some mail. He had missed the snow-bridge by which we had crossed the stream below our camp and, being unable to ford the latter, had tied the mail bag to a stone and flung it across the stream. He was now wandering disconsolately up the other side of the stream. It seemed probable that he would not be able to join us until we came to the glacier whence issued the stream, and we were surprised therefore to see him an hour or two later on our side of the stream. Doubtless, his native cunning had found him a place where it could be safely forded. The stream was a nuisance, and where a sheer cliff fell into it we were forced to make a toilsome ascent and traverse.

We lunched on a patch of moss and turf gay with flowers, set like a little park amidst a city of grey boulders. Above this point the main valley forks into two. The south branch contained a glacier covered in rusty red moraines suggesting ironstone. Occasionally, through rifts in the clouds, we discerned ice-clad peaks hemming in the head of this valley. The west branch, which bent round in a northerly direction, was the more important of the two and we determined to follow it.

We turned a corner and saw that the west valley branch was sub-divided into two more glacier-filled valleys. We had marched for only three hours when we decided to camp near the junction of these valleys. During the afternoon grey wreaths of monsoon mist concealed the peaks, and a slight drizzle of rain fell. We turned into our sleeping bags resolved to learn something on the morrow of the country we were in before pushing forward another camp towards the watershed of the range.

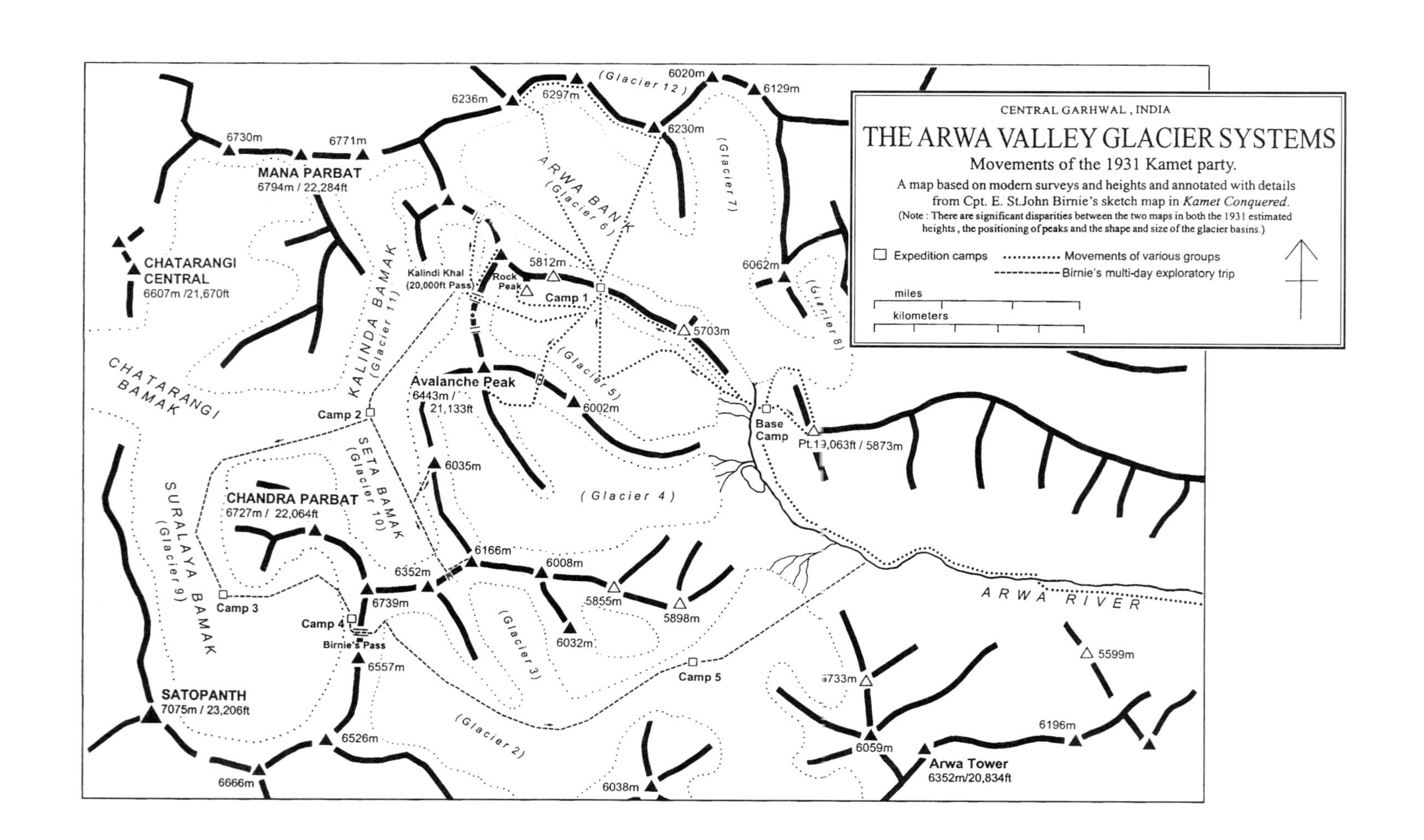
CENTRAL GARHWAL , INDIA
THE ARWA VALLEY GLACIER SYSTEMS
Movements of the 1931 Kamet party.
A map based on modern surveys and heights and annotated with details from Cpt. E. St.John Birnie's sketch map in Kamet Conquered.
(Note : There are significant disparities between the two maps in both the 1931 estimated heights , the positioning of peaks and the shape and size of the glacier basins.)
Expedition camps
Movements of various groups
Birnie's multi-day exploratory trip
miles
kilometers
6236m
6297m
(Glacier 12)
6020m
6129m
6230m
(Glacier 7)
6730m
6771m
MANA PARBAT
6794m / 22,284ft
ARWA BANK
(Glacier 6)
6062m
(Glacier 8)
CHATARANGI CENTRAL
6607m /21,670ft
Kalindi Khal
(20,000ft Pass)
Rock Peak
5812m
Camp 1
5703m
KALINDA BAMAK
(Glacier 11)
CHATARANGI BAMAK
Avalanche Peak
6443m / 21,133ft
(Glacier 5)
6002m
Camp 2
Base Camp
Pt.13,063ft / 5873m
SETA BAMAK
(Glacier 10)
6035m
(Glacier 4)
CHANDRA PARBAT
6727m / 22,064ft
SURALAYA BAMAK
(Glacier 9)
6166m
6008m
6352m
Camp 3
6739m
5855m
5898m
ARWA RIVER
Camp 4
Birnie's Pass
(Glacier 3)
6032m
5599m
6557m
Camp 5
SATOPANTH
7075m / 23,206ft
6526m
(Glacier 2)
6059m
6196m
Arwa Tower
6352m/20,834ft
6666m
6038m

CHAPTER TWENTY ONE

The Twenty-Thousand-Foot Pass

NIGHT SCAVENGED the mists from the sky, and the following morning dawned frostily clear. The sun was gilding the peaks as Greene, Shipton, Nima Dorje and I left the camp. Our plan was to ascend a peak and take stock of our position. Short of fording the ugly-looking glacier torrent, there was only one peak within easy reach – the one at the foot of which was pitched our camp. The steep mountainside was covered in loose boulders, and, to avoid accidents, we divided into two parties and ascended by separate routes. As we climbed we passed clumps of edelweiss growing in crannies of the rocks. Their altitude was fully 17,000 feet, and with the exception of lichens and mosses I have not seen flowers growing elsewhere at this height. We were at the top of our form and able to climb at the rate of 1,500 feet an hour. Such a pace is not to be despised in the Alps, and over 17,000 feet is indicative of perfect acclimatisation and physical condition. So far we had experienced little of the baneful effects of high-altitude deterioration. We did not long to return to civilisation, but were anxious to remain in this magnificent district and accomplish as much exploration and mountaineering as possible in the limited time at our disposal.

We did not rest until we were within a few hundred feet of the summit, for already the monsoon mists were gathering in the Arwa Valley. We had expected an interesting view, but the panorama exceeded our expectations. We gazed over a troublous sea of peaks, ridges and glaciers: peaks of ice and snow; rock peaks; aiguilles of splintered granite, spiking the blue sky; peaks possible, peaks impossible, and peaks at which even the hardened mountaineer might shudder on the threshold of his imagination; vast elevated snowfields, over which cloud shadows moved in slow procession; torrential glaciers crushed between rocky walls sinking green-lipped into the monsoon mists.

It was some time before we could sort out this complex and bewildering jumble of mountains, snowfields and glaciers into its individual components. When we were able to do so, we saw that the two valleys at the junction of which was pitched our camp contained snow-covered glaciers[1] of considerable size, enclosed by peaks and ridges exceeding 22,000 feet. These two glaciers were separated by a ridge of approximately the same elevation as the peak we were on. As regards the watershed of the Gangotri and Alaknanda Rivers, it was, unfortunately; impossible to determine whether or not the ridges bounding the heads of these two glaciers formed this, and we were, not high enough to see over them and beyond. The most striking peak of all those arrayed before us was an extraordinary fang of

[1] Glaciers 5 and 6.

ice and snow rising beyond the limiting ridges of the two glacier systems. This peak must be 23,000 feet high. Although a towering landmark, it was not marked in the map; we had, however, already come to the conclusion that the map was useless to us.

In the south and south-east were a number of high wall-sided peaks rising from glaciers that debouched into the Arwa Valley below our camp, whilst eastwards of these were several needle-like summits, grouped like the Chamonix Aiguilles round a massive rock mountain of savage steepness. We spent half an hour roughly sketching in the main features of the country and making prismatic compass bearings and panoramic photographs, and then continued on our way.

The mountain we were on was devoid of difficulty, and after scrambling over some boulders and toiling up a slope of soft snow we gained the summit ridge. The summit was separated from us by a snow-ridge, but as there was no particular hurry to reach it we sat for a long time on a rocky shelf and basked in the sun. The temperature for such an altitude was unusually high, and we found it unnecessary to don our spare clothing. Later we tramped leisurely up to the snowy summit, which the aneroid gave as 19,300 feet. The mists had risen, spoiling the view to the south and west, but we were rewarded by seeing some additional peaks to the north and north-west and a glacier,[2] some six miles in length, that flowed into the valley a mile above our camp. I do not know how long we spent basking in the sun, but it cannot have been less than three hours. Some imagine that Himalayan mountaineering is one continuous round of hardship and discomfort. So it is above 23,000 feet, for climbing at extreme altitudes is something more than toilsome; if he would enjoy himself, the Himalayan mountaineer should limit himself to peaks less than 23,000 feet; then sometimes he will be able to sit on his conquered summits, in the sun, heedless of the passing hours and mindful only of the beauties and grandeurs about him. We descended leisurely until we reached a snow-filled gully that connected with the northerly glacier, which we had noted from the summit. The snow was in perfect order, and we glissaded 1,500 feet in a minute or two.

On arriving back at the camp, we found that Beauman, Birnie and Holdsworth had also been busy. They had ascended the south valley fork[3] to about 19,000 feet and had found a camping-site on the ridge separating the two glacier systems. Like us, however, they had been unable to come to any definite conclusion as to which ridge constituted the watershed of the range. The only thing to be done was to establish a camp on the proposed site and explore the heads of the glaciers on both sides of it with a view to ascertaining whether any of the ridges bounding them formed the watershed of the range.

On the following day we set off to establish the new camp. Beauman, Birnie and Holdsworth had been forced to make a toilsome detour in order to cross the glacier torrent, but we discovered that it was fordable near the camp and, once a safety hand-rail of rope had been stretched across it, the porters were able to carry ourselves and the loads across on their backs. It was amusing to stand on the bank and watch Greene, almost completely enveloping the squat Passang, and Holdsworth, his inevitable pipe fixed firmly in his teeth, seated pick-a-back on his diminutive little Sherpa servant, Ang Nerbu, make the passage of the torrent.

[2] Glacier 8 [3] Glacier 5

With the exception of Holdsworth, who wanted to use his ski, and the porters, the remaining members of the party decided to reach the camping-site by traversing the ridge between the two glaciers. It was a delightful day; the weather was fine, there was no hurry, and we lounged along the ridge enjoying beautiful views. We came to the highest point, 19,000 feet, and, distributing ourselves on warm rock slabs, soaked in the sun.

Below, on the glacier, were our porters, a tiny string of specks toiling slowly upwards to the camping-site. Between the shifting mists opposite to us on the other side of the glacier rose a peak of about 22,000 feet.[4] It was the most graceful mountain in the vicinity of the camp, and we determined if possible to force a way to its summit. We could have stayed for hours on the ridge, regardless, of time, watching nature's scene-shifters of light and shadow going about their tasks, but it was necessary to establish the camp, so we plunged downwards through sun-sodden snow, gained the glacier, and plodded uphill to the site of it.

It was not an ideal spot on which to camp, and platforms had to be engineered for the tents between slabs of granite. We ate our evening meal in the rays of the declining sun. There was not a breath of wind. All nature was hushed, as though expectant of some calamity. Above us, the monsoon mists dissolved like foam into the deep green sea of the evening sky. Eastwards, between horizontal layers of cloud, the pyramidal summit of Kamet stood out like a geometrical proposition set by some heavenly Pythagoras.

The sun dipped behind the ranges. The peaks about us stood cold and immutable as marble and only Kamet continued to glow between long wreaths of ashen clouds. As we watched, mindless of the increasing cold, vast fingers of darkness reached out of the east. It was the same phenomenon as we had witnessed when descending to Camp Five on Kamet, the parallel shadows of peaks in the west, thrown hundreds of miles across the sky by the setting sun, seeming to unite in the east.

In the south rose a huge solitary pillar of thundercloud. Its foundations were sunk deeply into the foothill valleys; higher, it was livid and threatening; on its topmost minarets the day had spilt its wine. The lightning flickered about it, darting like serpents from one cloudy abyss to another or bursting upwards in fountains of mauve fire, but so distant was it that the silence remained unbroken by the faintest grumble of thunder.

For a while time stood still. The World was beautiful; her hair was spun from the golden clouds, her eyes were violet shadows, her breasts of purest snow. And Night, seeing her beauty, rushed eagerly from the east and threw his dark mantle at her feet. But beauty faded quickly from the World, and Night was left with a cold, dead thing in his arms.

A sickle moon shed a soft radiance upon the snows; near the moon blazed a great star. In the south, lightning quivered ceaselessly, and now and again, like the firing of some mine, there was an explosion that reached from the deepest chasms to the topmost pinnacles of the piled-up cumuli, so that their vaporous folds stood out from the night like the dun-coloured smoke of some bloody engagement raging over the plains of India.

[4] Avalanche Peak – 21, 600 feet.

Once I awoke in the night and, parting my frozen tentflaps, peered outside. The moon was declining and the camp was in deepest shadow. Eastwards, Kamet slept between two shawls of mist. The lightning had expended its energy and the pillared thunderclouds supported the starry arch of heaven.

We had previously decided to ascend the glacier above the camp and explore the ridge bounding the head of it in search of a pass leading over the watershed on to the Gangotri Glacier system. We rose early, but the monsoon mists rose earlier still from the southern valleys, and by the time we had started to trudge up the glacier they were pouring over the ridge we hoped to explore.

The morning was a warm one, and, although the sun seldom appeared, its rays poured down upon us through the blanketing mists with ferocious intensity. The snow was soft and laborious, but we marched steadily uphill, and in less than an hour gained the foot of the slope leading up to the crest of the ridge, which at this point rose 300 feet from the glacier. The slope was steep, but ribs of broken rock and screes led easily upwards. The ascent was not without its dramatic interest. We experienced a subtle thrill. We were about to see over an edge into new country. What were we going to see over that edge? Only snow and mountains, but snow and mountains never before seen by human eyes. We toiled upwards. A small cornice curled over the crest of the ridge. We advanced cautiously, driving ice axes deeply into the snow. A rock projected from the crest of the ridge – we made for it. One by one we gained the rock and halted there, gazing silently. At our feet, the ridge fell away in slopes of snow, ice and rocks – a steep slope, but in height no greater than the slope we had just ascended – and below, dimly seen through rifts in the surging mists, sun-chequered and mysterious, was a great glacier,[5] curving downwards in a westerly direction. It could only flow into the Gangotri Glacier. The problem was solved – we were standing on the watershed of the Alaknanda and Gangotri Rivers. Had we been devout Hindus, we should no doubt have fallen on our faces and made obeisance to the gods. As it was, we sat down and devoured a tin of sardines.

Our height was 20,000 feet by aneroid. The ridge on which we sat ran approximately due north-west and south-east. South-east of us it continued horizontally for some distance, then rose to the crest of a minor rock peak, fell again to a col, and finally merged into the snowy breast of the peak opposite to our camp. North-westwards, the ridge rose abruptly to the crest of a peak, the rocky summit of which was less than 1,000 feet above us. Two days previously, during the reconnaissance to the site of the 19,000-foot camp, Holdsworth had noticed an apparent pass from the head of the glacier[6] to the north of the 19,000-foot camp that appeared to lead over the ridge bounding that glacier. We decided, therefore, to continue with our exploration. Birnie and his servant, Dorje, were to descend the steep slope to the glacier on the far side of the watershed ridge and investigate Holdsworth's proposed pass. Shipton and I were to ascend the peak immediately to the north of the pass we were on. Holdsworth preferred to descend to his ski, which he had left at the foot of the ridge, and run back to camp on them.

Shipton and I were the first away, but as we scrambled along the ridge we saw Birnie and Dorje starting to descend the precipitous face of the ridge to the glacier.

[5] Glacier II. [6] Glacier 6.

Mist descended blocking them from our view, but once or twice we heard the thudding of their ice axes. Evidently the slope was hard and step-cutting necessary. The ridge Shipton and I were on, although steep and requiring care offered no difficulty. We were climbing between 20,000 and 21,000 feet, yet we progressed as rapidly and easily as though we were on an alpine peak of but half the height. In less than an hour we gained the summit, where we sat down on the piled-up boulders, warm and glowing from our exertions.

The weather appeared none too promising. Mists enveloped us, and particles of snow began to fall. The warmth was almost unnatural, and we should scarcely have been surprised had we heard the bellow of thunder. We occupied ourselves in building a large cairn, and then sat down hoping that the mists would clear. Our patience was rewarded; the mists drifted apart for a few instants. A peak was revealed the same matchless fang of ice and snow we had seen from the 19,300-foot peak two days previously. It is, as I remarked to Shipton, worth an expedition to climb. As though to emphasise the majesty of this splendid mountain and our own insignificance, the window in the mists lengthened and we saw the figures of Birnie and Dorje on the glacier at our feet. So minute they seemed – a snowflake might have covered them.

Snow was falling heavily as we descended, and visibility on the glacier above the camp was limited to a few yards. We experienced some misgivings as to Birnie and Dorje. From our peak we had seen the pass they hoped to cross. The descent on the Arwa side of the watershed did not look easy, and the route was liable to bombardment from hanging glaciers. It was a relief when, soon after reaching camp, the snowstorm abated and visibility improved. Later, we saw Birnie and Dorje descending the glacier[7] to the north of the camp. In order to reach the ridge on which was the camp they were forced to climb up a steep slope of snow, rocks and screes about 1,000 feet high, which must have come as a trying finish to a long day's work. As Shipton and I had suspected, the route was a dangerous one, and Birnie described how, when the mist and snow cleared for a few instants, he had seen huge walls of ice threatening them.

During our absence, the porters had erected several large cairns about the camp, on the summits of which they had placed rags as peace-offerings to the gods, an adornment calculated no doubt to inspire the deities with feelings of benevolence towards the expedition. Unfortunately, however, one of these cairns had been built on the ridge directly above the camp. It was a rickety structure with a pronounced lean towards the camp, and apparently needed but a zephyr of wind to ensure its destruction. I gave orders for its removal, and Ondi, who was both its architect and builder, reluctantly took it to pieces. One could only hope that the mountain deities would not regard this demolition as a disrespect and disbelief in their powers.

Whether or not the little incident two days later that I have yet to describe had any bearing on the matter I cannot say, but I suspect that our superstitious porters regarded it as a retribution for the insult tendered to the gods.

[7] Glacier 6.

CHAPTER TWENTY TWO

Avalanche Peak

ON JULY 21, SHIPTON AND I set out to attempt the peak opposite to the camp, taking with us Nima as porter. The weather boded ill, and scarcely had the sun flared up behind Kamet when it was extinguished by leaden clouds. The snow on the glacier was in an abominable state. It bore our weight for two or three steps, then its crust collapsed letting us sink deeply into the soft snow beneath.

The most promising route up the mountain was an upward traverse across the East Face to the South-East Ridge. We had noted this route from the 19,000-foot peak near the camp. To reach the northern end of the traverse meant a steep climb of 600 feet to a well-defined col in the north-east ridge of the peak. This slope was some 50° in angle, and at the foot of it was a bergschrund half choked with avalanche debris. The slope had been worn into a series of parallel runnels, scooped out by sliding snow. It is these runnels that lend the beautiful fluted appearance to Himalayan snow-slopes, and their formation is due to the heat of the sun and minor avalanches of soddened snow. In the Alps a slope of such steepness and continuity as that confronting us would almost certainly have been ice, but while we were in the Badrinath Himalaya we saw but few bare ice slopes, although of course, there were plenty of hanging glaciers forming ice walls.

The snow on the slope was in good order, and step cutting was unnecessary. We mounted quickly. The crest of the col was corniced, and some minutes were spent in hacking a way through the cave of overhanging snow. The weather meanwhile had been steadily deteriorating. As we put our heads over the lip of the col we were met by a biting wind and a scud of whirling snowflakes. On the slope we had been sheltered and warm, but as we stood on the col the wind blew the warmth out of us as a man blows the warmth out of a spoonful of soup. We sought shelter in the lea of a boulder. It was a dismal situation. We banged our gloved hands together and between whiles munched chocolate. We waited thus for fully three-quarters of an hour hoping for an improvement. But the sky darkened until the snows were dead white and lustreless. The wind growled past our rock, and snow began to fall heavily. Damp and shivering, we decided to retreat, and an hour later were imbibing some of Achung's choicest tea, a brew combining the flavours of tea leaves cooked to destruction, tin, juniper smoke, paraffin, and greasy dish-cloths. It had one virtue – it was hot. Achung was in a bad way, and suffering from his abnormally high blood pressure. Cause is allied to effect, and the badness of Achung's cooking was directly proportioned to the pressure of Achung's blood. It did not need Greene to tell us that Achung was afflicted by an abnormally high blood pressure even at the lowest elevation.

The day waned dismally, and snow fell intermittently till evening, when cooler and dryer airs mopped up the clouds. I lay in my tent reading my last mail over and over again. I read the newspapers until I knew all about bears, bulls and other commercial jargon. I became well versed in the latest divorces and murders, the probable winner of the three-thirty, and the reason why county cricket was dull. Later, when the snows were pallid in the after-glow of sunset, and frost had snuffed the warmth from the world, I remember wishing that a certain director of cinema films who had begged me to think out and engineer a "plot" during the expedition had been with us up there. I fear that he would have shivered, but he would have seen the universe's greatest plot, a plot hatched between day and night, enthralling sky and earth with its majesty and beauty.

Half the fun in mountaineering lies in being beaten or in the risk of being beaten. Not only does the mountaineer conceive an increased respect for his adversary, but he returns to the attack with a new zest. Should the citadel fall to his next assault he accepts its surrender not arrogantly, but humbly, for only by humility can the precious moments on the high hills be captured forever.

Despondence predominated as Shipton, Nima and I trudged once more across the softening snow of the glacier; already the morning sun was dulled by oily mists slinking up from the south.

The weather was warmer and the snow softer than it had been yesterday and everything pointed to a renewal of disappointment. Even our previous track could not support us, and we floundered deeply into the snow.

We gained the col. Sunlight glanced on the snow slopes we must traverse, seeming to beckon us onwards, and so we continued, hoping that the weather might hold.

We found to our disgust that a descent of over 200 feet was necessary before we could start ascending again. The snow on this descent was the worst we had yet encountered, unless it was some of that on the final slopes of Kamet. We sank in knee deep, and I reflected grimly that we should have to retrace our steps up that slope towards the end of the day. But no one who climbs with Shipton can remain pessimistic, for he imparts imperturbability and confidence into a day's work on a mountain that are in themselves a guarantee of success.

We took turns at track making. A quarter of an hour at a time was long enough, for the snow was that exasperating snow the mountaineer must expect to find during the monsoon season. Two or three steps are taken, the snow holds – will it hold another step? Apparently it will. The foot swings forward and the weight is gingerly transferred. Good! It holds. The other foot is swung forward, then – crunch! For apparently no reason save a certain cussedness, the crust has given way. The rear foot sinks deeply. Balance is regained only after an effort. Rhythm is lost. Mind and muscles must be braced anew. Imagine the same series of disappointments and mental and muscular recoveries repeated a thousand times at a height of 21,000 feet and the sum becomes a weary one.

Mists closed down upon us, the sun piercing them exact its own toll of energy. Difficulty there was none, and even when the snow steepened into an abrupt slope 200 feet high, leading to the crest of the north-east ridge, we had nothing to do but continue an unrhythmical, treadmill-like trudge which had now lasted for such a length of time that it seemed to me that my whole life had been spent in sinking into soft snow at a height of 21,000 feet.

We sat down gratefully on the crest of the South-East Ridge. Surely now the worst was behind us? Even if the ridge to the summit should prove difficult, we reflected that climbing difficulty was, up to a point, infinitely to be preferred, even at high altitudes, than the slavery imposed by crusted snow.

Our gaze passed along the ridge; it curved up into the mists like an icy scimitar; it was sharp and it was steep. If it was iced from top to bottom, we were likely to be defeated, for in that case many hours of step cutting would be necessary. There is one virtue in high-altitude mountaineering – little things may irritate and annoy to an extraordinary degree, but the big things do not matter until afterwards. They are accepted with an automatic resignation, partly owing to the numbing effect of high altitudes, which makes the brain incapable of appreciating them, and partly to the immensity of nature, for the forces among which the mountaineer moves are too vast to be translated into terms of temperament and temper. And so we sat in the snow, more concerned with the problem of opening a sardine tin than we were with the problem of ascending a peak on which we had set our hearts.

The day was a warm one – we were able to sit and eat our lunch in comfort; it was also depressing. The air was devoid of that essential *joie de vivre* that transmutes hard work on a mountain into joy of existence. It was heavy, stagnant, dead; it reeked of the humid far-off plains of India. The mists rolled sluggishly about us. Now and again they were parted by desultory airs. Peaks, ridges and glaciers were revealed, dim, almost unsubstantial, like phantasms in the steam from a witch's cauldron. The sun seemed to weigh on our eyelids, so that we found it difficult to interest ourselves in the scene about us. There was a glacier at our feet, bounded by a rocky ridge nicked by a well-defined col.[1] Beyond was a high peak, terraced with lateral bands of rock, wall-sided and massive. It appeared over 23,000 feet high, and was probably the peak marked in the map as 23,240 feet – the only measured point in this district.

Restlessness beset us, a restlessness forbidding long repose until the summit was reached. Time had slipped away and an hour had passed vengefully. Toil was renewed, but it was toil of a different nature from that necessitated by the wearisome snow slopes below. We had to climb a ridge, always a more interesting job than climbing a snow slope. A ridge, like virtue, is a narrow path, and virtue in this case is more interesting and amusing than the vice of wandering at will on a snow slope. But even the strait and narrow path has its pitfalls. The ridge was corniced. To avoid the cornices, we were forced off its crest on to the eastern face of the mountain. But luck was with us; what should have been a bare ice slope was conveniently crusted with snow. Yet, the slope was exceedingly steep and the snow covering the ice but a few inches deep, sometimes only an inch or so. We climbed carefully; a slip on the part of the leader would have meant disaster, for it was impossible to drive the ice axe into the ice and a fall would have been down the whole western face of the peak – 1,500 feet of ice precipices.

Altitude began to tell. We experienced the same old feeling that the body was a pump worked harder than it liked or was used to. Yet, we climbed that slope at a greater speed than I have climbed the last 1,000 feet of Mont Blanc.

The slope eased off and merged imperceptibly into a broad and comfortable

[1] Col 20,000 feet, between glaciers 4 and 10, visited subsequently by Birnie.

ridge. The ridge swept upwards into the mists. We passed easily along it, until presently it stretched away before us no longer, but fell away abruptly into nothingness. We had reached the summit.[2]

For a moment we felt no elation. As we gazed vacantly into the murk, dim shapes appeared like the shadowy manifestations of television. The mists were dragged aside. We saw the North-West Ridge of our peak sweeping away beneath us in a series of sharp ice ridges. Some giant had bitten the ridge, and the weather had piled ice and snow on to the bitten-out sections which had been chiselled and moulded by frost into parabolas with edges of delicate acuteness.

Sunbeams glanced through the shifting mists, illuminating glaciers and snowfields, peaks and valleys. Shadows chased across the snows like guilty consciences. There was much that was vague and little that was definite. We tried to disentangle the scene, but it was useless, and we resigned ourselves for a few minutes of quiet gazing, conscious only that we were on the summit of a great peak far removed from the world of men.

We might have stopped there a long time, for the weather was warm, but at the back of our minds was the uneasy thought that perhaps the crust of hard snow on the ice might melt, and we should have to cut many steps. Our fears were not entirely groundless. The snow-crust still held as we descended, but not so well as it had done during the ascent. The utmost care was imperative, and we moved one at a time, rope length by rope length. Birnie and Dorje were awaiting us on the col, having left the camp an hour or so after we and, on hearing how the snow was deteriorating, commenced to ascend. They disappeared into the mist, but as we sat on the col we heard the thud, thud, thud of their ice axes and knew that, unlike us, they were having to cut steps in some places for safety's sake. We waited some time for them, and only turned to go when we began to feel cold.

The descent was easy but unpleasant, and we fairly floundered in the abominable snow. The ascent to the lower col was fatiguing and we were glad to plunge through the cornice on the crest of the col and start down the steep slope to the main glacier. The snow on this slope was slightly crusted, for the sun had disappeared behind mists, and frost had frozen the surface of the snow.

We decided to glissade down the slope. I started off in a sitting position. Shipton and Nima Dorje followed some distance behind me. This was a mistake; all three of us should have taken separate lines, not followed one another.

As I shot down the slope the snow banked rapidly in front of me and spread out on either side in a small wedge-shaped avalanche, with myself as the apex of the wedge. This was nothing, for it often happens that a glissader down wet snow in the late afternoon pushes a small avalanche in front of him. In a few seconds, however, the avalanche in front of me attained formidable dimensions. There was no danger whatever, as I was above the avalanche, but I judged it advisable to stop. This I did without any difficulty by driving my ice axe into the snow. I had just brought myself to a standstill, and was watching the avalanche I had started careering away beneath me, when there came a sudden swish from behind and a mass of sliding snow struck me and carried me helplessly down the slope. I realised

2 The height by aneroid was 21,800 feet but in the map Birnie estimates it at 21,600 feet. Actually, I believe that both these are under estimates and that 22,000 feet is a closer approximation. The ascent from the camp was actually 3,000 feet.

at once what had happened. Shipton, behind me, had started to glissade and detached an avalanche on his own account. It was not a large avalanche, but it was a heavy one, composed of masses and lumps of sodden snow. My first feeling was one of annoyance – the annoyance of a man in a crowd who is carried by a press of people in the opposite direction to that in which he wants to go. Lying on my back, I drove my ice axe into the snow with all the force I could muster. For a moment I almost stopped, but then the weight of the snow piling up behind me shoved me brutally down the slope. It was that sudden brutal and irresistible force that caused mere annoyance to be replaced by apprehension. And then I remembered the bergschrund at the foot of the slope. We had crossed it without difficulty at a point where it was choked with former avalanche debris, but here and there it was not choked, and gaped widely. With desperate energy I drove my ice axe again and again into the firm snow beneath the avalanche. I could not stop myself, but I managed to slow myself down and allow a considerable quantity of the sliding snow to precede me. Had the slope been longer, I might have stopped myself altogether, for the avalanche was not more than a few yards in width. But it was too late. I saw the sliding snow in front of me shoot downwards and outwards over the upper lip of the bergschrund, with the lazy grace of water curving over a weir. Everything seemed to take place with incredible slowness. I remember no sensation of falling, no shock, but I found myself on the slope below the bergschrund. Then, without a pause, I was shot forward and downward again. I heard behind me a dull, heavy thudding as the tail of the avalanche continued to pour over the bergschrund. It was still pouring when the van of the avalanche stopped. My position now was that of a passenger in a telescoping train. My head and shoulders were free, but the lower portion of my body was in the avalanche. The sodden snow compacted. I experienced a terrible pressure – I thought my ribs were going to be crushed in like an eggshell – then, abruptly, the pressure ceased.

There was silence save for a slight hissing of laggard snow on the lip of the bergschrund. I struggled to free myself, and was able to do this without much difficulty. I stood up and gazed at the bergschrund. The difference in height between its upper and lower lips was fully fifteen feet, and such was the impetus of the avalanche that it shot clean over the crevasse beneath, which at this point was two or three yards wide. Had the avalanche slid slowly, or had the upper lip been less high, my grave would have been in the depths of the glacier, buried beneath tons of avalanche snow. I suddenly saw Nima gaily glissading, with a broad grin on his face, straight down the track left by the avalanche. With my remaining breath I shouted out a warning to him to go to the right, where the bergschrund was completely choked with snow, and then, feeling winded and a trifle sick, sat down. My hands were white and dead with cold and the numbing effect of driving them into the avalanche. Shipton and Nima massaged them, and circulation returned gradually and painfully.

It had been a narrow escape, and it was an example of how easily an accident may occur on a mountain. It was entirely my own fault. There would have been no danger if I had glissaded with caution, but I had not glissaded with caution, I had shot off down the slope without a thought as to whether Shipton and Nima were near to me or not. Actually, they had not started until some time after me, and the avalanche they detached had attained considerable volume and momentum by the time it reached me. As an avalanche it was so small as to be scarcely worthy of the name, yet it had carried me helplessly down the slope, and, had the fates not been kind, would have killed me. It is not the spectacular snow avalanche weighing tens of thousands of tons that causes mountaineering disasters, but the small, apparently inoffensive slide that buries the mountaineer in the depths of a crevasse or casts him over a precipice.

There were two interesting features about this accident. The first was the condition of the snow. It had a slight yet definite crust on its surface, formed by frost during the hour or so we had been descending the mountain. I have never seen wet well-crusted snow in the Alps slide,[3] and in the present instance sliding was not spontaneous, but due to our own sliding bodies forcing the snow apart and shoving it down in front of us as well as the sodden condition of the snow, which rendered it so heavy that the slight crust on its surface was unable to prevent its sliding when disturbed. The second interesting point is that it was not new snow that slid, but old snow. In the Himalaya during the monsoon season, so intense is the heat that snow becomes saturated with water, for perhaps the first foot or so of its depth, and these saturated layers periodically avalanche. It was an avalanche of this nature that carried down Doctor Longstaff and his Alpine guides on Gurla Mandhata. To climb safely the mountaineer must approach the Himalaya with an open mind prepared to amend preconceived alpine notions. Many conditions are similar, but others are dissimilar, and the possibility of old snow sliding away in large avalanches every day or two is a condition that seldom obtains in the Alps. Experience on a mountain is too often bought dearly; in the present instance it was bought with unusual cheapness.

It was a miserable trudge back to camp across the glacier. My body was aching from the crushing it had undergone, and every breath was an effort. If the snow on the glacier was soft in the morning, it was now a morass. We sank in half way to the knee at every other step. When at last we reached the camp, Greene diagnosed a broken rib. It was a simple and unimportant fracture, but it shows how near I came to being crushed in the avalanche.

Birnie and Dorje arrived an hour or so after us. They had reached the summit only after some heavy step cutting, for the thin crust that had so assisted us had melted too much to allow of safe footholds without a step being cut in the ice beneath.

While Shipton, Birnie and I were engaged in climbing Avalanche Peak, as we dubbed the 21,800-foot peak, Beauman and Greene had ascended a rock peak of 20,000 feet to the south-west of the camp which stands out, boldly, from the glacier. This peak presented no great difficulty, but they had enjoyed a pleasant day's climbing.

The day ended in a snowstorm. Snow fell heavily on July 23, and visibility was too poor for topographical work or for mountaineering.

During our forced inaction we made plans for the week that remained. In order to accomplish the maximum amount of work in that week we decided to split up into three parties. Birnie and I were to cross the 20,000-foot pass and explore the glaciers on the Gangotri side of the watershed, returning, if possible, across the

[3] Crusted or caked snow (wind slab) consisting of dry frozen snow can be exceedingly dangerous.

range by another pass. Shipton and Holdsworth were to make ascents from the 19,000-foot camp, whilst Beauman and Greene were to descend to Mana and make a reconnaissance up the Alaknanda Valley to the source of the Alaknanda River.

July 24 dawned depressingly – the slate-grey clouds were full of snow. My rib was not worrying me, but my bruised chest hampered my breathing to some extent. It would have been wiser to have remained at the camp, but I decided to accompany Birnie as arranged. If the weather was kind to us, it might be possible to return over the range via the Gangotri Glacier and a pass at the head of the Bhagat Kharak Glacier into the Alaknanda Valley.

Ten porters were selected to accompany us. We left the camp in drizzling snow. The snow on the glacier was in wretched condition, and we sank in deeply at every step. Almost at once I began to experience difficulty in expanding my lungs, owing to my bruised chest. As we slowly gained height, I found it harder and harder to breathe, and presently began to feel sick. I was suffering from an artificially induced anoxaemia.[4] I struggled on for an hour, but then could not advance another step. There was nothing for it but to return to camp. Although it was now snowing heavily, Birnie decided to cross the pass, taking with him seven porters. The remaining three porters started back with me to camp. It was a miserable descent – to be thwarted thus from fulfilling a cherished ambition was maddening. But soon I felt too ill to worry about anything. My legs would scarcely support me; my chest felt as though an iron band was being drawn more and more tightly about it. Once I dropped down into the snow exhausted and half-fainting. For the latter part of the descent the porters helped me along, and I was very glad to have them to lean upon. I arrived at the camp scarcely able to place one foot in front of the other. As I stumbled over the rocks near the cooking-tent, I saw something white in front of me. Thinking it to be a patch of snow, I was about to step on it when there was a cry from the cook. I paused – just in time to prevent myself stepping into the middle of an enormous number of eggs laid out in brave array on a slab of rock!

Later, as I lay in my tent feeling much better – for it was only exertion that produced a temporary anoxaemia – Shipton gloatingly told me about the eggs. He recalled to my mind how, before leaving Mana, we had detailed an old man, who was ever afterwards known as the "Egg wallah", to search for eggs. This search he had conducted with such energy that he had collected no less than a hundred eggs. To do this he must have scoured a considerable portion of the Central Himalaya. He had also found two chickens. One was dead – it had flown into a glacier torrent and been drowned. The other was looking none too happy. Apparently, like me, it was suffering from anoxaemia. The Egg-wallah had not known our route up from the Base Camp, and had ascended by a new and difficult route of his own from the glacier[5] north of the camp, yet, notwithstanding, he had delivered his precious burden intact. Perhaps the most charitable thing I can say about the eggs is that they varied from newly laid to nearly hatched. We ate them all, excluding of course those in the latter category, in exactly four meals, which works out at roughly six per man per meal.

[4] An effect produced by shortage of oxygen.
[5] Glacier 6.

Beauman and Greene had already descended to the Base Camp in the Arwa Valley, and had missed the Egg-wallah. It was arranged, therefore, that their share and my share of the eggs should be sent down with me. Four porters were detailed off for the task of helping me down. Although I felt perfectly well lying in my tent, I was still unable to imbibe enough oxygen when walking. It was necessary for four stalwart porters to half-carry and half-drag me down the glacier. The lower I got the better I felt, as, owing to the difference in altitude, the same limited expansion of the lungs would allow me to imbibe more oxygen. By the time I reached the Base Camp I was feeling almost fit again. This incident goes to prove how necessary is a good lung capacity for high-altitude mountaineering. Undoubtedly, there is no finer training for high altitudes than deep breathing exercises, as these expand the lungs and tend to help deep breathing to become automatic at high altitudes. Forcing oneself to breathe deeply at high altitudes is much more tiring than breathing deeply and naturally. That evening we feasted on eggs and eggs and then eggs.

Next morning we were delayed by the slowness of the porters bringing down loads from the upper camp and it was not until late in the afternoon that we set off down the Arwa Valley. The amount of snow that had melted in the past few days was amazing, and the whole appearance of the valley had changed. On the way we met the Dak-wallah with our mail, which included a large bundle of newspapers with little in them besides Indian troubles and financial crises. The world awaiting us was a gloomy one.

All next day we stumbled over stones, and it was not until late in the afternoon that we hurried across the dangerous terminal moraine. Barely had we passed the danger zone when some boulders thundered right across our track, leaving clouds of sulphurous dust in their wake.

It was good to exchange the blinding glare of the upper snows, and suns that seemed to wither the flesh, for flowering meadows and soft moisture-charged breezes impregnated with the sweet scents of turf and flowers. The walk to Mana on July 27 was a delightful one. Our way was carpeted with flowers. Since we had ascended the Arwa Valley, hosts of little white "everlastings" had arisen, whilst every emerald patch between the grey rocks was gay with red, yellow and white potentillas. We strolled into Mana in the golden calm of a perfect evening.

CHAPTER TWENTY THREE

Sources of the Ganges

BEAUMAN DECIDED to remain at Mana, but Greene and I were anxious to ascend the Alaknanda Valley and visit the source of the Alaknanda. We hoped, if there was time, to ascend some distance up the Bhagat Kharak Glacier and look for possible passes from its head into the Gangotri Glacier. It was scarcely probable that Birnie would attempt to cross one of these passes from the Gangotri side, for weather conditions, although good at Mana, were not good on the high mountains, but if he did we might meet him.

It was a misty morning as we walked up the Alaknanda Valley. The summits were concealed yet we could appreciate the magnificence of the portal of granite precipices through which we were passing. Our gaze paused appalled on sweeping walls of granite even while our nailed boots sank into soft turf, from which peeped the gay-eyed potentillas and gentians.

Once or twice we passed little caves beneath the crags with entrances partially sheltered by primitive walls. We could only conjecture that hermits had dwelt, perhaps even now dwell, in these, who had cut themselves off from the world to rest and meditate near the source of their sacred river.

On the pastures were shepherds minding their flocks. We passed the last of them; the hillsides became rockier; the mountains closed in about us.

We entered a stony waste of water-worn boulders washed down from the mouth of a side valley by spring floods. This valley contained a glacier, and, as we suspected, the glacier discharged a torrent of formidable size. We had been following a rude track to the edge of the stones, and hoped, therefore, to find a bridge across the torrent, but when we came to it, not only could we find no bridge, but we experienced grave misgivings as to the possibility of fording it. The mists had closed down upon us, and, as it was impossible to see far, Greene ascended the bank of the torrent in search of a bridge or a snowdrift, while I looked for a ford. The torrent was a steep one, and its waters tumultuous. In one place it was divided into two by a bank of boulders, and, as it was slightly less steep here, there seemed a chance of fording it. Presently, when Greene returned unsuccessful, we determined to try and effect a crossing. I went first, with a rope tied round my waist, held from the bank upstream, so that it would be of maximum assistance in preventing me from being washed off my feet. The depth of the torrent was not more than three feet, but what it lacked in depth it made up for in steepness and energy, and even with a rope it was all I could do to avoid being torn from my foothold. Green followed, likewise tied to a rope. Now that we had a handrail of rope stretched across, there seemed no need for each of the porters to be roped separately the handrail should suffice to prevent them from being swept from their feet.

The Old Soldier came next, carrying my tent, sleeping bag and other equipment. Although ungainly in appearance, his strength is prodigious, and he crossed with scarcely a pause, a broad grin on his face. Our old friend the Egg-wallah followed, carrying our box of provisions on his back. For a few yards he went well. He crossed one branch of the torrent to the central bank of boulders, and then essayed the other. He would have been all-right had he gone quickly, but he hesitated in the worst part of the torrent when he was about two yards from the bank. For a few moments he struggled to maintain his foothold, but the torrent was too strong for him and, though he clung tightly to the rope, he was swept from his feet. Even then, had he kept his wits about him, he could have reached the bank, by pulling himself a yard or two along the rope, but instead of doing this he clung helplessly to the rope without moving, petrified with fear. We yelled to him to advance, but he seemed incapable of doing anything. It was all over in a second or two. The torrent clutched and pulled at him remorselessly; first one arm gave out; he hung for a second or two by the other, then let go. In an instant he disappeared into the raging waters. He reappeared a few yards lower down on the edge of a vertical fall, quite ten feet in height, then vanished over it; almost before we had time to think, he was dashed over a lower fall, and another and another. It was a terrible spectacle. For a moment we paused, horrified, then raced down the bank leaping from boulder to boulder. It seemed certain that he must perish, dashed into pulp on the rocks, and we had given up all hope, when to our amazement we saw him crawl slowly out of a pool.

Greene was the first to reach him. At the best we expected to find many broken bones, but an examination disclosed nothing worse than severe bruising and superficial cuts. His escape had been a miraculous one, for he had been carried about a hundred yards down a raging torrent through a total vertical height of at least forty to fifty feet, and over a series of falls up to fifteen feet each in height. The poor old man's clothes had been torn from him with the exception of his shirt, and he was groaning and shivering in an access of terror and cold.

Naturally, we had given no thought to the load that had been carried down with him. We had seen it bobbing about for a few moments, but it had then disappeared, doubtless smashed to matchwood. Our attention was now called to it by two or three of our porters on the opposite bank, who were declaiming its loss. They had chased not the poor old Egg-wallah, but the load! To our Darjeeling men a few Egg-wallahs mattered but little, but the sahibs' food was of paramount importance. Such is their mental outlook, an inexplicable one to a European mind. It was a striking instance of the utter callousness of one Eastern race for another. The Egg-wallah was a Hindu, our Darjeeling men Buddhists. His life to them was worth no more than the snap of a finger. The sahibs' comfort and convenience was of greater importance. This incident by itself goes to show how deep is the gulf between East and West, and how abysmal is that other gulf between religion and religion in the East.

We rejoiced in the recovery of the Egg-wallah, but we bemoaned the loss of our food. It was best to return to the nearest pastures, where there was plenty of fuel. But how to get the Egg-wallah back across the torrent? He was in a state of collapse, and incapable of doing anything for himself. Luckily, higher up, there were two large boulders, one on either side of the torrent; between these we fixed a rope. From this the Egg-wallah was suspended by loops and hauled across the torrent without a further wetting. Greene, the Old Soldier and I followed, re-fording the torrent one by one, tied to ropes.

It was now late in the afternoon and chill mists enveloped us. We were soaked to the skin and shivering from inaction. It was a relief to find a grassy hollow around which dwarf juniper was growing in abundance. We made a great fire, and under its cheering influence even the Egg-wallah forgot his troubles and we ceased to remind each other of the delicacies now absorbed by Mother Ganges.

To our surprise and delight not only was our hunger appeased but our palates were titivated by Nima Dorje, who on Kamet had proved himself to be a far better cook than Achung, and who now produced unsuspected delicacies from the porters' food. He was a modest little fellow, and his aptitude for cooking had been obscured by his cinematographic activities. We vowed that Achung must go. His day of reckoning had come. No longer must he be allowed to spiflicate the digestions of the expedition. Nima Dorje should reign in his stead.

As the sun was setting, we decided to go for a stroll. We did not intend to go far when we left the camp, but the beauty of the evening tempted us on and on up the slopes above. As we climbed Nilkanta came into view. There are peaks in the Badrinath Range of greater height, but none to equal it in beauty of form and grace of outline. The sun had set, and its upper slopes were bathed in a cold pure afterglow. It is a peak built up of ice-ridges so fine and transparent that their edges merge imperceptibly into the sky, ice flutings, the continuous sweep of which emphasises height and steepness, and precipices crowned by ice-bastions that yield savagely to gravity in dreadful avalanches.

We scrambled on, mounting diagonally across the rough hillside. When next we paused we saw that the afterglow had ebbed from Nilkanta. The great peak was no longer queen of earth or sky, but ashen grey, nebulous – an afterthought, on the starry page of Heaven.

Before we turned campwards, we made a discovery. The torrent that had nearly caused the death of the Egg-wallah was securely bridged with snow avalanche debris! Greene must have got within a few yards of this natural bridge, but owing to the mist had not seen it.

We hurried downwards. Tropic night rushed to meet us, dragging by its locks a white mist. Into this mist we plunged. Soon it was dark, and we could neither see nor hear our camp. The hillside was indefinite and complicated, and it was difficult to maintain the right direction.

We began to experience doubts as to whether we should find the camp. We shouted. There came no answer. Suddenly, we smelt the familiar odour of burning juniper. Like bloodhounds we followed the trail, and in a few minutes rejoiced to see the dull glow of burning juniper through the mist.

And so the day ended by the campfire in companionship and happiness, warmth and comfort, while the light mists eddied and disappeared, and far away a dark ridge stood out from the night as a brilliant moon swung up into the stars. It was, nearly midnight when we turned into our sleeping bags. We were lulled to sleep by the deep voice of the Alaknanda speeding on its way towards the teeming plains of India.

The following morning we set out to visit the source of the Alaknanda, taking with us the Old Soldier and Passang.

Crossing the torrent by the snow bridge we had noticed the previous evening, we descended boulder-strewn slopes. Between these and an ancient moraine was set a little alp, a green oasis in the midst of the hungry rocks. There, to our surprise, we found a shepherd and his flock. How was he to descend the valley when the snow bridge melted or was washed away? Possibly, the villagers would make a bridge for him late in the summer, when the cold of autumn compelled him and his flock to retreat to lower levels. Why had he gone so far up the valley when he might have remained on one of the more fertile alps lower down? Was it because he wished to cut himself off from his fellows and while away the summer near the source of the sacred Alaknanda? He might have chosen a worse spot. How could such a man employ himself when he could neither read nor write? Some might envy him. Knowing nothing of the city, he was content. He had never heard the hammering of a typewriter, or breathed the stuffy air of an office. He recked nothing of financial crises; income-tax inspectors knew him not. His domain was the green pastures his walls were the mountain peaks, his roof the ever-changing sky. A handful of grain a day was all that he needed. Time was not something to be cajoled or defied – it passed.

We climbed the moraine, and, descending on the far side; found ourselves in a wilderness of boulders. Before us we could see the Alaknanda winding tortuously between its rocky banks. Up and down we toiled, up over stony ridges and down into little dells pink with willow herb. We breasted the last boulder-strewn ridge and gazed across at the muddy waters of the Alaknanda, surging from the combined snouts of the Bhagat Kharak and Satopanth Glaciers.

We had expected something beautiful; we had promised ourselves a thrill, neither expectation nor promise was fulfilled. As we gazed upon the rushing muddy waters beneath us, and the dirty ice of the Bhagat Kharak and Satopanth Glaciers, we felt that this was not a worthy setting for the birthplace of India's holy river. Here were no blue caverns of ice, but two torrents befouled with glacier mud, seeping unimpressively from beneath the snouts of two glaciers and uniting into one torrent a hundred yards lower. Yet, if beauty there was none, the scene was possessed of a certain wild impressiveness. Sheer desolation imparted a weirdness and magnificence into the landscape. Dimly seen through the swirling mists, dark precipices loomed forth. The air trembled with the thunder of the torrent. The huge boulders around, cast down by gravity and glaciation, were silent witnesses of forces ever at work fashioning the great peaks.

We returned by a different route, passing on our way a bank of strawberries, but their fruit was watery and tasteless.

We followed the Alaknanda until we came to the torrent in which we had lost our box of food. We ascended it in the hope of finding some of the food – possibly it might have been washed into backwaters. Soon our search was rewarded. We discovered tins of condensed milk, macaroni and tea, a large cabbage, a bag of very damp sugar, the Egg-wallah's trousers and one shoe. But, alas, of the delicacies, which included a tin of preserved ginger and half a bottle of rum, there was no sign. We did not think it worth while bringing back the Egg-wallah's trousers. Before their immersion they were none too savoury. During the interim they had certainly had a wash, but that was all that could be said for them. The Egg-wallah, however, had a different idea as to their value, and subsequently put in a claim for ten rupees, a claim which, to his intense surprise, was recognised, for, even though his trousers were not worth an anna, the poor old man deserved something for the fright and knocking about he had received in the torrent.

We spent the remainder of the afternoon lounging about in camp. The weather was clearer than it had been heretofore, and we could see a col at the head of the Satopanth Glacier. This must have been the col crossed by Meade when he explored the head of the glacier, and which apparently led, without difficulty, into the Kedarnath Valley system.

We spent another happy evening round the campfire, and next morning reluctantly packed up and started off back to Mana. Would that we had had a few weeks more left in which to explore the Badrinath Range and climb some of its magnificent peaks! We could only register a vow to return.

The weather was threatening as we descended the valley. On the way we met Beauman, who was coming up to visit the source of the Alaknanda, which he hoped to accomplish in one day from Mana, but, as the weather was deteriorating, he returned with us to Mana.

The same evening that we arrived back at Mana we were joined by Birnie, who had descended from the Arwa Valley. He told us that doubtful weather had rendered the original scheme of re-crossing the Badrinath Range by a pass into the head of the Bhagat Kharak Glacier inoperative, and he had been forced to keep within reasonable distance of the 19,000-foot camp, in order to have a base to retreat to in the event of really bad weather. He had crossed the 20,000-foot pass in a heavy snowstorm and descended some three or four miles down the glacier (11)[1] on the Gangotri side of the watershed, and made his Camp II some five miles from the junction of this glacier with the main Gangotri ice-stream. Next day he ascended a glacier (10) leading up to an apparent pass to the north-east of the 23,240-foot peak and reconnoitred the pass, which was forced up steep snow slopes. Descent on the far side was found to be possible but difficult. As the pass led back into the Arwa Valley, and not into the Alaknanda Valley, as he hoped, he returned. From the pass a view of several miles was obtained down the main Gangotri ice-stream.

He next ascended another glacier (9) leading back towards the watershed and partially reconnoitred an obvious pass at its head. Camp III was made at about 17,500 feet. On the following day, reconnoitring was continued with Gian Singh, a local porter. After some step cutting this second pass was reached. Descent on the far side was found to be steep but practicable. Unfortunately, however, the pass did not lead to the Bhagat Kharak Glacier and the Alaknanda Valley as hoped, but into a subsidiary glacier flowing into the Arwa Valley. The route over this pass is liable to be overwhelmed by ice-avalanches, but a safe camping-site (Camp IV) was found.

Next day, Birnie, with the whole of his porters, returned to the pass. The porters were lowered one by one through a cornice, and 2,000 feet of very steep snow-slopes were descended by the party. After a careful descent the easier glacier (2) was reached. Luckily, there was no ice to give trouble. This pass is only possible for laden men under good conditions, as ascent or descent on the Badrinath side of the watershed would involve too great a strain. Camp V was made at 16,700 feet. The local men showed up exceptionally well, and several of them became skilled in handling the rope and ice axe.

After a long, tedious march, Birnie found himself once more in the Arwa Valley on July 29, and descended to Mana.

Shipton and his porters were the last to return. He had climbed a peak estimated at about 19,000 feet, which rises directly above Mana. No great difficulties had been encountered. From the summit he had had a beautiful view of Mana Peak and its glaciers. Before leaving Mana, we conversed with an educated Hindu pilgrim who could speak good English. He seemed to have some doubts as to the source of the Ganges. The Sarsuti River was, he argued, with truth, considerably longer than the Alaknanda River, and therefore the true source of the Ganges must be in the glaciers near the Mana Pass. He told us something about a traditional pass said to exist between Badrinath and Kedarnath. By this pass it

[1] See map on p. 486.

was, he affirmed, an easy day's walk of three miles between these two places. The surveyors, however, think differently; the distance is over twenty mile on the map as the crow flies, and it would be necessary to cross several passes, the highest of which is the 20,000-foot pass reconnoitred by Meade. It is not wise to try to cross these holy snows of Himachal. A pilgrim had once attempted a passage of the range, but he had not got far up the valley leading towards Nilkanta when he was seized by the devil, who sank with him into the ground. His basket was left, on the hillside, and may still be seen. Possibly as a result of this outrage, there was a terrific fight between the god Vishnu and the devil, and the footprints of the combatants are visible now in the hillside. Vishnu won.

CHAPTER TWENTY FOUR

Down the Pilgrim Route

ON JULY 31 WE PACKED up our belongings and moved camp to Badrinath.

We pitched our tents near the dak bungalow opposite to the town, on pastures covered with edelweiss. The same afternoon we were received with much pomp and ceremony by the Rawal. An address was read to us by his interpreter from the foot of the temple steps. This address was couched so delightfully that I make no excuse for giving it here in full.

To Mr. F. S. Smythe and other members of the British Himalayan Expedition.

DEAR SIRS, – Please allow us to extend our most hearty and loyal congratulations to all of you – members of the British Himalayan Expedition – on your glorious achievement in successfully completing the conquest of Mount Kamet. It is probably the ninth occasion on which you and your honoured party have alone been privileged to set foot on the highest summit yet attained. It is indeed a matter of glory to you, not less to the Empire, to have opened a new chapter in the pages of history in this heroic direction. It is therefore no surprise to us to learn that your manly enterprise and commendable achievement is being deeply appreciated far and wide and is being applauded as the most gallant and daring expedition of the present age. Let us thank Almighty God for having accorded us this noble opportunity to thank personally the brave sons of a brave Empire to whom all heads bow in reverence. And speaking about ourselves, we need hardly assure you that our joy knows no bounds for more reasons than one, for we can with some pride express that Mount Kamet stands in a district to which we have the honour to belong. We are therefore extremely gratified to feel that this holy peak has achieved an International fame and distinction today which have certainly elevated our heads and existence in the eyes of the civilised world.

It is God's will that we have been honoured to welcome you here in this holiest place – the premier shrine of India – where every year during summer nearly 50,000 pilgrims yearly flock on pilgrimage with single-minded devotion and religious-vented mind. We need hardly mention that we are living in a district surrounded by a series of unsurmountable hills, devoid of almost all sorts of modern facilities, though it may be said to the credit of our benign Government that we are at least enjoying some of the facilities that were hitherto entirely unknown to us. But this unhappy district has frequently suffered from the severest type of famines in the past several years owing to the ridiculously poor condition of agriculture and lack of irrigation. It is only a few merciful showers of rain at times that save the inhabitants from regular starvation. Trade in the district is negligible, and whatever money we get from military and other Government services is barely sufficient for our living in view of the exorbitant rates of foodstuffs due to the lack of better communication in the district. The apathy of our miserable plight can better be illustrated from the fact that during the famine of 1918–19 grain could not be imported into the district from plains on any imaginable hire! Desperate efforts were then resorted to, and you will be agreeably surprised to know that we could get a little quantity of grain by post parcels only! Can anything be more deplorable and miserable? Some of the mule-carriers that volunteered to do the service could only reach up to Nandprayag – a place fifty-five miles below from here – on charging a hire of Rs. 24 a maund![1] Sirs, this is how we are living in this twentieth century! All over India we hear reports that the rates of grain have gone unprecedentedly low, but here in the hills we are getting it at the same old rates and that also of a bumper harvest, i.e., wheat 3 seers[2] and rice 2½ seers a rupee. We need hardly dwell upon the fact that this deplorable condition is all due to the absence of communication in the district for which we have long been striving hard.

The Government, realising the apathy of this country, surveyed the line from Rikhikesh to Hardwar for a railway some ten years ago, at an expense of a few lacs of rupees, but the idea of a railway line was probably dropped as it was not found remunerative. But the Government did not leave the matter altogether, for it then surveyed a line from Lansdowne to Karanprayag, via Vyasghat, Musagali and Adbadri for a cart-road some five years back, but owing to the financial stringency in the Government budget, the proposal could not as yet be taken in hand and nobody can say when it may ultimately materialise.

It is indeed a pity that the loyalty and services of Garhwalis was not adequately rewarded and respected. We may affirm here, without violating any canons of modesty, that the association of our community with the British Army has been long, and the meritorious services rendered by the Garhwali soldiers in every theatre of war both on the Indian frontiers and in the far-off climes in the service of His Majesty the King Emperor is now a matter of history. Our two gallant brothers obtained the coveted Victoria Cross for their heroic front; one of them died in duty and the other is fortunately living. This small district with its humble resources, out of loyalty and devotion to the Crown, wonderfully served the Empire during all periods of her crisis, but it is sheer misfortune to assert that our most legitimate and rightful demands in this respect have not yet been acceded to nor do we see chances of its adoption in the near future. In this way, obviously it appears to us that we are doomed to live in our present deplorable and helpless state for a number of years to come.

We fully trust, sirs, you have with deep interest sympathetically listened to this story of our poverty and backwardness. We re-affirm that the culminating point of our moral, material and economic progress solely depends upon the question of CART-ROAD.

Though we quite realise that the Government is at present running under great financial stringency, it cannot be concealed that the Government has unlimited resources at its disposal if it at all wills and cares for its poor and loyal subjects of Garhwal. The Government can conveniently earmark some money annually for the purpose, and we are sure, without any great embarrassment to the Government, the

[1] 80 lbs.

[2] One seer =2lbs.

work can be finished within a very few years. We need hardly impress upon you the fact that with the opening of this new line the number of pilgrims, besides local traffic, will increase many more times ahead, and will far improve the economic and commercial status of the district.

We therefore most earnestly and respectfully beg you to lend the weight of your influence to this demand to the Government when you come across with the higher authorities and thus considerably increase the chances of its fulfilment. We are convinced, sirs, that if you evince some real interest in the matter, the Government would in all likelihood pay more attention towards it. Let it be candidly said that our main purpose in bringing our standing grievance in this respect to your notice is fervently in the hope that you will leave no stone unturned to get it redressed, in order that peace and prosperity may as well reign in the district for the first time during the 130 years of the British rule in Garhwal.

We are afraid we have rather far travelled beyond the range of your active interest, for which you will very kindly forgive us, but in fact we could not resist the temptation of putting forth our humble yet acute case to your benevolent notice since we are positively certain that you will not fail to pay sympathetic and lively attention and care in this matter.

Lastly we beg to assure you, sirs, of our steadfast devotion to the Crown and our determination to continue to serve it as the sword arm of India.

With very best prayers for your long life and prosperity,

We have the honour to remain,
Dear Sirs,
Your Warm Admirers,

HIS HOLINESS THE RAWAL OF TEMPLE BADRINATH
AND THE PUBLIC OF BADRINATH
(GARHWAL DIST.).

Badrinath (U.P.),
August 1, 1931.

I fear it may be a long time before the Rawal and the people of Badrinath get their cart-road, for the expense of constructing and maintaining such a line of communication would be enormous.

We were scarcely fit subjects for such a flattering address. Our beards were long, our clothes worn; our nailed and granite-like boots seemed awkward and clumsy amid the barefoot or sandalled pilgrims. The local photographer, who had been summoned for the occasion, can be excused if the picture he took was tilted to one side.

After the address had been read, Birnie delivered a lecture in Hindustani on the expedition. No lecturer can have lectured to a more unusual audience. Pilgrims thronged the temple steps. The aged and the infirm were brought on litters to listen. The stone-paved square without the temple was thronged by the populace of Badrinath. They listened with the greatest interest as Birnie explained in detail how Kamet was climbed. He illustrated his lecture by producing various items of equipment. Our Darjeeling men swaggered nonchalantly through the throng, bearing with them tents, ice axes, ropes, sleeping bags and other expedition equipment. Great applause greeted the conclusion of this lecture. I made a speech in English, which was translated into Hindustani by the Rawal's secretary. From the impassioned harangue on the part of the interpreter, it was obvious that what I said was both ornamented and magnified – possibly just as well, for the flowery idioms of the East are outside my experience.

At the conclusion of these ceremonies we were entertained to lunch. The Rawal informed us that he himself was unable to attend, as he had to meditate and pray in the temple. After nearly three months of Achung, the lunch seemed a masterpiece of cookery. There were creamy rice, curiously flavoured and spiced, small pies, fruit, and many queer sweetmeats. These were washed down by "Himalayan tea", the flavour of which remains a unique and unhallowed memory. Replete to bursting-point, we tottered back to camp and spent the remainder of the day sleeping off our shameless gluttony.

Next day we were shown round the temple by the Rawal. Inside it is an inner shrine where reposes the sacred image of Vishnu. The idol is not more than three feet high, and it is made of a black stone and marble. It is clothed in a rich gold brocade. In order to see it, a large mirror was procured, and from this the sun was reflected into the temple. In front of the image are a number of lamps and a table also, covered in brocade. In the forehead of the image there is a solitary diamond of moderate size. It is said that the properties, such as dresses, eating-vessels, etc., belonging to the image are not worth more than 5,000 rupees owing to the fact that the original gold ones were stolen by some robbers, who made their way across the snows in winter. The idol is provided with a meal every afternoon. Dishes are placed before it, and the doors of the shrine closed, so that the image is left to consume its meals in quietness. Not until after sunset are the doors again opened. Attendants prepare the idol for bed, and the doors of the shrine are again closed until morning. There are many attendants, both male and female, and the usual dancing-girls. No one is allowed inside the inner apartments of the temple except the servants, and only the Rawal may touch the idol.

Many come hundreds and even thousands of miles to visit Badrinath and Kedarnath. What is the reason behind this long and toilsome pilgrimage from the plains of India? Some, who have lost their husbands, wives or children, believe themselves to be under a curse for some offence committed during a former existence, and undertake the pilgrimage to expiate their crime against the gods. There are many Yogis among the pilgrims who believe that only by pain and toil may they acquire merit or rid themselves of their sins. Many of these even renounce their names and identity. Included among them are those of noble family and the lowest of the low. These Yogis practise detachment and abandon everything in order to meditate, and it is their aim to rise superior to bodily needs or ailments. Some fast for weeks on end without clothing or shelter save rude caves in the mountainside. These ascetics cover themselves with ashes, whilst the Sanyasis and Gosains (devotees of Siva) wear a red wig of coiled and matted hair over their heads, which gives them a wild and ghastly appearance A leopard- or deer-skin is their dress. They carry a rind or a gourd, in which the charitable place gifts of food, a pair of tongs for making their fire and an Earthen water-jug. Another sect is the Kanphata Yogis.[3] These wear ochre-coloured garments. They dedicate themselves to Bhairava, a terrible mountain deity. The religion of some of these

[3] Kanphata means "ear split", because the lobe of the ear is pierced and a pendant of rhinoceros horn, agate or gold passed through.

Yogi sects is associated with indescribable rites. It is not long since human sacrifices were offered on the altars of the temples in Kumaun and Garhwal. Even nowadays the initiation ceremony into the Kanphata caste consists in drawing blood as an offering to their god. It is for this reason that they slit their ears. Unlike the Hindus, they do not burn their dead, but enclose them in a coffin in an upright position, or else throw the corpse into a river.

After visiting the temple we were conducted by the Rawal to an enclosed bathing which is fed by a hot sulphurous spring. This, like the waters of Lourdes, is reputed to be capable of cleansing and invigorating body and soul. In Europe its waters would probably be drunk for their medicinal properties, but at Badrinath they are used merely to bathe in.

Below the bathing-pool there is a flight of steps, worn by the tread of countless feet, that leads down to the Alaknanda. Where these steps disappear into the torrent there is an iron bolt, to which pilgrims cling while immersing their bodies in the grey glacier waters of their sacred river. Close by is another hot spring which issues steaming from a rock, whilst a few yards away, and projecting from the river water, is a large boulder pierced by a hole, through which the god Vishnu is reputed to have poked his finger.

In camp that evening we realised sorrowfully that it was our last night in the High Himalaya. The morrow would see us marching downhill into tropical heat. Had the weather been bad we could have turned plainwards without regret. But it was not bad; it was perfect. The sunset was a peaceful one. Our one regret was that a few clouds obstinately concealed Nilkanta. We knew that from our camping-ground there is a view of that marvellous peak, and it would be disappointing to leave Badrinath without seeing it.

The evening was cool, and we dined in the mess-tent. After dinner we came out for a final pipe and a stroll. The camp and the Alaknanda Valley were in deep shadow. The night was very still. We could hear the low thunder of the Alaknanda and the murmur of Badrinath. We could smell the sweet scent of pastures still warm from the sun. The moon was rising. Suddenly our attention was arrested. We saw Nilkanta. It was bathed in brilliant moonlight and was framed by the dark walls of nearer mountains. It was difficult to believe that it was a mountain and not some product of the infinite manufactured by the stars.

Later, when the camp was sleeping, I lay awake gazing through the doorway of my tent at Nilkanta: later still, in dreamland, I sought refuge on that serene summit from the uneasy phantasms that beset the wanderer through the valleys of sleep.

The dawn was sparkling and fresh, and we saw Nilkanta lit gloriously by the rising sun. Its snows were the last we were to see on our march back to Ranikhet. Just as we were about to leave, a local resident Pandit Nerian Dutt, who informed us that he was a retired banker, begged us to come and see his garden. We did so, and we were surprised at the number of flowers he had managed to cultivate in the rocky soil. He was a charming old gentleman of a type not often seen nowadays in India. He loaded us with fruit and other delicacies, and informed us that he had sent word down to Joshimath to inform the steward of his orchards there that we were coming.

That the path below Badrinath is dangerous and impassable in winter was evidenced by the avalanche snow lying in the Alaknanda Valley. The sun had been melting it for months, but in such quantities had it accumulated that in several places it still bridged the Alaknanda River. One bridge was an extraordinary freak of nature, and resembled a brickwork bridge, owing to the snow being curiously veined with streaks of dirt.

Down and down we tramped. Gusts of heat met us. The valley walls closed in upon us. Dust whitened our boots. Runnels of sweat coursed down our foreheads as we approached the dak bungalow at Pandukeswar.

During the past two months we had forgotten that flies existed. Now, as swarms of them settled on our food, we were disagreeably reminded of this curse of Himalayan travel in the lower valleys.

Night fell dark and ominous with a flicker of lightning to remind us that we were approaching the foothills. Insects whirred and fluttered about us and as we ate our dinner a hundred moths committed suicide in the candles.

We awoke next morning to hear a series of crashes. A huge boulder was falling down the opposite side of the valley. It bounded down in a series of leaps, plunging at last, with a splintering crash, into the forest beneath.

The path, in the way that Himalayan paths have, played a bad joke upon us that day. We were congratulating ourselves on having all but reached Joshimath when it turned uphill and we found ourselves confronted with an ascent of some 1,500 feet.

At Joshimath there is a hospital at which Lewa had been detained as his feet were considered too bad to allow of him being carried to Ranikhet. The hospital is under the charge of a native doctor whose cleanly methods and efficiency impressed us not a little. Poor Lewa's feet were not a pleasant sight. Mortification had set in: his toes resembled burnt cinders; on the edges of the affected areas cracks had opened up down to the bone, oozing blood and pus. But, despite the terrible appearance of his feet, Greene was satisfied that not only would they be saved, but that at the worst he was not likely to lose more than the top joints of his toes. A welcome surprise awaited us at Joshimath. Pandit Nerian Dutt had been as good as his word and we feasted on mangoes from his orchard. How good those mangoes were! We vowed that we had never tasted anything like them. Even to a sophisticated palate, a mango is a gift from the gods, but it must be perfectly ripe – not under-ripe, when it is disappointing, or over-ripe, when it tastes of paraffin, but ripe to the hour; it is then a peerless fruit.

As we descended the Lower Alaknanda Valley the heat became more intense. Pilgrims were toiling up the path.

Those who were too old or crippled to walk were carried on litters, whilst others rode ponies. They eyed us incuriously and apathetically. Many looked starved and worn out by their journey. We encountered also the postman. In order to ward off wild animals and evildoers, he carried a spear with a ring of bells round the shaft.

The farther we proceeded southwards, the heavier became the rainstorms, but by starting at dawn every morning we were able to avoid both the heat of the day and the torrential downpours which occurred almost every afternoon. The march

Right: Nilkanta 21,640ft/6596m, the fine peak above Badrinath. The peak is now called Nilkanth. *Photo: Yama Kei Archive*

was dull and uneventful. We managed to keep in good health save that for two days I suffered from an attack of fever.

On August 13 ponies carried us up the sun-baked hillside to Ranikhet. In the hospitable club there we soon forgot the toil, the heat, the flies and the smells of the past ten days. Our beards came off; we wallowed in hot baths; we ate well-cooked food; we slept between sheets. Civilisation claimed us, and at the time we would not have had it otherwise. A real appreciation of life is made up of contrasts. Civilisation cannot be properly appreciated unless you have lived in the wild. Comfort can only be judged by discomfort. No man can claim to be a gourmet until he has sampled native cooked food. For the past three months we had lived as men can only in the wilds. Our eyes had searched wide horizons; we had sweated and we had shivered; we had experienced comfort and discomfort; we had gazed upon ugliness and beauty; we had known comradeship; we had found peace.

A few mornings later I saw the Himalaya for the last time. The forest was whispering the secrets of the slow dawn wind; the call of a cuckoo came joyously from a distant ridge. Day was already fashioning her twisted pillars of cloud. Into the stainless air and at an immeasurable distance from the common things of earth rose the everlasting hills.

53, 54 The 1931 Kamet team at Raniket before departure: (*l to r*) standing: Raymond Greene, R.L. Holdsworth, Bentley Beauman, Eric Shipton and E. St John Birnie; seated: Nima Tendrup, Frank Smythe (leader) and Achung (cook). Lewa *(inset)*, the experienced sirdar, had taken part in expeditions to Everest (1921, 1922, 1924), Nanda Devi (1928) and Kangchenjunga (1929). In 1931 he reached the summit of Kamet but was badly frostbitten. He was later sirdar on Everest (1933) and Nanga Parbat (1934). *Photos: Smythe archive*

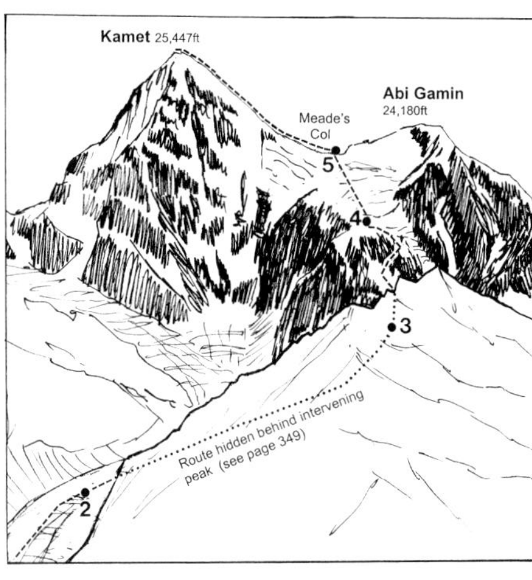

55 *(above)* C.F. Meade's photograph of the upper part of Kamet, which his party came so close to climbing in 1913. The difficulties are concentrated into rock and ice cliff above Camp 3 and the icefall below Meade's Col. Above the col the steep summit pyramid proved surprisingly arduous in 1931.

56, 57 *(far left)* Camp 2 on the East Kamet Glacier. A couloir in the right wall gave access to the snow basin seen in Meade's picture. *(near left)* On the summit of Kamet, the highest peak to have been climbed by 1931.
Photos: Frank Smythe

58 *(right)* The mixed face above Camp 3, dominated by the bastions of Abi Gamin.
Photo: Bentley Beauman

59, 60, 61 *(top)* Fording the Arwa River. *(right)* Avalanche Peak, the crosses mark the points where the climbers were avalanched. *(inset)* The Rawal of Badrinath and his retinue – in a long letter, he asked Smythe's group to press for better access to the region to ease the critical food supply problems created by the pilgrims to the source of the Ganges. *Photos: Frank Smythe*

62 *(right)* Porters climbing the steep ice bulges below the North Col of Everest in 1933. *Photo: Frank Smythe*

63, 64 *(left)* The leadership partnership forged between Hugh Ruttledge (far left) and Frank Smythe enabled the 1933 Everest expedition to mount strong summit bids despite difficult weather. With good morale and strategy the party (which included the core of the Kamet team) established and stocked two high camps (Camp 6 at 27,400ft!).

65 *(centre left)* Camp 5 in 1933.

66 *(lower left)* A still from Wyn Harris's film shows Jack Longland's team leaving Camp 6 after their major supply effort.

67 *(top right)* Wager and Wyn Harris descend from Camp 6 after their comprehensive examination of the upper difficulties of the mountain.

68, 69 *(lower right)* The upper slopes of Everest seen from the 1938 Camp 5. The heavy snow cover contrasts with the leaner 1933 conditions. On their 1938 summit bid Smythe *(inset)* and Shipton encountered deep powder snow above Camp 6 that made progress too slow.

Photos: John Morris (63, 64), *Percy Wyn Harris* (66), *Frank Smythe* (65, 67, 68), *Eric Shipton* (69)

70 *(right)* The upper slopes of Everest in 1933. X marks Smythe's high point at c.28,100ft (reported as roughly the same place as that reached by Norton, Wager and Wyn Harris).

71 *(left)* Smythe's photograph which was captioned in the *Alpine Journal* account (the first published record) as being taken from his highest point (in which case a hidden gully must break the obviously easy ledge leading into the right branch of the Great Couloir (see *Everest 1933* p.140 and p.631 in this book). *Everest 1933* has it captioned as showing the "Great Couloir at about 28,000ft" suggesting that it shows the access ledge to the left-hand branch. If the former is correct it seems likely that *two* roped climbers, with time in hand, would have gained the right branch and made progress up the rocks above. *Photos: Frank Smythe*

A NOTE ON EXPEDITION FOOD AND DIET

[abridged from the original expedition appendix]

MENTALLY as well as physically the mountaineer requires the best and most varied food that can be provided. Variety is as essential as quality, for lack of it inevitably induces boredom, and boredom on a mountain is tantamount to a defeatist attitude of mind.

An expedition must be fed first on its journey to Base Camp, and then above Base Camp on the mountain. Travellers who pass along the lower valleys and over the foothills of the Himalaya often suffer stomach disorders – colic, constipation, and diarrhoea. Anyone continuously afflicted is liable to impair his strength for the later high climbing, whilst his whole mental outlook may be changed with him becoming demoralised and "fed up". I believe the cause is mainly due to extraneous matter in the food and water, and poorly cooked food.

All water, particularly if it passes near houses or through cultivated land, should be boiled, if cholera, dysentery, typhoid and other diseases are to be avoided. This water should also be filtered, with either a portable filter or through linen cloths, to remove as much extraneous matter as possible.

Local flour should be avoided as it invariably contains dust and grit. Local rice should always be sifted. Another cause of stomach trouble is due to eating improperly cooked chupatties. If these are to be eaten, they should be as thin and crisp as a wafer biscuit. They should break, not bend, for it is their uncooked doughy centre that is responsible for the trouble.

The fact that we suffered for the most part from only minor disorders is, I believe, due to our avoiding local food so far as possible with the exception of fresh meat, which is unlikely to contain extraneous matter.

Another important consideration is an adequate supply of food containing the vital anti-scorbutic vitamin C. There is a strong probability that the mental and physical deterioration experienced by some Himalayan expeditions was partly due to lack of vitamin C. Polar explorers say that it is possible to go without fresh food of any kind for a considerable time. This may be possible at lower altitudes where the evil effects of deterioration are not so obvious, but over 20,000 feet, the slightest ailment is magnified many times. Failing fresh fruit, vegetables and meat, pure lime juice is probably the best and most easily assimilated anti-scorbutic.

We took lime juice, and this was taken regularly by all members of the expedition. We were also able to obtain wild rhubarb, bracken shoots, and on one or two occasions small wild onions. There seems no reason, however, why apples, green bananas, and lemons should not be taken by an expedition and eaten every day by its members. Fruit might also prove useful as supplying acid to the body as compensation for the lack of bodily acidity, which results from oxygen lack at high altitudes.

After bad experiences on two Himalayan expeditions I can only say that the importance of selecting a good cook cannot be over estimated, but even with the best cooks cleanliness should still be given serious attention.

If fresh meat is to be eaten, it may be from an old, hard-worked animal and thus lean and sinewy. In such circumstances a mincing machine is an essential item of culinary equipment. But if used it should be frequently cleaned to rid it of pieces of putrefying meat. Utensils, particularly aluminium pans, should also be periodically inspected.

We kept our tinned meats for use above the Base Camp and relied upon obtaining local mutton, chicken and eggs from the villages and pastures through which we passed, and on shooting bharhal (wild sheep).

Above the Base Camp the importance of its selection and supply cannot be over estimated. At high altitudes the body resembles an engine that must be constantly supplied with fuel for heating and running – ideally in small quantities at frequent intervals. This fuel is sugar. An excellent idea on a mountain is to carry a pocketful of lump sugar or sweets that do not induce thirst. I made the mistake of not estimating for enough sugar, but fortunately there was plenty of goa (native sugar) in the upper valleys of Garhwal.

The most valuable alcoholic drink is rum, because of the sugar it contains. During a climb, alcohol is more dangerous than useful, but as a night cap I know of nothing to equal a drink of hot rum. Unlike other alcoholic stimulants, it keeps the body in a warm glow for the remainder of the night, and best of all it induces sleep. Whisky and brandy are best kept purely as luxuries or for emergencies.

Fresh meat was taken up to Camp Three, 20,600 feet, and buried in the snow there, but above that point it was not easy to digest meats with the exception of tinned sausages, tongues, sardines, etc., and the craving for sugary foods became more and more pronounced. Jam, sweetened condensed milk, chocolate, sweets, tinned fruits, etc., all satisfy this craving. Hot chocolate drinks are excellent at night. Bovril pemmican represents the easiest way of taking meat, but should be well diluted owing to its essential fattiness. It is one of the most concentrated foods known and is an excellent standby in case of emergency. Porridge can be eaten at any altitude, and so also can eggs, which also supply any meat [protein] that the body may require.

Food on Kamet was carefully rationed and apportioned by Eric Shipton. As with cooking, the work of rationing is more likely to evoke blame than praise, and the fact that it worked without a hitch on this expedition points to the efficiency of Shipton's arrangements.

CAMP SIX

Camp Six

First published by Hodder and Stoughton, 1937

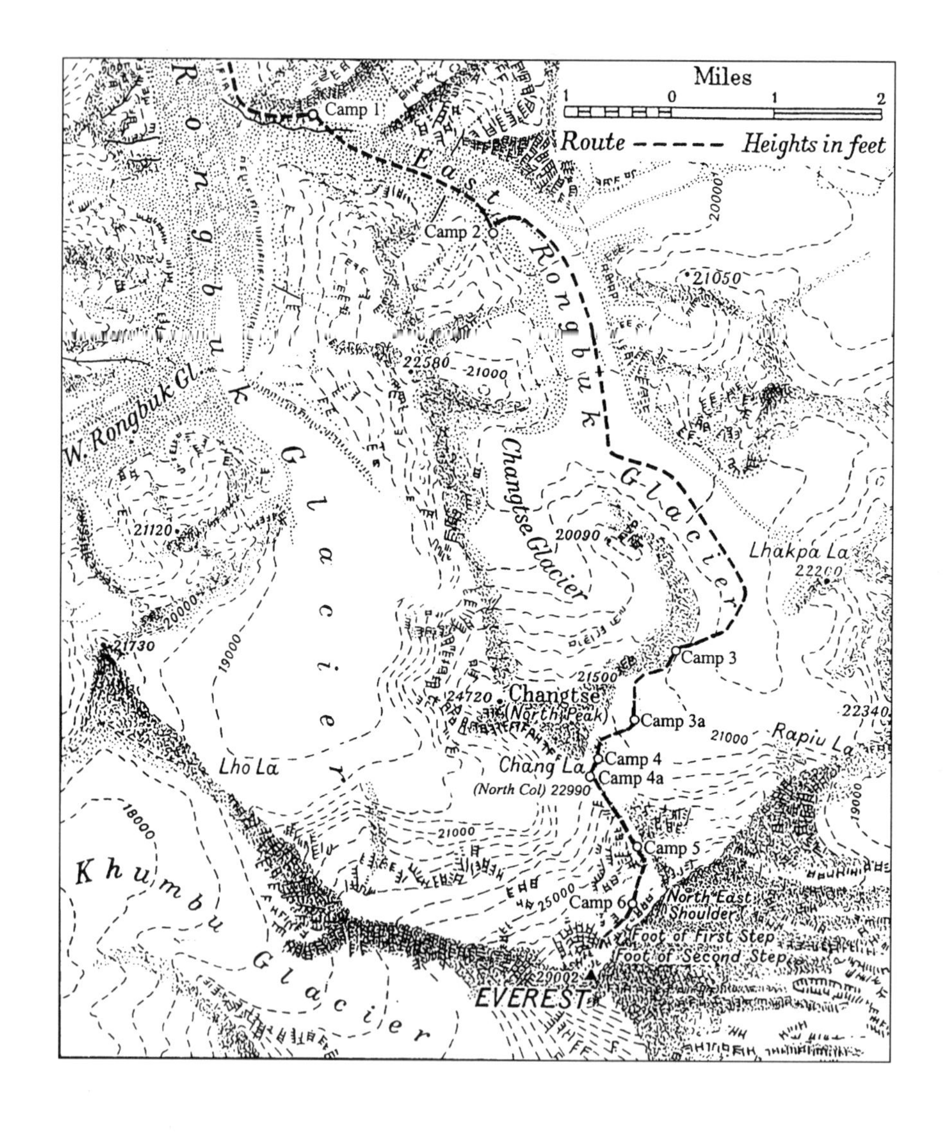

Contents

AUTHOR'S NOTE: This book is a personal account of the 1933 Everest Expedition, compiled from a diary which accompanied me to the highest camps, and is published by permission of the Mount Everest Committee. The reader who desires a more comprehensive account is referred to the official expedition book – *Everest 1933* by Hugh Ruttledge.

There have been six expeditions to Everest of which two were primarily reconnaissances and there is to be a seventh in 1938. The 1933 Expedition was the fourth and, like the 1924 Expedition, it came very near to success. Its members were:

Hugh Ruttledge (leader) [Hugh], E.O. Shebbeare [Shebby], C.G. Crawford [Ferdie], Captain E.St.J. Birnie [Bill]; Maj. Hugh Bousted [Hugo]; T.A. Brocklebank [Tom]; Dr. C. Raymond Greene, Percy Wyn Harris [Wyn], J.L. Longland [Jack], Dr. W. McLean [Willy], Eric E. Shipton, Lieut.W.R. Smijth-Windham [Smidge]; F.S. Smythe, Lieut. E.C. Thompson [Tommy], Lawrence R. Wager [Waggers], George Wood-Johnson.

The memories of physical hardship are fortunately so illusive that it almost seems to me that my diary exaggerates. Did we really have such an unpleasant time in 1933? Perhaps in this connection I may mention the diary of a former Everest climber. Above the Base Camp his description of the day's events is said to be prefaced invariably by the words "Another bloody day".

It is instinctive with man to want to dominate his environment and Everest is one of the last great problems left to him on the surface of this Earth. In solving this problem he adds to his scientific knowledge, and enjoys a physical and spiritual adventure.

That Everest will be climbed cannot be doubted; it may be next year or a generation hence. Every expedition adds to our knowledge of the problem, yet, in the end, the climber depends for success on the casting vote of fortune. There are three problems inherent in the ascent. Firstly, the difficulty of the mountain, which is considerable at a height of 28,000 feet; secondly, the altitude and, thirdly, the weather. Skill and knowledge may solve the first two, but the last will always remain an incalculable factor. The weather defeated the 1933 and 1936 expeditions, though it remains to be proved that men can live in the rarefied air above 28,000 feet without some artificial aid.

Lastly, no reference to the Everest problem, however brief, is complete if it fails to mention the Sherpa and Bhotia porters. Their work has brought us very near to success, and the story of their courage and devotion should stand out in letters of gold when the last chapter in the struggle comes to be written.

Publisher's Note for 2000 reprint: Unlike the earlier books in this omnibus, in *Camp Six* the author has adopted Christian names and nicknames to describe his companions. To assist the reader these are added (where necessary) after the names in the list above.

The disappearance of Mallory and Irvine in 1924 and the discovery of the ice axe in 1933, make *Camp Six* and the official account (*Everest, 1933*) of particular value. These carried the assessments of what might have happened in 1924 by the first climbers to revisit the scene. Their opinions may be more focused than those of modern commentators as they had similar equipment, food, fuel, and tactical perceptions as the 1924 climbers. Frank Smythe suggests, in the postscript, the ice axe position may point to an accident that took place during the ascent. The later discovery of what may have been a carefully stashed (rather than discarded) oxygen bottle *apparently* beyond (towards the summit) the ice axe site may weaken this theory. In 1999 the discovery of Mallory's roped body, suggested that he was linked to Irvine at the moment of mishap. This has, if anything, made the presence of the ice axe even more puzzling as the body and axe sites are a considerable distance apart, albeit generally in line. These more recent discoveries are of relevance to the debate in this book, so additional footnotes (denoted by asterisks) have been added where suitable.

CHAPTER ONE

Darjeeling

CALCUTTA IS HOT even in February. Though sorry to part from many hospitable friends, I was glad to begin the last stage of my journey from England to Darjeeling.

It was a stuffy night to begin with in the "Darjeeling Mail", and ravenous mosquitoes interfered with my slumbers, but towards dawn the temperature fell and cool, refreshing airs rushed in at the window.

As the train neared Siliguri the sky lightened with a quick rush of rosy tints and little pools of water opened calm eyes in the paddy fields of the Bengal plain.

I peered from the window into the dim hill-filled north, and there, high up in the sky, I saw a tiny point of golden light. During the few seconds that it was visible before a curve took it from sight it grew larger. It was the summit of Kangchenjunga, nearly one hundred miles distant.

At Siliguri, the foothills meet the plain, and the hillman the plainsman. Half of those on the platform were languid Bengalis, the other half energetic, slant-eyed, broad-faced, high-cheeked Tibetans; smooth-skinned, quiet-mannered Lepchas from Sikkim, and tough little Sherpas from Nepal, their brows furrowed as though from the strain of staring into great distances, and their eyebrows puckered from the snow-glare of the passes. Traders, beggars, Lama pilgrims, rickshaw wallahs from Darjeeling and little Nepali women from the tea plantations, with gay-coloured blouses and cone-shaped wicker baskets on their backs; all were cheerful, all ready to show their teeth in a broad grin.

I breakfasted, then ascended to Darjeeling by the world-renowned Himalayan Railway. So wide are the carriages that they seem likely to over-balance on the narrow-gauge line. A brave little engine draws the train, but it would not succeed in climbing the steeper gradients without two men stationed on the front to pour sand on the rails.

First along the plain, fussed the train, then into the sub-tropical forests that extend for scores of miles along the foothills of the Himalayas. One minute, we were on the level, the next we were climbing steeply uphill.

After the placid, less secretive beauties of English woodlands, these Himalayan forests are strangely impressive. Sunlight rarely penetrates their dense foliage, beneath which all manner of rank shrubs struggle despairingly upwards towards the sunlight; giant creepers embrace the moss-clad trees in an octopus-like grip, and epiphytic ferns, proof of the humid climate, hang from the branches in lank green tendrils, so that the traveller fancies himself walking on an ocean floor amid pendent masses of seaweed. In each great tree dwells a colony of birds and insects, and there is a constant whirring and humming as though countless sewing machines and sawmills were being worked by invisible hands.

Pantheists who can see only beauty and gentility in nature should visit a tropical or sub-tropical forest. Grossness and strife are the keynotes, and the predominant motif is death and the fear of death. Much has been written of the gentle beauties of the English countryside, but where are the poets of the jungle?

The train stopped to pick up a red-haired Irishman, who told me that he had been sitting up all night for a tiger, but without success. He also related the providential escape of a friend from an infuriated leopard. The would-be leopard killer fired one barrel of his gun – he was using a double-barrelled shotgun firing soft-nosed bullets – and missed. The other cartridge misfired. The next moment the leopard was on him. He ducked as it sprang and somehow – he was a powerful man – threw the beast over his shoulder. The leopard was so surprised at this "all in" treatment that it made off, leaving the hunter with a badly mauled arm which he subsequently lost through sepsis. The story ended romantically; he married his nurse.

Presently we emerged from the forest on to a hillside terraced with paddy fields. Even this foothill country is comparable with the Alps in scale. In one glance my eye passed from the steamy depths of valleys, little more than one thousand feet above the sea, to hills ten or twelve thousand feet high, and from these hills, to the distant snows of the Himalayas which were already half obscured by clouds rising in slow columnar masses from the ranks of blue foot-hills. I remembered Ruskin's majestic peroration:

> Out from between the cloudy pillars as they pass emerge for ever the great battlements of the memorable and perpetual hills.

Tom Brocklebank met me at the station and we walked up the steep streets of Darjeeling to the Planters Club, where I was most hospitably welcomed by the secretary and his wife, Mr. and Mrs. Wrangham Hardy. From the "quarterdeck", as the terrace outside the club is known, the visitor, seated in an easy chair with a drink by his side, can look out over the roofs of Darjeeling on one of the grandest views in the world.

Ruttledge and the others had been working hard for the past fortnight, and most of the porters had been selected and "wormed" at the hospital, a necessary operation accomplished by means of castor oil and santonin. Ruttledge's plan was for the expedition to move slowly across Tibet and establish the Base Camp on or about April 20, as he thought that this would help the party to acclimatise to altitude. To assist further in this process, an advance party in the charge of Ferdie Crawford – consisting for the most part of those without high altitude experience – would leave in advance of the main party and remain for a few days at Tsomgo bungalow, 12,000 feet. This is on the Sikkim side of the Natu La, a pass of 14,300 feet, by which we were crossing the Himalayas into Tibet.

The weather was already causing some anxiety as Dr. Sen, the Meteorologist of Alipore, who was supplying weather reports to the Expedition, had predicted an early monsoon. We knew that this was only a shrewd guess, based on a combination of different circumstances, but we knew too that so experienced a meteorologist would not hazard a guess without considerable data and forethought. It was worrying to our peace of mind, especially as the weather was unsettled along the Himalayas whilst the snow line was said to be abnormally low for the time of the year. Everything depended on our having a spell of fine, windless weather between the ending of winter conditions and the onset of the monsoon. In the absence of any such period we were doomed to almost certain failure.

The anxieties and responsibilities of the leader of an Everest expedition are many, yet, however carefully preparations may be made, success or failure in the end depends on a turn of Fortune's wheel. This is as well, otherwise mountaineering would be a dreary business.

Among our porters was Nima Tendrup, the "old soldier", who had been my servant on the Kangchenjunga and Kamet expeditions and had accompanied all three of the previous Everest expeditions. Only younger men were being chosen for our porter brigade, for "old soldiers" have a knack of grousing and imparting discontent to their fellows, whilst some of the men of past expeditions were still a prey to the superstitions woven about Everest, but in Nima Tendrup's case an exception was made. He was old as Bhotia porters go, probably over forty, though he gave his age as twenty-four, and would not be able to go very high, probably not above Camp 3, but he would do his best, that I could vouch for, and as a servant he would serve me well. Many of my Himalayan memories are inseparable from his solemn face with its permanently worried expression and its sudden broad smile.

Lewa was another veteran. He, also, had accompanied all the previous Everest expeditions, and had taken part in three Kangchenjunga expeditions. He had been sirdar of the Kamet expedition, and now he was to be head sirdar of an Everest expedition, a position coveted by all Himalayan porters. On Kamet he had lost all his toes through frostbite, but to a man of his calibre this mattered little. No stronger, more hard-bitten man ever trod a mountainside. When, high on Kamet, one of the porters dropped his load through sheer exhaustion, Lewa picked it up and carried it in addition to his own, a total weight of over one hundred pounds, to the highest camp at 23,300 feet.

One more veteran was Lhakpa Chedi, who carried a load to Camp 6, 26,800 feet, on Everest in 1924. He had a comfortable billet as a waiter in Darjeeling but was anxious to come as our mess-man and made no secret of his intention to go as high as anyone. And lastly, I cannot omit Ondi.[1] When I first saw Ondi in 1930 on Kangchenjunga, I thought I had never seen such a "tough", but I came to learn that beneath an almost blackguardly exterior, there reposed an unshakeable loyalty and a heart of gold. During that expedition he had fallen thirty feet into a crevasse and it was only by chance that I found him. He was badly knocked about and was sent down to the Base Camp and told to remain there by the doctor. This was not good enough; within three days he was up again, thirsting for further work.

The enthusiasm of the Sherpas and Bhotias for an Everest expedition is amazing. When word comes that an expedition is in being, they flock to Darjeeling from the remote villages of the Sola Khumbu valley in Nepal, or cross the high passes between Tibet and India. Accustomed as they are to poverty and hardship,

[1] Wangdi of "Everest 1933". I retain the spelling used in *The Kangchenjunga Adventure* and *Kamet Conquered.*

and to the carrying of immense loads, there is much more than the desire for lucre, good boots and warm clothing, in their anxiety to accompany an expedition; they are adventurers; it is a point of honour with them to see Everest climbed.

Certainly an Everest porter's pay is better than that of a tea plantation coolie, whilst the possibility of a substantial bonus should he be selected to establish a high camp is a powerful incentive, yet, a sudden accession of wealth serves only to bring out his happy-go-lucky nature, and he will gamble away a month's pay in an hour or spend it almost as quickly on a single colossal "blind". In these days of life insurances and "safety first" there is something refreshing in the spirit of these men. Their attitude to their employers is best summed up by the remark of one of them to Ruttledge. "We will carry as high as we can. It is up to the Sahibs to finish the job." Many of us hope that one day one of these men will be given the opportunity of standing beside his employers on the summit of Everest. It would be a fitting climax to the "job".

The days at Darjeeling passed pleasantly and quickly. Shebbeare, our chief transport officer, made arrangements with a Kalimpong mule contractor who agreed to convey our stores to Kampa Dzong in Tibet. Thenceforward we should be dependent on yaks and donkeys hired to us by the Dzongpens (Governors) of the districts through which we passed.

The expedition was provided with wireless, which was to be used to receive weather reports and transmit news to the press. There was a permanent station at Darjeeling under the charge of Mr. D.S. Richards, who had undertaken independently to organise this service, whilst two officers of the Royal Corps of Signals, Thompson and Smijth-Windham, were to accompany us to the Base Camp, whence it was hoped they would get into touch with Darjeeling, and be useful on Everest installing a telephone line between Camp 3 and the North Col.

Preparations were at last completed, but before the expedition left Darjeeling it was blessed by the Abbot of the local Buddhist monastery. It was a striking and picturesque ceremony held in bright sunlight with the shining snows of Kangchenjunga in the background. Each member was given a few grains of rice and a ceremonial scarf was placed around his neck. After an incantation the rice was tossed into the air as an offering to the gods. Finally, the Abbot blessed us and prayed for our success and safe return. The ceremony meant much to our porters and sent them off with brave hearts.

The advance party left Darjeeling on March 3. Crawford had acquired an immense, brilliantly striped umbrella, which almost concealed the "baby" Austin car in which he and some of his companions were to travel the first few miles. Amid ringing cheers from the assembled populace the umbrella and the "baby" Austin disappeared from view round a corner of the road.

The weather was bad along the Himalayas when they left and Kangchenjunga was plastered with freshly fallen snow. To appreciate fully the majesty and beauty of this marvellous mountain, visitors to Darjeeling should get up early and visit Observatory Hill, only a few minutes' walk from the centre of the town. From this vantage point, there is nothing to obscure the view of the snows fifty miles away in the north. The eye bridges at one bound the sub-tropical depths of the Rangit Valley, then passes over wave upon wave of foothill ranges, until brought up against the enormous barrier of the Himalayas.

On numerous occasions in the past I had stood on Observatory Hill and watched dawn or sunset on the crest of Kangchenjunga. So one morning a day or two before leaving Darjeeling I rose early and walked to the top of the hill. It was an absolutely still morning, but presently a light wind stirred a little grove of prayer flags arranged about a Buddhist shrine on the crest of the hill. It was a signal. In another instant Kangchenjunga was fired by the sun. For a few moments the light lingered there as though uncertain of its tenure, then swept downwards in a strengthening tide. One by one lesser peaks took up the tale, till a vast glowing curtain was hung in the dusky northern sky. So remote were these great mountains that it seemed strange to reflect that in a few weeks we should be among them. Then they would no longer be a spectacle to watch in warmth and comfort; we should feel their winds and their cold; and know the harsh strength of them and their brutality.

CHAPTER TWO

The March Through Sikkim

THE SECOND PARTY, of which I was a member, left Darjeeling for Kalimpong on March 8. A fleet of "baby" Austin motor cars and Shebbeare's lorry conveyed us some miles along the road towards the Teesta valley. Baby cars have done much to alleviate the loneliness of the tea planters in the Darjeeling district, and narrow, tortuous mule tracks of terrifying gradients, once deemed impassable to cars, are now traversed as a matter of course.

I was a passenger in Shebbeare's lorry and at first was tempted to shut my eyes and offer up fervent prayers as it whirled round corner after corner of a narrow and winding road with the edges of precipitous hillsides never far from the wheels. But I did Shebby an injustice; he was accustomed to hill roads and well acclimatised to the giddiest drops off hairpin bends.

At the village of Ghum we picked up three Gurkhas who had been attached to the expedition: Havildar-Major Gaggan Singh Pun, Havildar Lachman Singh Sahi and Naik Bahadur Gurung.

The first and last named were typical of their race: small agile little men, packed with muscle, vim and energy. Shy and nervous at first, they soon became their natural selves and there was always a grin handy on their broad faces. To such men hard physical work is a genuine pleasure, and if there is a spice of excitement or danger about it, so much the better. As with the Sherpa or Bhotia porter, life to the Gurkha is best worth while when it is adventurous.

Lachman Singh was, in appearance, a different type from his comrades. He was taller and slighter, and at first seemed to possess more of the characteristics of the plainsman than the hillman. There was thoughtfulness and breeding in his dark, lean face and large lustrous brown eyes; he was a good linguist and capable of assisting in the complicated monetary accounts of the Expedition.

The road, after passing through Ghum, crossed forest-clad hillsides. It was a cool morning on the heights and a damp mist mingled with the trees, but as we descended, coolness gradually gave place to warmth and we emerged from the mist into a torrid sun.

Beyond the eighth milestone from Darjeeling, the road was impassable even for Austin Sevens. Some of our porters were waiting for us there, among them Tsin Nurbu, who had been engaged to carry my photographic apparatus. I remembered him well as he was Kurz's servant during the 1930 Kangchenjunga Expedition, and had climbed Jonsong Peak, 24,344 feet.

Weeks of physical inactivity had softened my feet and a combination of rough hill track and new marching boots soon brought about blisters; my own fault, as it is one of the minor follies of life to set out on a long march in brand-new boots. Marching in the Himalayas provides the mountaineer with excellent opportunities for using up the retired climbing boots that clutter up the attic at home.

The path descended steeply and the heat in the Teesta valley seemed almost to leap up at us as we lost height. The hillsides were covered with tea plantations whose sombre green contrasted pleasantly with a shimmering mica-laden dust lying inches deep on the sun-scorched path.

We were not sorry to stop for a drink at Mr. Lister's tea estate. On the verandah wall of his bungalow he had inscribed the heights of members of previous Everest expeditions. Up to date Brigadier Norton had overtopped everyone, but he was now eclipsed by Raymond Greene. Regretfully we tore ourselves away from this pleasant place with its cool shady verandah and garden of colourful flowers.

Down and down the dusty path we tramped, and presently entered the jungle. If the sun was powerful on the open hillsides, the heat here was far more trying. The great trees with their moss-clad boles, the snakelike creepers and the dense undergrowth imprisoned a dank air, heavy with the fusty smell of rotting vegetation, which seemed almost to quiver with the whirring of insects and the insane clatter of frogs from every marshy place.

We passed through a filthy village, which might have been the capital of Beelzebub to judge from the hordes of pestering flies, to the suspension bridge spanning the Teesta River. The Teesta Valley at this point is only 600 feet above sea-level, but gusts of cool air from the hurrying torrent reminded us of the far distant snows.

To our relief motor cars were waiting to convey us to Kalimpong. A well-engineered road climbs a steep hillside to this village, but it merely served to emphasise the mechanical incompetence of our native drivers. The native can acquire road sense, but mechanical sense, never. As with a certain type of European driver, it is a point of honour (and laziness) with him to climb everything he can on top gear, and he changes down only when the car is in danger of stopping altogether, and the engine is straining and groaning like a damned soul.

A most hospitable welcome from Mr. and Mrs. Odling awaited us at Kalimpong, and soon we were comfortably installed in a bungalow which had been reserved for our use.

The doyen of Kalimpong is Dr. Graham, the founder of the world-renowned Kalimpong Homes, where half-breed children, many of them the illegitimate children of tea planters by Nepali women, are educated, taught various handicrafts and in general fitted to earn their living. In the extensive workshops all manner of useful things are made, from clothing and furniture to metalware and objects of art.

It was a calm, delightfully cool night, and I slept on the verandah in my sleeping bag. Nima Tendrup brought me a cup of tea early next morning and the sight of his broad smiling face somehow made me feel that the expedition had begun.

There was plenty to be done at Kalimpong, including much unpacking and sorting of equipment, in which work the transport officers were considerably harassed by the weird and wonderful system governing the identification of our stores. Various bands of colours had been painted on the boxes on the supposition that the contents could be instantly identified by comparison with the store book. In theory this was perfect, but in practice the colours quickly wore off or by merging into one another produced new and unidentifiable colours, and it later transpired that one of the transport officers was colour blind. A further difficulty arose from haphazard packing. Thus, a case containing, say, one dozen bottles of champagne, half a dozen pairs of snow goggles and three pairs of socks was not calculated to simplify the troubles of our long-suffering transport officers.

Ponies for the march were supplied to everyone, mine being purchased from Raja Dorje, a Kalimpong dignitary who represents the Bhutan Government in India. She was a high-spirited little beast named Relling and not even the brand-new saddlery, which Raja Dorje had generously included in the purchase price, allayed certain qualms I had at the thought of narrow mountain paths with precipitous drops below them.

On March 12 we rose early. The mules were ready for their loads, but as usually happens on these occasions, there were more loads than mules and additional animals had to be requisitioned. Before starting on the march we attended a service at the Mission Church which was conducted by Dr. Graham. Faithful to past habits I arrived late. Outside the church I had considerable difficulty with Relling, who bolted in a beeline for the open porch, so that, for a moment, I pictured myself making a dramatic entry and clattering down the aisle. Relling knew as well as I that her new master was no horseman. I quieted her at last, and slunk in at the beginning of the psalms.

Ruttledge read the first lesson and Shebbeare the second; it was impressive to hear them clattering up the slippery aisle in their nailed boots. Then Dr. Graham delivered an address which he concluded by praying for our success and safe return.

After the service, Dr. Graham invited us to his house, a delightful place looking out over the forest-clad foothills. Then, with the cheers of the mission children and the "good lucks" of many friends in our ears, we set out on our long march to Everest.

It is about twelve miles from Kalimpong to Pedong. The route is one of the main trade routes between India and Tibet and along it, supported by roughly cut posts, runs a solitary telegraph wire, Lhasa's sole link with the outside world. The path is roughly cobbled over long stretches, and very fatiguing to walk upon, and it lies along the side of wooded foothills, which gradually increase in height as the traveller progresses northwards.

The dak bungalow at Pedong is situated on an open slope looking over the valley of the Rangli Chu. Like most of the dak bungalows in Sikkim it commands an extensive and beautiful view, this being largely due to the foresight and unerring instinct for situation of a former political officer of Sikkim, Claude White.

There we were joined by George Wood Johnson and Boustead; the former had come from his tea plantation near Darjeeling, the latter from the Sudan.

The night was chilly and more than once I was roused by the grumblings of George, who was attempting to sleep in one of the woollen bags officially supplied for the march. Although heavier than the eiderdown bags intended for use above the Base Camp, these were unsatisfactory. For warmth and comfort there is nothing to better a double eiderdown bag, and it was found necessary to scrap the woollen bags in their favour at an early stage of the expedition.

Most of us slept on the verandah and we woke in the cool dawn to hear the bell-like notes of the Himalayan cuckoo sounding from the forest.

From Pedong the path descended steeply to the Rangpo River the boundary between Sikkim and British India, where our passes were examined by a smart and efficient-looking little Gurkha N.C.O. From the river a steep ascent through dense forest brought us hot and thirsty to the dak bungalow at Pakyong near a thriving bazaar where we purchased some oranges.

A little way from the bungalow is a grassy ridge commanding an uninterrupted view to the north and there Bill Birnie and I spent a lazy hour.

Some miles away across an intervening valley we could see the houses of Gangtok, the Capital of Sikkim perched on a ridge, and more distantly the Himalayas, half drowned in a dense blue haze whence rose columns of copper-coloured thunder-clouds. The haze deepened to an inky black as the afternoon lengthened and thunder grumbled over the ranges.

Nightfall quickly cleared the sky of thunderclouds and the moon rose over the Bhutan hills, lighting the wooded ridges and emphasising the profound shadows in the valleys between them.

The following morning was even more beautiful than the last. The atmosphere was limpid like a mountain-stream, the haze had vanished and in the north Kangchenjunga gleamed like an uncut jewel on a dark-blue cushion of foothills.

The march to Gangtok consisted once again of a long and steep descent followed by an equally long and steep ascent, where we were glad of our ponies. Relling was very suspicious of any unusual objects on or beside the path, but responded gallantly to "chu chu", the equivalent of "gee-up" in this part of the world. Shebby, I noticed, walked the whole of the way. He was determined, indeed, to walk to the Base Camp, a Spartan effort of self-abnegation.

Halfway up the hillside, where we halted for lunch, Ruttledge found a leech on the brim of my Terai hat. It was the only one of these pests we had so far encountered; we should see plenty of them during our return march in the rains.

Gangtok is ranged untidily on the side of a ridge, on the crest of which stands the Maharajah's palace; an unpretentious but attractive building constructed in the Chinese style, with a wide gently sloping quadriform roof and elaborate porticoes. The same pippin-faced Chowkidar, whom I remembered in 1930, welcomed us at the dak bungalow and being well versed in the thirstiness of mountaineers quickly procured beer from the bazaar.

There was a certain amount of work to be done, including the fitting of flannel linings to our twenty five high-altitude sleeping bags, but I remember Gangtok best for its beautiful situation, its healthy climate and the hospitality we enjoyed there. The dinner, Williamson the Political Officer for Sikkim, gave us that night was our last in civilisation for some time and we made the most of it. It is sad to think that none of us can again enjoy his genial welcome; he died in 1935 while on a visit to Lhasa.

CHAPTER THREE

The Natu La

THREE DAYS PASSED quickly and on March 16 we were off again. The porters realising, like us, the importance of making the best of civilisation, had a grand carousal in the bazaar the night before, and as we trudged uphill towards Karponang, I saw several with faces twisted in anguished headaches. Shebby and I kept together, both of us determined to walk the whole way to the bungalow.

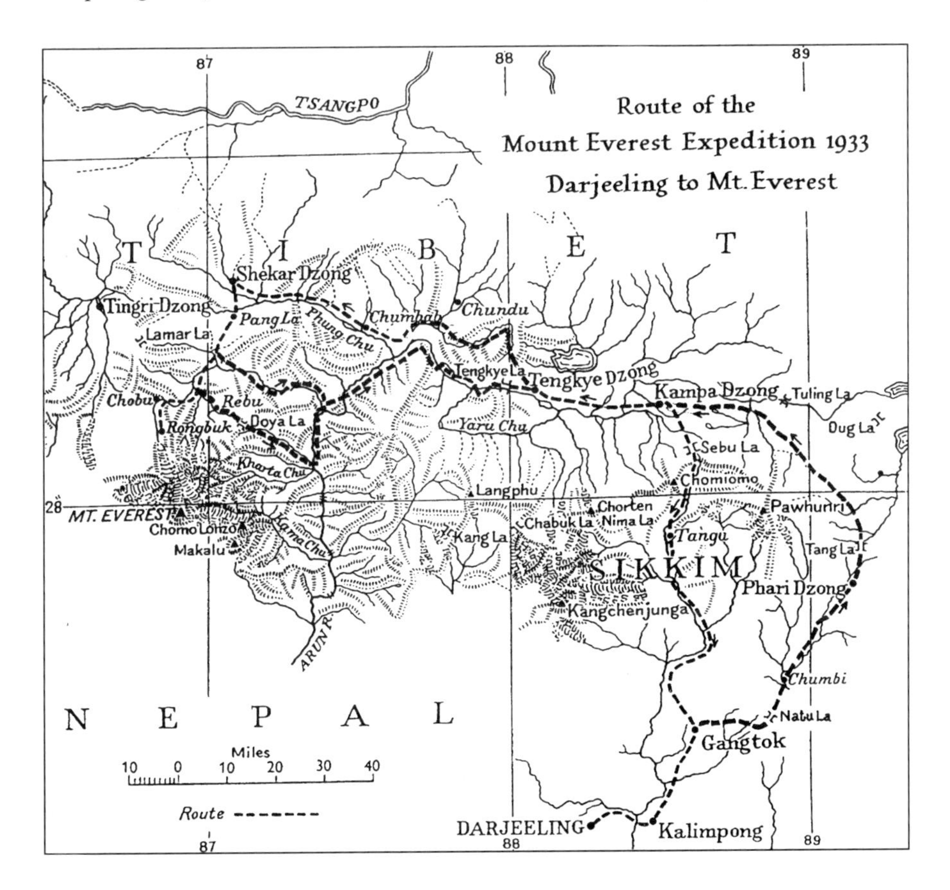

My feet were in better shape now, and I enjoyed walking, especially as we were nearing the high mountains.

The vegetation changed gradually as we ascended. Gangtok is just below the frost level and sub-tropical plants flourish, including orchids and tree ferns. Perhaps 1,500 feet higher the forest was snow-white with magnolias, and here and there we saw the delicate fronds of amaryllis swaying beside the path. Higher still, red rhododendrons were in bloom like splashes of blood amid the white magnolias.

We were soon reminded that we were following one of the principal trade routes into Tibet by meeting a convoy of mules and ponies laden with bales of wool; then an itinerant lama, dressed in dingy red, with a dry, puckered face which cracked into a smile when we greeted him.

The scene became alpine, and long before reaching Karponang we passed drifts of oozing snow whilst the damp, steamy odours of the lower valleys were replaced by the resinous incense of the heights.

So stimulating was the air that we covered the ten miles from Gangtok and ascended 4,000 feet in just over four hours. We paid for our energy in thirst; on arrival I drank ten cups of tea and ate an enormous omelette prepared by Lhakpa Chedi, who was there well ahead of everyone.

The Karponang bungalow with its covered-in verandah reminded me of an Austrian mountain hotel. It was chilly at 9,500 feet and we were glad of warmer clothing. One of our first jobs was letting air into the petrol and paraffin tins to prevent leakage due to the difference of pressure at the increased altitude. Incidentally, I have yet to accompany a Himalayan expedition which did not lose one-quarter to one-third of its petrol or paraffin during the march.

That evening we sat around a blazing log fire, smoked our pipes and discussed plans for the future.

The following morning I left in advance of the others with a new cameraman. Tsin Nurbu had proved unsatisfactory and had been replaced at Gangtok by Tensing, a short, sturdy little fellow with almost bandy legs and a naïve disarming grin.

For some distance, the path traversed a hillside, then turned northwards. I rode Relling for about half a mile, but she was too frisky that morning, so much so that she put one foot over the edge of a log bridge.

It was a nasty moment as there was a drop of about ten feet into a torrent. I walked for the rest of the day.

As we neared Tsomgo, it was apparent that Tibet was not far distant, for the valley in which the bungalow, 12,500 feet, is situated is as barren as the Grimsel Pass in Switzerland. In two days we had exchanged sub-tropical luxuriance for a stony, desolate waste. The snow had partially melted and lay in an ugly patchwork on the hillsides, whilst a Zen lake, lowering clouds and an occasional drizzle of snow presented a dreary scene. We were not sorry to escape into the cosy little bungalow and toast ourselves before a log fire.

The first party had left two days before and in a note to Hugh, Ferdie Crawford wrote that they had climbed Chomunko, a fine rock peak of 17,500 feet. There was some doubt at that time as to whether ascents during the march to Everest were beneficial, and I was one of those who believed in husbanding strength for the battle with high altitudes. My views have changed since. I believe now that acclimatisation should be gained, not on Everest where life is so wearing and uncomfortable, but on other mountains at an early stage of an expedition. It is only after several Himalayan expeditions that it is possible to formulate any logical opinions. It is easy to jump to conclusions, and a man on his first visit to the Himalayas is all too liable to do so. Climbing Everest is a science, and conclusions are only reached after numerous practical experiments.

Most of us were feeling the effects of altitude to some slight extent, for we had risen quickly from comparatively low valleys. My pulse-rate instead of its normal fifty or less had jumped to sixty, and I had the same feeling of tightness at my temples which I associate with the first climb or two of an alpine holiday.

One of the porters developed severe toothache and Raymond, deciding that the offending tooth would have to come out, extracted it with skill and dispatch. It was not the first time I had seen a native's tooth pulled out, and I have always marvelled at an apparent indifference to pain. In the present instance, there was not a murmur, and the toothless one walked happily away carrying his decayed property, anxious to exhibit it to his friends.

It was a cold evening and snowed a little, but at nightfall the mists cleared and stars appeared. Again we discussed ways and means on Everest. Two conclusions emerged: we must try to make Camp 1 virtually a Base Camp and possibly put an intermediate camp between Camps 4 and 5, for, as we all agreed, the long carry between these two camps was more likely than anything else to tire out the porters.

Owing to the altitude I slept badly that night. I shared a room with Hugh and the last thing he said to me was: "There's no one on this show I wouldn't like to see on the top."

We were off at 7.30 the next morning, March 18. The sky was a deep blue, and the sun brilliant and warm; far below, in the direction of the Teesta Valley, a sea of feathery clouds stretched southwards; it was altogether a morning to be up and doing and ideal for crossing the Natu La.

A long traverse across a hillside followed by a stiff ascent led to the pass. Enthusiasm for photography brought me there ahead of my companions. The shaley slopes were fatiguing, but it was stimulating to see a little forest of prayer flags, silhouetted against the deep blue sky, fluttering in the westerly breeze. It was the threshold of a new land.

Presently I stood beside the prayer flags and with their stiff, dry rustling in my ears gazed northwards into Tibet. The first thing I saw was Chomolhari, the sacred mountain of Eastern Tibet, rising from lower hills that faded from gold and brown in the foreground to a delicate blue in the far distance. A thin pennant-like cloud trailed from the summit and beyond it were other clouds, masses of slow-moving vapour, reflecting perceptibly the colour of the brown hills beneath. Distance and space were my first impressions of Tibet. We had climbed out of valleys clothed in luxuriant vegetation and here before us was a land utterly different, and profoundly peaceful.

Down we went, for some distance over slopes of soft snow. It was heavy work for the mules and some of them capsized, including the one carrying my bedding and other personal belongings. Half an hour later the snow was behind and we halted for lunch by a limpid stream decorated along the banks with prayer flags, placed there to propitiate the water gods. It was a depressing spectacle to watch our transport slowly filing past. These hordes of animals and hundreds of packing cases separated us from the simplicity of travel. I remembered a vow that one day I would travel in the Himalayas with the lightest and simplest of equipment; that I would be tied to no stages and committed to no plan; that I would wander where I chose. Somehow, this vast transport made Everest into an inexorable and rather dull duty. The companionship of the campfire was absent and in its place was a rowdy mess tent, which always reminded me of a Sunday-school treat. We had carried civilisation into the wilds, and civilisation is better left at home.

And what of ourselves? "Team spirit" is an ineffective link when a large number of men, some of whom have not even seen one another before, are gathered together from the corners of the Earth and sent off to climb Everest. I can visualise a small party of friends. There is no need to rant and rhapsodise to them on the merits of "team spirit", because friends do not need to be reminded of it any more than a true patriot needs to be reminded of his country's flag. They are friends, and therefore have that give and take between them, which is instinctive. That is the ideal mountaineering party. It is when people start to talk about "team spirit", thus implying something to be inculcated and remembered rather than something instinctive, that something seems wrong with this Everest business.

From our luncheon place a rough path descended to the Chumbitang bungalow. On the way I developed a splitting headache. It was a typical altitude head, aggravated by sun-glare, and every step on the stony track sent a jarring shiver of pain from the base of my neck to a point immediately above the eyes.

The bungalow is situated at 13,300 feet in a pine forest and must be one of the highest in the Himalayas. It was a cold evening with a hard frost, but once again we made ourselves cosy round a log fire. Shortly before turning in, Bill and Hugo Boustead discovered that the ponies' blankets were missing, the grooms having appropriated them for their own use. The miscreants were reprimanded, but thinking themselves safe, again purloined the blankets, but they reckoned without Bill, who repeated his visit of inspection. A "try out" such as this usually occurs during the early stages of a Himalayan expedition. The native, with his simple cunning, tries to get the better of his sahib. If the sahib is weak, so much the better, but if he is intolerant of "old soldierly" tactics, well, the "old soldier" must resign himself to the fact. Obviously, unless prompt and stern measures are taken to deal with offenders, matters quickly go from bad to worse. Hugh's first action the following morning was to dismiss the head groom and one of his assistants. Another groom when asked by "Shebby" why he had not covered his pony with a blanket ingeniously replied that he was trying to harden off the pony to the Tibetan climate.

During the descent into the Chumbi Valley, which is one of the few fertile and wooded valleys in this part of Tibet I saw a bullfinch, some edelweiss and several picas, quaint little rat-like animals, something like marmots.

On the way we turned aside to visit the Khajuk Monastery, which stands on a bluff overlooking the Chumbi Valley. Passing through a gateway and not forgetting to give some large cylindrical prayer wheels packed with tens of thousands of prayers a turn, we entered a courtyard decorated in red and yellow, the sacred colours of Tibet. There we were received by the abbot and were shown over the monastery. The temples and shrines were very dark and lit only by a few wicks floating in little bowls of butter. There were numerous images in niches, some of them beautifully carved and one, a pale-faced, white-clad female figure, was said to represent the Goddess of Everest; the porters lost no time in adorning it with propitiatory scarves. The abbot had himself executed some of the mural paintings. These represented various aspects of human life, and were of a frankness calculated to shock the more reticent Westerner. There were also numerous phallic symbols, emblems of mortal and earthly fertility. The monastery was pervaded by the smell of incense, butter and unwashed clothing.

The monks were very curious and some of them incessantly demanded baksheesh. They wanted to know why we were trying to climb Everest and I think suspected some material object, possibly a search for gold, even after Hugh had done his best to explain through Karma Paul our disinterested and idealistic motives.

A good path over a fir-clad hillside brought us to the floor of the Chumbi Valley. There we met Russell, the British trade agent, and a party of Tibetan dignitaries, all wearing dark glasses, who had come from Lhasa; one of them was the Dalai Lama's representative.

Just before reaching the bungalow at Yatung, we came upon an old man with a terribly lacerated back lying on a blanket by the wayside. He had been mercilessly beaten, and we learned, that he was a suspected murderer and had received 150 lashes as an inducement to confess. The villagers made no attempt to help him, but stood around grinning broadly. He was starving as well, and we sent him some food and did our best to find someone to care for him. This made us realise more than anything, that we were no longer in British administered territory, but in a country where prevails an age-long custom and summary justice.

Rain fell heavily shortly after our arrival at the bungalow. Smijth-Windham and Thompson with their wireless banderbast arrived a little later, having taken a different route over the Jelap La. They brought with them a case of whisky which was welcomed with acclamation. That evening the expedition gramophone was worked, hard and, I finished writing my diary to the strains of the latest rumba, a strangely incongruous noise in the solitudes of Tibet.

CHAPTER FOUR

To Kampa Dzong

THE RAIN CEASED in the night and the sun shone brilliantly next morning, March 20. The dark-green firs mantling the hillsides and the craggy mountain tops, set in a brilliantly blue sky, reminded me of the Tyrol, for the Chumbi Valley, unlike most of Tibet, is fertile owing to its southerly situation and its accessibility to the monsoon air current as well as to the rain and snow precipitated by the range of Pauhunri in the west.

After breakfast some Tibetans insisted on dancing outside the bungalow, obviously for baksheesh, but it was a poor performance and their scratch band had none of the resonance or rhythm of a properly constituted monastery band.

A small detachment of Indian infantry is stationed at Yatung to protect the trade route which, since Sir Francis Younghusband's Expedition of 1904 has been held by the Indian Government as far as Gyantse, and the Sepoys amuse themselves with football and hockey on their parade ground, a flat space liberally sprinkled with stones. As soon as George saw this he proposed a game of polo. Equipment was soon forthcoming in the shape of hockey sticks, lent by the soldiers and two polo sticks which George had cherished all the way from Kalimpong. Raymond and I being no horsemen, much less polo players, were content to watch, applaud and, if necessary, jeer.

It was a desperate affair, that game, and it was not long before Hugo came a nasty cropper, after being horribly fouled by George. Bill, however, was in his element, as he is an expert, and his skill in appropriating the ball probably went far towards saving others cracked skulls. For the rest it seemed that limbs must be broken sooner or later, but as often happens in such rough and tumbles, the game ended with nothing worse than bruises.

March 20 was a lazy day. The sun shone cheerfully and was pleasantly warm. That evening some of us dined with Russell, and the English doctor of the Chumbi Valley. Russell had made himself very comfortable in his official bungalow, and we envied him his pleasant retreat, so cut off from the outside world. We were thinking of bed when news came that some of our transport, which had been behind us, had passed through Yatung without stopping, apparently unaware of our arrival. It was necessary to prevent it getting too far ahead, especially as we needed some of the Whymper tents, so Bill bravely left at 10.30 on his pony in an attempt to stop it.

Next morning, March 21, we set off to Gautsa where the first party were awaiting our arrival.

There are numerous hamlets and villages in the Chumbi Valley. All seemed prosperous and some, with their wide chalet-like roofs weighted with stones, reminded me of alpine villages. The people were friendly and grinned and salaamed as we passed; no doubt they make an easier living than the people in the less fertile districts to the north.

The valley climbed steeply and presently we emerged from the forest on to open slopes where, in a sheltered nook away from a chill wind, some of us lunched and afterwards cantered over two miles of perfect turf.

The fine day was short-lived; clouds crowded up from the west and snow fell. As we neared the bungalow the second party gathered outside it and a dismal dirge-like song came to us through the snow. It seemed dimly familiar, then I remembered. I had heard it once before, during the general strike, sung by a motley collection of people in the street outside the T.U.C. Headquarters; it was the "Red Flag".

To divide an expedition up into two parties inevitably tends to produce cliques, and I suspect that members of both parties secretly wished in their hearts that things could have continued as they were. However, this feeling presently disappeared and we became one party again which, if too large for the liking of some of us, was at least as homogeneous as could be expected when a number of persons previously unacquainted with one another are brought together and directed towards a common objective.

Bill in spite of his night ride, had been unable to retrieve the Whymper tents and we had to make shift with the bungalow, which was too small for the whole party, and the mess tent. Owing to the limited accommodation of the former we dined on the verandah. It was snowing hard and for the first time I was glad of my thick llama wool coat. Afterwards we crowded into the little living room, and Ferdie Crawford, possibly inspired by the "Red Flag", discoursed at length on Russia and Bolshevism. The four relegated to the mess tent, of whom I was one, slept well but were awakened by a yell from Jack Longland when a chair fell on him in the night.

We remained at Gautsa during the whole of the following day. Hugh summoned the expedition together, and told us that he had made Shebby, the senior transport officer, second in command of the expedition.

Towards midday more bad weather blew up from the west, and snow fell heavily all the afternoon and evening. Next morning, March 23, it lay several inches deep, but the sky had cleared and the sun shone powerfully as we breakfasted.

Fortunately, not enough snow had fallen to impede our transport animals. The valley, at first sparsely wooded, became barer and bleaker in its upper reaches, and barren hillsides swept up on either hand.

The ease with which I walked uphill at a height little less than the summit of Mont Blanc proved that I was acclimatising well. Presently, to save energy I rode, but soon had an unpleasant experience. The path in one place was only a foot or two wide owing to drifted snow, and below were slopes and crags falling sheer to a river. Suddenly a small piece of snow dislodged by the sun rolled on it. This so startled Relling that she reared up on her hind legs and balanced for a moment on the very edge of the cliff, then bolted along the narrow path. I struggled to get my nailed boots out of the stirrups, but they had jammed. Eventually I managed to wrench her head towards the mountainside, and she plunged into a snowdrift and stopped quivering with fear.

Presently we emerged from the valley on to a wide plain bounded by low hills. There for the first time we experienced the full force of the Tibetan wind, a withering blast that made us pull on thick gloves and balaclava helmets.

The route lay through snowdrifts, slush and boggy ground. Sometimes at a bridge over a stream, there was an awkward jam of struggling mules, and woe betide anyone whose pony was caught in the maelstrom. Karma Paul accidentally got involved on one occasion. He was forced off his pony by the press and only the prompt action of a porter prevented him from being trampled under foot.

We were now on the Phari plain and could see Phari Dzong, a full five miles distant, but appearing much nearer in the brilliant atmosphere. Here was Tibet proper, and a bleak, inhospitable land it seemed, brown and desolate, unmoving and unchanging, except for the slow march of sun and cloud in the steadfast blue of the moistureless sky. Scarcely a blade of grass was to be seen, nothing but earth, sand and stones. Yet life was not altogether at a discount. There were birds, and popping in and out of their burrows scores of little picas.

As we neared Phari, we saw its Dzong (fort) towering above a huddle of mean houses built of earth, mud and stones. This village has an evil reputation for health, and former expeditions have contracted dysentery there. It is curious how humans maintain their diseases in a situation so open to the winds of heaven.

A redeeming feature of Phari is the view of Chomolhari, 23,930 feet. We had seen this mountain from the Natu La; now we had a closer and more impressive view. It reminded me of Kamet and should prove climbable by its long eastern slope.* The wind-driven snow was tearing from the crest in a great white plume, and I think the sight of this was the first intimation some of us had as to what we must expect on Everest. It was a sobering thought that this wind-swept summit was little higher than the North Col, our jumping-off point for the final ascent.

The inhabitants of Phari welcomed us noisily. Among them was the village madman, who proceeded to strip himself of his clothing, a feat which it is certain no sane person would care to emulate in the Tibetan climate.

Tents were pitched for the first time. Each of us had one to himself of the Whymper pattern, large enough to stand up in and with plenty of spare room for suitcases and kitbag. A certain amount of privacy is psychologically necessary during an expedition; privacy, to write, read and think. For the first time since leaving Darjeeling, I was able to unpack my personal belongings.

Russell arrived the same day. He was en route to Gyantse and dined with us in the mess tent.

Phari is not an ideal introduction to Tibet; in one matter only do I connect it with pleasure – sleeping for the first time in my own tent. Here was a space I could call my own, something to escape to at times from the crowded mess tent.

Owing to transport difficulties we had to spend two nights there. There was one exciting incident when Ferdie's servant managed to set his master's sleeping bag alight through carelessness with a candle. This in turn set alight to the tent, and only the early discovery of the accident saved a more serious conflagration as a strong wind might easily have driven the flames through the camp. I have often pictured the appalling consequences if some evil-disposed person were to set alight to the store dump of an Everest expedition.

Hugh spent much time composing a dispatch to the newspapers. This onerous work is one of the penalties of leadership of a large expedition. I speak from experience, as I have written the dispatches of two expeditions. Having to concentrate on a dispatch after a hard day's marching or climbing is a fatiguing job and not one that should fall on the leader of an Everest expedition, who is overburdened with responsibilities. One of the best things about travel in remote regions is that the traveller is cut off from the outside world. Such "splendid isolation" is not possible when an expedition is equipped with wireless and has by this or some other means to maintain touch with the press. A craving for isolation may sound selfish to those who like to follow an expedition in the spirit through the medium of print, but the true lover of travel hates anything extraneous to the job in hand.

Old Nima Tendrup was now in his element. He was never an efficient servant during the bungalow marches, but in camp life he excelled. In 1930, he had very soon discovered that if his hair and mine were not to be prematurely whitened,

* Climbed in 1937 by Fred Spencer Chapman and the inexperienced Passang, supported by C.E. Crawford, Pasang Kikuli and Nima Thundup [Tendrup?]. The climbers had a 300ft fall during the descent that was nearly terminal – a major epic!

some method must be evolved out of my natural untidiness. Everything, therefore, my clothes, and odds and ends, had to be packed methodically. This required considerable perseverance on his part, for I was wont to turn out my suitcase and scatter its contents on the floor of my tent. Yet, so strict was the discipline he enforced, I soon found myself automatically putting things in their right place, and I even, after a while, began to remember where they were. The net result was less trouble for Nima Tendrup, and it was no longer necessary for me to rout him out to find something. He always had an eye to the main chance and the main chance with him was the avoidance of unnecessary work. He would have made a captain of industry had he been born to that station of life.

Phari being interpreted means "Hog Hill", and the filth and smells of this village make it a singularly appropriate name, but during the two nights we spent there we were tempted to substitute Dog, for the number of these animals rivalled the number of inhabitants and they barked and yowled incessantly the greater part of the night. One reason for the unhealthfulness of Phari was soon apparent – the dust. The dry climate pulverises offal and filth of all kinds, and the prevailing north-west wind does the rest. During our two days there our tents, clothing and food were never free from this dust, and it was as well when eating a meal not to allow the imagination to dwell on its origin. There are two golden rules of travel in Tibet: firstly, boil all water and, secondly, camp to the windward of villages.

We left Phari thankfully on March 25. There had been 22° of frost in the night, and I had been kept awake till 2 a.m. by barking dogs. With a short march before us we did not leave until after lunch. Raymond and I rode together the first three miles, then dismounted and walked, as the wind was cold and snow beginning to fall. There were no syces (grooms) in view, but Nima Dorje, one of the assistant cooks, and a porter, appeared, and we handed over our ponies to them. Disobeying orders, the porter tried to mount Relling, but he was so clumsy that he fell off backwards, jamming one foot in a stirrup, and Relling bolted, dragging the unfortunate man violently along the rocky ground. We tried to get hold of the bridle, but Relling was thoroughly frightened. Luckily for the porter his foot came away from the stirrup. For a few moments he lay there, and we thought he had broken a bone; then he grinned broadly and scrambled to his feet. As for Nima Dorje, he appeared to consider the incident a huge joke.

Monotonous slopes led up the Tang La, 15,200 feet. The wind smote us vigorously and powdery snow mingled with dust swept stingingly into our faces. It was a dull pass, indeed scarcely a pass at all except in name. Its sole merit is its proximity to Chomolhari, and as we descended the far side to the camping place known as Shabra Shubra, the snow-laden mists thinned and we saw the great peak's brown-grey precipices; they might have been fashioned by a few careless slashes of a Titan's knife.

Shabra Shubra was a horribly uncomfortable camping place. The wind raged out of the west across the desertlike plain and it was all the porters could do to pitch the tents; the big mess tent in particular needed a dozen men to tame it. We had walked over the Tang La easily enough and most of us seemed to be acclimatising well, but we soon discovered that breath was easily lost when the body was called upon to wrestle with a large tent in a strong wind.

The conditions were bad enough to daunt any cook, but Tencheddar rose nobly to the occasion and produced a superb Irish stew. With this and some hot tea inside us we snuggled into our sleeping bags.

At sunset the wind slackened somewhat and I ventured outside my tent to take some photographs. The scene was indescribably bleak and magnificent. From the camp, the brown wind-bleached plain stretched for miles to the north and west, streaked and patched with snow and blurred here and there with hurrying squalls. Immediately to the east rose the precipices of Chomolhari with ragged wisps of cloud twisting slowly up them, whilst on the crest of the mountain a writhing sheet of wind-driven snow flamed in the setting sun.

So this was Tibet; incredible that men and women could dwell in such inhospitable surrounding; why had they not immigrated to the fertile valleys south of the Himalayas? Is there an instinctive love and reverence in their hearts for this brown wind-swept desert with its far blue hills and the southward glimmer of the Himalayan snows?

I took one or two photographs, fumbling with half-numbed fingers at my camera, then was glad to escape from the searing cold and burrow into my sleeping bag where I presently became warm.

Probably the dirt and germs of Phari had something to do with it but I had stomach pains that night and did not sleep until the small hours. The temperature fell to 4°F., and as I lay I could hear above the flurries of wind and snow the stamps and groans of the unfortunate mules and ponies. How they survive such nights in the open I do not know.

As the hours passed ice formed by my breath gathered on the mouth of my sleeping bag, and dogs barked dismally from a neighbouring Tibetan encampment. Once I struck a match and glanced at my watch. I worked out that at home (allowing the difference between English and Indian time) my wife was just sitting down to her dinner, and here was I uncomfortable without and within, wondering whether sleep would ever come to hasten the passage of the leaden-footed hours.

The sun struck the camp late next morning owing to Chomolhari. There is one consolation about camping in cold weather: the traveller sleeps in his underclothes; thus the agonies of dressing are obviated. My boots were like granite and I tried ineffectually to thaw them, first over a candle, and then in the sun. Finally I rammed my feet into them as best I could and for the next few hours my toes were kept fully occupied in thawing them. What I disliked most about the march to the Base Camp was having to breakfast in the open every morning. This was accounted necessary owing to the absence of the mess tent, which had to be sent on in advance to the next camping place, but I suspect that the real reason was a Spartan desire on the part of our leader to harden us off.

It was a picturesque company that assembled for breakfast. Everyone was muffled up to the eyes, and Willy McLean in a huge green canvas wool-lined coat, which had been given to him by General Bruce, reminded me of the well-known advertisement for Michelin motor tyres.

The morning was calm when we sat down, but before we had finished eating the wind was beginning to blow again. According to Ferdie, it was three hours too early and should not have risen in this part of Tibet until ten o'clock. It was obvious that we were in for in or a hard day's marching, and the mess tent was got off well in advance on the backs of Phil and Flo, the two mules specially selected to carry it. So also were the wireless petrol engine and generator, the most awkward load of all, which was valiantly carried by four porters.

We all rode, but I for one spent the first hour or two waggling my toes to and fro in my boots. The wind increased, as we progressed westwards, and the powdery snow was hurled across the plain in stinging clouds and it was all our ponies could do to face the blast, whilst here and there the snow had collected in drifts several feet deep, and several times I had to dismount and lead the floundering Relling to solid ground.

There were ten miles of this travelling across what, according to Wager, was very like Greenland. Then we halted in the shelter of a bank where the ground began to rise, and ate some chocolate and biscuits. After this the route led gradually uphill to a pass where there was a cornice overhanging a short, steep snow slope. I found a gap in the former and tried to urge Relling through it and down the snow slope, but the snow was so soft that she went in up to the girths and becoming frightened, plunged and reared; so I dismounted and dragged her down the slope, getting a kick on the shin for my pains.

Beyond this pass we came out of the snowy country into a stony, desolate valley, flanked by barren hillsides. On one occasion, it was necessary to cross the stream that flowed down the valley. I have reason to bless that stream. As the result of a motor accident four months before leaving England there was an adhesion in one of my knees that made certain movements painful and difficult, so much so that I wondered whether it would affect my climbing on Everest. Relling refused the stream so I dismounted and, holding the bridle in one hand, jumped across. I landed awkwardly on a loose stone and fell, twisting my knee as I did so. The pain was intense, and for a minute or two I sat there unable to move, but when I rose to my feet I found that the knee was working more easily than before, and from that time onwards I was no longer troubled by it. The sudden twist must have broken down the adhesion.

The camping place known as Lunge Bur was less exposed to the wind than Shabra Shubra, but it was only after a struggle that we pitched the mess tent. It had been a terribly trying day for the porters and transport animals, and Shebby said that it was the hardest march he had ever done. This was our highest camp so far, about 16,000 feet, and exertion of any kind made us puff hard. Late in the afternoon I strolled up an old moraine above the camp, and finding a sheltered spot, basked in the sun. It was the first time I had been warm and comfortable in the open since leaving Phari, and it was pleasant to feel the heat of the sun while listening to the disappointed roaring of the wind on a crest only a few yards above me.

There was a cheerful company in the mess tent at supper, for we all felt that the worst was behind us. The night was warmer, but the altitude bothered me, and I slept badly. To the misery of sleeplessness was added an infernal yapping of dogs the whole night through.

We rose at 6 next morning, March 27. The wind had fallen to a complete calm, and the warm sun made breakfasting in the open pleasant for once in a way. In spite of a bad night I felt fairly fit, and decided that a day's walking would help me to acclimatise. It was a long march for imperfectly acclimatised men, about 14 miles, and included three passes, the highest being nearly 18,000 feet, but I felt the altitude much less than I had expected and was able to enjoy the beautiful views. The atmosphere was crystal clear, and in the south the Himalayas rose in a great wall from the golden plains.

Most of the day I walked with Shebby, whose enthusiasm for nature and inexhaustible fund of good stories made him an interesting and entertaining companion. During the latter part of the march, I had a slight altitude headache and was glad to ride the last two miles on April the Fifth, a docile old pony who seemed as steady as a tank after the exuberant Relling. Subsequently at Bill's suggestion I took her over permanently whilst Bill, a splendid horseman, had Relling. From both points of view it was an eminently satisfactory exchange.

So far we had subsisted largely on fresh meat and vegetables, but so badly cooked was the dinner that night, possibly due to the altitude, that a difference of opinion already in evidence suddenly came to a head in a fierce argument as to which was preferable, badly cooked and indigestible fresh food, or more digestible tinned food. On this occasion I confined myself to chocolate biscuits and as a result slept well, but I was one of the few who did, for the combined effects of the dinner and a very cold night kept many awake. Raymond told me next morning that it was the coldest night he had known in the Himalayas. Only that tough old warrior Shebby seemed completely unaffected and he woke me before the sun had risen and it was still bitterly cold, as he wanted to know what exposure to give his 16 mm. cinema film.

We breakfasted off eggs purchased from a neighbouring village. They were about half the size of English eggs and their shells were so thin that they broke unless carefully handled. Some were of ancient lineage, but none were actually bad.

Miles of the pebbly plain over which we marched that day could have been covered by motor cars or used as a landing ground by aeroplanes. The weather was good and the Himalayas serene and unclouded. Among a host of great mountains Chomiomo and Kangchenjau were visible and later Kangchenjunga appeared.

In the north was a range of high brown, snow-capped hills. The highest had two huge scars in it, caused by landslips, which were so light in colour that they gleamed in the sun as though some fabulous hoard of silver had been laid bare.

We lunched out of the wind below some crumbling cliffs. Jack found them impossible to resist, and was soon disporting himself on some hair-raising "routes" whilst the rest of us basked in the sun.

Our camping place at Tatsang was beneath a crag crowned by a nunnery. The camp was on the leeside of the crag, but the wind, not to be so easily outwitted, veered quickly round and resumed its attack with renewed vigour.

The difference between sun and air temperatures in Tibet must be experienced to be appreciated. In my tent it was positively hot, but outside the wind was bitingly cold. This wind in combination with the sun dries the face until it cracks like the parched mud of a riverbed. The only way of preventing its depredations is to keep the skin moist and pliable with face cream, and I had nursed my own countenance with loving care, but even so, one corner of my lip was unpleasantly cracked. Others with a healthy disregard for cosmetics were in worse plight, and Tom Brocklebank's face had been reduced to a condition suggestive of a lunar landscape.

In the afternoon we climbed up a steep path to the nunnery where we were warmly welcomed by the nuns, who varied from mere children to old ladies so wizened that they seemed almost a part of the arid landscape. Their clothing was black with age and their smoke-darkened faces were almost concealed by immense mop-like wigs of greasy wool. By way of a jest, or perhaps for some religious motive, the body of a sheep had been nailed to the door of the nunnery. This instead of putrifying had merely dried and mummified in the dry air. The interior of the nunnery was dark and full of strange smells. Glass is seldom seen in Tibet, and light and ventilation are at a discount in Tibetan dwellings; no doubt after the relentless glare of the plateau, darkness comes as a relief. These nuns lead a life of almost unbelievable hardship. Their only fuel is shing (dried yak dung), and how sufficient crops to maintain them can be raised from the miserable soil of this district is a mystery. Probably some Tibetan Authority sees to it that supplies are sent. Prayer and contemplation are their principal occupations, and the view, at least, gives them scope for the latter, for the monastery commands a marvellous outlook over the brown plains to the Himalayas.

Almost the first thing that strikes the traveller in Tibet is the cheerfulness of the people. No hardship or discomfort could dim the smiles of the nuns as they posed for their photographs, and these smiles broadened, if that were possible, when we presented the nunnery with a gift of money, and they whipped off their woollen wigs and bowed low in gratitude. It was not a pleasant evening. The wind hurled itself furiously at the camp, and clouds of dust enveloped everything – our clothes, our hair, our sleeping bags, the food we ate, were covered with this abominable dust. Our porters, in a praiseworthy attempt to provide us with a change of diet, spent some time in snaring snow trout from a stream. They caught two or three, but they were small and bony and not worth eating. Such poaching was not favoured by the nuns, and we were told that destruction of these trout, which were evidently regarded as sacred, would bring us bad luck. This prophecy was fulfilled when one of our mules died suddenly and mysteriously in the night. Medical opinion, however, did not put any magical interpretation upon this, and the diagnosis was distended stomach and colic due to drinking too much snow water.

The dry air of the Tibetan plateau and the constant dust had already produced a crop of sore throats, and nasal douches and throat sprays were much in demand. I was fortunate as yet, but my throat was too dry and uncomfortable for cigarette smoking. Though dust, particularly germ-infected dust may by itself cause a congested throat, I am convinced that the intensely dry air of Tibet is mainly to blame. On Kamet, which is situated in a moister climate, none of us suffered, but on the North-West Face of Kangchenjunga, which is exposed in part to the dry north-west wind of Tibet, there were numerous sore throats.

The temperature fell to zero during the night, but that devilish wind dropped and the following morning dawned calmly. To reach Kampa Dzong we had to cross a pass of 16,000 feet, at the head of a gently sloping valley about nine miles long. On the way to it we saw a gazelle and several kyang (wild asses). Waggers, who had already found much to interest him in the geology of the country, passed me at a gallop as I was walking April the Fifth up the stony track, but he had not gone far when his pony stumbled and he took a nasty toss from which he was lucky to escape with minor cuts and bruises. I did not see him pocket any of the angular quartzites (or whatever they were) on which he landed.

It was obvious when we reached the pass that if we climbed a hill to the south we should obtain an extensive view of the Himalayas, and in all probability see Everest in the west. Our anticipations were fulfilled when, after an easy ascent of about 1,000 feet over stony slopes and screes, a wonderful panorama greeted us, extending from some far-distant peaks in Bhutan to Everest and the great massif to the north-west of it including Cho Oyu, and Gyachung Kang. Five of the ten highest mountains of the world were visible: Kangchenjunga 28,150 feet, Makalu 27,790 feet, Lhotse (the south peak of Everest) 27,890 feet, Everest 29,002 feet, and Cho Oyu 26,870 feet.

Everest nearly 100 miles away, beyond the Nyonna-ri range and the snows of Ama Drime, was unclouded, and we could distinctly see a thin stream of wind-driven snow trailing from the crest. We gazed long at it, for there was our goal, the end of our pilgrimage. Could we attain it? On the hillside we had puffed hard, and our hearts were still beating fast, and there were 11,000 feet still to go. The head of a pin held at arm's length would almost have covered the mountain, yet through a telescope magnifying 40 diameters every major detail was visible: the sweep of the north ridge from the North Col leading up to the ragged crest of the north-east shoulder and the north-east ridge separating the north rock face from the ice-clad south-east face; the second step in the ridge, on the possibility of which so much depended, and the little triangle of snow on the final pyramid tapering upwards to the summit.

South-east of Everest rose the graceful pyramid of Makalu, and eastwards of this the eye swept over a hundred lofty summits to the square-topped Jonsong Peak, 24,344 feet. The ridge we had climbed in 1930 was clearly visible, and I could see the snowy shelf where we had pitched our highest camp. Then came the massif of Kangchenjunga. Three of its five peaks were visible, and through the telescope the ridge connecting the east peak with the summit could be seen in detail, a thin blade of ice hacked into jagged towers and moulded by the wind into sickle-like curves, whence great cornices curled over like waves breaking against the blue firmament.

Almost parallel with the skyline of the East Ridge was the North-East Spur climbed by two Bavarian expeditions. This could tell much of effort, courage and tragedy. Where the spur abutted against the North Ridge, the avalanche-swept slope which finally stopped the second expedition was clearly visible.

Eastwards of Kangchenjunga, and just showing over Chomiomo, was Siniolchu, 22,600 feet,[1] with its ice-fluted ridges uniting with mathematical precision in a summit of surpassing delicacy and beauty.

Next came Chomiomo, Kangchenjau and Pauhunri, three sonorous names for three noble mountains, which are linked for all time with the name of Dr. A.M. Kellas, who had died on the very pass beneath us during the 1921 Everest Expedition.

Chomo Lhari was nearly fifty miles away now, and beyond it peak after peak ranged far across Bhutan into the blue hazes of illimitable distance where snowfields and peaks melted in mid-air like shimmering snowflakes.

To me, at least, it was very interesting to see again the two isolated summits I had seen in 1930 from Jonsong Peak. Their bearing, ascertained with a prismatic

[1] This peak was climbed in 1936 by a German party of Paul Bauer, Karl Wien, Günther Hepp and Adi Göttner.

compass, was 28° north of east. We were nearer to them than I had been on the Jonsong Peak, but only their summit snows were visible; and they were at least 150 miles away. There is nothing in the map to suggest the presence of high mountains in this direction, and these two peaks must be over 20,000 feet high and may exceed 23,000 feet. It would be interesting to know whether any traveller has seen them, and can throw light on their position.

We ate lunch and I busied myself with photography, until a cold wind forced us to descend. On the way down we saw several hares; how they live in this wilderness it is difficult to say, yet there is vegetation of a sort, brown and withered at this time of the year, but renewing its growth later when the moist air and rains of the monsoon arrive. There were also some curious marks on the sandy slopes consisting of ribbon-like tracks only an inch or two wide running as regularly and as straight as ski-tracks down the hill. These puzzled us; were they the tracks of snakes?[2]

We regained the pass in a few minutes and descended from it towards Kampa Dzong. It was pleasantly warm, indeed hot, in the valley, and for almost the first time in Tibet we discarded clothing on the march.

To judge from the herds of barhal grazing on the slopes above us, there would seem to be plenty of game in this district, but it is, of course, never shot, the taking of animal life being frowned upon by the Tibetans. Perhaps generations hence, when wild life has been exterminated in many parts of the globe, this will be appreciated.

We turned a corner, passed a primitive water mill and came within sight of Kampa Dzong. The fort stands on a rugged crag some 800 feet above the plain, a simple, beautiful citadel and designed by men with an instinct for architectural power and symmetry.

Camp was pitched on a level expanse of stubbly grass in the shelter of a low, sandy ridge, whence issued a spring of pure water, near a village of low, flat-roofed houses ornamented at every corner with bunches of willow wands to ward off evil spirits.

An inferior curry at dinner that evening was followed unexpectedly by a magnificent stew for which, alas most of us had no room – one of life's minor tragedies. After dinner Raymond, in response to many requests, told a long and amusing story of an acquaintance who is reputed to dabble in Black Magic. He is a born raconteur and from this point of view alone was an asset to the expedition. It was much warmer, and when we turned in at 8 p.m. the thermometer registered only 4° of frost.

Kampa Dzong is situated at about 12,000 feet, and I slept well. There were 14° of frost in the night, but the sun struck the camp early next morning. It was a lazy day for me, except for letter writing and photography, but the transport officers had plenty to do in checking over the dump of stores which had arrived in advance of the expedition, whilst the "Bijli Wallahs"[3] busied themselves with the petrol generator and charged up their wireless batteries. The generator made

[2] As far as I know no snakes have been seen in this part of Tibet. Have snakes ever been seen anywhere at such an altitude?

[3] Wireless officers: Smijth-Windham and Thompson.

little noise, merely a steady chug-chug, but it was an irresistible "draw" to the inhabitants of the village, who spent hours gazing at it with ill-concealed awe.

Part of the day was spent in a long and involved settling-up of accounts with the Kalimpong mule contractor, whilst Jack and Wyn identified loads, a process much complicated by the system of colouring. As Bill said, loads should be numbered straight through. This was the method we adopted on Kamet and it proved simple and successful.

Late that afternoon Hugh, Shebby, Wyn and I, taking with us Karma Paul, called on the Deputy Dzongpen, the Dzongpen (Governor) being away on a visit to Lhasa. We were ushered into a dark, earthy-smelling house and seated ourselves on a low, carpet-covered bench in a little space which was half courtyard and half room. Hugh, who was clad in a long embroidered Tibetan coat and an English opera hat, obviously created a profound impression. After an exchange of compliments, presents were presented to our host, in return for a gift of six dozen eggs, consisting of a Homburg hat, a pair of expedition goggles, a looking-glass, a flask of whisky and the usual ceremonial scarf. For one awful moment we thought that the whisky was not whisky but tea, as earlier in the expedition some practical jokers had substituted this in one of the flasks, but it happily proved to be the genuine article. After a further exchange of courtesies, chang (native beer) was served in wide, shallow china cups. Before sipping it, a little fingertip must be dipped five times into the cup and a drop flicked into the air, as a gift to the gods. The guests then take a sip and some more chang is immediately added. This ceremony of sipping and refilling the cup is repeated twice, but after the third time the whole of the contents may be consumed. Then Hugh demonstrated the capabilities for contraction and expansion of his opera hat, to the huge delight of everyone. He also promised to write from England, and our host promised to answer. After being invited to visit the Dzong on the morrow, we took a ceremonious departure.

Arriving back at the camp, we found ourselves transported from centuries-old custom to one of the latest products of Western civilisation – wireless, which had been installed in the mess tent. Unfortunately, except for a few odd scraps of telephony such as 'Hullo, Berlin. I want a line to London,' little was heard, but the inhabitants of Kampa, who crowded in at the door of the mess tent, were vastly impressed by the melancholy squeaks and howls emitted by the instrument they probably thought that we were invoking the spirits of the dead.

After breakfast next morning, I strolled up the ridge behind the camp, and seated myself on the sun-warmed sand. At my feet a slope littered with boulders fallen from crumbling sandstone crags, and patched with coarse yellow grass, sloped gently into the plain. Although I was only 200 feet above the plain, the view across it was extensive. Yellow and brown at first, it gradually lost its distinctive colouring in the distance. Beyond it, the Himalayan snows seemed suspended in mid-air above bands of purple haze. The white triangle of Everest and Makalu's symmetrical pyramid, were both visible, whilst to the south were Jonsong Peak and the complicated ridges of Kangchenjunga.

A little later the Deputy Dzongpen arrived to conduct us over the Dzong. He was attired in a plum-coloured robe surmounted by a blue silk waistcoat, and long strings of blue beads hung from his ears. A steep path led up to the Dzong, but before we entered the old building we turned some prayer wheels the size of beer barrels which must have sent out many thousands of prayers at every revolution.

Against primitive weapons, the Dzong could withstand an indefinite siege, provided it was adequately manned and provisioned, but a modern field gun would soon shatter its walls. We passed a heavy sealed door and were told that it guarded a granary; then groped our way up various other ladders in the dark interior and eventually emerged on to the flat roof. It was a sensational situation as only a low parapet separated us from a sheer drop of some hundreds of feet. Suspended from poles were various emblems: bunches of yak hair and sheaves of grass and willow. There was also a Buddha carved in a slab of rock and a wheel of life. Far below was our camp, with its doll-like tents, whilst the brown plain was dotted black with the yaks which were to transport our stores over the next stage of the march.

Descending from the roof, we visited the library. Tibetan books are so bound that it seems almost impossible to read them, but as Shebby said, few would understand them, for they are too deeply philosophical for any but advanced scholars of Buddhism.

Our tour of inspection over, we descended to the camp, where we were met by an aggrieved George, who told us that he had been bitten by the expedition dog when visiting the store dump. This dog, named Policey by the porters, had been recently acquired by the Expedition. She was a fierce Tibetan mastiff, and her job was to keep an eye on the stores. Obviously she had functioned all too well. Fortunately, it was not long before she was able to distinguish between authorised and unauthorised visitors to the store dump, but to begin with it was always a hazardous business to venture into her vicinity.

A mail arrived during the afternoon. In addition to some very welcome letters from home, it included a communication from a gentleman who styled himself "The Autograph King".

Before leaving Kampa we visited Dr. Kellas's grave. The inscription put up when he died in 1921 had fallen to pieces, so we erected a slab of sandstone and Shebby carefully measured and traced out an inscription,

A.M. Kellas,
1921.
Om Mani Padmi Hum[4]

which the monks of the neighbouring monastery promised to chisel out. Then Shebby, the oldest member of the Expedition, read Psalm 121, "I will lift up mine eyes unto the hills," while the rest of us stood by with bared heads.

On this morning of brilliant clarity, Chomiomo Pauhunri and Kangchenjau, the three peaks climbed by this great pioneer, were full in view beyond the brown plain. Few rest in such a place; it commands one of the grandest panoramas in the world.

During the day, Eric, Ferdie and I made an interesting little experiment. We

[4] It was thought that this Buddhist prayer, which means, "Hail to the jewel in the Lotus" would encourage the local inhabitants to preserve the grave.

climbed up the sandy slopes above the camp at the approximate rate of 400 feet an hour, the speed we expected to climb on the upper part of Everest. It seemed incredibly slow, and our pulses accelerated scarcely at all, and, when we stopped, almost immediately returned to normal. An interesting experiment: I wondered if we should remember it when we were gasping for breath thousands of feet higher on Everest.

CHAPTER FIVE

The Tibetan Plateau

THE MORNING of April 2 was cloudy. I rose early in order to hand my letters to Lobsang, who was taking the Expedition mail to Gangtok. Henceforward, yaks and donkeys were to be our transport animals, and it was a brave sight to see them lumbering off in detachment after detachment across the plain.

From Kampa Dzong to Lingga is a fatiguing march of about eighteen miles. Part of the way I walked with Hugo. We discussed plans, and he told me that he was in favour of parties of three on Everest, an arguable proposition as it meant a ruinous waste of manpower in the event of a reverse due to bad weather.

The wind rose at ten o'clock and as the day lengthened blew harder and harder, viciously whipping clouds of dust, mixed with an occasional stinging spatter of snow, into our faces.

At about halfway to Lingga, we forded the Yaru Chu, and on the far bank discovered the one sheltered place on this otherwise windy march. But if it was an unpleasant march for us, it was far worse for the animals. April the Fifth was in a sorry state and had to be led by the bridle; as for the poor woebegone little donkeys, although less than half the size of yaks, they were laden as heavily as the latter, and it was a pitiful sight to see them plodding along. Now and again their legs would double up under them and they would sink to the ground, and have to be lifted upright by their cursing drivers before they could continue.

One of them foaled, but the mother was on her way again within five minutes of the birth and was loaded up less than an hour afterwards. Tibet is a rough, hard country for the beast of burden.

The last five miles lay across a plain of dried-up mud and swamps. Here the wind was blowing a gale, and with heads down and goggles over our eyes we struggled on against the blast. Innumerable dust devils rushed across this weary expanse in whirling columns hundreds of feet high, whilst the distant ranges showed dim and murky through the same all-pervading substance. An appropriate name for this plain, which extends for a score or more of miles south of Tengye Dzong, would be "The Plain of the Dust Devils".

The village of Lingga stands in the heart of the plain, and it is hard to imagine a more dismal situation. The camp had been pitched nearby, and when at length I arrived there, limp and tired, I found others equally tired sprawled on the floor of the mess tent. Wind, more than anything else had taken it out of us that day.

There was a small lake close to the camp, and we saw bar-headed geese and Brahminy ducks. We would have shot a goose as it would have been a welcome addition to the cooking-pot, but it was part of our agreement with the Tibetan Government not to shoot wild life in Tibet.

It was a perfect night when I went to bed. The wind had miraculously fallen and the whole firmament glittered with hungry stars. Those who have only seen a night sky from lower and moister elevations can have no conception of its magnificence when viewed from the cold, moistureless "Roof of the World".

So far, I had not developed a sore throat as had several of the others, but I thought I was in for one that night, and in an endeavour to stave it off wore a Matthews respirator. Unfortunately I found it impossible to keep the mask on for long owing to a feeling of claustrophobia and, suffocation. The latter, as Raymond explained later, was entirely imaginary, for as much air as the lungs normally require can be inhaled and exhaled without effort through the forty layers of wire gauze. Be that as it may, I could never breathe comfortably through this apparatus, though this is not to say that it might not be very useful in preventing sore throats during the march across Tibet and keeping the climber warm in high camps.

The temperature fell to 6°F. in the night and ice an inch thick formed on the lake. An interesting question was; how did the geese and other waterfowl avoid being frozen in during the night? Shebby suggested that they migrate to the lower and warmer Kharta Valley, but this seems doubtful, as it is sixty miles away.

Following a chilly breakfast in the open, Shebby and I started off together at 7.30. The track between the marshes was in places hard and gravelly, and in others sandy and tedious, yet we averaged over three miles an hour, fair going at the height. According to Shebby, a procession of sick men had trailed across here in 1924, including Mallory, who was suspected of appendicitis, Beetham down with dysentery and Somervell with a very bad throat.

The morning was brilliant, and there was only one shining cloud, shaped like a long, thin dagger, with the point resting on Jonsong Peak. We expected the wind to rise at any moment, but scarcely a zephyr rustled the coarse grasses, or stirred the pools, which the hot sun had already freed of ice.

Everest was just in view over the Nyonna-ri Range, and between it and Makalu rose the peak of Ama Drime (pronounced Amadreamy) a mountain as beautiful as its name.

To walk with Shebby was an education, as he is an enthusiastic naturalist and particularly interested in ornithology. We saw and photographed a number of birds on the marshy pools, and none of them seemed in the least afraid of human beings.

I felt positively ashamed at walking so comfortably when the poor little donkeys were once again struggling valiantly along, yet collapsing frequently beneath their appallingly heavy loads. They reminded me so vividly of the donkeys I used to ride on the sands when I was a boy, but those were jolly, happy little donkeys, loving their fun, and these were poor, scared morsels of animals, doomed to slavery until exhausted nature caused them to collapse for the last time, never to rise again. Their bones whiten beside the trade routes in Tibet.

It was a longer march than the map seemed to indicate. After we had passed the marshes I got very thirsty, and when at last we saw Tengye Dzong shimmering above the plain all saliva had gone and my tongue felt like a strip of leather.

Our camp was pitched close to a fair-sized lake opposite to the old Dzong, which, if not possessing the dramatic qualities of Kampa Dzong, is nevertheless a fine building; the modern "jerrybuilder" who disfigures the British countryside should take a trip to Tibet; he might gain some constructive ideas.

One disadvantage of travelling in Tibet is that transport has to be changed every time an expedition comes within the province of a new Dzongpen, so again Hugh donned his Tibetan coat and opera hat to receive the Dzongpen of Tengye. This dignitary having arrived with his retinue of servants, there followed a long haggle as to the hire price of transport animals for the next stage of our march, an occasion calling for the consumption of much whisky. Finally everything was settled amicably, and the Dzongpen, appreciably mellowed, promised us a great feast if we returned successful.

Little wind rose that day and the temperature was well above freezing point when we dined. The gramophone as usual caused great astonishment and amusement, and a Sola Khumbu woman, a sister of one of our porters, who had joined the party, was especially intrigued by it, and on every occasion that it was played edged as near to it as possible, her broad face wreathed in delighted smiles.

Next morning, April 4, was so warm that some of us breakfasted in pyjamas and overcoats. Canvas baths had been provided, and I had a hot bath in my tent. During the morning I photographed the camp and the local inhabitants, of whom the women, with big hoops over their heads, made excellent subjects. The people of Tengye Dzong were very curious, and the camp was besieged by ragged beggars whom Nursang and Lewa violently ejected at intervals. The country in the neighbourhood, as well as the beggars, reminded me of Egypt; the arid hills are the same yellowish brown and rise like the ghosts of hills against a dark-blue sky.

Compared to the Phari plain, Tengye was almost tropical. According to local information, the winter had been unusually dry, and we asked ourselves whether it was going to be a season of seasons, or would it break later and give us hell? A burning question that only time could solve. As Hugh said, 'There is a tremendous spirit of optimism in this party.' It was a necessary spirit, for, in the words of Paul Bauer, speaking of Kangchenjunga, 'One has got to be an optimist to climb a great peak in the Himalayas.'

In the afternoon our old enemy the wind remembered us, and squall after squall of dust beat down on the camp.

Apart from checking over stores there were various odd jobs. Waggers who was attending to meteorology as well as geology, unpacked a barograph, but yak transport had reduced it to its component parts, and, although we tried to put it together, it was plain that it could never work.

For some obscure reason we were issued with crampons. I have found these useful in a cross-channel boat or customs queue, as attached points outwards to the back of a rucksack they save their owner from being jostled, but on Himalayan expeditions they are an unmitigated nuisance and invariably puncture everything within reach.

That afternoon the first Olympiad in the history of Tengye Dzong was held amidst the utmost enthusiasm. It included some spectacular pole vaults by Jack

Longland, an expert performer, the "pole" being a section of a wireless mast. Then Hugo Boustead, who had represented England at the (authentic) Olympic Games, demonstrated the art of boxing. He took on man after man among the porters. At first they were reluctant to hit a sahib, but soon warmed to the game, and Lhakpa Chedi attacked with great vigour; however, it was not long before Hugo proved to him that a little science is worth a world of unscientific attack, however vigorous it may be. But the real fun began when two porters put on the gloves; the scrap developed into a windmill-like affair and soon became so fast and furious that it had to be stopped. Finally, as a joke, various small Tibetan children were given the gloves and went for each other like true sportsmen amid roars of laughter. The football was also very popular and Nursang did his best to form the Sherpas into a rugger scrum; they and the Tibetans have the genuine sporting instinct.

After tea, Eric, Hugo, Bill and I walked about 1,500 feet up the hillside behind the camp, climbing some crags on the way, where we found a number of ammonites, evidence that this arid elevated plateau was formerly a sea-bed.

Tencheddar, the cook, once he was allowed to settle down in any one place for some days, usually managed to produce something good and for dinner that night we had a well-flavoured curry, followed by stewed apples. I suspect, however, that it was the bottle of sloe gin afterwards, combined with some previous entertainment given by the Dzongpen to Hugh, Shebby, Raymond and George, that contributed to the general hilarity with which the evening ended. The only absentee was Willy McLean, who was in bed with a chill,

With a seventeen miles march before us, and two passes to cross, we were away early next morning. Less than a mile from the camp we passed the village of Tengye, a tumble-down place with flat roofs and a young forest of willow wands to ward off devils. Presently we heard a harsh cawing from some crags and thought it was magpies, until we saw dozens of partridge-like birds, identified by Bill as chicaw. There were also numerous sleek, well-fed hares which regarded us with mild interest before loping up the stony hillsides.

The route lay up a rocky valley with reddish crags on either hand splashed with dark-green clumps of juniper, then over a col adorned with the usual cairns and prayer flags and down to another arid valley where we halted for a bite of food. On the way up to the next col the wind made itself felt and I waited an hour in a sheltered place for Tensing, who had my wind-proof suit. Then I mounted April the Fifth (incidentally it was April 5), but the poor old thing jibbed at the steep slope up to the 16,000 foot pass, and I ended by more or less pulling her up. On the pass the mail runner overtook us and forgetting the wind, we opened our letters on the spot and devoured the news from home.

On the far side of the pass, the route descended precipitous rocks and shale, then long, sandy slopes to another valley containing a dried-up, sandy watercourse, as wide and smooth as an arterial road. This valley debouched into yet another and wider valley, in which were some villages. At long last we saw the welcoming green speck of the mess tent and were soon supine within it out of reach of the abominable dust-filled wind, thankfully aware that a long, dull march, with quite 3,000 feet of ascent thrown in, was behind us.

Willy, who had not yet recovered from his chill and had ridden all the way, pronounced the local water as being unfit for human consumption, so we had to boil and filter it, a slow and tantalising process to thirsty men. In the matter of food we were even unluckier, for the transport animals had lagged behind and it was a long time before we had anything to eat. When at last some stores arrived, we had a gargantuan feast of ham and tea, biscuits, butter and jam. Supper was a scratch affair, but Tencheddar and Lhakpa Chedi rose to the occasion and produced some more ham, scrambled eggs and cocoa. Not all the transport had arrived, and for once we sat on the floor of the mess tent – which, incidentally, was far safer than the expedition chairs, which had a knack of collapsing and depositing their occupants on the floor without warning.

The night was warm, 4° above freezing, and a half moon shed radiance on the hills. I finished my diary in my tent with the barking of Policey in my ears. Night after night she rendered the landscape hideous; as, apart from George, she had already bitten four Tibetans, we wondered what her total bag would be by the end of the expedition.

Our next march to the village of Dochen was only nine or ten miles, but the wind made short work of any gratitude we might have felt. The valley was filled with whirling sand devils, and clouds of choking dust came rolling along like a series of gas attacks. Had it not been for this abominable wind we might have enjoyed the grassy camping place at Dochen, with its view of Shankar-ri, a thin, graceful rock peak 20,000 feet high. We camped early and after lunch Ferdie looked in at my tent and suggested a walk over the hill behind the camp. Two hundred feet up the hillside is a stone cell at the entrance to a small cave. It had no door and merely narrow slits in its walls. Possibly a hermit had sealed himself within it and the slits served the dual purpose of providing him with light and air and allowing the villagers to pass through food and drink. What unnatural things are done in the name of religion! That a creature of flesh and blood should shut himself away from the sun to brood in a gloomy cell a few feet square is an unconscious commentary on the ignorance of the human race and the darkness of the human mind.

To avoid the wind, we kept to the lee-side of a ridge, going very slowly as a high-altitude discipline, yet we climbed at about one thousand feet an hour, and found we could converse without effort or breathlessness.

The ridge led between a minor hill and a tall conical hill with a monastery perched high up on it, to a col whence we saw two high peaks in the north-west marked on the map as exceeding 21,000 feet. Considering their height, it was astonishing how little snow they carried. Southwards, the weather was in poor shape and the Himalayas were concealed by clouds extending to the Nyonna-ri Range in Tibet.

An easy scree-run took us rapidly down to camp. Arriving there, we found a surgical operation in progress. During the march the ponies of Karma Paul and Lobsang Tsering had fallen. Karma Paul had broken a little finger and Lobsang Tsering a collar bone. Owing to muscular contraction, it was found impossible to set the collarbone without an anaesthetic, and the mess tent was turned into a temporary hospital. Chloroform was administered by Raymond while Willy stood by to set the broken bone, but soon after he became unconscious Lobsang's heart stopped. The only hope of getting it going again, short of a massage involving a major operation, was an injection of coramine. This drug was in one of several medical boxes in Raymond's tent, and Raymond was not sure which one.

Happily, by great good fortune, Hugh, who hastened to look for it, found it in the first box he opened. The hypodermic needle was jabbed into the patient's heart, an upsetting process for a layman to watch, and the heart started to work again; it had stopped for about a minute and a half. As Lobsang was a strong fellow this was almost certainly due to the altitude, and Raymond said afterwards that in future operations at high altitudes he would administer oxygen with an anaesthetic.

Owing to dust suspended in the atmosphere, the sun had little power next morning and breakfast in the open was a shivery affair. Bill and I left camp together. The going was fatiguing owing to incipient sand dunes, but April the Fifth seemed in fine fettle. The river winds sinuously between earthy cliffs, deeply eroded in places, and the country in general was my conception of the Arizona desert.

After three miles we forded the shallow river, beyond which the country was rougher and the path wound over a barren, sandy hillside where a low, scrubby bush somehow managed to find nourishment. Finally, a steep descent over a slope of loose sand to a causeway and a bridge across the river brought us to our camping site, a flat space in a bight of earthy cliffs partially sheltered from the wind.

At lunch in the mess tent there was a discussion on leisure for the working-classes and what they should do with it, but my diary does not record any definite conclusions. Presumably they should do what they like with their leisure. Having no liking for the interminable arguments in the mess tent, I found it more amusing to sit on the hillside above the camp and send down miniature avalanches of sand, in the movement of which there was something equable, ordered and definite.

After tea, Hugh, Hugo, Eric and I scaled a hill directly above the camp. We went slowly enough to carry on a conversation, yet we climbed about 2,000 feet in one and half-hours and reached a height of about 16,000 feet. The wind was strong, but not excessively cold, and the rocks we scrambled over reminded me of the Crib Goch ridge in North Wales.

Eric and I went well together. His pace suited mine perfectly and I believe the opposite held true; we had climbed together on Kamet, I hoped we should do so again on Everest. One of the things that worried me slightly was not knowing for certain with whom I was going to climb on Everest. That few of us were used to climbing together was a serious weakness in the Expedition, and it was a pity that the years between 1924 and 1933 had not been profitably utilised in building up a homogeneous Everest party. To a mountaineer the possibility of having to climb on the highest mountain of the world with someone with whom he has never climbed before is disturbing. A party must move as one man to stand a chance of success.

We gained the summit of our hill as a red-rimmed sun was sinking behind blue dust-bleared ranges. The scene reminded me of a mist-haunted day in the Isle of Skye, and a silvery thread-work of rivers on the dim plain at our feet almost completed the illusion.

Hugh had been cogitating several problems for some days and he made known to us his ideas after dinner. The Camp 1 of former expeditions was to be virtually a Base Camp, Camp 4 on the North Col was to be made as luxurious as possible, and Ferdie was to be in charge of the glacier camps. A lengthy discussion followed on ways and means of climbing the mountain. The general opinion was that if an attempt failed before the monsoon we should wait to see whether another could be made during or even after the monsoon; at the same time the whole strength of the party must be devoted to a pre-monsoon attempt. There was some divergence of opinion on the problems of acclimatisation and deterioration. For my part, I was against remaining too long on the North Col. Eric and I knew that we reached the top of our form quickly and that once our peak of acclimatisation was passed we might deteriorate equally quickly if we remained at a high altitude. Some acclimatise early, others late; and some deteriorate earlier than others. It was a formidable problem with many unknown factors.

The wind was blowing gustily when I went to bed and Policey was making a throaty noise suggesting that she had just connected with someone's leg. For some reason I had an aching back, and was again upset internally, so that I did not sleep well. It was a windy night and the damp air from the river helped to chill the camp.

The march next day, April 8, was long and tiring. Some difficulty was experienced in getting the transport off. As usual the donkeys were grossly overloaded, but what could we do when no more transport was available?

We crossed one of the tributaries of the Arun River by a shallow ford. It is strange country hereabouts. The valley floor is flat, three or four miles wide and virtually a desert with innumerable sand dunes arranged in regular ranks by the wind. Many miles away in the south rose a high snow peak, probably Makalu, whilst to the east and south-east stretched the Nyonna-ri Range, not an impressive range from this direction as the higher peaks are mostly concealed by nearer ridges, except for the thin, wedge-like spire of Shankar-ri.

For five miles it was hard work over loose sand, a distance that had proved too much for the aged and exhausted donkeys of former travellers, for there were several bleached skeletons half-buried in the shifting sand, and we were glad to turn north-west up the valley of the Bhong Chu, where by the river there was a level expanse of warm turf. We sank down gratefully and ate our lunch. The sun was hot and there was no wind, and it was delightful to lie at our ease with the bells of the transport train tinkling from the plain behind us and the low music of the gently flowing river in our ears. To complete the idyll a skylark approached to within a yard of us and hopped along the line of our recumbent figures, narrowly inspecting each of us in turn, whilst a mouse hare came out of its hole a few yards away and, after satisfying itself of our peaceful intentions, began to burrow industriously in the dry soil.

The warmth had tempted numerous insects from their hiding places, but some met a premature fate in Raymond's poison bottle. Then some diving ducks moved leisurely down the stream until, disturbed by the passage of a stately lammergeier, they hurriedly rose and thudded away.

We had not rested long before our old enemy the wind discovered us, and the last part of the march to Trangso-Chumbab was in the teeth of dust-laden squalls. Camp was pitched on a dirty space where the wind raged, covering everything with clouds of filthy dust, doubtless infected by the neighbouring village. What a pity we did not camp on the clean sward where we had halted, but a large expedition is tied down to certain stages and the position of its camping grounds is dictated by the necessity for housing and feeding the yak and donkey drivers.

Before we turned in, Raymond, at Hugh's suggestion, read out aloud Norton's 1924 dispatch, in which he summed up the possibilities of climbing Everest.

Afterwards Hugh and I had a long discussion by candle light in Hugh's tent as to whether or not the first party should be devoted solely to reconnoitring the North-East Ridge to determine the possibility or impossibility of the second step. We both knew how difficult it was to decide anything at this stage; so much depended on the strength of the expedition when the time came for an attempt on the summit. Probably not more than six men would be able to go high, and of these not all would be capable of reaching the summit. On no account, therefore, must the two fittest men expend themselves on a reconnaissance. It was interesting to discuss quietly such complex problems, yet, when all was said and done, such discussions were purely academic. We must "wait and see".

CHAPTER SIX

Shekar Dzong

Punctually with the sun, old Nima Tendrup appeared bearing my canvas bucket of hot water. Being an Oriental, he always woke me gently. He would untie my tent, and his round, honest face like a blackened full moon would appear, then, if I was asleep, he would say, 'Sahib! Sahib! Sahib!' gradually raising his voice until I woke.

Our march to begin with was across an arid sandy plain, but, on turning a corner, we were astonished to look down a cliff and see the river flowing through a country as fertile as any we had yet seen in Tibet. There were even scraggy, ill-nourished trees and, on the far side of the river, small hamlets surrounded by fields which are tilled with a perseverance that wrests sufficient for bare existence, and no more, from a poor soil. What would these people think, living as they do on the verge of starvation, could they see food dumped into the sea, or left to rot, so that the "prices" of an outworn capitalist system might be further bolstered up? There are no false values in Tibet.

I was ambling along on April the Fifth with Ferdie when of a sudden there came a thudding of hoofs behind and, with a whoop, Willy and Hugo bore down upon us. The startled April the Fifth promptly bolted; one stirrup leather broke and away I went across the plain completely out of control, dimly aware that Ferdie's pony had bolted too. At length I managed to pull up and dismount, but next moment April the Fifth, now thoroughly roused, tore the reins out of my hand and took to her heels once more. It was surprising to see this unwonted energy in the old pony, and my initial annoyance was replaced by a roar of laughter.

The wind rose early and assaulted us vigorously for the greater part of the march. The landscape was almost lunar in aspect, and gaunt brown and yellow hills splashed with reddish crags shivered in a dust-filled sky.

We camped soon after midday. A rocky little peak rose immediately to the north and this Hugo and I climbed. We chose a steep route, and reached the summit buffeted by a strong and bitterly cold west wind. If the wind was as cold and hostile as this at 15,000 feet, what must it be like 10,000 feet higher on Everest? We agreed that a wind of equal force, at 28,000 feet would paralyse a party and defeat an attempt on the summit.

The view from our hill was extraordinary. In every direction rose brown, waterless hills, desolate, windswept hulks of hills possessing neither the beauty of fertility nor the grandeur of the sublime: it was a dead country, fit only for the Wandering Jew and the spirits of the damned.*

We looked in vain for Everest, but clouds filled the south; bad weather raged along the Himalayas. The sun was sinking in a fierce red glare as we descended in strange contrast to the moon, poised serenely on the quickening flood of night.

As we neared the camp, we saw the donkey and yak drivers congregated by their fires. They had piled boxes of our stores around them for shelter and these were now scattered liberally over the landscape, obviously accessible to thieves.

A doleful tale awaited us. One of the drivers had deserted with his animals, after abandoning their loads by the wayside. Thanks to the transport officers, the loads had been collected and fresh animals procured. It had meant hard work for Lewa, and he did not reach camp until long after dark, tired out and scarcely able to speak for the dust that choked his throat.

The morning of April 10 was chilly and again the sun shone with little power owing to the dust in the sky. Hugh, Shebby and I walked together the first hour or so, then I rode. April the Fifth was in splendid form; a week ago she had looked like dying and was stumbling dejectedly along, now she had quite recovered and her coat was becoming positively glossy.

At first we traversed a narrow, sandy valley enclosed by reddish disintegrating crags and slopes of screes. Moses might have passed through a similar valley on his way to the Promised Land, and with much the same primitive transport as ours, but not carrying the latest products of Western civilisation, such as wireless and the tinned products of Fortnum & Mason and the Army and Navy Stores. Then the path crossed a low pass, adorned with the usual cairns, Mani stones and prayer flags, and, after switchbacking over some small rises where the rising wind blew hard in our faces, finally debouched on to a gently sloping plain where the transport column stretched out like an attenuated dragon. Some miles distant rose a solitary yellowish crag with a little cluster of white objects on it – the famous monastery of Shekar Dzong, photographs of which are familiar to readers of Everest books.

We had heard stories of smallpox at Shekar and had decided to camp if possible two or three miles short of it, but after an hour or so, when we were rapidly nearing the village at the foot of the crag and there was no sign of the mess-tent, we suspected that Karma Paul, who was ahead, had thought otherwise.

A car could be driven for miles across the gently inclined plain, and old April the Fifth broke spontaneously into a trot, and raced a Tibetan dignitary, also bound for Shekar; a pleasant-featured, smooth-skinned little man in a red silk dress and finely embroidered hat. I tried to converse in broken Nepali as we rode side by side, but my best efforts elicited nothing beyond unintelligible grunts accompanied by broad grins exposing a set of remarkably white and even teeth.

* Here Smythe is quoting from *Scrambles Amongst the Alps* – see earlier reference on page 178.

As we neared Shekar we were astonished at the fantastic beauty of the monastery, which is lodged on the precipitous side of a rock some 1,200 feet high.

Possibly some enterprising builder, a lama perhaps, tired of the level places, and yearning for the heights, as well as security from marauders, fashioned a ledge whereon to build a dwelling, whence he could peacefully survey the world at his feet, and from this humble dwelling grew the great monastery. With its white walls ranged one upon the other; it is a stupendous feat of architecture and a grandiose gesture of defiance to the law of gravity. Above the monastery, a turreted battlemented wall rises almost vertically to the final extravagance; the ancient Dzong perched sublimely on the very pinnacle of the crag.

Karma Paul told us that there was no smallpox except in the monastery, and in a village to the north of the crag. Camp was accordingly pitched on some dried mud almost directly under the monastery. It was a filthy spot, the recipient of every wind that blew, and directly to leeward of the squalid village of Shekar, which deposited its infected dust straight on to the camp. Raymond was justly furious and disclaimed any responsibility for dysentery, smallpox, typhoid and any other disease the expedition might contract, but by the time he arrived it was too late to change the site, as the animals had been unloaded and the camp pitched.

Soon after we camped, the Dzongpen considerately sent his servants with a gift of tea, milk and chang, but we had scarcely had time to refresh ourselves before somebody discovered that the loads, which were still coming in on yaks, mules and donkeys, had been tampered with. Eleven pairs of porters' high-altitude boots, a tent, porters' windproof clothing and socks were missing and many ration boxes had been forced open and their contents rifled. The porters were furious at the loss of their kits, and before we could stop him Lewa violently set about one of the drivers. The four principal yak drivers were immediately arrested, tied up with leather thongs and handed over to the Dzongpen.

The thefts had been carried out with considerable ingenuity. In some cases lumps of turf had been substituted for the stolen articles to compensate for the loss of weight. Bottles of rum intended for the high camps had also been stolen, whilst many tins of food had disappeared or been slit open. Altogether about one hundred pounds' worth of equipment and food had been lost. A thorough check of stores was necessary and all the afternoon we laboured, beaten by the wind and half-choked by the acrid dust.

At supper we washed the filthy dust from our throats with a hot punch of whisky, water, sugar and lemon juice. As usual the wind dropped at nightfall, and before turning in George and I went for a short walk. The dust had settled and a brilliant moon drowned all but the brighter stars. High above our heads on the dark and apparently inaccessible precipice was the monastery, its white walls glowing ethereally as though transparent and lighted from within. As we stood watching this strange and beautiful sight, the silence was broken by a low dirge-like sound rising and falling; the lamas were praying. Then came the mournful note of a deep-toned horn, and the slow percussion of a great drum. Both epitomised this changeless, mysterious country of Tibet. In the West civilisations might wax and wane, kings and dictators come and go, but Tibet would remain the same. Fortunate land that none covet it; in its barrenness lies its strength, in its winds and cold its protection from the greedy progress of the West.

The last notes quivered and died away in the crags and there was silence, a profound, wonderful silence, and in that silence a glorious meteor fell slowly in the north-east sky and disappeared behind a distant range. Did the lamas see it, and was it an answer to their prayers?

Next morning, I was unwell with severe colitic pains and vomiting. I was a little anxious; to contract dysentery at this stage would be a serious matter, not only for me, but for the expedition, which would want both its doctors on the mountain. Raymond made me up a draught of bicarbonate of soda and later Willy gave me a tablespoonful of castor oil, which I somehow managed to keep down between mouthfuls of whisky. After this, I lay supine in my sleeping bag experiencing, every quarter of an hour or so, pains which seemed to twist me up inside into knots. Thanks, however, to these stringent measures, I was much more comfortable by lunchtime though decidedly empty.

In the afternoon, the four men arrested as suspected thieves were publicly flogged by order of the Dzongpen. Ruttledge in his official capacity of leader had to attend the ceremony and he was accompanied by various other members of the expedition. Three hundred lashes with rawhide whips was the portion of the unfortunate men. We were pretty sure that they were guilty, but to inflict punishment upon them without trial savoured too much of "Alice in Wonderland": "sentence first, verdict afterwards".

When the sightseers returned, they said that the beating was not a severe one as punishments go in Tibet – a hundred lashes apiece, which were received with stoical indifference. The object of the beating was to extort confession, but none of the four accused men would admit guilt. Doubtless a few pairs of good boots were worth a good deal more to them than one hundred lashes.

Quite a ceremony was made of the punishment, if it could justly be called punishment. It was administered in an open courtyard with the Dzongpen occupying one housetop and members of the expedition the other. There were two official whippers, and at the end of every ten strokes the accused men were asked if they wanted to confess. This would appear the usual procedure in Tibet, and a suspected criminal, whether innocent or guilty, is thrashed before his trial, just in case he happens to be guilty and confesses, thus saving the "court" a world of trouble. Whether he is sentenced to further punishment if he confesses I do not know. Flogging is a comparatively mild punishment in a criminal code which includes the cutting off of ears and limbs.

By the evening I was much better, but to make the cure certain Raymond gave me a dose of bacteriophage. As there was nothing whatever left in me I slept well, but woke once to hear some other unfortunate vomiting.

The morning of April 12 was cold and sunless; there was a slate-grey pall in the south and snow was falling in the Everest region. My sick partner turned out to be Tom Brocklebank, another victim of the foul germ-laden dust.

Policey was doing her job well. During the morning more than one lama from the monastery, whose curiosity outran his discretion, had to flee for his life. At lunch there was a discussion as to whether alcohol should be taken to the high camps. The only contribution I could make to this was to point out that rum had proved successful as a warming nightcap on Kamet. On the question of spirits I agreed with Raymond that when a temporary stimulation has passed away, the body is left colder than it was before. I have noted this in the Alps. Probably the high sugar content of rum is responsible for its warming properties, and my experience is that a hot non-alcoholic beverage such as chocolate is as valuable in promoting a warm and comfortable sleep.

After lunch, several of us visited the monastery under the guidance of Sonam Topchi Lama, one of the under sirdars. After crossing a shallow river, which combines the functions of "company's water" and main drain of Shekar, we passed along a narrow lane bordered by Mani stones, then up a steep path, pausing to stone an aggressive dog *en route* (the fiercest Tibetan mastiffs are not proof against accurate stone-throwing) and through a massive gateway into the monastery. The first thing we noticed was the stink from the sewage which trickled down the slimy gutters of the narrow streets. Once used to this – and the traveller's nose soon acclimatises itself to the foulest smells – we examined with interest the massive buildings with their narrow smoke-begrimed latticed windows, rising tier upon tier on the steep face of the crag. Then, turning off the main street, we were conducted through another gateway gaudily painted with scenes from the life of Buddha into a rectangular courtyard whence rose two poles the height and girth of telegraph poles, adorned with prayer flags. A flight of stone steps led up to a temple, and at the foot of them some men were busily engaged in pouring tea from large buckets into beautifully chased silver teapots which, being filled, were borne with much pomp and ceremony down the courtyard to the far end, where about two hundred lamas were assembled, squatting on the ground.

The lamas were attired in dark-red habits, with one arm bare to the shoulder, the symbol of poverty. Their faces, necks, hands and arms were dark from the smoke of countless shing[1] fires, and each was provided with a brass teacup. The teapots were placed on the ground and the men deputed to pour out the tea prostrated themselves before them in prayer; then the lamas, still squatting on the ground, held out their teacups to be filled. As each lama received his portion, a priest who accompanied the pourer mumbled a prayer, which he terminated with a clap of his hands. It was a striking and picturesque ceremony, but I have no doubt that some of our Christian ceremonies would seem equally strange to a Tibetan.

After taking many photographs, to which the lamas did not object in the least, we were escorted up the steps into the main temple of the monastery. It was almost completely dark inside, and until our eyes accustomed themselves to the gloom we slipped and stumbled about on the uneven stone slabs forming the floor. Presently we made out a number of long benches raised a few inches from the floor, and covered with the same dull-red fabric as the lamas wear, arranged, not at right angles to the three sacred images at one end of the temple, but longitudinally. We mounted some steps to a chancel and examined the images, which were partially lit by a small window. They were gorgeously painted and bejewelled, the centre one having what appeared to be a magnificent diamond set in its forehead. Those to right and left were smaller than the central figure, and before all three were little butter lamps, placed between brass bowls containing water, on a shelf covered in red brocade. Behind and above these images loomed a huge and

[1] Dried yak dung in this instance; the only fuel in many parts of Tibet. Shing is a generic name in Tibet for fuel of any kind.

majestic Buddha. It was a pity that the many elaborately painted and embroidered prayer banners which decorated the temple should be wrapped in perpetual gloom. Why should religion and gloom be inseparably associated? Does gloom make worship easier? And if so, why? In one wall of the temple were hundreds of pigeonholes containing books, but we had no opportunity to examine these; doubtless they were philosophical works pertaining to Buddhism.

Next, we were shown another temple where the former abbots of the monastery were embalmed in wooden boxes. Finally, we were conducted to a room and invited to seat ourselves on cushions. A large number of curios and trinkets were then placed before us and offered for sale. I purchased a copper charm-box, a teacup in Chinese silver and an amulet inlaid with turquoises. It was very evident that the lamas had a keen eye towards business and had no objection to Indian money in exchange for their wares. I would have welcomed an opportunity of purchasing something really unique, such as one of the silver teapots, but nothing of this nature was forthcoming despite the requests of Karma Paul, who acted as bargainer in chief on our behalf.

Our purchases made, we climbed up the loose pastry-like rock above the monastery to the old fort crowning the crag. This had been long disused, and its crumbling walls leaned so precariously over the precipice that it seemed as though a good push would send them crashing on top of the monastery some hundreds of feet beneath.

We crept cautiously up steep flights of stairs, being careful not to touch broken beams and masses of tottering masonry, and emerged on to the roof. Once there our eyes turned instinctively in the direction of Everest. Immediately we saw it; there was no mistaking the huge, gaunt pile wedging the southern sky.

It was a stormy evening, with lurid banks of cumulus cloud piled on the Himalayas, but Everest stood a little apart from the storm centre and we could clearly distinguish the North-East Shoulder and the North Face falling towards the North Col, which was concealed behind a nearer ridge. Snow had fallen, but the wind was clearing it away and dark rock ribs projected like bones through a thin white skin. There was no light or shadow to relieve the harsh black and white of rock and snow, and in the dull light the great mountain looked forbidding.

As the sun dropped near the horizon the queer crumbling walls about us glowed a lurid red and the shadow of the rock on which we stood, with the Dzong clearly outlined and blunting its sharp point, crept across the plain.

The descent from the roof was unpleasant, as we felt that the unstable pile through which we crept by devious passages and stairways was ready to collapse on us at any moment, and it was a relief to tread the mountainside.

By the time we had regained the camp, the sunlight had passed from the Dzong, but some shining hills in the east cast a faint reflection upon it, so that it glowed faintly rose against a deep-green sky.

In the night there was a great commotion. The porters, not unnaturally, had made the most of their stay at Shekar and had quickly made the discovery that the local chang was particularly potent. Lhakpa Chedi, up to date a model of sobriety and discretion, had let himself go for once, and there was a tremendous hullabaloo when he and some of his friends returned to camp. But we could hardly blame our men; there was little jollity ahead of them.

CHAPTER SEVEN

The Rongbuk Valley to Base Camp

Five days only separated us from the Base Camp, and with feelings of thankfulness we saw the newly hired transport animals arrive on the morning of April 13, and knew we could leave Shekar; there is little doubt that a serious illness would have occurred had we remained in its filthy precincts.

From Shekar the route was first of all through a narrow earthy gully where the transport animals jammed and some of the loads suffered severely. It was a dull, grey day, and the high hills were veiled in drizzling snow, but we welcomed this as dull days are usually windless in Tibet.

I rode April the Fifth and was accompanied by Ferdie. In another narrow section of the path we got mixed up with a number of transport mules, one of which lashed out and caught April the Fifth a nasty smack on the muzzle. There was an awkward drop from the path into the stream, but the old pony took the blow in good part and did not bolt as Relling would have done.

After this the route followed a dry, sandy water-course, then passed over a brow and descended a shaley hillside to a bridge over the Bhong Chu. As usual, April the Fifth lagged behind. I was resigned to her snail-like progress and half asleep when suddenly she leapt forward with a bound that nearly unseated me and careered at a gallop of at least twelve miles an hour across the Bhong plain. Policey had come up behind and slyly seized her tail.

Camp was pitched on refreshingly clean turf near the village of Pangle. I arrived simultaneously with a snowstorm; in a few minutes the ground was white, then the clouds stole away and the sun came out.

After tea several of us climbed a hill rising about 1,000 feet above the camp, and from the summit looked westwards along the wide, irregular valley of the Bhong Chu with its queer little conical-shaped hills all steaming like volcanoes with wind-driven snow.

For dinner that evening Tencheddar produced some of the best coffee we had yet tasted. Why he could not always make good coffee was an unsolved mystery. But we were a shivering company in the mess tent, and were glad to escape from the bitter cold into our sleeping bags.

Hugh woke us at dawn next morning, April 14, in the hope that we would reach the Pangle La in time to see Everest before the clouds gathered. Unfortunately an earlier start than usual, even when notified to the cook the night before, is liable to upset kitchen arrangements, the Oriental being a slave to habit and unadaptable in the matter of time, and, after standing about and cursing in the cold, we ended by breakfasting at the usual time.

It was obvious when we began the ascent to the pass that we were unlikely to see anything owing to snow-charged clouds in the south. I began the day on April the Fifth, but the poor old thing seemed to think our way was downhill, and great was her surprise and chagrin when she found that she was expected to climb more than 3,000 feet. However I let her off lightly and walked most of the way with Waggers, though in point of fact she went well, despite her age, and did not blow like some of the other ponies, which were obviously feeling the altitude.

It was a tiring and monotonous trudge to the pass. The wind had formed little stilettos of ice on every projecting stone and the scene was desolate and bleak. The Pangle La is 18,000 feet and, as long as I made no conscious attempt to hurry, I found myself ascending at almost sea-level speed. It was a matter of rhythm and of adjusting each step to the lungs. On a hillside a song which fits the pace is immensely helpful, and often I discover some ditty to govern my legs and breathing.

Cairns and prayer flags adorned the pass. Of Everest there was nothing to be seen, and the southern sky was filled with leaden clouds and blue-grey curtains of falling snow. There was little colour and the view was a drab monotone like a fogged negative. The biting wind did not invite a halt, so Ferdie, Tom and I climbed a hill to the east of the pass. Easy walking brought us to the summit, which is about 600 feet above the pass. Beyond was a higher and more shapely summit which we climbed at our own speed: mine was certainly not less than 1,500 feet an hour, and possibly as much as 2,000 feet, and I felt extraordinarily fit and well acclimatised. The wind blew harder and harder as we gained height, and I was interested to see how my windproof suit would withstand it. It did so admirably, and it was a relief to know that in all probability it would be equally effective against the far colder winds of Everest. According to an aneroid, the second hill was 18,750 feet high. There was a cairn on the summit and a bunch of willow-wands and prayer flags which seemed to show that, like us, the Tibetans are not satisfied with merely crossing a pass and have an eye for a view. In clear weather there must be a splendid view of Everest, but on this occasion not a single high peak was visible. The clouds extended to the remote east and west and the low hills beneath them looked unusually dreary, whilst barren valleys without an apparent vestige of vegetation and unlit by sunlight stretched for miles.

There was no object in prolonging a halt in the icy wind, and I raced down slopes of snow and screes to the south of the pass where the transport was winding sinuously along. The donkeys were having something worse than a hard day, but fortunately there were spare ones, so that when one collapsed tired out, its load could be transferred to a fresher beast. We passed through a striking gorge and noticed a dizzy path high up on the cliffs of its west side leading to a hermit's cave. A pleasantly warm sandy valley brought us to a camping ground in a willow grove, hard by the village of Tashidzom, a charming spot where newly born lambs gambolled in the meadows.

Shebby and George had a gruelling time supervising the transport over the pass. George was almost always last in camp, which meant that he had to put up with more wind and dust than the rest of us, but he never complained and was always his cheerful exuberant self.

After the dust of Shekar plus laboured breathing in the cold, dry air when ascending to the pass, sore throats were very evident, and Shebby had a particularly nasty cough, which attacked him most of all at night and must have interfered with his sleep a great deal. I had much to be thankful for in having so far escaped the worst of the sore-throat curse. We arrived very thirsty at Tashidzom, and I drank enormous quantities of strong tea, and paid the penalty with a restless night, which Policey did not improve by barking for hours on end, so that I was tempted to retaliate with an ice axe on more than one occasion. Still, it was some compensation for lying awake to hear the sighing of the wind in the willows. On the march and later on Everest, I had many bad nights, yet at high altitudes the hours pass more readily than they do at low levels. Sleep does not seem so necessary; it is sufficient to rest the body. The most disagreeable effect of sleeplessness is a host of trivial yet worrying thoughts which are sometimes concentrated into fancied and absurd grievances. These in their turn are responsible for a deterioration of judgement and an upset of mental balance which can be a serious menace to the smooth working of an expedition. Such deterioration – "bloody-mindedness" is cruder but more descriptive – is best countered by experience and knowledge of high-altitude conditions, for this helps to maintain a sense of proportion. Thus, instead of loathing the method by which your companion imbibes his soup, you merely tell yourself that your loathing is inspired by altitude and that your own method is probably just as disgusting to him. Once this idea is planted in the mind, it will never cease to bear the fruit of tolerance, sympathy and understanding.

Next morning I was unwell. There were shivers down my back and my inside was all awry. I was not the only seedy one; the dust of Shekar had wreaked havoc on throats and many of the porters could only speak in whispers.

The march from Tashidzom to Chö-Dzong is about twelve miles and lies along a monotonous valley. It was a fine morning, but quickly forming clouds soon obscured the view we should have had of Everest, whilst plumes of wind-driven snow writhed from the hilltops.

The camping ground at Chö-Dzong was exposed to every wind that blew, and once again our belongings and food were covered with dust. Later in the day, Eric and I climbed a 17,000 foot hill to the north of the camp. My chill, or whatever it was, had passed away during the march and I felt fit and strong again. The clouds were dissolving and presently Everest showed over the snow-clad ridges. There were many fine summits in the south, but none to dispute this vast peak. For some time it was indistinct, but presently, when the sun sank, the mists clinging to it released their hold and floated away. We trained the telescope and were surprised to see how little snow had found refuge on the rocks. The northern face had been swept bare by a westerly wind that was still raging in unbridled fury and driving the snow from the North-East Ridge in a tenuous banner miles long. It was a fearsome sight, and not even the warm glow of the setting sun could mitigate its cold ferocity. We gazed intently at the upper part of the mountain, but our view was not encouraging. It was plain that the rocks were very steep, and that Everest was no easy mountain even by alpine standards. The Second Step looked uncompromising, but to the north of it we noticed a recess half-filled with snow, though neither of us liked the look of a long smooth-looking slab above it. When viewing a high mountain in detail from an elevation where comfortable breathing is possible, it is not easy to estimate difficulty, for difficulty cannot be dissociated from altitude. The final pyramid, which appears slightly foreshortened from the Base Camp, was seen in its true relationship with the rest of the mountain. If the Second Step could be climbed there was a choice of two routes: directly up a conspicuous triangular snow slope, or up the rocky North Face of the pyramid to the right of this. If, however, Norton's traverse route proved practicable, we should probably have a choice of three routes two of which finish up the summit ridge of the mountain from the north-east and the third up the North-West Ridge. I must confess to some pessimism on first seeing Norton's traverse. In the gathering shadows the head of the great couloir which it crosses looked very forbidding. How much better from a mountaineering standpoint was the ascent by the North-East Ridge as compared with this unpleasant-looking route leading far out on to the slabby face of the mountain.

As we gazed the last glow faded and Everest relapsed to an austere grey against a rapidly darkening sky where the first stars sparkled.

The descent was an easy scree-run, and soon we were telling Ruttledge what we had seen.

We were a cheerful company at breakfast next morning, knowing that in a few hours we should be camped in the Rongbuk Valley within sight of Everest. From Chö-Dzong, the valley gradually bends southwards, then it narrows and the hills on either hand become more precipitous, and the stream more turbulent. Presently we came to the two crags at the entrance of the Rongbuk Valley, dubbed by Norton "the gates of altitude", because the traveller who passes between them is immediately conscious of having left the plateau of Tibet and of being on the threshold of Everest. Beyond, the hillside is steep and craggy and the path narrow. It was heavy work for the donkeys, for their loads were continually bumping against out-jutting rocks and many of them collapsed from fatigue, only to be heaved on to their feet again and beaten and blasphemed into renewed activity.

We turned a corner; Everest should have been visible, but clouds filled the head of the valley. There had been a recent and severe blizzard, as in places snowdrifts concealed the path, whilst a bitter wind sweeping along the desolate valley whipped powdery snow into our faces.

The Rongbuk Monastery came into view, with its tiers of low buildings on a brown hillside. We pitched camp near it and were glad to escape into the mess tent from a searching wind. During the afternoon the mists slowly broke up and by tea-time Everest stood revealed, bathed in sunshine. Though the height of the north face is about 10,000 feet from the head of the Rongbuk Glacier to the summit, it was difficult to estimate the scale of the mountain. The North Peak approaches 25,000 feet in height, yet appears relatively insignificant beside its great neighbour. In colour Everest is an ochreish brown with a pronounced band of light-yellow sandstone traversing it horizontally 1,000 feet below the summit. Norton and Somervell's route was along this "yellow band" as it is now known. The two most prominent features of the mountain are the Great Couloir, which cleaves the northern face from the foot of the final pyramid almost to the Rongbuk Glacier, and the huge snowy plinth, which supports the north-west extremity of the mountain. In one respect Nature has sadly blundered; the North Peak, a massive, ugly mountain, conceals the sublime fall of the north face. Seen from this direction the highest mountain of the world deserves a finer setting.

We unpacked the astronomical telescope, and examined the mountain. Opinions formed a trifle hastily the previous day were discussed anew. There seemed just a possibility that the Second Step could be climbed directly from the crest of the North-East Ridge, for the telescope revealed the suggestion of a snow slope on the far side. Was it possible that the step was a fraud and that the crest of the ridge was continuous at this point? The evidence made this seem very unlikely. Once the Step was climbed the remainder of the ridge did not appear formidable, though the final snow slope on the face of the pyramid was steep. As regards Norton's traverse; if the head of the Great Couloir could be crossed and a conspicuous, sloping scree-covered shelf attained at the base of the final pyramid, the summit should prove accessible. An obvious place to pitch the highest camp was on a snow-covered ledge below the First Step at a height of about 27,800 feet.

Later, when a quick rush of sunset fired the great pile of rock, we forgot to consider detail and could only admire the fierce beauty of our adversary. Darkness fell swiftly, and when I turned into my tent the sky sparkled with innumerable stars and lightning flickered in the southern sky. The night was very cold, it seemed to me the coldest we had so far experienced, though the altitude, 16,000 feet, may have increased the apparent coldness and I for one shivered in my sleeping bag and woke with my beard icy from my congealed breath.

April 17 was Easter Monday; oranges and bottles on Hampstead Heath; for us, a blessing at the Rongbuk Monastery. We straggled to the monastery, armed with numerous cameras, passing en route a great chorten, which stands apart from the monastery and makes an impressive photograph with Everest in the background, and passed into a courtyard where two lamas were stationed, blowing for all they were worth into curiously shaped horns which made a noise reminiscent of the fog-horn near the Goodwin Sands. The walls of the courtyard had been recently painted in gaudy colours. To Western notions, some of the paintings were frankly obscene, but in Tibet it is the object of an artist to portray all aspects of human existence, not merely those calculated to pass muster with local watch committees. The God of War was particularly impressive, and the ruthless evilness of his countenance certainly symbolised the passions of combative men.

We were conducted through a doorway, and passing along a dark passage climbed two flights of steps, steep and slippery enough to merit considerable caution in nailed boots, on to a sort of roof verandah, at one end of which was a large glass-windowed cabinet, some eight feet in height and six feet in breadth, for all the world like a telephone booth. Within this cabinet the venerable Abbot of the monastery was waiting to bless the expedition, and he beamed upon us a welcoming smile so broad that his face seemed almost to divide into two halves. It did not take us long to realise that we were in the presence not only of a genial soul, but one of the great personalities of Tibet; humour, wisdom, kindliness, sympathy and understanding all shone in his large and mobile face.

Hugh tendered the respects of the expedition through Karma Paul, and presents were ceremoniously given and received. Ours were two finely brocaded cloths, a tea set and a leather suitcase. The last made the greatest impression, and we could only hope that it would prove useful. The Abbot's gift to us consisted of two dried sheep and a bag of meal, valuable commodities in this barren valley.

After these exchange of gifts he asked after the health of the "General Sahib": General Bruce is well remembered here. Then he wished us complete success and enjoined caution. If only, he said, we remembered to pray we should succeed.

Next came the blessing ceremony. The porters had been provided with a rupee each to present to the monastery and the usual ceremonial scarves, but many added their own money to the official gift, whilst some who had no scarves were given back those already presented so that they might present them in their turn. As the men approached the cabinet, they salaamed profoundly, many going down on hands and knees and touching their heads thrice on the stone floor. Then they presented their scarves and money, whereat the Abbot responded with a muttered blessing and touched each man's head with a small prayer wheel, whereupon the supplicant backed away, receiving as he did so a ribbon and a packet of sacred seeds from one of the attendant lamas.

When our turn came, for some reason, which my friends could doubtless explain, my appearance provoked a roar of laughter from the Abbot; indeed the old man chuckled and trembled to such an extent that I thought he would have an apoplectic fit. All of us had to say "Om Mani Padmi Hum", but the Abbot was not at all satisfied with my pronunciation of the prayer and made me repeat it several times. Finally he consented to be photographed and posed before a battery of cameras and cine-cameras.

From the Rongbuk Monastery to Base Camp is a walk of about five miles. We passed the village of Rongbuk, which must be one of the bleakest as well as one of the highest villages in the world, and followed the wide, gently sloping floor of the valley. That it is a holy valley is evidenced by the number of Mani walls, and in point of fact it is said that a former ruler of Tibet decreed that it should be preserved as a bird sanctuary, and that no life must be taken within sight of the sacred mountain of Chamolang (Everest).

To the west rises a finely shaped ice peak, reminding me of the Zermatt Weisshorn, whilst the eastern side of the valley is bounded by steep reddish crags. In one place an immense landslide had pushed a tongue over 100 feet thick some distance across the level valley floor, and piles of Mani stones had been placed at the edge of the debris, presumably to propitiate the mountain gods, whilst on the debris itself a hermit had constructed a cell, doubtless on the very reasonable assumption that another landslide was unlikely to occur at the same place.

After three or four miles of almost level going we came to the terminal moraine of the Rongbuk Glacier, and, passing between large mounds of stones, arrived at a strip of coarse grass by the side of a frozen pool which the old hands identified as the site of the 1924 Base Camp. At first sight it did not appear in the least comfortable, but later, when we were at higher and far more uncomfortable camps, we should probably compare it with the Elysian Fields.

The wind was blowing gustily up the valley from the north, so, while the porters busied themselves with pitching the tents, some of us crossed over the moraine ridge to the south of the camp, and basked in the sun on the windless side. The cairn commemorating the three previous expeditions had been built on this ridge in 1924, but it had since fallen down or, what appeared more likely, been deliberately destroyed by the superstitious Tibetans, and only a few scattered fragments with the remains of names upon them were to be seen.

The march across the plateau had told upon the party and several were unwell. Tommy was suffering from altitude more severely than anyone, and it was feared that he had strained his heart, Ferdie had developed lung trouble, whilst Wyn had a nasty chill, bad enough to be called influenza. Then there was a crop of sore throats and one or two could only speak in whispers. I was one of the few who could count themselves fairly fit, though an aching back, due possibly to my motor accident, made the carrying of a rucksack irksome.

Our arrival at the Base Camp coincided with Raymond's birthday, not a very happy anniversary considering the number of his patients, and we celebrated it that evening with a first-rate dinner on which Tencheddar was warmly complimented. Now that the kitchen was properly installed and feeding arrangements centralised, we looked forward to better meals than we had had during the march. The altitude, 16,800 feet, made sleep difficult that night, but there would be many worse nights in the future, whilst the thought that our long march across the dusty plateau of Tibet was over would have compensated for any discomfort. Now at last many plans were to be tested and many daydreams given a chance to materialise.

CHAPTER EIGHT

Camp 1 and the East Rongbuk Glacier

THE SUN TOUCHED the ridge of my tent at 7.15 next morning, April 18 and a few minutes later the whole tent was bathed in its warm light. No slog in the teeth of a biting dust-laden wind had to be done that day; our way lay upwards now, till the summit was reached, if the gods were kind.

The weather was perfect; not a cloud showed and Everest was without its usual plume of wind-driven vapour. There was plenty for all to do, as a vast jumble of stores and equipment had to be checked and sorted out for the high camps. My job was to ascend to the site of Camp 1 and ascertain how much room was available for tents, there having been some difference of opinion over this between the old stagers Shebby and Ferdie.

I set off with Nima Tendrup and trudged across a waste of glacier-borne stones to the shelf formed by the east-side moraine of the Rongbuk Glacier, a convenient route followed by previous expeditions which avoids a maze of moraines and ice.

Behind now were the dust-charged airs of the plateau; the atmosphere was crystal clear and the sun brilliant in an intensely blue sky, and only an occasional rush of cold air reminded us of more hostile altitudes.

As we progressed along the almost level shelf Everest slowly concealed itself behind the massive North Peak and peaks to the west of it were revealed, notably the shining ice-fluted ridges of Nuptse and the graceful cone of Pumori. What a district for a mountaineering holiday were it not for the gaunt wind-swept pile of Everest to awaken different thoughts.

To set off this noble background, the Rongbuk Glacier sweeps upwards in a serene curve broken in its middlemost portion by thousands of ice pinnacles arrayed like a march of giants solidified during a sortie from the heights.

About three miles from the Base Camp, the shelf peters out into boulder-strewn slopes. During the 1924 expedition, Captain Noel had managed to drive some mules to Camp 1, but the route was no longer possible for animals. Nima Tendrup had accompanied that expedition, but his memory of the route was vague and we kept too high round a corner, and had to descend several hundred feet to the camp site which is near the snout of the East Rongbuk Glacier.

A dozen or more stone sangers (shelters) erected by the previous expeditions were still standing, and it was evident that a thousand men could camp there if need be. The glacier stream a few yards from the camp was frozen over but some energetic work with the ice axe disclosed water and I had a refreshing drink. A cold west wind was blowing, but a sanger afforded protection and I spent a pleasant hour eating my lunch in the sun.

I had not finished when; chancing to glance upwards, my attention was caught by a tiny silvery object in the sky, apparently very high, moving rapidly from west to east. A second or two later it disappeared behind a shoulder of the range running southwards to the North Peak. Was it an aeroplane? If so, it must be a machine of the Houston-Everest Flight. But this was impossible; the last mail had brought us the news of their successful flight over the mountain. Was it a bird? But what bird could gleam so brightly?

It was pleasant to escape for once from the bustle of the expedition, and the afternoon was well advanced when Nima Tendrup and I strolled back to the Base Camp. There I related my experiences, but, in view of the fact that the first flight had been made, the others not unnaturally ridiculed the suggestion that I had seen an aeroplane.[1]

Next day, April 19 a party consisting of Shebbeare, Longland, Shipton, Birnie, Boustead, Wood-Johnson and Brocklebank, with a large number of our own porters and locally recruited Tibetans, all carrying heavy loads, established Camp 1, Meanwhile, Hugh and I worked hard at the stores. These were in boxes, coloured and marked for different camps, and it was merely a question of working out sufficient quantities for the first assault on the mountain. It looked very much as though difficulties were going to arise owing to the non-arrival of the porters, who had been sent for, from the Sola Khumbu valley in Nepal, and it was possible that the pass they must cross into Tibet west of Everest was still blocked with winter snow.

In the afternoon we made a minute examination of the upper part of Everest through the astronomical telescope. The mountain was in splendid climbing order and since our arrival at the Base Camp had showed few signs of wind. It was always a fascinating occupation to examine it through a high-powered telescope, and one productive of much argument, yet, as we all realised, time alone could prove the truth or otherwise of our theories and assertions. As that great mountaineer, the late Captain J.P. Farrar, was wont to remark, "You can't tell what rocks are like until you've rubbed your nose against them."

The Camp 1 party returned in the afternoon. One of the porters, Ondi, had been taken ill during the ascent, but with indomitable pluck had continued to

[1] A second flight was made on April 18 and Lord Clydesdale afterwards told me that the machines had silver dope on the wings, which would render them conspicuous at a great distance, especially in the clear Himalayan atmosphere. I cannot say the exact time that I saw the silvery object, but it must have been round about 11 a.m., though this is only a guess as I had no watch.

carry his load. Now he was in a state of collapse and came staggering slowly into camp helped by two of his comrades. He was immediately put to bed and within a very short time Raymond and Willy had diagnosed double pneumonia. Soon he relapsed into a coma and his one chance of survival depended on oxygen, for double pneumonia at an altitude of 16,800 feet must prove fatal unless oxygen can be administered.

That evening, I visited him in his tent; he was still unconscious. It was probably the last time I should see him alive and I remembered him with gratitude and admiration for the work he had done on Kangchenjunga and Kamet. The little toy whistle fixed to the valve of the oxygen apparatus, so as to make the flow of oxygen audible, sounded peculiarly pathetic, almost as though his life were escaping from him in a thin wail.

Later, just before turning in, I watched Smidge and Tommy, who had been hard at work all day erecting their wireless installation, trying to get in touch with Richards at Darjeeling, but without success.[2]

I woke at 4 a.m. Ondi's oxygen cylinder was being changed by the doctors and I heard Raymond tell Hugh that he was living but that his temperature was 104. At 7.30, when I got up, he was still alive, even better.

The condition of Ferdie was now causing anxiety. At such an altitude, there seemed little chance of recovery from his lung trouble, so it was decided to send him down with Ondi to the Kharta Valley for two or three weeks. It was a terrible disappointment for him, and we were all very sorry for his bad luck. If any expedition needed a professional "life and soul" he would fill the bill admirably. He was his usual cheerful self when he rode off on a pony. One danger of high altitudes is that once a man becomes seriously ill he is unlikely to recover unless he is sent down to a lower level. Everest is no mountain for invalids.

Wyn was still ill with influenza, but, fortunately, it was not considered necessary to send him down. At the same time, it was unlikely that he would be strong enough for work on the mountain for some time.

On April 21, Shipton, Longland, Birnie, Boustead, Wood-Johnson and I went up to occupy Camp 1. Eric and I started in advance of the others. We went deliberately slowly to avoid rapid breathing through the mouth, as Eric had a sore throat and an altitude cough, but we took only two hours to walk about four miles and climb 900 feet, Camp 1 being 17,700 feet.

It had been arranged originally that all six should sleep in one of the arctic tents, but when this was pitched we saw that it meant a crush, so Eric and I erected two small Meade tents and ensconced ourselves therein. These were tents of the same pattern that had proved so good on Kamet, homely, companionable little tents, yet capable of withstanding the worst weather.

We had not camped long before choughs appeared on the look out for scraps. They were quite tame and hopped about the camp eyeing us inquisitively, as though well aware that no animal life must be taken in the sacred Rongbuk valley.

The intensely dry air and hot sun were already ravaging our countenances. My lower lip had cracked so badly that I was careful to avoid hot condiments and foods. My beard, always a laggard, was coming on, but I was not yet accustomed

2 We heard afterwards that the Darjeeling station had been put out of action by lightning.

to the feel of it, and vowed I would shave it off at the earliest opportunity. A beard, of course, is an admirable protection against sunburn.

During the afternoon the weather threatened snow, but the clouds broke up later and the evening was calm. Increased height, coupled with the necessity for breathing through the mouth, had aggravated sore throats, whilst some were not yet well acclimatised; Jack, in particular, had a pulse of 130 when he arrived in camp and was breathing jerkily. In the end only George and Hugo slept in the Arctic tent, the others preferring Meades.

It was not until we unpacked the first of the glacier camp ration boxes that we discovered that instead of four pounds of sugar in each box there were only four ounces of this precious substance. This was a dreadful discovery, but, it was in part compensated for by the number of sugary foods. Many and terrible were the curses hurled at the firm responsible for the packing, but it was really the expedition's fault for not having supervised it. There was considerable grumbling also over the quality of the jam and sweets, and we found that the cheapest quality of Messrs. Crosse & Blackwell's jam, intended only for the porters, was preferable to that supplied by another firm to the Europeans.

My heart and lungs might be acclimatised to 17,700 feet, but not so my digestion. We had curry for dinner and it gave me hell. As I lay uncomfortably awake I remembered a notice I had once seen reproduced. It ran something like this: "A grand potato pie feast will be held for the brethren in the parish hall, after which Father O'Reilly will address the brethren, the subject being 'A Night in Hell.' "

The threatened storm broke during the night, and a fierce wind roared down on the camp, smiting our little tents. At 6 a.m., when I looked out, the sun was shining weakly, but an hour later the sky had clouded over. Then came a deep, long-drawn-out boom which I thought must be an avalanche, followed a few seconds later by another boom. It was thunder, an unusual occurrence on Everest. The storm lasted two hours, and seemed to concentrate on the range running south to the North Peak and on Everest itself. Later the wind dropped, and snow fell heavily.

I had never previously seen a thunderstorm at such an altitude and it would be interesting to know how far the thunderclouds extended up Everest. Before the monsoon, thunderstorms are usually confined to the warmer valleys south of the Himalayan watershed. The weather was in a surly combative mood, and it was impossible not to feel that Everest resented our coming and was giving loud tongue to that resentment. At all times a thunderstorm among high mountains is impressive and even at this altitude where the thin atmosphere tends to deaden sound the great chorus of echoes that reverberated from peak to peak was indescribably magnificent.

Long after the thunder had ceased, snow continued to fall; possibly the storm preluded a spell of bad weather, as is often the case in the Alps.

In spite of the snowing under of his kitchen Lhakpa Chedi, who was acting-cook, came up to scratch, and we breakfasted sumptuously on tea, porridge, fried ham and potatoes. Heavy snowfall is usually accompanied by passably warm conditions, but on this occasion it was so cold that when I cleaned my teeth the water in the tooth-mug froze in a few minutes. There was nothing to do except lie up for the day in our sleeping bags and listen to the dismal patter of the snow on our tents. For part of this dull time I busied myself writing a little description of this, our first camp, on Everest.

> A few minutes ago, the weather looked like clearing; the snow had almost stopped and there was a fierce white glare that seemed to presage the sun. Now the snow has started again, pattering on the roof of my tent. Sometimes when a gust of wind catches it, it hisses across the Willesden canvas like a snake; at other times, when the wind drops, it treads lightly, like a crowd of small, inquisitive people.
>
> It is 11 a.m. In England, the early workers will be breakfasting, men will be stoking up factory fires, the electric trains will be humming through the suburbs of London.
>
> Now and again a gust of wind shakes the tent, and the accumulation of powdery snow trickles off it to add to a rising drift. Occasionally, around me, I hear my companions cough or stir in their sleeping bags. By my side is my suit-case, and on it a miscellaneous collection of articles: a tin of throat pastilles, a pair of snow goggles, a pair of mitts, a candle-end, a knife, a map of Everest, a volume of *Pickwick Papers*, a pocket Testament, and a leather case containing photographs of my family. Near the end of the tent rests my green kit bag, a hat, a scarf, and a light rucksack intended for high altitude climbing. Over my double-layer, eiderdown sleeping bag is laid my thick llama coat, which I have never ceased to bless since we began to experience the Tibetan wind. Under my pillow are wedged sundry articles of clothing it is easier to sleep at a height with the head high.
>
> I am clothed in a pair of woollen combinations, a Shetland body belt, two pairs of Shetland pants, three Shetland pullovers, and a camelhair sweater. On my head is a woollen Balaclava helmet; the warmth of it round my ears and neck is most comforting. The tent is getting dark owing to the accumulation of snow. I bang the sides and the snow slithers off. How long will it continue to fall? Should the snowstorm develop into a severe blizzard and make life too uncomfortable in our Meade tents, we have always the arctic tent, the same pattern of tent in which Courtauld spent so many months on the plateau of Greenland.
>
> Still the snow falls, too regularly to hope for an early clearance. I have plenty of books to read, and *Punch* and the *Passing Show* arrived by runner only yesterday. How queer the little suburban jokes and tittle-tattle about actors and film stars seem here.
>
> Why are we lying here, when we might be eating and drinking in comfort at sea level? Yet, for some curious reason, I would not exchange the discomfort of Everest for the comfort of sea level. We curse our luck, we curse the discomfort, but we go on with it. Why? I wish I knew. My hands are ingrained with dirt, my face sun-scorched and sore, my cracked lips painful. 'Why do you do it?' How can we explain when we don't know? And we don't care whether or not we are understood – not a bit. We only know that in discomfort, in storm, in the beauty and grandeur of the mountains we have discovered something very much worth while.

The snow ceased falling in the afternoon and the sun showed through a thin mist. But the weather was still unsettled, and when night came the stars shone dimly. Dinner consisted of thick pea soup and Irish stew: a good meal, yet few of us slept well; I did not doze off until after 3 a.m.

April 23 dawned mistily. Snow lay several inches deep and the scene was bleak and wintry. Further inactivity was distasteful, and Hugo, George, and I decided to ascend the East Rongbuk Glacier towards the site of Camp 2. The new snow was deep enough to form bridges between the boulders of the side moraine of the glacier and we were continually breaking through and barking our shins. In such conditions rhythm was impossible and we jumped from boulder to boulder like paralytic cats, frequently sinking knee-deep into concealed ankle-twisting holes.

Presently we came level with the lowermost of the great ice pinnacles that are a feature of the glaciers in this region. How they are formed is still a matter for speculation among glacierologists, and there is nothing resembling them in the Alps. There are thousands of pinnacles of an average height of about 50 feet, some as high as 80 feet. Unlike the square-cut séracs of the Alps they are mostly tapering, some being amazingly beautiful and ending in crests of extraordinary fragility and delicacy. Here and there stones are embedded, but for the most part they are pure ice of a cold translucent green to which the deep blue of the sky contributes its own subtle tinge. To pass between their ranks is a fitting introduction to the highest mountain of the world, and he is unimaginative indeed who cannot feel the spell of this strange land.

We ascended the true left hand moraine, until a small glacier debouching from the west forced us on to a medial moraine which we reached by a simple but fatiguing traverse. The snow became steadily worse as we trudged along this, and a pitiless, nearly vertical sun resolved the landscape into a scorching, glaring expanse. Nothing was to be gained by exhausting ourselves and, at a point about a mile from the campsite, we decided to return: we had been going for about three hours. Finding a place more or less sheltered from the wind, which was beginning to blow venomously up the glacier, we lunched off sardines, biscuits, condensed milk and honey, concluding with a snowball treated with condensed milk, a passable imitation of a custard ice. We were tired, and my legs were like leaden weights, but as we descended we gradually regained strength and were once again able to interest ourselves in our surroundings, an interest too easily lost in the slogging work of mountaineering at high altitudes.

We could even muster sufficient mental energy to want to climb the fine peak north-west of the glacier, named by a previous expedition "Kellas's Dark Rock Peak",[3] which was subsequently to appear in the illustrated press on numerous occasions as "Everest".

On returning to Camp 1, we found Raymond and Tom, who had come up from the Base Camp accompanied by Policey. They told us that Waggers had been forced to remain there owing to stomach trouble. More welcome news was that Wyn was recovering from his chill and should be able to join us in a few days. Willy had accompanied Ondi, who was still very ill, as far as Rongbuk. On the way both sides of the stretcher had broken, and the sick man had fallen heavily to the ground. Raymond had some things to say about the manufacturer of this stretcher which I wish that gentleman could have heard. Incidentally, we were finding cases of food and equipment wrongly marked, and checking them made for a considerable amount of unnecessary work, which was doubly trying in the cold wind. The packing also in many cases did not correspond with the store book, and, to make matters worse, we found that some of our luxuries, including all the crystallised fruit, had been stolen, no doubt during the marches between Tengye Dzong and Shekar Dzong. The boxes had been so skilfully opened and closed that scarcely a trace of the tampering was to be seen, whilst to make up

[3] This peak, 23,180 feet high, was climbed by Shipton's party in 1935.

weight, stones had been substituted. It was infuriating to know that for many days porters and animals had been carrying boxes containing little beyond geological specimens from the districts where the thefts had taken place.

Wireless communication with Darjeeling had not yet been established, although Smidge and Tommy were working hard at the problem. It seemed strange that they should fail to get into touch with Darjeeling when they were able to receive the B.B.C. short-wave Empire broadcasts.

For supper that evening we had pea soup, baked beans and a little meat. Waggers had given me two thermometers to record maximum and minimum temperatures above the Base Camp, and the minimum recorded in my tent that night with the thermometer, which I forgot to put outside, only a foot from my body was 10°F. Yet, it felt a warm night; possibly we were becoming inured to cold.

I slept better, but lay awake for two hours, belching in a horrible manner, so too did others, judging from sounds from other tents, whilst often someone would have a coughing fit. Sore throats, coughs and "tummy troubles" are tremendous hindrances to climbing at high altitudes. The foul dust we had breathed for weeks on the march, combined with the cold, dry air and the necessity for breathing quickly through the mouth, had wreaked havoc on the membranes of our throats. To climb Everest we should have to rise superior to the many physical disadvantages of high altitudes.

CHAPTER NINE

From Camp 2 to Camp 3

We were glad of a rest day following our reconnaissance towards Camp 2. Next morning, April 24, the sun was shining from an unclouded sky. The minimum overnight temperature was –1° F. We did not turn out until 10 when we decided to complete the route to the site of Camp 2. Raymond and I started first and were followed by Eric, George and Tom. Walking was easier now that sun and frost had consolidated the snow; also we were better acclimatised. We reached our previous highest point in two hours; beyond this there was some heavy slogging through softer snow and we began to feel the altitude, not as a headache, but as an increasing tiredness and weakness in the legs. We were not sure as to the exact position of the campsite and as a result went too far up the glacier. Actually it was at the junction of a side glacier with the main glacier, on a slope of screes and ice beside a frozen glacier lake hemmed about on three sides by ice pinnacles. It was a weirdly beautiful place; the smooth snow-covered surface of the frozen lake might have been a dance floor for the mountain elves, and the ice pinnacles, slender and gleaming against the intensely blue sky, watchtowers to guard their revelries against intrusion. It was strange to think that the reeking chimney stacks of Lancashire and these shining spires of virgin ice were part and parcel of the same earth.

We were tired, a tiredness due primarily to sun and altitude, but once again our strength returned as we descended. We regained Camp 1, as the golden sunlight was relinquishing the peaks.

The temperature fell to –3°F. in the night, but owing to a strenuous day and improving acclimatisation I slept well and did not wake until the sun was up.

That day, April 26, Eric, George, Hugo and I with twenty Tibetan porters and four Sherpas, including Lhakpa Chedi, who was to cook for us, set off to establish Camp 2. Most of the snow, fallen during the previous storm, had melted and walking was comparatively easy. We improved on the previous day's route and for some distance followed the sharp crest of a medial moraine. The Tibetans were in good spirits and laughed and chattered gaily, apparently impervious to the effects of altitude in spite of their heavy loads. They included a woman who carried a load fully as heavy as any carried by the men; she seemed to enjoy it and her broad, smoke-begrimed face was one continual grin. These Tibetans seemed tireless, but it was noticeable that, although a mountain people, they had not acquired that slow, unhurrying labour saving pace so necessary in mountaineering. Their method was to hurry along for a short distance, then rest, but it is possible that their heavy loads, and the fact that they placed the greater part of the weight on their foreheads by means of a tump-band, had something to do with this.

On arriving at the camping site, Eric and I cut a hole into the frozen lake until the pure cold water bubbled up through the ice. The camp was well sheltered from the wind, but conditions were wintry, and when at 4.15 p.m. the sun disappeared behind the 22,000 foot peak west of the camp, the thermometer fell to 10°F. in a few minutes. The sun alone makes life possible at these altitudes. When there is no wind it is possible to bask thinly clad in its rays, but directly it disappears the cold from outer space seems to pour down on the earth. One moment we were strolling about warm and comfortable, the next we were wriggling into our sleeping bags.

The night was very cold and the temperature fell to –18°F. I slept little; I was warm enough, and could only blame the altitude for my insomnia. The hours, each longer and colder than the last, passed slowly. Once or twice I lit a candle and tried to read, but it was too cold, even with gloves on, to hold a book and my hands soon lost sensation and I was forced to replace them in the sleeping bag and restore circulation by rubbing them vigorously. There was dampness in the cold, and my breath congealed on the roof of the tent and on my sleeping bag in a thick rime.

Presently it was necessary to leave my tent. Extricating myself by slow degrees from the clinging folds of my sleeping bag, I huddled on my heavy llama wool coat, pulled on my camp boots, fumbled with cold fingers at the tapes closing the flaps of the tent and crawled outside. Among the pale, ghostly séracs beneath a myriad shivering stars an intense stillness reigned, broken occasionally by the pistol-like reports of splitting ice, and dull, tearing wrenches from the depths of the glacier.

Shuddering, I returned to my tent and with stiff fingers laced together the flaps and crept into my sleeping bag, where I spent the next quarter of an hour massaging the circulation back into my hands.

When I awoke next morning, April 27, the camp was quite silent; no one would rise until the sun arrived. And the sun was a long time arriving. Through the gauze-covered window of the tent I could see it shining brilliantly on the slopes above. It reached the ice pinnacles and a reflected opalescent glow invested the camp. Then a brilliant light was suddenly spilled on the ridge of my tent. Quickly it spread downwards, and the frost-stiffened fabric gleamed as though encrusted with powdered jewels. Soon the whole of one side of the tent was alight, and particles of rime began to fall from the roof, pattering on my frost-stiffened sleeping bag, lodging in my beard, exploring my face like cold finger tips.

The snow creaked to a footfall outside, a hand fumbled at the lacing of the tent, the tent flaps parted, and there was old Nima Tendrup, a grin on his face and a plateful of steaming porridge in one hand. How it went down, that porridge! I could feel the warmth of it spreading through my whole body, percolating to every toe and fingertip, the embodiment of life and energy.

It was a rest day; we were to remain at Camp 2 for a period to acclimatise and there was no object as yet in pushing on up the glacier. After breakfast Hugo and I climbed a slope of screes and snow behind the camp until we had a bird's-eye view of the East Rongbuk Glacier. Conditions were still very wintry, and powdery snow lay deeply in the hollows between the séracs. Above the level of the camp were thousands of séracs arranged in regular lines; then the glacier bent in a great S-shaped curve and disappeared between the East Ridge of Everest and the square, blunt mass of the North Peak. Camp 3 was to be pitched on the last bend of the curve, a shelter-less site and so exposed to north-westerly blizzards that the 1924 party was forced to retreat to the Base Camp. Perhaps with our arctic tents we should manage to weather the worst Everest might have in store for us there and at Camp 4 on the North Col. Today, with a clear sky, except for a diaphanous mist floating lazily from the summit ridge of Everest, the tale of storm and blizzard seemed remote.

Along the centre of the glacier runs a moraine forming a deeply cut channel or trough; up this trough former expeditions had passed, and the only problem was to discover the easiest route to it from Camp 2. Between it and the camp was another and less continuous trough, and it seemed best to follow this for some distance then traverse the glacier where it was least broken. We knew that once in the main trough we were unlikely to meet with difficulties. Unless it had changed materially since 1924, it would lead us through the tangle of séracs to the upper plateau of the glacier.

We descended to camp in time to join Eric and George at a lunch consisting of frozen turkey galantine and queer little balls of a doughy substance pronounced a great delicacy by Lhakpa Chedi, but which I for one found uneatable.

In the afternoon Ruttledge, Greene, Birnie, Brocklebank and Longland arrived. Tom had a slight chill whilst Jack was still unacclimatised to altitude; however, as I told him as he lay in his tent feeling pretty sorry for himself, he was probably another Odell.[1] Hugh, who was remarkably fit, said that Wyn and Waggers had recovered and were shortly coming up from the Base Camp to Camp 1. Shebby, after some stomach trouble, was also better and was at Camp 1 where nearly all our stores and equipment were now assembled. The "Bijli Wallahs" (Wireless

[1] N.E. Odell, after acclimatising very slowly in 1924, put up a remarkable performance on Everest.

Officers) were not yet in touch with Darjeeling and were experimenting with every conceivable combination of aerial and apparatus.

There was an argument that evening as to our dinner hour. Some wanted it early and others late. Early was taken to mean 4 p.m. and late 6 p.m. The cook and his assistants had to be considered, as the cold after sundown made it difficult to wash up. A compromise of 5 p.m. was finally agreed upon, with a hot drink in our sleeping bags at 6.

The sun disappeared at 4.15. The fall of temperature as it did so was extraordinary. At 4.10 the temperature in my tent was 65°F.; at 4.20 it was 20°F. and at 4.30 7°F.

There was another intensely cold night with the same disagreeable frosting-over of sleeping bags and tents, and the minimum temperature was –16° F. Perhaps 48° of frost does not sound much, but on Everest low temperatures are only half the story; the lack of oxygen must also be taken into account. Oxygen is fuel to the human body and without sufficient of it the body cannot maintain its warmth.[2] The most noticeable effect of oxygen lack at high altitudes is a quick loss of circulation in the extremities. Expose bare hands outside a sleeping bag when the temperature is round about zero and numbness supervenes in a minute or two, And once lost, circulation is difficult to restore, prolonged and vigorous rubbing is necessary and the process is painful.

The weather was uncertain next morning, April 28 the sky was half-filled with high clouds moving quickly from the west and a smother of snow was tearing across Everest. Hugh decided that George, Hugo and I should reconnoitre the glacier towards Camp 3. We left camp soon after 8 and, following the first medial moraine, made rapid progress. The moraine appeared continuous, though snow concealed it here and there, yet in one place there was a snow masked hole, it could hardly be called a crevasse, over which I stepped quite unaware of its existence. George, who was behind me, did not see it either, but accidentally put his ice axe through the snow-bridge. I had stepped unwittingly across a perfect death trap. It was only two or three feet wide at the top, but it was bottleshaped below and at least 100 feet deep to judge from the hollow sound of the stones we threw into it. After this we roped and, turning left from the moraine, and crossing a crevasse by a substantial snow bridge, passed between some minor séracs on to the uneven surface of the glacier. Here powdery snow lay deeply, concealing holes between slippery hummocks of ice. At first I led, and every time I floundered hip deep into an apparent crevasse, George yanked me backwards on the rope, as nonchalantly as a fisherman lands a sprat. So good did he prove at this that he was relegated permanently to second place whilst Hugo and I took turns at the track making.

Presently we crossed a minor trough in the glacier and, climbing a bank of glassy ice saw, framed between some ice pinnacles, a wide corridor thrusting its way up the glacier as far as we could see. This was the central trough, and our route towards Camp 3.

Threading our way between the pinnacles we descended into it without difficulty. Its floor was composed of scree alternating with soft, deep snow and

[2] It has been pointed out by scientists that somewhere near the summit of Everest, it is hoped *above* the summit, there is a critical altitude at which there is not sufficient oxygen to compensate for the loss of body heat due to breathing the intensely cold air. It is obvious that life cannot continue in such conditions.

progress was wearisome in the extreme. Furthermore, the sun was reflected from the pinnacles on either hand in a hot glare and we were soon troubled by the lassitude so often experienced by former Everest climbers, a mental and physical lethargy undermining all interest and determination. Had it not been for this we might have appreciated the beauty of this strange road, leading fairy-like through an enchanted forest of gleaming pinnacles.

We continued for another hour, then decided that further progress was unnecessary; the route was obvious enough, and it remained only to follow it.

A cool breeze was blowing up the trough as we descended, but on the snow-covered glacier there was such an airless blinding glare that our energy drained away like liquid through a funnel, and we were thankful to regain Camp 2.

Porters carrying more food and equipment, including an arctic tent had arrived from Camp 1. They had also brought with them Policey, who was noticeably feeling the altitude and panting rapidly; we could only hope that she would not have enough breath left for barking at night.

An arctic tent was pitched and we dined comfortably. As usual I slept none too well. At high altitudes a man breathes mostly through the mouth. This in my case used to result in an uncomfortable ring of ice round the neck of my sleeping bag, and on one occasion I woke, after a particularly vivid dream, under the impression that I was a small boy again and had just been kissed by one of my aunts.

Snow fell lightly in the night, but the weather was fine next morning and it soon melted and evaporated. I breakfasted in my sleeping bag and remained in my tent writing letters until lunchtime. Meanwhile Greene, Shipton, Birnie and Longland continued with the work of making the route to Camp 3.

During the day some porters arrived from Camp 1 in response to a note sent down by Hugh. It had been planned that they should spend a rest day at Camp 2, then go through with their loads to Camp 3, but, unfortunately, they brought up a number of unwanted oxygen cylinders instead of fuel. Fuel was of paramount importance, and its non-arrival delayed our start for a day. I had no objection to a rest day and lounged about in the sun listening to the vexed discussions of those whose job was to get up enough stores and equipment, so that we wretched climbers could assail Everest.

The latest news from below was that Wager, although at Camp 1, was still none too fit and that wireless communication had not yet been established between the Base Camp and Darjeeling. Apparently the mountains were blocking reception both ways. From all accounts the unfortunate Smijth-Windham and Thompson were almost in despair and were experimenting with every conceivable site for their aerial. Such was the first message, but a second, brought up by a porter only a few minutes later, said that communication had been established and that signals were at full strength. One problem at least was solved, but I suspect that Hugh hardly welcomed this news, as it meant he would now have to send telegrams to the newspapers.

Raymond and Jack of the Camp 3 party were back early, but Eric and Bill did not return till suppertime, when their absence was beginning to cause anxiety. In spite of soft snow in the upper part of the trough, they had got within a quarter of a mile of the camp site and had seen the North Col. There was nothing now to stop us from establishing Camp 3, and one immediate result of this good news was a cheerful company at supper in the arctic tent and a long tiger story from George, which was suitably capped with a jorum of hot rum punch.

Next morning, April 30, Hugh decided that George, Hugo and I should go through to the site of Camp 3, thereby completing the route for the porters, and examine the North Col through a telescope. We took with us two porters, Nima Dorje, the brother of an assistant cook, and Kitar, Hugh's servant. Because he was the Burra Sahib's servant, the latter was suffering from a swelled head, and had to be severely reprimanded more than once for disobeying orders.

There was now a well-trodden route up the glacier and we reached our previous highest point in half the time it had taken originally. Thenceforward we continued up the trough over stones and snow, then continuous snow, following the tracks of Eric and Bill. Higher up is a devil's garden of fantastic growths and profiles of gleaming ice; as though some Gothic designer had applied surrealism to an unusually vivid imagination yet never lost sight of beauty in his most extravagant constructions. Almost imperceptibly the trough peters out in the gently sloping uppermost reaches of the glacier. Here the ice pinnacles are evolved from the smooth surface of the glacier. To begin with they are mere nodules and low hummocks, then, as the glacier carries them down, they attain individuality and gain in height to become finally the noble structures with which we were familiar. Wind, evaporation, a great range of temperature and the movement of the glacier all play their part in shaping them, but it is a significant fact that they are only found in exceptionally dry climates and are not seen in districts where moister conditions prevail.

Wind had drastically denuded the glacier of snow, and we found ice of glassy hardness, indeed some of the hardest and most slippery ice I have trodden; it was here that several porters hurt themselves in 1922 and 1924. Nevertheless, we progressed fairly rapidly, aided here and there by patches of snow.

Presently we halted for some lunch. As we ate, the weather quickly deteriorated; a smooth, grey, fish-like cloud slid out of the west concealing Everest, and a strong wind rushed down the glacier, tearing up the loose snow and flinging it about in sheets.

We continued as quickly as we could, presently roping as a precaution against stray crevasses, but clouds gathered quickly, the sun weakened, shrivelled to a faintly glowing ball and vanished, and light, shadow and colour united in a single doleful monotone. The site of Camp 3 was obvious enough, but we should see nothing of the North Col if we reached it; there was no object in going farther, and we retired to Camp 2 in drizzling snow.

Towards evening the angry sky relented and, with an abruptness characteristic of high mountains, the clouds melted away, disclosing a colourful sunset. The stage was now set for the next act, the establishing of Camp 3 and the forcing of the route to the North Col. Mountaineering at last; an inspiring thought.

CHAPTER TEN

Below the North Col at Camp 3

I WOKE (MAY 1) with a feeling that this month would see the issue decided. The weather had regained its good humour and I spent the morning in my sun-warmed tent reading and writing. Some more porters arrived to help establish Camp 3, which Shipton, Birnie, Longland, Boustead, Wood-Johnson and I were to occupy on the morrow. Except for some very cold nights we had been moderately comfortable at Camp 2; discomfort on Everest begins at Camp 3. It would be good to be on the move again. Inactivity is worse than discomfort to a mountaineer, especially on Everest. The big task before us was never far from our minds, and it aggravated an impatience arising from the slow advance believed to be necessary for acclimatisation and the consolidation of camps with ample food and fuel. This slow progress was part of a prearranged scheme; the question is should a future expedition gain its acclimatisation on other mountains before reaching the Base Camp? If it did it would be spared much boredom, discomfort and deferred hope. There was the summit not very far away and we must wait and wait, and Everest is not a good mountain for a waiting game. Life at high altitudes is doubly trying to a civilised man. He ceases to appreciate beauty and becomes more and more crude in his thoughts and habits. He thinks for the most part of his comfort and of food and drink. He is a prey to a mental as well as a physical lethargy and gazes apathetically at scenes which he would be quick to understand and appreciate at lower levels.

During the day I washed for the first time since leaving the Base Camp and cut my fingernails, which were curiously dry and brittle. Much dirt was ingrained in my hands and only long scrubbing removed it. My moustache was long and straggled into anything I drank. I loathed the feel of it, and the feel of my beard, but both protected me a little from sunburn.

The sky clouded over in the afternoon and snow fell. During the snowstorm, which was not a heavy one, the dak runner arrived with letters from home. We grabbed our mail and retired to our tents like dogs to their kennels with succulent morsels. There was also a batch of newspapers, but their most startling headlines roused little interest: wars, revolutions, cabinet crises and the like – a cursory glance, nothing more; we were too concerned with our own small affairs, our own world of snow, rocks and weather. Were we parochial or did we look down like Olympian gods on the incredible follies of a far-distant world? Yet, this world ever reminded us of its manifold activities: clothing, boots, food, ropes, tents; its products were there to help us to the top of Everest.

Wyn and Waggers arrived during the day and we were glad to notice how much fitter they looked. Later it stopped snowing and the sun set frostily in a green sky.

After supper, Nima Tendrup brought me a hot water bottle, and with this warming my feet I told myself it was better to be a Sybarite and comfortable than a Spartan and uncomfortable. Life is too short not to make ourselves as comfortable as we can; there will be discomfort enough for some of us in the next world. Yet, in spite of this luxury I had a very bad night as something I had eaten died a lingering and agonising death within me. I did not sleep until 5 a.m., and was awakened at 6.30 by Hugh, who turned out in the bitter cold to hand over various items destined for Camp 3, including diaries in which meteorological notes were to be recorded. No leader ever rose earlier than he.

Feeling ill and disinclined to face the long slog to Camp 3, I somehow packed my gear and set off with Eric in advance of the porters. For the first mile or so I could scarcely drag one leg after the other, then the pain in my stomach gradually dissipated itself in a feeling of sickness which, in its turn disappeared.

The weather was good for three-quarters of the way, then degenerated into a desultory snowstorm. After nearly four hours we turned a corner beneath the crags of the North Peak and reached a side moraine where there was evidence of the Camp 3 of previous expeditions in the shape of old tins and expended oxygen cylinders. These last, we decided, would make excellent dinner gongs.

Nothing can exceed the efficiency of Sherpa porters when a camping site is reached. Within a few minutes they fashion a number of level platforms and erect the tents, which at once transform the stoniest waste into something sociable and homelike.

From the camp, the North-East Face of Everest was in full view. The mountain is not at its best from this direction. Much of the upper part of the North-East Ridge is concealed behind the North Ridge, whilst the final pyramid, although nearly 1,000 feet high, appears squat and unobtrusive, and it is impossible to estimate the width of the mountainside between it and the North Ridge.

The sun left the camp at 3.15 p.m., earlier than we had expected. As usual at the approach of night the snow ceased falling and the clouds quickly melted away, exposing the world to an intense cold, which seemed almost to flow down like some deadly liquid from the uttermost depths of space. Before turning in I walked out on to the glacier until the North Col was in full view. I had memorised photographs of it taken in 1924, and it was at once evident that the slopes had changed considerably during the past nine years. The ice chimney climbed by Mallory in 1924 had disappeared, whilst access to the Col via the easy but dangerous central route, the scene of the 1922 avalanche, was intersected horizontally by a formidable-looking ice cliff. The most conspicuous feature was an outward sloping shelf, slanting from low right to high left across the face of the Col. In bad snow conditions it would be exposed to avalanches, particularly in its lowermost portion, but there was ice there now; I could see its dull, lustreless gleam. Perhaps the best route to the shelf was the 1922 route, if the ice cliff could be climbed. Once gained, it should be possible to discover a moderately easy route to the crest of the Col.

We dined at 4 p.m. and afterwards had a hot drink in our sleeping bags. I slept well until midnight, when the usual ice forming round the neck of my sleeping bag, plus a rather sore throat, woke me. Snow was beginning to fall; I could hear the light swish of it on my tent.

I slept on and off until 7, when Nima Tendrup brought me my breakfast of porridge, tea, fried ham and biscuits. When I looked out of my tent I was astonished to see a mound of snow suddenly burst asunder, disclosing Policey busily wagging her tail and not one whit the worse for her temporary burial. She preferred to sleep in the open, and invariably refused the shelter of a tent.

The wind rose later and by sundown had reached gale force. This was our first taste of really bad weather. The little tents flapped wildly in the snow-charged gusts, but the porters had pitched them well and had tied the guy-ropes to large boulders and piled more boulders on the outside flaps.

The storm increased steadily during the night, and by midnight a hurricane was raging. I found sleep impossible until the small hours owing to dust-like snow infiltrating through the ventilator of my Meade tent and, as I noticed with considerable disquiet, through the tent fabric itself. This last was very serious. If our tents were not snowproof at Camp 3, how would they behave 6,000 feet higher where complete shelter and maximum comfort were vitally necessary? Fortunately we had some tents made of the same cloth as that of our windproof suits which so far had proved thoroughly satisfactory.

The worst nights pass. The wind dropped; dawn came and with it the sun. It was a fair morning, apart from smooth-looking reticulated clouds, lying in long regular lines from east to west, a portent of evil weather, confirmed by a low reading of the Watkins aneroid barometer. Some porters with more equipment, including arctic tents, from Camp 2, were expected, but they did not arrive; probably there was too much new snow in the trough and on the glacier.

We were tired of inactivity, and decided to reconnoitre the North Col. An easy but laborious side moraine led us up for about 800 feet to the upper plateau of the glacier. The wind had blown this almost completely free of snow, exposing ice as slippery as a skating rink, and most of us came croppers. Only Eric seemed unaffected; I think he had on a pair of new boots, with Tricouni nails, but he is one of those people who adhere to any surface. Crampons would have been useful, but they conduct cold to the feet and their straps impede the circulation.

We unanimously decided to attack the central route to the North Col. This meant scaling the ice wall, already mentioned and it looked a bad place for porters, but we remembered two rope ladders presented to the expedition by the Yorkshire Ramblers' Club. Once the wall had been climbed, one of these should suffice to consolidate the route.

In 1922 and 1924, Camp 4 had been pitched on a ledge only a few feet below the crest of the Col, but this no longer existed, and the only ledge we could see likely to prove wide enough for a camp was some 200 to 300 feet lower.

Before we could begin work on the slopes, Jack had to return to camp, as he was not yet well acclimatised. This left Eric, Hugo and myself to carry on, and an hour and a half after leaving Camp 3 we arrived at the foot of the slopes, a superb curtain of snow and ice apparently suspended from the dark-blue sky. Beneath them we felt very weak and small, and the summit of Everest was 7,000 feet higher – 7, 000 feet still to go.

Our way to begin with lay up a broad gully between two breasts of ice, a safe enough introduction as a slip or an avalanche could not carry a party over an ice wall or into a crevasse. The snow proved unexpectedly hard and wind-blown, and every step had to be kicked. We took it in turns to lead and after an hour and a half had gained perhaps 400 feet of height. Fixed ropes were unnecessary on this first section, but above it they would be essential for the porters.

We felt little wind but higher the snow was being driven across the North Face of Everest in great clouds, which writhed, far away from the mountain, vanishing like steam in the dark-blue sky.

The slope steepened gradually, and presently we were step cutting in icy snow. It was hard work and, as we were merely reconnoitring and had no wish to tire ourselves at such an early stage of our acclimatisation, we decided to return.

Mists gathered during the descent and we reached camp in falling snow. No one had come up from Camp 2, so George and Nima Tendrup descended that evening to find out what was happening there. The possibility of the monsoon arriving early was never far from our minds, and we felt that the sooner we got on with the job the better. One thing likely to delay us was that Camp 4 was to be occupied by the whole climbing party. This was accounted necessary in order that everyone should be acclimatised as soon as possible, but it would make porterage difficult and might delay the assault on the summit. Six climbers on the North Col should be ample: two for one attempt, two for another attempt, to act also as a support party at Camp 5, and two in permanent support at Camp 4.

It was a dull evening with a grey roof of clouds. We dined in the porters' tent pleasantly warmed by two Primus stoves. Pasang, the official cook, was suffering from altitude, but Lhakpa Chedi, who was full of energy, prepared a tasty meal.

That night I had a particularly vivid dream. My wife and mother had just sat down to dinner when I entered the dining room in my climbing clothes and gave them an account of our doings. It was one of the clearest dreams I have ever had and without a single fantastic feature, and I shall never forget their looks of astonishment. It was as though space had been annihilated for a few instants.

Altogether I had my best sleep above the Base Camp, eleven hours, but others were not so lucky, and next morning some complained of being kept awake by a feeling of suffocation. Yet, there were never any grouses and at times I felt almost selfish for the quick, easy way in which I acclimatised. Acclimatisation is purely a matter of luck, and it must be heart-rending to a man, who is a first-rate mountaineer and longing to put up a good show, not to be able to go well at high altitudes.

May 5 dawned mistily, but presently the sun struggled through. The peaks were dusted with freshly fallen snow and Everest looked very forbidding in its livid mantle with a dull white cloud clinging hungrily to the summit.

I breakfasted luxuriously in my tent off porridge, fried ham and tea and afterwards read *Pickwick Papers*, pausing now and then to anoint myself with face cream. My lips were now in a fair state of repair, thanks to frequent applications of cream, but my nose was very sore, particularly at the base of the nostrils and I had picked my face and ears till blood came: there is nothing more difficult to resist than the craving to accelerate the departure of flaking skin.

During the day, Ruttledge, Brocklebank, Greene and Wood-Johnson arrived from Camp 2 with a large body of porters; a heavy day's work as the snow had drifted deeply in the trough. The porters were in fine fettle, except for one grouser, my first cameraman and an "old soldier", Tsin Nurbu. It was important to keep an eye on grousers; pessimism has a knack of spreading rapidly on Everest.

A high wind rose at sunset and blew violently all night. Few slept owing to fine, powdery snow penetrating the tents, and my diary of May 6 begins laconically: "Another bloody day".[1]

The morning sky was cloud-streaked with a plume of furious wind-driven snow on every peak, and a huge one raging from Everest. We had hoped to continue with the work on the North Col, but it was the windiest morning we had yet had and to start was manifestly impossible.

As the day progressed, the wind increased in violence. Making a great effort during a lull, we erected an arctic tent on a small frozen pond, which formed a conveniently smooth floor. We did not expect Wager and Wyn Harris from Camp 2, but on the off chance that they might brave the gale several of us struggled down the glacier through the snow-laden gusts. Once round the corner of the North Peak we escaped the worst of the wind and saw them coming up the glacier. Policey was with them; she had descended with George and was now returning eager for the fray. It was a tough pull for their porters over the last mile, but with heads down and emitting shrill whistles between their clenched teeth they struggled to the camp and dumped their loads with tired but satisfied grunts.

That night Bill, Eric, Raymond, Tom and I slept in the arctic tent. It was a great improvement after a small Meade, but even so we woke in iced-up sleeping bags cursing an unpleasant rain of snow, formed by our condensed breath, falling from the sun-warmed roof. The minimum temperature was –12°F. in the night.

CHAPTER ELEVEN

The Ice Slopes to the North Col

THE 7TH OF MAY was another day of foul weather, and a high wind did its best to blow the camp away. How Policey survived such days and nights I cannot imagine. At 6.30 a.m. when I looked out of my tent she was almost a solid ball of snow and ice, but on seeing me her tail wagged, breaking loose from its icy bonds with an audible crack. In spite of the abominable weather, a day of complete inaction was not to be thought of, and Ruttledge, Birnie, Shipton, Longland, Boustead and I, accompanied by Nima Tendrup and Pasang carrying ropes and wooden hollow-spar pitons, set off for the North Col slopes.

The wind on the glacier plateau beneath the Col had stripped the ice almost completely bare of snow and it was difficult to keep on our feet. From the crest of the North Col pennons of snow were streaming far upwards into the blue. And, higher still, Everest was the embodiment of elemental fury. It reeked and smoked like a volcano, and its yellow crags and slabs showed dimly through writhing clouds of snow rushing along at a speed of fully one hundred miles an hour.

Long before we reached the foot of the Col it was evident that Pasang was not

[1] See Author's introductory note.

going well; he was stumbling on with a sort of grim determination painful to see. We divided his load between us and sent him back to camp. Old Nima Tendrup was, as usual, lumbering along with an apparently tireless gait, but he complained of cold feet and we noticed that he was not wearing his wind-proof suit. These porters are improvident fellows.

We had expected to find the slopes of the Col sheltered from the wind, but we were soon disillusioned. The wind poured rather than blew over the Col and the ridges of the North Peak and descended almost vertically into the glacier basin, whirling huge columns of snow before it. In places snow had been stripped from the face of the Col and a blue gleam here and there suggested some prolonged, step cutting before Camp 4 was pitched. At the same time, the steps we had made three days previously had vanished completely and would have to be re-made. Our original plan of establishing Camp 4 by May 10 did not seem likely to mature; in such conditions it would take three days at least to force the route and another day or two to stock the camp with provisions and equipment for the higher camps. It was even more doubtful whether all the climbing party would be able to live there as Hugh had planned, as owing to the non-arrival of the Sola-Khumbu men, we were short of porters.

The wind was too unpleasant for climbing on the slopes, and we dumped the ropes and pitons by a fallen ice block at the foot of them and returned to camp.

During the evening the wind dropped and the weather showed signs of improving. The night was calm and it was a relief not to be constantly awakened by the thrumming and drumming of the tents.

The morning of May 8 was fine; only a slight fuzziness remained in the sky to remind us of yesterday's hurricane, and the Furies, worn out after days of continuous exertion, slept. Nevertheless, it was very cold, the minimum temperature in the night being –20°F.

Something we never properly appreciated was the work of the cooks. These unfortunate men were the recipients of much abuse, yet however bad the conditions they almost invariably produced a good breakfast. One advantage they had over us was the warmth of the cooking-stoves, and they would keep them going all night unless carefully rationed. Fuel is precious at 21,000 feet.

Before breakfast Lhakpa Chedi sliced a finger badly with a knife, and Raymond was called from his sleeping bag to attend to him. The Sherpas and Bhotias are careless of wounds as a rule and appear to feel pain far less than a European. It is the prospect of injury rather than the injury that upsets them. Neither do they mind the nastiest medicines, and I have seen them swallow castor oil as if they liked it. Also they are careless of the cold and have not yet learnt to guard themselves properly against frostbite. Superstition and a cold wind are the two things that undermine their morale quickest.

With the exception of Tom, who was still able to enjoy smoking, there was not one of us now who had not an uncomfortably dry or sore throat. Some could only speak in husky whispers and many were racked by tearing coughs.

Hugh had decided overnight to send up a party of four, Eric, Raymond, Jack and myself, to pitch a camp on the glacier plateau near the foot of the North Col slopes, as this would obviate a fatiguing trudge up the moraine to the plateau, and economise the energy of the climbers, who were in for a tough piece of work on the slopes of the Col. This work was to be done in relays, and the first party who occupied this new camp, Camp 3a we called it, would be followed by a second party of four consisting of Wager, Wyn Harris, Birnie and Boustead.

The porters were in good form and Policey insisted on accompanying us, thus reaching a height of nearly 22,000 feet, surely a world's record for quadrupeds. She did not appear to mind the glacier in the least, and gaily leapt crevasses or floundered gallantly through patches of soft snow.

The glacier plateau was mostly bare ice, but there remained in one place an extensive and deep patch of windblown snow, of solid consistency that held tent pegs well. When we arrived, the sun, shining weakly through a deepening haze, was completely encircled by a halo; another blizzard was brewing.

The porters, together with Wyn and Waggers, who had accompanied us for exercise, returned to Camp 3, and we set about making ourselves as comfortable as possible. Eric appointed himself cook and a very good cook he proved. We had a Primus stove, and a fug of such density was created in the arctic tent that, as someone remarked: 'You could cut it up into pieces and throw it outside.' After lunch we decided to continue with the work on the North Col and fix the first of the ropes. The snow was in better condition than before, and kicking and cutting steps, we made rapid progress to the foot of a steep slope leading up to a great crevasse.

It was after 5 when we decided to turn back. The sun had long since vanished and a deathly cold was creeping down the slopes. We drove in one of the long wooden pitons and attached a rope, then descended, putting in intermediate pitons en route, until the full length of the two hundred feet of rope was out, after which the lower end of the rope was attached to another piton.

Our work done, we descended rapidly to the lower slopes, where it was possible to glissade. Here Raymond came a nasty cropper. He was sliding down hard snow when suddenly his feet dug into a patch of soft snow and he took an awkward forward toss, twisting a stomach muscle. Finally, Jack, who, in spite of a high altitude cough had done a full share of the work, offered up his all at the foot of the slopes. He was feeling far worse than anyone, yet it was natural for him to be in the van of the attack.

It was snowing heavily when we arrived back in camp, but in spite of this we had a cheerful evening, except that our dinner was spoilt by some atrocious tinned veal. It was the worst tinned meat I have ever tasted and, for once, I think that not even fastidiousness due to altitude was to blame for our dislike; I can only compare it to a mass of jellified string. The remainder went down the nearest crevasse; it must have given the East Rongbuk Glacier severe indigestion.

The arctic tent held four of us comfortably, and we slept with our feet towards the centre like spokes of a wheel.

Snow fell heavily all night, but we were warm and moderately comfortable, although the snow beneath the tent did not form such a soft bed as might be supposed, and became lumpy and uneven, due to the weight and warmth of our bodies.

It was still falling when May 9 dawned. Four to six inches had already come down and the weather seemed likely to double that quantity. Things looked black. It might be a long time now before we reached the North Col, as a heavy fall of snow would make the slopes impracticable owing to the danger of avalanches. There was nothing to be done except to hope for the best. Our remarks on the weather were terse and bitter. Luck was dead against us; neither in 1922 nor 1924 had such continuously bad weather been experienced. The only kick I got out of it was chaffing Raymond, who had decided to stop at the camp in spite of his damaged stomach muscle. Before starting on the Kamet Expedition he said that he always brought good weather, and on that expedition he certainly had, but Everest had defeated him. Fortunately there was not much wind, except for an occasional gust, but it was tedious lying in our sleeping bags listening to the snow hissing down the sides of the tent.

Meals took a long time to prepare. Once the "Primus" ran short of fuel, and when I went out to get some more paraffin I had difficulty in finding the tin as, it had been buried by snow. When at length I re-entered the tent, plastered with snow from head to foot, the others laughingly called me Captain Oates. Indeed, the scene outside might have been transported from the Beardmore Glacier. Nothing was visible save our solitary blister-like tent, looming fantastically through the driving snow, and the morning was as dark as an English November day.

We took turns at the miserable business of "washing up", which consisted of rubbing the plates and other utensils with snow, and at obtaining supplies of ice for cooking purposes. To get this last it was necessary to go some distance from the camp and shovel away the freshly fallen snow until the glacier was bared.

Lunch consisted of a galantine of chicken and veal frozen solid, a hot drink, biscuits and butter; then, once more, we settled down in our sleeping bags for the long afternoon and evening. The time was partly killed by a discussion on mountaineering ethics, whilst in the interludes would come in a hoarse whisper from Eric, "Oh, for a few dozen eggs!" Yes, we would have given much for fresh eggs, as already we were heartily tired of tinned food. It lacked the vital quality of fresh food; there was something dead about it.

Early in the afternoon there was a temporary weather clearance, but soon it was snowing again. At 3 p.m. we were surprised to hear voices. Wyn and Waggers, with Bill in charge of the transport, had arrived from Camp 3, bringing with them another arctic tent.

The day ended dismally, and snow was falling heavily as we cooked our supper. At 7 we drew our sleeping bags over our ears in preparation for another long night. It was a cold night, too; a pair of camp boots, which I used to heighten my pillow, remained snow-covered, whilst the neck of my sleeping bag creaked with the congealed moisture from my breath every time I moved. None of us slept well; to sleep well at high altitudes a man must be very tired and we had had no exercise.

I woke next morning, May 10, from a desultory slumber to see the tent glowing as though it were on fire; the sun had risen in an unclouded sky. It was a perfect day, but how could we utilise it? There was nearly a foot of new snow and streams of it were pouring like water over the ice cliffs of the North Col. Possibly, on the morrow when the snow had had time to consolidate conditions might be safe.

A calm dawn was succeeded by a wind that blew the snow about in clouds on the glacier. It was fearfully cold, and had it not been for the arctic tents we might have been forced to retreat before this, as no one can stick out such weather as we had experienced since arriving at Camp 3 without deteriorating unless he is warm and moderately comfortable. We were very depressed. Not only did the North Col appear more difficult than it had been in 1922 and 1924, but conditions remained continuously and obstinately wintry. With the non-arrival of the Sola-Khumbu men our transport might prove inadequate to take advantage of a short spell of fine weather, and we should be reduced to emergency tactics – a dash for the summit by an unsupported party handling its own transport.

We discussed many things but our thoughts always returned to the immediate problems. We agreed that our only hope of climbing the mountain was to take an arctic tent as high as possible and stick out the weather until a fine spell arrived. But could we stick it out? Life at high altitudes is exacting, both mentally and physically. Worn nerves, sore throats, and general debility including loss of weight and lowering of the whole bodily system must be expected. Altogether it was a gloomy prospect.

The night of May 10 was the coldest I ever remember – indeed, as we all agreed, the coldest of the expedition; but it is possible that the altitude intensified the cold and our camp was pitched on snow and ice, always a colder floor than rock. One thing was very evident: the wind was worse on the glacier plateau than at Camp 3. We had anticipated some shelter at least in the lee of the North Col, but as already mentioned the wind seemed to flow down from the Col and the glacier plateau formed a cauldron for its fury.

The morning of May 11 promised better weather, but optimism was at a discount; we felt that Everest was merely playing with us. Once again we set off, this time through deep and fatiguing snow, digging out en route a dump of ropes and pitons at the foot of the Col. Then again came the treadmill-like action of climbing slopes covered in powdery snow lying loosely on a hardened slippery substratum. The snow got worse and worse as we gained height, and by the time we reached a small crevasse, where the slope steepened considerably, it was obvious that to progress further meant risking avalanches. The snow had about it that smooth velvety appearance suggestive of wind slab, and with Alpine memories of this treacherous kind of snow at the back of my mind I had no hesitation in pronouncing for retreat.

Jack was again going badly. His altitude cough was so violent that it sometimes caused him to vomit his food. Nothing could be more weakening at a high altitude, but as before he gallantly insisted on accompanying the party. To cap our discomfiture, the weather showed signs of breaking. Grey clouds came flying out of the west and joined with the mists already streaming from the crest of Everest. On arriving back in camp I sent a note to Hugh telling him of the bad conditions and that all we could do was to play a waiting game.

In spite of reverses and disappointments and the general unpleasantness of life, we were a merry party that evening in the arctic tent, and Raymond, who had recovered from his stomach injury, once again entertained us with some of his stories, which not even an altitude of 22,000 feet could dull in the telling.

Another windy night followed, but it was some consolation to know that the wind, while doing its best to blow our tents away, was stripping the loose snow from the face of the North Col.

Breakfast next morning was the usual dreary affair. There were the plates with the remains of supper congealed on them, the knives and forks in a similar plight, the cups with their frozen dregs. Of course things should have been cleaned after supper; of course they never were; it was too cold; it was better to creep into one's sleeping bag and stay there. Then there was the usual wrestle with a recalcitrant cooker; an irksome job, accomplished with cold fingers to the accompaniment of many curses.

But there was at least cause for some satisfaction; the weather was definitely better and the sun shone hotly from an unclouded sky. Two porters arrived from Camp 3 to carry ropes and pitons, and with them we set off for the North Col. As usual, our steps had disappeared, and we had to dig out the fixed ropes. Kick-kick. Cut-cut. Waggers and Hugo shared the work of remaking the route – then Eric and I went ahead. Presently we came to the section suspected of wind slab. We halted and I went ahead on a belayed rope and sounded the slope with my ice axe. The snow varied in depth and hardness; sometimes there was a crust and sometimes not; it could be trusted not to avalanche.

We passed the uppermost limit of our previous reconnaissance. Next came the steep slope, leading up to the great crevasse. It was hard work climbing this as the axe had to slice through a superficial covering of powdery or wind-crusted snow into hard névé, and I soon discovered that to keep on step-cutting I must economise my energy, and that such economy could only be effected through a deliberate lung action in time with the swing of the ice axe.

The slope steepened, and during the last hundred feet to the crevasse we could stand upright in the steps and touch it with our hands. I have never worked out this angle, but it must be over 50°. It was a relief to gain the nearly level shelf formed by the lower lip of the crevasse. The scene here was superb. At our feet were the depths of the crevasse fading from sunlight to an iridescent green and deeper still to an impenetrable twilight, whilst on either hand rose walls of glistening ice. Fortunately at one point the crevasse was well choked by a mass of snow, possibly the debris of an avalanche. Immediately above it was a concave punch-bowl-like slope, bounded on three sides by ice cliffs, a place to distrust instinctively if only because of the moat-like crevasse at the foot of it.

We slumped down in the snow for a rest. For once we could rest comfortably; as yet no storm clouds had formed and the sun shone from a dark-blue sky with the lambent heat of an arc lamp. In the north-east were the brown expanses of the Tibetan plateau, and in the far east, in an atmosphere devoid of the slightest haze, the shining battlements of Kangchenjunga. Everest was still a weary way above us, and as I gazed at it I remembered something Mallory had written: "We expect no mercy". Neither did we. There is nothing merciful about these altitudes. You may sentimentalise over beauty afterwards, but beauty is far from the mind when you are toiling upwards through the thin, cold air. There is monotony in the snow, hostility in the ice cliffs, cruelty in the yellow outward-shelving slabs. The final pyramid is the inmost citadel of a Giant Grim whose lungs are filled with the breath of storms.

Slowly the warmth, drained away during the slow advance to the crevasse, returned to our feet and after a snack of food we drove in a piton and let a long length of rope down the slope. Then we continued with the ascent.

After crossing the crevasse and climbing a steep little bank we entered the punchbowl. Neither Eric nor I fancied the snow here, but after examining it carefully and prodding it with our axes we decided that it was too powdery to avalanche.

The final slope to the foot of the ice wall was steep and the snow upon it, though unlikely to avalanche, was fatiguing to climb owing to a slippery crust a foot or more below the surface. My first thought on reaching the foot of the ice wall was that at all events it was not so formidable as the one Hoerlin, Schneider, Wieland[1] and I had climbed on Kangchenjunga in 1930. My next thought was that, unlike the Kangchenjunga wall, it was perfectly safe from ice avalanches, and could not possibly break away.

At its lowest point the wall was about forty feet high, of which fifteen feet were vertical, possibly even overhanging. To right and left it rose abruptly, forming impassable ice cliffs over a hundred feet high, and in one cliff, fully fifty feet below the surface of the ice, we were surprised to see a projecting rope end, a relic of the 1922 or the 1924 expedition. It was a proof of the great quantity of snow which falls on the North Col and also of the rapid downward movement of the ice masses, as it is probable that this rope had been carried from the site of Camp 4 which in 1924 was on a ledge only a few feet from the crest of the Col.

Some loose snow that had poured down from above was piled fanwise against the foot of the wall, and this had to be trodden down and consolidated into some sort of a ledge. This done, I began to cut the first step. Directly I swung my ice axe I recognised the ice as the tough, almost rubbery stuff peculiar to the High Himalayas. Cutting steps in such ice is a tiring business, as often the pick sinks into it, as though into glue, without chipping any away, and has to be wriggled out.

At length the first step was made, but when I tried to stand in it, I found it impossible to keep my balance without support from Eric owing to the outward bulging ice. Jack and Waggers had now arrived, and Jack produced a piton from his rucksack. Although intended for rocks it would at least serve as a belay, and, supported by Eric, I reached up with both arms and, after one abortive attempt, managed to hammer it into the ice. Jack, an Admirable Crichton, had also brought a karabiner and this was attached to the piton ring and the rope passed through it. Provided that the piton would hold, I was now supported from above and able to continue step cutting without falling off backwards. With my left foot well planted in one step, I cut another step to the right above the overhanging bulge large enough for both feet. The difficulty now was to get first the right and then the left foot across to this step. But first of all a rest was essential as I was panting so rapidly that I felt quite dazed; also, in addition to footholds I had cut handholds and my hands were losing sensation. At the foot of the wall I soon recovered breath, energy and circulation. Then, feeling better, I set off again, but found that the only way of reaching the new step was to stand on the piton with my right foot. This was by no means easy in the broad, clumsy, high-altitude boot and at my first attempt my foot slipped and, being now without support from above, I was within an ace of toppling off backwards. Fortunately my left handhold and foothold prevented this, though the shortness of breath due to such an unexpected

[1] Uli Wieland died on Nanga Parbat in 1934. *Requiescat in Pace.*

exertion nearly caused me to come off anyway. A second attempt was successful, and once both feet were on the capacious hold the worst was accomplished.

Above was ice of an angle of about 70° covered in loose powdery snow which had to be shovelled away with the gloved hands and the head of the ice axe before steps could be cut. It was savage going. Every minute I had to halt and gasp for breath, and beat my frozen gloves together in an effort to keep the circulation going in my hands. At length, to my great relief, the ice axe no longer met pure ice, but hard névé. A few cuts now with the adze end sufficed for a step and progress was rapid. The névé gave place to pure snow, soft on top but well packed beneath, and it was enormously comforting to feel the foot sink deeply into it. I trod out a platform, plunged in the axe up to the head, put the rope round it and sank down for a rest. I was feeling pretty done and my heart was pumping as though it would burst; yet I remember a thrill of exhilaration. This was altogether different from the monotonous work we had so far endured; it was mountaineering.

Presently Eric, climbing in his usual effortless style, joined me. The others had not roped on to him, as they had decided to descend and fix ropes in the punchbowl and on the slopes below the crevasse.

From our position we were able to examine the slopes above. There was no sign of the ledge which accommodated the 1922 and 1924 expeditions, and the only ledge we could see likely to prove large enough for a camp was the one, already noted, some 200 to 300 feet below the crest of the Col. To reach it we first of all plodded across the wide, steeply inclined shelf which might be very dangerous in bad snow, whilst the route up the ice wall formed a natural channel for any avalanches that fell from it. Then we passed to the right of a detached sérac, and ascended diagonally beneath an ice wall to the left of a great blade of curiously stratified ice. Half an hour later we were on the ledge. It was formed by the lower lip of a half-choked crevasse, the upper lip being an overhanging ice wall some thirty feet high, whilst above it a very steep slope swept upwards to the crest of the Col. As far as it went it was a good site. There was a nearly level space some forty feet long and twenty feet broad for the tents, but an obvious disadvantage was the risk of an avalanche falling on to it; furthermore, the ledge was not as near the Col as we could have wished. It was just possible that there was a higher camping site, but we were too tired to explore further: my legs were unusually weak and my heart was still hammering unpleasantly against my ribs.

Murky clouds slid up over the snowy edge of the Col above; snow began to fall and the wind rushing round unexpected corners whipped it rudely into our faces. Down we went, visions of steaming tea in our minds.

In the fading light the ice wall looked terribly forbidding, but mercifully a length of rope attached to an ice axe now dangled over it. Eric went first and I gave him an additional rope as a safeguard. I could not see him and he could not let me know verbally when he had reached the foot of the wall as his voice had long since departed, but he jerked the rope as a signal for me to follow. It was an unpleasant descent. The wind racing along the crest of the wall whirled the snow viciously into my face, and I had to remove my iced gloves and grip the rope with bare hands: I placed it between my legs, under my right armpit and so over my shoulder and, hoping devoutly that Eric was holding it below so as to prevent any swinging, slid rapidly down through the smother of snow and alighted beside him.

It was now late in the afternoon and the cold was increasing. To encourage the circulation to return to our extremities we fairly raced down the punchbowl to the crevasse. The others had fixed ropes on the slopes below the crevasse, and aided by these we soon descended to the lower slopes. Back in camp our visions of tea materialised, and never did visions materialise more effectively.

That evening we felt more optimistic than we had done for some time; whatever the weather, there was a known route and fixed ropes to help us up it. But the weather, annoyed at our presumption, raised a gale in the night: Jack, Wyn and Waggers, who were to fix a rope ladder on the ice wall and rope up the remaining steep bits of the route on the morrow, would have a dismal time remaking the steps.

May 13 was a rest day for Eric and me, and we descended to Camp 3 to collect the gear we needed for Camp 4 and the higher camps. I was not feeling well; my heart was thumping quickly, and there was a dull, half-strangled sensation about the way it worked. We were greeted by Hugh, who was very pleased that the route to Camp 4 had at last been made. Ferdie had come up from Camp 2; he was much fitter, having recovered quickly from his chest trouble. Tom and George were also there, the latter very depressed at the thought that he was for the time being relegated to Camp 3 to organise the transport between it and Camp 4. He longed as much as anyone for a crack at the mountain and it was very hard luck on him, but as Shebby was too unwell with laryngitis to tackle the whole of the transport problem, somebody had to be sacrificed. We did our best to console him by telling him that he was doing as valuable work as anyone, as indeed he was. Hugh was not very fit and was obviously feeling the altitude. He had a very bad throat and on medical advice was about to go down to Camp 2 for a day or two. Bill had been hard at work planning a modified, scheme of attack which would make an assault possible with the minimum number of porters, in the event of the non-arrival of the Sola-Khumbu men. As we all agreed, there was little enough time in which to climb the mountain before the monsoon arrived. Two more weeks should see the fate of the expedition settled one way or the other.

Eric and I spent some pleasant hours at the camp, then tramped back to Camp 3a. Eric was going well, but I was very tired, and could scarcely drag myself up the glacier. The slightest exertion accelerated my heart and I wondered dismally whether I had strained it on the ice wall beyond all hope of immediate repair. Anyone who makes a severe physical effort over 22,000 feet has to pay for it afterwards.

On the way we met a party of porters returning from the camp after carrying up some more provisions. They grinned and salaamed as they passed us, striding downhill with the loose rolling gait of born mountaineers, and chattering gaily among themselves as though they had not a care in the world. What splendid fellows they were. It was heartening to see them. If it were humanly possible to establish a camp within striking distance of the summit they would do it. They made me feel very humble. Here was I trailing miserably up the glacier, with a bumping heart and weak legs, worn out after a single day's work, and here were they looking as though they were only at the beginning of the expedition, not with many days of exacting toil behind them.

I was thankful to reach camp and drop down on my sleeping bag too done almost for the hot drink prepared by some Good Samaritan.

There was a full gale that night, and sleep was impossible owing to the drumming of the tent, and sharp crashes due to the impact of sheets of thin ice whipped off the glacier by the wind.

The wind did not drop at dawn as it usually did, but went on for some hours. As soon as it abated Bill, Eric, Hugo and I, with twelve porters, set off to the site of Camp 4. Wyn, Waggers and Jack had done great work the previous day in roping nearly all the route and fixing a rope ladder on the ice wall. They had made the track anew, but as usual the gale had ruined it, and once again we had to kick it out; wretched work; how detestable those slopes had become. The weather was in a fiendish mood. It was putting every obstacle in our path, and doing its best to undermine the spirit of enthusiasm in the expedition.

I noticed grimly that the porters seemed almost to enjoy the ascent. After a few days, they would be as sick as we of the stamping, kicking and cutting. It was a slow job getting them, one by one, up the ladder, and took altogether one and half-hours. Hugo bravely remained at the top of the ladder for both their upward and downward passages, and as a result suffered severely from the cold, which gathered like some deadly liquid on the slopes when the sun disappeared behind the North Col.

From the camp site the North Ridge of Everest was visible and we gazed up a snow slope extending ribbon-like along the edge of the ridge. This ends at 24,300 feet, and above it is a long stretch of broken rocks leading up to the North-East Shoulder, whilst to the right of this is the band of yellow slabs. The North-East Ridge forms the uppermost limit of the Yellow Band and it was silhouetted sharply against a white cloud, streaming away to the south-east. After so many days of kicking, hacking, cutting and scraping in snow and ice, it would be good to feel firm rock beneath the feet.

The porters dumped the loads and we returned to camp. Except on the ladder, they descended unroped, aided by the fixed ropes, and we were soon back in camp. There, Raymond and Tom, who had come up for the day from Camp 3, had some good news for us. Shortly after Eric and I had left Camp 3 on the previous day, forty-eight Sola-Khumbu porters had arrived, having come straight through from the Base Camp without a rest, a magnificent effort indicative of the work they would do on the mountain. Our porterage problems were now solved, and it remained only to go ahead with the assault – weather permitting. A second piece of news was not so cheerful. Smidge and Tommy had received a weather report by wireless that the monsoon had reached Colombo. This meant an early monsoon, and we might have only ten days or a fortnight left in which to climb the mountain. Could we do it? Everything depended on the weather, and the weather was anything but kind.

CHAPTER TWELVE

Supplying Camp 4

DURING THE NIGHT of May 14 we had one of the worst gales I remember. The wind must have reached hurricane force, and how the tents stood up to it I do not know. At the height of the storm a gust lifted the arctic tent bodily in spite of its strong guy ropes and the weight of several men inside it, and for a moment we pictured it bowling merrily down the glacier like a captive balloon broken loose from its moorings. Fortunately only a strut was blown in and another forced out of place. Eric received the collapsed side of the tent on top of him, and it was pitiable to hear him give his opinion of the episode in a hoarse whisper, all that was left of his voice. What with the howl of the gale, the volleying snow and the pistol-like cracking of the canvas, sleep was impossible.

As before, the gale did not drop with the dawn if anything it increased, stripping the snow from the glacier in sheets and ruthlessly exterminating every step on the North Col slopes.

At 10 the wind abated, and Bill, Eric, Wyn, Hugo and I with twelve porters set off to establish ourselves at Camp 4. After our long, boring and uncomfortable time at Camp 3a, it was a great relief to leave it for a higher camp, and all of us hoped devoutly that we would not have to return to Camp 3a until someone had climbed the mountain.

The wind was still blowing hard enough to make the climb unpleasant, but once again the porters went splendidly. It was unthinkable convoying them one by one up the rope ladder in the cold wind, so a quicker method was evolved, and all of them were tied together on one long rope separated from one another at such intervals that there were never more than two on the ladder at the same time. Wyn bravely volunteered to see them down again, and I would have stopped to help him, but for almost the first time in my life I had lost all sensation in my feet. Fearing frostbite, I trudged up as quickly as possible to the camp and, finding the arctic tent already erected, pulled off my boots, which were frozen as hard as stones and began a vigorous massage. Circulation returned gradually and half an hour later all danger of frostbite had passed.

We all agreed that Camp 4 was preferable to Camp 3a owing to its more sheltered position, and our only anxiety was the possibility, at present remote, of an avalanche falling on to it from the steep slope immediately above. But our position, with its view along the Himalayas to Kangchenjunga and north-eastwards over the snow-covered peaks into the brown uplands of Tibet, more than compensated us for this hypothetical disadvantage.

Unlike members of former expeditions, we were able to enjoy food and had a substantial supper, but I did not sleep until after midnight, owing to the noise of small pieces of ice falling from the upper lip of the crevasse on to the tent.

I awoke before the others next morning, May 16, and coaxed a "Primus" into action. We were using a half-and-half mixture of petrol and paraffin, on the assumption that paraffin would not vaporise efficiently at 23,000 feet and higher, and once the "Primus" was well warmed it burned well.

The weather looked doubtful and again we felt anxious as to its intentions. True these had been made very plain since we left the Base Camp, but now that Camp 4 was established the operation scheme for the assault was ready to be put into action. Should it fail we might he reduced to an emergency scheme, meaning a rush for the top by an unsupported party, an alternative Hugh was anxious to avoid.

We lounged in our sleeping bags all the morning, then lunched off tinned kippers. For once the "Primus" was not functioning well. It refused to burn properly and emitted such noxious fumes that I was glad to escape from the tent into the open air and descend to meet the porters under the charge of Jack, Waggers and Raymond who were coming up from Camp 3a.

On the slopes of the North Col the atmosphere was moderately calm, but higher the wind was raising the loose snow, whirling it across the slabs of the Yellow Band and lifting it far into the air from the crest of the North Ridge. The porters were all very cheerful in spite of their 40-lb. loads, and I helped Waggers with them on the rope ladder.

Eleven men remained at the camp and were accommodated in a bell tent, and the remaining eight descended to Camp 3a. I manipulated the rope above the ladder and very glad I was to see the last man safely down, as a bitterly cold wind had seized the opportunity of bombarding me with powdery snow.

The weather had promised ill and Everest weather does not forget; snow fell throughout the night and continued to fall long after dawn. Nothing could be done; ascent or descent were likewise impossible. What wretched luck we were having; the number of fair days since we left the Base Camp could be counted on the fingers of one hand.

At 9 a.m. the sun tried to edge through, but it was a poor, weak sun, and we eyed it derisively. Another anxiety was the possibility of being cut off for several days from Camp 3a; however, we had food and fuel for Europeans and porters for a week. And the monsoon was coming; every day was precious now. Surely we could reasonably hope for a few days of good weather before it arrived? None of us had seen such continuously bad weather in the Himalayas, yet, in spite of all, the porters were of good heart; we could hear them chattering in their tent. What was the use of being pessimistic when we had such men to see us through with the job?

Some consolation was afforded by a magnificent lunch, cooked by Eric over two "Primuses", consisting of royans de la Bordelaise, tinned loganberries with condensed milk and cafe au lait; a princely repast, except that the acid juice of the tinned loganberries hurt my dry sore throat.

During the afternoon snow continued to fall heavily. Life was very boring. I amused myself with a minute examination of my face in a small pocket mirror. It had been wrecked by sun and wind. Where my beard did not protect it, the skin could be pulled off in large flakes, and my ears were beyond all hope of immediate repair. My nose was moderately sound except for the edges of the nostrils, which were raw and sore, whilst the constant need to wear woollen sweaters had saved my neck. In the matter of lips I was more fortunate than most, and by dint of constant greasing I had saved them from cracking too disastrously, but some of my companions had oozing crevasses and bergschrunds which were painful to contemplate. Worst of all it had become a habit with me during the night to remove scabs when half asleep, so that old cracks were being constantly reopened and were not getting a chance to heal.

The storm continued all the afternoon and, knowing that the snow was accumulating steadily on the slope above the camp, we were a trifle uneasy. We regretted our mail which was due that day, and we thought with envy of those at Camp 3 who in all probability were devouring theirs.

The weather became steadily worse during the afternoon, and by nightfall a blizzard of hurricane force was raging. How we blessed our arctic tent. No snow penetrated it except once or twice when the flaps were opened to allow people to pass outside, and then streams of fine powder would pour in. We were comparatively sheltered, but what was it like at Camp 3a? We heard afterwards that the arctic tent there had caved in and was nearly carried away.

Curiously enough, most of us slept well in spite of the blizzard but next morning, May 18, we discovered that a quantity of powdery snow had managed to creep in, between the flaps during the night, and our first job was to shovel it out. There was little improvement in the weather except for occasional gleams of sun, and above us we could hear the wind roaring across the North Col, like great waves on a rocky coast. Yet, for all its malignity, the bad weather appeared to be localised and confined to the Everest region, and now and then through the hurrying mists, ranges of sun-warmed hills appeared, and beyond them the amber-coloured plains of Tibet.

No one ascended from Camp 3a, the wind was too violent; but in the afternoon the weather improved, and we all set off to complete the route to the crest of the Col. First, at the end of the ledge supporting the camp, came a steep sérac, which had to be traversed diagonally. After our inactivity it was almost pleasant to wield an ice axe again. The surface of the sérac was composed not of pure ice, but of firm névé in which we cut bucket-like steps. Next came two snow-covered crevasses and a snowy trough. Still ascending diagonally, we reached the foot of an unbroken snow slope leading up to the crest of the Col. The shortest route to the lowest point of the Col was a nearly horizontal traverse, but, as the snow here was a doubtful proposition, we decided that straight up to the crest was the safest way. On this last slope the snow was soft and powdery at first, but higher, step cutting was necessary in windblown névé. One by one we popped our heads over the crest and congregated on a narrow edge of hard snow breathing hard. The North Col was won at last.

Immediately beneath was the upper basin of the main Rongbuk Glacier, bathed in brilliant sunshine, and above it the gleaming cone of Pumori, a splendid outpost to a tangle of giant peaks. Small fragments of silvery mist hung about the flanks of the nearer peaks, but in the north-west all was sunlit and serene. Only Everest still scowled, and from far above came the growl of the wind, a steady undercurrent of menacing sound. There was something implacably hostile about the great mountain, and in the absence of sun, with a wind-driven smother of flying snow, and a smooth, slate-grey cloud oiling along with extraordinary speed, yet ever forming so quickly as to remain clinging to the summit, it was possible to imagine a vengeful and terrible personality.

We were not on the lowest point of the North Col, and to reach it had to traverse a sharp ridge of hard snow. The wind was strong here, and we were glad of our axes to help balance us against the fierce gusts. It was a sensational crest; as Baedeker might have said: "Not difficult for adepts but requiring a perfectly steady head." For perhaps fifty yards it was nearly horizontal, then it descended, broadening out as it did so, to the lowest point of the Col. Here was a site sufficiently large for some tents should dangerous snow compel us to evacuate the ledge and move Camp 4 to a safer place, but one receiving the full force of the north-west wind which, compressed between Everest and the North Peak, charges across the Col. Above the Col rises the long, gradually steepening snow slope already mentioned ending at a height of 24,500 feet, with an easy looking broken rock crest, the true crest of the North Ridge, to one side of it.

So much we saw in a few hurried glances, then turned our backs on Everest and retired along the crest. It was late in the afternoon, and if only the wind had hustled us less, we might have halted to enjoy the splendid view. Pumori was cloud-girdled now, and the mist fragments of an hour ago had grown into stately pillars of cumulus which cast slow-moving shadows on the snowfields.

As we stepped into the welcome shelter of the leeside of the Col where our footsteps ran down in a steep, wavering line, there came a last vicious gust of wind that carried a handful of snow from the ridge and cast it rudely into our faces. Everest has no manners.

Kicking vigorously into the already good footholds to stimulate slackening circulation, we descended rapidly to the camp. A few minutes later we were untying our frozen boots in the arctic tent and the "Primus" was roaring with its promise of hot tea.

The sunset was quietly beautiful, and through the talc window of the tent we saw Kangchenjunga glowing above a level sea of cloud. Was it possible, faintly possible, that the weather was mending?

CHAPTER THIRTEEN

Blizzard at Camp 5

NO SNOW FELL during the night, but next morning (May 19) clouds were moving quickly across Everest from the north-west, whilst an ominous canopy of mist concealed the Arun Valley. Exercise and the need to acclimatise more than anything else decided Eric and me to reconnoitre the North Ridge.

Our first job was to fix a long length of line up the slope to the Col and to secure it to an ice axe driven into the hard snow of the crest. Once on the Col, we were careful to avoid the corniced eastern edge of the long snow slope already mentioned, as well as some minor crevasses, and at the first opportunity we made for the rocks at the side of the snow. To judge from our pace, we were well acclimatised, and we climbed nearly 1,000 feet in the first hour. On the Col the wind was merely annoying, but higher it was so strong that we could not have continued had the rocks been difficult. It was our first experience of a high wind above 23,000 feet, and it made us realise, even more than the battering we had already endured, the hostile nature of Everest. Except for the wind, there was nothing particularly malignant about the weather. The usual cloud plume was streaming from the North-East Ridge, but in other respects the weather was good, and the sun shone brilliantly. It was just wind, ceaseless, relentless, bullying wind. And wind on Everest is subtly demoralising. An upward step is no longer something interesting and worth doing, but something useless, and the final pyramid of rock with its writhing plume of wind-driven snow, the summit of Everest; it is the epitome of weariness.

I do not know whether pessimism is best countered by being in the front or the rear of a climbing party, but on this occasion when Eric's turn came to set the pace I discovered something reassuring in his beautifully balanced and rhythmical movements which even the wind seemed unable to affect.

At about 24,200 feet we halted and took stock of ourselves and each other. Eric's helmet and face were masked with ice. I saw a movement between an ice-encumbered moustache and beard, he was saying something, but the gale prevented me from hearing. As for me, my gloves were iced and my woollen balaclava helmet glued to my beard.

It was far enough, and I shouted to Eric. 'This — wind!' No further explanation or opinion was necessary; we turned and descended.

My legs were tired and it needed a conscious effort to control them, whilst now and then the wind sent us staggering. This wind was a supreme factor. We should court disaster if we tried to establish Camp 5 in a similar wind. The porters with their heavy loads could never face it. It would knock all the stuffing out of them, even if it did not inflict dangerous frostbite. Soon after we regained camp Jack and Waggers arrived from Camp 3a with additional stores and tents for Camps 5 and 6. After three days' isolation we were glad to see them and hear their news. Tom was fitter and had accompanied them to the foot of the ice wall where he had volunteered for the cold, disagreeable job of seeing porters up and down the rope ladder. Camp 4 was now stocked with enough provisions to withstand a siege and at the first opportunity, Camp 5 would be established and the assault begun.

The wind dropped that evening and for the first time since we arrived at Camp 4 the night was calm. I slept well and when I woke the sun was warming the tent and the sky cloudless. Had the Fates relented? Lassitude and pessimism were replaced by energy and optimism, and at 8.45 Wyn, Bill, Hugo and eleven porters set off to make Camp 5. The porters were in splendid fettle and grinned happily as they humped their heavy loads. They were as glad as we to be up and doing. Off they went and, lazily watching in the hot sun, I saw them climb round the icy corner near the camp, trudge slowly up the steep slopes beyond and disappear one by one over a distant edge.

I continued to bask in the sun, the first time this had been possible at Camp 4. The weather remained quiet and the sky unclouded except for the usual plume on Everest, though now and again a suspicious fuzziness appeared clinging to the crest of the north ridge.

During the afternoon Greene, Wager and Longland, and later Crawford and Brocklebank arrived from Camp 3a.

Meanwhile, the rest of us watched the progress of the Camp 5 party. They reached a long stretch of broken rock above the snow slope, and there halted for a long time. Why? What was delaying them? The site of Camp 5 was at least 1,000 feet higher. Bill and I had discussed it only the previous day, and had agreed that a break in the ridge at about 25,700 feet was probably the best place. We were still puzzling as to the reason for their non-advance when I had to descend to the ice wall and relieve Jack of the chilly business of bringing porters up the ladder. The sun had already left the slopes and a cold wind soon chased the warmth from my extremities. It was a relief when the porters were all up and I could trudge back to camp. Others had felt the cold during the last part of the ascent, principally because of the inevitable wait at the foot of the ice wall, and the circulation in Raymond's feet was only restored after a long rubbing.

Towards evening the porters of the Camp 5 party began to straggle in; they showed surprisingly few signs of strain or tiredness and fairly scampered down the slopes. We were in the arctic tent puzzling over their report that not only had Camp 5 not been pitched but the loads had been dumped on the rocks just above the top of the snow slope, fully 1,000 feet below the intended site, when Wyn thrust his head in between the flaps. His beard was stiff with ice and an icicle several inches long hung from his nose. He brought bad news. There had been a disagreement as to the camping site and Bill, fearing for the porters in the cold wind, had decided to dump the loads on the top of the snow slope and retreat, a decision supported by Hugo but not by Wyn. Each had decided as he thought best, and this failure to establish Camp 5 was primarily due to the fact that the members of the party had never previously climbed together. I think we all realised with some bitterness that we were nothing but a scratch party hastily collected together and sent to climb the highest mountain of the world. This and nothing else had resulted in the failure, and no criticism of the party or any member of it is permissible; indeed, only sympathy can be felt for men placed, through no fault of their own, in such a position.

Lastly came Bill escorting Hugo, who was very tired and going very slowly. The day ended dismally in unproductive argument, criticism and discussion. One unpalatable fact emerged from this: valuable, perhaps vital, time had been lost.

Ferdie and Tom returned to Camp 3a that evening, but Raymond, Waggers and Jack remained at Camp 4; it was obvious now that we should need all our available strength for establishing Camp 5 and launching an assault.

Next morning, May 21, Eric and I set off to make the route to the site of Camp 5, carrying a quantity of red bunting to mark the way for the party which, it was hoped, would finally establish the camp on the morrow.

The air was calm and warm on the slopes above Camp 4, but immediately we reached the crest of the North Col we were met by our inveterate enemy, the wind. We were both in good form, and quickly ascended the broken crest of the ridge, but the wind increased in force the further we advanced. On the Col there was nothing more than a strong breeze, but less than 1,000 feet higher it was blowing a gale. We could hear the gusts approaching and braced ourselves to resist them, but often they sent us staggering. More than once, as we toiled miserably upwards, I asked myself whether it was worth it; this horrible discomfort, these numbed feet, this wind-lacerated face, these cold fingers, this panting, sorely stressed body. I thought of English fields, warm brooks and trees bursting into bud, cricket pitches, the scent of new-mown hay. A useless toil, why endure it? Then I thought, with an inward grin, what a fuss there would be if we reached the summit. We would have to endure long adulatory speeches, our digestions would be ruined by innumerable dinners, and we would be pestered by autograph hunters. Here on Everest, at least, there was peace. The aloof pyramid with its flaunting cloud was somehow infinitely satisfying, inspiring and terrible. Those who climb on Everest see life as a mess of warring elements; they realise their completeness and their incompleteness, their nobility and their ignobility. Perhaps that is why men explore; in exploring the earth they explore themselves.

More often than not the thoughts of a climber at high altitudes struggle impotently in an ocean of weariness. Look at something, a rock perhaps; you see it, you may even remember it, but there is no instinctive analysis of shape and colour. It does not stimulate a sense of comparison, or set in action any train of deductive thought.

The wind was worse than ever on the top of the snow slope; it was impossible to turn the face into it – it seared the cheekbones. We crouched down, sometimes on hands and knees, to avoid being blown off the ridge. Finally, we halted and looked at one another; our beards, moustaches and balaclava helmets were thick with ice. An imperceptible nod – talking was impossible in the gale – and we began to fight our way downwards.

On the North Col there was little wind by comparison, and strolling along the sharp snow ridge it was difficult to remember the wind 1,000 feet higher. It is curious how quickly the brain forgets discomfort. If this were not so, I doubt if any sane man would return to Everest.

We did not linger on the Col – our toes were dead – and we hurried down to camp where we removed our boots and inspected the damage. It took a long and vigorous rubbing to restore circulation, particularly to my left big toe. Afterwards we both remarked that our toes were sore. We were lucky not to have been frost-bitten.

Hugh had come up from Camp 3 with the sad news that poor George had gone down with a stomach ulcer and had been sent back seriously ill to the Base Camp. He had insisted on descending the glacier unaccompanied by a European, a truly sporting effort. Knowing him better than the others I could realise to some slight extent what this meant to him. Everest had been a dream of his for many years, and he had taken on a tea-planting job to learn Nepali and be near the Himalayas.

That evening a long discussion took place in the arctic tent, and it was decided that a party consisting of Wyn Harris (in charge), Greene, Birnie and Boustead should establish Camp 5 next day, weather permitting. The following day, weather still permitting, they would establish Camp 6 whilst Birnie and Boustead would escort the porters down and remain in support at Camp 5. Among the porters selected for Camp 6 was Lhakpa Chedi, who was desperately keen to lead his companions to the highest camp, which he swore should be higher than in 1924.

Wyn and Raymond would then reconnoitre the Second Step and, if possible, attempt the summit. Eric and I were to be a day behind the first party, and would act as a support party to assist them in the event of emergency and afterwards make another attempt on the summit should they fail.

After supper, Hugh visited the porters' tent to explain the plan of campaign. He came back with the cheerful news that all the men were in great spirits. They told him: 'Don't be anxious, we mean to carry those loads as far as we possibly can, you will see tomorrow. Then it is up to the sahibs to climb the mountain.'

May 22 dawned fine. If only the weather continued fine we should have a crack at the top, and a spirit of optimism was present in all when Wyn, Raymond, Bill and Hugo and their porters set off, with Hugh, Jack and Waggers accompanying them for the sake of exercise. It was 7.15 when they left and, as far as we could see, little or no wind was sweeping the north ridge. Eric and I were thankful for a lazy day, for we were both a trifle weak in the legs; the struggle against the wind the previous day had taken it out of us and energy is not easily regained at 23,000 feet.

We were able to sit outside the arctic tent in comparative comfort and watch the party through the telescope as they climbed the North Ridge.

Hugh was the first back, having gone as far as the North Col, a great effort for a man of his age. He reported good weather, and that the porters were going splendidly. Then came Jack, with a porter who complained of stomach pains and had been unable to last the course. I went a few yards from the camp and helped to bring the sick man round the steep and awkward ice corner. During the day Tom and Smidge arrived, after laying a telephone line as far as the foot of the ice wall. Smidge, in spite of his lack of mountaineering experience, had climbed well. His arrangements were now nearly complete. At Camp 3 he had installed a wireless linking him with Tommy at the Base Camp, who in turn transmitted news to Darjeeling and received weather reports. Only a telephone wire between Camp 3 and Camp 4 was needed to complete the communications of the expedition.

Shebby, whose laryngitis was better, had accompanied the party to the foot of the ice wall, and when I descended to help with the porters' loads, he croaked up a hoarse but cheerful greeting.

At teatime Raymond arrived. He was very done. In his unacclimatised state, the task had proved beyond him, and we realised now that it had been a mistake for him to go through to Camp 5 without a longer halt for acclimatisation at Camp 4. His heart was beating irregularly and he thought it was dilated. Waggers had taken his place in the first party and everything had gone well, except for the sick porter whose load had been abandoned, and Camp 5 had been established at about 25,700 feet. On the way up, they had passed Finch's 1922 camp about 300 feet above the top of the big snow slope. It was in a comparatively sheltered position between two large boulders, but the wind had torn the tent to ribbons. Oxygen cylinders were scattered around, and one still contained oxygen although it had lain there for eleven years. So dry is the atmosphere on Everest that the valve was unrusted, and Raymond had given himself a dose of gas. He said it was so stimulating that for a time he regretted his decision to return. A spool of "Kodak" film was also found near the camp and we wondered whether development would reveal anything of interest.[1] Although feeling very tired, Raymond had taken samples of alveolar air. Only those who have climbed at high altitudes can realise what such devotion to science means. The porters were naturally tired after an ascent of nearly 3,000 feet, but Hugo had done much to help and encourage them during the descent, and those not retained at Camp 5 arrived back very pleased with themselves in spite of their weariness. What splendid little men they are; there are none to compare with them in hardiness and cheerfulness.

The stage was set for the attack. Everything now depended on the weather, and the weather that evening was not promising. We knew that the monsoon was slowly developing in India, and there were signs of it already in the Everest region. Ranks of cumulus clouds had formed in the trench-like Arun Valley, and far away in the south great anvil-shaped masses of false cirrus glowed a dull, fiery red at sunset.

I was roused in the night by a light rustling sound. Snow was falling. For a while I listened, then slept again. A good three inches had fallen when we poked our heads out of the tent next morning, May 23, and the sun was shining through the drifting mists with a hot, fierce glare. Worst of all the air was warmer, almost breathless it seemed, after the dry, cold air of the past few weeks. This must be the monsoon, or at all events the first breath of it. We were on the edge of things; we might have to race bad weather to the summit and such a race was not pleasant to contemplate. There was too much risk of being caught at a high camp by a heavy snowfall.

There was no wind at Camp 4, but it was blowing on the North Col and at Camp 5 the telescope revealed fluttering tents. Before the first party left, a signalling arrangement had been agreed to. If they had to remain at Camp 5, then Eric and I had to remain at Camp 4, but as far as we could see little or no snow had fallen at Camp 5 and there was every hope that the weather was good enough for them to establish Camp 6. We peered through the telescope until our eyes ached, but although we searched the rocks and the neighbouring snow patches, we saw no signs of the sleeping bags, which were to be displayed in the event of their being unable to start, and in the end we decided to ascend.

The steps below the North Col had been filled up by the freshly fallen snow, and had to be remade. This was hard work, and the forty minutes spent in reaching the Col came as a poor preliminary to the long grind up the North Ridge. Once again there was a suspicious weakness in our legs. Were we deteriorating? If so, this was partly due to lack of palatable foods and particularly meat at Camp 4. The high-altitude rations had been based on the experiences of 1922 and 1924, when men had found they could eat little or no solid food. We had been higher longer, and had acclimatised better, and as a result our high altitude rations had proved insufficient. Various notes imploring those below to send up more substantial food had gone down from Camp 4 but so far without result, for such food was mostly at Camp 2 and lower. Drastic reorganisation was necessary if the climbing party was to maintain its strength. A scientifically worked out rationing scheme had gone by the board, as it always will do on Everest. Calories and vitamins look charming

[1] It proved to be unexposed.

when set down on paper in England at sea level, but high on Everest a man eats what he wants to eat, and no power on earth can make him eat certain things because he ought to eat them unless he also happens to like them.

As we passed along the snow ridge of the Col, clouds flew out of the west borne on a cold wind; then, as we began climbing the rocks by the side of the snow-slope, snow began to fall. The wind increased as we ascended, and at the top of the snow slope we were climbing heads down in the teeth of a blizzard. We debated whether or not to turn back, but a gleam of sun through the hurrying mists suggested better weather higher. Perhaps, after all, the first party were on their way to Camp 6; in this case our job was to support them, and we decided to continue.

The rocks above the snow slope were easy, and it was only necessary to use the hands occasionally, but ice axes were invaluable in helping us to balance.

Presently we came upon the remains of Finch's tent, looking strangely forlorn with its tattered rags of green canvas flapping from the fallen tent poles, whilst the oxygen cylinders scattered around suggested the encampment of some strange beings from another planet. The ridge is broad hereabouts and less well defined than lower down and there is plenty of choice of route up the shattered rocks.

The wind continued to increase as we made height; once we halted for a rest behind some boulders, but it was seldom that we escaped one iota of its malice. It was snowing heavily now, and visibility was limited to a few yards; however, we were cheered now and again by seeing pieces of red bunting, weighted down by rocks, which the first party had left to mark the route.

The last 500 feet was a real struggle, principally because our legs were weak from the strain of maintaining balance in the wind and the consequent impossibility of progressing rhythmically. I noticed that I was taking two breaths for every step. A lead-like leg swung forwards and upwards, puff, puff; slowly, and with a conscious effort, the weight was transferred to the forward foot and another lead-like leg was thrust forwards and upwards, puff, puff. And so it went on.

We had seen no bunting for some time and were becoming anxious lest we should miss the camp, when we came to a slope of screes and snow above which something unnaturally clear-cut loomed through the blizzard – the camp. Hugo was the first to greet us; the Camp 6 party had been unable to start. For the moment we were too tired to grasp the significance of this. Then we saw that there were only two Meade tents, which could accommodate only two climbers apiece. As I realised this there came to me a feeling of more than ordinary fatigue; to return again to Camp 4 through the blizzard *might* be possible, but it would not be easy. But Wyn and Waggers realised the state of the case and at once volunteered to descend and relieve the congestion. It was unselfish of them, more unselfish than any of us realised at the time. It meant abandoning their attempt, and relinquishing altitude strenuously won. I do not believe Eric and I even thanked them. We accepted their decision as something inevitable, an instance of co-operation that neither expects recognition nor demands thanks. They told us that they had had a very bad night, and that the wind had hammered the camp and done its best to hurl it from the ridge on to the East Rongbuk Glacier; then they packed their rucksacks and a minute later disappeared into the blizzard.

With their departure we did our best to make ourselves comfortable. As already noted, two tents had been pitched for climbers, and a few feet lower were some porters' tents. To facilitate cooking and conversation the tents had been pitched entrance to entrance. This was satisfactory as regards the tent with the entrance away from the wind, but the tent occupied by Eric and me had its entrance facing the wind and, although partially sheltered by the tent shared by Bill and Hugo, was not proof against the fine powdery snow which penetrated the flaps, however carefully these were tied. We did our best to remedy this state of affairs, but without success. But what was much worse was the inability of the thin tent fabric to resist the finer particles of snow which hour by hour penetrated it and covered everything in the tent.

At sundown the wind abated somewhat, snow ceased to fall and the clouds vanished from the upper part of Everest. We had no thermometer, but the cold seemed greater than any we had yet experienced, and there is little doubt that the temperature rivalled the lowest recorded on the expedition.[2] There was a belated gleam of golden sunlight, and through the gauze-covered window of the tent we saw a clear sky, and below, a far-stretching sea of clouds from which the higher peaks stood out like islands. I was rested now and there was a hot drink inside me; interest revived and with it an ambition to take photographs. Here was a scene worth recording and I crawled out of the tent on to the scree-covered shelf. The wind met me immediately – embraced me is more descriptive, for it seemed to wrap itself about me with a deathly coldness. As quickly as I could I fumbled with my camera, and shot off two or three photographs. What a scene to step into out of a little tent! One peak, and one alone, challenged our altitude, Cho Oyu, 26,870 feet. Hard by rose another great mountain, Gyachung Kang, 25,990 feet. The sun was only a little way above the horizon and there was no warmth in it. There was no warmth in anything; the world was given over to an all-pervading cold. Emphasising our isolation were the clouds stretching in regular woolly waves as far as the eye could see. Even the North Col was below them, and our friends at Camp 4 could not have seen us even had they wished. We were alone; the eye might pass from horizon to horizon without seeing a single sign of man. The cloud crests were tinged with gold, and the troughs between were a pallid grey. North-westwards the peaks were indescribably savage, and their pitiless steepness was emphasised by scimitar-like blades of ice, reddened by the sun as though steeped in blood. And above rose Everest, bleak and pale, seeming almost to repel the golden sunlight. Little whorls of snow were hurrying across it, now rising upwards and vanishing into the deepening blue of the sky, now forming out of apparent nothingness, a constant transmutation of restless energy.

It was magnificent but deadly. Suddenly I realised that my camera was slipping from my numbed fingers. Clutching it, I crawled back into the little tent, where for the next hour I was occupied in restoring circulation.

The sun sank, and a pale afterglow invested the camp, quickly superseded by the night. With darkness, the wind rose again and the tents soon developed a steady drumming, and from drumming a pulsating booming and pistol-like cracking of their fabric. We were in for a bad night. We scraped together some snow and filled a saucepan which we placed over a Tommy's cooker, but it was an hour before we

2 –23°F. at Camp 2.

got a drink of tea, and this we failed to raise to boiling-point as there was a temperature at which the heat lost from the saucepan through contact with the cold air was equal to the heat gained. At this altitude solid methylated fuel is hopelessly inefficient.

Our supper consisted of condensed milk, "Ovaltine" and sardines. It was good as far as it went, but not solid enough, and there is something peculiarly unappetising about a frozen sardine in gelatinous oil at 25,700 feet.

Supper over we settled down for a long night. We were both fairly warm in our double eiderdown sleeping bag with spare sleeping bags in lieu of mattresses beneath us to insulate us from the cold of rocky ground. Unfortunately this last had not been properly levelled: the porters had been too tired, and the peaks, valleys and ridges beneath us were not conducive to sleep. In vain we tossed and turned trying vainly to discover some hollow into which we might wedge our sore hips. Finally, we found that the most comfortable as well as the warmest position was lying back to back pressed closely together.

Meanwhile the wind increased blowing the powdery snow through the frail canvas, miserable material for a job of this sort, while even more snow penetrated the flaps and the holes at each end of the tent, through which ran the ridge guy rope. In an hour we were liberally sprinkled with snow, in two hours we were covered by an inch or more of the same cold material. I tried in vain to escape it, by tucking my head into my sleeping bag, but soon had to withdraw, gasping from lack of oxygen. The snow accumulated in our beards, where our breath congealed it into ice; it covered our balaclava helmets, and penetrated the necks of our sleeping bags. So we lay, while the long, sleepless hours span out to a dismal dawn.

Our provisions in one corner of the tent had to be dug out of the snow before we could breakfast. Then we waited for the sun, and waited in vain. Instead, grey clouds came flying out of the west bringing a smother of snow. There was no question of further advance. Bill and Hugo had slept better than we, as not so much snow had penetrated their tent, and no movement came from the porters, whose tents were a few yards away; we hoped that they were warm and comfortable; at all events they were provided with equipment similar to ours.

Towards midday the sun put in a feeble appearance and there was some talk of setting off to Camp 6, but the wind settled that idea when it roared across the huge expanse of slabs and flung the snow it had collected upon the camp in a furious blizzard.

We talked little, our throats were too sore, and Eric could only speak in a hoarse whisper. What we did say was confined to our immediate comfort, of which there was a noticeable lack, and we agreed that it was the worst weather and the worst camp we had ever endured. Yet, somehow or other, time passed. In this respect high altitudes are merciful. A man is too lethargic to feel bored, and lethargy is the keynote in high-altitude mountaineering. On Everest it is an effort to cook, an effort to talk, an effort to think, almost too much of an effort to live.

Daylight failed. There was a faint golden gleam through the murk, Everest's one concession on a day of unmitigated ferocity.

The wind responded to nightfall by rising to a fury, such as I have never before experienced in a tent. The thin canvas flapped and cracked wildly, as though incensed with a thousand devils clutching gleefully at every fold. Each gust worked itself up into an orgasm of fury, only to be followed by an even worse gust. Three yards away was the edge of Everest's north-east precipice and the wind was blowing straight over it. Suddenly one guy rope tore loose. The side of the tent nearest to Eric billowed in. He endeavoured to press it back by lying against it with the whole weight of his body, but the fabric was held by the wind pressure as tightly as a football. If another guy went we might be blown, tent and all, over the precipice.

Somehow or other I extricated myself from my sleeping bag and dragged on my windproof trousers, then went through the usual exhausting acrobatics of getting my windproof jacket over my head and shoulders. Lastly I pulled on my granite-like boots. The tapes closing the tent flaps were frozen; it was impossible to unlace them in gloves, and by the time I had done so in bare hands, my fingers had lost sensation. This done I crawled out of the tent on hands and knees. It was not completely dark and the western sky was faintly green. A smother of snow was raging across the rocks, and through this I saw the errant guy. It had pulled away from two large stones to which it had been attached, and so great had been the strain that the stones, which cannot have weighed less than one hundredweight, had been shifted bodily. By dint of considerable exertion in a momentary lull, I managed to reattach it and tighten it. Then I crawled around on hands and knees – it was not safe to stand in the wind – and after some minutes managed to find additional stones with which to reinforce the guy. Finally, exhausted by the effort, I struggled into the tent and flopped down on my sleeping bag gasping for breath.

It was some time before I recovered sufficiently to get into my sleeping bag. Unluckily we had had our suppers before this episode, and brief though my excursion outside had been, it was long enough for the wind to subtract the warmth from my extremities. After an hour or so I managed to restore circulation to my fingers, but my feet remained like marble slabs all night, and partly for this reason and partly because of the storm, I did not sleep at all.

At midnight the wind suddenly dropped, and at 1 a.m. we discussed the possibility of starting at once and attempting to reach the summit the same day from Camp 5. There was nothing new in this suggestion, as we had already talked it over as a last alternative in the event of a failure to establish Camp 6, yet we both knew in our hearts that the chance of success was infinitesimal. The suggestion could not be taken seriously; it would be asking too much of ourselves after two wretched nights, and too much of the weather. Curiously enough, a little later Hugo crawled across from the other tent and made a similar proposal.

At 6 a.m. there did indeed seem some hope of pushing on towards Camp 6, and Hugo with grim determination roused the porters and told them to get ready to start. Splendid men, they at once responded. But then, yet again, came the wind. It was not so violent as before, but it was colder if that were possible. Even so, Hugo was still determined to push on, and got the porters out of their tents. It was a gesture, nothing more; to push on meant certain catastrophe. Although we did not know it at the time, four men were already frostbitten.

Retreat was imperative, so agreed Eric, Bill and I. Our plans had miscarried. For the time being we were beaten. There was no porters' food left – we had not bargained to keep so many men at Camp 5 for so long; and there was no disguising the fact that the battering had told upon us. The porters had retreated to their tents, and along with the others I went outside to persuade them to start down. The wind and the cold were dreadful, and in a few minutes my hands, although protected by heavy gloves, had lost all sensation, and I could not move them; they were stiff and dead and seemed not to belong to me. Unless I did something for them they would be dangerously frostbitten, so I retreated to the tent, and kneeling inside it feebly beat them together, gasping for breath the while. I had done this for some minutes without effect, when one of the porters – I wish I could remember which one, for I was too done at the time to take note of him – seeing how it was with me, came into the tent and for fully a quarter of an hour rubbed and pummelled them between his own until the circulation began to return. It was an agonising process, and I remember twisting and groaning with pain. His own must have been frostbitten at the time, as by this time all the porters were more or less frostbitten. Such is the spirit and devotion of the Sherpa porter.

We collapsed the tents by letting go the end guy ropes, or they would be blown away otherwise, then began the descent through the blizzard.

It was a miserable procession, and as I watched the dim shapes of my companions lurching slowly through the clouds of wind-driven snow, I reflected with a certain grim humour that this, May 25, was Ascension Day.

We had made a serious, well-planned attempt upon the mountain, and it had failed. We were all of us worn out with the strain, and some were frostbitten.

Both wind and cold decreased steadily as we descended. In comparison it was almost genial 1,000 feet above the North Col. Yet Hugh, describing his experiences of this same day in *Everest 1933* wrote:

> But the wind is a torture. It hurts the eyes in spite of protecting goggles. It imprisons the limbs in a grip like that of fast-running icy water, till every step upward is a battle. The fingers of the hand holding the ice axe stiffen under the glove and have to be prised open and beaten to restore circulation. Worst of all perhaps is the searing cold of the air drawn into the over-driven lungs. Movement becomes almost automatic …

To us, the conditions he described seemed almost genial after the blizzard at Camp 5.

On the rocks above the North Col we met a large party consisting of Hugh, Wyn, Waggers, Ferdie and Jack with ten porters who had come up to render assistance. There was no question of the ascending party going on to Camp 5 as had been originally planned, and the two parties joined forces and descended to Camp 4.

On the way down the long snow slope Bill had a narrow escape. To save time and energy he tried to glissade, but the snow was hard and icy, and he quickly got out of control. The snow not only slopes downwards towards the North Col, but outwards to the east, and ends above a precipice 2,000 feet high falling to the East Rongbuk Glacier. Towards this precipice he began to slide head downwards at an ever-increasing speed. Fortunately some porters were descending nearby and Da Tsering took a flying leap at him and managed to stop him. It was great presence of mind, but Da Tsering regarded it as a huge joke, and burst into a roar of laughter, as did the other porters. Bill's only damage was a strained leg, but it was a near thing. This was the only untoward incident, but before reaching Camp

4 Lhakpa Chedi and one or two others among the Camp 5 porters were on the point of collapse and needed assistance. Like us, they had shot their bolt. So at length we arrived at Camp 4, where the arctic tent seemed like a palace after the miserable snow riddled tents at Camp 5. Here we took stock of ourselves. We were a very different party from the party that had set out so confidently only a few days before. Of the porters all were frostbitten, two of them, Lhakpa Chedi and Pasang,[3] seriously. Only one, the lion-hearted little Ang Tarke (sic),* was likely to go high again, the rest would have to be sent down as quickly as possible to the Base Camp for medical treatment. That evening when they showed their toes and fingers to Raymond, who, in spite of his strained heart, had insisted on remaining at Camp 4, I think Hugh and the others were able to appreciate something of what they and we had endured at Camp 5.

The Europeans of the party had suffered less. Both my big toes were slightly affected and all the tips of my fingers, and when at length I managed to restore circulation I felt as though I had been kicking at a brick wall with bare feet, and holding on at the same time to a red hot oven with my fingers. We were all very tired, not ordinary fatigue, but that deadly sort of tiredness, which is as much mental as physical, and there was a weakness in our legs, which could only be the result of remaining too long at a high altitude. To fit ourselves for another attempt we must rest and eat.

There was a gloomy party at supper in the arctic tent. We had taken a knock and no mistake. Everest had proved merciless. In 1922 and 1924, the principal bogey was altitude; in 1933, it was the weather. We were determined to try again, but our determination was different from what it had been before; enjoyment and optimism no longer existed for us. Everest had become a job of dour and exacting work that had got to be done – somehow.

CHAPTER FOURTEEN

Camp 6

THE MONSOON was fast developing and a further complication was evident at Camp 4. The snow was accumulating on the slopes above the camp, and already small masses had slid over the ice wall immediately above the camp and landed beside the tents.

I slept like a log, but was rudely awakened next morning by a sudden rushing sound followed by a dull roar. An avalanche? No, nothing but a miniature slide weighing a few hundred weights and making a noise out of all proportion to its bulk.

According to some, who had slept less, several slides had come down, fortunately without striking the tents. Six inches of snow had fallen overnight, and there was

[3] Lhakpa Chedi subsequently lost two fingers and Pasang one.

* Ang Tharkay who later became famous.

a grave danger that an avalanche might obliterate the camp. Two courses were decided on: firstly, several would descend to Camp 3 to relieve the congestion, and secondly, the camp would be transferred to the crest of the North Col where it would be safe from avalanches. We might have to besiege Everest for some time, and it was inexpedient to tire out porters wanted for high camps, by making them carry provisions up to Camp 4 for any but the climbing and support parties. Whether there was time for another attempt on the summit depended on the monsoon, and there were ominous signs that the advance guard had reached the Everest region. The cloud in the valleys was increasing daily, snowstorms on or below the North Col were becoming more frequent, and there was a moist feeling in the air.

Wyn Harris, Wager, Birnie, Longland, Shipton and I were to remain at Camp 4 with provisions for two or three weeks, so that in the event of a fall of monsoon snow cutting us off from Camp 3 for some time, we should not be forced to decide between the evil alternatives of starvation or a dangerous descent. There was only one dissentient to this scheme: Hugo, whose military instincts were all against complete isolation eventuating from a breakdown of communications. As an alternative he suggested withdrawing to Camp 3, and attempting to climb Everest by its North-East Ridge. This suggestion could not be considered seriously: it was tantamount to another expedition and meant abandoning Camp 5 and the equipment there for Camp 6. Also, the North-East Ridge is a doubtful proposition; it is very long, and in places the difficulties are obviously formidable; any attempt to climb it would have to be prefaced by a reconnaissance.

During the day we moved the camp to the North Col. Fortunately, at its lowest point, the crest is broad, and here, after some laborious levelling, two arctic tents were pitched, one for the climbers and one for the porters.

It meant two carries by the porters to tranship the camp to the new site, and operations were hampered to begin with by the soft, freshly fallen snow and the need to remake the route.

During our absence at Camp 5, the telephone line had been connected to Camp 4, and an apparatus installed. It had now to be extended to the new camp, but unfortunately it was too short and ended on the crest of the Col about one hundred yards from the camp. It was the windiest possible spot for the world's highest telephone booth, and we devoutly hoped we should not have to visit it often. Our one consolation was that as it was only connected to Camp 3, we could not get a wrong number.

Meanwhile, Ruttledge, Crawford, Greene and Brocklebank descended to Camp 3, escorting the frostbitten Camp 5 porters. We heard afterwards that they had some difficulty in persuading the men to leave their tent; the strain had told hardly upon them, and one or two were well nigh demoralised. One, Tsin Nurbu, my first camera man, chewed a red sweet and then spat on the snow in an attempt to convince Raymond that he was suffering from some terrible disease of the lungs, whilst it took an hour or more to persuade two other men to move. At the same time it is worth mentioning that one of the Pasangs resisted all temptation to self-pity and roared with laughter at the sight of his frostbitten fingers, which were beginning to look like hideously distorted carrots, though they must have been paining him terribly. It takes a hero to rise superior to his physical frailties.

When we parted from Hugh he wished us good luck, and we knew that behind this banal expression there was a prayer for our safety and success. His was the hardest part, to lead and yet not be in the forefront of the battle. He would spend anxious days and nights at Camp 3. Neither he nor we had any illusions left as to what Everest could do, yet our attempt must never degenerate into a mere gamble with fate. Mallory laid down the code for Everest climbers when he wrote:

> Principles, time-honoured in the Alpine Club, must of course be respected in the ascent of Mount Everest. The party must keep a margin of safety. It is not to be a mad enterprise rashly pushed on regardless of danger. The ill-considered acceptance of any and every risk has no part in the essence of persevering courage. A mountaineering enterprise may keep sanity and sound judgement and remain an adventure.

We had expected wind on the exposed crest of the Col, but the evening was the calmest we had so far experienced above Camp 3. In the cwm formed by the head of the main Rongbuk Glacier clouds had gathered like a fleet of silvery airships. One lingered stationary on the icy cone of Pumori; and far beyond the labyrinth of peaks stretching north-westwards from Everest, copper-coloured masses of false cirrus were ranged like titanic anvils. As the shadows lengthened the folds and sinews of the snow were revealed. Slowly the colour of the clouds changed from silver and copper to grey. Some light mists on Everest melted away, and the final pyramid ventured a bleak smile in the westering sun. Westwards in a sky of vivid green, slender threads of cirrus scored red slashes in the sky, and eastwards Kangchenjunga was already drowned in the swift-spreading darkness.

Optimism revived that evening in the arctic tent. Our one grouse was food. Many messages had been sent down imploring our transport officers to send up something more substantial, but as yet little or nothing had been done. We had not foreseen, and were now unable to satisfy, our high-altitude appetites. Before he descended Hugh had promised to see to this matter personally. Meanwhile, we must continue to exist on the now utterly unpalatable "slops".

Our greatest craving was for fresh fruit and vegetables. In my imagination I used to picture an orchard of rosy-cheeked apples, plums and pears, and a green salad. We would have pawned our birthrights for a green salad. Raymond had urged that the expedition should be supplied with fresh fruit and vegetables from Kalimpong or Gangtok, and tentative arrangements had been made for their transport, but had later been cancelled on the score of extra expense. Yet, there had been some two dozen mules carrying wireless apparatus; wireless apparatus versus a green salad! At Camp 4 that evening we felt entitled to a good grouse.

Not all the equipment had been brought up; we had no mattresses, and as a result slept badly. I would not have slept at all had not Waggers insisted on tucking half a blanket beneath me. There was little or no wind, though our situation tempted every wind that blew.

The sun reached the camp early next morning, May 27. The air was calm, and we lay in our sleeping bags scarcely able to credit the fact. Then we ventured outside. The sun was hot, positively hot, and a deep peace had fallen on Everest. Gone were the clouds of wind-driven snow, and the yellow crags cut serenely into a dark-blue sky. Below, the clouds still concealed the valleys, but they had shrunk appreciably and were powerless to harm us; the slanting rays of the sun were just touching their topmost billows.

Someone carried the telephone box along the ridge after breakfast and, connecting it to the wire, rang up Camp 3. Hugh replied that a weather report received from Alipore said that the oncoming monsoon had weakened temporarily. This report, sent by telegraph to Richards at Darjeeling, had been relayed by wireless to the Base Camp and Camp 3, then by telephone line to the North Col.

It was necessary to rest the porters after their strenuous efforts of yesterday in carrying up Camp 4 to the Col, but it was tantalising, even exasperating, to do nothing save watch thin mists slowly floating across the face of Everest. We remained in our sleeping bags until the afternoon, when Eric and I descended to collect various things from the lower camp. There we met Ferdie, and Willy McLean, with some porters carrying five loads of food. Luxuries and solids at last! Hugh had done wonders at Camp 3. We grinned happily at one another and our mouths watered as we promised ourselves any number of gastronomical permutations and combinations. Ferdie and Tom had done magnificent work the past ten days. Nothing could be more boring or fatiguing than convoying porters up and down those monotonous slopes, yet here was Ferdie again, fresh as paint and full of vim and good cheer.

We were surprised to see Willy, as we had not expected him; he seemed much fitter and might be invaluable a little later, when the assault was renewed and exhausted or frostbitten men returned from the higher camps.

We climbed leisurely back to camp, for once without cutting or step-kicking, noticing, however, that Kusang, one of our best men, seemed very tired. Was the strain of prolonged residence at high altitudes beginning to tell on our porters? They would need to be at their best to carry a camp to 27,000 feet.

What a feast we had for dinner! As an hors d'oeuvre, biscuits and "Patum Peperium" then an old friend of the mountaineer, "Maggi" soup; the entree was beans; the joint, bully beef with mixed pickles and pickled walnuts; and the sweet, strawberry jelly; at least, it would have been jelly had it been given time to set. Odd corners were filled with biscuits, chocolates and toffee. And so to bed, but I for one had overeaten.

We should have risen early next morning, May 28, but our digestive processes had needed a long night, and it was not until 8 a.m. that Wyn, Waggers, Jack and Bill left for Camp 5 with their twelve porters. The morning was calm and brilliantly fine. Was this the long-hoped-for spell of quiescent weather prior to the monsoon when the north-west wind is held at bay by the strengthening southerly current of the advancing monsoon?

For some time Eric and I stood outside the tent in the sun watching, as slowly and methodically they mounted the ridge. We did not altogether like the look of the sky with its streaks of gleaming iridescent cirrus, whilst far below, a sea of cloud, which for the past few days had concealed the lower valleys, had increased in height a little. However, Waggers, always a cautious fellow as befits a meteorologist, had been almost optimistic.

At 10.30 I carried the telephone box along the ridge, connected it to the wire and, squatting down on the sharp snow edge, talked to Smidge, who gave me the latest weather report from Alipore, prophesying high cloud in the Everest region and snow showers on the morrow. Then Hugh came to the telephone and I described last night's dinner in detail, whereat I heard him chuckle. He said that a watch would be kept at Camp 3 on the upper part of the mountain during the assaults.

Soon after I returned to camp, Eric saw a solitary porter descending the ridge. As he was going very slowly and appeared exhausted, we went out to help him down. When we got up to him it proved to be Kusang. There was a drawn, staring expression in his eyes; he was completely done, and we had to support him between us; yet he never once failed to muster an invincible grin, although he scarcely seemed to realise where he was. He had not got very far, probably not higher than the top of the snow slope. We saw him into his sleeping bag and gave him a hot drink.

After this, we lunched and again enjoyed a princely feast. Indeed, my principal memory of that day is of the food we ate.

The weather remained quiet throughout the afternoon, and towards evening the three porters not retained for Camp 6 returned. Unlike Kusang they were little affected by their long, hard carry and were full of beans. They told us that Bill had gone badly owing to his strained leg, but had made a great effort and eventually reached the camp long after the others.

A calm evening was succeeded by a calm night. After the hurricanes we had endured it was queer to hear nothing but a desultory breeze rustling past the tent. For weeks, try as we would, we had been unable to escape the wind, and here we were on the North Col, the windiest place of all, in comparative peace. Everest is a mountain of weather paradoxes.

The morning of May 29 was fine and calm. Three good days in succession, it was more than we had dared hope for. Eric and I were early out of our sleeping bags; outside the tent the light was dazzling, and Everest lifted serenely into a sky of deep, pure blue.

There could be no error this time, Wyn, Waggers and Jack would establish Camp 6: it remained only to see how high they pitched it. We gazed upwards at the rocks. Camp 5 was invisible and we could see no sign of the party among the broken crags above it. The gods slept quietly, and in all the vast stage of peak and sky we could discern no movement.

Beneath, the valley clouds were much as we had seen them for the past two days and there was no upward stirring of their white billows. Yet it could only be a matter of days, perhaps hours, before the furies were unleashed again. We must take and enjoy the rare gifts of hope and pleasure when they were presented.

There was no hurry, and we breakfasted leisurely. It was likely to be our last comfortable meal for some days. After breakfast we packed our rucksacks. Apart from extra clothing we carried nothing save a small camera and one or two film packs; every extra ounce depletes the store of energy at high altitudes. Then, in the warm sunlight, we set out on the first stage of our journey.

It was the fourth time we had climbed the North Ridge. Previously we had made height at the rate of about 1,000 feet in the first hour, but now, to husband our strength, we climbed at about half that speed. At the same time I do not believe we could have climbed quickly even had we tried, as long residence at high altitudes and our experiences at Camp 5 had told against us. We were both of us a stone or so down in weight and as a result more vulnerable to wind and cold, whilst, in my case, my frostbitten toes were hurting when I put my weight on them. Lastly, our throats were in poor shape. Mine was merely sore, but Eric's was far worse; he was almost speechless, and it was obvious that his strength was being slowly worn down by the constant discomfort. By no stretch of imagination could we be said to be at our best. It remained to be seen whether acclimatisation – and we were splendidly acclimatised – could weight the scales against deterioration.

There is no man with whom I climb better than Eric. In pace and rhythm he is the beau-ideal of a mountaineer. He flows rather than climbs uphill and it is an education to climb with him. There was never any need to halt, and height was gained as calmly and inevitably as a clock hand mounts to the hour.

After less than an hour we began to feel the wind; it poured out of the west in cold douches which strengthened gradually as we gained height. The weather was breaking. The fine morning flickered and went out. Clouds formed above and below. By the time Finch's camp was behind a blizzard was threatening. Another blizzard at Camp 5, it was unthinkable. And the Camp 6 party? Were they doomed to fail without even reconnoitring the Second Step? We had left Camp 4 full of hope and now hope had been supplanted by the familiar feeling of advancing in opposition to something implacably hostile and relentless. Already a leaden rush of snow concealed the pyramid. Camp 6 must have been established by now, but Jack would be hard put to it to steer his tired men down the complicated mountainside.

In the dull light the crags between which we threaded our way assumed queer, even sinister shapes. I remember one that exhibited the profile of an old man with a great hooked nose and a leering grin. At high altitudes fancy weaves queer thoughts that come and go like timid ghosts on a formless background of inertia and fatigue.

A broken edge of decaying rock where a strip of red bunting rippled forlornly in the rising gale, a scree slope and the tents of Camp 5 appeared a few yards ahead through clouds of driving snow. The ascent of 2,700 feet had taken five hours.

We slumped down thankfully in one of the tents, too tired for the time being to unlace our boots or remove our ice-caked windproofs. Bill had been expecting us and had thoughtfully preserved a hot drink in a thermos flask. He looked very tired and worn. At the best of times he could ill afford to lose flesh and he was now, for all his layers of clothing, little more than a skeleton. Yet he told us of his determination to remain at Camp 5 as long as his support was needed. He knew what this meant, as he had already endured four nights there in the blizzard, which routed the first attempt. We admired his fortitude; what worse can a man endure than several nights at such an elevation in a small tent on an exposed and wind-swept ridge without any prospect of attempting the summit?

As we lay in the tent the blizzard steadily strengthened. Now and again we poked our heads outside, but nothing could we see but a few yards of mountainside where the driven snow rushed in whirling clouds. What of Jack and the Camp 6 porters? As the afternoon wore on we became more and more anxious. Bill told us that the party had set off from Camp 5 diagonally across the North Face, where there was nothing definite – nothing but a vast expanse of shattered outward-dipping slabs with patches of screes and steep little walls which would only complicate direction finding in thick weather. The party could not pass to the east of the camp where precipices fall to the East Rongbuk Glacier, but they might easily pass to the west of it without seeing it and descend unwittingly the steepening North Face of the mountain. If they did – it was better not to dwell on the thought, a thought of tired-out men lost on one of the greatest of mountain-sides, wandering helplessly and without sufficient strength to reascend and search for the right route.

The afternoon lengthened and a premature gloom gathered as the blizzard thickened. Suddenly we heard something above the roar of the wind. A dim figure showed through the murk, then another and another. There was a relieved shout and one by one the porters came scrambling down the rocks to the camp. Among them was Jack. He was unrecognisable his eyebrows, his eyelashes, his moustache were rimed and caked with snow and ice, his beard was a mass of ice; icicles inches long hung from his nostrils.

'A drink?' There was no need to ask. We had it ready and he gulped it down. His eyes were bloodshot and strained from the effort of peering into the blizzard. He spoke shortly, tersely, breathing hard the while; he was very tired but the fire of mental energy burned as brightly as ever. 'The camp?' Yes, it had been pitched on the Yellow Band at about 27,400 feet. It was splendid news. And the porters had climbed magnificently. He flung a flat object on to the floor – a folding lantern in a leather case. They had come across the remains of the 1924 Camp 6 and it was lying amid the debris. Also an electric torch – one of the porters brought it into the tent, an old-fashioned mechanical dynamo-driven affair[1] I picked it up and pressed the lever. Instantly the dynamo hummed and the bulb lit up. It had lain there for nine years and not a speck of rust adhered to it.

The party had descended by a different route. They had ascended the yellow band more or less directly, but on the descent Jack had discovered a ledge traversing horizontally towards the North-East Shoulder. From the end of this a short, steep descent brought them to easier ground. Thenceforward he decided to follow the crest of the North Ridge as, owing to the blizzard, a descent of the north face might involve them in difficulties. It was a wise decision.

Several rock towers barred direct access to the ridge, and they had to descend the north face some distance before they were able to traverse to the ridge crest below these obstacles. Here, all Jack's instinct for route finding was needed. A mistake would have brought them to one side or other of the ridge, which is never well defined but forms an obtuse angle between the North and North-East faces of the mountain. At this juncture the storm burst in full fury. As Ruttledge wrote:

> In a few seconds Nature seemed to go mad. The far horizons vanished as the voice of the wind rose to a scream and the snow tore past in blinding sheets. The effect upon tired men may be imagined. Their world disappeared, their goggles iced up till they had to be discarded, whereupon their eyelashes froze together, making it difficult to see at all. They were literally fighting for their lives. Well for them that they had a great leader and a great mountaineer at their head.

In Jack's own words: "Visibility suddenly narrowed to a snow-swept circle of some twenty yards – and I was taking a party down a ridge which I had never been on

[1] Manufactured by the General Electric Company.

before, but which I knew to be ill-defined and easy to lose, particularly in such conditions."

A fine morning – then this, Everest in its deadliest mood. Everything depended on keeping the men together. Had one collapsed through fatigue the result must have been disaster, but the Sherpas responded with that gallantry born of moral as well as physical courage. Heads bent to mitigate the cutting lash of the wind on their tortured flesh, they grimly fought their way downwards. They gained the ridge and a few feet lower came upon the remains of the 1924 Camp 6, some rags of green canvas and collapsed tent poles in a shallow hollow, slightly sheltered from the full force of the storm. Here they halted for a few moments and, their spirits revived by the discovery, rummaged about for "souvenirs" amid the pathetic remnants – the last camp of Mallory and Irvine.

They continued, but about 200 feet lower a terrible thought flashed into Jack's mind. Were they still on the North Ridge or had they been tricked into descending the North-East Face which lower falls in precipices to the East Rongbuk Glacier? If so, there was no hope of forcing the men back uphill to the ridge. They were too tired. Some were already halting to rest at intervals, and required continual encouragement. On no account must he let them see his doubts. The party continued clambering down slab after slab and over abrupt little walls where tired feet had to be placed with never-failing care, and at last, when it seemed they must go on and on forever, the tents of Camp 5 loomed through the whirling snow. It was a great moment – a supreme reward to hard-pressed men who had given their all that others might gain success.

All this we did not gather at the time, for tiredness prohibits lucid explanation, but we heard enough to realise that we had witnessed the end of another great struggle in the fight for Everest.

It was questionable whether Jack should continue the descent to Camp 4, but much revived by food, drink and rest he decided to carry on, although the hour was late, nearly 4 p.m. Even the weary descent to Camp 4 was worth while with a warm and comfortable arctic tent at the end of it, occupied by supports, who would have come up that day from Camp 3, to minister to his needs and those of his worn men.

Two men, however, were too exhausted to start, and as they might dangerously hamper the party, it was agreed that they should remain overnight at Camp 5. One of them was Kipa Lama, and it was apparent that the strain had affected him mentally as well as physically. He was a quaint, good-natured little fellow; sturdy and broad, with a face that was almost always creased in a simple, confiding smile. He was somewhat of a butt among his comrades, who never lost an opportunity of pulling his leg. It was always good-humoured chaff, but poor little Kipa had taken it to heart as a reflection on his ability. On arriving at Camp 6, therefore, he had dumped his load with a satisfied grunt and, turning with an inquiring expression to his sahibs, had demanded a "chit" – certificate of good conduct – on the spot! He was told that he would get it later, and was hurried off down with the other porters. He must have been proud to know that he was one of eight men specially selected to establish Camp 6 and had helped to carry it 600 feet higher than in 1924. There would be no more leg-pulls now.

In 1924 Norton wrote that the names of the men who carried up Camp 6 deserved to be inscribed in letters of gold. So do the names of the men in 1933.

They were:[2]

Ang Tarke [Tharkay]	Sherpa
Da Tsering	Sherpa
Nima Dorje	Sherpa
Ang Tsering	Sherpa
Kipa Lama	Sherpa
Pasang	Bhutia
Tsering Tarke	Bhutia
Rinzing	Bhutia

With the departure of Jack and his men, Bill, Eric and I settled down to make ourselves as comfortable as possible. There were the same two tents as during the first attempt, the Meade, in which Eric and I had spent two miserable nights, and a Burn's tent of "Grenfell" cloth which was snowproof and comparatively comfortable.

Unwilling to endure again the discomfort of the Meade tent, Eric and I decided to share the Burn's tent with Bill. Unfortunately, this only held two men comfortably; with three it rivalled the Black Hole of Calcutta. Before that night I had read with cynical amusement tales of mountaineers who described crowded Alpine huts in which if one man wanted to turn over his companions had to turn with him. Now I know these tales to be true. In theory the middleman should have been the most uncomfortable, but such was not the case. The outside men, and I was one of them, were wedged against the walls of the tent, and these were rather colder than ice owing to the blast outside.

More than once that night I tried to summon up sufficient resolution to extricate myself and complete the night's rest in the other tent, which, for all its infiltrating snow, could scarcely be less comfortable. I do not know whether any of us slept. I did not. I lay there semi-comatose, dimly aware of the wind, but as the hours dragged on even this tired and dropped to a calm. There was no sound then save the uneven breathing of my companions and now and then a long shuddering sigh as overworked lungs found temporary relief in the scanty oxygen. Cheyne-Stokes breathing is experienced by those who climb high. The breathing becomes shorter and shorter and there is a feeling of partial suffocation until the lungs automatically obtain relief in a long, deep breath. It is by no means an inevitable process, but when it occurs it makes sleeping difficult. The fact that at lower levels it is only seen in dying persons is proof in itself of the borderline conditions on Everest.

[2] It is interesting and in some cases tragic to recall the subsequent history of these men. Several of them accompanied the ill-fated German expedition to Nanga Parbat in 1934 when four Germans and six porters lost their lives in a blizzard. Nima Dorje was one of those who perished, whilst Ang Tsering was the last survivor. The fact that he lived five days through the blizzard with no food for most of that time and scarcely any shelter, and was then able to struggle down to safety after all hope of saving him and his companions had been abandoned, speaks for itself of his extraordinary powers. The same spirit drove him and his companions up to Camp 6 on Everest and down to Camp 5 through the blizzard. Ang Tarke and Pasang accompanied Shipton and Tilman on their expedition to Nanda Devi. In 1936 several of these men again distinguished themselves on Everest, especially Ang Tarke and Rinzing. Tsering Tarke died shortly after the return of that expedition.

With incredible slowness the tent lightened. Then there was a faint opalescent glow – the reflection of the sunlight stealing down Everest. Suddenly the ridge lit up and the frost-covered fabric sparkled like diamonds. The light crept down the tent, embracing it kindly. Golden at first, it soon changed to white and the warmth of it increased every minute.

Aching and stiff, we disentangled ourselves and set about the task of preparing breakfast. And what a disagreeable task this is in a small tent at 25,700 feet. At high altitudes refuelling the body is a sordid and distasteful business. Everything seems to conspire against it being performed quickly and efficiently. The tin opener has disappeared. Everyone last saw it in a different place; it would appear to combine the ingenuity of a Maskelyne with the elusiveness of a Houdini. It is found at last in the most obvious and conspicuous place of all where, of course, no one had thought to look for it. Its appearance is distasteful: a frozen mixture of various foods coats it, including, of course, sardines and condensed milk. It is driven with scant ceremony into another tin of frozen condensed milk and retaliates violently and does its best to rip the hand of its user. Curses are croaked at it.

The condensed milk is frozen solid and the whole top has to be removed from the tin, which resents this process in open and savage warfare. Then the stove. There was a pressure stove now at Camp 5 in addition to the solid methylated fuel. The latter, if showing a marked disinclination to heat anything, would at least condescend to light in a reasonable time, the former required coaxing, together with an infinite patience and the diligent application of the pricker, without which no self-respecting pressure stove would dream of functioning at a high altitude; and prickers, as everyone knows, are imbued with the same coyness and self-effacement as tin openers.

Then the labour. Every labour, however small at sea level, is magnified a hundred-fold at 25,700 feet. Cooking is infinitely distasteful, but the ultimate zenith as it were of hard work is reached in extricating yourself from the clinging folds of your sleeping bag and pulling on your windproof clothing and frozen boots. Some recommend that boots should be cherished all night in the sleeping bag, but I have always regarded such people as theorists who have never shared a sleeping bag with a pair of well-frozen boots. Yet, those who find such company distasteful have to pay for their exclusiveness in the morning. By then the boots are of granite-like consistency; they resist all attempts at coercion; nothing will console them for the indignity of being left out in the cold save a belated warm over a candle or a cooker. Picture then the spectacle of a climber grimly and carefully thawing a boot in a candle flame, turning it over and over as with a joint on a spit, like a priest engaged in some sacrificial rite of appalling significance and solemnity.

Once again the monsoon clouds had retreated, but not so far as on previous occasions. Over 5,000 feet beneath us was the Rongbuk Glacier, in some parts wrinkled and seamed and in others smooth and virginal. As yet it was in cold shadow, but above it the cone of Pumori was full in the sun, and beyond this graceful mountain, peak after peak was being slowly robed in brilliant light, whilst the icy edges of many a terrific crest cut like polished knives into the shadows. Far away in the west stood Gaurishankar, so often mistaken in the past for Everest, and nearer were the huge massifs of Cho Oyu and Gyachung Kang with their acres of shining snow.

At our feet was the East Rongbuk Glacier extending northwards in a serene curve, and we could clearly distinguish its complicated fretwork of ice pinnacles. Beyond it the earth wearied of its turbulence and the Himalayas gradually decreased in height and steepness, like waves about a harbour mouth, sinking finally into the honey-coloured uplands of Tibet. Closer at hand the North Peak lifted massively in a tent-like crest linked with the North Col by a series of scolloped elliptical snow edges of extraordinary sharpness. And closer still rose the summit of Everest. It looked absurdly near and easy to climb. A walk of an hour or two should take us there and back. Such was our first impression, but when we came to look closer we were disillusioned. Here was something built on a scale contemptuous of human judgement and the human eye. We stared hard at the brown rocks in search of Wyn and Waggers. Was it possible that they would succeed in settling not only the question of the route but of gaining the summit? This was scarcely probable. A singleness of route and purpose was vital to success. I could not help feeling that their energies would have been better directed into attempting Norton's route, for Norton had unhesitatingly pronounced in its favour, and there has never been a better judge of Everest problems. There had been too much argument already as to the relative merits of the two routes and now the strength of one party at least was to be dissipated on a reconnaissance. The clear issue was that, whereas Norton's route was practicable, it was obviously difficult and exacting and of a nature such as the mountaineer instinctively avoids.[3] The ridge, although a better route if it were practicable, was an unknown quantity. True, the First Step did not look difficult, but between it and the Second Step the telescope had revealed a narrow and broken rock edge. The Second Step was a sheer cliff some eighty feet high and appeared impregnable to direct assault, taking into account the fact that strenuous rock climbing is impossible at 28,000 feet. If it could be climbed there was no doubt that the difficulties would be shorter and the route less dangerous than Norton's traverse. Mallory had been in favour of it and had set out with Irvine to climb it but he had not returned and the matter was non-proven, as it is by no means certain that Odell saw them on the Second Step when he had that last dramatic glimpse of them between the mists.

This then was the problem and Eric and I were now in favour of attempting something which had been seen and judged to be practicable, especially as the monsoon was likely to break at any moment. It was understood between us that unless Wyn and Waggers discovered a practicable route up the Second Step we should, in the event of their failing to reach the summit, go "bald-headed" for Norton's route.

Breakfast over, we said goodbye to Bill and, leaving him to his solitary vigil, began the climb to Camp 6.

As far as Camp 5 the North Ridge provides nothing but the easiest of scrambling. Above the camp the rocks are easy, but in general angle appreciably steeper. We should have borne diagonally upwards at first, then doubled back to the blunt crest of the ridge, but we chose to ascend more or less directly from the camp, and this soon landed us on some awkward slabs and steep patches of frozen grit. It was a place demanding care, and it cost us both time and energy to traverse

[3] It is axiomatic in mountaineering not to leave the crest of a ridge in favour of a traverse across a face unless an insurmountable obstacle bars progress on the ridge. [Most modern ascents follow the ridge.]

first one way and then the other to avoid some abrupt little walls. Two or three hundred feet higher the going improved considerably and the ridge became more defined. Both of us were climbing better than on the previous day; we were on new ground, and had the stimulating feeling that every step took us nearer to our objective. Many uncomfortable weeks, many unprofitable ascents and descents were behind us. Now we were mountaineering.

Sometimes Eric led and sometimes I. It was a settled policy with us to husband every ounce of strength; so we went slowly, our object being to keep moving rather than halt at frequent intervals. Every step was a stage in the day's work and as such demanded all the concentration we could give to it. The man who wears himself out on a mountain is he who has never learnt to walk properly. At high altitudes every detail is magnified. At an Alpine level the mountaineer in good training needs to be told that an upward step of one foot in height does not involve merely twice the effort of an upward step of six inches but several times the effort, but at high altitudes this is painfully obvious. Taking short upward steps is one of the secrets of husbanding strength on Everest, and another is an aptitude for discerning the easiest route through a wilderness of broken rocks. Any jerky movement is fatal, for jerks mean sudden outputs of energy, which accelerate heart and lungs, as though the body was a high-powered racing motorcar engine with a sensitive throttle control. The summation of all these things is rhythm, and rhythm is an attitude of mind rather than any conscious physical control, included in which is confidence in one's companion and in oneself, a resolute refusal to be hurried by time or distance, and the elimination of all worrying thoughts.

We were climbing along the ridge at about 26,500 feet when Eric, who was leading, suddenly stopped and pointed: "There go Wyn and Waggers on the Second Step," he said. I joined him and we stared at the North-East Ridge, whence the Second Step lifts its steep prow. There were certainly two dots on a small patch of snow at the foot of the step, and as my gaze concentrated on them they seemed to move. Then, simultaneously, we realised that they were two rocks. And on a snow slope above the step were two more rocks which seemed to move too when we stared hard at them.

It was a strange experience, especially in view of the fact that it was hereabout that Odell saw Mallory and Irvine for a few moments between drifting mists. Was it possible that he was similarly deceived, especially in view of the mists, which may have enhanced the illusion of movement? I do not think he was deceived. His description is too detailed to allow of a mistake in the first place: most important point of all, he describes one figure as moving up to join the other. But I do not believe they were on the Second Step or that they climbed the step in the minute or so that he was able to watch them. The Step is fully eighty feet high, and they were carrying heavy oxygen apparatus. Assuming the ascent to be possible, it could hardly take less than half an hour with or without oxygen apparatus, and Odell did not see them for more than a few minutes. His view was between shifting mists, and it is probable that they were traversing one of two prominent rises in the ridge some distance below the First Step, or the First Step itself. It would be easy to mistake the position of a party on a misty day on a complicated peak like Everest.

A little higher the ridge flattened out. A few yards to the west was a shallow hollow, really the head of an ill-defined gully, with a sloping floor of screes and boulders. Here lay a little tangle of green canvas and tent poles – the highest camp of 1924. There was something inexpressibly desolate and pathetic in the scene. Time and weather had burst and ripped the frail shelter into fragments. And those who had last slept there, Mallory and Irvine? Where were they? Would Everest yield its secret?

A few yards higher we decided to halt for a rest and a bite of food. A scarcely perceptible breeze was blowing, but it was too cold to make a halt possible on the ridge; on the lee-side, however, was a ledge, the only one we had seen and to this we descended. It was an ideal spot, a suntrap quite sheltered from the wind. We seated ourselves side by side, our legs dangling over the depths of a gully descending towards the East Rongbuk Glacier. It was the first time we had halted in comfort above the North Col. The sun had been shining since we left Camp 5, but we had not noticed it. Now we could feel it; it penetrated our clothing and embraced our bodies; it was hot in our faces; we did not need to kick our feet together to keep the sluggish blood flowing; they became warm of their own accord. And warmth renewed interest and hope. The one thing that alloyed pleasure was the thought that presently we must force ourselves to go on.

We ate a little, not much, for our stomachs rebelled against food and eating was a duty not a pleasure, and at length summoned up the energy to continue. The cold breeze met us on the ridge, and in a few minutes we were back where we had been before both in temperature and weariness.

Above the 1924 Camp 6 some yellowish pinnacles of decaying limestone bar further direct progress along the north ridge, but we avoided them easily by a diagonal upward traverse across a slope of screes and boulders. This brought us to a great stretch of broken slabs, screes and patches of snow extending to the foot of the belt of steeper sandstone slabs already designated the Yellow Band. There was no difficulty in ascending this ground; we had merely to pick out a route that involved the minimum of effort; but it was a dull trudge, and doubtless because of this and the absence of any interest or difficulty to occupy our minds we both began to feel the altitude as we had never felt it before. There was another factor, which may have contributed to this. On the North Ridge there had been a breeze, but here, on the face of the mountain, the life had gone out of the air; it was heavy, dead and charged with some subtle quality of languor and fatigue.

On the ridge we had climbed slowly but continuously, but now, however slowly we climbed, we had to halt at intervals. Yet I suppose we made progress at the rate of three or four hundred feet an hour – we could scarcely have done less when the going was so easy. Like all tired climbers I was beset by futile little worries. Perhaps on some rocks a few feet high there were two routes, an upper and a lower. The lower merely deferred the issue and meant in the end a steeper and more fatiguing ascent; the upper, on the contrary, meant effort all the time and was obviously better inasmuch as the effort was more uniform, yet the mind boggled at the thought of effort at all; 'better defer it for a while,' it said. Yet the effort has to be made. Then would come a sudden spurt of determination, a whip-up of flagging energy, and I would take the upper route.

As soon as we came within view of the Yellow Band we halted. From Jack's description we knew roughly where Camp 6 had been pitched, but it was some time before we spotted the dark-green tent on the great expanse of slabs.

Not being by any means certain as to Jack's descending traverse route, we decided to climb directly up to it over the slabs. The camp was at the junction of two thin gullies which splayed out below in an inverted V, and one of these should afford us a convenient route. To enter it meant crossing diagonally a large bed of hard snow extending some distance along the foot of the Yellow Band. There were no signs of any steps made by the first party and step cutting was necessary.

Eric and I had both cut steps at 25,000 feet on Kamet, but this was nearly 2,000 feet higher. The snow was blue and icy, indeed almost névé, and several swings of the axe were necessary to fashion a step. To me, the sound of an ice axe meeting hard snow or ice is the sweetest of all sounds on a mountainside, but here each swing of the arms set loose a few more grains in the diminishing sands of energy. Half a dozen strokes, and heart and lungs were working intolerably fast, and it was necessary to lean on the axe and gasp for breath, oblivious to all else but the vital need of oxygen. Slowly the lungs eased their exhausting pumping; the hands gripped the axe shaft again; swing, swing, swing, and again the crescendo of heart and lungs. So it went on.

The slope was not more than 100 feet long, but it seemed interminable. It was behind us at last and we found ourselves in the mouth of the gully. Here the snow was the exact antithesis of the snow we had just crossed; less exposed to wind, it had collected in soft powdery masses, and from balancing upwards on firm steps we were reduced to wallowing knee deep and even thigh deep. There was no question of ascending it, and we floundered across diagonally to the rocks of its western side. Yesterday's blizzard had covered these in loose snow, but even so they were preferable to the gully. Free of snow they would have been easy enough, but now the ledges in the outward-dipping slabs were concealed, and the snow had to be shovelled away with gloved hands at every step. There was no suggestion of tying on the rope, for there was never a single projecting rock to hitch it round and it would have been merely a nuisance.

The climbing was difficult, far more difficult than we had anticipated. It occurred to us both that at sea level the ascent would have been reckoned as difficult, but now I am not so sure; on Everest, difficulty cannot be dissociated from tiredness and altitude. We were wondering dully whether we had missed the camp, when we clambered over a slab and saw the tent a few feet above us perched on a slope of scree. We, or perhaps only myself, as Eric had little voice left, let out a croak of relief. We could have continued had the need been great, but 'sufficient unto the day' – we were dog-tired.

There was no one to welcome us; Wyn and Waggers had not yet returned. Somewhere they were toiling, perhaps up, perhaps down. Had they reached the summit? When would they return? These questions could wait. We were too tired to do anything but attend to our own immediate needs, and of these the greatest were rest and a hot drink. The first was easily satisfied and unlacing the tent flaps we sank down on the sleeping bags within; and there we lay some time, too tired to move. Finally, we bestirred ourselves sufficiently to prepare the second. At this height the solid methylated gave off little warmth; the blue flickering flames seemed cowed and oppressed by cold and altitude, and a full hour elapsed before they had melted enough snow to lubricate our dried-up throats and leather-like tongues, and then it was only a cup of luke-warm tea apiece.

Suddenly we heard the scrape of boot-nails and a few moments later were welcoming Wyn and Waggers. We did not need to ask them whether they had reached the summit; their bearing was not that of successful men. The first thing Wyn did was to fling down an ice axe at the entrance of the tent. 'Found this,' he said.

'Must have belonged to Mallory or Irvine.'

They squashed themselves into the tent and seated themselves with the thankful sighs of tired men. We asked no questions but set about preparing a hot drink.

When they had rested a little we had their story. Wyn told it; and though for a tired man he was amazingly coherent and intelligible, we had frequently to interrupt him: 27,400 feet does not conduce to clear thinking or description. Yet in the end his story was clear in all its essential details. Following a miserable night, they had risen at 4.30 and, after a very poor meal and the usual exhausting ritual of thawing frozen boots and pulling on windproof clothing, left the tent shortly after 5.30. At this hour the sun had not yet risen above the North-East Ridge and the cold was so great that they feared frostbite. They traversed the slabs of the yellow band diagonally, gradually gaining height. An hour later, when the sun appeared, they halted and Waggers removed his boots and massaged his numbed feet. Fortunately, there was little or no wind; otherwise both must have been dangerously frostbitten.

Not far beyond this halting-place Wyn discovered the ice axe which can only have belonged to Mallory or Irvine. It was lying on the slabs, which are hereabouts inclined at an angle of 35°–40° unsupported by crack or ledge, and dependent on friction alone for its lodgement.

For the time being the axe was left where it was found and they continued traversing to the foot of the First Step. As we had suspected, it appeared possible to avoid climbing the two towers, which compose the Step by a traverse to the north of them. The ridge could then be gained above the step. But the objection to this, was that the 200 yards long section of ridge crest between the First Step and Second Step, a jagged saw blade of rock with abrupt gaps fifteen to twenty feet deep, looked difficult. The labour of traversing such an edge at 28,000 feet would be immense, and a gap fifteen feet deep, if the sides of it are vertical and unclimbable, is sufficient to stop a party at a much lower elevation. Norton and Somervell had much the same view in 1924, and were so impressed by the difficulty of the ridge and the second step, that they continued traversing the Yellow Band in the hope of circumventing the difficulties. So with Wyn and Waggers.

Their idea was to climb directly upwards, to the foot of the second step, thus short-circuiting the difficult section of the ridge, and with this in view they continued to traverse along the top of the Yellow Band. But the further they went the steeper and more difficult were the rocks above them. The telescope had revealed a chimney, which Wyn had noted as a possible line, but this they were unable to find. The sole possibility was an oblique gully, which appeared to cut through the steep belt of rock to a point above the Second Step. They reached the foot of this at 10 a.m. and tied on the rope for the first time. Wyn then tried to lead up it, but he found himself in one of the shallow scoops peculiar to the limestone, of which the rocks hereabouts are composed; there were no clean-cut edges, only round knobs affording the poorest of holds, especially as they were covered in snow. The climbing was very steep and at 28,000 feet, where gymnastics are impossible, and the climber cannot accomplish anything in the nature of a strenuous arm pull, it proved hopeless.

Four hours had flown and the net result was that careful examination and a determined attempt had disclosed the apparent impracticability of the ridge route. We could only speculate as to what the result would have been had they gained the ridge immediately above the First Step. The ridge *may* be practicable; the point is, can a party be spared in the future to prove this? They will have no time or strength left for an alternative route should it prove impossible.

Having failed to reach the foot of the Second Step, Wyn and Waggers were now committed to the sole alternative. Norton and Somervell's route; so they continued along the top of the Yellow Band with the steep rock band of the Second Step above them, and presently came to the head of the great couloir. This they crossed, finding like Norton before them treacherously loose snow in the bed of the couloir. On the rocks beyond, where the yellow band surges outwards in a buttress separating the main couloir from a subsidiary couloir, they encountered steeper and more difficult climbing. And the conditions were bad; the snow of yesterday's blizzard had accumulated on the sloping ledges and in every crack and chimney. Furthermore, Waggers was tired: he thought he might be able to continue for another hour not longer. Lastly, the time was 12.30 p.m. Even had conditions and the strength of the party rendered the summit accessible, it would have been impossible to return to camp by nightfall and for exhausted men benighted on Everest there is only one ending.

On the way back they again examined the possibilities of reaching the foot of the Second Step, but they were too tired to carry out their intention of gaining the ridge above the First Step. Finally, Waggers managed to reach the ridge below the First Step immediately above the ice axe,[4] whence he gazed down the stupendous ice slopes, of the South-East Face. In this connection it is interesting to note that ice is plastered to the south side of the Second Step, and it is just possible that the step can be avoided by an upward traverse on this side, though whether a climber can cut steps in an ice slope of 60° or more, as the angle would appear to be, at 28,000 feet is another unsolved problem of Everest. There are many problems, and each may use up a party, perhaps a whole expedition.

The full story, as I have given it here, Eric and I did not hear until afterwards, but we heard enough to convince us that we must go "all out" for Norton's route and not dissipate our energy between it and the ridge route, as Wyn and Waggers had so unfortunately had to do in their capacity as a reconnaissance party.

We listened to their story with that apathy peculiar to high altitudes. Even the finding of the ice axe, one of the most dramatic discoveries in the history of mountaineering, failed to evoke more than a passing interest.

By dint of a long and miserable effort the methylated cooker mustered sufficient energy to melt some snow. There was no time to heat up a good drink, for time was getting on, and it was essential that Wyn and Waggers should be off down to Camp 5. So contenting themselves with some lukewarm liquid they gathered themselves together and prepared to descend. It must have cost them more than

[4] Wyn Harris left his own in place of it.

an ordinary effort to face the weary descent, but what would the position have been if they had been too tired to descend, with one small tent at Camp 6, capable of accommodating only two men, and that uncomfortably? And what if there had been a sudden blizzard to make the descent impossible?

A minute or so later, I took a photograph of them; they were following Jack's downward route; their heads were bowed, and they moved in that heavy dragging way peculiar to tired men.

After their departure Eric and I did our best to make ourselves comfortable. Comfort was the only thing in our minds; all else, all plans and thoughts for the morrow could take care of themselves. And there was little enough comfort to be had in that small tent. No platform had been available for it, and one had been constructed of stones, but the party had been too tired to do this efficiently, or to level the floor of the platform, and the result was that the tent canted outwards, whilst sundry large and sharp stones beneath the thin sewn-in ground sheet reminded us forcibly of the hardness of things in general and of Everest in particular. In addition to this, the outer side of the tent was improperly supported and projected beyond the edge of the platform. This reduced the effective width and added greatly to the discomfort.

I do not remember that there was any discussion as to who should have the upper and who the lower position, I only know I found myself in the upper. The net result was that I spent the night rolling at frequent intervals on to Eric, whilst Eric spent the night being rolled on at frequent intervals by me.

Before trying to sleep, we cooked some supper. There was a little store of provisions, enough for three days, perhaps four at a pinch, and ten or a dozen tins of solid methylated fuel. We placed the cooker between us as we lay in our sleeping bags and investigated the provisions. There was condensed milk, sugar, drinking chocolate, tabloid tea, "Ovaltine", café-au-lait, Brand's meat extracts, sardines, cod roes, biscuits and sweets.

Hot drinks came before everything else and these the wretched little cooker resolutely refused to produce. At 27,000 feet water boils at a temperature many degrees below the boiling point at sea level, but not once during our stay at Camp 6 did we manage to get a boiling drink, and we had to content ourselves with lukewarm concoctions. Our language regarding the solid methylated cooker is unprintable, but it is far too much of an effort to be angry at 27,400 feet.

Our supper consisted principally of Brand's beef extract, which was frozen solid and had to be thawed out before it could be eaten. We had no desire for solids – indeed, no desire for food of any kind; eating was a duty. Drinking was a different matter. Our bodies were desiccated by the intensely dry atmosphere and craved for moisture, which also served as a palliative for sore and congested throats.

Our meal ended with café-au-lait and condensed milk, which was voted superb. Then, before settling down for the night, we unlaced the tent flaps and glanced outside; everything now depended on the weather.

The evening was calm, the calmest we had known above the North Col. The smooth, outward dipping slabs glowed in the fast setting sun and, at an immense distance beneath, clouds concealed the valleys and lesser peaks. There was nothing to obstruct the tremendous prospect. Seen from Everest, great peaks that dominate the climber as he toils along the East Rongbuk Glacier, and up the slopes of the North Col, show like insignificant ripples at the base of a great ocean roller. Even the North Peak was but a stepping-stone to quick-footed vision.

It was cold. Space, the air we breathed, the yellow rocks were deadly cold. There was something ultimate, passionless and eternal in this cold. It came to us as a single constant note from the depths of space. We stood on the very boundary of life and death.

The night spread out of the east in a great flood, quenching the red sunlight in a single minute.

We wriggled by breathless degrees deep into our sleeping bags. Our sole thought was of comfort; we were not alive to the beauty or the grandeur of our position; we did not reflect on the splendour of our elevation. A regret I shall always have is that I did not muster up the energy to spend a minute or two stargazing. One peep I did make between the tent flaps into the night, and I remember dimly an appalling wealth of stars, not pale and remote as they appear when viewed through the moisture-laden air of lower levels, but brilliant points of electric blue fire standing out almost stereoscopically. It was a sight an astronomer would have given much to see, and here were we lying dully in our sleeping bags concerned only with the importance of keeping warm and comfortable.

There is one blessing, if of a negative nature, in high altitude. The physical and mental processes are so slowed down by lack of oxygen that a sleepless night does not drag as interminably as it does at sea level. The climber, though awake, lies semi-comatose, scarcely heeding time's passage. The one thing that stirs his sluggish mental processes into activity is acute discomfort. At times we *were* acutely uncomfortable, and this was due, as already mentioned, to the uneven sloping platform beneath us and the ineffective width of the tent. Between spasms of rapid breathing, sometimes so acute as to amount to a feeling of suffocation, I would drop off into a light slumber only to roll on top of Eric and awake with a resentful elbow in the small of my back. Then we would curse bitterly, not each other but a common fate.

We slept with heads buttressed high by wads of rucksacks, boots, rope and windproof clothing, as this aids breathing at high altitudes. Balaclava helmets protected our heads, and only eyes, mouths and noses were exposed. We were reasonably warm and I felt myself to be resting in spite of my sleeplessness.

The night was calm until shortly before dawn. Then, for the first time, a gust of wind tugged at the tent. It was succeeded by another and stronger gust. By dawn a gale was blowing.

We had planned to start at about 5.30 a.m., but it was impossible; to have left the tent even for a few minutes would have meant certain and severe frostbite. It was terribly depressing to lie thus, our hopes destroyed in a single hour, but at the same time I could not suppress a feeling of relief that I did not have to endure the exertion of turning out of my sleeping bag and of struggling into my windproof suit and boots. Ours was not the disappointment of men eager and willing to set off for an unclimbed summit; we only felt that an unpleasant duty had been frustrated. I was tired too, and needed additional rest to recuperate from the exertions of yesterday. Eric felt differently about this. He told me afterwards that so far from recuperating, his strength deteriorated steadily during the day and that his chance of doing himself justice vanished when we were prevented from starting. This physical difference between us crystallised one of Everest's greatest problems – that of two men setting out for the summit both at the top of their form.

As daylight increased snow began to fall; we could hear the familiar yet ever hateful patter, swish and lash of it on the tent.

We breakfasted. The wretched business of having to replenish the saucepan with snow was scarcely compensated for by the lukewarm cup of tea apiece eventually produced by the cooker, yet it served to stimulate a discussion of the position as we lay side by side in our sleeping bags.

If the weather improved would the summit be possible on the morrow? The new snow, even though much of it blew off the mountain as it fell, would inevitably accumulate in every sheltered place, particularly in the vicinity of the Great Couloir. Neither of us voiced the thought to the other, but we knew that unless a miracle happened we were as good as beaten. However, we could at least go as far as possible when the weather mended. But would the weather mend? At the back of our minds was always the thought of the monsoon. At any moment now it might burst on Everest in full force and snow fall for days on end. What then? We had food for another three days, four at a pinch, maybe even five with the strictest rationing, but there was only fuel for another two days, reckoning the use of one tin of solid methylated per meal and three meals a day. Food is useless at 27,400 feet without fuel. Something to warm the stomach is the first essential; without warmth a man cannot live for long; he is too near the point where the oxygen he breathes is insufficient to counteract the cooling of the body by the cold air. For how many days a man can live at 27,400 feet in a small tent supplied with ample food and fuel is a matter for conjecture. I should say not longer than a week. In the event of a continuous snowstorm we should naturally try to descend, but I do not believe a descent from Camp 6 is possible through deep snow even in fair weather; the slabs of the Yellow Band would be impassable.

A heavy snowfall is a risk the climber will always have to face high on Everest, and it militates against a camp on the final pyramid to the west of the great couloir. Here it needs but a sprinkling of snow to render descent impossible, or at least desperately dangerous, and conditions which do not prohibit a descent from a point as high as the ledge beneath the First Step at nearly 28,000 feet, on which we had planned originally to pitch Camp 6, may well make impossible descent from a more westerly point. Yet, whether or not a camp should be pitched on the pyramid may have to be considered. The main point is that Everest cannot be climbed by any route or method, without risks far in excess of ordinary mountaineering risks, and the problem a mountaineer will always have to face is whether or not he is entitled to take risks overstepping the traditional standards of safety in mountaineering in order to gain success. My own belief is that the man who climbs on the upper part of Everest does overstep these standards, and that owing to the unique nature of the problem his conceptions of what is justifiable and what is unjustifiable cannot be based on Alpine standards of safety and danger. One thing only delimits reasoned adventure from unreasoned recklessness – the duty owed by an expedition to its porters. So long as these men are employed their welfare must always determine the manner of climbing

Everest, and this helps the climber to gauge his duty to his comrades, and those who anxiously await his safe return.

By the afternoon a full-dress blizzard was raging. We were far too lethargic to be alarmed at the possibility of being marooned permanently. Indeed, our discussion of the possibilities already mentioned was purely academic and on a curiously detached and impersonal plane, almost as though we were scientists discussing an immature experiment, yet our instincts were animal rather than human, inasmuch as we were concerned only with the present, and our complaints were against trivial things which loomed out of all proportion to the possible events of the future. It is probable that we remember each other's grouses without remembering our own – a happy dispensation. Eric had developed a "complex" relating to fresh food. All through the expedition he had been a protagonist of fresh food. The toughest and most indigestible piece of gristle from a Tibetan sheep of Marathon-like build was to him preferable to the most succulent product of Messrs. Fortnum & Mason that came out of a tin. Now in a hoarse, scarcely audible voice, he enlarged on the lack of fresh food at Camp 6. 'Oh, for a few dozen eggs!' was his constant plaint; or 'This — tinned muck' he would whisper bitterly. I could sympathise, at all events, with his craving for eggs. Certainly an omelette nicely fried and well buttered with a dash of *fines herbes*, would have gone down well, and one of those huge bilberry omelettes known as "palat-schinken" in the Tyrol would have been a welcome change from the frozen corpses of sardines in congealed oil.

As I felt I ought to contribute a grouse of my own, I conceived a more and more bitter hatred for a sharp stone beneath the tent. This had been placed at the exact point most convenient for my hipbone. I made a few futile tugs and jabs at it, but it was evidently a large, well-wedged stone and refused to budge. My remarks concerning it were rich in those hyphens and asterisks whereby the deserving printer tries to conceal, and yet, paradoxically, to reveal the niceties of the English language.

Towards evening there was a sudden gleam of light. We looked outside. The clouds had parted, revealing the rapidly declining sun. Its pale light accentuated rather than mitigated the bleakness of the prospect. The wind was still volleying across Everest, raising spirals of loose snow, which hurried in an endless procession across the slabs. Every crack and cranny held its salt-like snow and only the more exposed slabs had been swept clear. In between the flying rags of mist the sky was green, not the warm green of grass and trees, but a cruel feline green utterly unmerciful. Yet the sight of it rekindled a spark of hope. If we could do nothing else on the morrow we might once and for all dispose of the problem of the ridge route and the Second Step.

The wind was moderating as we prepared our meagre supper, and only an occasional squall worried the tent. The night was no more comfortable than the last, and to describe it would be to repeat a catalogue of discomforts. Now and again would come a fierce squall succeeded by a period of calm, then another squall. But as the night wore on the calm intervals lengthened and the squalls were less violent. Perhaps, after all, we should be able to attempt the summit. In the conditions we could not hope to succeed; we could only do our best.

CHAPTER FIFTEEN

The Assault

THE SKY WAS clear at daybreak. We had resolved overnight to leave at 5, but a rising wind and intense cold made this impossible. Cold we could have faced, but the addition of wind is too much for mere flesh and blood on Everest.

Matters appeared hopeless until an hour later when the wind suddenly fell to a complete calm. And it did not return. We listened expectantly for the hateful rush and tug of it, but the calm persisted.

Breakfast eaten, we extricated ourselves foot by foot from our sleeping bags and with much labour and panting pulled on our windproof suits.

Our boots might have been carved out of stone, and they glistened and sparkled inside with the frozen moisture from our feet. I made a vain attempt to soften mine over a candle, but it was useless, and somehow or other I thrust my feet into them, pausing at intervals to beat my bare hands together, or stuff them into my pockets.

We donned every stitch of clothing we possessed. I wore a Shetland vest, a thick flannel shirt, a heavy camel hair sweater, six light Shetland pullovers, two pairs of long Shetland pants, a pair of flannel trousers, and over all a silk-lined "Grenfell" windproof suit. A Shetland balaclava and another helmet of "Grenfell" cloth protected my head, and my feet were encased in four pairs of Shetland socks and stockings. Gloves are always a problem on Everest, and the ideal glove that is warm yet flexible and will adhere to rocks has still to be designed; in this instance, a pair of woollen fingerless gloves inside a pair of South African lambskin gloves, also fingerless, kept my hands moderately warm.

A slab of Kendal mint cake apiece sufficed for food. It was a mistake not to provide ourselves with more food but our repugnance for it had been still further intensified during our enforced stay at Camp 6. Apart from this we carried a length of light climbing line, whilst my "Etui" camera accompanied me as usual. (With one film pack this weighed one and a quarter pounds.)

At 7 we emerged from the tent and laced the flaps behind us. It was sadly obvious that Eric was far below his usual form. He had eaten less than I since we had arrived at the Camp, and now he complained of stomach pains, and asked me to go slowly – a request I might have made myself had he been fitter.

A shallow snow-filled gully took us diagonally upwards and across the Yellow Band for the best part of 100 feet. There was no difficulty, but every minute or two we had to halt and lean on our ice axes gasping for breath.

The gully petered out into a great expanse of slabs. Again there was no difficulty; advance was merely a matter of careful balance and choice of the easiest route; yet the angle as a whole on the Yellow Band is such that a slip would probably end in a fatal slide, especially as the climber would have little strength left to stop himself. Fortunately, our broad, lightly nailed boots gripped the sandstone well. The snow of yesterday's blizzard had been blown from many of the slabs, but here and there where it had accumulated on the shelving ledges we had to tread circumspectly.

Though we left the camp an hour and a half later than Wyn and Waggers had done, the cold was still intense and there was little warmth in the sun, which was just peeping over the North-East Ridge.

The first and most lasting impression of the climber on Everest will always be the bleak and inhospitable nature of the great mountain. On the Yellow Band no projecting crags, ridges or buttresses stimulate the interest or the imagination; there is nothing level and the climber must tread a series of outward-shelving ledges where the rope is useless to him. Never have I seen a more utterly desolate mountainside. And above, still a weary way above, was the summit pyramid set squarely at the end of this vast rocky roof; a last tremendous challenge to our failing strength.

Traversing, and ascending slightly, we made for the foot of the First Step which, from the moment we emerged from the initial gully, appeared close at hand. Its shape reminded me in some curious way of the summit of a Lake District hill, which I had climbed one dewy spring morning before breakfast to "work up an appetite". It had taken me an hour to scale 2,300 feet of turfy bracken-clad fellside, and now with eleven hours of daylight in hand I was doubtful whether we had the time or strength to climb and descend 1,600 feet. Yet, I was going better than I had expected. Exercise was loosening my cramped and stiffened limbs and for the first time since arriving at Camp 6 I was conscious of warm blood flowing vigorously in my veins. But, unhappily, this was not the case with Eric. He was going steadily, but very slowly, and it was more than ever plain that there was something wrong with him.

Not far from the First Step we crossed an almost level platform covered in small screes, a possible site for a future camp, then traversed almost horizontally. We were immediately below the Step when I heard an exclamation behind me. Turning, I saw that Eric had stopped and was leaning heavily on his ice axe. Next moment he sank down into a sitting position.

Many times during the march across Tibet we had discussed what to do in the event of one man of a party of two being unable to continue, and we had agreed that unless he was exhausted and unable to return alone safely his companion should carry on alone, in which decision he would be supported by the expedition and its leader. It was an expedition maxim that no man must go on till he reached a point of complete exhaustion, and Eric was far too good a mountaineer to do this. The saving grace in high-altitude climbing is that there is a point at which a man cannot continue to ascend but can still descend relatively easily and quite safely. This is Nature's automatic safety check.[1]

[1] I am convinced that this automatic check rules out the possibility of a man collapsing suddenly near the summit of Everest. Such a disturbing possibility has been mentioned as the result of tests carried out by the R.A.F. in a decompression chamber. These tests revealed that at a pressure equivalent to a height of 28,000-30,000 feet many

I asked Eric whether he felt fit enough to return to camp safely. He replied unhesitatingly, "Yes," and added that he would follow slowly. This last, though I did not know it at the time, was inspired by generosity. He had no intention of proceeding further and merely said that he would to encourage me and relieve me from all anxiety as to his safety. It was another example of that good comradeship which will one day take men to the summit of Everest.

Leaving him seated on a rock I continued. I looked back after a minute or so, but he had as yet made no move.

There was never any doubt as to the best route. The crest of the North-East Ridge, leading to the foot of the Second Step, was sharp, jagged and obviously difficult. As for the Second Step, now almost directly above me, it *looked* utterly impregnable, and I can only compare it to the sharp bow of a battle cruiser. Norton's route alone seemed to offer any chance of success, and it follows the yellow band beneath a sheer wall to the head of the Great Couloir.

At first there was no difficulty and a series of sloping ledges at the top of the Yellow Band took me round a corner and out of sight of Eric. Then came a patch of snow perhaps thirty yards wide. There was no avoiding it except by a descent of nearly a hundred feet, but fortunately the snow was not the evil floury stuff I had expected, but had been well compacted by the wind; indeed, such hard snow that step-cutting was necessary.

Step cutting at nearly 28,000 feet is a fatiguing operation, and the axe seemed unconscionably heavy and unready to do its work. In the Alps one powerful stroke with the adze would have fashioned a step, but sudden spurts of exertion are to be avoided at 28,000 feet, and I preferred the alternative of several light, short strokes. I must have looked like an old hen grubbing for worms, but even so I had to cease work and puff hard after making each step.

High altitudes promote indecision. Projecting through the snow was a rock and at first sight it seemed a good foothold. Then I thought it was too sloping and that I had better cut to one side of it. But I had no sooner changed my mind when I decided that perhaps after all it could be used as a foothold and would save me a step or two. I must have spent a minute or two turning this ridiculous little point over in my mind before doing what was the obvious thing – avoiding it. It is curious how small problems encountered during a great undertaking can assume an importance out of all proportion to their true worth.

When I had crossed the snow I again glanced back, but there was no sign of Eric following me, and I continued on my solitary way.

Contrary to accepted mountaineering practice, I found that the easiest as well as the safest method of traversing the slabs was to keep the ice axe in the outside hand as there were always little cracks and crannies to put it in. It was a

men faint suddenly and without warning. Such tests, however, are artificial inasmuch as they make no allowance for acclimatisation, and I do not believe they have any real bearing on the Everest problem. I cannot for an instant believe that under natural conditions nature acts in so arbitrary a fashion. Her processes lead slowly and unmistakably to a logical conclusion. It is only artificial conditions that she resents. Perhaps this is one of the deep-seated reasons why many Everest climbers abhor oxygen apparatus. There is something artificial, unnatural and therefore dangerous in its use on Everest. The argument that it is necessary in high flying, mines, etc., etc., cannot hold water inasmuch as such conditions are unnatural, men not being endowed with the capabilities of birds or moles, which do not, incidentally, require oxygen apparatus to sustain them.

third leg to me and an invaluable companion throughout the whole of the day.

Beyond the snow patch the slabs were covered here and there with loose, powdery snow. This had to be kicked or scraped away before I dared stand on the outward-sloping ledges. Progress was slow, though steady, and as I advanced and saw the final pyramid appear above the band of rocks beneath which I was traversing, there came to me for the first time that day a thrill of excitement and hope. I was going well now, better than when I had parted from Eric and for a moment there seemed a chance of success.

The bed of the Great Couloir was hidden, but a subsidiary couloir and a buttress separating it from the Great Couloir were full in view. Both were sheltered from the wind and as a result were still heavily plastered with the snow of yesterday's blizzard. My hopes were dashed as I gazed at the buttress. It was considerably steeper than the rocks I was traversing, and snow filled every crack and was piled deeply on every sloping ledge. Was it climbable in such a condition? In the Alps perhaps, but not at 28,000 feet by a man nearing the limit of his strength. And the subsidiary couloir? Even supposing the traverse of the buttress proved practicable, what kind of snow should I find in this narrow cleft? Most likely unstable powder affording no certain footing and impeding every movement. True, it might be possible to avoid it by climbing the rocks at one side, but these, in their turn, were mostly snow-covered.

Instinctively I looked for an alternative. Could I climb directly upwards to a point above the Second Step and attack the final pyramid without having to continue this long, wearisome and unprofitable traverse? The wall rose above me like a sea cliff, in places it overhung, and every hold, every wrinkle and crack held its quota of snow. There was no visible break in it until the buttress where there was a gap, possibly the point reached by Norton in 1924, which might prove a feasible alternative to the subsidiary couloir. At all events direct ascent was impossible. One thing alone gave me hope: once the subsidiary couloir had been climbed and the rock band passed there seemed every reason to suppose that the principal difficulties were behind. I could see the face of the final pyramid and it did not look difficult. There was a scree slope at the base of it and higher a slope of light-coloured boulders. Energy alone would be required to surmount it. Of course, it may hold its surprises, for Everest will remain a stubborn opponent to the last; but I feel confident that once the rock band is below, the change from difficult and dangerous climbing to safe and easy climbing will inspire the climber to outlast fatigue and altitude over the remaining 600 feet to the summit.

The angle of the Yellow Band steepened gradually as I approached the Great Couloir. In general direction the ledges were parallel with the Band, but they were not always continuous, and once or twice I had to retrace my steps for a yard or two and seek an alternative route. But the climbing was never difficult – it required only unfailing attention to the planting of each foot on the sloping ledges, especially when these were masked by loose snow.

Presently the bed of the Great Couloir became visible. It was shallow enough not to necessitate any steep descent into it, and was filled with snow, perhaps thirty to forty feet wide, which ended beneath the rock band. Several hundred feet lower was a pitch of unknown height, beneath which the couloir widened out into a small hanging glacier, then fell steeply towards the Rongbuk Glacier, a total height from my position of about 8,000 feet.

It was a savage place. Beyond was the steep and snowy buttress separating me from the subsidiary couloir, and hemming me in above was the unrelenting band of rock, and higher still the final pyramid, a weary distance away, cutting aloofly into the blue.

I approached the couloir along a ledge, which bent round a steep little corner. This ledge was comfortably wide until it came to the corner, then it narrowed until it was only a few inches broad. As far as the corner it was easy going, but to turn the corner I had to edge along, my face to the mountain, in a crab-like fashion. The rocks above projected awkwardly, but it was not a place that would have caused a second's hesitation on an alpine climb. One step only was needed to take me round the corner. This step I funked. The balance was too critical. With arms spread-eagled above me I sought for steadying handholds. They were not essential; balance alone should have sufficed, but I felt I could not manage without them. I could find none; every wrinkle in the rocks sloped outwards. For a few moments I stood thus like a man crucified, while my heart bumped quickly and my lungs laboured for oxygen, and there flashed through my mind the possibility of a backward topple into the couloir an interminable slide into belated oblivion.

I retired a few yards and apostrophised myself as a fool. I knew that the traverse was possible, and if Eric had been there I should not have hesitated. Being alone made all the difference.

I tried again, and once more found myself in the spread-eagled position but without the courage to take the one step that would have placed me in safety round the corner.

The only alternative was a ledge about twenty feet below. I was loath to lose even twenty feet of height, but there was nothing for it but to descend.

The slabs separating me from the ledge were reasonably rough, and though there were no very definite holds there were wrinkles and folds. For the rest friction should serve. Facing outwards and sitting down I lowered myself gingerly off the ledge on the palms of my hands. The friction was even better than I had hoped for, and the seat of my trousers almost sufficed by itself to maintain me in position without the additional support of the palms of my hands. There was no awkward corner in the lower ledge; it was wide and honest, and though it sloped outwards and supported a bank of snow three or four feet deep, it brought me without difficulty to the snowy bed of the couloir.

Wyn and Waggers had found the same loose, disagreeable snow in the couloir as had Norton in 1924, but I suspect that they traversed the upper ledge and so crossed higher than I. The snow at my level, as a tentative forward dig with the ice axe revealed, had been hardened by the wind and step-cutting was again necessary.

One step, then a pause to gasp, while the snow at my feet and the rocks beyond swam uncertainly before me. Then another step and another bout of gasping.

The snow was very hard and the angle of the Great Couloir at this point fully 50°. About a dozen steps – I was across at last.

Next, how to traverse the buttress? I must climb almost straight up it for about fifty feet before continuing more or less horizontally towards the subsidiary couloir.

The rocks were steep and snow had accumulated on them untouched as yet by the wind. How had the wind swept the snow in the couloir hard and left the slabs at this side unaffected?

When these slabs are snow-free they are probably not much more difficult than the slabs to the east of the Great Couloir. There are numerous ledges, and though the general angle is appreciably steeper, there is no necessity for anything but balance climbing, and I confidently believe no insuperable obstacle will prevent the climber from reaching the subsidiary couloir. But now snow had accumulated deeply on the shelving ledges and it was the worst kind of snow, soft like flour, loose like granulated sugar and incapable of holding the feet in position. As I probed it with my axe, I knew at once that the game was up. So far the climbing had been more dangerous than difficult now it was both difficult and dangerous, a fatal combination on Everest. The only thing I could do was to go as far as possible, always keeping one eye on the weather and the other on the strength I should need to retreat safely.

The weather at all events was fair. In the shelter of the buttress and the wall beyond the subsidiary couloir there was not a breath of wind and the sun shone powerfully – too powerfully, for it seemed to sap my strength and my resolution. I was a prisoner, struggling vainly to escape from a vast hollow enclosed by dungeon-like walls. Wherever I looked hostile rocks frowned down on my impotent strugglings, and the wall above seemed almost to overhang me with its dark strata set one upon the other, an embodiment of static, but pitiless, force. The final pyramid was hidden; if only I were on it away from this dismal place with its unrelenting slabs. The climber who wins across the slabs to the final pyramid must conquer a sickness of spirit as well as a weariness of body.

With both arms at breast-high level I began shovelling the snow away before me; it streamed down the couloir behind me with a soft swishing noise. Several minutes elapsed before a sloping ledge was disclosed, then I heaved myself up, until first one knee, and then the other, were on it. In this position, like a supplicant before a priest, I had to remain while my lungs, intolerably accelerated by the effort, heaved for oxygen. Then with another effort I stood cautiously upright.

More snow had to be cleared before I could tread a smaller ledge on the slab above; then, to my relief, came a step unattended by this prodigious effort of clearing away snow. But relief is short-lived on Everest and the ledge that followed was covered several feet deep in snow bevelled into a steep bank, yet without the slightest cohesion.

Presently I had to stop, as apart from the need to rest overstressed heart and lungs, immersing my arms in the snow brought such numbness to my hands, gloved though they were, that I feared I might let slip my ice axe.

So slow and exhausting was the work of clearing the snow that I began to rely on feel alone. That is to say, when I could I trusted my foot to find holds beneath the snow rather than clear the snow away from the slabs until I could see the holds. I realised full well the danger of this, and whenever possible used my ice axe pick as an extra support by jamming it into cracks. This last precaution undoubtedly saved me from catastrophe. There was one steeply shelving slab deeply covered with soft snow into which I sank to the knees, but my first exploring foot discovered a knob beneath it. This seemed quite firm and, reaching up with my axe, I wedged the pick of it half an inch or so into a thin crack. Then, cautiously, I raised my other foot on to the knob, at the same time transferring my entire weight to my front foot. My rear foot was joining my front foot when the knob, without any warning, suddenly broke away. For an instant, both feet slid outwards, and my weight came on the ice axe; next moment I had recovered my footing and discovered another hold. It happened so quickly that my sluggish brain had no time to register a thrill of fear; I had acted purely instinctively and the incident was over almost before I knew it had occurred. I did not even feel scared afterwards as I was climbing now in a curiously detached, impersonal frame of mind. It was almost as though one part of me stood aside and watched the other struggle on. Lack of oxygen and fatigue are responsible for this dulling of the mental faculties, but principally lack of oxygen. It is a dangerous state of mind and comparable to the mental reactions of a drunken man in charge of a car. He may believe that his judgement is unimpaired, even that he can drive more skilfully than usual; in point of fact, as statistics and the police court news reveal, he is much more prone to an accident in this condition.

Just before crossing the Great Couloir I had looked at my watch; it was 10 a.m. Now I looked again. An hour had passed, and I had made about fifty feet of height, not more. At least 300 feet of difficult rocks, all deeply snow-covered, remained to be climbed, before easier ground on the final pyramid was reached. Perhaps I could do another hour or two's work, but what was the use of it? I should only exhaust myself completely and not have the strength left to return.

I shovelled away the floury snow until I had made a space on which I could stand; though I did not dare to sit.

I was high up on the buttress separating the Great Couloir from the subsidiary couloir. Above me was the band of rock beneath which I had been, and was still, traversing. It looked impregnable except where it was breached by the subsidiary couloir, and the place already mentioned a few yards to the east of this couloir. For the rest it is Everest's greatest defence, and stretches unbroken across the north face of the mountain. The striated limestone rocks composing it actually overhang in places, and the section above the Great Couloir reminded me of the well-known pitch in the Central Gully, on Lliwedd, in North Wales.

It is possible, indeed probable, that weariness and altitude distorted my judgement, but there are two things I believe to be true. Firstly, that Norton's route is practicable, and that when the "tiles", as he calls the slabs, are free of snow, they can be traversed without excessive difficulty to the subsidiary couloir, and this can be climbed on to the face of the final pyramid. Secondly, that it is not a practicable route when snow covers the slabs. But there is no doubt that even in the best conditions this part of the climb will tax a climber's powers to the uttermost. The unrelenting exposure of the slabs, dependence on the friction of boot nails for hours on end, added to the physical and mental weariness and lethargy due to altitude, will require something more than strength and skill if they are to be countered successfully. The summit was just in view over the rock band. It was only 1,000 feet above me, but an aeon of weariness separated me from it. Bastion on bastion and slab on slab, the rocks were piled in tremendous confusion, their light-yellow edges ghostlike against the deep-blue sky. From the crest a white plume of mist flowed silently away, like unending volcanic steam, but where I stood there was not a breath of wind and the sun blazed into the hollow with an intense fierceness, yet without warming the cold air. Clouds were gathering, but they were thousands of feet below me. Between them I could see the Rongbuk Glacier, a pure white in its uppermost portion then rugged and uneven where it was resolved into a multitude of séracs and, lower still, a gigantic muddle of moraines as though all the navvies in the world had been furiously excavating to no logical purpose. Beyond it, the Rongbuk Valley stretched northwards towards the golden hills of Tibet, and I could make out the Rongbuk Monastery, a minute cluster of minute buildings, yet distinct in every detail through the brilliantly clear atmosphere. With this one exception, I remember no details. My position was too high, my, view too vast, my brain too fatigued to register detail. There was nothing visible to challenge my elevation. The earth was so far beneath; it seemed impossible I could ever regain it. The human brain must needs be divinely inspired to comprehend such a vista, and mine was tied to a body fatigued by exertion and slowed down in all its vital processes by lack of oxygen. Somervell's description of the scene is simplest and best "A god's view".

More by instinct than anything else, I pulled my camera out of my pocket. The photograph I took is pitifully inadequate.

I cannot enlarge on the bitterness of defeat. Those who have failed on Everest are unanimous in one thing: the relief of not having to go on outweighs all other considerations. The last 1,000 feet of Everest are not for mere flesh and blood. Whoever reaches the summit, if he does it without artificial aid, will have to rise godlike above his own frailties and his tremendous environment. Only through a Power within him and without him will he overcome a deadly fatigue and win through to success.

Descending even difficult ground at high altitudes is almost as easy as descending at an alpine level, and within a few minutes I regained the Great Couloir. Recrossing it, I halted on the broad, comfortable ledge to take a photograph. It is curious that I did not remember taking this photograph or the one from my highest point until the film was developed, so I think my action at the time was more automatic than reasoned, as before starting on the expedition I told myself many times that I must take photographs whenever possible. This lends colour to a theory I have long held, that in climbing at great altitudes, when mind and body are in the grip of an insidious lethargy, it is on the subconscious, rather than the conscious, that the climber must rely to push him forwards. Therefore, it is essential that the will to reach the summit of Everest be strengthened by a prior determination to get there. Perhaps it is not too much to say that Everest will be climbed in England.

After taking this photograph it occurred to me that I ought to eat something. I was, not in the least hungry, indeed the thought of food was utterly repugnant, especially as my mouth was almost dry, and my tongue leather-like, but in duty bound I pulled a slab of mint cake from my pocket.

And now I must relate the curious incident described in "Everest 1933".

After leaving Eric a strange feeling possessed me that I was accompanied by another. I have already mentioned a feeling of detachment in which it seemed as though I stood aside and watched myself. Once before, during a fall in the Dolomites, I had the same feeling, and it is not an uncommon experience with mountaineers who have a long fall. It may be that the feeling that I was accompanied was due to this, which, in its turn, was due to lack of oxygen and the mental and physical stress of climbing alone at a great altitude. I do not offer this as an explanation, but merely as a suggestion.

This "presence" was strong and friendly. In its company I could not feel lonely, neither could I come to any harm. It was always there to sustain me on my solitary climb up the snow-covered slabs. Now, as I halted and extracted some mint cake from my pocket, it was so near and so strong that instinctively I divided the mint into two halves and turned round with one half in my hand to offer it to my "companion".

It was apparent when I recrossed the couloir that I would do better to return across the Yellow Band by a lower route. The angle of the band west of the First Step is very slightly concave, and on such slabs a degree or two in angle makes all the difference. The western end of the band terminates below in a great cut-off, a sheer precipice which carries the eye in a single bound to the Rongbuk Glacier. My return route lay a few yards above and parallel to the edge of this precipice. There was no difficulty whatsoever. Care alone was needed, especially when crossing some patches of snow which, unlike those on the upper part of the band, were treacherously soft and unstable.

Very soon I found myself below the point where I had parted from Eric, but on looking up, could see no sign of him. I now had to make the choice between climbing up at least 100 feet and joining the ascending route or of traversing directly to the camp. To ascend again at this stage was utterly distasteful. I was too tired, and my legs were leaden; they would descend easily enough or traverse horizontally, but I doubt whether I could have dragged them uphill unless hard pressed. A temptation I had to resist firmly was to slant off down the Yellow Band by Norton and Somervell's route. This was a far easier line than the long, wearisome traverse across a series of shelving ledges to Camp 6. In two or three hours I could have reached Camp 5, even continued on down to the comfort of the arctic tent at Camp 4. Unfortunately, Eric was waiting for me at Camp 6, and if I did not turn up he would naturally assume an accident.

The climbing was simple enough at first, but presently became more difficult. Instead of the easy slabs, which had led us upwards from the camp to the foot of the First Step, I found myself on a series of narrow outward-sloping ledges separated by abrupt little walls. These ledges were never continuous for long, and it was necessary when one petered out to descend to another. However, I could still afford to lose height without descending below the level of Camp 6.

This route took me across the band some distance below the place where Wyn and Waggers found the ice axe, but I did not see any further traces of Mallory and Irvine. I remember glancing down at a wide, gently sloping expanse of snow, screes and broken rocks below the band and thinking that if the ice axe indeed marked the point where they slipped, it was possible that their bodies might have come to rest there.

Some of the ledges were wider than others and I paused to rest at intervals. It was during one of these halts that I was startled to observe an extraordinary phenomenon.

Chancing to look over the North-East Shoulder, now directly in front of me,

I saw two dark objects in the sky. In shape they resembled kite balloons, and my first reaction was to wonder what on earth kite balloons could be doing near Everest, a certain proof that lack of oxygen had impaired my mental faculties; but a moment later I recognised this as an absurd thought. At the same time I was very puzzled. The objects were black and silhouetted sharply against the sky, or possibly a background of cloud my memory is not clear on this point. They were bulbous in shape, and one possessed what looked like squat, underdeveloped wings, whilst the other had a beak-like protuberance like the spout of a teakettle. But what was most weird about them was that they distinctly pulsated with an in-and-out motion as though they possessed some horrible quality of life. One interesting point is that these pulsations were much slower than my own heart-beats; of this I am certain, and I mention it in view of a suggestion put forward afterwards that it was an optical illusion and that the apparent pulsations synchronised with my pulse-rate.

After my first reaction of "kite balloons" my brain seemed to function normally, and so interested was I that, believing them to be fantasies of my imagination, I deliberately put myself through a series of mental tests. First of all I looked away. The objects did not follow my vision, but when my gaze returned to the North-East Shoulder they were still hovering there. I looked away again, and by way of a more exacting mental test identified by name a number of peaks, valleys and glaciers. I found no difficulty in Cho Oyu, Gyachung Kang, Pumori and the Rongbuk Glacier, but when I again looked back the objects were in precisely the same position.

Nothing was to be gained by further examination and, tired as I was with the apparently endless succession of slabs, I decided to carry on to Camp 6. I was just starting off when a mist, forming suddenly, began to drift across the North-East Shoulder. Gradually the objects disappeared behind it. Soon they were vague shadows, then as the mist thickened, they disappeared altogether. The mist only lasted a few seconds, then melted away. I expected to see the objects again, but they were no longer there; they had disappeared as mysteriously as they came.

Was it an optical illusion or a mirage? It may be of interest to state that my height was about 27,600 feet and that the objects were a few degrees above the North-East Ridge about half-way between the position of the 1924 Camp 6 and the crest of the North-East Shoulder. This gives their height as about 27,200 feet, and a line connecting me with them would have ended not in a background of sky, but of clouds and mountains. It is possible, therefore, that imagination magnified some strange effect of mist, mountain and shadow, yet whatever they were, it was a strange and altogether uncanny experience.

The first light mist was a forerunner of other mists, which quickly gathered and drifted across the mountainside, concealing familiar landmarks. It might not be easy to find Camp 6 among the wilderness of slabs in a mist and I began to feel anxious, especially as I could not see the tent. Fortunately, however, two prominent towers on the North-East Ridge, which I knew were directly above the camp, showed now and then.

In places the sandstone slabs were intersected horizontally by slippery belts of quartzite. The first intimation I had as to how slippery they were, was when I lowered myself down a steep little wall on to an outward-sloping quartzite ledge.

It was far more slippery than the sandstone ledges, and I did not dare trust my bootnails upon it. There was no alternative but to climb up to a sandstone ledge, and this ascent, though it cannot have been more than twenty feet, made me realise how tired I was.

Presently the two rock towers were almost immediately above me and I halted and looked round expectantly for the camp. It was still not visible. Was I above it or below it? Had my route-finding been at fault? All about me was a vast labyrinth of outward-dipping slabs. Now and then a puff of icy mist would float out of space and pass djinn-like up the mountainside to the crest of the North-East Ridge where it shredded out and rushed away to join in the ceaselessly moving vapour that boiled upwards and outwards from the south-east precipice.

A few more steps. There was something familiar now about the rocks. Suddenly I came to a shallow, gently sloping gully filled with snow. There were footmarks in the snow; it was the gully immediately above the camp. Next instant I saw the little tent snugly bedded in a corner; small wonder I had not seen it before. What a relief! I let out a hoarse croak of joy and quickly scrambled down to it.

Eric was there. It scarcely needed a word on my part to tell him of my failure; he had seen enough to gauge the conditions. He had descended without difficulty and his stomach was much better. We both talked in whispers, for my mouth and throat had been dried up by the cold air. A hot drink was the first thing; I had not known how thirsty I was, for the intense desiccation of high altitudes takes the body a stage beyond the mere sensation of thirst. And the warmth of it; there was life in that drink.

We discussed plans. Now that we had failed our one desire was for comfort, and there was no comfort at Camp 6. Eric was well rested and strong enough to descend to Camp 5; I, on the other hand, felt very tired; that hour of climbing beyond the Great Couloir had taken it out of me more than many hours of ordinary climbing. We agreed, therefore, that Eric should descend whilst I remained at Camp 6 and descended next morning. It was not a good arrangement; men should not separate on Everest, but another miserable night wedged together in that little tent was not to be borne.

An hour later, at about 1.30 p.m., Eric left. The weather was fast deteriorating, mists had formed above and below and a rising wind was beginning to raise the powdery snow from the face of the mountain. For a few minutes I watched him methodically traversing the sloping shelf, following Jack Longland's descending route; then a corner hid him from sight and I lay back in my sleeping bag for a much needed rest.

For the next hour I lay semi-comatose from fatigue.

I may even have slept. Then I became suddenly conscious of the tent shuddering violently in a high wind. The rest had refreshed me greatly and my brain was beginning to reassert itself over my tired body. I unlaced the tent flaps and looked outside. A blizzard was blowing; nothing was to be seen but a few yards of slabs over which the snow-laden gusts rushed and twisted. Rapidly the wind increased. I could feel the little tent rising and straining against the guy ropes, and in between the thudding and cracking of its sorely stressed cloth hear salvoes of driven snow spattering viciously against it.

Eric? I was very anxious. He must be having a horrible descent. He would do it all right; he was not one to associate with mountaineering accidents; his calm, detached confidence was a passport to safety in itself. Still, I could not rid myself of anxiety or of a succession of futile yet worrying pictures that flashed through my mind: snow and wind; wind, relentless, battering, snow-filled wind; wind as cold as death; and a lonely, toiling, ice-encrusted figure.

Towards sundown the wind fell appreciably and the clouds blew clear of Everest. Again I looked outside. Every other peak was concealed beneath a roof of clouds stretching in every direction. At that level a tempestuous wind was blowing and now and then a mass seethed upwards as though violently impelled from below and shrivelled into nothingness. The sky above was blue-green, never have I seen a colder colour, and the declining sun was entirely without warmth. Now and then little twisting devils of wind-driven snow scurried past: small wonder that the Tibetan believes in a cold hell; here were its very flames licking across the slabs of Chamalung.

There was little fuel left and half of it went to cook my supper. It was 6 p.m. when I had finished. I exulted in my comfort. There were now two lots of sleeping bags to keep me warm and I was soon snug with enough below me to defeat the sharpest stone. It did not occur to me that I was spending a night higher than any other human being; I was purely animal in my desire for warmth and comfort. Neither did I feel in the least lonely; in this respect it seemed as natural to spend a night alone in a tent at 27,400 feet as in an hotel at sea-level.

I remember nothing more until the following morning. Something heavy was pressing on me when I awoke, and I was astonished to find a snowdrift covering the lower half of my body, reaching almost to the ridge of the tent. How had it got there? Then I remembered a small hole which Eric and I had accidentally burnt in the side of the tent during our cooking operations. It was only an inch or so in diameter, yet large enough for the powdery snow to pour ceaselessly through all night like sand through an hour glass, gathering in a drift which filled nearly a quarter of the tent. There must have been a more than usually severe blizzard.[2]

I looked at my watch: 7 a.m.; I had slept the clock round for the first time since leaving the Base Camp, if not for the first time during the whole expedition. And I was greatly refreshed; as long as I lay without moving I felt almost as though I were at sea level; my heart was beating slowly, steadily and rhythmically, and my brain was more active than it had been since leaving Camp 4. Perhaps I might be able to settle once and for all the vexed question of the Second Step before descending to Camp 4. With this idea in my mind I heaved myself up into a sitting position and began energetically to push away the snow. Instantly the familiar panting supervened, and at the same moment I was aware of the intense cold, the greatest cold I remember during the expedition. Within a few seconds sensation had left my hands and I had to push them into the sleeping bag and put them between my thighs.

The sun had not yet reached the tent, possibly it was behind clouds, and it was useless to think of doing anything until it arrived. It struck the tent a few minutes later, and putting on my gloves I rummaged among the snow for fuel and

[2] The weather both at Camps 5 and 4 was very violent that night.

provisions; it was some time before I found a tin, the last tin, of solid methylated and could prepare a cupful of café-au-lait. I loathed the sight of food, but I managed to force some down. Then I looked outside. One glance was sufficient: even if I had the strength or inclination (and the latter was now at a low ebb) for a reconnaissance, the appearance of the weather, to say nothing of the lack of fuel, made an immediate descent imperative. High grey clouds were stealing out of the west and overhead a formless murk was gathering in which the sun was struggling with fast diminishing power, whilst the freshly fallen snow had a dull lifeless look. Another blizzard was brewing.

Collecting my few possessions together, I crawled outside and hooked together the flaps of the tent. Then crossing a snow slope I commenced to work along the shelf towards the North-East Shoulder. One backward glance I took at the little tent: it looked strangely pathetic perched amid the desolate rocks and I felt almost as though I were abandoning a friend. It had served us well.

The air was calm and the monsoon clouds thousands of feet beneath almost stationary. This was fortunate, as the shelf proved none too easy. The wind in the night had been too high to allow much snow to collect, but such snow as there was had firmly cemented the screes masking the slabs, and in places, where there were no screes, the slabs were thinly veneered with ice. It was the only time I had seen this disagreeable condition, known to alpine mountaineers as verglas, above the North Col, and it may have been caused by the sun of the previous day warming the rocks so that the first snow melted and froze, or it may have been due to wind pressure.[3]

Near the North-East Shoulder the shelf petered out into a slope of soft powdery snow resting upon shelving slabs. Except that it was not so steep, it was a replica of the place beyond the Great Couloir. My first impulse was to descend as directly as possible, but I noticed that by descending diagonally across it I would come to some rocks leading down to the screes below the yellow band. The snow here had been little affected by the wind and covered the rocks two or three feet deep, and at every step I sank in above the knees. Also, like the snow beyond the Great Couloir, it was so loose that it could not have held me in the event of a slip, and I had an unpleasant feeling that the whole lot might pour off the slabs at any moment, carrying me with it.

After a very slow and careful descent, I reached a shallow chimney by the side of the rocks. The way now was obvious and relatively easy, and I paused for a rest. As I did so I saw a curious fuzziness in the north-west. Quickly it concealed the final pyramid and advanced along the slabs. Scarcely before I had time to

[3] On thinking this matter over subsequently it has occurred to me that an increased humidity in the air due to the monsoon current may have been responsible. On the other hand, melting and freezing cannot take place on the North Face of Everest, otherwise far more snow would adhere to it. That the air must always be extremely dry is borne out by the fact that the ice axe discovered by Wyn Harris and Wager was quite unrusted. Possibly, therefore, wind pressure alone may have been responsible. The hard icy snow on Norton's traverse can only have been formed by this, and it may be that sometimes it forms a glaze of ice on the rocks, especially when the air is moister than usual during the monsoon season. Even at high altitudes the monsoon air current must appreciably increase the percentage of humidity. In humid conditions wind alone is sufficient to plaster rocks with a thick coating of ice. Evaporation as well as wind plays a large part in keeping the North Face of Everest free of snow and any ice glaze forming must soon evaporate. I doubt whether climbers will ever encounter ice on the rocks above the North Col prior to the advent of the monsoon air current, which in the present instance had undoubtedly reached the mountain.

realise what it meant, a gust of wind nearly blew me from my holds. Then came another gust and another, and before I had time to move a hurricane was raging.

The situation changed with almost ridiculous suddenness. From climbing slowly, but reasonably comfortably in a still atmosphere, I was reduced to clinging on to the rocks for all I was worth, whilst great waves of wind tried to sweep me from the mountain. Fortunately, easy ground at the foot of the yellow band was only about fifty feet below and somehow or other I managed to climb down the rocks to it. But any relief I felt at treading a gentler slope was quickly offset by the hurricane. Muffled up though I was in all my clothing with two helmets on my head, it was impossible to face the driven snow, and with my goggles almost useless I could see little or nothing. So fierce was the wind that there were times when I could only progress on hands and knees, and even so I was several times swept from my balance and only managed to stop myself with my ice axe. All the malignity and intolerance of Everest were concentrated in that withering blast. And the cold was proportional to the wind, the most paralysing cold I have ever known. It was not content merely to numb my hands and feet; it seized my whole body in a merciless grip.

I have a dim memory of passing the foot of the yellow pinnacle above the 1924 Camp 6 and of bearing instinctively to the right towards the crest of the north ridge. Here with nothing to break its rush, the wind was at its worst, and for minutes at a time progress was impossible. I could feel a kind of deadness creeping up the lower half of my body, something I had never known before, and I remember thinking vaguely that the end would come when it reached my heart. My legs were stiff too, and seemed scarcely to belong to me. The struggle could not be kept up for much longer.

Suddenly I found myself on the crest of the North Ridge and in a familiar place. A few feet below me was the ledge where Eric and I had rested during our ascent to Camp 6; the only place sheltered from the wind.

Slowly and stiffly I half climbed, half slid down to it. There was no wind there and I could actually feel the sun shining dimly through the clouds of wind-driven snow.

For a while I sat too numbed and exhausted to move. Then I began to beat and kick my lifeless hands and feet together. Slowly the dead feeling left my body and circulation painfully returned except to my fingertips and feet, which no amount of kicking could restore to life.

It was astonishingly warm on the ledge, but on the crest of the ridge above me the wind roared ferociously, striking the rocks now and then with a noise like a thunderclap and the clouds of wind-driven snow whirled over my head.

Half an hour later the first fury of the storm had spent itself and I was ready to face the remainder of the descent. I would have remained longer, but the sun had disappeared and with it the warmth.

It was an effort to clamber back over the ridge and endure the wind again. To follow the ridge was impossible, and after passing the remnants of the 1924 Camp 6 I kept below it to the west where the wind was not so strong; even so I had frequently to cling on to the rocks to prevent myself from being blown away, and progress was very slow, especially as the rocks are steeper here than those above the camp. Providentially, the wind lessened considerably as I lost height. At about

26,000 feet it was blowing nothing worse than an ordinary gale and visibility had improved to such an extent that there was no risk of missing Camp 5 as I had feared at one time.

Progress should have been more rapid, but if anything it was slower. I was very tired and every wall and slab took a long time to negotiate. By the time the tents of Camp 5 came into view I was descending at a snail-like pace and my legs seemed scarcely to belong to me. I was about 300 feet above the camp when I first saw it, and was just congratulating myself on the prospect of rest, shelter and a hot drink when two figures emerged from one of the tents. I shouted and waved, but even in my own ears my voice sounded a thin, hoarse wail. They did not hear me; instead, and it was tragic to watch, they busily set about collapsing the only tent left standing.

I shouted again, angrily this time – fate was playing me a scurvy trick – but they neither looked up nor heard me, and a minute or two later set off down to Camp 4 and vanished from sight.

Cursing bitterly, I continued, and it may have been due to this disappointment but I experienced considerable difficulty in descending some steep slabs interspersed with abrupt little walls. There was one place in particular which I remember vividly where I had to let myself down by the arms on to a snow-covered slab in an angle of which was a bed of hard snow. The lower part of the slab was too steep to descend and I had to cut steps down the snow; it was all I could do to cut them, and they cost me much of my dwindling reserve of strength. Once at the camp and with nothing but the easiest of scrambling before me I decided not to halt and re-erect the collapsed tent, but to continue the descent to Camp 4. I learned later that if I had looked inside the tent I should have found a "thermos" of hot tea, which Bill had considerately left there.

I was feeling considerably stronger now, owing no doubt to the loss of altitude, and the only thing that bothered me was a curious weakness in my legs, which had developed an annoying habit of giving way under me every few yards. The strange part of it is that I do not remember feeling tired, yet I staggered down the rocks like a Saturday night "drunk".

A miserable descent: well-known landmarks were reached and passed with nightmare-like slowness: a small piece of red bunting; two big blocks of rock; Finch's 1922 camp with its tattered green canvas and scattered oxygen cylinders.

At last the top of the long snow slope; and there I was cheered by seeing some figures issue from the two blister-like arctic tents at Camp 4 and begin slowly to mount the ridge.

It was easy enough descending now, but I could not glissade in my weak condition and had to follow the rock crest all the way, and an incredibly laborious crest it seemed. However, my legs were in better shape; I rested rather than collapsed every few yards, yet, paradoxically, I felt more tired than before, and the explanation of this must lie in the difference between ordinary physical tiredness and exhaustion due primarily to altitude.

Of those who ascended from the camp some stopped with Eric and Bill to assist them down, whilst one came on for me, and after climbing some distance up the ridge halted to wait for me. When I got to him I saw it was Jack. He was half frozen, but he greeted me cheerfully and produced a "thermos" full of hot tea laced with brandy. The effect was nothing short of miraculous, and within a minute or two my whole body was charged with warmth and renewed strength. Thenceforward there was no need to halt and I was able to keep going continuously.

What a scene when at last we popped our heads in at the arctic tent. Eric, and Bill were there in their sleeping bags, both very tired, whilst Willy was bustling about preparing hot drinks and food, and in general doing all he could for everyone.

In a minute or two my ice-stiffened wind-proofs and boots were off and my dead feet were being energetically rubbed by a porter. I had not escaped unscathed. Some toes were frostbitten and all my fingertips were without feeling. Time would show the extent of the damage.

Not content merely to cook and supply food and hot drinks, Willy examined us all. He declared me to be perfectly sound except for frostbites, that my pulse-rate was only sixty-two, and that my heart showed no signs of strain. Meanwhile Jack telephoned the news of our arrival and our failure to Camp 3. Hugh would be glad to hear we were safely down, far too glad to worry about our failure; still it was terribly hard luck not to be able to send back better news to England. For the moment Everest had won. There was no one else fit enough for another attempt. We had shot our bolt and must go down for a rest. Perhaps, with luck, we should have another crack later.

There were a number of oxygen cylinders in the tent and as an experiment I dosed myself with the gas. As I was now acclimatised to a far greater height, the only beneficial effect was a slight increase of body warmth. Apart from this it made my throat drier and sorer than ever, and I was glad to remove the mask from my face.

Eric had had a terrible descent from Camp 6. The wind was so fierce that at one point he was tempted to return. Fortunately he decided to struggle on; he could never have fought his way back across the Yellow Band in the teeth of the hurricane. Lower, on the awkward slabs above Camp 5, which had given me so much trouble he was nearly killed when a patch of snow gave way beneath him as he was lowering himself on to it from an abrupt little wall. He could find no foothold and had to haul himself back, a supreme effort to an exhausted man at that altitude. He reached Camp 5 absolutely played out.

Although it was a stormy night and snow battered the tent, we slept the sleep of exhaustion; all save Bill, who was in severe pain. How he stuck it out alone at Camp 5 I do not know; the strain had told on him severely and he was frostbitten in both feet and fearfully emaciated. Everest had had the last word and we were a very worn-out party; I doubt whether any of us could have survived more than a day or two longer at or above Camp 5.

CHAPTER SIXTEEN

Retreat

THE MORNING of June 3 was reasonably calm though it was blowing hard on high and the usual sheets of snow were tearing across Everest. After breakfast our first job was to collapse the two arctic tents, leaving sufficient food and oxygen apparatus in them for another attempt, should this prove possible.

Willy, now a sick man, was very unsteady on the sharp crest of the Col and tottered along scarcely able to keep his balance. In one respect we were lucky; no avalanches had occurred as yet on the slopes of the Col, though it was obvious that with the new snow accumulating and the strengthening of the warm monsoon air current they must be expected in the near future.

At the site of the first Camp 4 we were surprised to meet Shebby. It had always been his ambition to reach the North Col and that day he realised it, a fine performance for a man of his age. He had brought up a number of porters and it was thus possible to retrieve everything except the tents, food and equipment for the next attempt.

On the rope ladder and the slopes below it Willy petered out completely and required continual assistance. Eric too was in poor shape. He had a terrible headache, due he thought to sun glare, which so affected him that he was incapable of coherent speech. It was a descent of broken men.

Tired as we were ourselves, it was not the occasion to stand on ceremony, and when we had supported Willy between us to the lower slopes and all danger was over we let go of him and he shot down the snow to the glacier like a sack of coals. It did not occur to me then what a brutal thing it was to do. Afterwards we had almost to carry him into Camp 3, where we were greeted by the grinning Nursang, who had thoughtfully prepared a meal. We left him there to be brought down later by some porters and carried on to Camp 3.

Eric was still very queer whilst Bill was on the point of collapse, and it was a sick little procession that trailed into camp. I shall never forget the greeting we had from Hugh and the others; it made everything we had gone through, even our defeat, worthwhile. After the high camps, Camp 3 was a Capua of comfort and luxury and soon we were stretched out in the arctic tent, imbibing hot drinks and being pampered in every possible way.

Willy arrived later after being helped down by two porters. He was fighting for breath; there was something very wrong with his lungs and heart. Eric too was temporarily knocked out, whilst it was obvious that Bill, apart from his frostbitten feet, which were paining him greatly, would not be fit to go high again; he was a mere shadow of his former self.

Wyn and Waggers were among those at Camp 3, and we heard about their descent from Camp 6. Wyn had a very narrow squeak when attempting to glissade down a short humpbacked snow slope near Camp 5. The snow was so hard that he lost control and began to slide towards the 4,000-foot precipice falling to the East Rongbuk Glacier. It was a desperate moment, and he did the one thing possible to save himself by turning on to his face and driving the pick of his ice axe into the snow. It was a question whether he could stop in time, as he did not dare force the axe too deeply into the snow at first, otherwise it would have been snatched from his hand. He said he would always remember the little spray of snow flung up by the pick as it bit into the slope; it seemed an interminable time before he slowed down and stopped a few yards from the edge of the precipice.

There had been only one fatality, but a sad one – Policey. Eager to be in at the death, she had gone up to Camp 3a and had not been seen since. A crevasse must have engulfed her. Probably she wandered away from the camp and trod through a snow bridge. We hoped that her death was swift and merciful. She had been an institution, for all her shyness and independence, and we missed her.

These and many other things were related and discussed in the arctic tent that evening. What a change it was after miserable confinement in a small tent – cold, uncomfortable and with no interest in life beyond its immediate necessities. True, the wind was roaring outside in disappointed fury, as though baulked of its prey, but it was powerless to harm us now, it merely played an appropriate accompaniment to a happy reunion and a great occasion.

No expedition without some element of good fortune in attendance could have come through such weather as we experienced safely. Perhaps, as Wyn once suggested, we were not really alive, and it was merely a collection of ghosts, yet it was a queer kind of ghost that ate so many pickled walnuts, as he did that evening. We were alive, and 'damned lucky' was the general opinion, though in our hearts we knew that luck was only another word for Providence. What a pleasant sound a "Primus" makes – I never realised how pleasant before. And the steaming chocolate, we could smell it again and taste it, incense was never sweeter, nectar never more gracious to thin, tired bodies. But there was something even sweeter than this – the knowledge that we had done our best; this elevated failure almost to success.

Of all parts Hugh's had been the hardest. Could any have guessed his feelings as he saw his climbers disappear into the clouds? Then no news save hour by hour a tale of storm from Camp 4, while he waited at Camp 3 doing nothing, because there was nothing he could do. A lonely task this leadership of an expedition, none can know how lonely save the leader himself, for his is the responsibility, his the blame when things go wrong. He is the Aunt Sally of thoughtless critics. In war and peace, in politics, and religion, it is always the same; the leader, never the led, must shoulder the responsibility and the blame.

There are lucky leaders and unlucky leaders, and I shall always remember Hugh Ruttledge as a lucky leader. Twice now he has led Everest expeditions in conditions of exceptional difficulty and danger, and he has brought them back safely.

Having compared experiences, our next thought was of the future. The party was in no condition at the moment for another attempt, and a wireless message from Raymond, who was at the Base Camp, strongly urged withdrawal. There were two schools of thought: one was in favour of descent to the Kharta Valley for a complete rest; the other, believed that a short rest at the Base Camp would suffice to make some of us fit for another attempt; it would also enable us to keep an eye on the mountain, which would be impossible from the Kharta Valley. Wyn strongly supported this last scheme, doubtless because he and I were at the moment the two fittest, though he had strained his heart slightly. What we felt was – get it over one way or the other and go home. Whether or not an attempt could be made once the monsoon had broken remained to be seen. The matter was settled when Hugh pronounced in favour of the Base Camp scheme.

At this time I supposed I was the fittest, inasmuch as my heart was sound, whereas most of those who had gone above the North Col were suffering from enlarged hearts, but I was more badly frostbitten than the others, with the exception of Bill, and another attempt might result in the loss of some toes. However, "sufficient unto the day ..." The main thing was a few days' rest at the Base Camp.

Next morning, June 4, was the warmest so far experienced at Camp 3, and we toasted ourselves in the sun before starting for the Base Camp. Obviously the monsoon was close upon us, for only this could account for the lack of wind and the unusual warmness of the air.

It was a sad little procession down the glacier. Bill was quite broken up and could scarcely walk; his frostbitten feet were troubling him a great deal and were very painful. Eric was still suffering from his head and with one or two others remained at Camp 3 for one more day. For the rest of us it was a pleasant stroll, except that my toes were beginning to bother me and sent sharp pangs of pain through my feet at every step.

Conditions were very different from what they had been when we ascended to Camp 3. Streams of water were running down the trough and in one place a lake about a hundred yards long had formed. Its green waters, with a forest of giant ice pinnacles rising out of them, were a pleasant sight for eyes wearied with the glare of high altitudes. Most of us halted by it and lounged on the sun-warmed boulders.

Where the route left the trough a new route had been made by Lachman Singh, which brought us quickly across the glacier. At Camp 2 Lachman Singh was delighted to see us. It had been a lonely time for him, but he had done valuable work in supervising the dispatch of stores to Camp 3. Instead of a snow floor, there was now a little lake, whilst all the snow had melted from the vicinity of the camp, leaving screes.

So delightful was it that Bill, who had only got there with considerable difficulty, decided to stop until Shebby arranged to have him carried down to the Base Camp. The remainder of us also spent the night there – a night, which proved unexpectedly cold, so that more than once I woke shivering; there was not enough flesh left to keep me warm.

June 5 was another perfect day with little or no wind on Everest. If only we had been up there then perhaps we might have had better conditions and a greater measure of success.

After a leisurely breakfast, Wyn, Waggers, Jack and I strolled down to Camp 1 but it seemed a long way and the miles of screes were trying to my frostbitten toes. Yet any discomfort we may have had was more than compensated for by a descent to more genial levels. All our physical and mental senses, dulled by weeks of residence at high altitudes, were quickened; it was like emerging from a smoky ill-lit room into a sunny and fragrant garden. To the mountaineer descending from Everest:

> The common air, the earth, the skies,
> To him are opening Paradise.

At Camp 1 the meal prepared for us by Nima Dorje tasted as a meal never tasted before. The effect on me was to make me forget my frostbitten feet and descend the remainder of the way to the Base Camp in an hour and twenty minutes.

What a bleak place the Rongbuk Valley had seemed when we left it, and now the air was moist and balmy and, miracle of miracles, shy little saxifrages and crucifers were peeping up from between the stones like clusters of forgotten stars.

Tommy was at the Base Camp to welcome us, and he had a gargantuan feast ready, luxuries he and Smidge had ordered from Darjeeling. Our appetites had returned and we suddenly realised that we had starved for the past weeks. We sat down in the mess tent and guzzled shamelessly. Fresh mutton and fresh vegetables from the Sola Khumbu valley, turnips and onions: fresh food after living for weeks on "tinned muck"; words cannot describe the beatitude of that meal.

George was also at the Base Camp. Poor chap, he was very ill with his gastric ulcer. To one so full of life and energy it had been past all bearing to miss it all.

Nima Tendrup greeted me full of smiles; I learned that after doing well at Camp 3, and even carrying to Camp 4, he had been taken ill and had been sent down to the Base Camp.

That night I slept warmly, comfortably and soundly, a sleep untroubled by the fitful waking periods that had become a part of life at high altitudes, and did not wake until the sun was well up and old Nima Tendrup was ready with a cup of tea and my hot washing water. But the supreme climax came after breakfast when I had a hot bath, my first for many weeks. What a blessing to rid the skin of the ingrained dirt. I remember thinking as I wallowed in it, that it marked the end of a stage. What of the future?

CHAPTER SEVENTEEN

The Final Attempt

RAYMOND WAS right to urge a withdrawal to the Base Camp. At Camp 3 we felt that another attempt might be possible after a short rest, but the Base Camp supplied a necessary contrast which enabled us to take stock of ourselves and the situation. Of those who had gone high only Eric and I had sound hearts. Bill was a wreck, and both he and Willy had to be carried down the glacier. Willy especially was very ill, though he had only been to the North Col, and Raymond diagnosed a patch of pneumonia on one lung; he was given oxygen for many hours on end. Eric, on the other hand, although a sick man when he arrived at Camp 3, should recuperate quickly, and the same might be said of Wyn if only his heart would stay "put" when it returned to normal. Waggers had strained his heart badly, but he was a tough fellow and there was no knowing what he might do. The same applied to Jack, who, although, like everyone, he was many pounds down in weight, had "guts" to the nth degree. Ferdie and Tom were obviously ready for more work even after their strenuous efforts on the North Col – a gruelling, unselfish job. Lastly, Hugo's leave had expired and he had gone posthaste to Darjeeling before the attempts on the summit.

As for myself, although my heart was sound and I felt fit enough for another attempt, I was, like everyone else, very thin. I shall never forget my first complete view of myself as I sat in a bath the morning after our arrival at the Base Camp. I could nearly encircle a thigh with the thumb and fingers of one hand. As someone suggested, we ought to take a photograph of ourselves and send it to the newspapers as "Starving Russian Refugees". The effect of prolonged residence at high altitudes – we had spent a month above 21,000 feet – had been to reduce not only flesh but muscle, and I suffered badly from muscle collapse in my legs, and for the first day or two could walk only a few yards at a time. It was probably this more than anything else that made my descent from Camp 6 such a rickety affair. Yet, according to Raymond, I had lost less flesh than most people. As regards my frostbitten toes, the two big ones were the worst. They were nearly black and one was full of pus, but Raymond told me I should lose only the nails. Fortunately my fingers were not bad, though the tips were raw and painful. Why I was not more badly frostbitten during my descent from Camp 6 I do not know. Good boots, and my habit of moving my toes about inside them, were primarily responsible.

Altogether there was no disguising the fact that the odds were several thousand to one against our reaching the summit, even supposing that conditions proved possible and there was a break in the monsoon. Our descent to the Base Camp had coincided with the arrival of the moisture-charged monsoon clouds; they had wrapped themselves about Everest and within a day or two the mountain was like a sugar cake with scarcely a rock visible. According to the inhabitants of Rongbuk the north-west wind reasserted itself and blew it black again. The sun could have little to say in the matter, otherwise the snow would consolidate and Everest would turn into a snow mountain permanently, so the snow above a certain level, probably that of the North Col must remain powdery, and in such a condition the mountain is inaccessible. Our one hope, therefore, was that there would be a break in the monsoon coinciding with a strong wind, which would temporarily clear the mountain of snow.

On June 12 Bill, George and Willy left the Base Camp for Chö-Dzong where a hospital camp was being established. At this lower level they should recover more easily than at the Base Camp. Poor George was very depressed, but derived some consolation from the fact that the mountain was unlikely to be attempted again for some time at least. We were seated in the mess tent when he said: 'I don't mind going, for you're not going to get up, and I'll tell you why – the weather's too bad.' At this there came in a hoarse whisper from Eric, who was still almost speechless, 'I never thought of that.' It was indeed what Mr. Punch would call "a glimpse of the obvious". Our hopes were at zero.

On June 11 Ferdie and Tom left to reconnoitre the North Col and if possible reopen the route to Camp 4, and on the 13 Hugh, Raymond, Eric, Jack and Tommy followed. A week at the Base Camp had worked wonders. Good food, and long refreshing sleep had revived interest, hope and energy. Some had even bathed in a pool of icy water and all had spent lazy hours revelling in the sun and the warm, moist air.

The following day Wyn and I set off to Camp 1. We both felt astonishingly fit; Wyn's heart had apparently returned to normal and the muscular weakness had left my legs; my frostbitten toes alone annoyed me. The weather was typical of the monsoon with high clouds beating up from the south, concealing Everest and the head of the Rongbuk Glacier, and snowstorms every afternoon.

We reached the camp in two hours, having walked at almost sea-level pace, where we were welcomed by Bahardur Gurung, who had some tea ready. It was a beautiful afternoon with scarcely a breath of wind, but occasional fleeting snow showers reminded us that the monsoon was active and that in all probability snow was accumulating deeply on Everest.

Nima Dorje cooked us a good supper, and when we turned in the night was so warm that my tent seemed positively stuffy and I could not sleep except with both door flaps wide open.

An unclouded sky next morning roused our latent optimism. Was there really a chance of a break in the monsoon? I wished I could feel as optimistic in my heart as I pretended to be; many days of fine weather would be necessary to clear the snow from Everest.

Three hours' easy going in still, warm air brought us to Camp 2, and the porters arrived only a few minutes later; they were in splendid form and as eager as we for their revenge if only conditions allowed.

Once again I slept badly at Camp 2. Though perfectly acclimatised, I felt much as I did when I first reached this altitude. It seemed a critical height with me and above it or below it I always felt fitter. As I lay experimenting with all the usual sleep-wooing artifices, I noticed a light in Wyn's tent; he too was wakeful.

Before continuing to Camp 3 we examined Everest through the telescope. There appeared to be as much snow on it as on an alpine peak in mid-winter, and here and there were avalanche tracks, long, narrow furrows suggesting slips of loose, powdery snow, particularly on the slabs of the Yellow Band and Norton's traverse. The tent at Camp 6 was still standing but looked as though it were practically buried. The result of this examination was a renewal of pessimism. Only a sprinkling of snow was needed to render the slabs impassable, and now there was at least two or three feet of the very worst kind of snow, and there was as yet no sign of any break in the monsoon.

Snow began to fall soon after we left the trough and fell more and more heavily as we approached Camp 3. Those ahead of us were congregated in the arctic tent and the first news we heard at the camp was that Ferdie and Tom had failed to reach Camp 4 owing to dangerous snow conditions on the slopes of the North Col. They had managed to excavate the lower ropes, but those above the crevasse were buried beneath several feet of snow. An avalanche had swept over the rope ladder and the snow in the punch bowl was too unsafe to meddle with.

After some discussion it was decided provisionally to remain at Camp 3 till the end of the month. If a break in the monsoon occurred it might be possible to reopen the North Col route by climbing it at night when the snow was safely frozen, but I do not think any of us seriously believed there was any chance of attempting the mountain for several weeks at least.

It was still snowing when I went to bed, and snow continued to patter on my tent until long after midnight; I knew this because I was kept awake for part of the night by my aching frostbitten toes, whilst later I was awakened by the thunderous roar of an avalanche.

Next morning June 17 was fine. The mornings are usually fine during the monsoon season, and it is not until midday that clouds gather and snow begins to fall. The porters were all very cheerful and there were unlimited volunteers anxious to go high again. Perhaps the bonus was an incentive; those who went to Camp 5 got 30 rupees each, and those to Camp 6 60 rupees. News was received by wireless from Smidge at the Base Camp that Willy had got Pleurisy. If it was serious Raymond would have to descend, which meant weakening the party still further.

All the afternoon and evening snow fell heavily on Everest, but the clouds dissolved during the evening, and when I turned in the sky was alive with stars and the Milky Way was hung like a spectral banner across them, whilst from the south came an uneasy flickering of sheet lightning. Owing to a dull throbbing ache in my toes, I was unable to sleep, so for the first time I had a drug, allonal I think. This sent me to sleep for some hours, but I woke soon after midnight and remained awake until dawn. There is no doubt that this inability to sleep well at high altitudes is the most depressing factor in high-altitude mountaineering. A man must be tired by a hard day's work before he can sleep, and inactivity at high altitudes is wearing on physique and nerves.

Next morning, in perfect weather, Ferdie, Eric and Tom visited the Rapiu La, a col little if any higher than Camp 3, between the North-East Ridge of Everest and a peak of 22,950 feet on the ridge separating the East Rongbuk and Kangshung Glaciers. They reported a superb view of the south-east face of Everest and of Makalu and Chomolönzo.

So hot was the sun during the morning that the eye of faith perceived the snow melting from the rocks of Everest, but as usual clouds formed at midday and snow fell in the afternoon. A dreary time it was lying up every afternoon for hours on end in the arctic tent with nothing to do. The warm, moist monsoon air was rapidly healing our throats. Eric's voice had returned and he was making the best of it in an argument with Wyn on relationships in Kenya between planters and government officials. This argument lasted for hours on end and the protagonists returned to it each day like giants refreshed. It eclipsed all other arguments, and before its torrents of invective and abuse the rest of us remained silent except for an occasional sly dig of the partisanship poker when the fire showed signs of smouldering. The impression I formed of Kenya is that it is populated exclusively by government officials who make life as difficult as they can for planters and planters who – but I cannot do justice in mere words to the iniquities of the planters.

Eric woke me next morning, just as it was getting light, and at five he, Hugh, Ferdie, Tom and I set off to the Rapiu La intending to climb the 22,950-foot peak to the north of it. An hour's easy walking took us to the col, where we were greeted by a marvellous view of Makalu and Chomolönzo. The latter peak reminded me of the Aiguille Verte possibly because to the left of it stands a huge rock pinnacle not unlike the Dru: magnificent, terrible mountains and apparently unclimbable, at all events from the west and north. Close at hand was the South-East Face of Everest. There can be no more terrific series of ice cliffs and ridges in the World. One subsidiary ridge rises fully 7,000 feet from the Kangshung Glacier in a sublime sickle-like curve of gleaming ice. Its crest is razor-like and from it fall other crests equally sharp, divided and subdivided into delicate flutings separating icy channels formed by the constant downrush of avalanches, which even at this early hour were falling one after the other with scarcely a pause, so that this vast mountainside seemed to stir and grumble uneasily in the searching rays of the sun.

In the far distance, south of the silver and blue snows of Kangchenjunga, a wall of dun-coloured monsoon cloud spanned the horizon and closer at hand a sea of woolly mist extending for scores of miles concealed the Arun Valley and its tributaries, its topmost billows brilliant in the sun and the deeper troughs a dark brownish-purple.

The snow slopes of Peak 22,950 feet rise immediately to the north of the Rapiu La and after a short halt we set off to climb them in the hope of an even finer view. The snow was very soft and from its condition it was obvious that we must expect much the same conditions on and above the North Col – impossible conditions for climbing at high altitudes and dangerous because of avalanches on any but the gentlest of slopes. At every step we sank in up to the knees and the leadership changed hands at frequent intervals. There was no difficulty, and after an hour or so's hard work we arrived on the indeterminate summit of the mountain. The monsoon mists were rising, but between their sluggish folds there were enchanting glimpses of dark-green upland pastures thousands of feet beneath in the direction of the Kharta Valley. Grass again; it seemed scarcely possible in this frigid land. Then, piercing the sluggish mists, the beautiful little peak of Khartse, 21,390 feet, stood draped in ice delicately modelled into thin flutings uniting in a precise summit.

But it was at Everest that we looked longest. From this direction the great North-East Ridge is seen almost end on. It has its origin in the Rapiu La and rises 7,000 feet to the North-East Shoulder and thence to the summit, a distance as the crow flies of nearly three and a half miles. Finch suggested it as a possible line of attack in 1922, but compared with the route so far attempted via the North Col and North Ridge it would seem to have little to recommend it. Length alone is against it and too many camps would be required, whilst the difficulties, if not excessive in the first 2,000 feet, are obviously great below the North-East Shoulder, whilst the shoulder itself with its spiky pinnacles might prove impassable.* Still, it was intriguing to speculate on the possibilities of forcing a route. If Everest could be climbed entirely over a ridge an attempt in the monsoon would be justifiable, for Bauer and his Bavarian party had boldly attacked Kangchenjunga during this season and by overcoming great difficulties had proved it to be the

* This was the area where Pete Boardman and Joe Tasker disappeared in 1983. The link-up with the Shoulder was made in 1991 by an Anglo/NZ party and the full ascent of the mountain by the complete North-East Ridge was made in 1995 by six members (including four sherpas) of a Japanese Expedition led by Tadeo Kanizaki.

best for tackling an ice ridge. But face climbing, particularly on a slabby face such as the North Face of Everest, is impracticable in conditions of monsoon snow. Warmth and the absence of wind make the monsoon season ideal for mountaineering on peaks of moderate elevation and it is a matter for regret that Everest cannot be attempted then, as the climber would meet with almost genial conditions and would seldom be exposed to the risk of frostbite or sudden wind storms.

Two weeks of reasonable weather between the ending of impossibly cold and windy winter conditions and the monsoon is all the climber can expect on Everest, and there will be seasons when he does not get even this.[1] The highest mountain of the world dictates its own conditions and the mountaineer would scarcely have it otherwise, for however much he may bemoan his luck, he knows in his heart that uncertainty is the spiritual essence of mountaineering.

We were beaten and Everest had no further use for us. Standing humbly on the summit of a peak nearly 23,000 feet high, we could only admire the beauty and splendour of our adversary. Everest had been hostile towards us and we had felt that there was something almost personal behind this hostility, in the bitter cold and sudden smiting storms. The thin air through which we had toiled so painfully had been imbued with some intangible quality opposing our progression, thwarting us with an insidious lethargy, blunting the fine edge of our first enthusiasm. We had felt we were unwanted; perhaps because we were unworthy.

But we could no longer associate our own puny qualities with Everest, for Everest had withdrawn from us and only our vision could win to that far summit where the clouds paced slowly.

There was no break in the monsoon. Day by day snow fell. Avalanches rumbled and smoked from Everest, and at nights soundless lightning set the south sky trembling. And the weather reports held out no hope. Nothing was to be gained through staying at Camp 3, and on June 21 we withdrew to Camp 2 and on the following day to the Base Camp. There, once again, our appetites returned and we slept. How we slept! I had never before appreciated properly this satisfying blessing of sleep. There was nothing to do but discuss the future. Was it worth while waiting on through the monsoon? This was argued ad nauseam by us all. And, meanwhile, Everest covered itself ever deeper in monsoon snow until only avalanche tracks were to be seen where boulders ten or fifteen feet high were known to exist. In the mornings the sun shone warmly and we stretched ourselves out on the warm turf where the saxifrages bloomed in their galaxies of starry blooms, but most afternoons clouds gathered, hailstorms trailed their slate-grey skirts over the hills and the silences of the Rongbuk Valley were awakened by peals of thunder.

In the evenings there were other and unusual noises from the wireless tent; the Savoy Orpheans and the notes of Big Ben. A strange thing that all the world should be whispering over the solitudes of Tibet: with us the eternal rumble of the glacier torrent and the snows of Everest pale beneath the stars, and in England the multitudes of escaping workers hurrying over Westminster Bridge.

[1] As in 1936.

There was a case of champagne; we could not drink to success, so we celebrated Jack's birthday. Even at that height the corks flew skywards and the champagne gushed out like a fountain; a pail was the only receptacle that coped with its exuberance. Then, as we had half expected, the word came from England ordering our withdrawal; also a telegram from the King, who shared our disappointment and hoped we would have better luck next time.

Would there be a "next time?" It was a sad morning when our tents were collapsed; they seemed by now almost to have rooted themselves into the brown earth. Then, once more the long trains of lumbering yaks and thin-legged, quickfooted little donkeys, patient as always beneath their loads and the curses of their drivers; but this time Everest was behind us. Warm sun and deep-blue sky – it seemed absurd to leave.

A day later we said goodbye to the Lama of Rongbuk. Clouds, congregating at the head of the valley, concealed Everest. An hour later I looked back for the last time. The air was still and warm and filled with the scent of flowers which had everywhere sprung up between the stones. It was July 3. Two and a half months ago we had trudged up the track in the teeth of a bitter wind. There had been a powdering of snow on the ground and drifts across the path; Everest had risen starkly before us. And now, flowers and warm moist air and Everest buried in snow. The great mountain was invisible, holding court to the clouds. It had let us all go; Providence had been kind. The old Lama of Rongbuk had prayed for our safety and his prayers had been answered.

And now we must think of the future. Perhaps one day we would tread again the stony path beneath the deep blue of the Tibetan sky and see that yellow pyramid with its white plume writing the endless message of the west wind.

POSTSCRIPT

The Ice Axe found on Everest

SO MUCH controversy has raged around the ice axe discovered above Camp 6 that it may be of interest to restate the facts and the theories put forward to account for its presence. The axe was found about sixty feet below the crest of the North-East Ridge and about 250 yards east of the First Step, lying on the slabs unsecured by either ledge or crack and dependent on friction alone for its lodgement. Though an ice axe offers little resistance to the wind, it is astonishing that it should have remained there, for winds on Everest are known to exceed 100 miles per hour. It is quite likely, however, that nothing approaching such a velocity is reached near the surface of the slabs, and it is possible that the place where the axe was found is never visited by winds of hurricane force owing to the formation of the mountainside. How did the axe come there? It has been suggested that it was deliberately left there by Mallory or Irvine, as it would impede their progress over the rocks to the summit. All who have climbed above 27,000 feet on Everest are agreed that an ice axe is necessary. Not only is it a useful prop when traversing the slabs, but it is essential when crossing patches of snow. Had Mallory and Irvine climbed the ridge they would have had to cross numerous snow patches, whilst on the North-East Face of the final pyramid there is a snow slope several hundred feet high which might well provide a quicker and easier route to the summit than the rocks to one side which can only be reached by an awkward-looking traverse by a climber approaching the final pyramid over the Second Step. Lastly, the concluding section of the North-East Ridge, i.e. the summit ridge of the mountain, consists of a snow and rock edge some 200 yards long, which no mountaineer would dream of traversing without his axe. If Norton's route is followed an ice axe is even more essential. I had to cut a number of steps across beds of hard snow and across the great couloir. If I had reached the subsidiary couloir it would have been equally essential, whilst there are some large patches of snow on the north face of the final pyramid which the climber may have to climb or cross en route to the summit. Quite apart from its usefulness when crossing snow, I found it to be nothing short of a third leg on the outward-shelving ledges of the Yellow Band. No mountaineer of Mallory's calibre would have deliberately discarded so vital an aid to success.

Was the axe dropped accidentally? If so, the party could only have dropped it somewhere between the point where it was found and the ridge, and it would have been a simple matter to descend and recover it.

The most tenable theory is that the axe marks the scene of a slip. The climbing is easy at this point, yet once a climber slips he would be unlikely to stop himself, and with a heavy oxygen apparatus on his back he would have no chance at all: it may be that the oxygen apparatus was the primary cause of the disaster, for unimpaired balance is necessary even on the easier slabs of the Yellow Band.

It is likely that the two were roped together indeed, this may be regarded as certain, as Mallory would have considered it his duty to rope himself to his less experienced companion though he knew that in the event of a slip he was unlikely to hold him. They were traversing the slabs, in preference to the broken and probably more fatiguing crest of the North-East Ridge, when one of them slipped. The other instinctively dropped or put his ice axe down and seized the rope in both hands in an endeavour to check the fall of his companion. He failed and was pulled off by the rope. This is no abstract theory. In 1934 I accompanied a party of guides on the south side of Mont Blanc in search of the bodies of two Oxford undergraduates. The first intimation we had of an accident was finding an ice axe marking the scene of a slip, which occurred, on rocks no more difficult than those at the point where the axe was found on Everest. The second man had discarded his ice axe in a vain attempt to stop the leader and had been pulled off.

Another debatable point is whether the accident to Mallory and Irvine occurred during the ascent or descent. If Odell saw them on the Second Step, then it occurred during the descent; yet in view of the difficulty of the ridge below the Step and the formidable nature of the Step itself it appears more likely that it occurred during the ascent and that Odell saw them on one or other of the two rock towers below the First Step as already suggested.[1] In support of this theory is the unlikelihood of the First Step yielding to direct assault from the ridge. It appears necessary to turn it on its north side, the south side being a sheer ice slope so far as is known. Now supposing the two were descending after having negotiated the First Step, it is unlikely that they would traverse so near the crest of the North-East Ridge, especially when Mallory must have been well aware of the line taken by Norton and Somervell which slants diagonally downwards across the Yellow Band (i.e. well below the point where the ice axe was found). A descending party on Everest is concerned to lose height as quickly as possible, and it is hardly likely that Mallory and Irvine would continue an almost horizontal and wearisome traverse on or near the crest of the North-East Ridge when an obvious and quick route down the Yellow Band was open to them.

A last hypothesis. Supposing, like Norton and Somervell, they had been impressed by the apparent difficulty of the North-East Ridge and the impossibility of carrying an oxygen apparatus weighing about 35 pounds up the nearly vertical cliff of the Second Step – a formidable proposition at sea-level and most likely an impossible feat at 28,000 feet, taking into account the clumsiness and inefficiency of the 1924 apparatus – and had followed the traverse route, then it is practically certain that they would, like Norton and Somervell, have taken a lower line when descending and passed well below the point where the axe was found.

All mountaineers hope that Mallory and Irvine reached the summit of Everest, yet it cannot be denied that the facts are against their having done so. If, indeed, the ice axe marked the point at which an accident occurred, then it is possible that further traces may be found on the slope of broken rocks, snow and screes, at the foot of the yellow band.*

[1] See page 616.

* These assessments can now be reviewed in the light of the discovery of an oxygen bottle, of 1924 vintage, seemingly closer to the First Step than the ice axe site. Mallory's body, discovered in 1999, was found considerably lower suggesting that there was no link between the ice axe and the incident (presumably a slip and fall) that led to Mallory's demise. These matters are discussed in detail in *Ghosts of Everest* (The Mountaineers, Seattle/Macmillan, London 1999).

THE VALLEY OF FLOWERS

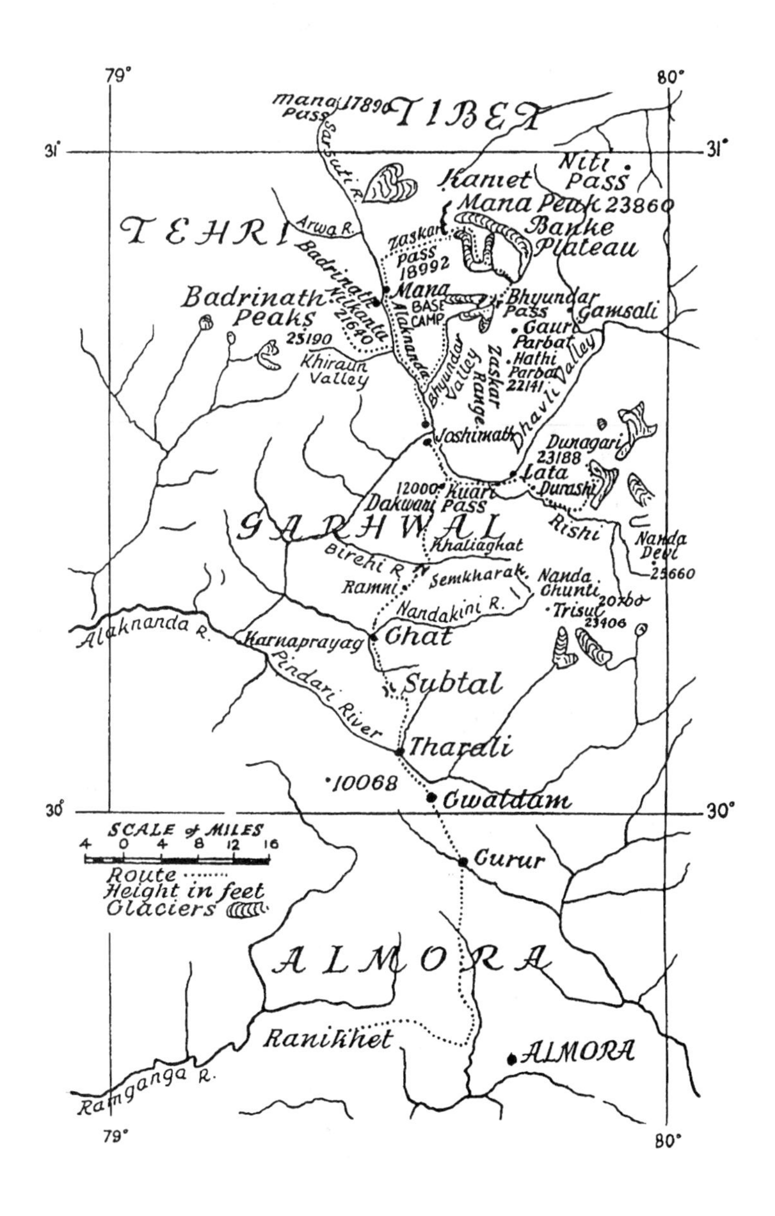

The Valley of Flowers

First published by Hodder and Stoughton, 1938

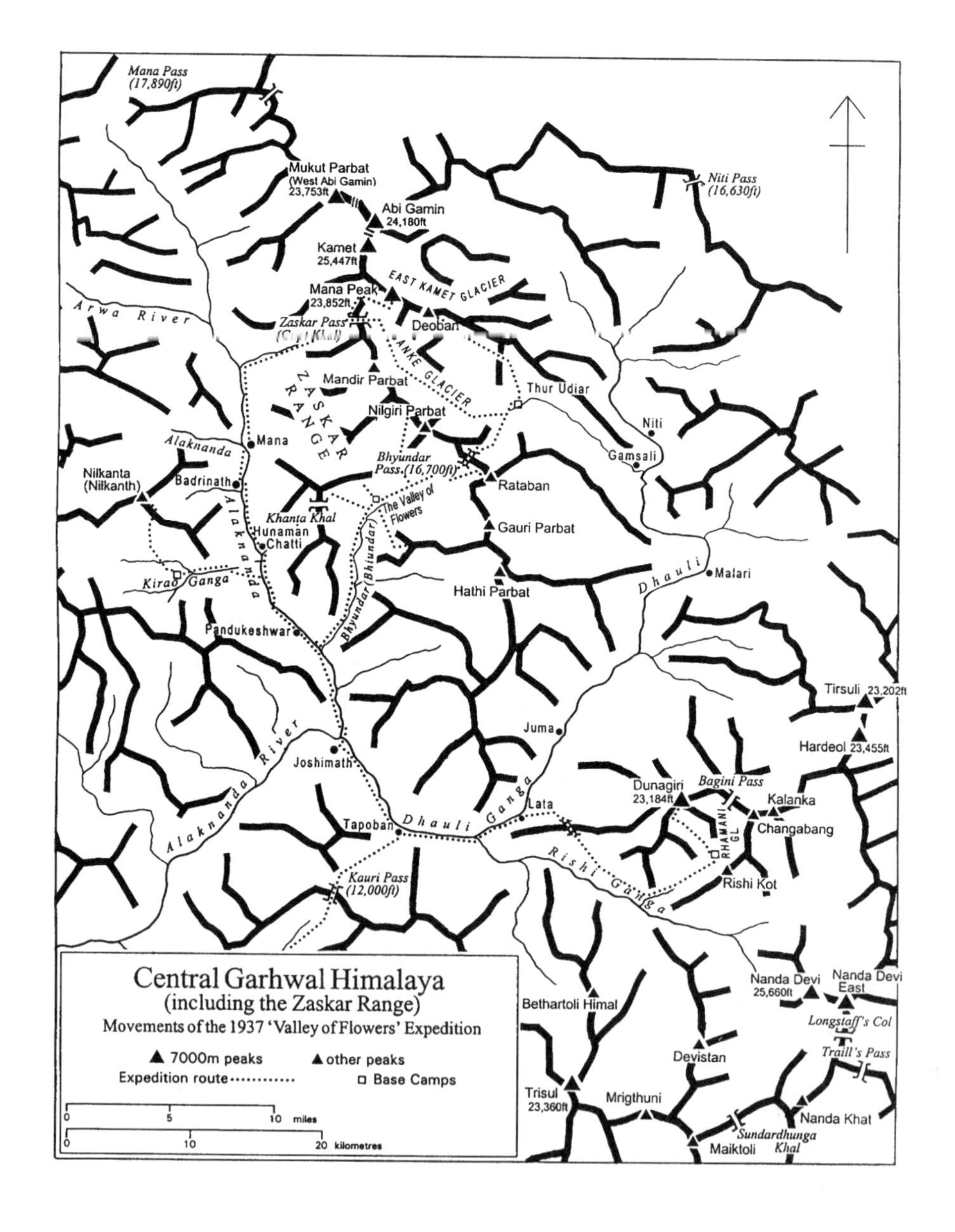

Contents

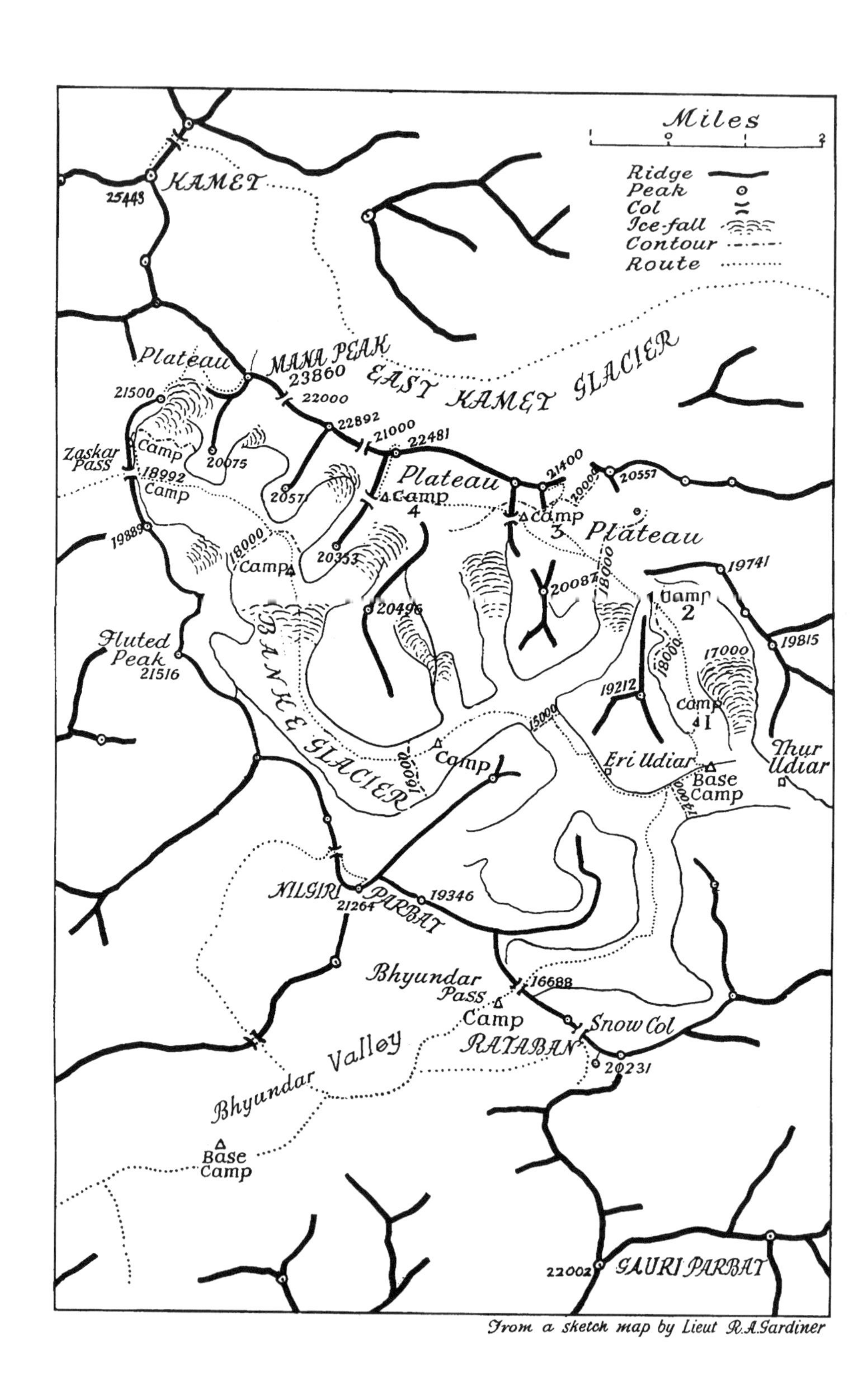

From a sketch map by Lieut R.A.Gardiner

CHAPTER ONE

The Valley of Flowers

THIS IS THE STORY of four happy months spent amidst some of the noblest and most beautiful mountains of the world. Its inception dates back to 1931. In that year Kamet, a mountain 25,447 feet high, situated in the Garhwal Himalayas, was climbed by a small expedition of six British mountaineers of whom I was one. After the climb we descended to the village of Gamsali in the Dhauli Valley, then crossed the Zaskar Range, which separates the upper Dhauli and Alaknanda Valleys, by the Bhyundar Pass, 16,688 feet, with the intention of exploring the mountainous region at the sources of the two principal tributaries of the Ganges, the Alaknanda and Gangotri Rivers.

The monsoon had broken and the day we crossed the pass was wet, cold and miserable. Below 16,000 feet rain was falling, but above that height there was sleet or snow. A bitter wind drove at us, sheeting our clothing with wet snow and chilling us to the bone, and as quickly as possible we descended into the Bhyundar Valley, which bifurcates with the Alaknanda Valley.

Within a few minutes we were out of the wind and in rain which became gradually warmer as we lost height. Dense mist shrouded the mountainside and we had paused, uncertain as to the route, when I heard R.L. Holdsworth, who was a botanist as well as a climbing member of the expedition, exclaim: 'Look!' I followed the direction of his outstretched hand. At first I could see nothing but rocks, then suddenly my wandering gaze was arrested by a little splash of blue, and beyond it were other splashes of blue, a blue so intense it seemed to light the hillside. As Holdsworth wrote: "All of a sudden I realised that I was simply surrounded by *primulas*. At once the day seemed to brighten perceptibly. Forgotten were all pains and cold and lost porters. And what a *primula* it was! Its leek-like habit proclaimed it a member of the *nivalis* section. All over the little shelves and terraces it grew, often with its roots in running water. At the most it stood six inches high, but its flowers were enormous for its stature, and ample in number – sometimes as many as thirty to the beautifully proportioned umbel, and in colour of the most heavenly French blue, sweetly scented."

In all my mountain wanderings I had not seen a more beautiful flower than this *primula*; the fine raindrops clung to its soft petals like galaxies of seed pearls and frosted its leaves with silver.

Lower, where we camped near a moraine, were *androsaces*, *saxifrages*, *sedums*, yellow and red *potentillas*, *geums*, *geraniums*, asters, gentians, to mention but a few plants, and it was impossible to take a step without crushing a flower.

Next day we descended to lush meadows. Here our camp was embowered amidst flowers: snow-white drifts of *anemones*, golden lily-like *nomocharis*, marigolds, globe flowers, *delphiniums*, violets, *eritrichiums*, blue *corydalis*, wild roses, flowering shrubs and rhododendrons, many of them flowers with homely sounding English names. The Bhyundar Valley was the most beautiful valley that any of us had seen. We camped in it for two days and we remembered it afterwards as the Valley of Flowers.

Often, in dark winter days, I wandered in spirit to these flowerful pastures with their clear-running streams set against a frieze of silver birches and shining snow peaks. Then once again I saw the slow passage of the breeze through the flowers, and heard the eternal note of the glacier torrent coming to the campfire through the star-filled night.

After many years in London I went to live in the country, where I set to work to make a garden out of a field of thistles, ragwort and dandelions. I had looked on gardening as an old man's hobby, and a dull and unremunerative labour, but I came upon something that Karel Capek had written:

> You must have a garden before you know what you are treading on. Then, dear friend, you will see that not even clouds are so diverse, so beautiful and terrible as the soil under your feet. ... I tell you that to tame a couple of rods of soil is a great victory. Now it lies there, workable, crumbly and humid. ... You are almost jealous of the vegetation which will take hold of this noble and humane work which is called the soil.

So I became a gardener. But I was profoundly ignorant. Two and a half years ago I did not know the difference between a biennial and a perennial. I am still ignorant, for there is no limit to ignorance or knowledge in gardening. But I discovered one thing; that there is a freemasonry among gardeners, which places gardening on a pinnacle above jealousy and suspicion. Perhaps this is because it is essentially a creative task and brings out a fine quality of patience. You may hasten the growth of a constitution but you cannot hasten the growth of an alpine plant.

In 1937 the opportunity came to return to the Bhyundar Valley. I travelled alone for several reasons, but it was arranged that Captain P.R. Oliver of the South Waziristan Scouts should join me towards the end of July and that he and I should spend two months mountaineering in the Garhwal Himalayas, after which I should return to the valley to collect seeds, bulbs, tubers and plants. Thus, I should have six weeks on my own before and during the monsoon season, and to help me I engaged, through the kind offices of Mr. W.J. Kydd of Darjeeling, four Tibetan porters of whom the Sirdar, Wangdi Nurbu (or Ondi), was an old friend of mine.

One reason for this small party was that, after four large and elaborately organised Himalayan expeditions, I welcomed the opportunity of taking a Himalayan holiday, a very different affair from an attempt to climb one of the major peaks of the world and involving an entirely different scale of values both human and material. The ascent of Everest has become a duty, perhaps a national duty, comparable with attempts to reach the Poles and is far removed from pleasurable mountaineering. Mountaineering in the Garhwal and Kumaon Himalayas more nearly resembles mountaineering in Switzerland, for here are mountains and valleys like Swiss mountains and valleys but built on a greater scale. But, unlike parts of Switzerland, the country is unspoilt by commercialism.

There are no railways, power lines, roads and hotels to offend the eye and detract from the primitive beauty and grandeur of the vistas, and there are peaks innumerable, unnamed and unclimbed of all shades of difficulty, and valleys that have never seen a European, where a simple, kindly peasant folk graze their flocks in the summer months.

Then the flowers. From the hot valleys in the south, moist and humid during the monsoon season, to the golden hills of Tibet with their dry, cold winds, there is much to tempt the imagination of the gardener and the botanist, Yet, strangely enough, little collecting has been done since the years between 1846 and 1849 when Sir Richard Strachey and J.E. Winterbottom made their famous collection of specimens. It was left to R.L. Holdsworth in 1931 to point out the potentialities of this floral storehouse and in *Kamet Conquered* he wrote:

> There are many enthusiastic gardeners who, I feel sure, would welcome these Himalayan high alpines, and I write this in the hope that some enterprising philanthropist will go and get us seed or plants, not merely of the easier, bigger species from comparatively low down, but of many a shy *primula* and gentian which haunts the more austere heights of that wonderful world.

It was my privilege to undertake this work and the reader, while remembering, and I hope generously, my ignorance, must judge for himself whether the Bhyundar Valley deserves its title the Valley of Flowers. Others will visit it, analyse it and probe it but, whatever their opinions, to me it will remain the Valley of Flowers, a valley of peace and perfect beauty where the human spirit may find repose.

I arrived at Ranikhet on June 1 after a stay in Naini Tal with Sir Harry Haig, the Governor of the United Provinces and Lady Haig. Sir Harry was then President of the Himalayan Club and he very kindly promised to do everything in his power to help me, whilst Lady Haig, who is an enthusiastic gardener, has done much to beautify the already beautiful surroundings of Government House at Naini Tal.

Ranikhet is a hill station situated at about 5,000 feet on a foothill ridge, which commands a view of the Central Himalayas, from the peaks of western Nepal to the snows of Badrinath and Tehri Garhwal, comparable in beauty, grandeur and extent to the celebrated view of Kangchenjunga, from Darjeeling. In a single sweep the eye ranges from east to west past Nanda Kot, 22,530 feet, climbed in 1936 by a Japanese expedition; Nanda Devi, 25,645 feet, the highest peak in British administered territory and thus strictly speaking in the British Empire, which was climbed in 1936 by the Anglo-American Expedition; Trisul, 23,360 feet, climbed by Dr. T.G. Longstaff in 1907, and which remained the highest summit to have been reached until 1930 when Jonsong Peak, 24,344 feet, was climbed by the International Kangchenjunga Expedition; then the great massif of Hathi Parbat, 22,070 feet, and Gauri Parbat, 22,027 feet, with Nilgiri Parbat, 21,264 feet, behind and slightly to the west ; Mana Peak, 23,860 feet, and Kamet, 25,447 feet, nearly 100 miles distant; and so westwards to the snows of Badrinath, 23,420 feet, with Nilkanta, 21,640 feet, one of the most beautiful peaks in the Himalayas, standing alone, and the far snows of Tehri Garhwal, where much interesting exploration remains to be done.

This vast wall of mountains is best seen in the clear atmosphere of morning before the clouds, formed by the hot, moist air currents from the valleys, have obscured it, and many a time I have risen early to look over the foothills, dim and shadowy in the twilight, to the snows, hung like a glowing curtain across the whole width of the northern sky, yet so remote it seemed no human foot could tread their auroral steeps.

It is in these moments of awakening, when not a bird twits from the forest and the sun steps from peak to peak slowly and in splendid strides, that the sage's words ring true: "In a hundred ages of the Gods I could not tell thee of the glories of Himachal."

At Ranikhet I was joined by the four Tibetans from Darjeeling. I have already mentioned Wangdi Nurbu. He will be familiar to some readers as the man who fell into a crevasse on Kangchenjunga and remained in it for three hours before he was found. He was badly knocked about and was sent down to Base Camp to be cared for by the doctor, but two days later insisted on returning to the highest camp. Then, on Everest in 1933, he was taken ill with double pneumonia and was sent down to a lower valley in an apparently dying condition, only to reappear at the base camp one month later carrying a heavy load on his back and clamouring for work on the mountain. Such is the spirit of the man. He is a little fellow, all bone and wiriness, who does not carry an ounce of superfluous flesh and has one of the hardest countenances I have seen; he looks a "tough", but in point of fact he is sober and law abiding. He has less pronounced cheekbones than many Tibetans and his lips are thinner and firmer. His eyes are usually slightly bloodshot in the whites, which gives them a ferocious, almost cruel look, but Wangdi is not cruel; he is merely hard, one of the hardest men I know, and fit to enter a select coterie of Bhotia and Sherpa porters which includes men such as "Satan" Chettan, who was killed on Kangchenjunga, and Lewa, the Sirdar of the Kamet Expedition, not to mention that pock marked piece of granite, Lobsang, who distinguished himself on Everest and Kangchenjunga, but who has, unhappily, since died.

Wangdi is illiterate, but in addition to his native language he can speak fluent Urdu and Nepali. He is quick and jerky in action and in speech; it is as though some fire burns within him, which can never properly find a vent. Like many of his race he is an excellent handy-man but failing his kukri (curved Gurkha knife) prefers to use his teeth, and I have seen him place the recalcitrant screw of a camera tripod between them and turn the tripod with the screw as an axis until the latter was loosened, then calmly spit out such pieces of his teeth as had been ground off in the process. Last, but by no means least, he is a fine climber. On Everest in 1936 he jumped automatically into the lead of the porter columns on the North Col and was never so happy as when exercising his magnificent strength and undoubted skill.

Pasang, with his high cheekbones and slanting eyes, is a true Tibetan type. A tall stringy man with thin spindly legs, he somehow suggested clumsiness, and undoubtedly he was clumsy on a mountain, particularly on snow, so that when climbing with him I had always to be on my guard against a slip. I think he must have been something of a fatalist, for whenever he did slip the first thing he did was to let go of his ice axe, the one thing by which he might have stopped himself, and leave it to God or his companions to decide whether or not he should continue to slide into the next world. But though this passivity was exasperating at times

I liked Pasang. He might give the impression of being a lout, but there was plenty of common sense packed away behind his ungainly exterior, and he was to be trusted on any other matter but climbing. His naive awkwardness, and I can think of no better way of putting it, betokened a nature free from all guile and he was ever ready and willing to do his best, however uncomfortable the conditions in a rain-soaked camp or on a storm-lashed mountainside. He was no leader and had none of the fire, vivaciousness or conscious toughness of Wangdi – where others went he was prepared to follow – but there was something solid and enduring about his character, and the quick smile that unexpectedly illumined his normal solemn countenance was a sure indication of kindliness.

Tewang was an old stager and one of the men who climbed to Camp V on Everest in 1924. Hugh Ruttledge wrote of him in *Everest 1933* that: 'Efficient, completely reliable, and never idle, he performed every office from porter messman to nurse, in a manner beyond praise.' Undoubtedly he was ageing, for he had become heavy, and it was apparent that he would be of little use in difficult mountaineering and would have to be relegated to Base Camp as sheet anchor of the party. Age tells quickly on Tibetans, perhaps because they wear themselves out when they are young, or it may be that the height at which they live has something to do with a rapid deterioration in their physique at a period when a European is in his prime. He was of an even quieter disposition than Pasang and in all ways slower than his companions; you could see this in his heavy face and lumbering gait. I scarcely ever saw him smile, but there was a natural fatherliness about him which would have chosen him automatically as a nurse, as it did in 1933, had there been any nursing to do.

Nurbu was the youngster of the party. He had been Major C.J. Morris's servant on Everest in 1936, and the training he had then received had stood him in good stead, for he was the most efficient servant I have ever had. A good-looking lad, with a round, boyish and remarkably smooth skinned face, he was invariably cheerful and quick to seize upon and remember anything to do with his job. He had had little or no mountaineering experience and came to me as a raw novice at the craft, but he was a natural climber, neat and careful, particularly on rocks, on which he was cat-like in his agility and, unlike many of his type, quick to learn the finer points of mountaineering, such as handling the rope and cutting steps in snow and ice. Himalayan mountaineering will hear more of him in the future and I venture the prophecy that he puts up a good showing on Everest in 1938.

Such were my companions – I cannot think of them as porters – and I could scarcely have wished for better. They contributed generously and in full measure to the pleasure and success of the happiest holiday of my life. Three days at Ranikhet sufficed to complete my preparations, but I might not have got away so expeditiously had it not been for the help given me by Mrs. Evelyn Browne, whom many Himalayan mountaineers will remember with gratitude, whilst my short stay was rendered additionally pleasant by the kindness of Major Browne, the Secretary of the Club.

On June 4 my arrangements were completed and eleven Dotial porters, of a race indigenous to southern Nepal, had arrived to carry my heavy luggage to Base Camp. So at last the dream of several years was on the verge of practical fulfilment.

CHAPTER TWO

The Low Foothills

EVERYTHING WAS READY on the morning of June 5 and the lorry which was to convey me the first part of my journey was packed to capacity with fifteen porters and some 1,000 lbs. of luggage. This journey, of some fifty-five miles from Ranikhet to the village of Garur, was along narrow roads, the hairpin bends in which were innumerable and acute and the driver drove on the principle that no obstacle was to be encountered on the corners, and if it was, Providence must decide the issue. Fortunately Providence was well disposed and, apart from some hectic encounters with stray cows and bullock carts, the drive was uneventful.

The foothills of the Himalayas provide the perfect introduction to the "Snows" and their gentle forest-clad undulations lead the eye forwards to the background of gigantic peaks which distance serves to increase, not diminish in beauty.

After following for some miles the clear-running Kosi River and passing numerous villages and Government resin-collecting stations, the road climbed over a high ridge, where I saw several tree rhododendrons and the distant snows of Trisul and Nanda Devi, then wound sinuously down to the level floor of the wide Sarju Valley.

Garur, the terminus of the motor road, is a sordid little place, like any native place to which "civilisation" has penetrated disguised in the form of motor cars. Flies swarmed over the offal in the street, beggars whined for alms, and from one of the single-storey hovels a cheap gramophone wheezed drearily. There is no doubt that the farthest-flung tentacles of civilisation debase, not improve human conditions. However, like Mr. Gandhi, I might damn motor cars, but I had not hesitated to employ one. I turned my back gladly on the place with its smells, the immemorial and "romantic" smells of the East, which are compounded quite simply of the effluvium from an inadequate drainage system and unwashed human bodies, mingling in the present instance with a reek of oil and petrol, and set off on the first stage of my march. For the next few months I should neither see, hear, nor smell a motorcar or aeroplane; it was a stimulating thought.

Beyond Garur, the path crosses the Sarju River by a well-built suspension bridge, then, after sundry ups and downs, begins a long climb to the Gwaldam dak bungalow.

It was a hot march – the temperature cannot have been much less than 100 degrees in the shade – and the Dotials poured with sweat. How they managed to carry their 80-lb. loads I do not know. I felt a slave driver, but it is possible I estimated their efforts by my own incapacities, for I had left Ranikhet with a temperature of 101 degrees and a feverish chill. This may have been unwise, but I am convinced that the best way of ridding myself of a chill is to walk it off and sweat it out; I certainly must have accomplished the latter as I was fat and flabby after many months of sedentary living.

The foothills of the Central Himalayas are poor in flowers owing to forests of chir (*Pinus longifolia*), which cover the ground in a carpet of needles, thus preventing the growth of plants or the germination of seed. Yet these forests have a charm of their own, for the chir is a fine tree and though it has few branches and casts little shade, grows straight and true to a considerable height. Furthermore, trees are well spaced and owing to the absence of clogging undergrowth or lank grass, the country resembles a well-kept parkland. Lastly, the chir is highly resinous and the air is fragrant in its neighbourhood.

In normal circumstances it is an enjoyable walk to Gwaldam but that day it was a matter of setting my teeth and plugging on with a bursting head, aching limbs and a thirst which I satisfied recklessly at every spring.

So, at last, after a ten miles' walk and an ascent of some 4,000 feet I emerged from the forest on to the ridge where the bungalow stands overlooking the haze-filled depths of the Pindar Valley to the remote gleam of the Himalayan snows.

Two Englishmen were encamped near the bungalow, Mr. G.W.H. Davidson, the Headmaster of Colvin Taluqdars College, Lucknow, who had with him one of his Indian pupils, and Major Matthews of the Royal Engineers, and their kindness and hospitality had much to do with my rapid recovery from my chill, for I went to bed with an excellent dinner and a considerable quantity of whisky inside me and woke miraculously better next morning.

From Gwaldam a forest path descends steeply into the Pindar Valley. We were away early, soon after the sun had fired the snows, and an hour later had descended 3,000 feet to the Pindar River.

About half-way to the village of Tharali I met with another Englishman, Corporal Hamilton, a member of a party of soldiers of the East Surrey Regiment who were at this time attempting the ascent of Kamet. Unfortunately, he had damaged his arm, which had become poisoned. As I had with me a comprehensive medical kit I was able to disinfect and bind up the wound, which had already been treated by an Indian doctor.

The expedition in which he took part is one of the most remarkable in the annals of Himalayan mountaineering. The soldiers, who were led by Corporal Ralph Ridley, after an expedition the previous summer to the Arwa Valley glacier system, boldly decided to attempt Kamet in 1937. Their organisation was admirable and they failed primarily through lack of sufficient porterage after overcoming the greatest difficulties of the route and reaching a height of 23,700 feet. At the same time to attempt a major peak, even though it has been climbed before, is unwise without adequate mountaineering experience; there are peaks of all heights and shades of difficulty in the Himalayas where the novice may learn the craft. Nature is intolerant of ignorance, and he who attempts the greater peaks of the Himalayas without having acquired that delicacy and acuteness of perception, that instinctive *feeling* for his task, will sooner or later blunder to disaster. This is not meant to detract from the merit of an expedition which was conspicuous for the initiative and self reliance displayed, but merely to point out the advisability of preliminary preparation in mountaineering. It is to be hoped that future mountaineering expeditions will receive the encouragement of the High Command.

Tharali huddles at the foot of a knoll thrusting forwards into the Pindar River, which narrows considerably at this point. The village was devastated by a flood in the summer of 1936. Twenty inches of rain fell in one day and the Pindar River, unable to discharge its surplus waters through the narrow portion of the valley, rose and flooded the village, destroying a number of houses and drowning forty of the inhabitants.

The usual camping ground is a strip of sun-scorched turf by the river, but I preferred the partial shade of some pines on the knoll near the village school, which sports large notices over every approach to the effect that all are welcome; ineffective propaganda to judge from the absence of pupils, but perhaps it was a holiday.

The afternoon was the hottest I ever remember. My tent, which was only six and a half feet long by four feet wide, was intolerable, so I lay outside it on a mattress in the scanty shade of the pines, plagued by innumerable flies.

Evening brought little relief, and the sun set in a furnace-like glare. The night was breathless but I managed to sleep, only to be awakened shortly before midnight by flickering lightning and reverberating concussions of thunder. The storm was confined to the hills and passed after an hour, leaving a dull red glow in the sky, presumably the reflection of a forest fired by lightning.

I breakfasted early and was away at five o'clock, anxious to break the back of the long march to Subtal, which entails some twelve miles of walking and 5,000 feet of ascent.

The storm had done nothing to clear the air and the forests were charged with damp enervating heat, so that it was a relief to emerge from them after two hours' uphill walking on to more open slopes, where the village of Dungri perches below a basin-like rim of hills. The air here was cooler and men and women were working energetically in the terraced fields or scratching shallow furrows with primitive wooden ploughs drawn by oxen or buffaloes. The men greeted me in a friendly way, and the children gazed at me curiously, impudently or shyly in the manner of children the world over, but the nose-beringed women I met with on the path hastened by with averted faces. At one hamlet a man ran out of a house, saluted with military precision and offered to carry my rucksack. Doubtless like many another in this country, he had served with the Garhwal or Kumaon Rifles.

Forests of chir, open country artificially deforested, then rhododendrons, deciduous trees, spruces and firs is the natural upward order of growth in the lower foothills, where crops flourish best in the temperate zone from 4,000 to 8,000 feet. I entered the cool forest above Dungri and seating myself on a mossy bank ate my lunch of biscuits and potatoes. I was far ahead of the porters; the forest was profoundly silent, and great clouds were slowly building up in a sky of steely oxidised blue. Not even in the Sikkim forests have I seen finer tree rhododendrons, and there was one moss-clad giant, which cannot have been less than five feet in diameter. For how many centuries had these trees endured? Long before the wooden ships of "The Company" sailed to India they must have established themselves on the knees of the Himalayas.

Beyond my luncheon place I had a glimpse of a brown bear as it leapt from the path – a little fellow who was gone in a flash. After this the path mounted at a restful angle and passing over a brow descended to a stream issuing from a rocky rift. There was a deep pool and I stripped and bathed, gasping at first in the ice cold water then dried myself on a flat rock in the sun. While I was engaged in this a small boy passed and catching sight of me bolted precipitately up the path; then halted to eye me with fearful curiosity. Probably he had never seen a European before and at all events anyone who bathed, and in ice cold water, was indubitably mad.

The camping ground at Subtal, the name given to an extensive pasture, is a sparsely wooded ridge, which rises on either hand to hills densely forested in spruce and the Himalayan oak, which is a narrow spreading tree as compared with the English oak. To the north the ridge falls away into a branch valley of the Nandakini Valley, through which the western glaciers of Trisul pour their waters into the Alaknanda River.

It was not yet midday, but the sky was thick with clouds and the earth lay still and silent beneath a weight of lurid haze. The porters were long in arriving, but it was a marvel that they should arrive at all considering the weight of their loads, the distance and the climb. If my mathematics are not too rusty the energy required to lift a human body plus an extra 80 lbs. of weight through nearly a mile of height comes to well over 1,000,000 foot pounds of which the load amounts to about 400,000 foot pounds. In terms of the load alone it is equivalent to shovelling about 75 tons of coal into a furnace.

Meanwhile, a party of traders with a dozen ponies had halted close by and lit a fire after carefully stacking their merchandise under a tarpaulin. Presently one of them, seeing that I was alone, asked me if I would care for some food. It was a generous thought, but I had no need to deplete their probably slender supplies. This was only one instance of the kindliness of the people of this country and it seemed to me that the human atmosphere of Garhwal and Kumaon was very different to what it had been in 1931. Is Mr. Gandhi's creed of non-violence bearing the fruits of sympathy, tolerance and understanding or is a more positive and less vacillating British rule responsible? Whatever it is, one thing is certain: only through co-operation, friendship and mutual respect between the British and Indian races is any real and lasting benefit for either to be achieved in India in that distant future when education and evolution will have emancipated the Indian peoples from their strangling social and religious prejudices.

The early afternoon darkened gradually and in the close sultry atmosphere flies attacked me venomously. The haze deepened until it was difficult to perceive where the hills ended and the clouds began. A rust-coloured light invested the forest, then faded as the last oases of blue sky were swallowed up by chaotic and enormous thunderclouds, and the far north where the Himalayas lay began to shudder with long muffled reverberations of thunder.

At two o'clock the porters straggled into camp, soaked with sweat and very tired. As the Darjeeling men pitched the tents, one for me and one for themselves, heavy drops of rain were splashing into the forest and the thunder was rumbling continuously as though a column of tanks and guns was crossing a hollow-sounding bridge.

Soon lightning was flickering and stabbing through a blue wall of advancing rain, smeared dull white with hail, and the thunder was tearing overhead like a giant rending endless strips of calico. Then above the thunder I heard a dull roar, rising in strength and pitch every instant, and almost before I had time to realise its meaning the thin-topped spruces a hundred yards distant bent like whip-lashes and a terrific squall of wind and hail, rifted by mauve swords of lightning and fearful explosions of thunder, burst in wild fury on the camp.

This first blast of the storm did not last long and half an hour later the rain stopped and the wind died into a damp calm, smelling of wet earth and vegetation. Though the storm had retreated from the immediate vicinity of Subtal the thunder continued, coming from every direction and without pause in a single tremendous sound that grew and ebbed and grew again in concussions that seemed to shake the hills to their foundations.

The storm was working up for another climax when Nurbu brought me my supper, which Tewang had artfully cooked in the shelter of a hollow tree. Afterwards I lay in my sleeping bag and watched through the entrance of the tent the finest display of lightning I have ever seen. The whole sky was continuously blazing with mauve fire and it was possible to read uninterruptedly from a book. Slowly the lightning grew in brilliance, if that were possible, and the thunder in volume. This was no ordinary storm, even in a district where storms are frequent, and I wished I had moved the tents after the first storm, though with the ridges on either side of the camp there did not seem any likelihood of danger. There was no time to do anything now and at nine o'clock the storm was upon us in a hurricane of wind, hail and rain, punctuated every second by blinding lightning and terrible explosions of thunder.

Lightning when it strikes close to the observer does not make the noise we conventionally term "thunder", or even the rending, tearing noise already mentioned, but a single violent explosion, a BANG like a powerful bomb. I have no hesitation in admitting that I was thoroughly scared, and as I lay in my sleeping bag I could have sworn that streams of fire flickered along the ridge of the tent and down the lateral guy rope.

The worst was over within half an hour and I went outside to see how the Dotials had fared, for I half feared that one or other of the trees beneath which they were sheltering had been struck. To my great relief they were all safe, though even the irrepressible Wangdi, who together with Pasang, Nurbu, and Tewang had been in the other tent, seemed a trifle shaken by the experience.

This was the last of the storm so far as it concerned us, but long afterwards the sky flamed with lightning and thunder serenaded the ranges. I am not exaggerating when I state that I do not remember a second's pause in the sound of the thunder during a total period of eight hours.

The sky next morning was cloudless, but dense haze concealed the view I had hoped to obtain of the snows. We were away as the sun touched the camp and descended through cool and fragrant forests, alive with the song of birds, to cultivated slopes and small villages; then into a wooded valley with a stream of clear running water. Here at about 7,000 feet on an open slope I saw the first of a little *iris* (*I. kumaonensis*), which I knew I would meet with later on the Kuari Pass and in the Bhyundar Valley. I also came upon hundreds of the largest cobwebs I have ever seen. For a mile, the trees and shrubs had suspended between them vast nets, wet and shining after the rain, with the spider waiting for his breakfast in the centre of each. So strong were the webs that stout twigs to which they were affixed were bent at right angles, whilst the largest was stretched between two trees fully twelve feet apart and had as its spinner a spider about six inches in width from tip to tip of its hairy legs.

At the village of Ghat, which is situated in the deep Nandakini Valley, a single room dak bungalow destitute of furniture did not attract me and I preferred to camp by the river. The tent had scarcely been pitched when thunder began to growl again and a mass of inky clouds advanced quickly down the valley. A few minutes later I was astonished to see a writhing column of spray appear round a bend of the river and descend on the camp. Next moment up went my tent, wrenching the metal tent pegs away as though they were matches, and swept along the ground towards the river. Yelling to the men I threw myself on it and a few moments later was joined by Wangdi, Nurbu and Pasang, all shouting with laughter, evidently convinced that a whirlwind was a huge joke.

Later the weather improved and I supped in the calm of a perfect evening. I had no official cook. Experience has taught me that official cooks are to be avoided in the Himalayas as they are almost invariably dirty and are born "twisters" and "scroungers"; worst of all they are impervious to insult, sarcasm, or righteous anger, and like their European prototypes, resent the best intentioned suggestions and advice. Furthermore, they are set in their habits, and their habits are vile, and, lastly, they are invariably bad cooks, or so my experience goes, and are largely responsible for the stomach troubles that beset Himalayan expeditions.

Therefore, I had left it to the men to decide between themselves as to which of them should cook for me, and Tewang had elected himself or been elected to the post. To write that he was a good cook, which implies the exercise of imagination and a fertility of invention, would be to overstate his abilities. He was simply a plain cook, so plain that his cooking would have palled at an early date on an appetite less voracious than mine. His most artistic culinary flight was rissoles, and he would produce these with one of his rare smiles creasing his broad face and an exaggerated pride worthy of a conjurer who has out-Maskelyned his own professors. But he cooked what he did cook well and I seldom had cause to reproach him on this score. So having seen that he was clean, that doubtful water was boiled, and that dishcloths were used in preference to the tail of a shirt, I left him to his own devices.

The Dotials were averse to proceeding to Joshimath via the Kuari Pass. As they justly pointed out the route from Ghat via Nanda Prayag and the Alaknanda Valley is considerably easier. I had, however, no intention of proceeding by that route, which is very hot and at times fever-ridden, in preference to the cool, healthful and beautiful high-level route via the Kuari Pass, and when I pointed out the disadvantages of the former route, their objections soon resolved themselves into good-humoured grumblings.

From Ghat the path crosses the Nandakini River by a strongly built suspension bridge, then zigzags up a steep and arid hillside. Some 2,500 feet up this, perched on a grassy spur, is a small village, the inhabitants of which greeted me cheerfully. Their lives are spent, like the lives of most people of this country, in agricultural pursuits. A spring and summer of intense activity, devoted to the task of levelling their little fields on the steep hillsides, removing innumerable stones and building them into walls so that the monsoon rains do not wash the precious soil into the valley, turning the thin soil with wooden ox-drawn ploughs, sowing, reaping and threshing, is followed by a winter of comparative inactivity. Scarcely less strenuous is the work of the shepherds deputed to drive the flocks to the upper pastures, which are so few and scanty that owners must take it in turns to graze them. Theirs is the life of the mountain peasant the world over; a struggle against adverse forces, yet forces that once tamed will yield, if not bountifully, at least enough to maintain a fit and hardy race. A dull, monotonous life perhaps, a minute cycle of work and rest, but running through it all the never-ending thread of human propagation and continuity. These dour peasants may be outwardly insensible to their tremendous environment, but the vast hills that everlastingly mock their puny efforts, the deep valleys with their rush of glacial waters bearing onwards to the far-distant plains, the remote glimmer of the high snows have become a part of them, and deep in their inmost selves must rest a love, respect and reverence for their unrelenting taskmasters, the Himalayas.

From the village, the path mounted an open hillside to a ridge clothed with oaks and tree rhododendrons. I lunched in a glade which commanded a view between the trees of Trisul, a vast barrier of shining snow at the head of the deeply cut Nandakini Valley, whose ribbon-like stream thousands of feet beneath me twisted and turned between bare shoulders of the hills. The air was fresh, and only the whirring and humming of insects fell on a profound stillness. All around me grew a pale mauve daisy, whilst on the slope below was a cat mint with rosette-like silvery foliage and blue flowers, some of which were already in seed.

Presently the porters appeared. They were singing, and their simple little song, echoing through the silent glades of the forest, somehow partook of the beauty and majesty of the surroundings; complicated music would be out of place where everything is simple and sublime.

Beyond the glade, the path traversed a forest clad hillside, then emerged on to open slopes terraced with fields where the little village of Ramni perches. Our camping place was on turf close-cropped by the village animals but not eaten so short as to destroy the brilliant blue flowers of a tiny gentian (*G. capitata*). In 1931 we had been pestered by flies at Ramni, but on this occasion a mosquito net over the entrance of my tent enabled me to escape their hateful attentions.

It was a hot afternoon, but the evening was delightfully cool; the flies disappeared and, with no midges or mosquitoes to take their place, I ate my supper in peace beneath the accumulating stars.

CHAPTER THREE

The High Foothills

THE FOLLOWING morning was cloudy, but the clouds soon dissolved in the sun. As I walked up the forest path to the next ridge I felt myself to be nearing the threshold of the high hills. The *anemones* increased in number as I climbed, whilst hosts of buttercups spread a golden carpet over the dew-drenched turf.

Many sheep and goats laden with grain were following the same path on their way to the upper valleys of Garhwal, where the grain is transferred to yaks and jhobus (half-breed yaks), then taken over the high passes into Tibet. Ponies are sometimes employed for load carrying, but the bulk of the grain is carried in little bags, reinforced with leather, on the backs of sheep and goats, the sheep carrying some 20 to 25 lbs. and the goats as much as 30 lbs. The drivers are ragged, picturesque, friendly fellows, some with long curly hair. They walk with a shambling flat-footed gait something like that of the Alpine guide, and two or three of them will share a long water-pipe with a wide, shallow bowl, which they fill with villainous tobacco, mixed with charcoal, or when no tobacco is available, charcoal alone. Smoking one of these pipes is something of a ritual. A man takes two or three rapid puffs, then hands on the pipe to his neighbour, so that the pipe soon goes the round of a dozen men. In this way asphyxiation or carbon monoxide poisoning is avoided.

Thunder was rumbling in the west as I breasted the ridge above Ramni, but the north and east were clear and Nanda Ghunti stood revealed in all its beauty. This peak is 20,700 feet high, and is so beautifully proportioned that it appears almost as high as its greater neighbour, Trisul.

On the far side of the ridge the path descended through forests, crossing occasional glades. I remembered that Holdsworth found *Paeonia Emodii* hereabouts, and I kept my eyes open. But I did not see one until I was within half a mile of the camping ground; then, suddenly, in a shady place, and close to the path, I saw a clump of them. The day was dark now, for a storm was brewing, but even in the gloom of the forest, their cream-coloured blooms shone out as though retaining the recent sunlight in their petals. The clump was the only one in bloom, as the rest were already seeding. This place must be a marvellous sight in April and the first weeks of May, for this paeony blooms early, pushing its way, like the Alpine crocus, through the edge of the retreating snows.

I remembered Semkharak as one of the most delightful camping grounds we had seen during the march to Kamet, but now hills and forest were burdened with impending storm, and the little alp seemed dreary and forlorn. Thunder was growling about the hills when I arrived, but I did not have to wait long for the men, who were just in time to pitch the tents before rain fell in torrents.

For the next two hours lightning darted viciously at the forest-clad ridges and the thunder reverberated from lip to lip of the cup-shaped hills, then, towards evening, with that suddenness peculiar to mountainous countries, the rain and the thunder ceased and the clouds vanished as though absorbed by some invisible vacuum cleaner.

The men collected wood from the forest and soon a great fire was blazing. It was my first camp fire, and I sat by it contentedly while the golden sunlight died on the nearer heights, then fired the distant snows of Nanda Ghunti. Nothing had altered since we camped here in 1931 and there was even the same half-burnt tree-stump where our fire had been lit. Possibly the slender oaks and conifers had added a few inches to their stature, but for the rest Semkharak was the same. Things do not change quickly in the East.

Raymond Greene, a born raconteur, had kept us amused with stories throughout the evening. Six years had passed, but I could not regret them, for the peace and beauty of the hills was mine that evening. The last cloud vanished, the last glow faded from Nanda Ghunti, and the sky lit up with stars. Not a breath of wind stirred in the treetops. Darkness fell. I ate my supper, then smoked my pipe and dreamed, until the fire had died down to a heap of glowing embers and the dew lay hoary on the grass.

Next morning I descended into the Bireh Valley, passing through hundreds of acres of paeonies in seed. The seed was unripe, but I gathered some, hoping to ripen it later; I know now that this is difficult if not impossible in the case of the paeony, for the seed shrivels, and becomes valueless. It must be gathered when it is perfectly ripe and ready to fall out of the pod.

The path crossed a small log bridge over the river near a vertical crag of crumbling rock, beneath which some drovers, disregarding the law of gravity, had camped for the night. We exchanged greetings and, as is customary in this country, they inquired as to where I was going and from whence I came.

From the river the path zigzagged steeply upwards, then traversed the hillside almost levelly, through forests of tree rhododendrons, roses and a white sweet-scented flowering shrub to the camping ground at Kaliaghat, which is in an open grassy place, sprinkled with large boulders. Adjoining it are cultivated fields, beyond which rises a vast wall of forest, broken high up by gigantic crags. Many queer noises came from this forest, including the whistle like cries of a bird, and once I heard a coughing sound, which was probably made by a bear or panther.

The afternoon was hot and fly-ridden. It was impossible to sit outside my tent without being pestered by innumerable flies, whilst inside it was like an oven, so I occupied myself with collecting flowers for my press. It was a beautiful evening, but the flies, as is usual in Garhwal, were replaced by midges, which although small seemed capable of biting through the toughest skin, to judge from the exasperated scratchings of the porters.

From Kaliaghat a pleasant path across meadows, then through rhododendron and oak forest, led to a wide alp gay with white and blue *anemones* (*A. obtusiloba*) within view of the Kuari Pass, which cuts a notch in a ridge. Thenceforward the route lies across steep craggy hillsides, then past an impressive gorge, where a stream spurts out of a narrow cleft to form a perfect bathing pool, and finally, after sundry ups and downs, mounts towards the pass.

As I was well ahead of the porters I seated myself with my back to a mossy bank, where grew the delicate sprays of a beautiful little *androsace* (probably *A. rotundifolia*), and ate the lunch provided by Tewang. I had not been there long before I heard a footfall, and looking up saw a wild-looking fellow with a long-handled axe over his shoulder regarding me with the greatest curiosity. As soon as he saw that I was disposed to be friendly he squatted on the ground and burst into an unintelligible gabble. Probably he had seen no one to talk to for some time and was making the best of his opportunity. My very limited stock of Urdu elicited that he was there with his flock for the summer and that he lived at Kaliaghat. Apart from this, our "conversation" was limited to gestures and smiles, which, however, are very good substitutes for speech in the wilds. I gave him some tobacco and he departed beaming.

Presently along came the Dotials. As usual, in spite of their heavy loads, they were happy, and were singing their rhythmical little songs. We lunched at Dakwani, a fertile alp 1,000 feet below the Kuari Pass. There I saw many *Iris kumaonensis* in bloom. This little *iris,* a miniature edition of the English garden *iris*, grows on hot, well-drained sunny slopes. All it asks for is a cool root run. Then, when the winter snow melts, it pushes out its thin leaves and a little later its spire of purple blooms, which partake in colour of cold shadowed snow and rich blue sky. It grows well in England and I have one in my own garden, which brings to me every spring a memory of the Himalayas.

Dakwani is the usual camping ground, but I determined to push on and camp on the pass, for this is a renowned view-point and commands a prospect extending from the Nanda Devi group to the peaks of Badrinath. Accordingly, I left the main transport at Dakwani and with three Darjeeling men and four Dotials climbed a zigzag stony track to the pass. The crest is not the best viewpoint, and I camped on a rocky ridge some distance to the east, where there are no near hills to interfere with the panorama. Unfortunately clouds and haze concealed most of the peaks, but I hoped that the following morning would afford a clear view particularly of the Zaskar Range, into which the Bhyundar Valley cuts, and the peaks I hoped to climb during the next few weeks.

The evening was dark and dense clouds massed along the haze-filled Alaknanda Valley. We hoped that no thunderstorm was brewing as the camp was in an exposed position and we had no wish to repeat the experience of Subtal. The men had carried up some wood from Dakwani, but there was plenty of dwarf rhododendron available, the sight of which delighted the Tibetans as it reminded them of their native land in many parts of which it is the only fuel, apart from dried yak dung.

Winter snow still covered large areas of the hillsides, but already a tiny gentian with daintily frilled petals carpeted the ground.

At sunset the dark clouds delivered a sharp hailstorm but later the sky cleared somewhat, revealing scattered stars. After the hot marches across the foothills, it was good to feel the need of a sweater and the warmth of an eiderdown sleeping bag. Better still, there were no flies or midges and I could sleep with the tent flaps wide open.

The tonic of the high places was in the air. So far, I had lived with little thought of the future, my thoughts circumscribed by the day's march, but now for the first time I experienced that feeling of expectancy which every mountaineer has when approaching high mountains.

A restful sleep and I awoke as usual with the first light. But there was no view; above and below, sluggish vapours concealed the glorious panorama, which I had seen in 1931 from the same place. The Tibetans were as disappointed as I, for they were anxious for a glimpse of the peaks we hoped to climb.

Presently the main party joined us and we descended towards the Dhauli Valley, at first over open slopes, then into pine forest; and there at the upper limit of the trees I came upon an old friend, which I had photographed in 1931, a solitary sentinel gnarled and weather-beaten by countless storms. It was decaying, for to judge from its appearance it had been maltreated by lightning, but it still stretched gaunt, hard branches against the sky, an embodiment of that enduring force which epitomises, in material form, the spirit of the hills.

As we came out of the upper forest on to a wide alp, the clouds parted, revealing the great massif of Gauri Parbat and Hathi Parbat; then almost before I had time to take in the grandeur of this sudden revelation, a terrific icy spire, shining and immeasurably remote, thrust itself through the clouds, Dunagiri.

The Dotials said they were certain of the path to Joshimath. It is true there was a path at first, but it soon petered out in the forest. We kept on for some distance through a tangle of vegetation; then it was brought home to us that we were lost. I was well ahead of the men and stopped. The forest was very quiet; not a sound, not a breath disturbed the serene silence. Above, the great trees formed a canopy with their interlacing branches, and at my feet the deep shadows were accentuated by pools of sunlight.

Wangdi joined me and we yelled lustily until all the men were assembled; then we struck straight down the hillside, forcing our way through undergrowth, and at length, to our relief, came to a path leading in the direction of Joshimath.

I halted for lunch by a leisurely little stream, fringed with marigolds that wandered into a sun-drenched glade. After this the path wound sinuously across the hillside, descending gradually as it did so into a forest of chir, hot and resinous in the nearly vertical noonday sun. Thenceforward it was a somewhat weary march, but enlivened at one place by a number of lemurs playing about on a boulder. They allowed me to approach within a few yards of them, but looked so hostile that I felt glad of my ice axe. Beyond were numerous hamlets whose inhabitants were working industriously on their small terraced fields of grain and vegetables. I asked one of them how far it was to Joshimath, and he replied two miles, but it was more like four or five; these people have small regard for distance, and measure it in time rather than mileage.

The path divided, and not sure as to which branch to take, I waited until a small woman driving some oxen appeared. She seemed terrified when I questioned her and hastened by with averted eyes. How many decades will there be before the Indian woman is emancipated from the mental, moral and physical slavery she has endured for countless generations?

Joshimath is perched on a hillside some 1,500 feet above the junction of the Alaknanda and Dhauli Rivers. It is a halting place of pilgrims who journey to Badrinath during the summer months to pay their respects to Mother Ganges, and worship at the shrines of deities associated with the sacred snows of Himachal (Himalaya). Unhappily, they bring with them many diseases from the plains, and cholera, dysentery, typhoid and malaria exact their toll from the devout, whose notions as to sanitation, cleanliness and hygiene are at constant variance with the well-intentioned preventive and remedial efforts of the Indian Government. All along the road infection is spread by hordes of flies and he is a wise traveller who boils every cup of his drinking water.

The village is an ugly little place with slate or corrugated iron-covered, two-storeyed houses, straggling unbeautifully over the hillside. Primitive little shops displaying sweetmeats, vegetables and other commodities line the main street, which is roughly paved in places and in others has been deeply channelled by the monsoon rains. The pilgrims spend the night in single-storeyed rest-houses, not unlike the hovels provided for the Kentish hop-pickers of former days, some of which are situated in narrow passages running off the main street, and are filthy, and evil-smelling. Such pestilential conditions have little effect on the pilgrims and scores were to be seen, many being naked save for a loincloth, seated in meditation, their thoughts fixed on the shrine at Badrinath, their sacred destination.

There are numerous temples dedicated to various gods, principal among them being Vishnu, who is represented by an idol carved from black stone. Joshimath was at one time the capital of the Katyuris, the rulers of western Kumaon and Garhwal, and the successors of the Buddhists, who were driven out of Nepal, Kumaon and Garhwal by Sankara, the indefatigable destroyer of Buddhism in India, who is thought to have lived in the seventh or eighth centuries. It was he who advocated pilgrimage to the shrines of Shiva and Vishnu at Kedarnath and Badrinath. His disciples were established in these ancient shrines and the consequent influx of pilgrims prevented a reversion to Buddhism. Owing to religious quarrels between followers of the two deities, Joshimath was abandoned by the Katyuris, whose kingdom was broken up, forcing them to establish themselves as independent rajahs. Since it was first instituted, the pilgrimage to Badrinath and Kedarnath has increased in importance and nowadays some 50,000 or 60,000 pilgrims from all parts of India, including the remote south, make their way every year up the Alaknanda Valley. Even the pilgrimage to Benares is not so beneficial to the soul as that to the snows of the Himalayas, which bestow so bountifully their sanctity and bliss to the heart of man. It is written in the Skanda Purana:

> He who thinks of Himachal though he should not behold him is greater than he who performs all worship in Kashi (Benares). In a hundred ages of the gods, I could not tell thee of the glories of Himachal. As the dew is dried up by the morning sun, so are the sins of mankind by the sight of Himachal.

Doubtless some of the old Buddhist demonolatry is responsible for the veneration in which the snows are held. It may be that the European mountaineer has something of the same superstitious instinct handed down from the days of sun and moon worship, when the hilltops were the abiding places of gods and devils; and not long ago Mount Pilatus was reputed to be haunted by the uneasy ghost of Pontius Pilate. Understanding has replaced fear, but it may be that the shadows of ancient mysteries remain, so that the sight of high mountains rekindles in a different guise the same feelings of awe which our remote ancestors had in their presence. That Kumaon and Garhwal should be especially consecrated to the gods of Indian religious mysticism is easily, understandable. Is there any region of the Himalayas, or even of the world, to excel this region in beauty and grandeur? Where else are there to be found such narrow and precipitous valleys and gorges, such serene vistas of alp, forest, snow-field and peak? This "abode of snow" is rightly the goal of the heat-enervated people of the plains. Never was a pilgrimage of finer accomplishment. It is the perfect antidote to a static life, and it cannot fail to inspire in the dullest a nobler conception of the universe.

Below Joshimath, sins are purified by the swift-running waters of the Alaknanda River. From the shrine at Vishnu Prayag the pilgrims descend a flight of steps and dip themselves in the ice-cold torrent; they ascend rejuvenated in mind, and it must be in body, ready to tread the stony path that leads through the gorges to Badrinath, along the "great way" to final liberation of spirit.

There is a bungalow at Joshimath perched on the hillside above the village, and containing one living room and a bathroom with the usual zinc hip-bath, the servants quarters and kitchen being in a separate building. In the living room are some book shelves, the last resting place of a number of volumes of great antiquity, among them Blackwood's Magazines, the Christian Science Monitor, and works of Victorian and Edwardian novelists, all of which form a restful home for small beetles, "silver-fish" and numerous unidentifiable insects. In these respects the bungalow is similar to others in the district, but in one other respect it is remarkable, as being the home and breeding place of the largest spiders I have ever seen, not excluding the tarantula of South America. The bathroom is their happy hunting ground, and I bathed that evening with one eye on the dilapidated ceiling lest some huge brute, six or seven inches across, should descend upon me.

The men had marched well, so I rested them for a day, which I devoted to letter writing. Joshimath boasts a post-office, a curious ramshackle little building, with a doorway so low I had to stoop to enter. In this lair, surrounded by the usual appurtenances of his craft, a morse key, ledgers, pigeon-holes and official notices innumerable, I found the Postmaster and his assistant.

In 1936, during the Everest Expedition, the letters sent back by members mysteriously disappeared, to reappear some six or eight months later in England bearing the following typewritten notice:

> Suffered detention in Gangtok post office owing to the postmaster's failure to affix stamps and to forward them in time. The Postmaster has been sent to jail for his offence.

But any doubts I may have entertained as to the efficiency of the Indian Posts were dispelled by the Postmaster of Joshimath, who proved not only courteous, but helpful and efficient.

Later, the local Bunnia (storekeeper), a comfortable looking person who beamed amiably through thick spectacles, put in an appearance and I ordered sattoo (parched barley, a staple food in the Central and Eastern Himalayas), rice, gur (native sugar, which is purchased in lumps resembling solid glue), tea, curry ingredients, atta (flour), spices, potatoes and onions. I bought enough to keep the four Darjeeling men for a fortnight, allowing two pounds of food per man per day, and the cost worked out at roughly 6 annas per man per day. Eggs I failed to secure, although a man was sent to scour the country for them.

Late in the afternoon there was a thunderstorm, but towards sundown the clouds melted away, and with my work done and arrangements completed for the morrow's march, I reclined in an easy chair on the verandah, while a gentle breeze stirred an apricot tree above me, then fell gradually to a complete calm. A rosy glow invested the great rock faces opposite and dusk gathered in the deep Alaknanda Valley. The last mist vanished in a sky of profound green, and the first star shone out.

Little did I know, but this was the evening before the great tragedy on Nanga Parbat, 400 miles to the north-west, where seven German mountaineers and nine Sherpa porters were settling down to a sleep from which they were destined never to awake.

At Joshimath the evening was supremely peaceful, and there came to me, for the first time since leaving Ranikhet, an indescribable exaltation of spirit, which most travellers experience at one time or another in the Himalayas. For days past I had walked over the foothills, rejoicing in the scenery; yet never for one moment had I escaped civilisation; it had been always at my heels, and I had walked with one eye on time and another on distance, my mind occupied with futile matters. Now I had in some way escaped from this slavery to schedule and was free to enjoy some of the grandest country of the world.

CHAPTER FOUR

Approach to the Bhyundar Valley

WE WERE AWAY at 6 next morning. One of the porters was leading a goat which I had purchased at the last moment for the exorbitant sum of 9 rupees, a fine beast with a long clean shaggy coat which reminded me vaguely of those curious little doormat-like dogs that trail behind amply-proportioned females in Hyde Park and Kensington Gardens. I dubbed him Montmorency, but why I cannot for the life of me recollect. I liked Montmorency, and had not known him above an hour before I regretted his fate; he was very intelligent, very affectionate, very fond of human society, very docile at the end of his lead, and he had a most pathetic expression, as much as to say, 'Please don't kill me yet. Let me enjoy for a little longer the sun, the air and the luscious grass.'

From Joshimath a steep path, a preferable alternative to the long tedious zig-zags of the pilgrim route, descends 1,500 feet to Vishnu Prayag, the junction of the Alaknanda and Dhauli Rivers. Perched on a spur between these rivers is a hamlet and a little square-walled temple whence a flight of stone steps descends to the Alaknanda River, here known as the Vishnu Ganga, for the benefit of the pilgrims who wish to immerse themselves in the sacred waters.

Above Vishnu Prayag, the pilgrim path enters a gorge with sheer precipices on either side, which echo the thunder of the Alaknanda River as it rages furiously over its steep rock-strewn bed. It was a cool still morning and already the path was thronged with pilgrims. They were an amazing assortment of men and women: fakirs, with wild, haggard, sunken faces and unkempt beards, clad only in a loin-cloth, their bodies smeared with ashes, and fat bunnias, squatting like bloated bull-frogs on charpoys borne by sweating coolies, their women-folk plodding dutifully in the rear, carrying the family bedding, cooking-pots and food; and, queerest sight of all, little old men and women, so old it seemed impossible that life could persist within their fragile shrunken bodies, hunched uncomfortably in wicker baskets on the backs of coolies. But most were on foot: first father, striding unencumbered along, and wrapt in meditation, then mother, often as not a weak little creature perhaps fifteen years of age, bowed down beneath an enormous burden, sometimes with a baby in addition on her shoulder.

So they venture on their pilgrimage, these pilgrims, some borne magnificently by coolies, some toiling along in rags, some almost crawling, preyed on by disease and distorted by dreadful deformities. And the stench! Fifty thousand pilgrims for whom sanitation and hygiene have no place in the dictionary. And not least the flies, millions upon millions of flies. Small wonder that cholera; dysentery and typhoid are rife along the route.

Something sustains these pilgrims; few seem to enjoy their pilgrimage, yet their faces are intent, their minds set on their goal. They are over-awed, too, by their stupendous environment; you can see this in their faces. Europeans who have read and travelled cannot conceive what goes on in the minds of these simple folk, many of them from the agricultural parts of India. Wonderment and fear must be the prime ingredients. So the pilgrimage becomes an adventure. Unknown dangers threaten the broad well-made path; at any moment the gods, who hold the rocks in leash, may unloose their wrath upon the hapless passer-by. To the European it is a walk to Badrinath; to the Hindu pilgrim it is far, far more.

The path, after crossing the Alaknanda River by a well-built suspension bridge, traversed a craggy hillside to a small village where the porters halted to refresh themselves. A mile beyond this village, a rocky bluff marked the entrance to the Bhyundar Valley. Except for the size of its stream, which suggested an extensive glacier system, there was little to distinguish the valley from other side valleys of the Alaknanda Valley. A disreputable little suspension bridge spans the Alaknanda above the confluence of the two rivers, and near it I waited for the porters. The sun stood high, and the heat filled the valley like faintly simmering liquid. Pilgrims were plodding along the path. Most were clad in white, but here and there were splashes of vivid colour. Old and young, feeble and infirm, plod, plod, plod. They passed in their hundreds.

I smoked my pipe in the shade of a boulder and ruminated. Why? What was the force that impelled them from their homes on the far-off plains to the Himalayas? What was the force that had impelled me? No concrete religious motive, but something far more complex and indefinable. Perhaps the answer lay in this upward bending valley with its dark forests and the distant glimmer of the high snows.

The porters appeared and one by one crossed the shuddering little bridge, then halted on the green slope beyond. A rough track passed a small hamlet at the entrance of the valley, a filthy little place with ankle-deep mire like an Irish farm-yard, then mounted through woods by the side of the sun-wickered torrent, which rushes impetuously over great boulders under a lacery of spreading trees. Soon the Alaknanda Valley was well behind and the air partook of a new freshness.

After a steep climb the path emerged from the forest on to cultivated fields, presided over by a small village. Here a stinging nettle introduced itself to my bare knees. I do not know its botanical name but it springs up in Garhwal wherever cultivation upsets the natural order of things. It defends itself with light coloured stiletto-like spines, sharper than the sharpest needle, and is altogether more vicious than the English species.

This village is typical of many in Garhwal. The houses for the most part are single-storeyed, and their rough stone-tiled roofs are strengthened by additional stones placed upon them, so that with their wide eaves they resemble in a remarkable degree the chalets of the upper alpine pastures. They are fronted by roughly paved yards in which much of the work of the household is carried out, such as threshing, weaving and wool spinning. Most of the population were working in the fields, but here and there women squatted engaged in weaving on a simple hand frame helped by their children who, when they had overcome their fear of the white-skinned stranger with his stubbly red beard, were all agog with that excitement and curiosity which is the prerogative of children the world over. These Garhwalis affect dark-coloured workaday costumes, which on occasion, are brightened with coloured shawls, aprons and bandeaux. Like the Tibetans they are fond of ornaments and trinkets and there is a distinct similarity in the costumes of the two peoples, a similarity which becomes more marked as the Tibetan frontier is approached. As might be supposed, extensive trading between Garhwal and Tibet over the Niti and Mana Passes has resulted in a fusion of blood, and the people of the upper valleys of Garhwal, though Hindus by religion, are partly Tibetan in origin. Unlike some half-breeds the Marcha Bhotias, as they are called, combine many of the best qualities of the two races. Some of them are shepherds and are used to scrambling about on steep hillsides, so that they make excellent porters, and with mountaineering training should rival the Bhotias and Sherpas, who have done so well on Everest and other high peaks.

Beyond the village the path entered dense deciduous forests, and the valley narrowed into a gorge with vast sheets and curtains of rock on either hand, shimmering here and there with gauzy waterfalls. The heat tempering breeze died away as the afternoon lengthened, the sun disappeared behind the hills and not a leaf stirred in the shadowed forests.

We camped in the riverbed on a sandy place, which is only covered when the snows are melting fast or the monsoon rains are torrential. It was my first camp in the high mountains and I could hardly have chosen a better site. A few yards away the river hastened through a shallow channel and beyond it was forest, riven in places by gullies littered with stones and broken trees brought down by avalanches ending in terrific crags stained black with seeping water whilst far up the valley a snow-robed peak shone between the dark precipices of a distant gorge.

It had been a long hot march, but the porters were in great fettle, and busied themselves collecting driftwood and building a large fire of which the core was a tree trunk weighing the best part of a ton, deposited near the camp by some flood. Dusk fell. The sunlight died on the far peak, and between the precipices the stars shone out one by one. Nothing moved except the river. Then, in this profound calm, a small bird in a tree above my tent broke suddenly into song, a queer little song, plaintive, very sad and very sweet. It had none of the throaty luxuriance of the nightingale, or the optimistic pipings of a song thrush; it was an unhurried little song, a tweet-tweet or two, then silence, then a sudden trill, then a slow sad note. For a full half-hour this bird sang its evening hymn, until darkness had thickened in the valley and the sky filled with stars.

I dined off soup and vegetable curry by the fire; afterwards the men threw log after log into the blaze until the flames stood high and the tents and nearby forest were illumined. Presently the moon appeared and transmuted to the purest silver the torrent and the far snow peak at the head of the valley. Long after the men had wrapped themselves in their blankets I sat by the glowing embers in a great peacefulness of spirit.

CHAPTER FIVE

Bhyundar Valley: Base Camp

NEXT MORNING, as usual, I breakfasted luxuriously in my sleeping bag. There is no better preliminary to a day's marching than a plateful of porridge. For the rest, biscuits, butter, jam or marmalade with plenty of tea or coffee made up my normal repast. Eggs and bacon were lacking, but so also was my craving for this peculiarly English dish at five in the morning.

The weather was cloudless and the air deliciously cool. This march, I hoped, would take me to my base camp. The path lay through dense jungle and as I walked several pheasants flew up in front of me and twice I heard crashing sounds as of some large beasts making off. Then the path descended to the riverbed, where to my astonishment we met with a snake. It was curled on a flat stone and at first sight I took it for a strip of cloth dropped by a villager. I was about to step on it when it moved and raised an ugly little head in readiness to strike. It was a brown snake; perhaps fifteen inches long, with banded markings. The men said it was poisonous and one of them killed it, but probably it was harmless for, contrary to popular opinion, harmless snakes form by far the larger percentage in the Himalayas and, for that matter, on the plains of India.

Some two miles above the camp was a side valley ascending towards Hathi Parbat. Seen against the brilliant morning light this great mountain appeared magnificent, and its massive, wall-sided precipices support a remote little snowfield tapering languidly into a snowy summit. If the col between it and Gauri Parbat could be reached both mountains should prove accessible, but it appears totally inaccessible from the west owing to steep icefalls exposed to ice avalanches from hanging glaciers.

Having passed a small village at the junction of the two valleys, populated by cheerful peasants and shepherds, the path crossed the river by a bridge consisting of two tree-trunks held in position by cross-pieces, the interstices of which were filled with stones. Here I was met by a Sikh surveyor, who was camped in the side valley, a fine-looking man attached to Major Gordon Osmaston's party, which was engaged in re-surveying Garhwal and Kumaon. He showed me some of his work, which seemed to me to be careful and well drawn, but I am no judge of draughtsmanship. He had discovered that the side valley, instead of ending under Hathi Parbat, as delineated in the old maps, bends southwards, parallel to the watershed of the Zaskar Range, and continues for several miles. I asked him whether he thought that Hathi Parbat could be attacked from the west, but he did not think it was possible from this side though, as he told me with a smile, he was as yet no mountaineer, and was only a beginner in the art – a very necessary art when surveying such rough steep country as this.

The junction of the two valleys is only about 7,500 feet, and beyond it is a forest of oaks, tree rhododendrons, chestnuts, bamboos and willows, to mention but a few trees, densely undergrown with shrubs and briers. Abundant proof of a moist climate is afforded by epiphytic ferns suspended in delicate tendrils from the trees, but of flowers there were few, though here and there I noticed an arum (*Arisaema Wallichianum*), which I had seen already on the foothill ridges, a plant which is more striking than beautiful, with an evil-looking, cobra-like head, whilst in open places were many strawberries, daisies and buttercups. Yet there was so little of floral interest or beauty in the lower and middle sections of the Bhyundar Valley that I began to wonder whether my memory had tricked me and coloured falsely something that was dull and uninteresting. However, I could scarcely grumble: there was no carpet of flowers to beautify my way, but there were forests, cool and shadowed, and above the forests remote hills, and higher still a sky of gentian blue untenanted by a single wisp of vapour.

The path climbed steeply, and presently the deciduous trees gave way to conifers and the cold smell of dank vegetation and decaying leaves was replaced by the warm incense of resin. Then it came to a wide sloping alp. The grass here was less lank and had grown little since the winter snow left it, but already it was being grazed upon by sheep and goats, whose shepherds had quartered themselves in stone huts. The height must have been nearly 10,000 feet, and from peaks on either hand, tongues of snow descended far into the valley.

Beyond the alp was a forest of firs growing between enormous boulders, the debris of a great rock-fall. The difference between the lower and upper forests of the Himalayas must be experienced to be appreciated. The lower forests, jungles that extend upwards to some 7,000 feet, are full of insect and animal life, the upper forests are characterised by their silence. My footfalls were hushed by a carpet of needles, and as I walked I became gradually aware of this silence, so that when I seated myself on a moss-clad boulder, I was already accustomed to it. There was no wind, not a whisper in the pine-tops, and the only sounds were my heart pumping audibly in my ears and the steady thunder of the valley torrent. Here and there the sunlight had slipped between the treetops, and cast brilliant pools amid the shadow, revealing moss-plastered boulders and a delicate tracery of ferns. These pools of sunlight and the shadows of the trees were the only things that moved and that very slowly, as the day lengthened.

The path emerged from the forest on to another alp, a favourite haunt of shepherds to judge from the well-built huts. Here were innumerable blue and white *anemones* (*A. obtusiloba*) and in between them *Primula denticulata*, many of which were already in seed.

I crossed two streams and on a high bank beyond the second came on a monkshood (*Aconitum heterophyllum*) with dark green-purple blooms, and a host of pink rock jasmine (*Androsace primuloides*), lovely little flowers which never ceased to fascinate me. This *androsace* is a common enough plant. You can buy it in England for nine-pence and it is described in nurserymen's catalogues as "pretty and easy", but to appreciate its true worth, you must see it tumbling over grey boulders in a rosy cascade under the deep blue of the Himalayan sky, revelling ecstatically in the beauty and grandeur of its home, eager to perpetuate itself, and sending out its runners in all directions, each with a little rosette of leaves ready to root in any scrap of soil or earthy crack.

As I walked across this last alp, I saw that beyond it the valley narrowed into a gorge finer than any I had yet seen. The forest was compressed between immense walls of rock of which one was nearly vertical and the other, that to the east, actually overhung and was fully 1,500 feet high. Even the noonday sun, only a degree or so from the vertical at this time of the year, could not relieve this gorge of its austerity or impart kindliness into the stern-visaged crags.

Through the gorge loomed a wall of high rock peaks, and had it not been for my previous visit to the Bhyundar Valley, I might have concluded that the valley ended abruptly at the base of these peaks.

At the entrance to the gorge the path zigzagged steeply downwards to a log bridge spanning the river between two large boulders. Over this frail structure, which is prevented from falling to pieces by bamboo thongs, the shepherds drive their flocks to the upper pastures of the valley. Any domestic animal save a hardy Garhwali sheep or goat would be appalled by such a passage, for the river issues with savage force from the jaws of the gorge and to fall into it would mean for man or beast instant destruction.

With the thunder of the torrent in my ears, I ascended steeply through a pine-forest, and presently came to open slopes where the gorge widens. Here were two gullies filled with hard snow in which I had to cut steps with my ice axe; I cut large ones for the benefit of the porters as a slip would have precipitated a man into the torrent several hundred feet lower. Beyond the second gully I regained the path, which traversed a steep grassy hillside where the valley widens out and bends eastwards almost at right angles under the wall of peaks that from below the gorge seems to form an impasse.

Since leaving the village I had been alone, having outstripped the porters. For weeks and months past I had visualised the Bhyundar Valley as I had seen it in 1931, but so far I had come upon few flowers. Beauty and grandeur I had seen in plenty; valleys, rivers, mountains and vistas such as only the Himalayas can show, but of floral beauty comparatively little, but now, as I turned a corner of the path, I saw out of the corner of my eye a sheet of blue on the hillside. It was a blue fumatory, the *Corydalis cashemiriana*. I had seen it once before in Sikkim, or a flower like it, growing here and there between boulders, but here was a whole slope of it, a colony of thousands. It is a small plant with a stem six inches high, and flowers an inch long, narrow, pipe-like and tipped in dark-blue, and so delicate and beautiful they might have been made for the lips of Pan.

A great avalanche, thousands of tons of snow, had fallen into the valley just above the gorge and covered the streambed a hundred feet deep for several hundred yards. I have never seen the debris of a bigger avalanche and as it had descended from a peak of not more than 16,000 feet, it was the proof of an abundant winter snowfall. Passing it and keeping to the west of the main torrent, I presently crossed a steep little subsidiary torrent, after an awkward jump between two boulders, and continued round the bend until I reached a point where there was a view up the valley to its end. It was the same view as in 1931, but with a difference. In that year, we had visited the valley during the monsoon season, when the peaks for the most part were concealed by clouds and the atmosphere was moist and warm by comparison with the dry, cold Tibetan winds we had experienced on Kamet; but this was a pre-monsoon day – the sun shone from a moistureless sky, only the lightest of fleecy clouds rested on the peaks, and the air was imbued with the vigour of spring.

In this part of the valley there were camping places innumerable, yet none of them satisfied me completely. I had several weeks to spend in the valley and desired perfection. My camping site must be so beautiful that I could never tire of it, a site where the march of light and shadow would charm me the day through, where there was shade from the noonday sun, and fuel unlimited for my camp fires. My eye was caught and arrested by a shelf on the far side of the valley, an alp that sloped green and smooth, with birch forests above and below, ending in an almost level lawn. Here if anywhere was the perfect place. I retraced my steps to the avalanche, crossed the torrent, and ascending to the lower end of the shelf sat down to await the porters.

Base Camp was pitched at the uppermost end of the shelf, and within a few minutes the men, with that peculiar facility of Tibetans for digging themselves in, had converted a nearby hollow into a kitchen, and collected firewood and water; so that within a quarter of an hour I was comfortably ensconced in my rickety folding chair drinking a cup of tea.

There was no doubt about it; here was the ideal camping site. On three sides it was bounded by silver birches with a lower frieze of purple- and white-flowered rhododendrons. Never have I seen finer birches. In the westering sun their brilliant foliage and silver bark seemed to partake of the purity of earth and sky, whilst their leaves, rippling in a light breeze, suggested some pebble-floored pool of shimmering water. The valley meadows were 500 feet beneath, and beyond them stood the great wall of rock peaks now revealed in all its magnificence, a wild uprush of giant crags biting into the slow pacing clouds.

After this dizzy climb the eye turned almost with relief to the soberer peaks at the head of the valley, past a torn glacier and subsidiary buttresses, to the snow-crowned crest of Rataban. Of the gorge there was no sign, it lay concealed round the bend of the valley, so that to all intents we might have been cut off from the lower world in some exit-less valley inaccessible to men. Immediately above the camp lay masses of avalanche snow, that had swept through channels in the birch forest and strewn timber upon the alp, enough to keep our fires lighted for weeks, without the necessity of cutting down a single living branch. Spring had only recently come to the alp, but already the moist turf was pulsing with life. Between the lank dead herbage of the previous summer innumerable shoots were pushing upwards, some fat and stumpy, others thin and spear-like, some uncurling as they rose – countless plants anxious to perpetuate themselves before the summer was done and winter's grip closed in once more.

A few plants were already in bloom. A minute blue gentian spread its tiny frilled blooms over the turf, just above the camp were hundreds of purple *Primula denticulata* and here and there a white *allium* was clustered – a graceful plant with a bulb which, as I soon discovered, was excellent to eat.

One of my first jobs was to pay off the Dotials. It is usual in such cases for the native to assume at the outset that his employer is out to do him down and the foreman, having been summoned, squatted before me with such an expression of mingled distrust, cunning and relief (at being paid at all!) on his wizened pippin-like face that it was all I could do not to laugh. However, the business was settled amicably and without the usual corrosive and entirely unprofitable arguments, which result from the payee's primitive knowledge of arithmetic. One rupee per man for each day's outward march, half-pay for the return journey and some "baksheesh", minus such advances of pay as had already been made. It was perfectly simple but it took an hour of noisy argument between the Dotials to convince themselves that they had not been swindled; then the pippin-faced foreman, doubt and suspicion removed from his beaming countenance, returned and expressed himself as satisfied and more than satisfied; if the sahib wanted him and his men for the return journey, well, he had only to send word to Ranikhet.

By the time these financial details had been settled and the stores unpacked and arranged in a spare tent it was evening. A warm light filled the valley and the lengthening shadows revealed unsuspected grandeurs and beauties in the great rock walls opposite. The light breeze had fallen to a complete calm and not a leaf of the birches quivered. Quickly the sun dipped behind the Khanta Khal pass, which we had crossed in 1931 from the Bhyundar Valley to the Alaknanda Valley. Best of all the men were contented. Wangdi came up to me with a happy grin on his hard face. He swept his arm in a single comprehensive gesture over the birches and across the valley, past the glowing snows of Rataban. "Ramro, sahib!" He was right; it was beautiful. While Tewang cooked the supper, Pasang, Wangdi and Nurbu collected wood, so that by the time the sun had set and a chill crept into the air I was comfortably seated by a roaring log fire.

Let me confess at once that I am an incurable romantic. Since the days when I devoured G.A. Henty and Fennimore Cooper I have looked upon the campfire as a necessary adjunct of enjoyable travel. What is the charm of it? Is it because it panders to deep-seated hereditary instincts? Are we for all our central-heated homes and "no draught" ventilation system essentially primitive at heart? Have our cavemen ancestors handed on to us an animal-like love of its warmth and light, and safety from bestial marauders? And has such love been transmuted to something purely romantic? Will civilisation grind out of man all his ancient qualities, his fierce unreasoning passions, his hopes and fears, his love of nature and primitive things? Does peace and security spell effeminacy and deterioration of the virile qualities? What will we become when the need to struggle for our existence is banished from the perfect world promised us by philosophers, economists and pacifists? Perhaps in this a reason is to be found for all forms of physical adventure. The qualities that have given us domination over the beast, that demand safety not as a dead level of existence but in opposition to danger continue to find an outlet for their activity in sports labelled dangerous, useless or unjustifiable. Peace between men is not incompatible with maintenance of physical virility when so many adventures are possible in the open air. Whether it be the cricket or rugger field or the heights of the Himalayas there is enough to satisfy this adventurous spirit of ours without resort to the soul-deadening work of killing our fellow men. It remains to be seen how our inherited instincts are to be adapted to our need of peace and happiness, the two things which men crave most. I am sure myself that they are to be found in the open air, and that the present movement in this direction, not only in Britain but in many other countries, is an unconscious revolt against the primaeval desire to kill in order to maintain physical safety and virility. This development represents the growth of the human intelligence towards a new and happier conception of the universe and human relationships. Most of all does it indicate a Divine desire for the physical, mental and spiritual progress of mankind. Who are we to talk of degeneration and retrogression in a God-made world?

It was the first time I had travelled alone in the Himalayas and the experience after the last two caravanserais to Everest was more than refreshing. For the first time in my life I was able to think. I do not mean to think objectively or analytically, but rather to surrender thought to my surroundings. This is a power of which we know little in the west but which is a basic of abstract thought in the east. It is allowing the mind to receive rather than to seek impressions, and it is gained by expurgating extraneous thought. It is then that the Eternal speaks; that the mutations of the universe are apparent: the very atmosphere is filled with life and song; the hills are resolved from mere masses of snow, ice and rock into something living. When this happens the human mind escapes from the bondage of its own feeble imaginings and becomes as one with its Creator.

My pen has run away with me; it often did when recording my impressions in the Valley of Flowers, for it is impossible to continue along conventional channels when the country on either side is so fair, so even though I am not understood or at risk of being labelled "sentimental" – a red rag this word to the bull of materialism – I must endeavour to record my impressions during my sojourn in this valley.

That first evening I sat long by the camp fire until the talk in the porters' tents had dwindled away and the silence was complete save for the light, almost imperceptible hiss of the burning logs. Presently even that died and the fire shrank to a heap of glowing embers. The cold stole up behind me; suddenly I was chilly and my pipe was out. A few minutes later I was warm in my eiderdown sleeping bag. The last thing I saw before closing my eyes was a bright star poised on a distant ridge looking at me through the door of the tent.

The sun rose above Rataban at 6.20 next morning. I awoke to birdsong – a great chorus from the surrounding birch forest and rhododendron brakes. Most prominent was a small undistinguished brown bird, of the corncrake family I should say. I dubbed it the zeederzee bird for this most nearly describes its song. It was a perfect morning, not a cloud, and the dew-soaked grass shone like a pavement of frosted glass in the brilliant sunlight.

Nurbu brought me my breakfast as I lay slothfully in my sleeping bag. Occasionally Pasang officiated, but more often it was Nurbu, and his cheerful smile was a happy beginning to a day.

As I ate the usual porridge, biscuits and jam there seemed to be something missing, pleasantly missing. Then I remembered – the flies. Except for the camp on the Kuari Pass, flies had been with me all the way from Ranikhet; they had become a part of the natural order of things. And now there were no flies; it seemed almost too good to be true.

After breakfast the Dotials, who had bivouacked close by, left for Ranikhet. They seemed well contented and the pippin-faced foreman, for about the tenth time, announced his readiness to return with his men.

Leaving Tewang to mind the camp, Wangdi, Nurbu, Pasang and I set off on a tour of inspection.

Immediately below the camp we found a rough sheep track running downwards through the steep birch forest. It was partly overgrown with vegetation but some vigorous work with a kukri soon cleared a way. Here, as on the alp above, *Primula denticulata* was growing. This plant seems to like shade and sun almost equally well so long as it receives plenty of moisture at the roots, but a moist place in the sun is probably ideal.

Below us we could hear the roar of the torrent and soon we were slithering down a snow-slope between it and the lowermost edge of the forest. Immediately to the east of the camp was a wide gully, and a huge spring avalanche pouring down this had bridged the torrent so that we were able to cross without difficulty to the other side of the valley. Here on well-drained south-facing slopes many plants were already in bloom. As we scrambled up a steep grassy buttress between clumps of dark green juniper I saw growing on a skyline above, the same dark purple monkshood I had seen below the gorge; then the white umbels of *Anemone polyanthes* which is closely allied with *Anemone narcissiflora*, with *Corydalis cashemiriana* brilliantly blue in between.

A steep scramble and we stood on a wide shelf littered with boulders and there grew a plant which is one of the rarest and most beautiful of its family, the lily-like *Nomocharis oxypetela*. In colour this *nomocharis* is very different to the *Nomocharis nana* which also grows in the Bhyundar Valley; the latter is blue, the former rich daffodil yellow. Obviously it revels in the sun on well warmed, well-drained meadows and slopes where there is plenty of fibrous material and rocks to feed its roots with moisture.

I set the men to work to collect bulbs and presently they had dug up two or three dozen with their ice axes. It was not easy work, for the *nomocharis* bulb grows a full six inches deep and its favourite habitat is a dense matting of bracken roots and sometimes juniper roots and between boulders and stones.

Another plant in bloom was a purple *orchis* one to two feet high, whilst the ubiquitous little *Iris kumaonensis* was approaching its best – thousands of blooms on the stony hillside. Then, over the rocks, the pink *Androsace primuloides* was fast spreading its silver-green rosettes and pink flowers.

A light breeze had sprung up and before it the *nomocharis* nodded and bowed their golden heads. In slow waves it rippled across the slopes, bringing an indescribable scent of plant life with now and then a breath of delightful thyme-like perfume which I soon found emanated from a purple-flowered plant that creeps over the sunny faces of boulders and dry slopes.

We returned to camp for lunch, after which I busied myself pressing the specimens collected during the morning. I had never pressed flowers prior to this expedition and I must confess I found it an irksome and finicking task. The remainder of the afternoon I spent collecting in the vicinity of the camp. Among the plants I discovered was a fleshy leafed *bergenia* (*B. Stracheyi*) growing between moss-clad boulders on a northern slope, and in the forest behind the camp a wood lily, *Trillium Govanianum*. Not far from the camp was a bank facing south already gay with flowers, including *Nomocharis oxypetela*, whilst on the edge of the gully east of the camp a creamy dwarf rhododendron common throughout the Himalayas and many parts of Tibet was in bloom together with the delicate little creamy bells of a *cassiope* (*C. fastigiata*).

At tea-time Tewang announced that he had a bad foot and that it was now hurting him up the leg to the groin. He had blistered it during the march and the sore had festered, but like any other happy-go-lucky Tibetan it had never occurred to him to mention it until his whole leg was poisoned. Before I could treat him I made him wash his foot. I do not suppose he had ever consciously washed in his life and he performed the ablution with a sort of pained surprise and indignant resignation. Needless to say his foot was filthy, the dirt of years being caked between the toes. It would seem an impossible task to make the Tibetan realise the connection between dirt and disease, the one is just dirt, the other an affliction meted out by the Gods. This done, I scraped and probed the wound with a scalpel until blood and pus flowed in generous quantities, afterwards bandaging it with lint. The sight of the blood heartened Tewang and his broad flat face broke into a beaming smile. 'Now I shall be all right,' he declared. And so indeed he was, for in a few days the trouble had cleared up completely.

That evening I supped again by a great fire. During the heat of the day a breeze flowed up the valley, but it dropped at sundown to a complete calm so that I could light my pipe with an unshielded match and the sound of the stream served only to emphasise the profound stillness. The clouds ebbed fast from the peaks and a silent rush of mist swept up through the gorge and passed across the opposite hillside. The sunlight died and the night came swiftly; in less than half an hour from the time the sun set it was dark except for the coldest and faintest of after-glows on the high peaks, a light matching the pale brilliance of the stars.

The fire of birch logs burned perfectly, red and blue flames with scarcely any smoke, and in its light the faces of the men stood out from the darkness against a still darker background of forest.

The moon became apparent, a brilliant crescent riding high overhead; it silvered the snows and glaciers and lit the gathering dew with a cold fire.

Slowly, as the air required equilibrium, the low valley mists dissolved until by 8.30 not one vestige remained.

A bird sang during the first hour of darkness, a curious song that I had not heard before; chuck, chuck, chuck, chuck, eee, chuck, chuck chuck, chuck, eee; something between that of a nightjar and a corncrake, but presently it stopped and all that remained of sound was the steady rumbling of the glacier torrent.

CHAPTER SIX

A Minor Climb

IMMEDIATELY above the camp the birch forest swept up in an unbroken sheet for some 500 feet. Above it were open slopes still snow-covered, whence rose the steep ridges of a peak about 17,000 feet high. This peak I decided to climb, for not only would it provide an admirable training expedition, but also it should command a panorama of the Bhyundar Valley and its surroundings. So on June 19, after an early but leisurely breakfast, Wangdi, Nurbu, Pasang and I set off to exercise our climbing machinery. We avoided the fatigue of forcing our way through the forest by ascending a grassy ridge bounding the gully to the east of the camp. Two hundred feet higher, this ridge tailed out into snow-slopes broken only by occasional rocky outcrops and incipient ridges. The snow was hard frozen and we made rapid progress. We were passing one of the rocky outcrops when a flare of imperial purple caught my eye and I halted to admire a superb *primula*. Fully ten inches high, it rose in regal dignity from a centre of thin mealy leaves, rooted in a moist crack generously fed by snow water, which oozed over a slab in convulsive jerks beneath a film of ice. I think it was the dark blue form of *Primula nivalis macrophylla*.

Above this point the slope steepened and presently we were forced to kick, and sometimes to cut steps. Here, for the first time, I was able to observe the different climbing styles of my companions. Wangdi was the most experienced of the trio, but he had not learnt to move rhythmically, and put a great deal of unnecessary effort into his climbing, kicking his steps with a restless, untiring vigour and so viciously he might have had a grudge against the snow. Nurbu followed docilely, obviously intent on learning all he could about the finer points of mountaineering. Pasang, on the other hand, had not the remotest idea of rhythm or co-ordinated movement. He moved jerkily and in rushes, breathing heavily the while, and appeared incapable of transferring his weight gradually from one foot to the other so that it seemed he might slip at any moment. After a while I made him lead in the hope of teaching him the art of walking up a snow-slope, but it was all in vain; he was wedded to his own method, or lack of method. So I left him to his own devices and he went rushing on ahead, kicking steps as though his life depended on reaching the summit in the least possible time, and of course soon had to stop for a rest. It is indeed curious that these Tibetans, and the same applies to the Sherpas, who spend their lives among the hills, have never learned to walk uphill easily; they have to be taught this art by Europeans with not half their experience of hill-walking.

As we mounted, making height at the rate of nearly 1,500 feet an hour, the green valley fell away, shrinking as it did so, and the wall of rock peaks opposite increased in apparent stature and grandeur. Presently a peak well to the north-east came into view, an isolated, pyramidal, wall-sided mountain rising head and shoulders above its neighbours that reminded me of photographs of Mount Robson in the Canadian Rockies. Later, I learned that Lieutenant Gardiner, who had been surveying the district, had named it Nilgiri Parbat, and had placed its height at 21,264 feet. Could it be climbed? Certainly not from the Bhyundar Valley, though to judge from the general angle of its ridges, the North Face was probably less formidable. At all events it would be well worth reconnoitring, though to approach it from the north would mean forsaking the Bhyundar Valley in favour of a parallel valley, to reach which it would be necessary to force a pass over the wall of rock peaks, separating the two valleys.

Without any difficulty we gained the crest of a minor spur. Barhal (wild sheep) had been there before us, and their tracks zigzagged aimlessly about the snow-slopes. Kicking steps, we advanced steadily, and within three hours of leaving the camp had gained the East Ridge of our peak at a point about 500 feet below the summit.

A brisk little wind was blowing across the ridge, but we sheltered from it under some sun-warmed rocks a few feet below the crest and ate a meal. It was a beautiful morning, and the sky in our vicinity was unclouded. In the south, dense pillars of cumulus were rising from the valleys, and between them we discerned the snowfields of Trisul and the massive spire of Nanda Devi. Separating us from these two great mountains were the subsidiary spurs and ridges of the main Zaskar Range, a bewildering labyrinth of rocky edges, and uptilted strata over which the eye wandered restlessly, seeking lodgement but finding none until, wearied of sheer savagery, it passed to the west where Nilkanta stood solitary and serene, the undisputed queen of the Badrinath Peaks. The mists were slowly embracing it, but before they concealed it I examined the final pyramid through my monocular glass. The only route that seemed to offer the remotest chance of success was the South-East Ridge. The lower part of this was hidden behind nearer mountains, but if in the upper part a rock step several hundred feet high could be surmounted, the upper slopes of snow and ice should prove feasible.

After a halt of half an hour in the sun, we continued on our way. From the point at which we gained the ridge, the peak springs up steeply in a serrated edge of reddish rock. It was possible to avoid this obviously difficult crest by scrambling up the disagreeably loose South Face, but for the sake of exercise and training I determined to attempt it. To begin with, there was little difficulty, but presently we came to a steep slab. Here I had a further opportunity of observing the methods of my companions. Wangdi made light of it but did not scruple to use the rope as a handhold, although the holds, if small, were sufficient. Pasang, though more at home on rocks than on snow, was very ungainly, and inclined to pull himself up by strength of arm. Nurbu was the best of all, and his swift effortless agility convinced me then and there that in him were the makings of a first-rate mountaineer.

Above this preliminary slab was a wall which I found distinctly trying. Furthermore, a tightness in my head, that had accrued during the past hour or so, was rapidly developing into one of those jarring headaches which result from lack of acclimatisation to altitude.

From the top of this second pitch, the ridge rose in an overhanging tower culminating in a fang-like point and was completely inaccessible. The alternative, as already mentioned, was the South Face. To reach it, we had to descend an unpleasantly loose chimney where Pasang, now the last man down, managed to dislodge an angular block of rock weighing a fair hundredweight, which flew close to those below before shattering itself into fragments. Then tongues wagged and hard things were said, and it was a very abashed and painfully careful Pasang who descended the remainder of the chimney.

A traverse across some rickety ledges, and a scramble up the decaying face brought us to the summit. Mists were forming, but between them the nearer mountains showed and, more distantly, the buttresses of Gauri Parbat and Hathi Parbat. The day was now windless and warm, but I was in no mood to appreciate this or the grandeur of my surroundings, for my headache had become worse and every movement sent a thrill of pain from the base of the skull to a point just above the eyes. The descent was a purgatory. I could scarcely see straight and vomiting supervened, but this did not relieve the headache – it increased it, if that were possible. After what seemed an age, owing to the clumsiness of Pasang and the consequent necessity to move one at a time, we got off the rocks and began the descent of the snow slopes. Had it not been for my mountain sickness I should have enjoyed the longest glissade of my experience, as it was possible to descend about 4,000 feet of snow slopes to a point within two minutes' walk of the camp. Wangdi glissaded expertly, and Nurbu was a trier, but Pasang was hopeless and it was not long before he slipped and descended ungracefully on his back for some hundreds of feet, dropping his ice axe, which the good-natured Nurbu recovered. Except for Wangdi, who was soon out of sight, it was a melancholy procession. First of all myself, able to glissade only a few yards at a time owing to the pain in my head, then Nurbu, and lastly the unfortunate Pasang, scrabbling about like a beetle on a sheet of glass. And so at length to the camp, where Wangdi and Tewang greeted me with broad, unsympathetic grins and a mugful of steaming hot tea. My first peak had not been enjoyable.

CHAPTER SEVEN

The Snow Col on Rataban

THE TWO DAYS following the ascent of the minor peak I devoted to flower collecting. The weather was already appreciably warmer, and at night lightning flickered in the south. The monsoon was approaching, and as though in anticipation of its warm, life-giving breath, plants sprang up everywhere with astonishing rapidity. Already the green bells of a fritillary (*F. Roylei*) surrounded the camp. This is an unobtrusive flower, but it has a charm of its own, a delicacy surpassing that of many more showy flowers. As the green bells on their springy stems nodded and dipped vivaciously in the light breezes, I half expected to hear the tinkling of fairy chimes over the alp. Maybe they sounded, but not to mortal ears.

By the stream I came on a bank blue with *cynoglossum* (*C. glochidiatum*), a blue that matched the midday sky. Then there was a moist place on the opposite side of the valley, yellow and purple with marigolds and *Primula denticulata*. It was an incongruous combination of colours which would look out of place, perhaps ugly, in a garden, yet if Nature is sometimes reckless, her taste is unerring. Picture a golden carpet quivering ceaselessly in the wind, with violet splashes between and the clear waters of a stream lapping over the grey boulders, in little collars of foam, or reposed in deep quiet pools that mirror the peaks and sky. In the middle distance the valley-sides sweep upwards, green at first, then blue, breaking on high in bleak and desolate crags, and beyond, the massive buttresses of Rataban, their harsher details softened by distance, supporting snowfields and silver-edged ridges etched against the intensely blue sky.

In Britain the atmosphere subtly deceives our estimation of height and distance, but in the moisture-free atmosphere of the Himalayas the peaks look high because they are high. At midday they gleam like polished steel under a nearly vertical sun and the eye sinks with relief to the green valley floor. Yet, if in the matter of detail and height little or nothing is left to the imagination, the colourings compensate; in this brilliant atmosphere they are celestial. Possibly the ultraviolet in the light at high altitudes has something to do with this. Take a knot-weed, the little *Polygonum affine*, one of the representative plants of the Central Himalayas: it colours the hillside in millions upon millions of rosy blooms, and the glow of it may be seen a mile away, lighting the slopes. Yet in England, it is a poor, dull-coloured flower, and becomes lank and attenuated in our soft climate. Even such an unpretentious flower as a yellow violet (*Viola biflora*) imparts to itself some quality of sun and atmosphere, for it shines like a star from the coarser herbage.

The second day saw the death of Montmorency. I was loath indeed to kill him, for he had become an institution, but fresh meat was necessary. For nearly three weeks I had lived on a vegetarian diet, and though it suited me admirably in some ways I discovered that I was not going as strongly on hills as I should have done, whilst my craving for meat, which had remained temporarily in abeyance, had returned with twofold force. I was tired of vegetable curries, so I cast hungry, predatory eyes on poor Montmorency and ordered his execution. It was a grisly business. The men, unwilling to lose any of his blood, scraped and cleaned a large rock slab, then trussing Montmorency's legs together, they laid him on the slab like a sacrifice and a moment later a razor-edged kukri had severed his head from his body. But if goats have souls, then perhaps Montmorency looked down with a certain complacency on the subsequent proceedings, for his meat, having been buried in a snow-drift, lasted for more than a fortnight, whilst his skin, after being well scraped, afforded an excellent carpet for the floor of the porters' tent. For the remainder of the day the men scraped and flogged it, and even put it in their tent with them at night. But here Montmorency got something of his own back. Even the Tibetans have a power of smell, though it is seldom obvious, and in the night I woke to hear a chorus of oaths, then the sound of something being hurled into outer darkness. It was the skin of Montmorency.

One of my memories of 1931 was of a col at the head of the Bhyundar Valley. It is a col that no mountaineer could look at without wanting to ascend; a parabola of pure snow, between Rataban and a minor unnamed peak to the north. I determined therefore, to pitch a camp on it and, if possible, attempt the ascent of Rataban, via its steep North Ridge.

After a night of distant lightning, Midsummer Day dawned with a murky, watery sky. We were off at 6.30, leaving Tewang at the Base Camp, carrying five days' food, and light equipment. The men were lightly laden, but soon they began to make heavy weather of the march up the valley. It was obvious that they had been over-eating themselves with the innards of Montmorency. The Tibetan is perforce normally a vegetarian, but when he can get meat he stuffs himself until he is scarcely able to move. I was not exactly comfortable myself, having dined very heartily off Montmorency's liver, and this heavy meat meal, after nearly three weeks' abstinence from meat, had put a strain on the digestive organs; so our progress was slow and subject to many halts.

Having crossed the snow-bridge below the camp, we ascended along the northern side of the valley. It was easy going, at first between boulders, then along the wide, dry stream-bed, which was littered with the remains of avalanches fallen during the spring. I was surprised to notice that the northernmost slopes of the valley had been extensively burned. Wangdi explained that this had been done by shepherds the previous summer, presumably with the object of improving the fertility of the ground, and of destroying numerous juniper bushes which encumbered the slopes. This burning could only have been accomplished some time after the end of the monsoon season or during a spell of very dry weather.

On the way up the valley we passed two shepherds' huts. It is the practice in these mountains for the shepherds to let their flocks wander over the hillsides during the daytime, but to round them up at night in a space near their huts to prevent them from straying or being attacked by bears. These rounding-up places are distinguishable by the weeds that grow on them. It was also very noticeable in Garhwal that where extensive grazing is permitted, the smaller and tenderer plants are soon eliminated and in their place spring up a tall knot-weed (*Polygonum polystachyum*) and an even taller balsam (*Impatiens roylei*). Once these two plants have got a hold of the ground, pastureland is permanently ruined and I noticed a number of places in the Bhyundar Valley where this had occurred.

Beyond the second shepherds' hut, the flowers were abundant. In a marshy place where a stream seeped between cushions of bright green moss, grew a tall white *primula* (*P. involucrata*), and near by was a small dank alcove in the rocks, padded with moss, where a trickle of water fell like liquid silver into a pool girt around with rosy knot weed. This pool emptied in its turn into a larger stream with rocky banks, already gay with white anaphalis, an everlasting flower with a golden centre, whilst on higher, drier places, yet with their roots well down in moist fissures, *Androsace primuloides* grew in thousands of pink blooms, exuding a sweet, almost musky scent impossible to analyse or describe.

We next crossed a hillside and there on a corner I came on the bright blue *Eritrichium strictum* which, in my ignorance, I mistook at first for a forget-me-not. It is a cousin of that alpine king of flowers, the *Eritrichium nanum*, but unlike the latter is comparatively easy to cultivate in England. Its colour reminded me of an *eritrichium* I had seen in Tibet during the 1936 Everest Expedition. We were crossing the Doya La, a pass of about 16,000 feet, into the Kharta Valley when we came upon a cushion-like plant covered in almost stalkless brilliant blue forget-me-not-like flowers. I have never been able to discover its name, nor is there any mention of it in any list of plants collected during the various Everest expeditions.

Our route was the same as that followed by shepherds who cross the Bhyundar Pass, and presently we came to the place where the Kamet Expedition had camped in 1931. The tent platforms in the grass-slope were still visible and though the flowers were not as advanced as they had been then, there were enough to remind me of what Holdsworth had written:

> Where we pitched our tents it was impossible to cut a sod of turf from the ground without destroying a *primula* or a fritillary.

To gaze upon an old camping site years after is like returning to the scenes of one's youth. It inspires a sadness as well as an interest. Six years had passed since we camped there and now we were scattered about the world. Life is too short, its memories too evanescent; I was the only one to return to the Valley of Flowers.

Above this camping place the glacier forked into two glaciers, one of which originates on Gauri Parbat, the other on Rataban and Nilgiri Parbat. Both are extensively moraine-covered, and with the winter's snow half-melted presented a dreary appearance. The fast melting snow on the peaks was bringing down many stone-falls; a steep rock buttress at the junction of the glaciers grumbled ceaselessly and although half a mile from the base of it, I could distinctly hear the hum and whine of falling rocks. But the most impressive rock-fall came from a peak to the south of the main glacier, and must have weighed hundreds of tons. Not content to follow any prescribed route the stones leapt furiously down the mountainside and across the lower grass-slopes, leaving long scars in their wake. Among them was a block the size of a house, which took the side moraine of the glacier in its stride and rushed a full hundred yards out on to the ice.

Where the rough shepherds' track passed beneath a crag, I saw a small yellow flower which I dug up with my ice axe and discovered to be bulbous. It proved to be the yellow star of Bethlehem (*Gagea lutea*). Beyond this crag the track mounted a gully, then climbed steeply to a turfy shoulder. There were juniper bushes here, so we were able to collect some fuel. The men were in better form now, having to some extent walked off the effects of Montmorency, and while they collected wood I wandered about the hillside collecting specimens. I had not to look far before I saw a minute and almost stemless *primula* with a pink star-shaped flower, peeping up from densely clustered masses of foliage. This was *Primula minutissima*, one of the smallest of *primulas*. Then there was a cinquefoil, the yellow variety of *Potentilla argyrophylla*, which at this height is considerably smaller than its wine-red brother. I also found a cross between it and the red variety, and this is perhaps the most beautiful of all, for in colour it reminded me of a yellow sunset splashed with scarlet, the whole uniting to form a superb deep orange.

Having loaded ourselves with wood, we followed the crest of a side moraine. Here, growing among the grit and stones, were numerous rock plants, among them *sedums* and what I knew from Holdsworth's description must be *Androsace poissonii,* a little white flower that grows from cushions of silver wool-like foliage. But as Holdsworth wrote, "It spreads into big masses in open peaty places and seems to need no stone," and I found it later covering such ground.

Presently we left the moraine in favour of the snow-covered glacier. This glacier, like the main Bhyundar Glacier, bifurcates in its turn. The easternmost branch, which has its origin under Rataban and the snow col, forms in its lowermost portion an impressive ice-fall, bisected horizontally by a belt of cliffs over which the ice is precipitated every minute or two, recompacting itself on the glacier beneath. This ice-fall is inaccessible to direct attack, but can be outflanked by following the route towards the Bhyundar Pass almost to the pass, then traversing to the south-east on to the snowfield above it.

A prominent buttress to the west of the ice-fall affords a good approach to a steeply sloping snow-covered shelf, which I knew must be traversed before a direct ascent could be made to the Bhyundar Pass. As I scrambled up it, well ahead of the men, I came once again upon the dark blue *Primula nivalis macrophylla*. Every moist place held its quota of these glorious flowers which charged the still afternoon air with their subtle fragrance, whilst a little higher grew the light blue variety, which seems to combine the colours of earth and sky, the blue of the Himalayan sky and the duskier blue of the valley.

We camped on a shelf formed by an overhanging crag. All around, between clumps of dwarf rhododendrons, the turf was starred with *Primula minutissima*, and close by was a small cave whence a rivulet trickled down a mossy gully gay with *androsaces*. The icefall was close at hand and every minute or so there was a harsh roar of falling debris, with now and then the thunderous crash of a larger avalanche.

Mist had formed during the afternoon, but at sundown it melted away at our level and we looked across a sea of vapour, its topmost waves reddened by the declining sun to a snow-peak south of the Bhyundar Valley. The base of this peak was mist-shrouded, but the summit stood out sharply against a green sky. It was of pure snow, and there was a beautifully moulded ridge that ran straight as a die to the crest. The map does not indicate its presence, but that was not surprising. Was it climbable? If so, from which valley? It would be necessary to reconnoitre the approaches to it. Mountaineering difficulties in the Himalayas are two-fold: that of climbing a mountain, and that of finding a route to one or other of the ridges of that mountain; and the second difficulty is sometimes greater than the first.

As the sun sank it lit Rataban, which I examined with interest through my monocular glass. The North Ridge rising from the snow col looked formidable, if not impossible, in its lowermost portion, and about 800 feet above the col was an overhanging nose that appeared entirely inaccessible to direct attack. The east face of the mountain was not visible and failing a route on it the most hopeful alternative was a route up the North-West Face. There were two or three minor rock-ridges and though the face as a whole looked steep and complicated, there seemed reason to suppose that with good conditions it could be ascended to a point on the North Ridge above the overhanging nose. Once on the snow-covered uppermost portion of the ridge, the summit should prove accessible. Even as I gazed at the great mountain the sunlight moved quickly up it to be superseded quickly by the cold night shadow.

The men cooked a tasteful supper, but I had scarce time to eat it before a violent wind rose. To sleep afterwards was impossible owing to the wildly flapping canvas of my tent, but the rising moon came as a signal and with that incalculable suddenness peculiar to atmospheric conditions in high mountains this ephemeral wrath of the elements ended as abruptly as it began.

Pasang awakened me soon after five next morning. I wish I could muster the vim and cheerfulness of a Tibetan at this drear, cold hour. When he attended to me he always did so clumsily and with a take-it-or-leave-it manner, but this last was only a mannerism.

Our way lay diagonally upwards across snow-slopes and two wide gullies. The snow was frozen and a slip would have precipitated a man over the cliffs below; so we roped up at the camp. So hard was the snow that in many places it was necessary to cut steps, but apart from this there was no difficulty and presently, when we came to a ridge of broken rocks, we advanced unroped. The rock-ridge ended a short distance below the Bhyundar Pass and we roped up again for the traverse, which took us across the snowfield above the icefall. In a very short time we were at the foot of the final slopes leading to the col. The weather was now uncertain and mists had already formed. We were unable to see clearly and because of this I disliked the look of a snowy corridor between some séracs and the slopes of the minor unnamed peak to the north-west of the col, as the debris of avalanches was lying there and I could not tell whether it was of snow or ice; if the latter, we would be well advised to avoid it.

The alternative route, which I decided, was the safer, went straight up through the séracs, and provided us with some pretty ice-work. In one place we had to descend into and climb out of a wide crevasse well bridged with snow, with a steep upper lip forty feet high. It was fatiguing work, especially for laden men, and we were glad to reach unbroken slopes above. Thenceforwards it was a monotonous plug up steep slopes in thick mist to the crest of the col where the two tents were pitched, partly on stones and partly on snow and ice.

It had been a short and in the main, easy ascent, and after lunch clearer weather tempted me to work off my superfluous energy in scaling the minor unnamed peak of about 19,000 feet to the north-west of the col. A ridge, at first of broken rock, then of snow, leads to the summit, and as there was no difficulty or danger about the climb I decided to go alone and was on the summit within an hour of leaving the camp.

The view of Rataban across the col confirmed the conclusions I had already reached. It was useless to attempt the North Ridge directly from the col, whilst the East Face was entirely impracticable owing to sheer precipices swept by avalanches from a hanging glacier perched on the uppermost slopes of the mountain. The North-West Face however, was more hopeful, and provided that a belt of steep rocks about two-thirds of the way up it could be climbed, it should be possible to reach the North Ridge and follow it over snow to the summit.

In other directions the view was partially obscured by clouds, but I could see the Banke Glacier 5,000 feet beneath to the north-east, and beyond it a complicated muddle of rock peaks. The view to the north and north-west was totally obscured and I was disappointed at not seeing Mana Peak and Kamet. It was pleasantly warm on the summit, but there was something about the atmosphere I did not like, an indefinable feeling of impending storm.

I descended leisurely to the camp where Wangdi welcomed me with a cup of tea. The remainder of the day passed uneventfully, except that now and then an ice avalanche thundered down the eastern precipice from the hanging glacier already mentioned. Towards sunset a chill wind rose and it was apparent from the sky that a storm was about to break. The west was filled with boiling clouds, but to the north-east I could see the distant rust-coloured plateau of Tibet beyond ranges of snow-streaked peaks. More to the east, a storm was centred on the Nepalese border, and a vast anvil-shaped cloud was linked with the earth by steel-blue rain streaked grey with hail and snow, whilst other clouds were scattered like glowing embers along the Himalayas.

It was a magnificent but desolate scene, and a biting wind soon hustled us into our sleeping bags. I slept lightly but moderately well, only to wake at 3 a.m. with a sense of impending danger. There seemed no reason to suspect danger of any kind, but presently I noticed a curious feeling as though a cobweb covered my face. At first, in my drowsy condition, I thought it was a cobweb, and several times put up my hand in an attempt to brush it away, but presently, when I was fully awake, I realised that it was an effect of electrical tension, for I had experienced the same sensation on several occasions in the Alps. It is not a happy situation lying in a tent pitched on the very crest of a ridge knowing that an electrical storm is brewing, and ever since I was struck on the Schreckhorn I have dreaded lightning, for it is the least compatible of all Nature's forces on a mountain.

During the next minute or two, the feeling of tension increased rapidly, then, suddenly, there was a mauve glare, a pause of less than one second and a muffled roar of thunder that seemed to come from every direction like some subterranean explosion. Then came the wind, blasting across the ridge with such force that it threatened to tear away the camp and hurl it down the precipice. But the tents had been well pitched, for with memories of what Himalayan gales may accomplish on Everest such an important detail was not to be overlooked.

Happily there were no more lightning discharges, but snow fell so heavily that by five o'clock it was clear that not only must our attempt on Rataban be postponed, but that we would be well advised to retreat, before it accumulated to such a depth as to render the slopes below the col dangerous from avalanches. So I shouted to the men and eventually succeeded in waking them. They must have thought me a fool not to wait until the blizzard abated, for the Tibetan, though he may be a good climber, has little or no conception of the finer points of mountaineering and cannot appreciate danger until it occurs. However, after I had done my best to explain the position, they showed alacrity in packing up the camp.

In the matter of sheer unpleasantness breaking camp on an exposed Himalayan ridge in a howling blizzard at 5 in the morning must be hard to equal. Such an occasion always discovers Wangdi at his best. He seems everywhere at once; lion-like in strength and active like a cheetah. His grim little face becomes even grimmer. There is a job to be done, an unpleasant job; no use fiddling with it, get it done and quickly. So it came about that within a very short time the frozen, wildly flapping tents were smothered and subdued, and sleeping bags, cooking utensils and food rammed into rucksacks.

It was impossible to see more than a yard or two in the blizzard; our upward track had vanished beneath six inches of snow, and it was more by luck than judgement that we steered a course, which avoided awkward crevasses. Visibility improved as we descended, so abandoning our upward route in favour of the suspected corridor, which we now knew to be perfectly safe we slid pell-mell down easy slopes to the snowfield.

Henceforward the descent was uneventful, except that Pasang slipped twice on the snow-slope above the lower camping place. The second time this happened I was nearing a boulder projecting through the snow, so jumped forward to get the rope round it, in doing which I caught my shin violently against a projecting flake of rock. This inspired me to such a flight of oratory that the unfortunate Pasang moved with unexampled care for the remainder of the descent.

We breakfasted in rain at the lower camp; higher, however, it was still snowing hard, and I wondered whether the storm heralded the monsoon.

With most of the day before us, we descended leisurely, and I took the opportunity to collect further plants. When we left the snow covered glacier in favour of the moraine, and came a little later to flower covered slopes it was brought home to me how supremely delightful mountaineering in Garhwal can be. On

Everest, a climber may be for weeks above the plant level, and he longs for a sight of grass and trees until even the Rongbuk Valley with its dwarfed herbage and wilderness of stones becomes desirable. Climbing in Garhwal is altogether different. There the climber is never far from green valleys, indeed little or no farther than he is when climbing in the High Alps. Thus he is able to spend the morning on the snows and the afternoon amid the flowers. In such contrast lies the spiritual essence of mountaineering. The fierce tussle with ice-slope and precipice and complete relaxation of taut muscles on a flower-clad pasture; the keen, biting air of the heights and the soft, scented air of the valleys. Everest, Kangchenjunga and Nanga Parbat are "duties", but mountaineering in Garhwal is a pleasure – thank God.

Ere we reached the uppermost shepherds' hut, the scowling cloud roof broke up, and the sun poured into the valley, lighting the rain-soaked pastures, so that every flower and blade of grass shone with a marvellous purity.

So unsuccessfully, but delightfully, we returned to the base camp.

CHAPTER EIGHT

On Doing Nothing

THE DAY following our unsuccessful attempt to climb Rataban was brilliantly fine. I did nothing, not because I was tired, but because I was lazy. By nature I am a lazy person, but, unhappily, I seldom have the opportunity of being lazy, in which I do not differ from any other father of a family who has to earn his living. And now there were heaven-sent opportunities. Why had I sweated up to the col on Rataban, when I might have been lazy? I could see its serene and shining curve against the deep blue sky, distant and remote above the silver birches. In that answer lay the answer to "Why do you climb?" Mountaineering madness no doubt, but assuming that this madness (call it sublimation of sex or atavism or anything you like) is impossible to eradicate, how is mountaineering to be enjoyed best?

Amid a welter of conflicting philosophies, I have always clung to one idea – that to get a kick out of life, a man must sample the contrasts of life. And so it is with mountaineering. The positive ceases to exist when there is no negative. Activity can only be measured against inactivity; therefore, to appreciate the joys of activity it is necessary to practise passivity. Hence the off day. Now an off day is not something to be indulged in grudgingly; it is a necessary and integral part of mountaineering, the essential complement of the "on-day". I can sympathise with the man who with only a short holiday scales all the peaks he can in the time; yet, if he neglects inactivity, he neglects contemplation and we cannot appreciate Nature otherwise.

There are many who climb and enjoy climbing for exercise, fresh air, good health and relaxation from a sedentary life, yet Nature is discernible in part only through the medium of physical exercise. A superman may be able to divorce his spiritual consciousness from his physical make-up at all times, but there are few supermen, and most of us must strive physically and mentally to discern the verities of creation.

The West assumes its superiority over the East primarily because it is further advanced in mechanical matters, but woe betide it should it continue to associate mechanisms with spiritual progress. In Garhwal I met a true civilisation, for I found contentment and happiness. I saw a life that is not enslaved by the time-factor, that is not obsessed by the idea that happiness is dependent on money and materials. I had never before realised until I camped in the Valley of Flowers how much happiness there is in simple living and simple things.

By the standards of the West I led a life of discomfort, and I frankly admit that I should not be content to lead such a life in England, for it is necessary to conform to the standards of one's environment. A large majority of people do not realise how necessary it is to conform to these standards and for this reason look aghast on the "discomforts" endured by explorers. Genuine discomforts of fatigue, heat and cold are common enough in mountaineering and exploration, but the largest part of so-called "discomfort" is not discomfort at all except when measured against a different standard and a different environment.

To my mind, the acme of mental and spiritual discomfort would be to live in some super-luxury hotel in the Valley of Flowers. Happiness is best achieved by adapting ourselves to the standards of our environment. For this reason I suspect that cranks and extremists are essentially unhappy persons and symptomatic of a life that has become socially and mechanically too complex for its environment. In Garhwal I found no red, green or black shirts, no flags or emblems, no mechanisms, no motor cars or aeroplanes, but I did find a happy and contented people. I think the attitude of Himalayan peoples to western progress is best summed up in the words of a Tibetan, and Tibetans consider themselves superior to Europeans in spiritual culture. He said: "We do not want your civilisation in Tibet, for wherever it is established it brings unhappiness and war." It is a terrible indictment and it is true.

During the morning I lounged about the camp. It was a morning like other mornings, quiet and seeming scarcely to breathe. Dew lay thick on the flowers; birds sang in the forest and the air was sweet and charged with pleasant smells.

I reclined on a bank below the camp. Presently a gentle breeze began to blow, touching the flowers with light fingers. Smaller flowers such as the blue *corydalis* quivered a little but the taller flowers, the white *anemones* and golden *nomocharis*, nodded in slow undulations as though conscious of their grace and dignity.

During the afternoon clouds gathered; building up slowly, column by column and mass by mass. There was a wild sunset with fingers of lurid light but, as usual, evening established equilibrium in the atmosphere, and the stars shone out in their thousands as night spread from behind the ashen snows of Rataban.

We were very content. I knew the men were content because they used often to sing their simple Tibetan melodies. This is one, a great favourite with Wangdi when he was climbing a hillside, as well as I can remember it.

Lento.

In immeasurable contentment I sat by the fire.

CHAPTER NINE

The Snow Peak

DURING OUR ATTEMPT to climb Rataban, I had been much impressed by the beautifully proportioned snow-peak to the south of the Bhyundar Valley, and had decided to attempt the ascent. It might prove accessible from the southernmost branch of the main valley glacier, but this route would involve at least two camps, and at the moment I had no intention of making lengthy expeditions. Could it be approached from the Bhyundar Valley? It should be possible to examine it by climbing some distance up the northern side of the valley, and such a reconnaissance had the advantage of including botanical work. So two days after our retreat from Rataban, Nurbu and I crossed the valley and after mounting grass-slopes scrambled up a steep craggy buttress on which our handholds consisted for the most part of juniper roots.

We did not pause until we were nearly 2,000 feet above the floor of the valley, when we seated ourselves and I examined the mountain through my monocular glass. From this direction it appears as a rock-peak rather than a snow-peak, built up of striated cliffs dipping sharply from south to north. The snow-ridge we had seen consists of névé resting on the uppermost of these striations. Between the peak and a minor rock peak to the north overlooking the Bhyundar Valley is a wide gully; if this could be entered from a little valley branching off at right angles from the Bhyundar Valley it seemed as though the ridge could be approached over one or other of a series of sloping snow-covered shelves. The lowermost portion of the gully was concealed behind the shoulder of the minor rock-peak we had already climbed, but I came to the conclusion that serious difficulty was unlikely.

These points settled, Nurbu and I spent two or three hours scrambling about for flowers. We were climbing a steep ridge when I came on the first blue poppy (*Meconopsis aculeata*) I had seen in bloom. It was growing solitary in a rocky sentry box, its roots and foliage protected from the sun, yet adequately nourished by a slow seep of water.

Holdsworth described this flower as being the colour of the sky at dawn, and so, indeed, it is. As I pulled up on to a ledge out of breath after a stiff scramble, it confronted me not more than a yard away, lighting the dark-shadowed rocks behind it. Like most poppies, it is open and wide, droops slightly, has a centre of many golden stamens, and is so fragile that its petals are detached merely by brushing against them. It protects itself with sharp spines arranged on the stem and buds, which penetrate the skin like so many minute spears.

We were crossing a gully, when my companion pointed upwards, and I saw not more than 400 feet higher, on a snow-bed in the gully, a herd of about a dozen barhal. For a few moments they did not see us, then the leader, a grand old beast with a splendid head, gave a shrill whistle, and away they went, helter-skelter over the snow and in an incredibly fast rush across the steep wall of the gully.

When they penetrated the Nanda Devi basin, Messrs. Shipton and Tilman found herds of comparatively tame barhal. It is possible that the absence of bears as well as of humans accounted for this. In the Bhyundar Valley there are bears and the barhal are very wary; this is the only explanation I can give for their timidity in a district which, as far as I know, has never been visited by sportsmen. In Tibet I have seen almost tame barhal, and during the 1933 Everest Expedition they grazed near the Base Camp. No bears have been observed in the Rongbuk Valley and the Tibetans take no wild life.[1] Tameness and timidity in wild life is a study of considerable interest. Where small beasts are hunted or preyed upon by larger or fiercer beasts, they must of necessity become timid and wary, but in districts where no hunting occurs and there are no ferocious beasts, it is reasonable to suppose that creatures should be less timid.

June 26 dawned with an evil sky. Far above the highest peaks lay a roof of slate-coloured cloud, and in the valley livid mists had already congregated. I was doubtful whether it was worth while setting off to climb the snow-peak, particularly as a drizzle of rain was falling, but the men settled matters by pulling down my tent and packing it up. As I had sent Pasang down to Joshimath for my mail I took with me only Wangdi and Nurbu, which meant that I had to travel with light equipment.

Descending into the valley we walked along the south bank of the stream and, after forcing our way through some dense vegetation, entered the side valley already mentioned. The weather improved visibly as we ascended this and we were trudging up the terminal moraine of the small glacier which fills most of it, when the mists parted and the snowy summit of our peak stood out full in the sun. As quickly as possible I climbed the moraine, arriving on top as the last mists were vanishing. Now I could see what I had not seen before, that the base of the gully could be approached without difficulty over a level and uncrevassed glacier.

I had already noted a possible camping site on a ridge between the gully and another gully to the south of it, which formed a channel for ice avalanches from a conspicuous hanging glacier far up on the face of the mountain. As the main gully was exposed to falling stones we mounted for some distance by the side of it, then crossed it quickly where it was comparatively narrow. Although the

[1] It is possible, however, that snow leopards are to be found and these would prey on barhal and other wild life. There are also wolves in Tibet.

crossing only took a minute or two, we did not care for it, as now and then stones came skidding down the hard snow.

Our camping site was by a large overhanging boulder, perched on the crest of the ridge, which formed an excellent kitchen. It had cracked above and appeared insecurely poised, but Wangdi laughed away my faint protests and proceeded to pitch the porters' tent under the overhang, after levelling a platform for my tent immediately above the boulder.

The cooking fuel was dwarf rhododendron collected on the way up. It was necessary first of all to construct a little trench of stones; in this an empty cigarette box and sundry pieces of dried grass were placed to provide the nucleus of the conflagration. Pieces of dwarf rhododendron were then arranged on top, after which Wangdi and Nurbu lay flat on their stomachs at either end of the trench and taking it in turns, blew energetically at the smouldering wood. It was an exhausting process and soon their eyes were streaming from the acrid smoke which issued in suffocating clouds from the "kitchen", but they were undaunted and an hour later with a grin of triumph Wangdi brought me a cup of tea. It was well-nigh undrinkable, but so much hard work had gone to the making of it that I could not in decency refuse it or even surreptitiously throw it away, so summoning up all the fortitude of which I was capable I gulped down what was virtually liquid rhododendron smoke.

A hundred feet above the camp was a steep crag forming a projecting buttress, which would deflect down the gully to the south of us any ice avalanches falling from the hanging glacier. I had already seen *Primula nivalis* on the way up, so to work off the baleful effects of the tea, which promised to be both peculiar and distressing, I climbed up, ostensibly to look for flowers. I had not gone far when I saw, spreading from a thin crack above me, a little clump of densely clustered light blue flowers, still shining with the morning rain. I had an awkward climb, as the rocks were nearly vertical at this point, but when at length I succeeded in reaching the plant I recognised it as a *paraquilegia* (*P. grandiflora*) which I had seen once before during the 1936 Everest Expedition. It would be difficult to find a more genuine rock plant than this, or a more delightful contrast to the stern crags. One blast of cold wind should suffice to wither and shrivel it, a single frost to burn its tender foliage, yet it grows; a miracle of growth, battered by storm, scorched by sun, the prey of hail, storm and blizzard. Heaven knows how it grows, and that I think is the correct answer.

The weather, having cleared up to a point, remained undecided until sunset, when there was a further turn for the better, and in the west, Nilkanta appeared, cutting sharply through long thin lines of mist. Ours was an impressive situation. On the one hand was the wide gully by which we must commence the ascent on the morrow, with an icy channel down the middle, cut by falling stones; on the other hand, the ice-swept gully ending beneath a precipice, crowned by a great mass of shattered ice, fully 300 feet thick. No ice fell, but there were numerous rock-falls, among them a block weighing at least a ton, which tore down the gully, hit a projecting crag, and flew far out into the air, disappearing from sight with a deep droning hum.

Just before dark, our boulder gave two or three such ominous creaks that Wangdi and Nurbu thought better of camping immediately beneath it, and hastily excavated a platform to one side. For supper I had the cold remains of Montmorency, a couple of potatoes, biscuits, jam, and a cup of "Ovaltine". This last named beverage, which in happier circumstances makes an excellent night cap, had been ruined by the all-pervading smoke of dwarf rhododendron. I threw it away, when the men were not looking, but did not fail to compliment Wangdi; poor man, it had cost him and Nurbu fully an hour's energetic blowing to produce it.

The night was calm and warm, too warm for the height, which cannot have been less than 14,500 feet. We breakfasted at the late hour of 5.30 instead of 4.30 as planned, everyone having overslept. The tea was undrinkable and the porridge barely edible. However, this had the effect of hastening us on our way, and we were off at six o'clock.

The snow, although only slightly frozen, was hard, and step cutting or kicking was necessary all the way. To avoid falling stones we kept to the edge of the gully, and there was only one place, where we had to turn a projecting corner of rock, that was in the least dangerous. It was a calm morning, but there was a certain amount of cloud about, whilst the southern sky was heavy with dense masses of cumulus, backed by tall anvils of false cirrus; in all probability the monsoon was already drenching the plains and foothills.

Having passed a precipitous belt of rock above the camp, we abandoned the gully in favour of a snow-shelf, which slanted steeply towards the upper névé. In gaining this shelf we came upon a glorious display of *Primula nivalis*, growing in thousands on ledges watered by the melting snows. There can be little or no earth in such a situation and there is no doubt that this is the hardiest of all *primulas*, rejoicing as it does in barren rocks, running water, and coarse grit.

Without pause we climbed up and along the shelf, presently passing above the hanging glacier. I was now reaching my best mountaineering form, and it was no longer a fatigue but a joy to climb. This stage is reached when muscles are entirely under control, and rhythm, without which it is impossible to enjoy mountaineering, has been acquired. Wangdi was also fit; else he could not have sung without pause a monotonous little ditty, which lasted him only two or three steps before it had to be repeated.

Presently the slope steepened into an ice-bulge, to avoid which we mounted close to the rock wall bounding the uppermost edge of the shelf, Above the bulge we saw that in order to gain the snow-slopes leading to the upper névé we must either work through an ice-fall, up slopes which would almost certainly become dangerous later in the day, or climb the rock-wall immediately above us to the crest of a ridge. I decided upon the latter course as the wall was breached at one place by a gully of no particular difficulty. At its base the gully was defended by a bergschrund (marginal crevasse), but this was well bridged with avalanche debris and we crossed without difficulty to the snow-slope above. The snow was in good order, and we mounted quickly to where the gully ended under some rocks. These proved loose but not difficult, and within a few minutes we had climbed them and were seated in the sun on the ridge.

We had been going hard and it was time for a rest and a meal. From our position we looked along an easy, almost horizontal ridge, ending in the glacier-clad face of the mountain, which we must scale before gaining the upper snow-crest. It was a straightforward climb, except at the point where the ridge abutted against the face. Here a wall of ice about fifty feet high would have to be surmounted in order to gain the easy-looking slopes running up to the summit ridge.

Twenty minutes later we set off again and scrambled along the broken rocks of the ridge where I had to tell Wangdi, who was at the end of the rope, that he must not attempt fancy routes of his own. He was an independent fellow and always imagined that he knew best; occasionally he did, but generally he did not, and he would waste valuable time in climbing up a bit of rock by a different route simply because it was a different route.

The ice-wall was not as formidable as it looked, but it presented a pretty problem in step cutting up a broken corner. I enjoy ice-work and solving this alone made the climb worthwhile. Furthermore, it was a sensational place, as the corner overhung a sheer drop of two or three hundred feet where the glacier broke away to the left. To a lover of ice-craft there is something peculiarly satisfying in the hard clean thump of an ice axe pick meeting ice, and step-cutting brings the same sort of satisfaction that a sculptor experiences when working with his chisel. Cutting steps is not a matter of brute force but an art to be performed with the minimum expenditure of effort and the maximum of enjoyment. A good ice axe is not merely a shaft of wood with a steelhead at the end of it, but something that lives, and is for the time being an essential part of the mountaineer. The feel of it and the balance of it, contribute in some subtle way to enjoyment: to get the best out of it, you must treat it gently, deliberately and rhythmically, not blindly and forcefully. To the layman this may seem unnecessarily lyrical and even ridiculous. What is there, he asks, in cutting a step in ice? If you would answer this, watch one of the Oberland guides at work. "Easy", you say – then try it for yourself. There is Sonja Henie's skating – easy, but …

Presently we were on the slope above. At first we had to steer a devious course between crevasses, but once these were passed the slope stretched unbroken before us to the summit ridge. The climbing now was the antithesis of the work on the ice-wall; dull, slogging work of no interest whatsoever. Light mists had formed and the sun shone through them with a hot suffocating power that sapped our energy. I was not altogether happy about the snow, for that fallen during the recent bad weather had not consolidated perfectly as yet, and the general formation of the slope made it an avalanche trap; so at intervals I kicked and prodded it with my axe in order to determine its consistency. The surface layer of new snow was about eight inches thick; beneath this was a breakable crust, and beneath that granular snow. It was in the surface layer that danger lay, if any. At present it was adhering firmly to the old crust beneath, but later, when the sun grew hotter, it might slide. It was essential, therefore, to reach the summit and return as quickly as possible.

Our pace was very slow on the last part of the slope, for the sun was well nigh intolerable and the snow very soft, and it was with considerable relief that we reached the ridge leading towards the summit. The summit was not far distant, or so we thought, and was separated from us by a sharp snow-edge. After the slogging work of the snow-slope, this edge was delightful to tread. With renewed energy we pressed on, and some twenty minutes later trod the point we had seen. It was not the summit; beyond, stretched the ridge, at first almost horizontally, then steeply, disappearing into the mist. I heard a groan of disappointment from Nurbu. I could echo his protest, as we had climbed fully 4,000 feet in three and a half hours and I was now very tired. It was a pity to be so tired; otherwise we might better have enjoyed this splendid ridge. When I had first seen it from our camp under the Bhyundar Pass it had looked magnificent, and it was magnificent, the beau ideal of snow-ridges, not too soft and not too hard, with an edge moulded by wind and storm into a perfect blade.

We had not advanced far when a strong cold wind forced us to halt to put on our spare clothing and Balaclava helmets. This wind had only one thing to be said in its favour: it would prevent the lower snow-slopes from becoming dangerous; for the rest it was bitterly cold and though it had little effect on the grim-visaged Wangdi, it was fast knocking the stuffing out of Nurbu.

The ridge seemed interminable, for mist always adds to the apparent length of a ridge. I had assumed that it stretched unbroken to the summit, but such was not the case. There was a break in it, a curious rift where the lowermost part had separated from the uppermost and sunk, leaving an almost vertical wall about twenty feet high. No doubt the mist and our fatigue magnified this wall out of proportion to its true size; at all events, the sight of it was too much for Nurbu. 'Tik nay, Sahib! Tik nay' ('No good, Sir! No good!') he ejaculated. But strangely enough this unexpected difficulty had the opposite effect on Wangdi and myself; it stimulated our flagging energy. I shouted at Nurbu through the rush of the wind, a villainous mixture of English and Urdu – we were not going to lose the peak now. At the same moment I saw through the ice-rimmed oval of Wangdi's Balaclava a sudden grin; the next moment, like the mountaineer he is, he had driven in his axe, and given the rope a turn round it, prepared for my advance.

The wall was composed of hard névé not pure ice, and a few slashes with the adze end of the ice axe were sufficient for a step. In a few minutes we were up. The summit could not be far off. Of a sudden the mists swirled asunder. Ahead of us, the snow-ridge swept up in a perfect curve, to end in a perfect point, sunlit and infinitely beautiful, against a pool of blue sky.

Ten minutes later, at 10.50, we were there. Strangely enough the air was calm although the wind was tearing across the crest a few feet below: not an unusual phenomenon on mountains. My principal memory is of my feet, which were very cold. On the lower slopes my boots had leaked in the wet snow and the cold wind on the summit ridge had completed my discomfiture. Thus, much of my time on the summit was spent in waggling my toes about in my wet half-frozen socks in an attempt to restore circulation. Apart from this, I mustered up sufficient energy to take a photograph, or rather to set the delay-action release in the shutter so that all three of us could be included, as a memento of the occasion. This, when printed, showed Wangdi posed in the manner of some Grecian athlete about to do his stuff, looking his very toughest and grimmest, with a long, bamboo cigarette-holder projecting defiantly from his lips. Nurbu, also, had so far forgotten his tiredness as to smoke a cigarette, whilst I am chiefly remarkable for my head-gear which consisted of a Balaclava helmet to protect my ears and face from the cold wind, and on top of that a double Terai felt hat put on during our stay on the summit to protect my head from the sun. Such are the peculiar conditions at high altitudes.

The peak we had climbed must be about 19,500 feet. As our camp was between 14,500 and 15,000 feet, we had climbed between 4,500 and 5,000 feet. The climb had taken, including halts, four hours and fifty minutes, which must be accounted fast going at this height.

With the possibility, ever present in my mind, of the lower snow-slopes becoming dangerous, I gave the order to descend after a stay of ten minutes. Even at great altitudes in the Himalayas, it is possible to descend at an alpine speed and within half an hour we were off the snow-ridge. The slopes below had not changed appreciably, and were still safe, and we raced down them to the ice-wall. Here an unpleasant incident occurred. Wangdi was first down, then came Nurbu, and lastly myself I was reasonably well placed to check a slip, but when Nurbu decided to jump down the last six or eight feet without saying anything to me as to his intention, he nearly pulled me after him. I should be very surprised if he ever did such a thing again, for what I had to say about it at the time must have impressed itself indelibly on his memory. We regained the camp at one o'clock, having descended in two hours, and after drinking some dwarf rhododendron tea, set off an hour later to the base camp.

As we passed along the riverbed, we came on a bird's nest in a hollow between two stones, containing four eggs of a greyish-blue colour. It was a foolish place for a nest as it was only an inch or two above the stream level and would certainly be inundated when the monsoon broke. And there was every sign that the monsoon was about to break, for the sky was dark with impending storm and heavy drops of warm rain began to fall shortly before we reached the base camp.

At 6 p.m. it rained heavily, and soon after nightfall there was a fall little short of a cloudburst. As I lay in my sleeping bag, writing up my diary by the light of a candle, lightning began to flicker, and above the bombardment of the rain on the tent I heard the thunder growling on the peaks. The sound of the torrent rose to a roar, and I thought of the bird's nest; by now it must have been destroyed. Finally I slept, drummed into oblivion by torrential rain.

CHAPTER TEN

The Second Base Camp

THE MONSOON had broken. It was still raining when I awoke on the morning of June 28. Yet breakfast appeared as usual. With that aptitude for overcoming apparently insuperable difficulties, Wangdi and Co. had rigged a rough canopy of sacking over the hollow forming the kitchen; some wood, kept dry in their tent overnight, had done the rest. Further to assist them, I gave them the jaconet outer cover of my sleeping bag and this, when cut up and spread out, made an excellent waterproof canopy some six feet square beneath which and the other pieces of sacking, culinary operations were carried out.

I had decided, before climbing the snow-peak, to shift my base camp to the floor of the valley. There were two reasons for this: firstly, it would be central for botanical work and, secondly, the snow-bridge beneath the camp was rapidly disintegrating. True, there was another snow-bridge near the new camping site, which would last a fortnight at least, but on the whole the north side of the stream was more convenient.

At ten o'clock the rain stopped and a watery sun appeared. I decided, however, to postpone moving the camp until the morrow in order to search the neighbouring woods for plants. This work was delayed by the arrival of Pasang with the mail, and a local coolie carrying a maund (80 lbs.) of coolie food. Among the mail was "The Times" Special Coronation Supplement. The men were vastly intrigued with the pictures.

'That I suppose is your Potala?' said Wangdi, pointing to a drawing of Westminster Abbey. 'And that is the King and the Grand Lama about to crown him?'

I agreed that the Archbishop of Canterbury was in fact our Grand Lama.

Wangdi had already spoken to me about the abdication of Edward VIII. In spite of my very limited knowledge of Urdu, I could follow him when he said that if a King was indeed king, how is it that he cannot marry the woman of his choice? Either he does his work well or badly. And whom he marries is his own affair and his own choice. And what has woman to do with kingship? I think this may be said to sum up the feeling of the Indian peoples towards the abdication.

Later in the morning, the men spotted a black bear on an alp across the valley. At first, in spite of Wangdi's pointing finger, I could not see it, and when I did I needed my monocular glass to confirm that a tiny black spot was indeed a bear. These Tibetans have eyes like hawks.

It was only twelve days since I had arrived in the Bhyundar Valley, but time and the warm breath of the monsoon had wrought marvels to the flora. All around my tent were the nodding bells of *Fritillaria roylei* and hosts of a white-flowered onion (*Allium humile*), whilst on a rocky slope above the camp was a huge *megacarpaea* (*M. polyandra*) with stately spires of yellow flowers that exuded a sweet musky smell. In the woods were many white *herminiums* and I found another *primula* with a mealy purple flower which seemed to like the shade in a cool mossy place under rocks. Then there was a *clematis* (*C. grata*) not yet in flower, rambling over the bush rhododendrons, and on a bank near the tents a small shrub with charming bell-like, pink-white flowers, which I learned later was a *gaultheria*, and another shrub with long spikes of bloom which I could not for the life of me identify, not even its family. Indeed, my ignorance was pitiable. I was like a Cockney in a museum of precious things, only too eager and willing to acquire knowledge, but so confused and dazzled by the splendours about him as not to know how and where to start his quest. My sheet anchor was Dr. Ethelbert Blatter's book *Beautiful Flowers of Kashmir*. It had been given to me by that great gardener, Mr. G.P. Baker, and was invaluable in helping me to identify specimens, but even so there were many occasions when I was not even able to relegate a flower to its family. However, when the worst came to the worst I could always collect a specimen for my press and leave it to be named by the experts.

The afternoon I spent wandering about the woods where I found various ferns, including such homely species as the maidenhair and oak ferns. There is something blithe-some and gay about a birch forest; it is not jealous of the sun or dank with rotting vegetation. I well remember a little glade in which I spent some time reclining on a bank with my back to a moss-clad boulder. It was an absolutely still afternoon, for the warm breath of the monsoon seemed to have stifled the usual breeze. Above the tree-tops the peaks showed, dusted with freshly fallen snow between woolly masses of cloud, and from all around came bird song. Close at hand the notes of individual birds were discernible, and I heard from the alp the grating trill of the "Zeederzee bird", but the songs of more distant birds were indistinguishable from a chorus that resembled music played very softly in a vast cathedral.

When I came out of the forest I saw the lower slopes of the shelf dotted black and white. The sheep and goats, which I had been expecting for the past few days, had arrived. I did not welcome them, for they would eat the flowers, but I comforted myself with the reflection that there was plenty of room in the Bhyundar Valley and that they could do comparatively little damage.

Two of the shepherds called on us that evening and were entertained by the Tibetans. They were dressed in some dingy woollen material, with a plaid of sackcloth over their shoulders. Their features were of a Semitic cast with well formed aquiline noses and, like most Garhwalis, they had allowed their hair to grow long and had bobbed it in a becoming manner.

Rain fell during the night, and did not stop until after breakfast the next morning, when we packed up and moved the camp to the new site, a level meadow immediately above the stream, which had carved for itself a deep channel at this point. A short distance from the camp a huge avalanche, composed partly of ice, had fallen from the wall of peaks to the north of the valley, and after pouring through a gully in the gently sloping floor of the valley, had spread itself across the stream to a depth of fully fifty feet. It had shrunk considerably during the past few weeks, for it had originally extended 300 yards down the stream, after being bent at right angles from its original direction. This avalanche must have weighed many tens of thousands of tons, and the wind of it had snapped off short a number of birches along the edge of the meadow.

There was an abundance of birch and juniper for fuel, whilst a few paces from the camp a stream of crystal clear water meandered down a gentle slope, then splashed over some rocks into a little flower filled valley.

It was a beautiful camping place and from a floral point of view more interesting than the original Base Camp. The tents were pitched in the midst of flowers, prominent among which was the *Anemone polyanthes*. In between grew thousands of yellow *Nomocharis oxypetala* and here and there the blue *Nomocharis nana*. There were two kinds of *geraniums* and a blue *delphinium* (*D. brunnianum*). One of the loveliest of the taller plants was the *Polemonium caeruleum*, with wide flattish flowers of amethyst blue. The fritillaries were short-lived and in their place *potentillas* were springing up in their millions. It was remarkable how one plant replaced another as the summer wore on. When the fritillaries were in bloom, it seemed impossible that anything else could grow, so closely packed were they, yet here were *potentillas* equally closely packed. Only an uninterrupted cycle of growth can maintain such perfect balance. Would it were possible to perfect this cycle in our gardens. It is not possible in a cultivated garden where the balance is artificially maintained by constant weeding and thinning, but it may be possible in a wild garden provided that the cycle of growth and relationship of plants one to the other are made a scientific study. I believe that Rudolph Steiner has approached nearer to the problem than anyone. He has devoted his life to the study of rhythm in nature, and it is only through rhythm that harmony and beauty are achieved in the garden of flowers or in the garden of the human mind.

I spent the afternoon pottering about the camp. The little valley and a knoll close by the camp were rich in plants, though it would be a fortnight or more before many of them bloomed. Close to the stream was a drift of blue *cynoglossum* and on the slope above the tall spires of a stately pink-flowered, thistle-like plant, subsequently identified as *Morina longifolia.* At the head of the little valley, to one side of the tumbling stream, was a overhanging rock and under it glowed a single blue poppy, whilst on the steep bank above the river were many shrubs, including a pink rose and a bush rhododendron not more than five feet high which edged the meadow with crimson flowers. Scarcely less colourful was a mass of *Androsace primuloides*, falling over a large boulder perched near the edge of a dry and sunny bank, where various rock plants grew, including a yellow flowered *saxifrage* (*S. flagellaris*), which sends out long questing tendrils in all directions, and a little yellow *potentilla* (*P. eriocarpa*).

That evening the men collected an abundance of firewood, which Nurbu arranged with loving care; he is a connoisseur of camp-fires. Before the monsoon I had need of an eiderdown jacket in the evening but now is was unnecessary, for the air was warm and mild like an English July. I sat in my rickety camp chair, which had been artfully and ingeniously repaired by Wangdi to prevent it falling to pieces, and read Shakespeare's sonnets. What would he have written had he been there that evening? What message would he have carried from the flowerful meadows and dim forests? What language would he have garnered from the paling snows?

When night fell I continued to sit without reading and the pale faces of the *anemones* looked at me without moving, out of the darkness.

Rain fell in the night, but next morning was fine. I was off at eight, taking with me Nurbu, who usually accompanied me on my botanical expeditions, and who had become expert at pressing flowers and rigging the camera; furthermore, he took a genuine interest in the proceedings and often pointed out a flower which he thought might interest me.

The lush vegetation was wet and soon we were soaked to the hips. On the floor of the valley I saw nothing I had not seen before, except a *ranunculus*, but it was a different tale on a buttress. We had mounted perhaps 500 feet without seeing anything of special interest, when we came on a beautiful rose-coloured *cypripedium*, which could be none other than the *Cypripedium himalaicum* mentioned by Holdsworth. This little flower fully earns its popular title of lady's slipper, but it would be a very small lady who could fit it to her foot. It is not more than six inches high, but there were so many that the slope was imbued with a rosy glow. Nearby I saw a white flower with a golden centre at the end of a single stem. I identified it as a *lloydia* (*L. serotina*), also found by Holdsworth. This was an advance guard of millions, which later covered the ground at the base camp. The red *potentillas* were now at their best, huge flowers the size of half crowns, and in between them was a purple orchis, which almost always grew in association with thistles. Higher up, we had a stiff scramble on some rocks where a neat little *draba* ornamented the crevices and ledges, whilst a creeping knotweed was spreading over a weathered slab. Only a few sprays of this (*Polygonum vacciniifolium*) were in bloom, but I saw it later in many places, and came to the conclusion that it is one of the most beautiful of Himalayan flowers. When fully in bloom it cascades over the rocks in a rose-coloured flood and is visible from afar.

We ate our lunch on a juniper-clad ledge. Fifteen hundred feet beneath was the camp, a cluster of minute tents and beyond it the ragged shining line of the stream. It was a typical monsoon day; damp clouds were clinging to the peaks, or suspended in a sky of watery blue, their shadows almost stationary on the green valley floor; slate-coloured nimbus was gathering in the south and, as we ate, a dense mist oozed through the gorge into the upper part of the valley and congregated on the hillsides above and below.

We retired but not in time to escape the rain which fell with drenching force. It persisted until 8.30 p.m. when the stars shone out through an atmosphere sweet with wet turf and flowers, but this was only a temporary fine spell and rain set in again later and fell without pause until the late afternoon of the following day.

There was nothing for me to do but lie in my sleeping bag, write up my botanical notes, read, and in between whiles eat chocolate. This chocolate was remarkable, inasmuch as the makers presented with each packet half a dozen pictures of film stars. Presumably this was intended to increase sales, but unhappily the Indian hot weather had caused the chocolate to sweat, and beauties such as Greta Garbo, Bette Davis, Charles Laughton and Al Jolson presented a sadly debauched appearance.

Among the papers I had received by mail were copies of the *Spectator* and *The Times*. The news of the day was, as usual, depressing, but I got a certain amount of kick out of literary reviews, especially as regards one book which *The Times* praised highly, and the *Spectator* damned to perdition. Such contentiousness seemed to me symbolical of the distant combative world. Another paper, an illustrated weekly, told me with a wealth of detail and many diagrammatic drawings how to make my house gas-proof, but it said nothing about tents. It all seemed utterly fantastic viewed from the Valley of Flowers. It was as though I were looking down on an ant-heap that had gone completely crazy. That men and women should have to know how they can make their houses gas-proof before they can live at peace and charity with their neighbours is something so fantastic that the perpetrators of the joke should be locked up in an asylum. I tried to explain the idea to Wangdi but he looked at me so strangely that I desisted.

CHAPTER ELEVEN

The Belvedere

THE MORNING of July 2 was overcast and grey but I decided, more for the sake of exercise than anything else, to take a camp up towards the Khanta Khal Pass. From this pass, over which a route lies to the village of Hanuman Chatti in the

Alaknanda Valley, a gentle sloping valley extends some distance before falling sharply into the Bhyundar Valley. There is excellent grazing for sheep and goats and a well defined track zigzags up a steep lower pitch in the valley by the side of a waterfall. I remembered the valley well as Holdsworth had found many flowers there in 1931.

There was little of floral interest to begin with except that the edges of the birch forest were blue with *cynoglossum*, but higher up, where the path emerged into the open upper part of the valley, the slopes were brilliant with flowers and I found a *geum* (*G. elatum*), and the first *campanula* (*C. cashmiriana*) I had seen, a small flower like the English harebell. Then there was a collection of large boulders where I came upon a fine display of blue poppies; each boulder affording shelter for one and in rare cases, two plants. Even on that dull morning they seemed to shine as though capable of retaining the sunlight and blue skies of two days ago. At the back of my mind was the possibility of attempting a peak of about 20,000 feet, to the north of the Khanta Khal Pass, but new snow had fallen during the recent bad weather and I now realised that an attempt would have to be postponed until conditions improved. The alternative was to camp on a ridge to the south of the valley, and on the morrow attempt the ascent of a rock peak of about 17,000 feet, which overlooks the gorge of the Bhyundar Valley. So we crossed the stream by a convenient snow drift, and mounted slopes still bright with the blooms of a cream-white rhododendron, but had not got very far when rain fell heavily. The ridge for which we were making ends in a birch and rhododendron-clad knoll, overlooking the Bhyundar Valley. It was a perfect belvedere and I decided to camp on it. There was snow close at hand and the men, miracle workers where fires are concerned, somehow contrived to light the wet dwarf rhododendron wood under a convenient overhanging boulder.

At tea-time we were able to get a larger fire going and dry our clothes, but the weather relapsed again later, and at six o'clock torrential rain fell and continued until after dark, when a perfect cloud-burst descended. Never in my life have I camped in such rain, and I lay in my sleeping bag wondering whether the tent would be flattened beneath an apparently solid waterfall. To sleep was impossible, but shortly before midnight the rain ceased, leaving a calm atmosphere in which the roar of swollen torrents sounded a deep chorus, broken by a peculiar rushing and tearing sound, coming from a high waterfall on one of the rock peaks to the northern side of the valley.

No rain was falling when we awoke next morning, but the sky was packed with moisture-laden mist. The men had had an uncomfortable night. They are usually adept in the art of selecting a tent site, but on this occasion had chosen a hollow for their tent and had been flooded. It was some time before they could get a fire going, and breakfast was a scratch affair. In such weather a long or difficult climb was out of the question, and I decided to ascend the ridge from the camp in search of flowers and turn back if and when difficulties were encountered. We were away before seven, and scrambled up the ridge through dwarf rhododendrons and over big boulders. To judge from the amount of moss this portion of the Bhyundar Valley receives more rain than the upper portion. Doubtless its proximity to the Alaknanda Valley has something to do with this. At all events, there was a marked difference in the vegetation as compared with that of the upper end of the valley.

Soon we came on a host of *primulas* of the dark blue *nivalis* section, looking wonderfully fresh and clean after the rain. I found also a *codonopsis* (*C. rotundifolia*), many *bergenias*, which like a moist situation among rocks and, here and there, *geums*.

Presently, after a scramble up some moss-covered slabs, we reached a minor summit. Beyond it, the ridge crest consisted of enormous boulders piled upon one another with formidable drops on either hand. We advanced cautiously, and a few minutes later reached a slightly higher point. This was the end of our climb, for further progress was barred by a gap fully 150 feet deep with vertical or overhanging, slimy, moss-covered walls. In any event there was little object in continuing farther as once again the weather was spoiling, and dense mists already enveloped us. On this minor summit I was interested to notice a round burnt patch of grass. Lightning alone could have done this; indeed the rocks in the vicinity looked as though they had been frequently struck. Doubtless it was auto-suggestion, but I had a distinct feeling of electricity in my hair and beard and as it was not very dark, and we had no wish to offer ourselves as lightning-conductors, we descended to the camp.

Nothing was to be gained by staying in a particularly damp situation, so we packed up the sodden tents and descended; and as we descended the weather, with that perverseness peculiar to mountain weather, suddenly mended; the sun appeared, spilling brilliant light on the birch forest, and in less than half an hour the sky was almost unclouded and brilliantly blue.

It was a scene to make a photographer's mouth water. On high, the peaks dazzlingly white in freshly-fallen snow; beneath, the emerald green valley, the green of an Irish landscape in springtime, and closer at hand the wet-leafed birch forest quivering and dancing with reflected light. Flowers are most beautiful after rain, and I strolled down the hill enchanted, through drifts of blue *cynoglossum* and regiments of pink knotweed, pausing every few minutes to photograph some new and intriguing composition of flower forest, hillside and peak.

CHAPTER TWELVE

The Bhyundar Rock Wall

As already mentioned, the Bhyundar Valley is bounded on the north by a wall of rock-peaks which rises to a maximum height of about 20,000 feet. I had often looked at this wall with the idea of ascending one of the peaks on its crest. The difficulties were obviously formidable, for the wall is steep and complicated, and consists of rock buttresses, with precipitous little glaciers perched on shelves in between, except to the east, where it is breached by a glacier pass of about 16,500 feet which Wangdi told me was sometimes crossed by shepherds en route to the village of Mana. It was a pretty mountaineering problem, and as such appealed to me enormously.

The day after our descent to the base camp, Nurbu left for Joshimath to collect my mail and some more coolie food; the men took turns at this work which helped to relieve the monotony for them. Thus, I was left with Wangdi, Pasang and Tewang. The same day I took Pasang with me on a little expedition up the side of the valley which had as its objects flower collecting and an examination of possible routes up the wall from Base Camp. The former yielded nothing of especial interest. There seemed at this period to be a halt in floral growth, the earlier flowers having passed their best while many of the later flowers were not yet in bloom. During the ascent of a grassy buttress we disturbed a nestful of young pheasants which scattered in all directions. They could barely fly, but had learned to glide with considerable skill, though their take-offs and landings were deplorable and reminded me of my own first solo efforts in the Air Force. Pasang was unwilling to let them escape so easily, and after a horrible grimace at me, intended to convey the fact that they were good to eat, he went hurtling down the steep unbroken hillside. He aimed a number of stones but not accurately enough, and with shrill derisive squawks the pheasants disappeared into the depths of the valley.

As regards the second object, the most likely route appeared to follow first a grassy ridge then a series of rock buttresses to a small glacier, whence it should be possible to mount to the crest of the wall by means of a slanting ridge and a snow-filled gully.

We commenced the ascent next day. As it was high time Tewang had some exercise I took him in addition to Wangdi and Pasang. He did not get very far. We had climbed less than a thousand feet, when I noticed that he was slipping about in a positively dangerous manner on the wet and slippery grass. He had no nails in his boots! In a laudable (to him) desire to take back his climbing boots new and unworn to Darjeeling, where they would doubtless command a good price, he had substituted a pair of boots so decrepit that a tramp would have scorned them. I ordered him to descend to camp at once, put on his climbing boots and return, but when I saw him painfully and slowly descending the slope, obviously tired and perhaps still feeling the effects of his poisoned leg, I relented and told him to remain at Base Camp.

We camped at the foot of the first rock buttress to one side of a narrow gully protected from falling stones by an overhanging rock. On a wall of the gully was a bird's nest, which Wangdi managed to reach after some sensational gymnastics, followed by a still more sensational, not to say dangerous, downward leap into the bed of the gully. He said that it contained young, but what manner of bird it was I could not tell, as I did not see the mother.

While Wangdi and Pasang were pitching the tents, I scrambled up the gully over a couple of easy pitches on to the sloping crest of the buttress. This led to the foot of another buttress where the rocks were much steeper. At first sight it appeared as though a route might lie up the rocks to the east of this, but when I attempted to climb them I found that they were both smooth and steep.

An alternative was straight up the nose of the buttress, and here, entirely through my own fault, I got into trouble. By dint of an awkward bit of climbing, I reached a juniper-clad ledge, only to find that further progress was impossible, or at least desperately difficult. I had no option but to return and it was during this descent that I encountered an unexpected difficulty. On the ascent I had utilised an apparently firm hold in the middle of a slab, though being a staunch believer in the three points of attachment theory I had also utilised good handholds, but when I descended this hold broke away beneath my exploring foot. It was possible to descend the slab without it but very difficult, and it was half an hour before I succeeded in finding the right combination of finger holds. Climbing alone in such circumstances is a trifle too exhilarating.

In safety once more at the foot of the buttress, I investigated the west side of the buttress, and here there appeared to be a route, although not an easy route. As a last alternative, I traversed across the mountainside to determine whether or not the glacier was accessible to the east of the route originally planned. There may be a route here, but it is not a justifiable route, as the lowermost tongue of the glacier is loaded with stones and boulders of all sizes which it precipitates at intervals down the mountainside, and I soon decided against any further reconnaissance. I was returning when of a sudden there was a crash, and above a crag to my right, turning over and over against the blue, there appeared a block of rock the size of a grand piano. Without touching anything for several hundred feet, it descended with a noise like a shell, struck the rocks with another crash and burst into fragments, which hummed and whistled through the air before plunging into the snow-slopes below.

After lunching in camp, Wangdi and I set out to scale the upper buttress. The climb began with a steep pitch with undercut holds; then it was easy going to a wall about twenty feet high on which there was an awkward move diagonally upwards to the left. There was only one satisfactory hold, and getting on to it, while being pushed outwards at the same time by an overhanging rock, was not easy, so critical was the balance. I managed it with Wangdi waiting below to field me in the event of a slip. This wall was the only serious difficulty and above it a series of easier pitches and grassy ledges brought us to the crest of the buttress.

The usual afternoon mists had formed, so we waited in hopes of a temporary clearance. It came, and we saw before us a slabby ridge, running up to the left of the glacier. As we were merely reconnoitring we left the rope and followed the ridge as far as the slabby portion, then traversed off it on to a snow-slope which should afford an alternative route in the event of the slabs proving impracticable. Well satisfied with our reconnaissance we returned to camp.

There was plenty of juniper handy and to counteract the evening chill we built a large fire. If Base Camp life was remote from civilisation, this life of the bivouac camp was remoter still. There was not a breath of wind and the smoke of the fire curled lazily up the cliff to vanish in the deepening blue of the evening sky. From our position, which must have been about 2,500 feet above the base camp, we gazed down the lowermost portion of the Bhyundar Valley to the hills of Joshimath and the Kuari Pass. A vast range of cloud lay athwart the foothills, glowing so brilliantly that the shadowed hillsides in our vicinity reflected a faint opalescence. But the splendour of these cloudy citadels was short-lived, and half an hour after sunset night had fallen.

There is nothing that promotes an intimacy of spirit better than a camp-fire. He is dull and unimaginative who cannot sense the spirit of comradeship that persists within this warm circle of dancing light. Wangdi talked to me of Nanga

Parbat, and though my Urdu was execrable I could understand very well what he said, for there are occasions when language is no bar to understanding. He had taken part in the 1934 Expedition, which ended disastrously when three Germans and six porters lost their lives in a blizzard. After describing it he said:

> I have always felt that Nanga Parbat is different from other mountains. There is something there that will kill you if it can. It is a cursed mountain. I was asked to go again this year, but I said no, I would rather come with you, because I am quite sure there will be another accident and that many lives will be lost.

I can see him now, cross-legged on the ground, the red firelight on his hard face, his lips clenching the inevitable cigarette holder.

Pasang woke me next morning at 4.30 and at 5.15 Wangdi and I were away, leaving Pasang at the camp. Now that we knew the route we made rapid progress. The slabby ridge proved practicable and ended in a moraine where many primulas were growing, although the height cannot have been less than 16,000 feet.

A sloping shelf led without difficulty across the glacier to a snowfield whence the rocks rose sheer for fully 3,000 feet. Only at one point was there any hope of scaling them without excessive and, to judge from the amount of fallen stones on the glacier, unjustifiable difficulty, and that was where the ridge already mentioned slanted steeply upwards towards the crest of the wall.

Unfortunately the ridge ended in formidable cliffs. We tried at first to climb these but after wrestling with a loose gully and looser rocks above it, were forced to retreat and seek an alternative. This was by no means obvious until we discovered a snow-filled gully leading through the rocks to the crest of the ridge. The unpleasing feature of this gully was a wide crevasse at the foot of it, which had to be crossed by a snow-bridge. The crevasse was wide and abysmally deep and with two on a rope the fragile snow-bridge spanning it had to be treated with circumspection. Wangdi did not like it at all, but then he had spent three hours in a crevasse on Kangchenjunga, so some prejudice against crevasses in general must be allowed him.

Once on the crest of the ridge, the going was straightforward for a time up broken rocks and sharp snow edges, but the general angle increased gradually and with it the difficulties, whilst the weather was now brought to our attention by a drizzle of snow.

The crest of the wall was now not far above us, but the rocks leading to it were much steeper than I had supposed; in fact, where the rib ended, they sprang upwards in an almost vertical wall on which the snow, fallen during the recent bad weather, had accumulated to a considerable depth.

Our objective was a conspicuous rock-peak immediately to the west of a snowy gap, whence falls the snow-filled gully previously noted, and our one chance of success lay in crossing this gully and climbing directly up the steep face of the peak. It was an impressive place and obviously extremely difficult. Wangdi did not like the look of it and was, like myself, unfavourably impressed by the snow-covered slabs we should have to traverse in entering the gully. Fortunately there was an excellent block of rock around which the rope could be placed to secure the party, and with this to hearten me I embarked on the traverse. It reminded me strongly of the slabs beyond the Great Couloir on Everest. True, the angle was steeper and the snow, instead of being loose and powdery, was wet and heavy, but in the feeling of insecurity there was a remarkable affinity between the two places.

When at length I reached the gully, my doubts were resolved into certainty. The angle was steep and the snow so soft that at every step I went in above the knees. True, there was a slight crust due to the over-night frost, but even if we succeeded in crossing safely, what would it be like when we returned? It would certainly avalanche. And there was no security; the gully was too wide to allow of enough rope to secure one man to the rocks while the other man crossed. To add to the jest, snow suddenly began to fall thickly and the wind rose, sending it scurrying across the already snow-plastered crags.

'This is no good. Let us go down.' Wangdi's voice was urgent. He was right. Nothing was to be gained by reconnoitring further.

I rejoined him and we descended as quickly as possible through the snowstorm. Lower, it was raining and we arrived back at the camp soaked through. But we soon forgot our misery and sense of failure when some hot tea prepared by the thoughtful Pasang was inside us. Thus ended a climb, which, by alpine standards would have been accounted a difficult expedition. Our highest point was about 18,500 feet, which meant that we had climbed 4,000 feet from our camp.

It was still raining when an hour later we descended to Base Camp. I was first down and as I neared the camp, I saw Tewang, who was seated near the fire, suddenly dart into the porters' tent. He reappeared just before I reached the camp and came out a few yards to greet me. There was a smirk of righteousness on his broad face. He was wearing his climbing boots.

CHAPTER THIRTEEN

A Rock Climb

THE MORNING following the unsuccessful attempt to climb the rock wall, Nurbu arrived with the mail and news of the terrible disaster on Nanga Parbat – the worst disaster in the history of mountaineering. It occurred on the night of June 15, when an avalanche overwhelmed the camp, killing seven Germans and nine Sherpa porters. The news cast a gloom over our small camp, for my men had all lost friends. I had known the leader, Dr. Karl Wien, and had felt confident that he would lead his party to success. From the first newspaper reports it appeared that he had escaped, but these were false; he had died like Willy Merkl, the leader of the 1934 expedition, amid the snows of that most terrible and death-dealing of Himalayan peaks.

The weather was in poor shape, but not bad enough to prevent flower hunting. The abundant rain and warmth of the past few days had had the effect of bringing many plants into bloom. The wide stony riverbed a mile above the camp was coloured a brilliant magenta by a willow herb (*Epilobium latifolium*) which flourishes on a diet of river-borne grit. In much the same situation grew two *allardias* (*A. glabra* and *A. tomentosa*). *A. tomentosa* grows six or eight inches high and resembles a miniature marguerite, delicate pink in colour and with silvery foliage scarcely less beautiful than its flowers. *A. glabra* is much smaller and its almost stalk-less blooms grow close to the gritty ground. At the sight of such flowers, I used sometimes to experience a feeling almost of despair. How could I ever hope to grow them in England as they grew here? Would they not lose their delicacy and become coarse and lank in the damp British climate?

But the a*llardia* represented only one species in the vast family of Compositae, now in bloom. In stony places, and particularly along the tops of banks, was a white foam of *anaphalis*, and I remembered that after the Kamet Expedition, when its members re-united at a dinner, Raymond Greene, who had brought a number home, presented each of us with a little bouquet – a happy thought.

All over the lower slopes of the valley a little *senecio* had put in an appearance. It reminded me a trifle distastefully of its bigger brother, the ragwort, which is a pest of the British countryside. There is a field of it near my home and my garden receives annually some millions of its seeds, a large proportion of which germinate. There was also an *artemisia* (*A. roxburghiana*) a member of a family which must have one of the largest distributions in the world, except for the daisy and buttercup families, an *inula* (*I. grandigora)* which resembled a small sun-flower, and a tall *solidago* (*S. virgaurea*), a species of the golden rod or Aaron's rod of British gardens, whilst the erigeron family was represented by a charming purple daisy (*E. multiradiatus*).

Montmorency had come to an end, but now that there were sheep and goats in the valley it was easy to procure fresh meat. A mile from the base camp an old shepherd had taken up his abode in a stone hut which he had roofed cunningly with strips of birch-bark, and from him I purchased a sheep for five rupees. He was a fine looking old chap, and his deep-set eyes, seamed at the corners with innumerable tiny wrinkles, had that far-away look acquired by eyes used to searching far horizons. His clothes and footgear would not have fetched sixpence in the Commercial Road, but he had discovered something that untold millions cannot purchase – peace and happiness.

Every day he used to bring me sheep's milk in a little brass bowl. He asked for and expected nothing in return, but Wangdi told me that any empty tins I had to give him would be much appreciated, so I presented him with a biscuit tin. He was delighted; that biscuit tin might have been a golden casket filled with precious jewels.

During the afternoon and evening of July 9, the weather improved and the following morning was cloudless. On the spur of the moment I decided to camp below the glacier pass which, as already mentioned, leads over the range of peaks to the north of the valley about two miles to the east of the route described in the last chapter.

A mile or so up the valley the flowers were at their best and I shall never forget the scene where a clear-running stream meandered down to join the muddy glacier torrent. Millions upon millions of the little knotweed, *Polygonum afine*, covered the ground so densely as to form an unbroken carpet of rosy bloom, whilst scarcely less prodigal were the white everlastings, rivalling in their matchless purity the fleecy clouds already gathering about the peaks. The hillside was red with the

Potentilla argyrophylla, blue with *cynoglossum* and purple with *geraniums*, and on the flat stony floor of the main stream bed were acres of puce willow herb.

A little distance farther on we turned up flower-clad slopes which increased in steepness the higher we climbed. Here grew a large purple aster with widely separated petals, which I recognised at once from Holdsworth's description as *Aster diplostephioides*; a noble flower, not growing in colonies but scattered singly over the slopes. As a contrast to these more obvious beauties was a tiny blue forget-me-not-like flower, growing on sheltered gritty slopes where it could not be over-run by larger plants, but the most delightful plant of all, if comparisons are permissible, was a *cremanthodium* (*C. decaisnei*) which I found in the shelter of a rock at about 14,000 feet, a comparatively low elevation for this height-loving plant. Its little golden flower reminded me of the Alpine *soldanella*, for it is about the same size and droops its head in the same way; a very coy and shy little gem of the high mountain.

After climbing slopes so steep that we were glad of our ice axe picks on the slippery turf, we gained a ridge sloping at a moderate angle. Some distance up this was perched a huge boulder, forming a cave on the lower side, which, to judge from the sheep droppings, was a favourite pull-in for shepherds and their flocks. The men welcomed it, as it reminded them of a Tibetan camping ground, and wanted to pitch my tent on a solid mass of sheep droppings, being genuinely surprised when I objected. Otherwise, it was a charming spot. Close at hand was a stream, which cascaded down some rock slabs fringed with marigolds, whilst the turf all around was packed tight with innumerable little plants.

Soon after we camped rain fell heavily, but it ceased later, disclosing a lurid sunset. Himalayan sunsets are seldom as colourful as alpine sunsets, and in atmospheric beauty not to be compared with those of Britain, but this was an exceptional occasion, due no doubt to an excess of water vapour in the atmosphere, and Gauri Parbat glowed like a forging just withdrawn from a blast furnace, and continued to glow long after the first stars had appeared.

As I lay in my sleeping bag, I could watch through the door of the tent the upward creeping tide of purple shadow, an iridescent opal at its edge, slowly engulfing the glowing precipices until only the final crest was left to the sun. This faded and the purple deepened; then, unexpectedly, and it must have been due to the reflection from some high and far distant clouds, the glow returned, not as brightly as before, but of sufficient strength to lift the great mountain out of the night for a few moments in an unearthly splendour. This was the last of the day and was quickly superseded by the usual pale after-glow that invests high snow-peaks in a light infinitely cold so that they resemble icebergs floating on a dark sea.

I woke in the night with a start to hear a dull roaring sound and above it a succession of sharper crashes. A fall of stones was descending in a neighbouring gully, and looking out of the tent I saw a long line of scintillating sparks as the boulders collided with one another or struck against stationary boulders, an unusual sight which I have seen only once before.

It was a fine morning when Pasang woke me at four o'clock, except that the dawn light was diffused by high mists. From the camp a grassy boulder-strewn ridge took us easily upwards to a small snow-field sloping to the crest of the pass, which we reached within two hours of leaving the camp. The shepherds who cross this pass to Mana face considerable risks, as the northern slope of the pass consists of a steep and crevassed glacier which forms a tributary glacier of a much larger ice stream in the valley descending towards that village.

The weather was threatening, and the light early mists had deepened into an opaque pall beneath which the peaks and ranges to the south stood stark and forbidding. More for the sake of exercise than anything else, we scrambled up a minor rocky eminence immediately to the east of the pass. I had hoped for a view of Mana Peak but it and the nearer ranges were concealed by clouds. Our intention was to climb something if possible and my attention was immediately arrested by a striking rock-peak to the east of the pass, which forms an outpost, some 19,000 feet high, of Nilgiri Parbat. To climb it from the pass would mean a climb of great difficulty, but the formation of the mountain suggested that if the ridge between it and Nilgiri Parbat could be reached, the summit should prove accessible. To do this, it was necessary to traverse steep glacier slopes for some distance, then climb directly upwards. At the same time we must keep an eye on the weather and be prepared to retreat quickly in the event of a storm.

In the Alps mountainsides usually turn out to be less steep than they appear, but the reverse applies in the Himalayas, and we found ourselves on slopes far steeper than they had appeared from the pass. Fortunately, the snow was in good condition, but was not more than a few inches deep and rested on hard ice. A fall on a slope of this kind must be checked at once, as it is not possible to drive in the ice axe deeply enough to form a good belay for the rope, and I kept a watchful eye on Pasang. He, however, was going better than usual, probably because he was unladen, and he accomplished the passage without the semblance of a slip. Next came a scramble up some rocks to a snow-slope, which brought us to an almost level snowfield immediately beneath the ridge for which we were aiming. At the sight of the ridge our hopes of reaching it easily were immediately dashed, for a face some 1,000 feet high and defended at its base by a bergschrund (marginal crevasse) separated us from it. To the left was a belt of overhanging slabs, but to the right of these there was a chance of climbing an exceedingly steep slope to a point on the ridge about a quarter of a mile from the summit. It was no place for a large party, so leaving Pasang and Nurbu on the snowfield, Wangdi and I set out to attempt the summit.

The bergschrund was bridged with snow in many places and we crossed it without difficulty. From the snowfield the slope had looked steep and it proved even steeper than it looked. Prior to the recent snowfall it had been a sheet of ice, but six inches of snow now adhered firmly and had frozen so hard that step cutting was necessary. We had not progressed far when the sun appeared; the weather was improving, but we did not altogether welcome this as it meant that sooner or later the snow would soften on the ice. It behoved us to move quickly and we did not pause until we had reached the first of the rock slabs. These were awkward to negotiate, for they were smooth and without belays for the rope. With any other porter I would not have attempted them, but Wangdi had already proved that he could climb safely and steadily on really difficult ground.

As we reached the ridge, a burst of song fell on our ears and looking to the left we saw three or four little brown birds perched on a boulder, all singing lustily and very sweetly. This desolate ridge over 19,000 feet above the sea was a strange place to find songbirds. What were they doing there? Could it be that, like us, they were impelled to this high and lonely place by the spirit of the hills?

The ridge stretched almost horizontally to the foot of a rock step fully 100 feet high. There was no turning this either to the right or to the left as far as we could see, and the only chance of climbing it was to tackle it *en face* where there was a crack, which widened out higher into a chimney. The rock was excellent, a rough clean granite that reminded me of the Chamonix Aiguilles.

Having seen to it that Wangdi was securely placed and well belayed by the rope to a bollard of rock, I essayed the crack. This was awkward and strenuous rather than technically difficult, but strenuous climbing is tantamount to difficult climbing at high altitudes where even an ordinary arm pull is exhausting; indeed, of Everest it can be said that if the climber nearing the summit encounters a rock, be it only eight feet high, where an arm pull is necessary he will, failing an alternative route, not succeed in reaching the summit.

From the crack there was an awkward step on to the slab at its side a balancing movement which I could only accomplish when I had completely recovered my wind. The chimney above had to be climbed by means of back and knee work which involved such a strain that I had to halt and rest after every upward shove of my feet and arms. It was overhanging and roofed above and I had to leave it in favour of the right hand wall, to do which, I had to balance round a corner on small holds. I now found that above me was a slab about fifteen feet high, leading to easier rocks. It needed only a strenuous pull on my arms to take me up this, but I had discovered already that strenuous arm pulls were to be avoided at all costs. The alternative was a route to the right. This was not so strenuous but it was much more difficult, yet tired as I was by the struggle in the chimney, there was no alternative but to follow it. I had taken two steps, and was in the middle of a third, when there was a tug at my waist and a shout from Wangdi announcing that I had run out the whole of our eighty-foot rope. I was within an ace of climbing the slab, but there was nothing for it but to retreat and bring up my companion to the foot of the chimney. I had no belay for the rope and was standing on inch-wide holds, so I shouted down to Wangdi, illustrating my meaning by gesticulating with one hand while holding on with the other, that on no account must he use the rope as a handhold and, even more important, that he must not slip as I could not possibly hold him. But Wangdi was always the one to rise to an occasion and within a minute or two I heard him panting hard at the base of the chimney. There were now thirty feet of spare rope available, just enough to allow me to climb to the top of the step, where Wangdi, now well secured by the rope, presently joined me. It had been a hard piece of rock climbing, the hardest I had ever done at the height.

A little higher, the ridge looked so difficult that, as we were in no mood for further strenuous climbing if it could be avoided, we followed an easier line across the East Face of the mountain until we were able to climb directly upwards over steep and broken but not especially difficult rocks to a point above the difficulties. The top of the peak was only a few yards away and soon we were seated on a slab with a detached boulder, the actual summit, resting upon it.

It was 10.30 a.m., five hours since we had left the camp. Wangdi was delighted and full of grins. The first thing I did was to take off my boots and rub my feet, which had become wet, cold and numbed during the ascent of the snow-slope. This did not satisfy my energetic companion who, seizing some snow, proceeded to massage them vigorously. If mountaineers have nightmares, the nightmare of the lost boot or boots must surely take precedence over all other nightmares. On this occasion Wangdi, deciding that my boots were not in a safe place, suddenly lifted them over his head and deposited them in a niche behind him. He did it so quickly that for one awful moment I thought he was going to drop them.

There was little view owing to mists, but 1,500 feet beneath us we could see Nurbu and Pasang waiting patiently. As a reminder of our success Wangdi, who had already let out stentorian yells, prized some rocks away which raced down the slabby face and ice-slopes, leapt the bergschrund and finally came to rest only a few yards from the pair, who jumped up and bolted to his huge delight.

The weather was windless and the sun warm, but these very conditions made an immediate descent imperative; so after Wangdi's rubbing had restored the circulation to my feet and my waterlogged socks had been wrung out and partially dried, I replaced my boots whilst Wangdi occupied himself in building a commemoratory cairn, after which we commenced the descent.

I must confess that I disliked intensely the prospect of descending the 100 foot step, although, as I knew from experience, descending difficult rocks in the Himalayas is far easier than ascending them, so when we approached the step I looked for an alternative. There was only one possibility, a diagonal route down the face to join our ascending track at about two-thirds of its height, and this I very unwisely decided to take.

In order to reach the snow-slopes about 100 feet of rock slabs had to be descended. These were not only steep but singularly holdless. Wangdi went first, firmly held by me from the ridge. Having run out the full length of the rope he called on me to follow. I did so, devoutly hoping that he was well placed. He was not and when, after a very careful descent, I reached him, I found him perched on a tiny ledge supporting himself with one hand whilst taking in the rope with the other. It was a miserable stance, with no vestige of a belay and I implored him to climb very slowly and carefully. He did so, and when at length he reached the foot of the slabs I breathed a sigh of relief. But my relief was short lived, for in another moment he began to cut steps and it was only too plain from the sound of his blows that he was cutting into ice, not snow as I had anticipated. He progressed with painful slowness and appeared to have such difficulty in planting his feet firmly that, standing as I was on small holds and powerless to check a slip, my anxiety was intensified every moment.

Once again the rope ran out and Wangdi called on me to follow. I shouted to him to drive in his ice axe, and place the rope round it, but this he seemed unable to do. The reason was made plain to me when I descended. The slabs did not end as they appeared to end, but continued covered by a sheet of ice about one inch thick, which in turn was covered by an inch or so of powdery snow. All Wangdi had been able to do was to cut nicks in this ice plating just large enough for the extreme toes of his boots. It was the most evil place I have ever climbed and was fraught with every potentiality for disaster.

I realised now what a mistake I had made to leave the ridge; however, there was nothing for it but to continue and hope that within a few yards we should come to good snow. Driving in the pick of my axe as best I could and trusting that the toes of my boots would not slip from the minute holds, I descended to Wangdi, who seemed to be standing on nothing in particular. Once again he descended and once again I abjured extreme caution, for I doubt whether he realised what a horribly dangerous place it was we were climbing. And yet he was skill and caution personified: a Knubel or a Lochmatter[1] could not have descended more confidently. Forty feet more and up came a reassuring shout – he was on the good snow. It was not so hard as formerly, but this was to our advantage, for we were able to face inwards to the slope and kick steps. Moving without pause and both together we presently rejoined our upward track, and half an hour later came up to Pasang and Nurbu, who had throughout watched the proceedings with great interest, but without understanding the difficulties or dangers we had endured.

The snow of the traverse was in good condition and soon we were back on the pass, whence a series of glissades and a downhill run took us in little over half an hour back to the camp, where we had a long rest and a meal.

An hour or two later as we dawdled along the Bhyundar Valley I was able to appreciate once more the joys of climbing in Garhwal. A little while ago we had been straining every muscle on as steep and difficult a peak as I have ever climbed in the Himalayas, and now we were among the flowers; the perfect mountaineering contrast. It had been a great day's climbing.

CHAPTER FOURTEEN

The Lower Alp

SO FAR MY FLOWER hunting had been confined to the upper part of the valley above a height of 11,500 feet. I now decided to camp below the gorge and explore the pastures of the middlemost portion.

The day following the ascent of the rock-peak I spent resting and attending to correspondence. I had been looking forward to a visit from Mr. P. Mason, the Deputy Commissioner of Garhwal, and Mrs. Mason, but a coolie arrived with a note to say that Mrs. Mason was ill at Badrinath and that their visit would have to be cancelled. They sent with the coolie a gift of apples, eggs and onions. The eggs I especially welcomed, as since leaving Ranikhet I had been unable to purchase one, the reason being that the Brahmin regards chickens as unclean.

The following morning, July 13, I descended the valley with Wangdi and Nurbu. We camped on the alp below the gorge, where the flowers, if nothing like so abundant as they were in the upper part of the valley, at least justified an investigation. I found a purple *orchis* and a small *arum* I had not seen before, whilst the

[1] Josef Knubel and the late Franz Lochmatter: two of the finest Swiss guides of their generation.

camp was surrounded by the white *Anemone obtusiloba*, and innumerable strawberries, which carpeted the ground so densely it was impossible to take a step without crushing a dozen or more. Nurbu soon collected a hatful, and I had them for lunch crushed up in sheep's milk, but they were lamentably tasteless, not to say indigestible.

After lunch I wandered off on my own up the side of a gully, where some monkshood was already in seed. I was not hopeful of finding anything of interest and I was about to turn back when in a moist, mossy place under some rocks above me, watered by a tiny spring, I saw a gleam of pure white. I scrambled up the slope and came face to face with one of the most beautiful little *primulas* (*P. wigramiana*) I have ever seen. There were a score or more altogether nestling amid cushions of bright green moss. They were white, with a soft butterfly-like bloom on their petals, and they shone out of that shadowed place like stars fallen to earth. I had not seen this *primula* before, nor did I see it again.

Thus encouraged, I climbed out of the gully into the forest above it. This consisted partly of deciduous trees and partly of conifers; there was also a flowering shrub with a syringa-like flower. I ascended, sometimes having to force my way through undergrowth, till I neared the foot of the great cliff which forms one of the jaws of the gorge. Then I stopped. I cannot quite explain *why* I stopped, but immediately I did so, I became aware of a stillness in which not a single leaf quivered. There was one sound: a tree cricket somewhere, droning out a single monotonous note which rose and fell like the hum of a distant sawmill, but suddenly this ended and after that the silence closed in upon me. And with the silence there came to me a curious and wholly inexplicable dread. Dread of what? I am imaginative but not, I believe, nervous, but when I advanced a step and a twig cracked like a pistol shot beneath my foot, I jumped violently and I could not explain why.

I climbed for a few minutes more until I was not fifty paces from the foot of the great cliff, which loomed above me and above the forest, projecting here and there in black, slimy bulges, whence water dripped with an occasional furtive patter into the forest. Perhaps it was this cliff with its potent and somehow relentless force that impressed itself upon me, that and the silence of the forest. Then I saw that beneath the cliff there was a cave and that all around the cave the damp ground was trampled and crushed as though by some heavy beast. I looked at the dark mouth of this cave, and though I could see nothing, I felt that there was something looking at me – something malevolent. Had I stumbled on a bear's lair? If so, it were better not to investigate further; I was alone, and an ice axe is a poor substitute for a rifle.

So I retreated, and I do not mind admitting that I cast a glance or two backwards over my shoulder. I had seen nothing and heard nothing, yet some primitive instinct told me that I had been in danger. Was it imagination? If so, why did that great mountaineer, C.F. Meade, write:

> The mystery and thrill of travel is always upon one in the Himalayas, but the mystery is awful, and the thrill is sometimes a shudder.

Heavy rain fell in the night, but next morning was bright and clear. The atmosphere had been scoured of water vapour, and the distances had that brilliant electric-blue tinge, common to mountainous regions after bad weather. The pastures were a vivid green, the forests by contrast dark, the peaks blue and remote against a bluer sky.

We were early astir and after breakfast Nurbu and I descended the valley in search of flowers. Below the alp, a stream hurrying downwards to join the main torrent had been bridged with logs, faggots and stones by the shepherds; beyond it was a slope speckled red with the largest wild strawberries I have ever seen, and beyond this again pine forest. A forest is very beautiful on a fine morning after rain. The sombre shadows cast by the trees emphasise the pools of light spilled by the sun. Here is a mossy place, hoary with dew and lit by a shaft of sunlight, and here a graceful fern frond in sharp and shining relief against the shadow. On such a morning the gloomiest forest seems charged with laughter, the whisper of falling water drops, the breeze in the treetops, and the cadence of a small stream the pipes of Pan sound sweet-noted down the dim sun-flecked aisles.

There were few flowers, and many ferns, but where the path emerged from the forest on to a lower alp, I found a tall *euphorbia* (*E. pilosa*), a yellowish-green undistinguished plant and a purple-flowered, many-headed daisy. The alp had no novelties, but was bright with *potentillas* and *anemones*. I had better luck at the lower end of it, for here I discovered the first *aquilegia* (*A. vulgaris*) I had seen in Garhwal, a blue flower which was growing in one place only, an area of not more than twenty yards square. I never saw it again, and when I returned in the autumn for its seed I found that the sheep had eaten it.

We descended towards the torrent and there, in an alcove formed by two boulders, I found a blue poppy. The altitude was not more than 9,000 feet, which is unusually low for this flower. Then there was a host of rosy *Androsace primuloides* running riot over the boulders, a blue *lathyrus*, a purple motherwort (*Leonurus*) and a white-flowered shrub with singularly long and sharp spines. But the most remarkable plant was a bright pink *Eritrichium strictum*, which must have been a freak, as this flower is normally blue. How did this come about? Was it due to some chemicalisation of the soil, or to some unusual cross-pollination? It is interesting to note that the colour was precisely similar to that of the *Androsace primuloides* which was growing in its thousands a yard or two away.

The monsoon warmth and rain, particularly the heavy rain of the previous night, had roused the torrent to fury. In its presence it was almost impossible to hear oneself speak and as Nurbu and I stood close to it, the raging water ejected a stone weighing several ounces which just missed my head. I have never known such a thing happen before and it was obvious from Nurbu's expression that he placed a magical interpretation on it; doubtless some disgruntled river god was having a pot at me.

On the way back to camp we collected a large number of strawberries which compensated in some degree for a joint full of maggots provided by Tewang. After lunch we returned leisurely to Base Camp, arriving there in a rainstorm, which however, ceased later, allowing me as usual to enjoy my supper in peace and contentment by the camp-fire.

CHAPTER FIFTEEN

The Abominable Snowman

SINCE I HAD FIRST seen that grand mountain Nilgiri Parbat, 21,264 feet, named by Lieutenant R.A. Gardiner of the Survey of India, I had on several occasions turned over in my mind the possibility of an ascent. I had examined the mountain from the west, south and east and from these directions there did not seem the least hope of an attempt proving successful. The sole remaining possibility was a route from the north or north-west. There were two possible lines of approach: one via the Bhyundar Pass and the Banke Glacier and the other via the snow pass, which I had already visited [Chapter 13], and the glacier-filled valley which runs in its uppermost portion roughly parallel with the Bhyundar Valley. I decided on the last-named approach, as it involved the exploration of a valley the upper portion of which, as far as I knew, had not been visited by Europeans.

On July 16 I left Base Camp, taking with me Wangdi, Pasang and Nurbu with light equipment and provisions for five days. The past week had seen many more flowers come into bloom, prominent among which was the *pedicularis*. This plant goes by the unpleasant popular name of lousewort, from the Latin *pediculus*, a louse, as one of the species, *Pedicularis palustris*, was said to infect sheep with a lousy disease; but it would be difficult to associate the beautiful *pedicularis* of the Bhyundar Valley with any disease, particularly the *Pedicularis siphonantha* with its light purple blooms. There were also many dwarf *geraniums* and the *saussurea*, which grows in an astonishing variety of forms, varying from wide-spreading, flattish leaves with purple cornflower-like blooms rising almost stalk-less in the centre, to curious balloon-shaped plants and little balls of silver-grey wool that grow high up above the snowline.

Gentians, formerly conspicuous by their absence, with the exception of the ubiquitous *Gentiana aprica*, were also in bloom, and I came across a plant (*G. venusta*) like a small edition of that well-known denizen of the Alps, *G. acaulis*. It seems very shy of opening its petals and its little flower is almost stalkless. There was also growing in moist mossy places among the rocks *Primula reptans*, which rivals the *Primula minutissima* in delicacy. With so much beauty and interest attached to the ascent I scarcely noticed that I was walking uphill.

As we passed near some boulders, there was a sudden startled squawking and half a dozen or more young pheasants flew out from a small cave. Wangdi was greatly excited at this, and said that the birds would return to roost. I must confess that my mouth watered so much at the thought of roast pheasant as a change from sheep and goat that then and there I consented to a most nefarious expedition, which was planned to take place after dark.

In order to shorten the morrow's march we camped several hundred feet above our former camping place by the edge of a snowdrift amidst hundreds of *Primula denticulata*, many of which were still in bud. As I had found the same species of *primula* in seed five weeks previously, this struck me as remarkable. As late as October 7 I found flowering plants in ground where avalanche snow had recently melted. It would be interesting to know what process takes place in a plant that is covered for a year or more by avalanche snow, as must often occur in this country. Does it continue to live? Presumably it does, as even compacted avalanche snow contains an appreciable quantity of air. Small wonder that in England gardeners experience difficulty in growing a high Alpine or Himalayan plant, for these supposedly hardy plants are not really as hardy as plants that grow at much lower elevations, which are exposed to climatic conditions all the year round. It is nothing short of miraculous that a plant which lies dormant, protected by a covering of snow for six months of the year, should deign to grow in our bewildering climate.

It was almost completely dark when Wangdi poked his head in at the door of my tent and with a wicked grin announced himself as ready for the murder of the innocents. Together with Nurbu and Pasang, who were armed with blankets, we descended the boulder-clad hillside. A few yards from the cave Wangdi whispered to me to wait; then he and the other two conspirators crept forward as softly as cats. The next moment there was a concerted rush and both entrances to the cave were stopped by blankets. There was no answering scurry of startled birds, so Wangdi crawled under one of the blankets and groped about inside. There were no pheasants roosting there, and he retired into the open, saying things in Tibetan, which doubtless exercised the nuances of that language, but at the meaning of which I could only guess. For a few moments I was as disappointed as he, then the humour of our attempted murder struck us both simultaneously and we burst into a roar of laughter.

Next morning we were away in excellent weather. Being lightly laden, I was well ahead of the men. On approaching the pass, I was surprised to notice some tracks in the snow, which I first took to be those of a man, though we had seen no traces of shepherds. But when I came up to the tracks I saw the imprint of a huge naked foot, apparently of a biped, and in stride closely resembling my own tracks. What was it? I was very interested, and at once proceeded to take some photographs. I was engaged in this work when the porters joined me. It was at once evident when they saw the tracks that they were frightened. Wangdi was the first to speak.

'Bad Manshi!' he said and then 'Mirka!' And in case I still did not understand, 'Kang Admi (Snowman)'.

I had already anticipated such a reply and to reassure him and the other two, for I had no wish for my expedition to end prematurely, I said it must be a bear or snow leopard. But Wangdi would have none of this and explained at length how the tracks could not possibly be those of a bear, snow leopard, wolf or any other animal. Had he not seen many such tracks in the past? It was the Snowman, and he looked uneasily about him.

I am not superstitious. The number thirteen even in conjunction with a Friday means nothing to me. I do not hesitate to walk under a ladder unless there is the danger of a paint pot falling on my head. Crossed knives, spilt salt, sailors drowning when glasses are made to ring, black coats, new moons seen through glass, chimney sweeps and such like manifestations leave me unmoved. But here was something queer, and I must admit that Wangdi's argument and fear was not without its effect. The matter must be investigated. So I got out of my rucksack a copy of the *Spectator* and with a pencil proceeded to mark the size and stride of the track, while the men huddled together, a prey to that curious sullenness which in the Tibetan means fear.

About four inches of snow had fallen recently, and it was obvious that the tracks had been made the previous evening after the sun had lost its power and had frozen during the night, for they were perfect impressions distinct in every detail. On the level the footmarks were as much as thirteen inches in length and six inches in breadth, but uphill they averaged only eight inches in length, though the breadth was the same. The stride was from eighteen inches to two feet on the level, but considerably less uphill and the footmarks were turned outwards at about the same angle as a man's. There were the well-defined imprints of five toes, 1½ inch to 1¾ inch long and ¾ inch broad, which unlike human toes were arranged symmetrically. Lastly there was at first sight what appeared to be the impression of a heel, with two curious toe-like impressions on either side.

Presently the men plucked up courage and assisted me. They were unanimous that the Snowman walked with his toes behind him and that the impressions at the heel were in reality the front toes. I was soon able to disprove this to my own satisfaction by discovering a place where the beast had jumped down from some rocks, making deep impressions where he had landed, and slithering a little in the snow. Superstition, however, knows no logic, and my explanation produced no effect whatever on Wangdi. At length, having taken all the photographs I wanted on the pass, I asked the men to accompany me and follow up the tracks. They were very averse to this at first, but eventually agreed, as they said, following their own "logic", that the Snowman had come from, not gone, in that direction. From the pass the tracks followed a broad, slightly ascending snow-ridge and, except for one divergence, took an almost straight line. After some 300 yards they turned off the ridge and descended a steep rock-face fully 1,000 feet high seamed with snow gullies. Through my monocular glass I was able to follow them down to a small but considerably crevassed glacier, descending towards the Bhyundar Valley, and down this to the lowermost limit of the new snow. I was much impressed by the difficulties overcome and the intelligence displayed in overcoming them. In order to descend the face, the beast had made a series of intricate traverses and had zigzagged down a series of ridges and gullies. His track down the glacier was masterly, and from our perch I could see every detail and how cunningly he had avoided concealed snow-covered crevasses. An expert mountaineer could not have made a better route and to have accomplished it without an ice axe would have been both difficult and dangerous, whilst the unroped descent of a crevassed snow-covered glacier must be accounted as unjustifiable. Obviously the "Snowman" was well qualified for membership of the Himalayan Club.

My examination in this direction completed, we returned to the pass, and I decided to follow the track in the reverse direction. The men, however, said that this was the direction in which the Snowman was going, and if we overtook him, and even so much as set eyes upon him, we should all drop dead in our tracks, or come to an otherwise bad end. They were so scared at the prospect that I felt it was unfair to force them to accompany me, though I believe that Wangdi, at least, would have done so had I asked him.

The tracks, to begin with, traversed along the side of a rough rock-ridge below the minor point we had ascended when we first visited the pass. I followed them for a short distance along the snow to one side of the rocks, then they turned upwards into the mouth of a small cave under some slabs. I was puzzled to account for the fact that, whereas tracks appeared to come out of the cave, there were none going into it. I had already proved to my own satisfaction the absurdity of the porters' contention that the Snowman walked with his toes behind him; still, I was now alone and cut off from sight of the porters by a mist that had suddenly formed, and I could not altogether repress a ridiculous feeling that perhaps they were right after all; such is the power of superstition high up in the lonely Himalayas. I am ashamed to admit that I stood at a distance from the cave and threw a lump of rock into it before venturing further. Nothing happened, so I went up to the mouth of the cave and looked inside; naturally there was nothing there. I then saw that the single track was explained by the beast having climbed down a steep rock and jumped into the snow at the mouth of the cave. I lost the track among the rocks, so climbed up to the little summit we had previously visited. The mist was now dense and I waited fully a quarter of an hour for it to clear. It was a curious experience seated there with no other human being within sight and some queer thoughts passed through my mind. Was there really a Snowman? If so, would I encounter him? If I did an ice axe would be a poor substitute for a rifle, but Wangdi had said that even to see a Snowman was to die. Evidently, he killed you by some miraculous hypnotism; then presumably gobbled you up. It was a fairy-tale come to life.

Then at last, the mists blew aside. At first I could see no tracks coming off the rock island on which I was seated and this was not only puzzling but disturbing, as it implied that the beast might be lurking in the near vicinity. Then I saw that the tracks traversed a narrow and almost concealed ridge to another rock point, and beyond this descended a glacier to the east of our ascending route to the pass. Whatever it was, it lived in the Bhyundar Valley; but why had it left this pleasant valley for these inhospitable altitudes, which involved difficult and dangerous climbing, and an ascent of many thousands of feet?

Meditating on this strange affair I returned to the porters, who were unfeignedly glad to see me, for they had assumed that I was walking to my death. I must now refer to the subsequent history of this business.

On returning to the base camp some days later, the porters made a statement. It was witnessed by Oliver and runs as follows:

> We, Wangdi Nurbu, Nurbu Bhotia and Pasang Urgen … were accompanying Mr. Smythe on July 17 over a glacier pass north of the Bhyundar Valley when we saw on the pass tracks which we knew to be those of a Mirka or Jungli Admi (wild man). We have often seen bear, snow leopard and other animal tracks, but we swear that these tracks were none of these, but were the tracks of a Mirka.
>
> We told Mr. Smythe that these were the tracks of a Mirka and we saw him take photographs and make measurements. We have never seen a Mirka because anyone

> who sees one dies or is killed, but there are pictures of the tracks, which are the same as we have seen, in Tibetan monasteries.

My photographs were developed by Kodak Ltd. of Bombay under conditions that precluded any subsequent accusation of faking, and together with my measurements and observations, were sent to my literary agent, Mr. Leonard P. Moore, who was instrumental in having them examined by Professor Julian Huxley, Secretary of the Zoological Society, Mr. Martin A.C. Hinton, Keeper of Zoology at the Natural History Museum, and Mr. R.I. Pocock. The conclusion reached by these experts was that the tracks were made by a bear. At first, due to a misunderstanding as to the exact locality in which the tracks had been seen, the bear was said to be *Ursus Arctos Pruinosus*, but subsequently it was decided that it was *Ursus Arctos Isabellinus*, which is distributed throughout the western and central Himalayas. The tracks agreed in size and character with that animal and there is no reason to suppose that they could have been made by anything else. This bear sometimes grows as large, or larger, than a grizzly, and there is a well-grown specimen in the Natural History Museum. It also varies in colour from brown to silver-grey.

The fact that the tracks appeared to have been made by a biped, is explained by the bear, like all bears, putting its rear foot at the rear end of the impression left by its front foot. Only the side toes would show, and this explains the Tibetans' belief that the curious indentations in reality superimposed by the rear foot, are the front toes of a Snowman who walks with his toes behind him. This also explains the size of the spoor, which when melted out by the sun would appear enormous. Mr. Eric Shipton describes some tracks he saw near the peak of Nanda Ghunti in Garhwal as resembling those of a young elephant. So also would the tracks I saw when the sun had melted them away at the edges.

How did the legend originate? It is known over a considerable portion of Tibet, in Sikkim and parts of Nepal, including the Sola Khumbu valley, the home of the Sherpas on the south side of the Himalayas. The reason for this probably lies in the comparative ease of communication on the Tibetan plateau, as compared with that in the more mountainous regions south of the Himalayan watershed where it is known only to peoples of Buddhist faith, such as the Sherpas of Nepal and the Lepchas of Sikkim. The Snowman is reputed to be large, fierce, and carnivorous; the large ones eat yaks and the small ones men. He is sometimes white, and sometimes black or brown. About the female, the most definite account I have heard is that she is only less fierce than the male, but is hampered in her movements by exceptionally large pendulous breasts, which she must perforce sling over her shoulders when walking or running.

Of recent years, considerable force has been lent to the legend by Europeans having seen strange tracks in the snow, sometimes far above the permanent snowline, apparently of a biped. Such tracks had in all cases been spoiled or partially spoiled by the sun, but if such tracks were made by bears, then it is obvious that bears very seldom wander on to the upper snows, otherwise fresh tracks unmelted by the sun would have been observed by travellers. The movements of animals are incalculable, and there seems no logical explanation as to why a bear should venture far from its haunts of woodland and pasture. There is one point in connection with this, which may have an important bearing on the tracks we saw, which I have omitted previously in order to bring it in at this juncture. On the way up the Bhyundar Valley from Base Camp, I saw a bear about 200 yards distant on the northern slopes of the valley. It bolted immediately and so quickly that I did not catch more than a glimpse of it, and disappeared into a small cave under an overhanging crag. When the men, who were behind, came up with me, I suggested that we should try to coax it into the open, in order that I could photograph it, so the men threw stones into the cave while I stood by with my camera. But the bear was not to be scared out so easily, and as I had no rifle it was not advisable to approach too near to the cave. Is it possible that we so scared this bear that the same evening it made up the hillside some 4,000 feet to the pass? There are two objections to this theory: firstly, that it appeared to be the ordinary small black bear, and too small to make tracks of the size we saw and, secondly, that the tracks ascended the glacier fully a mile to the east of the point where we saw the bear. We may, however, have unwittingly disturbed another and larger bear during our ascent to our camp. At all events, it is logical to assume that an animal would not venture so far from its native haunts without some strong motive to impel it. One last and very interesting point – the Sikh surveyor whom I had met in the Bhyundar Valley was reported by the Postmaster of Joshimath as having seen a huge white bear in the neighbourhood.

It seems possible that the Snowman legend originated through certain traders who saw bears when crossing the passes over the Himalayas and carried their stories into Tibet, where they became magnified and distorted by the people of that superstitious country which, though Buddhist in theory, has never emancipated itself from ancient nature and devil worship. Whether or not bears exist on the Tibetan side of the Himalayas I cannot say. It is probable that they do in comparatively low and densely forested valleys such as the Kharta and Kharma Valleys east of Everest and it may be that they are distributed more widely than is at present known.

After my return to England I wrote an article, which was published by *The Times*, in which I narrated my experiences and put forward my conclusions, which were based of course on the identifications of the zoological experts.

I must confess that this article was provocative, not to say dogmatic, but until it was published I had no idea that the Abominable Snowman, as he is popularly known, is as much beloved by the great British public as the Sea-serpent and the Loch Ness Monster. Indeed, in debunking what had become an institution, I roused a hornet's nest about my ears. It was even proposed by one gentleman in a letter to *The Times* that the Royal Geographical Society and the Alpine Club should send a joint expedition to the Himalayas in an attempt to prove or disprove my observations and conclusions. It was obvious that the writer hoped that this expedition, if it took place, would not only disprove them, but would prove the existence of the Abominable Snowman. I can only say in extenuation of my crime that I hope there is an Abominable Snowman. The tracks I saw were undoubtedly made by a bear, but what if other tracks seen by other people were made by Abominable Snowmen? I hope they were. In this murky age of materialism, human beings have to struggle hard to find the romantic and what could be more romantic than an Abominable Snowman, together with an Abominable Snow-woman and, not least of all, an Abominable Snow-baby?

CHAPTER SIXTEEN

Nilgiri Parbat: My Finest Snow and Ice Peak

WANGDI AND CO. had obviously been severely shaken by the events narrated in the last chapter, and it was a subdued little procession that crept down the north side of the snow pass. For a while the descent lay over easy slopes, then the glacier suddenly broke away in a steep icefall, and we had to descend carefully, cutting steps now and then, so that I marvelled at the hardihood of the shepherds who traverse this pass, presumably without ropes and ice axes, and relying for their safety on an instinctive rather than a reasoned knowledge of mountain-craft. In one or two places, I had to keep a careful watch on Pasang, for there were crevasses below waiting, as Professor Tyndall might have said, for an erratic body.

Having passed the crevasses we came to an unbroken snow-slope, descending in a steep concave curve to the main glacier. There we unroped the better to glissade. Wangdi descended skilfully, whilst Nurbu at least managed to get down without spilling himself, but Pasang, of course, could not kick more than a few steps before he slipped. As usual he let go of his axe, with which he could easily have stopped himself. His hat flew off, his load wound itself round his neck, and down he came like an attenuated bag of coals, his long limbs spread out like a starfish, whilst those below roared with unmerciful laughter. It is a hard world for Pasangs.

Wangdi having good-naturedly retrieved the errant ice axe and hat we continued on our way. The valley in which we found ourselves contained a long glacier, which like all long glaciers in the Central Himalayas at this time of the year, was largely denuded of snow and consisted for the most part of dirty stone-covered ice. As we turned the corner, where the glacier from the snow pass debouches on to the main glacier, Nilgiri Parbat came into sight at the head of the latter. It had looked magnificent from the south, east and west, and it was no less magnificent from the north-west. Built up on terrific precipices, its summit cut knife-like into the blue. There was no hope of climbing such precipices, yet there was one possibility, the North Face. Only the edge of this was visible, but it showed in profile, the best angle of view when gauging the difficulties of a mountain. It was certainly steep; I should not care to estimate its angle, but it cannot have been less than 40°, on the average. How to get on to it? That problem would have to wait until we could proceed across and over a muddle of icefalls that formed a half circle at the head of the valley.

I was anxious to push on as far as possible that day, but it was plain that the men had lost all interest in the proceedings. The Snowman had knocked the stuffing out of them, and they lagged limply and sullenly behind as though they fully expected Snowmen to leap out at them from behind every large boulder. There is no dealing with the Bhotia or the Sherpa when he is in this condition; superstition has much the same physical effect on the native as the fear of high altitudes had on the early climbers of Mont Blanc. My annoyance increased and finally when, after strolling ahead at a snail-like pace, I had to halt and wait for over an hour to allow them to catch up with me, I told Wangdi what I thought about him. But it was no use; he and the others were tired, prematurely worn out by the terrors of the day: so we camped on the side moraine below, not above the main icefall of the glacier as I had hoped, at a height which cannot have been more than 15,000 feet and may have been less, to judge from the vegetation in the vicinity.

After tea I scrambled up some rocks until I could look over the lower icefall of the glacier. What I saw was magnificent, but scarcely encouraging. Above the icefall there is an almost level glacier plateau, and above the plateau a semi-circle of precipices and icefalls. It was a savage and awe-inspiring place and reminded me of that terrible cirque of Kangchenjunga from which we had vainly tried to force a way in 1930. As regards Nilgiri Parbat, I could now see that the uppermost part of the North Face was glacier-clad. The slope was steep and intersected in many places by ice-cliffs, but once on it, there seemed a chance that the summit might prove accessible. About 2,500 feet below the summit the mountain is linked by a ridge to a neighbouring peak of about 19,000 feet, but any direct approach to this ridge was out of the question owing to cliffs and icefalls. In one place only was there the remotest hope. This was where a long snow-crested buttress ended against the North-West Face of Nilgiri Parbat. If the crest could be gained, it should be possible to traverse a shelf across the face between broken ice to the foot of a steep snow gully ending on the ridge connecting the mountain with an unnamed and unmeasured peak on the range extending from it to the north-west. It is a complicated piece of topography and difficult to describe. As for the North Face of Nilgiri Parbat, this also is very complicated, so much so that it was impossible to determine whether or not a route could be made up it. But was the climb at all practicable? The camp was 15,000 feet or less and Nilgiri Parbat is 21,264 feet. We should have to descend some distance from the initial buttress in order to traverse the North-West Face towards the snow gully. Assuming such a descent to be 200 or 300 feet it meant a climb from the camp of about 6,500 feet, a tremendous climb in one day in the Himalayas, even on easy ground, and one which in all likelihood would prove too long should the climbing prove difficult. So depressing was the prospect that it seemed best to devote ourselves merely to a reconnaissance and return later with more food and equipment for a higher camp.

I cannot sleep well when a problem is weighing on my mind and that night constant and vivid lightning contributed to my wakefulness. Once I roused myself to look out of the tent. To the west over the Alaknanda Valley an intense electrical storm was raging. Towering clouds were piled far up in the sky and these were illuminated every second by fountains of mauve lightning. The storm was not far distant and every now and then the hollow rumble of thunder echoed along the glacier. If anything was likely to settle the issue it was the weather. But the lightning died away with the dawn and the day broke calmly and with it the conviction came to me that we must attempt Nilgiri Parbat, so at five o'clock I roused the men and we breakfasted. I was not sure of their temper after the previous day's experiences and I did not tell Wangdi that I intended to attempt the mountain. I left Pasang at the camp to the mercy of the Abominable Snowmen.

At 6 we were off. A tongue of ice led conveniently through the icefall. Here and there step cutting was necessary and we had to circumvent some wide crevasses, but there was nothing to cause us more than a moment's pause, and within half an hour of leaving the camp we were on the plateau.

The buttress, which is sharp-crested above, splays out below into precipices, which can be out-flanked by a snow-slope and snow-ridge. Crossing the plateau, we ascended this slope in a diagonal line designed to keep us out of range of a mass of unstable looking ice pinnacles. The snow was hard frozen and step-cutting was necessary. I always welcome step-cutting at the beginning of a climb, as there is nothing like it to instil vitality and set the sluggish blood circulating. I had no need to look back to see how Wangdi and Nurbu were faring; in some telepathic way I could feel them through the rope. A night's rest, coupled with that power possessed by the Oriental for forgetting unpleasant experiences, had worked wonders. Fire, dash and energy had returned to them.

The slope narrowed into a ridge. Swing-swish. Swing-swish. There is heavenly music in the sound of an ice axe slicing into hard-frozen snow. The morning was still and cold and the great cirque, out of which we were climbing, silent and immobile. On our left was a steep and narrow gully, polished by falling debris, and bounding it an enormous mass of cold green séracs, tinged with a pale opalescent light reflected from some sunlit snow peaks down the valley.

The ridge petered out into gently sloping snow. Immediately above was a crevasse with a beard of icicles on its lip and above that a steep snow-slope leading up to the sharp crowning ridge of the buttress. The crevasse was choked with snow in one place, and well held on the rope by Wangdi I gingerly crossed the bridge and cut steps up the lip. The slope above was steep and consisted of ice covered with a skin of well-frozen snow. Later in the day, when the sun had softened the snow, it would be impossible to descend it without cutting steps in the ice, but there was a rock rib to the right, which should serve as an alternative route. Chopping steps and moving all together, we were soon up the slope on to a ridge above. Here the sun welcomed us and we halted for a short rest. It was now no longer necessary for me to keep the men in the dark as to the objective, and I told them that we would go to the summit if possible. Their reply was laconic and typical. 'Tikai, Sahib.' ('All right, Sir.')

So far the weather had been good, but now mists began to form. Above us we could see the ridge rising in a parabolic curve to a rocky shoulder, then in another curve which disappeared into the mist. A few minutes' rest and we recommenced the ascent. The snow was in good order and to make a step needed only a single vigorous kick. In places the ridge was sharp and needed care, but there was no difficulty and presently, it must have been about 8.30, we stood on the blunt topmost crest of the buttress. As we reached it the mist cleared a little and we could see above us a series of huge ice-walls and square-cut séracs. To the left was the shelf I had already seen. It was comfortably wide, which meant that we need not pass dangerously near to the séracs, but it was downward sloping and traversing it involved the loss of quite 300 feet of height; not much, but discouraging when so many thousands of feet remained to be climbed.

It did not take more than a few minutes to reach the end of it and the foot of the snow gully already mentioned, which is about 400 feet high and is bounded on one side by séracs and on the other by rock cliffs. At its base it was defended by a bergschrund well choked with snow, so that although some cutting was necessary to climb over the lip, we were soon on the slope above. This was steep, hard and icy. Every step throughout the whole of its height had to be cut and each step took several chops with the axe. It was hard work, but exhilarating work too. Wangdi and Nurbu were going splendidly and had the bit between their teeth. As for me, I had never felt fitter in my life, and was enjoying every minute of as fine a snow climb as I had ever had. The gully was in shadow, but the sharp thin snow-ridge in which it ended was lit by the white fire of the sun. Slowly we approached that ridge; then, held by Wangdi on the rope, I went ahead driving in my ice axe as I approached the crest, in order to determine whether or not it was corniced. It was not, and soon we were all moving along the blade-like crest, which ended after about 100 yards in a little plateau beneath the final ice face of the mountain. There we halted for another rest. It was ten o'clock and we had climbed about 4,000 feet in four hours; fair going considering the difficulties.

My mouth was very dry and I longed for a drink. I moistened it with snow and ate some chocolate, though, as is usual during a hard day in the Himalayas, I had no desire whatever to eat. Wangdi and Nurbu both refused food, but I told them that if they did not eat we should not be able to reach the top, to which Wangdi replied, 'Of course we shall reach the top!'

As we sat in the snow, the mists parted sufficiently to enable us to see the face of the mountain. As already stated, this consists of a steep slope of névé some 2,500 feet in height which ended to our left and at about our level in a line of ice-cliffs overhanging precipices about 3,000 feet high falling to the Banke Glacier. Had its angle been a degree or two steeper it must have been rock like the south face of the mountain. As it was, the downward movement of the névé had broken it up into séracs of which the largest formed a wall of ice 100-200 feet high which intersected the face for about three-quarters of its breadth. I had planned to ascend the face by its westernmost edge, but this was not practicable owing to broken ice. The sole remaining hope was to make a route diagonally upwards across it to the North-East Ridge. At first sight this did not seem a feasible alternative; for one thing it involved a long and complicated climb and for another it meant passing beneath numerous séracs and the frowning ramparts of the great ice wall. Since the recent snow fall there had been two small falls of ice, but the clean cut nature of the séracs and the ice wall suggested that avalanches only broke away very occasionally. The last and most important point to be considered was the condition of the snow. In no circumstances could an avalanche be risked, for with precipices below, the end of a party would be swift and certain. At present it was in good order, and the danger, if any, would occur later in the day when the sun had worked on the slope, though at present mist partially screened the mountain from that destructive agent.

My examination concluded and my decision made, we recommenced the ascent. First came a steep snow-slope, which we climbed diagonally to the left. The snow was hard frozen and vigorous kicking was necessary. Curiously enough, step kicking tends to make the feet colder rather than warmer, possibly because the vibration deadens the toes. I notice that the same thing happens to the hands when holding the vibrating wheel of a badly sprung motorcar.

For this reason I varied the work by cutting with the axe.

We had not advanced far when the mist closed in, this time more densely than before. Nothing saps the energy more quickly than steamy mist at a high altitude. The sun was scarcely visible, yet its heat was suffocating and the absence of a breeze contributed to our inertia. We were experiencing glacier lassitude, often referred to in connection with Himalayan mountaineering but which may be experienced on lower snow-mountains such as Mont Blanc and Monte Rosa. The physical cause is said to be an excess of water vapour in the atmosphere, but the mental factor enters into it also, for there is nothing more boring or fatiguing than climbing a long snow-slope in a mist. I began to go slower and slower and to breathe more and more heavily; and my legs were tired, a dead weight of tiredness due no doubt to my having kicked or cut every step since leaving the camp.

At this critical juncture, the mists again parted. We had been climbing for over an hour and traversing to the left at the same time, and I had anticipated seeing the ice-wall well to our right and but little above our level. Far from it. As the sluggish mists slowly and reluctantly released their hold, it loomed out like a vast sea cliff stretching to right and left as far as we could see and still a long and weary way above us. I had underestimated the scale of the face and it seemed that we were beaten: time and fatigue had tipped the scale against us. I turned to Wangdi to give the order to retreat, but at sight of the grim-visaged little man standing there imperturbable in his steps, as though his whole life had been spent in climbing arduous snow-slopes; the words on my lips changed themselves into:

'Go ahead, and take a turn, at the leading.'

I spoke in English, but Wangdi understood. He was at the end of the rope and it was only necessary to reverse the order.

There is nothing Wangdi likes better than leading on a mountain, for he is a leader, with the instincts of leadership, and he went at the slope with a tireless energy which, if not rhythmical, was nevertheless inspiring to watch. It was foolish of me not to have made him lead before, and I at once realised the difference between making steps and walking up steps already made. Quickly my energy returned to me and with it hope and optimism. Fatigue alone had made the ice-wall seem far away; actually it was not more than 300 feet above us and we were soon beneath it, close to its easternmost extremity. To outflank it we had to climb round a steep corner to the left, the approach to which involved the only really dangerous climbing we met with during the whole ascent. Some fifty yards from the corner a piece of the wall had become partly detached, forming a flake of ice about 100 feet high, weighing several hundred tons, which overhung and threatened the route for about thirty yards. Had we traversed the slope some distance below the foot of the wall, we should have been out of the danger zone quickly, as here the angle was less steep than it was immediately beneath the wall, but Wangdi, never a good route-finder, chose a more difficult line at the base of the flake where steps had to be cut. I did not notice what he was doing until it was too late, as I was still recovering from my fatigue at the rear of the rope. Not that it made much difference, for it meant that we were only two or three minutes longer in the danger zone; yet two or three minutes when the sun is threatening to dislodge a piece of ice the size and weight of a fortress wall can seem an unconscionably long time, and I was heartily glad when we were out of range.

The corner was steep and icy and was intersected horizontally by an awkward little crevasse with a vertical upper lip, so I went ahead again and, well belayed by the rope round Nurbu's ice axe, traversed to the left, then made straight up to the crevasse, cutting steps all the way. I got up at last after some heavy work and was presently joined by my companions. We had turned the ice wall, the crux of the ascent.

An unbroken but steep snow slope leading up to the crest of the North-East Ridge now remained to be climbed. The snow here was much softer than the snow beneath the ice wall, as it had been exposed to greater cold, and at every step we went in halfway to the knees, so that even the indomitable Wangdi had to halt and puff for breath every three or four paces. Meanwhile, I kept a sharp look out for wind-slab, but presently came to the conclusion that the slope was unlikely to avalanche, owing principally to the fact that the snow was not of the same consistency throughout.

Nevertheless, it was a relief when the slope steepened into a face of well-compacted névé; step-cutting was arduous work, but it was consoling to know that an avalanche could not possibly occur. Maybe, I was over-anxious as to avalanches; though I have never been in an avalanche, except for a very minor slide of wet snow during the Kamet Expedition, I have a profound respect for Himalayan snow, which I have always regarded as far more dangerous and less easy to estimate than Alpine snow. Such snow must, of course, observe the same laws as Alpine snow, but the conditions in which it exists are extreme and the changes of temperature, due to the greater height of the sun and colder nights, more variable than in the Alps. It behoves the mountaineer, therefore, always to proceed with the utmost caution and pessimism is better than optimism when climbing on it.

The slope seemed interminable but at length the angle eased off and with great relief we stood at last on the crest of the North-East Ridge. This was comfortably broad and inclined at a moderate angle, and moving very slowly, for we were now very tired, we tramped along it. Ahead of us the ridge rose to a point. We could see nothing higher; surely this must be the summit? It was not. As we toiled up to it, we saw beyond, a long and weary way beyond, another point. Disgusted, we slumped down into the snow, breathing heavily, then, a minute later, I glanced cautiously over my shoulder; the summit was not nearly as far away as we had supposed. Distance and fatigue are inseparable at high altitudes. Nothing can appear more remote and inaccessible than the summit of Everest seen by an exhausted climber from a point only 1,000 feet below it, but at 28,000 feet the climber is permanently weary and rest has little effect on him or on his estimation of distance.

We heaved ourselves to our feet and recommenced the ascent; but we had not proceeded more than a few yards when a strong wind suddenly rose. So bitter and penetrating was it that we halted to huddle on every stitch of spare clothing, gloves and Balaclava helmets; thus muffled up we continued slowly to advance along the ridge, which had now attained to the quality and dimensions of a nightmare ridge along which the mountaineer is doomed to climb without ever getting to the end.

During the past hour the clouds had vanished from the immediate vicinity of

Nilgiri Parbat, and we became dimly aware of a superb vista extending in all directions. Hustled and blasted by the wind, we toiled on, but the mountain had one more surprise in store. As with leaden legs we breasted the top we had seen, once again it sprang up before us. But this time there was no mistake; the ridge stretched almost level for perhaps 200 yards, then suddenly narrowed into a blade, which swept upwards in a shining curve to end in a perfect point.

Once more we plumped down in the snow for a rest and once more we heaved ourselves to our feet and continued towards our goal. But there was now a different feeling – that snowy triangle lifting with mathematical exactitude into the blue was assuredly the summit.

We came to the point where the ridge narrowed and steepened. It was impossible to traverse a crest so delicate and thin, so driving in our ice axes and shuffling along sideways, with toes dug well in at every step, we advanced one by one. Thus we came to the summit. There was room on it for but one of us at a time. I well remember standing in the snow with my arms resting on it while surveying for a few moments a marvellous panorama. My memory is of an isolation and height comparable with far higher summits, for Nilgiri Parbat, like the Matterhorn, stands alone and there is no peak exceeding it in height within three or four miles. The atmosphere that day, probably because of an excess of water vapour, was blue; everything was blue, the sky profoundly blue, the hills, the shadows and the distances. In the north, storm clouds were banked up along the edge of Tibet and beneath them I could see the Tibetan plateau, and that was blue and level like an ocean, except for one minute point of white bisecting the horizon. The same ridiculous thought occurred simultaneously to Wangdi and me, but Wangdi was the first to voice it. 'Everest'. And indeed the peak, which cannot have been less than 200 miles distant, bore a strange resemblance to Everest.[1]

The wind was blowing hard across the ridge a few feet below the summit, but the summit itself was windless. In this oasis of calm we would willingly have lingered, but there was a long descent before us with the possibility of bad snow. Five minutes we spent on that fragile, unearthly crest, the most beautiful mountaintop I have ever visited, then began the descent.

Now that the need to lever our tired bodies uphill was done with we could appreciate the splendours on either hand: the great precipice which falls to the south and the walls of ice leaning over to the north, seeming almost to overhang the Banke Glacier thousands of feet beneath. The wind was no longer a tormentor and the sun smiled kindly as we strolled along the ridge, and on either side of our splendid path peaks and clouds glowed radiantly in the afternoon sun with an unsubstantial, ethereal beauty. We trod the very parapet of heaven.

And so, at length, the snow slopes. The upper snow was unaltered, the lower snow softened by the sun, which was now shining on the ice wall. We hurried past the lurching flake and made all haste to the plateau. Once Nurbu slipped – he was very tired – but Wangdi and I drove in our axes and stopped him before he had slid more than a few feet. On the edge of the plateau we found some rocks with a small trickle of water and I filled my cup again and again, for we were all terribly thirsty.

[1] Everest is about 400 miles distant from Nilgiri Parbat and would not, of course, be visible.

After a short rest, we traversed the ridge and descended the gully, and here we had a foretaste of what to expect lower down. On the way up we had cut steps, but now we sank almost to our knees into soft wet snow. With the possibility of an avalanche in my mind, I insisted on every precaution, and we descended one at a time keeping as close to the rocks as possible. The snow on the slopes below still retained a crust which would bear for a step or two if trodden very gently; then it broke and in we would go, knee-deep and often thigh-deep. We had not realised before this how tired we were, but the climb of 300 feet to the crest of the buttress was the hardest work of the day. Wangdi and I took turns at leading, but even Wangdi's amazing strength was on the wane, and he was as glad as I to relinquish the lead after a few minutes' ploughing through the waterlogged snow. The snow was even softer on the buttress crest, indeed so soft that, as it could hardly become worse, we halted for half an hour on some sun warmed rocks where Wangdi and Nurbu at last condescended to eat something, while I wrung out and attempted to dry my socks, which as usual had become sopping wet.

The sun was fast declining when we set off again. Wangdi wanted to descend the slope up which we had come from the bergschrund, and would not believe me when I told him it was dangerous, so, as an illustration; I rolled a snowball down it. In a yard or two this had attained to the dimensions of a cart-wheel, the weight of which set a wedge of snow in movement. The wedge widened and widened and within a second or two a slice of the slope fifty yards wide was sliding down to the bergschrund in a formidable avalanche, leaving bare ice in its wake. Wangdi was suitably impressed, at least I hope he was, and made no demur about descending the rock-ridge to one side of the slope. This was easy until we came to the bergschrund, above which it broke off in a steep little wall. But the rocks were not as difficult as they looked, and soon Wangdi, whom Nurbu and I let down on the full length of the rope, had found a bridge over the rift. That was the last difficulty, and the ridge and slopes to the glacier proved so easy that we were able to glissade part of the way.

As we walked across the little plateau above the ice fall, the shadows were creeping up the cliffs and séracs with the stealthy haste of sub-tropical night, but above and around was a rampart of sunlight, whence the great peak we had climbed stood up from a labyrinth of ice to cut a glowing wedge in the darkening blue.

At 7 p.m. we were welcomed by Pasang, who had thoughtfully prepared some tea. We could drink indefinitely, but none of us could eat; neither could we sleep, we were too tired, and hours later I lay awake going over in my mind the events of the day. We had climbed nearly 7,000 feet up a peak which remains unique in my recollection for its beauty and interest, indeed the finest snow and ice peak I have ever climbed. Much that is worthwhile in life had been packed into the space of thirteen hours, but from all that I remember the summit stands pre-eminent and I can picture it as though it were yesterday, simple, beautiful and serene in the sunlight, the perfect summit of the mountaineer's dreams.

CHAPTER SEVENTEEN

A Second Attempt on Rataban

AFTER OUR exertions on Nilgiri Parbat, we arrived tired at Base Camp on July 20: there I slept the clock round, that deep refreshing sleep that comes after the first effects of exceptional exertion have worn off. July 21 was the date that Peter Oliver was to join me, but he had written that he would probably be a day late. However, I decided to descend the valley a short distance to meet him in case he should be up to time.

Various flowers had put in an appearance during the past few days. Near the stream was growing a campion (*Silene tenuis*) and another plant very similar in appearance which turned out to be a *lychnis* (*L. apetala*) with a Chinese-lantern-like flower pendant on a thin stalk, whilst a creeping bellwort (*Codonopsis rotundifolia*) was twining itself about the stalks of large plants.

The *anemones* were past their prime, but a multitude of *geraniums*, *delphiniums*, *polemoniums*, *potentillas* and many smaller flowers filled my garden, as I had come to look upon it, with glowing colours.

It was a perfect morning as Nurbu and I strolled over the meadows. Arriving at the lower end of the gorge we scrambled up to the right through dense undergrowth, then over a series of striated slabs until we were able to see far down the valley. A little ledge formed an ideal belvedere and we spent three delightful hours basking in the sun and lazily watching the slow lights and shadows as the clouds passed.

Rhubarb grew near by and Nurbu munched away whilst I photographed a yellow shrubby *potentilla* (*P. fruticosa*) which grew in cracks and crannies of the neighbouring crags. A botanical miracle of high mountains is the manner in which every vestige of decay is seized upon by the roots of plants. Presumably birds have much to do with the distribution of seed, but the strong upward rising air currents from the valleys must play a major part in clothing the crags and mountainsides and account for the presence of flowers amid the eternal snows far from alp-land and meadow. The study of air currents and plant distribution in the Himalayas should disclose some interesting facts.

As Peter did not put in an appearance we returned to camp where I spent the remainder of the day attending to my pressed specimens, some of which had been affected by the monsoon damp. After so many delightful weeks, I felt almost depressed at the thought of leaving the Valley of Flowers, for I had discovered a never-ending delight in the growth of the marvellous garden that surrounded me. There are many virtues in wandering about the Himalayas, but to me the ideal life will always be a flowerful country where I can pitch my camp and settle down to observe all that happens about me. To the botanist there is a realm of interest and potential exploration in half a mile of hillside. I had not realised this before, and I remember with regret how often I hastened unseeing through valleys, my eyes fixed on the hilltops when at my feet was lying one half of interest and beauty.

Peter arrived next morning, having accomplished the march from Ranikhet in nine days. He had brought with him two Darjeeling men, in addition to the Dotials who had carried his heavy baggage. These were Tse Tendrup, a Tibetan, and Ang Bao, a Sherpa. Ang Bao (or "Babu" as his comrades called him) I remembered well, as he had carried my photographic apparatus during the 1936 Everest Expedition. He was the only Sherpa of the party and this was to his disadvantage, for though the Sherpas of the Sola Khumbu valley in Nepal are closely related to the Tibetans and are Buddhists by religion, there is nevertheless a subtle difference. The Sherpas are Tibetans who have emigrated from Tibet into the fertile valleys of northern Nepal close to the southernmost flanks of Everest. They are an exceptionally hardy race and natural mountaineers who have put up a magnificent showing on Everest and other Himalayan expeditions, but it is possible that the Tibetan, wedded to his bleak windswept plains, scorns these emigrants to warmer and pleasanter climes.

It may be that Ang Bao's youth, for he was little more than a boy, and natural willingness and good nature, made him the hewer of wood and drawer of water of the party; at all events the gulf between him and the Tibetans was manifest, and on more than one occasion we had to interfere to prevent the wholly unscrupulous Wangdi from saddling him with more than a fair share of work.

He was a little fellow with a round boyish face and somewhat sly eyes; but he was not in the least sly, and it was merely an ingrained diffidence and nervousness that caused him to falter in his gaze and look uneasily about him. He was not a great mountaineer, being naturally timid and clumsy, but he was a trier and a sticker to the nth degree. In one way he scored heavily over his companions, for he had acquired, probably at Ranikhet, a brand new pair of khaki riding breeches. They were fearfully tight at the knees and must have caused him prolonged suffering when marching or climbing, but if they did he never gave a sign, and whatever the menial tasks foisted upon him or the leg pulls he had to endure, there is no doubt that these breeches and their obvious superiority over all other garments possessed by the party preserved in him a feeling of superiority which stood him in good stead on many trying occasions.

Tse Tendrup I find difficult to describe, for he was one of those men who psychologically and physically are somehow always in the background. In a word he was unobtrusive. You could not imagine him being the focal point of a row or being riotously drunk or being unconventional in the smallest particular. He did his work well, but somehow one never thought about his doing it: I suppose it was because he did it well. He was a fair mountaineer, not rankly bad like Pasang or brilliantly good like Wangdi. Everything that he did was fair; he gave no trouble; he commanded no especial praise. Had he been born a European he might have lived in a suburb and travelled up to "Town" by train every day, worked at the same office, lunched at the same restaurant, and spent his fortnight's holiday at the same place, playing golf at the same handicap. It is strange to write of a Tibetan thus, for most people associate Tibet with strange and weird practices, and think of Tibetans as an altogether exciting not to say uncanny race. But I suppose there are ordinary conventional Tibetans just as there are ordinary conventional Englishmen and Tse Tendrup was one of them.

I have hesitated to describe my companion because a hide bound convention which surrounds mountaineering literature, perhaps more so than the literature of any other subject under the sun, decrees that your companion on a mountain shall remain only a name, a mere cypher which climbs to the summit and back again. On this occasion, however, I am going to violate convention, not to say tradition.

I have accompanied Peter Oliver in the Alps and on Everest. My most vivid memory is of climbing behind him while he cut or kicked steps up the slopes of the North Col in 1936. I remember thinking at the time that here was a man endowed with the physique and spirit of a George Leigh-Mallory. There was the same restless force and fine attunement of the nervous senses to the work in hand, the same exercising of imaginative and artistic qualities, always a surer passport to success in mountaineering and exploration than brute force. I have not the slightest doubt that many have eyed his spare frame, as they have eyed mine disparagingly, and wondered why something beefier and stronger could not be found for Everest. For the old traditions die hard and to the uninitiated the mountaineer is broad, strong and heavy, with the bunched and knotted muscles of a Sandow, and if he be naturally endowed with a beard of Assyrian luxuriance so much the better. It is hateful to debunk such cherished traditions, but the fact is, it is the lean, spare man who climbs best. Lastly, Peter is a genuine lover of the mountains and on such the mountains confer their greatest gifts.

That evening we discussed plans. Our main objective was Mana Peak, 23,860 feet. This is a near neighbour of Kamet and during the Kamet Expedition it had been the most striking peak of any in view. Now that Nanda Devi had been ascended by the Anglo-American Expedition, Mana Peak was the highest unscaled peak in the Garhwal Himalayas with the exception of the East and West Abi Gamin which form a part of the Kamet massif and are dull looking, somewhat shapeless mountains. But height alone did not influence our decision; Mana Peak is an outstandingly fine mountain, a great pyramid of red granite splendid to look up from all directions and conspicuous even from Ranikhet, some 100 miles distant. It is a difficult peak too, not only because of its steepness but because of the complex nature of the ridges and glaciers surrounding it. In 1931 it was agreed that to climb it from the East Kamet Glacier would involve an expedition with a greater number of camps than were required for Kamet, and that the ascent from this direction would be difficult, perhaps impossible. The remaining approaches are from the west, south and east, and of these that from the west, from the Saraswati Valley to the north of Badrinath and Mana, was evidently steep and intricate, whilst the report of members of the Kamet Expedition, who had explored some distance up the Banke Glacier to the south-east of the mountain, was scarcely encouraging.

Some weeks previously, however, I had received a very interesting letter from Lieut. R.A. Gardiner of the Survey of India, who had been surveying in the Banke Glacier area. He wrote that he had discovered a glacier system between the East Kamet and Banke Glaciers, of which the old map gave no indication, consisting in its uppermost portion of a series of snowfields forming what was virtually a plateau some six miles in length. Though he had not visited the westernmost snow fields he had climbed to a height of 20,000 feet on the ridge between the plateau and the East Kamet Glacier and was of the opinion that if three peaks on this ridge, of 21,400 feet, 22,481 feet and 22,892 feet, could be outflanked from the plateau and the East Ridge of the mountain reached, the summit should prove accessible. We decided, therefore, to follow his suggestion and first of all attempt the mountain from this direction, to do which it was necessary to cross the Bhyundar Pass, 16,688 feet, at the head of the Bhyundar Valley, and establish a base camp in the Banke Valley at about 14,000 feet. This plan, incidentally, would enable us to diverge *en route* to the snow col I had already visited and attempt the ascent of Rataban, an unwise suggestion on my part because Peter had only recently been at sea level and Rataban is a difficult mountain, 20,231 feet high, not an ideal training expedition for an unacclimatised mountaineer. Apart from this last scheme the proposed visit to the Banke Plateau had the advantage that, even if we failed to climb Mana Peak, there were some fine and probably accessible peaks in the vicinity of the plateau.

We estimated that we should require between two and three weeks' food, some of which, such as fresh meat and vegetables and coolie food, could be obtained from the village of Gamsali, at the junction of the Banke and Dhauli Valleys. With only five porters at our disposal, we had to jettison every unessential, with the exception of cameras and films, which I for one regard as essentials in mountaineering and exploration. It must, however, be added that some whisky which Peter had brought with him was also translated into the same category.

The smallness of our party was dictated by the cost of porterage. Also a small party accompanied by first-rate Sherpa or Bhotia porters is the superior of a large party, even on the greater peaks of the Himalayas, by virtue of its mobility and power to change plans at a moment's notice, thus seizing its opportunities without delay. Shipton is the high priest of the small Himalayan party, and certainly his expedition with H.W. Tilman in 1934 in the same district was an example of how much may be accomplished.

The flurry of packing and sorting over, the Dotials were sent off down the valley, and the Darjeeling men dispatched with the first relay of loads with instructions to dump them somewhere near the place where I had camped previously below the Bhyundar Pass, leaving Peter and myself to enjoy a lazy afternoon. The men were late in returning, so late that we became anxious for their safety, and went out to meet them. It was a pitchy night, but they arrived at last, having found the glacier very wearisome to negotiate owing to the snow having melted, exposing moraines and ice.

Next morning we left with the remainder of the loads. Despite the first relay, there was enough over to necessitate everyone carrying a heavy burden. I have never taken kindly to load carrying in the Himalayas and prefer to leave it to men who are used to it and think no more of 60 lbs. than I would of a day's food and equipment in the Alps. In a word, I prefer comfort to discomfort whenever possible. Hugh Ruttledge summed me up during the 1933 Everest Expedition when he called me a "blooming sybarite", only he did not use the word "blooming". No doubt I am, though I do not altogether fancy one dictionary definition of sybarite, "An effeminate voluptuary". In the present instance I was consoled to some extent by some pointed remarks of Peter's on the subject of his own load. It is always comforting to know that others are suffering too.

It was brilliantly sunny when we left Base Camp, but within two hours clouds had formed and a drizzling rain set in. The porters had dumped their loads at the foot of the slopes leading to the Bhyundar Pass and not at the old camping site, as they said that there was now no water there. As we were very damp outside we decided to counterbalance this by becoming equally damp inside, so we sat under a boulder and consumed an appreciable portion of the necessity already mentioned. The effect of this upon me was to make me sing. Fortunately no avalanche occurred.

Towards sunset the rain stopped and the mists cleared, revealing the rocky pile of Nilgiri Parbat, glowing in a green sky at a seemingly impossible height above us. Then Rataban appeared over the ragged lip of the nearby ice fall, but it was on the former peak that the sun lingered, and long after dusk had fallen and the stars brightened it continued to shine, at first gold, then silver, then miraculously gold again, as though the earth had reversed its rotation for a few minutes.

The following morning was warm and calm and we made rapid progress to the Bhyundar Pass, finding it unnecessary to rope for any part of the way. Just below the last gentle slope leading to it, we discovered a pleasant place which needed little preparation in order to pitch the tents. There were numerous flowers in the vicinity, including a yellow *corydalis* (*C. govaniana*) with slender feathery foliage, yellow *androsaces* and a number of golden-brown *sedums*.

In the late afternoon there was a heavy hailstorm accompanied by thunder. Thunderstorms are frequent in the foothills in the Himalayas, but seldom occur among the high mountains.

The weather did not recover its good humour during the night and the following morning was misty and grey. We waited some time for an improvement, but as this did not materialise, set off to the snow col, taking with us Wangdi, Pasang, Tewang and Tse Tendrup and leaving Nurbu and Ang Bao to bring up the remaining loads from the lower camp. We had not gone far before Tewang began to show evident signs of fatigue. Since I arrived in the Bhyundar Valley, he had had little or no exercise and I thought he was merely out of training, but when we got to the ice fall he suddenly collapsed and we then realised that he must be in a bad way to judge from the greenish colour of his face and his racing pulse. There was nothing for it but to send him back to the camp escorted by Wangdi and Pasang, while we carried on with Tse Tendrup.

The ascent was complicated by mist and drizzling snow, whilst the col, when at length we reached it, was bleak and bitterly cold with a mixture of hail and snow, carried along by a strong wind rushing across it. The three of us crowded into the single tent until Wangdi and Pasang arrived with the remaining tent and equipment, when we were able to warm our chilled bodies with a hot drink.

It was a miserable afternoon. We lay side by side in our sleeping bags in our little Meade tent which measured approximately six and a half feet in length and four feet in breadth, whilst the wind and snow drove furiously at the camp. The porters fared worse than we did, as their tent leaked, wetting their sleeping bags. This tent, which was strongly made and of thick material, had served its turn on Kamet, but as it was evidently unfit for further use at high altitudes we decided to scrap it at the first opportunity. Tents, like wind proof clothing, need to be replaced every season in the Himalayas, for the intensely powerful sun at high altitudes quickly damages canvas, whilst rapidly alternating heat and cold, dampness and dryness, put a considerable strain on any finely woven material.

At sundown, to our relief, the weather moderated and we were able to enjoy some pemmican soup cooked over a "Primus". After my luxurious days and nights in the Bhyundar Valley I cannot say I took kindly to sharing a tent, even with a boon companion, for there are certain penalties and restrictions attached to this: one cannot, for instance, light a candle in the middle of the night and charm away some sleepless hours with a book, whilst kicking or tossing about is regarded unsympathetically; but thank heavens for one thing, neither of us snored.

The eastern sky was clear at dawn, but heavy clouds were massing over the Alaknanda Valley and the Badrinath Peaks. However, there was no immediate reason why we should not attempt the ascent of Rataban, the summit of which cannot be more than 2,500 feet above the col. With the prospect of some difficult climbing and in all probability iced rocks it was inadvisable to start too early, and we did not leave the camp until eight o'clock, when the weather was excellent.

As already mentioned, the direct ascent of the north ridge from the snow col is impracticable, or at all events desperately difficult, and the one possibility of climbing the mountain from this direction is to force a route to the upper part of the ridge by one or other of a series of rock ribs on the steep North-West Face. With this end in view we traversed more or less horizontally from the camp, making for a rib which I had previously decided, when examining the peak, was the most likely line of attack. To gain this we crossed a bergschrund, which offered little difficulty, then climbed diagonally over a steep slope of well-frozen snow. The rib to begin with was not particularly difficult and the rock, a granite material, was firm and delightful to climb, but it was slow going on the whole and for the most part we could move only one at a time.

The ridge ended against a rock band, perhaps 200 feet high and slanting from west to east across the face of the mountain. The rocks were sheer, even overhanging, and their yellow and red edges bit brutally into the sky. The one possibility of climbing them was to the right; once above the band a minor rib should lead up to the crest of the North Ridge above the impassable section whence the climbing lies over snow to the summit. It was a difficult and exposed traverse. Moving one at a time and belaying carefully at every rope length, we edged along a series of minute ledges until we came to a well-defined chimney. This we attempted to climb, but it was altogether too strenuous, whilst an overhang at the top demanded a pull on the arms on to unknown and doubtful ground, a pull which would be unjustifiable at any altitude let alone at nearly 20,000 feet. The alternative was to cross the chimney and continue the traverse past a corner. It was an awkward movement and meant edging along in the position of a man crucified. Thence after a steep climb we came to an ill-defined ridge of snow and rock that appeared to lead continuously to the crest of the North Ridge. The greatest difficulty had been overcome and it now remained to be seen whether there was sufficient time to reach the summit and return.

As Peter followed round the corner I noticed that he was climbing slowly and with increasing effort. It was no surprise to me, therefore, when he announced that he was feeling very tired and that he did not think he would be able to continue if the difficulties persisted. He suggested, however, that I should carry on for another rope length to determine whether we could reach the ridge without great difficulty, for once on it he felt that he might be able to continue to the summit should it prove merely a snow-plug. I followed his suggestion, but merely with the idea of prospecting the route for a future occasion, as I knew there was no justification for continuing in such circumstances and, incidentally, we were climbing for pleasure.

After kicking steps up steep snow, and climbing an awkward rock pitch, I saw from the crest of the latter that the rib we were on continued to the North Ridge of the mountain and that while there were no insuperable obstacles the difficulties were considerable. Having noted this, I returned to Peter and we rested for a few minutes. It was disappointing to fail when the peak was almost within our grasp, but it was no fault of Peter's; the fault was mine and mine alone. I do not suppose any mountaineer has tackled such difficulties at a similar altitude within a fortnight of being at sea level, and it was foolish of me to suggest the climb, though in my own defence I must state that I had not for a moment anticipated such difficulties as we had encountered. As it was, Peter had put up a magnificent performance in reaching a height of about 19,500 feet after an outstandingly difficult and exacting climb.

Providence walks in many guises. As we slowly descended the sun vanished in a chaos of leaden vapour and within half an hour snow was falling heavily. Had this storm overtaken us near the summit we should have been hard put to it to retreat safely; as it was the snow filled the interstices of the rocks of the lower rib and rendered the climbing unpleasant, not to say difficult.

When ascending a peak, the mountaineer tends to underestimate the steepness of the climbing, and his mind, particularly when he is on new and intricate ground, is occupied with the technical details of his craft, but during the descent he is better able to appreciate the steepness and grandeur of a mountainside. The present instance was no exception, and I do not believe either of us realised until we descended the formidable nature of the face we had climbed. Peter said that it was the hardest and steepest climb he had done in the Himalayas.

The hour or two of warm and sunny weather we had enjoyed during the ascent had softened the snow on the slope by which we had ascended to the rib, and as there was ice below it, to have descended safely would have meant much step-cutting. We abandoned it, therefore, in favour of continuing down the rib. This last part of the descent was disagreeable, for the rocks were not only running with slush and water, but shaley and loose into the bargain. Furthermore, we were wet and cold and the rope had become exasperatingly stiff and sodden with water. To Peter, who was feeling very tired, it must have been a very trying descent, but he gave no hint of this and was a pillar of strength on more than one awkward slope where everything was loose and there were no belays for the rope.

As we neared the foot of the rib, we heard distant shouts from the porters intended to guide us to the camp through the snowstorm. The rib, which had seemed interminable, ended at last, and to our great relief we were able to cross the bergschrund without difficulty. Thenceforward we ploughed through the soft snow of the glacier and preceded by loud and oft reiterated demands for chha (tea) eventually reached the camp, soaked and bedraggled.

It had been a hard not to say anxious climb and we were thankful to be off the mountain. We agreed as we poured steaming tea into our chilled bodies that everything had worked out for the best. Nothing was to be gained by prolonging our stay, especially as the snow col formed a natural funnel for every wind that blew, and after a meal we packed up the wet tents and hastened down to the camp near the Bhyundar Pass.

Thus ended my second attempt to climb Rataban. It may be that the mountain is more easily accessible from the south or east, though from what I have seen this appears very questionable, but if it is ever my fortune to attempt it again I should follow the same route; although very steep and difficult, it is, I am convinced, entirely practicable and will afford a magnificent climb to the summit of this grand peak.*

CHAPTER EIGHTEEN

The Banke Plateau

AFTER OUR unsuccessful attempt to climb Rataban we proceeded to carry out the next part of our programme, and it was decided to cross the Bhyundar Pass without delay and pitch a base camp in the Banke Valley from which to push up a series of camps on to the plateau whence we hoped to attempt the ascent of Mana Peak.

When we returned to our camp near the Bhyundar Pass we found that Tewang had not recovered from his indisposition and was now complaining of a pain in his chest. I took his temperature and was aghast to find it only 95.2° He must be seriously ill if not at death's door. To make certain, I took it again and the laggard mercury rose to normal. This little medical detail satisfactorily settled, the patient was ordered to remain in his sleeping bag and the onerous task of cooking was handed over to Ang Bao.

All the stores were now at the camp. We had planned to relay them over the Bhyundar Pass into the Banke Valley, but the men were very averse to this, as they did not want to return to the pass, and next morning Wangdi said that they would prefer to carry double loads. This meant well over 100 lbs. per man; it also meant that Peter and I had to carry as much as we could manage and we eventually set off with at least 60 lbs. apiece.

The passage of the Bhyundar Pass is not difficult, but care is necessary when descending the icefall on the east side. Here Wangdi attempted, as usual, to make a better route than we, and proceeded to lead the men across a dangerous ice slope seamed with crevasses and loaded with loose stones. We shouted to him to

* Rataban was climbed on August 8, 1939, from the Kosa Valley to the east, by Ernst Huber, Nima VI and Mourcoulia, members of a Swiss expedition led by André Roch. This expedition also climbed Gauri Parbat, Hathi Parbat and six other summits in the Kosa/Rataban cirque.

return and follow our route, which he eventually did, and when he came up with us Peter gave him a dressing down, which I fear was entirely without effect as Wangdi is constitutionally unable to differentiate between safety and danger on a mountain.

Below the icefall we descended a slope of screes where we came across a beautiful *delphinium* (*D. densiflorum*) growing in close-packed spires of flowers not more than a foot high. How it lodged in this desolate situation with nothing but stones to root in is a mystery.

From the screes a steep snow-slope led down to the glacier well below the icefall where, as was only to be expected, Pasang did his inevitable *pas seul*, or his famous imitation of a sack of coals sliding down a chute into a cellar. Once on the glacier we had a dull and fatiguing trudge over ice and moraines to its junction with the Banke Glacier. Here there was a marked change in scenery. The Bhyundar Valley is moist and fertile, but the Banke Valley is drier, stonier and barer, and its ochre-coloured rock reminds the mountaineer that he is only a few miles south of the main Himalayan watershed and the Tibetan border. Without a doubt it receives much less rain than the Bhyundar Valley, the reason being that the latter runs from south-west to north-east and is linked with the Alaknanda Valley, which forms a natural channel for the monsoon air current, whereas the Banke Valley runs east-south-east to west-north-west and is linked with the upper part of the Dhauli Valley, into which the monsoon current does not penetrate with the same power that it does into the Alaknanda Valley. I expected, therefore, to find a less luxuriant plant life and one characteristic of a drier climate.

The Banke Glacier, like the majority of the main Himalayan ice streams, is covered in moraines for the greater part of its length and presents a dreary but not unimpressive spectacle of mountain decay. We followed to begin with a side moraine of the glacier we had descended, a delightful bank forming a home for innumerable *potentillas*, *androsaces*, *saxifrages* and *sedums*. I found nothing new until I came to some little rosettes of fleshy leaves, from the centre of which flower shoots were emerging, which I knew must be a house leek (*Sempervivum mucronatum*). I selected a specimen for my press, and so potent was the power locked up in this little plant that it continued to send out its flower shoot for a full two or three more inches in spite of the weight and pressure applied to it.

It was a tedious crossing of the glacier, over innumerable mounds of moraine, some of them fully 100 feet high, but it was made interesting by the plants which grew even in this barren wilderness of shattered rock, and I came upon many *allardias*, both the large and small varieties, their pink flowers warm and cosy amid silver cotton-wool-like foliage.

By the time we had reached the other side of the glacier our loads seemed even heavier than before and we were thankful to pitch the base camp on a shelf at about 14,000 feet, between two shepherds' bivouacs known as Thur Udiar and Eri Udiar (Cold Cave). There was plenty of fuel in the shape of juniper bushes close at hand, and it was altogether a delightful spot as the ridge immediately above the camp formed a natural rock garden.

Soon after our arrival a shepherd, Alam Singh by name, appeared with the remains of two sheep, which he explained had been killed by a rock fall. As the meat appeared quite fresh we purchased it and afterwards, having discovered that he had an assistant to mind his flocks in his absence, sent him down the valley to Gamsali to purchase vegetables and, if possible, milk.

Tewang, unfortunately, was still unwell and once again the cooking fell upon Ang Bao, who, unexpectedly, proved capable of turning out excellent chupatties. As a rule I find this particular form of unleavened bread exceedingly indigestible and for that reason had provided myself with biscuits for my stay in the Bhyundar Valley, but it was now necessary to live as far as possible off the country. I think it was General Bruce who once remarked that chupatties made of native flour acted like sand paper on the inside, though whether he intended this eulogistically or as a warning I did not discover. At all events I have never eaten sandpaper so am not in a position to judge. The General had visited Garhwal in 1907, accompanied by Dr. T.G. Longstaff and the late A.L. Mumm, and his name is legendary along the Himalayas, particularly among the Gurkhas. In such veneration is he regarded that a story is told of an old lady of Mana who asked to be allowed to drink the water he had washed in, as by so doing she would acquire merit and be cured of her various ailments.

Next day was necessarily a rest day, for we had worked hard, and it was only fair to the porters after their great effort. To save time on the morrow, when we hoped to push the first of our camps up towards the Banke Plateau, I spent the afternoon reconnoitring the approach.

Lieut. Gardiner had written that the only practicable route to the plateau lay to the east of Peak 19,212 feet, climbed by Eric Shipton in 1931. The plateau is cunningly concealed, and the only indication that an extensive glacier system exists to the north of the Banke Glacier is afforded by a steep and broken icefall, which descends to join the glacier. Thus it is easily understandable why no one had previously suspected the existence of the plateau. Gardiner had given no exact details as to the route to be followed, but from the camp it appeared as though this must lie to one side or the other of a steep and narrow gorge. The crags immediately above the camp were disagreeably loose and shaley, so I climbed the slope to the west of the gorge, halting on the way to admire a large white anemone with a golden centre (*A. rupicola*) which covered the hillside in its millions. The slope ended in a ridge clad in juniper against the dark foliage of which galaxies of flowers; *potentillas*, *androsaces*, *anemones*, *polygonums* and *geraniums* made brilliant splashes of colour.

From this point I was forced into the upper part of the narrow and wall-sided gorge and, following a little break across the cliffs, was presently able to make my way almost directly upwards over a series of awkwardly dipping slabs, which were broken at about two-thirds of their height by a small wall.

There were good handholds and I was soon up, emerging from the gorge on to a beautiful little alp, ablaze with flowers, of which *geraniums*, *potentillas* and *polygonums* formed the majority. But the rock gardener must needs turn from such flamboyant beauty to the humble little plants that seek refuge amidst the crags, and on the crest of the cliff I had climbed I found a cushion-plant with a host of white flowers with yellow and red throats (*Androsace Chamaejasme*). For my part, I would not readily exchange the exotic gardens of a Mogul Emperor for a sight of these little plants that lift their starry heads close to the eternal snows.

It was a beautiful afternoon, for the weather had recovered its good humour, and I spent a delightful hour on the alp, lounging on my back amid the flowers and looking across the Banke Glacier to the ice-crowned precipices of Rataban gleaming in the afternoon sun as though built of liquid but immobile silver.

I did not return by the way I had come, but by another route, which crossed the alp above the gorge, and after traversing a narrow ledge, descended pastry-like rocks and steep screes to the camp.

That evening we made ourselves comfortable round a fire of juniper. This shrub has a smell, which I shall always associate with travel in the Himalayas, and I have only to sniff the smoke of it to be transported in an instant back to the campfire. Someone threw some branches into the centre of the fire, and with a roaring crackle a great gust of flame illumined the faces of my companions. The tents stood out sharply and in the background the dim hillsides rose on their long climb towards the stars.

Alam Singh arrived back soon after dark, bringing with him onions, flour and a spinach-like vegetable, but alas no chickens or eggs. More porters' food was required, and it was arranged that Tewang, who was obviously unfit for high altitude work, should descend to Gamsali for it and hire a porter to carry it up, whilst Alam Singh was engaged to transport wood to the lower camps, as it was necessary to husband our petrol and paraffin.

We were off at 7 next morning in doubtful-looking weather. On the slopes below the gorge we halted to collect juniper, after which I ascended the side of the gorge, taking some rope with me, whilst Peter remained below to shepherd the men, whose heavy loads made the ascent very awkward for them. It was not thought necessary to rope them until they reached the point where the route lay straight up the wall of the gorge, but I realised that this was a mistake when I saw Ang Bao struggling to hoist himself and his load up a place which was entirely without difficulty for an unladen man. Peter could not see this from his position, nor could he hear my shouts, owing to the roar of the torrent. With great anxiety I watched the little man striving, desperately to balance up on a foothold over a sheer 200-foot drop, and great was my relief when I saw him reach safety. He was evidently a poor rock climber or else overloaded, for the other men made light of the place. Peter roped the men together and I threw them down the end of the 100-foot rope. After this it was plain sailing and at length everyone was on the alp, except Alam Singh, who resolutely refused to have anything to do with the rope, for which he obviously entertained the gravest suspicion, and who eventually succeeded in scaling in his bare feet an entirely different route to the right over some smooth and awkward slabs.

The ascent to the alp had occupied well over two hours, as against the half-hour I had taken when climbing by myself. Such transport difficulties all too often lead to modification of plans in the Himalayas, and so it was in this instance. The preliminary difficulty seemed to have taken the heart out of the men and they climbed very slowly up the easy slopes above the alp. Alam Singh was even slower, and found it necessary to sit down and rest about every fifty yards. It was exasperating when we were anxious to get on and place our first camp as near to the plateau as possible. Presently, mists gathered, and drizzling rain began to fall.

The flowers were interesting and beautiful. I well remember a rocky place, where water seeped over some slabs, tufted a brilliant green with moss between which, in cracks of the rock, bloomed thousands of yellow *androsaces*. Then, in the screes, were many plants of the same *delphinium* we had seen below the Bhyundar Pass and in turfy places numerous *sedums*, with here and there a woolly *saussurea*. But the most striking flower of all was a *pleurospermum* (*P. candollii*). An illustration, even a coloured illustration, would probably convey the impression that this flower is interesting rather than beautiful yet of the many flowers that I saw in Garhwal, there was none that attracted me more. It is one foot or less in height and at the end of a stout and hollow stem the flower stalks branch outwards in all directions, supporting wide-open white flowers delicately frilled at the edges and with numerous stamens ending in dark-coloured anthers. Nothing remarkable you may say, but you must see this plant on a misty day, when it seems to attract the distant sunlight to itself, so that its thin almost transparent petals glow as though illumined from behind. Even if you have little or no interest in flowers, it demands that you pause and pay tribute to its beauty and to the Divinity that raised it among the barren rocks.

We camped at about 15,500 feet, much lower than we had hoped, on a stony desolate place near the steep tongue of a minor glacier. Everyone was wet and miserable, and Peter and I came to the conclusion that we should have to lighten the loads considerably on the morrow and work out in detail a system of relays, else we should not succeed in getting anywhere near Mana Peak. Rain continued to fall steadily for the remainder of the day, but we had a tent each, which was some comfort. I lay in my sleeping bag reading Mr. Richard Aldington's cynical book "Death of a Hero". It is an admirable work but I should have preferred Mr. P.G. Wodehouse on this occasion. Ang Bao evidently found the conditions equally depressing, for he did not shine as a cook that evening and the formless lumps of mutton he produced were only fit to strop a kukri. As a result Peter and I had a bad night; I did not sleep at all but lay awake, as I often used to lie awake on Everest at much greater heights, marvelling at my folly for voluntarily exchanging the comforts of civilisation for the discomforts of the high mountains. Many have marvelled thus, yet they return; no one has ever satisfactorily explained why.

The weather was still misty next morning but the rain had stopped. Having sent back Alam Singh, who was more of a hindrance than a help, and sorted out the food and equipment we were to take on with us, we set off to the plateau.

Our way lay up a bold moraine on which numerous plants grew, including *Androsace chamaejasme* and a delightful *saxifrage* (*S. hirculus*) with yellow petals red at the base and stems covered in rust-coloured hairs.

The moraine ended in a snowy corridor which brought us without difficulty to the foot of a glacier tongue of bare ice, where Peter, who was thirsting for some step-cutting, went ahead and hewed out a staircase. It took an hour to get the men up, after which we found ourselves on a snowfield. Ascending this we halted for some food on a patch of rocks then continued across another snowfield, which is separated from the main icefall of the plateau by a ridge where we saw a cairn, evidently erected by Gardiner. We followed this ridge for a short distance, then traversed horizontally to the plateau, which is here considerably crevassed and broken and which as already mentioned, is a glacier system with a series of snowfields at its head. We were able to avoid the crevasses by ascending snow-slopes under an overhanging rock face and presently came to a shelf formed by the lower lip of a wide crevasse, a short distance below the first major snowfield. Here we decided to camp, as the day was well advanced, the weather was once again deteriorating and the men had to return to the first camp by a route which might be difficult to follow in the event of a blizzard. Our tents were pitched entrance to entrance for the sake of convenience, and after we had collected some water from a stream on the neighbouring cliff we retired to our sleeping bags.

Snow fell lightly for the remainder of the afternoon. I cooked the supper. I cannot remember exactly what I cooked, but I suspect it was a hash of some kind. I am rather good at hashes. There is nothing difficult or niggling about them, no take this and take that and weigh this and weigh that; yet there is a complex grandeur in my hashes which Mrs. Beeton at her best could hardly hope to emulate. My record hash was compounded of eighteen ingredients; I remember it well because I was sick afterwards.

Cooking in a small tent is a filthy business. To begin with, it has to be performed while lying in a sleeping bag. This affords scope for a professional contortionist, and it often happens that when balancing some tinful of liquid in an awkward and constrained position, one is seized by a violent attack of cramp. But I anticipate; first of all the stove must be lit, and not only lit but kept alight. We had a "Primus" with a burner adapted for use at high altitudes. A "Primus" is far and away the best cooker for Himalayan mountaineering and is infinitely better than a methylated or solid methylated cooker, but good though it is, it is subject to its high altitude tantrums, and if you endeavour to light it too soon, it fills the tent with noisome fumes which send you coughing and choking into the open air. The tremendous temptation to pump it vigorously to start with must be resisted, for this is a cardinal mistake; the burner fights for a fleeting instant then goes out and a vast cloud of smoke rises like a volcanic blast from the apparatus: strike a match incautiously and the tent is liable to explode. A "Primus" must be humoured, and be worked up gently to do its job. It may be cajoled, but never bullied. It suffers from only one ailment, a more or less chronic quinsy, and it is advisable to have an instrument known as a pricker handy in case, at a critical moment when the hash is nicely simmering, it chokes and suffocates. Its digestion is remarkably good, and it can assimilate with equal ease paraffin, petrol or a mixture of both these fuels. Whether it is as accommodating as a Diesel engine I do not know; I have not yet tried one with whisky, brandy, lubricating oil or treacle.

After dark the sky cleared suddenly, revealing a starlit expanse of glacier, and the dim forms of peaks beyond it. The night was very cold, the coldest we had yet had, and a damp chill struck up from the snow through the floors of our tents.

At 4 a.m. I set the "Primus" going and we breakfasted. The sky was unclouded and dawn showed calmly behind a range of sharp rock-peaks. The sun struck the camp at 5.15, and a few minutes later we left, intending to reconnoitre and if possible climb an unnamed peak of 21,400 feet on the ridge separating the plateau from the East Kamet Glacier, the view from which should enable us to form an opinion as to whether the two higher peaks of 22,481 feet and 22,892 feet between it and Mana Peak could be outflanked.

After zigzagging between crevasses we came to the first of the major snowfields, whence we saw that the peak was obviously accessible from a col immediately to the east of it and between it and Peak 20,557 feet. We were now able to appreciate for the first time the beauty and extent of the plateau. Westwards it stretched beneath Peak 21,400 feet to the foot of an icefall above which there was evidently a further snowfield, and southwards we looked over a snowy rim and the concealed Banke Valley to Rataban, Gauri Parbat, Hathi Parbat and the far blue ridges of Trisul, Dunagiri and Nanda Devi.

Having crossed the snowfield, we followed a ridge of broken rocks where we came upon one of Gardiner's camp sites, and a two-gallon tin of petrol more than half full. This was a godsend as it meant that fuel rationing was no longer necessary.

From the surveyors' camp we ascended some rocks and trudged up a snow-slope. Conditions were excellent and we climbed fast, perhaps too fast for I developed a headache and felt slightly sick, though I suspect this was due to the fumes of the "Primus" which filled my tent while I was cooking the breakfast.

Although the surveyors had ascended these slopes several weeks previously their tracks were still distinct, a proof that only a small quantity of snow had fallen in this district during the early months of the summer. At the head of the snow-slope on the ridge overlooking the East Kamet Glacier is a small island of rock which had been visited by Gardiner and had probably served as one of his survey stations, as it commands a superb view. From it we looked down a precipice over 3,000 feet high to the East Kamet Glacier, which, with its sinuous curves and level lines of moraines, resembled some vast arterial road. At the head of it stood Kamet in all its superb beauty and majesty. It was the finest view I have ever had of the mountain and I could trace out the route by which we had climbed it in 1931. Five of a party of six Europeans had reached the summit, together with two porters of whom the Sirdar, Lewa, had been so badly frostbitten that he had lost all his toes. That was the only unhappy memory, but it would take more than the loss of toes to dishearten or incapacitate a man of Lewa's calibre and he had accompanied the 1933 Everest Expedition.

I had not anticipated when I climbed Kamet that a few years later I should be attempting the equally fine Mana Peak. From our position the peak was plainly visible beyond three intervening peaks, the 21,400-foot peak which rose immediately above us, and the two peaks of 22,481 feet and 22,892 feet. As we had anticipated, there was no hope whatever of outflanking these to the north for all fell sheer to the East Kamet Glacier thousands of feet below. The wall bounding that glacier to the south extends for a distance of seven or eight miles, and is unassailable from the north. Ours was a unique position on the crest of it, yet in a depression which enabled us to appreciate to the full the grandeur of ice-cliff and precipice down which avalanches roar and smoke, whilst close at hand was the névé of Peak 21,400 feet, riven and rent into square-cut turrets the size of cathedrals – altogether a splendid scene of mountain savagery and frigid beauty.

A cold little wind presently decided us to continue with the ascent of Peak 21,400 feet. There was no difficulty whatsoever in the climb, which lay up a slope of snow about 1,200 feet in height. As we had ascended very quickly to the ridge we decided to go slowly, and taking turns at the step-making mounted at the rate of about 1,000 feet an hour. As we climbed the sky clouded over and by the time we reached the summit, which consists of an almost level snowfield an acre or two in extent, a level canopy of cloud truncated all the higher peaks to the south and east. Yet if the view in most directions was disappointing, there was one mountain, which showed to great advantage, Nilgiri Parbat. Only the uppermost portion was visible, the great slope on which Wangdi, Nurbu and I had laboured so long, but it seemed to float up in the mist sunlit and serene, as though annexed permanently to the heavenly regions.

Unfortunately we could see little of the plateau or the ridges to the west of our peak. Soon mists began to form about us, and a cold damp wind rustled across the snow. There was no object in prolonging our stay and in five minutes we pelted down slopes that had taken over an hour to climb, then strolled back to the camp.

It was typical monsoon weather: a fine morning, then rapidly forming mists, and a snowstorm in the afternoon, which rendered the remainder of the day in camp thoroughly disagreeable. As previously arranged, three of the men, Wangdi, Pasang and Tse Tendrup, had ascended from the first camp with a second relay of loads, leaving Ang Bao and Nurbu to descend to the base camp for the extra coolie food which was being brought up from Gamsali.

The advent of the porters meant that we needed no longer to cook for ourselves. The chief objection to cooking in the high Himalayas, apart from the work it involves, is the mess and the dirt, and the floor of a tent soon becomes filthy with congealed samples of various foods. The carbon formed by burning petrol and paraffin is peculiarly obnoxious in this respect. Washing is impracticable, as water obtained by melting snow over a cooker is far too precious to be used thus, and the skin quickly becomes ingrained with dirt whilst fingernails go into profound mourning. But my most disagreeable memory in connection with this business of eating and drinking at high altitudes is of washing up. This is accomplished by rubbing the pots, pans, plates and other utensils with snow, a chilly, uncomfortable and altogether loathsome task. Sherpa and Bhotia porters, on the other hand, regard cooking from an entirely different angle. Like children they love to be given opportunities of making a first class mess. I honestly believe that these men are positively unhappy if accommodated in a clean tent and told not to dirty it, in which respect they resemble the slum-dweller, who when transferred to a new tenement promptly proceeds to use the bath as a convenient receptacle for coal. Another thing that the Himalayan porter loves is a fug in his tent, and there is no doubt that cooking greatly assists in the formation of this. On such an occasion, the interior of a porter's tent must be experienced to be believed, for the atmosphere generated is of such density that it seems almost possible to cut it up into lumps and throw it out of the entrance. This love of a fug is common among mountain folk and mountaineers. To my mind, people who pretend to revel in draughts and cold rooms, who impinge on their friends at the breakfast table with a horrible heartiness and in general adopt such manners and costumes as are most likely to impress on all and sundry their hardihood and devotion to the open air, ought to be put away in some special fresh air asylum where they may indulge their horrid practices to their hearts' content.

Perhaps the greatest menace of all is the man, and not infrequently the woman, who insists on filling an already freezing railway carriage with a violent draught, then revels like the sadist he is in the acute discomfort of his fellow passengers. The Direktion of the Lindenalp Railway settled this vexed question once and for all when they put up the notice:

> In the event of a dispute between passengers as to whether the window shall be open or shut, the dispute shall be referred to the conductor, and the window then shut.

I think it was Dr. Howard Somervell who told me that he was once travelling in comfort with the window shut when an old gentleman got in at a station and, after fidgeting and shuffling in that manner peculiar to a fresh air fiend, said irascibly: 'I really must insist on that window being opened.' Had he spoken politely, no doubt a compromise would have been effected: as it was the window remained shut. This led to a tirade in which such expressions as 'Degenerate young men of the present day' were employed freely. It is a pity that this indignant old gentleman got out at the next station without knowing that he was speaking to one of the toughest and finest mountaineers of the post-war era who had only recently returned from an Everest Expedition. If he has not since died of chronic bronchitis, pneumonia or rheumatic fever, I hope that he will chance upon these lines.

Next morning, August 2, we set out to establish another camp. The weather was in poor shape and in a thick mist we groped our way up the first snowfield, steering with the aid of a compass and a detailed and excellent sketch-map supplied by Gardiner. Without the latter, it is probable that we should have kept too far to the south and have got into difficulty on Peak 20,087 feet, which rises, from the southernmost edge of the plateau. As it was we were able to make our way through the icefall above the first snowfield to another snowfield, which lies to the south of Peak 21,400 feet. Now and again, when the mists thinned, we could see the slopes of this peak to our right, and were careful to keep well away from the base of it, in case of ice avalanches.

We took it in turns to lead and Peter steered a skilful course through the crevasses of the icefall, but when my turn came on the snowfield above, I was soon told that I was describing a circle. One reason for bearing off the compass course was the unexpected presence of steep slopes where we had expected none. There was no debris on the glacier to indicate that ice avalanches fall from these, but it seemed advisable to keep well away from them. Up to this point we had made, as was revealed later, an excellent line, but we were now beyond the point we had seen during the previous day's climbing and also, we believed, beyond the farthest point reached by Gardiner. All about us was mist and a waste of snow, and not a landmark was to be seen. Our position was analogous to that of a blind man searching for a black cat on a dark night. Nothing was to be gained by blundering on, and we decided to camp until the weather cleared, so our single tent was pitched and the porters sent back to the second camp.

It was an unusual experience, to camp without knowing in the least where we were, and we awaited the lifting of the mists with a feeling akin to that of a child who is all agog for the curtain to rise on the first act of a pantomime. We had not very long to wait.

At 4 p.m. the mists began to break up; a rift of sky showed and against it a sunlit edge of snow. Quickly now the mists melted away, and the almost level snowfield on which we were camped shone out in virgin splendour and beauty.

Immediately to the west of the camp was a snow-ridge easily accessible at one point where it sank down almost to the level of the snowfield, and we set out to investigate what lay beyond it.

The sun was fast sinking as we mounted a slope to a shallow col in the ridge. The view from this col is forever impressed on my memory. The ridge runs roughly from north to south and is interposed between the snowfield on which our camp was pitched and a snowfield enclosed between Peaks 21,400 feet and 22,481 feet. The last mentioned snowfield is not part of the glacier up which we had come, but forms the head of a glacier descending to join the Banke Glacier.

From the col, a slope about 200 feet in height falls to an extraordinarily steep and broken icefall in which the snowfield breaks away at its southernmost edge. Mist still lay below our level and now and then tongues of it licked up the ice-fall between towers of ice to be illumined suddenly and brilliantly by the reddening sun, so that the ice-fall flamed and smoked like a witch's cauldron.

The snowfield above the icefall afforded a superb contrast to this savage and uneasy scene, for its level and unbroken expanse stretched calm and serene like a cloth of pure silver. At its westernmost extremity Peak 22,481 feet stood deeply shadowed with a thin wispy cloud, brilliantly sunlit, stealing across it. Here and there other clouds were stationary in a sky of turquoise-blue, like yachts waiting for a fair wind, and in the south enormous masses and banks of monsoon cumulus were ranged along the distant foothills and the peaks of Nanda Devi.

As the sun slipped down behind Peak 22,481 feet the vast snowfields about us glowed with an unearthly light. It was a scene that might have been borrowed from an Antarctic plateau and we had much the same feeling of remoteness that the Polar explorer experiences, for no valleys were visible and we gazed over unending wastes of snow and ice, a superlatively majestic vista as restful to the spirit as it was cruel and hostile to the flesh.

We returned to camp moderately satisfied with our reconnaissance. The snowfield we had seen was easily accessible, but as to what lay beyond it and whether Peak 22,481 feet could be turned to the south, we could only conjecture. Was there another snowfield between it and Peak 22,892 feet? If so, would it be possible to traverse this to the East Ridge of Mana Peak? It was evident that we should have to lengthen our communications considerably and another two camps at least would be necessary. Taking all in all our chances of climbing Mana Peak from this direction were now very remote.

CHAPTER NINETEEN

Peak 22,481 Feet

THE IMPROVEMENT in the weather was only temporary, and next morning mist again concealed everything. Inactivity was distasteful, and though we should not in any event be able to pitch a fourth camp until the morrow, as the porters would be occupied in relaying stores from the second camp, we decided to make certain of the route to the snowfield. Accordingly, we re-ascended the col and followed the sharp crest of the snow-ridge to the north of it until we came to a place whence it was possible to descend to the snowfield above the icefall.

The porters arrived during the day, so that everything was ready to advance the camp on the morrow. Once again the mists cleared and a calm evening was succeeded by a night of intense frost. August 4 dawned brilliantly clear and we were off at 6.30. An inch or so of snow had fallen in the past two or three days, and this had frozen into a light crystalline powder that glittered and sparkled in the sun. It was a morning to delight a photographer, and Peter and I busied ourselves with our cameras during the traverse of the ridge on to the snowfield. Every vestige of haze had disappeared and all of the greater peaks were visible, including Trisul, Nanda Devi and the mountains in the neighbourhood of the Milam Glacier. The finest of all the peaks in the vicinity of the Banke Glacier was Nilgiri Parbat. Mists swathed its lower shoulders, but the upper ice-slope, now so familiar, stood out above them like a tempestuous wave, frozen as it was about the curl over and break. Seldom is the photographer presented with such perfect lighting and beautifully arranged composition and though no photograph can do justice to the grandeur and ethereal beauty of such a scene the photograph I was able to secure does suggest the splendour of this noble mountain.

As we trudged across the snowfield I was reminded of a similar trudge early one morning in the Bernese Oberland over the Ewigschneefeld, for there is a strong similarity between the "Field of Eternal Snow" and this Himalayan snowfield.

The snowfield sloped gently to the west for three-quarters of the distance, then more steeply to another minor ridge at the foot of Peak 22,481 feet. We gained the ridge without difficulty, and looked expectantly beyond it to the west. We hoped to see another snowfield enabling us to outflank Peak 22,481 feet, but in this we were disappointed. From the ridge, steep snow-slopes fall to the west, and it would be necessary to descend these for some distance before continuing the traverse. Then came a ridge with a steep ice-slope, which could not be avoided. Was there an easy route beyond it and was it justifiable to force a route over such difficult terrain? To do so would mean cutting ourselves off from our base for an indefinite length of time and extending our communications to an unjustifiable length. What would happen in the event of bad weather preventing a retreat for several days? We were a light party with neither sufficient food nor equipment for prolonged siege tactics. I think we both realised that the game was up and that Mana Peak was inaccessible from the east.

The sole remaining hope was a higher route past Peak 22,481 feet. We had taken only two and a half hours to the ridge, so decided to camp in a sheltered hollow, and the same day attempt the ascent of this peak, the view from which should reveal once and for all whether or not there was a hope of approaching Mana Peak from the east.

It was not an ideal site for a camp, for the slopes of the hollow reflected the sun with terrific heat, so that we felt like flies beneath a burning glass, but it was better than the wind-swept crest of the ridge. A drink of tea and we were ready to begin the ascent. Meanwhile, the men returned to the third camp with instructions to return with the remaining food and equipment on the morrow, though in case bad weather should isolate us at this camp we had brought up food and fuel for several days.

The easiest route to the top of Peak 22,481 feet is along the South Ridge. Unfortunately, with that perverseness characteristic of the monsoon season, mists were already gathering and by the time we had climbed 500 feet of easy slopes we were unable to see whether or not it was possible to continue the route in the direction of Mana Peak. For 1,000 feet there was no difficulty whatsoever, then the ridge narrowed and rose in an unclimbable rock step. To avoid this we had to ascend an ice-slope to the right. The ice was steep and peculiarly glutinous and many strokes of the axe were required to fashion a step. But if it was hard work for me, it was an equally tedious business for Peter, who for the next hour had to stand in his steps while paying out the rope inch by inch.

Not far from the top of the slope was a shallow scoop that had to be crossed diagonally. In negotiating this my arms became tired and my axe seemed very unready to do its work, but the steps were made at last, and with a feeling of intense relief at having accomplished as strenuous a piece of ice work as I have done in the Himalayas, I secured myself to a rock and, seated in comfort, took in the rope as Peter ascended.

Thenceforwards the ridge consisted of broken rocks and snow. The mists gathered more densely as we climbed and we reached the shoulder in a desultory snowstorm. The final ridge, which runs almost due west from the summit, is broken up into minor pinnacles. For the most part we were able to follow the crest, but in one or two places were forced to forsake it and traverse to one side or the other of the pinnacles. There was no great individual difficulty, but the sum of all the difficulties made a formidable total for a climb at this altitude.

The rock-ridge abutted against the final peak, which, though steeper, was less difficult. We climbed slowly, for we were tired, and it was a relief when at length the ridge no longer rose before us but eased off gently into a horizontal snow edge forming the summit [of Peak 22,481 feet – now known as Deoban].

There was no view, yet we were conscious of standing on a high and isolated peak. We could not see, but we could sense, the precipices that fall for thousands of feet to the East Kamet Glacier. With a chill little wind blowing, there was no inducement to stay, and with common accord we turned and commenced the descent.

The sole difficulty was the ice-slope, where seeping water had damaged the steps. The arduous task of cutting them anew was undertaken by Peter, whom I held from the rocks above while seated in a cold wind, which bombarded me with hail and snow. When my turn came to descend I found that already many steps were unsafe owing to the rapid flow of water, and I must have exasperated my companion by re-cutting them. Descending steep ice is never pleasant when the legs are tired, and the slow balancing movement from one step to the next imposes a greater strain on the knee than in any other form of climbing. The reader can verify this for himself by standing with the toes of one foot on the extreme edge of a high step for a minute or two, then very slowly stepping down with the other foot and gradually transferring the weight. To do this for an hour or two not only provides an excellent illustration but is one of the best training exercises for mountaineering I know.

Back at the camp we imbibed pints of tea and were soon telling one another what a grand climb it had been. Fortunate indeed is man that he can forget so soon the physical stresses of life and remember only the greater blessings of his strenuous endeavours.

Once again the mists cleared in the night and next morning, August 5, in fair weather we retraced our steps up the lower slopes of Peak 22,481 feet until we were about 500 feet above the camp, then traversed horizontally across a broad ill-defined ridge to a corner, whence we were able to see all that lay beyond.

Mana Peak is not accessible from the east. We stood on the edge of a semicircle of precipices, enclosing the head of a deeply cut glacier, on the far side of which rose Peak 22,892 feet, a fang of ice cutting sharply into the morning sky. There was no possibility whatever of further advance, for the precipice fell sheer at our feet to the glacier in vast sheets of ice broken by belts of rock slabs. Even supposing that the col between Peaks 22,481 feet and 22,892 feet could be reached, the traverse of the latter peak would be by itself a long and difficult expedition. We were beaten and must attempt Mana Peak from some other direction.

Now that there was no further need to concentrate on one task we were able to take stock of our surroundings. A labyrinth of peaks lay before us, sharply cut wall-sided peaks with razor-like edges rising from unseen glaciers. Over them our vision passed to the peaks of Badrinath, and the glorious isolated pyramid of Nilkanta. Fleecy cloudlets were slowly sailing along the Alaknanda Valley and in the south a great wall of luminous monsoon mist rested on the foothills. Over 4,000 feet beneath was the Banke Glacier, banded with orderly moraines, sweeping round in parabolic curve between ranks of splendid peaks whose innumerable edges, domes, towers and spires shone serenely in the warm sunlight.

We had failed to climb Mana Peak from the Banke Plateau, but we had been richly rewarded in other ways and the interesting and beautiful views we had enjoyed during the past few days amply compensated us for any momentary disappointment.

The porters arrived at the camp soon after we returned. It was sad to tell them when they had carried up so many heavy loads that we had failed, but I think they accepted failure as inevitable, for so experienced a mountaineer as Wangdi must have realised already that we were still far from Mana Peak.

It was necessary to evacuate the camps as quickly as possible, and this meant that everyone must carry a very heavy load. A drink of tea and we set about the task of packing up the tent and stores. This done, we set off to the third camp, at which a single tent was added to the loads. Some lunch, and we continued down to the second camp. None of us were enamoured of this cold desolate site, and Wangdi suggested that we should add still further to our mountainous loads and carry on down to the ridge where the surveyors had camped, though Peter and I felt as though our necks and shoulder muscles had been branded with red-hot irons.

After several days camping on snow, it was a relief to camp on rocks, for these are always warmer than snow and usually less exposed to strong winds. There were plants on the ridge: a little *draba* (*D. incompta*) and a *saussurea*, with a purple flower in the midst of silvery wool-like foliage. As the men pitched the tents, we spied the unfortunate Nurbu and Ang Bao, toiling up the glacier with additional stores from the base camp, but I suspect that any grief they may have felt for a day of useless work was mitigated by the thought that they would have to go down, not up, on the morrow.

The difference between camping at 20,000 feet and camping at 17,000 feet in the Himalayas is astonishing. An appetite for food, and a capacity for sound, restful sleep, are possible at the lower altitude whereas both are absent at the higher. Medical authorities have put 21,000 feet as the highest altitude at which it is possible to live for a considerable time without serious physical or mental deterioration, but I would place 19,000 feet as the limit in this respect, at all events as regards my own capacities. A great deal of nonsense is talked about the effects of altitude, such as the Italian contention that Addis Ababa is too high from a physical standpoint as their capital in Abyssinia, though undoubtedly the palm must be given to the dear old lady who came fluttering up to Mr. Hugh Ruttledge after his return from Everest, exclaiming: 'I can understand what you have gone through at those terrible heights. I live at Crowborough.'[1]

Next day we descended to the base camp, and very pleasant it was to get down to the flowers and the balmy air of the Banke Valley. After so many strenuous days, a rest day for the porters, at least, was essential. Both of us had been burned, in spite of copious applications of face cream, for several days on Himalayan snowfields under almost vertical suns would cause discomfort to an armadillo, and our throats were a trifle sore, due possibly to breathing continuously through the mouth.

Tewang was no better. He was occasionally spitting blood and there was something evidently seriously wrong with him. We decided to send him down without delay to Joshimath, where there is a hospital whence he could be forwarded to Ranikhet and Darjeeling.[2] As we would have to engage a substitute at the first opportunity we were forced to deprive him of his climbing boots. As already mentioned, he had cherished these with an abounding love, and it went very much against the grain to surrender them. He was allowed, however, to keep his climbing suit, as we had enough spare clothing to equip his successor. The remainder of the Darjeeling men were remarkably callous as to the plight of their companion. They do not understand sickness until afflicted themselves and Wangdi, although he had gone down with double pneumonia on Everest in 1933, despised the invalid for an indisposition that did not allow him to take part in the more strenuous affairs of the expedition and more than once darkly hinted that he was shamming.

So ended our first round with Mana Peak. We had been afforded an example of the necessity for prolonged reconnoitring in the Himalayas before attempting the ascent of a major peak, and reconnoitring is half the fun and interest of Himalayan mountaineering.

[1] This reminds me of another dear old lady who said: 'So you are going to Everest; it must be *quite* in the wilds.'
[2] His trouble turned out to be a mild but chronic bronchitis.

CHAPTER TWENTY

Mana Peak: Reconnaissance

GARDINER HAD written that he did not think Mana Peak was accessible from the south; therefore, all we could hope for was a reconnaissance from the head of the Banke Glacier. We would then follow his route across the Zaskar Range via the Zaskar Pass, 18,992 feet [now called Gupt Khal], to the south of the mountain, and descend to Badrinath. For this we needed about one week's food, and the day after we returned to Base Camp Wangdi descended to Gamsali for some more sattoo for the porters, and two men to help carry the loads over the pass.

Two days at Base Camp gave me time to examine and collect plants in the Banke Valley. As previously mentioned, the climate of this valley is distinctly drier than that of the Bhyundar Valley, as it is less exposed to the monsoon current. Actually I observed few plants which I had not already seen, or was later to see, in the Bhyundar Valley, but it was noticeable that the flora was more advanced than in the latter valley and that flowers which do not normally bloom until late August or early September in the south of Garhwal, bloom here in late July and early August. The valley's proximity to Tibet must have something to do with this, for in that arid country it is remarkable how plants leap into growth during the early part of the monsoon, and it needs but a fortnight of moist warm air to convert an apparently barren waste into a carpet of flowers. This haste in plants to perpetuate themselves is doubtless because of the shortness of the summer season between the cold winds of spring and autumn. Well to the south of the Himalayan watershed the summer is longer and plants need not hasten to complete their cycle of growth.

I found an excellent instance of this in a lettuce (*Lactuca lessertiana*). I was nosing about some rocks not far from the camp when I noticed a purple flower on a cliff above me. Not having seen it before, I climbed up to it over steep and difficult rocks. I need not have given myself so much trouble, for six weeks later when I returned to the Bhyundar Valley, I found it growing in its millions on a slope near the base camp where it had but recently come into bloom. Another proof of the greater dryness and possibly windiness of the Banke Valley as compared with the Bhyundar Valley was afforded by the large number of cushion plants such as *saxifrages* and *androsaces*. Except at greater elevations I did not see such compact foliage in the Bhyundar Valley. It is impossible that these little cushions covered all over in almost stalkless starry flowers can retain their delightful characteristics in the warm moist climate of Britain; they must inevitably become lank and attenuated. Yet the gardener can scarcely grumble; that a plant flourishing at a height greater than Mont Blanc should grow at all in our climate pertains to the miraculous.

The weather was now excellent and Peter and I spent two delightful days at Base Camp. Late the second day, when night had fallen and we were enjoying the warmth of a fire, Wangdi reappeared together with two men he had secured at Gamsali. It had not been an easy task to find porters and these two had only consented to come when he had promised them that they would be engaged for the remainder of the expedition, and be provided with boots and equipment at Badrinath, promises he had no authority whatsoever to make and which as he knew could not be kept. At all events here they were and everything was now ready for our first march up the Banke Glacier on the morrow.

The weather was in cheerful vein when, on the morning of August 8, we began the ascent of the glacier. A rough shepherd's track followed along the northern bank, sometimes on the crest of the side moraine and sometimes in a corridor, gay with *potentillas* and *allardias*, between the glacier and the hillside. This track continued as far as the shepherds' highest bivouac place, Eri Udiar, but beyond this there is no track and the traveller must fend for himself in a wilderness of stones and moraine.

We made excellent progress, but had to halt many times for the porters, who were continually retarded by the slowness of the two local men. At his best, the Marcha Bhotia is slow compared with the Sherpa or Bhotia (Tibetan). Instead of completing a march in a reasonable time and enjoying a long rest during the afternoon and evening, he prefers to loiter along throughout the day regardless of rain, snow or any other inconvenience. This may suit his book, but it is exasperating to his employers, and I know of no sterner test of patience than to travel with these men.

About Eri Udiar, the Banke Glacier sweeps round almost at a right angle, and the traveller leaves the side of it in favour of a route, which cuts across the perimeter of the bend. The ascent was unexpectedly easy, though there was a good deal of up and down going on mounds of moraine which varied from 50 to 100 feet in height. By the time we had turned the corner it was evident that bad weather was brewing, but not even the eloquence of Peter, who has a fluent command of Urdu, could coax the two Gamsali men and they became slower and slower and their halts more frequent. I was ahead, finding the best route through a tangle of moraines, when a shout announced that they had halted once and for all. It was impossible to persuade them to continue. Not for any quantity of clothing, boots or baksheesh would they have ventured farther. They were beyond the grazing grounds; no one from their village had ever penetrated so far up the glacier; it was a country of spirits, demons, dragons and psychic phenomena of all kinds. There was nothing to be done; they returned and their loads were distributed between us and our own long-suffering porters. Wangdi was furious, and if looks could have killed Gamsali would have been two short in its population register. So once more Peter and I trudged along with well-filled rucksacks, and I remember thinking then, and on other occasions too, that the cult of the small expedition can be overdone and that there are occasions when it has its distinct disadvantages.

The mists drooped lower and a blue veil of rain swept down the valley. It was gone within half an hour, leaving the sun to shine brightly through heaped-up masses of cloud. We camped where the surveyors had camped on a medial moraine of the glacier and were cheered a little at finding a load of wood they had left there. But I for one was in a thoroughly bad temper. Perhaps the stones had something to do with this, for nothing is more trying to the temper than a day spent pounding over loose stones. I have never forgotten Bentley Beauman's remarks on this subject in 1931 when for two days we marched up the stony floor of the Arwa Valley. Shakespeare could not have surpassed him in adjectival or epithetical force on the subject of stones.

There was more desultory rain, more doubtful sun and swirling mists, then with magical suddenness the evening cleared, the mists vanished into a frosty atmosphere and, far above, the great boiler-plate precipices the ice-cliffs of Nilgiri Parbat gleamed in the setting sun.

The night was cold and was rendered uncomfortable for me by the puncturing of my air mattress. Air mattresses are very light and provide an excellent insulation between the body and the ground, but once they are punctured, they are very difficult to repair, as not even immersion in water will reveal a small hole. Furthermore, it takes time to become accustomed to them, as, if they are blown up too tight they are very uncomfortable, whilst if they are not blown up enough the ground impinges on the hips. Now that I was on the ground, I found it uncommonly hard, and spent a good part of the night fiddling about trying to remove innumerable angular stones from beneath the floor of the tent.

The morning was cloudless and had it not been for our heavy loads we might have enjoyed better the day's march. Beyond the camp, we passed beneath Nilgiri Parbat, the tremendous cliffs of which are crowned by immense walls of ice, which now and again collapse and send avalanches roaring and smoking towards the glacier. Four miles to the north-west of Nilgiri Parbat, and on the same ridge overlooking the Banke Glacier, is an unnamed peak of 21,516 feet, which is characterised by a fluted ice face. Ice flutings are common in the Eastern and Western Himalayas, but are seldom seen in the Central Himalayas. They are formed by a constant down-rush of avalanches, which carve out parallel channels separated by thin edges of ice: the effect is very striking and adds greatly to the beauty of a mountain. In the present instance, however, the flutings had been weathered into parallel series of ice-pinnacles, in much the same way that earth-pinnacles, of which there are excellent examples in the Alps, are formed by denudation and weathering. The pinnacles were remarkable for their height, which cannot have been less than 100 feet and must have been more in a great many instances, and for the manner in which they clung to the steep face of the mountain. With the sun shining upon them, they presented a strange scene and reminded us of the ice-pinnacles of the East Rongbuk Glacier, between which the mountaineer passes on his way to Everest. It would be interesting to know why this is the only fluted peak in the district. The pinnacles were on a north-facing slope, and but little exposed to the full power of the sun. Possibly some air-current was responsible, but I could think of no complete explanation for their presence.

It was a relief when after a march of three miles the moraines petered out at the foot of an icefall. The latter was not in the least difficult, and soon we were above it on the uppermost ice of the glacier, whence it is nothing but a walk to the Zaskar Pass.

As we had planned to reach the pass on the morrow there was no object in proceeding farther, and we camped on a convenient side moraine. Mana Peak was in view and exhibited its south ridge almost in profile. If the crest could be gained there was a possibility that the summit would prove accessible, but we disliked the look of an apparently vertical step about 1,000 feet from the summit. There was no hope of gaining the ridge from the Banke Glacier as it ended in a buttress, really a separate point of 20,675 feet, whence impracticable precipices fell sheer to the glacier. It was equally inaccessible from the south-east or east, for there, apart from terrific steepness, hanging glaciers swept every line of approach with their avalanches. As to what lay round the corner to the west of Point 20,675 feet we could only guess, but from Gardiner's letter we knew there were steep ice-falls barring all direct approach to the mountain.

The weather was still improving. No rain or snow fell that day and the evening was cloudless with Nilgiri Parbat glowing like a vast sail down the valley, and casting an opalescent light on the camp long after the sun had left the glacier. Shortly before sunset we strolled across the glacier to the moraine on the far side on which the surveyors had built a large cairn. From this point Mana Peak appeared totally inaccessible, and we neither of us felt that we stood the remotest chance of success. Yet on this beautiful evening a mundane matter such as climbing a particular mountain could not intrude for long on the mind and we returned to camp through a motionless, frosty atmosphere, which was already forming a film of ice on the pools of the glacier, with the great peak we hoped to climb hard-cut against a deep green sky at a seemingly immeasurable distance above our heads.

In hard frost we set off next morning to the Zaskar Pass. It was all easy going, and we did not need the rope until we came to a few small crevasses. A scramble up a slope of snow and shale and we stood on the pass. Nilkanta rose to greet us beyond the unseen Alaknanda Valley, and to the north of it the snows of the Badrinath Peaks glowed serenely in the calm morning air.

Our first impressions had been confirmed during the walk to the pass that a direct attack on Mana Peak from the head of the Banke Glacier was out of the question. Between the lower buttress of the South Ridge and the ridge on which we now stood was an impassable icefall, which descended from a recessed plateau enclosed between the South and North-West Ridges. I have never seen a more formidable icefall. It was a full 3,000 feet high: wall upon wall, tower upon tower, the ice rose, riven and rent in all directions as though by an earthquake, whilst tongues of debris stretched far on to the Banke Glacier. One glance was sufficient; there was no hope there.

But there was one slender chance of success and this was to follow the ridge from the Zaskar Pass over a subsidiary peak of about 21,500 feet to the plateau already mentioned. It would be necessary to descend from the peak to the plateau, and such a descent might well prove impracticable, but once on the plateau there was a possibility of reaching the long North-West Ridge of the mountain which connects with Kamet, three miles to the north-north-west, and of traversing it to the summit.

It was a theory, and fact often jostles uncomfortably on the heels of theory. The Zaskar Pass is 18,992 feet, Mana Peak 23,860 feet. Allowing for a descent of several hundred feet from Peak 21,500 feet to the plateau, this meant a climb of well over 5,000 feet in a distance of about three horizontal miles. And incidentally, there was Peak 21,500 feet, a formidable climb in itself. From the Zaskar

Pass the ridge, after running more or less horizontally for a short distance, springs up in a sharp and steep snow-ridge which ends against a rock face about 500 feet high, obviously very steep in its uppermost portion. Above this rock face the ridge bends almost at right angles in a snow crest which appeared very narrow, might necessitate much step-cutting, and which eventually ends in the summit of Peak 21,500 feet. Furthermore, we were a small party with provisions and fuel for not more than four days, and it was probable, even supposing that the traverse of Peak 21,500 feet was practicable, that at least two camps, and possibly three, would be needed before an attempt on the summit could be made. On the face of it, all we could hope for was a reconnaissance, which would disclose the possibility or impossibility of the route. Should it prove possible, we could descend to Badrinath and return with the necessary sinews of warfare.

Such were our conclusions. It remained only to carry the first part of the programme into effect and reconnoitre the route. Accordingly when the porters arrived we told them to pitch the camp just below the crest of the pass; then, having provided ourselves with some food, we set out at ten o'clock to climb Peak 21,500 feet.

Although at this stage there seemed no chance whatever of attempting Mana Peak in the near future we were both of us fired with an optimistic energy; and it was impossible not to feel optimistic on a morning when there was scarcely a cloud in the sky, and only the lightest of winds rustled across the ridge. We had experienced some dull and misty days on the Banke Plateau, but now the weather was perfect. Perhaps the fact that we had now only a little food and a camera apiece contributed to our lightness of foot and spirits.

After passing along an easy crest of snow and screes we came to the point where the ridge springs up in a series of snow bulges, before tapering into a sharp edge. The first of these bulges was of ice, covered with snow, which varied from the merest sprinkling to several inches in depth. Our problem was to find a route, which involved the minimum of step-cutting, and though in this we were only partially successful, the step-cutting was speedily accomplished by Peter.

The second bulge was very similar to the first and was followed by snow-slopes, above which the ridge narrowed and rose steeply to the foot of the rocks, where we suspected the crux of the ascent must lie. It occurred to us here that we might be able to outflank this difficult upper portion and possibly Peak 21,500 feet by a traverse to the west and an ascent to the plateau. In this, however, we were mistaken and after a walk across snow-slopes we were brought up short on the edge of impassable ice-cliffs.

Before retracing our tracks we glanced down into a glacier some thousands of feet beneath on to which an ice avalanche had fallen with such force and momentum that the debris had swept along for a distance of nearly half a mile. It was a grim reminder of the fate that had overtaken the Nanga Parbat Expedition, regarding which the Editor of the *Alpine Journal* wrote: "It lies beyond any man's power to calculate the forces of Nature and their effects on the hanging glaciers and vast snow-fields suspended from those mighty slopes and precipices." It is indeed only possible to climb safely in the Himalayas by keeping not only out of the obvious range of ice avalanches but, out of seemingly impossible range, and parties that attempt such routes as that on Nanga Parbat will always risk destruction. To what extent such a risk is justifiable or unjustifiable must depend always on the climber himself and the store he sets on his life and the lives of his porters balanced against the possible fulfilment of his ambitions.

Having returned to the ridge we recommenced the ascent. Two or three hundred feet higher we came to a point where the ridge was intersected horizontally by a crevasse, the upper lip of which formed an ice-wall about thirty feet high. Before crossing the crevasse we halted to admire the icicles which were suspended from the lip; gleaming in the sun and with a background of snow-peaks and deep blue sky they made a magnificent spectacle.

The ice-wall was by no means as difficult as it appeared, but even so a number of steps had to be cut before we were able to gain the slope above. We now climbed diagonally upwards and regained the crest of the ridge, which proved so sharp, steep and icy that steps had to be hewn all the way up it. This arduous task was undertaken by Peter, who now seemed at the top of his form. It is a privilege to follow behind a first rate ice-man and during this part of the ascent I had little to do but step up in the excellent steps made by my companion. When you do not have to make steps yourself there is something very pleasant and lulling in the sound of an ice axe cutting into snow and ice, and the lazy swish of the dislodged fragments as they skip and spin into the abyss.

At length the snow-ridge levelled out and ended abruptly against the rocks. These proved easier than anticipated, for they were well broken and consisted for the most part of firm material, reddish in colour; but here and there were loose rocks, including one slab wedged insecurely in a chimney over which we climbed as gingerly as cats on a glass-topped wall. A little way above this was a steep sheep's back of slabs with small holds, which necessitated a long run out of rope for the leader, but apart from this and a short ice-slope with a treacherous covering of snow there was nothing to give us more than momentary pause until we came to a vertical cliff about 50 feet high immediately under the sharp upper ice-ridge leading towards the summit. The rock here was dark and striated and none too firm as compared with that lower down. There was no possibility of climbing directly over the cliff as the crest overhung so, well held by Peter, I moved along a little ledge to the right until I came to a corner beyond which a narrow ice gully descended towards the Banke Glacier. This was the crux of the ascent; if we could climb up and round this corner there seemed every chance of circumventing the obstacle. There were good holds, but a severe arm pull must be avoided at a height of over 20,000 feet. A step or two upwards, then one to the right and my exploring hand was able to touch a small, sloping, scree-covered ledge. This was covered by a film of ice, which I cleared as well as I could with one hand while supporting myself with the other. Having at last decided that a step was justifiable I balanced up with the delicacy, but scarcely the grace, of a Blondin and a moment later was on the ledge. But this was not the end of it; the rocks still forced me to the right into the ice-gully, which was here so steep and narrow that it more nearly resembled a chimney. Retrieving my ice axe from my rucksack in which I had carried it, I cut two or three steps in the ice until I was able to balance across to a hold on the far side. Then, after climbing upwards for a few feet, I cut back across the gully on to a sloping ledge immediately under the crest of the ridge, and above the rock wall, where I could not resist a triumphant shout of 'Done it!' to Peter.

Soon we were together at the commencement of the ice ridge. Himalayan ice ridges are notorious for their sharpness and there are few edges in the Alps to equal these fragile crests that lift into the blue with fairy-like and ethereal beauty. This ridge was no exception.

To the right it fell away in tremendous precipices to the head of the Banke Glacier; to the left we looked down one of the longest and steepest ice slopes of my experience. Indeed, I cannot recollect how or where the slope ended; it dropped and dropped for apparently thousands of feet. Along the crest formed by the intersection of these two slopes we had to make our way; a crest so thin and knife-like that Peter remarked that it was the sharpest ridge he had ever trodden.

The crest consisted of ice, covered with several inches of snow, which varied in depth so that sometimes it was impossible to drive in our ice axes deeply enough to form a firm belay for the rope. Thus it was necessary to cut good steps. Moving one at a time and taking turns at the work we advanced slowly, keeping just below the crest, which was slightly corniced in places. It was exhilarating work. A Himalayan mountainside often seems to stifle ambition and all those qualities that go to make for success on a mountain, but a ridge is different; here is a celestial pathway, with nothing to oppress the climber and only the blue sky above.

An hour passed; the slopes to the north-west were now appreciably less steep and the ridge less acute. Presently we came to a broad snow slope. Up this we trudged very slowly. To carry heavy loads up to a camp, then indulge in difficult climbing, is a tax on strength, and we were tired. However, what we lost in energy we made up for in rhythm. Nothing is more fatiguing than to climb behind a man who has never learned the art of rhythmical climbing on a snow slope. Peter is by instinct a snow- and ice-man, and when he led I found myself following docilely in his wake, and with that minimum of effort which is linked inseparably with a rhythmical uphill pace.

So at length we reached the summit of Peak 21,500 feet. It consisted of an almost level ridge and we trudged along to the far end until we could look down to the plateau. We were only about 300 feet above it and a broad and easy snow ridge, a mere walk, linked it with the summit on which we stood. Beyond the plateau was the North-West Ridge of Mana Peak, a long, gently sloping and apparently easy crest, an obvious route to the summit. The sole remaining problem was how to reach it from the plateau. In one place it sank down, forming a shallow col not more than 1,000 feet above the plateau, and linked with the latter by a slope which from our position seemed inclined at a moderate angle. If this slope, which as far as we could judge was composed of snow, could be climbed and the ridge gained there was every hope of reaching the summit.

The South Ridge on the other hand looked far more difficult and the rock step near the top was obviously very steep and likely to prove an insuperable obstacle. And there was no means of reaching the ridge easily, for the one and only route from the plateau lay up a subsidiary ridge, which was not continuous but petered out high up against a steep face. The North-West Ridge was the easier of the two routes if the slope leading to it could be climbed.

We returned to camp through the usual afternoon mist, well satisfied with our reconnaissance.

Perhaps it was the hardness of the ground beneath my punctured air mattress, or maybe something I had eaten, but I was unable to sleep well that night. I lay restlessly turning over the events of the day in my mind. Mana Peak was accessible, or at least there was a reasonable chance of this, and the weather and snow conditions were ideal; and we were descending to Badrinath on the morrow; this meant the loss of a week and it was unlikely that the weather would remain good during the height of the monsoon season.

Had we enough provisions and fuel for an immediate attempt on the summit, and was an attempt possible with only one additional camp? We had no time for more than one camp and in any event it would be difficult to convoy laden porters over Peak 21,500 feet, whilst an ill-provisioned camp in such a remote situation was out of the question. For several hours I lay cogitating the problem and the more I cogitated, the more clear did the issue seem; we must push up a camp to the lower rocks of Peak 21,500 feet and the day after attempt the summit. This point decided, I slept.

CHAPTER TWENTY ONE

The Ascent of Mana Peak

WE AWOKE next morning, August 11, to perfect weather and as usual breakfasted in our tents. Meanwhile, the men packed up ready to descend to Badrinath. After breakfast I tore myself reluctantly from my sleeping bag and crawled out of my tent. The sun was shining from a cloudless sky and not a breath of wind stirred in all that vast arena of glacier, peak and sky. This decided me. I lifted the petrol tin; there was a full half-gallon of petrol left. Then I approached Peter and with some trepidation put the proposal to him, that instead of descending we should take a camp as far up the ridge as possible and on the morrow have a crack at the top. I did not expect him to acquiesce, but he did; the amount of fuel left was the strongest argument. He was not enthusiastic to begin with, for he is a sound and cautious mountaineer, but it was the weather that decided him. We should have to eke out our slender resources with coolie food, but even so there would be plenty left for the men. So it was agreed.

Wangdi was informed of the change of plan. I do not know what he thought, but to judge from his expression I can hazard a shrewd guess. He had been counting the hours till we should arrive at Mana, where there is excellent marwa (native beer) and now this and other pleasures were to be postponed. Undoubtedly the Sahibs were mad and especially Ismay[1] Sahib. Gloom settled on his hard face, but it presently vanished. It was a *fait accompli* and must be accepted as such; he would see us through with the job. So the tents and stores were unpacked, re-sorted and repacked, and an hour later we set off up the ridge.

Climbing even moderately easy snow and ice with laden porters is a very

[1] The nearest the Tibetan can get to my name.

different matter to climbing without them, and it was necessary to enlarge considerably the steps we had already made. Then, of course, there was Pasang, who might slip at any moment, whilst of Tse Tendrup and Ang Bao it cannot be said that they were pillars of strength to the party. However, Wangdi and Nurbu were well able to take care of their less competent companions and Nurbu, in particular, had acquired a knowledge of rope craft which was astonishing, considering that less than two months previously he was a raw novice unversed in the finer points of mountaineering.

Two hours later we reached the uppermost limit of the snow ridge and cast around for a place to pitch the tent. There was only one – immediately beneath the crest on the precipice falling to the Banke Glacier. At first sight it seemed an impossible situation, but nothing is impossible to the Tibetan or Sherpa when it comes to pitching a tent and in a few minutes the men had descended a wall of snow and ice fifteen feet high and were busy excavating a platform at the base of it where it rested on some rocks. An hour later the tent had been pitched, the sleeping bags arranged inside, and a pan filled with water from a drip nearby. This done, some tea was prepared for the men after which they set off down to the Zaskar Pass, having previously had instructions to return on the morrow and await our arrival.

Perched on the rocks we watched their descent. It was a ragged little procession. Pasang and Tse Tendrup in particular seemed to regard their feet as the least important part of the anatomy, and contrasted oddly with Wangdi and Nurbu, who moved with the confidence of experienced mountaineers, plunging in their ice axes at every step and belaying the rope in readiness to check a slip.

Having seen them disappear in safety we surveyed our surroundings. It was certainly the most sensational camping site of my experience. Like certain houses of ill design and antique origin it was possible to step straight out of the bedroom and down the stairs, only in this instance there was a 1,500 feet precipice in lieu of stairs. Immediately behind the tent the ridge crest concealed the view to the west, but to the east we looked across a precipice crowned by an ice wall from which were suspended huge icicles gleaming in the sun like sheaves of Titanic spears. Beyond this was the edge of the plateau with a frozen cataract of ice descending from it towards the Banke Glacier which stretched south-eastwards in two great curves before disappearing behind a distant shoulder under the shining snows of Nilgiri Parbat. Immediately beneath was an ice-sheeted gully scored and seamed by stones which, dislodged by the fierce sun from masses of decaying crags, never ceased their whirring and humming, with now and then the resounding crash of a bigger block, until the evening frost had set its seal on the mountainside.

The weather was good and not even heavy mists charged with desultory hail squalls could dim the optimism we now felt about the outcome of the morrow's climbing. We spent the afternoon lounging about the warm rocks and in my case collecting flowers, for even at this inhospitable altitude, far above the permanent snowline and the nearest alps and meadows, plants had obtained a lodgement on the crags. I found the same little woolly *saussurea* I had already seen on the edge of the Banke Plateau (*S. bracteata*)[2] and a beautiful little yellow-flowered

[2] Unfortunately I lost my specimens of this plant.

saxifrage growing from woolly, densely tufted foliage which clung close to cracks and crannies of the rocks (*S. jacquemontiana*).

During the afternoon I lost my pipe and spent a considerable time searching for it. No doubt it fell from my pocket and descended the gully to the glacier, from which it will emerge a century or so hence above Gamsali to gladden, I hope, one of the inhabitants of that village. This was a tragedy and Peter commiserated suitably with me on my loss; at the same time I suspect that as a non-smoker he was secretly relieved because it was a particularly foul pipe and the tent we shared was very small.

Our eyrie lost the sun early and the increasing cold forced us to seek the shelter of our sleeping bags. From this vantage-point we looked out through the entrance of the tent on the glories of a monsoon sunset. At this season, when there is an abundance of water vapour in the atmosphere, sunrise and sunset are far more colourful than in the dry periods before and after the monsoon. The clouds bear witness to this and the towering masses of cumulus that are built up during the afternoon glow with a fiery splendour at sundown. That evening the colourings were especially fine. Shortly before sunset we witnessed the phenomenon known as the Brocken Spectre, the conditions for which are a low sun and a wall of mist. There was a point not far from the camp still bathed in sunlight and standing on it I saw my shadow surrounded by a halo of prismatic colourings cast on the mists that lingered in the gully to the east of the camp. I attempted to photograph it, but though I was using panchromatic film the attempt was unsuccessful.

Soon after this the mists rapidly cleared from the vicinity of Mana Peak and lying in our sleeping bags we gazed out of the tent on to the group of snow-peaks south of the Zaskar Pass and far beyond them to a vast range of cloud, sunlit above and shadowed below, spanning the distant foothills. Quickly white changed to amber and amber to gold as peaks and clouds reflected the enormous conflagration of the setting sun. Then, even more quickly, the shadows welled upwards, a delicate opalescent blue at their edges where they met the sunlight, and within a few minutes the peaks had gone out and only the cloud mountains were left to carry the day to its peaceful ending. A little later when I looked out of the tent entrance the world had been drained of all sunlight and was pallid and deathly cold.

We supped off pemmican soup thickened with the porters' sattoo. Soup is perhaps scarcely descriptive for Peter, ever a lover of the latter commodity, which to me tastes like pulverised blotting paper, added so much that the resultant mess was practically solid and to assimilate it needed all the gastronomical fortitude of which I was capable.

My last memory before attempting to sleep is of the stars. Those who have only seen stars through the dense atmosphere of low levels cannot conceive their grandeur when viewed through the thin keen atmosphere of the High Himalayas. The firmament is crowded with innumerable archipelagos of brilliant fire shining undimmed from horizon to horizon, except when the Milky Way interposes a spectral luminescent veil, apparently so near that a hand outstretched could tear it down from heaven. Beneath these serene eyes the mountaineer must needs forget his little woes.

73 In July 1937, making use of the information gathered by the official Indian survey teams, Frank Smythe and Peter Oliver and their sherpas explored the enchanting Banke Plateau at the centre of the Zaskar Range. This area of high snowfields is flanked by several 6000m peaks, one of which, Deoban (Deovan) 22,484ft / 6855m was climbed to assess the best way of tackling Mana Peak. The views hereabouts are extensive with *(l to r)* Tirsuli, Hardeol, Pt.6992, Kalanka, Changabang, the two Nanda Devi peaks, Dunagiri, Durpata, Rataban, Hathi Parbat and Gauri (Ghori) Parbat seen in this early morning view to the south-east. *Photo: Frank Smythe*

73 The view north from the crest of the Kauri Pass

74 *(centre right)* The dead pine on Kauri Pass – Smythe's nostalgic sentinel landmark.

75, 76 *(above)* The Alaknanda feeds the Ganges and Hindu pilgrims *(right)* trek to its source near Badrinath.

77, 78 Frank Smythe's 1937 "Valley of Flowers" trip was his personal "pilgrimage" to a mountain region on the fringes of the monsoon area *(left)*. It was a time for photography, plant collecting, writing and reflection on his life all set against an ambitious climbing agenda. Every few days he returned to Base Camp for rest and contemplation.
All photos: Smythe

79 Looking south-west from the Gupt Khal to Nilkanta and Chaukhamba.

80 *(below)* Investigating "bear"(?) tracks crossing a high snowy ridge.

81 *(lower right)* The rocky cwm on the northern side of the Bhyundar Valley.

82 *(right)* Rataban and its col.

83, 84 One of Smythe's best climbs of 1937 was the first ascent of Nilgiri Parbat 21,264ft, situated between the Bhyundar and Banke Valleys. He was accompanied by the sherpas Wangdi (Ondi), and Nurbu. After a 4000ft climb on the west side they reached the ridge on the right at 10 am. A diagonal line up the sunlit slope gained the upper part of the left-hand ridge which led to the summit by 2pm – a 6000ft climb in eight hours. The inset shows the jubilant Wangdi and Nurbu, on the top. Nilgiri Parbat looks particularly fine from the Banke Plateau to the east from where Smythe took this and other greatly valued pictures of a peak which gave him his 'finest ascent on snow and ice'.

A HIMALAYAN MOUNTAINEER ENCOUNTERS A UNIQUE OBSTACLE

A Giant Boulder of Monumental Dimensions that All but Prevented F. S. Smythe's Conquest of the Mana Peak

BARRING THE WAY TO THE SUMMIT: Mr. F. S. Smythe approaching the great tunnelled boulder and (*inset on left*) attempting to regain the ridge on emerging from the tunnel which debouched on the very verge of a 4,000 ft. precipice. How he had to swing across this Mr. Smythe describes below

THIS diagrammatic drawing illustrates a perilous phase seemingly barring the way to the summit and presenting that the hole did not end on the crest of the ridge but to

85, 86, 87, 88 *(above)* A view from the Gupt Khal to Mana Peak (23,825ft.), the highest unclimbed Zaskar summit in 1937. Smythe and Peter Oliver *(inset)* approache[d] by a ridge and satellite peak (off picture to the left). From the high glacier shelf the sunlit ridge led to the obvious forepeak on the right. Oliver (feeling fatigued) decided to stop at this point so Smythe continued alone up the final 800ft buttress *(right)* to complete the climb. At one point the way was barred by a perched boulder that formed the subject of a vivid press story on his return *(left)*. *Photos: Frank Smythe (2), John Morris (ins[et])*

90 *(above)* Smythe and Oliver then attempted Nilkanta, the arresting peak above Badrinath. Difficult climbing on the South-East Ridge led to the upper buttresses where a sudden hailstorm forced a retreat. *Photo: Graham Little*

91, 92 Their final objective was the South-West Ridge of Dunagiri (below – the left hand skyline) which had been attempted by Oliver and Campbell (1933) and Eric Shipton and Ang Tharkay (1936). Smythe and Oliver climbed to the top of the initial steep shoulder but made no further progress along the vertiginous continuation ridge *(inset)*. *Photos: Joe Tasker and André Roch*

> Sit, Jessica. Look how the floor of heaven
> Is thick inlaid with patines of bright gold.
> There's not the smallest orb which thou behold'st
> But in his motion like an angel sings,
> Still choiring to the young-eyed cherubims;
> Such harmony is in immortal souls;
> But whilst this muddy vesture of decay
> Doth grossly close it in, we cannot hear it.

Neither of us slept much. I doubt whether I slept at all, but my memory is vague on the point. It is easy at high altitudes for a man to wake up in the morning convinced that he has not slept at all. But the bogey of sleeplessness is not as formidable as it is at sea level; deprivation of oxygen results in the mountaineer lying in a semi-comatose condition and the hours pass quickly, not drag by on leaden feet as they do at sea-level. I remember clearly the silence; there was not a breath of wind or the rumble of an avalanche the whole night through. I remember too in more wakeful and alert periods turning over again and again in my mind the fortunes of the morrow, for this was likely, as we both realised, to be the greatest mountain day in our lives.

At 3 a.m., I got the Primus going after some ineffectual attempts, which filled the tent with fumes. It was bitter cold at that hour and everything that could freeze had frozen, including our boots, but a hot porridge of sattoo and a cup of chocolate put life into us.

At five o'clock the light was sufficiently strong to permit of our starting. Stiffly we mounted to the ridge and began the ascent of the rocks. The stars were paling rapidly in the fast-strengthening light, and the weather was perfect, not a cloud.

As we climbed, at first up the chimney and broken rocks, then over the slabby section where my hands, which I had to remove from my gloves to grasp the small holds, became very numb. Our muscles soon lost their stiffness and we began to enjoy the ascent.

We made good progress to the foot of the wall immediately beneath the ridge but here we were checked. The trickles from the snow melted by yesterday's sun had frozen in ugly sheets of ice on the holds and on the scree shelf above, and the ice axe pick had to be requisitioned to clear the rocks, an awkward business when only one hand was free, the other being occupied as a support.

The landing on to the frozen scree-covered shelf was particularly delicate, but at length we were over the obstacle and on the snow ridge above. Here, thanks to the steps cut two days, previously, we made rapid progress and at 6.30 were on the summit of Peak 21,500 feet.

A downhill walk of about 300 feet brought us to the plateau which was still in shadow and very cold. Crossing this and ascending gently we made for the North-West Ridge; but the nearer we approached the slope leading to it, the more formidable did it appear, and it soon became evident that we had been misled as to the angle.

Splitting the base of it was a bergschrund, half choked with snow. Peter crossed, held on the rope round my in-driven ice axe, and cut a step or two over the shallow lip of the crevasse to the slope above. Once on this I hoped to see him advance quickly, kicking or slicing out steps in frozen snow, but instead he cleared away what was evidently a surface layer of loose, powdery snow and swung his axe; it met the slope with a dull thud – ice. And ice of the toughest quality to judge from the time it took to fashion a step. Two or three steps and he called on me to join him. I did so. There was no mistaking the fact that the slope was an ice-sheet from base to crest, covered not with a layer of firm well-consolidated snow, as we had hoped, but in snow of the consistency of flour or castor sugar. To climb the slope would involve the additional labour of clearing this surface snow away in order to cut a step. And the slope was about 1,000 feet high; it meant a day's work at least, in all likelihood two days' work, even supposing we had the strength to do it at a height of nearly 22,000 feet. There was nothing for it but to descend.

Having returned to the plateau, we discussed the situation. The game was up, but was it quite up? There was one possibility, a very remote possibility – the South Ridge. We had already agreed that it could in all probability be reached from the plateau along a subsidiary ridge ascending to a point about 1,500 feet from the summit of the mountain, but we had also agreed that the ridge was more difficult than the North-West Ridge and that the rock step some 800-1,000 feet from the summit appeared very formidable. Still, it was the only alternative open to us and we decided to attempt it, though I do not believe either of us had any hope of ultimate success.

To reach the foot of the subsidiary ridge we had to cross the plateau and descend some 300-400 feet, which descent increased twofold the work of the day.

There was no difficulty in approaching the foot of the subsidiary ridge but to reach the crest we had to clamber up a steep little gully with an awkward rock step. The ridge consisted of a thin edge of icy snow sweeping up like the blade of a scimitar before petering out in the west flank of the South Ridge about 400 feet from the crest.

Sometimes step-kicking was permissible, but for the most part it was safer and less fatiguing to slice steps out of the ridge crest. Peter did most of the work and we progressed steadily along this sensational edge with feet turned outwards like a pair of Charlie Chaplins.

The angle of the ridge increased the higher we ascended so that by the time we got to the point where the ridge ended in the face it cannot have been less than 50 degrees. Much depended on the condition of the face; if there had been the least possibility of the snow sliding we should have had no option but to retreat; but the slope was in good order, a hard slope of compacted snow and ice; mostly ice. It was also very cold, being as yet untouched by the sun, and we gazed longingly at some sun-warmed rocks on the ridge crest far above us.

From the point of view of sheer hard work this last 400 feet was one of the toughest jobs I have ever engaged in and there is no doubt that Peter, who rose splendidly to the occasion to do a lion's share of step cutting, although he had already worked hard on the ridge below, must attribute his failure to reach the summit to the energy he expended at this stage of the climb.

Here and there were rock slabs, which afforded welcome resting places but seldom security for the rope. At length the angle eased off a little and a minor rib of rocks and snow led up to the crest of the South Ridge which we gained with a vast sense of relief at ten o'clock.

Here the sun met us for the first time and we plumped down on a rock to revel in its warm rays. Peter's feet had become numbed with cold during the ascent and the first thing he did was to take off his frozen boots and restore the circulation with a vigorous massage. If I remember aright we tried to eat some chocolate but with little success; after breathing hard through the mouth in the cold dry air there was little saliva in our mouths and our throat muscles would not function efficiently. This disability is common at high altitudes and is, I believe, partly responsible for loss of appetite when climbing. For this reason liquid food is far to be preferred to solid food.

From our position the South Ridge stretched roughly horizontal for some distance, though considerably broken up into minor points, crests and rock towers; then it sprang upwards in a steep rock ridge alternating with occasional snow edges to the sharp-pointed summit. We were looking at it *en face* so could not estimate the difficulty of the rock step which we knew was likely to be the crux of the climb.

Had we been climbing in the Alps we might have appreciated the grandeur and complexity of the edge along which we scrambled, but at nearly 23,000 feet these qualities are seldom appreciated by mountaineers who have already expended much energy in overcoming initial difficulties.

For the next hour we made little or no height and in several instances lost it when descending some rock tower or snow point. In places the ridge was a snow crest, sometimes corniced on its eastern side, and we traversed cautiously one at a time across the steep western slope; in other places we moved both together over broken rocks.

This horizontal section ended in two or three little rock towers more formidable than any yet encountered and we had to descend some fifty feet to the west and traverse across the face to avoid them. Fortunately the slope we traversed was composed of hard snow, not ice, and we were presently able to regain the ridge without difficulty at the point where it swept steeply upwards to the summit, which now seemed close to us but was in reality a full 1,000 feet higher.

Now at last we were at grips with the final problem, and what a splendid problem it was. I shall always regret that we were too tired to enjoy those red granite slabs that lifted up and up in a great sweep towards the finely tapered summit edging proudly into the blue. Here was something to warm the heart and blood: clean, firm granite and a perfect day with not a breath of wind to chill us; what more could we have desired in different circumstances? But now a weight of tiredness opposed us and out of the tail of my eye I could see that my companion was climbing with increasing effort and that every upward step was a painful weariness to him.

We came to a sloping platform on the crest and there Peter seated himself wearily and told me that if he continued he would become unsafe as he was now very tired. He was not exhausted but might become so with further effort. It was a terrible disappointment to us both. Seated side by side we discussed the situation. There was no doubt that he was suffering primarily from the effects of altitude. As long as he rested he felt fit and strong, but directly he exerted himself uphill intense fatigue supervened. To climb downhill is, as I knew from my experiences on Everest, easy, even to a man who cannot muster the energy for another upward step. I asked myself, firstly, was it justifiable to leave him resting at that point and, secondly, was I justified in making a solitary attempt on the summit? Had the weather been anything but perfect there would have been no choice in the matter we should have had to descend. But the weather was perfect; although it was nearly noon the sun was shining with unabated fierceness and the rocks even at this great elevation were warm to the touch. So I asked him if he minded my carrying on alone. Though he gave no positive indication of his feelings I do not believe he liked the idea; it was not the prospect of being left alone but my safety that worried him, and afterwards he told me how anxious he had been, which is typical of him – the most unselfish man I have ever climbed with. So it was agreed and, leaving him seated on the platform, I recommenced the ascent.

A few feet above the platform the ridge narrowed into an awkward bank of snow overlying a length of slabs tilted downwards to the east and projecting as a thin flake over the precipice to the west. Along the uppermost edge of the slabs the snow had melted, leaving a high bank of snow on the one hand and on the other a drop so sheer there was nothing a falling object could touch for some hundreds of feet. The strange little path thus exposed, which was never more than two feet wide, continued unbroken for twenty or thirty yards and reminded me of the ledge on the Grépon euphemistically known as the "Route aux Bicyclettes".

At the end of the ledge was a low wall and beyond this broken rocks and snow leading to the foot of our *bête noire*, the step in the ridge. I should estimate this as 150 feet high, and at first sight it appeared a formidable obstacle. It was built up of horizontally stratified rocks and overhung in places, but the fact that the strata were well defined and dipped if anything slightly inwards encouraged the hope that perhaps a way could be made up it from ledge to ledge. A direct approach from the ridge crest was out of the question, but immediately to the right of the step was a shallow, ill-defined little gully, and it occurred to me that if this were climbed a horizontal traverse could be made across the face of the cliff to a point whence the upper portion was practicable.

To my relief the snow of the gully was in excellent order and though so steep that I halted to rest at every step with my chest against it, the fact that I could drive in my ice axe to its head gave me a feeling of security. After about 100 feet of this arduous work I was able to step to the left on to a ledge a few inches in width which traversed the cliff more or less horizontally. Edging sideways along this under some impassable overhangs I reached a point where a series of rock leaves projected from the face. Although fragile in appearance they were perfectly firm and climbing slowly up them with some halts for breath I presently found myself at the top of the step. The worst had been accomplished – or so I thought – and I shouted joyfully to Peter, who was now busying himself with his camera.

Above the step the going was easy until I came to a slab about 25 feet high. There was no avoiding this and it had to be climbed. There were few holds, but a tongue of snow well frozen to the rock afforded an excellent purchase for the ice axe and by utilising the friction of my knees I was soon at the top.

After this the climbing was more laborious than difficult and with nothing to occupy my full attention I realised how weary I was and that every step involved a conscious effort of will power. As I have discovered on many occasions, easy climbing can seem more fatiguing than difficult climbing, though, of course, this only applies up to a certain point in tiredness beyond which difficulties become insuperable owing to sheer muscular weakness.

Going very slowly, with halts to rest every few steps, I approached the most remarkable obstacle I have encountered on a mountain. By some extraordinary geological chance a boulder the size of a cottage had wedged itself athwart the ridge. There was no climbing over the top of it for it overhung, nor could I see a way of clambering over a vertical wall of rock to one side, really a tongue of the boulder. Had I been climbing in the Alps I might have scaled this wall, but it meant an upward pull on the arms alone and for this I had insufficient strength; gymnastics are not possible over 23,000 feet. There was no hope of turning the obstacle to the left, for here the precipice fell with appalling steepness, but there was one way – and it is this that makes the obstacle unique in my recollection of Himalayan climbing – there was a way under it.

The boulder was hollowed beneath and this hollow persisted from one side to the other. The cave thus formed was perhaps five feet high at its entrance but it was more than half choked with ice, leaving just room for a man prepared to crawl.[3] Stooping down I looked through a little funnel of glistening black ice and perceived a gleam of light at the far end. It was a last hope and I crawled inside.

Describing these events now makes them seem straightforward enough, but at the time they possessed a queer dreamlike quality, which is consonant with my former experience of severely difficult climbing at high altitudes. I believe the absurdity of the situation must have struck me because I remember halting my crawl to laugh aloud, but my laugh deteriorated into a gasp; laughter is hard work at high altitudes.

I had hoped that the hole would end conveniently on the ridge above the boulder but this was too much to expect. It ended to one side – the side overlooking the western precipice.

Crawling forwards, I looked out through the ice-encumbered exit. Once again Fortune smiled. The precipice beneath was sheer but there was a ledge half-hidden by snow and ice running forwards beneath the boulder towards the ridge. The difficulty was to get out of the hole on to this ledge. Having got my head and shoulders out; I twisted to the right until I could grasp satisfactory handholds, then half-pushed with my knees and half pulled with my arms. For a moment my full weight came on my arms, then I was in safety on the ledge. It sounds a sensational manoeuvre; at the time, however, it seemed obvious and straightforward. But it was very exhausting and when, a minute later after a short pause, I regained the ridge I had to rest before I could summon up the energy to continue.

As to the ridge immediately above the boulder I have the vaguest recollection; I think it was easy snow and rock, but I do remember that the snow was softer and more powdery than lower down. I remember too looking up and seeing the summit apparently an immeasurable distance away, just as the summit of Everest had appeared from over 28,000 feet in 1933.

Then to my dismay I came on yet another obstacle – a step in the ridge some fifty feet high. Had I been stronger I might have climbed this, for the rocks, though steep, were broken, but I had no further strength for strenuous rock-

[3] When free of ice at the far end and with snow-free rocks at the exit this passage would be comparatively easy.

climbing and was now fast drawing on my last reserves of energy.

The alternative was a snow filled gully to the left. This lay on the south-west face of the mountain and was exceedingly steep. At its base it narrowed into what was virtually a chimney, but above it broadened out into a snow slope, which I told myself must surely lead to the summit. It was the sole alternative, the one breach in the topmost defences of the mountain.

Traversing horizontally to the left I entered the gully. Thank heavens it was filled with snow, not ice, but deep soft powdery snow into which I sank almost to the knees. Fortunately there was well compacted snow beneath and I was able to drive in my ice axe to the head, which gave me a feeling of security, especially when the surface layer poured off in loose streams and hissed down the gully and out over the precipice.

Once or twice I was able to use rocks, including a little outcrop where the gully broadened. It was funereal going; at every step I had to halt and rest before I could muster sufficient energy for the next step.

As the gully broadened the angle of the slope lessened. I now saw the ridge to my right; it was unbroken snow, but I did not venture too close to the crest for fear of cornices. It ended at a point of snow, but I scarcely dared believe that this was the summit. I trudged towards it. There was no cornice and a few minutes later, at about 1.30 p.m., I sank down in the soft snow, Mana Peak beneath me, after the hardest solitary climb of my life.

For a minute or two I was too fatigued to do anything but sit breathing heavily, blissfully conscious that whatever else befell me I had no longer to lever myself uphill. Then as my speeding heart and lungs quieted I became gradually conscious of my position and the view.

Since I left Peter I had been concerned with climbing and my whole physical and nervous energy had been concentrated to that one end, but now that the deadening work of hoisting the weight of my tired body uphill was at an end my mental faculties were released from physical bondage. The one concession of high altitudes is that as soon as the climber rests for any length of time he is enabled to forget his physical weariness. To me that day it was as though I had been led blindfold up the mountain and that the bandage had been removed on the summit. It was this more than any sense of "conquest" or achievement that made my few minutes on the summit unforgettable, so that if I live to be old and feeble I can still mount the golden stairs of memory to inspiration and contentment.

The summit of Mana Peak is the highest and southernmost point of an undulating snow ridge about 200 yards long which extends northwards in the direction of the group of peaks known as the Abi Gamin. Kamet is immediately to the west of this group, and the first object I saw when I had recovered from my fatigue was its huge reddish pyramid, to which clung a vast banner of cloud floating slowly westwards yet ever forming against the mountain as it did so.

It would be easy to reel out a string of names of ranges, peaks, glaciers and valleys, but to occupy the mind with trifling topographical details on the summit of a great Himalayan peak is a petty anticlimax to weeks of reconnaissance, strenuous work, and a final glorious scramble. On a mountaintop time's sands are grains of pure gold; must we then obscure their brightness with a leaden mess of trifling detail? After Kamet I remember clearly but one detail in all that enormous landscape, the plateau of Tibet. I saw it to the east of the Abi Gamin, a yellow strand laid beyond the Himalayan snows, shadowed here and there with glowing clouds poised in a profound blue ocean like a fleet of white sailed frigates. For the rest there were clouds and mountains; clouds alight above, blue caverned below over the deeper blue of valleys, citadels of impermeable vapour spanning the distant foothills, and mountains innumerable snow mountains, rock mountains, mountains serene and mountains uneasy with fanged, ragged crests, beautiful mountains and terrible mountains, from the ranges of Nepal to the snows of Badrinath and the far blue ridges of Kulu and Lahoul.

Would that Peter had been there to share this with me.

But of all my memories, distinct or vague, one memory stands pre-eminent: the silence. I have remarked before this silence of the high mountains. How many who read this have experienced silence? I do not mean the silence of the British countryside or even of the northern hills and moorlands, for though we may strain our ears and hear nothing there is always life not far distant. I mean the silence of dead places where not even a plant grows or a bird dwells. That day there was no wind, not the lightest breathing of the atmosphere, and I knew a silence such as I have never known before. I felt that to shout or talk would be profane and terrible, that this silence would shatter in dreadful ruin about me, for it was not the silence of man or earth but the silence of space and eternity. I strained my ears and heard – nothing. Yet, even as I strained, I was conscious of something greater than silence, a Power, the presence of an absolute and immutable Force so that I seemed on the very boundary of things knowable and things unknowable. And because I have felt this more than once before on the high mountains I know that death is not to be feared, for this Force is a part of Heaven and a part of us; how else should we be aware of it? From it we have been evolved; into it we quietly and peacefully return.

The minutes passed. Presently I mustered up the effort needed to take some photographs; then I began the descent.

The ascent had been hard work; the descent was absurdly easy by comparison. My strength returned with each downward step and once again I realised, as I had realised on Everest, that altitude alone is responsible for exhaustion on high Himalayan peaks. To judge from the speed at which I descended the difficulties of Mana Peak are also primarily dependent on the altitude, but it was a steep descent nevertheless and the reverse passage of the hole under the boulder, while being considerably easier, especially as I discovered more holds, was awkward, and so was the slab below it and the big step in the ridge.

An hour later I rejoined Peter, who had regained his strength so well that he had scrambled about to take photographs and had ascended the ridge for a short distance. No time was to be lost if we were to get back to camp before dark and we descended without delay.

All went well till we turned off the ridge on to the ice slope, but here we had to re-cut many steps which had been damaged by the sun and lost much valuable time in regaining the lower snow ridge. Such work coming after a great climb is particularly irksome and it is on such occasions that risks are taken and accidents occur, but Peter rose nobly to the task and deepened the steps with unfaltering precision.

At last we were on the plateau. The afternoon mists had risen and we passed along the crest of Peak 21,500 feet in a desultory hailstorm. Before turning off it we shouted to the porters, who should be awaiting our arrival at the camp, in the hope that they would hear us and prepare some tea and were relieved to hear a faint response.

At 6.15 the camp loomed out of the mist and a few minutes later hot tea was moistening our parched throats. How good it was, no nectar is more revivifying at the end of a hard day on the mountains.

A few minutes' rest, while the men packed up and we set off once more, down the ridge to the Zaskar Pass. At last the snow and ice were behind us; no longer was it necessary to place each foot with exact care; through the dusky mist we moved shadow-like along the easy scree ridge. Already the strenuous events of the day were in the remote past, no longer linked to us by any thread of difficulty or danger. Trudging along, very weary now, through the swift gathering darkness we came at 7.15 to the camp.

So ended the longest, grandest and hardest mountain climb of our lives.

CHAPTER TWENTY TWO

A Hailstorm on Nilkanta

ON AUGUST 13, the day following the ascent of Mana Peak, we reached Badrinath after a fatiguing march from the Zaskar Pass, and there remained for the next two days comfortably ensconced in the little rest house.

Kedarnath and Badrinath are the two goals of the pilgrims who throng annually to the Himalayas to worship the five deities of Hinduism, Siva, Vishnu, Devi, Genesa and the Sun, Kedarnath being dedicated to Siva, the Destroyer, and Badrinath to Vishnu. The Rawal, or High Priest of Badrinath is a Brahman from Southern India, and the temple of which he is the keeper, a little building with a gilded roof, contains the image of Vishnu carved in black stone. From the temple a flight of steps, polished smooth by the feet of innumerable pilgrims, leads down to the Alaknanda River in which the devout dip themselves, holding on to ring bolts to prevent the swift torrent from sweeping them away. There is also a hot spring believed to be very efficacious, especially every twelfth year when the planet Jupiter is in the sign of Aquarius.

Architecturally Badrinath is a mean little place being composed for the most part of single-storied houses which display a wealth of corrugated iron roofing, and its situation in a barren boulder-strewn valley almost completely destitute of trees adds still further to its ugliness. Its greatest interest lies in its proximity to the source of the Alaknanda River, the "true source" of the Ganges, which issues from the Bhagat Kharak and Satopanth Glaciers a few miles distant, though a nearer and remarkable waterfall is acknowledged to be the stream mentioned in the Skanda Purana, "where the Ganges falls from the foot of Vishnu like the slender thread of a lotus flower."

The pilgrimage is not undertaken merely for abstract religious reasons but in many cases as deliberate self-immolation and penance for sins, and this accounts for the presence of many ascetics, Yogis, Bairagis and Sanyas. The Yogis come from all classes of the community, from the noblest Rajput families to the lowest castes, and having renounced everything material, except the barest necessities of life, strive towards Nirvana through mortifying the flesh. To what extent a man is justified in severing all social ties and battening on the charity of his neighbours in pursuit of selfish, yet in one sense selfless, ends, is only one of the innumerable social and religious problems of India. At least he sets an example in simplicity of living, the secret of earthly happiness.

Only one great mountain is visible from Badrinath, Nilkanta. This peak is associated in Hindu mysticism and mythology with Siva, for Nilkanta or Nilakantha, the Blue-necked, is an allusion to the god whose matted locks are represented by the torn glaciers and eternal snows. It is easy to understand why Nilkanta should be held in superstitious awe and reverence by the pilgrims, for there is no more majestic and awe-inspiring peak of its height in the world. It rises 21,600 feet above the sea and its summit is only five miles from Badrinath, 10,159 feet. Like the Matterhorn it stands alone and has no rival within eight miles, and is beautifully proportioned, being pyramidal in form with a graceful ice-clad summit whence sweep down three great ridges, of which the south-east terminates in the Alaknanda Valley at an elevation of only 7,000 feet.

My first view of the mountain was as dramatic as it was beautiful. The Kamet Expedition, after exploring the Arwa Valley, descended to Badrinath en route to Ranikhet. We knew that Nilkanta is visible from Badrinath but were frustrated by monsoon mists from seeing it during the day. But as we dined the mists cleared, revealing it full in the light of the rising moon. Of many moonlit views I have seen, the snows of this glorious peak framed between the dark walls of a gorge was the most beautiful.

Peter had also seen the mountain and it was agreed before I left England that we should attempt the ascent. Such views of the mountain as we had already seen had convinced us that the only possible line of approach was via the South-East Ridge. Though the longest of the three ridges, it seemed likely that it was accessible from the Khiraun Valley which bifurcates with the Alaknanda Valley four miles below Badrinath and which, as far as we knew, had not been entered previously by a European. If the crest of the ridge could be gained at a point within reasonable distance of the summit, there appeared to be a possibility of climbing the mountain.

Our first concern at Badrinath was to engage some more porters. So far we had managed with our five Darjeeling men, but they and we had carried very heavy loads, and for peaks such as Nilkanta, which are within easy reach of villages, the ultra-small party loses its point and inadequate porterage merely complicates an expedition. So word was sent to Mana and soon a number of Marcha Bhotias arrived from that village. Several had "chits" from former expeditions and one produced a recommendation given him by Mr. C.F. Meade in 1913. We engaged four of them, picturesque fellows with wild locks and dressed in a weird and wonderful assortment of costumes.

Two days passed restfully and pleasantly during which time we received generous gifts of fruit, vegetables and sweetmeats from Pandit Neryan Dutt, who befriended the Kamet Expedition in 1931, whilst I must record here the courtesy of the postmaster who, although suffering from malaria, put himself out to further our arrangements.

By the evening of August 15 our "banderbast" was complete and we left next morning after seeing over Pandit Neryan Dutt's garden, which contrives to exist and flourish miraculously in this stony valley and includes fruit trees, although snow lies for several months of the year and winter temperatures must fall well below zero.

Unfortunately the weather was bad. Since we arrived at Badrinath rain had fallen almost continuously and the monsoon was now very heavy. There is no doubt that we should have remained in the north of Garhwal near the Tibetan frontier, where the monsoon air-current is sheered away by the dry winds of the Tibetan plateau, but we were encouraged to attempt Nilkanta by the success of the Anglo-American Expedition which succeeded in climbing Nanda Devi during the height of the monsoon season.

The bungalow at Pandukeshwar is four miles south of the Khiraun Valley but it was necessary to spend a night there in order to pick up some more food and equipment as well as leave certain items which were not needed for Nilkanta. This done, we set off on the following morning, August 17, for the mountain.

Retracing our way up the Alaknanda Valley we crossed the Alaknanda River by a primitive little bridge, built however on the correct cantilever principle, and entered the Khiraun Valley. The impression we had gathered from the map was of a steep-sided valley narrowing into a gorge, for Nilkanta rises 10,000 feet out of the valley in about two horizontal miles, a steep angle even in a country of tremendous mountainsides. Such, however, is by no means the case and on entering the valley we found ourselves amid fields and woodlands watered by clear running streams.

For a little distance we followed a rough shepherd's track but presently lost it and had to force our way through a wilderness of pink-flowered balsam (*Impatiens roylei)* growing fully eight feet tall. Had it not been for the labour we might have appreciated the beauty of these flowers which covered acres of the valley floor in a sheet of bloom, as it was, we were heartily glad to regain the path, dripping with sweat after the unusual exercise.

Crossing the valley torrent, which by its size suggested a considerable glacier system, we climbed a steep track to a hamlet set amid cultivated fields on a sloping shelf of the valley-side. Europeans were evidently something of a curiosity here and I nearly scared a small girl out of her wits when I attempted to take her photograph.

We camped half a mile beyond this village at a height of about 9,000 feet, a pleasant peaceful spot within sound of several streams.

Rain fell in the night and the morning of August 18 was dull and misty. After wading through dripping vegetation, which included thistles fully seven or eight feet high, we traversed forest-clad hillsides, then climbed steeply up the northern side of the valley. The local men were so slow that we began to wonder whether we should ever get on to our mountain. Every boulder, ledge and terrace was a potential halting place for a prolonged puffing at their pipe, which had to be passed from hand to hand, and even Wangdi soon abandoned all hope of persuading them to move until the ritual was ceremoniously and inflexibly fulfilled; this was their method of travel and the immemorial customs of the country were not to be violated by impatient Europeans.

To judge from its vegetation, the Khiraun Valley receives an abundant rainfall and enjoys a warm climate due to the proximity of the deep Alaknanda Valley, which is a natural funnel for the monsoon current, and I noticed oaks growing at between 11,000 feet and 12,000 feet, an unusual height for this tree. There were also many plants, including an annual blue gentian (*G. tenella*) which a week later covered the upper slopes with innumerable blooms, and the curious woolly spires of a *saussurea*.

At length, and quite unexpectedly, we arrived at a most beautiful alp, hundreds of acres of perfect turf grazed over by flocks of sheep and goats. There was a stone shepherd's shelter and the shepherd came forward to greet us, a soldierly looking fellow who told us that he had served for ten years with the Garhwal Rifles and that we were the first Europeans he had ever seen in the valley.

We camped on the alp and it would be difficult to imagine a more delightful spot for, as Peter remarked, good turf is rare in Garhwal and here were hundreds of acres of fertile meadows where we had anticipated finding steep and barren hillsides. Indeed it was difficult to imagine that we were on the slopes of one of the steepest and most formidable peaks in the Central Himalayas, especially as we had seen nothing of it as yet owing to mist.

Next morning we awoke to hear the patter of rain on our tents. Mist shrouded the hillsides but the shepherd accompanied us some distance to direct us to a higher alp. After scaling about 1,500 feet of grassy hillside we traversed horizontally and eventually came to a little shelf with plenty of dwarf rhododendron at hand for fuel, whilst juniper was not more than half an hour away. As we were unable to see more than a few yards owing to mist and were quite unable to estimate our position in relation to the south-east ridge, of which we had seen nothing, we decided to camp, having estimated our height as being close on 15,000 feet.

So dense was the mist that when Peter ventured away from the camp on a tour of inspection he lost his bearings and only found his way back with difficulty; such dense and persistent mist is rare in the Himalayas and for all we could see of our surroundings we might have been camped on an English fell-side.

The mist cleared from our vicinity at nightfall, revealing the Khiraun Valley, and eastwards, far beyond the Alaknanda Valley, the dim forms of Gauri Parbat and Hathi Parbat, the massive bulk of Dunagiri and the thin keen peak of Nanda Devi. For a minute we gazed at these great mountains, then, instinctively, our eyes passed upwards. Immediately above the camp was a hillside, its wet herbage white and frosty in the moonlight, ending in a dark shoulder; above and beyond the shoulder a slender ribbon of snow tailed upwards into the stars – Nilkanta.

The following morning was fine but did not appear likely to remain so for long, and at 6.30 we set out on a reconnaissance which would, we hoped, determine whether or not we could reach the crest of the South-East Ridge, and if so whether the ridge afforded a practicable route to the summit.

The hillside was unexpectedly easy and after mounting over grass and boulders we approached a small glacier descending into the Khiraun Valley. As this was apparently un-crevassed and the snow was old and well compacted, we proceeded to cross it, but had not gone far when we came to an unpleasant bottle-mouthed hole of unknown depth which had remained invisible until we were within a yard or two of it. After this we did what we should have done before, roped together, and without further incident crossed the remainder of the glacier to a broken rock face leading up to the crest of the ridge. The rocks were not in the least difficult and presently we stood on the ridge.

Considering the general angle from which Nilkanta rises from the Khiraun Valley we were not surprised to find that the ridge was very steep; at the same time it was broken up in its lowermost portion into a complicated mass of rock pinnacles: could these pinnacles be outflanked and, if so, was the ridge above them less broken and complicated? Only through practical trial could we determine this and we decided to push forward with our reconnaissance as far, as was possible in the day.

Immediately above us the ridge broadened out to form a commodious camping site; then, after continuing almost horizontally for another hundred yards, sprang upwards towards the first of the rock pinnacles. Seen *en face* the rocks appeared very difficult; actually they were well broken up and we proceeded unroped. It was an enjoyable scramble for, although mists had again gathered and there seemed every prospect of a snowstorm, the weather was windless and warm.

Climbing rapidly, we followed the ill-defined ridge crest for a short distance, then traversed to the right above the depths of a gully, stepped round a corner, and scrambled up a series of slabs and ledges interspersed with screes, steering as well as we could in the mist for a point on the ridge crest above the initial group of pinnacles.

After several hundred feet of this work a fault in the cliff tempted us still further to the right along a ledge, but this proved a mistake as the ledge petered out in an impassable precipice, so retracing our steps we climbed directly upwards and presently gained the ridge crest above the more formidable of the lowermost pinnacles.

The rock here was mostly firm and plentifully supplied with holds and we progressed rapidly over a minor pinnacle, descended from it into a gap, and climbed up to the right of the ridge over broken ground towards the next pinnacle. And here we encountered the first serious difficulty.

The pinnacle we were aiming for was thin and sharp and the gap beyond it deep. We decided that it must be outflanked if possible. To the west was a narrow gully leading down to broken rocks but it was an unpleasant place, loose and with a mixture of grit and snow resting on slabs. The alternative was a traverse on the East Face. The rock here was firmer but the climbing, technically speaking was more exposed and difficult and we had to descend greasy rocks down and round a nearly vertical corner overhanging a terrifically steep gully cleaving the East Face of the mountain.

After this came a long stretch of easy rocks and once more progress was rapid; indeed the climbing on the whole had been much easier than anticipated, though the route finding throughout had been tricky and we were lucky to have discovered at a first attempt a comparatively easy breach in the lower defences of the mountain.

But Nilkanta had a surprise in store, and we had not advanced far when there rose before us a thin and elegant pinnacle with sheer sides falling into unknown depths and so formidable in appearance that it seemed our reconnaissance had come to a premature end.

At such moments it is a sound plan to stop and eat, for rest and food have an optimistic effect on a mountaineer, but in this instance the more we stared at this hard faced sentinel of the ridge the less we liked it.

One thing was in our favour, the rock. The best that Chamonix can muster is no better than the clean-cut granite of this part of the ridge.

For the first rope length all went well and the climbing while steep was more strenuous than difficult. Then we came to a little corner immediately under an overhanging slice of rock. It was only twenty-five feet from the crest, but there was no climbing the overhang. To the left ran a ledge which appeared to tail out in the precipice; but to the right there seemed just a chance that we might work across the face of the pinnacle and regain the ridge beyond it.

Well held by Peter – the belays for the rope were splendid throughout this part of the climb – I edged along an outward sloping gangway and after a delicate traverse to the right and an awkward movement round a corner, made principally on the hands, and a further traverse, reached a little recess under an overhang beyond the pinnacle. The only hope of regaining the ridge was to climb a curiously grooved slab to the left. The holds were sloping the wrong way, but by getting my feet on the slab and lying back with my hands grasping an edge – in technical parlance a "lay-back" – I was able to work my way up, a very exhausting manœuvre at nearly 19,000 feet which I could not have done without the climbing and acclimatisation to altitude of the past few weeks.

Twenty-five feet more of steep climbing, this time on good holds, and I reached the crest of the ridge above the pinnacle which proved to be more of a step on the ridge than an isolated point.

Peter joined me, and in so doing douched with cold water any little vanity I might have felt at overcoming a difficult obstacle by loitering negligently up the rocks. However, on such occasions it is possible to repair injured pride by reflecting that there is a right and a wrong end to a climbing rope.

The ridge now continued almost horizontally for a short distance, then rose abruptly in another step formed by a wall several hundred feet high, of which the lowermost 200 feet consisted of a belt of very steep slabs.

Here in all probability was the crux of the climb. We could not tell what lay above, but hoped that once up this step, if it were practicable, we should find ourselves on the upper snow and ice-slopes of the mountain.

There was no time for a further reconnaissance for the afternoon was well advanced, and after examining carefully this next problem we began the descent convinced that we must contrive to pitch a camp as near as possible to the foot of the step, though, as we had already agreed, it was beyond the scope of our small party to convoy laden porters up the difficult place we had just climbed: it would mean fixing ropes and indulging in "siege tactics" for which we were ill-equipped and incidentally had no intention of undertaking.

In the hope of finding an easier alternative route past the pinnacle we explored downwards to the west and there, as luck would have it, discovered that the ledge I had rejected on the way up was a fraud and continued on out of sight round a corner to end in easy rocks. We had put ourselves to a great deal of unnecessary trouble by selecting the other and much more difficult route. Nevertheless, it was a sensational little causeway. We had to crawl along a narrow sloping shelf over as sheer a drop as any seeker of the sensational could wish to experience, then lower ourselves on to some footholds and in spread-eagle fashion edge round a corner.

The lower traverse and the slimy corner were also avoided by the gully we had looked down, but this, though technically easier, was an unpleasant alternative as the rocks were loose and covered with a treacherous mixture of snow and grit.

For the rest, the descent was uneventful until we came to the complicated hillside above the camp, where the mist was so dense that we could see only a few yards. Every now and then we paused to shout in the hope of attracting the porters' attention. Our shouts were heard and answered, but even so it was difficult to find the camp, and when at length we reached it, the light was rapidly failing.

The weather was in a sullen mood and it was no surprise when heavy rain set in soon after our arrival. But we could hardly grumble; whatever Nilkanta had in store for us, we had enjoyed a splendid day's mountaineering and we celebrated the occasion with a feast of "Maggi" soup, mutton, potatoes, onions, delicious wild rhubarb gathered near the camp and "Ovaltine" after which a certain bottle husbanded by Peter at Pandukeshwar circulated steadily between the tents.

It is seldom that bad weather fits in with a plan on a mountain, but heavy rain next day not only offered no temptation to push up a camp but enabled one of the local men to descend to Pandukeshwar for another pair of boots for Peter who had lost many nails from his present pair. Still, if I had to choose where to spend an "off day" would not select a small and leaky tent battered ceaselessly by torrential rain.

Fortunately, Peter had plenty of reading matter and he loaned me "Dr. Johnson". As I lay in my sleeping bag listening to the dreary sound of the rain on the canvas and occasionally making vain attempts to check a steady drip on to my sleeping bag, I tried to picture the worthy Doctor. Under similar circumstances would he have written something such as this?

> Sir,
> I address you from within the miserable confines of a tent, a leaky, plaguy structure into which a proportion of moisture finds its way with a scurrilous persistency. This inclemency of the elements is as irksome as it is irritating and taxes considerably the moral fortitude while imposing discomfort on the human frame. In a word, Sir, it is shrewish weather and foully damp.

The rain continued until the afternoon of August 22, and the temperature fell sharply, so that when the mists cleared the peaks showed heavily plastered with freshly fallen snow.

The following morning was bright and as further inactivity was thoroughly distasteful we decided to push up the camp to the site we had already noted, taking with us the five Darjeeling men and three Mana men, Kharak Singh, Mangal Singh and Nater Singh.

Mana men jibbed at crossing the little glacier, except for Nater Singh, whom we had already marked out as exceptionally keen and willing, and it was some time before Peter's fluent Urdu could persuade them to continue.

Several inches of snow had fallen and this and stones had to be cleared away before level platforms could be made for the tents. Meanwhile the weather quickly deteriorated; snow fell heavily and the atmosphere both in gloom and dampness did its best to emulate an English November day.

The camp having been pitched Mana men were sent down, after which we settled into our damp sleeping bags to continue a dreary and apparently useless vigil.

Fortunately the snow did not accumulate deeply on the rocks and under the influence of the sun next morning melted so quickly that we decided to push forward our next camp.

It was essential to load the men lightly for steep rock climbing and we cut down equipment to the minimum. Thus we made rapid progress, climbing for the sake of speed and convenience in two parties widely separated, so that the second was in no danger from stones dislodged by the first.

But the dice were still loaded against us, and a heavy snowstorm broke before we reached the awkward slimy corner of the first difficult pinnacle, quickly covering the rocks with slush. There was nothing for it but to camp, as it was out of the question to allow the men to return unaccompanied in such conditions from anywhere beyond this point.

There was no semblance of a ledge on the steep and broken mountainside, but after an hour's work a little platform was built up just large enough for our single tent. This done the porters returned to the lower camp, leaving us on our damp and uncomfortable little eyrie.

My memories of this camp are exclusively of dampness and discomfort. The reader of travel books expects and demands that the traveller should endure hardship and discomfort; but these make a weary catalogue, and I will content myself by remarking that the tent leaked freely, that our sleeping bags were wet, and that the only means by which we could dry our underclothing was to sleep in it. Is it not a strange thing for men to endure such discomforts for the sake of climbing a mountain? I have often asked this of myself but have never been able to find an answer. Let there be no mistake; the true explorer or mountaineer derives no feeling of superiority over his fellow men from his achievements; his "conquests" are within himself and over himself alone.

A space of six and a half feet by four feet, when occupied by two men and an assortment of foods, food utensils and cooking apparatus, tends to become a trifle cramped and is not conducive to restful sleep. In such circumstances it is a major folly to broach a tin of condensed milk and expect what is left to remain within the tin, and when next morning came the sight of the tent floor afforded convincing testimony as to the volatile qualities of this substance. It was no hardship, therefore, to wriggle out of our steam filled sleeping bags and after a melancholy breakfast set off on what we realised could only be a forlorn-hope attempt on the summit.

The sun was shining brightly when we started and the view from our lofty perch ranged from Kamet and Mana Peak to Dunagiri and Nanda Devi, but we had no illusions left as to the unsettled state of the weather or the rapidity with which a fine morning deteriorates during the monsoon season

The condition of the mountain was now far worse than it had been before and we had a foretaste of what to expect when, instead of climbing round the steep corner of the initial pinnacle, we elected to descend the narrow gully, where snow several inches deep and frozen stones and grit made a disagreeable and dangerous combination. We moved with the greatest care and were unanimous in condemning the place when at length we reached the safety of the gap beyond the pinnacle.

After this the climbing was easier despite the freshly fallen snow on the rocks and we made good progress over the thin pinnacle to the foot of the step in the ridge.

Already the weather was breaking. Within an hour the brilliant morning had been snuffed out by fast gathering mists and the great crags above us loomed cold and hostile through the thickening vapour. Our attempt was doomed to failure; the condition of the mountain alone warranted that assumption; still, we determined at all events to climb the step and reconnoitre as far as possible towards the summit.

If the rocks of the thin pinnacle were firm and delightful to climb the rocks at the foot of the step were the exact reverse, for here we found a flaky pastry-like substance. Moving one at a time and very carefully we edged across a series of rickety ledges, then clambered upwards to a sloping scree covered shelf which traversed the band horizontally. The belt of rotten rock ended here and above the shelf were firm slabs broken here and there into projecting crags and seamed with incipient gullies.

Our first attempt to climb the slabs failed. Then we attempted to follow a shallow scoop-like gully. This quickly steepened into unclimbable rocks, but there seemed just a chance of forcing a route out of the gully over the slabs to the left.

It was a bad place. Peter had no belay worth speaking of and was standing on small holds as I slowly worked my way out across the slabs. The climbing reminded me of the harder routes on Lliwedd in North Wales; there were the same small slabby holds and unrelenting exposure except that on Nilkanta the climber who "comes off" falls, not hundreds, but thousands of feet, not that the result in either case is likely to be different.

There was one particularly awkward place where a long step on tiny toeholds had to be made. I hesitated a long time before making it for the reason that to return would be even more difficult; however, I decided to "burn my boats" in the hope that the climbing would become easier beyond. The climbing did not become easier; indeed, after running out about sixty feet of rope, I found further advance impossible. I remember very well clinging to the tiny rugosities of the rock and wishing devoutly that instead of nailed boots I had on felt soled shoes. Then, at this critical juncture, when I knew that retreat was inevitable, a terrific hailstorm burst on us.

One moment the rocks were warm and moderately dry, the next they were cold and streaming with slush and water. So violent was the storm that soon our situation became dangerous owing to the torrents of hail that poured down the slabs.

I have a vivid recollection of my retreat, but it must have been equally painful for Peter, insecurely placed as he was and powerless to check a fall.

Soon my fingers lost sensation on the slush covered holds, but there was no opportunity to warm them, nor was it possible to wear gloves when handling such small holds. The stride was the worst as I had to rely on wet finger holds which I was totally incapable of feeling, but it was done at last and I rejoined Peter thankfully, after one of the nastiest bits of rock climbing of my experience.

The hailstorm ended a few minutes later. There was one last possibility of climbing the step, by a line to the right of our last line. The rocks here were steeper, but they were more broken, and this time we were successful in forcing a route after a difficult and exposed climb.

The upper portion of the step consisted of broken slabs and snow on which we were able to move both together for the most part. Making rapid progress, though we were both feeling tired after our strenuous efforts, we scrambled to the crest of a conspicuous point, which forms the uppermost limit of the step. Here we rested and lunched.

There was no question of proceeding further. We were fully 2,000 feet below the summit of the mountain, the weather was against us, the day well advanced and the mountain in impossible condition: at this height, which cannot have been more than 19,500 feet, fully a foot of new snow was lying, and higher the conditions were manifestly worse.

From our position a snow ridge rose parabolically to a point on the ridge beyond which another snow ridge swept up to the foot of another and, as far as we could judge, very formidable step. If this last could be climbed the summit should be accessible via snow and ice slopes.

There is no doubt that we had underestimated the length and difficulty of the South-East Ridge. To climb Nilkanta another camp or possibly two camps will be necessary, one at our highest point and another above or below the final step. To carry up camps over rocks such as we had encountered will be no easy task, and a week of perfect weather may be required for the job.

But whatever the trials and difficulties the prize will be well worthwhile, and the climber who eventually treads the crest of this peak will be conscious of having climbed one of the most beautiful peaks of its elevation in the Himalaya.*

Much splendid mountaineering awaits the climber who, sick and tired of high altitudes and the spirit of nationalism and competition which surrounds the highest summits of the world with an atmosphere more stifling than the oxygenless air, turns his attention to peaks such as Nilkanta. At moderate elevations he is able not only to test himself to the uttermost of his strength and skill but also to appreciate the beauties of Nature and enjoy the same thrills that the pioneers of alpine mountaineering enjoyed. It will be a happy day for Himalayan mountaineering when the "conquest" of high altitudes is achieved.

We returned to camp drenched by hail, rain, sleet and snow. There was nothing further to be done and the following morning we signalled to the porters at the lower camp to ascend and carry down the camp, which they did so expeditiously that we were able to descend the same day to the lower alp. Next day we descended to Pandukeshwar and on August 28 arrived at Joshimath.

* Nilkanta (now known as Nilkanth) was first climbed in 1974 by Sonam Pulzor, Kanhiya Lal, Dilip Singh and Nima Dorje, members of an Indian Tibetan Border Police team led by S.P. Chamoli. In the same year ITBP teams also climbed Kedernath and Shivling. Claims to the first ascent of Nilkanta had been made by an Indian Army expedition led by Colonel N. Kumar but these were considered unreliable after an official investigation prompted by Himalayan Club experts.

CHAPTER TWENTY THREE

Defeat on Dunagiri

AFTER NANDA DEVI, the undisputed goddess of the Central Himalaya, one of the finest peaks in the group of mountains between the Milam and Dhauli Valleys is Dunagiri, 23,180 feet, which is situated to the north-west of the Nanda Devi basin. For many years past it has attracted the attention of mountaineers, and there is no grander sight in Garhwal than its ice-clad summit soaring in a tremendous sweep out of the Dhauli Valley which, at the confluence of the Dhauli and Rishi Rivers, is only 6,170 feet above the sea.

Dr T G Longstaff, who in 1907 crossed the Bagini Pass to the east of Dunagiri, was of the opinion that the mountain was accessible from the south. Acting on this Peter Oliver and D. Campbell attempted to reach the South-West Ridge from the west but were barred by precipices and hanging glaciers. It was left to Eric Shipton to find a route to the ridge from the east in 1936, and to reach the shoulder of the mountain at a height of about 22,000 feet accompanied by one Sherpa porter. From this shoulder, knife-like ice edges lead for nearly a mile toward the final peak.*

Peter was naturally anxious to attempt once again this splendid mountain and it was the lodestone which drew us south after our failure on Nilkanta. We had hoped also to attempt the unclimbed East Peak of Nanda Devi, but as there was no time for this we resolved to devote the whole of our energies to Dunagiri.

The mountain is more difficult of approach than Nilkanta, and the climber must work his way up the great Rishi Valley before entering the Rhamani Valley which leads up to the South-East Face. We estimated that three weeks' coolie food, weighing about 350 lbs. would be required, and to carry this eight local porters were engaged, including Nater Singh, who had proved his worth on Nilkanta. As it was necessary to retain two men for work on the mountain, Nater Singh and a youth named Dharam Singh were selected and provided with boots and other equipment. Dharam Singh, who to judge from his appearance had more Tibetan than Indian blood in him, had served with the Nanda Devi Expedition, and had become possessed of an ice axe of which he was inordinately proud. In build and manner he suggested an experienced mountaineer, but in point of fact he was not, and though cheerful and willing, proved the least competent of our new recruits.

After some uncomfortable days and nights on Nilkanta, Joshimath seemed a haven of rest and repose and the two days that we spent there were devoted almost exclusively to eating and sleeping. It was an effort to tear ourselves away from the dak bungalow, but on August 31 we set off up the Dhauli Valley.

* See account in *Nanda Devi: Exploration and Ascent* by Eric Shipton and H.W. Tilman, Bâton Wicks / Mountaineers, 1999, pp. 275–78 – an article originally published in *A.J.* 49, pp. 27–40.

We had hoped that the weather would improve, as it must do if we were to stand the smallest chance of success, and there certainly did appear some prospect of this when we left Joshimath.

At the village of Tapoban we had a stroke of luck in being able to purchase seven eggs. Some eggs had been bought at Joshimath, but as half of them were bad we were taking no chances. Accordingly, a bowl of water was requisitioned and the eggs tested: if they sank all was well, but if they swam the reverse was the case. These proceedings were watched by the inhabitants of the village with the greatest curiosity and astonishment, including the vendor, who obviously looked upon them as impugning his good faith and the faith of his hens. Happily all sank. In addition to the eggs we acquired an aged rooster and thus set up for one meal at least proceeded cheerfully on our way.

Once again the weather was profligate, and rain set in later, so that we arrived at the village of Lata damp and cheerless. There was no camping ground and we pitched our tents on a path near the village. But we reckoned without the cows coming home from the upper pastures and a mêlée ensued in which the opposing forces were the cows, whose inflexible determination was to proceed as they always had proceeded along the path, and ourselves, who strove to make them realise the wisdom of by-passing a crowded thoroughfare.

The inhabitants of Lata are cheerful, friendly people and soon called on us with gifts of vegetables. Among them was an old shikari who had accompanied Dr. Longstaff in 1907 and Peter when he climbed Trisul in 1934, a charming old gentleman armed with an antique rifle which projected through the medium of caps and gunpowder, an assortment of ironmongery and stones. He was particularly anxious that we should assist him in stalking a bear, which had recently killed one of the cows of the village, but as we had left our rifle at Joshimath we were unable to accept this invitation, no doubt he would be able to deal with it effectively if he could get within close enough range for a blast of nails and pebbles. There was also an impression abroad that I was a doctor and I was called on to treat cases of conjunctivitis and blood poisoning. On this, as on other occasions. I was amazed at the implicit and touching faith in the Sahib. It was no use telling my patients that they must go to the hospital at Joshimath to be treated by the Indian doctor there; no, the Sahib was worth a thousand Babu doctors, however well qualified.

During the night we were plagued by mosquitoes, which if not malarial at this altitude, were so venomous that I woke next morning scarcely able to see out of my eyes.

From Lata to the alp known as Lata Kharak a steep track scales 5,000 feet of hillside, at first through dense sub-alpine vegetation, then between pines, birches and rhododendrons. The morning was showery, but the weather improved later and we spent the remainder of the day pottering about the camp collecting seeds or gazing on the stupendous panorama of mist-swathed ridges, deep blue valleys and the remote snows of Hathi Parbat shining through windows in slow-moving columns of thundercloud.

Rain fell in the night but the morning was fine. Our route lay along the north-west side of the Lata Ridge to a grass pass south-west of Tolma Peak. We now entered the Rishi Valley and at once had a foretaste of the next three days' travelling in a goat track, which wound sinuously in and out of gullies.

Before we had gone far the weather broke in a sharp hailstorm, which cleared as we breasted a ridge and saw at our feet the bright green alp of Durashi. Down we went over slopes blue with gentians and frosted silver with edelweiss, just in time to pitch the tents before hail and rain again deluged the valley. Wet mists surrounded us for the remainder of the day, but when night fell the stars shone out and through the clear air we saw the twinkling light of a shepherd's fire on the slopes of the Kuari Pass many miles away.

We left early next morning and walked up slopes of grass and boulders to the ridge we must cross to the alp, Dibrugheta. Immediately ahead, towering from the jaws of the Rishi Valley, was Nanda Devi with light mists stationed on its dark precipices. Small wonder that until Shipton and Tilman penetrated the tremendous gorges of the valley to the inmost sanctuary of the goddess, this district was reputed locally to be the abode of demons and dragons, for there can be no more awe-compelling scenery in the world than the vista of gorges framing this glorious mountain.

The weather was perfect and we were able to enjoy to the full the beauties of Dibrugheta, which Dr. Longstaff described as a "horizontal oasis in a vertical desert". Our tents were pitched on a sward of flowers with forests above and below, and in the background the sunlit slabs known as "The Curtain"; a peaceful, beautiful place where we rested through the sunny afternoon in lazy contentment.

Unhappily the fine weather did not last; rain fell during the night and we set off next morning in mist and drizzle. In the dripping forest above the alp we disturbed a black bear, who quickly made off. A red currant grows here but, like the Himalayan strawberry, it is almost tasteless. After climbing some 1,500 feet we emerged from the forest on to a shoulder where I found monkshood in seed, then traversed steep hillsides covered here and there in juniper and *berberis* (*B. aristata*). There were also numerous flowers, including *lloydias*, *potentillas*, *anemones*, gentians, *saxifrages* and *androsaces*. I noted the seed of *nomocharis* and was able to collect some when we returned. There is no doubt that the Rishi Valley and the Nanda Devi basin would well repay botanical exploration.

The Nanda Devi Expedition had made a well-defined track, which we followed without difficulty. Yet even so progress was slow, for the track was seldom level and to travel one mile takes two or three hours in this valley with its innumerable gullies and buttresses.

Two goats had been purchased; one had been slaughtered at Durashi and the survivor now accompanied us. It was a cause of much tribulation to the man leading it, but all my sympathies were with it. Twice it escaped and was recaptured with difficulty after an exciting scramble across the hillside.

Shortly after midday we came to two draughty caves where the Nanda Devi Expedition had camped, but we were determined to make a longer march, and Peter eventually persuaded the local men to continue despite a good deal of grumbling.

Just beyond this place a steep stream rushes down a series of slabby scoops and falls. From sheer laziness we tried to cross too high instead of at a safe and easy place a little lower. The agile Wangdi got over, but the next man failed although assisted by an ice axe. Then I tried. There was a small hold in the middle of a smooth, water-worn slab, and I managed to get one foot on it, but when I tried to raise myself my foot slipped and down I went. Fortunately the stream narrowed into a scoop and in this I wedged above a drop of fully fifty feet with water cascading over me. I managed to force my way up against the torrent until one of the men grasped my hand and dragged me to safety, soaked to the skin, with one elbow skinned and feeling something worse than a blithering idiot.

The remainder of the march was miserable, but I obtained a grain of vicarious comfort in the torrential rain, which was now falling; it was impossible for me to become any wetter.

We found a camping place near a trickle of water and levelled tent platforms on the steep hillside. Everything was damp and the tents being muddy leaked like sieves. Our luck with the weather could scarcely be worse, and conditions for the porters were wretched in the extreme as they had no spare underclothing to change into; their cheerfulness under such conditions is inspiring.

A supper of dhal (lentils) and rice curry made the world seem a better place and it became positively rosy after a jorum of whisky. The night that followed is memorable to me above many nights. With us we had a two pound tin of black treacle. This had been drilled through the top with the usual holes to allow of the treacle coming out and the air going in. The tin was placed in my tent, but deliberately turned itself upside down and oozed all night over the floor, my sleeping bag, mattress and sweaters. The last mentioned article does not combine harmoniously with black treacle and I shall never forget the anguish on Nurbu's face when he looked in next morning.

It was a dull, sullen morning and snow was falling down to the 17,000-foot level. For a few minutes there was a suspicion of sunlight then, inexorably, the mists shut down and rain began to fall.

The going was easy on the whole and we reached the entrance of the Rhamani Valley earlier than expected. The mist made the way up this difficult to find, but we ascended a gully and traversed hopefully along hillsides considerably less steep than those of the Rishi Valley. Presently, after crossing two streams, we came to a grass slope where there was a large overhanging boulder, the ground beneath which showed evident signs of former occupation. This was Shipton's camping place and it was remarkable that we should come across it after groping our way up the valley and over complicated hillsides in a thick mist.

Here we camped. There was juniper handy and soon Ang Bao had contrived to light a fire in the shelter of the boulder and brew tea. We next dismissed the local men, with the exception of Nater Singh and Dharam Singh, and settled down to make ourselves as comfortable as possible.

Any optimism we might have had as to climbing Dunagiri had long since evaporated. It was now September 6 and since August 13 when we arrived at Badrinath there had been only one completely fine day. There is no doubt that had the Nanda Devi party experienced similar weather they could not have succeeded, for snow had fallen every day, and the mountain had been continuously plastered. Yet there is no reason to suppose that we experienced especially bad monsoon weather, and mountaineers visiting Garhwal during the monsoon season should keep as far north as possible until the monsoon ends, as it usually does, in September.

Rain fell most of the night and as usual we dressed next morning in damp clothing. Once again it was a day of continuous mist and rain, and as we had little idea as to where we were we steered by Peter's compass, making more or less directly up the valley to begin with, then in the approximate direction of Dunagiri. In good weather it would have been a delightful walk as we passed many slopes and lawns bright with flowers, some of which were now in seed, including *allardias*, yellow *potentillas* and *primulas* of the *nivalis* section.

Then we made uphill by the side of a moraine. We could see little or nothing and presently when sleet and snow fell heavily we decided to camp, for there was no object in continuing on what might well prove to be a wrong route to Dunagiri. Three men were retained and the other four sent back to Base Camp. As for the remainder of the day, my diary records simply, "Rain, sleet, snow. Tent leaking."

Six inches of snow fell in the night, but next morning when we looked out of our tents the weather was clear, and we saw the long summit ridge of Dunagiri, white and brilliant in the sun, peeping over a nearer ridge.

To reach the col at the foot of the South-West Ridge we had to cross two intermediate glaciers and ridges. Just beneath the crest of the first ridge we had an inkling as to the snow to expect on the mountain when a little snow slope peeled off in a miniature slab avalanche. Tse Tendrup, who was holding me on the rope from the ridge crest, apparently thought I was in great danger (there was none as the slope was not fifty feet high and ended in screes) and planting both heels in the snow pulled for all he was worth. A volley of half strangled curses was his sole reward for an action which, on the face of it, was entirely praiseworthy.

The second ridge involved us in a steep descent of some 300 feet, but at length we stood on the glacier immediately beneath the slopes running up to the col. Mists had again formed, but the day was warm and the snow soft and unpleasant to tread. As far as we could see the best route to the col was to one side of a wide and steep bulge of ice. At the foot of the slope was a partially choked bergschrund, which we crossed without difficulty. We had progressed less than 200 feet and I who was leading was cautiously prodding the snow with my ice axe when there was a dull thump. We came to a sudden halt; then, through the mist and above us, we heard the unmistakable rushing sound of an avalanche. There was a slight hesitation, then we turned and fled making for the shelter of the ice bulge.

It was a nasty moment, for we could see nothing in the mist, only hear that ominous grating rush of sliding snow. As we ran, balls of snow scampered past us, nothing more.

The main body of the avalanche stopped just above our farthest point. It was a small one, an affair of an inch or two of surface snow, scarcely enough to have carried us down with it, much less buried us, but it gave us a fright and with common accord we turned our backs on the slope and after some little trouble found a camping place on the glacier, well protected from avalanches by wide crevasses. The porters were then sent back to the lower camp with instructions to return on the morrow with food, fuel and equipment for the camp we had planned to pitch on the col.

It was a desolate situation. All about us was snow and ice, great crevasses, frowning séracs and the mist wreathed precipices of Dunagiri. Our height was about 19,000 feet, and as this is equal to approximately half atmospheric pressure at sea-level, we found it impossible to cook potatoes and after boiling them for over an hour gave them up as a bad job and ate them hard.

There was a sharp frost during the night, and next morning we climbed quickly up hard snow to the col. A biting wind was blowing across the crest, but even this could not detract from the grandeur of the view. I know of few situations where the climber is more conscious of his height. He stands on the edge of a labyrinth of snow and ice, looking down into fertile valleys and away over ranges of low hills towards the distant plains. No human brain can take in the immense panorama, and it was almost a relief to turn to objects more easily calculable: the glorious twin spires of Nanda Devi and the terrible precipices of Changabang, a peak that falls from crest to glacier in a wall that might have been sliced in a single cut of a knife. No journey is more sublime than this visual journey from the remote depths of sub tropical valleys to the terrific summits that girt about the "sanctuary" of Nanda Devi.

From the col the South-West Ridge of Dunagiri springs up in a series of sharp snow edges to a rock band about two-fifths of the way to the summit ridge. Above this band the ridge is flattened to the east and forms an edge rather than a ridge between the South-East and West Faces of the mountain. Thus the climb above the rock band is more of a face climb than a ridge climb until the South-West Shoulder of the peak is reached, whence a series of sharp edges lead towards the final snow cap of the mountain.

Shipton found ice above the col, but when we set off to prospect the route we found soft snow on the initial ridge and the climbing was wearisome rather than difficult.

Perhaps an hour later we reached a little plateau at the foot of the rock band, an obvious site for a camp, though it was doubtful whether the summit was accessible in one day's climbing from this point, taking into account the length of the final ridge.

The rock band was still plastered by recently fallen snow, which had melted here and there to form an ugly ice glaze. Our first attempt to climb it round a corner to the left was unsuccessful, and we found ourselves in an uncomfortable position on snow covered rocks with, in my case, boot soles caked with ice and numbed fingers. After this we did what we should have done before, tackled the problem frontally; and after a difficult and exacting piece of work succeeded in climbing it.

Thenceforward the ascent was comparatively easy until the ridge petered out in the face of the mountain, judging from photographs, this face is some fifty degrees in angle in its lowermost portion and steepens several more degrees before connecting with the south-west shoulder. In good conditions it should be possible to climb it over rocks, but these were now buried beneath snow or glazed with ice and we were forced to the east on to a snow slope.

Whether further advance was justifiable depended on the condition of this slope. At the point where the ridge merged into it the snow was suspiciously wind-rippled, and held by Peter I went a full rope length ahead to test it. Wind ripples inevitably suggest that deadliest form of avalanche trap, wind slab. The climber is proceeding on hard and apparently safe snow when the surface layer cracks and sweeps down, carrying him with it. A slope of two or three hundred feet may well prove fatal as the snow, which has been compacted by the wind, splits up into hard blocks.

The two essential conditions for wind slab are a slope, which permits of the snow accumulating on the lee of a ridge or buttress and a humidity of the atmosphere not less than about 80 per cent. These conditions persist on the North Col of Everest during the monsoon season, and combine to render the east side a death trap. On this slope of Dunagiri, however, though the required degree of humidity was certainly present in the atmosphere, the slope was exposed to the wind, which instead of indirectly depositing snow on a lee had directly compacted it by pressure. Yet, when all is said and done, and the mountaineer has taken into account the implications of weather, snow, temperature and position of the slope, the casting vote between safety and danger must as often as not be based on intuition, a *feeling*, as Mr. Winthrop Young would have it, for the mountains, just as the old sailor can "smell" bad weather or danger in his environment, so can the mountaineer sense danger on a mountain. This intuition is the product of experience and a love for the mountains; it springs from something far deeper than superficial logic or rule of thumb; no text books can analyse it, nor words describe it; it is the still small voice of Nature, and woe betide him who turns a deaf ear.

The slope was safe, but it was steep; not until we approached the shoulder did we tread rock, then there was an awkward little wall and an icy gully. Meanwhile the weather had steadily deteriorated and the signal for our arrival on the shoulder was a sudden snowstorm, accompanied by a strong and bitterly cold wind. We paused just long enough to see the first of a series of sharp snow edges leading towards the summit. There was no question of advancing further as, apart from the bad weather; we were both tired after a climb of well over 3,000 feet on snow, which reminded me of midwinter snow on a high alpine peak.

The porters meanwhile had carried up the camp to the col and by the time we had descended through mist and snow the tents had been pitched.

September 9 dawned clear after a cold night and soon after the sun had risen we packed up preparatory to carrying the camp up the ridge. In such unsettled weather and difficult conditions there was no possibility of taking it beyond the little plateau at the foot of the rock band. From this point retreat is possible in bad weather, but a camp above the band might be isolated for a considerable period, quite apart from the difficulty of pitching it on the steep and exposed slopes beneath the shoulder.

Our steps of yesterday had been filled up with snow and had to be made anew, and with laden porters the ascent took nearly twice the time previously taken by Peter and myself.

Except that there was a nearly level platform for the tents the site had nothing to recommend it, for it was fully exposed to the wind. Our advent was the signal for the worst Himalayan weather I have known, except for the storms on Everest in 1933. My diary is terse on the point.

> *September 9.* Pushed camp to plateau below rock step. Blizzard at 11 a.m., lasted 22 hours. Terribly cold. Zip fastener broke and powdery snow invaded tent (Peter and I were sharing his tent). The coldest night I've ever spent bar high camps on Everest.

10th. Wretched day. Blizzards. Descended to col for more provisions. Snow one to two feet deep on ridge and avalanches peeling off the slopes; steps had to be remade. We were working with two porters, Tse Tendrup and Ang Bao, the remainder having returned to the lower camp for more provisions and equipment.

11th. Clear early. Gale later, then blizzard. Lightning at night. Hopeless conditions.

12th. Clear morning but snowstorm in afternoon. High wind blowing clouds of snow off mountain. Sun cleared some of the snow from rocks above the camp.

In such conditions there was little hope of reaching the summit and we were not in the position to play a waiting game. We determined, however, to push an attack through as far as possible, in which we were encouraged to some small degree by the quantities of snow stripped from the mountain by the wind. If we could regain the shoulder there was a chance we might find the summit ridge in fair condition.

The night of September 12 was starlit and calm and at 4 a.m. on September 13 we roused ourselves and began the wretched business of cooking a meal. The cold was intense; our boots were iron-like, and as usual the condensed milk had spilt overnight, and frozen in a horrid mess to the floor of the tent.

We were off at 6. The rope, which had become wet, had frozen and was as intractable as a steel hawser. The cold was still intense, and my toes soon became so numb that nothing I could do would restore circulation. The one thing in our favour was the weather, which was clear and calm.

If the difficulties had been considerable before they were now far worse, and it was all we could do to force the ice- and snow-plastered rocks immediately above the camp.

We led in turn. The upper snow slope had been safely swept by the wind, but our former steps had disappeared and had to be made anew. The shoulder is about 1,500 feet from the plateau, but it took three and a half-hours to reach. As we climbed, the fine morning quickly deteriorated; mists were forming as we trod the first of a series of snow crests leading towards the summit, and a rising wind carried powdery snow into our faces.

The ridge rises and falls in a series of scallop-like edges. Of the precipices on either hand, that to the south-east is a mere 4,000 feet, but that to the west is appalling in its steepness and magnitude. At first sight it seems to fall direct into the Dhauli Valley, 15,000 feet lower; actually, however, the *sheer* drop into a side glen of the valley cannot be less than 8,000-10,000 feet and constitutes one of the highest mountain walls of the Central Himalayas.

We had hoped against hope that we would find the ridge in good condition, but in this we were disappointed.

The fierce blizzards of the past few days, instead of sweeping it bare had accumulated loose snow upon it, building it up in the process to a razor-like edge.

The first crest was merely fatiguing, as at every step we sank deeply into the soft, floury snow, but on the second we encountered cornices which increased in size the farther we advanced. And they were cornices of the most treacherous type. The ridge crest was continuous in appearance and it was the *undercut* that varied in width. Thus in one place the undercut would be practically nil, and in another place a few yards away, eight or ten feet, without any perceptible difference in the run of the ridge crest to indicate this variation in the overhang.

The solution to such a problem is, of course, to traverse a ridge at a safe distance from any possible cornices, but in the present instance the steepness of the south-east slope, coupled with the loose deep snow, made such an alternative disagreeable, not to say dangerous.

The wind increased steadily as we advanced, and the ridge reeked and smoked with blown snow, so that it became more and more difficult to estimate our position in relation to the cornice. These conditions contributed more than any negligence on our part to a narrow escape from disaster.

We were taking it in turns to stamp out a track through the loose snow, and Peter was in the lead. He was some thirty feet ahead of me and half concealed every few moments by clouds of wind-driven snow, when without a sound the ridge crest peeled off beneath him. As the loosely packed snow collapsed the wind caught it and whirled it upwards, so that it seemed almost to explode. For a moment he disappeared from view, then I saw him; he had been at the edge of the break, and though he had fallen with the cornice he had landed on the true crest of the ridge a few feet lower.

It all happened in a second. He stopped, while the collapsed cornice went smoking down the ice-slopes, then scrambled back to the ridge and safety.

A question I have often asked myself since is would I have been able to stop him had he followed the cornice down the ice face? I could only have done so by throwing myself down the other side of the ridge. Once in the Alps I had to do this, but that was to check the fall of a companion, and I had a second or two in which to decide upon a course of action. Here I had less time and at high altitudes the brain works slowly. I can only *hope* that I would have done the right thing.

We were shaken by the experience, and when Peter regained the ridge, almost exhausted by the effort, the one thing I could think of to say, and it flashed illogically, absurdly and brutally into my mind, was, 'You have been warned!'

After this little misadventure we traversed the south-east slope some distance from the ridge, but we had not gone far when it was brought home to us that we were beaten. I was now taking a turn ahead and so steep was the slope that I was edging along sideways. Worse than this was the loose snow; at every step we sank in to the knees; and beneath the snow was ice, so that it was impossible to secure ourselves by driving in our axes, and we felt that the snow might cascade off at any moment and take us with it. Our attempt had been pushed to the limit of justifiability. There was nothing for it but to retreat.

We had traversed about one-third of the ridge, and beyond our highest point there appears to be no insuperable obstacle. Given good conditions Dunagiri is a safe climb, but it will never be an easy one, especially if much ice is present.

The descent was a miserable experience. I did not realise until we retired how cold I was. Never have I felt so cold; my feet were without feeling and my fingers so numb and stiff that I could scarcely grasp my ice axe. To halt on the ridge was impossible, but a short distance below the shoulder we found a partially sheltered place under a rock where I removed my boots. My feet were white and entirely without feeling, so Peter set to work to rub them. For half an hour he worked away and I can never be sufficiently grateful to him; there is no doubt that he saved me from serious frostbite.

As we sat on an uncomfortably sloping rock we were able to take stock of ourselves and of what we had endured on the wind blasted ridge. We were caked with ice, and our faces looked out from the midst of a solid mass of ice – matting our beards, moustaches and Balaclava helmets.

We turned back at 10.15 and regained the camp at 1.15, after a descent complicated by yet another snowstorm. There Tse Tendrup and Ang Bao set to work on my feet. Their skill was surprising; an experienced masseuse could not have done it better. No doubt Tibetans are used to dealing with frostbite, and experience in treating it is hereditary with them. It was an agonising process when the circulation began to return, and so prolonged was the rubbing that raw patches appeared.

There was no question of a further attempt on Dunagiri, and we packed up the camp and descended through weather that was working up for another blizzard. On the col we collected the remainder of our gear and hastened down to the glacier, meeting Nurbu and Pasang on the way, who relieved us of some of our loads.

Wangdi had pitched a camp on the glacier, and there my feet had another rubbing which restored the circulation, except to my big toes which had already suffered on Everest, and which continued to remind me of Dunagiri for some months to come.

Altogether we were thankful to be off the mountain safely, for what with avalanches, blizzards and collapsing cornices, we felt that we had had more than our fair share of excitements. I remember coming across a copy of *Punch* which had arrived by a previous mail. In it was a questionnaire entitled, "Are You Alive?" I read it very carefully and decided that we were, but only just.

Snow fell heavily at the lower camp, and the weather increased in spitefulness during our return through the Rishi Valley, reaching a climax the day we marched from Dibrugheta to Durashi, when rain fell in such torrents that the stream between the two alps had to be forded one man at a time tied to a rope.

But this day, September 16, was the last day of the monsoon. As I lay shivering in a soaked sleeping bag I saw the stars shining steadily and next morning the alp lay white and frosty beneath a cloudless sky. The fine weather lasted, and all day as we marched to Lata Kharak the sun blazed with a new found vigour. The monsoon had ended as though turned off by a tap.

We had been beaten, soundly thrashed, by Dunagiri, but it was an experience we could hardly regret. Within the space of three weeks we had tasted all that mountaineering has to offer in the Himalayas. Swiftly perish the memories of failure and success; imperishable are the memories of good adventuring.*

* The first ascent was completed on July 5, 1939 by the Swiss trio of André Roch, Fritz Steuri and David Zogg, from a high camp cut out of the South-West Ridge in the vicinity of the shoulder. The less steep continuation ridge was found to be very difficult by this experienced alpine ice-climbing team. The route was attempted again in 1975 by an Austrian team led by Erich Vanis. On this occasion only the shoulder was reached. On October 15, 1976 four members of an American expedition, attempting to repeat the South-West Ridge, fell to their deaths from the steep slopes below the shoulder (Graham Stevenson, Arkel Erb, John Baruch and Benjamín Casasola). There were two separate falls (during their descent) from roughly the same spot. Treacherous ice conditions seem to have been the cause. The various failures by very experienced climbers, together with this accident, surely emphasise the difficulty of this climb?

The second ascent of the mountain was made in October 1975 by Joe Tasker and Dick Renshaw who established a new route up the South-East Face. In 1976 six members of a Japanese expedition led by Anitake Makinouchi made the third ascent by way of the North Ridge.

CHAPTER TWENTY FOUR

Autumn in the Valley of Flowers

ON SEPTEMBER 21 Peter and I parted at Joshimath, Peter to return to Ranikhet and I to return to the Bhyundar Valley to complete my botanical work. So ended the happiest mountaineering partnership of my experience.

It was a perfect morning as I strolled along the Alaknanda Valley. The air was charged with a new sweetness and strength. The humid, waterlogged vapours of the past two months had been replaced by an atmosphere of crystal clarity; the sun was no longer a fierce despotic tyrant but warm and genial.

The last of the pilgrims were descending from Badrinath, and they too seemed imbued with the vigour of the atmosphere and greeted me cheerfully. In a week or two Badrinath would be evacuated for the winter, when snow accumulates to a great depth and renders the Alaknanda Valley inaccessible.

The cycle of life and growth had entered a new phase. Here and there were fields of millet ripening to a deep magenta, and the hillsides were tinted with brown and gold. The predominant note was the intense stillness. The streams after their turbulence had regained tranquillity; the weather, freed from its recent passions, had lapsed into a profound peacefulness; the air was entirely without movement, and a great hush had fallen on hill and valley.

Once again I crossed the crazy little suspension bridge over the Alaknanda River and climbed through the forests to the same camping place at the edge of the Bhyundar River.

Nothing had changed since I entered the valley three months earlier. The remains of the half-burnt tree-trunk were still lying there; the evening was the same with the distant peak alight between the walls of the gorge. Then, miracle of miracles, and I must ask the reader to accept this as true; the same little bird sang the same little hymn from the tree above my tent. In this changelessness lies Nature's greatest message to men. Beside it our hurly-burly of rush and bustle can be viewed in its true proportions; our little snobberies, our puffed up self-importance, become as naught when viewed against this supreme indifference of Nature. Yet the message is not purely negative; it should not inspire hopelessness or passivity. In Nature we see a force building up from limitless materials to some unimagined end; we are part of a growth infinitely serene; why then should we not partake of serenity?

At the upper village next morning I met the old shepherd who had supplied me with milk. He and the other shepherds had driven down their flocks and were about to descend to the Alaknanda Valley for the winter. The grain had been reaped, and lay in golden piles on rushwork mats or in the flagged courtyards of the houses.

Above the village I saw no one, until I came to the pastures below the gorge where some goats were still grazing. Beyond these alps the valley was deserted, and it seemed strange that it should have been abandoned thus early; probably there are seasons when snow falls deeply early in October and the shepherds dare not risk their flocks later than the third week in September.

On the last occasion I had crossed the bridge below the gorge the torrent had raged furiously, but with the ending of the monsoon it had shrunk to peaceable dimensions, for winter cold was now gripping the high snows.

It was good to pass through the gorge into the upper meadows. Peter and I had left them under scowling skies, but now the sky was the colour of the gentians that were blooming in their millions at Base Camp, except where a few light plumes and tufts of glowing cloud clung to the peaks or floated lazily between them. When I had left, green was the predominant shade, now it was brown and gold; the floor of the valley was enriched with soft colourings, varying from tile deep red of the *potentilla* leaves to the yellow of the withering grasses and the faintest tinge of russet in the birch forest. Here and there drifts of white everlastings matched the snows on high, and down by the stream blue *cynoglossum* and deep red *potentillas*, growing from turf only recently evacuated by avalanche debris, were in bloom, hastening to complete their cycle before winter should come.

The predominant note was peace not the faintest breeze ruffled the herbage and the silence was the silence of a vast ocean utterly calm, though always the sound of the streams came to the ear as a soft almost imperceptible cadence.

The evenings were cooler now and frost rimed the herbage at nights, so that I was glad of a fire. Otherwise there was little difference. The same evening mist swept up through the gorge, hurried along the valley and melted away as quickly as it formed, and the same stars looked down when the snows of Rataban had flamed and paled in the swift tide of night.

The morning after our arrival I set the men to work to dig up *nomocharis* bulbs. It was no easy task, as the *nomocharis* seems to prefer the company of bracken roots and grows a full six inches deep; ordinary forks and spades were useless, and ice axes had to be employed.

Meanwhile I collected seeds. Unfortunately the sheep had done considerable damage and numerous plants that I had carefully marked had been nibbled down to the roots. Thus I had great difficulty in finding such plants as the *Cypripedium himalaicum* and even the *Polemonium caeruleum*, which had flourished in the vicinity of the camp.

Thanks to a friend of Peter's, Lieut. Robertson, I now had a rifle with which to stalk the Abominable Snowman. Alas, at Joshimath I had received a telegram from London which read "Tracks made by bear" so all that remained to be done was to search for the bruin. It was sad to have my romance rudely shattered, for I had long nourished the secret hope that there really was an Abominable Snowman and that he lived in the Valley of Flowers. I had wondered, too, what my legal position would be were I to shoot him, and had pictured an intricate argument in the Law Courts hinging in all probability on whether the Snowman was the man-eating variety or merely a devourer of yaks. If the former I could at least plead justifiable homicide, but if the latter my position would be intricate and difficult and I might have to face a charge of snowmanslaughter at the very least.

So far from being grateful to the scientists who had elucidated my measurements and photographs, I cursed them roundly as destroyers of my romantic illusions. I endeavoured to explain to Wangdi that the tracks had been identified as those of a bear by the scientific pandits in London, but he dismissed their conclusions contemptuously and said something in Tibetan which I was unable to understand, but which I am certain was derogatory to zoological science. He even evidenced a scepticism as to the power of the rifle and explained that even if I did not drop dead before I had time to fire it the bullet would pass straight through the Abominable Snowman without incommoding him in the least. It says well for his bravery that he did not hesitate to accompany me on my stalk.

It was a perfect morning when we left Base Camp, with hoarfrost on the ground and the sun rising in a cloudless sky from behind Rataban. My plan was to climb the hillside to the east of the base camp, then to traverse more or less horizontally across the end of the glacier into which the tracks had descended.

Our best route lay up a steep and broken ridge, and we were scrambling up this and had arrived at the foot of a little rock step perhaps fifteen feet high, when of a sudden there was a rushing sound from above. Thinking for a moment that a stone was coming, we ducked in close to the rocks and next moment a musk deer jumped over our heads and was gone in a flash. I had a momentary glimpse of it as it bolted down the ridge with incredible surefootedness and speed, before disappearing from sight over a brow.

A few yards higher we found its cave, which was full of droppings and highly charged with musk. Except for this incident the ascent was uneventful, and we came at length to a boulder-strewn shoulder where we were surprised to find a cairn, which had probably been built by the Sikh during his survey of the Bhyundar Valley. A little higher, the ridge ended against a sheer rock face, two or three thousand feet high. Here we halted, for the ridge was an excellent viewpoint and commanded a view of the glacier and mountainside to which the tracks had descended.

Needless to say there was no animal life to be seen not so much as a barhal, though we had seen their tracks during the ascent, so we divided our time between scanning the hillside through my monocular glass and collecting seeds from various small plants which included *androsaces*, everlastings, dwarf *potentillas* and gentians.

Light mists had formed in the valley and between them the stream showed, a straggling silver line, but the sky was unclouded, a deep royal blue into which the snow laden peaks rose unfuzzed by a single breath of wind. Gauri Parbat in particular loomed spectacularly magnificent, whilst the snow peak we had climbed lifted a gleaming crest on dark-banded precipices dusted with winter snow.

There seemed little object in pelting across hillsides after a bear or even an Abominable Snowman when we could lie at our ease on the warm sun-soaked turf, and it was a full two hours later before we bestirred ourselves from our lethargy to continue with the hunt.

Having descended from the ridge we crossed the tongue of the glacier and traversed steep hillsides, buttresses and gullies until we came to another grassy ridge, which rose to a craggy top. It was a perfect luncheon place, whilst many plants in seed more than compensated me for any regret I may have felt at not sighting our quarry. So for the next sunny hour or two we rested there or filled envelopes with seeds, and what better way is there of spending an autumn afternoon on a hillside? Which would you prefer: a flower in your garden or a mouldering head on your wall?

Before returning to Base Camp we descended to the buttress beneath which was the cave into which I had seen a bear retreat. The bear had left or was not at home, but on the buttress I discovered a gentian I had not seen before, light purple in colour and with a light green throat which I decided was worth any number of bears.

We arrived back at Base Camp without having fired a shot, and for this I am glad. Long may the peacefulness of the Valley of Flowers remain undisturbed.

The days passed all too quickly and with their passing the autumn hues brightened until the valley glowed golden in the sunlight. Twice showers fell in the late afternoon and once thunder rumbled among the ranges but the weather otherwise remained perfect. I wish that I could convey some picture of this perfection. The sun shone daily from unclouded skies of indescribable purity, all Nature slept and dreamed and the very spirit of Peace pervaded the still atmosphere. As I had felt on Mana Peak so did I feel now, that to shout would be profane, that this peacefulness in which we lived was a precious experience.

A clever friend once told me: "The trouble with you is that you feel more than you think." If this is so, thank God for my disability. For solitude in the Valley of Flowers taught me the insignificance and incapacity for happiness of thought as compared with a meditation that knows no intellectual limitations but is content to accept with childlike faith and delight the infinite beauties and grandeurs of the universe. So limited is the scope of thought when brought to bear on the splendours of the Universe that we must first of all rid ourselves of its ensnaring tangles before we can turn our eyes to heaven and read the message of the hill and the stars. What a man gains in cleverness he may lose in spiritual perception; he, is indeed great who can conquer his own cleverness.

The day came when the Dotials arrived to carry my loads to Ranikhet. This was September 29, my last day in the Valley of Flowers, and that evening I sat late by the campfire. The night was supremely still and the smoke of the burning juniper stood straight up into the stars. The porters had long since ceased talking and were fast asleep and no sound came to me but little hissing whispers from the fire and the eternal note of the stream. All about me was the great peacefulness of the hills, a peacefulness so perfect that something within me seemed to strain upwards as though to catch the notes of an immortal harmony. There seemed in this peace and quietude some Presence, some all-pervading beauty separated from me only by my own "muddy vesture of decay".The stars and the hills beneath the stars, the flowers at my feet were part of a supreme Purpose, which I myself must struggle to fulfil. Poor little man, from ignoble depths to starry heights, from hill top to valley in a reckless run; poor, slogging little man, how hard and wearisome the climb, how besetting the winds and difficulties. Surely the hills were made that we should appreciate our strength and frailties? The stars that we should sense our destiny? Yet through all this tangled skein of earthly life must run the golden thread oι beauty. Beauty is everywhere; we need not go to the hills to find it. Peacefulness is everywhere, if we make it so; we need not go to the hills to seek it. Yet because we are human and endowed with physical qualities, and because we cannot divorce ourselves from these qualities we must needs utilise them as best we can and seek through them beauty that we may return refreshed in mind and spirit. So we go to seek beauty on a hill, the beauty of a larger freedom, the beauty that lifts us to a high window of our fleshy prison whence we may see a little further over the dry and dusty plains to the blue ranges and eternal snows. So we climb the hills, pitting our strength against difficulty, enduring hardship, discomfort and danger that through a subjugation of body we may perceive beauty and discover a contentment of spirit beyond all earthly imaginings. And through beauty and contentment we gain peace.

It is the ugliness man creates that leads to discontentment and war; the ugliness of greed, and the ugliness that greed begets; a vast ocean of ugliness in which he perishes miserably. It is because men are beginning to realise this that they long to escape from an environment of mechanical noises, of noisome fumes and hideous arrangements of bricks and steel into the beauty and quietude of the countryside, to carry themselves naturally on their legs, not artificially on wheels, to travel at God's pace, to listen to the song of Nature, the birds, the streams and the breeze in the cornfield, to look upon beautiful things, flowers, meadowlands and hilltops, to live for a time simply and rhythmically in airs untainted by factory smoke, to discover the virtues of simplicity and goodwill.

Beauty, health, good comradeship, peace, all these had been mine in the Valley of Flowers. For a while I had lived simply and happily and I like to think, indeed I know, that those about me had been happy.

Such memories are imperishable for they rely on their perpetuity not on physical action, but on a contemplation that reaches into the very soul of beauty. For I had seen many beautiful things and not least of these the loyalty and devotion of my companions, those hard bitten men who were ready to dare all and risk all if by so doing they could further my plans and ambitions. Such loyalty as this is rarer than gold.

So I spent some of my last hours in the Valley of Flowers, seated by the camp fire, until the flames died down and the stars brightened beyond the hill tops and all about me was the serenity of God.

MOUNTAINEERING HOLIDAY

Mountaineering Holiday

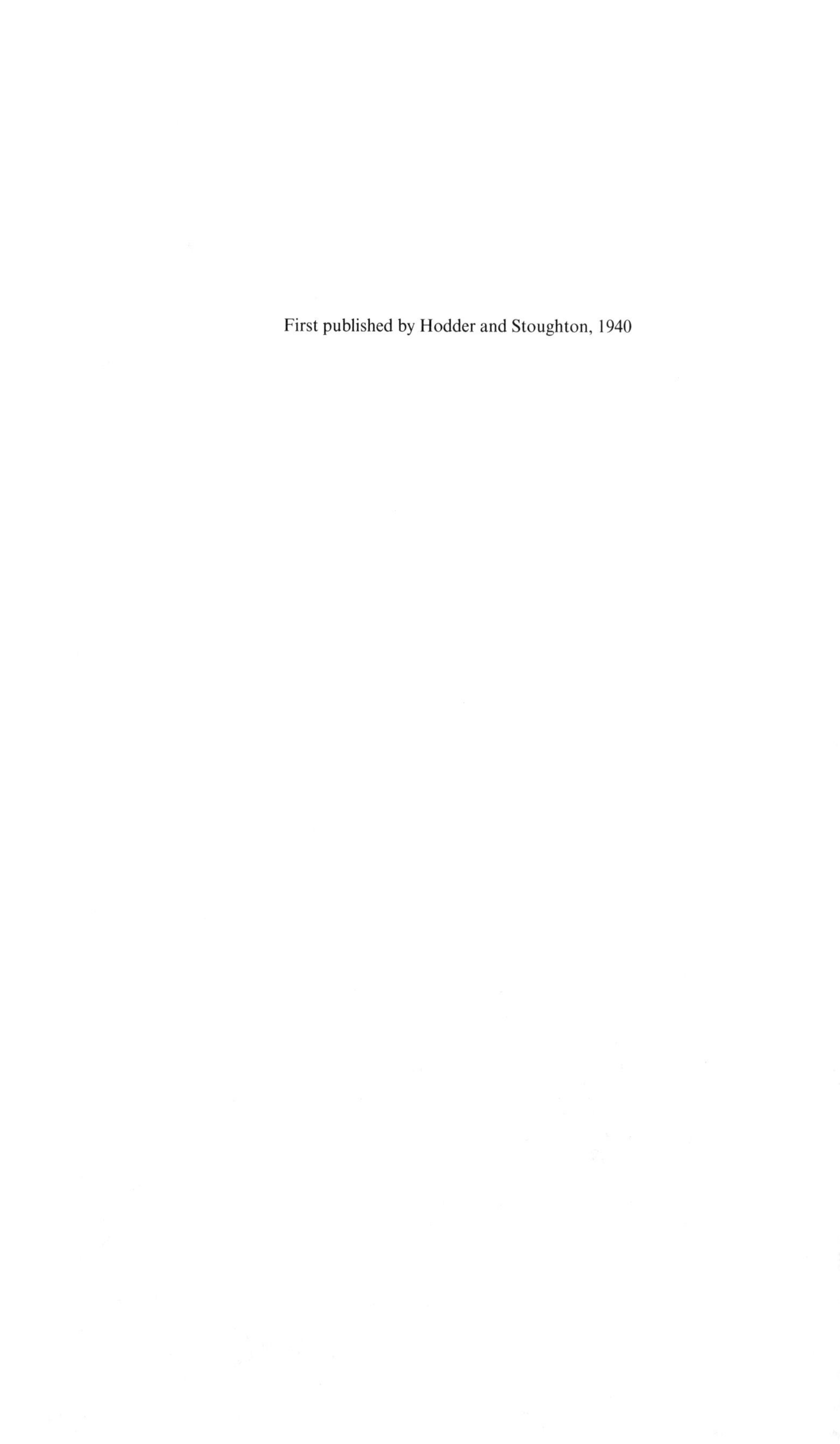

First published by Hodder and Stoughton, 1940

Contents

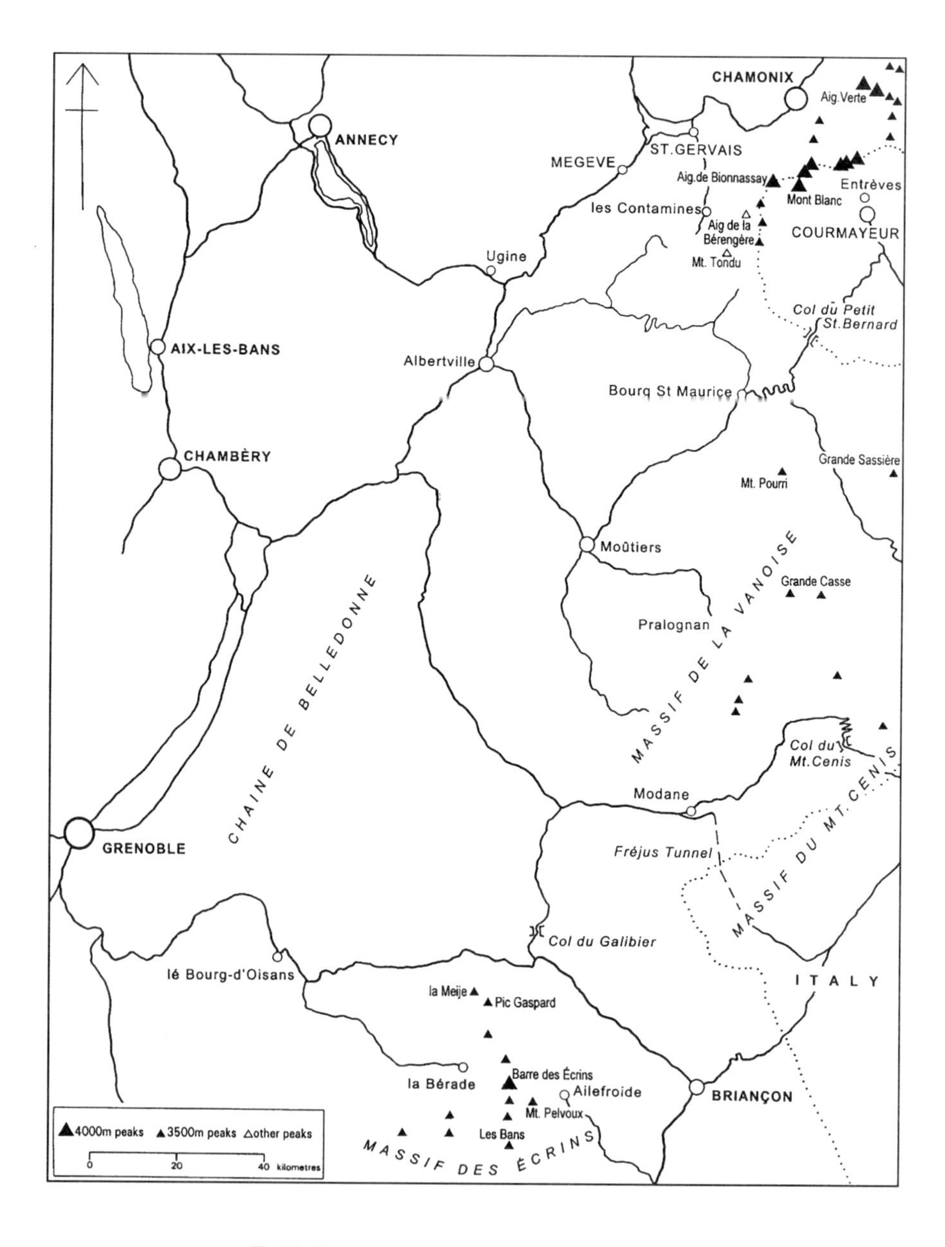

THE FRENCH ALPS

CHAPTER ONE

To the Alps

THERE IS NO HOLIDAY like a mountaineering holiday. For eleven months the mountaineer has lived, perhaps in a city, perhaps amidst fields and hedges, on ground tamed, cultivated, and built upon by the hand of man; and he has sighed for a glimpse of mountains, for the mountain wind on his cheek, keen, pure, and cold, for the lilt of the mountain stream, for the feel of rock in his hand, for the crunch of frozen snow beneath his feet, for the smell of mist and the fragrance of alp and pine forest.

In his spare moments he has read about mountains, pored over maps, and studied guidebooks. Then comes the day when he inspects his boots, his ice axe, and his rope. He packs his suitcase and his rucksack. He buys his railway ticket. The incredible has become credible. For two weeks, three weeks, or a month he will escape from civilisation and all its works; he is off to the mountains.

Jim Gavin and I met at Victoria Station on the afternoon of July 29, 1939. The rush to the Continent was at its height, and the platform was crowded with holidaymakers. I remember that, as I stood watching the bustle, I longed for the quiet silent places, where I should not have to listen to the explosions of the internal combustion engine, breathe the sickly fumes of petrol, jostle my way along crowded pavements, eat in the glare of electric light, wake up to an array of chimney-pots crouched beneath a looming pall of smoke.

A boat train is an interesting spectacle, collectively and individually. Many curious types and conditions of English people venture abroad for their holidays. Gentlemen, who normally only wear plus fours when playing golf, feel compelled to don them when visiting the Continent. Perhaps they want the foreigner to recognise them as Englishmen, and the foreigner, be he Frenchman or German, Turk or Italian welcomes them. He knows instinctively, and from long experience, that they may be imposed upon in all manner of ways. In the tourist business the plus-foured Englishman is a palpable means of wealth.

Then there is the hiker who dresses himself in his oldest, shabbiest, and dirtiest clothes. He will be seen any day during the tourist season at Victoria attired in a pair of filthy shorts or stained flannel trousers, an open-necked shirt, and a tattered sports coat. On his legs are a pair of gaudily-topped stockings, on his feet a pair of clumping boots, and on his head a felt hat, the appearance of which suggests that it has been previously kicked for some miles through the streets of London. Lastly, on his back is an enormous rucksack, which in age, condition and appearance matches itself perfectly with the items already described. Further to prepare for his Continental holiday, he has omitted to shave for the past few days.

Certain questions inevitably occur. Why is it necessary for him to start his holiday in this condition? What will be his appearance at the end of the holiday, and what will be the reactions of those among whom he spends his holiday? Is it his intention to impress the foreigner by the "toughness" of his demeanour and appearance, or is it simply a manifestation of the Englishman's innate love of hard living, open air, cold baths, roast beef, etc. etc.?

Then there is, I regret to state, a certain type of mountaineer, whose objects appear similar to those of the hiker. He is wreathed around with ropes; crampons and ice axes radiate from him at uncomfortable and dangerous angles; his boots, armoured with sharp saw-edged nails, are a source of constant anxiety to others less heavily shod in passport and customs queues, and a perpetual menace to parquet and polished floors. His clothing exudes a peculiar stale, musty odour. He has a lofty and superior mien, and looks superciliously at those not similarly attired and equipped, as much as to say: 'I am better than you. I am tough, a he-man. Look at my rope, my ice axe, and my boots. I am a mountaineer; as for you, you are kittle-kattle, mere tourists.'

These strange personages are happily in a minority, if a very evident minority. The majority of the travellers consist of ordinary tourists. Some of these would not like to be described thus, for they are bound for places, expensive places, where ordinary tourists do not congregate. They are select, well groomed, languid, and they exude, in contrast to the mountaineer already mentioned, expensive perfumes. They are experienced travellers, and one feels instinctively that the hotel labels on their luggage are genuine, and not purchased as a mixed bag in Paris.

Then there are genuine tourists, those incapable of fending for themselves, the products of Messrs. Cook, Lunn, Frame, and other agencies. Their centre of gravity is a courier, a harassed, nervous person usually to be seen hurrying about with folios of tickets in his hand, whose life is spent in constant fear lest something go wrong, whose mind is a sort of perpetual motion machine of time-tables, reservations, passports, and landing tickets. It is interesting to speculate as to what would happen to his flock were he to be taken ill, fall overboard, go on strike, die, or simply, to vanish.

Off at last! Waving hands and a flutter of handkerchiefs, a last barrage of kisses, and the packed train steals out from beneath the grim, smoke-grimed vault of Victoria. The holiday has begun.

The train does not get very far. After labouring heavily for some ten minutes it comes to a halt in a suburb of London. There it waits for five minutes, then continues for a short distance, only to come to another halt in another suburb. We remember that we are on the Southern Railway and take stock of our surroundings.

The foreigner's first entry into London must be a depressing experience. He sees suburbia, an expanse as monotonous as any desert, but without a desert's charms of distance and serenity. As Karel Capek wrote in *Letters from England*:

> The train flies past a whole town, which is beset by some terrible curse; inexorable Fate has decreed that each house shall have two pillars at the door. For another huge block, she has decreed iron balconies. The following block she has perpetually condemned to grey brick. On another mournful street she has relentlessly imposed blue verandas. Then there is a whole quarter doing penance for some unknown wrong by placing five steps before every front door. I should be enormously relieved if even one house had only three.

Yet if Fate has condemned man to be the slave of outward appearance, signs of diverseness in his character and intellect are discernible in the gardens that adjoin the railway. Some are desolate wastes in which dustbins stand in sordid repose, and a few blades of grass eke out a grimy and a precarious existence, but others bear evidence of his struggle to preserve a feeling for beauty amid the uglinesses of his own construction, and cheek by jowl with a patch containing nothing more exciting or original than a few cabbages blackened by the smoke and soot of passing trains, exists a well tended lawn, with perhaps a surround of flower beds together with one or two shrubs, a sundial, a bird bath, and a tiny greenhouse.

High up on the embankment, the passer-by looks down dispassionately on this evidence of human activity. He may feel sad or glad according to his mood, but for the most part he will gaze unseeing, for suburbia has come to be an accepted part of the twentieth century system. Yet the struggle goes on. Every flower that is planted in these little gardens is indicative of some flicker, some spark to set the human soul afire.

The countryside, when at last the train has struggled through the suburbs, inspires altogether different reflections. Foreigners regard it with horror. 'Why,' they say, 'in our country this would be cultivated. Here it is mostly going to waste.' And they gaze from the windows of the train at the broad acres of Kent as though at a criminal who stands morally and socially condemned. To such outspoken condemnation, the Englishman replies lamely that industrialisation is responsible and that the yeomen of England have gravitated to the towns. He goes on to explain that it is cheaper to import butter, eggs, and bacon from Denmark and Holland, meat from New Zealand and the Argentine, that farming doesn't pay, that agricultural wages are too high to make it pay, and so on and so forth. To all this the foreigner listens politely but without much attention. His eyes are fixed on the fields that flash by, upon the derelict-looking farms, upon tracts of coarse sedge grass and deserted grazing-land.

'But you could be self-supporting if you cultivated this. In my country ...'

Sevenoaks marks the limit of suburbia, though some would maintain that Tonbridge is now within the grip of Greater London. Beyond Tonbridge there is indisputably country. When I was a child I lived near the railway between Tonbridge and Paddock Wood, and the Continental expresses held an irresistible fascination for me. I used to ask myself whether I should ever travel in one and cross the sea to a new land.

For a few instants I saw the house where I lived between the trees. The trees were a little higher, but the house was unchanged, and so were the oast- houses beyond it. Here I was, *en route* to the Continent and the Alps. I was thirty-nine years of age, but for a split second I lay again on the same daisy-sprinkled bank, my chin cupped in my hands, and watched the Continental express roar past towards new lands.

Marden, Staplehurst, Headcorn, Pluckley – these are sleepy little villages on a long straight stretch of railway between Tonbridge and Ashford, where engine-drivers of Continental expresses do their best to make up for lost time. They do not appear to have changed, nor does the Weald of Kent. The fields, the copses, the woods, the oast houses are much the same as they used to be, and in the north beyond the Weald, loom hills in the same blue line. This is the real England; this

England changes little; this England is not concerned with a hurrying industrialism; it is slow, and essentially conservative; in this lies its strength, its beauty, and its happiness. If you were called upon to think of some scene, some vista typical of England, of what would you think, what picture would form in your mind? I have sometimes asked myself this and the answer is always the same. It is a simple English countryside, the countryside seen from the window of any train. I come from Kent, and I think of the Kentish countryside. For all the aeroplanes that drone overhead, the motors that rush along the roads, it is very peaceful. It calls to mind the pealing of church bells through a still air, the rushing of water over a millstream sluice, a chorus of rooks from tall elms, the scent of new-mown hay, and freshly gathered hops.

Through such memories men best discern the meaning and the value of their native land. The English tradition lies not in towns, coal mines, and factories, but in fields, hedges, woods, and slow running streams; in mellowed bricks and ivy; in tall trees and smooth green lawns; in smoke-blue distances and soft grey skies.

Beyond Ashford, through which the train jolts at high speed with a tirade of wailing and whistling, the character of the country changes. For a few miles it is undulating and wooded, then, suddenly, like a single bold stroke of a pen, come the South Downs. Here is something different from the trim and fertile Weald. The latter is circumscribed by hedges, fields, ditches, and roads, the former knows no such restrictions or limitations. The Downs are not mere earthy undulations, they are hills. They inherit the same freedom as the sea, the freedom of wind, storm, and sunshine, and they share with the sea an uncompromising simplicity of design. The face of the Weald changes according to the whims and fancies of man, but the Downs remain aloof and uncultivated, and because of this changelessness they epitomise the spirit of the past. In the Weald a man may escape back into the Middle Ages, but in a fold of the Downs he can travel farther than this; he can hear the tramp of Roman legions and the twanging of Saxon bow-strings, and he will feel deep down within him a heritage of hard-won experience, a pride, a solemnity, and a tradition.

The train passes between the shoulders of the Downs and the house-tops of Folkestone come into view, rows and rows of them slated and grey, with a single hideous gasometer brooding over them like some Cyclopean pillbox. Beyond the houses is the quivering glint of the sea.

When an Englishman is safely back in England from the Continent and the horrors of the Channel crossing are forgotten, he will exclaim, 'Thank God for the channel!' In crossing those twenty miles of water he way lose the contents of his stomach but he will gain a wonderful feeling of security. When leaving England the sensation is different. Though he be under the aegis of Thomas Cook & Sons with his fare paid from beginning to end (including tips), he becomes an adventurer. For a few days or weeks England will know him not. He will see no English policeman; he will drink no English beer; he will eat no English beef; he will not hear 'Paridownercarplee' and other English sounds.

Between Folkestone and Dover it is possible to examine the state of the sea and estimate the chances of internal survival. On the present occasion they seemed excellent. Only the gentlest of waves lapped the chalk cliffs and the Channel stretched level and unheaving beneath a sky of pale hazy blue. As we emerged from the last tunnel Dover's stately castle came into view frowning down on the mean, ugly little town at its feet.

In another minute we arrived at the harbour station. The porters here are for the most part taciturn, grim-visaged men. Doubtless they have much to endure at the hands of excitable foreigners with a limited command of the English language. Having exchanged our luggage for a numbered token we took our places in the passport queue. Many uncomplimentary things, some deserved and some undeserved, have been written, and will yet be written, about the passport and customs arrangements at Folkestone and Dover. I have stood in the same puddle of water described by one infuriated writer to *The Times*; on the other hand, I have found the customs officials invariably courteous and scrupulously fair. For some reason they always seem to believe me, and I can only suppose that this is because I always tell them the truth. On one occasion only have I experienced trouble and that was when I forgot to declare an article of silk because I had forgotten its existence. The manner, in which the officer divined that I had got such an article and ferreted it out, had in it more than an element of the occult. There is, however, the story of the old gentleman in the top hat. One day a stately old gentleman attired in a frock coat, and an unusually tall and glossy silk hat, presented himself at the customs. His luggage was duly examined and found to be devoid of dutiable articles. The examining officer's attention was then drawn to the unusual size of the silk hat.

'Would you mind removing your hat, sir?' he asked.

At once the old gentleman bridled up.

'Certainly not,' he replied. 'What nonsense! I refuse to do any such thing.'

This naturally aroused the official's suspicion and he said:

'I'm sorry, sir, but I must insist that you remove your hat.'

'I will do no such thing,' returned the old gentleman angrily.

This put the customs official in a quandary and he went off in search of a higher authority. In the end, the old gentleman was taken to the Chief Customs Officer, but declined as resolutely as before to remove his hat, and to the threat that it would be taken off by force replied that to do so would be an assault on his person. Finally, a police warrant was procured and the hat removed. There was nothing inside it. After that, there was, of course, a blazing row. The police blamed the Chief Customs Officer, and the Chief Customs Officer blamed his underling. After that, at odd intervals, the old gentleman used to be seen attired as usual in his frock coat and tall silk hat. He became quite a well-known figure and none of the customs officials had the temerity to ask him to remove his hat a second time. One day, however, there was appointed a new junior customs official, a short tempered and abrupt young man. To him the old gentleman presented himself, and to his intense astonishment was asked for the second time to remove his hat. He was even more indignant than on the previous occasion and worse than that, he was rude, very rude.

His rudeness was too much for the customs official. He was short tempered himself, and he had had a trying day. Leaning across the counter, he deliberately knocked the silk hat from the old gentleman's head. It was packed with drugs.

Passengers often complain bitterly of queues. A voluntary queue is distasteful to most freeborn Englishmen, but to be compulsorily herded is peculiarly galling. The young men who examine passports at Dover are as efficient as they are nonchalant. One flicks open the document and takes a peep, then passes it to another who takes another peep, shuts it up and hands it to the owner. In addition, there are sometimes to be seen men in Burberrys whose sinister and watchful mien indubitably classes them as detectives.

If I were a spy I should write my notes on the pages of my passport. As it is, I reserve these pages for the names and addresses of people I meet on my travels, hotels, prices, rates of exchange, notes on wines and eatables, mountaineering details, articles to be purchased, etc. etc. Only once have the defaced pages aroused suspicion in the foreign breast and that, of course, was in Italy where everything unorthodox is suspicious to the Fascist ear or eye.

The voyage was uneventful. I am bound to admit that on the whole the Channel has been kind to me, but there have been times when it has not. I have tried most of the seasick remedies. One preventative of seasickness is to get thoroughly drunk, taking care, however, not to mix the drinks. Another effective method is to get a friend to knock you on the head at the commencement of the voyage. A third, and infallible, cure is to tie a handkerchief round the neck, insert a walking stick, and twist.

The English Channel is no respecter of persons. A friend of mine was once crossing it on a very rough day. He is one of those disgusting fellows who strolls about smoking a large cigar when everyone else is wishing that he was dead. As he was promenading the deck, he espied a small man with a very green face huddled in a corner. My friend recognised him, and going up to him exclaimed with horrible heartiness: 'Hullo, Admiral, what are you doing here?' The Admiral, for such indeed he was, gave a gulp, looked up, recognised my friend, and whispered, 'For God's sake, don't call me Admiral here.'

When the Channel is smooth I am glad to have been born an Englishman. I promenade the deck, thinking of tall ships, Nelson, and our heritage the sea. I look at the receding cliffs of Dover and thrill with patriotic pride and insular superiority. But when the sea is rough, I wish I had been born in Switzerland or Tibet, and creep away into a corner vainly hoping for a swift and merciful death.

To outward appearance Calais is no more exciting than Dover. However, the trains run about the streets in a most intriguing manner and the railway porters carry loads which would make a British railway porter shudder. It is apparent also to the traveller that he has set foot on the Continent because of the tendency to wear uniforms. No longer is he in an atmosphere of nondescript shop keeping. He has entered the zone of efficient militarism, even though it is a democratic, and therefore benevolent, brand.

French customs officials are as courteous as British customs officials. Nevertheless, they have their foibles and weaknesses. At Dover, scents and cameras are greeted with hostility and suspicion, but at Calais and other French ports, an object of far less value titivates the official zeal and rouses the Gallic passion. New clothes, cameras, films, whisky, poufft! – They are nothing; half a pound of tobacco is dismissed with a wave of the hand; but stay! What is this? Yes, it is, incredible, unbelievable, a packet of one dozen boxes of matches, costing eightpence at the local grocer's. Alack and alas, it is borne off in triumph. Sadly we realise that we shall never see it again. In future, we must light our pipes and cigarettes with French matches. If we are lucky we get matches which when struck merely project molten sparks into the eyes. Remember, therefore, always to close the eyes when striking French matches. But if we are unlucky, we get matches which exude horrible sulphur fumes for some fifteen or twenty seconds, matches that in South America are called "Stinkerados" and not without reason. Matches are the price the English pipe smoker must pay for a holiday in France. It would appear that the whole vigilance of the French customs is directed in a never-ending search for matches. Bold and fortunate indeed is he who can smuggle a few boxes past them, and in particular, past the women examiners whose whole feminine acuteness and perception seem to be directed in search of matches.

Nothing here need be written about French railway trains, except to state that they are bigger, more comfortable, more efficiently heated, and are said to have more accidents than English railway trains. Notices on them are presented to the traveller in three languages, not including English, and the schoolboy translation of the most prominent of these is: 'It arrives frequently that the agents travelling on the line are blessed by bottles or other objects solid.'

A French line "talks" differently to an English line. The English line says, 'Rumpety-rump, rumpety-rump' in a slow traditional English way; the French line says, 'Rumpty, rumpty, rumpty, rumpty' in a hurried, impatient manner. The French countryside between Calais and Paris is altogether more spacious and more sensible from an agricultural point of view than the English countryside between Dover and London. The ploughman does not have to about turn so frequently, and can make a furrow half a mile or more in length. Also, of course, more land is under cultivation. It tells, as eloquently as any countryside can tell, of a thrifty, hardworking people, a people who do not play at farming as a side-line to industry, but whose life and livelihood are linked with the soil. Human efficiency, however, seldom spells beauty when applied to Nature, and it is natural for the Englishman to prefer his own countryside of useless acres and hedges behind which he revels in his privacy. Yet this countryside of northern France possesses a grandeur, a beauty, and a dignity. It is just such a countryside as Constable loved to paint, rolling in long undulations, with wide horizons, blue distances, and towering, slow-strolling clouds.

Paris is in odd contrast to the French countryside. If it were representative of France as a whole it would be spacious, staid, and dignified. It would go to bed early, get up early, and be thrifty and hard working. The great mass of Parisians are staunch to the standards set by France as a whole, but the Paris seen by the visitor is merely cosmopolitan. Precisely the same criticism may be levelled at the West End of London but not, I think, with the same justice. The garish ugliness of Piccadilly Circus finds its counterpart in Paris, but it is doubtful whether the country-folk who visit the West End of London find even that portion of the city quite so unrepresentative of national life and manners as French country-folk find the centre of their capital city. To the resident Londoner, there is, of course, nothing artificial in London; it is just London, and no doubt the same applies to the Parisians' attitude towards Paris, yet the gulf between the French countryside and its capital always seems to me far wider than that between the English countryside and its capital. Possibly this is due to the difference in size between the two countries. To country-folk born and bred, a great city inevitably seems strange, bewildering, and exotic, yet it would be difficult to imagine a greater contrast than that between the midinette of the Paris boulevards and the simple, patient, hard working, peasant wife of France.

For the first time in my experience there was a dearth of porters at the Gare du Nord, due to the fact that France was steadily mobilising. I do not propose to enlarge upon the excitement of a taxi drive from that station to the Gare du Lyon, for this is a stock tourist subject. Suffice to say, that in spite of the driving, which appeared to border upon the miraculous, we arrived safely. There are fewer accidents in Paris than in London, and this is probably due to the quick reaction time of the Latin temperament.

While waiting for our train to Grenoble, we dined at a restaurant opposite the station. It is always a source of wonder to the visitor to Paris that so many restaurants can not only exist but also apparently thrive. It would be interesting to know how many Parisians eat their meals under their own roofs. The Englishman is often accused of lack of imagination, but to my mind nothing can be more unimaginative than a Parisian restaurant. I do not mean in the matter of food, for he would be a brave man who criticised French gastronomy, but in the surroundings in which food is eaten. No doubt the French love of food is responsible for the mirrors which surround the diner. Everywhere he looks he sees, actually or reflected, other people eating, and he is able in various directions to observe himself similarly occupied. French restaurants exist simply and solely to cater for the science of eating. In England, however, eating is not so much a matter of gastronomy as atmosphere. It is of more importance to the Englishman to know that Dr. Johnson once dined in the same establishment than to know that the beefsteak is succulently cooked and tastefully embellished, and he is only too glad to pay for the privilege. Artfully shaded lights, old oak beams and tradition mean far more to him than scientific and imaginative cooking. He takes what he gets; the rest is atmosphere and tradition.

Such reflections inevitably lead to the conclusion that the Frenchman is a realist. Realism is fundamental in the French character. When the Frenchman eats he is concerned only with eating, when he loves he is concerned only with loving, and when he makes war he is concerned only with making war. The talk about Latin sentiment is nonsense; the French are the least sentimental of all races and the greatest realists. Hence the Maginot Line.

The journey through the night towards Grenoble was not very comfortable, for we had decided, on grounds of economy, not to book a sleeping compartment, and in addition to ourselves our compartment contained a young French artillery officer and a sailor, which made it impossible for us to put our feet up. Frenchmen, I have always noticed, slumber peacefully in any position, and appear never to want to put their feet up. Englishmen, however, endure agonies if they cannot raise their feet above floor level. Possibly the British climate and a heritage of gout and rheumatism have something to do with this?

Although we travelled on the P.L.M. Railway, which I have been told on good authority stands for Pour la Morgue, the night passed without accident. Truth compels me to admit that I have only been in one French railway accident. This took place near Lyon. I was slumbering peacefully when I awoke to find myself on the floor of the compartment beneath a pile of other passengers and luggage from the racks. Among the passengers was a tall, sad faced young man, a courier as it transpired, and when we had sorted ourselves out, and tended to our bruises and abrasions, he said quite calmly: 'Don't bc alarmed, ladies and gentlemen, this is nothing. A little while ago I was travelling in the Riviera when there was a serious collision. I was among the survivors and was being transferred from the scene of the accident in another train when the engine of that blew up.' English people are a trifle unfair to the French in the matter of their railways. I have travelled from Marseilles to Paris at night through almost continuous dense fog and have arrived on the stroke of time. What English train could perform this feat? It goes to show that French signalling arrangements are highly efficient, though certain cynical persons have affirmed that I was lucky.

The night was pleasantly cool and, to our unbounded surprise, the window was not only opened but allowed to remain open. Thus I am debarred from making any of those time honoured witticisms which have to do with the conflict of opinion between the fresh air loving Englishman and the fun loving foreigner as to the ventilation of a railway compartment. Truth further compels me to state that the French sailor left the corridor door wide open, and that I, feeling chilly, stealthily closed it. I feel that I must endeavour to rehabilitate the self respect of the British nation by quoting a notice which I suspect is entirely fictitious. It runs: 'In the event of a dispute between passengers as to whether the window shall be opened or shut, the dispute shall be referred to the conductor and the window then shut.'

Dawn found me stretching my legs in the corridor. The train was passing across a well-cultivated plain intersected with the usual rows of poplars, and dotted with crinkly tiled farmsteads and cottages. In the middle distance, a smooth surfaced river threaded level water meadows. Here and there lay drifts of thin white mist, and these added to the impression of distance, so that the plain seemed to stretch endlessly eastwards. As I gazed, the glowing disc of the sun rose into a cloudless sky. It leapt up beyond a high irregular edge forming the crest of a great line of hills, spanning the whole width of the eastern horizon. It came to me with a sudden queer thrilling feeling that I was looking at the Alps. I remembered then, as though it were yesterday, how, as a boy, I had gazed thus from the window of a train and first seen the Alps. Age and experience may dim the vision of high mountains, but I never fail to recapture something of that initial exaltation when for the first time in a mountaineering holiday I see the far-off loom of the high mountains.

It is a queer thing this feeling men have for mountains. How is it that some can look unstirred upon a scene that will rouse emotion in others? How is it that some are alive to beauty, and others are not? Is not the Buddhist theory that we go from life to life retaining not memory but instinctive knowledge the most logical explanation? Some have gained knowledge; others have yet to gain it. If this is so, then I am thankful that I have gained this knowledge of beauty, that I can gaze at a high hill and its beauty, and sense my destiny in the quietness and peace of Nature. If this is spiritual progress then ours is a gracious and glorious journey, and ugliness is but a passing phase to set off beauty and render its value perceptible to the spirit, just as strife and unhappiness are the perfecters of peace and happiness, a paradox which when understood lifts one edge of the veil from the mystery of human existence.

Quickly the sun lifted over the Alps. The mists were infused with opal, the river was transmuted to a stream of gold and distantly the great hills grew and grew in the eastern sky.

An hour or two later we were past Lyon and among the foothills of the Alps. This is a curiously tip-tilted country of stratified limestone; the earth has been eased up in bits and pieces so that one may walk up a slope of pasture and forest only to be brought up short by a sheer precipice. These first uplifts of the Alps have a charm of their own, and for anyone who wishes to walk and camp, here is a district open in nature, and commanding varied and beautiful views.

Grenoble is one of the finest cities in France. It is built of a light-coloured stone, and is tidy and neat. Its position at the junction of the Isère and Drac valleys makes it an important military centre. It is strongly fortified and any army that managed to force the alpine passes would be hard put to it to break through to the French lowlands.

As we had several hours to wait for a motor bus to La Bérarde, we refreshed ourselves first of all with a bath at an hotel. Selling a bath to an Englishman is, on the Continent, still in the nature of a ritualistic procedure. First of all the bath must be ordered and booked at the bureau. The bather is then passed on in turn to the concierge, the lift man, a "boots" and finally to the corridor woman in whose domain the bathroom is situated. I have had some remarkable baths in my time, but the most remarkable of all was at an inn in the Austrian Tyrol, in1922. There my demand for a bath produced, first of all, incredulity and amazement, then amusement, and finally a resigned determination, as much as to say, 'We have heard, even read, that Englishmen must have baths. Well, here is an Englishman, he wants a bath he shall have it!' An hour or so later, I was conducted down to the cellar. In the floor of this there was a hollow, into which a quantity of hot water had been poured. Undeterred I had my bath, but I had an uneasy feeling at the same time that more than one pair of eyes watched the operation, and I fancied I heard titterings.

In the matter of baths and five-o'clock tea, the Englishman is gradually coming into his own on the Continent, where both of these functions are regarded as lucrative side-lines by hoteliers, who know very well that, although they may charge exorbitantly for a bath, the Englishman must still have it. In this connection, I recollect the tragic story of a Scotsman. With native canniness he compounded for his baths over a lengthy period. Unhappily, however, he had to return home after only a few days. The hotel proprietor was ready and willing to meet him over the matter of pension terms, but resolutely declined to refund his bath money.

The ceremony of the bath over, we watched the world go by from an out-of-door cafe. Grenoble is a famous tourist centre and we saw numerous English people. Amongst them was a fashionably dressed party in an immaculate Rolls Royce, complete with chauffeur, cigars, and vase of flowers. They alighted, languidly sipped coffee and departed. Then came a group of British cyclists, members of the Cyclists' Touring Club, sunburned and fit. They chaffed the waiter, ordered their drinks in Cockney English, which was immediately understood, and departed amid broad smiles. I dare say they were better ambassadors of Britain than the exquisites in the Rolls Royce.

After lunch we ascended by *téléférique* to Fort Rabot, which is a thousand feet above the town, and enjoys an extensive panorama of the neighbouring hills and mountains. Mont Blanc, which is visible from this belvedere in clear weather, was concealed by haze, but we saw the outpost peaks of the Dauphiné Alps and noted that the snow line was unusually low, this being due to storms during the spring and early summer.

Then we boarded the motor coach, which for the sum of sixty francs conveys the traveller from Grenoble to La Bérarde, a distance of fifty miles. It was an ancient open type of vehicle, and the driver appeared also to be the proprietor of the small café from which it started. We both had a profound respect for the skill of the French driver and this was increased a hundred-fold during the journey. In outward appearance there was nothing remarkable about our chauffeur. He was a short, podgy man, attired in nondescript clothing and a faded cloth cap. The stub of a cigarette was parked behind one ear, and he had a lazy confiding smile. But beneath a very ordinary outward appearance lurked a driving skill and verve, which would have turned the countenance of many a driver in the Brooklands Mountain Handicap, a pea-green with wondering envy.

On the road to Le Bourg-d'Oisans, there was little opportunity for him to display his skill, except in a solitary encounter with another car which cut in recklessly and maliciously, for this is a wide and well-graded thoroughfare, linking Grenoble with Briançon. Jim and I had previously pictured the Dauphiné Alps as a primitive region of primitive roads, into which only the more enterprising amongst tourists venture. The journey to La Bérarde completely disillusioned us. For one thing, the road as far as Le Bourg-d'Oisans resembled in its traffic density one of the great British arterial roads, for another, the Val Romanche is a dull valley at the best of times, and acrid smoke from numerous factories pollutes the atmosphere. It was a dismal introduction to the wildest mountain group of the Alps.

Le Bourg-d'Oisans is a popular tourist resort and its narrow streets were crammed with motor cars of every type, horsepower, and description. We halted there for refreshments, then, continuing on our way, passed from the Val Romanche into the Val Vénéon at the head of which is situated La Bérarde. There is no through route in this valley, and the road is narrow and tortuous. Providence undoubtedly watched over our driver. His usual method when rounding a corner on the narrow road was to go as fast as possible and rely on his horn, regardless of the fact that anyone coming in the opposite direction would be sounding *his* horn for all he was worth. It was only by sheer luck that we did not meet another car on a corner. We did, however, encounter a motor-coach shortly after turning a hairpin bend and were only able to pull up with a yard or two to spare, after which it was necessary to back, in order to allow the other coach to pass, to the very edge of a precipitous drop, a performance which evoked our unqualified admiration.

The scenery conformed closely to our expectations. The Val Vénéon is typical of the district, a narrow valley with precipitous craggy sides rising towards rugged rock peaks. Stunted pine-trees derive scanty nourishment from the stony soil, and torrents dash furiously down the steep hillsides. Jim summed it up very aptly when he said, 'It reminds me of a scene from "Dracula"; only the bats are missing.'

Grandeur, sublimity, austerity, wildness, these were our first impressions of the Dauphiné Alps. It was not until later that we began to appreciate the beauty of this country, which is unlike any other Alpine district, not excepting some of the sheer-sided valleys of Canton Glarus and the Bernese Oberland.

I should not like to live in a Dauphiné valley. I should feel shut in and depressed. I should want to climb out of it in order to see a little further than the rift of sky vouchsafed by the towering mountainsides and rocky defiles. Yet people do live in the Val Vénéon, and not only live, but enjoy the process, to judge from the smiling faces we now and again met with along the road. At various villages and hamlets we stopped for passengers and refreshments. I do not know whether it was the refreshments, or the nature of the road, but our driving approximated more and more closely to the Brooklands tradition, and we began heartily to wish ourselves at La Bérarde.

The most dangerous section of the road was inappropriately the last five miles between St. Christophe and La Bérarde. Here, after a steep climb, which had the comforting effect of reducing our speed, the road traversed the mountainside in a manner analogous with that of a serpent. We could have borne this had there not been sheer drops from the edge of it. Our driver took it flat out; he would rush at terrifying speed towards a bend, round would come the wheel, round would go the heavy coach with shrieking tyres, then, almost before he had finished twisting the wheel one way, he had to twist it the other way for the next curve as hard as he could, and round we would screech, our wheels a few inches from the edge of the precipice.

I shall never cease to admire my companion's behaviour during this nerve-racking time. Lifting his eyes from the terrifying prospect of immediate and violent death, and apparently releasing his mind from all trivialities such as a possible error of judgement, a burst tyre, or the failure or the steering gear, he enquired in measured accents the names of certain peaks that were visible up the valley.

Then, lo and behold, the last curve and the last precipice were safely behind! The road lay along the floor of the valley and ended in a little village of tall, whitewashed houses, La Bérarde.

Profoundly thankful to Providence we clambered out of the motor-coach, and stealing one last look of awe at our driver, who had removed the cigarette stub from behind his ear and was puffing at it with an expression of bored detachment, made haste to seek for accommodation. We had anticipated no difficulty in this respect when we left England, but we had already learned that Dauphiné is one of the most popular holiday districts in France, and a glance at the parked masses of cars was sufficient to assure us that beds were doubtful in the extreme. So it proved. We made for the principal hotel, only to be told in that lofty manner which characterises the hotel proprietor who is complacently aware that all his rooms are full up with guests that there was not a bed to be had. It was my badge of honorary membership of the French Alpine Club that saved us. The manager's eyes strayed to it and he was visibly affected.

'Yes, Messieurs, I think it may be possible to give you a room, that is, if you do not mind sharing one, and have no objection to the annexe.'

We assured him we had no objection to the annexe and were forthwith escorted thither. It is often the mountaineer's lot to sleep in an annexe, for when he moves about he is not able to book accommodation in advance. In this respect, he who plants himself at one centre scores heavily.

It would appear that the principal object of an hotel proprietor who builds an annexe is not merely to cater for an overflow, of guests, but to impress upon his guests by contrast how desirable are the amenities of the hotel.

So it was in this case, and I will content myself by remarking that the annexe in which we found ourselves was that kind of annexe where you dare not look under the bed. One word alone of A.D. Godley's verse need be changed:

> They will dine on mule and marmot
> And on mutton made of goats
> They will face the various horrors
> Of Dauphiné table d'hôtes.

Two other British mountaineers, Messrs. David Cox and Peter Lloyd, were present and to them we recounted our impressions of the motor-journey. They replied that when they had travelled along the road, the motor coach had narrowly escaped being struck by falling stones. Mountaineering is certainly not the most dangerous of alpine pastimes.

The surroundings of La Bérarde bear out the reputation of Dauphiné for stoniness. There are a few pastures wrested from the stones by the industrious peasants, but these only serve to emphasise the harsher features, the tumbled boulders, scree slopes, crags, and precipices. Our first impression of the Val Vénéon was of a valley similar to that in which Sinbad found his diamonds; a closer look, however, revealed that Nature had done her best to beautify the barrenness. She had sown innumerable flowers, and so well had she succeeded in this pleasant task that my later impressions of Dauphiné came to be not stones but flowers.

We dined in a fly-blown, low-ceilinged room in which were some two dozen guests. On the walls were various advertisements and some cheap German lithographs of pre-war vintage, one depicting wasp-waisted ladies and bearded gentlemen admiring a vista of Mont Blanc, not an inspiring picture and one which became depressing when gazed at too long.

Why is a French roll delicious and French bread abominable? This does not apply to all French bread, but it does to the bread of Dauphiné, and, unhappily, rolls and coffee of a quality that makes breakfast a meritorious function in many parts of France are lacking in the smaller Alpine resorts, where even the butter has a flavour of goat about it, and the honey is no less synthetic than it is in Switzerland. Primitivism may or may not be desirable, but primitivism which apes civilisation is undesirable. The early mountaineers in the Alps were undoubtedly flea-bitten, but at least they had the satisfaction that the primitive brings to civilised man. The modern Alpine mountaineer has often neither the one nor the other, and has to go far afield to discover the joys of simple living, unless he is sufficiently enterprising to render himself independent of inns and hotels by camping.

After dinner we refreshed ourselves with a stroll. The weather during the past few days had been fine in Dauphiné. It was still fine although we did not entirely approve of a smooth-looking cloud in the north. The moon was rising, and though its rays had not yet penetrated into the valley, they lit the great crags opposite, which hung in the stars like a spectral curtain.

When travelling it is impossible to be peaceful, for rapid motion, whether on land or through the air is inimical of true peace. Haste is synonymous with worry and impatience, and these, in their turn, are scarcely compatible with the greater human qualities of patience, thoughtfulness and consideration for others. It is pleasant to arrive in the mountains after a rapid journey by rail and road. For a day or more the traveller has seen the countryside flash past him as a welter of fleeting and illusive impressions. There is something unreal about rapid transit from one place to another, except in the ultimate change of scene. He who girdles the world in a fast-moving aeroplane sees less than he who sits himself down in a quiet country place.

Jim and I had come to a halt among the mountains. They were around us, unmoving, looming against the stars. We could hear them, a soothing note of running water, constant and enduring; we could feel them, not only beneath our feet, not only their cold breath, but as a presence, not the mere presence of so many tons of rock and snow, but a spiritual balm, the blessing and benediction of changeless things.

CHAPTER TWO

Les Bans

WE AWOKE next morning to hear a peal of thunder and a patter of hail. Our suspicions of the previous evening had not proved unfounded. Slate-coloured clouds were oiling up from the west and crackling concussions of thunder reverberated amongst the peaks.

In the matter of alpine weather, I consider myself a Jonah and I remarked as much to Jim, with a sort of gloomy satisfaction. His reply was: 'Well, I'm usually lucky, so perhaps we shall cancel each other out.' I could only hope that what he said was true, for I had come to look upon my ill luck with alpine weather as proverbial and inevitable. What usually happens is that I arrive in the Alps at a time when everyone is complaining of the drought. On the evening of my arrival, dark clouds gather and on all sides I hear people say, 'At last we shall have some rain.' It is true, there is rain, and snow, and every kind of climatic unpleasantness, continuing without intermission for the next two or three weeks. In disgust I return to England, with the idea of finishing my holiday in North Wales or the Lake District. I arrive back to find that there has been a drought ever since I left. Headlines decorate the newspapers – farmers, it is said, are frantic and prayers for rain are being said in the churches. A day or so later I arrive at Seathwaite or some such normally wet place in the hills, to find every marsh and stream dried up. It has not rained for over two months the inhabitants tell me with a gloomy despair. 'Don't worry, it will now I've come,' I answer. They look at me unbelieving and incredulous, but sure enough that self-same night rain begins to fall and continues to fall without intermission for the remainder of my holiday. Soon after returning home I receive post cards from friends still in the Alps, the Lake District, or North Wales. 'Why on earth did you go back to England?' enquire the former.

'The weather has been marvellous since you left.' 'What a pity your holiday came to an end!' write the latter. 'We are having perfect weather.'

It was therefore, with feelings of surprise and amazement that I noticed a distinct improvement in the weather towards midday. The thunderclouds receded with baffled growls, the sun broke through, and a rainbow arched itself prettily across the valley. Was it possible that my Jonah had met its match in Jim? At all events it had received a temporary set-back, and I agreed enthusiastically with Jim's suggestion that we should set off immediately towards the Pilatte Hut with the idea of climbing Les Bans, a peak of 12,040 feet, on the morrow. I even went so far as to suggest in my turn that, instead of spending the night in the crowded hut, we should sleep in the open, taking with us our bivouac tent and sleeping bags for the purpose, a proposal to which he acquiesced with enthusiasm.

The weather had almost completely cleared when, shortly after lunch, we set out from La Bérarde, and only an occasional drift of warm rain added its pearls to the herbage as we trudged up the valley.

Now that our mountaineering holiday had properly begun, my first reaction was not, I fear, that of *joie de vivre* and unbounding energy; but a loathing for my rucksack which seemed unconscionably heavy; furthermore, as I laboured up the path, I seemed to melt all over like an ice cream on a summer's day. In three words, I was out of training. Let me express at once my unbounded admiration for those persons who are always in training, who skip, run, and jump before breakfast, who plunge themselves in ice cold water, who cut out this and that in the matter of food and drink, who stride over miles and miles and miles of the countryside every weekend, passing every public house with an air of insufferable self-denial and virtue, who twist and writhe their stomach muscles and add knobbly inches to their biceps. I do none of these things, I am much too lazy; therefore, for the first day or two of an alpine holiday, I am out of training and a peak of 12,000 feet and a walk of not more than twelve hours is as much as I can comfortably manage. Jim, being in the army and incidentally twelve years younger than me, was, of course, in training. He had suggested Les Bans as our first expedition, and had obtained details from a climbing friend, who described the ascent as an excellent little training climb. All the same, Les Bans is 12,040 feet high and is described by Baedeker as "very difficult; descent nearly as long", and I began to wonder what schemes were afoot for the mortification of my untrained flesh.

The worst of being out of training is that there is a lack of co-ordination between mind and muscle. The untrained one proceeds uphill in fits and starts, not with that slow, deliberate, rhythmical output of energy and movement which is the sure sign of good training. The feet are not put down exactly where it is intended they should be, and a really stony slog is productive of many unshed tears. So it was on this occasion; the path seemed exceptionally stony and rough; my rucksack grew steadily heavier, and through eyes smarting with salty sweat, I watched Jim enviously as he strode uphill with never a drop of moisture on his brow, serenely unconscious of his labouring companion.

An hour later the path debouched on to the Alp de Carrelet. The weather had almost completely cleared now, and only the thinnest of thin blue showers was being wafted by the warm west wind across the precipices of the Ailefroide. Is there a nobler view in Dauphiné than that from the Alp de Carrelet? Imagine a meadow of brilliant green, all the more brilliant by contrast with the savage surrounding precipices, dotted with small feather-like pines, which unite to sweep up a hillside in a full-fledged forest. Beyond this gentle foreground is a background of precipice, a huge, rust-coloured curtain 6,000 feet in height, mellow and remote in the afternoon sun, crested by a thin ribbon of silvery, wind-turned snow.

On the Alp de Carrelet there is a hut at which climbers spend the night before undertaking one of the numerous expeditions in the locality. Experience of the Alps had taught us to associate good viewpoints with refreshments, and a few minutes later we were seated in the hut, a rough stone dwelling resembling a hop picker's hut, drinking light French beer at the moderate sum of three francs a bottle. A number of tourists were doing much the same thing. Most were possessors of ice axes. The ice axe has taken the place of the walking stick and alpenstock with the modern tourist. It is true that it is neither so useful as a walking stick, nor so impressive as an alpenstock with a spiral of place-names and heights engraved on it, but it confers on its owner a certain distinction and separates him from that other kind of tourist who does little walking, and thus does not need even an ice axe. From an ice axe to a pair of crampons is another step, and though the latter may never be used, except perhaps as a substitute for socks over the boots on the slippery ice of a glacier, their ferocious appearance is worth something to their intrepid owner and they are distinctly useful when placed points outwards on the back of a rucksack in a customs or passport queue. A length of rope completes the equipment. I wish I knew how to coil a rope as neatly and as beautifully as the tourist does. I wish, too, that I could get the same thrill out of mere possession and exhibition, but ever since a rude fellow called out to me on the first occasion that I carried a rope, 'Goin' to 'ang yourself, guv'nor?' I have sedulously sought to conceal this damning evidence of mental instability. Far be it from me to gibe at these proud possessors of ice axes, crampons, and ropes, even though they do no more than walk up to a hut, spend the following day admiring the view, and walk down again, for I know full well that I too, went through the stage of owning but not using the tools of mountaineering.

We continued on our way greatly refreshed. After proceeding for a short distance, we came to a point where the path divided. Both branches appeared to continue up the valley, so we took the right hand one, which contours along the mountainside to the west of the stream. I am glad we did so because we entered upon some of the most flowerful slopes I have ever seen in the Alps, indeed I do not recollect seeing elsewhere in that range so varied and concentrated a number of rare and lovely species.

It was now late in the afternoon and the shadows were gathering in the valley. There was no further doubt as to the weather's immediate intentions; the storm clouds had all dissolved and we were assured of a fine day for our climb.

Presently we reached the limit of burnable vegetation and cast around for a bivouac site. After scrambling for some time over the steep hillside we found an overhanging boulder, the size of a cottage, which formed a shallow cave, twenty yards from a tumbling stream arched over with an immense drift of avalanche snow. I could see that Jim's professional zeal was aroused by sundry inequalities in the ground, so leaving him to engineer a comfortable platform, I went in search of fuel.

It was the first time I had ever bivouacked at a moderate altitude in the Alps, and I was reminded of camping in similar situations in the Himalayas. I returned with an armful of juniper to find that my companion had excavated and levelled a sleeping place. Water was not so easy to get. We had to crawl under the vaulted avalanche snow in order to reach the stream, an uncomfortable process, as the packed snow above weighed many tons.

At length all was ready for a meal. Before leaving England, we had weighed the pros and cons of a pocket "Primus" but had decided against it on the score of weight. Instead, we had provided ourselves with a methylated cooker of a type, which has a burner consisting of a number of holes round a central orifice into which the methylated is poured. The scheme is that having three-quarters filled the orifice, the methylated is lit; this heats the burner until presently the spirit vaporises and jets of flame emerge from the holes. It is a simple contrivance and reasonably efficient, except in a wind; then it is the very devil. On this occasion there was no wind, and we vowed that the tea we brewed was perfect.

There is no doubt that mountaineering, or for that matter any hard exercise, in the open air makes a man appreciate his food and drink, and the most ordinary tea acquires a bouquet and fragrance undreamt of in civilisation.

Tea was followed by soup. In the matter of soup, I am not only knowledgeable, I am expert. Once, when staying at a hut, I made a soup that contained sixteen ingredients. My climbing companion who partook of it said that it was unique, but a little later after looking at me for some time without saying a word, tersely remarked that it was a beautiful night outside and went out to look at it. I was only too glad to follow him.

On this occasion I was circumscribed in the matter of ingredients, and the soup consisted merely of a packet or two of "Maggi" powders. But for all that it proved excellent, and we vowed that our bivouac was superior in comfort to any hut.

Our supper eaten, we lit our juniper fire, and lolling back in our cave smoked our pipes. The evening was supremely calm. On high, the crest of the Ailefroide was pink, against a sky of deepening blue, and at the head of the valley beyond the serene curve of the Pilatte Glacier stood Les Bans, a graceful mountain built up of sweeping ridges, aglow in the declining sun. As we watched, peaceably puffing at our pipes, the golden tide ebbed heavenwards. As the dusk gathered the light breezes died away and the smoke of our fire stood up with scarcely a quiver. There was no sound save for the constant percussion of the glacier torrent. It seemed scarcely credible that little more than forty-eight hours ago we were in the maelstrom of London. In retrospect civilisation seemed strangely futile and purposeless. I remembered the remark of a Himalayan native. He said: 'We have heard of your wonderful machines that go very quickly through the air and across the earth. But tell me, does it make a man happier to go from one place to another quicker than we go on a pony?'

The mental reactions consequent upon spending one day in London and the next day in the High Alps are curious. It would be difficult, to begin with, to imagine a more abrupt change of scene. Then it is undoubtedly true that during the first few days of his holiday, the mountaineer tends to be obsessed by the time factor, the predominant factor of civilised life. A great many mountaineers never escape from time, and that this is so is proved by a slavish adhesion to it when making or subsequently recording a climb. A glance at any climbing publication will prove the truth of this assertion. There is, of course, a certain technical interest about "times" in mountaineering. Furthermore, some attention to time is necessary for reasons of convenience and, on occasion, safety, but I have never been able to understand the type of mind that cannot escape from time on a mountain, and that must needs climb pocket book and pencil in hand noting the time at which such and such an object is reached. For me, perhaps the greatest enjoyment in mountaineering lies in escaping from my normal enslavement to time. The fact that I may have crossed the bergschrund at 3.15 a.m., reached the ridge at 6.25, traversed the first gendarme at 7.10, and gained the summit at 9.42 is of little or no interest, nor does it interest me to know the time of someone else on the same route. I suspect that this abhorrence of watch-in-hand climbing is due to the fact that I enjoy the scenery of mountains as much as I like climbing mountains. I am, however, bound to admit that were the world made up of people like myself, it would be an impracticable sort of affair, and from a material standpoint decidedly primitive. It would rub along in a happy-go-lucky mañana manner; but it would at least be contented, happy, and without wars, for no one can fight a war nowadays who is not a slave to time.

In the present instance time as an associate and reflection of human activity no longer mattered. It was measured only by the deepening dusk and the kindling stars. There was no time in the constant note of the glacier torrent, nor was time measured by a multitude of trivial thoughts. We were content to meditate, to allow ourselves to assimilate without effort, the beauty and peace of eventide.

Meanwhile our fire flamed and crackled merrily, and as daylight waned, lit up our cave with its ruddy glow. The fragrant smell of the burning juniper transported us back to the early days of alpine climbing, the days of Edward Whymper, Leslie Stephen, John Ball, and A.W. Moore. Perhaps the pioneers shared our campfire. It needed little imagination to picture ourselves bivouacking, not for a popular expedition, but an unclimbed peak, thrilled with the subtle joy that comes to a man on the eve of new adventure into the unknown, the prospect of setting foot where no human foot has trodden before.

The fire died down and the moon rose. The crags high above us shone against the stars then slowly the pale radiance crept valley-wards. It brought with it a chilling feeling, a promise of frost, and we made haste to get into our sleeping bags while still warm. There was no occasion to employ the tent, which was intended only for an emergency and we used it as a coverlet.

Jim had engineered a wide platform, and we lay side by side in perfect comfort. Presently I heard him breathing deeply and regularly and knew he slept, but it was a long time before I followed suit. I did not even want to sleep; I was content to gaze upwards at the stars, and the brilliant orb of the moon sailing its precise course through the heavens. Gradually, with increasing sleepiness, there came to me a feeling of unreality as I contemplated the mysteries of space; the mountains seemed to shrink and recede and the roll of the glacier torrent was resolved into celestial music ...

We both awoke later, in my case a trifle chilly as I had the outside berth, and the earth beneath me was damp. It was midnight or thereabouts and much of the romance had vanished from the proceedings. Jim presently went off to sleep again, but I lay awake for the remainder of the night. I have had many sleepless nights in the mountains, particularly on Everest, and very long some of them seemed. The present night was no exception and, as I lay awake with a cold spine and stiff shoulder blades, the world no longer appeared so beautiful as it had done when my stomach was warm and well filled. There is a sordid fact connected with all human activity; it is that aesthetic enjoyment is dependent on a warm and well nourished body, and that failing this condition the loveliest mountain views may be contemplated with a cold loathing. This was a case in point; I longed for dawn and activity, and thought wistfully of those civilised comforts which I had affected to despise.

Dawn came at last; the faintest paling of the sky behind the moon-bathed cliffs of the Ailefroide. In happier circumstances I should not have noticed it, but now I roused my blissfully slumbering companion.

'It's getting light,' I told him.

He received this intelligence with an incredulous grunt, gave a snort and a heave and settled down once more to slumber.

But I had had enough of bivouacking and went off to get water. After a tricky scramble in the dark under the snow arch I filled the saucepan, only to slip on the way back and upset it. By the time it had been refilled the remarks I had to make about breakfasting in the dark, with particular reference to saucepans, had effectively roused Jim into a show of activity.

Hot tea was good; it was more than good, indeed beyond the range of laudatory adjectives. It put life into our cold stiffened limbs and rekindled the damped fires of optimism and enthusiasm.

By the time we had finished our breakfast it was light enough to see, so packing our rucksacks we set off for Les Bans, having cached our bivouac equipment under a boulder.

The moon showed shrunken and pale as we trudged up the stony path towards the Pilatte Hut, and ahead the crest of our peak shone with the first cold pallor of day. We both felt in that stupid, drowsy state peculiar to the early hours of the morning, when vitality is at its lowest. Many writers have enlarged on the excitement of an early start in the Alps, I have been guilty of this myself, but years of indiscretion, if I may put it thus, now compel me to state emphatically that not only is there nothing exciting or romantic about it, but that it is a thoroughly disagreeable proceeding which I associate with a stomach that complains bitterly for not being allowed to complete its normal digestive processes in peace, and a certain mental state best described as fedupness with everyone and everything.

However, it will be inferred that if mountaineering happiness is primarily a matter of efficient circulation and unimpaired digestion, then there is nothing like a good brisk walk for setting things right. So it proved in the present instance; an unqualified gastronomical gloom presently disappeared, and was superseded by intelligent interest and even mild enthusiasm.

An hour after leaving our bivouac we came to the Pilatte Hut. Outside it was stationed a solitary tourist of doleful demeanour who growled a surly 'bon jour, Messieurs,' which greeting we returned with, what to him must have seemed, a hateful heartiness.

Purely as a matter of interest and inquisitiveness we opened the door of the hut and glanced inside. At least Jim did while I peered over his shoulder. Next instant he staggered back, pulling back towards the door as he did so. I have never been in a submarine unable to rise from the bed of the sea with the air becoming fouler every minute, but I should imagine that the experience would closely resemble a night spent in the Pilatte Hut during the holiday season. Our feelings were summed up by Jim, who turned to me and said in a voice vibrant with emotion, 'Thank God we bivouacked, Frank.'

A few minutes later we trod the frozen surface of the Pilatte Glacier. We were still in cold shadow, but we could see the sun shining on the upper séracs of the glacier, which were silhouetted against the blue sky in all manner of strange poses. We could also see another party evidently bound, like us, for Les Bans.

Tramping uphill over board-hard snow through motionless frosty air was a pleasant preliminary to the more serious work of the day. The glacier was larger and more complicated than we had suspected, but tracks of previous parties obviated the need for route finding, and we mounted in that preoccupied yet negative frame of mind which I always associate with long and uninteresting ascents on easy snow.

Higher up, the glacier was considerably broken and the ice scenery varied and beautiful, broken walls of gleaming ice alternating with widely rifted crevasses. We had to zigzag through the latter, crossing numerous well-frozen snow bridges, and pass beneath a tottery wall of ice some eighty feet in height, which appeared ready to crumple up and fall at any moment.

Presently we came out of shadow into brilliant sunlight and plumped ourselves down in the snow for another meal; it was several hours since we had left our bivouac and the inner man had long since passed from active resentment into a dull despair and from dull despair into renewed resentment.

Second breakfast, as all mountaineers know, is a solemn and time-hallowed rite. It marks a transition stage in the day's work, a ceremony differentiating the cold hours of dawn from the exciting prospects of a day's mountaineering.

I forget what we ate, but I believe sardines, raisins, and chocolate were on the menu; and I can never eat the first named without thinking of a friend of mine whose favourite mountaineering diet is sardines and honey, spread together on bread and butter.

Our halt span out into a full half-hour. As we sunned ourselves we noticed with an interest that verged upon incredulity living creatures emerging from the Pilatte Hut some 2,000 feet or more beneath us, and remarked that the peaks of Dauphiné, with the exception of the glacier-clad mountains we were climbing, were fully as stony and precipitous as we had anticipated.

Continuing on our way, we made some more zigzags through the intricacies of the glacier, and arrived an hour later at the foot of an ice slope which ended in the East Ridge of Les Bans. At its foot this slope was rifted by a formidable bergschrund separating it from the Pilatte Glacier on which we stood. The rift was bridged by a tongue of snow at one place, but its upper lip was some fifteen feet high and vertical if not overhanging. The party ahead of us had crossed the snow bridge, scaled the lip, and cut steps up the ice slope. There seemed, therefore, every reason for us to do likewise and profit by the steps they had cut. But to my shame I must record that not only did we not do this, but that we avoided their route altogether and climbed up by an easier way. I, not Jim, was responsible for this decision. I crossed the snow-bridge and tried to climb the ice lip, and because it was steep and strenuous work, and because I was hopelessly out of training, I returned to Jim and declared myself in favour of an easier route if such existed. I have not the slightest doubt that Jim could have romped up the ice lip, but he unselfishly agreed with me that we could get up more easily on the left. Our "slink round", as I termed it later, meant traversing horizontally until we were almost beneath the Col de Pilatte, crossing the bergschrund at an easier place, climbing some rocks and snow to the col, and doubling back along the ridge from the latter to the final rocks of Les Bans. In the course of this entirely unnecessary manoeuvre we at least had the satisfaction of treading classic ground, for the bergschrund we crossed was that associated with a dramatic episode during the first passage of the Col de Pilatte by Edward Whymper's party in 1864. The bergschrund was more formidable then and the party, who had crossed the pass in the reverse direction, had to jump down fifteen or sixteen feet, and forward at the same time some seven or eight feet, alighting on a narrow ridge of ice. The first three made the leap successfully. Then came the turn of Whymper's friend Jean Reynaud. The episode is best described in Whymper's own words:

> He came to the edge and made declarations. I do not believe that he was a whit more reluctant to pass the place than we others, but he was infinitely more demonstrative – in a word, he was French. He wrung his hands. 'Oh, what a *diable* of a place!' 'It is nothing, Reynaud,' I said 'it is nothing.' 'Jump,' cried the others, 'jump.' But he turned round, as far as one can do such a thing in an ice step, and covered his face with his hands, ejaculating, 'Upon my word, it is not possible. No! No!! No!!! It is not possible.'
>
> How he came over I scarcely know. We saw a toe – it seemed to belong to Moore; we saw Reynaud a flying body, coming down as if taking a header into water – with arms and legs all abroad, his leg of mutton flying in the air, his bâton escaped from his grasp; and then we heard a thud as if a bundle of carpets had been pitched out of a window.

No such excitement befell us, and a little later we found ourselves on the sharp snow crest separating the Col de Pilatte from the rocks of Les Bans. The party ahead of us had climbed the mountain and were descending, and we paused to watch them. There were three of them, one, the middlemost man on the rope, being both bulky and clumsy, so much so that we watched almost anxiously. Largely because of him, the party was moving slowly, and the loose rocks they knocked down more than deterred us from attempting the climb until they were safely off the mountain. Seen *en face* the rocks appeared well nigh vertical, but the lie to their steepness and difficulty was given by the climbing method employed by the party we were watching, particularly that of the fat man, a method destructive to the seat of the trousers. It was not an inspiring spectacle and it became positively alarming when the fat man's feet shot from under him on a patch of ice and he subsided with a jolt on some rocks. However, as I told myself, who were we to criticise? I, at least, should put up an equally undignified performance on this, my first expedition of the season.

They were down at last, and after exchanging greetings, and seeing that they were out of range of any stones *we* might knock down, we moved along the ridge to the rocks and began to ascend.

The climb proved an excellent first expedition of the season, and the rocks, though steep in places, were neither too difficult nor too sensational and were excellent in promoting that harmony of mind and muscle which is the hallmark of skill and practice in mountaineering.

Unhappily, the pleasure of the ascent was marred by severe altitude headaches. I have suffered from these headaches before, both in the Alps and Himalayas, and they always result from a climb to an elevation in excess of 10,000 feet the first day. I do not know if they are peculiar to mountaineers because, while many members of Everest expeditions have been prostrated by them on arrival at Thangu bungalow in Sikkim, which is situated at a height of only 11,000 feet, tourists frequently visit the bungalow without similar ill effects. If there is a worse form of headache I do not know it. It begins at the base of the skull and drives knives of pain through the head to the eyes. Every movement, every jar of the foot on the ground, is agony, and when vomiting supervenes it does little or nothing to alleviate the pain. My only consolation was that Jim complained of a similar headache. This sounds a selfish statement, but there are few human beings, however Christian or humane, who do not derive a vicarious satisfaction from knowing that their ills are shared by a companion. Therefore while I said 'Bad luck' to Jim, when he complained of his headache, I was secretly glad that I was not the only one to suffer.

Had it not been for our headaches, we should have enjoyed better than we did the scramble to the summit. Fortunately memory has the inestimable advantage of eliminating physical sensation and promoting to the fore, often in false perspective, latent mental and spiritual enjoyment. Thus I remember the climb as interesting, the weather as perfect, and the views as extensive and beautiful. Memory tells me that the rocks were pleasant to handle, that they were soaked with sun, and seemed almost to breathe warmth as we climbed up them. What memory does not tell me is that at the time I had a bursting head, and that I swore to myself over and over again that come what might never would I climb a peak as high as Les Bans the first day of a mountaineering holiday.

Moving for the most part both together we progressed rapidly, at least Jim did, while I laboured in the rear, a prey to my lack of training which transformed an easy and pleasant rock climb into a sweating, puffing, unharmonious labour.

My head was feeling like a Mills bomb which has just had its trigger released when, of a sudden, rocks no longer loomed above, and we trod with dramatic unexpectedness the level summit of Les Bans.

Headachy and sick we sank down on sun-warmed slabs of schistose. 'That's that,' said Jim, with the air of one to whom the climb has seemed unexpectedly and disappointingly short. 'Thank heavens!' I replied fervently.

A few minutes' rest improved our malaise and we were able to take stock of the view. The Dauphiné Alps certainly confirmed our first impressions of wildness and grandeur. What we saw was not fantastic and bizarre like the Dolomites, nor serene and well ordered like the principal ranges of the Alps, but something in between. There were glaciers to be seen, in particular the Pilatte Glacier which curved away at our feet, but these were incidental to the main theme, which was an intricate jumble of savage rock peaks, not peaks with sweeping ridges and faces like those on the main watershed of the Alps, but mountains whose principal characteristics are steepness and complexity. To an orthodox mountaineer the view from Les Bans is depressing rather than elevating. It is uneasy and somehow incomplete. It is neutral in colour; there are no green alps and smiling pasturelands such as the mountaineer gazes upon from the heights of the Oberland or Mont Blanc; there are no gentle and gracious forms, no shining snowfields and remote wind-fashioned snow edges. Order and methodicity is lacking and, instead, there is a vast untidy mess of rocky mountains and narrow tortuous valleys. The Dauphiné massif is a by-product, a collection of shattered peaks arranged any-how, not in supreme disregard for ordinary laws like the Dolomites, but rather as an untidy afterthought to the Alps. It is as though Nature had said, 'Well, there are the Alps, they look all right, but there's a vacant space here, and I've a lot of stuff left over, not much snow and ice but any amount of rock; I'll plonk it down here and make the best job I can with it.'

But already I can sense my mountaineering friends writhing inwardly. To say such things about Dauphiné! Look at the Meije, the Écrins, they say; graceful mountains, splendid climbs; this fellow, confound him, is only writing to annoy – deliberate contentiousness! Therefore, let me hasten to add that the Dauphiné Alps grow on the mountaineer. I have recorded here faithfully my first reactions to these mountains, but later, only a little later, I came to like Dauphiné better. A conventional mountaineer requires some time to accustom himself to the unconventional, and unconventional from an architectural standpoint Dauphiné certainly is. During my few days in this country I came to learn the charm of its stony valleys, where little flowers peep out in unexpected places, and the untamed splendour of its peaks and precipices. I learned that it is a range of unsuspected views and odd and delightful corners, as many of both in a mile as in any other mountain country I know. Then there is the spell of the unknown. In point of fact there is nothing unknown about the peaks of Dauphiné, though there are many new routes to be made up them, but the early reputation of inaccessibility gained by this labyrinth of ridges, gorges, and valleys has never been quite dispelled. It is accurately and meticulously mapped, but the mountaineer feels that to him personally it is *terra incognita*, and that he must explore it: in the course of his explorations he will experience much the same feelings that the pioneers experienced who first worked their way from valley to valley over the intricate ridges. Such then is the charm of this strange country, and if the charm is at first not apparent it becomes perceptible with increasing knowledge and experience.

Apart from general impressions, what did we see from the summit of Les Bans? First and foremost our gaze sought out the Meije, 13,065 feet which, except in the matter of height – Barre des Écrins, 13,450, is the highest summit in Dauphiné – is the undisputed monarch of the district. It also enjoys the distinction of being the last great alpine peak to have been climbed and this not so much on account of its forbidding appearance as the sheer difficulty of the climbing. The Meije is unmistakable from any direction, a square-built mass with a long summit ridge bristling with towers, with one conical-shaped point, the Grand Pic, at the western-most end, to complete the resemblance to a Norman fortress. Les Écrins was not seen to advantage because of the interposing mass of the Ailefroide. Les Rouies, 11,775 feet, and the Pic d'Olan, 11,740, are the highest peaks to the west, the latter a beautiful wall-sided mountain renowned among rock climbers.

Yet we were little concerned with topographical details. For one thing we were too headachy and tired; for another the sun blazed down with lambent intensity, and there was not a breath of wind to temper its heat. It is not often that the mountaineer finds himself frizzling on an alpine summit 12,000 feet high, and Jim, feeling that he had done all that was required of him in the matter of the view and topographical identification, settled himself back to a boulder with his handkerchief over his face and fell fast asleep. I would have followed his example had it not occurred to me that if I did so we might both of us continue to sleep for hours and be benighted in consequence. Therefore I contented myself with a doze.

In this way over an hour passed. It is a curious experience dozing or sleeping on a mountaintop. The mountaineer, half drugged by the sunlight, rouses himself by slow degrees. He sees before him peak, range, and valley shining and unsubstantial like a vision, so much so that it is difficult to separate reality from unreality, and it requires a conscious mental effort to face up to the hard fact that a long, toilsome and difficult descent has to be negotiated. Sleeping on a mountaintop is not always a safe luxury, and I can recollect more than one occasion when I have set off down a difficult climb, yawning and drowsy and an incomplete master of myself for the first minute or two. It is in such moments of physical and mental inertia that accidents may occur.

The descent proved easy, and we rattled down the rocks. Our headaches were finally dissipated by the loss of height, and we both felt in good fettle by the time the ridge was regained. There we decided to descend the ice slope we had avoided on the way up. It was easier than expected, though the vertical lip of the bergschrund needed delicate balance. Jim went first, and after asking for plenty of slack rope, jumped the last ten feet or so down and across the rift, alighting gracefully on a snow ridge forming the lower lip, whence he skidded off down the slope below for a yard or two before coming to a halt in the soft snow of the glacier. I followed, and if my performance was not so dramatic as that of Reynaud's seventy-five years before me, I felt equally ridiculous as I sailed through the air, to alight with an undignified thump, and shoot down pell-mell to my laughing companion.

Thenceforwards we ploughed and glissaded rapidly down the sun-softened snow of the Pilatte Glacier. The séracs and the crevasses were behind, or so we thought, and we were on smooth unbroken snow when of a sudden down went my feet into a concealed crevasse. It was not a wide crevasse, but wide enough for a lissom mountaineer, and I had a momentary vision of sombre bottle-green depths before I struggled out. The rope was by no means taut, and Jim told me afterwards that he was over the same trap. It was a lesson to us both; nothing could have seemed more innocent than the snow slopes we were on when the incident occurred, and we apostrophised ourselves as fools.

The shadows were lengthening as we passed the Pilatte Hut, and scampered down slopes of scree and snow to our bivouac place. We retrieved our equipment and strolled down the flowerful slopes to the Alp de Carrelet, where we quenched our thirst with beer.

Forgotten were our headaches and fatigue as we lolled contentedly outside the Carrelet Hut in the late afternoon sun. Life was very good; the clock had moved on a few hours; another mountain memory had been gained. In any dark or evil hours that might lie ahead we could return in spirit to a star-filled night by a

Juniper fire, sun-warmed rocks and the meadows of the Alp de Carrelet. Such memories endure.

So we lingered a while on the Alp de Carrelet. The sun slipped lower and lower in a cloudless sky and cool shadows gathered in the valley. Peak and precipice stood immobile in a silent air. Only the stream continued its litany and birds twittered in the hushed pine forest. At such moments earthy man is aware of something greater than his earthiness.

Dusk was falling as we walked down the path to La Bérarde.

CHAPTER THREE

Barre des Écrins

OUR LUCK with the weather was in the ascendant, and immediately after our return to La Bérarde from Les Bans we determined to climb the Barre des Écrins, the highest peak in Dauphiné; after this ascent we should be in sufficiently good training to traverse the Meije.

Since Edward Whymper's party made their classic first ascent and traverse in 1864 a number of routes have been made up the mountain. The most popular of these is that by the south rock face from the Col des Avalanches, the descent to La Bérarde being made via the north-west ridge, the Col des Écrins and the Glacier de la Bonne Pierre. This expedition is usually made from the Temple-Écrins Hut above the Alp de Carrelet, but enquiry elicited the information that the hut had been destroyed by an avalanche, and that another hut was being constructed but was as yet uninhabitable. We determined, therefore, to bivouac in the neighbourhood of the hut.

With only a short walk in prospect it was unnecessary to leave La Bérarde until after lunch, and we spent the morning following upon our ascent of Les Bans idling about the village.

Not so very many years ago La Bérarde was unconnected with the outside world by a motor road and delightfully primitive. The Swiss very wisely have deliberately sought to exclude motor cars from some of their valleys, and one of the charms of Zermatt is that it is possible to walk in the street without being threatened by motorists who nowadays appear to imagine, and not without reason in view of the timorous behaviour of pedestrians, that a road confers on them a divine right of progress. The French, however, possibly for military reasons, have of recent years constructed motor roads in many valleys hitherto only accessible by mule track. It may seem bigoted and die-hard conservatism to denounce motor cars out of hand, but the sad fact remains that of all man's inventions the internal combustion engine has been put to the lowest uses. Furthermore, it is smelly and noisy, and the particular brand of tourist it conveys to the Alps often reflects its vulgarity and noise. One immediate effect of an influx of motorists, as opposed to those who spend their holidays in the mountains for the sake of peace and quietness, is on the economic and social life of a small community. The peasant, who previously lived simply and happily is apt to become cunning and discontented when absorbed by civilisation. Catchpenny phrases such as "standard of living" engage his attention, and he presently becomes imbued with that restless kind of striving after an ephemeral "something", which characterises those who live and work in cities, without realising that in so doing he is jettisoning contentment and happiness. An Alpine village which is being "developed" by motor car and tourist would make an interesting sociological study.

La Bérarde is an example of an essentially primitive Alpine hamlet that is being rapidly "developed" by tourism. There is one comparatively new hotel, a pleasant structure built in the chalet tradition; for the rest the village houses have been converted into (it would be more truthful to say have become) hotels, whilst there is, of course, the inevitable shop selling picture postcards and trinkets, the trashy nature of which bears testimony to the type of mind that purchases them, and the decline of art in general. At frequent intervals cars and charabancs arrive; they disgorge their passengers who, after refreshing themselves at one or other of the hotels, walk a few hundred yards (the more energetic among them), buy postcards and trinkets (made anywhere but in Dauphiné), and depart in a cloud of dust, happily conscious that they have "done" the Central Alps of Dauphiné, a fortunate illusion which no true lover of that country would want to dispel.

After lunch, we shouldered our rucksacks and set off to the Alp de Carrelet and our bivouac place. The weather was now perfect, and after the usual pause for refreshment at the Carrelet Hut we mounted leisurely through a forest of small pines towards the site of the Temple-Écrins Hut.

It was a pleasant walk, and we paused more than once to contemplate the beauty of the view, which included Les Bans set gracefully at the head of the curving Pilatte Glacier, and the abrupt rocky pile of the Pic Coolidge, a peak Dolomitic in aspect by virtue of its yellowish colour and formidable appearance.

As we neared the limit of the forest we cast around for a bivouac site, but as there was no level place, continued, until we were above the forest and on open ground below the Temple-Écrins Hut. Here we came upon some almost level turf, complete with a small stream and, best of all, a quantity of firewood in the shape of the remains of the former hut which had been swept down by the avalanche. In Scotland or Switzerland we might have entertained doubts as to the legality of burning even the debris of a hut, but we felt that there was unlikely to be any officious person in the vicinity, and that no one would worry over the destruction of a few planks.

In order to save weight we had left our sleeping bags at La Bérarde and had brought with us only the tent. This we erected, and uncomfortably low it seemed when the two supporting ice axes had been affixed to either end. However, we consoled ourselves with the thought that we should start shortly after midnight.

The sun set soon after our arrival, but we counteracted the chill that came quickly to the air with a roaring fire of hut debris. 'It is,' as Jim remarked, 'an ill avalanche that blows nobody any wood.'

The evening was serenely calm. During the day, cumulus clouds, the products of moist valley air, had gathered about the mountains, but towards sundown they began slowly to break up, until only a few thin wisps were left, a delicate pastel pink, against a green sky. The most striking object in view was the Pointe du Vallon des Etages in the south-west, a peak bearing a striking resemblance to the Matterhorn. Eastwards, the topmost crags of the Écrins were visible, glowing in the sun's last rays. The stars waxed gradually brighter and the light from our fire grew on the gentian-carpeted turf.

Many a time I have pondered over the peace and tranquillity of the hills. It seems that man when he treads the city street treads some lower spiritual level and that on the hills he meets with something better than the mere negation of noise and haste. There is spiritually a positive quality about Nature, just as there is a negative quality about the centres of civilisation. The artificial and the superficial tend to promote evil rather than good; the natural, though it may be disregardful of life, is essentially good because it teaches restless, striving, and unhappy man the virtues of order, rhythm, and tranquillity. Nature seldom takes life except to perpetuate her species, whereas men take life for motives of anger, greed, power, selfishness and jealousy. There seems inherent in hills a Presence of Peace, and this Presence is perceptible to those who listen with all ears. To the true philosopher Peace is discernible anywhere, but for most men this is impossible because of their physical environment, and they must seek it in quiet places far removed from the activities of their fellows. It is from this lower grade that, the hermit, the monk, and the nun come. Theirs is a confession that they have failed to find spiritual peace, because of their own incapacity to do so. They are afraid to face up to the problem of finding it in the company of their fellow men, and prefer to seek peace rather than to make it.

The modern escapist is in temperament and desire something between the peace finder and the peacemaker. He seldom understands his own motives; in his desire to escape for a while from the noise and confinement of the city he accedes to a blind and sometimes selfish instinct. He may delude himself with talk of sunlight, hard exercise, and fresh air, but the real reason for his escape is a search for peace. Peace is the natural, not the unnatural end of human progress, and its evolution is to be discerned not only in Geneva and the correspondence columns of newspapers, but in the heart of every man who seeks the solace of a quiet and restful hour, and in every man whose scale of values is not rooted in a purely material conception of life.

The escapist is a glowing spark from the anvil where man is being forged. Perhaps decades hence a race, living let us hope in amity amid beautiful surroundings, will examine critically present day man's spiritual yearning for a peace of mind and body that at the moment of writing seems as far out of his reach as ever. They will discern a growing revolt against ugliness, and social and economic misery, and the dawn of a new era, the beginning perhaps of a Romantic Age in which beauty and the creation of beauty will find a new scope and a new recognition.

If the mountains do nothing else they at least tend to promote thought, for only the fool or the dullard can stand on a high hill without sensing a destiny and a peace in which earthly death is the merest incidental.

Darkness was gathering as we prepared and ate our supper. This, as at first planned, was to be a single course of soup with trimmings, but Jim presently remembered that among our provisions were some dried apricots and suggested that these might be improved and rendered succulent by immersion in boiling water. This was no sooner said than done and our aluminium pan was placed over the fire on two stones so arranged as to form a small trench. All went well until the pan was retrieved from the fire. Jim did this, but it was a delicate operation as the pan had no handle, and in the middle of it something went wrong and our precious sweet was distributed over the grass and among the ashes of the fire. Jim was deeply chagrined, and on several subsequent occasions referred to the incident in scathing self-condemnatory terms. Fortunately the damage was largely repaired by our scooping up the apricots and eating them; they were pronounced to be excellent, in spite of ashes and other foreign matter adhering to them.

By the time we had eaten our supper, darkness had completely fallen. We piled wood on to the fire and sat by a great blaze smoking our pipes; and a pipe never tastes so good as when it is smoked in the open by a wood fire. As we sat we talked. I asked Jim whether younger officers in the army still cherished illusions as to the manner and meaning of war. His reply was that none, not even those too young to remember the last war, had any illusions, war was an unpleasant and bloody business.

At that moment the thought of war seemed unreal and fantastic. The moon was rising behind the Écrins and its rays shone on the rock peaks opposite to us across the valley. One great lesson Nature has to teach man is methodicity. On mountains the rhythm of the universe is appreciated more easily than it is at lower levels. From the high and lonely outposts of the earth the mountaineer gazes with humble awe outwards and beyond the hilltops into space. And as he gazes he senses an answer to the meaning of life. He looks down dispassionately upon human strugglings and sufferings, yet knows full well that presently he must descend among them, taking his part in the world of men and affairs. Yet when he does so he carries down with him, as a pilgrim might who visits a shrine, a measure of the peace and serenity of spirit he has gained on the hills. He appreciates better the value of the essential, and the valuelessness of the unessential. Nature has taught him contentment and simplicity, that to overburden the mind with material matters is to incur discontentment, complexity, and unhappiness, that some detachment of mind and spirit in the midst of everyday affairs is the key-stone of genuine happiness. He is able to appreciate the value of meditation and the dangers inherent in the spiritual quagmires of rush and speed, for speed more than anything else is synonymous with selfishness, callousness, and inconsiderateness. Thank God, machines are seldom seen on mountains. The Tibetans believe that to dig for minerals is to let loose devils. They have good cause to do so if it be remembered that the aeroplanes now raining destruction upon men are made from minerals dug out of the ground. Love of Nature is man's spiritual armour against the Moloch of the Machine. Through his sense of beauty in natural things he struggles to escape from a self-constituted and self imposed enslavement. Nazi Germany is symptomatic of a spiritual enslavement. We are fighting to control materialism and its spawn, the machine.

Soon after moonrise, mists gathered above and below. This was due to a sudden lowering of temperature and presently, when equilibrium was established in the atmosphere, they dispersed and the peaks shone out clear and unclouded. The cold increased quickly and we were soon reduced to that state, which visitors to the average English hotel will readily recognise, of being scorched by an open fire from the front and withered by a cold draught from the rear.

Shortly after ten o'clock, we decided to seek refuge in our tent and try to sleep a little. As it seemed likely that the one farthest from the entrance would be asphyxiated during the night, we tossed for the privilege of outside berth. I won, and Jim had to take the risk.

Having insinuated ourselves through the small sleeve opening we lay down side by side. We had previously prepared a platform for the floor and this proved moderately comfortable, but because of the close confinement and lack of ventilation we found it impossible to sleep, and soon came to the conclusion that although the tent might prove its value in an emergency, it was otherwise to be avoided. Jim was the first to rebel and announced his intention of spending the remainder of the night by the fire. I was glad to follow suit, and we remade the fire and settled down as near to it as we dared, now and again turning our backs to the blaze, in the manner of grilling chops. So the night passed. We nodded and drowsed, and alternated between being roasted and frozen. Tent and turf were white with frost when at half past two we stiffly roused ourselves to prepare our breakfast. Hot tea put fresh life into us, and an hour later we packed up the frost-stiffened tent and set out for our climb.

The night was cloudless, and as we breasted the slopes above our bivouac we saw before us the summit crags of the Écrins bathed in the moonlight, floating like some ghostly vision in the stars.

For a while we trudged over loose stones, but presently came to a path zigzagging up the slopes between the glacier and the Pic Coolidge. The excellent state of this path proved that the ascent of the Écrins from this direction is popular among climbers. Following a path uphill is a good preliminary to a day's mountaineering. It needs no skill and little effort, yet the exercise is sufficient to loosen the muscles, quicken the blood in the veins, and in general prepare the mountaineer for the more serious work of the day.

Dawn came as we passed beneath the ferocious north-west precipice of the Pic Coolidge. Slowly the shadows cast by the waning moon were absorbed by the increasing light. It was a glorious morning. For some time past, as we had mounted the path, I had speculated half sleepily as to the nature of a luminous white cloud hovering in the north-western sky, but as the light grew I saw that it was the great snow field of Les Rouies.

Daylight came as we trod the frozen surface of the glacier. We had to pass beneath the mouths of some stone-swept couloirs falling from the Pic Coolidge, but at that hour the mountain artillery was silent and nothing fell. A little later we crossed the southernmost branch of the glacier and mounted some rocks to the northernmost branch, which ends in the Col des Avalanches under the south wall of the Écrins. We already knew that there were others ahead of us, and as we turned a corner and came within sight of the cliffs of the Écrins, we saw and heard two parties, the first of two, and the second of four men. They were already on the rocks, and must have started at least an hour before us, after sleeping in the half-built hut. This was annoying, as we realised that it would be inadvisable to follow them for some time owing to stones they might knock down on us. We decided therefore, to mount to the Col des Avalanches, find some spot out of reach of a light but bitterly cold wind and breakfast. This decision was soon proved to be right, as presently we heard excited shouts and the rattling of stones.

We had no difficulty in reaching the col but to descend on the other side of it out of the wind was a different matter. Shivering in an icy blast we gazed down a sheer precipice falling for many hundreds of feet into an icy stone-scarred gully, descending with terrific steepness some 3,000 feet to the Glacier Noir. There was, however, one ledge which appeared large enough for our purpose and, while Jim held me on the rope, I descended from the ridge to investigate it. It proved to be only two feet in breadth; I edged and shuffled along it, but had not gone far when I realised that it was by no means safe. The rocks above and below were unstable and I could feel the whole mountainside tremble slightly, or so I imagined. I was about to retrace my steps when out of the corner of my eye I saw a patch of blue. It was a cushion of the Alpine forget-me-not (*Eritrichium nanum*), and near it were growing other cushions covered with stemless blue flowers, a blue matching the sky and, in brilliance and purity, seeming to partake of the very atmosphere. Here was an example of Nature's adaptation to circumstances, for the Col des Avalanches is 11,515 feet above the sea. These little plants had weathered and endured countless storms and freezing cold, yet in their close packed foliage, set tightly and snugly in niches and crannies of the rocks, was the will and the capacity to exist and to endure.

I rejoined Jim and we decided to wait at the foot of the rocks on which the other two parties were climbing. As we approached the rocks we heard warning shouts and then the whizz of stones. We made haste to make ourselves as small as possible under a vertical wall, and there we had to remain for the next hour or more. It was a depressing situation for, if we were safe from stones, we were assaulted by the bitterly cold wind and were in shadow out of the sun, which shone, as it seemed to us, with fulsome self esteem on the cliffs of the Fifre, a peak of 12,075 feet to the south of the Col des Avalanches. How we longed for its warmth as we beat and kicked our hands and feet together, while listening to the humming and whining of the stones dislodged every few seconds by those above us. Why couldn't the two parties get a move on? we asked ourselves time and again. What the deuce were they doing? We could hear their voices, but presently they ceased and with them the stone falls. I ventured forth from the protective rocks, and gazed up the gully to the left. I was about to tell Jim that it was safe to advance when once again came the rattling of stones and I just had time to scurry back like a rabbit into its burrow when down they came with a vicious clatter, clatter, and whizz, whizz, flying and ricocheting like bullets.

There was another long and disagreeable wait, but at length it seemed that the stones really had ceased to fall and gingerly we forsook our shelter and, with many an anxious glance upwards, proceeded to follow tracks in the snow up the gully to our left. This divided above into two chimneys. The right hand of these was glazed with ice and looked so repulsive that we decided that the left-hand one was the route of ascent. In deciding this we made our first blunder. As was obvious from the tracks in the snow, the other parties ahead of us had attempted the same route and we assumed, with what justification I do not know, that they knew the way. In point of fact, they knew it no better than we, and we were led into an impossibly difficult chimney. We retreated, baffled. As already mentioned the right hand of the two chimneys looked equally unattractive, and to avoid it we attempted to scale the rocks to one side of it. Our manoeuvres were so varied and complicated that I am entirely unable to remember them in detail. I have a vague recollection of climbing some steep and difficult rocks to the left of the ice-glazed chimney and of trying to traverse into the latter above the icy section. This failed and, eventually, after over an hour's work, we retired to the snow, where we indulged in a good grouse against everyone and everything, excluding, of course, ourselves who were really to blame. I will spare the epithets, and economise in the asterisks, and will only remark that the things we had to say about the parties in front of us were excusable having regard to the provoking circumstances.

Were we to be beaten before we had begun? Were we to creep ignominiously back to our bivouac place and La Bérarde? It was not to be contemplated for a moment. Get up we would, come what might. 'I am sure the route must lie up that chimney,' said Jim, pointing to the unpleasant ice-glazed rift already mentioned. 'The guidebook says ...' But we had already read our fill of the guidebook, and, had come to the conclusion that it was wrong in every particular. 'I'm going to try it,' continued Jim imperturbably, in response to my growl of scepticism, and without further ado, he set about wrestling with the intricacies of the cleft. And he *did* do it. It was a good lead, and he had to surmount one particularly wicked bit some distance up. The chimney was long, but proved easier than anticipated; it is probably not difficult in normal conditions; but the presence of ice may turn the easiest route into a struggle, and we realised as we mounted one reason for the slow progress of the parties in front of us.

The chimney slanted from left to right across the face of the mountain. It provided a sufficiency of resting places, and Jim seldom had to run out more than fifty or sixty feet of rope. He was in good form and climbed confidently and well, but I was the reverse and put up a sorry performance on the cold ice-sheeted rocks. It is worse than disagreeable climbing steep rocks when you are out of form; physical unfitness interposes a barrier between the climber and the mountain so that the latter seems remote and hostile. In such circumstances climbing is the reverse of enjoyable; it approaches too near to the borderline of fear. Climbing when in good form is a very different matter. There is no physical or psychological barrier between man and mountain. There is no "dithering", no indecision, no vacillation; calmness, confidence, and enjoyment are experienced by the climber, who is physically and mentally fit; there is harmony. This applies to most forms of human activity. It is no good trying to do a job of work for which there is not the requisite knowledge, skill, and capacity. The work retaliates on the worker. So it is in mountaineering, as the annual accidents list reveals. Mountains are apt to retaliate on those who approach them without skill, knowledge, and humility.

The chimney petered out into debris-covered rocks and patches of snow. We paused and searched the cliffs ahead of us. The guidebook said that it was necessary to bear to the right, then mount some difficult rocks by means of a fixed cable. The route, however, was not visible. Immediately above us was a deeply cut snow-filled gully, ending in sheer overhanging precipices. There was no way here that we could see, and in any event to mount directly upwards seemed contrary to the instructions of the guidebook; nor could we see any sign of the parties ahead of us.

I suggested to Jim that we must look to the right and that I would go ahead and prospect. He agreed, and I set off up some slabby rocks to one side of a shallow scoop. Here and there these rocks appeared scratched as though by boot-nails, but there was otherwise no definite indication of a route in this direction. A long wait at the foot of the precipice had chilled us to the bone, and climbing the icy chimney in the shadow had done little to improve our condition. But now we were in the sun and the rocks were warming every instant. For the first time that day I began to extract some pleasure from the climbing. It was a sensational position in which I found myself after an ascent of some forty or fifty feet. Immediately above me was a thin chimney, a ferocious overhanging rift, with some loose rocks wedged insecurely in its uppermost portion. Surely the route could not lie there; the difficulties were as obvious as they were desperate. On both sides of the chimney the cliffs were patently unassailable, vertical or overhanging walls of yellowish rock. Was there a route still farther to the right? If so, it could only be gained by traversing at a lower level. I decided to investigate and commenced to descend some steep rocks which formed the left-hand wall of the chimney, my plan being to cross the latter lower down, turn a rock nose and examine what lay beyond. Before doing this I brought up Jim, so that I was well held from above. It was an awkward descent; the rocks were not sound, and I had to test every hold; the precipice below was abysmal.

Thirty or forty feet lower I became convinced that we were hopelessly off the route. The proposed traverse across the chimney to the right was as difficult as it was dangerous, and I knew that neither extreme difficulty nor danger are met with on the south face of the Écrins if the proper route is followed. So I shouted up to Jim, 'It's no good, I don't think we can get round there, it's a horrible place. We had better get back. I can traverse from here,' to which he replied cheerfully, 'All right, I'm not very well placed but I can hold you.'

A nearly horizontal traverse was the shortest way back to the point from which we had started, but it was undoubtedly "thin" and exposed, the holds being small, and I was glad to regain the debris-covered rocks. Jim returned by my route of ascent and presently we were reunited. More than an hour had passed and we were no wiser than before.

Our next move was to attempt a traverse at a lower level; but this proved equally futile. We found ourselves on treacherously loose rocks of tremendous steepness and were glad to beat a retreat. Two hours had now passed and time was galloping. If we did not at once find a route we should have to retreat. We were puzzled and angry with the guidebook and with ourselves. We had seen some steps in a patch of snow near the mouth of the "impossible" gully, but had dismissed the latter out of hand. Could it be that the route followed this gully despite all appearances to the contrary? Was it a case of the "second degree". We had been misled by our predecessors at the commencement of the climb and had believed, when we saw their traces the second time, that we should be misled again if we followed them, especially in view of the apparent impossibility of climbing the gully. Was it possible that on this occasion they were right, and that we must follow the evil looking rift?

At this point in our dilemma we heard voices and next moment the familiar rattling of stones, a few of which came flying past us out of the mouth of the gully. We beat a hasty retreat, then paused and looked up. The problem was immediately solved when we saw three figures descending a fixed cable into the gully from the rocks to the right of it. The cable was obviously that mentioned in the guidebook. But why was the party descending? What had gone wrong? These questions could only be solved by personal contact. At all events, there was the route plain to see, and we were going to climb it.

Shouting up a warning that we were in the line of fire from stones, we rapidly climbed up into the mouth of the gully. As we did so, doubt and indecision vanished like snowflakes in the sun. We had been tricked and bamboozled; our blood was up; for the first time that day we climbed quickly and confidently.

Soon we were at the point where it was necessary to leave the gully in favour of the rocks to the right. Down these rocks extended a stout steel cable attached at intervals to iron spikes. Three Frenchmen were descending it. They were painfully slow and for some inscrutable reason were using a doubled rope in addition to the cable. It was no use waiting for them. They would take half an hour at least to get down, and we set off up the cable.

Climbing which entails mere gymnastic strength and agility is not the most enjoyable kind of climbing, and ascents such as the Dent du Géant and the Italian side of the Matterhorn, where hundreds of feet of fixed ropes or cables must be scaled, are more strenuous than meritorious or pleasurable from a mountaineering standpoint. Not only is such climbing artificial, but there is always the disquieting thought at the back of the mind that perhaps the ropes or cables are insecurely attached or have rotted or rusted away. On this section of the Écrins, the rocks are less difficult than those we had been climbing in our attempt to discover the route and the cable is therefore unnecessary. Time, however, was now of such vital consequence that we did not hesitate to shin up as quickly as possible. *En route* we passed the three retreating climbers and asked them why they had abandoned the climb. Their disconsolate and scarcely encouraging reply was, 'We lost the way and we are too slow,' an inadequate explanation in view of the fact that they were climbing behind another party who had not retreated, having apparently found the route. I fear that we did not feel charitably disposed towards them, for we had spent much time in dodging the stones they had knocked down; also it was their initial blunder that had led to so much wastage of time. On a complicated mountainside like the South Face of the Écrins, it is unwise to assume that a party in front of you is right or wrong unless it is known to be accompanied by someone who knows the route. Failing such knowledge he is a wise mountaineer who adheres unswervingly to his own judgement.

Above the fixed cable were some steep but comparatively easy rocks. These brought us to a corner and an incipient ice-filled gully, which we crossed to a rocky rib. And here again we went wrong. We should, I believe, have made a further traverse to the right, but we elected to climb directly upwards. For a few feet the rocks were practicable, then they rose in an overhanging nose, which forced us back into the gully we had just crossed. At this point the gully was ice filled and exceedingly steep for a few feet, but a little higher the ice gave place to rocks set at an even steeper angle, smooth slabby rocks, oozing with melted snow water. We had both of us now completely recovered from our former despondency, and I, who was then in the lead, was feeling more energetic, yet, in my semi-trained condition, this section of the climb taxed me severely. The rocks showed no signs of nail marks, and it seemed certain that we were again off the route, but it was obvious that if they could be climbed we would gain easier ground above.

The holds were small, and few and far between; it was possible to get the first joint of the fingers and the tip of a boot on them and no more. An additional disadvantage was that Jim was some distance below, having secured himself to a belay on the easier rocks, there being no stance in the gully; thus a slip would have involved flying like a bullet from a gun down the icy gully, which in steepness and appearance resembled a frozen waterfall.

Climbing those wet slabs was a horrid experience. I was not at all sure of myself, and my movements were jerky. I put strength rather than skill into the work, as a climber does when he is not in training. The rocks were cold and wet, and I felt my fingertips becoming numb. Halfway up it suddenly came to me that I should be hard put to it if I had to retreat. Had I the reserve strength? Perhaps I had; it is amazing how much strength a man can muster to meet real emergency; but at the time I felt that I had not; I felt that at any moment my legs would start that horrid uncontrollable trembling which arises simply and solely from lack of training. I have never fallen off rocks when leading a climb, but I understood then how and why this may happen. It may arise from lack of strength and skill, or from fear, or from a combination of all three, and it was from that detestable combination of weaknesses that I suffered on that occasion. Imagination can be a blessing and a curse on a mountain; it was a curse on that occasion. I pictured all too vividly the results of a slip: the slide with desperately grabbing hands down the rocks, the fearful velocity of the fall down the ice chute of the gully, the rope snapping on the belay like a piece of thread.

Jim had no inkling of my malaise, for he was in good training and came up like a bird. I remarked casually that I thought it was a bad place and he agreed. He complimented me on my lead, but I knew myself that I had climbed very badly. Had I failed to climb the last bit I might not have been able to retreat safely. I had taken a chance, and the chance had come off. But the fact that the chance had come off does not absolve me from a charge of reckless climbing and bad mountaineering.

We were now above the lower rock cliffs and on a great slope of snow set at a high angle, leading up for several hundred feet towards the crest of the Écrins. The slope is intersected by various minor rocky ribs and we mounted by one of these without much difficulty, though the climbing was continuously steep. My memory, usually retentive of the details of a climb, is strangely vague as to this section of the route. What I do remember was an increasing anxiety as to the state of the weather. The early morning brilliance had been dimmed as we climbed, but so engrossed were we with the work that we scarcely noticed this. Now, as we toiled upwards, the sun disappeared behind formless grey mists drifting quickly out of the south-west. It was long past midday and it was necessary to hurry – above everything we must hurry.

There were rocks ahead; shattered crags ending in the summit ridge of the mountain, with little surges of mist moving along them like lazily propelled smoke.

Our rib ended and we had to ascend some snow diagonally to the right. There were steps here, evidently those of the party which had not turned back. Had the snow been in good condition we could have followed these steps and mounted over it most of the way to the summit ridge, but we were too late to do this; the snow was soft and concealed ice; to have climbed it, much step-cutting would have been necessary. So we took to the rocks on the right of the snow, loose, disagreeable rocks, yet safer and quicker than the snow. Up and up we progressed, rope length by rope length; extreme care was essential and every hold had to be tested.

The last bit was the best. Here the rocks, though steep, were firmer. The cliff ended with dramatic suddenness on the summit ridge. A strenuous scramble and we arrived there breathing hard, and with something more than a feeling of ordinary thankfulness.

We looked at our watches and were astonished to see that they registered 3.15 p.m. The climb had taken eight and three-quarter hours from the Col des Avalanches, of which three to four hours had been spent in waiting for the parties ahead and in finding the route. We vowed that it was the most complicated climb that we had ever done, and certainly I cannot recollect a climb of similar character in which so much time was spent in route finding. We had no cause for self-congratulation.

The actual summit of the Écrins was a short distance to the east, but the lateness of the hour and the ominous weather made it imperative to descend immediately. Before doing so, we paused for a few moments to take stock of our surroundings. Had it not been for the delays we should have enjoyed a magnificent panorama, but the brightness of the morning had gone out and the ranges loomed dull and indistinct beneath a lowering pall of slate-coloured cloud. As we stood, a few hail-stones fell on the rocks at our feet with dry rustling whispers, and out of a still and silent void came a little wind that hissed a threatening whisper and was gone.

Our descent lay first of all over the Pic Lory, which is some sixty feet lower than the summit of the Écrins, then down the ridge towards the Dôme de Neige, the route descended by Whymper's party in 1864. From Whymper's description, which was the only one I had read, I expected to find dangerously loose rock. Actually, the reverse was the case, and the passage of many climbers had deprived the route of ill-attached fragments, leaving a core of sound rock. There was no real difficulty in following the ridge, and we moved both together all the way, yet it was a beautiful and unique edge of rock, so thin in some places that it resembled a narrow wall splintered and breached by a cannonade.

For the most part we kept to the east side, and clambered along, holding on to the knife-like crest of the ridge with our hands. The climbing aroused all Jim's enthusiasm. 'What a grand ridge!' he exclaimed on more than one occasion; and so it was, but like all grand things in life, it ended all too quickly, and we came to the point where a staircase cut out by the feet and axes of many climbers descended towards the Glacier Blanc. Down this we went without pause and, like Christian Almer seventy-five years before, found that the bergschrund at the foot of the slope could be jumped without difficulty.

Half an hour only had elapsed, and we lost no time in descending the upper slopes of the Glacier Blanc.

In order to reach the Col des Écrins, we had to run the gauntlet of ice avalanches for a distance of about one hundred yards. Two had fallen and we lost no time in threading our way between the fallen blocks. We were soon out of range of the threatening masses of séracs, and trudged wearily through soft snow to the col. We had cheated the weather, but only just. As we stood on the col, we were enveloped by a thick drift of hail and a spiteful volleying wind; then from our left, high up amid the crags of the great peak from which we had descended, came a crackling growl of thunder.

The descent from the Col des Écrins to the Glacier de la Bonne Pierre is simplified by the presence of numerous steel cables, and we devoutly hoped that the thunderstorm, raging on the Dôme de Neige immediately above us, would avoid our vicinity. The position of a climber who descends a wire cable on a mountain in a thunderstorm is analogous with that of a person who elects to scale a factory chimney in similar weather conditions by means of a lightning conductor. However, any fears we might have entertained on this score were allayed, as the thunderstorm devoted itself exclusively to the Écrins, doubtless under the mistaken belief that we were still on that mountain.

The descent was enlivened for me at one place by my ice axe doing its best to pitch me down the mountainside. This occurred on the steepest section of the cable. I had put the axe through my waist loop of rope and, as I was shinning hand over hand down the cable, its point caught on a rock, so that for a short time I was unable to move either up or down, a disagreeable situation when the weight is dependent on the arms alone.

As we descended, we were interested and puzzled by the behaviour of two climbers on the snow slopes at the foot of the col. For a long time they were stationary, but at length succeeded in crossing the bergschrund on to the Glacier de la Bonne Pierre. The mystery was partly solved when we reached these slopes and saw the mark of an obvious and unpremeditated slide, which ended on some rocks just above the bergschrund. The latter proved a formidable obstacle, but, after climbing down some rocks, we trod gingerly across a rickety-looking snow bridge spanning the gulf.

Snow was falling heavily as we slid and slithered down the upper slopes of the Glacier de la Bonne Pierre. Little was visible in the mist and gloom, but we followed the tracks of the two climbers we had seen and presently came up with them, two young Frenchmen who were sheltering from the snowstorm under a boulder. They generously offered us a drink of rum, which we gratefully accepted. Then they told us that one of them had slipped and fallen several hundred feet when they were climbing unroped down the slopes of the col. He had managed to stop himself at the rocks already mentioned a few yards short of the bergschrund. They had been the party in front of us all day, and it seemed strange that, having successfully accomplished a difficult traverse, they should nearly come to grief on the easy slopes of the Col des Écrins. But that is the way mountaineering accidents so often happen, when the difficulties are behind and easy climbing alone remains to be done. Reaction, inattention, carelessness, these are the prime psychological causes of the great majority of Alpine disasters.

I do not know how or why the Glacier de la Bonne Pierre got its name; its moraines are not such as to merit this distinction, and a number of harsher terms occurred to us as we descended. But the merit of Dauphiné Glaciers is that they are small, and their disagreeable features proportionately so; we emerged from the mist and snow and were soon in the valley that unites with the Etançons valley less than a mile from La Bérarde, the scanty pastures of which presently shone out from the rocky valley beneath.

Jim, true to that great British tradition of always descending from a mountain in time for table d'hôte, hastened on ahead with one of the Frenchmen, while I accompanied the other, a pleasant red-haired youth who talked so rapidly and so unintelligibly that I was content to reply, "Oui, Oui" or "Non, non" when an answer seemed indicated, a procedure which greatly impressed him with my conversational powers and knowledge of the French language.

What a delightful experience it is to descend from the high mountains after a hard day's climbing. One hour the mountaineer is among dead things, ice, snow, and rock, frozen, silent, and utterly indifferent to life, the next he is among life. First of all, he sees compact little plants set snugly in the stones of the moraine, anemones, saxifrages, drabas, and androsaces, their blooms silken and shining, then, as he descends, he enters into the kingdom of growing things. He sees water, that was higher frozen and silent, and hears the lilt and talk of it as it descends the hillside in rivulet and torrent, in ripple and rill, and glimmering pebble-floored pool. The air is soft, moist, and warm, not hard, dry, and cold, as it is on the heights, and charged with subtle and illusive fragrances, the smell of moist moss and herbage, the breath of flowers, warm resinous drifts from the pine forest. To appreciate to the full this beauty of living things it is necessary to spend some weeks on the blizzard-swept slopes of a Himalayan peak, then to descend from the scorching sun glare, and the desiccating cold of flesh-shrivelling storms, to growing things. Never does the world seem so beautiful, and never is the meaning of life so evident, as it is at that glorious moment when the descending mountaineer first sees the starry blooms of a saxifrage or androsace peeping up at him from the stones of the moraine.

My companion presently wearied of a conversational monologue and at my frequent halts to examine flowers, and hastened on, leaving me to descend, as I always like to do, at my own slow pace.

Jim had good-naturedly waited for me and together we strolled through one or two little fields, almost ready to be cut for a second precious hay-crop, and re-entered La Bérarde, sixteen hours after we had set out that morning from our bivouac. We were well satisfied with a great day's mountaineering.

CHAPTER FOUR

Interlude

THE MORNING after our traverse of the Écrins we woke to find rain falling heavily and thunder reverberating from the heights. In the British hills, little account need be taken of rain; it is part and parcel of our soft island climate, and he is a faint-hearted climber who is deterred by it from making ascents. There is something stimulating rather than depressing about a rainy day on the Cumbrian fells. No clothing yet devised can prevent the walker or scrambler from becoming soaked to the skin; yet the antidotes, a hot bath, an open fire, a saddle of Herdwick mutton, and a glass of hot grog induce a feeling of wellbeing that must be experienced to be believed.

In the Alps, however, rain is a malefactor, an unwelcome intruder upon the domain of sun and blue sky, and it usually means snow on the mountains, which may rule out difficult ascents for a day or two after the weather has improved.

Alpine hotels are ill adapted for rainy days. To an Englishman, veal, veal and yet more veal is a poor substitute for Welsh mutton or ribs of Scotch beef. There was not a hot bath to be had in the annexe of La Bérarde, whilst open fires and comfortable chairs are, of course, unheard of on the Continent. Much criticism has been levelled at the ghastly discomforts and horrible cooking of English hotels. It is the Englishman's privilege to criticise his own institutions, and he can do so without fear of incarceration in a concentration camp. The foreigner does not realise that such criticism is in ninety-nine cases out of a hundred a kind of inverted sentiment; therefore, he assumes that when a patriotic Englishman grumbles about his own institutions, those institutions must, in truth, be appalling. The Germans, more than any other people, are prone to make this psychological blunder; they have yet to learn that open grumbling and criticism are the hallmarks of Freedom and the guarantees of improvement. For myself, I have come to the conclusion, after travelling in various parts of the world, that there is no hotel quite so bad as a bad English hotel, and no hotel so good as a good English hotel.

During the two days that Jim and I were forced to remain inactive, we came very near to being bored. As both days were similar in their general characteristics, it is only necessary to describe one. We awoke and looked out of the window. Clouds were low on the mountains, and rain was falling steadily on to a tin roof with a depressing sound, which reminded me of Somerset Maugham's play "Rain". One or two disconsolate tourists were standing about in the village street, clad in mackintoshes or capes, whilst the whitewashed houses, patched and streaked with damp, presented a somewhat debauched appearance. We dressed and came down to breakfast, banging our heads as usual against the floor of the landing as we descended the stairs, which had apparently been constructed for the passage of persons not exceeding five feet in height.

We entered the *salle à manger*, steeling ourselves to resist unflinching an atmosphere that never knew an open window, and was charged with the smell of stale tobacco smoke, mingling with a curious and indescribable drift from the kitchen, compounded apparently of dirty dishcloths, grease, smoke, garlic, coffee, and various unidentifiable substances and liquids. Continuing to steel ourselves we approached our table. On it we perceived the debris of last night's supper, together with an ashtray piled with cigarette ends, the usual toothpicks and the usual tablecloth.

We took our seats and awaited the advent of "Jules". We liked Jules and we felt sorry for him. He was always working and always over-worked, a satellite that revolved unceasingly about Madame who seldom appeared to the public gaze. Like the servitor of old, he went about his duties in a waistcoat and shirtsleeves with a green apron tied to his waist. He was not above seventeen or eighteen years of age, and he had a thin body and a thin, white face surmounted by thin, lank, dark hair. In outward appearance he was always exactly the same, which suggested that he never went to bed, or if he did go to bed had no time to take off his clothes.

He was a timid, friendly fellow, and, as we felt instinctively, only existed to be "put upon"; that it was a case of 'Jules will do it', and 'Leave it to Jules'. He was at once the "Bill" and the "Smike" of the establishment.

Jules presently appeared and, having cleared the debris of dinner away, but leaving the usual toothpicks and the usual tablecloth *in situ*, brought us a *café complet*, which, being interpreted, meant almost stone cold coffee, and milk, topped with a dense skin of revolting appearance, thick crusty doorsteps of sour bread, pats of butter, which in taste and aroma suggested the goat, and a glutinous yellow substance which we agreed was probably apricot jam.

We shouted to Jules, and Jules reappeared. We mustered all the French at our command. Why was the coffee cold? It was disgusting. We sought for other and equally appropriate adjectives: and the milk: in future, a strainer must be provided to separate the liquid from the solid.

Up went Jules's shoulders and eyebrows in the expressive French manner, as much as to say, 'These Englishmen, *parbleu*! They are particular. There is no satisfying them. Why cannot they be content with a crust of bread and a sip of coffee?'

He smiled bleakly. Yes, it was even as Monsieur said, the coffee *was* a trifle cold. It would be heated again, and if Monsieur desired to strain the milk, a strainer would be provided. Off he went, his mind dwelling on the curious idiosyncrasies of Englishmen, in particular their tendency to regard with disfavour skin on the milk, when other and more sensible people looked upon it as a delicacy, especially when spread upon bread.

A long interval, and the coffee reappeared, two or three degrees Fahrenheit warmer. Is the sour, hard, crusty bread, which it is necessary to tear like a wolf before it can be eaten, really palatable to Frenchmen? Presumably it is, and that soft, fine-grained English bread is obnoxious to a Frenchman. Tradition and custom are, of course, everything in the matter of food; I have given a Tibetan a tin containing a choice product of Messrs. Fortnum & Mason, seen him make a wry expression, empty the contents on to the ground and make off with the empty tin, smiling happily. Yet it might be supposed that in bread-eating countries there would be some common standard.

During the morning we watched the rain falling, wrote letters, and perused sundry magazines, deposited by former travellers, of dentist waiting-room vintage. Lunch was much better than breakfast, for the Frenchman's appetite rouses itself by midday. During the afternoon we saw various parties of tourists arrive in motor cars and charabancs. They alighted, ate a meal, stood about in the rain for some minutes, then re-entered their vehicles and departed. They had "done" La Bérarde and it is only logical to assume that La Bérarde had "done" them. Why they came to that village must remain a mystery, for there was absolutely nothing to be seen except low clouds, stony hillsides, and rain.

At the sacred hour of five o'clock we retired to our bedroom, bumping our heads as usual during the ascent of the stairs, and brewed some tea over our spirit cooker, consoling ourselves still further with a home-made cake that had accompanied us from England. Had it not been for tea, we might well have embarked on some desperate and lawless action, but it enabled us to maintain that equanimity and contentment of spirit that is possible with the Englishman who, though he may have lost all, yet still has his five o'clock tea.

The second day was precisely similar to the first, except that the rain descended with ever-greater ferocity, and the snowline crept down to within 3,000 feet of the village. At the end of it, while we were eating the inevitable veal, Jim suddenly said, 'What about the Pâtisserie des Alpes?' He referred to the well-known tea-room at Chamonix, and I was quick to catch his meaning.

'Right,' I said, 'we'll go to Chamonix tomorrow.'

It was a grey, drizzling morning when we boarded the motor bus for Grenoble. We felt rather like a man who, having been to the dentist and had one extraction, must needs return for another. We were relieved, however, to note that the bus was a modern and less decrepit vehicle than that which had transported us to La Bérarde. Also our former driver had been superseded by a tall, lean man with a long, thin, lantern-shaped face and prominent nose, who wore a beret cocked at a rakish and decisive angle and a cigarette, which he transferred from one corner of his mouth and back again with a single and miraculous facial contortion. We gazed at him earnestly; realising that upon him our safety depended. Here, we told ourselves, was the Frenchman of fact and fiction, the nonchalant Frenchman, magnificent in war, supreme in emergency, the Frenchman who drives a super-charged Bugatti round the Montlhéry circuit without turning a hair at a speed bordering upon the impossible. He seemed unconscious of our scrutiny, and seated himself at the wheel with our former podgy driver at his side.

I have already exhausted my adjectives in describing the drive from Grenoble to La Bérarde and have none left for the return journey. I can only say that it was terrific, and that the driving would have prematurely whitened the hairs of Sir Malcolm Campbell. When we came, as we soon did, to the snake-like portion of the road, we rounded the corners by the simple process of skidding them, our wheels never more than a few inches from the edges of precipitous drops.

Our descent put me in mind of a story told about the late Sir Henry Segrave. He was given a bus to drive during the General Strike, but to his chagrin and disappointment, found that all he could get out of it was fifty-five miles an hour, to do which he put it in neutral on Hampstead Hill. It is said that he was surprised and pained when all the passengers got out at the first stop.

During the whole of this tremendous descent, our driver engaged in animated conversation with our ex-driver; and would now and again turn in his seat and pass some quip over his shoulder to the passengers, returning to his driving just in time to skid the next corner. I can still see the profile of his long, lean, melancholy Gallic countenance, engaged in the endless pursuit of transferring a cigarette stub from one corner of his mouth to the other, and feel the motor coach rocking beneath me as it tore down the narrow mountain-road towards some corner, skirting an abysmal drop round which it seemed humanly and mechanically impossible to go.

We arrived in safety at Le Bourg-d'Oisans. The worst was over and we regarded with neutral feelings a change of drivers, the bandit, as we called him, being replaced by the podgy man. After this, the wide Route des Alpes was a bagatelle and the seventy or eighty kilometres per hour with which we traversed it, a snail's crawl.

At Grenoble we had several hours to wait for the train and occupied ourselves with wandering about the town. It was Sunday and, although no Continental city can ever hope to emulate the awfulness of a London Sunday, Grenoble is imbued, in the morning at least, with a certain atmosphere of propriety; that is to say, some of the shops are shut; there are fewer passers-by in the streets than during weekdays; and many persons have seen fit to clad themselves in black clothing, a trait which the respectable French bourgeoisie share with the Swiss, in addition, of course, to the carrying of umbrellas.

From Grenoble we travelled to Chambery and Aix les Bains, and there changed into a train for Annecy. The bad weather seemed to be limited to the High Alps, for the weather in the foothill region was perfect. This last, as already mentioned, is an ideal country for a walking or camping tour, and I made a resolution to return one day to the Grande Chartreuse. When I am too old and feeble to scale high mountains, I shall be well content to gaze from a distance upon the snows and wander amongst the green hills, the woods, and the flowers of the lower alps. In the first flush of youth, and in active middle age, it is not easy to picture physical feebleness and a curtailment of activity, yet the very nature of mountains helps to instruct a man in the art of living, which is to be spiritually contented. As the train lumped along towards Annecy I gazed up at the high green hills and tried to imagine myself years hence ensconced on one of their summits, gazing towards the distant snows. Even if I had not the strength to climb a low hill I should still go to the mountains, in order to be among them, and feel them about me, as I have always known them. I should no longer know a fierce desire to grapple with rock, snow, and ice, but would be content merely to gaze upwards between the clouds at their precipices and their remote shining snow. No regretful or jealous pangs would be mine. Vision alone would content me. Physically, all I should ask for would be to feel the cool breath from the snows tempering the heat of the summer sun, to listen to the same glacier stream, to smell the same smells, of hushed pine forests, of warm shower soaked turf, of flowers and fresh cut hay. What matters age or feebleness when so much is left?

At Annecy, a clean, flourishing little town at the northernmost end of the lake of the same name, we gravitated automatically to a *pâtisserie*, and endeavoured, not without success; to compensate the inner man for the Spartan living imposed on him at La Bérarde.

Replete with ices of various flavours, and dangerous looking pastries, we climbed into the motor bus that was to convey us to Chamonix. We had become inured to French driving, and our progress on this occasion seemed devoid of excitement. It is true that Jim lost his hat overboard, and that we nearly crushed a corpulent old gentleman in a straw hat against a wall, but the mere fact that we took corners fast and blind in the traditional French manner, seemed small beer after the Brooklands-cum-Montlhéry descent from La Bérarde.

How many centuries will elapse before man learns to be considerate to his fellow men when in charge of a vehicle? It would seem that speed and mechanisation have an adverse effect on the human intellect. Men and women, who are otherwise courteous, considerate, and kind, become rude, inconsiderate and utterly callous at the wheel of a motor car. Why is this? What is the psychological explanation? Is speed a drug or a stimulant like morphia or cocaine, stifling the best and bringing out the worst in man? If so, the Church would do well to recognise the fact. A sermon on the sin of speeding would at least be stimulating and controversial, and a change from dissertations on other and more conventional forms of sin.

Lack of education and imagination is at the root of many evils. The man who drops a bomb from an aeroplane sees merely a blob of smoke on a large map; something so remote from his action that the two seem scarcely connected. In another minute or two, the smoke blob is far behind and out of sight. He has not the imagination to picture the damage and misery he is causing. Eliminate machines and explosives but leave civilisation in its same state in other respects, and it is doubtful whether war, if fought by cold steel alone, would be fought at all; its incongruousness would be brought home to man. The paradoxical thing about civilisation is that it has perpetuated the possibility of war through its creation of the machine, and precisely the same callousness that obtains on the roads of Europe today, makes possible the pressing of a button as a result of which men are killed and maimed miles away. If education is to be effective, it must above all things cultivate imagination in youth, for without imagination, the possibility of waging war, which will become easier as machines are improved, will only increase. In the meantime, the psychology of speed, and the relationship between man and machine, provides a study for the best brains of the age, for if man is allowed to speed unchecked on his mad rush he must head for destruction. *Diabolo ex machina*

The Lake of Annecy is a favourite rendezvous of French people from Lyon, and other cities, and its banks presented a gay spectacle this sunny afternoon. After passing the lake, the road mounted through a forest to the village of Ugines, then followed the Arly Valley to Mégève. At one village, I forget which, we stopped, in order to allow the passengers to visit some gorge, waterfall, or other natural attraction. Jim and I meanwhile enjoyed a drink, and agreed over it that organised sightseeing was not for us. Why was this? Was it mere superiority on our part that prevented us from jostling along with a crowd of other people to gape and stare at some waterfall or fairy-glen (admission two francs), or was it boredom, or some other horrible human characteristic? I have often asked myself why I dislike "sights", why I detest accompanying a crowd of goggling and gaping trippers, and listening to a raucous-voiced guide, expatiating on the merits, beauties, and historical interests of the said "sights". A star in Baedeker is sufficient to send me post-haste in the opposite direction, except, of course, in the matter of hotels.

For me Nature when commercialised becomes dull and tedious to witness. Turnstiles and a fairy-glen are incompatible associates, and even a high and magnificent waterfall becomes a sad, shamefaced affair when viewed from behind an iron railing with a row of parked charabancs in the background. Beauty and grandeur in nature lie primarily in exclusiveness, remoteness, and unexpectedness. A countryside is infinitely more alluring when you have not read about it in guidebooks, and told which parts of it are admirable and which are not. Even in mountaineering I regard guidebooks with a certain hostility and innate suspicion. I do not want to be told where to climb and how to climb. I want to climb and find out things for myself; it is much better fun and, incidentally, better mountaineering.

Continuing on our way, we passed through Mégève. Not so very many years ago, I spent a night at an inn in this village, a simple charming inn, where I was entertained by some strolling minstrels. Mégève then was a sleepy little village of no particular importance, but it has since become a fashionable winter-sports resort. It is unjust to condemn a place merely because it has become popular and been transformed from a village into a "resort", yet I can never repress a certain feeling of sadness when I see an Alpine village that I had formerly known as simple, "old world", and primitive, "discovered" by the outside world and transformed into a venue for film stars. However skilfully this transformation may be effected, it reflects industrialism and all that industrialism means when applied to Nature. Private enterprise more often than not produces architectural uglinesses. Only socialisation in its best sense is going to save Nature from spoliation, for to money-grubbing man left to his own devices beauty in Nature means little or nothing. I was glad when Mégève was behind, and its barren piles of hotels, cable railways, and other appurtenances of tourism out of sight.

As we approached St. Gervais, we had to join a queue of vehicles, whose progress had been blocked for some unexplained reason. The motoring temperament reacts in a curious manner to an obstruction on the road, and the immediate Latin reaction is to press the horn and keep it going. I once worked in an office above the principal thoroughfare of Buenos Aires. Near-by was a crossroad, and when the policeman held up traffic, every motorist when his car came to a halt proceeded to blow his horn until the policeman lowered his hand. The noise was terrific and interfered considerably with business in the neighbouring blocks, yet it had come to be regarded as a custom of the country. It may be that to a citizen of Buenos Aires the failure of motor drivers to blow their horns in a London traffic block is equally inexplicable.

It was evening as we entered the Arve Valley and approached Chamonix. Over the foothills the sky was clear, but Mont Blanc was concealed behind mists, yet, as we turned a corner, there came into sight a point of radiant sunlit snow. It was so high that the neck had to be craned to look at it, and seen through the misty window it appeared unearthly and unreal. What is the spell of a mountaintop that it should cause men and women to rise electrified in their seats and exclaim, "Wunderschön!" "Magnifique!" or "Wonderful!" according to their kind? Is it mere size? Is it colour? Is it shape? Is it remoteness? What link was there between that shining point and human emotion? Do men perceive through a high hill, through physical form and outward appearance, an all-pervading spiritual force?

Beneath Mont Blanc on the hem of its robing forests lies Chamonix. For me this place epitomises more than any place I know among mountains, the vulgarity of man. What is vulgarity in the mountains? It is not merely some effect produced by a large number of persons congregated together, it is not merely noise, untidiness, or architectural monstrosity; it is incompatibility, incongruity. Nothing is ugly except as a combination or a relationship with surrounding objects, Chamonix does not harmonise with its surroundings, nor for that matter does any city. But there are degrees of harmony, and standards, which by custom come to be accepted, and Chamonix, I think, outrages these standards. The Alpine village before the advent of tourism became through custom and tradition an accepted and therefore harmonious part of the Alpine scene. This was due to centuries of slow growth and development, in which the prevailing motif was a profound conservatism. An Alpine village has not sprung up in a year, or in a decade; it has grown slowly. Tourism is a recent product and its growths are mushroom-like. Architecturally, it all too often outrages tradition, and produces in the minds of those who respect tradition a reaction of ugliness. This applies in smaller or greater degree to all Alpine villages that have been developed as tourist centres, though there are places in Switzerland or Austria where an honest attempt has been made to perpetuate tradition outwardly, while abandoning it inwardly for modern requirements in the matter of comfort, sanitation, etc. No such attempt has been made at Chamonix. It would appear that the private property owner and the city dweller who know nothing of Alpine architectural tradition are allowed full scope for their money-making propensities. That is the tragedy of Chamonix, and it is the tragedy of much of Europe. Mankind pays for the democratic system with ugliness, and will continue to pay so long as that system in its present form survives, so long as individual greed is allowed to trample upon public interest. It will occur under a socialist regime, and indeed under any regime so long as commercialism is considered to be of more importance than the preservation or construction of beautiful things.

Chamonix was crowded, but we managed to obtain accommodation at the Hôtel des Etrangers near the station, the cleanliness and good food of which contrasted agreeably with the annexe of La Bérarde, this being due to an enterprising proprietor, who spoke excellent English, an acquirement which in most Alpine hotels is usually responsible for a substantial bill.

That evening we amused ourselves by visiting a variety entertainment at the Casino, where we heard a number of comic songs, which we did not understand, and witnessed some convincing trouser-pulling.

Further, to improve our knowledge of the night life of Chamonix, we took a peep at the gambling where that depressing game of chance called Boule is played, depressing because there is even less chance of winning than there is at roulette and because gambling is, like alcohol, essentially a depressant in the long run.

Next we dived down for five minutes to an underground dance hall to emerge with smoke-smartened eyes into the starry night. As we agreed, nightlife is all very well in Paris or London, but it is out of place at Chamonix under the snows of Mont Blanc, at all events to the conservative mountaineer.

We had previously planned to climb one or more of the great routes on the south side of Mont Blanc, but these ascents demand perfect weather and conditions, and the weather was now unsettled. So we pored over the maps and eventually I suggested that we should postpone crossing the range into Italy and visit its western extremity, which neither of us had seen.

The best centre for climbing hereabouts is the Trélatête Hotel, situated at the end of the glacier of the same name at a height of 6,450 feet, and enquiries elicited the fact that it was clean and comfortable. Should the weather improve we agreed that it would be good fun to traverse Mont Blanc from this hotel and descend to Courmayeur in Italy, thence returning to Chamonix over the mountain by one of the southern routes.

This decided upon, we spent the morning after our arrival at Chamonix purchasing provisions, and shortly after midday boarded the motor bus to Les Contamines and Notre-Dame-de-la-Gorge.

The drive was a pleasant experience and unaccompanied by excessive speed or reckless cornering. Although it was a grey day with a sullen cloud roof, the bus was crowded with tourists who obviously extracted plenty of enjoyment out of the ride in spite of the depressing weather. It is of course, usual with that haughty and aloof person the mountaineer, to scorn and deride the foibles, eccentricities, and naïveties of the tourist. There is without doubt a certain insincerity about the "Wunderbars" and "Magnifiques" with which the tourist greets the Alpine glow and other phenomena, and the impact of such a chorus upon the splendour of Nature is to create an atmosphere of vulgarity, so that even the Alpine glow is relegated to the status of a picture postcard. A crowd of human beings and the sublimities of Nature simply do not mix; there is something aesthetically and spiritually wrong just as there is in a mixture of vintage port and Scotch whisky. For me it is impossible to enjoy natural scenery in the company of a number of my fellow men, and this prejudice applies to mountaineers as a whole. There is something essentially individualistic in man's relationship with, and appreciation of Nature. Yet the mountaineer who sneers at the herds of tourists lays himself open to the charges of snobbery and intolerance. Far better if he sees in the rowdiest of paper strewing picnic parties a glimmering of an idea that may eventually emancipate mankind from the purely materialistic conception.

It may be that some who visit Nature's sanctuaries do so merely because it is fashionable; that is the lowest and most ignorant form of travel, degrading to the finer sensibilities and destructive of those powers of self determination and discrimination which separate mankind from the beast. But the great majority of those who spend their holidays in the mountains, whether singly or in groups, do so because they extract a genuine enjoyment from natural scenery. Their sentiments may seem cheap and stereotyped, and they never stop to question themselves as to why they enjoy this or that; their manners are sometimes abominable, and they strew their sandwich papers about the landscape, yet, though they do not realise it, they are responding automatically and without thought to the immemorial call of Nature: they are escaping from something which they cannot define, not merely bricks and mortar, smoke, and noise, but something artificial, and at variance with man's natural heritage which is Nature and the fruits of Nature. Will this revolt lead eventually to a decentralisation of mankind? Ages hence, will the inhabitants of this planet look back upon this age as an age of material enslavement? Will they see in its wars and tyrannies, in its economic miseries, the by-products of a strangling material existence into which even the sun is denied an entry? Industrial centralisation and the manner in which it has been carried out without regard for the spiritual, mental, and physical well being of man, was the danger of the nineteenth century and is the curse of the twentieth century. These tourists who escape from it for a week or two in every fifty-two weeks are the pioneers of a new decade in which art, literature, and knowledge will enrich the human mind.

Bigotry is not the least of human failings. Merely to climb mountains is not to enjoy mountains. There was more than a germ of truth in Ruskin's contention that mountaineers regarded mountains as greasy poles, for some mountaineers do regard mountains in this light; they see in Nature only a field of physical endeavour; mountain summits to them have the same worth as scalps to a Red Indian; they are concerned only with their own feats and their superiority through muscular strength and skill over the tourist who is content to crawl about the lower slopes; yet, they are escapists, too, driven by some subconscious urge from the city into the open air and the sunlight. My own experience, included in which is public lecturing on mountaineering subjects, goes to show that there are more people outside the trade unionism of mountaineering, who extract a genuine spiritual enjoyment and inspiration from the mere presence of mountains and from being among mountains, than there are in that trade unionism. All too frequently, the sport of mountaineering tends to destroy the love of mountains. This may seem paradoxical, but I believe it is true. It may be argued in defence of mountaineers that they are inarticulate, yet even this cannot wholly explain the appalling literary mediocrity of climbing club publications, and the predominance of the objective over the subjective. Of all God's creatures, the mountaineer who describes his climb in a mountaineering publication is in many ways the most stereotyped. If he feels anything he is afraid to express it. His horror of sentiment would be laughable were it not tragic. He is a slave to fashion. His descriptions are merely so many permutations and combinations of facts and observations. Above all, he gives the reader the impression of a fatuous and dreadful self-complacency. Perhaps he assumes that what he has seen and what he has felt has been seen so often and felt so often before by other people that any attempt at description is unnecessary; if so, this is a lazy habit of thought, a negation of individualism and a moral cowardice; the man who shrinks from expressing his thoughts and sentiments only does so because he is afraid of being laughed at.

Among what has been contemptuously referred to as the proletariat, in other words tourists who are content to spend their holidays walking in the valleys and over the lower slopes, I have met more genuine lovers of mountainous scenery than I have among mountaineers. Undoubtedly the physical act of climbing a mountain is a sport, yet to define mountaineering as a sport only is to omit incentive, cause, and effect, for the true mountaineer does not climb for the sake of physical exercise alone, but to establish some mental and spiritual contact with Nature. Therefore the sport of mountaineering, unlike most other sports, has a philosophical background, to neglect which is to neglect its *raison d'être*. In the same way a man does not go yachting merely for the sake of manoeuvring a yacht, he goes because he loves the sea and rejoices in the freedom of wide horizons.

Ruskin was right when he wrote that the beauty of mountains is best appreciated from the valleys. He might have said that beauty is better appreciated through inaction than through action. The mountaineer, who is interested in getting up and getting down a mountain as expeditiously as possible, and who in the matter of time and speed is concerned only with the competitive aspects of the sport, necessarily misses beauty. The true mountaineer is the one who climbs mountains for spiritual as well as for physical reasons, is not concerned with haste except in the interests of safety, and likes to spend as many hours as possible on a mountain in order to contemplate the scenery. This is not to say that long and difficult climbs on which speed is essential are not part and parcel of the mountaineer's philosophy. They are a very necessary part because they provide a contrast as well as a test, and mountaineering is in the nature of a test between man and mountain. To enjoy mountains and mountaineering to the full a compromise must be effected between the active and the passive make-up of a man. Ruskin did not get all he might have done out of mountains because he was content merely to contemplate them, but the mountaineer who rushes up and down mountains gets far less. To appreciate mountaineering to the full it is necessary correctly to assess the relative needs and merits of the physical, mental, and spiritual qualities, and he is a connoisseur of life who recognises this.

From the hamlet of Notre-Dame-de-la-Gorge, where the road ended, we proceeded on foot up a steep, roughly-cobbled path to the Chalets de Nant-Borrant. This was also the goal of the tourists in the motor coach, and it was interesting to note the speed with which they walked. For our part we trudged slowly along and presently overtook them. They were all puffing heavily. It is a peculiarly distressing form of progression, this rushing and puffing uphill; not one person in a hundred knows how to climb with the minimum of effort. It is perfectly easy. Firstly, go slowly. Secondly, go steadily and do not stop, except when you want to for reasons of sightseeing. Thirdly, do not walk on the toes, but endeavour to place the whole foot on the ground. Fourthly, transfer the weight from foot to foot deliberately and rhythmically in a slow easy action devoid of any spring or jerking. Fifthly, take short steps. It is a case of the tortoise and the hare; you will be surprised how easily you overtake those who have passed you in the first place, arriving at your destination almost as fresh as you were when you started.

A pleasant path through cool woodlands took us uphill towards the Trélatête Hotel. The afternoon was overcast and oppressive, and the silent forest held a threat of storm. Whether on foot or on ski, there is something peculiarly enjoyable about ascending a path through a pine forest. Pines are restful trees, and the resinous smell that permeates the still atmosphere beneath them is very soothing. A pine forest speaks and breathes of hills. To some people it is sombre and sad, full of furtive whisperings and dismal sighings. It is true there are occasions when it gathers to itself the quintessence of solemnity and gloom, but unlike some forests, it is seldom menacing and threatening. There is in it an atmosphere of peace and tranquillity.

When mounting through a pine forest the walker is scarcely conscious that he is gaining height except in terms of effort. He may mount for hours and see little, except occasional glimpses of distant hills between the branches. Then, and the transition is abrupt, the character of the forest changes. He sees through the dim aisles brightness, which is resolved as he climbs into blue sky. Then, suddenly, the trees thin out and he steps from the forest on to an alp, where a few outpost pines stand, gnarled weather-beaten trees, that embody in their heroic force the steadfastness and endurance of the hills. On the wiry turf of the alp, he pauses, and gazes outwards and downwards along the way he has come. The view is beautiful and dramatic. His vision swoops in an instant down green sheets of forest into a valley and beyond it over range upon range of hills. For the first time he feels the cold breath of the snow on his cheek, a vital, exhilarating breeze. One stage of the way to the mountaintop is behind.

The Trélatête Hotel is situated a few yards above the tree line on a grassy neck connecting a spur with the hillside. It is not a beautiful building and consists simply of a rectangular box, a dirty white in colour in which are inset numerous windows. The proprietress was a middle-aged woman, a typical French housewife, always working, always cleaning, always cooking and always good-natured. I take off my hat to the thrifty, hard-working, cheerful housewife of France. She is the mainstay, the prop, and the backbone of that country. French Governments may come and go, there may be war and rumours of war, but the French housewife goes on for ever. She is the spirit of France.

We asked whether Englishmen often visited the hotel; her reply was, very seldom, but there was a Mr. X, who ran the skiing course for English visitors; he was a *gentilhomme*, an altogether estimable gentleman. Did we know him? Had we met him? We had to admit that we had not, and felt that our stock was lowered in the eyes of Madame by our not being acquainted with so distinguished a personage. We excused ourselves by telling her that this was our first visit to the western end of the Mont Blanc range, that we thought it very beautiful, very interesting that the hotel was admirably situated, etc. etc., which went some way towards counteracting our ignorance in the matter of Mr. X. I take it that Mr. X. is an *habitué* of this part of the world. Many who read this will have encountered the hotel *habitué*. I remember on one occasion visiting an hotel in a remote Scots village. There were two *habitués* there, which is an unusual circumstance. When I entered the lounge I saw them seated in state on either side of the fire, crusty old gentlemen who stayed there every summer for the fishing. There they sat, each in his own chair, and I shuddered inwardly to think what might have happened had I inadvertently sat in one or other of the chairs. They were entrenched behind *The Times*, and were not on speaking terms, because each considered himself more of an *habitué* than the other; I could almost feel them glowering through the columns of print. As for me, I was the only other visitor and because I was not a fisherman was beneath contempt.

Then there is the story of an elderly member of the Alpine Club who was an *habitué* of a certain hotel in the Valais. It was the unwritten law at that hotel that guests should not change into evening dress. For years this law had been obeyed and no one had dared to break it. But one day there came to that hotel a visitor so ignorant that on the evening of his arrival he assumed a dinner-jacket. He was preening himself in the lounge, apparently under the impression that he was the only gentleman present, when the *habitué* entered. He paused horror-struck, then giving the perpetrator of the outrage a pulverising glare, walked up to him, and said in a voice loud enough to be heard by everyone present: 'I have to inform you, sir, that dinner-jackets are not worn in this hotel.'

There were few guests at the Trélatête Hotel, and the *salle à manger* was forlorn and a trifle chilly. The dinner, however, was excellent, and the wine moderate in price, considering that it had to be carried on mule-back from the valley.

An overcast afternoon had turned into a sullen evening, and when we went to bed, in a clean and comfortable room, rain was falling heavily. It was still raining the following morning and continued in torrents all day. We agreed that it meant quantities of snow higher up, and that our plans of traversing Mont Blanc, and making an ascent of the south side, had gone awry. I told Jim, with a sort of gloomy satisfaction, that my bad luck with the weather was stronger than his good luck, to which he replied with invincible optimism that perhaps, after all, his good luck might win through.

The Trélatête Hotel, like all mountain hotels, is ill-adapted for a stay in bad weather. There are no comfortable chairs, in which last respect the foreigner is more fortunate than the Englishman, inasmuch as he can sit for hours on end on a hard chair, long after the Englishman has been reduced to furtive writhings and wrigglings. To the mountaineer bad weather is worse than tedious; he sees his precious holiday slipping away, hour by hour, and day by day. He becomes restless, and crotchety. He reads, he writes, he has an occasional drink; at frequent intervals he consults the barometer, tapping the unfortunate instrument in an aggressive manner suggestive that it, and it alone, is responsible for the weather. Jim, a man of infinite resource, managed to unearth a set of draughts in which game we were joined by a cheerful young Frenchman, a university student who was spending his vacation wandering about the mountains. Finally when even fox and geese had palled, we were reduced to talking politics and discussing the possibilities of war occurring in the near future. An evil cloud was darkening over Europe. I had never been conscious of war clouds on mountains, but I was aware of them then. It was not a fever like that of 1914 but a disease, a malignant growth, which mankind seemed unable to stem. A passionless, cold-blooded catastrophe was about to break on the world.

And all day long the rain poured down.

CHAPTER FIVE

Mont Tondu

THE RAIN HAD CEASED when we wakened next morning. Unwilling to waste another day, we decided to attempt the ascent of Mont Tondu, 10,485 feet, which stands at the westernmost extremity of the Mont Blanc range. It is not a long climb from the Trélatête Hotel, and we did not leave until eight o'clock. After the past five days of mountaineering inactivity, it was good to be on the move once more and we both felt blithesome and gay as we mounted the path towards the Trélatête Glacier. It was a pleasant introductory walk and the slopes were bright with flowers, shining in the luminous atmosphere. Our guidebook mentioned a *mauvais pas* which had to be crossed before reaching the glacier, but we did not see anything of the kind, and within half an hour of leaving the hotel were treading the ice of the latter.

The Trélatête Glacier is less popular with tourists than the Bossons Glacier or the Mer de Glace, but it is much frequented. Tourists who only visit the lowermost portions of alpine glaciers must return sadly disillusioned, for, more often than not, they see the rubbish chutes of the mountains, a muddle of terminal moraines and melting dirt-riddled ice, scenes not of pure ice and snow but of decay, ruin, and destruction. The lower part, of the Trélatête Glacier has little to commend it in beauty or interest. The ice is dirty, so are the patches of snow in its hollows, and the slopes on either side are monotonous and shapeless. Sluggish mists contributed to this effect of dreariness, and it was a relief when between them we saw a glint of sunlight on the distant snows of the Aiguille des Glaciers.

Presently we came to an icefall, where the glacier flows over a steep step in its bed. We ascended this without difficulty, zigzagging between crevasses. As we did so, we noticed curious puffs of warm air seeming to emanate from the crevasses.

I have noticed this before in the Alps and it is difficult to explain, seeing that air in crevasses should be cold.

The icefall was soon negotiated, and we emerged on to the almost level ice above it. Here snow was lying, and we paused to put on the rope. After crossing the level stretch, we mounted slopes of scree and snow to the tributary glacier, which descends from the Col du Mont Tondu. Here we came to new snow, which became progressively deeper as we ascended, so that presently we were sinking in well above the boot.

Ahead of us was Mont Tondu, an indeterminate looking mountain. The obvious way to it was to continue up the glacier to the right of the col, but the slope here was steep and with much new snow on it might avalanche, so we decided to make for the col and follow the ridge from it to the summit

It was monotonous treadmill-like work. Trudging uphill roped to a companion is less fatiguing than trudging uphill alone unless of course, that companion has a pace entirely different from your own, when it is the reverse. The secret is to go slowly enough to allow the mind to detach itself from physical exertion, for it is a profound truism that when exertion is of such a nature as to occupy the mind to the exclusion of everything else, it is fatiguing. I do not mean, however, that the mountaineer should drift so far from his work as to be unready to meet a sudden emergency, such as his companion falling into a crevasse; he is not a good mountaineer who has not learned to react instinctively to sudden danger.

There is something very soothing about a long walk uphill, when heart and lungs are functioning with a minimum of effort and the pace is unhurried and rhythmical. The mind is disengaged, and free to contemplate with dispassionate detachment any subject it chooses, from metaphysics to the cut of a companion's trousers. Such contemplation, not being within the fixed time limits so often demanded by the exigencies of civilisation, prescribes a serenity in which time ceases to be of account. On many occasions I have walked up two thousand or three thousand feet of mountainside and found myself at the top wondering how I got there. I seemed to have been transported thither by some magic carpet. The Easterner has translated in more practical fashion this detachment of the mind. He is able to exist without always doing something, or seeing something, or being amused, and he exists happily. To the Western mind, such browsing is ox-like, yet how simple and peaceful life in the West would be if we cultivated detachment. I suppose that we should revert to the primitive in many respects because with the time factor ceasing to matter, the whole economic and social fabric would tend to disintegrate. Yet, it is certain that if peacefulness and happiness were the aims of humanity we would attain them.

We stood on the Col du Mont Tondu and behind us was a thread-like track curling down the snowclad glacier. Except for that visible and outward evidence of our progression I should have suspected some satanic agency as responsible for our elevation.

It was warm and sunny on the col and we descended a few yards on the south side to a sloping ledge whence the new snow had melted, exposing rough warm rock. There we lunched. From our belvedere we looked down on grassy slopes to the west of the Col de la Seigne, a pass 8,245 feet high on the frontier between France and Italy. To emphasise this last fact there came from the Italian side of the pass the sound of gunfire, a vengeful growling which, amid the peacefulness of the hills, was as inappropriate as hiccoughs in a cathedral.

This would be a beautiful world were it not for the inclusion of man. What singular chance, what interpositioning of Providence led to his inclusion? The sound of guns, the ridiculous little uniformed men swarming on both sides of the Col de la Seigne, was it to suckle these that Providence created the World? Why is it that everything in nature is appropriate except man; man the invader and destroyer of beauty, with his smoke, his smells, his noise, his nonsensical, illogical lust for killing his fellow men, his unquiet, his savagery, his defilement of nature and of beauty, and most of all his conceit and inappropriateness to the scene in which he has been cast? Has it ever occurred to philosophers that perhaps man is not indigenous to this planet, but arrived through some means from another planet where he was more appropriate, and that ever since he has been striving, without success, to adapt himself to conditions, which are fundamentally at variance with him, except in the matter of physical tolerance?

It was a delightful half-hour in the sun, and had it not been for my energetic companion, I might have remained there for the rest of the day. However, inexorable fate decreed that we must climb Mont Tondu, so languidly re-packing our rucksacks, we set off up the ridge. It was mostly easy going, except for one steep place where the holds were concealed beneath new snow and some loose rock had to be negotiated with care.

Presently we came to a flat snowy shoulder on which some foolish person had erected a large cairn. Beyond this the ridge suddenly narrowed and became more interesting. It was never difficult, but the crest was sharp and the drop on either side formidable.

Much of the freshly fallen snow had melted from the rocks and we scrambled leisurely along, until presently we came to the summit of the mountain. It was windless and warm there and the sun shone hotly through a blanketing mist. It was disappointing to have no view, and we decided to wait some time in the hopes of seeing one. My own experience of waiting on a mountaintop for a mist to clear usually resembles that of the man who stands watching an excavation being made in a road; nothing whatever happens except that the hole gets deeper. This occasion, however, was an exception, and we had not been seated for more than a few minutes when the mists parted abruptly and swept back like a curtain. In the gap thus formed Mont Blanc stood out radiant in its robes of freshly fallen snow, a spectacle as beautiful as it was dramatic.

We spent an hour or more on the summit and although there was little to be seen time passed like magic. Time usually seems to pass quickly in mountaineering. Human conception of time is based not so much on the movement of the earth round the sun as on personal interests, and if we separate these interests from the purely quantitative conception of time it is possible to glimpse dimly a fourth-dimensional state in which time as a measure of events and activity does not exist, and where events occur unaccompanied by and unrelated with that physical change which is essentially the bedrock of the human time factor; for time is a measure of life as we know it in this world. I have felt this very strongly on more than one occasion when climbing mountains; a sequence of events was in a curious way dissociated entirely from any sense of time. Thus, presupposing a survival of personality, it is possible to envisage dimly a state of existence which being related only to quality and dissociated entirely from all quantitative conceptions as we know them here, is timeless. Thus a sequence of events is timeless, even though remaining a sequence because no quantitative conception exists in the personality which experiences it. It may be that sleep and dreams give us some inkling as to the nature of this state, for it is possible in a dream to break free from time and to be conscious only of a sequence of events which have no relation to time as a fixed quantity, whilst sleep, and for that matter unconsciousness, are timeless to the sleeper, and for this reason suggest a temporary dissociation of the spiritual and the physical, which is not memorable afterwards, when the association is resumed under the different order of conditions obtaining on this planet.

This may seem very far removed from the subject of this chapter, but I am sure that others who read this have had similar experiences with regard to time, not only when climbing mountains, but in many other walks of life, and it is interesting to delve into the subject, even if such delving leads only to suggestions and inferences of the vaguest nature.

We retired languidly along the ridge. On the snowy shoulder it occurred to us to see whether or not our previous determination to ascend by the ridge from the Col du Mont Tondu in preference to the glacier slopes was justified by the condition of the latter. So when we came to the rocks at the lower end of the shoulder we dislodged a boulder on to the slopes. Instantly the layer of new snow, perhaps a foot thick, began to slide. At first it was a small section a yard or two in width, but quickly the snow on either side began to slide too, forming an ever widening wedge, so that in a matter of seconds hundreds of tons of snow were in motion. At first the slide made a gentle serpent-like hissing, but as it increased in weight, volume and speed the hissing was resolved into a harsher sound, as though a giant were sand papering a piece of wood, and we saw the avalanche, for such it was, pour down the slopes with gathering momentum, and spread out in a mass of snow blocks three or four feet in depth on the glacier hundreds of feet lower.

It was an ordinary wet snow avalanche, and although we might well have escaped had we been overtaken by it when ascending from below, we might on the other hand have been overwhelmed and suffocated, for it is possible, as many disasters have proved, for a man to be buried and suffocated beneath an avalanche only a foot or so in depth owing to the manner in which snow consolidates when it comes to rest. For this reason the best chance of survival lies, not in trying to oppose an avalanche, or letting it knock you off your feet head downwards, but by endeavouring to keep on the surface by lying on the back and making swimming movements with the arms and the palms of the hands.

It was with great satisfaction that Jim and I watched the avalanche, for the mountaineer is only human, even if a trifle mad, and enjoys being proved right in his decisions. Thus we descended the ridge, pausing now and then to detach other slides, feeling unusually self-virtuous.

Back on the Col du Mont Tondu we halted for a rest and refreshment. The weather was still misty, but unquestionably on the mend, and we watched and photographed some effects of mist, light, and shadow, which dignified the little mountain we had just climbed into a giant of seemingly immeasurable height and remoteness. During the descent to the Trélatête Glacier we indulged in the luxury of glissading, but because of crevasses deemed it advisable to retain the rope. Glissading on a rope closely resembles skiing on a rope. It is first of all necessary that the glissaders should be approximately equal in skill. Even so it often happens that one man sets off, and is proceeding at speed down the slope before the other man is properly under way, the result being that the rope tightens with a jerk which tugs the second man forward on to his nose. This halts the first man who waits resignedly for the second man. But the second man's blood is now up; he is out for revenge; with tremendous speed he shoots past the first man so that precisely the same thing happens in the reverse order.

Jim and I managed a trifle better than this, and slid down without misadventure until we came to a point where a diagonal descent had to be made. Here the snow petered out on to a small patch of ice above some stones and rough bare glacier. When I came to this, my feet shot ungracefully from beneath me and I skidded on my back down the ice. There was no danger – I could have stopped myself easily enough on the stones – but Jim, very wisely, thought otherwise, and drove his axe into the snow above, halting me almost at once with an unpleasant jerk. He was right to do this, for there were crevasses below, and in mountaineering what may seem a joke at first may well have disastrous consequences.

Heavy mists still hung over the Trélatête Glacier as we descended, but on leaving the glacier we emerged into bright afternoon sunlight. For half an hour we remained seated on a flower-covered bank then strolled down to the hotel.

As an introduction to the western end of the range, the ascent of Mont Tondu had proved admirable. We had seen enough to convince us that this region is beautiful and interesting. It now remained with the weather to determine whether or not we should be able to make other and finer ascents, including the traverse of Mont Blanc on which we had set our hearts, a descent into Italy, and a return over the south face of the mountain. There seemed every reason to suppose that it was improving; and the barometer, the most reliable prophet of all, and the most reviled, was rising, not abruptly and jerkily, but in that slow, steady, assured manner which presages a general improvement of weather conditions.

That evening the mists thinned and vanished and the sun set peacefully behind the hills. We decided that another day of fine weather was necessary before setting off for the traverse of Mont Blanc, and that we would spend the morrow in making a second expedition from the Trélatête Glacier.

When we went to bed the whole sky was brilliant with stars.

CHAPTER SIX

The Tête Carrée

We were roused at dawn next morning. Other mountaineers staying at the hotel had been called long before and had left for their climbs, but we saw no reason to start especially early for the Col Infranchissable, our first objective, and it was not until six o'clock that we packed the food provided by our hostess and set off for the climb.

In cold shadow we trudged up the Trélatête Glacier and mounted the icefall, which a hard frost had rendered so slippery that we regretted not having provided ourselves with crampons.

Continuing up the glacier we presently overtook the first of the parties that had left before us, a man and a boy who were going very slowly and were already tired. The uppermost portion of the glacier provided pleasant walking over hard frozen snow, and we mounted rapidly, passing another party bound like ourselves for the Col Infranchissable.

Presently we emerged from shadow into sunlight and paused for a rest. It was a brilliantly clear morning, and the peaks of Dauphiné sixty miles distant stood out hard and clear with every detail distinct, the pinnacles on the ridge of the Meije, the graceful summit of the Écrins, and the narrow rift of the Coup de Sabre. The first halt on a snowfield in the sun is one of the best hours in mountaineering. Later in the day the sun pours down a furious glare, but early in the morning the sunlight is gentle and welcoming and in pleasant contrast with the numbing shadows. It reveals delicately, not harshly: long thin shadows and shining drifts of light, hollows and ripples, edges and ridges, the curves and volutes of the snow-field, the lacery and tracery of crevasses. Sunrise in the Alps is a slow awakening, not an abrupt and dramatic rousing as in the Tropics, and the mountaineer who treads the snows at this hour is conscious of some heritage of beauty, the purity of space, and elemental changeless things translated into visible and tangible form. Mountaineers are not the only ones to see beauty in snow. What is it that drives men to the polar regions? It is snow, the simplicity of snow, the sublimity of snow. What is it about the great elementals of the earth that appeal to men, the sky, the desert, the polar wastes, the mountains? It is only the fool who can look at snow and pronounce it to be nothing but frozen water.

The Col Infranchissable is situated at the head of the Trélatête Glacier and to reach it involves nothing more than a walk. Intent on escaping from a chilly wind that poured through the gap, we mounted to a rock spur projecting from the north-west ridge of the Tête Carrée and there found a moderately sheltered place from which to enjoy the view. And the view surpassed all our expectations. It commands the whole of the South-West Face of Mont Blanc, from the Brouillard Ridge to the ridge on which we stood, on the main watershed of the range, which extends westwards from Mont Blanc to the Aiguille de Bionnassay, and thence to the Tête Carrée, the Aiguille de la Trélatête and the Aiguille des Glaciers. From the Aiguille de Bionnassay the ridge bends south, and we looked across the South-West Face of Mont Blanc. If the height of this great wall be taken from the Val Veni in Italy, it is some 11,000 feet, but from our position only the uppermost portion was visible, that above the Glacier de Miage Italian which is some 6,000 feet in height. This is without a doubt the most complicated mountainside in the Alps, more intricate even than the East Face of Monte Rosa. From our position we looked down to the Glacier de Miage Italian and, as we gazed at the tremendously steep stone-scarred couloirs that descend from the Col Infranchissable on this side, we marvelled at the temerity of the parties that have traversed the pass. It is true, of course, that seen from above a route always appears more formidable than it does when seen from below, but even so the ascent of the Col Infranchissable from the east must be one of exceptional difficulty and danger in all but the best conditions of snow and weather. Looking down the cliff at our feet we saw thousands of feet beneath the broken surface of the Miage Glacier. High up, this glacier divides into three branches, all steep and tremendously shattered and broken. Between these are complicated rock ribs, and to the east of the easternmost branch rises the great Brouillard Ridge, which with the even greater Peuterey Ridge buttresses Mont Blanc to the south. So much for bald detail, yet it is not detail with which the mountaineer, who sets eyes on this amazing view, is concerned. There is too much to be seen, a veritable labyrinth of rock and ice. I remember looking and wondering how climbers manage to reach the Quintino Sella Hut, then cross the icefall to the east of it into the long couloir that runs up to the Col Emile Rey from which the ascent of the Brouillard Ridge is made. Seen from the Col Infranchissable the whole route looks hopelessly impracticable, and the view was an example of that mountaineering maxim that until a route is actually attempted, always supposing that it is not positively and patently dangerous, it is impossible to estimate its difficulties with any degree of accuracy.

There is nothing serene about the view of the south side of Mont Blanc except the summit of Mont Blanc itself. The mountainside before us was uneasy and threatening and in marked contrast with the snowfields over which we had ascended; it suggested not permanency but decay, ruin, and destruction. From our lofty perch we could see every detail; processions of lurching séracs, ice-swept couloirs with tongues of debris at their feet, and everywhere the marks of avalanches. And we could hear the processes of destruction in active operation, even though the falls of stones and ice were invisible to the eye, a clattering and growling rising on occasion to a reverberating thunder that echoed and re-echoed round the cirque. It was almost with relief that the eye passed from this unbridled mountain savagery to the south, where placid hills receded towards the snows of the Grivola and the far distant heat hazes of the Italian plain.

From our vantage point the Aiguille de Bionnassay was in full view and we examined it with interest. There are few alpine snow peaks to equal and none to exceed this mountain in beauty. From the Col Infranchissable it resembles the Obergabelhorn as seen from the Wellenkuppe – there are the same sweeping edges, the same elegant summit, and the same superlative simplicity. The rocky section of the South Ridge up which the route lies from the Durier Hut on the Col de Miage was heavily plastered with snow but another day of the same hot sun we were now experiencing should put the mountain into safe condition.

Having assured ourselves on this point we turned our attention to the Tête Carrée. The mountain rises directly from the Col Infranchissable, and we had merely to follow the North-West Ridge to gain the summit. This ridge was in a wintry state. The recent falls of snow had not accumulated to any depth, but had been blown by the wind to form plumes and cornices on the south-east side. The sun was shining almost directly down the ridge, and the fragile eaves and feathers of snow glowed with unearthly beauty.

The climb was not difficult. We began the ascent with some strenuous step-kicking on the west flank of the ridge then mounted some rocks to a small shoulder. Above this the slope was icy enough to necessitate step cutting. Jim made short work of this, and we ended the climb with a plug up soft snow to the roughly horizontal summit edge.

Apart from Mont Blanc, the view of which was essentially the same as that from the Col Infranchissable, we could now see the Aiguille de la Trélatête, the most popular peak of the district. A party was in the act of reaching the summit, and we could see their tracks on the long steep snow-slopes above the Trélatête

Glacier. We pondered on the possibility of continuing along the ridge from the Tête Carrée to the mountain, but decided against it on account of the steep slopes we should have to descend; the Aiguille de la Trélatête is decidedly not a peak to descend in the afternoon soon after a heavy snowfall. The same considerations forced us to cut short our stay on the summit of the Tête Carrée and after a quarter of an hour we set off down.

Another party had climbed the peak by a different route from ours direct from the Trélatête Glacier, and we followed their tracks. It was a steep but easy descent, but it was made disagreeable by soft snow and a sun glare of withering, scorching intensity. In vain we searched for trickles of water, but in the end had to content ourselves with picking up handfuls of wet snow and squeezing out the moisture.

When at length, after a cautious descent, we reached the Trélatête Glacier, we found that the hard frozen surface over which we had walked in the early morning had softened and refused to support our weight. The sun glare here was worse if anything and we ploughed down feeling like flies trapped in the globe of a powerful light. Thankfully we reached the side moraine and there imbibed copiously of a stream; how good was the feel of that cold pure water in our parched mouths!

I have one more memory of that climb; in some ways the most outstanding memory of all. It is that of a little shelf bright with thousands of creamy *Ranunculus glacialis* with silken petals and golden stamens, a compact colony of plants in the midst of a stony desolation high up amid the permanent snows. It was an example of the tolerance of Nature, and of the unending adaptations that go to make this World. Life had breathed on that spot and, lo, it had been made beautiful.

Back at the Hotel we met with a fellow member of the Alpine Club, Dr. N.S. Finzi, and his Swiss guide, Franz Biener, and spent an enjoyable evening in their company. Franz Biener comes of a famous family of guides, and his is a name associated with many great ascents. There is no finer type of man than the first class alpine guide. First and foremost he loves the mountains, not as a means of livelihood but for themselves. He is quiet, gentle, and unassuming, for it is only inferior guides, or the money-grubbing type, who suffer from braggadocio and intolerance. There is much in common between the alpine guide and the seaman; the serenity of their environment is reflected in their faces and in their character. The guide is a simple man, with a simple philosophy based on understanding, not cleverness. He has deep down within him an inarticulate faith in Providence, he is steadfast in purpose and a sense of responsibility is fundamental in his character. He possesses an instinct and an intuition for his work, which comes only of long apprenticeship in mountain craft.

Only once have I climbed with a guide. That was during a search party, and I was impressed, not only at the skill and speed with which he climbed, but at the margin of safety that in some indefinable way characterised his every movement. He who climbs with a first rate alpine guide not only feels safe, but is safe. The measure of the worth of mountaineering lies not only in accomplishment, but also in the margin of safety over and above that accomplishment.

The weather was now set fair and we decided to traverse the Aiguille de Bérangèr and the Dôme de Miage to the Durier Hut on the morrow, and the Aiguille de Bionnassay the following day to the Vallot Hut. Then if the weather remained fair we would traverse Mont Blanc and descend to Courmayeur.

CHAPTER SEVEN

Aiguille de Bérangèr and Dôme de Miage

A DISLIKE of an early start delayed our departure until 5.45 next morning. We had enjoyed our stay at the Trélatête Hotel, and were sorry to take leave of our hostess who, as a last *beau geste*, unhesitatingly accepted English money, together with the rate of exchange we quoted, although it was obvious that she knew nothing of the latter.

The sun was gilding the mountaintops as we passed along the now familiar Trélatête Glacier, and there was a promise of perfect weather in the sky, which was unclouded, except for a few long drawn filaments.

We were uncertain as to the point where the glacier is left in favour of the slopes of the Aiguille de Bérangèr. It often happens in such a case that two men take slightly different routes, each convinced that his particular route is the best. So it was in this instance, and it was with selfish satisfaction that I seated myself on a stone after a twenty minutes' scramble to await Jim, who had become involved in some awkward climbing up steep slabs. It is easy to preach against the evils of the competitive instinct in man, but however much a man may try to convince himself that he is above such feelings, if he is honest he will admit to a certain sensation of satisfaction as he watches a companion labouring up a hillside by a more difficult route than the one he has chosen. He may say, 'Bad luck, old fellow,' but what he really means is, 'What a blithering idiot you were not to come up my way; it was a much better way than your wretched way.'

The Aiguille de Bérangèr is one of the easiest peaks in the range of Mont Blanc, and one of the best viewpoints. Grass, gently inclined slabs, and patches of snow took us rapidly upwards. We halted for a meal below a snowy shoulder, assimilated the ubiquitous sardine and toasted in the sun. The weather was perfect. Not a breath, not a whisper disturbed a profound quietude. And peaks and ranges rose unruffled by wind or cloud. The distant Dauphiné, with every detail distinct, glowed in the morning sunlight and opposite, across the Trélatête Glacier, we could discern the marks of the avalanches we had detached on Mont Tondu, elongated smudges on the immaculate snow of that mountain.

It was evident that we were in for another grilling, and we smeared our already ravaged countenances with glacier cream. Sunburn can be a great leveller of persons. I have seen strong men, usually novices, scorn to smear themselves with cream. 'What, put on that stuff, me!' they exclaim, as though it had been suggested that they should eat bread and milk in lieu of beef-steak, and they labour across the snow all day with an air of insufferable superiority, obviously contemptuous of "tenderskins". They return home triumphant, but with a red-hot countenance and a vague but dawning doubt at the back of their minds. The doubt becomes more pronounced that night as they feverishly toss and turn, with burning face and neck, unable to sleep a wink. They appear at the breakfast table next morning short of temper and in colour resembling lobsters. But that is not all. Horror piles on horror. Their skin swells in bubbles until it resembles the peaks and craters of a lunar landscape. Then it cracks all over, even in the corners of the lips, so that a smile becomes an agony and talking an effort, until finally their countenances are reduced to a state of complete ruin. Then they growl at you with horrid imprecations (taking care not to open their mouths too wide) and say, 'Why the blazes didn't you warn me about the sun?'

Continuing on our way we passed along a gently sloping snowy shoulder. The view from this is as beautiful as it is dramatic. For a few yards we looked down snow, then the eye passed from a gleaming edge, where the snow-slope bent out of sight, and in a single leap came to rest on hamlets, villages, and pasturelands 8,000 feet beneath. Such views are not so commonplace as might be imagined in the Alps. They may be enjoyed at their best from the northern wall of the Oberland, and the greatest charm when climbing, say the Guggi Route on the Jungfrau, is to glance down on to forest-clad hills and meadows. Himalayan views are sometimes even more dramatic, and I remember well the amazing downward plunge of the eye from a height of 22,000 feet on Dunagiri into the Dhauli Valley 15,000 feet lower.

It is possible to climb mountains without being especially conscious of the altitude when the climber is on peaks surrounded by glaciers, but he who climbs the Aiguille de Bérangèr in clear weather cannot fail to be impressed by his height and position, and the snow on which we walked seemed to be poised like some magic carpet in mid air above the foot hills.

The aeronaut has little impression of height because he is completely detached from the earth, whereas the occupant of a captive balloon is much more conscious of his position and altitude. Doubtless there are many who, if transported to such a position, would experience giddiness or sickness, accompanied perhaps by a desire to throw themselves over the edge. Yet, it is not justifiable to assume that looking down from a mountain is disagreeable because of a dislike of looking down from a tall building or a sea cliff. For me the last two experiences are distinctly unpleasant, and anyone who can gaze unmoved upon the sea from the edge of Beachy Head need have no qualms as to his reactions on the most sensational of alpine precipices.

It was a glorious pathway up which we walked. The sun was warm without being fierce and scorching; it lit the snow until it shone like pure silver; it revealed every detail of the slopes, every fold, hummock, and ripple, and cast blue shadows filled with reflected opalescent light.

What an excellent thing it is to stand on a mountain, conscious that your muscles have carried you thither without the aid of any mechanical contrivance; to feel superlatively fit; to be clear of eye and head, and strong of leg and arm; to breathe deep breaths of keen cold air and in each breath discern the power and beauty of the Universe; to know a contentment untrammelled by any anxiety, and a peace of mind and spirit which is true happiness.

The shoulder levelled out and we came to the foot of the final steep snow slope, which ends just below the summit of the mountain.

We climbed leisurely, but it was warm work nevertheless, for the sun was full on our backs, and we were glad to make across to some rocks and drink from a trickle of water.

Others had already ascended the peak, and as we refreshed ourselves we saw them descending the slope a few yards away. There were several parties, some with, and some without guides. Their descent was not an inspiring spectacle, as few of them had any notion of glissading; the more venturesome went head over heels down the slope and the less venturesome subsided on to their seats. Unquestionably the alpine guide earns his pay, even on such an easy mountain as the Aiguille de Bérangèr, and our sympathy went out to the guides, who were not only denied a safe and easy glissade, but had, in addition, to restrain the antics of their charges, who even on that safest and easiest of snow slopes were fully capable of hurting themselves.

The most striking spectacle of all was the descent of a woman who, having abandoned all hope of retaining her balance, was content to be lowered down on her back. In the pioneer days of mountaineering women wore skirts. Nowadays, and doubtless very sensibly, they wear trousers or breeches, but this does not alter the fact that the female form is in shape singularly ill adapted for the wearing of men's attire, and presents the most ludicrous appearance when clad in breeches. Trousers are a little better, but it must be a source of wonder to many that winter sports resorts are alluded to as "romantic" or potentially "romantic". It would be more logical to associate them with broken romances, for to the aesthetic or the romantically inclined there can be surely no more unromantic spectacle than that of a be-trousered woman tumbling about a snow slope on a pair of ski. It is scarcely possible to picture a Romeo wooing a be-trousered Juliet on the snows of Mont Blanc or Mürren.

Twenty minutes later we sat sunning ourselves on the summit of the Aiguille de Bérangèr, devoutly thankful that we had arrived late enough to avoid sharing it with a crowd. As it was, the crowd had left tangible evidence behind it in the shape of sandwich papers, chocolate wrappings, and orange peel. Such is the fate of the better known and easily accessible viewpoints of the Alps.

We were not long by ourselves, for presently another party approached by the ridge, which connects the Aiguille de Bérangèr with the Dôme de Miage. Accordingly, we continued on our way towards the latter peak, which we had to traverse in order to reach the Durier Hut on the Col de Miage.

The descent to the col between the two mountains was over snow covered rocks of little difficulty. Here we passed the party we had seen. They were all wearing crampons and for that reason were progressing with difficulty on the rocks. These adjuncts to climbing have become a fetish with a certain type of continental climber. Whatever the nature of the terrain, whether hard snow, soft snow, snow covered ice, or rocks, crampons are worn, and what is more are worn in many cases before experience has been gained of climbing in nailed boots. Hence there are many accidents directly attributable to climbing on ground where crampons are not only unsuitable but also dangerous. Soft snow, which balls between the spikes, is always treacherous, whilst such snow when it conceals ice is nothing short of a death trap. Regarded as an adjunct to climbing, crampons are valuable, but as a substitute for the nailed boot they are a snare and a delusion.

As far as the col we met with soft snow, but it was apparent that the long steep slope leading up to the summit ridge of the Dôme de Miage was frozen hard. Here crampons would be of real service and we halted to strap them on.

The slope as anticipated was icy and we mounted rapidly in short zigzags dictated by its steepness and the necessity to ease our ankles, which had to be considerably flexed on account of the angle. It was a long slope ending below not on the col we had passed, but on the Glacier de la Frasse.

If I had to be killed by a fall on a mountain I should not choose a snow slope ending in a precipice or ice cliffs; there would be too long an interval of anticipation. Yet there have been instances of climbers falling great distances down steep snow slopes and escaping with their lives, though I have heard it said that if the slope is icy and rough it strips a man first of his clothes and then of his flesh, a process altogether too mediaeval in character to be contemplated with equanimity.

However, no such thoughts entered our minds as we stepped steadily up the snow, for it was impossible to entertain morbid thoughts on that day of bright sunlight and exhilarating activity.

At length the slope eased away and we trod soft snow, which continued without difficulty over a minor eminence to the summit of the Dôme de Miage.

So far so good, and having cautiously cast around for a possible cornice, we seated ourselves in the snow and lunched. We had not been long engaged thus when we were joined by another party, a Swiss and his guide, who approached from the opposite direction. It was a pleasant encounter, not only socially but also gastronomically, as the Swiss generously insisted on giving us handfuls of prunes. 'I do not need them,' he said, 'for I must go down. I should like to go to the Durier Hut with you and climb the Aiguille de Bionnassay, but it is not possible; my wife awaits me.' Then, in reply to further thanks on our part, he said, 'After all it is good, is it not, to give and to share? It is the comradeship of the mountains that matters.'

He was right. 'It is the comradeship of the mountains that matters.' He spoke a profound truth. Laugh at mountaineers and mountaineering if you will, decry the dangers, stigmatise the risks as absurd and unnecessary, but remember that there is no sport which better promotes international friendships than mountaineering, for it is dissociated from those national rivalries and jealousies which so often prostitute other sports when transferred to the international arena or Olympiad. Mountaineering has its black sheep; it is capable of producing thoughtless and callous acts, but there is no sport so productive of that goodwill and unselfish co-operation, which all people of faith know must in the end triumph over the material greeds and frailties which are responsible for the unhappiness of man today. I hope our Swiss friend will read this; if so, he will say to himself, 'Well, at all events, it was worth a few prunes!'

There was no immediate hurry, and for an hour or more we lounged at our ease on the summit. Curiously enough, I remember little of the view. In memory's eye I can see the Aiguille de la Trélatête across the Trélatête Glacier, and dimly discern some small dots on it, two of which were probably Finzi and his guide. I can remember also the Aiguille de Bionnassay, now close at hand, and the summit of Mont Blanc with a smooth cloud capping it, a cloud neither of us fancied. Then there was a glimpse down to the fields of St. Gervais and Sallanches. But what I remember best was the sun. The mountain world that day, and on succeeding days, was soaked in sunlight. There was sunshine everywhere, on the heights and in the depths, on the columns of afternoon cloud ranged over the valleys, on the warm red granite of Mont Blanc, on the ice, and on the snow. The mountains were celestial, brilliantly lit, and superlatively calm. The sun shone through an atmosphere unbroken by any wind, and it was in this sun-drenched silence that our way lay then and on other days.

On such an occasion it is impossible to think of men in stuffy cities engaged in encompassing the ruin of other men. It was impossible to picture misery, to envisage the spectre of war on those sunlit heights. There is a lesson for all men to see, in the hills and in the stars above the hills, and in smaller things also, in trees and fields, streams and flowers. There is a great question mark in the sunny heights, in the purity and beauty of snow, earth, and atmosphere. We talk of heaven, as though it were some place better than the World. Is not that an insult to the Creator of the World? There is a peace in Nature, a peace in which death seems trivial and meaningless, a transition in some evolutionary process of which man is an unending part. But why hasten death through strife and suffering? The true index of war is not death, it is the misery and suffering it creates, which renders man incapable of appreciating the beauty of his environment.

The traverse of the Dôme de Miage is a fine expedition. The route lies for the most part over snow and is devoid of difficulty, yet it is always interesting and the views are magnificent. From the summit we continued over some minor summits to the rocky point where the ridge bends almost at right angles and falls steeply to the Col de Miage. The climbing here was more difficult, and to descend the snow covered rocks needed care. It was chilly on this sunless northern side of the peak and we were glad when, after a downward clamber of 1,000 feet, the ridge levelled out into the rudely horizontal crest of the col. We wondered where the Durier Hut was, there being no tracks of previous climbers to guide us, but could see no sign of it. It was a long ridge and we passed over various snow edges and rocky bumps until the ground began to rise towards the Aiguille de Bionnassay. There was still no sign of the hut, and our guidebook, a German publication, was annoyingly vague as to its exact position. Then, suddenly, just as we were becoming really puzzled and despondent, we saw it perched on the rocky slopes that descend to the Glacier de Miage Français about one hundred feet below the crest of the col. Only one end was visible; the remainder being buried beneath an accumulation of snow.

We had to dig away a snowdrift with our ice axes before we could release the door. Inside we found a single room about twelve feet long and nine feet wide, three quarters of the floor space being taken up by a bunk. The interior was filthy. The floor was covered with a black slush compounded of dirt and snow water that had seeped through the walls. It needed fortitude and determination to look under the bunk, where there reposed debris of all kinds, ranging from pieces of paper to mouldering scraps of food and verdigris-coated tins. The bunk was equipped with dirty straw palliasses, pillows greasy with the hair oil of past visitors, and about fifteen blankets, some old, tattered and threadbare, some comparatively new and thick, but all exuding a smell suggestive that they had been employed for an indefinite period in the deepest and dampest dungeon of a mediaeval fortress.

The cooking arrangements were simplicity itself; there were none. It is true that a stove had once been installed, but what terrible fate had overtaken it we could only conjecture. At all events the remains of it red with rust stood pathetically against one wall of the hut, whilst on the floor lay a dejected-looking length of iron piping which had been intended originally to conduct the smoke into the open air.

Such was our abode for the night, and we could only pray that the weather would not change and confine us to it for a longer period. If it did we could certainly exist for some time on our own provisions, and on the scraps of bread left by former climbers, but we shuddered at the thought of this last, for the bread was green with age and as hard as granite. There was one thing in our favour; we had the hut to ourselves.

Fortunately we were able to economise our methylated spirit by collecting water that fell from the snow on the roof instead of having to melt snow. As economy in fuel is important it would be convenient to climbers if huts such as this were equipped with guttering a pipe from which water could be collected. As it was, we had to employ a variety of receptacles to catch the desultory trickles.

The position of the Durier Hut enables it to receive the whole of the afternoon sun, and we spent a pleasant hour or two outside, during which we took the opportunity to dry our socks, puttees, and boots. As we did so, we gazed down the broken rock face and shattered icefalls that drop to the Glacier de Miage Français. The route up to the hut from this direction looked both difficult and dangerous, especially in view of the recently fallen snow that still cloaked the rocks, and we felt that our privacy was assured. In this last we were mistaken.

The sun was fast sinking when, to our astonishment, we heard a distant shout. Peering over the edge of the little shelf on which the hut stands we saw four climbers toiling up the snow covered rocks. They seemed to be making heavy work of the climb, which was not to be wondered at considering the state of the mountainside, and when they approached the rocks immediately below the hut we shouted down to ask them whether they would like the assistance of a rope over the last steep section. They refused this and presently arrived climbing unroped but evidently tired.

The party consisted of three Frenchmen, one young, one middle-aged, and one elderly, and a guide. The last named was a member of the old school. He did not wear the usual beret of the Chamoniards but a grey cloth cap. Like most guides, he was attired in a thick cloth suit, with coat, waistcoat, and drainpipe trousers. Alpine guides are for the most part intensely conservative in the matter of clothing and rely not unreasonably, on their physical powers to withstand cold and exposure, yet it is an undeniable fact that two or three layers of knitted wool and a light windproof suit, weighing in all two or three pounds, are warmer than a broadcloth suit four times the weight. In support of this contention there are many instances of guides feeling a cold wind while their more sensibly clad charges proceeded in comfort.

He was a simple, friendly, unostentatious man, this guide, with a pink boyish complexion, blue eyes, and a moustache of imperialist dimensions, and his first thought on arriving at the hut was to provide for the comfort of his employers.

Our immediate reactions to the entry of the party were similar to those of any Englishman whose railway compartment is invaded by an excursionist family, but a friendly atmosphere was soon established. We had set about making the Frenchmen tea when we saw them labouring up the slopes, but water took a long time to heat over our spirit cooker and our visitors substituted a small primus, which we were told to use whenever we liked, a graceful and generous act.

They had come, they told us, from St. Gervais and, like us, intended to traverse the Aiguille de Bionnassay on the morrow, though, as they confessed, it was their first climb of the season and they were not yet in training.

An area approximately twelve feet in length by three feet in width, which represents roughly the floor space of the Durier Hut, when occupied by six men needs managing, if there is not to be frustration and irritation, particularly as regards culinary matters. Thus, while the middle-aged Frenchman and I cooked, the remainder occupied the bunk. The sun was setting as I heated a stew consisting of soup powder, bread, and pieces of bully beef, and peering through the little window, which admitted a modicum of light into the box-like building, I saw the sky afire, and the northern ice face of the Dôme de Miage glowing like a tumbling torrent of purest gold.

Cooking operations and the enjoyment of an Alpine sunset are scarcely compatible, and I had the uneasy feeling that Jim was hungering for his stew, and that any inattention on my part in favour of the sunset, resulting in an upset of our saucepan, which was perilously perched on a small and decrepit table liable to be jolted at any moment, would be visited by the wrath it deserved.

The operation was successfully completed thanks to the primus cooker, and seated on the bunk we devoured with a feeling of gastronomical ecstasy a stew, which was solid in all but name. 'A grand stew, Frank,' was Jim's verdict; it is a remark that I treasure.

Supper eaten, we prepared for bed. This involved some preliminary mathematics in the matter of blankets. Six men into fifteen blankets do not go, but my companion, a brilliant mathematician, solved the problem with the suggestion that each man should have two blankets and each pair of men one blanket.

Though an excellent sleeper as a general rule. I did not do myself justice that night. I lay awake and listened to a gradually rising crescendo of snores, punctuated at frequent intervals by violent upheavals and stifled groans from the younger of the Frenchmen, who fortunately was two removed from me: it seemed that in his dreams he suffered tortures, and more than once I was tempted to wake him and put him out of his misery. Meanwhile Jim, always a sound sleeper, gradually appropriated more and more of the communal blanket, until I found myself engaged in a tugging match to retain my share. I was tempted to expostulate, but he slumbered so peacefully that I did not have the heart to do so. In any event, I was reasonably warm, and lay comfortably enough, having become accustomed to the smell of the blankets, my head separated from the greasy odorous pillow by a spare sweater.

It was a quiet night, except for a vagrant wind soughing past the hut and occasionally, from the direction of the Dôme de Miage, the muffled growl of an ice avalanche. Through the narrow window, now laced with frost, I could see the glint of a star, and all about our small abode reigned the peace of the high mountains.

CHAPTER EIGHT

Aiguille de Bionnassay

WE WERE awakened by the Frenchmen getting up. It was 4 a.m., and there seemed no occasion to follow their example, as the guidebook time for the ascent of the Aiguille de Bionnassay from the Durier Hut is four to six hours, and we did not wish to spoil the pleasure of the ascent by climbing in cold conditions. However, they were so slow that nearly an hour later when we rose there seemed no prospect of them starting.

It is disagreeable to prolong the agony of an early start in the Alps and an hour sufficed for breakfast and climbing preparations. At six o'clock we sallied forth, just as the Frenchmen were strapping on their crampons, and set to work to climb the ridge.

The morning was clear and cold and our crampons bit with comforting assurance into hard frozen snow. We mounted quickly and without difficulty, first of all up a broad snow-slope, then over a mixture of snow and rocks, which presently thinned out into a sharp crest. This last brought us to a shoulder from which the ridge sprang up steeply in a rock edge defended in its lowermost portion by smooth slabs of formidable appearance.

The previous evening the guide had assured us that the best route lay to the west of the ridge crest via a snow-filled chimney, but this side of the ridge was out of the sun and the chimney was a cold, inhospitable-looking rift. If we traversed to the east over some slabby ribs we should reach snow which, to judge from the snow we had already climbed, should be in excellent condition; and our climb would be made in sunlight. It is true that this variation was unorthodox, and well removed from the usual route, but that made it all the better fun and we determined to attempt it.

From the shoulder a nearly horizontal traverse across snow brought us to the first of some slabby rock ribs, which we planned to cross diagonally. The rock was by no means firm, and climbing it in crampons was neither easy nor pleasant. It would have been better to have removed crampons, but this is not easy on steep ground, and in any event the rock climbing promised to be of short duration. To begin with, we made the mistake of keeping too high, and involved ourselves in considerable difficulties on the slabs. This was my fault; I was leading at the time, and I must have wasted a precious twenty minutes in what is best described as "messing about". Finally we crossed the first rib at a lower point, then traversed an incipient icy gully and another rib, after which we mounted at a steeper angle, until we saw a promising snow-slope above us to the right. We made for this slope; it was fully fifty degrees in angle, but we were relieved to find the snow in safe condition. There was no time to be lost as the slope was full in the sun, and would become impossibly dangerous in another hour or so, and we climbed at top speed.

The slope narrowed, and was finally strangled into a shallow chimney between rocks. So far, so good; except for the loss of time on the ribs at the beginning, we had made height quickly, and the conditions had been ideal for crampons. But now came ice. The hot sun of the past two days had melted the new snow on the rocks, water had trickled into the gully and there frozen during the night. Thump, thump. Later in the day the sound of an ice axe pick meeting ice may become dull and monotonous, and a measure of weariness, but early in a climb, when the air is frosty and the sun warm, there is no more inspiring sound in the ear of a mountaineer.

We were soon up. Then came rocks and snow; there was some steep climbing, but nothing to hinder us unduly. The slope lifted at an ever-increasing angle, ending in a delicate little scroll of wind-turned snow, a small cornice on the south ridge close to the final snow slope of the mountain.

Up and up we laboured, our crampon points driving well home. Now the cornice was immediately above us. A pause to flog it clear and we stepped on to the narrow crest of the South Ridge at a point well above the steep rocky section.

The snow was untrodden; the Frenchmen were below engaged in climbing the rocks. We hallooed and heard a distant response. A short pause to rest, and we continued towards the summit.

The way now was clear. We had to follow the snowy crest of the south ridge, then climb a final snow-slope, which ended at the summit of the mountain.

It was a simple and beautiful finish to a mountain climb. The slope was concave in form; a parabola of unbroken snow lifting to a fragile crest, a celestial, wind-tossed roller frozen and motionless.

As we climbed I remember looking to the right and seeing Mont Blanc shining and serene in the morning sun, then glancing down to the left across the snowy wave to the meadows of St. Gervais and Sallanches 10,000 feet beneath.

And so to the summit, a tent-like edge of snow, a summit almost as beautiful and dramatic as that of Nilgiri Parbat in the Garhwal Himalaya, which I remember as the *beau ideal* of mountain tops. The Aiguille de Bionnassay was won.

We arrived there almost simultaneously with a party of two women and a guide. Our French friends were half an hour behind us and presently joined us. It was nine o'clock when we reached the summit, and I for one would gladly have spent the next two or three hours there. A long stay, however, was out of the question. One glance at the route we must follow to gain the Col de Bionnassay disclosed enormous cornices. These would force us to traverse the south facing slope, on which the sun was shining so fiercely that it was only a matter of time before the snow softened on the underlying ice. The guide of the first party was fully alive to the danger and after pausing a few minutes left with his charges.

We waited until our French friends arrived, in order to photograph them, then set off down in the track of the other party. It was not long before we came up with them. The guide was taking no chances, and we realised directly we trod the slope that it was one demanding unremitting caution. A little earlier it would have been possible to have walked across it in crampons, but the brilliant sun had softened the snow, and beneath this, as already mentioned, was ice. It is on slopes of this nature that accidents are most likely to happen, for crampons, though valuable if used with circumspection, may easily become death traps on the feet of the inexperienced. The climber must estimate where it is necessary to cut steps into the underlying ice. If there is any doubt that the snow will hold his foot *in situ* then he must cut steps; he must also remember to kick any balling snow away from his crampons every few steps. To the inexperienced such slopes often seem simplicity itself to climb or traverse, but it must be remembered that snow usually varies in depth and that, whereas it may be deep and comparatively firm on the ice for a few yards, the next few yards may be the reverse. For this reason the weight cannot safely be transferred to the front foot until it is certain that the snow is firm and deep enough to hold. The skill involved in crossing such slopes lies in knowing where, and where not, the snow is to be trusted, and the experience required to determine this is considerable.

We felt profoundly sorry for the guide. His was the unenviable task of conducting two women across a slope that had in it every element of treachery and danger. Had his charges been experienced mountaineers all would have been well, but it was obvious from the way they climbed that they were raw to the job. They carried their ice axes in their outside hands, and leant towards the slope clutching at it with their inside hands, while the rope drooped down between them in a melancholy loop. Had the woman last on the rope slipped, she would have slid some distance before the rope tightened on her companion who would inevitably have been dragged from her steps. Could the guide have held both when it was seldom possible for him to drive his ice axe into the slope for more than one-third of its length? I am certain he could not.

So impressed were Jim and I with the weakness of the party that we offered to rope on to them, which would have meant that the two women were between experienced companions, but this offer was curtly refused by the guide, possibly because he thought that we wanted to rope on to his party for our own safety and that our presence would further endanger it! It might surprise him to learn that we were extremely relieved at his refusal!

The cornices were some of the largest I have met with in the Alps, indeed so extensive that the leading party had difficulty in avoiding them. Meanwhile the snow became worse and worse as we descended, and we did not hesitate to enlarge the steps made by the guide. It was a relief when we came to some rocks and saw that little more of the ridge remained to be descended to the col. The guided party halted here and we went ahead thanking the guide for his steps as we passed him.

A few feet from the col the cornices petered out and we were able to tread the crest of the ridge, the whole way to that point having lain on the south slope. We were in need of a rest and food and to escape a cutting north wind excavated a platform in the snow just below the ridge. We had been going hard, and it was pleasant to relax taut limbs in repose, whilst a few sardines slid down our throats with the greatest of ease.

As we ate, the first of the guided parties passed, but our French friends were a long way behind and were going laboriously and slowly.

Continuing on our way, we mounted a steep but easy snow ridge, passed over a subsidiary shoulder of the Dôme du Goûter, and joined the well trodden Dome Route which various Italian parties were descending after climbing Mont Blanc.

Never before had I been on Mont Blanc in such perfect weather. We were overcome by laziness and the warmth of the sun, and easily succumbed to the temptation of a siesta. So hot was the sun that when we came to some rocks we had only to plaster a slab with snow to obtain a trickle and a drink. For a long while we sat and toasted. Even the cold north wind had died away and Mont Blanc dreamed, as I have never seen it dream before, under a gentian sky. So still was the atmosphere so silent the great mountain, there seemed something almost unreal in our situation. We stretched out our limbs and gazed languidly upon the tremendous prospect of dazzling snow, deep blue sky, woolly white clouds, and violet valleys. Such peacefulness as this inspires the question as to the reason for the interposition of quarrelsome man, into the beneficent scheme of Nature, and the thought of war, which, had we but known it, was only a few days' distant, seemed so absurd, so fantastic, so completely and utterly inappropriate as to be unbelievable. Why live in cities? Why not enjoy the sun and the air? Why not exist simply and happily without the need always to be amassing needless materials? Is it not better to see and feel the brown soil and be a part of living, growing things than ensconced amid dead bricks and mortar? Is not the soft grass better than the hard unsympathetic street? Is it not man's true heritage the scents of the earth, moist turf, a woodland after rain, new mown hay on a June evening; to see beauty; flowers opening their petals, blue hills and horizons overhung with tall clouds. Why has progress, civilisation, religion, doomed mankind to enclosures and cities, where he must needs crowd into communities so closely set as to deprive him of the sight of a patch of grass or a glimpse of blue sky? This is the question mark of the age. If this is progress then God save man from it; if this is living then it is better to be dead; if this is what is meant by man being made in the image of God, then Hell is preferable to Heaven. We talk of war as though it were a misfortune. Modern war is mass suicide, the result of unhappiness and frustration which produce in their train greed and hatred, the product of an environment so artificial and complex that it foredooms happiness (which is the child of simplicity) in advance. Who are we with our factories, our "Black Country", our coalmines, our grimy smoke-canopied cities, and our slums, to air our innocence and preach our virtuousness? War is like a disease that manifests itself on the skin, but it is not the skin that is wrong, it is the blood. Not until man reverts to simple living in natural surrounding and gains contentment will he free himself from the germs of unhappiness and frustration, which produce the particular fever of war.

It is perhaps curious that mountains should inspire such thoughts, but a mountain is only one manifestation of Nature. Mountains are simple things; they have not been rendered into complex objects by the hand of man, they are too big to be spoiled. Life in the mountains, or for that matter in any wild place far from cities, teaches over and over again that human beings to be happy need only bare and simple necessities, and that directly this teaching is lost, and necessities become associated with unnecessary adjuncts, economic factors intrude which make for complexity, and ultimately for unhappiness and strife.

It was nothing but a walk to the Dôme du Goûter. There was no need to hurry, and we lounged uphill enjoying every step of the ascent. But slow as we were the French party were slower still, and we presently came to the conclusion that they were very tired.

The Dôme du Goûter shoulders the final peak of Mont Blanc, and it is easy to understand how and why parties lose their sense of direction in thick weather on its complicated slopes, but on this most brilliant of summer afternoons not a breath of wind ruffled the immaculate snows, and the many tragedies that have taken place hereabouts seemed distant and remote.

From the Dôme du Goûter there is a descent of a few yards, then an ascent of two or three hundred feet to the Rochers Rouges, on which stands the Vallot Observatory. This is now used solely as a hut and recently the French Alpine Club constructed another hut close by, an all-metal building which gleams incongruously against the snows of Mont Blanc.

My memories of the Vallot Hut are pleasant and unpleasant. I have had reason to bless it when descending late from Mont Blanc after a long climb up the South Face of that mountain, yet its cold and dirty interior remains a disagreeable memory. To tourists ascending Mont Blanc by the ordinary route it is a longed for halting place at which to have a hot drink and be comfortably sick. In this connection I recollect being aroused early one morning after a chilly night by a party consisting of two guides and a tourist. The last named was a tall, thin, lugubrious looking man who, for some inscrutable reason, carried a thermometer attached to a ribbon round his neck. As he stood in the doorway, looking the picture of misery he managed to gulp out, 'Bon jour, Messieurs' – then he was violently ill.

Undoubtedly the tourist who assails Mont Blanc without some preliminary training is a brave man, for mountain sickness, which in the Alps is more often than not a product both of imperfect physical condition and altitude, is as bad or worse than sea sickness, perhaps worse, for in sea sickness the victim can lie down, whereas in mountaineering he has to keep on his legs.

Since those days a hut keeper has been installed at the Vallot Hut and home comforts may be enjoyed. We entered a warm little living room with a stove at one end, and bunks at the other, to be welcomed by the guardian, a phlegmatic, broad faced man, an ex-guide of Chamonix.

We were very thirsty and drank quantities of a pale coloured liquid re-heated for the occasion and described as tea, which, as we subsequently discovered, was regarded by the hut keeper as being worth almost its weight in gold, for we were charged seven francs a cup and drank between us some ten cups in as many minutes.

Nevertheless, we were glad to have such comforts, and when it is considered that the Vallot Hut is the highest building in Europe with the exception of the hut on the Italian summit of Monte Rosa, and that everything must be carried up to it on men's backs, the visitor must expect to be charged high prices.

It was late in the afternoon when our French friends arrived. They had altered their original intention of descending by the Aiguille du Goûter route, and leaving their guide to go down to St. Gervais had struggled on to the Vallot Hut. They were, all three of them, very nearly exhausted. The youngest man was the most, and the oldest man the least affected. It was impossible not to speculate as to what might have happened to them had the weather changed during the traverse of the Aiguille de Bionnassay. It is probable that had it done so and a blizzard developed Mont Blanc would have added to its long death roll.

The evening was bitterly cold, for the Vallot Hut is the recipient of every wind that blows, and a strong breeze tore past, finding its way under the door with a vicious whoo, and discovering various creaks and groans in the weather-beaten building. It denied to us the beauty of the sunset, as it was impossible to remain outside for long, though I managed to take two photographs with half-frozen fingers.

Yet the evening sky promised good weather for the morrow. The sun set in a lake of gold, shot with green, saffron, and blue, behind the serrated summits of the Chaine des Aravis. Long belts of haze below, and fine drawn tendrils of cloud above, were filled with splendid colours, so that earth and sky were suffused for a few minutes with light, and Mont Blanc seemed to float in luminescent space.

The hut was crowded, for others were present in addition to the three Frenchmen and ourselves. Fortunately plenty of blankets were forthcoming as the night was intensely cold and our boots froze hard, but any possibility of a restful sleep was sabotaged for me by the youngest of the three Frenchmen. It was my misfortune to be next to him, and he was unable to keep still for two consecutive minutes. All night he was engaged in desperate combats with imaginary enemies, and entreaties and curses proving ineffectual, I was forced to resort first of all to nudgings, then to joggings, and finally to kickings, and while he was composing himself to a further nightmare, endeavour to snatch a few minutes' sleep myself.

CHAPTER NINE

Mont Blanc and the Brenva

I WAS THANKFUL when dawn broke, and I informed Jim with an ill grace that he had been slumbering like a hog, but that I had had scarcely a wink, whereat he, in the manner of a man who has enjoyed a sound and refreshing sleep, was suitably sympathetic and commiserating.

At breakfast we had more tea at seven francs a cup, then having thawed our boots over the stove and strapped on crampons, we paid a staggering bill and sallied forth on to the snows of Mont Blanc.

After the close, steamy interior of the hut the keen frosty air was wonderfully invigorating, and my grumpiness, consequent on a wretched night soon vanished. The promise of a golden sunset had been fulfilled and Mont Blanc rose serene into a cloudless sky, yet it was no morning on which to linger and a bitter little breeze spurred us into activity.

Other parties from the Grands Mulets were arriving at the hut as we left, and we were thankful that we were first away, and did not have to shove and jostle our way to the summit through the hordes that were congregating to ascend to it.

At first we were thankful for gloves and balaclava helmets but we soon warmed up as we climbed, and were able to appreciate our surroundings.

It has been said that the traveller should make a point of witnessing two sights, the Taj Mahal by moonlight, and sunrise from Mont Blanc. I had some years previously witnessed the first of these and now had the privilege of witnessing the second. So much has been written by abler pens than mine about sunrise seen from Mont Blanc that I hesitate to enter the descriptive lists. That morning we saw to perfection the shadow of the mountain cast upon a sea of mist lying some thousands of feet beneath and extending westwards as far as the eye could see. We also experienced the same sensation of isolation and elevation so frequently commented on by former travellers without however, suffering from the disagreeable symptoms of mountain sickness, which can ruin the aesthetic pleasure of ascending Mont Blanc.

The ascent of the mountain by the ordinary route from Chamonix has often been associated with the treadmill. Physically it is undoubtedly a wearisome affair, without any saving grace of climbing variety. The walker has merely to follow a deep groove worn in the snow by the feet of his predecessors and he is certain to arrive on the summits, unless he tires of this proceeding and wanders aside to fall into a crevasse, becomes sick or otherwise incapacitated, or decides to give up and go home, which is what I should do if I were a tourist. There is, however, much in the way of beauty to be noted. This beauty is perhaps not always perceptible when viewed in the company of a pair of guides whose sole object is to hustle their charge as expeditiously as possible to the summit and down again to Chamonix, in order that further employment may be obtained with the minimum of delay. Beauty and commercial bargains are uneasy bedfellows at the best of times; on a mountain they are positively murderous. But anyone, who is content to spend a night at the Vallot Hut, as we did, and lounge up to the summit next morning, can hardly fail to enjoy the experience. He will, if he has never before scaled a high mountain, see beauty previously undreamed of. It will be borne home to him that snow is not a white substance without form or void but the petrifaction of grace and purity, a celestial coverlet capable, like marble in the hands of a craftsman, of being moulded by sun and wind into delicate, fragile and unearthly forms. Therefore, go slowly up Mont Blanc and see the day strengthen on the snow, watch the stealing shadows, the glowing highlights; snow set brilliant against cobalt blue; snow in waves and ripples; snow in long gentle undulations; snow in serene plains and shining edges; snow in slopes, crests and cornices; snow in smooth lofting domes and steeply pointed spires. Watch how this snow sparkles and glitters as though strewn with diamonds, how it varies in shade, reflecting the tones of the sky, the gathering, dispersal, and passing of clouds. See how it moulds itself in heaven, matchlessly pure, infinitely tender in form and colour.

An hour's walking and we stood on the summit.

The view from the summit of Mont Blanc is notoriously unsatisfactory from an artistic standpoint. The Alps lie far below and the eye, ranging over a multitude of mountains and valleys, is totally unable to appreciate the extent and magnificence of the panorama. The view resembles that from an aeroplane; the earth is too remote, too detached, too flattened; there are no outstanding objects to provide foregrounds and middle distances to set off depths and backgrounds, and height instead of being a stimulus is a drug. Great mountains are best viewed from below or, perhaps best of all, from points halfway up them, whence depth and height are equally obvious, each a complement and a help to the other.

Yet that morning it was possible to appreciate the beauty of the view from the snowy crown of Europe. The morning was calm, but now and then there was a slight stirring of the atmosphere, a bitter little breath that came and went, the merest hint of the deathly cold that reigns wherever eternal snow has its being. All else was light. The atmosphere was brilliant, the snow like light liquefied and frozen; the sun poured light into the World and we who stood on that high point were invested and permeated with light.

Then there were clouds. The south was given over to clouds ranged over the violet depths of the Italian valleys, citadels of vapour apparently as solid and impermeable as the snowy dome on which we stood, clouds in woolly masses with blue chasms deep in their glowing folds, bronze-coloured clouds in vast anvil-shaped wedges, lifted beyond the blue ranges out of the far distant Plain of Lombardy. And between these clouds, with their shining domes and arches, their uplifted cupolas, airy minarets and unsubstantial pillars, was the blue of the hills; and higher still, above their topmost edges, dominating their furthest reaching tendrils and fingers, like a myriad upraised shields, gleamed the eternal snows.

Here was fantasy and reality, fantasy in the misty convolutions of the atmosphere suggestive of strange dreams, queer imaginings, and untranslatable phenomena, reality in the lift and loom of cold snow and hard rock.

We saw the Grivola and Paradiso, the well-remembered forms of Dauphiné and the serried ranks of the Graians, in the east the up-jutting Matterhorn side by side with the glowing snows of Monte Rosa, and north-westwards the clustered summits of the Oberland.

And now I suppose that I had better admit that I am writing from memory. Did I really appreciate what I have tried to describe, or am I at this moment vicariously enjoying the view from the summit of Mont Blanc? I remember that I photographed Jim and that Jim photographed me, and that my photographic enthusiasm was aroused by the marvellous lighting effects, and in particular by the clouds. But supposing I had been given a pencil and paper and told to jot down my impressions there and then on the summit of Mont Blanc, what would I have written? I doubt if I would have written anything; my fingers were too cold; I had to stuff them into my pockets after taking photographs, and I remember that the returning circulation hurt abominably. What a miserable thing the human body is when it comes to enjoying a view from a high mountain. How it puffs and pants, how it aches and complains, how wretched it can be. The Tibetan philosophers declare that it is unnecessary to ascend Everest when it can be climbed so easily in spirit, but there is an abysmal gulf between the Eastern philosophy of material and physical *laissez-faire* and the Western cult of material gain and physical experience. Possibly the desire to climb mountains arises from a desire to effect a compromise. If so, it is the most effective compromise I know, and it has this inestimable advantage; it enables the mountaineer to accumulate memories, and the outstanding power of memory lies in separating and eliminating the physically unpleasant from the mentally and spiritually inspiring. Thus in this book I am able to live again, and in a different manner, the experiences of my mountaineering holiday. On this basis the philosophy of a mountaineer should be that a spiritual and physical compromise makes for a well-balanced philosophy. Yet there are some to whom mountaineering spells only physical exercise, and who pass unseeing and uncomprehending the beauties of the hills. There has, for instance, been applied to the attempts to climb Everest a stark materialism out of keeping with the idealistic nature of that enterprise, and it is impossible not to feel, however illogical it may seem in view of the bad luck with the weather that has so far dogged expeditions, that the mountain will not be climbed until it is approached in a different manner. To climb mountains safely and successfully it is necessary to possess something more than activity and skill; we must have what Mr. Winthrop Young terms the "feeling" for mountains, and this "feeling" has a spiritual rather than a material basis and significance.

Mountains, perhaps more than any other aspect of Nature except the sea, bring men into touch with those universal forces, which in their summation men call God. On them we are able to review our physical selves and glimpse the hidden regions of the spirit. We are brought in some inexplicable manner into closer touch with the creative forces out of which we have been evolved, and the experience is refreshing and inspiring. It enables us to view and review the material aspects of life for what they are worth, and they appear small and ephemeral when seen in association with the grandeurs of the hills. Small wonder that the Tibetan on his windy plateau has few material ambitions, as we plain-dwellers know them. To him a manufacturing district would be nothing short of a hell on earth. In the same way the mountaineer, freed for a time from life in a city, looks down on the plain and wonders why he and his fellow men congregate amid smoke and noise, and what lasting happiness is to be gained from the struggle to accrue materials other than the essentials of existence. He sees in the quest of unessential things a false measure of human progress, and his mind is filled with wonder that mankind should neglect the simple enjoyment of the fruits of the earth and the possibility of happiness and peace.

We had decided overnight to descend to the Torino hut by the Brenva route and the Col de la Fourche. The ascent of Mont Blanc from Italy via the Col de la Brenva is a classic climb which was immortalised by Mr. A.E.W. Mason in his book *Running Water* and it occurred to us that it would be an interesting route down Mont Blanc.

The descent from the summit of Mont Blanc to the Col de la Brenva, between Mont Blanc and Mont Maudit, is nothing but a walk down a slope of snow, which furious winds have carved into ripples and crusted "soup plates". The Brenva route terminates a little above the Col, and shortly before reaching the latter we turned to the south towards the edge, where the gentle snows of Mont Blanc break away in a tremendous face, falling towards the Val Veni 10,000 feet beneath.

It was likely that the past days of good weather had been utilised by parties in ascending the Brenva route, and it was no surprise to us to see tracks. We followed these, first of all down easy snow, then over steepening slopes. The Brenva route once possessed a great reputation for extreme difficulty on account of the séracs that defend the exit on to the col, but for many years past they have given little trouble, and have yielded to frontal attack without the necessity of making a difficult and exposed traverse on ice as was sometimes the case. Thus, in 1927 when I climbed the Brenva, I remember nothing worse than a steep little wall of ice about twenty feet high at the top of the climb, though the slopes below the séracs are always long and steep, and when icy may tax severely the powers of a strong party. Even so, there are few great alpine routes to equal the Brenva in grandeur and sublimity.

Soon we saw the tracks of our predecessors bend sharply round a corner and vanish beneath a line of ice cliffs. Before embarking on the traverse we paused to take a photograph. I have seen many beautiful and dramatic scenes among the mountains, but none to surpass the view we had that morning from the Brenva. The photograph I took gives no more than a hint of this. It shows in the foreground a wall of ice stippled in sunlight like the facets of some immense diamond, then the depths of the Aosta valley 12,000 feet lower. The cloudscape was, if possible, even more ethereally beautiful than that seen from the summit of Mont Blanc. Diaphanous fragments of mist swam in mid-air between us and the dim blue depths where Courmayeur lay, and in the background huge cloud pillars were ranged along the hills and valleys with the ever lovely Grivola enthroned amidst their luminous folds.

The depths at our feet were impressive beyond description. We were perched on the edge of a cloudy abyss, which seemed almost to breathe up at us catching us coldly by the throat. In one downward glance, in one swift glimpse, there came to us the realisation of height and depth. Grandeur, beauty, exhilaration, even for one fleeting moment, terror, was concentrated in that downward plunge of the eye.

From snow we passed to ice, a parabolic, bowl-shaped slope of it which had to be crossed diagonally. It was as well that we wore crampons, for without them we should have had to cut many steps. It was no place in which to linger. The route passed along the base of an ice cliff fifty or more feet in height. It was clean cut and firm, except in one place where a piece had partially detached itself and hung in a menacing flake, a hundred tons or more in weight, athwart the route. Sooner or later it would fall and sweep the slope below with irresistible force and anyone who chanced to be in the way would be trodden out of existence like a beetle.

This is the kind of risk inseparable from mountaineering. Whether it be falling stones or ice, the risk has sometimes to be accepted by the mountaineer. But it is not accepted rashly or heedlessly, for he is a fool who climbs heedless of risk. There is a subtle dividing line in the matter of justifiable and unjustifiable risks. Climbs undertaken nowadays in the quest for new alpine routes are often unjustifiable and outrage mountaineering practice and tradition. It behoves the mountaineer to distinguish between fair risks, which involve only a remote chance of accident and unfair risks where there is a strong probability of disaster. It may be argued by non-mountaineers, 'Why climb at all, there is an inevitable risk, the risk of falling, attached to the simplest ascent?' To this the mountaineer may reply, 'Why venture on the roads of England, there is always the risk of meeting with an accident!' This, the non-mountaineer counters with, 'But I must, it is necessary that I should take that risk.' – 'Well, then,' retorts the mountaineer, 'do without motor cars; our ancestors lived comfortably enough without these death-dealing contrivances. You are prepared to take your risk in order to conform to civilisation with its unnecessary luxuries, you must therefore, allow me to take my risk in pursuit of my unnecessary luxury of climbing a mountain.'

The traverse brought us to an ice rib sloping steeply down to some rocks. Other parties have climbed these rocks, but the route on this occasion avoided them in favour of the slope to the west. This slope consisted of well-frozen snow, fully a foot in depth, resting on, and well adhering to, ice. There was a veritable staircase up it, made by parties who had ascended during the past two or three days, and though the angle was high we had only to walk down it, moving both together.

It was an altogether different occasion to my ascent in 1927. Then, the snow was thin on the ice and step cutting was necessary on the uppermost portion of the slope, but now we descended with almost ridiculous ease, merely having to take care that we did not trip over our crampons, or allow their points to catch in our breeches or puttees.

As we descended we met two ascending parties of two men each. The first consisted of moderately experienced mountaineers, but the second, composed of two youths, was putting up a pitiable exhibition of mountaineering incompetency. As is usual in such cases the rope was a curse rather than a blessing, and merely ensured the death of both climbers in the event of a slip by either. They were evidently tired too, to judge from their slow and laborious progress, and we wondered how they would be going by the time they reached the top of the climb, or what would happen to them should the weather change for the worse.

At length we came to the commencement of the well-known ice ridge. This is the *bonne bouche* of the Brenva route, and the subject of some stirring descriptions by the pioneers. Yet, like the uppermost part of the climb, it seems to be easier than it used to be, and there is no record, as far as I know, of a party in recent years encountering a blade of ice so sharp as to necessitate an *à cheval* method of traversing it.

There was no urgent hurry and we paused for a rest and a bite of food. A glance at a watch disclosed that no more than one and a quarter hours had passed since we left the summit of Mont Blanc, of which less than one hour had been expended on the Brenva route itself.

Ours was a splendid breakfast place. Before us stretched the ice ridge a hundred yards in length and level like a tent ridge. Beyond it was the dark peak of the Aiguille de la Brenva with its slender pencil of rock, and beyond that the luminous depths of the Aosta valley in which silver-lit clouds floated lazily. As though to emphasise the fact that we were now in Italy, the sun blazed down with a new-found power, so much so that we decided not to prolong our halt unduly in case we should encounter soft wet snow.

The ice ridge was easy enough; at the same time it was exceedingly sharp and required a fine balance and steady nerves.

We were soon at the end of it. There I was surprised to find that the route, instead of continuing along the rocky ridge, which falls to the Col Moore at the foot of the Brenva route, branched off down a snow rib to the right, and after descending a gully, traversed the mountainside almost horizontally to the col.

In 1927 the route I had followed kept close to the ridge crest, so that here was a new invention which, as it was probably easier than the ridge, we decided to follow.

The snow was none too good on the initial rib, for already the fierce sun had eliminated all traces of the overnight frost and we had to keep a careful watch on the possibility of an avalanche occurring. After following it for perhaps a hundred feet the tracks bore to the left down steep snow to some rocks at the side of the gully. Neither of us fancied the snow, and we took every precaution when descending it. It proved safer than it looked and we reached the rocks without misadventure. Here it was obvious that, while the parties we had passed had walked up the east side of the gully, then crossed it horizontally to the rocks with

93 *(previous page)* The Innominata Ridge which divides Mont Blanc's Brouillard and Frêney Faces. The sunlit Col du Frêney is behind the foreground snow blade. Adolphe Rey's skill during the first ascent of the ridge (1919) brought success after several earlier failures. *Photo: Bradford Washburn*

94 *(below)* Adolphe Rey - his Innominata and Hirondelles leads solved two difficult rock problems of the day. Rey and Smythe climbed together in 1934 in a search for two climbers missing on the Innominata Ridge.

95 *(right)* The victims, recovered from the Frêney Glacier by the guides, are carried down to Courmayeur.

96 *(top right)* Adolphe Rey, Frank Smythe, Camille Grivel and Edouard Bareux (or Baroux)* at the Gamba Hut after they had discovered the bodies.

97 *(lower right)* The Courmayeur Guides attended the funeral service. On the front row, Grivel, a guide injured during the recovery, Bareux and Rey are on the left. Giuliano Rey, the warden of Gamba Hut, is standing on the far right and the tall man just to his right is Mr J.S. Hoyland, the father of one of the victims. The uncertainty of "adventure" is symbolised by the memorial cross to Felix Ollier who was lost during the Duke of the Abruzzi's North Pole attempt in 1900. *Photos (taken with Mr Hoyland's agreement): Frank Smythe*

*Edouard Bareux was Una Cameron's guide during her successful East African trip in 1938 when ascents were made on Mts Kenya and Kilimanjaro and in the Ruwenzori Range.

98 *(above)* Jim Gavin, Smythe's alpine partner in 1939. They had previously climbed together around Zermatt in 1935 and on Everest in 1936. In an eventful military career Gavin (with the rank of Major General) ended as a N.A.T.O. Intelligence expert at the height of the Cold War. *Photo: John Morris*

99 *(top right)* Gavin moves across the rocks of Les Bans – 'neither too difficult nor sensational, excellent in promoting that harmony of mind and muscle which is the hallmark of skill and practice in mountaineering.'

100 The camp near the Temple Écrins Hut prior to the traverse of Barre des Écrins – warmed by the wreckage of the old hut where Gavin noted 'it's an ill avalanche that brings nobody any wood'.

101, 102 Pictures taken during the traverse of the Aiguille du Bionnassay. A guided party preceded them during the descent of the East Ridge in the rapidly deteriorating snow conditions *(right)* – 'We felt profoundly sorry for the guide … had his charges been experienced all would have been well but it was obvious that they were raw to the job.'

Smythe and Gavin were able to linger on the slopes of the Dôme de Gouter and enjoy the views back to their route of ascent. 'Never before have I seen Mont Blanc in such perfect weather … we gazed languidly upon the tremendous prospect of dazzling snow, deep blue sky, wooly white clouds and violet valleys. … the thought of war, which, had we but known it, was only a few days distant, seemed so absurd, so fantastic, so completely and utterly inappropriate as to be unbelievable.'

103 'I have seen many beautiful and dramatic scenes among the mountains but none to surpass the view we had that morning from the Brenva. The photo gives no more than a hint of this ... in the foreground a wall of ice stippled in the sunlight like the facets of some immense diamond.'

104 On the descent of the Old Brenva Route – '... before us stretched the ice arête, a hundred yards in length and level like a tent ridge ... beyond was the dark peak of the Aiguille de la Brenva and ... the luminous depths of the Aosta Valley in which silver lit clouds floated lazily.

105, 106 On the Innominata Ridge: a pinnacle high on the ridge *(left)* and a view down on the German climbers grappling with the poor snow conditions on the upper slopes *(below)*.

All photos in this section except 93 and 98: Frank Smythe

'We paused to photograph the Germans as they mounted the rib. I believe they were as thankful for our steps as we had been for theirs in the couloir. As we watched them it was brought home to us how steep was the slope: they were emerging from an abyss thousands of feet deep ...'

ease in crampons, the sun had already softened the thin layer of snow clinging to the ice. There was nothing for it but to cut steps. The work was rendered additionally unpleasant by the possibility of falling stones from the crumbling crags that overlooked the head of the gully. I was, therefore, delighted when Jim expressed a desire to go ahead and perform this onerous task; it appeared that he wanted some practice in step-cutting. I fear that from my demeanour he must have guessed the relief I felt at not having to labour and sweat in the sun, which now bore down on the mountainside with a ferocious power, for I agreed with alacrity, belayed myself to an excellent spike of rock, sat down with a contented grunt, and cheerfully bade him go ahead with the job.

He did so, while I yielded myself up, while paying out the rope yard by yard, to that sloth and laziness which is especially pleasurable when the other fellow is doing all the hard work. At the same time I kept a sharp lookout for falling stones; but only one or two harmless pebbles slithered down the gully, and he was left uninterrupted to his task of step cutting. So quick was he that I had scarcely time to make myself really comfortable, or remove sundry intrusive stones from beneath me, when he had accomplished the traverse and was cutting down the far side of the gully.

Inexorably the rope ran out until at length I had to call a reluctant halt and stir myself into sufficient activity to follow him down the steps he had made, a disagreeable descent as the ice was running with water.

This done, we bore round a corner out of the gully on to a long traverse of the mountainside, substantially the same route as that followed by Professor T. Graham Brown and I, when we ascended the Brenva Face of Mont Blanc in 1927 and 1928. It was comparatively easy going, and half an hour later we stood on the Col Moore at the foot of the Brenva Route.

A steep little ice slope brought us down to the Brenva Glacier. Except for the passage of the gully the descent had been accomplished with astonishing ease, so much so that my companion must have formed an erroneous impression as to the merits and difficulties of the route. The difficulty of a rock climb is easily assessed, but such assessment is not possible in the case of snow and ice climbs where conditions vary from year to year, and it would be rash to label the Brenva as anything but a great climb which may, under certain conditions of ice and snow, be easy, and may, under other conditions, be both difficult and dangerous. It is in their capacity to change from year to year, and even from day to day that the charm of such routes lies.

The walk across the head of the Brenva Glacier to the ridge of the Tour Ronde was a sheer purgatory, for the sun blazed with relentless power into the snowy hollow between Mont Blanc and Mont Maudit, and the snow was so soft that at every step we sank in almost to the knees. A sorry anticlimax it seemed after our stroll down the upper slopes of the Brenva, and it was with relief that we gained the foot of the slopes leading up to the Col de la Fourche which we had to cross to the Glacier du Géant.

Neither of us fancied the ascent to the col. The snow was in reasonable condition, but the route brought us under a threatening cornice and the rocks hereabouts are disagreeably loose.

Of recent years numerous miniature huts have been built on the range of Mont

Blanc for climbs inaccessible without bivouacking, and one constructed of iron now stands a few yards from the Col de la Fourche, semicircular in shape like a Nissen hut, and capable of accommodating with reasonable comfort some four to six climbers. A party of two was in possession, one of them being Armand Charlet, the most enterprising and energetic of the younger generation of Chamonix guides. They were there with the object of ascending the Brenva Face of Mont Blanc on the morrow by the route made by Professor Graham Brown and myself in 1928.

An hour later, after a welcome drink of tea, we took our departure and having clambered up to the Col de la Fourche set off down the far side to the Glacier du Géant. Here, quite unexpectedly, we encountered the most difficult and strenuous climbing of the day, for the heat of the sun had turned the snow into running slush, and it was necessary to cut steps into the ice beneath for the greater part of the descent.

Once again Jim craved for some practice in step cutting, and this time he got it in good measure. For my part, I remained happily ensconced on the crest of the col in the sun paying out the rope as he worked his way down. When the time came for me to follow I passed him and we descended rope length by rope length, taking advantage of sundry rocks as halting places and belays for the rope, until we came to the lowermost section of the slope, where the route traversed the slope almost horizontally above a gaping bergschrund. At one point only was it possible to cross the schrund. Here a downward jump of ten or twelve feet, and a forward jump of seven or eight feet, had to be made. It was an exposed descent to the jumping off point, and every step in the water-soaked ice had to be made anew. Jim did this, and to safeguard us both from an unpremeditated slide into the cavernous maw of the bergschrund, cut out a bollard of ice round which the rope could be securely passed, a neat piece of sculpture which evoked all my admiration. Then he descended to the lip of the schrund, called for extra rope, and took a flying leap on to the lower lip whence he skidded down the slope below into soft snow. It was skilfully done, and when he had risen to his feet and brushed off the wet snow from his person, he ironically invited me to follow.

I did so. It was not a particularly difficult jump, but I have never been enamoured of such leaps; they produce momentarily a queasy feeling in the pit of the stomach similar to that sustained during the first moment in a descending lift, or the rapid fall of a ship into the trough of a wave. Even twelve feet seems a formidable height when viewed from above and gravity an obnoxious thing in that moment or two of hesitation preparatory to making the leap. Yet when the leap is made and the landing achieved, then, of course, the leaper vows it is nothing.

Thenceforwards we had to endure the dullest and most fatiguing of plugs through soft wet snow over the Glacier du Géant while our countenances were scorched and shrivelled by the afternoon sun, which was reflected with a dry, merciless intensity from the snowfield.

On the way to the Col du Géant we met a party of some dozen Germans all bound for the bivouac hut on the Col de la Fourche. Hefty, sweating fellows they were, and we wondered what Charlet and his "Monsieur" would have to say when they appeared. A sardine tin would be sparsely populated compared with that bivouac box, and we wondered whether the unfortunate pair would come through the ordeal alive enough to deal with Mont Blanc on the morrow.

Near the Col du Géant we passed a disconsolate looking Italian tourist who asked us whether we had seen a friend of his anywhere. We replied that we had not unless, as we endeavoured to explain in French, of which language the Italian understood a few words, he was among those present on the Brenva route, whereat our interrogator brightened visibly and declared with relief that perhaps he was.

This incident reminds me of a story I once heard. Two Germans set out from a certain German town for a climbing holiday in the Alps. During their first climb together one fell and was killed. The other, having assured himself that his companion was indeed dead, said to himself, with true Teutonic philosophy, 'Well, he is dead, poor Hans – I weep for him one tear!' Then, having dried the tear, he continued, 'Hans would not wish me to spoil my holiday by telling anyone that he is dead, and to have him carried down and buried very expensive will be. I will therefore continue with the holiday and climb all the mountains that he and I were going to climb.'

He proceeded to do so and had a most successful and enjoyable time. Then he returned home. A few days later he was walking in the street when he was stopped by a friend who, after asking after his health, enquired as to the whereabouts of the missing Hans. 'Hans?' said the climber. 'Hans? Let me see now, Herr Gott, yes! Hans, poor Hans, he fell and was killed on that first mountain we climbed!'

The Col du Géant is the easiest pass across the range of Mont Blanc. A large hut-hotel is situated on the Italian side easily accessible from Courmayeur by a rough path, which avoids permanent snow. It is usually crowded with Italian tourists and climbers during the summer months, and we arrived to find it packed out. While waiting for beds, we had no option but to find a corner in the *salle à manger* and have a meal, a scarcely enjoyable function in view of the fact that our clothing had been soaked during the descent from the Col de la Fourche. However, the world assumed a brighter complexion after some soup, poached eggs, and a flask of Chianti, which last, coming after a heavy day, had the effect of making us so sleepy that we could scarcely muster up the energy to climb the stairs to the dormitory in which two beds were eventually reserved for us.

The night was not enjoyable. Some fifty or more persons of both sexes slept in the dormitory on beds arranged in tiers; the roof was low and a single window, a foot or two square, was totally inadequate as a ventilator. Furthermore, our underclothing was soaked, and the only way we could dry it was to sleep in it. We also suffered from an intense thirst, which, however, was slaked by my enterprising companion, who deftly insinuated himself through the narrow window and returned with a cupful of snow gathered from a drift. For the rest, we tossed and turned in an atmosphere which increased during the night to a pitch of tropicality, which no one but an Italian could have endured without complaint. Altogether, it was a sorry climax to a grand day's mountaineering, and I remember lying in a clammy bath of vapour from my wet underclothing, vowing, as I have often vowed before, that I would avoid alpine huts for the rest of my days.

CHAPTER TEN

The Rochefort Ridge

WE ROSE EARLY next morning in order to carry out an ascent that we had planned overnight. This was the Aiguille de Rochefort, a peak to the east of the Col du Géant and the Dent du Géant and to approach it along the ridge connecting it with the Dent du Géant is a fine expedition involving the passage of an unusually sharp snow crest.

We breakfasted in an atmosphere stale with food and tobacco smoke, and it was a relief to step out into the frosty air.

The light grew rapidly as we trod the frozen snow of the Col du Géant, and we had not gone far before we halted to watch the light of the rising sun creep down from the summit dome of Mont Blanc to the precipices of the Brenva and the summits of the Peuterey Ridge.

I have seen Mont Blanc from the neighbourhood of the Col du Géant on numerous occasions, and experience of its difficulties and intricacies has only served to consolidate the feeling of wonder I always have when gazing at the great mountain. Whether or not a view impresses the viewer depends on many factors. The beauty of a mountain view would seem to depend to a large extent upon the disposition of the main lines. Nature as a designer prefers elliptical lines to straight lines; the World is curved and so, if we are to believe Einstein, is the Universe itself. This is not to say that Nature is invariable in her preferences; she has erected the Dolomites, which to my mind are bizarre and picturesque, but not beautiful. But the beauty of the High Alps depends primarily on curves and the arrangement and grouping of the resulting forms. Eliminate the curves from the ridges of the Weisshorn and what remains? A simple pyramid, a poor substitute for that sublime mountain.

Mont Blanc, for all its complicated bulk, is a mountain on which curves predominate. It is also a mountain of many contrasts and the beauty of the view from the Glacier du Géant depends on these as well as upon gracious contours. The whole extent of the mountain is embraced by the eye, from the meadows of Entrèves and the forests of the Val Veni to the final dome of pure snow 12,000 feet higher. In a single sweep the vision traverses the Peuterey Ridge, the greatest of all Alpine ridges, first of all over the peak of the Aiguille Noire set darkly against tender blue hills, where Mont Blanc shakes itself loose of forest, meadow, and upland; then the angular teeth of the Dames Anglaises, which fill the gap between the Aiguille Noire and the Aiguille Blanche; then in another lift to the crest of the Aiguille Blanche with its two points linked by a graceful parabolic snow edge followed by another and lesser drop to the Col de Peuterey; and finally a glorious sweep, beginning in rock and ending in unbroken snow, to the summit of Mont Blanc de Courmayeur and the supreme snowy cupola. But this is not all: the eye continues, travelling along a skyline of snow to the Col de la Brenva, climbing again to the sharp point of Mont Maudit, sinking yet again to the Col Maudit with its defending bastions of ice, to end its journey in the splintered towers of Mont Blanc du Tacul.

Is there another view in the Alps to surpass this in beauty and grandeur? The eye can scarcely comprehend the soaring peaks, the frozen torrents of ice, the avalanche-scarred gullies, the gleaming steeps constituting the mighty wall. Bewildered, it descends to find lodgement on the intervening ridge of the Tour Ronde, which separates the Glacier du Géant from the jumbled ice that laps against the Brenva Face of Mont Blanc. It is a fine ridge yet it appears insignificant in contrast with Mont Blanc. Perhaps it ought not to be there; it conceals the torrential Brenva Glacier, yet it provides a sense of scale, which would otherwise be lacking in the vista. Lastly, and this is the loveliest contrast of all, comes the westernmost bay of the Glacier du Géant, a shining unbroken snow field where the shadows of the bounding peaks grow and shrink, and silver lit clouds pass in the arms of straying winds.

The view to the east is altogether different in character. Here there is a muddle of broken rocks on which is set, in defiance of all orthodox mountain architecture, the queer spike known as the Dent du Géant. It was a fitting name to bestow on this rock. There is nothing beautiful or elegant in the tooth of a giant, and there is nothing beautiful or elegant in this rust-coloured pinnacle: it is perhaps fortunate that the giant in question lost his other teeth and has only this one left with which to bite the clouds and sky. As with a Dolomite pinnacle, it is impossible not to feel that the Dent du Géant was accidental to the scheme of things; it is brutal, not graceful, and would have been better left out. Even as a scramble it would be no particular loss, as to climb it, it is only necessary to swarm up a series of fixed cables, though in fairness it must be stated that there is a first rate route unattended by such abominations on the North Face. However, there it is, and unless it falls the victim of an earthquake, or is blown up by Signor Mussolini, there it is likely to remain for some very considerable time.

Our route lay up broken rocks to the southern base of the tooth. It was on these lower rocks that the greatest guide of his generation, Emile Rey, fell and was killed when descending unroped; in addition broken heads are not unknown hereabouts, as the Dent du Géant is ascended every fine day by hordes of people and the rocks of its plinth are dangerously loose.

To gain the West Ridge of the Aiguille de Rochefort it is only necessary to walk across a snow slope at the foot of the Dent du Géant. Here we strapped on crampons, then proceeded up frozen snow to the crest of the ridge.

Numerous parties had traversed the ridge during the past few days and we followed a track, which in places amounted to a deep furrow. Even so, the climb was in every way worthy of its considerable reputation. I have traversed more difficult alpine snow ridges, the North Ridge of the Bietschhorn for example, but I cannot recollect any to surpass the Rochefort in beauty and acuteness, added to which is the fact that it is several hundreds of yards in length, and maintains its sharpness for nine-tenths of the distance. We agreed that the ice ridge of the Brenva was not to be compared with it.

On a previous occasion I had retired defeated from the ridge because of a wind, but on this occasion scarcely a zephyr stirred, and we had merely to exercise continual caution with our crampons, so as to avoid catching their points in clothing or puttees when swinging the leg forward.

Traversing the ridge was an altogether delightful experience, and Blondin, engaged in his culinary operations in mid air above Niagara, can scarcely have experienced a greater thrill than we.

For the most part we moved both together, but there were one or two places where the ridge was so thin and unstable, and our balance so delicate, that we deemed it advisable to move separately; there were places also where the crest was undermined by small cornices which the tracks of our predecessors did not always wholly avoid.

The ridge was by no means level; it lifted up and down in an irregular wavy fashion, and was broken near its easternmost end by sundry small rock towers. All who delight in snow climbing; all who love an airy edge, all who revel in the niceties of balance should visit the Rochefort Ridge. The traverse was over far too soon, and we found ourselves beneath the culminating rocky tower of the Aiguille de Rochefort. What a wretched anti-climax this proved, a crumbling shaley ruin of a peak, a disagreeable curmudgeon of a summit, which except for the view, is worthless as a climb. A *via splendida* had ended in a *via dolorosa.*

A party of two, an Italian lady and her guide were in front of us, and we waited while they descended, because of the stones they were unable to avoid dislodging. They halted to give us their opinion of the climb, and to enjoin caution on the treacherous rocks.

Having removed our crampons we tackled the rocks. They were not difficult, but certainly needed care because of their unstable nature; it is impossible to clean such rocks by removing the loose fragments because the rock underneath is equally unsound.

Twenty minutes later we were sunning ourselves on the summit of the Aiguille de Rochefort. The view was little different from the one we had enjoyed on the snow ridge, except that we now saw the Grandes Jorasses in the east. Parties were on the summit of the Dent du Géant, and the still morning was rendered hideous by triumphant catcalls and other offensive noises in which the vulgar delight to indulge on the summit of a mountain.

There were two good reasons why we should not linger on the summit. Firstly, climbing on the loose rocks beneath the Dent du Géant in the company of the hordes descending from that peak would be both disagreeable and dangerous, and, secondly, we had previously decided to descend to Courmayeur with a view to traversing Mont Blanc by one or other of the routes on the south side of the mountain. Therefore, after a few minutes we set off down.

An hour later we were back at the Dent du Géant. I think that Jim had some idea of adding the peak to the day's bag, but he thought differently when he saw the queue waiting to ascend the fixed ropes, and heard the shouts and screams of the ascending and descending climbers. Of all Nature's works, mountains are least suited to human gregariousness, noise, and vulgarity, and we were thankful to leave the peak behind us and descend the lower rocks out of earshot.

On the way down we were afforded one of those spectacles of human foolishness and incompetence which are nowadays all too common on mountains. The route from the Glacier du Géant up the initial rocks was obvious; it could have been followed by a blind man, yet a belated ascending party had already missed it and had managed to get themselves into unnecessary difficulty and danger. For some inscrutable reason they had elected to climb not the rocks to the left of an introductory gully, which entail only a simple scramble, but the gully itself, which is a natural chute for falling stones. For a time we saw them labour up directly in the line of fire. Then they came to ice. This decided them to leave the gully in favour of the rocks to the right of it. To do this they had to cut a dozen or more steps in ice. The leader accomplished this somehow or other, but the steps were probably poor ones, for the second man slipped out of them and very nearly pulled his two companions with him. Had the party fallen they might not have hurt themselves; on the other hand, there was a fair-sized bergschrund at the foot of the slope waiting, as Professor Tyndall would have put it, for an erratic body. To us, as we rattled down the easy rocks on the other side of the gully, the procedure of the party appeared so foolish as to be almost beyond the range of criticism.

Half an hour later we were back at the Torino Hut where we paid our bill, had our passports examined and stamped by the resident gendarme, a phlegmatic little fellow, attired in the uniform of an admiral, then set off to Courmayeur.

It is a fearsome experience to ascend from Courmayeur to the Col du Géant on a hot summer's day, but the descent is merely boring and annoying, and the path curvettes and zigzags down a hillside, which for ugliness and looseness resembles a gigantic slag-heap. On the way down I stupidly managed to turn my foot on a stone and sprain my ankle. It happened in a moment and I cursed myself as every kind of an idiot as I slowly hobbled along, wondering disconsolately whether the damage would render our future plans inoperative.

There are, I understand, two treatments for a sprained ankle. One is to rest it and the other is to exercise it. I determined to persevere with the latter treatment. It was successful, though the ankle remained swollen and subsequently took two months to recover completely.

Once the tree line was reached the descent was delightful; there is no pleasanter mountaineering contrast than to exchange the scorching glare of the high snows for a cool resin-scented pine forest.

The shadows were lengthening as we emerged from the forest on to the meadows of the Val Ferret, but what should have been a pleasant stroll to Courmayeur was rendered horrible by innumerable motor cars that hooted viciously at us, then, to add insult to injury, raised clouds of choking dust in our faces.

Courmayeur is a popular holiday resort, crowded out in July and August with Italian trippers, yet it contrives to maintain something which its opposite number, Chamonix, is fast losing, the atmosphere of the past. If civilisation included only amenities such as cleanliness, hygiene, good food, and comfortable accommodation all would be well, but unhappily civilisation to many people nowadays is synonymous with the motor car and the aeroplane. The one brings its stink, noise, and dust to formerly peaceful alpine valleys; the other renders hideous the quietness of the mountains impinging its brutal row on the ears of those who climb to escape for a time from the former. Is it too much to hope that some future generation of men will regard with disgust that horrible instrument of mental and physical torture, the internal combustion engine, which has brought so much unquiet and unhappiness to the world of today?

We had evidently arrived at the height of the Italian national holiday, and accommodation for the night was problematical; however, we managed to secure beds at the Hotel Savoia where I had formerly stayed. At first we were refused accommodation, but luckily the proprietor remembered me, and we were given beds in a large basement apartment in which a chauffeur occupied a third bed.

That evening at dinner we drank Asti Spumanti, which perhaps more than any Italian wine loses its flavour and bouquet when transferred to foreign climes; I have never met with a satisfactory Asti Spumanti in England.

For many mountaineers Courmayeur recalls pleasant memories. It would be difficult to imagine a greater climatic contrast than that between this village and the snows of Mont Blanc. The climber may fight his way down through a blizzard in the afternoon and spend the evening at his ease under the trees of an out-of-door cafe listening to an orchestra or dance band. In such abrupt and pleasant contrasts lies one of the charms of mountaineering.

Unhappily our appearance was scarcely appropriate to the fashionable company in which we found ourselves. We had achieved a bath, and had shaved with a razor borrowed from the "Boots" but, for the rest, we had only the clothes we stood up in, and they were already dilapidated by the strenuous climbing of the past fortnight; thus our appearance was a trifle unsavoury, and there were no other climbers present to provide the necessary moral support. We were made fully conscious of our sartorial shortcomings when the head waiter placed us at a table in the company of two English ladies who, if I may venture upon such a speculative statement, were occupied between their holidays with the teaching of the young. With the most honourable and politest of intentions I ventured upon a 'Good evening' and accompanied this remark with a reference to the settled state of the weather. But my greeting was received with a disapproving pursing of lips, a non-committal sound, and a haughty glare, which meant, as well as any glare can, 'Who are you? I have never been introduced to you. I have no desire to know you. I don't like the look of you.' In a word I was put thoroughly, conclusively, and convincingly in my place, so much so that for a few frozen moments it needed little imagination to replace my immediate environment with a suburban drawing room complete with lace curtains, china cupboard, aspidistra, and goldfish in a bowl.

CHAPTER ELEVEN

The Innominata Ridge

OUR IMMEDIATE PLAN was to ascend to the Gamba Hut and climb Mont Blanc by either the Peuterey or the Innominata routes. Next morning, however, I felt far from well; I had contracted a chill, probably as a result of not changing my wet clothing on arrival at the Torino Hut and sleeping in damp underclothing, and fits of shivering alternated with a burning fever, the whole being accompanied by a bursting head. This, together with a swollen and painful ankle, scarcely seemed a happy preliminary for an ascent of Mont Blanc. However, acting on the same principle already applied to my ankle, I told Jim that we would go up to the hut, and that the mountain air, the panacea of all ills, would soon oust the germs.

Accordingly, after collecting some provisions, and assuring ourselves at the same time that further food was to be obtained at the hut from the resident hut keeper, we set off along a dusty road blaspheming the innumerable motors.

It was a relief to turn aside into the Val Veni, though even here we encountered many cars and had to keep a wary look out. Such activity seemed unusual even in holiday time, but we realised, when we came to the first restaurant in the valley, that we had inadvertently strayed down to Courmayeur on the Italian equivalent of a bank holiday. At all events, the scene that met our eyes was the nearest approach to Hampstead Heath that I have witnessed in the Alps: there was everything appropriate to such an occasion from orange peel and sandwich papers to accordions and performing monkeys. And upon this scene, between the pines, shone the snows of Mont Blanc. Here was one answer to those who ponder on the whys and wherefores of successful dictatorships, the gregarious instincts of man, and the mob that cannot divest itself of its mobbishness even in the presence of mountains and in the quiet sanctuaries of Nature.

This was not the only mob. There was another near the Hotel Purtud, a quieter and, to judge from the private motor cars, more exclusive mob. We lunched at the hotel and afterwards decided to spend the night there on account of my chill, which made me feel unequal to the ascent to the Gamba Hut. I fear this hiatus in our plan must have been irksome to Jim, but he generously made the suggestion in the first place, and expressed his enthusiasm for the spot. 'Why climb every day,' he said, 'when there are pleasant places like this?'

The Purtud Hotel is indeed a pleasant place. It stands amidst meadows and pine forest on the floor of the Val Veni beneath the precipices of the Aiguille Noire de Peuterey, where the Peuterey Ridge makes its first lift towards the distant summit of Mont Blanc. It narrowly escaped destruction from an enormous rock fall when the crest of the Col de Peuterey and a chunk of Mont Blanc de Courmayeur itself, fell down in 1920 on to the Brenva Glacier. So great was the weight and momentum of the avalanche that the torrent of rocks poured down the whole length of the glacier into the Val Veni, to the consternation of the populace of the district, who thought that Mont Blanc itself had fallen and that their last hour had come. Yet, by some miracle, no loss of life occurred and the rock blocks many of them the size of houses, were halted, almost on the threshold of the hotel.

The holidaymakers all left that evening and we dined in comparative peace. In an attempt to stifle my chill I swallowed a large quantity of Chianti, and followed up the wine with some quinine provided by the management. It was a pleasant and effective treatment, except for the quinine, and next morning, in spite of a feverish night, I was sufficiently recovered to ascend to the Gamba Hut.

It was a perfect morning when we set off. The dew-soaked pastures were laced with a filigree of shining cobwebs, and far above, light evanescent mists clung to the precipices of the Aiguille Noire, a happy augury of settled weather.

As we strolled up the valley we passed various military encampments, the tents being camouflaged and concealed in the pine forest in such a manner that it would be well nigh impossible to spot them from the air. The Col de la Seigne at the head of the valley is an easy grass pass, but the cost of forcing it in either direction, even if this proved strategically practicable would be prohibitive in men and munitions. Students of military history and tactics believe, not without reason, that in the event of war between France and Italy the former country would have a topographical advantage along the Alpine frontier, as the Lombard plain is more easily accessible from the watershed of the Alps than the lowlands of France. It is probable that this consideration, coupled of course with the question of Mediterranean Sea power, proved a decisive factor in favour of Italian neutrality at the outbreak of the present conflict.

Apart from these military eyesores the walk along the Val Veni was delightful. The path led us through a pine forest, then over a wooden bridge spanning a glacier torrent, where we were accosted by an officer who was inquisitive as to our destination.

Leaving aside militarism there is something wonderfully restful about this fertile valley beneath the precipices of Mont Blanc. Even though I were transported thither by some magic agency I believe that I should know instinctively that I was in the presence of mountains. What is this "presence" which the sensitive so easily perceive in the neighbourhood of high mountains? Is it due to some atmospheric resonance imposed almost imperceptibly on the ear, the product of stream and precipice? Is it sun-warmed turf and the scent of pines permeated by refreshing draughts from the snows? Or is it something subtler, and less readily explainable, something perceptible only to the innermost consciousness? Do the hills bring us into closer and more evident touch with spiritual forces? Why did Christ go up on to a hill to pray and meditate? Was it simply a desire for mental calm, or did His elevation bring Him into closer touch with inspirational forces? Many men have asked themselves these questions; the answer lies in their own inexpressible feelings.

After a rest in the shade of the pines we set off up the open mountainside with the fierce southern sun on our backs.

There is no deception about the path to the Gamba Hut; it means to go uphill and does so with continuous effectiveness. Some distance below the hut it mounts steep rocks. When I last came this way it was necessary to climb these rocks, but now steel cables make it possible for any reasonably active person to visit the hut. This is a pity, for the Gamba Hut is essentially a climbers' refuge, a starting point for difficult routes, and tourists, especially Italian tourists with their habit of sitting up late and love of clamorous nights, destroy the rest of those who start off for their climbs in the early hours of the morning, and are an unmitigated nuisance.

A band of some dozen or more tourists, male and female, were just leaving the hut when we arrived, and it was with considerable thankfulness that we witnessed their departure. They had, as was only to be expected, left a considerable mess behind them, and the temporary absence of the hut keeper, who had descended to the valley to procure fresh supplies of food, had led them into breaking into the locked kitchen and rifling the stores of food and wine.

Water is some distance from the hut, but by throwing snow from a nearby drift on to the sun-warmed roof we soon induced trickles and filled our saucepan preparatory to making tea. We were engaged in this when two parties of Germans, one numbering four climbers, and the other three, returned from a reconnaissance of the Peuterey and Innominata routes on Mont Blanc. They were all young fellows, and the leader of the latter party, who was a commander of Alpine troops, insisted on our sharing their food, and presented us with biscuits and Pumpernickel which he assured us his party did not require. It was a generous action and we were grateful. These Germans were all fit, active young men, and their leader was of that strikingly handsome type that Germany so freely produces; a lean, sun-bronzed fellow with a hawk-like countenance and piercing blue eyes. If these were representative samples of the German youth of today, then it is one of the greatest tragedies the World has seen that a political ideology, based on the Divine right of force and fatherland, should imbue such men with its vicious principles. In those young fellows, all ardent Nazis, yet patently wishful to be friends with us Englishmen, despite the poison assiduously pumped into them for years, we could sense something of the tragedy that was being enacted in Europe.

The rest of the afternoon we passed basking in the sun outside the hut, and when that beneficent orb, which we had come to regard almost as an institution, disappeared behind the Brouillard Ridge, a warm glow on the cliffs of the Aiguille Noire de Peuterey assured us of a continuance of fair weather.

Meanwhile the hut keeper arrived, a youth of some twenty years, who was accompanied by his mother, a little old lady with a pippin-like face and a pair of shrewd bright black eyes. Both carried tremendous loads, and we marvelled at the strength and activity of the woman, who had borne upwards of fifty pounds on her back from the valley.

Great was their consternation when they saw the forced lock of the kitchen door and the rifled pantry, and it was interesting to note that, although we were automatically dismissed as possible malefactors, the Germans came in for some sharp questioning and had to exculpate themselves. However, it was soon made clear that the tourists were the culprits for, to do them justice, they had left some money behind as payment for the food and wine they had consumed. It was plain, however, that this did not go far towards mollifying the indignant hut keeper and his mother, who could not reconcile themselves to the fact that the kitchen and living room sacred to themselves had been broken into, and loud and voluble did they wax on the iniquities of tourists.

We dined well that evening off spaghetti soup, fresh veal chops, and vegetables. Afterwards we shared a fiasco of Chianti with the Germans, who told us that they had come from Germany by car, and were returning after ascending Mont Blanc because they had no money left and prices in Italy, particularly of petrol, were high. They planned to bivouac on the morrow and complete the climb via the Innominata Route the following day.

Most of the parties who have climbed Mont Blanc by the Innominata route have bivouacked in the neighbourhood of the Pic Eccles, where the ridge separating the Frêney and Brouillard Glaciers abuts against the south face of Mont Blanc, but Jim and I were not enamoured of a bivouac; it is all very well to spend the night by a comfortable fire within the fuel line, but it is an altogether different matter to sit shivering at a height of 12,000 feet or more on Mont Blanc. We determined, therefore, to carry through the ascent in one day from the Gamba Hut. The hut is situated at a height of about 8,000 feet and Mont Blanc is 15,810 feet; therefore some 8,000 feet had to be climbed, a long ascent for a single day's work over difficult ground. We considered it essential to arrive on the Col du Frêney 12,000 feet, at dawn, and we decided to reconnoitre the route before attempting the climb.

The Germans recommended that instead of ascending the Brouillard Glacier to the Col du Frêney we should follow a route they had made during their reconnaissance. This was to ascend the Châtelet Glacier for a short distance, then cross the rock ridge between it and the Brouillard Glacier.

The weather was still perfect when we set off on our reconnaissance the next morning. Leisurely mounting the little Châtelet Glacier, which lies directly above the hut, we came to tracks in some snow where the Germans had descended from the ridge. Any liking we may have entertained for their route in the first place soon evaporated on the disagreeable slopes of shale and loose rocks, which we had to climb in order to reach the ridge, and an additional unpleasantness was falling stones to which the lowermost part of the route is exposed.

Apart from these disadvantages the climb to the ridge was easy enough, and the descent on the far side to the Brouillard Glacier proved only about fifty feet in height, the ridge being almost flush with the glacier on that side.

Once on the glacier we again followed the tracks of the Germans, but presently came to a point where they turned off to the right, and after mounting straight up, traversed horizontally the steep slopes above the glacier under the rocks of l'Innominata, the peak immediately to the south of the Col du Fresnay. There seemed no particular reason why a direct and easier route to the col should not be made through the séracs of the glacier, and I suggested to Jim that we should make one in preference to the Germans' route, which might be awkward to follow in the dark. Accordingly, we mounted the glacier, crossing numerous crevasses and threading our way between some formidable séracs.

The Brouillard and Frêney Glaciers bear witness to the steepness of the south side of Mont Blanc, and there are few alpine glaciers to equal them in angle. They are both tremendously broken up, the icefall of the Frêney Glacier in particular being notorious among mountaineers for its complexity. It would be difficult to picture a scene more savage than that where the Brouillard Glacier originates. The glacier begins its uneasy journey towards the pastures of the Val Veni from the foot of the final wall of Mont Blanc de Courmayeur, and is enclosed for the greater part of the way by the Innominata and Brouillard Ridges. In appearance it resembles a pavement of immensely thick marble blocks upheaved by earthquake, and on three sides, in sombre contrast with the dazzling disarray of shattered ice, huge precipices rise, a whispering gallery that echoes and re-echoes the cavernous thunder of falling ice as the unstable séracs lurch over to destruction. Here is Nature at her starkest and grandest. There is nothing gentle, except for the graceful snow-crest of the Col du Frêney and the summit snow of Mont Blanc de Courmayeur set in high and serene detachment above its pillared precipices of red protogine. All else is unbridled savagery; the loom of precipice, the slow downward jerking glacier with its constant outbursts of titanic energy, the clattering of stone-falls, the roar of avalanches, the grinding split of gravity-tortured ice. It was long after the major routes on Mont Blanc had been climbed before mountaineers set foot hereabouts. Not until 1919 was the southern wall of Mont Blanc, between Peuterey and Brouillard Ridges, climbed by Capt. S.L. Courtauld and Edmund G. Oliver, with their guides, Adolphe and Henri Rey of Courmayeur, and Adolf Aufdenblatten of Switzerland. They bivouacked on the Col du Frêney and next day reached the summit of Mont Blanc after a climb of eight hours. They were followed in 1921 by three famous Italian climbers, G.F. and G.B. Gugliermina and Francisco Ravelli, who made a slightly different route up the face. They bivouacked twice, the higher bivouac being on the precipice of Mont Blanc de Courmayeur, an exposed resting-place from which it would have been difficult or impossible to have retreated had the weather broken. Since 1921 the route has been followed by numerous parties, for the most part with guides.

In 1934 the climb was the scene of a tragedy. Two young British mountaineers, John Hoyland and Paul Wand of the Oxford University Mountaineering Club, attempted it. Hoyland, in particular, had shown great promise on the British crags, but he and his companion did not possess the requisite Alpine experience for an ascent of such magnitude. They were missing a month before they were found on the Frêney Glacier having fallen from the rocks immediately above the Col du Frêney. To me fell the task of organising the search party, when it was at length discovered that they had set off from the Gamba Hut. The leading guide was Adolphe Rey and his quick eye discovered the extreme point of an ice axe pick projecting from recently fallen snow. It was on ground so easy, it seemed impossible that a slip had occurred, but it had, and we followed the line of the fall down a couloir to the Frêney Glacier. I shall never forget the speed and energy with which Rey cut down and across a stone swept ice slope above a bergschrund at the foot of the couloir. We were only just in time to escape disaster. Rey went first down a deep groove of polished ice worn out by falling stones that intersected the uppermost lip of the bergschrund. He jumped out of the groove on to some avalanche snow that choked the bergschrund and I followed, not a second too soon, as next moment the groove was swept by a cataract of stones.

It only remains to be said that the dangerous task of conveying the bodies down the icefall of the Frêney Glacier was carried out by a number of Courmayeur guides, two of whom were slightly injured by falling ice and stones.

In order to reach the Col du Frêney we had to dodge between séracs and crevasses. The crevasses were abysmal and insecurely bridged with sun softened snow, but it was all plain sailing except for one awkward passage, where an insecurely bridged rift had to be crossed, and lodgement effected on its uppermost lip, and presently, after plugging up a snow slope, we stood on the col.

The ascent of 4,000 feet from the hut had taken only a little over three hours. Nothing was to be gained by continuing the climb, for the route towards the Pic Eccles was obvious, and we could scale the first two or three hundred feet of snow in the dark, if need be.

The day was windless and hot and we halted for a meal. It was an impressive situation, and savage precipices enclosed us except to the south where, beyond the sabre-like snow edge that sweeps up from the Col du Frêney to the rocks of l'Innominata, hazy blue hills and the violet depths of the Val Veni showed in pleasant contrast.

The descent was unexpectedly easy. We discarded the Germans' route to the Châtelet Glacier, and followed the Brouillard Glacier. There were fewer crevasses in this than anticipated, in spite of its steepness, and we enjoyed some exhilarating glissades. A final jog down screes and boulders brought us back to the Gamba Hut little over an hour after leaving the col, well satisfied with our reconnaissance, and thoroughly convinced that the Innominata Ridge could be climbed in one day from the hut and that a bivouac was unnecessary.

The Germans had all left before us that morning for their bivouacs, one party of three being bound for the Pic Eccles, and the other party of four for the Col de Peuterey, and except for a couple of Italians we had the hut to ourselves.

We spent the remainder of the day at our ease in the sun. Experience has taught me that to fill every day of a mountaineering holiday with strenuous climbing is a mistake. Climbing, interesting and thrilling though it may be, is best valued and enjoyed when measured against periods of rest and inactivity. A thing I have often noticed is that mountaineers who attach importance to an off day, not as a necessary rest but as something to be enjoyed for its own sake, like the mountains better than those who regard mountaineering primarily as a gymnastic exercise. Of course, if a man merely wishes to climb mountains and has no other interest in mountains there is nothing to be said, yet it is impossible not to feel that there are many who enjoy mountaineering who are never able to appreciate the beauty of mountains because of a notion that to get the most out of their holiday they must climb all the time. Let me declare at once that I am an essentially lazy mountaineer. As a rule when I get to the top of a peak I find that I have a great desire to rest there in the sun and admire the view. Spending every hour of every day in scaling mountains has a drugging effect on my mind, and I no longer enjoy the beauty and peacefulness of the hills. An off day comes as a pleasant oasis in a desert of physical effort. It is then that the beauty of mountains is best perceived. To extract the best from mountaineering it is necessary to strike a balance between the physical and mental powers. And the same principle applies to life in general. Is not the present state of the World proof that mankind is unbalanced in this respect? Material matters, and the mental efforts necessary to foster and maintain them, have led to a neglect of those spiritual considerations on which happiness and peacefulness so largely depend. The man who climbs mountains continuously and energetically usually has no time or inclination to appreciate beauty; he is concerned only with the physical interpretations of mountaineering. Similarly, to rush through life, to be occupied always with material affairs, is to miss a happiness and a well being that is man's spiritual birthright.

It was pleasant to spend the remainder of a sunny day on the turf of the alp where the hut stands. Dense clouds that had formed in the Val Veni nosed their way up the Brouillard and Frêney Glaciers, but they were harmless vapours and the sun declined in a clear sky. After life in a great city it is a queer experience to recline thus and watch clouds and mountains; there is something restful and soothing in the spectacle; the mind relapses into a half waking, half sleeping condition that has in it a quality seldom perceptible amid the rush and bustle of civilisation, a quality of oriental detachment and repose.

As the sun dropped towards the Brouillard Ridge the clouds ceased to grow out of the valleys. Nature became quiescent and breathless as though awaiting some revelation. The breeze died away; an opalescent light pervaded the atmosphere, subtly separating the ranges with its luminous breadths. There was no sound save for the constant percussion of glacier streams.

As the sun sank, radiating great arrows of light, and casting the shadows of every pinnacle and minaret on the Brouillard Ridge far across the dusky sky, the cold shadow tide swept upwards, yet long after it had passed I could feel warm fragrant breaths from the turf at my feet.

The Peuterey Ridge reddened and reddened until its details were merged into a single plane of light and colour: buttress, rib, and gully were no longer distinct; solidity was lost and the whole of Mont Blanc's greatest battlement was transformed into a glowing unsubstantial splendour hung like an auroral curtain in the deepening green of the evening sky.

Assured of good weather for the morrow we turned in early and slept an untroubled sleep, until shortly after midnight when the hut keeper and his mother roused us. Sleepy and glum we clambered down from the bunk. Meanwhile the hut keeper had taken a glance out of the door. 'Is it fine?' I asked him. 'No, Monsieur,' was the reply, 'there is mist.' This was bad news. Was the weather breaking? We went outside to look for ourselves. He had spoken the truth. Mist enwrapped the hut and the moonless night was pitch dark, only a few of the brighter stars being faintly discernible. Surely it was only a low mist? As long as the stars were not obscured by high cloud there was a prospect of fair weather. In any event there was no reason why we should not start. By the time we reached the Col du Frêney the weather should be showing its hand, and we could always retreat from there safely in the event of a storm.

The hut keeper's mother was particularly solicitous for our safety. 'You will turn back if the weather is bad?' she begged us. We promised her that we would and for my part it was a promise that I had every intention of keeping: I had been caught before by bad weather on the south side of Mont Blanc, on the Peuterey Ridge, and it was an experience I have no wish to repeat. Mont Blanc may spare once, but to expect generosity a second time is asking too much.

Bowls of steaming coffee, bread, butter, and jam put new life into us, and at a quarter-past one, we left our kindly hosts and trudged out into the night.

The mist was thick and we were thankful that we had gone to some pains the day before to memorise the route over the boulder-strewn slopes between the hut and the Brouillard Glacier. In addition, Jim had erected small cairns with pieces of paper in the top of them, and helped by our electric brooch lamps we lost no time in picking them out.

The night was ominously warm, but this was probably due to the blanketing mist and the latent heat of the rocks, which for the past fortnight had been absorbing the heat of the sun, for when we came to snow we found it hard frozen.

Our decision to mount by the Brouillard Glacier, instead of by the short cut advocated by the Germans, proved the right one, and with crampons on our feet we made rapid progress.

Normally there is little pleasure to be derived from an early start in the Alps, yet on that occasion we enjoyed the trudge through the darkness. We were bound for a great climb, and were hoping to carry through in one day what normally takes two days; thus an early start was essential. Then the way had been prepared to the Col du Frêney, and no route-finding or temper-provoking contretemps were to be expected up that point; we had merely to go steadily ahead up well-frozen snow wearing crampons; and, lastly, there was no need to hurry; we could go slowly and economise energy for the more serious work of the day, thus giving the inner man, who had been disturbed from his digestive processes at an unconscionably early hour, time to adapt himself to the proceedings.

In such circumstances there is a sense of adventure which neither time nor custom can stale. The mind occupies itself with the strangest imaginings and fantasies. There is nothing to see but the little pool of light cast by the lamp, the moving feet and legs of your companion, if he chances to be in front of you, and the dark forms of the mountains reaching up into the stars. Time, as a quantity measurable in terms of ordinary civilised existence, simply ceases to exist, and fancy places all manner of interpretations on the adventure: an essay perhaps in search of some sleeping dragon, the surprise of a citadel, the rescue of an imprisoned damsel or some such commendable and exciting project.

The mist, as we anticipated, did not reach far above the hut, and for the greater part of the way we climbed beneath an unclouded star-filled sky. Though we progressed easily and, as it seemed, slowly, three hours sufficed for the climb to the Col du Frêney.

Dawn was breaking as we reached the col, and in the half-light the scene appeared inexpressibly dreary, so much so that I found it impossible to rid my mind of the grim purpose for which I had visited the col five years before. I said so to Jim, and I think he felt the same about it as I did, for he said, 'Let's get on.'

We disconnected our brooch lamps, which had served us so well, and mounted the snow ridge above the col, our crampons driving into steep icy snow. All went well for a time, and moving both together we made height quickly. As we did so the light increased behind the sinister-looking mass of the Aiguille Blanche de Peuterey, which loomed opposite to us across the tangled ice of the Frêney Glacier, and soon the rocky mass of Mont Blanc de Courmayeur ahead of us was tipped with gold by the rising sun. It was some time before the sun reached us, because of the intervening Peuterey Ridge, but a sea of mist, which lay below extending southwards as far as the eye could see, was lit up in crest after crest and billow after billow. For much of the day this mist remained cloaking the valleys, and it added to our sense of height and the isolation on the flanks of Mont Blanc.

Yet we had little time or inclination then to admire the march of the sun over mist and mountain; we were too much taken up with the details of the climbing, and the necessity to combat time which, on a climb of this nature, wings its way swallow-like through the day.

107 *(above)* A winter view of the South Face of Mont Blanc showing the Innominata Ridge standing out clearly under snow with the oblique and low evening light. *Photo: Leo Dickinson*

Scenes on the Innominata Ridge: 108 *(left)* A tiny figure can be seen moving across to the Great Couloir. The escape couloir leading to the notch on the skyline can be seen. *Photo: Will Hurford*
109 *(above)* A wide-angle view of the face from the summit of Pic Eccles showing the Frêney Face (right) and the Brouillard Face (left). 110 *(below left)* Crossing Col Eccles.
111 *(right)* Julie-Ann Clymer leading the Grade 4 crack by the First Tower. *Photo: Roger Payne*

112, 113 Entering the escape couloir from the Great Couloir of the Innominata Route. On this South Face meltwater turns (at night) to icicles hanging from the upper headwall. These spears and falling rocks, loosened by the morning sun, strafe the couloir creating a hazardous passage for all but the earliest climbers. The escape couloir *(inset)* veers away from the fall line. *Photos: Roger Payne*

114 *(right)* Moving up to the Twisting Rib on the Sentinelle Rouge Route. The Red Sentinel itself stands out below with the (Brenva) Great Couloir to its right. *Photo: John Allen*

115 *(above)* A view from above the Red Sentinel Buttress across the subsidiary couloir to. the Twisting Rib. The Great Couloir and the buttresses of Route Major are further left.
116 *(below)* Looking down the ice ridges of Route Major to Col Moore. *Photos: John Allen*
117 *(right)* The final buttress and ice cliffs of Route Major seen from the Twisting Rib on the Sentinelle Rouge Route (refer to photo 31 for the line of the route). *Photo: Wil Hurford*

118 Moving up the Route Major's ice ridges towards the final buttresses. *Photo: John Allen*

The ridge above the Col du Frêney presently merged into a steep snow slope which ended in its turn against the rocks of the Pic Eccles. Our guidebook described the route as going to the west in the direction of the Brouillard Glacier, then up the rocks to the summit of the Pic Eccles. We accordingly made diagonally upwards in that direction. There was no sign of any track made by the Germans *en route* to their bivouac, but we continued hopefully to a corner, only to find ourselves on the edge of a sheer cliff falling to the glacier. At the same time the rocks immediately above us appeared unpromising, and it seemed unlikely that the route lay up them.

After a discussion we agreed that we must retrace our steps for a short distance. This we did, and after losing about a hundred feet of height turned upwards on to steep broken rocks. The climbing was not difficult, but it was sufficiently strenuous to make us realise that we were likely to encounter difficulties before reaching the summit of the Pic Eccles. These forebodings were fulfilled. We gained the south-west edge of the peak and continued over increasingly difficult rocks, until we came to a point less than one hundred feet from the summit, where further progress was barred by a wall of steep rock. It now appeared that had we gone to the right instead of to the left in the first place we would have encountered little difficulty; thus by following the directions of the guidebook we had involved ourselves in much unnecessary trouble.[1]

It was a sensational place where we stood. Immediately above us the rocks swept up in a vertical wall. To the left the cliff fell sheer to the Brouillard Glacier, and to the right slabs slanted steeply towards the Frêney Glacier. The only way of avoiding the impasse appeared to lie in a flanking movement to the right, which meant a descent towards the Frêney Glacier, and an ascent to a point above the wall, and I suggested to Jim that he should hold me on the rope while I investigated the route. He did so, and I climbed down a shallow groove for about fifty feet, traversed horizontally out of it, turned an awkward corner, and climbed slabs of moderate difficulty, until I found myself directly above him. As he was now well held I called down to him that to save time he should climb the wall with the assistance of the rope. This he did. It was exceptionally strenuous climbing, but he accomplished it so skilfully that I gave him nothing more than a tight rope on the most difficult section of all, where he had to climb an overhanging crack by means of a "lay-back" which, being interpreted, means that the weight of the body comes wholly on the hands and arms.

A few feet more of easy going and we stood on the summit of the Pic Eccles. The Germans had bivouacked on a small platform there and almost immediately we saw them. To our surprise they were only a short distance away on the far side of the Col Eccles which separates the Pic Eccles from the cliffs of Mont Blanc de Courmayeur: they must have left their bivouac not above half an hour before, probably on account of a cold night, and the necessity to warm themselves in the sun before undertaking difficult climbing, and we felt more than ever thankful that we had enjoyed a comfortable sleep in the Gamba Hut in lieu of a chilly and

[1] Capt. G.I. Finch has since informed me that his party avoided the Pic Eccles by traversing to the left a short distance from the Col du Frêney on to the Brouillard Glacier. It seems probable, therefore, that we, not the guidebook, were wrong, and that we made the mistake of attempting to traverse to the Brouillard Glacier too high above the Col du Frêney.

uncomfortable bivouac. The sight of them made us feel generously disposed towards everyone and everything, and we decided to halt and have our second breakfast, as there seemed little likelihood of finding an equally comfortable resting-place on the great face ahead.

The time was now 7.30; the sun was well up above the Peuterey Ridge and scarcely a breath of wind disturbed a serene and perfect morning. The other party of Germans bound for the Peuterey Ridge had bivouacked on the Col de Peuterey; they were still in cold shadow and were only just setting off for their climb. We could see their bivouac place, a scooped out hole in the snow, protected from the wind by a circular wall of snow blocks. They must have had a wretched night.

So warm was the sun and so excellent the delicacies in our rucksacks that the next hour passed like magic. It was with regret that we tore our gaze away from the glorious panorama of cloud and mountain, and it was a shock to find that the minute hands of our watches had spun through a whole circle. I recollect a feeling of resignation, coupled with a distinct tiredness and disinclination to continue, as we swung our heavy rucksacks on to our backs and set off for the serious work of the day.

The snow ridge linking the Pic Eccles and the rocks of Mont Blanc de Courmayeur is an airy affair, a blade so sharp and narrow that we did not hesitate to employ an equestrian mode of advance.

We were now on the rocks of Mont Blanc de Courmayeur. The ridge from the Col Eccles continues up these for some distance, more as an edge than a ridge, then loses itself in the immense red cliffs that dominate the upper part of the mountain.

Above the col there was no great difficulty for the first hundred feet. Then the rocks steepened and we presently came to the foot of the greatest single difficulty of the climb. This is where the ridge abruptly rises in a step some sixty feet in height. The only way of scaling the obstacle is to climb a more or less vertical crack. The difficulty of the crack had already been made evident by the time the Germans had taken to climb it, and it was no surprise to us when we were confronted by a rift of unusually repulsive appearance.

For my part, I was thankful that my companion was in good form, for I had little inclination for gymnastics that day. He climbed in brilliant manner, without hesitation, without delay, and as actively as a cat. As I watched the patch in the seat of his breeches growing rapidly smaller and finally vanishing from sight I wished devoutly that I felt in better form for such work.

It was as I suspected. When a cheerful shout came down inviting me to follow, my strength was entirely unequal to the task, my ankle rebelled at the strain imposed on it by anything in the nature of a wedging action, and my heart, which normally jogs along at a leisurely forty to fifty beats a minute, felt as though it were trying to burst from my chest. Altogether I was very glad of something better than the conventional tight rope above me, thankful indeed for some lusty pulls.

Winded and weak I at length arrived at the top of the crack, which in point of fact is more strenuous than difficult. My form was so poor that when I had at length recovered we discussed the situation. Jim was rightly doubtful as to whether I ought to continue and suggested an immediate retreat. I would have agreed with him had we been faced with continuously difficult rock climbing, but from what

I had read about the climb the crack we had just scaled was the most strenuous portion of the route. Therefore, I told him that I was prepared to continue. The strange thing is that, although I continued to feel weak for the next hour, I later improved to such an extent that I felt stronger, as we neared the summit of Mt. Blanc, than I did at the commencement of the climb, and was going as well as Jim.

Above the crack we bore slightly to the left. Some easy climbing for a few minutes brought us to another vertical rise in the ridge. This was not so difficult to surmount as the crack, as there was a sufficiency of holds, but it was strenuous going, and again I was glad that the rope was above and not below me.

We now came to a shoulder topped by a roughly horizontal snow edge. The situation of the climber here is amazing and we paused to take photographs. We looked along the gleaming snow then down into an abyss filled with glowing clouds from which rose the gleaming summits of the Grivola and Paradiso. To the left loomed the Aiguille Blanche de Peuterey, its immaculate snow summit linked to a secondary rock tower by a curving ice edge. It is through such glimpses, caught and registered by eye and brain in the heat and stress of a great climb, that the mountains best communicate their beauty and majesty to the climber. Memory in mountaineering is a capricious thing. Stupendous panoramas pass unheeded and unremembered, yet little glimpses of comparatively insignificant detail are caught and registered: the small window in the fleeing mist with its momentary view of shining snow; the dewy petals of an upland flower; the morning sun on a granite slab; a stream glinting out of smoke-blue depths. Smell also is a potent factor in assisting memory. What mountaineer is there who does not recollect some subtle odour? The curious, undefinable smell of a quickly forming mist; the warm breath of distant pastures and pine woods coming unexpectedly out of the ice-cold depths; the smell of moist turf and flowers on the edge of the moraine; the sulphurous cannonade of falling rocks. And in sounds: the hollow croak of a raven echoing across the cliff; the whisper of an unexpected wind, the sudden reverberation of avalanche or thunder; the hiss of skidding ice fragments; the harsh clattering of falling stones; the intimate talk of a stream; some tone or inflexion in the voice of a companion. These, and many other things besides, may be caught and stored for no apparent reason in the memory.

The shoulder we had reached juts from the precipices of Mont Blanc de Courmayeur. No argument is possible with these plaques of red protogine. Smooth and sheer they lift into the blue, and not even the warm southern sun can soften their austerity. The climber can no longer advance; he must go right or left; he can only go left. The rocks he must pass over at the foot of the precipice are in strange contrast to the firm protogine above; they were loose and shaley and unpleasant to tread, and demanded especial care and watchfulness because of the wet snow that partially concealed them.

The traverse brought us to a corner beyond which a huge couloir fully fifty yards in width cuts into the mountainside, a natural rubbish shoot which empties the stones from a wide range of cliffs over precipices on to the Brouillard Glacier. Courtauld and Oliver when they discovered the Innominata route in 1919 crossed the couloir and mounted by the rocks of the west side, but the Gugliermina brothers in 1921 preferred the rocks of the east side until the cliffs of Mont Blanc de Courmayeur forced them to cross the head of the couloir.

As we approached the corner we heard the clatter of falling stones and an instant later a volley of missiles flew past, hitting the rocks and flying far out into space with a vicious whirring. At the same moment we heard voices and realised that we were closing up with the Germans. They had decided to follow the Gugliermina route, and there was nothing for it but to wait until they ceased to dislodge stones, which was worse than annoying as all our mountaineering instincts urged us to climb as quickly as possible. As we waited we noted that stones, other than those detached by the Germans, were continually falling down the bed of the couloir, some in, and others outside, a deep groove that had obviously been worn in the ice by their predecessors.

Several minutes passed: presently stones ceased to hum and whizz past the corner and we ventured out of cover. Popping our heads round a rock we saw the Germans. They were engrossed in climbing the steep slabs at the side of the couloir. We realised at once that crossing the latter was the crux of the climb. It was a difficult and dangerous traverse, difficult because of its great steepness, and dangerous because of its exposure to falling material. And this material consisted not only of stones, but of ice. The night had been cold and huge icicles, yards in length and as thick as a man's thigh, had formed on the precipices overlooking the couloir. Now under the influence of the sun they were being detached from the rocks and were falling like huge javelins sufficient in size and weight to constitute a real danger.

Our first care was to climb to a safer position, and we shouted up to the Germans a warning not to dislodge stones. They obeyed, and a few minutes later we were in comparative safety. Then we paused to watch the Germans.

They were as anxious as we to cross the couloir with the minimum of delay. At first sight it seemed that the best way of doing so was to make for some rocks about midway across, climb these, and complete the traverse where the couloir was narrower.

The leader of the German party was of the same opinion, and began to cut steps in the bed of the couloir. He did not get very far. Stone after stone was racing down the rift; they fell every few seconds and, apart from those that careered down the groove, there were others that swept the rocks he was making for. Furthermore, the couloir was wide at this point and its bed consisted of a thin layer of slushy snow resting on ice. The dangers were great, so great that to brave them was unjustifiable. The Germans soon realised this: the leader cut a dozen or so steps, then he halted, and after exchanging shouts with his companions retreated to the comparative safety of the slabs.

Both parties ought to have reached this section of the climb earlier. There was no excuse for delay in the case of the Germans; they had bivouacked and should have been hours ahead of us, yet they had left their bivouac too late and had climbed too slowly. Possibly, part of their trouble was that, like most German climbers, they were burdened with unnecessarily heavy rucksacks. They would have done better to have gone either lightly laden with little in the way of bivouac equipment, and carried through the climb with the utmost possible speed, or have taken elaborate equipment and bivouacked again. The Gugliermina brothers were exponents of the latter technique and bivouacked twice on the climb. Jim and I, however, prefer to travel light and fast, for apart from its rigours and discomforts, a bivouac in the High Alps asks a great deal of the weather.

The leader of the Germans now decided that the only course open to him was to continue on up the slabs and cross the couloir at its head where it was comparatively narrow, even though the traverse involved risk from the icicles pendant on the cliffs above.

There was nothing we could do but wait until the Germans had climbed the slabs and crossed the couloir: we had already lost well over an hour, and with the danger of falling stones and ice increasing every minute as the sun poured its heat on to the face, the delay was exasperating in the extreme.

Presently the slow-moving Germans reached the point where it was necessary to cross the couloir and we were able to advance. It is possible that the enforced rest had enabled me to recuperate my strength; at all events I was now as anxious as Jim for action and went ahead up the slabs.

As far as possible I followed the edge of the ice, keeping a sharp lookout for stones and falling icicles. Both were now raining from the cliffs into the couloir, and the prospect of having to cross the danger zone was not one to evoke enthusiasm.

There was one awkward bit where a projecting rock tongue forced us into climbing the slabs. Crampons are dangerous in such circumstances, for the reason that it is difficult to determine whether or not the foot is likely to slip: the closer the foot is to rocks the greater is the security.

As we approached the Germans they began to cross the couloir. The ice at that point was softer than it was lower down, and the leader cut steps quickly across to the rocks at the far side. He was followed by his two companions, who lost no time in crossing the danger zone. Soon they were all across, and we prepared to follow their example. At that time we were halted on the slabs, I being some fifty feet above Jim. There was little or no security owing to the absence of hitches for the rope, and we had had abundant evidence as to the continuous steepness and exposed nature of the climb. I was on poor holds and was preparing to take in the rope while Jim advanced when of a sudden there was a shout of "Vorsicht!" from the Germans and the swish of falling ice. Instinctively I ducked in my head. Next moment the mass of javelin-like icicles hit the rocks just above me, burst into fragments and swept past me. The larger fragments missed me but a few of the smaller rapped me sharply about the body. It was a nasty moment and a further hint, if any were needed, that the sooner we were out of harm's way the better.

Jim soon reached me and a minute or two later we were at the edge of the couloir, ready to cross in the steps cut by the Germans. The distance was not great, and our eighty-foot rope sufficed to cover it; thus there was no need for us both to be on the ice at the same time, and some measure of security was possible. The most dangerous section of the traverse was near the far end. There the steps crossed the mouth of a ferocious chimney cutting deeply into the cliff above which was choked with ice and formed a natural chute for stones which fell every few seconds into the main gully.

The non-mountaineering reader will suppose that crossing an ice- and stone-swept couloir is a nerve-racking business, but the fact is that dangers encountered on a mountain usually induce a curious fatalism far divorced from any sensation of physical fear. It is much more nerve-racking watching a companion cross a danger zone than to do so oneself. It is, however, quite another matter deliberately to follow a route where the dangers outstep a reasonable margin of safety. The man who climbs the Grépon runs the gauntlet of falling ice from a hanging glacier for a hundred yards but experience has established this risk as a fair risk. On the other hand, the man who essays to climb the Eigerwand exposes himself to an unfair risk and lays himself open to a charge of recklessness. It is in undertaking unjustifiable climbs that fear is most likely to occur. I have never been so frightened in my life as when climbing the ice wall on Kangchenjunga, for I knew I was doing something that was unjustifiable and that outraged not only the traditions of mountaineering but Nature herself. It is difficult to explain what I intend by this last statement, but mountaineers will understand my meaning. There is in mountaineering some point at which Nature passes out of sympathy with the climber and becomes directly and uncompromisingly hostile to him. When a man feels this, and to the sensitive man it is very evident, it is time to look out or to turn back; a frontier has been crossed, a territory violated, and the penalty is likely to be heavy.

The crossing was soon made, and having safely established myself on the rocks, I called upon Jim to follow. He did so, while I kept watch on the beetling cliffs above and in particular the threatening ice-charged chimney. Nothing fell, and a minute or so later we were reunited, feeling that the worst was behind us.

We found ourselves at the base of an ill-defined buttress, bounded on one side by the ice-filled chimney, and on the other by a wider and less formidable rift. The latter appeared climbable if need be, but its loose rocks contrasted unfavourably with the firmer rocks of the buttress.

After the slabs and ice of the couloir it was good to feel firm rough rocks, with a sufficiency of holds and belays to hand, and we mounted quickly in the wake of the Germans. The climbing as before was continuously steep; indeed when we later reviewed the climb we agreed that our predominant impression was the exacting steepness of the face and the absence of ledges and resting places; there was not one place where it was possible to halt in comfort between the point where the traverse into the couloir begins and the summit ridge of Mont Blanc de Courmayeur.

It was not long before we again overtook the Germans. They preferred to make to the left into the couloir already mentioned, while we continued up the rocks to the side, only traversing into the rift a few yards from the point where it ended. Owing to some loose rocks we waited until the Germans had climbed out of the couloir. Then we carefully crawled over some precariously poised blocks to the head of the latter. We came to a curious snow mass and squeezing round it found ourselves on the crest of a shallow col separating a projecting buttress from the main mountainside. Above were slopes of rock and snow sweeping up to the crest of the Brouillard Ridge, which leads without difficulty to the summit of Mont Blanc de Courmayeur. Route finding was virtually at an end, hard work alone separated us from the summit of Mont Blanc.

The Germans had halted on the col. There was no room for us, but as we passed they good naturedly offered us some candied fruit, which we accepted gratefully as our mouths were unpleasantly parched.

A little higher we halted on some rocks. It was 2 p.m. Five and a half hours had elapsed since we left the Pic Eccles of which time an hour at least had been lost by the delays already narrated. However, there was plenty of time in hand; we anticipated no further great difficulties, and promised ourselves a comfortable night at the Grands Mulets; or, with luck, at Chamonix.

The ocean of mist, over which we had gazed at dawn, had risen, breaking up as it did so. Its steamy folds enwrapped us for a few minutes, then drew aside, disclosing a glimpse of toy-like woods and pasturelands at an immense distance beneath. There was no wind, no movement, no sound; Mont Blanc was sunk in profound sleep this serene and peaceful afternoon.

We roused ourselves from our lethargy and turned once more to the work in hand. We were on a slope of perhaps forty-five degrees in angle. In its lowermost portion, immediately above the precipices we had just scaled, were incipient rocky ribs, higher, these merged into unbroken snow, which swept up uninterruptedly for some hundreds of feet to the crest of the Brouillard Ridge.

Much depended on the state of the snow. All day the hot southern sun had blazed on it. We might have guessed it would be bad snow, and it proved to be in the worst possible condition, sodden through and through and in texture resembling a conglomeration of wet hailstones. Worst of all, it rested on ice, and was ready to avalanche. The one thing in our favour was that it was so waterlogged that it tended to slide in streams rather than *en bloc*, though these streams, as is usual in the case of wet snow, widened as they descended gathering mass and momentum as they did so.

The slope was a perfect crampon trap. This is not to say that it was easier to climb without crampons, in point of fact crampons were an advantage, but that something more than ordinary care had to be exercised with crampons. The snow resting on the ice varied in depth from a few inches to about two feet. Where it was thin, step cutting was obviously necessary, but where it was thicker it was not so obviously necessary. Yet the temptation to trust to the snow to hold the foot had to be rigorously resisted; the snow had to be cleared away and steps cut into the underlying ice. It is true that there were sections of the slope where the snow was deep enough and firm enough to mount without the need to cut steps, but for the greater part of the way step cutting was essential.

The non-mountaineering reader may exclaim impatiently, 'Why all this fuss? If there is any doubt why not cut steps all the way?' He must try to picture to himself the circumstances attendant on the problem. A long bout of step cutting, when it comes after many hours' hard work and thousands of feet of exacting mountaineering demands determination as well as physical strength. Furthermore, time is of vital consequence. It is so easy to take a chance on a mountain; nine times out of ten the chance will come off, but the tenth time it will not. Most mountaineering accidents, and almost all crampon accidents, are due to the tenth chance. They are the result of trying to save time and energy, or simply because of impatience, the kind of impatience that is bred in an age of speed and impatience. Above all things, it is necessary to approach mountaineering patiently: never hurry for the sake of hurrying, never subordinate the mind to the fatigues of the body; practice always a detachment of mind in which chances, difficulties, and dangers are weighed as dispassionately as the scientist weighs chemicals on a knife-edge balance.

We shared in the work and hard work it proved. In some places the ice was soft and waterlogged, which meant that a larger step than usual had to be made; in other places, it was of that tough, tenacious quality often found on slopes at a great altitude, which face south and are exposed to extremes of temperature. We cut straight up the slope, as this was safer than zigzagging or traversing in the avalanchy conditions. The slushy snow had to be cleared away before step cutting was possible and streams of it went swishing down the slope on to our German friends, who stoically endured the bombardment.

It was weary work. When we were resting on the rocks the slope had seemed short and easy; half an hour's work would land us on the ridge; but it seemed to become longer and longer as we flogged and hacked our way up it. Meanwhile the sun beat down upon our backs with an intensity that deprived us of much of our energy, and I well remember how the salty sweat stung my eyes when my turn came to cut steps.

About half-way up we bore slightly to the right on to an ill-defined snowy rib. This was better; the air here seemed cooler and less stagnant. Up and up we cut with a constant serpent-like hissing of down-rushing snow in our ears. We should have felt some excitement as we neared the long desired ridge, but I remember only a profound relief; that slope was too long and too exacting to foster either interest or excitement; it simply represented a job of gruelling work that had to be done.

Jim was in the lead as we approached the ridge. He was full of beans, swinging his axe with a ceaseless and untiring energy as skilfully as any guide. Hack, hack, swish, swish, the last step was made. He plunged his ice axe deep into the snow of the ridge. We were there.

Only an easy edge of rocks and snow separated us from the summit of Mont Blanc de Courmayeur.

We moved a few yards along the ridge, then paused to photograph the Germans as they mounted the rib. I believe that they were as thankful for our steps as we had been for theirs across the couloir. As we watched them it was brought home to us how steep was the slope; they were emerging from an abyss thousands of feet deep, and the first objects visible beyond them were the moraines of the Miage Glacier, 9,000 feet lower.

We were in need of some more food, so we scrambled along the rocky crest of the ridge till we came to a ledge wide enough to sit upon in moderate comfort. There we halted for half an hour until a chill little wind drove us on again. The Germans meanwhile passed us, but we overtook them a little later on Mont Blanc de Courmayeur.

We enjoyed the climb to Mont Blanc. After the blazing sun and motionless air of the south face, the atmosphere on the summit snows seemed charged with vigour; indeed, so cold was the breeze that we were not again encouraged to halt.

As we neared the summit of Mont Blanc de Courmayeur we saw the tracks of the party which had climbed the Peuterey Ridge. They had completed their climb several hours earlier, which seems to point to the fact that of the two routes the Innominata is the harder.

At 6.30 p.m. we stood on the summit of Mont Blanc. The last tourist caravan had long since descended, and the declining sun cast long shadows across the wind-rippled snow. A thin cold breeze was blowing; a shrivelling little blast that did not invite more than a few moments' halt.

As an end to a great climb the summit of Mont Blanc is ideal. No difficult ground separates the climber from the Vallot hut and Chamonix, yet the highest mountain of the Alps is a worthy climax to one or other of the great climbs up its southern flanks. For all the hordes that tread it on a summer's day, for all the sandwich paper and orange peel that desecrate its summit snows, there is an aloofness, a remoteness, and a serenity about the great mountain unequalled by any other Alpine peak. Mont Blanc is the King of Mountains, and, like a king, rises above small vulgarities.

I remember shuddering in the bitter cold while Jim manipulated his camera; I remember the golden sunlight, and a multitude of glowing clouds, dusky valleys and snowy mountaintops. I remember a feeling of unreality; we did not tread mere snow, nor a high point of the earth; we seemed uplifted in space. Here were no intricate mechanisms, none of those material things with which men surround themselves; here was nothing false or shoddy, nothing mean or ugly, nothing complex or difficult to understand. Here was no strife, no pettiness, no malice, and no uncharitableness. Here was beauty, and a superlative simplicity, a dome of glowing snow immobile in the firmament. Here dwelt the Spirit of Peace and the serenity of God.

Leisurely we made our way down the well-trodden ordinary route, past the Rocher de la Tournette and the Bosses du Dromadaire. The snow was molten, the western sky aflame with gorgeous lights, the depths on either hand profound wells of deepest purple; overhead the first stars shone like a dust of pearls; and all about this celestial path was the frigid silence of an alpine evening.

It was a wretched anti-climax to arrive at the Vallot Hut and find it virtually full of climbers. We were compelled to spend the night in the new structure where everything is metal except the blankets and pillows. This hut has double walls which are supposed to promote warmth but we found it icily cold, a night spent in a refrigerator at the North Pole could not have been less comfortable. The hut is entered through a trap door designed to keep out driven snow and this gives the inmate a feeling of imprisonment. The windows are of opaque glass and it is thus impossible to see any view or observe the weather. It is depressing as well as uncomfortable to sit on metal chairs, food eaten off a metal table is strangely unappetising, and there is something cold and unsympathetic about a metal floor. In general, confinement to this hut suggests incarceration in a submarine, but without the latter's saving grace of warmth and creature comforts.

Fortunately sufficient blankets were available and we slept moderately well, but breakfast next morning and a struggle with frozen boots was a wretched experience.

In fairness to the designers it must be stated that the hut had not then been fully completed, but when it is, it is difficult to see how it will ever be anything but depressing. Wood is a friendly, homely substance and metal is the reverse; nothing can alter this psychological fact.

The sun was shining brightly when we emerged from our steel box and set off down to Chamonix, yet there were signs that the weather was at last deteriorating and heavy, pillar-like cumulus clouds, with backings of lurid false cirrus were gathering in the west and north.

When we were presented with our bill at the old hut we found that we had not enough money to pay for our extravagances in the matter of tea the previous evening. However, among the parties which had arrived from the Grands Mulets, was an English lady who kindly loaned us one hundred francs.

Mont Blanc is pleasanter to descend than ascend by the ordinary route and its long snow slopes are delightful to stroll down in the morning when the snow is hard frozen and the sun not too glaring and hot. Even the ordinary route is not entirely free from objective danger, and on the Grand Plateau we came on the debris of an ice avalanche covering the track for fully one hundred yards, which had fallen from the séracs of the Dôme du Goûter. There is no need for the route to keep close to the Dôme du Goûter, but the Chamonix guides are nothing if not conservative, and prefer the remote risk of an avalanche to making a divergence, which would avoid the principal danger zone, at the expense of a few extra minutes of walking.

It was a charming descent. Before us were the smoke-blue depths of the Chamonix valley, and hills deeply shadowed with growing thunderclouds. We met with various ascending parties, among them a solitary climber who seemed already tired. We passed the Grands Mulets and thought of the pioneers who had slept there before embarking upon the great adventure of climbing Mont Blanc with their cohorts of peasants, their enormous quantities of meat and drink, and their perpetual fear of mountain sickness. To them it must have seemed a far greater adventure to tramp up the glacier to the summit, than it does for the climber of today to scale the southern precipices of the mountain. Is modern life tending to make men blasé in the search for adventure? What will happen when every square mile has been explored and mapped, when every Andean and Himalayan summit has been trodden and the World, in terms of speedy travel, reduced to the dimensions of an English county? Will man's adventurous instinct and his virility find sufficient scope and variety of experience in following where others have trodden or will he seek new worlds to conquer in interplanetary space?

There is little more to relate. We trudged down the Bossons Glacier, zigzagged through the glittering séracs, hurried beneath the stone-swept cliffs of the Aiguille de Midi, drank beer at the Pierre Pointue and descended lazily into the Chamonix valley by the *téléférique*.

We lunched late at Chamonix, and as we did so the clouds thickened and thickened on Mont Blanc. Thunder began to growl. The weather was breaking. We had a day or two of our holiday left, but why wait? It would be a sorry anti-climax to struggle up some peak in the teeth of bad weather. Might it not efface the memories of the past glorious fortnight? It would have been inartistic, a careless daub smeared on a picture of limpid beauty. That evening in sullen ominous weather we set off for England. Our mountaineering holiday had ended. A few days later Europe was at war.

APPENDICES

APPENDIX I

Smythe's Mountaineering Articles

Three mountaineering episodes not described in the main mountaineering books

RETREAT FROM MONT MAUDIT

From *My Alpine Album* (1947). This describes the attempt to make the first ascent of the South Face of Mont Maudit c.August 1, 1929. The first ascent followed a few days later when the face was climbed by the Italians Lino Binel, Renato Chabod and Amilcare Cretier.

Mont Blanc [and its outliers] makes its own weather, and more than anything else I associate it with storms. One of my most unpleasant experiences occurred during an attempt on the then unclimbed South Face of Mont Maudit. This was made with two companions Messrs. A. Harrison and C.W. Parry. The weather was perfect when we left the Torino Hut, and we crossed the ridge of the Tour Ronde to gain uppermost basin of the Brenva Glacier confident that it would remain settled. The Mont Maudit's great face proved steep and difficult, but we made good progress to a bivouac place we had previously noted. It was not the ideal bivouac, as it was necessary to excavate a platform in a slope of ice and huddle together on it as best we could. At sunset everything seemed propitious, but when the stars appeared we noted that they were not as steady as they should have been. This indication, slight though it was, of the weather's bad intentions, caused us to keep a particularly careful eye on the sky. Our forebodings were fulfilled. At about midnight it began to snow and continued to snow with increasing heaviness throughout the night. By dawn the best part of a foot had come down, and more was being added to the already vast accumulations on the mountain.

There was no question of continuing the climb; the immediate and urgent problem was whether we could retreat safely. On the way back we had to cross a wide gully of great steepness. In the middle of this falling stones had worn out a groove in the ice some six or eight feet deep. To the natural difficulty of the place was now added danger. Every few seconds avalanches of snow came rushing down the groove, soft loose snow that poured down like water. These avalanches sometimes continued for minutes at a time, and the intervals between them were perilously short. However, the gully had to be crossed, and it was decided that Harrison should go first. All went well until he was in the centre of the groove. He was cutting steps when with a swishing hiss a stream of snow descended the groove There was no time to avoid it, and all he could do was to drive the pick of his ice axe into the ice and brace himself in his steps as best he could. Next instant he almost disappeared beneath the rushing snow and Parry and I momentarily expected to see him swept away. If he had been, we could have held him on the rope, but for Harrison the position would have been similar to that of a trout hooked and suspended in a waterfall, and there was a strong possibility that he might have been suffocated or crushed to death by the strain on the rope.

The avalanche must have lasted a minute or more, but at length it tailed away. Harrison was still there. By an extraordinary feat of strength and endurance he had managed to resist the torrent of snow. But he was too exhausted to continue cutting steps, and had to retreat to where Parry and I were standing.

The position was getting more serious every instant. The gully must be crossed; there was no alternative route. Accordingly, we decided to wait until another avalanche had fallen; then, immediately it had ended I was to go ahead and complete the step-cutting. Very soon another slide came hissing down. It ceased presently and I hastily descended into the groove and racing across the steps already cut by Harrison, proceeded to hack out the remainder with the utmost speed and energy I could muster. The work was finished not a moment too soon. The last step had been cut and I was halted panting on the bank of the groove when an avalanche far larger than any we had yet seen came rushing down completely filling the groove.

After this it took only a few seconds for my companions to join me. But danger was not at an end. The great quantities of snow that had fallen, and were still falling, were resulting in avalanches of increasing power and size. It was vital to reach the Brenva Glacier without delay. Fortunately, we had with us an ice piton, and when we came to a long ice slope above the bergschrund we attached a rope to this and descended quickly without cutting steps.

A jump over the bergschrund and with profound thankfulness we trod the Brenva Glacier. We were not a minute too soon. We had just turned our backs on the snow-wreathed mountainside when there came a thunderous roar and a great avalanche poured down the cliffs and flung itself athwart the route we had descended. Had we delayed a few minutes we must have been destroyed.

In the heavy snowstorm it was impossible to retrace our steps over the Tour Ronde to the Col du Géant, and we were forced to descend the Brenva Glacier to Courmayeur. In snow and mist the way was not easy to find, but at length we emerged from the bad weather. But Mont Blanc had another unpleasant surprise in store for us. We were descending the easy Brenva Glacier unroped when Parry incautiously walked across a. load of boulders perched on the crest of an ice slope. Instantly the boulders collapsed beneath him and carried him with them down the slope. It was a terrible spectacle; he was engulfed by a swarm of rolling sliding boulders, and it seemed certain that he must be crushed to death. Harrison and I raced down and found him lying semiconscious, apparently badly injured. We carried him to a place of safety and there it was decided that I, who knew the route, should descend to Courmayeur for help while Harrison remained.

I shall not easily forget my dash down some 4,000 feet of steep glacier. I missed the way, and became involved in awkward climbing on glaciated slabs, to negotiate which I had to remove my boots and climb in stockinged feet. But I got down at last, and feeling pretty done, reached the little restaurant near the end of the glacier. Everyone there was kind and helpful; a boy was dispatched to Courmayeur on a bicycle whilst I sat down to a badly needed meal. I had barely finished when the search party arrived complete with a doctor, an amazingly smart piece of work. I accompanied them back up the glacier, and a weary climb that 4,000 feet seemed after the events of the day and past night. Parry had partially recovered, but was unable to walk, and had to be carried to Courmayeur which was reached the same day. He was not seriously injured, and had had a remarkable escape.

This was not the only occasion on which I have been associated with a search party on the south side of Mont Blanc, and no words of mine can do justice to the work of the Courmayeur guides who are always ready to go out at any time and in any season to rescue stricken climbers.

The foregoing narrates only a few isolated incidents. It is not possible here to describe the range of Mont Blanc in detail. My own memories of it are many and varied. I have been chased from the summit of Mont Blanc by hurricane and blizzard, and I have lingered on the ridges of the great mountain beneath unclouded skies when not a zephyr stirred. Is there a finer approach to any mountain than that to Mont Blanc over the wave-like crest of the Aiguille de Bionnassay? Is there any mountainside in the Alps where the feeling of height and isolation is more complete than that experienced by the climber who ventures upon ice slopes of the Brenva Face or the cliffs of the Innominata Route? Is there any beauty to excel that final dome of pure snow?

I would end these fragmentary notes, these anecdotes these tittle-tattle of personal experience, with the reminder that amid the shifting quicksands of this unhappy age beauty shines as it never shone before. For never has there been so obvious a contrast between good and evil as at the present time. To many, and I am one, beauty and peace are most easily perceived through Nature. On the high hills men enter upon a new kingdom of thought and inspiration, a new plane, a new level of spiritual contentment and happiness. When a man treads a high hill distrust and despair depart and indecisions vanish like snowflakes in the Sun.

CLIMBS ON THE JÄGIHORN AND THE BIETSCHHORN

First published in the 1932 *Alpine Journal* (Vol.44, pp277-282). The climbs are situated in the western Bernese Alps and as they have been little frequented by British and American climbers in recent years.

The South East Ridge of the Baltschieder Jägihorn, 3416 m.

This magnificent expedition, which Monsieur Paul Montandon justly considers to be one of the finest rock climbs in the Alps – an opinion that I can heartily endorse – deserves to be better known, for in itself it justifies the eight to ten hour trudge from Visp to the comfortable little Baltschieder Hut. This is situated on the southernmost spur of the Jägihorner between the two main tributaries of the Baltschieder Glacier. Suffice to say, it is a route comparable in interest, difficulty and soundness of rock with the best of the Chamonix Aiguilles.

H.B. Thompson and I had been unable to procure a guidebook to the district when driven out of Zermatt in 1932 by continuously bad weather. We knew nothing of the Jägihorn or its history. Owing to mist the Baltschieder Hut was not left until 6 a.m. on July 18. The weather was then very good. The initial rock cliff immediately above the hut was turned by a traverse across broken rocks and slabs to the terrace sloping up in a north-westerly direction.* The terrace was followed to the foot of a conspicuous pinnacle abutting against the south-west slope of the South-East Ridge. A crevice to the east of the pinnacle and some slabs brought us to the foot of a chimney which continued for about 250 ft. This chimney afforded some fine climbing, including one section resembling the Râteau de Chèvre on the Grépon, where at the chimney's termination a holdless rib had to be climbed. It should be noted that the routes of former parties to the ridge start farther up the terrace, are shorter and probably easier, and lead up to the S.E. ridge some distance nearer to the summit than the point on the ridge gained by us. This difference of route explains to some extent the discrepancy in time between us and the Richardet-Chervet party. Having no idea of the length and difficulty of the South-East Ridge – we deliberately chose a difficult route to its crest!

The chimney led up into a small amphitheatre, above which easier rocks brought us to the crest of the ridge. The arête very broken in its lower section, does not fall very steeply on either side. Gendarme succeeds gendarme, all of perfect red granite, with only an occasional loose block. Were a few parties to climb this ridge, it would rival the Grépon for soundness of rock. Half an hour was spent in a second breakfast on a flat slab. Beyond this point the gendarmes are higher and more difficult, whilst the precipices on either hand are sheer. The Grey Gendarme was turned on its eastern flank up steep but not very difficult rocks; Knubel's lead of this gendarme direct was a fine piece of climbing. The weather now became misty and visibility was limited. No rock step in a ridge that I have seen is more forbidding at first sight than the Great Step. Being ignorant of its previous history, we sought first of all to avoid it, as did the Richardet/Chervet party, by turning it on its eastern flank. But the smooth slabs looked unpromising, and deteriorating weather made us look for the quickest way. This is direct up it by the route attempted by Montandon's party and down which they

* On October 9, 1920, Paul Montandon with Josef Knubel made an attempt to climb the ridge. This was before the Baltschieder Hut had been built. They had previously prospected the route, and had climbed directly up the steep cliff rising immediately above the site of the present hut which. They also discovered an alternative way to the right (east) which avoids the steep initial cliff and follows a terrace sloping up approximately parallel to the crest of the S.E. ridge. The crest of the ridge was gained in two hours by this easier variation. The party then traversed the crest, the gendarmes on which steadily increase in height and difficulty. After having traversed a difficult fifty-foot gendarme (The Grey Gendarme) they found themselves confronted by the Great Step (Grosse Abbruch) the rock of which is curiously grooved. The lower portion of this was climbed to the foot of an overhang but the party proceeded no further and retreated from this point,

On August 12, 1923, Montandon returned to the attack with Otto Fahrni and F. Ösch. The southern peak of the Jägihorn 3416 m., was climbed from the north-west in four hours from the Baltschieder hut (P. Dubied died while attempting a solo ascent of this climb sixteen days later), and the South East Ridge descended. The "Yellow Wall", which is perpendicular, was roped down, though Montandon thought that it might be turned. The Great Step was also descended on ropes (two rappels of thirteen and twenty-two metresrespectively). The Grey Gendarme, which Knubel had climbed direct in 1920, was also descended on the doubled rope. The descent took 8–9 hours from the summit to the hut.

The first ascent of this ridge was made on June 10, 1924, by the late Willy Richardet and D. Chervet in just four and a half hours. The Grey Gendarme (climbed directly by Knubel in 1920) was turned on its eastern flank. The Great Step was also turned on the east by a shallow couloir, then up a crack for a few metres, then by slabs between the crack and the couloir, and finally up the couloir to the ridge. The Yellow Wall was climbed on the left (west) by a difficult overhanging crack, though they thought (as we subsequently proved) that there was an easier route still farther to the left. The Grey Gendarme and the Great Step offered no extraordinary difficulties, but the Yellow Wall they found exceptionally hard.

roped in 1923. About seventy feet of steep but not excessively difficult climbing brought us to the foot of the overhanging section which cuts partly across it. Here we found the piton of the descending party.

The face above this is practically if not actually vertical and is curiously grooved. So difficult did it appear that I took off my boots and left my rucksack behind. The ascent of the grooved face provided a most exposed piece of climbing of some forty-five feet. Progress was made by wedging the stockinged feet in the grooves, while grasping the thin edges of the flutings between the grooves and leaning well outwards to prevent the feet from slipping in the said grooves. In the upper part small holds manifested themselves, but it was with a certain feeling of relief that the sharp crest of the ridge above was grasped. Thompson, although burdened with my boots and carrying two rucksacks, made light of it in nailed boots, so that it is undoubtedly possible to lead it otherwise than in stockings. In its exposure and steepness I should class it with the right variation of the Winkler Riss (Vajolet) and the top of the Zdardansky Kamin (Langkofeleck).

A very sharp section of the ridge led us to the foot of the Yellow Wall, the crux of the climb. Here a heavy hail and snowstorm commenced, and in a minute the rocks were streaming with slush. Two overhanging cracks were attempted, one of which was probably that climbed by the Richardet/Chervet party, but neither proved possible. The storm increased, and soon the holds were concealed. An attempted traverse to the west proved also impossible. Traversing back to the ridge, we were greeted by unpleasant electrical tension where hissing axes caused us to descend a short distance on its western side. The storm, which lasted nearly an hour, then eased and the rocks quickly began to dry. A crack on the western flank of the wall was the sole remaining possibility. To reach it it was necessary to descend diagonally some fifty feet from the ridge below the impasse. The crack was of the typical granite type, and took us quickly up the western flank of the Yellow Wall to the ridge above. The arête here is again extraordinarily narrow and progress à cheval was painful. Another gendarme, turned by the previous parties on the east was traversed direct, but descent on the far side necessitated a short rappel (there are, however, undercut holds invisible from above). The summit was reached at 2.30 p.m.

Descent was made by the North West Face to the Baltschieder Glacier. The way marked in the Climbers' Guide is via a couloir under the South-West Face of the northern peak (3510m) of the Jägihorn. We descended broken rocks and steep snow from the depression between the north and south summits. Below these rocks, unclimbable slabs necessitated a traverse to the south. Another heavy snowstorm supervened, but we found it possible to force a way down slabs to the bergschrund, which was crossed without difficulty, though the snow bridge was in a dangerous state. The hut was regained at 7 p.m.

I have been unable to find any mention of any party climbing this ridge between the years 1924–1932.

The East Face of the Bietschhorn

In his admirable monograph on the Bietschhorn (*AJ* 42, 1931, pp236–241), Dr. Hans Lauper describes in detail the two routes that had been made up the East Face prior to 1930 – the East Spur and the East Ridge. Oskar Supersaxo, who with James Alexander first ascended the East Ridge (September 2, 1927), stated that he thought that the more northerly ribs were possible but would most certainly be no improvement on the existing routes.

Thompson and I found a copy of Dr. Lauper's article in Baltschieder Hut, and this, coupled with the fact that in 1925 J.V. Hazard and I had descended the East Spur, decided us to attempt the East Face between the East and North Ridges.

Of all the ribs that descend the East Face from the summit ridge one only extends as far as the bergschrund, the others petering out in steep ice slopes some hundreds of feet higher. This rib is not, however, continuous and loses its individuality in the upper slopes. It would be necessary to leave it and traverse a couloir to gain a well-defined rib to left. Examination disclosed the fact that at the point where the initial rib loses its individuality it bends to the left (south). At this point not only is the couloir less than one hundred feet wide but is sheltered for half of its width by the rocks of the initial rib.

The Baltschieder Hut was left in bright moonlight at 3 a.m. on July 22. Owing to the dangerous condition of the glacier and very bad snow, the bergschrund was not reached until 6 a.m. The latter was crossed without difficulty and the rocks of the initial rib gained. These proved easy, and progress to the point where it was necessary to traverse the couloir was rapid. Owing to the snowy conditions nothing was falling down the couloir, which, set at 60° necessitated step-cutting in ice for half of its width. It was only after a difficult climb, owing to snow and verglas covering the sunless rocks of the northern side of the rib, that the crest of the latter was gained. On the crest of the rib the rocks were dry. As height was gained the climbing became progressively more difficult. The rock on the whole is sound, but detached blocks require care where they are poised on the sharp crest of the rib. A vertical step curiously cleft by an overhanging chimney was turned by a steep crack on its southern side. Higher up, another step proved impossible to climb direct and had to be turned on its northern slope. Over an hour was spent here climbing 100 ft., as every hold in the nearly vertical face had to be cleared of snow and sheets of verglas. The crest of the rib above this step is extraordinarily sharp. The upper rocks were in bad condition, and much time was spent in climbing them.

The summit ridge was gained near the point of junction with the West Ridge. Few rocks were to be seen, and the red tower on the West Ridge was coated in snow and ice. The summit was gained at 2 p.m. Even under normal conditions this route would be more difficult than the East Spur, but subsequent parties – climbing under better conditions – should halve our time.

Descent was begun by the North Ridge. This proved to be in the worst possible condition – I have, in fact, never seen a snow ridge in such a dangerous condition. Two feet of loose powdery snow resting on hard snow, ice, or ice-glazed slabs. was bevelled into a knife-edge. Cornices, of a most formidable nature, decorated the ridge on both sides, so that it was sometimes necessary to traverse below the crest – a procedure necessitating the utmost precautions. Throughout almost its entire length above Pt. 3712 m. it was necessary to move one at a time. At Pt. 3712 m. a snowstorm supervened accompanied by wind, reducing visibility to a yard. Where the North Ridge bends north-eastwards we were unable to find the route, and it was only regained after a long bout of step-cutting in ice. The ordinary route to the Baltschiederjoch and the rock rib utilized by some parties to the south of it were alike impossible, the rocks being plastered with snow. The only remaining alternative was a direct descent of the East Face to the south of the rock rib. The face here consisted of sodden snow, well crusted by the wind but ready, nevertheless, to avalanche.* It was found possible to descend safely by causing a snowslide and descending in the track of the resulting avalanche.

This is the only occasion that I have seen wet snow in the Alps well crusted but in an avalanchy condition; in the Himalaya, the contrary often prevails. It can only result from exceptional weather conditions, and the conditions in July 1932 were exceptional, the Föhn having blown continuously for the past two weeks.

The avalanche thus detached was a huge one and covered an area of at least 100 yds. square, with debris piled six to eight deep.

The bergschrund was crossed as darkness was falling, and the Baltschieder Glacier descended by compass. The Baltschieder Hut was regained at 8.30 p.m.

[Note: These routes are described in *Bernese Alps Central* (Alpine Club 1979) but not in the current AC guidebook (*Bernese Oberland*). There is now a bivouac hut below the South-East Ridge of the Stockhorn to use as a base for the Stockhorn/Bietschhorn traverse – an extended rock ridge (Grade 4/5) followed by an alpine descent (see *Extreme Alpine Rock*, Granada, London, 1979).

ACCIDENT ON THE SOUTH FACE OF MONT BLANC

Smythe's account of this accident was published in the 1934 *Alpine Journal* (Vol 46, pp.415–419). It marks the one occasion that he climbed with guides, notably the redoubtable Adolphe Rey, the key figure on the first ascents of the Innominata Ridge (1919) and Hirondelles Ridge (1927). John Hoyland will be remembered for his early repeats on Clogwyn Du'r Arddu (see *The Black Cliff*, p14). Smythe's criticisms of the precocious first alpine season plans of Hoyland and Wand (leading figures in the Oxford University M.C. during one of its active periods) might be applied to many university groups in subsequent years, where major projects are talked up in advance and a programme of basic training climbs is often either neglected or truncated by the most ambitious members. The lessons of this accident are as applicable now as on the day they were written: long alpine apprenticeships, in a variety of seasons and conditions, are desirable for anyone hoping to climb the great routes with any degree of control and competence.

On August 21, 1934, a party, consisting of J.D. Hoyland and P. Wand, aged 19 and 23 years respectively, arrived at the Torino Hut on the Col du Géant from a camp near the Montenvers, which they are presumed to have left either on that or the previous day. On the following day they descended to Courmayeur, and were seen leaving that village at 2 p.m. They arrived at the Gamba Hut at 10 p.m., the guardian stating that they were very tired and carrying extremely heavy loads. They had thus taken eight hours for an ascent that can be accomplished comfortably in five hours.

They left the Gamba Hut at 9 a.m. next day, having informed the guardian (and recorded in the hut book) that they intended bivouacing on the Col Eccles and ascending Mont Blanc de Courmayeur by the Innominata Route. Again, according to the guardian, they appeared tired and when last seen were going very slowly. The weather, unsettled at that time, broke next day, snow falling on

* Reminiscent to the conditions encountered on Avalanche Peak in the Arwa Valley. See pp 495-496.

the hills in the immediate vicinity of Courmayeur, whilst the general conditions were also bad, there being a considerable amount of snow resting on the face of Mont Blanc de Courmayeur and the Innominata Arête.

Owing to the fact that letters were not expected, no anxiety was experienced in England until it was learnt that their camp near the Montenvers had not been reoccupied, and it was not until the middle of September that Dr. C.A. Wiggins, the guardian of Wand, arrived at Chamonix. There he ascertained that the party had left for the Col du Géant. Engaging guides, he went up to the Torino Hut where he found a record in the passport register to the effect that they had descended to Courmayeur. On arrival at Courmayeur he learnt that the party had left the Gamba Hut as already stated. He therefore engaged the guides Guillaume Rey and Baroux and, on September 20, sent them up to the Gamba Hut with instructions to commence a search.

Meanwhile Mr. J.S. Hoyland, the father of J.D. Hoyland, asked me on September 18 to travel out with him from England and institute a search. At that time he was unaware of the movements of Dr. Wiggins. We arrived at Geneva on the following afternoon, where we were met by M. Charles Gos, to whom Mr. G. Winthrop Young had previously sent a telegram. M. Gos accompanied us to Chamonix the same evening and was most helpful. At Chamonix we found that the guide Armand Charlet was ready to begin the search, having been engaged by M. de Ségogne, who had kindly wired on behalf of the C.A.F. His services, however, proved unnecessary, as at Chamonix we discovered that Dr. Wiggins was in Courmayeur and had traced them to that village, though, owing to poor telephone link between Chamonix and Courmayeur, intelligible conversation with him was impossible. Gos accordingly returned to Geneva, and Mr. Hoyland and I motored to Courmayeur (September 20).

At Courmayeur I engaged Adolphe Rey and Camille Grivel (porter), and on the 21st ascended to the Gamba Hut, Mr. Hoyland accompanying us for part of the way. In the afternoon Guillaume Rey and Baroux returned from Col Eccles after an unsuccessful search. They reported two metres of avalanche snow choking the bergschrund at the foot of the Innominata Face and the slopes of Col Eccles, and considered a further search useless. I decided, however, to search next day and, if it proved unavailing, to abandon it as there seemed small likelihood of finding traces – a month having elapsed since the accident. A search high up on the Innominata Route, supposing they had bivouacked and died in the storm that would most likely have overtaken them during their ascent, was, owing to recently fallen snow, out of the question. Guillaume Rey was sent down to Courmayeur and Baroux retained.

Next morning, September 22, we left the Gamba hut at 3.15 a.m., and climbing on two ropes, Rey and I, Baroux and Grivel, reached the Col du Frêney at 6.15. A good deal of step-cutting was necessary in the icefall of the Brouillard Glacier, and some time was spent in searching crevasses.

Some 100 to 150 ft. above the col on the ridge, which at this point consists of rocks and snow inclined at a moderate angle, Rey discovered an ice axe, the point of the pick being just visible above the snow covering the rocks. Descending from the ridge to the east, we found an old bivouac site which, as it proved, had no connection with the accident. Looking down the rock couloir leading to the

Frêney Glacier we could see an object on the surface of the latter which did not possess the appearance of a stone.

Unfortunately, I had neglected to provide myself with a telescope. Some time was spent in probing the snow which lay two or three feet deep on the ledges and on the ridge. Rey wished to push on a little, but before we did this I sent Baroux and Grivel down to a ledge from which a better view was obtainable of the couloir. From this vantage point they saw a balaclava helmet lying on the rocks, some 100ft. lower. Rey and I descended to this spot down steep but not difficult rocks, and then perceived other articles and clothing on the rocks below. There being now no further doubt that they had fallen from the ridge, it was decided to follow the line of their fall to the Frêney Glacier. We accordingly descended the loose rocks of the couloir, climbing at our utmost speed, owing to the possibility of falling stones being detached by the sun, which was rapidly gaining in power. During the descent various items of equipment were found, and it was obvious from these, which included full-size table forks and spoons, heavy skiing gloves, heavy woollen sweaters, guidebook and underclothing, a condensed milk tin, a bivouac tent weighing at least 6 lbs., etc. etc., that the party had been grossly overloaded.

Owing to falling stones, the descent of the ice slope at the foot of the rocks as well as the crossing of the bergschrund by an ice groove was dangerous. It was only an exceptionally speedy piece of step-cutting by Rey that prevented an accident, since shelter had but just been gained under the lip of the bergschrund when a fall of rocks occurred, which swept the steps and the ice shoot. The bodies were lying about fifty yards beyond the bergschrund, and it was obvious from the nature of their injuries that they had been killed instantly – they had fallen about 1800ft. Stones were falling, so we placed the bodies in a less exposed position. They were wearing crampons, which would have been more dangerous than useful on the ridge where the slip occurred, particularly in conditions of soft snow which, according to Rey, prevailed at that time.

The descent of the Frêney Glacier was rendered difficult and dangerous on account of the broken nature of the ice and the number of unstable séracs. Furthermore, the hanging glacier between the Rochers Gruber and Pic Eccles was discharging some immense avalanches, which were sweeping far down the glacier. Rey led with great skill and speed, but even so it took three hours to reach the slopes below the Col de L'Innominata. The Gamba Hut was regained at 2.15 p.m. Later Rey and I descended to Courmayeur, leaving Mr. Hoyland, at the hut (he having climbed up from the valley during our absence).

On September 24 twelve Courmayeur guides accomplished the difficult and dangerous task of recovering the bodies. By means of fixed ropes a route was forced up the side of the Frêney Glacier, thus avoiding the greater risks of falling ice. Two men were, however, slightly injured by falling stones in the couloir below the Col de L'Innominata. Thanks to the courtesy of the Italian military authorities, motor vehicles were provided to bring the bodies and the guides down the Val Veni. Nothing could have exceeded the kindness and sympathy experienced at Courmayeur. It will remain an enduring memory. The funeral was attended by many of the local inhabitants, nearly all of whom brought flowers. The coffins were borne by guides. The Prefect of Aosta was represented, as, were also the military and civil authorities. Signor Bertolini was the representative of the C.A.I.

Comment on this sad disaster would seem scarcely necessary; the facts speak for themselves. It is only because of Mr. Hoyland's earnest desire that his son's death may prove a warning and a deterrent that I should like to mention a few facts.

The original party which left England had announced that they intended to attempt routes among which were the Grépon, the traverse of the Drus, the East Ridge (Ryan/Lochmatter of the Aiguille du Plan (stated by Franz Lochmatter to be the hardest climb he ever did in the Chamonix Aiguilles), the Peuterey Ridge and the Sentinelle Rouge route on the Brenva face of Mont Blanc. That such expeditions particularly the last two, should be planned for a first season in the Alps is almost beyond belief. The Grépon was climbed, but owing to the inclusion of an almost complete novice [Jocelyn Bodilly] in the party, they were all benighted on the Nantillons Glacier and had to sleep in the little shelter placed on the rocks there. They had also planned to attempt the East Face of the Grépon, but whether this climb was carried out or not is uncertain. [Hoyland and Wand climbed this – Hoyland leading the Knubel Crack using a jammed axe for aid.]

A number of experienced mountaineers had warned them against attempting such routes as the Peuterey Ridge. It is even very doubtful whether a British-trained rock climber is justified in attempting such a climb as the traverse of the Drus in his first season, because the longer Aiguille climbs call for reasonable speed and a different technique to British rocks. The East Ridge of the Plan is certainly not a climb for any but a mountaineer, whilst it seems scarcely necessary to state that routes such as the Peuterey Ridge and the Sentinelle Rouge call for long experience in all the branches of mountaineering.

A broken watch that had stopped at 3.52 was found on one of the bodies. This, taken in conjunction with the fact that their bivouac sack had obviously not been used, that their stock of candies was also unused, as was apparently their lantern, suggests that the accident occurred during the ascent. If this was so, they took nearly seven hours to climb from the Gamba Hut to the Col du Frêney, as against the three hours taken by the search party. This time also speaks for itself. Had the accident not occurred it is very doubtful whether they could have traversed Mont Blanc in one day from Col Eccles. Apart from the fact that conditions were very bad at that time, they would almost certainly have been caught by the bad weather that broke in the afternoon or evening of August 24, in which case disaster must have overtaken them.

There is one last point on which comment should be made. The discovery of the ice axe reminded me immediately of the similar find on Everest last year. What most probably happened was that the leader slipped, and the second man having no firm snow into which to drive his axe put it down in order to seize the rope in both hands and, failing to stop the leader, was himself dragged down, leaving his axe behind him.

[The *AJ* Editor, Edward Strutt, added the following footnote: 'All mountaineers will concur with Mr. Smythe's comments. A few words of praise and thanks are due to him and that great guide, Adolphe Rey, for the skill and success of the admirably conducted search party.']

APPENDIX II

Mechanised Mountaineering

First published in the 1942 *FRCC Journal*. The North Face saga of the 1930s, in which the Germanic countries and Italy had played so prominent a part, suggested that climbing had become an extension of fascism. The early North Face attempts did seem to attract a procession of reckless young men bent on nationalistic fame, and the deaths on the Eigerwand (8), the Badile (2), the Grandes Jorasses (3) caused great concern. Added to other tragedies, in particular the incredible death toll on the German Nanga Parbat expeditions, these events appeared to indicate that normal climbing judgements had become distorted by other factors.

British, French, Swiss and American activists of the day, thus clung to proven traditional values. Smythe's comments, made during the height of the war, should therefore be seen in that context. In the post-war years mountaineers slowly began to realise the quality of those great climbs. Indeed Smythe's own comments about the Schmid brothers betray a certain ambivilance and it is difficult to imagine him being unimpressed with Heckmaier and Cassin had he known more about their abilities and motivation. Nevertheless the taint of fanaticism still persists and as yesterday's political goals are replaced with today's equally brazen pursuits of fame and fortune (by some), the comments still have relevance.

Smythe's comments on oxygen use in the Himalaya have a very contemporary ring and his sarcastic observations on piste skiing also have a sharp topical edge.

As a nation we have always jealously preserved the spirit of good sportsmanship, and of late we have watched with growing uneasiness certain Continental practices tending to debase mountaineering.

But before examining these it is interesting to trace briefly the growth of mountaineering. Mont Blanc was climbed as long ago as 1786, and the pioneers of that age safeguarded their progress over glaciers by clinging to long poles whilst a short-handled "meat-chopper" did duty as an ice axe. Britons were responsible for mountaineering for its own sake, as apart from a field science or a fashionable adventure like the ascent of Mont Blanc, and it is generally held that Mr Justice Wills' ascent of the Wetterhorn in 1854 heralded, or at least hastened its development. The Golden Age of Mountaineering lasted from 1854 to 1865, when the Matterhorn was climbed, but the disaster attending that most dramatic of alpine exploits put mountaineering back, in the words of the late Captain Farrar, 'half a generation of man'.

During the Golden Age implements were quickly improved and developed. The former clumsy ice axe evolved into an efficient instrument which now handles like a cricket bat or a fishing rod made by a master craftsman; special nailing was introduced for boots, and ropes strengthened and lightened. Apart, of course, from the appropriate clothing and sundry items such as a map and compass, those three are all the implements needed today in Alpine climbing.

Thus far British and Continental mountaineering had progressed in perfect accord. It was the introduction of crampons that started a cleavage which steadily widened into what is now a formidable rift between the British and German schools of thought. A form of crampon was worn by Alpine peasantry many generations ago, but the twin spikes clamped to the instep to help a man up an icy track are very different from the ten or twelve-point crampon of today. A.F. Mummery was one of the first to develop the crampon idea, but his screw-in spikes never proved really satisfactory, and it was left to Oscar Eckenstein and others to develop the modern crampon.

We invariably regard with suspicion any innovation in a game, and we are wont to make sure that it is an advantage before we will accept it. Even today a search through the back numbers of the Alpine Journal reveals an innate dislike for the crampon, and that is because crampons are abused by Continental mountaineers, many of whom learn to climb in them before accustoming themselves to nailed boots. The result is an increase in accidents, for of all the implements in mountaineering the crampon is the one that lends itself most readily to abuse. It is not, as some suppose, an alternative to step-cutting in steep ice, and it becomes positively deadly in conditions of soft wet snow, particularly when such snow rests on ice. With a boot it is possible to feel and gauge the state of the snow or the nature of the ice, but with a crampon between the boot and the ice, this is often difficult or impossible. A crampon is valuable on frozen snow, on dry glaciers, and ice of moderate steepness; and it can be useful also on steep ice when used in conjunction with ice pitons, but on soft snow and rocks it is more dangerous than useful. Had it never been invented it is certain that hundreds now in their graves would be alive today.

The use of the rope has progressed on more or less logical lines. There is no rope so good as the best British rope. Our seafaring experience is doubtless responsible for this. A good new rope is the physical safeguard of the climber, and its moral value is immense. Without it a party is simply a collection of individuals, with it an added strength, cohesion and security is gained. The mountaineer learns to use is rope for all manner of purposes. If the rope has been abused, apart from the ignorance and carelessness of the inexperienced, it is because nowadays it is too frequently used for freak descents of otherwise unclimbable precipices though, of course, it is perfectly justifiable to use it on difficult or impassable ground as a means of descent on a route. All that is really necessary on the hardest Alpine climbs is a spare rope for double-roping purposes, together with one or two slings through which the rope can be passed so as to obviate any tendency of it to jam when the time comes to release it from below.

If the crampon began a cleavage between British and German methods and ideals, piton technique went far to widen it. ... If climbing be regarded as a pursuit in which personal skill is the prime factor and simplicity, not expediency the motive, then the piton is permissible only as a safeguard on climbable faces, and is undesirable as a means of climbing otherwise unclimbable rock. This is the British view. The German technicians think otherwise. To them Nature only exists to be bludgeoned into submission, and if a precipice is reputed to be unscaleable then it must be climbed, if not by fair means then by foul. One may admire the courage of the performers, while deprecating the spirit in which the performance in undertaken; it is the same spirit as that which dynamites a trout pool or massacres tame pigeons. It is neither mountaineering, nor is it sport. Worse than this, the German technique in the years before the present war became tainted with nationalism. Desperate ascents in which pitons were driven into otherwise unclimbable rock were undertaken for the honour and glory of Germany, to prove that Germans were not only good sportsmen, but the best sportsmen, actions which signally failed to convince others.

British climbers may justly consider themselves free from these taints of mechanisation and nationalism. For the most part they have always looked upon mountain climbing as a sport in the purest sense of the word, a test of strength and skill in surmounting natural obstacles undertaken in accordance with traditional rules, and governed by a love of the thing for its own sake. At the same time, they cannot be wholly absolved from a charge of expediency. There exists, or has existed, a school of thought that Everest must be climbed, if not by traditional methods … then by the employment of oxygen breathing apparatus. It is true that the diminished oxygen content in the air near the highest summit of the world suggests the use of such an apparatus; there is little enjoyment to be had out of climbing without it at the highest altitudes of the Himalayas. At the same time, there would to my mind, be singularly little satisfaction in reaching the summit of Everest with oxygen apparatus. It is certain that were Everest to be climbed with oxygen apparatus, mountaineering tradition – were it worth anything – would very soon demand a non-apparatus ascent. This cult of expediency, as exemplified by the scientific experts, is to my mind one of the evils of the present age. Let us keep mountaineering clean and undebased even on the highest peaks of the Himalayas. Let us win through to the top of Everest for the love of the thing, not because it is expedient to get there. Expediency and good sportsmanship simply do not go together.

If any charge can be preferred against mountaineers as a whole it is that they have taken their achievements too seriously. I have been as guilty as any in that respect. I now realise that it is the joy, the good comradeship, the climbing that matter most in mountaineering, not the attainment of the objective. Mummery was the great apostle of the joy of mountaineering. It is impossible to associate such a character – bubbling over with irrepressible gaiety, conscious always that it was the game that mattered and not its prizes – with the dour exponent in mountaineering today, with his pitons, his oxygen apparatus and, not least, a nationally-minded Press to spur him on to some fresh "conquest" for the fancied honour and glory of his Fatherland. It is essential to the well-being of mountaineering not to overburden it with mechanical aids but to keep it as simple as possible.

There is one implement of mountaineering not so far touched upon, the ski. Skiing, yachting and gliding have something in common, but skiing is the simplest and, to the skier at any rate, the finest and most thrilling form of locomotion known to man. It is also, despite its inherent simplicity, one of the most difficult arts to learn; perfection indeed is unattainable. Crampons and pitons are mere accessories to mountain climbing, but the advent of the ski opened up an entirely new field to the mountaineer … Ski have not only opened up the Alps in winter, but they have done useful service in increasing the mountaineer's knowledge of snow conditions.

Finally, it may be of interest to particularise on some of the foregoing points. As already indicated, the greatest gulf between the British and German techniques is to be found in rock climbing. The most British climbers have done is to concede the justifiability of "Kletterschuhe" (felt-or rubber-soled shoes) when used in preference to nailed boots. Statements in the past as to climbing having reached the limit of possibility have so often proved fallacious that I hesitate to believe that rock-climbing in this country has reached that limit. At the same time, there would appear in the Lake District at any rate, little else than either minor variations of routes or very severe new routes left for the inventive genius of the modern school of climbers unless the German technique be copied. I hope this last will never come to pass. I have only once seen a piton on a British climb and that was on a route known as the Piton Climb above the Idwal Slabs on Glyder Fawr. Here the piton was used solely as a safeguard for the leader in the absence of a natural belay for the rope on a steep and exposed rock face. It has now been removed. [A piton was also used on Longland's Climb in 1928 and on Scafell's Overhanging Wall (1934) and three on May Day Climb in 1938.]

The German, on the other hand, has done much to ruin rock climbing in the Eastern Alps, for he has turned pleasant climbs into boring gymnastics, and I know of nothing so unsatisfactory in mountaineering as pulling up on wire cables or stepping from one iron spike to another. The Italians who, it would appear, are ever imitative of the worst practices in others, have vied with the German technicians in scaling otherwise impossible rock faces by means of enormous numbers of pitons. The North Face of the Grosse Zinne [Cima Grande] in the Dolomites is an outstanding example of such engineering. This 3,000-foot precipice was finally "conquered" after immense labours extending over months, the "conquest" being acclaimed by the Italian Press as another great achievement of Fascism. Comment would seem superfluous: it was neither mountaineering nor was it magnificent. Many similar climbs have been performed by the do-or-die Nazis in the Eastern Alps, in the Kaisergebirge, Karwendel and elsewhere. It was inevitable that the greatest of the Alpine faces should be similarly attacked. The North Face of the Matterhorn was the first to fall, then came the North Face of the Grandes Jorasses, and finally, the notorious Eigerwand.

It is impossible not to admire the skill and courage of the contestants [in this North Face quest]. The brothers Franz and Toni Schmid, who climbed the North Face of the Matterhorn, were first and foremost mountaineers. They were also modest young fellows, and the ascent though received in Germany as another indication of nordic toughness and superiority, was certainly not undertaken by the Schmids for motives of national aggrandisement. Nor was their achievement in the same category as the feats of the Italians on the Grosse Zinne; it was an ascent in which the odds between life and death were roughly equal. The same cannot be said of the Grandes Jorasses and the Eigerwand. Here again, skill and courage may be admired, but the artificial nature of the climbing as exemplified by the use of large numbers of pitons, the lives lost, and the national feeling behind the ascent, served to condemn these feats in the eyes of British mountaineers. We believe that in mountaineering as in other things, it is necessary to draw the line somewhere. Exactly where that line is to be drawn depends on temperament as much as on tradition. Irresponsible gambles with death, and risks undertaken from motives of national glorification are not in our climbing philosophy. Let us above all things oust the expedient from mountaineering, and keep this grand pursuit as simple and enjoyable as possible.

APPENDIX III

Frank Smythe (1900–1949)

by Arnold Lunn

First published in *A Century of Mountaineering*, Swiss Foundation for Alpine Research, Zurich, 1957; Allen and Unwin, London, 1957. The book celebrated the activities of the Alpine Club.

There was no British mountaineer between the Wars who was better known to the general public than Frank Smythe. His fame, solidly based on a foundation of achievement, was reinforced by the fact that he was also a popular lecturer and a skilful journalist.

Smythe was born on July 6th, 1900, and resolutely resisted Berkhamstead's attempt to educate him.* He was said to have a weak heart and was not allowed to play football. Raymond Greene writes: 'Physically on his mountains, intellectually in his books, he strove always to attain heights which were just a little beyond his powers, great though these were.'

At the age of fourteen, he cycled all the way to Wales to climb, and from then onwards insisted that all his holidays should be spent among the mountains.

In 1926 Smythe joined the R.A.F. and went to Egypt. He was not suited to that type of life and after several months he became very ill, and in the letters to his mother the doctors write: 'He has all the signs and symptoms of typhoid and we fear his heart may be considerably affected.' He was invalided out in 1927.

For a year he accepted an appointment with Kodak, and for the rest of his life he supported himself by books, articles and lectures on mountaineering. From 1930 onwards he was *The Times* correspondent for mountaineering.

Nobody assumes that a great scientist is only or mainly interested in his salary, or that judges have only a minor interest in justice, but there are people who make an analogous assumption in the case of a man who derives most of his income directly or indirectly from a particular sport. It was for the benefit of such critics that Raymond Greene thought it as well to refute in *The Alpine Journal* the view that Smythe 'climbed mountains not for the love of mountains but for the love of gain.' Smythe, as a professional writer and lecturer on mountains, was the precursor of guides like Rébuffat who have become professionals because they were impelled into this way of life by the flame of a devouring mountain passion.

Smythe was a competent but not a brilliant rock climber. The Mummery Crack, according to a climber who led him up the Grépon, was just above the limit of what he could lead, but he was a safe and seasoned cragsman capable of leading on most classes of rock found in the Alps. [He may have been unfit at the time.]

It was in the 1933 attempt on Everest that Smythe 'showed to the full', according to Raymond Greene, 'his superb icemanship. His approach to the

* Berkhamstead School, Hertfordshire. Smythe's fellow pupils included H.W.Tilman (who was several years older) and the Greene brothers – Graham and Raymond.

North Col seems to me the finest piece of ice-climbing I have ever seen.'

Smythe never climbed with a guide until he joined a guide on a search party. He learned to mountaineer by mountaineering. Dr. Graham Macphee writes:

> Although physically of light build, he had amazing powers of endurance, and could carry a heavy rucksack all day without apparent fatigue. A careful perusal of the accounts of the great climbs he did on the South Face of Mont Blanc reveals the hours of step-cutting he carried out. He was extremely good on snow and ice, with a wonderful knowledge of varying conditions, and had an uncanny sense of direction in difficult route-finding.
>
> It was my good fortune in my first Alpine season to accompany him on the Peuterey Ridge. Surprised by sudden bad weather soon after leaving our bivouac high on the Aiguille Blanche, he never faltered, and led the first successful descent on the Rochers Gruber from the Col de Peuterey in a storm I have never since seen equalled. Descending and crossing the complicated and difficult Frêney Glacier, he was never once at fault and unerringly attained the foot of the couloir leading to the Col de l'Innominata in dreadful weather conditions, so that we safely returned to the Gamba Hut thirty-six hours after setting out from Courmayeur.*

As a skier he was steady but by no means accomplished, somewhere between the standards of the British Third and Second Class tests. His ski-mountaineering record is relevant to the question of his position in Alpine history. His record of exploration in distant mountain ranges was exceptionally good. His pioneer ascents in the Alps, notably the new routes on Mont Blanc [with T.Graham Brown], are among the very few great climbs which have been first accomplished by an all British *guideless* party. If his claims were based solely on his record as a summer mountaineer it would not be easy to prove that any other British mountaineer had a finer record between the Wars, but what establishes Smythe's position as perhaps the best all-round British mountaineer of this period is the fact that he knew the mountains not only in summer but also in winter and in spring, and had mastered the techniques of *modern* mountaineering, ice-craft, rock-climbing and also skiing which is more and more being recognised as an integral element in the education of the all-round mountaineer.

I must not omit a tribute to his skill as a mountain photographer. Some day, we shall, I hope, be given a book containing the best of Frank Smythe's writings and the best of his photographs. Such a book should be a very good book indeed.

Of his leadership on the Kamet expedition, Raymond Greene writes:

> He was the best kind of leader for such an enterprise, the leader who makes all the plans with meticulous care and having, as it were, created the world leaves it to run itself, giving it only a gentle push if it slows down or begins to wobble on its axis, but remaining personally inconspicuous.
>
> At great altitudes a new force seemed to enter into him. His body, still apparently frail as it had been in boyhood, was capable of astonishing feats of sudden strength and prolonged endurance and his mind, too, took on a different colour. At sea-level the mistaken sense of inferiority so unfairly implanted by his early experiences rendered him sometimes irritable, tactless and easily offended. The self-confidence which flowed into his mind and body, the emanation as it were of the mountains whose strength he so greatly loved, changed him almost beyond recognition. It seemed impossible above 20,000 feet. to disturb his composure or his essential quietism. I

* Geoffrey Young has paid tribute to the characteristic that made Smythe a great mountaineer, 'the slow inner flame that burnt the fiercer as things went wrong and contrary winds blew up'.

> remember the Kamet expedition as a period of calm, unbroken by more than a rare small ripple of disagreement, and the calm was the result of Frank's confident but always modest and unassuming leadership.
>
> In the Himalaya he was equally good as a follower. Under Ruttledge on Everest he was as imperturbable, reliable and good-tempered in circumstances far harder and consequently more troubled.

Smythe was not indifferent to his fame, but I, who knew him well, am convinced that he was at heart a genuinely modest man, who found it difficult to believe in his own achievement.

Eric Shipton told me that he had been particularly impressed by a kind of Yogi-like power which Smythe seemed to possess to detach himself from his surroundings. 'There is something inevitably squalid', said Shipton, 'about a high camp in the Himalaya ... and climbers are often too weary to keep things ship-shape. On Everest one might have to remain some days on the North Col, but Smythe never got impatient or irritable, he preserved a complete detachment.'

No British mountaineer of the period was read more widely than Smythe. It was his particular merit to convey to those who had never climbed something of his own passion for mountains. He was admirable as an interpreter of mountain adventure, less admirable in his attempts to construct a religion out of his mountaineering experiences.

'Mr. Smythe's observations on life, death and judgment', wrote Lord Schuster ... 'are neither as original nor as profound as he seems to think'.

But it would be a mistake to assume that Smythe wrote for effect or invented emotions which he did not feel. Like the poets who

> Mar their mortal melodies
> With broken stammer of the skies

Smythe often failed to find the right words to describe a genuine spiritual experience. And the kind of remark which provoked Schuster's dry comment was largely due to his resolute refusal to read anything which other explorers of the borderland between the natural and the supernatural had troubled to report. 'I avoid reading that kind of book', he once remarked to me, 'because I want to be sure that my interpretation of the mountains is my own and is not confused or influenced by anything I might have read about religion or mysticism.' In those days he was not prepared to consider the possibility that a study of the subject might have clarified rather than confused his beliefs, and might, for instance, have helped him to distinguish between the worship of mountains, which is silly, and the worship inspired by mountains which is anything but silly. In the late twenties he sent me a succession of indignant epistles in which I was upbraided, much as an apostate might be upbraided by an apostle, for perverting the true mountain faith. I had been infected, so he believed, by the heresy of "Downhill-Only", and instead of insisting that young men should climb up mountains was actually encouraging them to race down them. 'Don't you realise', he pleaded, 'that mountains are meant to be worshipped, not treated as slides?'

But the worship of limestone and granite is – in the exact sense of the word – idolatry.

It is odd that Smythe, and those mountaineers who agreed with him, did not realise that they had adapted Ruskin's taunt for use against skiers. Ruskin accused mountaineers of treating mountains as if they were greased poles; Smythe attacked skiers for treating mountains as greased planes.

Smythe was a man who matured late. One of his earlier mountaineering companions once remarked to me that 'he thought in clichés'. When I first met him he was something of a monomaniac for whom history seemed to begin with the beginnings of Alpine exploration, but his strong prejudice against reading gradually disappeared. Towards the end of his life he was a voracious reader of history, biography and even of religious literature. His work as a photographer had educated his eye for colour and line, and he had begun to make a collection of reproductions of Alpine paintings from the Middle Ages onwards. I was impressed by his erudition and flattered that he should have asked me to collaborate in a book on mountains in art.

I have mentioned his modesty. Of other personal traits I must not forget his good humour. He was often in the centre of controversy, but he was incapable of malice. Our own friendship was founded on the two poles of firm agreement and no less firm disagreement. I recall no hour spent in his company which I did not enjoy.

APPENDIX IV

The Smythe/Graham Brown Feud

Despite a successful mountaineering partnership during 1927 and 1928 resulting in two great Brenva Face climbs, two of the most important interwar alpine first ascents, Frank Smythe and T. Graham Brown were soon locked in controversy. Shortly after the Route Major ascent Smythe had reason to privately criticise Graham Brown. From that point Graham Brown, who was, by all accounts, extremely touchy, developed a bitter animosity towards Smythe that tarnished their joint achievement and was a "problem" for their colleagues in the Alpine Club.

In the following years both achieved distinction, Graham Brown as an alpine explorer (with the assistance of guides) and an editor of the *Alpine Journal*, Smythe for his great climbs and expeditions and his many books. Yet whenever there was reference to the Brenva climbs, particularly by Graham Brown, the arguments resurfaced and their friends in the Alpine Club were dragged in to arbitrate and calm things down. Their basic disagreement was about who did what on the climbs, and who made the greater contribution to success. The following commentary traces some of the main episodes of the saga drawing on articles, books, and correspondence in the Alpine Club archives and other sources. Readers who might question the length and detail of this appendix are reminded of the huge historical significance of Brenva Face climbs. Despite Smythe's mixed feelings about the ascents they did form a launch pad for his mountaineering career. The subsequent wrangles illustrate how the participants in a major climb (or indeed any creative enterprise) can so easily fall out in the fame and publicity that inevitably follows.

THE INITIAL ARTICLES ABOUT THE BRENVA FACE CLIMBS

Smythe and Graham Brown appear to have enjoyed an amicable relationship in between the alpine seasons 1927 and 1928 signified by their involvement in the Clogwyn Du'r Arddu explorations prior to the ascent of Longland's Climb (p. 939).

The first accounts of the Sentinelle Rouge (Smythe,) and the Route Major (Graham Brown) were published in the *Alpine Journals* of 1928 and 1929 and the absence of subsequent correspondence or comment in the Journal suggests that their accuracy was broadly accepted by both climbers at that time. The captioning of a photograph in Smythe's article "Brenva Face ... Showing Mr Smythe's route" might well have been an initial irritant for Graham Brown however.

Smythe's account, written 'in collaboration' with Graham Brown (*AJ* 40, 1928, pp 68–77), noted that he had a number of new climbs in mind 'the greatest by far was an attack on the unclimbed Brenva Face of Mont Blanc'. The account is essentially the same as the account in *Climbs and Ski Runs*. He noted that many leading climbers had considered the various ways of tackling the face. He then stated that the Red Sentinel itself was agreed with Graham Brown as their base of operations with the Twisting Rib as the target, the more ambitious plan of the buttress left of the Great Couloir (the Route Major) being shelved because of the uncertain finish. Smythe, the far more able and experienced climber, was naturally cautious about embarking on such a dangerous mountain face.

According to Lord Tangley in his article about Graham Brown (*AJ* 71, 1966, pp 51–57) Graham Brown, though inexperienced, was keen to make the first ascent of the Brenva Face and saw the Route Major line as the logical route.

Tangley also noted that Graham Brown had 'a touchiness that made him, at times, a difficult companion, and resulted in interruptions in friendship. [There was also] a soaring ambition which made him wish the world to know that the great Brenva climbs were his.'

Graham Brown was eighteen years older than Smythe, a Fellow of the Royal Society and a Professor at University College, Wales. He had come to climbing late and become accustomed to using guides. In 1927 Tangley and Graham Brown had resolved to attempt the face but the weather was unsuitable. In his article Lord Tangley describes how Graham Brown came to be paired with Smythe:

> During the winter [1926/27] he [G.B.] had read all the alpine literature there was on the subject. This crystalised the route in his mind and when we met at Simpson's in the Strand to make plans … he was anxious that we should attempt the route [the Route Major line] … he was quite certain that under the right conditions there would be no stonefall and that it would be entirely free from falling ice provided the foot could be reached early in the morning.

The pair, with their guides, waited at Montenvers for a change in the weather and here Tangley [his holiday at an end] introduced Graham Brown to Smythe:

> I felt extremely sorry for Graham Brown that his dream should not have come true, and when Smythe came back to the Montenvers from his ascent … of the Old Brenva Route, it was with a good deal of pleasure that I introduced him to Graham Brown. I had known Smythe well for some years although I never climbed with him, believing (quite rightly) that I was nowhere near his class. Seeing him and Graham Brown left at the Montenvers, each at a loose end, I believed that Smythe was competent to lead the new climb and Graham Brown to follow him. Graham Brown's heart was set on Route Major but he knew nothing, any more than I did, about the state of the ground between the Torino and the foot of the climb. Smythe had recent knowledge of the section between the Torino and the start of the Old Brenva, but so far as I could judge, had never looked at or interested himself in anything beyond.

Tom Blakeney, responding to Lord Tangley's article (*AJ* 72, 1967, pp 135–136) stated that Smythe was far more informed about the lines on the face than either Tangley or Graham Brown supposed. Smythe knew about the possibility of a totally independent line between the obvious (but dangerous) Route Major line and the Old Brenva Route:

> His apparent disinclination to discuss these Brenva Face routes … was, I imagine, due to his never having met G.B. before, and regarded it as imprudent to embark

on so considerable a climb as the Route Major with an unknown quantity as a companion. Hence his preference, in 1927, for the Sentinel route … I do not attach much importance to merely thinking up routes; it is carrying them into execution that matters …

Graham Brown's paper, describing the Sentinelle Rouge and the Route Major ascents, was read to the Alpine Club in November 1928. In this he noted that when considering which way to try first the Route Major line, the Twisting Rib line and the right slanting rib line above the Sentinel were all considered and that they 'compromised' on the Twisting Rib. He noted that they had 'the good fortune to discover the Sentinelle Rouge route'. He recorded that they studied the final difficulties of the Route Major from the top of the Twisting Rib. 'We *then* saw that the serac wall could almost certainly be surmounted … we then and there resolved that the route must be attempted.' [The italic "*then*" is from the original article … being Graham Brown's own emphasis.]

Graham Brown went on to describe the ascent of the Route Major in much the same way as Smythe (in *Climbs and Ski Runs*), making several references to Smythe leading. Smythe downplayed his leading role in his accounts of the climbs.

The critical section of the Route Major in Graham Brown's account is as follows:

Smythe attempted the chimney [later called the "Unclimbable Corner"] without success and then I tried and similarly failed. Yet it looked as if this was the only way. Neither of us wished to retreat, and it was doubtful if the south side of the buttress could offer an easier way or if there was now sufficient time to get round to ascend by it. I must say I shuddered at the suggestion of descending into the Great Couloir, crossing it and attempting the summit by way of the "Sentinel" route.

It is difficult to believe that Smythe would have made such a suggestion seriously as at this height such a traverse would have involved crossing the Great Couloir immediately beneath the ice cliffs. It does however indicate the growing sense of tension that was developing as the consequences of failure or a benightment became apparent, particularly if the weather deteriorated. Graham Brown continues:

It was this alternative, I think, which prompted me to offer Smythe my back in the recess. You may wonder why the offer was a tardy one – but we were wearing crampons and could not take them off. Smythe accepted the offer: tried the chimney again, and again failed to overcome it. He came down on my back with unfortunate effect, for my side pocket was ripped open and I lost my pipe – a sad discovery only made later at the Vallot Hut. Smythe then gallantly offered me similar aid. Again lodgement above the chimney was found to be impossible … I descended and, I am thankful to say, with less destructive effects. There is an advantage (sometimes) in a small and light build! Again the horrible alternatives presented themselves to us and drove me to suggest an attempt to get round the descending tongue of rock and traverse still further to the right … near the edge of the rock down steep ice … as I rounded the corner I saw to my amazement that, on the other side of the rocks and some way above, the ice slope merged into a broad couloir set at an easier angle and filled with good snow ….

The accounts in both *Climbs and Ski Runs* and *Brenva* confirm that Brown led this critical section protected, initially, by Smythe's high belay at the foot of the corner. Graham Brown's *AJ* account is from then much the same as Smythe's. At the crevasse he noted 'Our plan had been to make this new ascent a route to the summit of Mont Blanc de Courmayeur' with no mention of crossing the Col Major or any half-formed plan to do so or to bivouac there (though this may have been to protect a future ambition). Smythe's account in *Climbs and Ski Runs* finishes on the summit of Mont Blanc whereas Brown takes it a little further:

> On the summit of Mont Blanc the wind had fallen somewhat in strength, and now – thank goodness! – blew steadily. We reached the Vallot Hut at exactly 9.a.m. and descended next morning by the Grands Mulets and Pierre Pointue. Thence we walked to the Montenvers. Happy and contented we lingered on the way.

There is thus no sign in these accounts of any falling out between the two climbers. Indeed, (in a letter to his mother) Smythe noted that next day they traversed the Grands Charmoz and on September 10 did 'another new route'. In *Climbs and Ski Runs* Smythe reported (p.54) that they set out from the Lognon Hotel on September 9 to attempt Les Droites (maybe the then unclimbed North Face?). On reaching the Argentière Glacier unsettled weather dictated a change of plan and they attempted Aiguille d'Argentière – a bid that ended 1,500ft below the summit. Such actions are hardly indicative of a divided team.

LATER DISAGREEMENTS AND DISPUTES

An early dispute concerned Graham Macphee. Smythe had to end his holiday prematurely for family reasons but Macphee was coming out to join them both. Smythe wrote to Geoffrey Winthrop Young in 1928 describing what happened:

> I suggested that G.B. might care to join forces with Macphee. This he was glad to agree to. Now Zürcher, Josef Knubel and Leyen were at the Montenvers and it was therefore, to my amazement, that I was informed just before I left ... that G.B. had tacked himself on to them. When I pointed out to Graham Brown what was to happen to Macphee I was informed that I had no right to make arrangements and to interfere with his "plans". Though it is a little difficult to understand what his "plans" were had he not met Zürcher. Macphee meanwhile turned up at Courmayeur ... – I take full responsibility for letting him down .... Zürcher and G.B. meanwhile went round to Courmayeur. Now comes something that you will find hard to believe but it is nevertheless true. Zürcher – an awfully nice chap – seeing Macphee stranded naturally invited him to join the party but *Graham Brown refused* [Smythe's emphasis].

Writing again to Young in 1933 Smythe added more:

> I was very surprised therefore to hear later from Macphee ... that [Graham Brown] would not climb with [him] ... and did not hesitate to write to G.B. and tell him what I thought about it. G.B.'s attitude was that I had forced a quarrel on him and he never forgave me. I did my best to patch things up later and wrote positively abasing myself as I did not like to feel I had made an enemy – the only one I have ever made. But it was useless and G.B. remained my implacable enemy ever since ...

The paper Graham Brown read to the Alpine Club in 1928 is notable in its moderate and unhostile tone in view of this Macphee spat and his later pronouncements – though it implied that he "steadied the ship" at the crucial moment after the failure to climb the corner – something Smythe particularly resented as he felt he had done so much of the leading and step-cutting to that point.

Relations between the two men must have deteriorated further in the early thirties, possibly aggravated by Smythe's growing fame following his high profile Kangchenjunga and Kamet ventures. A page from a letter he wrote to Graham Brown in 1932 adds an important new dimension to the Route Major ascent and suggests that both Smythe's and Graham Brown's accounts of the climb were both diplomatically sanitised.

> ... I began to get anxious as I saw ourselves faced with a second bivouac which might well have been fatal and would certainly have been fatal had the weather broken.
>
> Then we reached a chimney [the "Unclimbable Corner"] in the buttress. You bravely offered yourself as a footstool and I stood on you in crampons. I did my best to get up but it proved an impossible place. My arms were naturally tired with the hours of cutting in the tenacious ice but it is untrue to say that I fell out. Had I done so nothing could have saved us as you were standing in ice steps. I remember however landing awkwardly on you and tearing your coat with my crampons. Then you tried but also without success and your crampons in turn made holes in my coat when you returned.
>
> I then said that our only alternative was to descend and traverse round a corner. This meant an extremely hard bit of cutting on excessively steep polished ice which coming so late in the day and after so much previous cutting was a bit of work that called for resolution on my part [here Smythe seemed to forget that Graham Brown led this critical passage as he described in *Climbs and Ski Runs*]. It is possible that the chances of success and retreat were debated at this point for a great deal depended on doing the right thing and it was definitely the point at which a decision to go on was made but I fear I must say in that very arduous ice work that followed I remember no encouragement. After cutting round the corner – a traverse where a slip by either of us could only have ended in disaster, we found ourselves on easier rocks. There was a chimney – not very hard – but it had a pitch in it that required an arm pull. My arms were tired from the hours of cutting and you led the pitch very well indeed. At length we came to the upper ice wall – quite easy – up which I cut and then easy slopes to the ridge between Mont Blanc and Mont Blanc de Courmayeur. On the final easy ridge to Mont Blanc de Courmayeur you led. We were climbing both together. You were about twelve feet above me on a gendarme. Suddenly with a shout (you would have called it a scream in my case) you came off. I had no belay whatever but as you came sliding off the gendarme I took in as much of the rope as I could. You fell onto the ice slope and shot down it. I thought everything was up with us but I scrabbled the rope up against the rough rock and by a miracle though you had fallen well below me and were rapidly gathering pace the rope by the grace of God caught and held on a small knob. So great was the jerk that as you may remember it was no easy job getting your knot undone when we reached the Vallot.
>
> That is the true account of our climb up the Brenva face of Mont Blanc and I think the aspersions you cast ... [are] unjust and unfair in the extreme.
>
> I wrote you a letter about two years ago, not an 'abject apology' and not intended as such but a genuine desire on my ... [rest of letter lost?]

What Graham Brown had written to trigger this response is not clear. It may have been his first account summarised above.

THE BRENVA FACE CLIMBS ARE REPEATED

In as much as Graham Brown tended to think of the Sentinelle Rouge as mainly Smythe's creation and the Route Major as his, he was also perturbed by the instant popularity of the former and the relative neglect of the latter, the superior route, and this is indicated in *Brenva*. In 1933 with his now regular guiding team of Alexander Graven and Alfred Aufdenblatten, Graham Brown, by then a very experienced climber (albeit invariably guided) and something of a Mont Blanc expert, repeated the Route Major and added a new route – the Via della Pera (Pear Buttress Route) to complete a trio of routes on this great face. Graham Brown was particularly concerned to popularize the Route Major and wished to photograph it and write about it with that intent. The accompanying table shows the pattern of ascents of these great routes during the 1930s.

Graham Brown's article on the Route Major repeat appeared in the *Alpine Journal* of 1933 Vol. 45, p.366 and here he discussed the Col Major for the first time. He also noted that the snow in the "Unclimbable Corner" was three feet higher than in 1933. Graven led it directly but still found it hard.

In March 1939 Graham Brown read a paper to the Alpine Club entitled *The Brenva Face* (*AJ* 51, p181-200). In this he sharpened his criticisms of Smythe noting that 'Smythe [in 1927] was emphatic that the final buttress [of the Route Major] was impracticable'. He also noted 'I traced the route [Sentinelle Rouge] and eventually proposed it to Smythe.' He then stated that they had ascertained the feasibility of the Route Major during the ascent of the Sentinelle Rouge but

Early Ascents of the Brenva Routes (based on T. Graham Brown's researches in *Brenva*) (g) = guide

Sentinelle Rouge ascents

Date	Climbers
1927	
Sept 1/2	Frank Smythe, Thomas Graham Brown
1929	
Sept 6/7	Ludwig Hall, Walter Stösser
1930	
July 31/ Aug 1	T. Beeringer, Hans Huber, Gustav Kröner
1932	
July	Hermann Bratshko (g), Karl Schreiner, Emil and Karl Rupilius (poor weather necessitating a 2nd bivouac on the face)
1933	
Aug	Günther Hepp, Martin Pfeiffer, Heinz Tillman
Aug 17/19	L. Gillarduzzi, E. Rent
1935	
Aug 1	Una Cameron, Édouard Bareux (g), Élisée Croux (g) (first one day ascent from the Fourche bivouac hut)
Aug 8	Robert Greloz, André Roch (too late a start from the Torino Hut led to a steady change of plans as the climbers were forced right to avoid avalanche couloirs. They eventually exited near the Old Brenva)
July 18/21	Stephano Bizio, Romeo Salesi
1937	
Aug	F Peringer and party
Aug	Ludwig Steinauer and party
Aug	Dr. A Glanzmann, Joseph Lerjen(g), Joseph Aufdenblatten(g)
1938	
July 20	Paul Aschenbrenner, K. Deutelimoser, Wastl Mariner, T. Plattner
July 21	Loulou Boulaz, Pierre Bonnant
July 28	Lucien Devies, Jacques Lagarde
July 28	M. Berghartswieser, H. Lobenhofer, F. Punz, V. Surrer
Aug 2/4	Three German climbers
Aug 25	Baron Georges de Golcz, Z. Zorosdowicz, W. Zulawski
Unplaced ascents	
c.1935	Wilhem Diehn, Joseph Lerjen (g), Adolf Schaller(g)
c.1939	Rudolf Faissi and party

Route Major ascents

Date	Climbers
1928	
Aug 6/7	Frank Smythe, Thomas Graham Brown
1933	
July 26	Alexander Graven (g), Thomas Graham Brown, Alfred Aufdenblatten (g), The party descended the South-West Face
1937	
July 24	Dr. A. Bauer, Hermann Steuri (g)
Aug 6	Paul Hagenbach, André Roch
Sept 2/3	P. Gazzana Priaroggia, G.P. Guidobono Cavalchini
1938	
July 25	René Auber, René Dittert
Aug 2/3	Una Cameron, Édouard Bareaux(g), Élisée Croux (g)
Aug 14	Maurice Renard, Armand Charlet(g)

Via della Pera ascents

Date	Climbers
1933	
Aug 5	Thomas Graham Brown, Alexander Graven (g), Alfred Aufdenblatten (g)
1937	
July 24	Robert Greloz, André Roch

that 'my suggestion that we should return to the Torino Hut and try it was vetoed.' The article also noted that Percy Farrer had suggested the crossing of the "Col Major" during the winter of 1927/28, and that:

> ... the great pass was therefore the chief of our projects of 1928 when our plan was to bivouac on the pass after ascending Route Major, so as to descend the other flank next morning. We were successful on the route, but the bivouac was vetoed and the crossing of the pass was abandoned. For the next five years the completion of the pass my hopes shared my hopes with the Via della Pera.

Graham Brown also claimed planning for the Pear Buttress at that time and broaching it to Smythe noting the Aiguille de la Belle Étoile as a focal point and objective of the route. 'Smythe was willing to try to get to the small aiguille from above but not from below.'

Thus in this single lecture, with its follow up *AJ* article, Graham Brown claimed inspiration for the Sentinelle Rouge route, introduced the concept of the crossing of the Col Major with a bivouac on the summit ridge of Mont Blanc, and the first ascent of the Pear Buttress. In both of these grandiose projects he suggested that Smythe was unenthusiastic. Neither of these projects were mentioned in his 1929 *AJ* account of the Route Major ascent. He accused Smythe of 'vetoing' both ideas.

THE PUBLICATION OF *BRENVA*

Graham Brown resurrected these assertions in 1943 in the drafts for his book *Brenva*. The publisher wisely took the precaution to send the proofs to Smythe who was in Canada at the time. He was so perturbed when he saw the proofs that he threatened legal action as described by Lord Tangley in his *AJ* article.

In a letter to Graham Brown's publisher (E.F. Bozeman of J.M. Dent) Smythe complains bitterly:

> ... [Graham Brown] didn't want to lead on steep ice. He carefully does all he can to ignore, minimise, and decry all the ice work I had to do ... On the ice I led every foot – cut every damn step – big buckets too because he was unhappy. I was amused too to read how a gust of wind blew him over on the summit ridge of Mont Blanc de Courmayuer in 1928. There was no wind. He wanted to lead the easy ridge to the top and did so. He came off twelve feet above me, fell past me on to the ice slope – hit it on his back and went off like a bullet. I had no belay ... I scrabbled the rope up agains the rock and miraculously it caught on a minute knob and held. The nearest thing [escape] I have ever had. I wonder how he can write what he does when I saved his life.
>
> But enough. The whole thing is more than distasteful. 1927 and 1928 are seasons I want to forget. If after all I have told you, you can reconcile what I've written with your conscience then publish the book. But I do ask you to see Edwin Herbert [later Lord Tangley]. He's my solicitor so you can show him this letter if you like, but I do ask you to help me out in this miserable business. I like the mountains too well to want to be involved in one of these quarrels which only discredit our sport.
>
> Since I have been out here I have seen a lot of the Rockies. You can probably guess my job: a grand one. Sandy Wedderburn, Peacocke, Pat Baird and various others are out here.
>
> Yours ever
> Frank Smythe

Smythe's bitter criticisms about Graham Brown are not reflected in his going out with him again on the Droites/Argentiere trip two days after their Route Major ascent, particularly if the Droites North Face was the objective (though the easier Col du Droites might have been the target). It may be that he felt compelled to make this trip because of Graham Brown's complaints about his disrupted holiday.

The problems created by the *Brenva* book proofs were reduced by Lord Tangley's arbitrating skills as described in his article. In a letter (probably to Dent) he gave an explanation of the background to the dispute:

> It is to be regretted that these two climbers quarrelled. Although other causes operated [the Macphee incident] ..., at the root of the break was their difference in technical skill as mountaineers. The Professor was to attain, in the 1930s and outstanding record of climbs in the Alps with guides ... Smythe on the other hand, had grown up as a guideless climber. ... In a guideless party of two, it is necessary that each should be able to do his share of the leading. Frank never begrudged doing a large share of the leading, but it was putting too unequal a strain on him to have to do virtually all the leading on such long climbs.
>
> As Frank sometime said, it was often quite minor irritations about a companion that produced friction in a climbing party and these, combined with the great strain of continual step-cutting produced a good deal of the temperament on his side of which the Professor complained. It is not a very rare thing for a highly strung climber, who is inwardly determined to go all out for a climb, to let off steam by saying it looks hopeless and they will certainly have to abandon it ...
>
> From all accounts Frank was in a temperamental mood in 1928; he told a friend later that year that he had a conviction all along that he was going to be killed and that it preyed on his mind. He was gloomy of the prospects [for the Route Major] though 1928 was a wonderful year in late June and early July. There is no doubt that he felt too much would devolve on him, and that part of his nerviness and want of confidence was due to that. He greatly resented, however, the Professor having said in Courmayeur, after the climb, that Frank had wanted to throw it up and only the Professor being present saved a retreat. He knew, too, that on Mont Blanc, as on earlier climbs that season, the Professor had taken no lead and had been virtually a passenger, if not a hindrance. But it was contrary to Frank's mentality to nurse enmities: in private he might express strong opinions on Graham Brown's claims to have led largely on Mont Blanc, but he said nothing openly until faced by the Professor's deliberate statements.

Graham Brown climbed with others during the 1930s. Most notably he had a fine season with Charles Houston in Zermatt in 1934. Houston invited him to join his father's Mount Foraker expedition in 1935 and on Houston's prompting Graham Brown was invited to join the 1936 Nanda Devi expedition but he did not perform well as Houston noted in *Nanda Devi: Exploration and Ascent*:

> We ... were well acclimatised, except for Graham Brown who was bluer and more short of breath than the others. More disturbing was how unaware of his condition he was and, indeed, rather paranoid. It was obvious that he could go no higher ...
>
> Graham Brown didn't fully recover even at Base Camp from his altitude related paranoia. This was my first experience with what today would be called High-Altitude Cerebral Oedema (HACE) ... When I did not invite him to K2 in 1938 he went to Masherbrum instead where a similar episode developed, ending in failure and bad frostbite for him and some of the party.

On Masherbrum, Robin Hodgkin confirms that he was not a success becoming more difficult as height was gained, imperious and inflexible about route-finding and being notably unsympathetic about his and Harrison's frostbite injuries.

Lord Tangley's observations on the basic incompatibility of the "pairing" that he had arranged are probably correct. A tense young amateur, who had learned his climbing from youth, is hardly a suitable partner for an inexperienced but ambitious middle aged "gentleman" climber who is used to being conducted up his routes by efficient professional guides.

Tom Blakeney, in a letter to Nona Smythe in 1950, was savage in his condemnation of Graham Brown, accusing him of consistent lying to boost his role in routes in which he was little more than a passenger. Nevertheless Blakeney conceded that Smythe was in a nervy state in 1928:

> I have no doubt that with G.B. in the party he knew it would devolve too much on him. He bitterly resented G.B. having said, in Courmayeur after the 1928 climb, that Smythe had wanted to throw up the climb, and only G.B. being present saved the retreat. On the other hand, in fairness to G.B., I must add that the latter told me that he only spoke of the matter after their rupture and then because Smythe was (so he says) going on about G.B. being a burden on the climb.
>
> G.B. told me that Smythe had a complete breakdown and wept; and that later he wrote to G.B. begging him to draw a veil over the whole business and asking to be friends again. I think the vendetta between them was probably due to awareness on G.B.'s part that he had played a very meagre role on the climb ....

Yet, notwithstanding Graham Brown's apparent lack of awareness of the potential dangers of the enterprise, these two climbers established two fine climbs on the greatest face in the Alps. They took part in one of the great episodes in Alpine history and it is sad that they were unable to jointly bask in the glow of their success.

APPENDIX V

Smythe's Books, Articles and Photographs

Books originate in London unless otherwise noted. The term "reprints" refers to all subsequent editions. All books are credited to "F.S. Smythe" except *The Mountain Vision*, *Again Switzerland*, *A Mountain Top* and *Rocky Mountains*, *Climbs in the Canadian Rockies* and *Mountains in Colour* ("Frank S. Smythe") and *Mountaineering Holiday* is given "Frank Smythe" on the jacket and "Frank S. Smythe" on the title page.

Frank Smythe was one of the most prolific of all mountaineering authors. He produced twenty-seven books and wrote numerous articles for both the popular, photographic and mountaineering press. The books can be split into various groups:

NARRATIVES The straight reports of periods of climbing or specific expeditions – the six books in this collection plus *Alpine Journey* (1934), *Over Tyrolese Hills* (1936), *Again Switzerland* (1947) and *Climbs in the Canadian Rockies* (1950).

PHOTOGRAPHIC BOOKS Smythe produced ten elegant photographic albums – a series developed with his friend Jack Newth of A. and C. Black and launched in 1937 with *The Mountain Scene*. As a keen photographer Smythe assiduously recorded his travels. He excelled in carefully-composed landscapes of a type that was much imitated in the succeeding years. The books adopt a general formula: the initial photographs depict mountain detail – rivers, trees, snow scenes, mountain chalets etc – followed by high mountain landscapes, sometimes with posed figures. Each image has an accompanying commentary containing both historical, topographical and photographic, compositional and technical observations.

Though his photographs rarely convey the "power" of that of the greatest mountain photographers the *body* of his work is an achievement of great distinction. Many of his images impress for their subtle lighting, classic composition and accurate reflection of the turbulent weather conditions of the mountains. There is however a dearth (in the published work) of intimate snapshots and good portraits – gritty pictures high on Everest of Wyn Harris, Wager and Shipton (for example) are notable by their absence.

ANTHOLOGIES, BIOGRAPHIES, FICTION Another sub-group of books are anthologies of episodes drawn from the earlier books – *The Spirit of the Hills* (1935) and *Adventures of a Mountaineer* (1940) – which developed into books of general reminiscence and reflection with a neo-philosophical bent – *The Mountain Vision* (1941), *The Mountain Top* (1947). This latter trend is also reflected in the commentaries in his photographic books. In combination these messages reveal Smythe as having a very individual approach to mountaineering – sensitive, not at all competitive and characterised by an underlying humility. These messages were not to everyone's taste – the more critical Oxbridge aesthetes of the Alpine Club regarded some of his writing as "purple prose". Yet other respected critics, such as Winthrop Young, Amery, Busk and Lunn, remained consistently supportive.

The biography *Edward Whymper* (1940) is a valuable record of the life and climbing of Smythe's great mountaineering hero. The slim *British Mountaineers* (1942) is a more modest excursion into biography.

Smythe's one novel (thriller), *Secret Mission* (1942), received good reviews.

The Kangchenjunga and Everest exploits had catapulted Smythe into a high public profile which he and his publishers were not slow to exploit. Thus, by the late 1930s, Smythe was evolving into a mass communicator about the mountains. His climbing activity and book production at that time was prodigious with major expeditions in 1937 and 1938, an alpine season in 1939 and an astonishing thirteen books published between 1937 and 1942. They were incredibly popular and many were reprinted several times. It is may be argued that Smythe's love of the hills, and the way he communicated it, established a bedrock of public understanding and acceptance of mountaineering that remains to this day.

The twenty-seven books are listed in their order of publication:

Climbs and Ski Runs (Blackwood, Edinburgh, 1930; reprinted: 1930, 1931, 1933, 1934 (Toronto) and 1957) Early climbs in Britain, the Dolomites, Corsica and the Alps.

The Kangchenjunga Adventure (Gollancz, 1930) A full expedition account. Thoroughly illustrated with mountain action and many local genre photos in Nepal and Sikkim.

Kamet Conquered (Gollancz, 1932; reprinted: 1933, 1938, 1947) The official expedition account. Fully illustrated. The book includes the exploration around the Arwa Valley to the west.

An Alpine Journey (Hodder, 1934; reprinted: 1940, 1941) A solo traverse of the Swiss Alps (Silvretta to the western Bernese Oberland) during the Spring of 1934. The final chapters cover Bernese Oberland reminiscences during seasons in the 1920s and 1930s.

The Spirit of the Hills (Hodder, 1935; reprinted: 1937, 1938, 1941, 1946, 1950) Climbing reminiscences and comparisons, with reflections on the meaning and impact of climbing.

Over Tyrolese Hills (Hodder, 1936; reprinted: 1936, 1937, 1938) A complete summer traverse of the Austrian Alps with Campbell Secord. A high quality, well-illustrated, narrative.

Camp 6 (Hodder, 1937; reprinted: 1938, 1941, 1956) The author's personal account of the 1933 Everest Expedition following, after a suitable delay, the official account (*Everest* 1933 by Hugh Ruttledge).

The Valley of Flowers (Hodder, 1938; Norton, New York, 1949; reprinted in 1947 and 1986) A major Garhwal exploratory trip. A book with a strong botanical image with virtually all the illustrations depicting flora. The trip had both botanical and mountaineering aims but unfortunately the former appears to predominate, superficially disguising the notable mountaineering saga that forms its core. Smythe and his companions conducted a very thorough exploration of the Bhyundar and Banke valleys, with important first ascents and attempts. These activities are obfuscated by an almost complete absence of action and mountain photographs. The missing photographs were published in *Peaks and Valleys*.

The Mountain Scene (A. and C. Black, 1937; simultaneous editions in the Dominions, MacMillan; reprinted: 1938) This was the first in a series of photographic books printed in gravure with cloth binding.

Peaks and Valleys (A. and C. Black, 1938 and simultaneously in the Dominions. The second photographic volume.

A Camera in the Hills (A. and C. Black, 1939; reprinted: 1942, 1946, 1948). A third photographic book.

Mountaineering Holiday (Hodder, 1940, reprinted: 1941, 1943, 1950) A well-illustrated (in the first edition only) narrative account of the author's 1939 alpine season in the French Alps.

Edward Whymper (Hodder, 1940) A biography of Smythe's mountaineering role model.

My Alpine Album (A. and C. Black, 1940; reprinted: 1947). The fourth photographic collection with a mix of detailed aesthetic views and landscapes including winter scenes.

Adventures of a Mountaineer (Dent, 1940; reprinted: 1941, 1945, 1949) An anthology of the author's mountaineering experiences selected from his earlier books with some new chapters.

The Mountain Vision (Hodder, 1941; reprinted in 1942, 1946 and 1950) A neo-philosophical treatise.

Over Welsh Hills (A. and C. Black, 1941; reprinted in 1942 and 1945) A fifth photographic book depicting (mainly) Snowdon and the Carneddau in winter conditions during December 1940.

Alpine Ways (A. and C. Black, 1942; reprinted: 1945, 1947). The fifth photographic album. The author pines for a return to the fabled mountain villages and ranges – 'For the present they must remain memories, but there will come a time, when this foul plague of Nazism is nothing but an evil dream. Then rucksacks will be packed and boots tended, and the eternal snows will rise out of the south in welcoming array as the Oberland or Valais Express breasts the wooded heights of the Jura.'

Secret Mission (Hodder and Stoughton, 1942) In his *AJ* review Teddy Eaton enthused – 'I could not go to bed until I had finished it ... unqualified praise both as mountain literature and as a thriller'.

British Mountaineers (Collins, 1942; reprinted: 1946) A slim historical treatise about the "Golden Age".

Snow on the Hills (A. and C. Black, 1946; reprinted: 1948) A larger photographic album, printed in good quality letterpress, which enhanced the Everest pictures and powerful Canadian/Alaskan mountain images.

The Mountain Top (St Hugh's Press, 1947) A miniscule reflective anthology.

Again Switzerland (Hodder, 1947) A ski mountaineering holiday in 1946 with trips around Adelboden, the Lötschental, Verbiers and the Swiss section of the Haute Route.

Rocky Mountains (A. and C. Black, 1948) Another photographic collection, printed in letterpress.

Swiss Winter (A. and C. Black, 1948) A photographic book aimed at the tourist and winter sports market.

Mountains in Colour (Max Parrish, 1949; Chanticleer Press, New York, 1949) Scotland, Lakeland and Wales, the Swiss Alps, the Canadian Rockies and some Himalayan scenes.

Climbs in the Canadian Rockies (Hodder, 1950; Norton, New York, 1950) The author's wartime training work, climbs on the great peaks and an exploratory trip to the Lloyd George range.

Journal Articles by Frank Smythe and others (during the 1930s Smythe was also the mountaineering correspondent of The Times, *writing numerous articles and features):*

Rock Peaks and Snow Peaks by Howard Somervell (*AJ* 35, 1923)
A Traverse of the Langkofel by the North-East Ridge by F.S. Smythe (*YRC Journal*, Vol.5, 1924)

Thunderstorms in the Alps by F.S. Smythe (*AJ* 38, 1926)

The North-East Face of the Klein Fiescherhorn by F.S. Smythe (*AJ* 38 1926)

The West Buttress of Clogwyn Du'r Arddu by F.S. Smythe (*YRC Journal*, Vol 5, 1927)

The Col de La Brenva; The Aiguille de Leschaux by R.Ogier Ward (*AJ* 40, 1928)

The First Ascent of Mont Blanc direct from the Brenva Glacier and other Climbs in 1927 by F.S. Smythe (*AJ* 40, 1928) The Sentinelle Rouge chapter was written in collaboration with T.Graham Brown yet the caption to the Mont Blanc topo notes "Showing Mr Smythe's route" (the Editor was Strutt).

Some Physical Characteristics of Avalanches by F.S. Smythe (*AJ* 41, 1929)

The First Direct Ascent of Mont Blanc de Courmayeur from the Brenva Glacier and Other Climbs by T. Graham Brown (*AJ* 41, 1929) – deals with the ascent of both the Sentinelle Rouge and the Route Major – the first printed account of the latter ascent.

The Assault on Kangchenjunga, 1930 by F.S. Smythe (*AJ* 42, 1930) Includes photos not in the book.

The Kangchenjunga Diary by George Wood Johnson (*FRCCJ* 25, 1931) A significant memoir from Smythe's main climbing partner on the expedition who gives greater stress to the risks and difficulties involved in moving the whole expedition over Jonsong La (20,080ft).

Chetin [Chettan] Obituary by Hugh Ruttledge, Edward Norton and Geoffrey Bruce (*AJ* 42, 1930)

The Assault on Kangchenjunga, 1930 Letters from Professor G.O. Dyhrenfurth, Frank Smythe and George Finch commenting on the boots, tactics and fatality (*AJ* 43, 1931).

Mountaineering Films Unattributed critique of the 1930 Kangchenjunga Film (*AJ* 43, 1931).

The 1931 Kamet Expedition by F.S. Smythe (*AJ* 43,1931) Includes several additional photographs.

The Jägi and the Bietschhoerner by F.S. Smythe (*AJ* 44, 1932)

The Mount Everest Expedition, 1933 by Hugh Ruttledge (*AJ* 45, 1933) With photos not in the books.

Col Major by T. Graham Brown (*AJ* 45, 1933, pp.365–372) Brown reclimbs the Old Brenva and Route Major with guides.

Everest 1933 by J.L. Longland (*FRCCJ* 27, 1933) An amusing and trenchant commentary on the risk of high-altitude climbing, acclimatisation and sherpa management.

Lessons from the Mount Everest Expedition of 1933 by T.G. Longstaff with contributions by Raymond Greene and C.G. Crawford (*AJ* 46, 1934) The final part is a chronicle of Crawford's diary entries: 'Shipton and Smythe at last arrived. The former was suffering from aphasia. Smythe doesn't think Norton's Route will go – he wants to apply siege tactics to the Second Step. They had a lot of snow to contend with on Norton's Traverse. Longland and Harris want to try again as soon as possible. … There is no doubt that [Smythe] is an extraordinary good high-altitude subject.'

Everest: The Final Problem by F.S. Smythe, plus follow up papers from Odell and Wakefield (*AJ* 46, 1934, pp.442–446). An exhaustive discussion on strategy. Smythe notes that the extra day spent at Camp 6 (27,400ft) left him stronger for the rest. Odell discusses the finding of the axe and the likely scenarios that stemmed from that discovery.

Accident on the South Face of Mont Blanc by F.S. Smythe. The Hoyland/Wand tragedy (*AJ* 46, 1934).

Mount Everest: The Sixth Expedition by Hugh Ruttledge (*AJ* 48, 1936).

Garhwal: 1937 by F.S. Smythe (*AJ* 50, 1938) Contains a full compliment of mountaineering photos.

The Brenva Face by T. Graham Brown (*AJ* 51, 1939) Graham Brown claimed the inspiration for both the Sentinelle Rouge and Route Major and that the crossing (after a bivouac) of Col Major had always been part of the Route Major plan.

Everest 1938 by H.W. Tilman. (*AJ* 51, 1939) The book was published in 1948!

Dauphiné and Mont Blanc: 1939 by F.S. Smythe (*AJ* 52, 1940) With high-quality photo reproductions.

Garhwal 1939: The Swiss Expedition by André Roch (*AJ* 52, 1940) Includes the first ascents of Dunagiri and Rataban, peaks than had defeated Smythe and Oliver in 1937.

Mechanised Mountaineering by Frank S. Smythe (*FRCCJ* 36, 1942) A strong denunciation of the use of pitons and other mechanised techniques (including oxygen use) in mountaineering.

Brenva A book review by Bentley Beauman (*AJ* 54, 1944).

Second Thoughts by H.E.G. Tyndale (*AJ* 55, 1945) Includes two rare Smythe photographs.

Training in the Canadian Rockies by T.A.H. Peacocke (*AJ* 55, 1945) Training mountain troops under Smythe's command.

Ernest Alexander MacLagan Wedderburn 1912–1944; Peter Oliver 1909–1945 Obituary notices by F.S. Smythe (*AJ* 55, 1945). Wedderburn, a Major in the Lovat Scouts, died on Christmas Eve, 1944, in a freak hotel accident in Italy. Smythe paid tribute to their mountain training work together.

Oliver, a Lieut-Colonel with the Frontier Rifles, was killed in action in Burma. Smythe noted that their Mana Peak ascent 'was comparable in length, difficulty and variety with the great routes on the south side of Mont Blanc'. He also comments on Oliver's role on Dunagiri ('he massaged my feet for an hour and saved me from frostbite') and Nilkanta ('he was at the top of his form ... as good on really difficult rocks as he was on snow and ice.').

Some Experiences in Mountain Warfare Training by F.S. Smythe (*AJ* 55, 1947, in two sections).

An Expedition to Lloyd George Mountains of British Columbia by F.S. Smythe (*AJ* 56, 1947)

The First Ascent of the Innominata Face of Mont Blanc, 1919 by S.L. Courtauld (*AJ* 57, 1949). The first article on this major first ascent (a short factual notice having been published in *AJ* 33, 1921). The author was on the Western Front from 1914–1918 which created a five-year break between attempts and ascent. The Gugliermina (1921) and Smythe/Gavin (1939) ascents are discussed.

Francis Sydney Smythe 1900–1949 Obituary notices by Anon (T.Graham Brown was the *AJ* Editor at the time), Bentley Beauman and Raymond Green. (*AJ* 57, 1949, pp 230–235). The main notice lists the salient mountaineering facts and (if written by Brown) is not ungenerous, Beauman discusses his literary/communication skills and Greene goes into detail about his education and various personal observations. In referring to his final 1933 Everest push Greene noted it was Smythe's 'final triumph of judgement when ... the day still young and his body still able, knowing the powdery monsoon snow too great a handicap, he turned his back on the goal of his ambitions.' Tom Longstaff, in his subsequent Presidential valedictory address noted Smythe as 'a tireless traveller, a giant on Everest, better known to the public than any other living mountaineer and withal a very charming character.'

Route Major by Moonlight by F.R. Brooke (*AJ* 57, 1952). An interesting alternative strategy.

Between the Wars, 1919–1939 by Jack Longland (*AJ* 62, 1957, pp 83–97).

A Century of Climbing Photography by C. Douglas Milner (*AJ* 62, 1957) Contrasts the photography of Smythe and Graham Brown.

Thomas Graham Brown, 1882–1965 Obituary notes by R.C. Evans and Basil Goodfellow (*AJ* 71, 1966).

T.Graham Brown, F.R.S., 1882–1965 Obituary note by Robin Campbell. (*SMCJ*, 1966). Includes information about Brown's retired life in Edinburgh including his friendship with Robin Smith.

T.Graham Brown by Lord Tangley (*AJ* 71, 1966). The author's role in the Brenva affair.

Frank Smythe and Graham Brown by T.S. Blakeney (*AJ* 72, 1967). A brief corrective note to the previous article reporting Smythe's awareness of the Sentinelle Rouge and the Route Major possibilities.

Francis Sydney Smythe: Mountain Photographer by Nona Smythe (*AJ* 81, 1976). With a poor representation of photographs, this article failed to advance his reputation as a notable photographer.

Relevant Books by Other Authors

Arranged in order of publication

Everest 1933 by Hugh Ruttledge (Hodder, 1934; McBride, New York, 1935 as *Attack on Everest*). The official 1933 expedition book.

After Everest by Howard Somervell (Hodder, 1936). Describes the 1923 Langkofel ascent.

Everest: The Unfinished Adventure by Hugh Ruttledge (Hodder, 1937). The official 1936 account.

Everest: The Challenge Sir Francis Younghusband (Nelson, London and New York, 1936).

Approach to the Hills by C.F. Meade (John Murray, 1940). Covers his Kamet explorations.

Upon that Mountain by Eric Shipton (Hodder, 1943. Collected in *Eric Shipton: The Six Mountain-Travel Books*, Diadem/The Mountaineers, 1985). Describes his three Everest trips with Smythe.

Brenva by T. Graham Brown (Dent, 1944). An exhaustive account of the exploration of the face. Magnificently illustrated with very specific topographical photos that typify the author's attention to detail.

Kingdom of Adventure, Everest by James Ramsey Ullman (Sloane, New York, 1947 / Collins, 1948).

Mount Everest, 1938 by H.W. Tilman (Cambridge University Press, 1948; Collected in *H. W. Tilman: The Seven Mountain-Travel Books*, Diadem/The Mountaineers, 1982). The official account.

A Progress of Mountaineering by J.H.B. Bell (Oliver and Boyd, Edinburgh, 1950).

Mountains with a Difference by Geoffrey Winthrop Young (Eyre and Spottiswoode, 1951). Contains an elegant tribute to Smythe (pp 143–144).

The Story of Mount Everest by W.H. Murray (Dent, 1953). Discusses Great Couloir strategies.

Abode of Snow by Kenneth Mason (Rupert Hart Davis, 1955; reprinted with extra illustrations and corrections: Diadem 1987 / The Mountaineers, Seattle, 1987).

To the Third Pole by G.O. Dyhrenfurth, with Erwin Schneider (Nyphenburger, Munich, 1952 as *Zum Dritten Pol*; first English edition, translated by Hugh Merrick – Werner Laurie, 1955). Contains Schneider's account of the ice avalanche on Kangchenjunga and other comments about that trip.

A Century of Mountaineering by Arnold Lunn, Allen and Unwin, 1957).

That Untravelled World by Eric Shipton (Hodder, 1969; Scribeners, New York).

Moments of Being by Raymond Greene (Heinemann, 1975). Contemporary observations of Smythe with amusing and penetrative accounts about the Kamet and 1933 Everest expeditions.

Life is Meeting by John Hunt (Hodder, 1978). Contains notes about Smythe's wartime activities.

Everest by Walt Unsworth (Allen Lane, 1981; Houghton Mifflin, Boston, 1981. Subsequent editions: The Oxford Illustrated Press, Yeovil, 1989; retitled – *Everest: The Mountaineering History*, The Mountaineers, Seattle, 1999 / Bâton Wicks, 1999). Contains a comprehensive summary of Smythe as a mountaineer plus much tactical and background information about the various Everest expeditions.

Smythe's Mountains by Harry Calvert (Gollancz, 1985). A valuable mountaineering biography.

Hands of a Climber – The Life of Colin Kirkus by Steve Dean (The Ernest Press, Holyhead, 1993). Describes Smythe's 1935 alpine training expedition for 1936 Everest contenders.

Geoffrey Winthrop Young by Alan Hankinson (Hodder, 1995). Contains critical reports about Graham Brown's "disputatious" nature.

Eric Shipton – Everest and Beyond by Peter Steele (Constable, 1998; Mountaineers, Seattle, 1999). Many references to Smythe on Kamet and Everest in Shipton's letters to Pamela Freston

APPENDIX VI

Smythe's Mountaineering Record 1909–1939

This may not be a complete record. There are a number of alpine and winter seasons where information is unavailable. On the expeditions those marked [d] are the expedition doctors. Pages in this book, or other books by Smythe and others, where the climb/expedition/season is described, are noted.

1909

First Climb La Pointe de Cray above Chateaux d'Oex, Switzerland, climbed with a 16-year old local youth. Oberland walks, with his mother, on the hills opposite the Eiger.

1914–17

School years Scrambling at Tintagel and on Penmaenmawr Mt.; a solo attempt on a gully on Moel Hebog; Cnicht; Bristly Ridge and Tryfan in a solo round from Pen yr Gywrd; solo ascent of (probably) Lliwedd's W. Buttress during which a sheep jumped to its death.

1919–1920

College years at Bradford Joined Yorkshire Ramblers Club where Ernest Roberts, C.D. Frankland and Howard Somervell were his mentors. He climbed on Almscliff, and in the Lake District and Wales: climbs on Pavey Ark and Gimmer Crag (including Little Gully – and a lead of Gwynne's Chimney); a solo ascent of Eagle's Nest Ridge Direct (VS) in stockinged feet; a solo attempt on Napes Needle on Great Gable; in Snowdonia explorations (with Roberts or solo) on Llechog and Clogwyn Du'r Arddu (including solo ascents of Far West Buttress and the grass terrace traverse of East Buttress at two thirds height).

1921

May Wasdale with J.H.B. Bell and A.B. Roberts. Climbs: Pillar's North Climb, Scafell Pinnacle Direct; Napes Needle and Eagle's Nest Direct – Smythe led though Bell later overtook him in rock-climbing ability.

September Clogwyn Du'r Arddu with Ernest Roberts: *Giants's Trod* on Steep Band, and *Non Such* – the first ascent of Far-East Buttress (neither route is identified in the guidebook); repeated East Wall Climb; attempted Chimney Route (then unclimbed); identified start and line of the future Longland's Climb.

December Moved to Innsbruck for Engineering studies. Began solo ski mountaineering trips. Attempted Gross Venediger with G.N. Hewett and Hewett's sister.

1922

Austrian Alps c. January–March Solo ski ascent of the Kraulspitze (Stubaital), and an attempt on the Olperer (Zillartal), with an unnamed American ending in a harrowing retreat.

Swiss Alps, Canton Glarus c. May A solo ski ascent of the Claridenstock. June An ascent of Tödi from the Grünhorn Hut with G.N. Hewett. pp 22–27

Austrian Alps and Dolomites c. July First conventional alpine season, with J.H.B. Bell. The N.W. Ridge of the Gross Venidiger followed by the Langkofelkarspitze and the Fünffingerspitze. pp 27–33. Moved to Switzerland for further engineering studies.

1923

Arlberg May Solo ascents of Faselfadspitze, Scheibler and Küchelspitze. pp 41–48

Silvretta Group c. May A solo ski mountaineering expedition. Tallispitze, Piz Buin and Signalhorn from the Silvrettahaus; traverse of the Silvrettahorn to the Wiesbadener Hut; traverse of the Dreiländerspitze (North and East Ridges) and the Vorder Jamspitz to the Jamtal Hut; ascents of the Hinterer Augenstenberg and Fluchthorn.

Dolomites Kleine Zinne and the Croda da Lago (Pomaninkamin) with Howard Somervell. The Zahnkofel and the N.E. Face of the Langkofel, with Howard and Leslie Somervell; the Grohmannspitze, and other "difficult" climbs with Ernest Roberts. pp 33–37.

Bernese Alps Ascents of Mönch and Finsteraarhorn with Colonel P. Neame. Traverse of the Eiger with Howard Somervell, Bentley Beetham, W.V.Brown and A.J.Rusk (West Ridge/South Ridge) testing the 42lb oxygen equipment sets being prepared for the 1924 Everest expedition (p79). Returned to Austria to complete engineering studies.

1924

Skye: The Black Cuillin July – with J.H.B. Bell. Cuillin Ridge, Cioch Direct, Crack of Doom; and pioneered West Trap Route *A Progress in Mountaineering* by J.H.B. Bell

1925

Ben Nevis Easter – with J.H.B. Bell. Retreat from Tower Gap during Tower Ridge attempt.

Bernese Alps July–August Schreckhorn, South West Ridge and a traverse to the Lauteraarhorn with J.H.B. Bell, followed, two days later, by a repeat attempt on the Schreckhorn with Alexander Harrison and C.M.K. Douglas with arduous retreat from high on the route during a prolonged thunderstorm, pp 48–55. Jungfrau, Guggi Route with J.H.B. Bell (a stormy ascent); Ochs (Klein) Fiesherhorn, North-East Face – first ascent with J.V. Hazard (after a previous attempt ten days earlier with Bell. A traverse of the Bietschorn with J.V. Hazard – ascent by WSW Ridge, descent by the East Spur.

1927

Corsica May – with F.H. Slingsby. Ascents of Mont d'Oro, Punta Orientale, Paglia Orba by South Face (after East Ridge attempt) and Monte Cinto. Solo ascents of peaks north of Paglia Orba and the North Summit of Capo Tafonata. pp 55–63.

French Alps July–August Mont Blanc, Brenva Spur with R. Ogier Ward and George Bower; Aiguille du Grépon (with Nantillons approach) with George Bower, who led the

Knubel Crack (with Scafell CB-type combined tactics) following an earlier failure; attempt on the North-East Face of the Paine de Sucre with T.S. Blakeney; second ascent of the East Ridge of Aiguille du Plan (Ryan/Lochmatter Route) with J.H.B. Bell – Smythe had a forty-foot fall in the Plan/Crocodile Couloir; Mont Blanc, Mont Maudit and Mt.Blanc du Tacul from the Torino Hut via the Col Maudit (third ascent) with Graham Macphee; August 10–11 – Aiguille Blanche with Graham Macphee during an attempt on the Peuterey Ridge. An incipient storm prompted an arduous retreat down the Rochers Gruber; Petit Aig.Verte with T. Graham Brown; Sept 1–2 – Mont Blanc, Brenva Face with Graham Brown; the first ascent of the Sentinelle Rouge route; Grandes Charmoz and Les Courtes (new route on the SSW Buttress) with Graham Brown. pp 88–117

1928

Bernina Alps January A winter ski ascent of Piz Bernina via the Labrynth and the Spallagrat with Bentley Beetham and Warren Homer (US).

Snowdonia: Clogwyn Du'r Arddu Easter and Whit. The first ascent of the West Buttress – an enterprise seemingly inspired by Smythe after his earlier explorations. Participants included Smythe, Jack Longland, C. Wakefield and T. Graham Brown on an Easter attempt Later Smythe with, variously, Graham Brown, Claude Elliot and R. Ogier Ward made two inspections of the final wall. At Whitsun a large party approached the cliff to encounter a rival Rucksack Club group of Fred Piggot, Morley Wood and Bill Eversden. Longland and Smythe joined with them to make the first ascent (led by Longland). pp 63–70.

Bernese Alps July Training climbs in the Blumlisalp group with T. Graham Brown.

Mont Blanc Massif July–August Aiguille du Grépon by the Nantillons Route with Ivan Waller (leading) and Graham Brown; Aig Verte, Moine Ridge with Graham Brown; Petits Charmoz with T.S. Blakeney and Graham Brown; Trident de la Brenva with Graham Brown and Blakeney prior to an abortive Brenva Face attempt; Dent du Geant with Graham Brown (July 5); Brenva Face, Route Major with Graham Brown (approached via the S.E. Ridge of Tour Ronde, August 6–7) – the first ascent with the summit reached after 8 pm and a descent via the Vallot Hut and Bossons Glacier (pp125–138);Grands Charmoz traverse (Aug 8) and Aig. du Argentiere (attempt) with Graham Brown (August 10) – attempt aborted when a storm threatened (p 54).

Bernese Alps December–January Ski mountaineering trips with Graham Macphee (Gespensterhorn and Mönch) and an attempt to climb the Eiger via the Eigerjoch with T.Y. Kagami – repulsed by difficulties on the South Ridge pp 70–83

1929

Mont Blanc Massif, Mont Maudit August – with Alexander Harrison and Charles Parry. They attempted a new route on the South-East Spur (the line climbed a few days later – August 4 – by Lino Binel, Renato Chabod and Amilcare Cretier). After a bivouac 1000ft up the face, bad weather forced a retreat during which Parry was injured. T.J. Kagami was his replacement but bad weather followed and Smythe and Harrison returned to Britain. In mid September Kagami and his guide Gottfried Perren completed a second line up the face right of the Binel/Chabod/Cretier route. pp 907–909

1930

Nepal/Sikkim: International Kangchenjunga Expedition March–June Günter Oskar Dyhrenfurth (leader), Hetti Dyhrenfurth, Marcel Kurz and Charles Duvanel (Swiss), Ulrich Wieland, Helmuth Richter[d] and Hermann Hoerlin (German), Erwin Schneider (Austrian), Frank Smythe, George Wood Johnson, J.S. Hannah and H.W. Tobin (British) with Narsang (sirdar), Naspati (sirdar), Chettan, Ondi, Lewa, Lobsang, Nemu, Tsinabo, Nima Tendrup, Nagpa, Tencheddar and others. From Darjeeling (April 7), they crossed the Kang La to Nepal. Base Camp was established (April 26) by the Kangchenjunga Glacier. The route was advanced (with two camps) to the lower left corner of the N.W. Face where the barrier ice cliffs involved technical ice climbing. During the push to establish

Camp 3, a section of the ice cliff avalanched and Chettan was killed. The party then attempted the N.W. Ridge of Kangbachen but this proved too difficult. On c. May 18 Schneider and Smythe made the first ascent of the nearby Ramthang Peak (23,310ft). The expedition then crossed the Jonsong La (20,200ft) and established a new Base Camp on the Lhonak Glacier. The first ascent of Jonsong Peak (24,344ft) was made on June 3 by Schneider and Hoerlin. A few days later Kurz, Tsinabo, Smythe (his second attempt), Wieland, Dyhrenfurth and Lewa made a second ascent. Meanwhile Schneider and Hoerlin climbed Dodang Nyima (23,620ft). Schneider (with Wieland in support) also climbed Nepal Peak (23,560ft) (c. May 23). The party then returned through Sikkim. pp 145–345.

1931

India, Garhwal (Zaskar Range). The Kamet Expedition May/August Frank Smythe (leader), Eric Shipton, Wing Commander E.B. (Bentley) Beauman, Raymond Greene[d], R.L. Holdsworth, Capt.E. St John Birnie, Lewa (sirdar), Achung, Nima Tendrup, Nima Dorje, Nima, Ondi, Passang, Ang Nerbu, Dorje, Budhibal Gurung, Randhoj Kan, Keser Singh and others. The party left Ranikhet (May 18) and established Base Camp (June 9). Camp 5 was established near Meade's Col (June 20). On June 21 Shipton, Lewa, Holdsworth and Smythe, supported by Nima Dorje, reached the summit (25,447ft) – the highest peak climbed at that time. Lewa sustained frostbite injuries, necessitating later finger and toe amputations. On June 23 Greene, Birnie and Kesar Singh repeated the ascent. The party then moved to Mana, via the Bhyundar Khal. Base Camp was established at the head of the Arwa Valley (July 17) from where various passes were crossed and seven first ascents were made – notably Pt.6443 / 21,133ft (Avalanche Peak) by Smythe, Shipton, Birnie, Dorje and Nima. Birnie, Dorje and six porters explored on the Gangotri side of the watershed regaining the Arwa side by a c.21,000ft pass. pp 353–514

1932

Bernese Alps July – with H.B. Thompson. Jägihorn, South-East Ridge and Bietschhorn, by a new route up the East Face (pp 909–912). Elected Honorary Member of C.A.F.

1933

Tibet: Everest Expedition March–June Hugh Ruttledge (leader), Frank Smythe, Percy Wyn Harris, Lawrence Wager, Jack Longland, Tom Brocklebank, Colin 'Ferdie' Crawford, E. St.J. Birnie, Raymond Greene[d], George Wood Johnson, W. McLean, E.C. Thompson, Hugh Bousted, E.O. Shebbeare, W. Smijth-Windham, Karma Paul, Lhakpa Chedi, Lewa, Nursang, Sonam Topgye, Nima Tendrup, Pasang Bhotia, Pasang Kikuli, Pasang Dorje, Kusang, Da Tsering, Angtharkay and others. Camp 6 was established at 27,400ft. in late May and two summit attempts followed (by Wyn Harris and Wager, and Smythe and Shipton). Both attempts reached the Great Couloir at about 28,100 ft., the first aborted because of fatigue and lack of time, the second stopped by poor snow conditions and soloing risks. At the end of the expedition: Ruttledge, Smythe, Crawford, Shipton and Brocklebank climbed Peak 22,340 ft. above the Rapiu La. pp 521–651

1934

Swiss Alps March–April Solo ski journey through the Silvretta Group to Arosa and Chur. From Flums he traversed of the Glarus mountains past Tödi to Andermatt and the Furka Pass. The Rhone Valley was taken to Brig and thence via the Gemmi Pass to Kandersteg, and Gstaad to finish at Montreaux. *An Alpine Holiday*

Switzerland, Pennine Alps August with Graham Macphee and Charles Parry. Traverse of the Matterhorn from the Schönbiel Hut via the Col Tournanche and the Italian and Hörnli Ridges. The traverse was made in unsettled weather forcing a two night stop at the Solvay Hut during the descent. *The Spirit of the Hills*

Mont Blanc Massif September 18–25 Smythe (on the instigation of Mr J.S. Hoyland) led a search party (the guides Adolphe Rey, Baroux and Camille Grivel) to discover John

Hoyland and Paul Wand. The bodies were found on the Frêney Glacier. Stonefalls and avalanches posed a continual risk to all involved. pp 913–916

1935

Austrian Alps June/July – with Campbell Secord (a noted Canadian climber). They traversed the Silvretta, Ötztal, Stubaital, Zillertal, Reichen and Hohe Tauern. Peaks ascended included: Bieltalspitze, Fluchthorn, Glockturm, Fluchtkogel, Wildspitze, Zuckerhutl, Wilder Freiger, Fussstein, Olperer, Hochfeiler, Furtschagl Spitze, Gabelkopf, Reichenspitze, Wildergloss Spitze, Rosskar Scharte, Simony Spitze/Dreiherren Spitze ('one of the finest expeditions in the Eastern Alps') to finish on the Gross Venediger. *Over Tyrolese Hills*

Switzerland, Pennine Alps August A 1936 Everest Training/Selection Meet under the leadership of Smythe with Jim Gavin, Peter Oliver, C.R. Nicholls, Oakes Smith and Colin Kirkus. Climbs included: Adlerhorn/Strahlhorn, Dom/Täschhorn traverse; Zumsteinspitze, a night in the Margherita Hut then Lyskamm, Castor, Pollux, Breithorn thence to the Gandegg Hut (8pm) and Zermatt (11pm) (all six climbers); Zinal Rothorn, Wellenkuppe, Obergabelhorn and Weisshorn.

1936

Tibet: Everest Expedition March–June Hugh Ruttledge (leader), Eric Shipton, Frank Smythe, Percy Wyn Harris, Edwin Kempson, Edmond Wigram, Charles Warren[d], Peter Oliver, Noel Humphreys, John Morris, Jim Gavin, W. Smijth-Windham, Karma Paul, Jemadar Lachiman Singh, Pasang Bhotia, Tsering Tarkay, Rinsing, Ondi, Tewang, Ang Tsering, Nursang, Ang Tharkay, Da Tsering and others. Attempt failed at North Col due to repeated heavy snowfalls. *Everest: The Unfinished Adventure* by Hugh Ruttledge

1937

India, Garhwal Byhundar and Banke Valleys in the Zaskar range and other areas June/September. Frank Smythe, Peter Oliver, Wangdi Nurbu, Pasang, Tewang, Nurbu, Tse Tendrup and Ang Bao, plus (on Dunagiri) Kharak Singh, Mangal Singh, Nater Singh. From the Bhyundar Valley ascents were made of several rock and ice peaks by Smythe with Wangdi, Nurbu and others. There were attempts on Rataban (Smythe, Wangdi, Pasang and Oliver). The most important climb in the first part of the expedition was the first ascent of Nilgiri Parbat [Parvat] (Smythe, Nurbu and Wangdi). In August the party made the first ascents Peak 22,481 (Deoban) (Smythe and Oliver) and Mana Peak by South-West/South Ridge by (Smythe and Oliver, Smythe soloing the last 800ft). Elsewhere in the region Smythe and Oliver, with their support team attempted the S.E. Ridge of Nilkanta (August 4) and Dunagiri by the S.W. Ridge (Sept 14–16) pp 659–800

1938

Tibet: Everest Expedition April/June H.W.Tilman (leader), Noel Odell, Charles Warren[d], Peter Lloyd, Peter Oliver, Frank Smythe, Karma Paul, Ang Tharkay, Kusang, Pasang Bhotia, Tensing Norgay, and others. Another abortive attempt. The North Col was reached from the Rongbuk Glacier to the west. The mountain was swathed in soft snow but Camp 6 was established at 27,200ft below the Yellow Band. The attempt on the following day (Shipton and Smythe) made little progress in the deep power snow. *Everest, 1938* by H.W. Tilman and *Upon that Mountain* by Eric Shipton

1939

The Dauphiné and the **Mont Blanc Massif** (August) – with Jim Gavin. In the Dauphiné they climbed Les Bans and traversed the Barre des Écrins, (start up the South Face). The Mont Blanc Massif ascents were Mont Tondu, Tête Carrée, Aiguille de Bérengèr, Dômc du Miage, Aiguille du Bionnassay, Mont Blanc – descent by Brenva Spur, Aiguille du Rochfort. Finally Mont Blanc was reascended by the Innominata Ridge. pp 807–906

Smythe continued to climb during the war and post-war years until his death in 1949 (to be summarised in a later volume).

Index

(abridged)